For Duane and Gina,
Longtime friends, with
Best regards of the author

Pierre

April 2016

#152/302

Tragic Truth

Oswald Shot Kennedy by Accident

Pierre Sundborg

CreateSpace Independent Publishing Platform,
a DBA of On-Demand Publishing, LLC
North Charleston, SC. Made in USA

This book was printed and is distributed by the CreateSpace Independent Publishing Platform. It is available for sale on Amazon.com and through traditional bookseller channels. Almost all text is set in the CGTimes typeface, which I consider to be improved from Times New Roman by Compugraphic Design Studio. CGTimes is available and was purchased from Monotype.

The front cover photo, apparently the only color photograph of Lee Harvey Oswald while alive (there are color photos of him dead and of his remains when dug up years later), was taken in the Dallas City Jail in the middle of the night when he was charged with murdering President Kennedy. It was purchased from, and is shown through the courtesy of, the Dallas Municipal Archive and Records Center. Photos, maps, documents and other images within the book have adjacent endnote numbers pointing to sources, credits and copyrights in NOTES AND SOURCES at the back, just ahead of the INDEX.

CREDITS AND PERMISSIONS

The author is a retired engineer, writing my first and only book. Not an established historian, I have included 1,327 direct quotations from 188 different reputable sources. I intend to fully comply with all applicable copyright laws, and believe I have done so, seeking and, when asked, paying for permission to include pictures and quotations. Elevated numbers such as [1122] refer to the 3,481 same-numbered entries in NOTES AND SOURCES at the back. There you will learn whether I obtained explicit permission to use and/or quote, for some how much I was asked to pay and decided to do without, and in a few vexing cases where it was impossible to identify or find a copyright holder or receive any reply, a description of that attempt. I agreed to many contracts with copyright holders, some specifying maximum numbers of print copies. If more than those are required, I will inform and re-negotiate. Any infringement by me on any rights of others is entirely innocent and unintentional. If any claim copyright where I have not obtained their permission, please know that my three skilled and experienced researchers and I performed dedicated due diligence before I claimed fair use. I promise to act honorably and will respond if contacted at either address above.

GRATITUDE FOR TEAMWORK

No author is an island. As I wrote for four years, invisible friends were near my ear, quietly whispering. Some know of their contributions, most don't. I first look back more than seventy years to the roots of my love of English. I am indebted to my journalist-editor-author father George Sundborg who gave me respect for the language in genes and by example; then to dedicated world-class teachers, the Sisters of St. Ann;[A] followed by Juneau-Douglas High School's Minna Lee Coughlin, June Dennison, Viola Dunckley and Iris Kirkpatrick; finally to Caltech historian, inspiration and gentle friend Dr. Rodman Paul.

When I set to work after almost a half-century of thinking, the only author who had written meaningfully on the subject, James Reston, Jr., became a dependable resource and cheerleader. The gods of good fortune smiled again when I found Gina McNeely to research sources and obtain permissions (and bargain down some exorbitant price demands!) for the 278 pictures in this book. A true professional and personal delight, she also referred me to graphic designer Mark Drefs who cleaned up old photos and showed that a palimpsest didn't work on the back cover, and to editor Nan Siegel who inspired some of the words distilled there.

In Seattle where Jean and I live, fortune also gave me brother-in-law David Muerdter to expertly execute the cover design, then future lawyer Corey Dong to be my copyright agent to obtain permissions to quote, and intellectual property attorney Lauren Kingston to advise and assist with one difficult but essential source.

Saving the best for last, I lovingly note the assistance of Jean Louise Penrose Sundborg, my bride of 49 years, who heard my intent to write this even before we married, and has not only put up with stacks of books and years at the computer, but has listened as I wrestled with problems, always suggesting and encouraging in her gentle way. Jean helped toward the end, promising that four months of indexing (Yuck!) would eventually end; she was right (Yay!).

Some authors write many books. I have only this one in me. It's the best work of my life, I am proud of it, and very happy to be finished. As the book goes off to the printer, you may be interested to know that in addition to almost fifty years of thinking and researching followed by fifty months of dedicated writing and obtaining necessary permissions, I have also spent $61,471 out of pocket — before purchasing 294 copies to give to family and friends.

Adding my special author-publisher's price from the printer, that works out to be over $225 that I have paid for the one copy you hold. If and when you are finished with your book, please consider donating it to a favorite library. If the public buy any copies, I may receive some offsetting royalties, but will then have to renegotiate and pay more to many sources from whom I've purchased limited-quantity rights to photos and quotations. Oh well, there's always something! Jean and I are comfortable with the expenditure of time and money, and we hope you will find this result to be worthy of your interest.

Pierre Sundborg, Seattle, Feb. 29, 2016

[A] All from Quebec, they learned English as a second language, which I believe gave them a greater command of the rules and spellings, which they enforced with rulers rapped on knuckles. Ouch!

CONTENTS

EVIDENCE

VERDICT

APPENDIXES

PREFACE

> "The mind stretched by a new idea
> never returns to its original shape."
> — **Ralph Waldo Emerson** [1]

CHRISTMAS WAS THE BUSY SEASON at Alaska Music Supply in Juneau. The weekly steamship from Seattle had offloaded its cargo, so I picked up guitars and TVs at the dock, then went to the post office for boxes of records and music books that had come on the same ship, but more cheaply. With them were two heavy cartons for me from my parents in Washington, D.C.

Dad, George Sundborg, administrative assistant to Senator Ernest Gruening of Alaska, knew of my interest in the *Warren Report* printed three months earlier on September 27, 1964. He easily chose and paid $86 for an excellent Christmas present, the twenty-six Government Printing Office books titled *Hearings Before the President's Commission on the Assassination of President Kennedy*, published on November 23. [2] [B]   That evening, I eagerly opened the boxes in my bachelor's pad in the basement of the Governor's Mansion. [C] Entirely at random, I pulled out volume XIX and soon it was open, also at random, to page 713, filled with a photo of a handwritten letter, blandly captioned "FOLSOM EXHIBIT NO. 1—Continued (p. 65)".

The letter from "Lee H. Oswald" to "Sectretary [D] of the Navy John B. Connally Jr." had been mentioned in the *Warren Report*, but that night I read it fully in its original form and was amazed. Connally had been wounded by an Oswald bullet in Dallas in November 1963. Until that night near Christmas 1964, I assumed as did almost everyone that Texas Governor John Connally was only an innocent victim of Oswald's shooting at Kennedy. But there in the letter pleading for Connally's help to improve his undesirable discharge from the Marine Corps, Oswald wrote: "I shall employ all means to right this gross mistake or injustice to a boni-fied U.S. citizen and ex-service man. The U.S. government has no charges or complaints against me. I ask you to look into this case and take the necessary steps to repair the damage done to me and my family." [3]

Delving back into the *Warren Report*, I found those words, [4] evaluated in the opinion of the head of the U.S. Secret Service. [5] Chief Rowley noted "Oswald's demonstrated hostility toward the Secretary of the Navy in his letter of January 30, 1962", testifying that under new rules, that clear threat "would have resulted in the referral of Oswald to the Secret Service." [6] Despite that, the *Report* included a Warren Commission conclusion: "Even with the advantage of hindsight, this letter does not appear to express or imply Oswald's 'determination to use a means, other than legal or peaceful, to satisfy [his] grievance'". [7]

That disdain was at odds with my reading of Oswald's words, a threat to take action if his discharge was not revised; so back into the *Warren Report* where it dealt with Oswald and

---

[B] Only 1500 sets were printed. Most are in libraries and universities, few are privately owned.
[C] That's another good story, but not for this book, which will be long even without enticing digressions.
[D] Oswald was a great reader but a miserable speller; no attempt will be made to correct what he wrote.

Connally, where I found this in an earlier *Report* section: [E] "Connally's connection with the discharge, although indirect, caused the Commission to consider whether he might have been Oswald's real target. In that connection, it should be noted that Marina Oswald testified ... that she thought her husband 'was shooting at Connally rather than President Kennedy.' In support of her conclusion Mrs. Oswald noted her husband's undesirable discharge and that she could not think of any reason why Oswald would want to kill President Kennedy." [8]

That seemed to be reasonable, but the *Report* countered that Oswald waited to fire until his bullets would have to go through Kennedy to hit Connally, and if Oswald had truly wanted to shoot Connally, he would have done so a minute earlier, as their limousine approached him. Was that true? [F] I dug into volumes of the *Hearings* to read what Chief Rowley and Marina had testified, and quickly realized that the Commission had it wrong. My belief then in late 1964 and 51 years later in 2016 is that Oswald's intended target was Connally, and as usual with almost everything throughout his life, inept Oswald messed up and killed the wrong man!

For most of my life I expected to read that, written by some scholar; but despite a few false starts — there's a chapter for them: 21 – OTHERS ON THIS TRAIL — there has never been a complete, definitive statement of a reality that seems obvious. I long held the thought that I should write it if nobody else does, but many appealing things got in the way: [G] I met, loved and married Jean Penrose, then also married IBM for thirty wonderful years. This subject was always in the back of my mind, being tested and refined. After retiring and checking off many "bucket list" items, I spent much of 2011 browsing my library of several hundred books about Kennedy, Connally and Oswald, and at year-end decided it was my duty and pleasure to begin full-time work writing this. It has turned out to be a big project resulting in a big book. As another writer wryly noted: "When I start out, I don't know if it's a short piece or a long piece. After three or four years, it becomes obvious that it's a long piece." [9]

In 2013, the 50-year anniversary of the Dallas event, I feared a tsunami of Kennedy assassination books. There was a trickle. September brought the first book squarely on the mark, by skilled historian and author James Reston, Jr. He had written that Oswald meant to kill Connally in his 1989 biography of Connally and in an excerpt in *TIME* magazine. *The Accidental Victim: JFK, Lee Harvey Oswald, and the Real Target in Dallas* was perfectly on target, but of somewhat limited caliber. With large type on small pages, it rephrased the 1989 expositions. Described in chapter 21, Reston's book did not make best-seller lists and seems to have disappeared without a ripple. His effort was noble; the subject deserves another try.

Rational people have thought long and hard about the matter, but can't answer a simple question: "Why did Oswald want to kill Kennedy?" The answer is that he had no such intent, and that's why there is no answer — it's the wrong question.

Oswald is dead, and with him died what we want to know: "What were you thinking?" Although I concede in advance that there is no absolute proof of this book's conclusions, one may take comfort from a wise observation by Norman Mailer: "If half the pieces in a jigsaw puzzle are missing, the likelihood is that something can still be put together. Despite its gaps, the picture may be more or less visible. Even if most of the pieces are gone, a loose mosaic

---

[E] This author, as did the Commission, finds that telling this story sometimes requires going A-C-B-D.

[F] Jumping way ahead: The most conclusive proof that what Oswald wanted was a shot at Connally is the mighty array of evidence near the end of this book, in chapters 18 through 20.

[G] John Lennon famously noted: "Life is what happens while you're making other plans."

can be arranged of isolated elements. The possibility of the real picture being glimpsed under such circumstances is small but not altogether lost. It is just that one would like to know if the few pieces left belong to the same set." [10] In this case, as you will see, all the pieces fit.

More than seventy years ago, Francis Wilson ended the preface of his book about John Wilkes Booth subtitled "Fact and Fiction of Lincoln's Assassination" with these words:

> "Much has been written to prove and to disprove this [disinformation], and, as is common with most celebrated cases, much fable has grown up around the Lincoln-Booth tragedy. Simple presentation of the facts, the proofs and warranted inferences should be sufficient to dispel all doubt as to the true story of this exceedingly dramatic event, perhaps the most dramatic in all American history, and, at the same time, clear it completely of any suggestion of fiction." [11]

Replace "Lincoln-Booth" with "Kennedy-Oswald" and you have this author's earnest ambition for the book you hold. That having been said, there is a problem:

In 2003 as I drove my Dad, then 90, to California for his final visit with many cousins, I mentioned that I was still thinking of writing this book. He asked me to restate for him — it had been decades since I had first told him — my belief and the facts on which it was based. When I had finished after about an hour, the trained journalist, newspaper editor and published author asked for a few minutes to reflect. Then he said very carefully: "Well, son, what you say makes sense, and certainly better sense than I have ever heard about the JFK assassination. I believe you have reasoned it out correctly, and I am so proud that my first son seems to be the first person in the world to have done so. If you have the ambition to write what you have just said to me, then you have an obligation and must do so. But, do that only for your own satisfaction. I must assure you that the world does not want to know; it's just too terrible to think that our wonderful President Kennedy was killed by accident. Nobody wants to hear that! So, I would encourage you to put it all down on paper, especially if you feel a sense of duty to do so, but I warn you, do not expect anyone to thank you. That will be the reality."

He was correct. I have gone ahead because of my sense of duty, and will be entirely satisfied to finish this writing, then buy and send copies to family and friends. And, I must admit it has been a pleasure to work through this for four solid years, six days a week, and find that it all seems to hold together, at least to me. My Caltech education in science likens this to a tested hypothesis that has passed all tests, so therefore is probably correct.

To conclude, I make the same pledge as was written by Arthur Schlesinger, Jr., in the Foreword to his 1960 campaign-season book *Kennedy or Nixon: Does it make any difference?* "I do not pretend impartiality in this matter. But I will rest my argument whenever possible on hard and verifiable facts; and my way, I hope, will be the way of reasoned analysis, and not of appeal to prejudice or emotion." [12]

"I carry my thoughts with me for a long time, often for a very long time before writing them down. I change many things, discard others, and try again and again until I am satisfied; then, in my head, I begin to elaborate the work and its breadth, its narrowness, its height, its depth, and because I am aware of what I want to do, the underlying idea never deserts me."

— **Ludwig van Beethoven** [13]

READER'S GUIDE

> "This book was OK, but it told me more about
> penguins than I really wanted to know!"
> — **Young lady's book report**

THIS IS A LARGE, COMPREHENSIVE BOOK. You may prefer to begin by skimming, perhaps to decide whether it's really worth reading. To assist, here are brief pointers to the highlights among its 405,780 words. (On average, each of the seven full-size Harry Potter books contained 157,143 words.[14]) Cut to the bone, here are recommendations of what to consider, with what I think most revelatory first:

1. Chapter 22 – A TRAGIC REALITY summarizes the key evidence and conclusions.

2. Chapter 20 – OBSTRUCTION OF BEST EVIDENCE relates amazing direct evidence, known for years only to a few students in Texas, and now by all who will read this chapter.

3. Chapter 19 – THE SHOT NOT TAKEN has the foremost piece of circumstantial evidence.

4. Chapter 18 – CONNALLY WILL RIDE argues strongly as to intent, from Lee Oswald's delay in acting, and the facts that he did not have his pistol or a full clip of bullets.

5. Oswald's pleading-but-threatening letter to John Connally, on pages 88 and 89.

6. Chapters 4 – MINSK and 5 – MISFIT display the multitude of Marine Corps and Navy documents deciding and affirming the hated change of his discharge to Undesirable.

7. Chapters 15 – REGARDING KENNEDY and 16 – REGARDING CONNALLY reveal, from everything he ever said, his attitudes about the two men in the limousine in Dallas.

8. Chapter 14 – TOO CLOSE TO CALL demonstrates that result does not illuminate intent.

9. Chapter 17 – POLITICAL PROCLIVITY, explains that the man who provably shot at a hated far-right-wing conservative was not also prone to shoot a like-himself liberal.

10. Every chapter ends with a brief summarizing box. The book's important points are summarized in those twenty-two boxes.

If you think I'm an isolated nut, please look to respectable persons with the same idea on pages 566, 583 and 591. At minimum, I hope you will come to doubt the "common knowledge" that Oswald must have intended to assassinate Kennedy because that's what he accomplished. No, for the reason that James Reston, Jr. titled his path-breaking book *The Accidental Victim*, Kennedy did not die of deliberate intent, but through inadvertence. In accidentally killing our President, as throughout his life, Oswald was an inept failure. That is our tragic truth.

> Key points of this guide:
> **Chapters 1 – 13 present a foundation of events and facts for the**
> **Chapters 14 – 22 evidence, analysis and tragic conclusion.**

MOTHER

1939 October 18 — 1956 October 24

> "[I]f you disagreed with her or if you expressed an opinion that she didn't agree with, then she would insist that you were wrong. ... [W]e get along very well, if one or the other don't say nothing. ... I am forgiving, but she is not. ... [I]t didn't seem like she could forget about anything."
> — **Marguerite's sister Lillian** [15]
>
> "[Lee] had to contend with her. She was so strong-minded on every point, no matter how large or how small. She was right and everybody else was wrong. I think she was the most influential individual in his life."
> — **Marguerite's son Robert** [16]

WHAT WAS LEE HARVEY OSWALD'S INTENT on November 22, 1963? The purpose of this book is to answer that question, rationally and supportably. For readers too young to have lived through the events of that time, and for others to refresh what they once knew about the death by shooting of John F. Kennedy, the first seven chapters are a condensed chronology of EVENTS. Then six chapters will perform ANALYSIS, followed by another seven considering the EVIDENCE to reach a fully-informed, sensible and defensible VERDICT in the final two chapters.

For those troubled by a basic question, "Did he do it?", EVENTS and the first two chapters of ANALYSIS should answer a certain "yes!" But most have known that for years, and still are uncomfortable. Their discomfort is probably rooted in the simple question, "Why?". Why did Oswald kill our President? [A] His motive was a mystery to the Warren Commission in 1964, and it remains just as much a mystery more than half a century later — but only if one believes he intended to shoot Kennedy.

This book's goal is to find Oswald's motive, to go inside his mind there on the sixth floor of the Texas School Book Depository as he waited for the motorcade to come around the

---

[A] Style manuals and linguists are divided on capitalizing "president". Chief Justice Warren's secretary, Mrs. McHugh, sent a typed note "**The President was shot** ..." into a closed conference of the Supreme Court justices. This book will also capitalize "President" when it refers to Kennedy.

corner into his 4-power sight. This book intends to offer a reasoned, sound and documented understanding of the troubling question: What did he think he was doing? To answer, we have to understand his mind, and that journey must begin with his mother.

There are two villains in this story, one who fired the rifle and one who taught him to demand undeserved respect. Lee Harvey Oswald's perverted sense of justice was nourished by Marguerite Claverie Oswald's example. Until he became a Marine at 17, she was the only formative influence on his life and development. Marguerite is primarily responsible for the unusual character of Lee, the strange views he adopted, and the terrible vengeance he sought.

As happened to me, other writers came to despise her. William Manchester in *The Death of a President*: "Marguerite Oswald often saw herself as the target of nameless forces; she was a woman of many resentments and felt them all keenly. [S]he was highly vocal on status and money, each of which she coveted and lacked." [17] Norman Mailer in *Oswald's Tale: An American Mystery*: "Marguerite has taken sufficient blame, scorn, and ridicule from other people (including the barely concealed animus of the Warren Commission) [B] that there is no need to depict her in one more unfavorable light—it seems certain at the least that every malformation, or just about, of Lee Harvey Oswald's character had its roots in her." [18]

Fifty-plus years have produced no compilation more complete or valuable than 1964's *Report of the President's Commission on the Assassination of President John F. Kennedy*, familiarly known as the *Warren Report*. Among its treasures is Appendix XIII, "Biography of Lee Harvey Oswald". Those 72 pages provide a well-documented foundation for this book's EVENTS in chapters 1 – 5. Endnotes in this book are referenced by superscript numbers in the text; e.g. [267] means that note 267 in NOTES AND SOURCES documents the material's source. With the *Warren Report*'s biography as base, here is the sad story of Marguerite and her sons.

Briefing Marguerite's background and Lee's 17 years under her influence require all of the next eleven pages. Questioning her, Warren Commissioner Hale Boggs pleaded: "Suppose you just make it very brief." Characteristically, she shot back: "I cannot make it brief. I will say I am unable to make it brief. This is my life and my son's life going down in history." [19]

Marguerite Francis Claverie [20] was born in New Orleans on July 19, 1907,[21] into a family of French and German extraction.[22] Her mother died a few years later, leaving six children in the care of their father, a streetcar conductor.[23] Marguerite describes herself as "a child of one parent", "one of the most popular young ladies in the [grammar] school", and her childhood as a "very full happy" one.[24] Her older sister, Mrs. Lillian Claverie Murret, who will play her part in 1963 when Lee moves to New Orleans, remembers Marguerite as "a very pretty child, a very beautiful girl." [25] They were poor but, Lillian said, a "happy family . . .[C] singing all the time." [26] Marguerite had only one year of high school [27] — as will her third child, Lee. Shortly before she was 17, she went to work as a receptionist for a law firm in New Orleans.[28]

Jean Stafford noted in her insightful *A Mother in History*: "To begin with, the record of Mrs. Oswald's matrimonial misfortunes shoots off at a forty-five degree angle from the norm." [29]

[B] Rounded (parentheses) are in the source, whereas [square brackets] indicate a change by this author.
[C] When a source omits, their . . . or * * * is shown. This author omits with ... in quoted material.

There will be three brief marriages. In 1929 at age 22, she married a shipping clerk,[30] Edward John Pic, Jr.[31] The marriage was not a success; in two years they separated.[32] Marguerite was then 3 months pregnant; she told her family that Pic did not want any children and refused to support her.[33] Fortunately for us, Pic was able to speak for himself thirty-three years later; he alone of three husbands was alive. Marguerite's sister Lillian, testifying to the Warren Commission, dropped the nugget that her husband Dutz Murret regularly saw Pic on the New Orleans wharves.[34] The next day, first husband Eddie Pic appeared before the Commission in New Orleans and explained himself to assistant counsel Albert E. Jenner, Jr.:

> "Mr. JENNER. I must confess candidly that up until yesterday I was under the impression that you were deceased, or at least no one knew where you were, and then a witness whom I examined yesterday told me, to my surprise, that you were very much alive.
>
> Mr. PIC. I certainly am." [35]

After questions about Pic's life and situation, and establishing the facts of the 1929 marriage:

> "Mr. JENNER. Now, at a point in your marriage to the then Mrs. Pic, who is now Mrs. Oswald, there was a time when you didn't get along; is that right?
>
> Mr. PIC. Yes.
>
> Mr. JENNER. ... Just tell me in your own words what difficulty you had with her.
>
> Mr. PIC. Well, we just couldn't put two and two together and make it come out four. ...
>
> Mr. JENNER. You just figure you were two persons who couldn't jell; is that just about a fair statement of your situation at that time?
>
> Mr. PIC. That's right. We couldn't make it. We just couldn't get along, you know, so we finally decided to quit trying and call the whole thing off; which we did." [36]

A boy was born on January 17, 1932, whom Marguerite named John Edward Pic.[37] All her sons will receive their fathers' names or (as here) permutations. Edward John Pic contributed to his son John Edward's support for 18 years.[38] Eddie Pic (the father) probably learned of Marguerite's charge that he had abandoned her because he didn't want children, so two months later he augmented his Warren Commission testimony with a written affidavit, including:

> "Marguerite's pregnancy with my son John Edward Pic was not the cause of our separation. I had no objection to children. It was a coincidence that about that time we had reached the point that we could not make a go with each other any more. Our separation which was amicable and which was arranged through an attorney would have taken place irrespective of Marguerite's pregnancy with my son John Edward Pic." [39]

Marguerite saw a great deal of Robert Edward Lee Oswald, an insurance premium collector [40] known to most as "Lee" [41]. He also had been married but also had separated.[42] In 1933, both Marguerite and Robert divorced [43] and they married.[44] Marguerite has described her marriage to Oswald as "the only happy part" of her life.[45] A son born on April 7, 1934, was named Robert Edward Lee Oswald, Jr.[D] after his father.[46] In 1938, the Oswalds purchased a small house [47] in what John thought was "a rather nice neighborhood," [48] New Orleans' Ninth Ward, to be ravaged by Hurricane Katrina in 2005.[49]

On August 19, 1939, a year after the Oswalds bought the house, sister Lillian recalls: "Mr. Oswald was cutting the grass, I think, and he took a severe pain in his arm, and she gave him some aspirin, and in the meantime she called the doctor, and he said that was the right thing to do,

---

[D] He was "Junior" for five years, but did not need or use that appellative suffix after "Senior" died.

to give him aspirin and to rub his arm, so then it seemed like he got worse, and while she was calling the doctor to come out, he just toppled over." [50] Robert Oswald died suddenly of a heart attack. [51] Two months later, on October 18, 1939, his second son was born, [52] and also named for his father, but because "Robert" had been assigned to the older son, he was "Lee". "Harvey" was the maiden name of his father's mother. [53] Lee would not normally use the middle name during his life; Ruth Paine, the English-speaker who knew him best in his final year told the Warren Commission: "I knew he had a middle name, but only because I filled out forms in Parkland Hospital. It was never used with him." [54] For some reason, criminals seem to be identified in full, so most came to know him as "Lee Harvey Oswald".

For a while after her husband's death, Marguerite did not work, probably living on his life insurance proceeds. [55] In 1940, she rented out their house, [56] moved herself and Lee into a rented house, but placed the two older boys in the Infant Jesus College Home, [57] a Catholic boarding school. [58] Boys and mother disliked this arrangement, [59] which John thought was done to save money. [60] John would testify: "Robert and I ... we hated the place. ... [U]s not being Catholics they lowered the boom on us." [61] In less than a year the two older boys returned to their mother and little brother. [62]

The photo of Lee, [63] marked "Age 2", was taken in 1941. Robert said that John, then he, had worn the same "baby suit". [64] When Marguerite purchased another house [65] in the

Ninth Ward, [66] she opened "Oswald's Notion Shop" [67] in the front room, selling "candy, needles, thread, ribbon and other sewing materials", [68] but it failed to make money [69] and she sold the house. [70] She applied to the Evangelical Lutheran Bethlehem Orphan Asylum Association for admission of her two older sons to their orphan asylum, the Bethlehem Children's Home. Her application stated she could contribute $20 per month to their maintenance and would supply shoes and clothing. [71] John told the Warren Commission: "[S]he constantly reminded us we were orphans, that she didn't have the money to support us ..." [72] She inquired also about Lee, but he was too young to be admitted. [73] John and Robert were accepted and entered the home in January 1942. [74] [E]

Mrs. Oswald moved to an apartment [75] and returned to work as a telephone operator. [76] She left Lee much of this time with her sister Lillian Murret, his aunt, who thought him a good looking, friendly child, but could not devote a great deal of attention to him because she had five children of her own. [77] Lee was next watched for several weeks by a woman who lived in the same house as the Oswalds, [78] but she said Lee was a bad, unmanageable child who threw his toy gun at her. [79] Marguerite Oswald "said a two-year-old baby couldn't be that bad." [80] Soon after the incident, she and Lee moved again, [81] this time to live close to the Murrets. [82]

Aunt Lil cared for Lee several more months. Near his third birthday, Marguerite again inquired about putting him into the orphanage, [83] perhaps because a disagreement with her sister made it impossible to leave him with the Murrets any longer. [84] One day after Christmas in 1942, Marguerite turned over her youngest, Lee, then 3, to the Bethlehem Children's Home. [85] She agreed to contribute $10 per month and to supply shoes and clothing, as for the other boys. [86] Lee was to remain in the home about 13 months. [87] Oldest step-brother John ruefully

---

[E] For younger readers, a reminder of the time: The U.S. entered World War II in December 1941.

recalled for the Warren Commission: "At Bethlehem they had a ruling that if you had a younger brother of sister there and they had bowel movements in their pants the older brother would clean them up, and they would yank me out of classes in school to go do this and, of course, this peeved me very much ..."[88] Aside from that, John and Robert have pleasant memories of the home,[89] which apparently gave the children a good deal of freedom.[90] Mrs. Oswald visited them regularly and they occasionally visited her.[91]

In 1943, Marguerite met Edwin A. Ekdahl, an electrical engineer older than herself who was then working in the New Orleans area.[92] They saw each other often, and by January 1944, had decided to marry.[93] She withdrew Lee from the Children's Home[94] and moved to Dallas, where Ekdahl expected to be located.[95] They planned to postpone the wedding to the end of the school year so the older boys could complete their year at the home.[96] In the meantime, she would care for Ekdahl,[97] who was recovering from a serious illness, probably a heart attack.[98] Mrs. Oswald decided when she arrived in Dallas that she did not want to marry Ekdahl after all.[99] Using proceeds from selling the New Orleans house,[100] she purchased a house in Dallas,[101] a portion of which she rented out.[102] In June, John and Robert left the Children's Home and joined their mother and Lee in Dallas.[103]

Ekdahl visited on weekends.[104] By 1945 she resolved her doubts about marrying him, influenced in part by his substantial income.[105] Explaining that she expected to travel a great deal, Marguerite tried unsuccessfully to return the older boys to the home in February 1945.[106] She and Ekdahl married in May 1945,[107] then lived together in Dallas.[108] The photo[109] is of their wedding day. Lee was 5½. Ekdahl got along well with the boys, on whom he lavished much attention.[110] John testified the step-father treated them as if they were his own children and that Lee seemed to find in Ekdahl "the father he never had"; John recalled that on one occasion he told Lee that Ekdahl and his mother had reconciled after a separation, and that "this seemed to really elate Lee, this made him really happy that they were getting back together."[111]

In September 1945,[F] John and Robert were put into a military academy in Mississippi,[112] where they will remain for three years.[113] Mrs. Myrtle Evans, who had known both Marguerite and Ekdahl before their marriage,[114] testified that Marguerite insisted on keeping Lee with her. Mrs. Evans thought Marguerite was "too close" to Lee and "spoiled him to death," which hurt her marriage.[115] With John and Robert away at school, the Ekdahls moved to Benbrook, a Fort Worth suburb.[116] All of Lee's schooling will be erratic and chaotic. This began with first grade in Benbrook after Marguerite falsely stated his birth date as July 9, 1939, which would make him 6, presumably to meet the usual "6 by September 1" requirement for first-grade entrants.[117]

Robert wrote of Lee's early experience with firearms: "The first time John and I came home from military school for a visit we brought our wooden practice rifles. They didn't fire, but we were taught how to hold them. At home we taught Lee how to hold a rifle and how to follow commands. He had a fine time, right-facing and left-facing and marching around with my rifle. ... Later, when we learned to shoot, we passed along our knowledge to Lee."[118]

[F] The war had ended in August when thousands died from A-bombs, bad enough, but it was not the millions who would have died if the U.S. and its allies had to invade and fight across Japan.

The Ekdahls' marriage broke down within a year. She suspected him of infidelity,[119] thought him stingy [120] and they argued frequently.[121] In summer 1946 she left Ekdahl, took John (14½) and Robert (12) out of the military academy, and moved to Covington, La.[122] G It is revealing to consider Robert's testimony to the Warren Commission in 1964. When he stated conservative political views and 100% respect for the U.S. Constitution and laws,[123] Commission member Representative Gerald R. Ford, to become President in ten years, asked: "Did you say that was your mother's philosophy, too?" Robert replied: "[M]y mother didn't actually bring me up too much. The orphan home and the military academy, and I believe there my basic philosophy was formulated. It was a very good school." [124]

Lee's record at Benbrook had been satisfactory, but he had not completed first grade, so he now started for a second time in September, enrolling in the Covington school.[125] But, he was withdrawn from that school in January 1947 [126] when the Ekdahls reconciled and moved to Fort Worth.[127] He enrolled in his third school, his third first grade, which he completed in May 1947.[128] In the fall, he entered the second grade, but relations between his parents deteriorated again and he was withdrawn before any scholastic grades were recorded.[129]

The Ekdahls, now in Fort Worth, continued to argue. According to eldest son John, "they would have a fight about every other day and he would leave and come back." [130] Robert reports: "Mother often nagged Mr. Ekdahl until he began to spend more and more time away from home." [131] When Earl Warren invited Marguerite to tell the story of her life, she chose to begin with 1½ pages of fine-print testimony about how she had cleverly obtained proof that Ekdahl was having an affair. At a time when he was supposed to be out of town,[132] she went with John and his friends to an apartment in Fort Worth; one of the boys posed as a telegram carrier, shouting "Telegram for Mrs. Clary". When the door opened, Marguerite pushed her way into the woman's apartment "and Mrs. Clary had on a negligee, and my husband had his sleeves rolled up and his tie off sitting on a sofa, and he said, 'Marguerite, you have everything wrong ... Listen to me.' I said, 'I don't want to hear one thing. I have seen everything I want to see, this is it.'" [133] H

Despite her confirmed suspicions, Marguerite lived with Ekdahl until January 1948,[134] when she "directed . . . [him] I to leave the home immediately and never to return".[135] He left and filed suit for divorce.[136] His complaint alleged that Marguerite constantly nagged, argued, accused him of infidelity, threw things at him, and finally ordered him out of the house; that these acts were unprovoked by Ekdahl's conduct toward her; that her acts endangered his already impaired health; and that her "excesses, harsh and cruel treatment and outrages" toward him made it impossible to live together.[137] She denied all these allegations.[138]

Now comes one of those coincidences that inspire conspiracy theorists. To represent her in the divorce proceedings, Marguerite hired Fort Worth attorney Fred Korth. Fourteen years later, Navy Secretary John Connally will resign to run for governor of Texas. Lyndon Johnson will recommend one of his supporters to be the replacement, and on January 4, 1962, President Kennedy will appoint Fort Worthian Fred Korth to the position. Shortly after that, in a miracle of timing, Lee Oswald in Minsk will mail an appeal to Connally for help

---

G This is the way we used to abbreviate state names, before the Post Office chose all-caps, such as LA.

H That last isn't important to this book's subject, but it's here so you can amaze your friends by stating, then proving, that there's a negligee in the *Warren Report*. Endnote [133] tells you where to read it.

I Words I inserted to replace several words or otherwise simplify quotations are in [square brackets].

upgrading his discharge from the Marines. Connally will forward Oswald's letter to Secretary of the Navy Fred Korth, who was Lee's mother's divorce attorney. There's really nothing devious or profound here — sometimes, quite simply, "It's a small world after all!"

John testified at the trial, and he later recalled that Lee was called to the stand but was excused without testifying "being he was under age." [139] The jury found that Marguerite was "guilty of excesses, cruel treatment, or outrages" unprovoked by Ekdahl's conduct. [140] In June, the court granted the divorce, and at her request, restored her former name, Marguerite C. (for Claverie) Oswald. [141] After three husbands, Marguerite will now have years of hardship and struggle that will embitter and age her into an unhappy old woman before her time. Good brother Robert reflected that: "The divorce was a blow to Lee. It meant the end of the only father-son relationship he would ever know." [142]

Marguerite moved to a house "right slap next to the railroad tracks." [143] Robert said: "it seemed prisonlike to John and me. [John] said it meant we were 'back down in the lower class.'" [144] Lee moved to yet another new school, his fourth, and completed the second grade. [145] Mrs. Oswald then purchased a small house in Benbrook [146] with a single bedroom in which Lee slept with his mother, and a screened porch where John and Robert slept. [147] "After all, Lee was the son she really cared about. The baby of the family. The one who slept in the same bed with her until he was eleven." [148] (There will be testimony about this on page 8.) Marguerite left the boys home alone while she worked at a department store in Fort Worth. [149]

"Lee was apparently Marguerite's favorite. In any dispute among the boys, she always sided with Lee." [150] According to an FBI report for the Warren Commission, "One night [a neighbor] was in the living room of the Oswald home talking to Mrs. Oswald ... Lee Oswald, the youngest boy, came running through the kitchen door and was chasing John Pic, his older brother. Lee Oswald had a long butcher knife in his hand and he threw the knife at John Pic but missed him, and it hit the wall. Mrs. Oswald only made the remark that 'they have these little scuffles all the time and don't worry about it.'" [151] Lee will seriously alienate his brother John because of a knife in a few years.

"John and Robert felt like strangers to Marguerite, as if she did not know them very well and as if they, too, were unaccustomed to her. ... But their alienation went deeper. They had left home at the ages of six and eight and, apart from one interruption, they had been away for eight years. Exposed to values vastly different from hers, they had adopted them and acquired a detachment that was to protect them from her and her claims. By the time they came home, they were lost to Marguerite forever." [152] That will not be the case for Lee.

As 1948's summer ended, Marguerite sold the Benbrook house. [153] The family returned to Fort Worth to facilitate Marguerite's, and now John's, employment. [154] She bought a house from which Robert and Lee walked to school. [155] John, 16, wanted to finish high school, but she advised him to leave school and work as a department store shoe stockboy to help support the family. [156] He gave her $15 per week from his $25 salary. [157]

Lee entered third grade [158] and, at last, was in one school an entire year, earning A's in social studies, citizenship, science, art, and music, but a D in spelling. [159] He transferred to a different school in 1949, where he remained three years. [160] His record there is not remarkable in any respect, mostly B's and C's, [161] with D's in spelling and arithmetic. He had C's for Spanish, [162] which may account for his rudimentary familiarity with that language in 1963. [163] His IQ was recorded as average, 103; on achievement tests in three years, he twice did best in reading and twice did worst in spelling. [164] This will be his life-long pattern; Lee will never learn to spell reliably, but will always be an avid reader. He was generally characterized as an unexceptional but rather solitary boy during these years. A fourth grade teacher described him as a lonely boy, quiet and shy, who did not easily form friendships with other students.[165] As his mother worked in a variety of jobs,[166] he returned home alone after school.[167] Lee's relationship with his brothers was good but limited by their difference in ages.[168] A neighbor thought Lee was an intelligent child, who picked things up easily, but regarded him as "a bad kid," who was "quick to anger" and "mean when he was angry, just ornery." [169]

John Pic, the eldest, joined the Marine Corps Reserve in October 1948; "my mother thought it would be a real good way to supplement the income ..." [170] He was only 16, but she "signed an affidavit saying that he was born ... a year earlier that his actual birth," [171] so John falsely "was 17." [172] He returned to high school in January 1949, while working part time and also attending reserve drills.[173] Shortly before he would graduate from high school, he enlisted in the Coast Guard "because it was the hardest service to get into." [174]

John's departure in 1950 meant a major change for Lee.[175] Robert wrote in 1967:
"In recent years I have read statements by psychiatrists and other experts who say that Lee may have suffered psychological damage because he shared a bed with his mother until [then]. I can't make any expert judgment about that, but I do know that Lee shared a double bed with Mother in the Benbrook house and, later, when we moved into Fort Worth. When John left for the Coast Guard in January, 1950, a few months after Lee's tenth birthday, Lee moved into John's bed. At the time, I didn't attach any particular importance to the sleeping arrangements. We were always short of space, and it seemed perfectly logical to me that John and I would share one bedroom and Mother and Lee the other. If this had a bad effect on Lee, I'm sure Mother didn't realize it. She was simply making use of all the space she had." [176]

John was asked, fourteen years later, to sum up for the Warren Commission:
"Mr. JENNER. Did you live in an atmosphere in which your mother directly or indirectly indicated to you that she thought she had been unfairly dealt with in her life?
Mr. PIC. Yes, sir.
Mr. JENNER. You had that very definite impression?
Mr. PIC. Yes, sir. ... I did not have this impression. She related this to me, sir. I didn't feel she had it any tougher than a lot of people walking around.
Mr. JENNER. That is what I am getting at, this was an impression she was seeking to create.
Mr. PIC. That is right, sir.
Mr. JENNER. You felt she did not have it any tougher. She was creating an impression that did not square with the facts?
Mr. PIC. Yes, sir. Every time she met anyone she would remind them she was a widow with three children.
Mr. JENNER. Do you have an opinion also as to whether this atmosphere in which Lee lived had an effect upon him and his personality?
Mr. PIC. I am sure it did, sir. Also, Lee slept with my mother until I joined the service in 1950. This would make him approximately 10, well, almost 11 years old.
Mr. JENNER. When you say slept with, you mean in the same bed?
Mr. PIC. In the same bed, sir.
Mr. JENNER. As far as you know or say when Lee came and stayed with you a short while in 1952 did he likewise sleep with your mother?
Mr. PIC. No, sir; he did not.
Mr. JENNER. He had reached a measure of independence by that time?
Mr. PIC. Well, when I left and went into the service there was a vacant bed in the house." [177]

The middle son, Robert Oswald, left school soon after John's departure, to work full time, contributing most of his earnings to support the family.[178] After a year, he returned to high school in 1951, completed his junior year, and joined the U.S. Marine Corps in July 1952.[179] The Warren Commission will ask him: "Were you unhappy with the manner and fashion of life that you had led up to that moment?" He replied: "Not in the manner or fashion, sir. I objected quite strongly to the apparent efforts of our mother to control me completely in all respects." [180] Thus far, two sons have abruptly hastened into the military without completing high school. As she had lied to get too-young Lee into first grade, Marguerite has done again to enlist John in the Coast Guard. This will all repeat for her youngest, Lee, in a few years.

In August 1952, Marguerite and Lee went to New York City, where John lived with his young wife and baby in her mother's apartment.[181] The "visit" began well, but when it became obvious that Marguerite intended to stay, the atmosphere changed. She quarreled frequently with Mrs. John Pic.[182] There was difficulty about not contributing anything toward her own and Lee's support.[183] Marge Pic liked Lee and would be glad to have him alone stay with them, but felt his mother set Lee against her.[184] The visit ended when Lee threatened Marge with a pocket knife during a quarrel over TV watching.[185] Eleven years later, FBI agents wrote: "Mrs. Pic stated that after the incident wherein Lee Harvey Oswald threatened her with the knife, she told Mrs. Oswald to either get out of the apartment or she would have her brothers come and have her thrown out and this precipitated further immediate bitterness during which Mrs. Oswald threatened to jump out of a window." [186]

Marguerite, ever the querulous contrarian, had an entirely different explanation for the Warren Commission: "My daughter-in-law was very upset. ... She didn't like me and she didn't like Lee. ... We were not wanted, sir, from the very beginning. ... So she hit Lee. So Lee had the knife ... in his hand. He was whittling, because John Edward whittled ships and taught Lee to whittle ships. ... So when she attacked the child, he had the knife in hand. So she made the statement to my son that we had to leave, that Lee tried to use a knife on her." [187]

John told the Warren Commission how Lee's knife threat changed the relationship between the brothers: "When Lee visited us in New York he came there a friendly, nice easy-to-like kid." [188] "[P]rior to this particular incident, I would consider us the best of friends as far as older brother - younger brother relationship. My wife always says that he idolized me and thought quite a bit of me. ... [A]fter I approached Lee about this incident his feelings toward me became hostile and thereafter remained indifferent to me and never again was I able to communicate with him in any way. ... Personally, I didn't know if he was more hostile towards me or my wife. I still don't know this fact." [189] "Lee did not speak another word to John for ten years" [190] until good brother Robert brought them together for Thanksgiving.

Marguerite and Lee moved uptown to a one-room basement apartment in The Bronx.[191] She began a series of low-paying jobs in department stores and ladies wear shops.[192] Lee was enrolled in the seventh grade of a junior high in the Bronx [193] until January 1953.[194] Of his 64 schooldays there, he was present only 15 full and 2 half days.[195] He received failing grades in most courses.[196]   [197]

In January they moved again within the Bronx,[198] where Lee's truancy increased. He was now in the area of PS (Public School) 44 but refused to go to school there.[199] An attendance officer located Lee at the Bronx Zoo and testified that Lee was clean and well dressed, but was surly and referred to the officer as a "damned Yankee." [200] Several truancy hearings were held [201] and it was decided to commence judicial proceedings if his truancy continued. [202] In February, the Pics visited. John testified that his mother told him about Lee's truancy and asked how she could get Lee to accept psychiatric aid. Nothing came of these discussions. [203]

In March, an attendance officer filed a petition in court alleging that Lee had been "excessively absent from school," he had refused to register at or attend school, and he was "beyond the control of his mother insofar as school attendance is concerned." [204] Marguerite went to court alone and informed the judge that Lee refused to appear in court. [205] Evidently impressed by the proceedings, Lee registered at PS 44, [206] but the judge declared him a truant, and remanded him to three weeks of confinement in the New York City Youth House [207] for psychiatric observation. [208] This is the first of four incarcerations during Lee's short, troubled life. The next will be seven weeks in a Marine brig in Japan, then an overnight in the New Orleans jail, and finally the weekend of death in Dallas.

Lee was tested, then he and Marguerite were interviewed by a probation officer and a staff social worker. [209] Dr. Renatus Hartogs, M.D., PH.D., Chief Psychiatrist of Youth House, carefully examined Lee and wrote a considerable report, summarizing:

> "This 13 year old well built boy has superior mental resources and functions only slightly below his capacity level in spite of chronic truancy from school which brought him into Youth House. No finding of neurological impairment or psychotic mental changes could be made. Lee has to be diagnosed as 'personality pattern disturbance with schizoid features and passive—aggressive tendencies.' Lee has to be seen as an emotionally, quite disturbed youngster who suffers under the impact of really existing emotional isolation and deprivation, lack of affection, absence of family life and rejection by a self involved and conflicted mother." [210]

Judging that evidence and the testimony he heard, Earl Warren summarized clearly in layman's terms: Lee was "a seriously detached, withdrawn youngster—detached from the world because no one in it had ever met any of his needs for love. He admitted to fantasies about being powerful and sometimes hurting and killing people ..." [211]

Dr. Hartogs continued to be active in psychiatry, and in 1965 wrote his book *The Two Assassins*, assessing the natures and causes of the abnormalities of both Lee Oswald and Jack Ruby (actually, both were murderers, not assassins) with this relevant re-evaluation:

> "Nine years and seven months before Lee Harvey Oswald assassinated President Kennedy, he sat in my office at Youth House, detention home for New York City's juvenile delinquents. ...
>
> I would describe Lee Harvey Oswald at the time I saw him as being potentially explosive. I suggested that he receive psychiatric treatment so that his inner violence—what might be called his silent rage—would not later erupt and cause harm. I handed in my recommendation, hoping it would be carried out. I gave little, if any, further thought to the fate of Lee Harvey Oswald until November 22, 1963." [212]

Psychiatrist Hartogs in 1953 recommended probation and help from a child guidance clinic, with his mother being urged to get help from a family agency. [213] The judge released Lee on parole for out-patient treatment, [214] but agencies turned down his case because of full loads and the intensive treatment likely required. [215] Lee attended school the few remaining seventh-grade weeks, completing with low but passing marks. [216]

"During his time in New York, Lee had apparently also become interested in politics. He later claimed that his involvement with Marxism had begun with a pamphlet protesting the execution of Julius and Ethel Rosenberg for wartime espionage. This pamphlet, printed by the

Communist Party, was handed to him by an old woman on a New York street corner." [217] Perhaps the direction that piece of paper gave his life is what influenced Lee, ten years later, to hand out Marxist pamphlets on the streets of New Orleans — and again wind up in custody.

The disdain of sons for mother was demonstrated in September when the Coast Guard transferred John Pic and family from New York to Portsmouth, Virginia. John said "I did not make known to my mother our whereabouts or our address." [218]

Also that September, Lee entered eighth grade at PS 44. [219] When his parole was about to end, Marguerite told the probation officer there was no need for her to appear in court, since Lee was attending school regularly and was now well adjusted. [220] The parole was extended until the school submitted a progress report, [221] which was highly unfavorable. Although Lee was in school regularly, his conduct was unsatisfactory; teachers reported that he refused to salute the flag, did little work, and seemed to spend most of his time "sailing paper planes around the room." [222] The judge extended parole. [223] Lee received passing grades in most subjects in the first marking period, but his report also contains notations by his teachers that he was "quick-tempered", "constantly losing control", and "getting into battles with others." [224] Lee appeared in court in November 1953 — ten years before he will die. Despite Mrs. Oswald's request that he be discharged, the judge stated his belief that Lee needed treatment and continued his parole until late January. [225]

On January 4, 1954, a caseworker visited their home [226] and was told that continued counseling was unnecessary. Marguerite declared her intention to return to New Orleans and was advised to obtain Lee's release from the court before leaving. [227] In the next two days, she was again instructed by the probation office and by the caseworker not to take Lee out of their jurisdiction without the court's consent. [228] Through all these contacts, Mrs. Oswald showed reluctance to bring Lee into court, probably prompted by fear that he would be retained in custody as he had been for three weeks. [229] Without further communication to the court, "they left ... either on the fifth or the seventh of January 1954" [230] and returned to New Orleans. [231] Learning this, the court dismissed the case [232] and that ends the unhappy New York episode.

In New Orleans, Lee and his mother stayed briefly with her sister and husband, the Murrets. [233] Lee completed the eighth grade [234] without any apparent difficulty. [235] He entered ninth grade in September and again received mediocre but acceptable marks. [236] In the photo [237] of his ninth grade classroom at Beauregard Junior High School, Lee is the "wise guy" in the back row who acts up and pays little attention. At the end of the school year in June 1955, he filled out a "personal history": Subjects he liked best were civics, science, and mathematics; least liked were English and art. His vocational preferences were listed as biology and mechanical drawing; plans after high school, however, were "military service" and "undecided." In response to the question whether he had "any close friends in this school," he wrote, "no." [238]

Those who knew Lee in New Orleans remember a quiet, solitary boy who made few friends. [239] He seems to have had few contacts. He read a lot, starting at some point to read Communist literature found at the public library. [240] Except in his relations with his mother, he was not unusually argumentative or belligerent, but he seems not to have avoided fights if they came; they did come fairly frequently, perhaps in part because of his aloofness and the traces of a northern accent in his speech.[241]   Friends of Mrs. Oswald thought that he was demanding and insolent toward her and that she had no control over him.[242]

Marguerite worked at two shoe stores.[243]   At one she was a cashier and salesclerk,[244] and Lee worked part-time about ten weeks in 1955.[245]   On the "personal history" he filled out in school, he claimed he had been a "retail shoesaleman";[246]   but his employer said they had tried with no success to train him as a salesman, and that he had in fact been a stockboy.[247]

Leaving the Murret house, Marguerite and Lee had moved to an apartment owned by Myrtle Evans,[248] who had known them ten years before. Relations between the women became strained,[249] so in the spring of 1955 the Oswalds moved to a French Quarter apartment.[250] During the summer of 1955, Robert left the Marine Corps, spent a week with his mother and Lee in New Orleans, then settled in Fort Worth, Texas.[251]   That seemingly inconsequential choice by the older brother is what will attract Lee, seven years in the future after his time in Minsk, to Fort Worth and Dallas rather than New Orleans, with tragic consequences.

Within a month of entering the 10th grade,[252] Lee presented to the school a note written by himself to which he had signed his mother's name. Dated October 7, 1955, it read:[J]

```
"To whom it may concern,
     Becaus we are moving to San Diego in the middle of this month Lee
must quit school now.  Also, please send by him any papers such as his
birth certificate that you may have.  Thank you.
                              Sincirely
                         Mrs. M. Oswald"
```
[253]

He dropped out of school shortly before his 16th birthday,[254] anxious to get away from home, as had both older brothers. Rather than John's Coast Guard, Lee chose Robert's Marine Corps. Robert testified: "He was very proud of my service record and it would so indicate that I conducted myself in the best tradition of the United States Marine Corps; not that I was any lily white, but I was never in any serious trouble and I progressed in rank ... I feel very surely that the reason that Lee joined the [Marines] was because of my service ... and he wanted ... to follow in my footsteps, in that same service ..."[255]   But, there was the problem that the Marines required enlistees to be at least 17. Marguerite supported his early departure from being her dependent, and helped by forging an alteration to his birth certificate.[256]

A few days after turning 16, he tried to enlist, using his mother's false evidence that he was 17.[257]   (Lee had entered first grade a year early,[K] and John Pic had joined the Marine Corps Reserve by means of his mother's false affidavit that he was 17.)[258]   Lee's attempt failed, and, according to his mother's testimony, he then: "read Robert's Marine manual back and forth. He knew it by heart. ... In fact, he would take the book and have me question some of the things. ... I even said, 'Boy, you are going to be a general, if you ever get in the Marines.'"[259]   The dropout worked the rest of the school year as a messenger boy for a shipping company, then briefly as an office boy, finally as messenger for a dental laboratory.[260] His military record subsequently showed his account of prior civilian jobs as follows:

"Performed various clerical duties such as distributing mail, delivering messages & answering telephone. Helped file records & operated ditto, letter opening & sealing machines."[261]

[J] This book provides Oswald with a virtual typewriter because of his hard-to-decipher penmanship.

[K] Your author began in second grade because first grade had one student more than it had desks!

Marguerite anticipated that Lee would join the Marines as soon as he was 17, thus leaving her alone. So, she moved them in July 1956 to Fort Worth because older son "Robert was raised in Texas, and has his girl friends and all his friends in Texas. So when Robert got out of the Marines, he wanted to live in Texas" [262] — thus so did his mother. In September, Lee enrolled in the 10th grade at Arlington Heights High School [263] but attended classes only a few weeks. He dropped out of school on September 28. [264] His erratic attendance at a dozen schools was at an end; he had achieved only the completion of grade 9.

Five days later, he wrote to the Socialist Party of America:

```
                                         "October 3, 1956
Dear Sirs;
    I am sixteen years of age and would like more information about your
youth League,  I would like to know if there is a branch in my area,
how to join, ect.,  I am a Marxist, and have been studying socialist
principles for well over fifteen months I am very interested in your
Y.P.S.L.

                                    Sincerely
                                    /s/  Lee Oswald" [265]
```

Accompanying the letter he mailed an advertisement coupon, on which he had checked the box requesting information about the Socialist Party. [266]

When Lee turned seventeen, he immediately enlisted in the Marine Corps — and this will be important — for six years: three years of active duty followed by three years in the reserve. On October 24, 1956, he took a bus to Dallas, passed his physical exam, was sworn in, then flew to San Diego. Robert would write: "When he left, I think Mother felt relieved. She knew he would be fed and clothed. I would be leaving her in November [to marry girlfriend Vada], then she would have only herself to worry about. Lee was more than relieved. On his own for the first time, he was looking forward to an adventure." [267] Lee later explained his leaving Marguerite at the youngest possible age, having completed only one year of high school: "My brothers left home as soon as they could. So did I. And that was fine with her." [268] Lee's step-brother John spoke to the Warren Commission for all three boys:

"Mr. PIC. Of course, I knew he would do it as soon as he reached the age.

Mr. JENNER. Why did you know he would do it and tell us the circumstances upon which you, the facts upon which you base that observation?

Mr. PIC. He did it for the same reasons that I did it and Robert did it, I assume, to get from out and under.

Mr. JENNER. Out and under what?

Mr. PIC. The yoke of oppression from my mother." [269]

Nearing the end of his testimony, John was questioned about Marguerite's communications:

"Mr. JENNER. That is about enough. Did your mother write you a letter that had good news in it?

Mr. PIC. I never recall one, sir.

…

Mr. JENNER. I haven't found a single letter yet, Sergeant, in which your mother fails to mention the subject of money.

Mr. PIC. You may find a Christmas card, 'Love, Mother,' sir.

Mr. JENNER. A letter?

Mr. PIC. No, sir; I don't think you will." [270]

••• ••• •••

A thoughtful summation of these formative years was offered by Lee's good, caring brother Robert in 1997, when interviewed by Michael Leahy of the *Arkansas Democrat-Gazette*:

> "Robert still thinks history has missed the brother whom he knew, the one bereft of a father and mistreated by a mother, a blank slate that got filled in with the wrong things. ... 'If you don't know what Lee missed, you don't know the key part of the story.' What he missed was Robert Oswald Sr., who died of a heart attack in 1939 at the age of 43, two months before Lee was born. A life-insurance salesman, the senior Oswald typically finished his days by sitting with Robert on the porch of their small house in New Orleans. Robert's older half-brother, John ... would join them, happy to have a devoted stepfather. ... 'I had 5½ wonderful years with Father and I had memories; Lee had zero time, OK?' he says, repeating the figures — *five, zero.* 'I don't think we'd be having this conversation if Father [had lived] and Lee had had him around. ... We all know that lots of people do OK with just one parent, one good, loving parent. ... But let's just say we had a situation that was different.' The 'situation' was their mother, Marguerite. ... The day after Christmas in 1942, Marguerite Oswald turned over her youngest son, Lee, then 3, to Bethlehem Orphanage Home. Lee lived at the orphanage for more than a year, sleeping at night on a small bed alongside Robert's in a large room crowded with other children. Five years older, Robert served as his baby brother's protector along with John ... 'John was my rock,' [Robert] recalls, 'and we were Lee's.' In the years that followed, something went terribly wrong with Lee." [271]

••• ••• •••

As he leaves home and mother, take note of these shapers of the character of Lee Oswald:

- He had not been influenced by any significant male presence. His father died before he was born. His older brothers were banished to orphanages, children's homes and a military academy. A much older step-father entered when Lee was 5½ and departed when he was 8. So, he grew up without learning, from men, how to be a man.

- Instead of constancy, he knew continual and frequent change. As he left school to enlist in the Marine Corps, according to Bill O'Reilly and Martin Dugard in their *Killing Kennedy*, he had lived at twenty-two different addresses and attended twelve different schools. [272] Lee had neither roots nor friends for when he would need them — absolutely none.

- He knew rejection rather than inclusion. John remembered: "[S]he constantly reminded us we were orphans, that she didn't have the money to support us ...". [273] Robert reflected: "[I]n the orphan home ... you get a sense of rejection. I did. I'm sure he did." [274]

- He learned to prevaricate and aggrandize, traits he would use attempting to appear what he is not. The teenage stockboy styled himself a "retail shoesaleman". In the last year of his life, he will make himself the "president" of a non-existent group in New Orleans.

- He learned from Marguerite to omit and augment, whichever was needed, to get anything not achievable with truth. She forged false birthdates to get him into school, then a dozen years later in a failed attempt to get him into the Marines before he was eligible. While young, he wrote notes and signed her name. Older, he will invent false identities.

- "He lied pointlessly, to no purpose and all the time, even when he had nothing to hide. Marina says Lee told three kinds of lies. One was *vranyo*, a wild, Russian, cock-and-bull lying that has a certain imaginative joy to it; another was lying out of secretiveness; and still another was lying out of calculation, because he had something to hide. Lying claimed much of Lee's energy and complicated his life a great deal." [275]

- Lee saw and learned from Marguerite that one must not forget or forgive an argument, lack of respect, imagined wrong or grudge. Her sister Lillian testified that "it didn't seem like she could forget about anything." [276] Lil's educated, articulate daughter Marilyn testified that aunt Marguerite "had a very curt tongue, and she doesn't forget very easily." [277]

- The complete rupture by Lee of his previously warm relationship with brother John after the New York TV-wife-knife incident, with Lee shunning John from 1952 through 1962, shows the extreme to which Lee held and extended a grudge built upon a thin foundation, as will be the case when he appeals to John Connally for help and does not receive it.

- Robert wrote: "Mother always detected hidden motives in people's behavior and suspected people of carrying on secret activities. She loved mystery, and I saw this trait reflected in Lee—just as he reflected her feeling that the world should recognize her as somebody special and important." [278]

- John and Robert matured into responsible men, whereas Lee was habitually undependable. Robert ("I have never been in any serious trouble in my life." [279]) knew the difference: The older boys were brought up more by the orphanage and military school, where they learned the solid values Lee was deprived of. Marguerite, his only model and touchstone, was primarily responsible for his turning out so differently from his upright brothers.

- "Again and again, faced by a choice between what was unhealthy and what was healthy for her son emotionally, Marguerite reached for the unhealthy. ... Lee did not have a single antisocial impulse to which she did not ... one way or another, lend her sanction." [280]

- At the time of the assassination, Jim Bishop deftly summarized her bad karma: "Years ago she had married three times and had three sons. One of the husbands died. The others left her. The sons enlisted in military services early. None of them ever came back." [281]

- Marina testified: "It seemed peculiar to me and [I] didn't want to believe it but he did not love his mother, she was not quite a normal woman. Now, I know this for sure." [282]

- A wise old immigrant from Russia, Peter Paul Gregory, was asked, "After you met Mrs. Marguerite Oswald, and had a chance to observe her, did that further your judgment of Lee Harvey Oswald in any way?" He responded, "Yes, sir. I felt that ... many of his peculiarities possibly were brought on by the influence of his mother. She impressed me as being not necessarily rational. She is quite clever, but certainly is most peculiar." [283]

- Mother and son Lee "also shared an uncanny constellation of emotions which had its outcropping in an extraordinary congruity of behavior. Feeling, as they did, that 'the world owed them a living,' they both carried around with them a prickliness, a miraculous capacity for ingratitude." [284]

- Taken altogether, the sad truth was that the only person near him was Marguerite, and it was from her narrow, egocentric, petulant, quarrelsome, narcissistic personality that he developed his own. She taught her Lee to expect more than he really was owed, and to demand respect where he deserved none. Because of that, he will kill, and be killed.

> Key point of this chapter:
> **The original villain, Marguerite Oswald, the greatest influence on son Lee, brought him up to demand undeserved respect.**

MARINE

1956 October 24 — 1959 September 11

> "Lee was in the Marine Corps, Lee was
> very happy to be in the Marine Corps,
> Lee was proud to be in the Marine Corps.
> Lee loved the Marine Corps."
> — **Lee's brother John Pic**[285]

YOU MAY CHOOSE TO SKIP THIS CHAPTER. Oswald was a lousy marine, learned little, was convicted in two courts martial, worked to get out early — and this was the proudest chapter of his life! When he applies for early discharge to care for his "wounded" mother, the Marine Corps will be relieved to see the last of him. Chapter 11 – FAILURE lists his significant lifetime successes and failures. You may skim that to quickly learn of Oswald the Marine.

If you read this chapter, your reward will be knowing the reasons for his two courts martial, his proficiency on the rifle ranges, and about how the boy-man practiced the traits he'd learned from his only significant adult model, his mother. For three years he will be in close company where others will observe and testify; where milestones will be meticulously recorded into military archives for our examination.[286]

On October 26, 1956, Lee Harvey Oswald reported to the Marine Corps Recruit Depot in San Diego.[287] He was 68 inches tall, weighed 135 pounds, had no physical defects.[288] On a series of aptitude tests, he scored significantly above the Marine Corps average in reading and vocabulary and significantly below average in arithmetic and pattern analysis. His composite score was 105, 2 points below the Corps average.[289] He stated a preference for duty in Aircraft Maintenance and Repair, for which he was recommended.[290]

Oswald was trained in use of the M-1 rifle.[291] He fired for record on December 21 and scored 212, 2 points into "sharpshooter" on a scale of marksman, sharpshooter, expert.[292] Later, he practiced with a .45-caliber pistol but no scores were recorded.[293] He was given his first ratings, the highest possible being 5.0: 4.4 in both conduct and proficiency. A minimum average of 4.0 will be required for an honorable discharge.[294]

On January 18, 1957, he reported to Camp Pendleton, California, for 5 more weeks of training.[295] A fellow recruit said Lee was generally unpopular and his company was avoided by the other men.[296] When his squad was given short leaves, he separated and spent his time alone.[297] At the end of this training he was rated 4.2 in conduct and 4.0 in proficiency.[298]

On March 18, he reported to the Naval Air Technical Training Center in Jacksonville, Florida,[299] to attend Aviation Fundamental School for 6 weeks of basic instruction in radar theory, map reading, and air traffic control procedures.[300] This course and the next in Biloxi required him to deal with confidential material.[301] He was granted clearance to "confidential" level "after careful check of local records had disclosed no derogatory data."[302] On May 1 he was promoted to private, first class (PFC), his highest Marine position.[303] On completing the course, he ranked poorly, 46th of the 54 students,[304] while receiving the highest ratings he will ever attain: 4.7 in conduct and 4.5 in proficiency.[305]

Oswald then went to Keesler Air Force Base in Biloxi, Mississippi,[306] for an Aircraft Control and Warning Operator Course with instruction in aircraft surveillance and the use of radar.[307] A senior marine in charge of his group[308] remembered Lee as "a somewhat younger individual, less matured than the other boys ... normally outside the particular group of marines that were in this attachment,"[309] with the nickname "Ozzie Rabbit."[310] He generally stayed to himself, often reading, did not play cards or work out in the gym with the others.[311] He finished 7th in a class of 30[312] and was assigned an MOS (military occupational specialty) of Aviation Electronics Operator.[313] His ratings were 4.2 in conduct and 4.5 in proficiency.[314]

On July 9, he reported at the Marine Corps Air Station at El Toro, California,[315] where his photo[316] was taken. Six weeks later, he departed for Japan,[317] arriving at Yokosuka on September 12.[318] He was assigned to Marine Air Control Squadron No. 1 (MACS-1) at the Atsugi Naval Air Station, 20 miles west of Tokyo.[319] The function of MACS-1[320] was to use its radar to direct aircraft.[321] The squadron also watched for incoming foreign aircraft, such as straying Russian or Chinese planes, so they could be intercepted by American planes.[322] Tensions were high there, as in most of the world of 1957.

Lee was a radar operator, scanning air traffic around the Atsugi field. Most was routine, with one major exception. He saw on the runway a strange unmarked black jet with long droopy wings that took off, reared back and shot almost straight up, out of sight[323] and beyond even radar's reach.[324]

The U-2 spy plane was designed to take high-resolution photos of military installations and important sites in hostile countries. It could fly at altitudes above 70,000 feet, above the reach of Soviet weapons of the time. NAF Atsugi was the U-2 base for the Pacific, from which they spied on China, Korea and Russia's Siberia. "The U-2 program was Top Secret and more, but it was no secret to the marines in Oswald's unit. They saw the planes, they tracked them, and they even communicated with them."[325] Despite rumors, the U.S. would not acknowledge having such a plane. Oswald knew of it in 1957, knowledge that he expected should be of great value to him in Moscow in 1959, to be described in the next chapter.

On October 27, when he opened his locker, a pistol fell to the floor and discharged. The .22 caliber bullet hit him above the left elbow.[326] Fellow marines found him sitting on the locker looking at his arm. Without emotion, Oswald said, "I believe I shot myself."[327] He was in the naval hospital at Yokosuka until November 15.[328]

The Judge Advocate General concluded that Oswald had "displayed a certain degree of carelessness or negligence" by storing a loaded revolver in his locker, but that "does not of itself constitute misconduct."[329] He was, however, charged with possession of an unregistered privately-owned weapon in violation of general orders. At court-martial he was found guilty and sentenced "To be confined at hard labor for 20 days, to forfeit $25.00 per month for two months and to be reduced to the grade of private."[330] The confinement was suspended. If he stayed out of trouble for 6 months, that part of the penalty would be cancelled.[331]

Some in his unit suspected Oswald had injured himself purposely to avoid the next deployment,[332] but if so, it didn't work — immediately upon his release from hospital, MACS-1 sailed to the Philippine Islands for maneuvers[333] and to be near during a political crisis in Indonesia. The squadron debarked at Subic Bay and set up a temporary radar installation.[334] While there, Oswald passed a test of eligibility for the rank of corporal.[335] In a semiannual evaluation, he was given his lowest ratings thus far: 4.0 in conduct and below-minimum 3.9 in proficiency.[336] The photo[337] was taken as the unit waited to sail back to Japan; Lee is nearest the camera.

Oswald biographer Priscilla Johnson McMillan writes:

"While Lee was stationed in the Philippines, a second curious episode occurred. Private First Class Martin E. Schrand was found shot to death one night while on guard duty outside a hangar that could have been sheltering a U-2. Lee knew Schrand well. They had been part of a small group of men who started radar training in Jacksonville the year before, and had been together most of the time since. A Marine Corps investigation in 1958 established that Schrand's death was accidental and self-inflicted, and yet a rumor arose among the men that Lee Oswald was responsible.

The rumor is notable for two reasons. Lee had considered himself a Marxist for two years. And at Subic Bay he had become sympathetic to what he called 'Communist elements' among the Filipinos. Afterwards, speculation arose that Lee wanted to break into the hangar and learn something about the U-2 so that he could use the information later on. Although the speculation appears to be groundless, the rumor is still notable as a measure of Lee's unpopularity among his fellow Marines."[338]

The rumors, reported to and considered by the Warren Commission, are probably wrong. This author tends to agree with McMillan: Lee didn't do it, but he was surely disliked.

Oswald was court-martialed a second time, for the offense of using "provoking words" to a sergeant at the Bluebird Cafe in Yamato, then assaulting that noncommissioned officer by pouring a drink on him.[339] Mates suspected Lee acted in revenge; the sergeant had assigned him to mess duty rather than radar monitoring.[340] The findings were that Private Oswald spilled the drink accidentally, but when the sergeant shoved him away, Oswald invited him outside in insulting language.[341] Oswald was sentenced to forfeit $55 and to be confined at hard labor for 28 days.[342] His previously suspended 20-day sentence for possessing the pistol was reinstituted,[343] so he spent 48 days in the brig,[344] June 27 to August 13, standing at rigid attention most of the time.[345] His qualification for corporal was voided.[346] "[H]is request for extended overseas duty was denied."[347] He was given terrible ratings: 1.9 in conduct and 3.4 in proficiency.[348] This nadir was probably when Lee decided to escape from problems in the United States to promise in the Union of Soviet Socialist Republics.

When Communist Chinese on the mainland began firing at insignificant offshore islands Quemoy and Matsu defended by Nationalists from Formosa, Oswald's unit sailed to the South China Sea, camped at Ping Tung, Taiwan,[A] then returned to Atsugi.[349] In October, he was transferred out of MACS-1 and put on general duty in anticipation of return to the United States.[350] His last oversea ratings were 4.0 in both conduct and proficiency.[351] Lee was regarded by his fellows overseas as an intelligent person who followed orders, did his work well, but complained frequently.[352] One testified that Oswald could speak "a little Russian" while he was overseas,[353] the first mention of that interest or ability. He sailed from Yokosuka on November 2, arrived in San Francisco 13 days later,[354] then took 30 days' leave.[355]

In December 1958, he was assigned to Marine Air Control Squadron No. 9 (MACS-9) at the Marine Corps Air Station at El Toro, where he had been before going overseas.[356] The aircraft surveillance [357] work gave him access to classified call signs and radio frequencies, which will be changed after his defection to Russia.[358] The officer in command of the radar crew, Lt. John E. Donovan, found him "competent in all functions," and observed that he handled himself calmly and well in emergency situations.[359] Donovan thought Oswald was not a leader but that he performed competently.[360]

This estimate was generally shared by his fellows. Most thought that he performed his assigned duties adequately but was deficient in disciplinary matters and such things as barracks inspection.[361] Oswald's Quonset mates complained and secured his transfer to another hut.[362] He was thought to be intelligent, somewhat better educated and more intellectually oriented than others on the base.[363] A few thought it more accurate to describe him as someone who wanted to appear intelligent.[364] He had a pronounced interest in world affairs, in which he appears to have been better informed than some of the officers, whose lack of knowledge amused and irritated him; he evidently enjoyed drawing others, especially officers, into conversations in which he could display his own superior knowledge.[365]

It seems clear from the recollections of those who knew him at El Toro that by the time Oswald arrived back in the United States, he no longer had any spirit for the Marines; the attitudes that had prompted his enlistment were entirely gone, and his attention had pivoted from the Marines to Russia. Priscilla Johnson McMillan, who will interview Lee in Moscow in a year, then later write the indispensable biography *Marina and Lee*, says he now arrived at his decision: "He made up his mind that he would go to the U.S.S.R."[366]

Most of the marines were aware that he had begun studying Russian [367] in Japan,[368] probably after his horrific seven-weeks locked in the brig after the second court martial.[369] He told a date who also studied Russian "that he had 'taught himself' by listening to Radio Moscow."[370] While at El Toro, he subscribed to a Russia-connected newspaper.[371] He had studied Russian enough by February 1959 to request a foreign language qualification test; his rating was "poor".[372] We know of his life-long inability to spell, so it seems likely he was probably better at listening and speaking than on paper.

[A] The main island was named Ilha Formosa (beautiful island) when discovered by Portuguese in 1544.

Many told anecdotes suggesting he desired to publicize his liking for things Russian, sometimes in good humor and sometimes seriously. Some called him "Oswaldskovich," to his pleasure.[373] He wrote his name in Russian on one of his jackets;[374] played records of Russian songs;[375] made remarks in Russian,[376] used expressions like "da" or "nyet";[377] and was pleased to be addressed as "Comrade".[378] Priscilla Johnson McMillan thought: "It was the behavior, one would guess, not of a spy but of a slightly egregious schoolboy hungry for attention." [379]

Oswald's inclinations must be viewed in context of 1959. In January the Soviets flew a Lunik satellite past the Moon and into orbit around the Sun, bragging that hapless American rocket failures proved the balance of power had shifted in their favor. In July, Vice President Richard Nixon and Soviet Premier Nikita Khrushchev clashed in "The Kitchen Debate" at an exhibition in Moscow. In October, Russia proudly showed the world photos of the back side of the Moon. The U.S. had little to show for the year except new states Alaska and Hawaii.

Connected with Lee's Russophilia was an interest in and acceptance of Russian political views and, to a lesser extent, Communist ideology, which led him into serious discussions at El Toro.[380] Lieutenant Donovan, a graduate of the School of Foreign Service of Georgetown University,[381] thought Oswald was "truly interested in international affairs" [382] and "very well versed, at least on the superficial facts of a given foreign situation." [383] He said Oswald had a particular interest in Latin America,[384] a good deal of information about Cuba in particular.[385] Oswald expressed sympathy for Castro.[386] Donovan believed that Oswald subscribed to the Russian newspaper—which Donovan thought was a Communist newspaper—not only in order to read Russian but also because he thought it "presented a very different and perhaps equally just side of the international affairs in comparison with the United States newspapers." [387]

Private Oswald may have been more open with a fellow private, who corroborates Lt. Donovan's testimony but thought Lee definitely believed that "the Marxist morality was the most rational morality to follow" and communism, "the best system in the world." [388] He described Oswald as "idle in his admiration for communism",[389] and attributed the decision to go to Russia to a growing disillusionment with the United States, especially its role in the Far East, and a conviction that communism would eventually prevail.[390]

Oswald enjoyed trying to speak Spanish with Nelson Delgado, an El Toro marine who spoke it fluently.[391] Delgado regarded him as a "complete believer that our way of government was not quite right." [392] Their discussions were concerned more with Cuba than Russia.[393] Shortly before, on January 1, 1959, Fidel Castro's revolution had succeeded in replacing the corrupt American-backed Batista government of Cuba. The two marines favored the Castro government and talked about joining the Cuban Army ... and perhaps leading expeditions to other Caribbean islands to "free them too." [394]

The Warren Commission wanted to know about Oswald's interests in Cuba and Russia, so called Delgado to testify in April 1964, by which time he had left the Marines to join the Army to be a "messhall first cook".[395] He didn't have much to tell about the conversations mentioned above, but when the questioning turned to attitude, this spilled out:

"Mr. DELGADO. He was basically a man that complained quite frequently.

Mr. LIEBELER. Do you think he complained more than the other Marines?

Mr. DELGADO. Well, yes; a little bit more. Anything, anything that they told him to do, he found a way to argue it to a point where both him and the man giving him the order both got disgusted and mad at each other, and while the rest of us were working, he's arguing with the man in charge. For him there was always another way of doing things, an easier way for him to get something done.

Mr. LIEBELER. He didn't take too well to orders that were given to him?

Mr. DELGADO. No; he didn't. ... I would say, 'Oz, how about taking care of the bathroom today?' Fine, he would do it. But as far as somebody from the outside saying, 'All right, Oswald, I want you to take and police up that area.' — 'Why? Why do I have to do it? Why are you always telling me to do it?' Well, it was an order, he actually had to do it, but he didn't understand it like that." [396]

Then the discussion turned to what Delgado had seen Oswald do next to him on the firing range, and that will be told where it will be most useful, in Chapter 13 – THE SHOOTER.

Lee's interest in Russia and ideological attachment to theoretical communism apparently dominated his stay at El Toro. His reading acquired direction; books like *Das Kapital* by Karl Marx, the father of Marxism, and Orwell's *Animal Farm* and *1984* were mentioned to the Warren Commission.[397] Playing chess,[398] he chose red pieces, preferring the "Red Army." [399]

For a short time, he played on the squadron football team,[400] but was not very good; he lacked team spirit and often tried to call the plays, which was not his job.[401] In January 1959, Oswald was given his semiannual ratings, scoring 4.0 in both conduct and proficiency.[402] On March 1, he was promoted back to the rank of private, first class.[403] Having dropped out of the 10th grade in Texas, he took high-school-level general educational development (GED) tests and received an overall rating of "satisfactory." [404]

In March 1959, Lee applied to Albert Schweitzer College in Switzerland for admission in 1960.[405] Schweitzer is a small school specializing in religion, ethics, science and literature. He claimed a proficiency in Russian equal to one year of schooling [406] and falsely said he had completed high school by correspondence with an average of 85 percent.[407] He claimed special interests in philosophy, psychology, ideology, football, baseball, tennis, stamp-collecting; plus writing short stories as his vocational interest.[408] He listed Jack London, Charles Darwin and Norman Vincent Peale as favorite authors.[409] He claimed membership in the YMCA and the "A.Y.H. Association", and said he had participated in a "student body movement in school" for the control of juvenile delinquency.[410] Most of that was complete garbage! On the basis of these representations, his application was approved.[411] He then sent a registration fee of $25, saying he was "looking forward to a fine stay." [412] He never made any actual move to attend, and his mother's later attempt to retrieve the $25 was denied.

In May, Oswald's ability with an M-1 rifle was tested for the second and last time in his Marine career. Firing 200 rounds, he scored 191, barely into the "marksman" range. The Corps' head of records wrote to the Warren Commission: "The Marine Corps considers that any reasonable application of the instructions given to Marines should permit them to become qualified at least as a marksman. ... Consequently, a low marksman qualification indicates a rather poor 'shot' ..." [413] This will be explored in detail in Chapter 13 – THE SHOOTER.

On June 6, Lee wrote to brother Robert (we continue to provide a virtual typewriter):

`"Well, pretty soon I'll be getting out of the corp and I know what I`
`want to be and how I'm going to be it, which I guess is the most`
`important thing in life."` [414]

He was less than half-way through the six-year hitch for which he enlisted, and early for a normal December 8 transfer to reserves (3 years active duty plus the 48 days of confinement that does not count as service). It seems certain he had decided to go to the Soviet Union, but that would not inspire the Corps to release him early. He could not forge a letter as he'd done to leave the 10th grade, so he needed a good reason, and fortune had smiled in December 1958.

Mother Marguerite had been working in a department store. One day in the King Candy department, she reached for a box of candy on a high shelf, which fell onto her nose.[B] She saw several doctors but none thought her problem was serious until, she wrote, one "advised me to apply heat to the swollen area around an eye and at that time one-half cup of infection drained out. 'Everyone got scared' and realized that, although there was no fracture of the nose, I've not been well after all." [415] [C] She did not return to work, and that provided Lee the fortuitous opportunity he required. He could not let anyone know his intention to go from the Marines to Moscow, so he appealed to her, holding out a false offer of help, coaching with this letter she saved and gave to the Warren Commission:

```
"Dear Mother
     Recived your letter and was very unhappy to hear of your troubles,
I contacted the Red Cross on the base here , and told them about it.
They will send someone out to the house to see you, when they do please
tell them everything they want to know, as I am trying to secure an
Early (hardship) discharge, in order to help you. such a discharge is
only rarely given. but If they know you are unable to support yourself
than they will release me from the U.S.M.C. and I will be able to come
home and help you .  The Red Cross cannot give you funds of any kind
they can only give you me.  and only If you make to right impresstion
on them. only if they know you cannot and are not reciving help from
any other kin, and only if they know you are in dire need now!  please
the tell them I will be able to secure a good job, as this is
important, also send me the names of some actual business's that I may
write Them and get an acceptance letter.  This last point is not
required but it would help my case for a hardship discharge if and when
I bring it before my commanding office,  Just inform them I am your
have been your only source of income. Lee" 416
```

This author looks at the letter, especially the promises he underlined to help his poor dear injured mother, and sees Lee crassly using her to get an early discharge and be on his way to glorious Marxism in the Soviet Union, which is precisely what he did. Marguerite, as would most mothers, thought much better of her boy, and told the Warren Commission:

"This is the letter which shows the different character of the boy tha[n] the newspapers are making of him—when I wrote and told him I had sold my furniture, and that my compensation and medical was stopped, immediately my son sends a special delivery letter, and that is the letter 'received your letter, was very unhappy. I have contacted the Red Cross, and they will contact you.' This is a nice boy to do this immediately, when he finds his mother is in trouble. He is not a louse, like the papers have been making him out. He might have some bad points, but so do all of us." [417]

On August 17, Lee requested a Dependency Discharge on the ground that his mother needed his support,[418] attaching affidavits from Mrs. Oswald, an attorney, a doctor, and two of her friends.[419] "Marguerite, who in the past had supplied her sons with false documents so that

---

[B] Other reliable sources say it was "a can of candy" or "a large glass jar of candy". I choose to reflect Marguerite's sworn affidavit: "some boxes fell on my face". Some researcher with tolerance for ambiguity may wish to wrestle to the ground what it was that fell onto her nose.

[C] Reminiscent of the fine tombstone epitaph: "I TOLD YOU I WAS SICK!"

they could enter the service before they were of eligible age, now supplied documents attesting that she was disabled and unable to support herself." [420] She swore:

> "Due to an accident in December 1958 I have been unable to work because some boxes fell on my face, as I was reaching for them off a high shelf. I am not able to work a full day as I have much discomfort from my sinus, as they are completely congested at night and I must apply steam to drain them during the day. When my disability insurance was discontinued I sold all my furnishings of my home and have been living off that, but now these funds have exhausted." [421] She soon added: "... my furniture ... sold for less than $200 and during this time, my cocker spaniel dog had puppies which I sold for $55. This has helped me, but now my funds are exhausted and I have no income and am unemployable since I am under the care of two doctors and must go every day." [422]

Son Robert Oswald testified to the Warren Commission in 1964 that he

> "was aware that she did have an accident [423] ... I asked her about it, or she volunteered the information of how the accident occurred, and that she had been seeing doctors, and so forth. And I did recall her stating to me that she had been to either two or three doctors, and none of them had said anything was wrong with her, and then she was insisting that there was definitely something wrong, and she was continuing to see other doctors." [424]

In his book *Lee*, Robert was less generous in 1967:

> "Her nose looked all right to me, so I thought maybe she was exaggerating the seriousness of the injury in the hope of collecting money from the company that insured the Fair store against such claims." [425]

Unfortunately for Lee — and tragically for the United States — sensible Robert was not in California to advise his little brother. He did not know of the early discharge until Lee was in Fort Worth (very briefly, while secretly on his way to Moscow):[426]

> "Mr. JENNER. Was there any discussion between you at any time during that period of the reason, if any special reason, for his discharge from the Marine Corps, earlier than he might have been discharged in normal course, which as I understand would have been in December of that year?
>
> Mr. OSWALD. I believe, sir, we had a brief discussion on that.
>
> Mr. JENNER. Who initiated it?
>
> Mr. OSWALD. I feel certain like I did.
>
> Mr. JENNER. And what did you do? ... just tell us what you asked him.
>
> Mr. OSWALD. To the best of my memory, I asked him—because I was aware of ... his regular date of discharge ... why he was discharged or released earlier than that date. And his reply was that mother had written the Red Cross and requested that he be released earlier.[427] ... And I might add I pointed out to Lee why did you accept this early discharge, since he only had a few months more, I believe it was, to go. Because it had been my experience in the service that when I ran across somebody who, for one reason or another, was going to get out a little bit early, I understood that they perhaps were subject to recall for that period at a later date, or something along that line. And I thought it was unwise.
>
> Mr. JENNER. Is this what you said to him?
>
> Mr. OSWALD. Yes, sir. I pointed out ... that it would have been the wise thing to stay in." [428]

But that solid brotherly advice came after Lee was out and on his way to Russia, after he had already made the fateful decision to evade his remaining obligation to the Marine Corps Reserve. And, although Robert thought that Marguerite instigated the early discharge process, it had in fact been Lee's idea, as seen in his prodding letter to her on page 23.

The August 28 report of the 3rd Marine Aircraft Wing Hardship or Dependency Discharge Board found:

"a.   Private First Class Lee H. OSWALD, not married, on his initial three (3) year enlistment in the Marine Corps is obligated to serve on active duty until 7 December 1959.

b.   The Marine submitted his request for a dependency discharge in order that he may provide physical and financial assistance to his invalid mother residing in Fort Worth, Texas.

c.   The home situation of Private First Class OSWALD has been aggravated subsequent to his enlistment date through incapacitation of this mother as a result of an industrial accident. The mother is no longer gainfully employed due to her physical condition and has no source of income. The presence of her son, Private First Class OSWALD, is required for physical and financial assistance." [429]

After its findings, the Board ruled:

"In evaluation of all facts available, it is the opinion of the Board that Private First Class OSWALD meets the requirements of paragraph 10273 MCM for release from active duty." [430]

In a formidable coincidence of timing, just as Oswald was working to leave the Corps, the president made an appointment that will change the fortune of the luckless private, and inevitably, the history of the United States. It was in August 1959 that five lieutenant generals and four major generals learned that President Eisenhower had jumped David Monroe Shoup, junior to all of them, over their heads to become the new Commandant of the Marine Corps. [431] After congressional hearings, Shoup will take command on January 1, 1960. When Oswald's purpose in fleeing from the Marines becomes known, Shoup will be what President George W. Bush (#43) termed himself, "the decider". This is the character of the man:

A contemporary article sized him up: "The U.S. Marine Corps breathes fire, thrives on tradition, and rests on a solid throne of legends. One of its greatest legends is David Monroe Shoup. For those who don't recognize the name, Shoup has achieved the pinnacle of success in his chosen field. He is, at fifty-six, a lieutenant general, holder of the Medal of Honor, and 22nd Commandant of the Marine Corps. In his compact, 175-pound body, Dave Shoup combines the heart of a soldier with the brain of a mathematician; the tactics of a drunken dockworker with the manners of a foreign diplomat; the vocabulary of a gunnery sergeant with the sentimentality of an aging Shakespearean actor." [432]   [433]

"As a colonel in World War II, General Shoup earned the Nation's highest award, the Medal of Honor, while commanding the Second Marines ... at Betio, a bitterly contested island of Tarawa Atoll. The British Distinguished Service Order was also awarded him for this action. The following citation accompanied his award of the Medal of Honor:

'For conspicuous gallantry and intrepidity at the risk of his own life above and beyond the call of duty as commanding officer of all Marine Corps troops in action against enemy Japanese forces on Betio Island, Tarawa Atoll, Gilbert Islands, from November 20 to 22, 1943.

'Although severely shocked by an exploding shell soon after landing at the pier, and suffering from a serious painful leg wound which had become infected, Colonel Shoup fearlessly exposed himself to the terrific relentless artillery, and rallying his hesitant troops by his own inspiring heroism, gallantly led them across the fringing reefs to charge the heavily fortified island and reinforced our hard-pressed thinly-held lines. Upon arrival at the shore, he assumed command of all landed troops and, working without rest under constant withering enemy fire during the next two days conducted smashing attacks against unbelievably strong and fanatically defended Japanese positions despite innumerable obstacles and heavy casualties.

'By his brilliant leadership, daring tactics, and selfless devotion to duty, Colonel Shoup was largely responsible for the final, decisive defeat of the enemy and his indomitable fighting spirit reflects great credit upon the United States Naval Service.'" [434]

In his 1969 retrospective, Ted Sorensen, the aide closest to President Kennedy, wrote in *The Kennedy Legacy*: "Marine Commandant Shoup had all the charisma of a Treasury clerk. Seemingly colorless, shy, and reticent, and not as outspoken in private as he has since become in public, he was nevertheless both candid and concise in his blunt advice to the President." [435] Highest-standard hero Shoup will deal with lousy embarrassment Oswald in chapter 4.

Oswald's request for early discharge sailed through. It was approved by the Wing Hardship or Dependency Discharge Board; [436] then gained six (!) endorsements by ever-higher levels of USMC command, [D] until finally approved in less than a month. [437] This author has no evidence, but suspects each level's endorsement may well have been accompanied by an unofficial note to the next higher level along the lines of "Good Riddance!" [E] Oswald's final ratings were 4.0 in conduct and 4.2 in proficiency. [438]

On September 4, Lee applied for a passport at the Superior Court of Santa Ana, Calif. His application stated that he planned to travel "4 months" to attend Albert Schweitzer College in Switzerland, the University of Turku in Finland, and also to travel in Cuba, the Dominican Republic, England, France, Germany, and Russia. [439] The Warren Commission noted: "At the time, the United States proscribed travel to none of the countries named …" [440] It is evident he had already formed his intent to stop only very briefly with his mother. Under Proposed Travel Plans on the application, he wrote he would leave Port of Departure "New Orleans" via "Grace Lines" on "Sept 21, 1959". [441] That is very close to the actuality, described in the next chapter — he will indeed sail from that port, on a different shipping line, one day earlier.

Consider the hidden agendas documented here. Both the Marines and Marguerite believed he was responding to a hardship, going to Fort Worth to take care of his injured and destitute mother, based on his letter on page 23. But the passport application said his purpose was to study in Europe; and Lee knew he would deceive them all by going directly to Russia. The passport was routinely issued 6 days later (such things were quite speedy in the old days before computers brought "efficiency") on September 10. [442]

The next day, September 11, he was released from active duty. A key document was the Notice of Obligated Service, completed in quadruplicate:

"You, having assumed the 6-year military service obligation prescribed by law upon your enlistment in the U. S. Marine Corps on 24 October, 1956, and having served in the United States Marine Corps from 24 October, 1956, to 11 September, 1959, are hereby released from active duty and transferred to the Marine Corps Reserve for the remainder of that 6-year period which ends on 8 December, 1962, unless sooner discharged. During that period you are deemed by law to be a member of the Marine Corps Reserve and will be subject to such training and service as is now or may hereafter be authorized by law for members of the Marine Corps Reserve." [443]

[D] During this escalation, Marguerite's nose injury somehow also elevated into an "industrial accident".

[E] *American Heritage College Dictionary*: "riddance *n.* A deliverance from or removal of something unwanted or undesirable." Note the "undesirable" harbinger of a discharge status to come!

A lieutenant signed, then Lee signed under "I hereby acknowledge receipt of the Notice of Obligated Service" [F], then the lieutenant signed again that he had given PFC Oswald his copy. Lee also signed an agreement to "retain all articles of individual uniform clothing" for use in his reserve duties or upon reenlistment. He will soon leave the uniform with his mother.

Lee was issued two wallet-size cards; both will be in his pocket when he is arrested in Dallas. The "Certificate of Service" on the left,[444] certifies that he "HONORABLY SERVED" in the Corps. The DD1173 "Uniformed Services Identification and Privilege Card" at right,[445]

Expiration Date "7 Dec 1962" will be an ever-present reminder that leaving active duty in California in 1959 did not end his obligation to military duty. He had not been discharged from the Marines; he was only transferred from active duty into the reserve, to serve in that capacity the next three years, until December 1962.

Another document signed that day, his Security Termination Statement, will become important when Oswald vows to violate it while trying to become a Soviet citizen, then will cause him justifiable concern of prosecution when he decides to return to the United States:[446]

> "I shall not hereafter in any manner reveal or divulge to any person any information affecting the National Defense, Classified, Top Secret, Secret, or Confidential, or which I have gained Knowledge during my employment (duty), except as may be hereafter authorized in writing by officials of the Naval Establishment empowered to grant such authority.
>
> "I, LEE HARVEY OSWALD 1653230 have been informed and am aware that 18 U. S. C., 1946 ed., Sup. IV, 792-797 and the Internal Security Act of 1950 prescribe severe penalties for unlawfully divulging information affecting the National Defense. I certify that I have read and understand appendices B, D, E, F, and H of the U. S. Navy Security Manual for Classified Matter, I have been informed and am aware that certain categories of Reserve and Retired personell [sic] on inactive duty can be recalled to duty, under the pertinent provisions of law relationg [sic] to each class for trial by court-martial for unlawful disclosure of information. I have been informed and am aware that the making of a wilfully [sic] false statement herein renders me subject to trial therefore, as provided by 18 U. S. C., 1946 ed., Sup. IV, 1001."

The lieutenant signed, and PFC Oswald signed to assume a very clear legal obligation that he will threaten to violate, in the Soviet Union, even before the year 1959 will end. One day later, El Toro reported his release to the Pentagon:[G]

[F] His signature here has become a hot item for those who somehow believe there are "Two Oswalds", because presumably the Marine lieutenant knew who the Marine private was when they signed.

[G] This is the first of many reconstructions in this book of USMC messages, usually with poor legibility, contained in the *Warren Commission Hearings*. These are accurate and much easier to read.

1959 September 12: Separation Section to Commandant of the Marine Corps [447]

```
                                    26:AGA:hjk
                                    1900
                                    12 Sept 1959

SIXTH ENDORSEMENT on PFC (E-2) OSWALD's ltr of 17 Aug 1959

From:  Commanding Officer, Headquarters and Headquarters Squadron
       (Officer in Charge, Area Separation Section) MCAS, El Toro
       (Santa Ana) California
To:    Commandant of the Marine Corps (Code DGK)

Subj:  Discharge by reason of Hardship, request for; case of Private
       First Class (E-2) Lee H. OSWALD 1653230/6741 USMC

1.  Private First Class (E-2) Lee H. OSWALD 1653230/6741 USMC was
released from active duty and transferred to the Marine Corps
Reserve on 11 September 1959.

                             [signed by]
                             A. G. AYERS JR.
                             By direction
```

It is important to leave this chapter with a full understanding of what just happened. This book's thesis is that Lee Oswald will attempt to shoot John Connally in Dallas, in revenge for Connally's failure to "repair the damage" from the "gross mistake or injustice" of the coming undesirable discharge. That undesirable discharge will be based both on his defection to the arch-enemy Soviet Union in the depths of the Cold War, and on his failure to comply with the obligation to the Marine Corps Reserve he just signed for. As Lee leaves active duty and heads home, he has agreed to continue and behave as a marine for three more years.

When older brother John Pic had completed his very long day of answers to the Warren Commission's questions, he was asked: "Is there anything you would like to add ... that you think you would like to have on the record?" He responded with this carefully-considered widely-encompassing statement: "I believe that Lee Oswald did the crime that he is accused of. I think that anything he may have done was aided with a little extra push from his mother in the living conditions that she presented to him. I also think that his reason for leaving the Marine Corps is not true and accurate. I mean I don't think he cared to get out of the Marine Corps to help his mother. He probably used this as an excuse to get out and go to his defection. I know myself I wouldn't have gotten out of the service because of her, and I am sure Robert wouldn't either, and this makes me believe that Lee wouldn't have." [448]

Oswald's Notice of Obligated Service assigned him to the Marine Air Reserve Training Command located at the Naval Air Station in Glenview, Illinois, [449] about which there will be history-making developments in Chapter 4 – MINSK.

> Key point of this chapter:
> **Marine Oswald was uninterested and troublesome — and this was the
> high point of his life! The Corps was pleased to approve his false
> pretext to exit active duty, but he left with a solemn obligation.**

MOSCOW

1959 September 12 — 1960 January 6

> "You should not try to remember me in any way I used to be, since I am only now showing you how I am. ... I could never have been personly happy in the U.S."
> — **Lee to brother Robert** [450]

UPON HIS DISCHARGE, THE MARINES returned PFC Oswald to Fort Worth.[451] He arrived by bus on September 14, 1959, and stayed with his mother who set up a cot in the kitchen of her one-room apartment.[452] Robert recalled: "[O]nly during one of these day[s] do I remember seeing him. He spent the day at our house."[453] They went hunting for squirrels and rabbits. Robert would write in 1967: "Lee could see, as I did, that Mother was not really disabled, and he told her that he did not plan to stay in Fort Worth."[454] Lee told Robert "that he was going to New Orleans ... to visit my Aunt Lillian ... and at the same time find a job in New Orleans, and make his home in New Orleans."[455] The photo by Robert shows Lee holding his two-year-old niece Cathy that day in Fort Worth.[456] He shows no hint of deception, so the secret hidden behind the smile will surprise.

Lee went to the Fort Worth office of his Selective Service System board, where he and the registrar filled out a new, up-to-date registration card,[457] important because on it Lee signed to acknowledge that three days earlier, on September 11, when he separated from active duty, he had entered into the Marine Corps Reserve as a private first class assigned to "MARTC NAS Glenview, Ill".[458] That unit will change his Marine Corps status, and thereby will change history.

He told his mother he intended to get a job on a ship or in the "export-import business."[459] If he stayed in Fort Worth, he said, he would be able to earn only about $30 per week; on a ship, he would earn "big money" and be able to send substantial amounts home.[460] Marguerite recalled: "So on the third day ... he came with his suitcase in the room and he said, 'Mother, I am off.' So since his mind was made up, I told him goodbye." [461] Despite telling the Marines he needed an early discharge to take care of her, Lee gave Marguerite only $100 [462] and left. She phoned sister Lil in New Orleans to tell her to expect him, "but Lee never did stop at the house." [463]

On September 17 at a New Orleans travel bureau, Oswald filled out a "Passenger Immigration Questionnaire," stating his occupation as "shipping export agent" who would be abroad for 2 months on a pleasure trip. He booked passage to Le Havre, France, on a freighter, the SS *Marion Lykes*, for $220.75.[464] He stayed in a hotel for three nights,[465] and wrote his mother a letter [466] (we continue to give him a virtual typewriter for easier reading). It will be her last news of him until she is surprised by a newspaper in two months:

> "Dear Mother:
>   Well, I have booked passage on a ship to Europe, I would of had to sooner or later and I think it's best I go now. Just remember above all else that my values are very different from Robert's or your's. It is difficult to tell you how I feel, Just remember this is what I must do. I did not tell you about my plans because you could harly be expected to understand.
>   I did not see aunt Lilian while I was here. I will write again as soon as I land.
>   **Lee**" [467]

The freighter *Marion Lykes* sailed on September 20,[468] carrying only four passengers.[469] Oswald shared a cabin with Billy Joe Lord, just graduated from high school and going to France for more education. Lord testified that Oswald was "standoffish," but told generally about his background, mentioning that his mother worked in a drugstore in Fort Worth and that he was bitter about the low wages she received. He said he intended to travel in Europe and to attend school in Sweden or Switzerland if he had the funds.[470] The other two passengers were Lt. Col. and Mrs. George B. Church, Jr., who also found Oswald unfriendly and had little contact with him. Oswald told them he had not liked the Marine Corps and planned to study in Switzerland; they observed some "bitterness" about his mother's difficulties, but did not discuss this with him. No one on board suspected that he was headed to Russia.[471]

Lee disembarked at Le Havre on October 8 and left for England that same day. He told British customs officials in Southampton [472] that he had $700 and planned to remain in the UK for one week before proceeding to a school in Switzerland; but on October 10 [473] he flew to Helsinki, Finland.[474] He may have been playing his own secret-spy game. He probably applied for a visa at the Russian consulate on October 12, his first business day in Helsinki.[475] The visa was issued on October 14, permitting one tourist visit of not more than 6 days in the

Soviet Union.[476] He left Helsinki by train the following day, crossed the Finnish-Russian border at Vainikkala, and arrived in Moscow, the capital of both Russia and the U.S.S.R., on October 16.[477]

Much of the chronology in this chapter and the next comes from Lee's handwritten account of his life in Russia. Tightly penned onto 12 pages,[478] he titled it "Historic Diary" atop the first. Early entries were written somewhat after the events they describe; in Minsk he kept a more contemporaneous record.[479] The Warren Commission and this author use the diary, which Oswald may have written with future readers in mind, only as his record of private life and personal impressions as he sought to present them. Otherwise, for more date-accurate and evenhanded facts, we rely wherever possible on official documents, correspondence, and the testimony of witnesses.

He was met at the Moscow railroad station by a representative of Intourist, the state tourist agency, and taken to the Hotel Berlin where he registered as a student.[480] That day he met Rimma Shirokova, the young Intourist guide assigned to him for his stay in Russia. Almost immediately he told her he wanted to leave the United States and become a citizen of the Soviet Union. The *Historic Diary* records that when Lee told Rimma that he intended to defect she was "flabbergassted," but agreed to help.[481] She was "politely sympathetic but uneasy" when he told her that he wanted to defect because he was "a Communist, ect."[482] According to the diary, she later told him she reported his statement to Intourist headquarters, which in turn notified the "Passport and Visa Office", probably the Visa and Registration Department of the Ministry of Internal Affairs, the MVD.[483] She was instructed to help Oswald prepare a letter to the Supreme Soviet requesting that he be granted citizenship. His *Historic Diary* says they mailed such a letter that day, October 16, the same day he had arrived in Moscow.[484] He is not only impetuous, but also its close cousin, fast!

The suspicious Soviets must have suspected that Oswald was too good to be true, a "plant" by America at the peak of the Cold War. Former KGB agent Yuri Shvets explained: "The intelligence trade has a thousand-year history, but try as it might it has never succeeded in coming up with a foolproof method of verifying a person's trustworthiness."[485] About Americans recruited by the Soviet Union, Shvets wrote: "All of them, to a greater or lesser extent, exhibited certain mental anomalies that set them apart from what are generally perceived as normal persons."[486]   [487]

With his visa limited to a visit of six days, for the next few days Lee's primary concern was to become a Soviet citizen. He told his diary that Rimma felt sorry for him and tried to be a friend because he was "someth. new."[488] On his 20th birthday, 2 days after he arrived in Russia, she gave him Dostoevski's *The Idiot*.[489] She inscribed it: "Dear Lee, Great congratulations! Let all your dreams come true! 18.X 1959[A] Moscow Yours Rimma"[490] He kept the book and carried it home to Texas in 1962. Let us remind ourselves that he is still a young man, only 20, too young to drink or vote in the United States at that time.

The American defector in the Moscow hotel was quite a curiosity, and became a man of great interest to reporters, as will be seen in the next few pages. The first, Lev Setyayev,[B] came to his room on October 19, saying that he was a reporter for Radio Moscow seeking impressions of Moscow from American tourists.[491] Their interview was apparently never broadcast.[492] Two years later, Oswald told officials at the American Embassy that he had made

---

[A] The European style of dates is day-month-year whereas the American is month-day-year. This author and other professionals from the computer disciplines know that the only logical (Yes, we are truly Dilbert and the proud children and disciples of Mr. Spock!) expression is year-month-day.

[B] This is as good a time as any to share the thickets researchers must traverse to find information in the 26 volumes from the Warren Commission. Oswald's notebook page recording the man's name is sandwiched between a diagram drawn to show the 120.2 feet from assassination witness Howard Brennan's head to Oswald's sixth floor window, and 8-page article "Prelude to Tragedy" by noted author Jessamyn West about her fellow Quaker, Ruth Paine (chapters 5 & 6), in *Redbook* magazine of July 1964. The search can be frustrating, but sometimes surprises with delightful pots of gold.

a few routine comments to Setyayev of no political significance. The Warren Commission, one of whose senior members was Allen Dulles, retired Director of the CIA, noted that the interview with Setyayev may have been an attempt by the KGB, in accordance with regular practice, to assess Oswald or even to elicit compromising statements from him.[493]

The Russians recognized what they had. General Oleg Kalugin, once KGB Chief of Foreign Counterintelligence, later said: "Using a stick and a carrot, using all sorts of bugging and listening devices, they found out that he was not a spy. ... He is good for nothing. He is not good for spying. He is not a CIA. He will not do any job for the KGB because he is not that kind of a man. He will botch everything, he will louse up everything." [494]

Colonel Oleg Nechiporenko will meet Lee in Mexico City in 1963. Later retiring from a career as a KGB agent, he will thoroughly research the Soviet government's relations with the strange man, and will be quoted several times in this book. He dug out the archives of the several directorates who investigated Oswald, and summed up their joint decision in 1959:

> "Oswald did not create the impression of being a source of valuable intelligence information. Giving him Soviet citizenship and permanent residency in the USSR would provide the KGB no benefit. ... [T]he deputy head of the First Chief Directorate [intelligence] concurred with his counterpart at the Second Chief Directorate [counterintelligence] that 'it was not advisable to give [Oswald] refugee status in the Soviet Union.'
>
> [T]he Registry and Archives Department informed the secretariat of the Presidium of their conclusions ... [I]n the eyes of the Committee for State Security, the KGB, Lee Harvey Oswald had been declared a 'tourist non grata.' It is plausible to assume that most any other individual in his position would have quietly accepted his fate and returned to the United States to continue working on his mastery of Marxism. But this tourist turned out to be a tough nut to crack." [495]

The following day, Rimma told him that the "Pass, and Visa Dept." wanted to see him.[496] On October 21, he was interviewed by an official concerning his application for citizenship. The official offered no encouragement. Lee wrote in the *Historic Diary*:

```
"He tells me 'USSR only great in Literature wants me to go back home'  I
am stunned  I reiterate, he says he shall check and let me know weather
my visa will be (extended it exipiers today)  Eve. 6.00 Recive word
from police official.  I must leave country tonight at. 8.00 P.M. as
visa expirs.  I am shocked!!  My dreams!  I retire to my room.  I have
$100. left.  I have waited for 2 year to be accepted.  My fondes dreams
are shattered because of a petty offial;  because of bad planning I
planned to much!  7.00 P.M. I decide to end it.  Soak rist in cold
water to numb the pain.  Than slash my left wrist.  Than plang wrist
into bathtub of hot water.  I think 'when Rimma comes at 8. to find me
dead it wil be a great shock.  somewhere, a violin plays, as I wacth my
life whirl away.  I think to myself, 'how easy to die' and 'a sweet
death, (to violins)  about 8.00 Rimma finds my un-concious (bathtub
water a rich red color)  she screams (I remember that) and runs for
help.  Amulance comes, am taken to hospital where five stitches are put
in my wrist.  Poor Rimmea stays by my side as interrpator (my Russian
is still very bad) far into the night,  I tell her 'go home'  (my mood
is bad) but she stays,  she is 'my friend'  She has a strong will only
at this moment I notice she is preety
Oct. 22.  Hospital  I am in a small room with about 12 others (sick
persons.)  2 ordalies and a nurse the room is very drab as well as the
breakfast. Only after prolonged (2 hours) observation of the other pat.
do I relize I am in the Insanity ward. This relization disquits me." [497]
```

Oswald resented being in the psychiatric ward and wanted a transfer.[498] He was examined by a psychiatrist, who concluded that he was not dangerous to others and after three days could be transferred to the "somatic" department. Hospital records [499] correctly understood that "in order to postpone his departure he inflicted the injury upon himself." [500] They note "He claims he regrets his action. After recovering he intends to return to his homeland." [501]

Rimma the Intourist guide had been his only friend, and now he has another young lady visitor: "**Afternoon I am visited by Roza Agafonova of the hotel tourist office, who askes about my health, very beautiful, excelant Eng., very merry and kind, she makes me very glad to be alive.**" [502]

Lee appears to be relaxing now that his visa-expiration deadline has passed. Out of the psychiatric ward, he found the hospital more pleasant. The new ward, shared with 11 other patients, was "airy," and the food was good. His only complaint, according to his diary, was that an "elderly American" patient was distrustful of him because he had not registered at the American Embassy and because he was evasive about the reasons for his presence in Moscow and confinement in the hospital. [503]

Four years in the future, the FBI will ask Lee's widow, whom we will soon meet, "If she knew Lee had tried to commit suicide while in Russia prior to their marriage. She did not … and said that she had asked Lee two or three times what was the cut on his wrist, pointing to the cut on his left wrist. Lee would become very mad and tell her nothing." [504]

Released from hospital on October 28, [505] he registered at the Metropol [506] as Rimma directed. The *Warren Report* suggests the government dictated the change. [507] I add my speculation that the Soviets did not know what to make of this strange man, so moved him to a room pre-bugged with microphones. His visa had expired, his presence was illegal, he had received no hint that the mandate to leave might be reversed. Later that day, Rimma told him that the "Pass and Registration Office" wished to talk to him about his future. [508] There, he was asked whether he still wanted to become a Soviet citizen; he replied that he did. Although told that he could not expect a decision soon, Lee wrote in the diary that he stayed near the telephone, fully dressed and ready to leave immediately if summoned. The next three days in his room seemed "like three years I must have some sort of a showdown!" [509]

On Saturday,[C] October 31, he acted. He took a taxi to the ten-story apartment building that had been converted into the U.S. Embassy to the U.S.S.R. [510] and asked to see the

consul. [511] He lay his passport on the desk, saying he came to "dissolve his American citizenship." Richard Snyder, the senior consular official [512] who will play a large continuing part in this story for years, invited Lee into his office. [513] Oswald declared that he wanted to renounce his American citizenship, denounced the United States and praised the Government of the Soviet Union. "Snyder could see the tension in his pallid face: 'He was wound up like six watch springs and highly nervous'" [514] but sought to learn his motives and background, and to forestall immediate action. Oswald told him he had already offered to tell a Soviet official what he had learned as a radar operator in the Marines.

[C] Psychiatrists and psychologists: Please note that Lee will almost invariably approach embassies and government offices on closed or almost-closed Saturdays. That may be a clue to his cognition.

Warren Commissioners pressed Snyder about his reluctance to act on Lee's request. It was not said aloud, but perhaps some were thinking that if Lee had lost his citizenship, he would not have been in Texas in 1963. "Snyder said later, 'Particularly in the case of a minor, I could not imagine myself writing out the renunciation form, and having him sign it, on the spot, without having him leave my office and come back some other time, even if it is only a few hours intervening.'" [515] The hour of that day of the week excused some delay: "it was a little after eleven A.M., and on Saturdays the embassy always closed at noon." [516]

Allen Dulles and Gerald Ford asked Snyder to define Lee's motivation; his reply was insightful: "In the case of Oswald, a man who, for one reason or another, seemed to have been uncomfortable in his own society, unable to accommodate himself to it, and hoping he will make out better some place else." [517] Snyder found Lee to be "intense and humorless." [518]

"Snyder suggested ... that Oswald wait until he was assured of Soviet citizenship, or he would have no citizenship at all." [519] Lee persisted, and the interview ended when Snyder told him that he could renounce his citizenship on the next business day, Monday, when the embassy would be fully staffed, by appearing personally to do so. [520] During the interview, Oswald handed Snyder his passport and a note on Hotel Metropol stationery, so it must have been written during the last three days:

"I Lee Harvey Oswald do hereby request that my present citizenship in the United States of america , be revoked.
I have entered the Soviet Union for the express purpose of appling for citizenship in the Soviet Union, through the means of naturalization.
My request for citizenship is now pending before the Surprem Soviet of the U.S.S.R..
I take these steps for political reasons. My request for the revoking of my American citizenship is made only after the longest and most serious considerations.
I affirm that my allegiance is to the Union of Soviet Socialist Republics.
Lee H. Oswald" [521]

The Embassy took immediate steps that will push Oswald along his slide toward killing in Dallas. "Snyder sent a telegram to the State Department describing his interview with Lee. Copies were sent at once to the CIA and the FBI, who started their own investigations," [522] urged on by Snyder's: "SAYS HAS OFFERED SOVIETS ANY INFORMATION HE HAS ACQUIRED AS ENLISTED RADAR OPERATOR." [523] Back in his hotel room, Lee recorded in the *Historic Diary*:

"I leave Embassy, elated at this showdown, returning to my hotel I feel now my enorgies are not spent in vain. I'm sure Russians will except me after this sign of my faith in them. 2:00 a knock, a reporter by the name of Goldstene wants an interview I'm flabbergassed 'how did you find out? The Embassy called us.' He said. I send him away I sit and relize this is one way to bring pressure on me. By notifying my relations in U.S. through the newspapers. ... A half hour later another reporter Miss Mosby comes. I answer a few quick questions after refusing an interviwe. ... I feel non-deplused because of the attention" [524]

Lee's "Goldstene" was "Moscow bureau chief of United Press International (UPI), Robert J. Korengold". [525] Sensing there was a story but he would not get it, Korengold had immediately sent his young UPI associate Aline "Ellie" [526] Mosby, where she got just enough from Lee to put the story on the UPI wire to the U.S. [527] History's clock begins its tick toward doom.

Brother Robert was the first of the family to get the news: "I was at work before daylight, delivering milk on my route for Boswell's Dairy ... when a taxicab drove up [and a man] walked up to the open door of my truck. ... 'I have a report here that your brother is in Russia,' he said." [528] Robert read the wire service teletype. Eight years later, he wrote in his biography of his little brother: "I was totally surprised ... I never suspected, until he went to Russia, that he had the slightest interest in Communism." [529] Robert continues with the breaking news on Halloween, 1959:

> "Reporters kept us busy all day and I was trying to figure out how to get in touch with Lee. Finally I decided to send a telegram, using some family phrase or expression he would be sure to recognize and know the message came from me. When he was little, I used to tell him, 'Keep your nose clean.' So ... I sent Lee a telegram, to the Hotel Metropole in Moscow:
>
> 'LEE, THROUGH ANY MEANS POSSIBLE CONTACT ME. MISTAKE. KEEP YOUR NOSE CLEAN.'" [530]

On November 1, only one day after the encounter at the Embassy, a brief story ran in Sunday newspapers; in Fort Worth it was featured on the *Star-Telegram*'s front page. Four years later, his mother told how she learned where he had gone: "Tape recording of interview with Mrs. Marguerite Oswald, mother of Lee Harvey Oswald. Recorded on November 25, 1963. Interviewer is Special Agent J. M. Howard,[D] U. S. Secret Service, Dallas, Texas. This recording is being made at Six Flags Inn Motel, Arlington, Texas." [531] [Marguerite:]

> "Oh, in the meantime I was babysitting and this lady had a young boy and I was desparate [*sic*] financially and still ill (they still hadn't found my trouble), so since she was a widow and the boy was alone she offered me a home and paid me $5.00 a week. I was very happy to get it because even though I was ill, there was times when I could cook and manage when the face didn't spasm and bother me. ...
>
> At this home, I went out to get the Sunday paper and when I picked up the paper the headlines said, "Fort Worth Man Defected";[532] [E] the first paragraph, if I remember, "Lee H. Oswald of Fort Worth has defected." I said, "Oh, my God, that is my son." I composed myself and read the story. The story stated that he went to Russia, as we know it has been publicized, I can't remember all of that, and it appeared to be his own decision, according to the paper. So, again, respecting other peoples privileges or rights, I said, and later made this public, that if, according to the paper, he had studied Marxism and that was the life he wanted since he was not hurting anyone and it was a political, as far as I knew, I wasn't too much at the time on these things, but since it was his decision and that was what he wanted I believed it should have been his privilege as an individual to pursue the thing he wanted, and I admired my son for the statements because of racial discontent in the United States and treatment of underdog and so forth. If he felt that way, and the papers stated that was his feeling and reason for going into Russia that he had the courage not to stay in a United States, that he did not like and to leave because I do not approve of all these politicians and all of these people saying things about the United States, and yet being a part of it. In my own way, I think it takes courage to stand up for your convictions, and so I accepted the fact that that was what he wanted and that he had a right to what he wanted to do with his life. Naturally, the newspapers and all the reporters were coming around. The woman told me I would have to leave the house. I had no place to go. I

Ex-Marine Asks Soviet Citizenship

MOSCOW, Oct. 31 (UPI) Lee Harvey Oswald, 20, a recently discharged United States Marine from Fort Worth, Tex., disclosed today that he had taken steps to renounce his American citizenship and become a Soviet citizen. He said the reasons for his move were "purely political."

"I will never return to the United States for any reason," Oswald told a reporter in his room at Moscow's Hotel Metropole.

The young Texan declined to give any details on his background or the reasons for his decision. But a U. S. Embassy official said Oswald had told him he arrived in Moscow on Oct. 15 immediately after his discharge from the Marine Corps and had no regular job in the United States.

[D] This is Mike Howard, who after retiring was free to tell of a surprising find he and his partner made that week at the Inn, the highlight of Chapter 20 – OBSTRUCTION OF BEST EVIDENCE.

[E] The clipping is from a Warren Commission *Document*, none of which were printed in their 26 books titled *Hearings*, probably from disinterest, perhaps from inadvertence as they rushed to publish.

had no money. I called my son, Robert, and told him that she insist that I leave the house. He said 'Well, mother, come over here.' I have been the type mother since I had raised my children alone and had struggled, not only financially, but was always tired and had no life of my own. In other words, as soon as I came home from work, my children wanted their food, so immediately I started working again. I sort of lived for the day when my children would find a good woman and marry and somebody to take care of them, because it was almost impossible for me to do justice to these boys." [533]

As we note that Marguerite is constitutionally unable to speak on any subject in a manner that is either to-the-point or concise, and that any statement she makes has a strong tendency to twist and loop back until she talks only about herself and the many troubles she has endured, let us also award her full credit for a good memory. We don't know how many times she read or studied that 1959 article, but more than four years after it was published, she was quoting it with a surprisingly high degree of accuracy.

American newsman Seth Kantor presents an interesting insight into the dysfunctional relationship between youngest son and mother:

"The first time I was aware of Oswald had been [when] he had defected to Russia and his mother, Marguerite Oswald of Fort Worth, was trying to get him to come home. I was on Scripps-Howard's *Fort Worth Press* then and Kent Biffle, another reporter on the *Press,* spent hours one day setting up a three-way telephone call involving Mrs. Oswald, her son at the Hotel Metropole in Moscow, and our city desk. When Oswald at last got on the line and Kent shouted, 'Lee, your mother is on the line ... and wants to talk with you,' Oswald hung up." [534]

Lee rejected the Embassy's efforts to deliver or read by telephone the telegram from Robert. [535] The Embassy then used registered mail [536] to send to Oswald's hotel room both that telegram and a separate message Robert had sent to the State Department in Washington, requesting them to deliver it to his brother, asking Lee to contact him immediately. [537]

"A Foreign Service Dispatch, prepared by the State Department on November 2 ... asserted in pertinent part:

'Oswald offered the information that he had been a radar operator in the Marine Corps and that he had voluntarily stated to unnamed Soviet officials that as a Soviet citizen he would make known to them such information concerning the Marine Corps and his specialty as he possessed. He intimated that he might know something of special interest.'" [538]

Photographs of the Snyder and State Department documents show they were routed directly "to the CIA, FBI and Office of Naval Intelligence," [539] where those cleared for Top Secret must have thought, "U-2"! "This particular espionage weapon was then the single most important intelligence asset available to the United States." [540]

The Naval attaché in the Moscow Embassy on November 3 wired to the Chief of Naval Operations in the Pentagon, alerting the top brass to view the Embassy's dispatches, because 'OSWALD STATED HE WAS RADAR OPERATOR IN MARCORPS AND HAS OFFERED TO FURNISH SOVIETS INFO HE POSSESSES ON US RADAR." [541] The CNO sent back a message the next day to the attaché in Moscow: "Oswald is PFC Inactive Marine Corps Reserve with obligated service until 8 December 1962" and because "he may have had access to confidential info", Moscow should keep the Pentagon advised of "significant developments in view of continuing interest of HQ, Marine Corps and U. S. intelligence agencies". [542] This shows with a high degree of certainty that General Shoup, the Commandant of Marines, now knows that Oswald, still a duty-bound Marine for three more years, is in the capital of America's bellicose opponent, and has offered to tell that enemy what he learned during his active duty. The march toward a change of his status in the Corps, and thus and then onward to Dallas, is inexorable.

The Pentagon took the matter seriously. At Lee's last post, El Toro Marine Base, Nelson Delgado recalled: "a group of civilians in dark suits [arrived] with stenographers and literally [took] over their headquarters company to question marines about Oswald." [543]

"'Oswald was a very unpopular man that month', [John] Donovan told the *Washington Evening Star* in December 1963. As the former commander of Oswald's radar unit, Donovan knew Oswald's ability to handle radar equipment and radar-related information. 'Clearly, for dealing with aircraft going from 500 to 2,000 miles an hour, you don't fool with nitwits. ... He [Oswald] was a good man on radar, there's no denying it.' [544] Lee knew the types of aircraft that entered and left the Air Defense Identification Zone. According to Donovan, Oswald's defection 'compromised all our secret radio frequencies, call signs, and authentication codes.' Oswald 'knew the location of every unit on the West Coast and the radar capability of every installation. We had to spend thousands of man-hours changing everything, all the tactical frequencies, and verify the destruction of the codes.'" [545] Those "could be varied: the data Oswald might have amassed on [the U-2 spy plane] presented a more difficult problem." [546]

On November 6, the Embassy received a letter, handwritten on lined paper. Similar to the note of a few days before but more confrontational, it augments the evidence that Lee's nature was to belligerently hyperinflate every difficulty, problem or grudge:

"Nov. 3 1959

"I, Lee Harvey Oswald, do hereby request that my present United States citizenship be revoked.

I appered in person, at the consulate office of the United States Embassy, Moscow, on Oct 31$\underline{st}$, for the purpose of signing the formal papers to this effect. This legal right I was refused at that time.

I wish to protest against this action, and against the conduct of the official of the United States consular service who acted on behalf of the United States government..

My application , requesting that I be considered for citizenship in the Soviet Union is now pending before the Surprem Soviet of the U.S.S.R.. In the event of acceptance ,I will request my government to lodge a formal protest regarding this incident.

Lee Harvey Oswald" [547]

Asked by the Warren Commission whether Lee had the capacity to write this letter by himself, Snyder replied that he did, noting its "Oswaldish" "extremely strident tone" "pomposity" and "sonorousness" [548]. He knew his man — and could equally have been describing Marguerite!

Consul Snyder quickly replied by letter that Lee could renounce his citizenship by appearing at the Embassy and, under oath, execute the necessary papers. On the embassy copy of Snyder's November 6 letter is handwritten "Sent by registered return receipt with copy of tel[egram] from half-brother [John Pic] in Japan, Nov. 9, 1959." [549] The embassy typed Oswald's letter into an "Airgram" to the Secretary of State in Washington,[F] saying "Embassy replying Oswald by mail acknowledging his letter and reiterating right of Amcit to renounce as expressed section 1999 revised statutes. ..." [550] Intervening messages between Moscow and

---

[F] At the end of her commendable term in 2013, Secretary of State Hillary Rodham Clinton was scolded by Republicans for not acting on one message to her from the U.S. ambassador in Benghazi, Libya. She explained that all messages from abroad to the State Department in Washington are addressed "To: Secretary of State" and there are 1.43 million of those a year (5,720 every working day).

Washington had affirmed that an <u>American</u> <u>citizen</u> had an undeniable right to renounce his citizenship, but all agreed Oswald was acting rashly, so he would have to take the next step.

The Warren Commission took testimony from Frances G. Knight, longtime Director of the Department of State's Passport Office. She summarized the 1959 actions and inactions of Lee Oswald at the U.S. Embassy in Moscow: "My comments on the citizenship and expatriation phase of the Oswald case are these: Insofar as the Oswald citizenship status is concerned, it is my firm belief that Lee Harvey Oswald, despite his statement to the U.S. consul in Moscow, that he wished to divest himself of U.S. citizenship, did not do so. At no time did he sign the required documents which were available to him for that purpose. Oswald was a 20-year-old ex-Marine, and the U.S. consul made it quite clear in his despatches to the Department, that Oswald was arrogant and aggressive, and angry and unstable." [551]

Before moving on, these are the results of Lee's three weeks in Moscow: He applied to the Soviets, was rebuffed, ordered to depart, and has remained only by being in hospital. Almost certainly hoping to impress the Soviet watchers, he made one (only one) visit to the U.S. Embassy on a Saturday and left his passport. His presence in Moscow and threat to tell the Russians confidential information from his Marine duty is now well-known in Washington. He did not follow through on his professed desire to terminate his U.S. citizenship.

Oswald's diary describes the period from November 2 to 15, during which he continued to isolate himself, as 'days of utter loneliness.' [552] In reply to caring brother Robert's telegram, he wrote this snide letter in longhand, easier to read in this typescript:

```
                                                   "Nov.8,1959
"Dear Robert
    Well, what shall we talk about? the weather perhaps?  Certainly you
do not wish me to speak of my decision to remain in the Soviet Union
and apply for citizenship here, since I'm afraid you would not be able
to comprehend my my reasons.  You really dont know anything about me.
Do you know for instance that I have waited to do this for well over a
year, do you know that I [phrase in Russian] speak a fair amount of
Russian which I have been studing for many months
    I have been told that I will not have to leave the Soviet Union if I
do not care to.  this than is my decision.  I will not leave this
country, the Soviet Union, under any conditions , I will never return
to the United States which is a country I hate.
    Someday, perhaps soon, and than again perhaps in a few years , I
will become a citizen of the Soviet Union, but it is a very legal
process, in any event, I will not have to leave the Soviet Union and I
will never leave.
    I recived your telegram and was glad to hear from you, only one word
bothered me, the word 'mistake.'  I assume you mean that I have made a
'mistake' it is not for you to tell me that you cannot understand my
reasons for this very serious action.
    I will not speak to anyone from the United States over the telephone
since it may be taped by the americans.
    If you wish to corespond with me you can write to the below address,
but I really don't see what we could take about if you want to send me
money, that I can use, but I do not expect to be able to send it back.
                                                   Lee" 553
```

Lee's statement that he will not have to leave was not based on fact. He will hear in a week that he can remain temporarily,[554] then in two months he will be allowed to remain indefinitely, but not in Russia.[555] The next day, the Embassy tried to deliver a telegram from his brother John Pic. Lee refused to open his door, so the message was sent to him by registered mail.[556]

As he waited for a decision, United Press International reporter Aline Mosby, who had contacted him back on page 34, succeeded in interviewing Lee.[557] She phoned and was told to come right over; Oswald told his diary that he thought she might "understand and be friendly" because she was a woman.[558] She will be the first to get a full interview. Miss Mosby found him polite but stiff; she said that he seemed full of confidence, often showing a "small smile, more like a smirk," and that he talked almost "non-stop." Oswald told her his usual great exaggeration: he could remain in the Soviet Union while job possibilities were being explored. He admitted that his Russian was bad but was confident that it would improve rapidly. He based his dislike for the United States on his observations of racial prejudice and the contrast between "the luxuries of Park Avenue and workers' lives on the East Side," and mentioned his mother's poverty; he said that if he had remained in the United States he too would have become either a capitalist or a worker. "One way or another," he said, "I'd lose in the United States ... even if I'd be exploiting other workers. That's why I chose Marxist ideology."[559]

Oswald told her that he had been interested in Communist theory since he was 15, when 'an old lady' in New York handed him "a pamphlet about saving the Rosenbergs."[G] But when Mosby asked if he were a member of the Communist Party he said that he had never met a Communist and that he "might have seen" one only once, when he saw that "old lady." His only apparent regrets concerned his family: his mother, whom he had not told of his plans, and his brother, who might lose his job as a result of the publicity.[560] The strong probability is that these sentiments were a bid for Aline's sympathy, not true sympathy for his family.

The interview lasted about 2 hours. Oswald thought he had exacted a promise from Miss Mosby that she would show him the story before publication but she broke the promise; he thought the published story contained distortions of his words.[561] Her notes indicate that he called her to complain of the distortions, saying in particular that his family had not been "poverty-stricken" and that his defection was not prompted by personal hardship but that it was "a matter only of ideology."[562]

Miss Mosby's story was distributed worldwide by wire service UPI. Here we begin a practice, where it is helpful to show a clipping, letter or document. For many such items, this book will first display the source photo from the *Warren Commission Hearings* or other document. Then will follow a careful transcription, intended to be considerably easier to read. At right is the Warren Commission's clipping from the front page of the *Fort Worth Star-Telegram* of Sunday, November 15, 1959.[563] The same words are transcribed on the next page.

[G] Husband and wife Americans, convicted and executed in 1953 for passing atomic secrets to Russia.

Fort Worth Defector Confirms Red Beliefs

BY ALINE MOSBY.

MOSCOW, Nov. 14 (UPI). — Lee Oswald, still sporting the chop-top haircut he wore in the U. S. Marines, said Saturday that when he left America to seek citizenship in Russia "it was like getting out of prison."

But his dream of achieving Soviet citizenship in exchange for the U. S. citizenship he renounced went aglimmering. The 20-year-old Texan from Fort Worth said Soviet authorities would not grant him citizenship although they said he could live in Russia freely as a resident alien.

"Imperialism" and lack of money while a child were his main reasons for turning his back on his native land, he said.

A slender, well-groomed youth, he carefully thought out his phrases before speaking in an interview at a Moscow hotel.

He had announced on Oct. 31 that he had renounced his U. S. citizenship and was seeking Soviet citizenship "for purely political reasons."

He said he told the U. S. embassy he was a devoted believer in communism and had read books on the subject since he was 15. Memories of a poverty-stricken childhood played a part in his decision, he said. His father, he said, died before he was born.

"I saw my mother always as a worker, always with less than we could use," he said. He insisted his childhood was happy, despite poverty. He admitted his mother "would not understand" why he had fled to Russia.

"In the Marine Corps I observed the American military in foreign countries, what Russians would call military imperialism," he said.

"I was with occupation forces in Japan and occupation of a country is imperialistic," he said.

"I would not want to live in the United States and be either a worker exploited by capitalists or a capitalist exploiting workers or become unemployed."

"I could not be happy living under capitalism."

He said Karl Marx' work "Das Kapital" set him on the road to communism, and he began to read all he could find about it.

Oswald joined the Marine Corps at 17. During his hitch he learned to be a specialist in radar and electronics.

"I saved my money—$1,600—to come to the Soviet Union and thought of nothing else," he said.

Many things bothered him in the United States, he said—race discrimination, "harsh" treatment of "underdog" Communists and "hate."

Oswald's diary, as usual, records his dissatisfied view of the interview:

"Nov -2-15 Days of utter loneliness I refuse all reports phone calls I remain in my room, I am racked with dsyentary.   Nov 15 - I decide to give an interview, I have Miss Mosbys card so I call her. She drives right over. I give my story, allow pictures, later story is distorted, sent without my perrmission, that is : before I ever saw and O.K.'ed her story. Again I feel slightly better because of the attention" [564]

Lee wrote in the diary that he was told in mid-November he could remain "until some solution was found with what to do" with him.[565] With this "comforting news"[566] he granted a second interview, again to a young woman.[567] Miss Priscilla Johnson of the North American Newspaper Alliance knocked on the door of his room, and Oswald went to her room in the same hotel that evening for an interview lasting 5 hours. He repeated most of what he had told Aline Mosby,[568] then said "For the past two years I have been waiting to do this one thing. . . . for two years I was waiting to leave the Marine Corps and get enough money to come. . . . I spent two years preparing to come here. These preparations consisted mostly of reading. It took me two years to find out how to do it."[569] He said the Russians treated his defection as a "legal formality," neither encouraging nor discouraging it.[570] She suggested that if he really wished to renounce his American citizenship, he could do so by returning to the Embassy. He vowed he would "never set foot in the Embassy again," sure that he would be given the "same run-around" as before. He seemed to Miss Johnson to be avoiding effective renunciation, consciously or unconsciously, to preserve his right to reenter the United States.[571]

In the excellent dual biography *Marina and Lee* that she will write after Dallas, Priscilla Johnson McMillan (a married name having been added) characterized Lee during this interview. Her judgment has gravitas — she is one of very few who wrote about Lee after actually meeting him. "[H]e did not seem like a fully grown man to me, for the blinding fact, the one that obliterated nearly every other fact about him, was his youth. He looked about seventeen. Proudly, as a boy might, he told me about his only expedition into Moscow alone. He had walked four blocks to Detsky Mir, the children's department store, and bought himself an ice cream cone. I could scarcely believe my ears. Here he was, coming to live in this country forever, and he had so far dared venture into only four blocks of it."[572]

For the rest of the year 1959, Lee seldom left his hotel room except for a few trips to museums. "I have bought myself two self-teaching Russian Lan. Books I force myself to study 8 hours a day. I sit in my room and read and memorize words.[H] All meals I take in my room."[573] Isolation was relieved only by another interview at the passport office, occasional visits from Rimma Shirokova, and lessons in Russian from her and other Intourist guides.[574]

He wrote an eight-page letter to Robert stating he was a Communist, containing bitter statements against the United States, vowing to live "here in the Soviet Union <u>for the rest of my life</u>" and telling his loving brother "that my mother and you are (in spite of what the newspapers said) <u>not</u> objects of affection , but only examples of workers in the U.S."[575] Robert received a third letter, this one not dated, on December 17:

```
"Dear Robert.
     I will be moving from this hotel, and so you need not write me
here .  I have chosen to remove all ties with my post , so I will not
write again , nor do I wish you to try and contact me, I'm sure you
understand that I would not like to recive correspondence from people
in the country which I fled.  I am starting a new life and I do not
wish to have anything to do with the old life.
     I hope you and your family will always be in good health.
                                   Lee"
```
[576]

[H] At this time he also purchased a pocket notebook, in which he drew a map of his immediate area of Moscow and wrote Russian-language words. That notebook will be an amazing find in four years, to be featured in Chapter 20 – Obstruction of Best Evidence.

If Lee believed that all his letters, outgoing and incoming, were being opened and inspected in Moscow, as appears to be the case, this may well have been a final attempt to convince the Soviets of his intention to cut ties with America and become a permanent Russian.

His mother sent him a December 18 personal check for $20. He returned it to her, saying that he could not "use this check, of course"; he asked her to send him $20 in cash and added that he had little money and needed "the rest," presumably a reference to the $100 he had given her in September. Marguerite later sent him a money order for about $25.[577]

Meanwhile, the huge Soviet bureaucracy [I] had been investigating and cogitating, as reported by KGB Col. Nechiporenko:

> "The news of Oswald's visit to the embassy, in conjunction with his attempt at suicide, upset the people who ran Intourist even more. Now the Western mass media were clued in to events, which could lead to reports that in the Soviet Union tourists are 'driven to commit suicide.' This could damage the image and commercial interests of Intourist by scaring away potential tourists to the USSR. Therefore, the Intourist brass again began to sound all the alarms. This time it sent [a] message ... straight to Anastas Mikoyan,[J] deputy chairman of the USSR Council of Ministers.
>
> As first deputy chairman, Mikoyan was in charge of all Soviet foreign trade organizations, including Intourist. In this capacity he could issue orders to the Ministry of Foreign Affairs and the chairman of the KGB. Mikoyan forwarded the letter to the head of the Seventh Department of the Second Chief Directorate, the division of counterintelligence that handled tourists." [578]

Col. Nechiporenko tells us that the difficult decision went to high levels, and was finally made, jointly, by Andrei Gromyko, Minister of Foreign Affairs, and Aleksandr Shelepin,[K] Chairman of the KGB, who wrote "a top-secret joint memorandum to the Party's Central Committee":

> "Considering that other foreigners who were formerly given Soviet citizenship ... left our country after having lived here awhile and keeping in mind that Oswald has not been sufficiently studied, it is advisable to give him temporary residency in the USSR for one year, with a guarantee of employment and housing. In this event, the question of O.'s permanent residency in the USSR and granting of Soviet citizenship can be decided during this term." [579]

After the Soviet Union fell into disarray and he retired from the KGB, Nechiporenko became a historian, and judged:

> "In the conditions of the time, the proposal was 'Solomonic' in its wisdom: Mute the situation, which by now had received international publicity, remove the petitioner from Moscow, and observe him carefully for one year in order to understand just who he considers himself to be and how suitable he is for the role of 'builder of communism' which he so stubbornly persists in claiming to be." [580]

In 1964, the Warren Commission will ask the Soviet Union for their information on Oswald. The Central Committee of the Communist Party of the Soviet Union will then send much to the USSR's ambassador in Washington, including this explanation for the Commission:

> "The competent Soviet organs, which examined Oswald's petition, did not find convincing grounds which would allow them to conclude that he met the demands made by the Constitution and Soviet legislation on Soviet citizens. The motives which caused Oswald to petition were also unclear. That Oswald expressed himself critically in relation to the government, of which

---

[I] "Bureaucracy" is a word born in France, where the impenetrable institution has been perfected!
[J] He will be famous in diplomatic circles as "Stony Pants" for his ability to sit forever and give nothing.
[K] The uniqueness of Oswald's defection is illustrated by these leaders, all famous, making the decision.

he was a citizen, could not be a determining factor. For the reasons indicated, Oswald's petition for Soviet citizenship was rejected." [581]

1960 began with Lee still in the hotel, still waiting. On January 2, Senator from Massachusetts John Fitzgerald Kennedy [L] declared: "I am today announcing my candidacy for the Presidency of the United States." On January 4, Oswald was summoned to the Soviet Passport Office and handed this Identity Document for Stateless Persons No. 311479.[582]

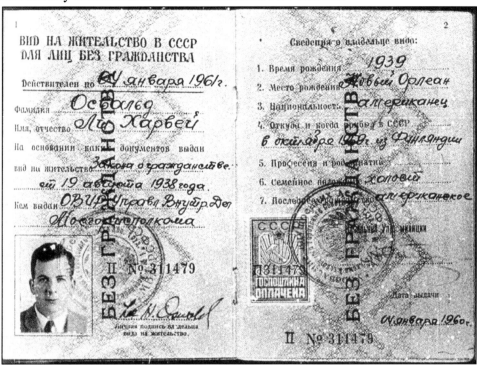

Nechiporenko's *Passport to Assassination* interprets: "Residency Permit issued to Lee Harvey Oswald on January 4, 1960, with an expiration of January 4, 1961. Oswald is listed as single, with no occupation." [583]

Officials told Lee he was being sent to Minsk,[584] an industrial city 450 miles southwest of Moscow, population 510,000.[585] His disappointment in not being granted Soviet citizenship was offset by relief that the uncertainty had ended. He told Rimma that he was happy.[586] The following day, he went to an agency the Russians call "Red Cross", in reality a front for the MVD, the Ministry of Internal Affairs.[587] It gave him 5,000 rubles,[588] of which he used 2,200 rubles to pay his hotel bill and 150 rubles to purchase a railroad ticket to Minsk.[589]

> Key point of this chapter:
> **Oswald arrived in Moscow with high hopes, but baffled the Russians,**
>   **irritated the American embassy, gave interviews that set off alarms**
>   **in the Pentagon, then was banished to inconsequential Minsk.**

[L] This book is only marginally about accidental victim JFK, making his first entrance here on page 43!

MINSK

1960 January 7 — 1962 June 13

> "He was nineteen when he went to Russia with such bravado and twenty-two when he returned, thoroughly disillusioned by his experience, but still not enamored of the United States ..."
> — **Earl Warren** [590]

LEE OSWALD WILL BE IN MINSK 2½ YEARS. Warren Commission member (and future president) Gerald Ford asked Moscow consul Snyder: "If you had known that Oswald was in Minsk, what would your reaction have been? Snyder: "Serves him right." Ford: "Why do you say that?" Snyder: "You have never been in Minsk." [591] During Lee's isolation there, events in the U.S. will propel him along the path to killing in Dallas. Important throughout this chapter are many documents relating to a Pentagon decision to downgrade his Marine Corps discharge. To truly understand his motive in Dallas in 1963, it is necessary to see and appreciate these documents, especially his plea to John Connally and the disappointing reply.

Lee arrived on January 7, 1960, was met at the station by "Red Cross" [A] workers who took him to the Hotel Minsk where Intourist employees speaking excellent English were waiting for him. [592] One of them, young Roza Kuznetsova, will become a close friend. [593] The next day, the 'Mayor' welcomed him to Minsk, promised him an apartment, and warned him against 'uncultured persons' who sometimes insult foreigners. [594]

Oswald had hoped to continue his education in Russia, so was disappointed by being assigned [595] to the Belorussian Radio and Television Factory, [596] where he reported for work on January 13. This major producer of electronic parts and systems employed about 5,000. [597] Oswald's union card described him as a 'metal worker'; [598] Marina testified that he fashioned parts on a lathe. [599] The 'experimental shop' [600] where he worked employed 58 plus 5 foremen. Work was assigned according to 'pay levels,' which were numbered from one to five plus a top 'master' level. A worker could ask to be tested for a higher level at any time. [601]

His salary varied from 700 to 900 rubles per month ($70-$90). [602] Although high compared with the salaries of professional groups in Russia, [603] it was normal for his type of

---

[A] As explained in the previous chapter, "Red Cross" was really MVD, the Ministry of Internal Affairs.

work.[604] It was supplemented by 700 rubles per month from the "Red Cross". His total income was about equal to that of the factory's director.[605] More noteworthy than his extra income was the attractive apartment he was given in March. A small flat with a balcony overlooking the river,[606] it cost only 60 rubles a month.[607] Oswald described it as "a Russian dream."[608] Had he been a Russian, he would have had to wait several years for a comparable apartment, and even then would have been assigned one only if he had a family.[609] The subsidy and apartment were the Soviet Union's favorable treatment of the defector.[610]

Lee enjoyed his first months in Minsk. His work at the factory was easy, coworkers were friendly and curious about the United States. Almost every night for two months, he took Roza Kuznetsova, his interpreter and language teacher,[611] to the theater, a movie or an opera. He wrote in his *Historic Diary*: "I'm living big and am very satisfied."[612]

In the previous chapter, Lee vowed at the U.S. Embassy that he was becoming a Soviet citizen and intended to tell the authorities what he had learned as a Marine. The embassy reported to the State Department; that went to the Pentagon's Office of Naval Intelligence and Marine Corps HQ. The USMC Discipline Branch then looked through his service record because, an expert testified, "they were trying to effect his discharge."[613] On March 8, 1960, the investigation resulted in a development of which he knew absolutely nothing at the time, but which will ultimately result in the death of President Kennedy. For easier reading than the exhibit in the Warren Commission volumes, here is a careful re-creation by the author:

1960 March 8: Commandant of the Marine Corps to MARTC, Glenview, Illinois [614]

NAVAL *SPEED*LETTER

(One box must be checked) REGULAR MAIL SPECIAL DELIVERY X AIR MAIL REGISTERED MAIL	CLASSIFICATION FOR OFFICIAL USE ONLY	IN REPLY REFER TO DK-MPV

	DATE 8 MARCH 1960
TO: COMMANDER MARINE AIR RESERVE TRAINING COMMAND NAVAL AIR STATION GLENVIEW, ILLINOIS	

ARRANGEMENTS BEING MADE WITH A FEDERAL INVEST AGENCY TO

FURNISH YOU WITH RPT WHICH RELATES TO PFC LEE HARVEY OSWALD

1653230 USMCR INACT CMM A MEMBER OF YOUR COMD X UPON RECEIPT

CMM YOU ARE DIRECTED TO PROCESS PFC OSWALD FOR DISCH IAW

PARA 10277.2.f MARCORMAN X

ADDRESS: COMMANDANT OF THE MARINE CORPS HEADQUARTERS, U. S. MARINE CORPS WASHINGTON 25, D. C.	←—SENDER'S MAILING ADDRESS Address reply as shown at left; or reply hereon and return in window envelope …

In plain English,[B] Commandant of the U. S. Marine Corps General David Shoup (introduced on page 25), ordered the officer in command of the Marine Air Reserve Training Command in Glenview, to which Oswald had been assigned for three years of reserve duty when he left active service:

> "Arrangements are being made with a federal investigative agency to furnish you with a report which relates to Private First Class Lee Harvey Oswald (serial number 1653230) USMC Reserve inactive, a member of your command. Upon receipt, you are directed to process PFC Oswald for discharge in accordance with paragraph 10277.2.f of the Marine Corps Manual."

The Marine Corps had at least five solid reasons for being displeased with Oswald, any of which would be sufficient cause to classify him as "undesirable" and throw him out:

- He wrote and signed a request for early discharge on the basis of "hardship", stating the need to return home immediately to care for, and pay for the support of, his wounded and impoverished mother. When he then quickly passed by her and went on to Russia using the passport obtained after he had made that request but before his discharge, it was provably certain that had been his objective all the while, so his reason for requesting early release was fraudulent.

- In his discharge documents, he signed the Notice of Obligated Service to acknowledge his understanding that he was still a Marine, now transferred to the Reserve, "subject to such training and service as is now or may hereafter be authorized by law for members of the Marine Corps Reserve" until December 8, 1962. In the depths of the Cold War, he then deliberately moved himself into Russia, beyond reach of the Marines, not only his physical body which could not now serve his Reserve obligation, but also for a communication path not secure from interception by the enemy, the Soviet Union.

- He had also signed the Security Termination Statement saying "I shall not hereafter in any manner reveal or divulge to any person any information affecting the National Defense, Classified, Top Secret, Secret, or Confidential, or [sic] which I have gained Knowledge during my employment (duty), except as may be hereafter authorized in writing by officials of the Naval Establishment empowered to grant such authority." He then bragged at the U.S. Embassy in Moscow that he had offered, and had full intention, to tell the Russians what he had learned as a radar operator, which would include information about radar capabilities, Friend-Foe identification codes, radio frequencies, and most harmfully, abilities and operations of top-secret U-2 spy planes.

- News stories about his defection highlighted the fact that he was a Marine, thus he was bringing discredit on his proud branch of service at this time when American patriotism was not only encouraged, but required.

- Even if any of the four above had been a close call, he had no offsetting credits in the bank, so to speak. He had been a lousy Marine, and the Corps owed him nothing.

[B] A grateful tip of the author's hat to Gunnery Sergeant Ruth Baker, USMC Recruiting Station in Seattle, for deciphering the SpeedLetter. Sgt. Baker quickly recognized that "**IAW**" expands to "in accordance with." She needed a few minutes of study for an "Ah Ha!" insight, based on knowing that "**X**" stood for a period, that "**CMM**" is not "command", "commission" or "communication" as I had guessed, but simply a little punctuation mark — a comma!

The specific authority to discharge was in paragraph 10277.2.f of the Marine Corps Manual:

"10277 DISCHARGE FOR REASON OF UNFITNESS

1. The Commandant of the Marine Corps and all Marine general officers exercising general court-martial jurisdiction, may direct the discharge or retention in the service of enlisted or inducted persons recommended for discharge by reason of unfitness, except that cases involving sexual perversion will be referred to the Commandant of the Marine Corps (Code DK) for decision.

2. The commander will recommend an individual for discharge for reason of unfitness when it is determined that his military record is characterized by one or more of the following:

[a. through e. covered sexual perversion, discreditable involvements with authorities, patterns of shirking, drug addiction, and failure to pay debts.]

f. For other good and sufficient reasons when determined by the Commandant of the Marine Corps or the Secretary of the Navy." [615]

The Manual defined five types of discharge to be given for various good and bad situations; the two best levels were Honorable and General; the two worst were Bad Conduct and Dishonorable. In the middle was this third of five levels:

"10254 UNDESIRABLE DISCHARGE

1. An undesirable discharge is separation from the service under conditions other than honorable. It is given for unfitness and misconduct." [616]

Putting it together, the Commandant ordered that Oswald be given an Undesirable Discharge by reason of unfitness because the Commandant had determined good and sufficient reason. The previous page suggested five such reasons — and they all gave reason to "get rid of him!"

In Minsk, Lee's spring and summer 1960 passed easily and uneventfully. There were picnics and drives in the country he described as "green beauty." [617] He obtained a hunting license under the name Aleksy Harvey Oswald. Because "Lee" sounded foreign (Chinese) and was difficult for them to pronounce, many Russians called him "Alek", "Aleck" or "Alik".[618] When he returns to the US, he will regularly use that as a false name.

He purchased a shotgun and joined a chapter of the Belorussian Society of Hunters and Fishermen, a hunting club sponsored by his factory, and hunted for small game in the farm regions around Minsk about half a dozen times in the summer and fall. The hunters spent nights in small villages; Oswald described the peasant life he saw as crude and poor.[619] Norman Mailer, in his wonderfully provocative *Oswald's Tale: An American Mystery*, used on-site interviews to relate one September incident:

"They were hunting for rabbit that day. ... Oswald was holding his gun crooked in his arm. Then, a rabbit practically jumped out from under his foot, and he went, 'Aooaoh!' and shot into the air. ... Later, he had another try, and missed again. The fact that he was a bad shot and could not fix his radio tended to alert [KGB agents in Minsk] Igor and Stepan. How was it that a former Marine with a Sharpshooter rating back in his U.S. Marine Corps — yes, KGB had information that he was not a bad shot — could miss his targets so? ... If [the KGB] had had any inkling that he would later be suspected of carrying out a crime of high magnitude — of highest magnitude! — they would have studied his marksmanship in a more detailed manner. As it was, however, what with everything else involving him, they made no special attempt to find out whether he was an excellent shot trying to create the impression he was a bad shot or had been naturally incompetent that day." [620]

Robert Oswald wrote of his little brother: "For the first time in his life he felt truly independent, with a place of his own, congenial friends his own age, enough money to live on, and two girls jealous of each other because of him. 'It brings a warm feeling to me,' he told his diary." [621] One of the "girls" was Ella German, a worker at the factory, of whom he said he "perhaps fell in love with her the first minute" he saw her.[622]

As introduced in the previous chapter, Dr. Cyril Wecht in his book *Cause of Death* stated that he "was able to review a thirty-five-page file that the KGB had kept on Oswald. ... The file said that Oswald was 'under constant surveillance' during his stay in Russia. Among those it identifies as KGB operatives informing the government of Oswald's activities were a neighbor in his apartment building, three co-workers at his factory, and two women with whom he had sexual relations. The file refers only briefly to Marina, and then only as a companion to Oswald. According to the typed notes, Oswald worked alone, or at least the KGB was unable to ascertain any contacts he made with known American agents living and working in the Soviet Union. The notes describe Oswald as 'anxious,' sometimes quick to anger, and with a weakness for liquor and women." [623]

●●● ●●● ●●●

On many pages to follow are letters and documents that will lead to Lee Oswald's discharge from the Marine Corps as "undesirable" because of "unfitness". Investigations, recommendations and orders will flow up and down the command chains, and between the Pentagon and the unit to which Oswald was assigned when he left active duty, the Marine Air Reserve Training Command in Glenview, Illinois. In the vortex of a whirlwind of paper is that unit's administrative officer, a first lieutenant. The first letter of many was sent by him to notify Oswald of what is to come, and inviting him to participate.

As we set out to follow the paper trail, keep in mind that Lee is isolated in Minsk. He will not see these letters and documents, and will not even know anything of the process that is about to begin, until January 1962 — 21 months after the next-page letter! — when Marguerite will be the first to notify him of the eventual result of a process he didn't know existed.

Some of the documents to follow are photo-like scans of exhibits in the Warren Commission's 26 supplemental volumes. When such exhibits are fuzzy or otherwise difficult to read, careful re-creations are displayed, as in the first example.

1960 April 26: Lieutenant M. G. Letscher to PFC Oswald [624]

UNITED STATES MARINE CORPS
HEADQUARTERS
MARINE AIR RESERVE TRAINING COMMAND
U. S. NAVAL AIR STATION
GLENVIEW, ILLINOIS

In Reply Refer to:
Code: 50/JET:rgr
1900
26 Apr 1960

CERTIFIED MAIL
RETURN RECEIPT REQUESTED

From: Commander, Marine Air Reserve Training
To: Private First Class Lee H. OSWALD 1653230 USMCR
       3613 Harley, Fort Worth, Texas

Subj: Discharge by reason of unfitness; recommendation for

Ref: (a) Para 10277.2f MarCorMan

Encl: (1) Statement of rights

1. Due to your recent activities, this headquarters will convene a
board of officers, to determine your fitness for retention in the
U. S. Marine Corps Reserve.

2. This Board will make a recommendation to the Commander, Marine Air
Reserve Training that you be separated by an Undesirable Discharge, or
retained in the U. S. Marine Corps Reserve.

3. You have the right to appear in person, or to be represented by
 counsel, and to present any evidence or statements you believe may have
a bearing on your case. If you do not desire to appear personally,
or be represented by counsel, you may submit to the Commander, Marine
Air Reserve Training such evidence or statements in writing as you desire the Board to consider.

4. If you decide to appear personally, and you desire military counsel
be appointed, please inform the Commander, Marine Air Reserve Training
prior to 14 June 1960.

5. Enclosure (1) is forwarded to you for completion and return to this
headquarters.

6. Your appearance, or that of any person in your behalf, will be at
no expense to the government.

7. If no answer is received within forty-five (45) days from the date
of this letter, your case will be placed before the Board for appropriate
action.

(signed)
M. G. LETSCHER
By direction

1960 April 26:   Enclosure from USMC to Oswald: "Statement of rights" [625]

```
From:    Private First Class Lee H. OSWALD 1653230 USMCR
         3613 Harley, Fort Worth, Texas
To:      Commander, Marine Air Reserve Training
```

1. I have been advised that I am being recommended for an Undesirable Discharge for reasons of Unfitness.

2. I understand that I will be afforded an opportunity to request or waive, in writing each of the following privileges:

    a. To have my case heard by a board of not less than three officers.

    b. To appear in person before such board, subject to my availability, e. g., not in civil confinement.

    c. That Military counsel of my choice will be provided if reasonably available, otherwise, military counsel deemed available will be appointed.

4. In view of the contemplated action and in accordance with my rights and privileges.

    a. I (do) (do not) desire to have my case heard by a Board of not less than three (3) officers.

    b. I (do) (do not) desire to appear in person before such Board subject to my availability at the time the Board convenes, e.g., (not in civil confinement).

    c. I (do) (do not) desire to be represented by a lawyer if reasonably available. If lawyer is not reasonably available I desire_____ _____to represent me if available. I understand that if I retain civil counsel it will be at no expense to the Government.

    d. I (do) (do not) desire to submit statements in my own behalf.

```
                              LEE H. OSWALD_____
                                   (Signature)

WITNESSED:


_____
        (Signature)


_____
          (Title)


_____
          (Date)

ENCLOSURE  (1)
```

The Warren Commission's display of this page shows that Oswald's rank, name, serial number and address at the top, then his name on the line above " (Signature)", were typed onto an existing form. The two pages (letter and attachment) were mailed on 'April 29, 1960' and "addressed to 'PFC Lee H. Oswald, 3613 Hurley, Fort Worth, Texas,'" in an envelope stamped 'Certified Mail No. 2180642.'" [626]

At exactly this time, on April 28, Marguerite was interviewed by FBI Special Agent John W. Fain. She told him "that all her letters [to Lee] had been returned undelivered, and she was worried over the safety of her son." [627] Receiving Fain's report from Fort Worth, Director J. Edgar Hoover wrote to the State Department and Director of Naval Intelligence, outlining a concern of the FBI's counterespionage section, because of Oswald's disappearance, that an imposter might acquire and use his identification for anti-American purposes. [628]

As Marguerite replies to the Marine Corps letter on the preceding pages, sharp-eyed readers may notice her reply is six weeks after Lt. Letscher's, unusual for the lady we know to be quick to take offense and return fire. The delay is almost certainly because of addressing problems. The letter to Oswald (on page 50) has his address "3613 Harley", but the envelope that carried it (on page 51) was addressed to "3613 Hurley", both in Fort Worth. Shortly before this, large cities had been divided into postal zones, as used in the following letter from Marguerite, from Fort Worth 4, Texas. Neither USMC letter nor its envelope used zones. To compound the mystery, in Fort Worth there were (and still are) both Harley Avenue and Hurley Avenue. They are residential, different and southwest of downtown. To further the confusion, as seen in her letter below, at this time Marguerite Oswald lived at 1410 Hurley!

It doesn't matter. The post office knew how to reach Marguerite, probably because she moved frequently and filed Change of Address cards with the Postmaster. Reach her they did, and she came in to their counter and although the Certified Mail label was checked to indicate "CHECK INDICATES DELIVERY ONLY TO ADDRESSEE", Marguerite signed as "AGENT", probably telling some poor PO clerk of her miseries because of a son missing somewhere overseas!

This book has given Lee Oswald a virtual typewriter to make reading his writing easier for you, so now also extends the same courtesy to Marguerite. Here is her reply:

1960 June 10: Marguerite Oswald to United States Marine Corps [629]

```
                                               1410 Hurley
                                               June 10, 1960

Reference Code: 50/JETIRGR 1900
26 April, 1960

United States Marine Corps

Dear Sir:

     I am writing you on behalf of my son Lee Harvey Oswald.  He
is out of the country at present and since I have no contact
with him I wish to request a stay of action concerning his
discharge.  Also, I desire to be informed of the charges against
him.  Please state reasons for such discharge.  After hearing
from you I will be willing to act in his behalf.

                              Sincerely,
                              (signed)
                              Mrs. Marguerite C. Oswald
                              1410 Hurley
                              Fort Worth 4, Texas
```

Marguerite's son is not only "out of the country at present", as she also told the FBI, but has been completely out of contact since late in 1959. She has no idea where he is, nor how to contact him, so she is plowing ahead on his behalf, doing what she thinks is right.

First Lieutenant Letscher, as will become quite clear on following pages, was the very model of a modern administrator. His reply was prompt, dated only one week later:

1960 June 17: Lieutenant M. G. Letscher to Marguerite Oswald[630]

UNITED STATES MARINE CORPS
HEADQUARTERS
MARINE AIR RESERVE TRAINING COMMAND
U. S. NAVAL AIR STATION
GLENVIEW, ILLINOIS

```
                              In Reply Refer to:
                              Code:  50/JET:erc
                                     1900
                                     17 June 1960
```

```
Mrs. Marguerite C. OSWALD
1410 Hurley
Ft. Worth 4, Texas

Dear Mrs. OSWALD:

    The letter of Commander, Marine Air Reserve Training, 50/JET:rgr
Over 1900 of 26 April 1960, to your son was prompted by his request for
Soviet citizenship.  An investigation concerning this matter has been
conducted by military authorities and the case will be placed before a
board of officers which will recommend that your son be retained in, or
separated from the U. S. Marine Corps Reserve.

    Your son, of course, has the right to appear in person or to present
any fact or evidence which would assist the board in reaching its de-
cision.  The letter of 26 April 1960, informed him of these rights.  In
view of the fact that he has not informed this Headquarters of his cur-
rent address and that he has left the United States without permission,
it is considered that a letter sent to the last address on file at this
Headquarters is sufficient notification.  A letter will be sent by
certified mail informing your son of the convening date of the board.

    Should you be aware of any facts or information which would assist
the board in evaluating your son's case, it is suggested that you for-
ward them to this Headquarters.

    It is regretted that action of this nature must be taken in your
son's case.




                   (signed)
                        M. G. LETSCHER
           First Lieutenant  U. S. Marine Corps
                   Administrative Officer
           Aviation Class III Reserve Section
```

One week after that, the letter adumbrated above was mailed to Lee at his last address on file:

1960 June 24: Lieutenant M. G. Letscher to PFC Oswald [631]

UNITED STATES MARINE CORPS
HEADQUARTERS
MARINE AIR RESERVE TRAINING COMMAND
U. S. NAVAL AIR STATION
GLENVIEW, ILLINOIS

```
                                     In Reply Refer to:
                                     Code:   50/JET:rgr
                                             1900
                                             24 June 1960

CERTIFIED MAIL
RETURN RECEIPT REQUESTED

From:  Commander, Marine Air Reserve Training
To:    Private First Class Lee H. OSWALD 1653230 USMCR
       3613 Harley, Fort Worth, Texas

Subj:  Convening of a Board; notification of

1.  A Board of Officers will convene to consider your case at 0900
on 4 August 1960.  They will meet at Headquarters, Marine Air Reserve
Training Command, U. S. Naval Air Station, Glenview, Illinois.

2.  You are encouraged to submit a statement or any pertinent infor-
mation concerning your case to this Headquarters, prior to the
convening of the Board.


                                     (signed)
                                     M. G. LETSCHER
                                     By direction
```

On May 1, 1960, the Soviet Union shot down an American U-2 reconnaissance plane and captured its pilot, Francis Gary Powers. Until then, the US had denied the existence of such a plane. Oswald, from his Marine stationing in Atsugi, Japan, knew of the U-2 and from his radar observations had a good idea of its capabilities. His presence inside the Soviet Union was thus a matter of grave concern at home, particularly to the CIA that operated the U-2.

Years later in his autobiography, supreme leader Nikita Khrushchev wrote that the Soviets saw President Eisenhower's U-2 affair to be a unilateral, unprovoked demonstration of supposed American superiority and outrageous treachery. He said it was a landmark event in the fight against imperialists who were waging Cold War. [632]

At this time there appeared Oswald's first signs of disillusionment with Russian life. On May 1 when the U-2 was downed, he noted in his diary that he felt "uneasy inside" after a friend took him aside at a party and advised him to return to the United States. [633]   A diary entry in June-July compared life in Minsk with military life:

"I have become habituatated to a small cafe which is where I dine in the evening. The food is generaly poor and always eactly the same, menue in any cafe, at any point in the city. The food is cheap and I don't really care about quiality after three years in the U.S.M.C." [634]

Ten time zones to the west, the Democratic National Convention met in Los Angeles to choose its candidates for national office. There were two top contenders. A lawyer from Fort Worth, John B. Connally, directed the campaign of the Senate Majority Leader, Lyndon B. Johnson of Texas. When it appeared LBJ was lagging behind Senator John F. Kennedy of Massachusetts, Connally called a press conference to warn that Kennedy was keeping secret his Addison's Disease, an incurable adrenal deficiency. Kennedy's campaign manager, brother Bobby, hotly denied that assertion as a despicable tactic showing the desperation of Johnson's adherents. [635] The episode had little effect, and on July 15 the Democrats nominated Kennedy to be their candidate for President. JFK did not hold grudges against Johnson, choosing him to run for Vice President; nor against Connally, as will be seen after the November election.

Marguerite Oswald asked many high-level persons to help locate and repatriate Lee, including Congressman from Fort Worth Jim Wright, Speaker of the House Sam Rayburn and Secretary of State Christian Herter. In the depths of the Cold War, she also appealed directly to the Soviet leader:

> "I also wrote to Mr. Khrushchev, July 19, 1960. I stated that Lee had gone to Russia in September of 1959 and that I had one letter from him in January, but my letter to him was returned and I never heard from him again. I asked Mr. Khrushchev to supply me with any information about his whereabouts, if he was working and so on and so forth, I said that I was much worried and deeply concerned as a mother would be. ... Now I did not receive an answer from Mr. Khrushchev ..." [636]

Marguerite complained that she did not receive replies from American officials, either.

———————————

This chapter displays re-creations of full-page documents. Showing them intact may leave spaces before or after, in which your author chooses to show interesting photos. Here is the first, printed by the Warren Commission with caption: "River view at Minsk taken from Oswalds' apartment." [637] One of the most remarkable attributes of Lee's apartment, uniquely opulent for a single man, which helped attract Marina to it and then to him, was this beautiful view of the bend in the Svisloch River. Marina kept the photo, stored it in Ruth Paine's garage, and gave it to the Commission. All that will be explained in later chapters.

Meanwhile within the Marine Corps, in the Pentagon and Illinois, records and rules were being examined and cited, and commands were issued:

1960 July 29: Lieutenant M. G. Letscher to Commander of MART [638]

UNITED STATES MARINE CORPS
HEADQUARTERS
MARINE AIR RESERVE TRAINING COMMAND
U. S. NAVAL AIR STATION
GLENVIEW, ILLINOIS

```
                                    In Reply Refer to:
                                    Code:    50/JET:cgm
                                             1900
                                             29 July 1960

From:  Mobilization Planning Officer, Mobilization Planning Branch
To:    Commander, Marine Air Reserve Training

Subj:  Discharge by reason of Unfitness; recommendation for, case of
       Private First Class Lee H. OSWALD 1653230 USMCR

Ref:   (a)  Para 10277.2F MarCorMan
       (b)  MARTCOM Order 1626.1
       (c)  CMC Spdltr DK-MDV of 8 Mar 60
       (d)  DIO, 9th ND confidential report serial 02049-E of 8 Jun 60
       (e)  DIO, 9th ND confidential report serial 02296-E of 27 Jun 60
       (f)  Para 4016.3b PRAM
```

Encl: [6 pages from Oswald's Service Record Book and 2 letters: 26 Apr 60 and 24 Jun 60] [c]

```
1.  It is recommended that the subject named marine be discharged from the
U.S. Marine Corps Reserve by reason of unfitness in accordance with refer-
ences (a), (b), and (c).

2.  References (d) and (e) contain reports of PFC OSWALD's activities.
Information contained in references (d) and (e) is also available in files
of the Office of Naval Intelligence.
```

3.   [4 items summarizing Oswald's Service Record]

4.   [statement that Reference (f) was complied with.]

```
5.  A letter informing PFC Oswald of his rights as outlined in ref. (b)
was receipted for by his mother, Mrs. Marguerite Oswald. An attempt was
made to inform PFC OSWALD of the convening of the board hearing his
case, however, the letter was returned marked "Unclaimed". See enclosures
(7)  and  (8)  [the 2 letters on line titled Encl:]

                                    (signed)
                                    M. G. LETSCHER
                                    By direction
```

---

[c] Reminder: This author shows simplifications by enclosing replacements in [square brackets].

The same day: An order was given to convene a board:
1960 July 29: Commander of MART to Board of Officers [639]

```
                                              04/FDS/rwm
                                              1900
                                              29 July 1960

FIRST ENDORSEMENT on Mobilization Planning Officer, Mobilization Planning
              Branch ltr 50/JET:cgm over 1900 of 27 July 1960

From:   Commander, Marine Air Reserve Training
To:     Senior Member, Hardship, retention and desirability board

Subj:   Discharge by reason of Unfitness; recommendation for, case of Private
        First Class Lee H. OSWALD 1653230 USMCR (Class III)

Ref:    (d) CPMART let 04/FDS/rwm over 5420 of 1 July 1960

1.   Reference (d) established a board to consider recommendation for
discharge due to unfitness.  Accordingly, you are directed to convene
to consider the recommendations contained in the basic letter.

2.   Upon completion of the board action, you will return all papers by
endorsement hereon.  The proceedings of the board will be made an enclosure
thereto.


                         (signed)
                         F. D. STICE
                         By direction
```

Ten days later: Reply to the order above:
1960 August 8: Board of Officers to Commander of MART [640]

```
                                              04/JEC/aeg
                                              1900
                                              8 August 1960

SECOND ENDORSEMENT

From:   Senior Member, Hardship, retention and desirability board
To:     Commander, Marine Air Reserve Training

Encl:   (9)  Proceedings of the Board

1.   Returned.

2.   Enclosure (9) contains the Proceedings of the Board for the subject case.


                         (signed)
                         J. E. COSGRIFF
```

1960 August 8: Proceedings of the Board of Officers [641]

```
Proceedings of the board to consider recommendations for the discharge
by reason of unfitness in the case of Private First Class Lee H. OSWALD
1653230 USMCR (Class III).

PRESENT   Lieutenant Colonel John E. COSGRIFF 016710 USMC   Senior Member
          Lieutenant Colonel Donald O. BRAZEAL 028340 USMCR Member
          Captain Harlan E. TRENT 052235 USMC           Member (Recorder)

The board met at 1000, 8 August 1960 at Headquarters, Marine Air Reserve
Training Command, U. S. Naval Air Station, Glenview, Illinois.

Private First Class OSWALD was not present and did not submit any evidence
or statements in his own behalf.

FINDINGS

1.  The Commandant of the Marine Corps Speedletter of 8 March 1960 to
Commander, Marine Air Reserve Training directed processing of Pfc OSWALD
for discharge in accordance with paragraph 10277.2f Marine Corps Manual.

OPINION

That references (d) and (e), which were reviewed by the Board, contain
information concerning the actions of Private First Class OSWALD which
warrants that he not be retained in the Marine Corps Reserve.

RECOMMENDATION

That Private First Class Lee H. OSWALD 1653230 USMCR be discharged for
unfitness in accordance with paragraph 10277.2f Marine Corps Manual.
```

[signed by all three]

```
JOHN E.  COSGRIFF      DONALD O.  BRAZEAL      HARLAN E.  TRENT
LtCol         USMC      LtCol          USMCR      Capt          USMCR
```

One day after that decision by the board:

1960 August 9: Commander of MART to Commandant of the Marine Corps [642]

```
                                          04/FDS/rwm
                                          1900
                                          9 August 1960

THIRD ENDORSEMENT on Mobilization Planning Officer, Mobilization Planning
               Branch ltr 50/JET:cgm over 1900 of 27 July 1960

From:  Commander, Marine Air Reserve Training
To:    Commandant of the Marine Corps (Code DK)

Subj:  Discharge by reason of Unfitness; recommendation for, case of Private
       First Class Lee H. OSWALD 1653230 USMCR (Class III)

1.  Readdressed and forwarded for review and final determination.  The
findings, opinion and recommendation of the board are approved.

                         (signed)
                         F.  E.  LEEK
```

Two actions subsequently occurred on the same day, a week later, within USMC headquarters: recommendation and final order (both sufficiently clear to be read without re-creation):

1960 August 17: Head of Discipline to Commandant of the Marine Corps [643]

RECOMMENDATION FOR DISPOSITION OF UNDESIRABLE DISCHARGE
NAVMC HQ 28-PD (REV. 5-59)

NAME (Last)	(First)	(Middle)	SERVICE NO.	RANK	COMPONENT	DATE
OSWALD	Lee	Harvey	1653230	Pfc	USMCR	17Aug60

DATE OF BIRTH	PLACE OF BIRTH	AGE	CURRENT ENLISTMENT DATE	PLACE OF DUTY
18Oct39	New Orleans, Louisiana	20	24Oct56	MARTC

PREVIOUS ACTIVE SERVICE	TOTAL SERVICE
24Oct56-11Sep59 USMC	3 yrs 10 mos

PREVIOUS OFFENSES

11Apr58 SCM viol art 92; 27Jun58 SCM viol art 117 & 128

BASIS OF RECOMMENDATION

See CNO ltr OP-921D/ck serial 015422P92 of 4Aug60 of which OSWALD is the subject

WERE SAMPLE CHARGES AND SPECIFICATIONS PREPARED AND SUBJECT CONFRONTED WITH SAME?	DID SUBJECT AGREE IN WRITING TO ACCEPT UNDESIRABLE DISCHARGE FOR THE GOOD OF SERVICE AND TO ESCAPE TRIAL BY GCM, AND THAT SUCH SEPARATION MAY DEPRIVE HIM OF VIRTUALLY ALL HIS RIGHTS AS A VETERAN UNDER FEDERAL AND STATE LEGISLATION?
☐ YES ☒ NO	☐ YES ☒ NO

MEDICAL OPINION	PENDING DISCIPLINARY ACTION (If any)
None	None

STATEMENT OF THE SUBJECT (Admission, Denial or No Statement)

No statement. Refused to answer correspondence

RECOMMENDATION OF SUBJECT'S COMMANDING OFFICER	ACTION AND/OR RECOMMENDATION OF COMMANDING GENERAL (If any)
Discharge IAW para 10277.2f MarCorMan Board concurs	Concurs

RECOMMENDATION

Discharge as undesirable for reason of unfitness IAW para 10277.2f MarCorMan

HEAD, DISCIPLINE BRANCH, PERSONNEL DEPARTMENT: _____ (Signature & Rank)

The Marines are ready for anything. Shown above is form NAVMC HQ 28-PD for an unusual, infrequent situation: "RECOMMENDATION FOR DISPOSITION OF UNDESIRABLE DISCHARGE". USMC headquarters in the Pentagon contains its Personnel Department, within which is a Discipline Branch, and here we see Colonel J. Twitchell, the head of that branch, giving the Commandant his final staff sign-off to order that Oswald be discharged as undesirable.

1960 August 17: Commandant of the Marine Corps to Commander of MART [644]

DISCHARGE ORDER
NAVPC 10113-PD

DEPARTMENT OF THE NAVY
HEADQUARTERS UNITED STATES MARINE COR.
WASHINGTON 25, D. C.

DMB-1-bco
DATE: 17 Aug 1960

TO: Commander, Marine Air Reserve Training, U. S. Naval Air Station, Glenview, Illinois

FROM: COMMANDANT OF THE MARINE CORPS (CODE DMB), WASHINGTON 25, D. C.

SUBJECT

Private First Class Lee H. OSWALD 1653230 USMCR; discharge of

REFERENCE
(a) PAR. **10254** MarCorMan
(b) PAR. **10277.2f** MarCorMan
(c) PAR. **10300** MarCorMan

(a)

1. Please discharge the subject-named, issuing the type of discharge certificate provided for in reference (c), by reason of **unfitness with an undesirable discharge, in accordance with the authority contained in reference (b).**

1960 August 29: Commander of MART to OIC, Reserve Records, Glenview [645]

```
                                        04/FDS/rwm
                                        1900
                                        29 August 1960

FIRST ENDORSEMENT on CMC Discharge Order DMS-1-bco of 17Aug60

From:  Commander, Marine Air Reserve Training
To:    Officer in Charge, Aviation Reserve Records Section, MARTC,
       U. S. Naval Air Station, Glenview, Illinois

Subj:  Discharge by reason of unfitness; case of Private First Class
       Lee H. OSWALD 1653230 USMCR (Class III)
```

1. You are directed to discharge the subject named man on the earliest practicable date, citing CMC Discharge Order DMS-1-bco of 17 August 1960 and reference (b) as authority for discharge. Upon discharge all obligated service is terminated.

2. Issue the type discharge provided in reference (a).

3. Upon discharge, this correspondence shall be endorsed to indicate the date of discharge, character of discharge and form number of discharge certificate issued and returned to this headquarters for filing.

4. The closed out service record book will be forwarded, under separate cover, to this headquarters for forwarding to the CMC (Code DK).

(undoubtedly signed – *WCH* shows a carbon copy)
F. D. STICE
By direction

At last: The final administrative action and entry into Oswald's Service Record Book, on the same day at the Headquarters of the Marine Air Reserve Training Command at the Naval Aviation Station, Glenview, Illinois:

1960 September 13: Administrative Remarks entered into Oswald's SRB [646]

1960 September 13: Final entries in Oswald's Service Record Book [647]

Oswald's "RECORD OF SERVICE" was brief, two pages, of which this is the second. The first two lines show his transfer into the "H. & H. Squadron", the administrative unit used only to complete the paperwork and discharge him from active duty at El Toro. The third line shows induction into the Reserve at Glenview Naval Air Station for what should have been three years. What ensued is not shown on this record — his travel to Moscow, his assignment to Minsk, and all the documents and processes we have seen that he still knows nothing about.

The fourth line is his discharge. On the last line, as part of the process, hard-working First Lieutenant M. G. Letscher, the Administrative Officer who prepared many of the documents that have been shown, recomputed his ratings, 3.94 for conduct and 4.1 for proficiency. The Marine officer who brought all these to the Warren Commission, Lt. Col. Allison G. Folsom, Jr.,[648] explained that "the markings are averaged at the end of the enlistment, and in accordance with existing regulations, the numerical quality of the markings determine the difference in the character of discharge".[649] The minimum requirement for an honorable discharge was 4.0. 3.94 may seem close, but is not the bare-minimum required 4.0.

A second endorsement soon followed; the reason for "Undesirable" discharge was changed from "unfitness" to "misconduct". It was signed by M. G. Letscher, who earlier in the year had sent the first letters addressed to Oswald, received and argued by Marguerite:

1960 September 15: Commander of MART to Commandant of the Marine Corps [650]

```
                                        In reply refer to:
                                        Code:    50/JET:nom
                                                 1900
                                                 15 Sep 1960

SECOND ENDORSEMENT on CMC Discharge Order DMB-1-bco of 17Aug60

From:   Mobilization Planning Officer, Mobilization Planning Branch
To:     Commandant of the Marine Corps (Code DK)
Via:    Commander, Marine Air Reserve Training

Subj:   Discharge by reason of misconduct; case of Private First Class
        Lee H. OSWALD 1653230 USMCR (Class III)

1.   Readdressed and forwarded.

2.   The subject named Marine was discharged from the U. S. Marine Corps
Reserve effective 13 September 1960.  He was discharged as Undesirable by
reason of misconduct, and was issued an Undesirable Discharge Certificate
(DD 258 MC).


                                (undoubtedly signed – WCH shows a carbon copy)
                                M. G. LETSCHER
                                By direction
```

Lee had no way of knowing it at the time — the process and every piece of paperwork we have seen above were completely unknown to him — but exactly one year and two days after his early release from active duty because of Marguerite's "hardship", he was discharged as "Undesirable" from the Marine Corps Reserve,[651] based on:

> "reliable information which indicated that he had renounced his U.S. citizenship with the intentions of becoming a permanent citizen of the Union of Soviet Socialist Republics. Further, that petitioner brought discredit to the Marine Corps through adverse newspaper publicity, which was generated by the foregoing action, and had thereby, in the opinion of his commanding officer, proved himself unfit for retention in the naval service." [652]

Because the Marines have no current mail address for him, the Undesirable Discharge Certificate referred to above will not be delivered to Lee until 18 months later, in March 1962. If you'd like to see it now, look ahead at page 98.

This was the height of the Cold War. On September 29, 1960, hearing a displeasing speech at the United Nations in New York City, Soviet leader Nikita Khrushchev wrote in his autobiography that his delegation, himself included, began making noise, shouting and yelling. "I took off my shoe and pounded on the desk. Obviously, our relations with the Americans were distant." [653]

On November 8, by a very narrow margin, John Fitzgerald Kennedy of Massachusetts was elected to be the 35th President of the United States, and Lyndon Baines Johnson of Texas was elected Vice President.

Lee wrote in the *Historic Diary* that he was becoming "increasingly concious of just what sort of a sociaty" he lived in.[654] He criticized the contrast between the lives of ordinary workers and those of Communist Party members. He complained about the lack of freedom in Russia,[655] the lack of opportunity to travel,[656] inadequate housing,[657] and the chronic scarcity of food products.[658] He observed that the party members were all "opportunists," who "shouted the loudest and made the most noise", but were interested only in their own welfare.[659]

Of his factory, he said that political considerations of which he disapproved dominated its operation. He attributed the lack of unemployment to the shortage of labor-saving machinery and the heavy load of bureaucracy, which kept "tons of paper work" flowing in and out of the factory and required a high foreman-worker ratio.[660] In addition, there was "a small army of examiners, committees, and supply checkers and the quality-control board."[661]

After returning to the US in 1962, Lee told Marina's student of Russian, Paul Gregory, about the factory, so Gregory was able to relate this incident to the Warren Commission, illustrating the importance of political correctness:

> "I know it was some kind of a shop and he ran some kind of a machine. Because he told me of some incident when he had to—the shop had to be changed, or they moved the equipment into another building, and the first thing they moved was the picture of Lenin and later they moved the equipment. It was heavy equipment, and they set the machines so that the men could work facing Lenin. And then they decided Lenin had to be hung in the most favorable place in the shop, and the Commissar came in and inspected the next setup and decided Lenin wasn't in the right place, and, therefore, they had to come back in and completely remount all the machinery and turn it around to face Lenin's new position."[662]

Lee wrote that life at the factory centered around the "Kollective." Meetings of the Kollective were "so numerous as to be staggering." In a single month he noted one meeting of the professional union, four political information meetings, two young Communist meetings, one meeting of the production committee to discuss ways of improving work, two Communist Party meetings, four meetings of the "School of Communist Labor" and one sports meeting. All but one of them were compulsory for Communist Party members, and all but three were compulsory for everyone.[663] Each lasted anywhere from 10 minutes to 2 hours. Oswald said that no one liked the meetings, which were accepted "philosophically"; at the political meetings especially, everyone paid strict attention, and party members were posted in the audience to watch for the slightest sign that anyone's attention might relax, even for a moment.[664] Oswald wrote that the "spontaneous" demonstrations on Soviet holidays or for distinguished visitors were almost as well organized as the Kollectivist meetings at the factory.[665] He noted that elections were supervised to ensure that everyone voted, and that they voted for the candidates of the Communist Party.

A remarkable result of his work at the plant — Lee made two friends! At best, when he returns to the US, there may be one more — but that is debatable. So, these are at least two-thirds of the only friends of his entire life. Alexander Ziger was the plant's deputy chief engineer. A Jew in Poland, he emigrated to Brazil to escape Hitler and WWII, then returned to live in Minsk in the 1950s. He and his family came to regret that decision[666] and applied to leave. Perhaps that helped cement his friendship with Lee. Also at the factory, Lee became a friend of Pavel Golovachev, the privileged son of a WWII flying ace who, like Lee, had his own apartment. "Marina believes that Pavel was far and away her husband's closest friend in Russia, and probably the closest friend he ever had."[667] Biographer Priscilla Johnson McMillan concluded: "Their friendships with him appear to have been genuine and spontaneous, and the two men, one perhaps a father figure, the other an older brother, were very likely the best and truest friends he ever had." [668] We may arrive at Lee's entire lifetime list of friends, birth-to-death, by adding his loving brother Robert, although as will be clear, Robert always loved Lee but Lee's response was unpredictable, sometimes hostile. That's it.

1961 began with Lee asking co-worker Ella German to marry him. She rejected him, saying that she did not love him and that she was afraid to marry an American. Oswald was "too stunned to think" and concluded that she had gone out with him only because she was envied by the other girls for having an American escort. [669] In one diary entry he attributed her failure to love him to "a state of fear which was always in the Soviet Union." [670]

On January 4, 1961, one year after he had been issued his "stateless" residence permit, Oswald was summoned to the passport office in Minsk and asked if he still wanted to become a Soviet citizen. He replied that he did not, but asked that his residence permit be extended for another year. [671] The entry in his diary for January reads: "I am stating to reconsider my disire about staying. The work is drab. The money I get has nowhere to be spent. No nightclubs or bowling allys, no places of recreation acept the trade union dances. I have had enough." [672]

On January 20, a bitterly cold but blindingly bright day in the District of Columbia: "I, John Fitzgerald Kennedy, do solemnly swear that I will faithfully execute the office of President of the United States ...". Then he asked us to ask what we can do for our country.

Chapter 1 – MOTHER demonstrated that Marguerite had the chutzpah to assert that she and her son Lee deserved assistance from all levels of society and government. Here's the "small world" example on January 26: "As Kennedy settled into office, the White House was inundated by phone calls, few of which reached [personal secretary Evelyn] Lincoln's desk. One of the few calls that did reach the president's office on his sixth day in office was from Marguerite Oswald [who] had come to Washington seeking help, and though ... the president did not talk to her, Lincoln noted the call in the official list of calls." [673]

Marguerite had spent three nights and two days sitting up in train coaches. "I arrived at ... 8 o'clock in the morning and I called the White House. A Negro man was on the switchboard ... I asked to speak to the President. And he said the offices were not open yet. ... So I called back at 9 o'clock. Everybody was just gracious to me over the phone. Said that President Kennedy was in a conference, and they would be happy to take any message. I asked to speak to Secretary Rusk, and they connected me with that office. And his young lady said he was in a conference, but anything she could do for me. I said, 'I have come to town about a son of mine who is lost in Russia. ... I would like personally to speak to Secretary Rusk.' So she got off the line a few minutes. Whether she gave him the message or what I do not know. She came back and said, 'Mrs. Oswald, Mr. Rusk'—so evidently she handed him a note—'[asks] that you talk to Mr. Boster, who is special officer in charge of Soviet Union affairs' ... And Mr. Boster was on the line. I told him who I was. He said, 'Yes, I am familiar with the case, Mrs. Oswald.' He said, 'Will an 11 o'clock appointment be all right with you?' This is 9 o'clock in the morning. So I said—this is quite an interesting story—I said 'Mr. Boster that would be fine. But I would rather not talk with you.' I didn't know who Mr. Boster was. I said, 'I would rather talk with Secretary of State Rusk. However, if I am unsuccessful in talking with him, then I will keep my appointment with you.'" [674]

Then she asked Mr. Boster to please recommend a hotel that would be reasonable, and he did, and she went and got a room by saying that "'the State Department recommended that I come here.' So they fixed me up with a room. ... I arrived at Mr. Boster's office at 10:30.

But before arriving ... I stopped at a telephone in the corridor, and I called Dean Rusk's office again, because I didn't want to see Mr. Boster, and I asked to speak to Dean Rusk. And the young lady said, 'Mrs. Oswald, talk to Mr. Boster. At least it is a start.'" [675]

So she met with Mr. Boster and two other officials, and undoubtedly with considerable rambling, told them, according to the Department of State's *Memorandum of Conversation*: "she thought there was some possibility that her son had in fact gone to the Soviet Union as a US secret agent, and if this were true she wished the appropriate authorities to know that she was destitute and should receive some compensation. Mrs. Oswald was assured that there was no evidence to suggest that her son had gone to the Soviet Union as an 'agent', and that she should dismiss any such idea." [676] They said that if his purpose was to defect, then that was his right; the U.S. would not stand in his way — a seeming echo of Lee asking the Marines for an early exit and their reaction: "Don't let the door hit you in the butt as you leave!" Finally, "It was agreed that the Department would send a new instruction to the Embassy in Moscow asking that the Soviet Foreign Ministry be informed that Mrs. Oswald had not heard from her son in several months and was very anxious to have word from him." [677]

Mrs. Oswald, despite having seen neither President Kennedy nor Secretary Rusk, went home rather pleased with the reception she'd been given. She told the Warren Commission: "[M]y trip to Washington—which was red carpet treatment. Let's say, gentlemen, if a woman gets on the phone at 9 o'clock and has an appointment at 11 o'clock with three big men, that is wonderful treatment. ... [T]hey were most gracious to me. The Administration was most gracious to me." [678] Chief Consul Rankin said: "I don't see why you should think that because they treated you nicely, that was any sign he was an agent." but good old Marguerite chided: "We'll, maybe you don't see why." [679]

Marguerite gave that Washington pilgrimage credit for a rapid result: "Approximately eight weeks later, on March 22, 1961, I received a letter from the State Department informing me of my son's address ... just eight weeks after my trip to Washington." [680] Her trip did cause a "Welfare-Whereabouts" memo to be sent to the American Embassy in Moscow, but Consul Snyder did not ask the MVD to help locate Oswald. By pure coincidence, as will soon be explained, Snyder had learned Lee's address. First, two other matters.

Four years later, Marguerite would bitterly complain to writer Jean Stafford against one of the most decent men who ever held high office: "Representative [Gerald] Ford ... said that I went to Washington ... which I did, when I was in dire need, which I was, but I went to petition President Kennedy to get my son to come home in order to support and help me, *not* to influence him [Lee]. What an injustice to a mother!" [681] Her complaint is quite obscure, but note that word "injustice" — it next appears in the threatening letter Lee will write to John Connally. The mother had taught the son that the two of them were treated unjustly.

An American TV analysis of Soviet files reported: "The KGB believed that, in time, Oswald would become disillusioned with Soviet life and leave on his own accord. They were right." [682] General Oleg Kalugin, KGB Chief of Foreign Counterintelligence, said: "Because he was a misfit, he found no home in Russia, and he started thinking of something else." [683]

The American Embassy in Moscow had not heard from Oswald in the fifteen months since his nasty letter of November 3, 1959.[684] "On February 13 [1961] ... Snyder found a letter from Oswald on his desk [and] was completely astonished to read that the young Marine, who had belligerently slammed his passport on the embassy desk fourteen months before and categorically stated that he never wanted to live in the United States again, was now writing in a very matter-of-fact tone" [685] to request the return of his passport and state that he wanted to return to the U.S. if he could "come to some agreement [with the American Government] concerning the dropping of any legal proceedings" against him. He noted that he had not become a Soviet citizen and was living in Russia with "nonpermanent type papers for a foreigner" and said that he did not appear personally because he could not leave Minsk without permission. The letter concluded: "I hope that in recalling the responsibility I have to America that you remember your's in doing everything you can to help me since I am an American citizen." [686]

Richard Snyder, who had briefly interviewed Lee at the Embassy in 1959, answered that Oswald would have to appear personally to discuss his return to the U.S. Snyder ended by stating that "the Department of State ... had received an inquiry from your mother in which she said that she had not heard from you since December, 1959 and was concerned about your whereabouts and welfare." [687] The State Department notified Marguerite of Lee's letter and address,[688] and as related above, she gave herself credit because of her appeal in Washington.

A reply from Oswald "asserted 'I cannot leave the city of Minsk without permission. . . I have no intention of abusing my position here, and I am sure you would not want me to.'" [689] He asked that "preliminary inquiries * * * be put in the form of a questionnaire" and sent to him.[690] Soviet authorities had undoubtedly intercepted and read the correspondence between Oswald and the Embassy, so knew of his plans.[691] Soon after the correspondence began, his monthly payments from the "Red Cross", in reality the MVD, ended.[692]

The Embassy wrote to Oswald on March 24, stating again that he would have to come to Moscow.[693] Later, the Department of State decided that his passport could be returned only if he appeared in person and the Embassy was satisfied, after exploring the matter, that he was really Lee Oswald, not an imposter, and that he had not renounced his citizenship.[694]

Oswald continued to chronicle his life in the *Historic Diary*. On the ninth page (headed "**DAiRY**") he recorded an event at the Palace of Culture for Professional Workers in Minsk:[695]

> "March 17 - I and Erich went to trade union dance . Boring- but at the last hour I am introduced to a girl with a French hair-do and Red-Dress with white slippers I dance with her . Than ask to show her home I do, along with 5 other admirares Her name is Marina. We like each other right away she gives me her phone number" [696]

Each had already lived the script of the other's life; her story is akin to Lee's sad childhood of instability, loss, only one part-time parent, repeated moving, few anchors.

Marina Nikolayevna Prusakova [D] was born on July 17, 1941, at Severodvinsk (formerly Molotovsk), Arkhangelsk Oblast', on Russia's far-north White Sea coast.[697] Her unmarried mother was Klavdiya Vasilievna Prusakova. When Marina was one, Klavdiya married Aleksandr Ivanovich Medvedev, an electrical worker.[698] Marina was told, falsely, that Medvedev was her biological father,[699] so she grew up with the Russian-style name Marina Alexandrovna Medvedeva. While still a young girl, Marina went to live with her maternal grandparents, Tatyana Yakovlevna Prusakova and Vasiliy Prusakov,[E] but he died when Marina

---

[D] Russian words and names use the Cyrillic alphabet. When transliterated into our Roman alphabet, spellings vary. My brother-in-law, professor Larry Penrose, a Russian language expert trained at the U.S. Army language school to sit in Japan and eavesdrop on Russia during the Cold War, says there is no one "right" spelling. When variations exist, this book spells as did the *Warren Report*.

[E] A wife or daughter uses her husband's or father's surname with "a" appended to show she's a she.

was about four years old. After three more years with grandmother Tatyana,[700] Marina moved to Zguritva, Moldavian SSR (formerly Bessarabia) to again live with her mother.[701] When almost ten, a friend burst forth, "Guess what? My mama was talking to your mama last night. And your mama said your papa isn't your real papa at all!"[702] Mother Klavdiya confirmed that the biologic father had been a soldier who died in the war. Marina's similarities are strongly like Lee's having a half-brother Pic with a different name, father Robert Oswald's death before Lee's birth, Marguerite's brief marriage to Ekdahl, the many moves she made with Lee, the young boy's frequent stays with aunt Lil, abandonment in the orphanage.

In 1952, the family moved to Leningrad[703] for Aleksandr to work in a power station.[704] Marina did well in school, and was eligible to "finish the full ten-year course that comprises a Soviet high-school education."[705] When she completed the seventh grade in 1955,[706] "a friend at school ... was about to take examinations for pharmacy school and Marina wanted to try, too. All her life, she told her mother, she had admired the white coats pharmacists wore and the spotless cleanliness of apothecary shops."[707] Klavdiya was ill and agreed because Marina might need a specialty to support herself. You can probably guess what happened: the friend failed the exam, but Marina, with no preparation, "passed with 23 of 25 possible points."[708] She entered the Pharmacy Teknikum for special training. After her mother died in 1957, Marina continued to live with her stepfather although they did not get along, she said, because she displeased him by her "fresh" conduct; she was not easily disciplined[709] and was a source of concern to him.[710] Marina regarded her childhood as unhappy. She was a teenager, 15 when her mother died and she will marry at 19 — the stars of this story are young people!

When she needed her birth certificate to "receive the internal passport for identification and travel within the country that is issued to every Soviet city dweller on reaching the age of sixteen ... Marina, her grandmother and the rest of her relatives ... were thunderstruck [when] from the registry office in Severodvinsk came the reply that there was no birth certificate or other documents for a Marina Alexandrovna Medvedeva, only for a Marina Nikolayevna Prusakova. (Marina's real father had been named Nikolai and her mother's maiden name was Prusakova. If the father does not claim, or the mother prove, paternity, a child born to an unmarried Soviet mother is given his/her father's first name as the patronymic [middle name] and his/her mother's maiden name as the surname.)"[711]

"This new discovery had humiliating consequences for Marina. Legally she had to take the name inscribed on her birth certificate. ... She had to change her ... school registration ... and endure the teasing of the other girls. As if this were not embarrassment enough, the space on her new passport for her father's name was left blank—to any Soviet child the ultimate token of illegitimacy, carrying a stigma of which he or she is painfully reminded on the innumerable occasions when the passport is presented as identification."[712]

Depressed and apathetic, Marina stopped studying and cut classes. "In May, only two weeks before the final examinations ... she was expelled for 'academic failure and systematic non-attendance at class.'"[713] Months of lassitude and non-skilled jobs ensued, after which she applied for reinstatement, worked hard, and graduated from the Teknikum with a diploma in pharmacy in June 1959. Two months later, Marina went to Minsk to visit aunt Musya, her mother's youngest sister, but she and Vanya and their four children were crammed into a small apartment. So, Marina went to her mother's eldest brother Ilya and aunt Valya,[714] who had no children, and with whom there grew a mutual affection.[715] Uncle Ilya Prusakov, a member of the Communist Party,[716] headed the Ministry of Internal Affairs' local bureau concerned with lumber, so had one of the best apartments in a building reserved for MVD employees.[717] [F] Ilya did not allow his family to take advantage of his high position, so "Marina went to the city and district militia headquarters to fill out countless questionnaires. After a suspenseful wait of two weeks, she received a permit to reside at her uncle's address, Apartment 20, No. 38-42 Ulitsa Kalinina. Without knowing it, Marina had vaulted from middle to the upper class"[718] and was already living on high-class Kalinin Street where she will make her first home in Apartment 24, No. 4, as the bride of a coddled foreigner — who has a private apartment!

Marina, only 18 when she arrived in Minsk, went to work in the drug section of the Klimincheskaya,[719] the Third Clinical Hospital.[720] Social life consisted of meeting friends, mostly students, in cafes to sip coffee, read newspapers, gossip, and carry on discussions. The group of friends "ran together," and Marina did not attach herself to a particular boyfriend. "[T]hey would dance to the music of Elvis, Eartha Kitt, or Louis Armstrong. 'A thing had only to be forbidden,' Marina recalls, 'for us to get hold of it somehow.'"[721] She enjoyed this life, which she had been leading for about 7 months when she met Lee.[722]

Lee asked if they could meet again, to which Marina suggested he return to the dance palace. He did, and after one week there she was![723] Marina told the FBI — only 2¾ years later — much will happen quickly! — "that Oswald's Russian, although good, bore a definite accent. She thought that he probably had come from one of the Russian-speaking Baltic countries."[724] She and all Lee's co-workers called him "Aleck" or "Alik", she explained, "because they did not like the name of Lee as it usually is connected with Chinese persons."[725]

Marina gave Lee her telephone number, and on March 30 he called her from the Fourth Clinical Hospital where he had an adenoid operation. Sympathetic because he was there alone, she visited him frequently. By the time he is discharged, Lee "knows I must have her."[726] He asked her to be his fiancée, and she agreed to consider it,[727] especially after "he said that his mother was dead [so] they were both orphans".[728] While they courted, there was a major development that will influence Oswald in two years: "about 1,500 CIA-trained Cuban exiles launched the disastrous Bay of Pigs invasion of Cuba in an attempt to topple Fidel Castro."[729] Castro led his troops in easily repelling and capturing the invaders, in only three days.

Lee visited Marina regularly at the apartment of her aunt and uncle, who were not disturbed by the fact that he was an American and did not disapprove of her seeing him. "Oswald showed her his apartment. She found it instantly appealing, 'a small darling one-room apartment with a balcony, a bathroom, gas kitchen and a separate entrance—quite enough for two, especially if they were young.' She had long admired this particular apartment house at the bend of the river and the view it commanded."[730]

He continued to ask her to marry, and on April 19, only one month and two days after they met, orphan Marina took "orphan" Lee to her uncle Ilya, acting *in loco parentis*, for the obligatory formal permission. Collaborating with biographer McMillan, Marina told the story:

> "The next day Alik put on his holiday best: a black suit, a white shirt and tie, even a dark blue hat. [H]e and Marina climbed the three narrow flights to Ilya and Valya's apartment, he stopped at nearly every step. 'Oh, my God, what will I say?' he groaned. 'Please help me out.' He was pale and his knees were shaking as he waited on the landing, summoning courage to ring the bell. ... Ilya met Alik in the living room and Marina went apprehensively into the kitchen with her aunt. Her cheeks flushed with embarrassment, she asked: 'Aunt Valya, is

---

[F] His work for the dread MVD will give conspiracy theorists a large pile to search through after 1963!

Uncle Ilya in a good mood today?' Valya nodded in the affirmative. 'Do you know what he's going to say?' Valya had no idea.

"Ilya, meanwhile, was asking Alik a battery of the usual questions. He said that Marina was still very flighty. She was fickle and immature, and she wasn't ready to get married. Then he asked Alik if he had the proper papers. Although he was an official of the MVD, Ilya, as he examined Alik's documents, overlooked a fact that might have been critical in giving his consent. Alik did not have a regular Soviet passport, but a special document for the so-called stateless person, the foreigner who does not have Soviet citizenship and may or may not have retained citizenship of another country. Ilya later explained that he was not expert in that type of document. He thought it was a special residence permit issued to a foreigner during his first three years in Russia, and he believed that Alik was already a citizen of the U.S.S.R. Had he had any other impression, he said, he would have withheld his consent to the marriage. As it was, he took the precaution of asking: 'And what about America, Alik? Do you intend to go back?' Alik swore that he did not, and Ilya took him at his word.

"After twenty minutes or so, Ilya called Marina in from the kitchen. 'So it's getting married you lovebirds have in mind. Alik, here, asks if he can marry you. I told him what kind of little bird you are and he has promised to reform you. Do you consent to marry him?' Marina answered that she did.

"'Marriage is a serious thing, Ilya said. 'Personally, I think it's too soon. But if I say No, Marina will blame me if her life is unhappy later on. If you think you'll be happy together, then it's not for me to refuse. Only, live with one another in peace. If you fight or if anything goes wrong, settle it yourselves. Don't come to me with your troubles.' Marina broke in like a little girl. 'Does that mean you are saying Yes, Uncle Ilya?' 'I am. Let's drink to it.' The four of them went into the kitchen and sat at the table, drinking cognac." [731]

Marina testified that when she agreed to marry him, she believed that Oswald could not return to the United States because he had told her he had no such intent, and had surrendered his passport in Moscow. She did <u>not</u> marry him in the hope of going to the United States. [732]

That "was only one of several lies he told her. She did not know that, even before they met, he had written to the American Embassy in Moscow to request his passport and help in returning to the United States. Nor did she know that he had lied about his age. He was twenty-one, not twenty-four. And he was not an orphan—his mother was alive." [733]

After filing notice of their intent to marry at the registrar, obtaining special consent for an alien to marry a citizen, and waiting the usual 10 days, they were married on April 30. [734] The "ceremony" was not much. They went by taxi with the necessary two witnesses, a lady who lived across the hall from Aunt Valya, and her boyfriend, "to ZAGS, the bureau where Soviet citizens go to register birth and death, marriage and divorce." [735] The same gray-haired old man who had taken their application ten days earlier sat them at his desk, had them sign his registry book, "and with a bit of a flourish, the old man placed the marriage stamp in Alik's passport. Then he admonished the bride: 'Be a good wife to him, now. No looking at the other boys!' With that he affixed the stamp to her passport. ... Marina peered over Alik's shoulder to inspect his marriage stamp. She noticed ... that his date of birth was 1939." [736] So, within minutes of marriage, she discovered one of his lies, about his age.

The *Historic Diary* entry for the wedding day reads:

"**We are married. At her aunts home we have a dinner reception for about 20 friends and neboribos** [neighbors] **who wish us happiness (in spite of my origin and accept** [accent] **which was in general rather disquiting to any Russian since for.** [foreigners] **are very rare in the soviet Union even tourist. After an evening of eating and drinking in which * * * ** [Marina's uncle] **started a fright** [fight] **and the fuse blow on an overloaded circite we take our leave and walk the 15 minutes to our home. We lived near each other, at midnight we were home.**"[737]

On back of the photo in Lee's handwriting is "April 30, 1961. Marina–Lee". Lee mailed the photo to brother Robert, who will give it to the Warren Commission in only three years.[738] The newlyweds both took 3 days off from their jobs, which they spent in Minsk [739] in their lovely apartment on Kalinin Street, as prized and cherished as Uncle Ilya's, but with a much better location, right on the bend of the Svisloch River, shown in a photo fifteen pages ago.

Oswald wrote in his diary for May 1, the day after the wedding and wedding night:

"**In spite of fact I married Marina to hurt Ella I found myself in love with Marina.**"[740]

The next entry, marked simply "**May**" reads in part:

"**The trasistion of changing full love from Ella to Marina was very painfull esp. as I saw Ella almost every day at the factory but as the days & weeks went by I adjusted more and more** [to] **my wife mentaly * * * She is maddly in love with me from the very start. Boat rides on Lake Minsk walks through the parks evening at home or at Aunt Valia's place mark May.**"[741]

And in June:

"**A continuence of May, except that; we draw closer and closer, and I think very little now of Ella.**"[742]

His mother, forever convinced he went to Russia as a secret government agent, told the Warren Commission her amazing belief: "I say—and I may be wrong—the U.S. Embassy has ordered him to marry this Russian girl."[743] The commissioners were perplexed; chief consul Rankin asked: "I am not clear about this being ordered to marry her. You don't mean that your son didn't love her." to which she explained: "Well, I could mean that—if he is an agent, and he has a girl friend, and it is to the benefit of the country that he marry this girl friend, and the Embassy helped him get this Russian girl out of Russia—let's face it, well, whether he loved her or not, he would take her to America, if that would give him contact with Russians, yes, sir. ... I know a little about the CIA, and so on, the U-2, [U-2 pilot] Powers, and things that have been made public. They go through any extreme for their country. I do not think that would be serious for him to marry a Russian girl and bring her here, so he would have contact. I think that is all part of an agent's duty."[744] Because Lee will die in Dallas before we can size him up, we must attempt to fathom Marguerite's style of thinking to have any hope of understanding his mind — she was his only mentor and model.

Shortly after their marriage, there are two major developments. Marina soon learns that she became pregnant in their first month; she will deliver a baby 9 months and 15 days after the wedding. And, Oswald surprised his bride — he is anxious to return to the United States! The diary says that he told her "in the last days" of June and that she was "slightly startled" but encouraged him to do as he wished.[745] Marina, never out of the Soviet Union, decides to take this unexpected chance with her strange American because she already knows that Lee Oswald is secretive, but bull-headed and bound to do whatever he wants, no matter what.[746]

The photo, probably taken by Lee, shows Marina on their apartment's balcony, with its prized view of the bend in the river.[747]

Lee notified the Embassy in a May letter that he was married and his wife would seek to accompany him to the United States.[748] "Since he still lacked the assurances he wanted, he reiterated, 'I wish to make it clear that I am asking not only for the right to return to the United States, but also for full guarantees that I shall not, under any circumstances, be persecuted for any act pertaining to my case.'"[749] The Oswalds also began to make inquiries in Soviet offices about exit visas.[750]

The young couple apparently enjoyed their new life.[751] They ate most of their meals in cafes or at restaurants.[752] For amusement, they went boating, attended the opera, concerts, the circus, and films; occasionally, they gathered with a group of friends for a cooperative meal at someone's apartment.[753] His Russian improved, but he retained an accent and never learned to speak with grammatical correctness, or to write well.[754]

Lee reopened correspondence with his family on May 5, with a friendly letter to his brother Robert. He said nothing about his contacts with the American Embassy, but mentioned that he had married, and that he had a job as a "metal-smith" and was living well. He asked his brother for their mother's address, and encouraged him to come to Minsk for a visit.[755] Robert answered the letter quickly — and here we mention that airmail took about a week each way, and that the Soviets probably read it all, both directions. On May 31, Lee wrote again, saying that before he could return he would have to obtain permission of the Soviet Union for him and Marina to leave and ensure that no charges would be lodged against him in the United States. In this letter, he mentioned that he was in touch with the Embassy in Moscow.[756]

A reminder of what was going on in the world: The next day, President Kennedy said to 400 journalists in France: "I do not think it altogether inappropriate to introduce myself. I am the man who accompanied Jacqueline Kennedy to Paris. And I have enjoyed it."[757]

Lee also wrote to his mother.[758] A couple of weeks later, Marina "saw him reading a letter from home with such a thoughtful expression that she asked whether it contained bad news." He then admitted it was from his mother, and had to admit that she was not dead. Thus Marina had learned the truth of all three pre-marriage lies described on page 69. Lee habitually lies — it's a defining characteristic of who he is. She had noticed the left-wrist scar from his suicide attempt in Moscow; he refused to explain it, never did, and Marina learned the truth only after his death. Now, when she also sees "the scar on his left elbow from the accidental discharge of a pistol while he was in the Marine Corps in Japan, ... he [says], falsely, that he had been wounded in action in Indonesia." [759]

As the second half of 1961 began, Lee had had no word since March concerning the return of his passport. Impatient for action,[760] "during his two-week vacation from the factory, Lee decided to fly to Moscow, without police permission." [761] He appeared without warning at the Embassy on July 8; it was a Saturday and the offices were closed.[762] [G] He used the house telephone to reach Richard Snyder, who came to the office, talked with him briefly, and suggested that he return on the following Monday.[763] Oswald called Marina and asked her to join him in Moscow. She arrived on Sunday, July 9,[764] and they took a room at the Hotel Berlin,[765] where he had stayed when he first arrived in Russia.

Lee returned to the Embassy on Monday. Snyder asked to see his Soviet papers and questioned him closely about his life in Russia and possible expatriating acts. Oswald stated that he was not a citizen of the Soviet Union and had never formally applied for citizenship, that he had never taken an oath of allegiance to the Soviet Union, and that he was not a member of the factory trade union organization. He said that he had never given Soviet officials any confidential information that he had learned in the Marines, had never been asked to give such information, and "doubted" that he would have done so had he been asked.[766] Some of his statements during this interview were clearly false. He had certainly applied for citizenship in the Soviet Union,[767] and had been disappointed when it was denied.[768] He possessed a membership card in the union organization.[769] In addition, his assertion to Snyder that he had never been questioned by Soviet authorities concerning his life in the United States is simply unbelievable. His wife knew the truth. "For Marina to perceive, at the youthful age of nineteen, that her husband told lies as a matter of character rather than of necessity was a feat of mature intuition." [770]

Lee showed anxiety, regularly displayed in his letters, that he might be prosecuted and imprisoned if he returned to the United States. CIA-conspiracy theorist John Newman opined: "From the available documents, a strong case could have been made—and Oswald knew and feared it—to prosecute him under military or civilian espionage laws." [771] Snyder told Lee informally that he did not know any grounds on which he would be prosecuted but that he could give no assurances.[772] Snyder wrote in his report to the State Department:

> "Twenty months of the realities of life in the Soviet Union have clearly had a maturing effect on Oswald. He stated frankly that he had learned a hard lesson the hard way and that he had been completely relieved of his illusions about the Soviet Union at the same time that he acquired a new understanding and appreciation of the United States and the meaning of freedom. Much of the arrogance and bravado which characterized him on his first visit to the Embassy appears to have left him." [773]

The passport that Lee had slapped down on a desk and left at the Embassy would expire on September 10, 1961.[774] He probably would not be able to obtain Russian exit papers by then, so he filled out an application for its renewal.[775] On an attached questionnaire,[776] he reiterated his oral statements that he had obtained only a residence permit in the Soviet Union and was still an American national. On the basis of the written and oral statements, Snyder concluded that he had not expatriated himself and handed his passport back to him,[777] "so that he could obtain the necessary exit visa from the Soviets, and wished him well." [778] Lee came

---

[G] Again! Arriving on weekends is his quirky habit. He did it in Moscow in the previous chapter, and will do it again in Mexico City in the next. It's always bad timing, and he doesn't seem to learn.

to the Embassy again the following day,[779] bringing Marina [780] to initiate procedures for her admission to the United States as an immigrant; they had a routine interview with Snyder's assistant, John McVickar.[781] "[T]he best was still to come. ... Marina had to go to the toilet. ... It was immaculate and as fragrant as a garden. There was even real toilet paper. Marina had seen that, instead of small squares of newspaper, only once in her life ... at the Hotel Metropole in Leningrad." [782] Three days later, they returned to Minsk.[783]

Lee wrote to his brother Robert that he had his passport again, and he and Marina were doing everything possible to leave the Soviet Union. The letter closed with an affectionate greeting to his brother and family.[784] Robert understood: "I knew he was trying to apologize, in his way. Lee never could say, in so many words, that he was sorry." [785]

Lee and Marina "discovered that their visit to the American Embassy was no secret."[786] Marina testified that she was dropped from membership in Komsomol, the Communist Youth Organization,[787] and that "meetings were arranged" at which "members of the various organizations" attempted to dissuade her from leaving the Soviet Union.[788] "But the more she was harassed, the more determined she became." [789] Her aunt and uncle did not speak to her for "a long time." [790] Paul Gregory, to whom Marina will teach Russian in the United States, testified that she referred to this period of her life in Minsk as "a very horrible time." [791]

The Oswalds began to work with local authorities for permission to leave the country.[792] His diary entry for July 16 through August 20 reads:

> "We have found out which blanks and certificates are nessceary to apply for a exit visa. They number about 20 papers; birth certificates, affidavit, photos, ect. On Aug 20th we give the papers out they say it will be 3½ months before we know wheather they let us go or not. In the meantime Marina has had to stade 4 differant meeting at the place of work held by her boss's at the direction of 'someone' by phone. The Young Comm. leauge headqutes also called about her and she had to go see them for 1½ hours. The purpose (expressed) is to disuade her from going to the U.S.A. Net effect: Make her more stubborn about wanting to go. Marina is pregnet. We hope that the visas come through soon." [793]

On August 13, 1961, East German soldiers hurriedly threw up a barbed-wire fence across Berlin, separating the U.S.S.R.-controlled sector from the western part of the city administered by the U.S., Britain and France. Within days, they backed the fence with an ugly tall concrete wall with armed guards on watchtowers overlooking a no-man's zone, and the Berlin Wall became a bleak reality, destined to imprison East Berliners until 1989.

For August 21 through September 1, Lee's diary reads:

> "I make repeated trips to the passport & visa office, also to Ministry of For. Affairs in Minsk, also Min. of Internal Affairs, all of which have a say in the granting of a visa. I extrackted promises of quick attention to us." [794]

Superpower tensions continue to increase. On August 30, the Soviet Union resumes its atmospheric testing of thermonuclear weapons, exploding a 150-kiloton hydrogen bomb over Siberia.[795] On September 5, after the Soviets tested two more H-bombs, President Kennedy announces he has ordered the resumption of U.S. nuclear tests.[796] In Lee's *Historic* Diary for all of September through October 18: "No word from Min. ('They'll call us.')." [797]

Oswald wrote to the Embassy on October 4, asking the U.S. Government to officially intervene to facilitate their applications for exit visas.[798] He stated there had been "systematic and concerted attempts to intimidate [Marina] into withdrawing her application for a visa" which resulted in her being hospitalized for a 5-day period for "nervous exhaustion." [799] When asked, Marina misunderstood "nervous exhaustion" and denied to the Warren Commission that she was hospitalized,[800] so the *Warren Report* says he probably lied to the Embassy.[801] "Like many of Alik's lies, there was a germ of truth in his claim. Marina had been hospitalized" [802] during her pregnancy after being overcome by gas fumes on a bus.

The Embassy replied that it had no way to influence Soviet conduct on such matters and that its experience had been that action on applications for exit visas was "seldom taken rapidly." [803] To expedite the exit visas, Oswald applied for an interview with Col. Nicolay Aksenov, a local MVD official, but was denied. He then insisted that Marina seek an interview, she agreed reluctantly, her interview was granted.[804] Marina thought this might have been due to the fact that her uncle was also a high-ranking official in the Minsk MVD, but she did not believe he used his position to obtain special treatment.[805] Colonel Aksenov questioned her about reasons for wanting to go to the US and, noticing that she was pregnant, suggested that she at least delay her departure so her child could be born in Russia. He told her many others were seeking visas; she and her husband would have to wait their turn.[806]

Lee again wrote to the Embassy, saying that if, as he anticipated, his residence permit was to be renewed in January for another year, it would be over his protest.[807] The Embassy replied that retaining his Soviet passport, "the type issued to persons considered by the Soviet authorities to have no citizenship, either of the Soviet Union or any other country ... does not prejudice in any way your claim to American citizenship." [808] The letter added that he could discuss renewal of his American passport when he next appears at the Embassy.[809] Although the letter certainly does not verify his US citizenship, Oswald will use it to support that claim in June 1962 when he petitions the Navy Discharge Review Board to retract his undesirable discharge that has already been in effect since June 13, long before this letter from the Moscow Embassy — and Lee still does not have any hint of that discharge or even its process.

Oswald is now hell-bent on returning to the U.S. Disabused of all Soviet enthusiasms, he portrays himself as an American who deserves his government's support. Unsuccessful in his attempt to inspire the embassy to "officially intervene" with the Russians to pry loose the exit visas, he does as Marguerite showed him by example, appealing to authority, and writes to U.S. Senator John Goodwin Tower of Texas. Lee probably chose Tower instead of any other senator or representative because of local name familiarity: Tower's home of Wichita Falls was near to, and affiliated with, the large city that was Lee's base in Texas, Fort Worth.[H] For several reasons, it is worth reading, then following this letter to conclusion:

- Lee will soon write his highly significant letter to John Connally. This is a preview opportunity to learn his style in seeking help from an official.
- Secondly, this letter's handling in Washington will leave a well-documented trail that will be quickly recalled and revealed on the day of assassination.
- The working style of the Warren Commission will be previewed in the final document in this series, when one of its Assistant Counsels studies the senatorial office staff and files.
- Finally, to avoid any intermixing with the many other letters in this chapter, they to be presented in chronologic order, it is simplest to take to conclusion this letter and the five documents it engenders. Therefore, in order from late 1961 to mid 1964:

[H] This author was IBM's Field Engineering Division Branch Manager in Fort Worth in 1974-1975, and regularly visited the Customer Engineers in Wichita Falls, the branch's northwestern outpost.

1961 December (day unknown): Oswald to Senator John G. Tower [810]

```
                                    Lee H. Oswald
                                    Ul. KALiNiNA 4-24
         Senator John G Tower          MiNSK,
                                            U.S.S.R.
          Washington , D.C.


           Dear Senator Tower ;
                     My name is Lee Harvey Oswald, 22,
         of Fort Worth  up till  October 1959 , When I came
         to the Soviet Union for a residenual stay . I took
         a residenual document for a  non-Soviet person
         living for a time in the USSR.  The American
         Embassy in Moscow is familier with my case
                 Since July 20th 1960 , I have unsucessfully
         applied for a Soviet Exit Visa to leave this
         country ,The Soviets refuse to permit me and
         my Soviet wife,(who applied at the U.S. Embassy Moscow,
         July 8 , 1960 for immigration status to the U.S.A.)
         to leave the Soviet Union. I am a citizen of the
         United States of America (passport No.  1733242 , 1959 )
         and I beseech you , Senator Tower , to rise the question
         of holding by the Soviet Union of a citizen of the U.S.,
          against his will and expressed desires.


                              Yours Very Truly
                              (signed) Lee H Oswald
```

The letter, as is usual with Lee, has problems with dates. It is undated, but must have been mailed in middle-to-late December. He dates Marina's application at the Embassy in Moscow as "`July 8 , 1960`", but July 8 was his attempt to visit the closed Embassy on a Saturday; she applied on July 11. Moreover, that was five months before this letter, in 1961, not 1960.

Using what would otherwise be blank space on this page, here is a photo taken in Minsk that Marina gave to the Warren Commission, which captioned it: "From left, Uncle Vasily, Aunt Lubova ("Valya") , Lee Harvey Oswald, and (standing) Marina Oswald." [811] Uncle Vasily Prusakov, brother of Marina's mother Klavdiya Prusakova, is the head of the local bureau concerned with lumber within the Ministry of Internal Affairs (MVD). If you see a resemblance to another Russian who rose through the ranks of the much more sinister KGB to become president of Russia, you are fully entitled to your opinion — and we agree.

Lee's plea was handled by one of the hard-working "case workers" so essential in every Congressional office. The euphonious Miss Linda Lee Lovelady "bucked" it:

1962 January 26: Senator John G. Tower to Department of State [812]

United States Senate

January 26, 1962

Mr. Frederick G. Dutton
Assistant Secretary for
  Congressional Relations
Department of State
Washington 25, D. C.

Dear Mr. Dutton:

Enclosed is correspondence I have received from a
Lee H. Oswald relating to apparent efforts on his
behalf to return to the United States, along with
his wife who is apparently a Soviet citizen.

I do not know Mr. Oswald, or any of the facts concerning his reasons for visiting the Soviet Union;
nor what action, if any, this government can or
should take on his behalf.

Quite obviously his inquiry should have been addressed
to the Executive branch. For this reason, I am forwarding this correspondence to you for whatever action
the Department may consider appropriate.

                    Sincerely yours,

                    John G. Tower

JGT/LL

Enclosure

Only two days later — I know from personal experience working in the office of Senator Long of Louisiana and watching my Dad's supervision of the office of Senator Gruening of Alaska that Executive departments were super-responsive — Miss Lovelady received her answer from the State Department and typed a brief "memo to file", an update for others in the office to read, and for improbable but possible later use:

1962 February 1: Memo to file within Senator Tower's office [813]

United States Senate

MEMORANDUM

2/1/62

Received a call from Mr. Stanfield
in Dept. of State regarding request
of Mr. Lee Harvey Oswald to return
to U.S. from U.S.S.R.

On November 2, 1959, Mr. Oswald
swore to the following affidavit:

"I affirm that my allegiance is to
the Soviet Socialist Republic"
He requested that his American citizenship be revoked.

He now wishes to return to U.S. with
his Soviet wife, who is pregnant.

His mother lives in Vernon and is
unable to pay for his return--state
dept. will probably finance this on
a loan basis.

Senator should not become involved in
such a case--therefore State will
report to us the course which they
follow regarding Lee Harvey Oswalt [sic]

Linda

Because the Senator's letter of January 26 had passed the buck to the State Department for any appropriate action, State's recommendation that the Senator not become involved was expected and undoubtedly welcome. No further action would be taken on Capitol Hill. An official "close-out" response from State arrived a week later:

1962 February 9: Department of State to Senator Tower[814]

DEPARTMENT OF STATE
WASHINGTON

February 9, 1962

Dear Senator Tower:

We enclose for your information copies of correspondence
containing the most recent information we have received
from our Embassy at Moscow regarding the case of Lee Harvey
Oswald, about whom you wrote me on January 26, 1962.

The correspondence sent to you by Mr. Oswald is being
returned. Should you wish to be kept informed of further
developments regarding Mr. Oswald an officer familiar with
the case may be reached on Code 182, extension 5340.

                    Sincerely yours,

                    Frederick G. Dutton
                    Assistant Secretary
Enclosures

The Honorable
     John G. Tower,
          United States Senate.

Enclosed were copies of two letters from Oswald to the Moscow Embassy and replies to him. And that was that. Oswald got no help from his senator, not even a reply. The senator's files rested quietly for 21½ months, until terrible news from Dallas sparked the excellent memory of Miss Linda Lee Lovelady, as shown on the next page:

Another photo[815] Marina gave to the Warren Commission shows the Palace of Culture, where Lee first met and danced with her in March 1961, halfway through his 2½ years of residence in Minsk, Byelorussia. They could see it from their apartment's balcony.

1963 November 22: Statement for the press from Senator Tower's office[816]

United States Senate

```
FROM THE OFFICE OF                    NOVEMBER 22, 1963

SENATOR JOHN G. TOWER


RE:  CORRESPONDENCE OF LEE H. OSWALD

1)  Oswald wrote to office of Senator Tower in January, 1962,

    per attached.  (Oswald letter from Russia is undated.)

2)  Oswald letter was sent to State Department.  State reply

    to Senator Tower shown in attached correspondence and in

    memo of phone call by State.

3)  State advised that the Senator not become involved in the

    case and at no time did the Senator correspond with Oswald.
```

Using space that is available so all full-page documents can be shown in large size, here is a photo given to the Warren Commission by Marina, taken during Lee's employment at Belorussian Gorizont Radio and Television Factory.[817] Eight male workers, all young, are relaxing in the sun. Lee is in the front-center, sporting dark sunglasses. Because no one else has such wonderful "shades", one wonders if they were not obtainable in the USSR, worn only by privileged Americans.

This photo may seem familiar because we saw a similar photo on page 19 of Lee sitting front-and-center among his fellow Marines in the Philippines.

During the Warren Commission's investigations in 1964, an Assistant Counsel went up Capitol Hill, got the entire story and wrote a report to the Chief Counsel:

1964 June 8: Warren Commission internal report [818]

```
                                        June 8, 1964


To:        J. Lee Rankin

From:      W. David Slawson

Subject:   Senator John G. Tower's contacts with Lee Harvey Oswald


This afternoon at 4:30 by prearrangement with Mr. Roland Kenneth Towery,
Press Secretary to Senator John G. Tower, I visited Mr. Towery at the
administrative offices of Senator Tower in the Old Senate Office Building.
After I arrived Mr. Towery called in Miss Linda Lee Lovelady, Case Worker
on the staff of the Senator.  In my presence Mr. Towery went through that
office's entire file relating to Lee Harvey Oswald and then gave me copies
of all the documents in that file.  I examined the copies and am satisfied
that they are in fact complete and accurate copies of the originals as
shown.  These copies are attached to this memorandum.

According to Mr. Towery and Miss Lovelady the events pertaining to these
documents occurred as follows:

On or shortly before January 26, 1962, Senator Tower's office received a
handwritten, undated letter from Lee Oswald.  Miss Lovelady, whose job
it was and still is is to take care of matters of this nature, routinely
sent Oswald's letter on to Mr. Frederick G. Dutton, Assistant Secretary
for Congressional Relations, Department of State, with an appropriate
cover letter stating that the Senator's office knew nothing about the
Oswald affair and was referring the entire matter to the Department of
State.  This cover letter purported to be signed by the Senator but
actually was "signed" by a machine which writes his signature.  Shortly
thereafter, on February 1, a Mr. Stanfield in the Department of State
telephoned the Senator's office and was referred to Miss Lovelady.
Miss Lovelady made a memorandum of Mr. Stanfield's call, and she
stated that to the best of her recollection that memorandum fairly
summarizes the contents of that call.

Subsequently, the Senator's office received a letter from Mr. Dutton
dated February 9, 1962, enclosing copies of the correspondence containing
the most recent information the Department of State had received from its
Moscow Embassy regarding Lee Harvey Oswald.  The letter from Mr. Dutton
stated that if Senator Tower wished to be kept informed of further develop-
ments regarding Mr. Oswald, an officer familiar with the case could be
reached on Code 182, extension 5340.  Miss Lovelady told me that neither
she nor, to her knowledge, anyone else in the Senator's office, specifically
including the Senator, ever had anything further to do with the Oswald case
or ever contacted the officer at Code 182, extension 5340 with regard to
```

Second page

```
                                       -2-


      the matter.  Furthermore, Senator Tower was not even aware of the
      Oswald matter and took no part in the actions of his office in the
      matter.

      Miss Lovelady and Mr. Towery told me that the foregoing disposition of
      the letter from Oswald was completed routinely and differed in no way
      from how that office handles other matters of a similar nature.  They
      also told me that the file shown me and the descriptions of the actions
      taken in respect to it constitute the entire dealings with or concerning
      Lee Harvey Oswald undertaken by the Senator's office except for two
      post-assassination matters.  The first of these concerns the attached
      document dated November 22, 1963, and entitled, "Re:  Correspondence of
      Lee H. Oswald."  It is a statement prepared for the press on November 22,
      1963.  The history of this is that as soon as Oswald's name was mentioned
      in connection with the assassination on radio and television Miss Lovelady
      remembered that the Senator's office had something to do with him in the
      past and, after an immediate file search, a statement to the press along
      the lines shown in this document was made.  The second matter concerning
      Oswald that occurred after the assassination is some correspondence with
      the Secretary of State for the purpose of clearing the Senator from some
      wild charges that had been made in the foreign and domestic press to the
      effect that he facilitated Oswald's obtaining a repatriation loan from the
      Department of State or otherwise helped him to return to the United States.
      Such charges have no basis whatever in fact, according to Towery and
      Lovelady.




                                       _____
                                               (signed)
                                        W. David Slawson


      Attachments
```

Only a staffer saw Oswald's plea for his senator's help. A machine "signed" the letter bucking the problem to the State Department. And "Dear Senator Tower" "was not even aware of the Oswald matter" until the afternoon of November 22, 1963, when, like most of us, he first heard of Lee Harvey Oswald. Thus ends the Oswald – Tower connection, or lack thereof.

In Minsk on December 11, 1961, the Plant Director and Personnel Department Chief of Radio Plant No. 5. on Krasnaya St. sent a report:

"Citizen Lee Harvey Oswald was hired as regulator in the experimental shop of the plant on January 13, 1960. During his employment as regulator his performance was unsatisfactory. He does not display the initiative for increasing his skill as a regulator. Citizen Lee Harvey Oswald reacts in an over-sensitive manner to remarks from the foreman, and is careless in his work. Citizen L. H. Oswald takes no part in the social life of the shop and keeps very much to himself. This report is issued for presentation to the Minsk City Militia Department." [819]

KGB agent Nechiporenko, writing his book in 1992, learned: "The KGB concluded that he was neither a spy nor a builder of socialism." [820] He interviewed KGB officials: "Both directorate heads briefed me on Oswald's complete history. It was clear that he was of no use as an operative. Their impression of him was that he was a gray, mediocre personality." [821]

"The Russians could have kept Oswald if they had wanted to, by granting him citizenship, by denying his request for an exit visa, or by simply ignoring his request. He was in their ... police state. But he was an 'unsatisfactory' and uncooperative worker of below-average skill, he was occupying an apartment that would otherwise have gone to a factory official, and until a few months before he had been receiving a financial subsidy. He was a drain on the country—and he brought no reward. If allowing Marina—who did not fall into any of the proscribed categories—to go was the price of getting rid of Oswald, why not?" [822]

On December 25, 1961, Marina was called to the Soviet Passport Office and told that exit visas would be granted to her and her husband; she was surprised, having doubted that she would be permitted to leave. In Texas, every member of the tight-knit Dallas-Fort Worth Russian exile community will be amazed that she was allowed to leave the U.S.S.R. One of those elders, Mrs. Dorothy Gravitis, testified to a conversation: "I was very surprised how did the Soviet Union let you out, I asked Marina. She said, 'We had a luck.'" [823] Oswald wrote to the US Embassy on December 27 that they would be given visas and asked that his American passport be extended. In his diary, he wrote, "It's great (I think ?)." [824] Shortly before the year 1961 ended, Marina went on maternity leave from her job. [825]

Lee wrote to his mother on January 2, 1962, telling her that he and his wife expected to arrive in the United States about March. He asked her to contact the local Red Cross and request that it put his case before the International Rescue Committee or some other group aiding immigrants to the United States. He told her he would need about $800, and she should insist on a gift rather than a loan; he told her not to send her own money. [826] Despite his instructions, she requested a loan from the Red Cross. [827] On January 13, Oswald wrote to the International Rescue Committee himself, asking for $800 to purchase two tickets from Moscow to Texas. [828] He wrote to the Committee again on January 26, this time asking for $1,000. [829]

January brought a burst of letters between Minsk and Moscow. On the 5th, Lee wrote to the Embassy, ending: "I would like to make arrangements for a loan from the Embassy or some organization for part of the plane fares. Please look into this and notify me." [830] A letter from the Embassy, [831] also dated January 5, crossed in the mail. It suggested that because there might be difficulties in obtaining an American visa for Marina, he should consider going alone to the U.S. and bring her over later. He replied that he would not leave Russia without her. [832] The Embassy replied that Marina did not yet have an American visa and that no evidence had yet been submitted that she would not become a public charge in the U.S. [833] It suggested that Oswald's mother or some other close relative file an affidavit of support in Marina's behalf. Before receiving this letter, Oswald wrote out such a document himself [834] and mailed it to the Embassy. [835] Upon receiving the Embassy's most recent letter, he wrote that his own affidavit should be sufficient, since he had been away from the United States for more than 2 years and could not be expected to obtain an affidavit from someone else. [836] But on the same day, he wrote to his mother asking that she file an affidavit of support with the Immigration and Naturalization Service. [837] On January 24, the Embassy acknowledged receipt of his affidavit, but again suggested that he obtain one from someone else. [838]

In the preceding pages, in addition to messages within the Corps, we have seen several back-and-forths between the Marine Corps and Marguerite, who appointed herself to handle the problem of his undesirable discharge, and told him nothing. Removed by 8 time zones — 1/3 of the way around the world — Lee Oswald has known nothing about that. *Nothing!*

> This is an important tipping point: To now, Lee Oswald has not had even any hint of the long process that changed his discharge. Now he first learns of his less-than-honorable discharge.

Late in January, Lee receives a letter from his mother bringing completely unexpected, very bad news. She wrote he has been given a dishonorable discharge from the Marines.[839] The discharge was actually "undesirable," a less derogatory category,[840] but isolated in Minsk, he does not know that. Afterward, he consistently said "dishonourable". It is not possible to ascertain whether the error was made by mother or by son, because her letter to him does not survive. This author lays odds it was Marguerite's mischaracterization.

Twenty-two months later, on the day Lee was buried, an FBI agent interviewed her at length (28 single-spaced typed pages), during which she related her reason for writing him, and what happened when he arrived in Texas:

"While Lee was in Russia ... in a brown official envelope from the Marine Department, was a letter addressed to Lee. ... I opened his mail which had been coming to the house. I didn't feel guilty about opening his mail because I had no way of knowing if he was even living. It was a letter from the Marine Corps ... stating that because of his defection to Russia, they have found it necessary to give him a dishonorable discharge ... I wrote Lee preparing him that he had had a dishonorable discharge and that it would be wise to return and face these things. So, when Lee returned from Russia I ... distinctly remember giving Lee the letter ... Lee says, 'Don't worry, mother, I will take care of this because I have been a good Marine and I have a good-conduct medal' which I saw with my own eyes that he had a good-conduct medal.[1] ... He, I know, felt that he didn't deserve the dishonorable discharge." [841]

When brother Robert testified before the Warren Commission in 1964, commissioner Gerald R. Ford asked: "When did you learn about the change in his discharge?" and Robert answered: "Sometime during the year of 1960, through my mother. She had advised me at that time she had received mail for Lee from the Marine Corps or from the Navy Department, stating that generally the reasons he had not notified them of changes of address, and perhaps even to the extent that he had left the country in the manner that he did, that it was going to go before a review board, and that he was to appear before this board to state his case, otherwise it would proceed without him. Then I became aware that the board's decision was an undesirable or a dishonorable discharge, I don't recollect which." [842]

What we now know about the content of letters is either feast or famine, depending on whether the recipient was a saver. The Warren Commission learned from Robert that Lee did not save letters he received. Asking about a letter Robert had written to Lee:

"Mr. JENNER.. Your reply—did you write him a letter?
Mr. OSWALD. Yes, sir.
Mr. JENNER. Do you have a copy of that letter?
Mr. OSWALD. No, sir; I do not have a copy of any letter that I wrote to him.
Mr. JENNER. You do not know the whereabouts of that letter?
Mr. OSWALD. No, sir; I do not, other than to say that I asked Mrs. Marina Oswald if Lee kept any of my letters and her reply was that 'No, he always threw them away.'" [843]

If a genie would offer this writer one item, I choose to have the letter Lee received from Marguerite in January 1962. After searching 26 volumes of addenda to the *Warren Report* and

---

[1] If he had such a medal, it was awarded before the Corps knew he had gone to the enemy USSR, or he had stolen or bought it at a flea market. The Warren Commission gives no hint of that "medal".

many other sources, I conclude that letter no longer exists. It must have been one of the letters about which Marina told Robert, "he always threw them away." All we know about it will be shown in the January 30 letters Lee will write to John Connally and to brother Robert. What we don't know, and apparently never will because mother and son are dead, is whether the bad-enough "undesirable" was wrongly changed to the worse "dishonorable" by Marguerite or by Lee. Because Lee will have her letter in front of him on January 30, and will write "dishonourable" (only he and Brits would put in that "u") in two letters, and from what she told the Commission, we are likely correct to believe Marguerite made the mistake.

Marguerite's letter was all that Lee knew about his discharge by the Marines. It was the worst possible news. Understanding Lee's values, we expect that if the letter had told of a death in the family, he would have shrugged and quickly dismissed it from mind. But this was monstrous! His adventure to Russia had not turned out well. All he could show for his life was honorable service as a Marine, plus, to a lesser degree, success in wooing and marrying Marina. Now that he was embarked on returning home, he was smart enough to realize that finding a job in the US would be imperiled by the deathly word "dishonorable".

There in Byelorussia, at the nadir of the Cold War, his options were limited. He was far away from the America where that week Jacqueline Kennedy recorded on a new wonder, videotape, a tour of the White House that would be shown in February on all three TV networks[J] to a record audience of 80,000,000.[844] In part, the Soviet authorities had sent him to Minsk because of its isolation. He might as well have been the Man on the Moon.

Lee Harvey Oswald sat down in his Minsk apartment to seek redress. He had only one option: write a letter. We don't know whether he pondered for long about whom to write. Appropriate addressees for an appeal might have been within the Marine Corps — anywhere from some junior officer in El Toro to the Commandant of Marines in the Pentagon. He probably rejected this immediately, realizing that the Corps knew he had been entirely deceitful in asking for an early "hardship" discharge to care for his mother. No, the USMC had been had and they knew it — his intent all along had been to go rapidly from Marine to Marxist.

Or, he could write to one of his representatives in Congress. But, he had appealed to Senator Tower more than a month ago (page 75) and had not had a reply, let alone any action "to rise the question of holding by the Soviet Union of a citizen of the U.S." Lee probably expected little chance of help, if he knew of them, from the other U.S. Senator from Texas, Ralph Yarborough of far-away Austin, or his Representative in Congress, James C. "Jim" Wright of Fort Worth, who had a long run in the House, from 1955 to 1989, when he was Speaker but had to resign because of scandal. Lee probably did not know or could not recall the name of either, having been absent from Texas since 1956.

He could have appealed to the President of the United States — lots of Americans with problems did that. But Dwight Eisenhower had been president during Lee's Marine years and when he went to Moscow. John Kennedy became President after Lee had been in Minsk a full year, so was an unknown. And, he was from Massachusetts, a foreign country in the eyes of Louisiana-born, Texas-reared Oswald. The Vice President wasn't any better — Richard Nixon when Lee entered the Soviet Union, and now Lyndon Johnson from far away Johnson City.

[J] Large cities had all three: ABC, CBS and NBC. In the author's hometown of Juneau, there was only one, which showed tape recordings, two weeks late, of old news and other programming.

He wrote to "Sectretary of the Navy; John B. Connally Jr.; Fort Worth, Texas". And — the hypothesis of this book — history was changed by the process begun that day in Minsk.

His choice of where to seek help may have been as simple as what was in his shirt that day, a pocket-size notebook Lee carried from his arrival in Moscow until two days before his death in Dallas.[K]   On its fourth page [845] are addresses for his peripatetic mother, a series of lines, crossed out as he wrote each new one.   Directly below Marguerite's addresses, on three lines: "John B. Connally | Fort Worth, Texas | Sec. of Navy."   Russian printing affirms that he bought the notebook in Moscow.   When he read or heard of Connally being appointed Secretary of the [L] Navy, he jotted it onto this page.

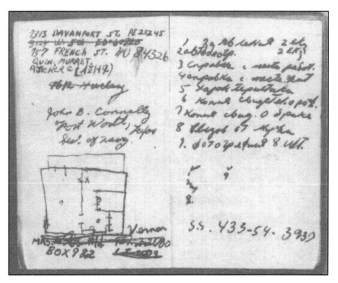

One matter is close to certain: the reason Oswald made that note and chose Connally to be his ombudsman is because both had lived in Fort Worth.

John Bowden Connally, Jr., a young lawyer from south Texas, served with distinction in the U.S. Navy during World War II, mainly in the South Pacific, earning both Bronze Star and Legion of Merit. A lieutenant commander when discharged in 1946, he returned to practice law until new senator Lyndon Johnson took him to Washington in 1949. They remained close friends and allies until Johnson's death. The photo is at the 1957 dedication of the Sam Rayburn Library.[846] Connally moved to Fort Worth to advise oil tycoons, made a fortune and learned the political ropes. As did many in Texas, he started as a traditional-liberal Democrat, then edged into being a new-style southern conservative.

In 1956, as Oswald was about to join the Marines, Connally led an effort to have a conservative Texas Democrat replace VP Richard Nixon as Dwight Eisenhower's second-term running mate. In 1960 he led supporters backing Lyndon Johnson for the Democratic presidential nomination, as told in the preceding chapter. Both efforts failed, but politics is pragmatic and forgiving. Despite his efforts against Nixon, in 1971 he will become Nixon's Secretary of the Treasury. Of more importance to this book, despite his energetic opposition to JFK at the 1960 nominating convention, Connally was appointed Secretary of the Navy

---

[K] The notebook is this book's treasure featured in Chapter 20 – OBSTRUCTION OF BEST EVIDENCE.
[L] Many writers leave out "the", but my bible of government, the *Congressional Directory*, requires it.

when JFK took office. There are three versions of how that came about, all from reliable sources who should know. All are described here because Connally's appointment will be important. It is what will cause Oswald to appeal to him; then, rejected, to take his tragic murderous revenge.

The first version is that V.P. Lyndon Johnson "was allowed only a few political appointments ... and one involved selection of the Secretary of the Navy. ... Johnson ... asked for the right to appoint one of his friends to the post. ... Connally was not only Johnson's long time friend, past campaign manager, and political ally, but he was also from Fort Worth, Texas." [847] Connally's autobiography captions the photo: "Vice-President Johnson and Defense Secretary McNamara congratulate the new First Sailor and his lady." [848]

A different version with a different champion came from Kennedy's "Irish Mafia" political advisor, Appointments Secretary Kenny O'Donnell, who wrote in his reliable (because he was there) memoir *Johnny, We Hardly Knew Ye* that McNamara "preferred John Connally, an appointment, incidentally, that Lyndon Johnson had nothing to do with, contrary to everybody's assumption at the time. Speaker [Sam] Rayburn [of Texas] had recommended John Connally in my presence, and President Kennedy readily agreed, as did McNamara." [849]

The legal assistant in the SecNav's office, US Navy Captain Andy Kerr, from whom we will hear more in a few pages, introduces the third version with an inside story:

"President Kennedy's favorite candidate for the ... spot was Franklin D. Roosevelt, Jr. [Secretary of Defense Robert] McNamara had insisted, however, that he be able to choose his own top people. Roosevelt was a close friend of the Kennedys. As navy secretary he would, therefore, have had direct access to the president, being thereby able to bypass the secretary of defense. McNamara would have found that prospect intolerable." [850]

The third version was documented by Kennedy's resident White House historian, Arthur M. Schlesinger, Jr., in his authoritative *A Thousand Days: John F. Kennedy in the White House*:

"The Navy Department presented a particular problem. Kennedy hoped that McNamara would accept Franklin D. Roosevelt, Jr., who not only was a close personal friend but had helped so much in the West Virginia primary. The Roosevelt record of association with the Navy was, moreover, long and formidable. Both Theodore Roosevelts, Sr. and Jr., had been Assistant Secretaries of the Navy; so too had been Franklin D. Roosevelt, Sr.; and there would be a pleasant historical symmetry in completing the quadrangle. Young Franklin himself had served with distinction in the Navy during the Second World War. But McNamara did not want him; and Kennedy, though regretful, accepted the decision without further question. (Perhaps feeling a little abashed, McNamara did accept Kennedy's old comrade from PT-boat days Paul Fay as Under Secretary of the Navy.) In the meantime, McNamara's personal talent search had unearthed the name of John Connally of Texas as a possibility for the Secretaryship. Late in December he called Kennedy at Palm Beach to clear an invitation to Connally. In view of Connally's Texas connections, he added, perhaps the appointment should be checked with the Vice President-elect. Kennedy said that Senator Johnson was sitting beside him and put him on the phone. Since Connally was one of Johnson's oldest political associates, Johnson was, of course, delighted. But this was all a happy coincidence, and, contrary to the speculation at the time, Johnson was not the source of the Connally appointment." [851]

Whoever championed or chose Connally, the die is cast for Kennedy's death because an inept malcontent will take umbrage at the Secretary of the Navy and attempt to shoot him.

The new President delighted in naming the Assistant Secretary of the Navy, choosing his wartime buddy, Paul "Red" (for his hair) Fay. They had met in WW II as PT-boat captains, and still enjoyed each other's company. Fay will play an innocent but essential role on the path to Kennedy's death, as will be seen in the next chapter when he, the ultimate authority, signs the final document rejecting Oswald's plea for an honorable discharge.

Photos of Connally were on the two previous pages; there will be more in chapters 6, 14 and 19. If you would now like to see Paul "Red" Fay, there are photos of him on pages 505 and 506 — and of great importance as the tragedy unfolds, his signature on page 143.

Many Americans think of the Marines as one of the military branches, comparable to the Army, Navy and Air Force. But no, the Marines are those members of the Navy who fight on land after being transported to a battleground by the floating Navy. Not a separate branch, the Marine Corps is part of, and under the authority of, the U.S. Navy.

Connally thus became the boss of the Commandant of Marines — and Oswald wanted him to tell the Marines what to do. Timing is everything, and unfortunately, as usual, it was not on Oswald's side. Connally was no longer in the Pentagon. He had resigned his position as Secretary of the Navy on December 20, 1961, after less than eleven months in that office, and had returned to Texas to run for Governor.[852] Lee did not know that — there was no way he could in the isolation of Minsk.

The important letter Lee wrote on January 30, 1962, will now be shown in four ways. Below at left is the clearest of three photos of the letter in the *Warren Commission Hearings*.[853] Because this is so important, my talented photo researcher Gina McNeely dug through the National Archives and found the better image below at right.[854] Following on full pages are the scan below at right after improvement by image expert David Muerdter, and then a careful transcription as if Lee had a typewriter, so you can readily understand every word.

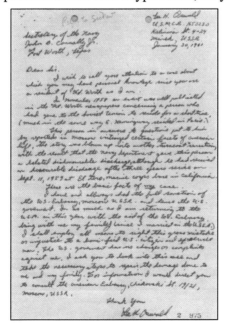 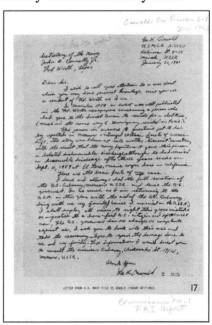

1962 January 30: Lee H. Oswald to John B. Connally Jr. [855]

Refer to Sec'tar

Lee H. Oswald
U.S.M.C.R. 1653230
Kalinina St. 4-24
Minsk, U.S.S.R.
January 30, 1961

Secretary of the Navy
John B. Connally Jr.
Fort Worth, Texas

Dear Sir.

I wish to call your attention to a case about which you may have personal knowlege since you are a resident of Ft. Worth as I am.

In november 1959 an event was well publisized in the Ft. Worth newspapers concerning a person who had gone to the Soviet Union to reside for a short time, (much in the same way E. Hemingway resided in Paris.)

This person in answers to questions put to him by reporters in moscow criticized certain facets of american life. The story was blown up into another "turncoat" sensation, with the result that the navy department gave this person a belated dishonourable discharge, although he had recived an hoourable discharge after three years service on Sept. 11, 1959 at El toro, marine corps base in California.

These are the basic facts of my case.

I have and allways had the full sanction of the U.S. Embassy, moscow U.S.S.R. and hence the U.S. goverment. In as much as I am returning to the U.S.A. in this year with the aid of the U.S. Embassy, bring with me my family (since I married in the U.S.S.R.) I shall employ all means to right this gross mistake or injustice to a bona-fied U.S. citizen and ex-service man. The U.S. goverment has no charges or complaints against me. I ask you to look into this case and take the neccessary steps to repair the damage done to me and my family. For information I would direct you to consult the american Embassy, Chikovski St. 19/21, moscow, U.S.S.R.

Thank You

Lee H. Oswald   2   975

As was done earlier with Oswald's letter to Senator Tower, here is the letter on the preceding page as if typed, so the reader may concentrate on what he wrote without having to decipher sometimes difficult handwriting. The spellings and spacings are his:

1962 January 30: Lee Oswald to John Connally — as if typed

```
                                     Lee H. Oswald
                                     U.S.M.C.R. 1653230
Sectretary of the Navy               Kalinina St. 4-24
John B. Connally Jr.                 Minsk, U.S.S.R.
Fort Worth , Texas                   January 30, 1961


Dear Sir.
        I wish to call your attention to a case about
which you may have personal knowlege since you are
a resident of Ft. Worth as I am .
        In November 1959 an event was well publicated
in the Ft. Worth newspapers concerning a person who
had gone to the Soviet Union to reside for a short time,
(much in the same way E. Hemingway resided in Paris.)
        This person in answers to questions put to him
by reporteds in Moscow criticized certain facets of American
life, The story was blown up into another "turncoat" sensation,
with the result that the Navy department gave this person
a belated dishonourable discharge,although he had recived
an honourable discharge after three years service on
Sept. 11, 1959 at El Toro,Marine corps base in California.
        These are the basic facts of my case.
        I have and allways had the full sanction of
the U.S . Embassy,Moscow USSR . and hence the U.S.
goverment.  In as much as I am returning to the
U.S.A. in this year with the aid of the U.S. Embassy .
bring with me my family (since I married in the U.S.S.R.)
I shall employ all means to right this gross mistake
or injustice to a boni-fied U.S . citizen and ex-service
man . The U.S . goverment has no charges or complaints
against me.  I ask you to look into this case and
take the neccessary steps to repair the damage done to
me and my family . For information I would direct you
to consult the American Embassy, Chikovski St. 19/21 ,
Moscow , USSR.
                        Thank You
                        (signed)
                        Lee H Oswald
```

Oswald made an error common in a new year's first month, dating it "1961", when it was really January 1962. At best, he wasn't good with dates. This was easily resolved; there was discussion between Marguerite and Warren Commission member Allen Dulles about another letter from Lee to her that he dated October 22, 1959, which was postmarked on arrival in the

U.S. October 30, 1961. She said: "Evidently Lee put the date incorrect ... I would say it was just an error, because the postmark proves the date." [856] Yes, it does.

Edward Jay Epstein, who spent as much time analyzing Oswald as anyone, terms this letter "angry", "betrayed considerable anxiety".[857] He submitted it to professional handwriting analyst Thea Stein Lewinson,[858] who opined "Oswald was under great pressure ... stresses in the handwriting suggest that he was venting considerable anger toward Connally." [859]

The letter eventually lodged in Oswald's Marine Corps personnel file, where it was found for the Warren Commission. With "Refer to SecNav" written at the top, it had been forwarded to the Secretary of the Navy, as instructed; we will soon see what action was taken.

With that important letter to Connally completed, Lee then wrote to his brother:

"January 30,1962

"Dear Robert,
    Well ,I have'nt heard from you for quite awhile either you're not writing or your letters aren't getting through to me.
    I told you in my last letter that we have finilly been granted exit visa's for leaving the Soviet Union we'll probably be in the states in the spring.
    You once said that you asked around about weather or not the U.S. goverment had any charges against me ,you said at that time "no", maybe you should ask around again, its possible now that the goverment knows I'm coming they'll have something waiting
    Mother wrote me a letter the other day in which she informed me that the Marine Corps had given me a dishonourable discharge in Nov. 1959 Did You know this?
    Of course , this is not too bad, since It relives me of reserve duty , but still I should take this into account.
    I wrote a letter to John B. Connally Secretary of the Navy who lives in Ft. Worth asking about my dishonourable discharge maybe you could ask him to look into the case since I don't know wheater the Russians will let that letter through.
    You said you were sending us something but be still having gotten anything don't worry packages are very slow coming and going.
    The Embassy said they will see about a loan for us when we leave so it seems our money problem will not be too acute.
    Marina Still has a month too go so by the time you get this letter you'll be pretty close too being an uncle . March 1 is the big day.
Marina sends her love to all,as I do hope to see you all soon
I really don't know where we'll settle I'd sort of like New Orleans.
  How's the hunting out at the farms?
  How the weather and all?
  If you find out any information about me, please let me know , I'd like to be ready on the draw so too speak We'll keep writing until We get ready to leave so don't quite writing
Your Brother
Lee&Marina" [860]

Robert saved both this letter and its envelope, which Lee had paid extra to register, probably to increase likelihood of delivery. Lee states that perhaps "letters aren't getting through" and "I don't know wheater the Russians will let that letter [to Connally] through." Lee's envelope, postmarked in Minsk at noon on January 30, arrived at the U.S. Post Office substation near Robert's house on February 6.[861] That was good speed then — and now.

Note that Lee accurately dated this letter — January 30, 1962 — as proven by the Minsk postmark of that date. And, he correctly spelled "Secretary". He was more controlled than earlier, when he wrote to Connally and, in his anger, got both of those wrong.

Oswald's letter with its "I shall employ all means" threat did not set off alarm bells in Fort Worth or at the Pentagon. It was not immediately made known to either the FBI or the Secret Service. However, in Chapter 16 – REGARDING CONNALLY will be testimony from the Chief of the Secret Service that he considered this letter to be Oswald's threat "that he would apply illegal means if he could",[862] and that the failure of this letter to ring alarms in 1962 was in part responsible for new inter-agency security rules put into effect in 1964.

Lee's envelope taking the threatening letter to Connally was most likely addressed as on the letter, simply to Connally in Fort Worth. There, the U.S. Post Office delivered to the Connally for Governor campaign headquarters, probably about February 7. Even in the midst of a hectic political campaign, Connally sent a reply in two weeks, as will be shown below.

This chapter will show the full path of Oswald's appeal, essential to this book's thesis. The *Warren Report*, dismissing it as unimportant, dispensed with it in only four sentences:
> "Connally referred the letter to the Department of the Navy, which sent Oswald a letter stating that the Department contemplated no change in the undesirable discharge. On March 22, Oswald wrote to the Department insisting that his discharge be given a further, full review. The Department promptly replied that it had no authority to hear and review petitions of this sort and referred Oswald to the Navy Discharge Review Board. Oswald filled out the enclosed application for review in Minsk but did not mail it until he returned to the United States." [863]

Back in Minsk, Lee had again written to the Embassy in Moscow, fretting about the delay in getting a visa for Marina to accompany him to the US. The consul advised that the delay was usual in the Immigration and Naturalization Service and counseled "it seems highly unlikely that the visa can be issued in time to permit her to travel before your child is born. Most airlines will not accept passengers during the ninth month of pregnancy. Therefore, it would seem advisable for you to plan for the baby to be born before you leave for the United States." [864] When Lee arrives in Texas, he will mail an appeal of his discharge, enclosing this letter from the embassy in an attempt to justify the length of time he stayed in the USSR.

The Department of State had notified Oswald's mother that it would need $900 to make travel arrangements for her son and daughter-in-law.[865] On February 1, Lee sent her a letter rejecting her suggestion that she try to raise money by telling newspapers about his financial plight.[M][866] Five days later, the Embassy wrote, asking him to make formal application for a loan.[867] Oswald wrote to his mother on February 9, reminding her to file an affidavit of support and asking that she send him clippings from the Fort Worth newspapers about his defection to Russia. He told her that he wanted to know what had been written about him, so that he could be "forewarned." Worried, he later repeated the request to his brother.[868]

Lee's prophecy in his January 30 letter to Robert, "**March 1 is the big day**" was a bit off, or the baby came a little early.[N] He took Marina to the hospital on the morning of February 15. A baby girl was born about 10 AM.[869] He had gone to the factory where news of the birth awaited him on arrival.[870] As was usually also the case with his mother, Lee's life

---

[M] If that was in fact her idea, well then, perhaps she was the inventor of today's "crowd sourcing"!

[N] An old aphorism: "The first one can come anytime; the rest take 9 months." The Oswalds had been married 9 months and 15 days. The author came a little faster, 9 months and 11 days.

had been one sad disappointment after another, so we must pay particular notice to his pride and joy as the new father shares the day's good news with his brother:

"Feb. 15,1962

"Dear Robert,

Well , I have a daughter, June Marina Oswald , 6 lbs. 2 oz. , born Feb. 15, 1962 at 10.AM. How about that?!

We are lucky to have a little girl, don't you think?

But then you have a head start . on me , although I'll try to catch up. Ha. Ha

This makes you an uncle, Congradulations!

The chances of our coming to the States are very good. as I already told you , we recived the Soviet exit visas. I can leave the country at any time. But there are still formalities concernig Marina's <u>entrance</u> <u>visa</u> into the U.S. These are granted by the U.S. goverment , and they have assured me they are getting all the papers together (they are quite alot) and certified accepted.

How are things ate your end? I heard over the voice of america that they released Powers the U2 spy plane fellow .[o] Thats big news where you are I suppose . He seemed to be a nice, bright ,american-type fellow, when I saw him in Moscow.

You woulde'nt have any clippings from the Nov. 1959 newspaper of Ft. Worth , would you .

I am beginning to get interested in just what they <u>did</u> say about me and my trip here.

The information might come in handy when I get back . I would hate to come back completly unprepared.

The American Embassy in Moscow has offered us a loan to pay for the price of the airline tickets,so we have nothing to worry about temporary along that line.

Have you heard from Pic at all, whats he doing now? still in the air force do you know ?

Well, I guess thats all for now.

P.S.   I recived a letter from you dated Jan. 3. I did not get it until Feb. 5 . The censors are so stupid over here it sometimes takes them a month to censor a letter before letting it through.

Love to Vada, Cathy and little Robert Jr . he and June will play together I'm quite sure .

Your Brother
Lee."[871]

Observing regular local practice,[872] Lee did not see the baby until Marina left the hospital.[873] The daughter was named "June Lee" in accordance with Russian custom and law that a child's second name must be the father's first name or a variation. He had wanted to name his child "June Marina," and protested the application of the law to her, since he had a United States passport. As was the usual habit, family and friends added "ka" to the child's name to signify "my dear little", so she was "Juneka" to some, and to those who could not handle the foreign-sounding name "June", she was "Marinka". Almost none could stand the proud father's Chinese-sounding name Lee, so he was "Alik". Marina, when they were not at odds, called him "Alka." His coworkers presented "one summer blanket, 6 light diapers, 4 warm diapers,

---

[o] In isolation, Lee keeps up with news by listening to radio. The Soviets traded downed-and-captured U-2 pilot Francis Gary Powers for their spy Rudolf Abel at the Berlin Wall on February 10. As this chapter receives its final edit, the movie *Bridge of Spies* portraying that has been released.

2 chemises, 3 very good warm chemises, 4 very nice suits and two toys".[874]

Marina and June came home from the hospital on February 23.[875] On that day an important letter was mailed to Oswald. It was delivered to his apartment, probably about March 1, in this envelope bearing Russian postal transliteration into Cyrillic:[876] [P]

Dedicated and gifted assassination analyst James Reston, Jr. points to the important:

> "[W]hat the ex-serviceman got from the ex-Navy Secretary … was a classic bureaucratic brush-off: a perfunctory promise to pass the problem on to his successor. Connally's letter to Oswald arrived in Minsk in a provocative, inflammatory package: a campaign envelope, with **JOHN CONNALLY** for **GOVERNOR** emblazoned on the front, and Connally's smiling face centered within a Texas star. Thus, at the beginning of this painful journey home, Oswald had been spurned by a fellow Texan, and he resented it deeply. The change in his discharge was only one, but perhaps the worst indignity that Oswald felt he had suffered. Now he had a face, in the middle of a star with a derisive smile, to go with his torment. Connally's face became the face of the U.S. government, and Connally's perfunctory snub fortified Oswald's bitterness against the country." [877]

As Reston tells the story, receipt of this envelope made such a strong impression on Marina that sixteen years later, testifying to the House Select Committee on Assassinations:

> "she told of how Connally's brush-off letter in February 1962, the origin of the grudge, had arrived at their Minsk apartment in a big, white envelope whose front flaunted the large, smiling face of John Connally, advertising his candidacy for governor of Texas." [878]

Lee must have deemed the envelope important, witnessed by the fact that he saved it, carried it to Texas when he returned home, and preserved it to be found after his death. The letter inside was not found among his possessions, and researchers have not seen an image of

---

[P] Your author knew about this envelope from Marina's testimony, searched for it for years, and found it in 2013 in *The Accidental Victim* by James Reston, Jr. In private correspondence, Reston wrote me: "On the Connally letter envelope, which I regard as clinching our case, I was thrilled to come upon it at the National Archives in a random folder, and simply xeroxed it. Hence, not a very good reproduction in the book, but good enough to knock your socks off. I made a specific request to the Archives to find the original, but I'm sorry to report that they never came up with it." I am greatly indebted to my kind friend Reston for finding it and sharing this reproduction.

the original he received, probably on fancy campaign stationery with more glorification of John Connally. We have only carbon copies that show the typed words:

1962 February 23: John Connally to Mr. Lee H. Oswald[879]

```
                                                   February 23, 1962




        Mr. Lee H. Oswald
        U.S.M.C.R. 1653230
        Kalinina St. 4-24
        Minsk, U.S.S.R.

        Dear Mr. Oswald:

             Your letter of January 30 has just been called to my
        attention.

             As I am no longer connected with the Navy, I have referred
        your letter to the office of the Secretary of the Navy in
        Washington, D. C.

                                        Sincerely,



                                        John Connally

        cc:  Honorable Fred Korth
             Secretary of the Navy
             The Pentagon
             Washington, D.C.

        BS/lh
```

The *Warren Report* does not mention this acknowledgement from Connally to Oswald, but two carbon copies are displayed in the *Warren Commission Hearings*, one from Marine Corps files, one from the Navy's. Connally's campaign office and the U.S. Post Office were efficient: The administratively correct but somewhat abrupt (Lee found it so) letter was typed on a Friday in Ft. Worth and its "cc:" copy was logged-in on Tuesday at the Pentagon. There, Oswald's letter to Connally (shown on page 88) and Connally's reply (re-created above) were both rubber stamped "2 975" at the bottom.

According to a fine memoir written by U.S. Navy Captain Andy Kerr, a long-time counsel in the SecNav's office, Fred Korth "was also a Texan and a lawyer. He came to the Office of Secretary of the Navy from ... army officer in World War II ... practiced law in Fort Worth before becoming a banker. He had not been noticeably involved in politics, nor did he appear to have political ambitions. Vice President Lyndon Johnson was his friend." [880] This is Fred Korth's second appearance in this book; way back in Chapter 1 on page 6 he was Marguerite Oswald's divorce attorney in 1948.

We and history are exceptionally fortunate that Captain Kerr wrote his autobiography, which he opened with the story of the letter from Minsk: [Q]

"One day we got a letter from Lee Harvey Oswald. The name meant nothing to us then. The letter was long and handwritten and was mailed from Russia ... It had been processed routinely in the secretary's mail room. Someone there decided that I, as special counsel to the secretary, should 'staff' the letter. The decision was logical because [it] had legal overtones. So it fell to me to decide what to do with the letter. ...

Those unfamiliar with the U.S. military services should know at this point that the Marine Corps is part of the Navy Department. Even the secretary of the navy needed to remind himself of this fact from time to time to avoid oversights damaging to delicate Marine Corps sensibilities. [There was] a sign over the door leading out of his office that read, "Remember the Marines." It reminded him to call the Marine Corps commandant to apprise him of important decisions before they became public. The flamboyant commandant at that time, General David Shoup, could become particularly peevish if this were not done.

When Oswald left the Marine Corps and went to live in Russia, he was given an administrative discharge that was less than commendatory ... "undesirable." He thought that characterization unfair. Later events were to prove the epithet to have been exceptionally mild. The letter was an attention getter. You don't find many Marines defecting to the Soviet Union.

I sent to Marine Corps Headquarters for Oswald's record, and studied the circumstances of his defection and subsequent discharge. There were no conflicts of fact between his letter and his record. A review of the statutes and regulations governing administrative discharges led to the conclusion that Oswald's discharge was in complete compliance with all legal requirements.

That, however, was not the end of it. The secretary can exercise clemency if he feels that there are strong extenuating circumstances. He may also intervene if an applicant's service was exceptionally meritorious.

Neither applied to Oswald. He had been a lousy Marine.

So I prepared the usual two papers that accompany all correspondence going into the secretary's 'action' basket. The first was a brief, setting forth everything I thought the secretary needed to know in order to make an informed decision. It concluded with a recommendation for action. The second was a paper for the secretary to sign that would put the recommended action into effect. [R]

In Oswald's case, my conclusions were that his complaint had no legal basis, his request was without merit, and that [new Secretary Korth] should not involve himself in any way. I recommended that he refer the letter to the commandant of the Marine Corps for 'appropriate action.' This phrase meant, in clear officialese, that the secretary was washing his hands of the case. The commandant could do with it as he wished. No one could doubt what the result would be. It was a kiss-off.

A day or two later, [Korth] called me into his office. He had obviously read the entire file and was intrigued. We discussed the case for half an hour or so, and at the end he said, 'I agree with you, Andy—this is the way we should handle it.' He then signed that second piece of paper that sent Oswald's letter on its way, we thought, to oblivion.

[Q] Kerr wrote "aboard our 43-foot sailing cutter *Andiamo* III at anchor in lovely Cook's Bay, Moorea, in French Polynesia ... from memory. ... Without access to ... files ... there are doubtless ... errors." There was one problem — Kerr confused the already-resigned Connally with the successor Korth. What you will read here has been corrected in that regard, otherwise it's as Captain Kerr wrote.

[R] Your author loves this explanation — it's precisely how I handled mail in an IBM military-patterned division headquarters in 1973-74 as the administrative assistant to a vice president.

But that's not exactly the way it turned out. On 22 November 1963, while riding beside President Kennedy in a motorcade in Dallas, John Connally, then governor of Texas, was shot through his arm and lung by Lee Harvey Oswald. President Kennedy was shot and killed in the same incident. The history books say it slightly differently—that Connally was wounded during Oswald's assassination of President Kennedy. The assumption is always that Oswald was shooting at Kennedy and that Connally was hit by accident or as a secondary target of opportunity. Could it not, however, have been the other way around? In spite of all of the investigations, including that of the Warren Commission, and the continuing fascination with and theories about the event, no one has yet come up with a credible motive for the shooting of Kennedy by Oswald. Against this, we know for a fact that Oswald once asked Connally for help in what may have been a *cri du coeur*. He was turned down flat. What greater motivation does a psychopath need?

Thus, by fortune I am able to provide a footnote to history." [881]

In Minsk, there was less urgency for departure after June was born.[882] Oswald wrote to his mother [883] and brother [884] that he would probably not arrive for several months. He wrote again to the Embassy, applying for a loan of $800;[885] the Embassy replied that it was authorized to loan only $500.[886] It had also decided that his own affidavit of support for Marina would be sufficient under the circumstances.[887] Meanwhile, the U.S. Immigration and Naturalization Service "after investigating Oswald's history, recommended that Marina be denied a visa because there was doubt as to Oswald's loyalty to the United States. The State Department intervened. In the opinion of the Office of Soviet Union Affairs, 'We're better off with subject in U.S. than in Russia.' Its ruling was based on a policy which held that it was potentially less embarrassing for the United States to have its unpredictables and malcontents at home than drifting about in foreign parts. In short, the State Department was not acting solely for humanitarian reasons. If Soviet authorities had granted Marina an exit visa partly to be rid of Oswald, American authorities were prepared to give her an entrance visa partly to get him back and out of harm's way. ... Oswald was considered an 'unstable character, whose actions are entirely unpredictable.' Like the Soviet authorities, the American authorities were afraid that he might do something politically embarrassing." [888]

On March 15, he received notice that Marina's visa application had been approved.[889] On March 24, he wrote in the *Historic Diary*: "Marina quits her job in the formal fashion." [890] Discussions with the Embassy to complete financial and travel arrangements continued through April and May.[891] The photo is in their Minsk apartment.[892]

In a few months at Thanksgiving dinner, Lee will say "he had had a hard time in Russia ... in the sense of earning a living ... he made about $80 a month, and it wasn't the money so much. It was the products were not available to him and also his wife to get even with the money, and they consistently ate cabbage and he was tired of cabbage ..." [893]

Oswald had complaints against the military, but not about any delay in answering mail. The *Warren Commission Hearings* show that a "UNSECNAV ROUTING SLIP" from the Office of the Under Secretary of the Navy referred his letter to "Commandant, Marine Corps", stating: "ROUTED TO CMC FOR APPROPRIATE ACTION WITH INFORMATION COPY TO CNO." [894] Oswald's pleading-threatening letter sped down the chain of command. Less than two weeks after it had been acknowledged from Connally's office in Fort Worth, the Marine Corps's Assistant Director of Personnel wrote this official reply:

1962 March 7: Brigadier General Tompkins to Oswald [895]

```
                                                   DKE-vhr
                                                   7 MAR 1962


     Mr. Lee H. Oswald
     Kalinina Street, 4-24
     Minsk, U.S.S.R.

     Dear Mr. Oswald:

     Your letter of 30 January 1962 addressed to the Secretary of
     the Navy concerning your separation from the Marine Corps Re-
     serve on 13 September 1960 has been referred to me for reply.

     A review of your file at this Headquarters reflects that a
     board of officers was convened by the Commander, Marine Air
     Reserve Training, Naval Air Station, Glenview, Illinois, for
     the purpose of determining your fitness to remain a member
     of the Marine Corps Reserve.  Referral of your case to this
     board was premised on reliable information which indicated
     that you had renounced your United States citizenship with
     the intentions of becoming a permanent citizen of the Union
     of Soviet Socialist Republics.  The Commander, Marine Air Re-
     serve Training, made reasonable effort to inform you of your
     right to appear before the board in person, representation by
     counsel of your choice and to present any evidence or state-
     ments you believed pertinent to your case.

     In the absence of reply from you concerning your rights as
     noted above, the board, nevertheless, convened and met on 8
     August 1960 at which time a recommendation was submitted that
     you be separated from the Marine Corps Reserve as undesirable.
     This recommendation was concurred in by the Commander, Marine
     Air Reserve Training and approved by this Headquarters.  Your
     discharge as undesirable was directed by this Headquarters on
     17 August 1960 and effected 13 September 1960.

     Your discharge certificate as undesirable is attached.  Ear-
     lier delivery of your certificate could not be accomplished
     since your whereabouts previously was unknown.

                                   Sincerely,


                                   R. McC. TOMPKINS
                             Brigadier General U. S. Marine Corps
                                Assistant Director of Personnel
     Encl:
     (1) Discharge Certificate
```

The Discharge Certificate enclosed with the letter was so important to Lee that he kept it close to him the remaining 20 months of his wretched life. Hours after his arrest, police will find it in his rented room. It then went to Dallas Police HQ, on to the FBI's Dallas office where it was carefully inventoried,[896] but then sank into oblivion and cannot be found.[897] Fortunately, a low-resolution and tilted microfilm was made in Dallas the week after the shooting. It is on the next page. Here is a best attempt to clean and straighten a restored certificate:

1960 September 13: Typed onto form DD-258-MC by Lt. M. G. Letscher [898]

UNDESIRABLE DISCHARGE

FROM THE ARMED FORCES OF THE
UNITED STATES OF AMERICA

THIS IS TO CERTIFY THAT

PRIVATE FIRST CLASS LEE HARVEY OSWALD 1653230

WAS DISCHARGED FROM THE

UNITED STATES MARINE CORPS

ON THE __13th__ DAY OF __SEPTEMBER 1960__

AS UNDESIRABLE

M. G. LETSCHER, FIRST LIEUTENANT, USMC

DD 258 MC   16—83083-2

Below are sources that led to the preceding restored certificate. At the left is the Web image most likely to be found, a "thumbnail" with very few pixels.[899] On the right is a higher-resolution version of that same image, purchased from the Dallas Municipal Archives:[900]

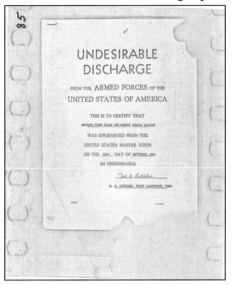 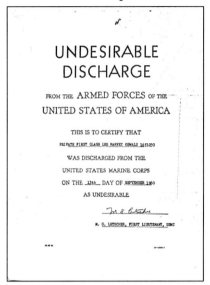

Lee now has the certificate shown on the previous page and knows that the changed discharge was not Dishonorable.   But in his prompt handwritten reply (we again supply a virtual typewriter for your reading convenience), he spells it "Undiserable":

1962 March 22: Oswald to Brigadier General Tompkins [901]

```
REPLY TO   DKE-VHR   7 Mach 1962.

                         LEE H. Oswald.
                         Kalinina ST.4-24,
                         Minsk  U.S.S.R..
R. McC. TOMPKiNS         March 22,1962
Brigadier Gen., U.S.M.C.
Ass. Direct. of Personnel


     Dear Sirs;
          In reply to your notification
of the granting of an Undiserable
discharge and your conveying of the
process at which it was arrived.
          I would like to point out
in direct opposition to your
information that I have never
taken steps to renouce my U.S.
citizenship,  Also that the United
States State Department has no
charges as complaints against
me   what/so ever.
          I refer you to the United
States Embassy, Moscow, or the U.S.
```

Second sheet

department of State Washington D.C.,for
the verification of this fact.
      Also, I was aware of the finding
of the board of officers of 8 Agust 1960.
 I was notified by my mother in
 December 1962.
      My request to the Secretary of
the Navy, his referal to you and
your letter to me, did not say
anything about a Review,which
is what I was trying to arrange.
     You mention "reliable information"
 as the basis for the Undiserable
discharge . I have no douth it was
newspaper speculation which foremed
your "reliable information ."
     Under U.S. law governing the
use of passports and conduct abroad
I have a perfect right to reside in
any country I wish too.
      I have not violated; Section 1544,
Title 18 , U.S. code , therefore you

Third sheet

have no legel or even moral right,
to reverse my honourable discharge
from the U.S.M.C. of Sept. 11, 1960,
into a undiserable discharge.
     You may consider this letter
a request by me for a full review
of my case in the light of these
facts, since by the time you
recive this letter I shall have
returned to the U.S.A. with my
family, and shall be prepared to
 appear in person at a reasonable
time and place in my area , before
a reviewing board of officers.
      If you choose to convene
a review board you may contact
me through the below address in
the United States after May 15th 1962.
    LEE H. Oswald
    7313 Davanport St.
    Fort Worth,
          Texas.   Sincerely
                  (signed)
                  Lee H Oswald

Lee learned about military paperwork in the Marines, evidenced by his printing atop the first page: "REPLY TO   DKE-VHR   7 Mach 1962." He continues to have problems with years. He dated his letter to John Connally 1961, although it was written in January of 1962. Here, he wrote on the second page: "I was notified by my mother in December 1962." — but this letter was written in March 1962, so he means her letter that he received in January 1962. On the third page, he tells of his discharge "from the U.S.M.C. of Sept. 11, 1960" — but it was that date in 1959. He has dyslexic tendencies, going both directions across year-ends.

Lee's pain is evidenced by his railing: "... you have no legel or even moral right to reverse my honourable discharge ...". It is abundantly clear that he hurts terribly because the Corps has snatched his greatest lifetime accomplishment from him, his successful completion of active-duty service as a Marine.

Oswald took pain to give an address where he expected to be in eight weeks. He must have imagined mail delivery slower than the actuality — from Minsk postmark to Navy receipt took only one week. Or, maybe he feared that a slow bureaucracy in Washington would take months to reply. The address he gave in Fort Worth, where he expects to be "after May 15th 1962" is the home of his brother, Robert. Characteristically and consistently, Lee manages to both misspell and mischaracterize Davenport Avenue as "Davanport St.", how Lee addressed his envelopes to Robert. It won't matter because the US PO delivers! — his letters to the States always arrived promptly.

Oswald's letter was rubber-stamped on arrival: **RECEIVED**
DISCIPLINE BRANCH
MAR 28   13 34   62 [902]

The answer came back to Minsk very quickly. Mailed on the third working day after receipt of his March 22 letter, it shows the Corps' determination to move his requested review from the headquarters of the Marines to a board of the Navy:

1962 April 2: Lieutenant Colonel Paul W. Seabaugh to Oswald [903]

```
                                          DKF-jcr
                                          2 Apr 1962


   Mr. Lee H. Oswald
   Kalinina Street, 4-24
   Minsk, U.S.S.R.

   Dear Mr. Oswald:

   This is in reply to your letter of 22 March 1962
   concerning your discharge as undesirable.

   This Headquarters has no authority to change the
   type of discharge issued in your case.  Your recourse
   is to the Navy Discharge Review Board, Department
   of the Navy, Washington 25, D. C.  I have therefore
   enclosed an information pamphlet describing the
   Board's function together with an application.

                        Sincerely,


                        PAUL W. SEABAUGH
            Lieutenant Colonel, U. S. Marine Corps
        Assistant Head, Discipline Branch, Personnel Department
           By direction of the Commandant of the Marine Corps

   Encl:
   (1) NAVEXOS P-70
   (2) DD Form 293
```

Oswald would not have been pleased with this sequence of events. He had appealed by writing to the Secretary of the Navy — and got back a reply from a mere Brigadier General. So, he wrote to the Brigadier General — and here's a reply from a lowly Lieutenant Colonel! He's the son of the mother who entrained to Washington DC and then phoned the White House to have a meeting with first-week President Kennedy, and only reluctantly agreed to meet with top-level Soviet experts in the State Department.

Lee set to work at once writing his appeal, five pages of "Brief" and "Statement". That document was completed and dated April 28. Perhaps because of expecting a quick exit from the USSR, or maybe to keep it all out of the hands of Soviet mail censors and spies, he held the application and attachments until he was in Texas, to mail on June 19. All are displayed in the next chapter, beginning on page 108.

April 29, 1962 brought a memorable "Camelot" event. Helen Thomas reported: "At a White House dinner honoring Nobel Prize winners, among the guests was theoretical chemist  and Nobel winner Linus Pauling,[S] who had spent the day picketing the White House in a ban-the-bomb protest.[904] [He] changed into a tuxedo and returned to the White House for dinner [and dancing with his wife, Ava Helen Pauling] [905] ... Kennedy greeted him with an appropriate sally: 'I'm glad you decided to come inside to dinner.'" [906]   That evening, Kennedy delivered a now-famous observation to the forty-nine Nobel laureates: "I think this is the most extraordinary  collection of talent, of human knowledge, that has ever been gathered together at the White House, with the possible exception of when Thomas Jefferson dined alone." [907]

On May 10, the Embassy wrote that everything was in order and suggested that Oswald come to the Embassy with his family to sign the final papers.[908]   At his request,[909] he was discharged from the Gorizont (Horizon) Electronics Factory on May 18.[910]   His work had apparently never been very good. Marina testified that he was rather lazy and resented having to take orders.[911] This estimate is confirmed by a report of the plant director and personnel department chief that he did not "display the initiative for increasing his skill" in his job, that he was "over-sensitive * * * to remarks from the foremen, and * * * careless in his work"; Oswald took "no part in the social life of the shop" and kept "very much to himself." [912]

In 1959 Lee had asked the U.S. Marine Corps for a discharge before the end of his enlistment commitment. The Corps, happy to see the backside of him, let him go. 2¾ years later the early-exit scenario repeats. He has gone downhill from radar operator-identifier to sheet-metal worker, and has not been up to the job in either. When this author was an IBM Corp manager, the departure of any employee for any reason required a form on which the final manager had to choose between "IBM sorry" and "IBM not sorry" about the departure, and thereon hung any possibility of re-hiring. It is perfectly clear that the USMC, and now the Belorussian Radio and Television Factory, chose "not sorry". He was a malcontent misfit.

On May 19, as the Oswalds prepare to leave Minsk, "Hollywood's most beguiling star was all whisper and curves and sex that night as she congratulated John Kennedy [in front of] fifteen thousand loyal Democrats at Madison Square Garden ... *Happy birthday . . . Mr. Pres . . . i . . .dent.* '" [913] Her dress was so tight she had been sewn into it. The President "quipped to the audience, 'I can now retire from politics having had 'Happy Birthday' sung to me in such a sweet, wholesome way.'" [914] Marilyn Monroe will be found dead in eleven weeks.

On May 22 — precisely 18 months before he will wound Connally and kill Kennedy — Oswald picked up his Soviet exit visa in Minsk;[915] he also had an interview with an MVD official to obtain final clearance for departure.[916] When they told uncle Ilya and aunt Valya that they had all the approvals and were really going, "Ilya spoke out again. 'He flits from side to side,' he said of Alik, 'and is unhappy everywhere. Maybe he'll go back and not like it there and then he'll want to come back here. But he'll never be allowed to come back. People are tired of nursing him over here.' ... Ilya's last utterance about his nephew-in-law had the tone of prophecy. 'He is,' Ilya said to Marina, 'a man who has lost his way.'" [917]

[S] Who taught this author freshman chemistry and chutzpah at Caltech — but that's a different story.

Lee, Marina and June Oswald departed by train from Minsk, going first to Moscow, then on to the U.S. These leaving-Minsk photos [918] were taken by friend Pavel Golovachev, who mailed the prints to Texas in care of brother Robert. Marina gave these and others, some of which you have seen in this chapter, to the Warren Commission. [919]

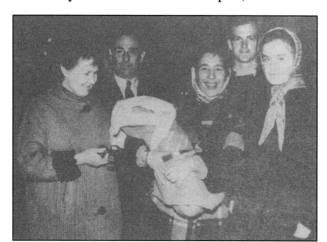

The Oswalds arrived in Moscow on May 24. [920] On that day, astronaut Scott Carpenter, a U.S. Navy test pilot, became the second American to orbit the earth, giving us slightly greater hope of catching up to the Russians. President Kennedy is trying to convince Congress of the need for affordable nationwide health care, [921] a full half-century before President Obama successfully battles to his greatest achievement, the Affordable Care Act.

At the American Embassy they filled out documents. [922] His new passport, limited for return to the United States, was issued that day, to expire on June 24. [923] Marina was given her American visa. [924] Final emigration arrangements were made with Soviet officials. [925] On June 1, Lee signed a promissory note at the Embassy for a repatriation loan of $435.71. [926] That purely humanitarian loan from the U.S. government later convinced Marguerite that her son was a spy working for the CIA, and conspiracy theorists that he was being brought home to murder the President on behalf of the CIA! The little family boarded a train for Holland, [927] passing back through Minsk during the night. [928] They crossed the frontier out of the Soviet Union the next day, June 2. In election news from Texas on that day, Secretary of the Navy John Connally won a runoff vote, becoming the Democratic Party's nominee for governor. [929]

Two days later, the three Oswalds sailed from Holland on the SS *Maasdam* of the Holland-America Line. [930] Onboard, they stayed by themselves. Marina testified that she did not often go on deck [931] because Lee didn't want her seen in public in her cheap dresses. [932] "He came to fetch her for meals, and it seemed to Marina that the other passengers were staring and laughing at her. She became self-conscious about her appearance and her clothes, unaware that it was the baby, swaddled from her waist to her toes, that was the object of so much attention. They had never seen swaddling before." [933] A photo of baby June encased in swaddling was on page 96. It didn't hurt the little girl — see her as a toddler on page 206, and on page 228 find a pointer to a photo of her, nicely grown, pretty and happy.

"Marina met only two people—the steward at the dining table and one gentleman whose father was Russian." [934] Lee spent most of the crossing in their cabin, writing pages and pages of political outrage onto Holland-America stationery taken from the ship's library. [935]

As the Oswalds sailed, a senior official in the Department of State sent a letter to Lee's anxious mother in Texas, not entirely concealing his exasperation with both mother and son:

1962 June 7: Department of State to Marguerite Oswald [936]

June 7, 1962

Dear Mrs. Oswald:

Miss James has brought to my attention the letter which you sent to her on May 25, 1962 reporting that your son, Lee, had informed you that he had not yet been able to complete arrangements for his departure from the Soviet Union to the United States.

Inquiry of the American Embassy at Moscow concerning your son's plans brought the reply on May 31 that your son and his family were leaving Moscow June 1 for Rotterdam and would leave Rotterdam June 4 on the S. S. MAASDAM for New York, arriving June 13. In all probability, by this time you have received this information from your son.

I am sorry you have been caused so much unhappiness as the result of your son's actions. You doubtless realize that his unfortunate situation was the result of his original decision to live in the USSR, and that the American Embassy at Moscow and the Department have made every effort to assist him. As you know, he originally informed the Embassy that he wished to remain permanently in the Soviet Union and never return to the United States. When he changed his mind later, the Embassy, regardless of his earlier actions, advised him regarding the procedure which he should follow to obtain Soviet exit permits for himself, his wife, and child; also the Department granted him a loan to pay for his transportation back to New York. I trust that your son is aware and appreciative of the assistance which has been rendered by the United States Government.

Sincerely yours,

Robert I. Owen
Officer in Charge
Political Affairs
Office of Soviet Union Affairs

The *Maasdam* docked at Hoboken, N.J., on June 13, 1962.[937] The Oswalds were met by a representative of the Traveler's Aid Society, asked to help by the Department of State. Lee claimed he had only $63. Marina "knew that he had had nearly $200 when he left Moscow and had spent hardly any of it since. To her, the mere fact that he claimed to have only $63 was prima facie evidence that he had more, since 'how could he live without lying?'" [938] Lee said they had no plans for that night or for travel onward to Fort Worth, and accepted help.[939] The society referred the Oswalds to the New York City Department of Welfare, which found them a room at the Times Square Hotel.[940] Oswald told representatives of the Society and the welfare department that he had been a Marine guard stationed at the American Embassy in Moscow. He also claimed that he had paid the travel expenses himself.[941]

Lee went out and Marina "decided to take a bath. But the letters on the faucets, 'H' and 'C,' were unfamiliar to her, and she decided to wait for her husband ... She longed to look out the window. But between her and the view were Venetian blinds, which she had never seen before ... He brought hamburgers and French fries, another new experience for Marina. ... Afterwards Lee explained about the faucets, and 'hot' and 'cold' became Marina's first words of English." [942]

The welfare department called Robert Oswald's home in Fort Worth. His wife Vada answered and said they would help. Robert sent $200 immediately.[943] Lee refused to accept the money, insisting the department itself should pay the fare to Texas; he threatened that they would go as far as they could on $63 and rely on local authorities to get them the rest of the way. In the end he accepted Robert's money.[944] On the afternoon of June 14, 1962, the Oswalds left New York by plane for Dallas and Fort Worth.[945] They flew from large Idlewild Airport, which will become JFK in only two years because Lee is back in the U.S.

Lee still had unpleasant business to finish. He carried with him his appeal to the Navy against the undesirable discharge, which he had already written but preferred to mail in the U.S. On this last day of travel, he made a final edit to a long plea, as will be seen in two pages when he mails it on his fifth day back in Texas.

Key point of this chapter:
Lee is soon disillusioned and unhappy. He marries a lovely girl, decides to go home, learns of the undesirable discharge, asks for help that is brusquely dismissed by Connally, battles the Pentagon, finally obtains loans and permits to flee the USSR.

MISFIT

1962 June 14 — 1963 November 21

> "Lee Harvey Oswald had been a misfit all his life. ... He was ... best described by his wife ... in her broken English: 'When Lee in the United States, he no like the United States; when he in Russia he no like Russia; when he come back to United States he no like United States; he like Cuba; when Cuba no take him, he no like Cuba. I guess he only like on the moon.'"
>
> — **Earl Warren** [946]

LEE OSWALD HAD GONE TO THE SOVIET UNION seeking happiness in a Marxist utopia. He was disappointed with a cold reception in Moscow and banishment to unimportant work in isolated Minsk. He now returns home hoping for better, but that is not to be. Chief Justice Earl Warren wrote a preview of this chapter: "[U]ntil the assassination, he lived a nondescript life, either quitting various jobs or being discharged for inefficiency or incompatibility. He lived largely on unemployment compensation, and often left his wife and child to the charity of friends. ... He was without friends or associates, an absolute 'loner' ..." [947]

Lee, Marina and June Lee Oswald arrived at Love Field in Dallas on June 14, 1962, met by older brother Robert Edward Lee Oswald, his wife Vada and their young children Cathy and Robert Lee. In an Affidavit of Support to the US Embassy in Moscow, Lee had written that they would stay with his mother in Vernon, Texas. [948] His changed decision to stay with Robert apparently had been prompted by his brother's invitation in a letter to Minsk. [949]

Robert testified that Lee had become rather bald, seemed to be somewhat thinner, had picked up "something of an accent," but was "the same boy" he had known before in 1959. [950] Disappointed with the muted reception, Lee asked: "What, no photographers or anything?" Robert explained, probably to Lee's displeasure, "No, I have been able to keep it quiet." [951]

Robert drove them all to his home in Fort Worth, where the brothers got along well. [952] They did not discuss politics, Robert said, because of a "tacit agreement" between them. [953] Robert testified that Lee quickly brought up the matter of his undesirable discharge. "He said he wanted to go down the next day to the Marine Corps office in Fort Worth, Tex., and discuss with them and perhaps find out what action he needed to take to have this corrected to an honorable discharge. ... My reply to him on that was that I thought that was a good idea and that ... if I could be of some assistance in writing the Marine Corps office directly on behalf of him. I do not recall any further conversation in reference to his dishonorable discharge." [954]

Lee immediately contested his discharge, without his brother's help. Using Robert's address, he now dated and mailed his application for review: [955]

1962 June 18: Oswald to Navy Discharge Review Board [956]

Page 2 of 2-page Application [957]

INSTRUCTIONS

Do not use this form if discharge by reason of sentence of GENERAL COURT MARTIAL - Use DD Form 149.

Attach original discharge certificate.

All evidence not already included in your military or naval record must be submitted by you before the date set for hearing. Since all evidence submitted will be retained on file with your application, it is suggested that extra copies be prepared for your information if you so desire. The Review Boards do not secure evidence for you.

Review Boards of the Army, Navy, Marine Corps, Coast Guard and Air Force convene in Washington, D.C. You may appear before the Board in person. However, this is not mandatory. (Your appearance and the appearance of witnesses in your behalf will be at no expense to the Government.) If you state on your application that you will appear before the Board in person and fail to do so without previous satisfactory arrangement with the Board, such failure will be considered as a waiver of appearance and your case will be reviewed on the evidence contained in your military or naval record.

If you wish to be represented by Counsel, you may:

1. Furnish Counsel at your own expense.
2. Choose a Counsel from the following list of organizations, any one of which will furnish representation at no charge to you.

Either of these methods will be at no expense to the Government. Government Counsel will not be furnished.

American Red Cross
American Legion
American Veterans of WW II
Catholic War Veterans, Inc.
Disabled American Veterans
Jewish War Veterans of the U.S.A.
National Association for the Advancement of Colored People
Veterans of Foreign Wars

UPON COMPLETION, MAIL THIS APPLICATION AS FOLLOWS:

ARMY	NAVY AND MARINE CORPS	COAST GUARD	AIR FORCE
The Adjutant General Army Records Center 9700 Page Blvd. St. Louis 14, Missouri	Navy Discharge Review Board Washington 25, D.C.	Commandant, (CBO) U.S. Coast Guard Headquarters Washington 25, D.C.	FORMER OFFICERS: Director of Military Personnel Hq USAF Washington 25, D.C. FORMER ENLISTED MEN: Air Force Records Center 9700 Page Blvd St. Louis 14, Missouri

If you make a change in residence, notify the appropriate headquarters immediately.

REMARKS

(A) I REQUEST THAT STATEMENT OF PLAINTIFF BE READ INTO RECORD.

(B) CORRESPONDANCE BETWEEN MCHQ AND PLAINTIFF MAY BE FOUND UNDER:
(1) DKC - VHR 7 MARCH 1962
(2) DKC GCR 2 APR. 1962

"Brief in Support of Application" [958]

Brief in Support of Application.

A review of my file, will show that a recommendation to separate me from the Marine corps. Reserve was concurred in by a board of officers at Glenview Illinois, to become effective from September 13 1960, or 1 year 2 days from the time I was honourably discharged from active duty at NAS1C, MCAS, El Toro calif. on 11 ... ... 1959.

Referral of my case to this board was promised on the proported fact that I had renounced my american citizenship with intent to become a permanent citizen of the Union of Soviet Socialist Republics.

Since this was the sole reason I was separated from the Marine corps. Reserve and summarily given a Undesirable Discharge I do hereby request:

That the Board does convene to review this case.

This is a case which comes under the heading: NAVEXOS 15(C)(4), i.e., a discharge improperly issued.

In this case there is no question as to service, which as the naval records show, was of a strictly honourable nature.

This case is a question of loyalty revolving out of my residence in the Soviet Union.

In requesting a review of this case, I can show; I had not violated any laws or regulations pertaining to my prolonged residence abroad and that I am a loyal U.S. citizen.

Page 1 of 4-page "Statement of Plaintiff" [959]

Statement of Plaintiff

(I request that this statement be made part of ....

I have been informed that a board of officers was convened at Naval Air Station, Glenview, Illinois to determine my fittness to remain a member of the U.S. M.C.R..

I was separated from the U.S.M.C.R. with a undisirable discharge superceding my original honourable discharge of 11 September 1959 given at NAS Marine corps air station, El Toro, Santa Ana, California.

This board was given to consider, weather I had gone to the Union of Soviet Socialist Republics with the object of becoming a permanent citizen of that country.

Since I was not in the United States at the time of the convening of the board and since I was completly unable to communicate with anyone in the outside world through the Iron curtain, this board found against me.

My relatives, who were notified of the convening of this board, could not conceivably present evidence on my behalf against such vangly defined charges, without any knowlege of my whereabouts.

It was only on July 8, 1961 that I was able to put in a appearance at the american Embassy, moscow after escaping from the disterduin

Page 2 of 4-page statement [960]

... from the disterdium of the city to which the Russian authorities had sent me. Subsequent events, through the active support of the U.S. Embassy, will see myself and my Russian wife in the U.S. very shortly.

As far as the case in question is concerned I can understand how, without any inquiry directed towards me, a conclusion of disloyalty might possibaly be arrived at.

However, weather my choice of permanent or temporary residence may be in the U.S.S.R.; or in the United States, grounds for such arbitrary action as was instigated against me cannot be judged as being fair or impartial.

I must point out, that I have not violated any laws under the U.S. Code Section 1544 title 18.

I may say, that even the most prolonged residence abroad is an accepted custom, and absolutly legal (so long as other pertinient regulations have not been violated).

In introducing the letter from the U.S. Embassy, moscow, I have it in mind the last paragraph nov. 13, 1961, which states: "meanwhile your retention of your present soviet passport or an extention thereof does not prejudice in any way your claim to american citizenship." signed Joseph B. norbury, american consulas.

Page 3 of 4-page statement [961]

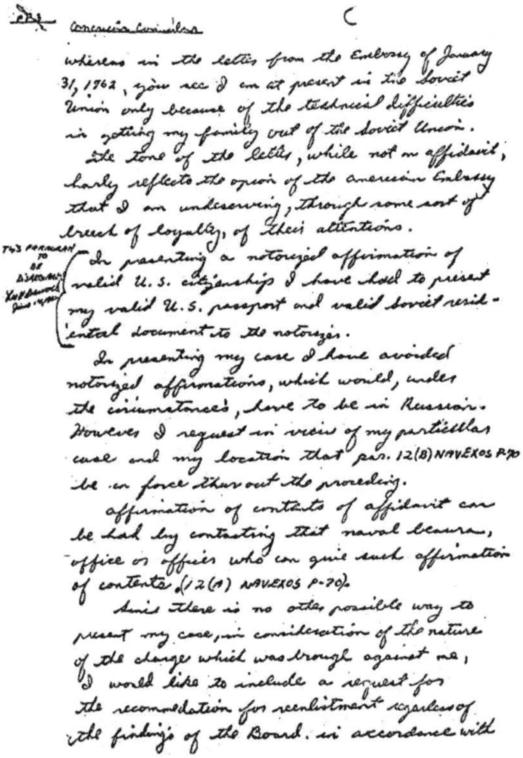
concurrence considerations

whereas in the letter from the Embassy of January 31, 1962, you see I am at present in the Soviet Union only because of the technical difficulties in getting my family out of the Soviet Union.

The tone of the letter, while not an affidavit, hardly reflects the opinion of the American Embassy that I am undeserving, through some sort of breach of loyalty, of their attentions.

In presenting a notorized affirmation of valid U.S. citizenship I have had to present my valid U.S. passport and valid Soviet resid-ential document to the notorizer.

In presenting my case I have avoided notorized affirmations, which would, under the circumstances, have to be in Russian. However I request in view of my particular case and my location that par. 12(B) NAVEXOS P-70 be in force thru out the proceeding.

affirmation of contents of affidavit can be had by contacting that naval bureau, office or offices who can give such affirmation of contents (12(A) NAVEXOS P-70).

Since there is no other possible way to present my case, in consideration of the nature of the charge which was brought against me, I would like to include a request for the recommendation for reenlistment regardless of the finding's of the Board. in accordance with

Page 4 of 4-page statement [962]

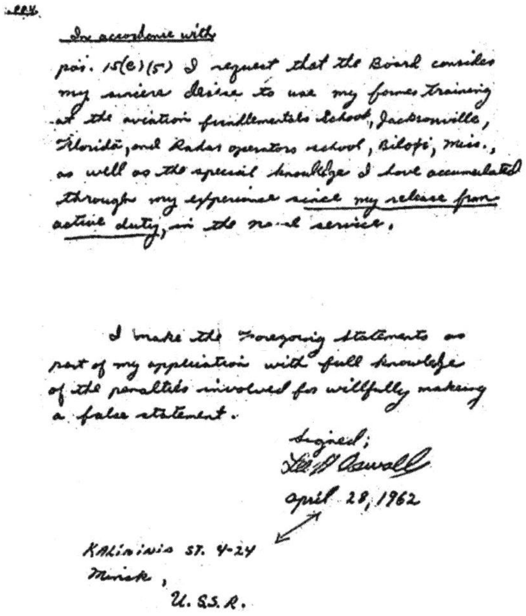
In accordance with par. 15(e)(5) I request that the Board consider my sincere desire to use my former training at the aviation fundamentals school, Jacksonville, Florida, and Radar operators school, Biloxi, Miss., as well as the special knowledge I have accumulated through my experience since my release from active duty, in the naval service.

I make the foregoing statements as part of my application with full knowledge of the penalties involved for willfully making a false statement.

Signed;
Lee H Oswald
April 28, 1962

Kalininia St. 4-24
Minsk,
U.S.S.R.

If he had a typewriter, this would be Lee's easier-to-read attachment:

"Brief in Support of Application .

A review of my file , will show that a recommendation to separate me from the Marine Corps. Reserve was concurred in by a board of officers at Glenview Illinois ,to become effective from September 13 1960 , or 1 year 2 days from the time I was honourably discharged from active duty at , H&HC , MCMS , El Toro Calif on 11 September 1959.

Referral of my case to this board was premised on the proported fact that I had renounced my american citizenship with intent to become a permanent citizen of the Union of Soviet Socialist Republics.

Since this was the sole reason I was separated from the Marine Corps. Reserve and summarily given a Undesirable Discharge I do hereby request:

That the Board does convene to review this case.

This is a case which comes under the heading:
NAVEXOS 15(e)(4) , i.e. , a discharge improperly issued.

In this case there is no question as to service , which as the naval records show , was of a strictly honourable nature.

This case is a question of loyalty revolving out of my residence in the Soviet Union.

In requesting a review of this case , I can show: I had not violated any laws or regulations pertaining to my prolonged residence abroad and that I am a loyal U.S. citizen ." [963]

"Statement of Planitiff

(I request that this statement be made part of my record.)

I have been informed that a board of Inquiry was convened at Naval Air Station ,Glenview, Illinois to determine my fitness to remain a member of the U.S.M.C.R..

I was separated from the U.S.M.C.R. with a undisirable discharge superceding my original honourable discharge of 11 Septemper 1959 given at H&HS Marine Corps Air Station , El Toro , Santa Anna , California.

This board was given to consider weather I had gone to the Union of Soviet Socialist Republics with the object of becomeing a permanent citizen of that country.

Since I was not in the United States at the time of the convening of the board and since I was completely unable to communicate with anyone in the outside world through the Iron Currtain ,this board found against me.

My relatives ,who were notified of the convening of this board , could not conceivably present evidence on my behalf against such vaugly definied charges, without any knowelege of my whereabouts .

It was only on July 8 , 1961 that I was able to put in a appearase at the American Embassy, Moscow after excaping from the dentention of the city to which the Russian Authorities had sent me. Subsequent events , through the active support of the U.S. Embassy , will see myself and my Russian wife in the U.S. very shortly.

As far as the case in question is concerned I can understand how , without any inquiry directed towards me , a conclustion of disloyalty might possibly be arrived at.

However , weather my choice of permanent or temporary residence may be in the U.S.S.R., or in the United States , grounds for such arbitary action as was instigated against me cannot be judged as being fair or impartial.

I must point out that I have not violated any laws under the U.S. Code Scetion 1544 title 18.

I may say that even the most prolonged residence abroad is an accepted custom , and absolutely legal (so long as other pertainent regulations have not been violated).

In introducing the letter from the U.S. Embassy , Moscow , I have it in mind the last paragrahp nov. 13 , 1961, which states: "meanwhile your retention of your present Soviet passport or an extension thereof does not prejudice in any way your claim to American citizenship." signed Joseph B. Norbury , American consular. Whereas in the letter from the Embassy of January 31, 1962 , you see I am at present in the Soviet Union only because of the technical diffculties in getting my family out of the Soviet Union.

The tone of the letter , while not an affidavit , harly reflects the opion of the American Embassy that I am undeserving , through some sort of breech of loyalty, of their attentions.

[The following paragraph is bracketed with a printed and signed note in the left margin:] "THIS PARAGRAH TO BE DISREGARDED Lee H. Oswald June 14,1962": In presenting a notorized affirmation of valid U.S. citizenship I have had to present my valid U.S. passport and valid Soviet residental document to the notorizes .

In presenting my case I have avoided notorized affirmations , which would , under the circumstances , have to be in Russian. However I request in view of my particular case and my location that par. 12(B)NAVEXOS P.70 be in force thur out the proceding.

Affirmation of contents of affidavit can be had by contacting that naval beaura , office or officer who can give such affirmation of contents .(12(A) NAVEXOS P.70).

Since there is no other possible way to present my case ,in consideration of the nature of the charge which was brough against me , I would like to include a request for the recommedation for reenlistment regarless of the finding's of the Board . in accordance

with par . 15(e)(5) I request that the Board consider my sincere
desire to use my former training at the aviation fundlementals School,
Jacksonville , Florida ,and Radar operators school , Biloxi, Miss., as
well as the special knowledge I have accumulated through my experience
since my release from active duty , in the naval service.

    I make the Foregoing Statements as part of my application with full
knowledge of the penalties involved for willfully making a false
statement.

Signed;
Lee H. Oswald
April 28, 1962

KALiNiNiA ST. 4-24
Minsk , U.S.S.R." [964]

Lee enclosed two letters to him from the U.S. Embassy in Moscow, quoting them as authority, a considerable over-reach in both cases. A letter of November 13, 1961, had reassured him that a Soviet passport for stateless persons would not affect the judgment yet to come about whether he was or was not still an American citizen, which was in question because of his attempts to renounce. He cited the letter of January 31, 1962, to justify the length of time he lived in Minsk, but it had simply advised him that Marina would not be accepted to fly during her advanced pregnancy, and they should remain on the ground until the baby was born.

From April 28 when he signed at the end of his "Statement" until he revised it by bracketing to disregard a paragraph, signing and dating that change on June 14, was a month and a half. It should be obvious that this appeal was quite important to him, as he had written then re-worked it from Minsk until the day they flew into Texas.

In Fort Worth on the day he mailed his thick application,[A] Oswald also took a step that will soon lead to contact with Russians in the Dallas - Fort Worth "metroplex", from them to an American lady learning to speak Russian, then to her garage where he will hide the rifle he will soon buy, until he suddenly needs it in November next year.

Lee phoned Peter Gregory, a petroleum engineer born in Siberia, who taught Russian at the Fort Worth Public Library as a "civic enterprise." [965] He asked Gregory to give him a letter testifying to his ability to read and speak Russian, so he can obtain work as an interpreter or translator. Gregory tested him and gave the letter,[966] and a week later took his son Paul Gregory, a college student, to the Oswalds. Paul arranged for Marina — not Lee — to give him language lessons during the summer.[967] "Her Russian would be fresh and up to date, whereas that of his father, who had been forty years in exile, might no longer encompass the idiom of young people in Russia." [968] "And when Paul ... shortly before leaving for college, handed her ... $35, she was overwhelmed. She had never in all her life had so much money. She felt that she did not deserve it. ... Marina knew what she wanted to do with it. She went across the street to Montgomery Ward and bought a pair of shoes for herself ($3.98), and for Alka green work pants, two flannel shirts, and another pair of shoes ($11)." [969]

Oswald's return from the USSR coincided with suspicion and hostility between the two superpowers, the years of the Berlin Wall and the Cuban Missile Crisis. The US government was not about to let Oswald wander around free of observation. FBI agents quickly found him

---

[A] Two 7¢ Air Mail stamps were postmarked on June 19; the Navy time-stamped arrival on June 20.
   Mail delivery in the U.S. (as in our mother, Britain) was and continues to be exemplary.

in Fort Worth in only his second week home.[970] An agent who interviewed him described Lee as tense and "drawn up"; he said Oswald "exhibited an arrogant attitude [and was] inclined to be just a little insolent." [971] At the end of the interview, Lee promised to notify the FBI if he were contacted by Soviet agents.[972]

To understand the FBI's interest, it is essential to recognize the strong anti-Communist compulsions of the 1960s. No better example exists than that of Lee's receipt of Communist and socialist publications, some from Europe. Always an avid reader, he subscribed, among others, to *Agitator*, *Krokodil*, *Ogonek*,[973] *Sovietskaya Byelorussia*,[974] *The Militant* and *The Daily Worker*. In the famous photo on page 129 that Marina will take of Lee holding his rifle in one hand, in the other he displays copies of the latter two, both printed in English.[975]

Analyst John Newman wrote: "Oswald's mail activity ... led to actions by the post office which Oswald protested. He had to execute a post office Form 2153-X, instructing them to 'always' deliver foreign propaganda mailings. He added this comment to the form: 'I protest this intimidation.'" [976] The form and his protest are in two "Warren Commission Documents", which were not put into the 26 supporting volumes published with the *Warren Report*: "The Warren Commission published 15 volumes of hearings and an additional 11 volumes of evidence. The published evidence was taken from a larger collection of what are called Warren Commission Documents, referenced by 'WCD' [in this book as "CD"]. There are 1,555 documents in all, encompassing roughly 50,000 pages. They consist largely of reports from the FBI and other agencies including the CIA, State Department, and other sources." [977] Newman tells the rest of the story in a *Note*, such as in my NOTES AND SOURCES section at the back of this book: "New York Customs received P.O. Form 2153-X from NYC P.O. which is executed by Oswald, Box 2915; CD 60, pp. 2-3; FBI reports Oswald's writing 'I protest this intimidation'; see CD 205, p. 157." [978]

Despised in the U.S.S.R., America was respected elsewhere. On July 1, "more than *two million* people ... lined the streets in Mexico City to see President and Mrs. Kennedy." [979]

Lee and family remained with Robert for about a month.[980] Marguerite Oswald visited, briefly, and was not invited to tarry. She told the Warren Commission she moved to Fort Worth because she thought Robert's house was too crowded and wanted to help them.[981] Lee, Marina and June moved into her apartment in July.[982] Marguerite described the period when her son's family lived with her as "a very happy month". According to her testimony, she and her son and daughter-in-law got along well. "From the beginning, however, this living arrangement strained Oswald's patience. For one thing, his mother, a very determined woman, insisted on speaking English to Marina and assumed that she understood.[B] His protests that she did not comprehend a word of English were to no avail. Marina did not seem to mind and went about the house cheerfully singing and helping with the housework." [983] Marina testified that Lee did not get along well with his mother and that he decided after several weeks that they should move to their own apartment.[984] Robert told the Commission: "[W]e have never really gotten along, she tries to dominate me and my wife, and I might say that applies to John and his family, and also to the extent that it applied to Lee and his wife ..." [985] Having now experienced the nature of her mother-in-law, "Marina was as anxious to get away from Marguerite as her husband was." [986]

[B] The author's father lived and died believing all foreigners secretly understand English — but it is necessary to yell it at them.

In August, Lee, Marina and June moved to a small one-bedroom furnished apartment in Fort Worth, cheap at $59.50 per month.[987] Robert helped: "When I drove up to Mother's apartment, I could hear Mother's voice before I got to the door. They were still quarreling as Lee and I carried the suitcases and boxes to the car. Marina just looked bewildered." [988] Marguerite "apparently felt that she had made a great sacrifice in moving to Fort Worth to help Lee, and now he suddenly was moving out, without even telling her where he was going to live. They drove to the new apartment—about one-half mile away." [989]

"Lee had liabilities in the job market. He had no high-school diploma. He had an undesirable discharge. And he had spent three years in the Soviet Union, a fact he probably did not confide to would-be employers, which left him with an abbreviated job history. The skills he had—radar training, the ability to speak Russian—were not in demand in Fort Worth. He did not want blue-collar work of the kind he had had in Minsk, yet he lacked the education for the white-collar work he would accept, to say nothing of the intellectual work he really wanted." [990] In July, the Texas Employment Commission referred him to the Louv-R-Pak Division of the Leslie Welding Co.[991] On his application he wrote falsely that he had had "2½ years experience" as a "machinist and sheet metal worker" in the Marines from which he had an "honourable" discharge.[992] As you know, his metal-working had not been in the Marines, but in Minsk. Because that would require difficult explanation and probably not get him the job, Lee twisted the past. As long as he was inventing, he decided under "MILITARY SERVICE RECORD" to promote himself: "Rating at time of discharge: SGT." [993]

Hired as a "sheet metal helper" at $1.25 an hour, he worked [994] "putting together aluminum windows and the kind of storm doors that have initials worked into them." [995] [C] On the job, he kept to himself and was considered uncommunicative.[996] Marina said he did not like his work.[997] Although Lee habitually lies and avoids, he honorably repays his debts: "From his earnings he began paying back the money he owed the State Department and his brother Robert, who had paid for his travel from New York to Fort Worth." [998]

Marguerite bought clothes for Marina and a highchair for the baby, but Lee told her not to buy "things for his wife that he himself could not buy." [999] He did not want his mother to visit the apartment and became incensed when his wife permitted her to visit despite his instructions.[1000] Witnesses described the apartment as "decrepit" and very poorly furnished.[1001] Acquaintances observed that Marina and the baby were poorly clothed, the Oswalds had little food, and at first there was no bed for the baby.[1002]

On August 1,[D] two days before moving into the apartment, Lee mailed an undated letter to the "NAVY DiSChARGe Reveiw BOARd". He had probably written it earlier but delayed the mailing so his new address would be correct for the Navy to use — this appeal against the undesirable discharge is important to him! The Warren Commission's copy is much too low in contrast to display for you; so, as if he had a typewriter:

[C] This is the first excerpt from Stephen King's book *11/22/63: A Novel*, a time-jumping fantasy but excellently researched and factually based, which I recommend for a subjective feel for the 1960s, for Texas, and especially for the plight of Marina at the hands and fists of her assaultive husband.

[D] The Navy saved and the Commission displayed the envelope, postmarked AUG 1.

1962 (mailed) August 1: Oswald to Navy Discharge Review Board [1003]

```
                                         H.Q.M.C.
   LEE H. OSWALD  (1653230)              Washigtion DC
   2703 Mercedes St
   Fort Worth , Texas

      Dear Sirs

         In regard to my request for a
   hearing by the "board" of review H.Q.MC ,
   of my discharge .
         I filled in a DD form 293 an sent in
      in early July
         Please notifie me of action taken
      in regard to my  request .

                              Sincerely,
                              [signed]
                              LeeHOswald
```

Lee did not point out his change of address, but the efficient Board noticed and replied to the new apartment on Mercedes Street. The Navy's reply of August 6, shown on the next page, acknowledges receipt of Lee's application on June 20, 6½ weeks earlier, and says, in essence, "Yes, we have yours, we're busy, we'll get to it when we can".

For younger readers, an explanation of "carbon copy" is in order. In the 1960s, there were no small office computers. The Xerox copier had been introduced in 1959, but was quite expensive and thought to be extravagant. To keep a file copy, the sender typed a letter with one or more pairs of very thin black carbonized paper and thin plain paper behind the original. Typewriters were either manual, with the fingers providing all the force to do the typing, or electric, in which easy-to-depress keys signaled a motorized system to assist by finishing the imprinting action. As the typebars or a typeball [E] hit a ribbon to type on top-sheet paper that had been pre-printed with a letterhead, the same slams made one or more carbon copies under that top sheet, by pressing the carbonized paper(s) onto the thin paper sheet(s), which were thence called "carbon copies". You knew a "cc" when you held it — somewhat fuzzy printing on plain (but usually lightly-tinted) thin paper with no letterhead.

The original letter that went to Oswald apparently does not survive. The Warren Commission obtained two carbon copies, one each from the Navy and from Oswald's Marine Corps file, and printed both in the twenty-six volumes that supplement the *Warren Report*.

To show you almost exactly what Oswald saw, this author made careful re-creations of three letters from the Navy Discharge Review Board, modeling those images on letterheads you will see later. Unfortunately, a Senior Assistant for Public Affairs Policy in The Pentagon, ruling for the Department of Defense's Branding and Trademark Licensing Program, forbade that, fearing "confusion" and "an implied endorsement as to the authenticity of the re-creation" by the Department of Defense. [1004]

[E] Probably not. The IBM Selectric was first sold in July 1961, but the government was a slow adopter.

To give a hint of the letter as Oswald received it, the carbon copy is shown below, beneath a scan of the Navy Discharge Review Board's letterhead, as used on a subsequent letter to Oswald, and very probably on this.

Navy Discharge Review Board letterhead in 1962: [1005]

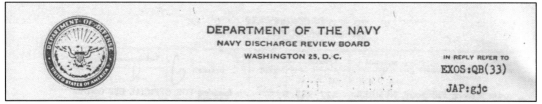

Here is a carbon copy of the first NDRB letter, probably typed on the letterhead above: [1006]

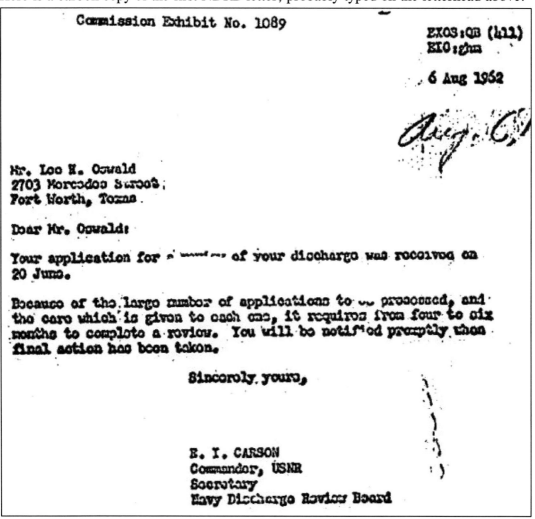

On August 16, the FBI again interviewed Lee: "[H]e denied, falsely, that he had either declared his intention to renounce his U.S. citizenship ... or told U.S. authorities that he was going to give the Russians secrets he had learned during his Marine Corps service." [1007] He still refused to discuss why he had gone to the Soviet Union, but was less hostile than during the previous interview. He protested his undesirable discharge from the Marines. [1008]

"Troubled by his flat denials of almost everything they asked, the agents asked, as suggested by Washington headquarters, if he would be willing to submit to a polygraph examination. Oswald categorically refused to take any such lie-detector test and excused himself from the interview." [1009] Marina testified he was very upset by the FBI's interest in him. [1010] The FBI "received a report from two confidential informants the next day to the effect that neither Lee nor Marina Oswald had anything to do with Communist Party activities in Fort Worth," [1011] so closed his file, noting he was "merely routine, unworthy of any further consideration." [1012] Lee never learned of this loss of interest — perversely, he would be greatly disappointed.

Before we travel into the small world of the Russian-speaking community of Dallas and Fort Worth, where Lee will gain acquaintances and possibly one friend, it is worth carefully considering a sage observation by one of the Warren Commission members, Representative Gerald Ford, who will become President of the U.S. in ten years. In 1965 he released a book, *Portrait of the Assassin*, retelling with his straightforward words the testimony by witnesses to the Commission. His book is particularly valuable for his ruminations on that evidence, and the conclusions he drew. Here's a beauty, applicable to this period of the Oswalds' life:

> "Many of the problems of the investigation could be solved only by meticulous inquiry into every last acquaintance and associate Lee ever had. The Commission staff compiled a list of hundreds of names of persons mentioned in one way or another in connection with Lee Oswald, and in turn checked acquaintances of acquaintances. One of the astounding conclusions was that, aside from his immediate family and a few relatives, Lee Oswald had no friends or acquaintances when he returned from Russia. There is no record in thousands of pages of testimony of his contacting a single person, other than his family, whom he had ever known before. If the important links in belonging to a place, a community or a nation are the personal ties and associations, the love of one's heritage, the faith in one's society and history, Lee Oswald in truth did not belong to this country. His family meant little or nothing to him; his mother eventually became anathema. In his writing he made it perfectly clear that he did not believe in his country's history or its institutions. Marina was right if she got the impression that he was a stranger in his own homeland." [1013]

As arranged (see page 112), Marina gave Russian lessons to Paul Gregory during August and September. Through Paul's father, Peter, the Oswalds became acquainted with a growing number of people of the Russian-speaking community in the Dallas-Fort Worth area, tied together socially by a common origin, language, and religion. [1014] In August, Peter Gregory invited the Oswalds and several members of the Russian community to dinner. [1015] One of those guests mentioned the Oswalds to George Sergei De Mohrenschildt, a petroleum engineer born in Russia, who visited them in September. [1016] (We are on the path to Mrs. Paine's garage.)

"Marina was the real sensation. Not only did she appear a childlike, innocent waif, but her use of Russian—and Russians tend to judge other Russians by the way they speak the mother tongue—was very cultivated. ... Marina was tiny and thin. ... She was well mannered and, above all, she spoke that pure Leningrad Russian, innocent of jargon or slang, that to them bespoke intelligence and education. She was like a fragile fossil, a relic of their old and much-loved homeland, that had suddenly been dug out of the Russian earth." [1017]

The Russian émigrés noticed significant problems between the young Oswalds. Elena Hall, born in Tehran to Russian parents, told the Commission: "I think she was stubborn, and he was just cruel to her, and they would argue for nothing, just nothing. And he would beat her all the time." [1018] "I think he talked very good Russian. He could read and write and everything. And he, in fact, a few times I told him, I said, 'Lee, why don't you speak in

English with Marina and let her learn English?' And he said, 'No. Then I am forgetting my Russian.' I said, 'You don't need the Russian language now in the United States. She needs English.' And he said, 'No, I won't.' He never will talk English to her." [1019]

Before leaving Minsk, Marina understood and spoke only the Russian language. She found herself isolated in Texas at first, with Lee the only person to whom she could talk. Then she made friends within Dallas's small Russian-speaking émigré community. The new friends considered Lee rude, but they delighted in conversations with Marina and her lovely pure Russian. For his part, Lee hates Marina's ability to talk with others, fearing he'll lose control over her. The couple had argued in Minsk, but that has now turned into fighting, sometimes quite violent. He plays out his need for any kind of power, unmet in his miserable life outside their home, so he hits and beats his wife in anger, attempting to control her. [1020]

The Russian community was interested in the Oswalds not only because they needed help, but also because they could provide the latest information about what was happening in Russia. [1021] Members of the group provided small amounts of money, groceries, clothing, and furniture, and occasionally visited the Oswalds, and the Oswalds in turn visited some of them in Dallas. [1022] It was evident that Lee did not appreciate the help of the Russian community. [1023] At least once he flew into a rage and shouted that he did not need any of the things that people were giving to him. [1024] Some, including his mother, felt that he resented the gifts because he could not give his wife what the others were providing. [1025]

Marguerite, the brood hen of his negative attitudes, told the Warren Commission: "The Russian friends, who were established, and had cars and fine homes, could not see this Russian girl doing without. They are the ones that interfered ... and within a short time, then, this Russian girl had a playpen, had a sewing machine, had a baby bed, and a Taylor Tot.[F] And this all came out in the paper—that they supplied this to the girl, because she was in need of these things. ... The point I am trying to bring out is that these Russian friends have interfered in their lives, and thought that the Russian girl should have more than necessary." [1026]

Oswald became increasingly unpopular with his Russian-speaking acquaintances, partly because of his resentment of their assistance. [1027] One stated that none of them cared for "Alik" "because of his political philosophy, his criticism of the United States, his apparent lack of interest in anyone but himself and because of his treatment of Marina." [1028] "There was something in Lee's attitude, moreover, which led them to believe that he hated anyone in a position of authority simply because he wanted to be there himself. ... He was, [one said], 'all anti, anti- the Soviet Union, anti- the United States, anti- society in general and anti- us..." [1029] Some believed that Oswald was mentally disturbed. [1030] However, they felt sorry for Marina and the child, so continued to help. [1031]

The Oswalds were having severe problems. [1032] The beatings, which began on a regular basis when Marina had opened their door to Lee's mother, now continued because of her friendship with the Russians. [1033] Marina had a blackened eye. [1034] She told her mother-in-law (whom she called "Mamochka" [1035]) and a Russian that her husband had struck her; [1036] it seems clear that Oswald had in fact hit her. [1037] Marina wrote and testified that this was a difficult period for them and that her husband was "very irritable" and sometimes some completely trivial thing would "drive him into a rage." [1038] "Robert Oswald saw Marina with a

---

[F] Like Kleenex and Xerox, this brand name of the Frank Taylor Company of Cincinnati came to be used for most prams and strollers, whether or not made by the Taylor company to carry little tots.

black eye but did not say anything." [1039] "Lee hit her again and again. ... The beatings were a humiliation. They devalued Marina in her own eyes, and she feared that they would devalue her in the eyes of anyone who knew of them. [But] she took the very Russian view that beatings are a private affair between man and wife, as private as sex." [1040]

Marguerite again perversely chose to support her Lee: "Now, this has been publicly stated by the Russian friends, that he beat his wife. I don't know if he did beat his wife. ... I went to the home and my son was reading, he read continuously—in the living room, and Marina was in the bedroom ... So I went into the bedroom, and she was nursing June with her head down. ... And I came around to the front and I saw Marina with a black eye. I happened to see the black eye. I know that he hit her and gave her a black eye. Marina said so, and my son has said so. But how many times does this happen, I don't know. ... Now, gentlemen, I don't think any man should hit his wife, as is stated in the paper, or beat his wife. But I will say this. There may be times that a woman needs to have a black eye. ... And then the children moved to Dallas. Now, this will end that part of the story. ... Now, that is the last contact I have had with Marina and Lee until the news broke in Dallas that Lee was picked up because of the assassination of President Kennedy." [1041]

Lee decided by early October to look for a new job, and discussed with some of the Russian community his lack of prospects. [1042] They advised him to seek employment in the Dallas area. [1043] Oswald failed to appear for work at the Leslie Welding Co. in Fort Worth on October 9 because he had already gone to Dallas. [1044] "The boss called Vada Oswald, looking for him because they were shorthanded, then called Marguerite." [1045] She recalled: "[T]he truth is, Lee and Marina left Fort Worth and didn't even tell me where they were. ... I was a little miffed. They left without telling me they were leaving. I was there that afternoon, and they left the next morning, and there's more to it than that, but never mind." [1046] Oswald did not see his mother or communicate with her in any way for 410 days, until she came to see him after the shooting. [1047] Leslie Welding soon received a letter from Lee stating he had "moved permanently to Dallas," and asking that the wages due him be mailed to Dallas. [1048]

On October 9, Oswald rented box 2915 under his own name at the main Dallas post office. [1049] This box will become infamous when a pistol and rifle are posted to it. He moved into the Dallas YMCA, paying $2.25 a night. [1050] With Lee gone to Dallas, Marina and little June were better off and safe living with Russian-community friends. [1051] Her support group now pitched in. [1052] One of them arranged for a friend in the Texas Employment Commission to help Lee find a job. [1053] Oswald told the lady-friend that he hoped to develop qualifications for responsible junior executive employment by a work-study program at a local college but this must be delayed because of his immediate financial needs and responsibilities. [1054] Having heard from the Russians how badly he needed money, she decided to get him any immediately-available job.

On October 11, he was referred to Jaggars-Chiles-Stovall Co., a graphic arts company, in response to a call from the head of the photographic department that needed a photoprint trainee. Oswald was enthusiastic about his prospects and apparently made a good impression; John Graef picked him over several other applicants. [1055] In 1964, Graef testified to the Warren Commission: "I asked him where his last position was, and he said, "The Marines," ... I said, "Honorably discharged, of course," as a joke, and he said, "Oh, yes," and we went on with other facts of the interview." [1056] This is the second instance of Oswald being hired without the prospective employer checking his "facts", or asking a former employer. There will be more.

On October 12 he began in his new position as a trainee making prints of advertising material. He worked 40 hours a week at $1.35 per hour [1057] "with equipment that reduced photographs, arranged advertising displays, and photoset type." [1058] Lee also "used the equipment to fabricate several pieces of false identification for himself, including a draft card under the name A. J. Hidell and a driver's license for an O. H. Lee." [1059] According to Marina, "he liked his work very much." [1060]

While Marina and June lived with friends in Fort Worth and Lee roomed at the Dallas YMCA, the world came close to nuclear annihilation. On October 16, photos from a U-2 spy plane convinced US analysts that Russia was installing missiles and atomic weapons in Cuba. In a chilling address, President Kennedy told us of the threat and his decision to place a naval blockade to intercept new shipments while demanding removal of the missiles already in Cuba. The most intense US-USSR confrontation since the 1948-49 Berlin blockade, this was worse because each side now had thousands of nuclear bombs and missiles ready to launch. [1061]

Mrs. Kennedy's Secret Service agent, Clint Hill, tried to prepare her for the worst: "'Well, I know this is a terrible thing to have to talk about, but I think it's important that I let you know what the Secret Service plans are in the event of an emergency. You know about the bomb shelter here, under the White House. ... In the event ... a situation develops ... we would take you and the children into the shelter for protection.'

"Before I could explain any further, she pulled away from me, in what can only be described as defiance, and said, 'Mr. Hill, if the situation develops that requires the children and me to go to the shelter, let me tell you what you can expect.' She was looking me straight in the eyes. She lowered her voice ... and with complete and utter conviction said ... 'I will take Caroline and John, and we will walk hand in hand out onto the south grounds. We will stand there like brave soldiers, and face the fate of every other American.'" [1062]

Robert Kennedy wrote of an incident on one of the darkest days of the crisis, involving the man who had ordered the change of Oswald's discharge: "General David M. Shoup, Commandant of the Marine Corps, summed up everyone's feelings: 'You are in a pretty bad fix, Mr. President.' The President answered quickly, 'You are in it with me.'" [1063] Kennedy held back his eager-to-attack military, making it possible for Khrushchev to back down without losing face, withdrawing his missiles in exchange for our public promise to not invade Cuba, and private assurance that we would remove US missiles from Turkey. "The crisis ... lasted [until Sunday] October 28, when the news came of Khrushchev's compliance with the American demands.[G] In ... Secretary [of State Dean] Rusk's words, 'We looked into the mouth of the cannon; the Russians flinched.'" [1064]

A lovely personal insight into JFK, "the man in the arena" in Theodore Roosevelt's phrase, was written by close assistant Ted Sorensen in his definitive biography *Kennedy*:

"[H]e was realistically aware of how limited an adult's influence is in the small child's world. Secretary McNamara liked to tell of the time he saw the President accost Caroline in the midst of the Cuban crisis just before her supper hour. 'Caroline,' he said, 'have you been eating candy?' She ignored him. The question was repeated and it was again ignored. Finally, summoning up his full dignity as Commander in Chief, he asked his daughter, 'Caroline, answer me. Have you been eating candy—yes, no or maybe?'" [1065]

[G] This is an event about which most recall how we heard the news. I had driven my '56 Chev east of Los Angeles to Covina, to work that Sunday on the Colorsound 3600 sound-light translator. After the radio gave the news, I did a U-turn and slept peacefully in my tiny Sierra Madre Canyon cabin.

The day the Cuban missile crisis ended, "Oswald visited Marina again and told her that he wanted her to come to Dallas to live with him." [1066] Two days later he wrote to join the Socialist Workers Party,[1067] which replied that he could not because "we don't have any branches at all in Texas." [1068] On November 3, Lee paid $68 rent for a three-room apartment in Dallas.[1069] With a rented trailer and Russian helpers, Marina and June moved there from Fort Worth.[1070] "Their first stop in Dallas [southwest of downtown, across the Trinity River in Oak Cliff] was a dump ... 604 Elsbeth Street ... actually made the Oswald's Fort Worth domicile look good." [1071] A friend who helped with the move describes: "It was a hole. It was terrible, very dirty, very badly kept, really quite a slum. ... The floor had big bumps in it, you know. It was like the building had shifted and you walked up hill, you know, to get from one side of the room to the other. It was not a nice place; no." [1072] Marina hated the filth so much that she stayed up until 5 AM, scrubbing everything.[1073] It was still a terrible dirty dump.

Lee sees her hatred for the best he can afford; they scream at each other for two solid days and the beatings resume. Having experienced kindness from her Russian friends, Marina became angrier than ever, finally leaving him to move in with gentle friends, the Mellers. She wanted to be so completely free of him that she didn't tell Lee where she had gone. When he tries to find her, the members of the Russian community, who never liked him at all, refuse to help. Lee thinks of himself as a great man, but now he finds himself alone, without a wife, daughter, or any friends.

"Nonetheless, Oswald persuaded her to come back after another week or so. Young, very pretty, with an infant in hand and an obviously difficult husband, Marina showed a knack for attracting sympathy and gifts in her new home country—a talent that Oswald clearly resented." [1074] Soon, marital difficulties started again. A friend who helped with the move was shocked when Lee "slapped her hard in the face twice [with] the baby in her arms" [1075] for not having the zipper on her dress completely closed.[1076] They argued over his refusal to allow her to smoke.[1077] There was also a quarrel when he told the landlady that Marina was from Czechoslovakia; in turn, he was angry when Marina, who disapproved of this deception, told the landlady the truth.[1078]

Several people tried to help Marina improve her scanty knowledge of English, but Lee discouraged this,[1079] probably hoping to limit her contacts. He apparently continued to beat her. Marina testified that when they moved into the Elsbeth Street apartment, her husband became "nervous and irritable" and was very angry over "trifles." She said that it was sometimes her fault that he beat her, for example when she wrote to tell an old boyfriend in Russia that she wished she had married him. She had begun: "Anatoly dear" and ended: "I kiss you as we kissed before." [1080] The letter was returned because of insufficient postage, and Oswald read it.[1081] "Lee's response was a good deal milder that she might have expected. ... [T]his time he merely slapped her ..." [1082]

"The Russian emigre community had found the girl-woman who would become their darling. How could she be anything else? She was young, she was a stranger in a strange land, she was beautiful. Of course, beauty happened to be married to the beast—a surly young American who hit her (bad enough), and who believed passionately in a system these upper-middle-class folks had just as passionately rejected (much worse)." [1083]

Because of this quarreling, acquaintances felt that Marina would be better off alone. In early November, Marina and June left Lee's apartment to take shelter with a series of Russian women married to American husbands. Marina first moved in with Anna Meller, saying she had no intention to return to Oswald. He was apparently quite upset and did not want Marina to leave him.[1084] Lee did not visit his wife at the Meller house,[1085] and for a short time did not even know where she was.[1086] Marina testified to the Warren Commission that he called her after she moved and they met at mutual-friend George De Mohrenschildt's house. Lee asked her to return home. She insisted that he stop quarreling and that he change his ways. He said that he could not change. Marina would not agree to return home with him and he left.[1087]

Marina then moved to Katherine Ford's house.[1088] She said she had decided never to return to her husband;[1089] it was Mrs. Ford's impression that Marina was going to stay at other people's houses until a permanent place could be found for her.[1090] Next, Marina and June moved to the home of Russian-origin Mrs. Frank Ray. That day, Lee called, asking to visit his wife, whom he had called and written. Mr. Ray picked him up and took him to Marina.[1091]

Marina wrote that at this meeting Oswald professed love for her: "I saw him cry * * *[H] [he] begged me to come back, asked my forgiveness, and promised that he would try to improve, if only I would come back."[1092] "* * * he cried and you know a woman's heart—I went back to him. He said he didn't care to live if I did not return."[1093] That day she decided to return to him. Mr. Ray helped pack and took her back to the Elsbeth Street apartment.[1094]

Members of the Russian community who had taken care of Marina so that she would not have to live with Oswald felt that their efforts had been in vain. Lee did not care for most of these people and made his feelings apparent,[1095] so contacts between Oswalds and Russians diminished.[1096] Mrs. Ford testified that Marina told her she contemplated suicide during this period because Lee was treating her badly and she had no friends; she felt that she had "no way out."[1097] Marina acknowledged to the Commission that she had had such thoughts.[1098]

Robert Oswald invited older half-brother John Pic and younger brother Lee, and their families, to dinner on Thanksgiving, which in 1962 fell on November 22, a date that exactly a year later will burn into our national memory alongside December 7 and September 11. In the biography *Lee*, Robert wrote: "I didn't invite Mother to the gathering. We wanted to be sure it would be a happy meeting for everybody, with no bitterness of unhappy reminders."[1099] Lee, Marina and June traveled to Fort Worth by bus, where John Pic and Robert met them at the Greyhound station.[1100] Pic had not seen his half-brother for 10 years, "since just after young Lee had threatened John's wife"[1101] with a pocket knife in New York City.

Robert captioned this photo in his book *Lee*: "Our Thanksgiving reunion on November 22, 1962, was the final family gathering for the three of us brothers—and the last time I saw Lee until exactly a year and a day later. Marge, John, and John Pic, Jr., are on the left; Lee and Marina on the right. I'm holding Robert Lee, Jr., in center foreground. Vada, far right, was almost crowded out of the picture."[1102]

The Warren Commission questioned John Pic extensively about that day's conversations. Two areas are relevant to this book. First came the matter of Lee's undesirable discharge:

"Mr. PIC. He did mention that because of his actions he had received a dishonorable discharge from the Marine Corps and that he was attempting to get this changed to an honorable

---

[H] * * * means words were deleted by the source. When this author deletes, the indicator is ...

status.

Mr. JENNER. Did he appear bitter about it?

Mr. PIC. He showed us his card which stated dishonorable or bad conduct, something like that. I think it was dishonorable. He showed it to me." [1103]

...

Mr. PIC. Then he told me he was attempting to get this changed, and he had written several letters to the Secretary of the Navy about getting it changed.

Mr. JENNER. Did he mention the then Governor Connally in that connection?

Mr. PIC. I believe he did, sir.

Mr. JENNER. Governor Connally was not then Secretary of the Navy. Did he express any resentment toward Governor Connally?

...

Mr. PIC. [W]hen he mentioned to me that he had written to get it changed, Governor Connally was the Secretary of the Navy. He did mention the name Connally.

Mr. JENNER. Did you have any feeling or get the impression that he was bitter toward Governor Connally as a person?

...

Mr. PIC. No, sir; just the fact that the man had the job and he was the man he had written to." [1104]

Further, "John Pic reportedly said Oswald [said that he] could not get a driver's license with his undesirable discharge ..." [1105] After dinner, talk was difficult because the family wanted to converse with Marina but Lee wouldn't let her speak English. Paul Gregory, Marina's student of Russian, arrived to drive Lee and family home. John told about meeting Paul:

"Mr. PIC. Now, my brother Robert, whenever he introduces me to anyone always refers to me as his brother. Lee referred to me as his half brother when he introduced me.

Mr. JENNER. On this occasion?

Mr. PIC. It was very pronounced. He wanted to let the man know I was only his half brother. And this kind of peeved me a little bit. Because we never mentioned the fact that we were half brothers. ... Right then and there I had the feeling that the hostile feeling was still there. Up until this time it didn't show itself, but I felt then, well, he still felt the same way." [1106]

"They had always stood together as full brothers and fellow sufferers at the hands of Marguerite. Suddenly, John was aware that Lee was still smoldering with the old antagonism. He was not one to forget." [1107]

After that family gathering, Robert spoke to Lee once by telephone and also received a post card and a letter, but he eventually lost contact and did not see him again until a year and a day later, in the Dallas jail. [1108] Robert wrote Lee two or three times, asking for the address of Lee's Dallas apartment(s) so he might visit the family, but Lee told Robert to write to him at PO Box 2915, and not to attempt a visit. [1109] John Pic never again had any contact with Lee — in fact, he will testify that the Secret Service did not permit him to attend Lee's funeral. [1110]

Despite his disillusionment with Soviet life, Oswald kept up his interest in Russia. He wrote to the Soviet Embassy in Washington for information on how to subscribe to Russian periodicals and for "any periodicals or bulletins which you may put out for the benefit of your citizens living, for a time, in the U.S.A." [1111] He subscribed to several Russian journals. [1112] Soon after his return to this country, Oswald had started to correspond with the Communist Party and the Socialist Workers Party. He subscribed to the *Worker* in August 1962. [1113] He continued to read a great deal on a variety of subjects: books by Marx, Lenin, "and similar things." [1114] Marina said that he read books of a historical nature, including H. G. Wells' two volume "Outline of History" and biographies of Hitler, Kennedy, and Khrushchev. [1115]

On January 25, 1963, the frugal and monetarily trustworthy Lee "sent $206 to the State Department, thus completing repayment of the $435 loan that had been made to him in Russia the previous spring. He was now free to seek a new passport and travel outside the United States." [1116] Having already repaid brother Robert for his $200 loan for airfare to Dallas, Lee was now free of debt.

Two days later, he sent a coupon [1117] and $10 cash toward the $29.95 purchase of a snub-nosed .38 Special (caliber) Smith & Wesson Victory-model revolver with barrel cut down to only 2 1/4 inches for easy concealment. In the NAME blank he entered "A. J. Hidell". He also wanted "AMMO" and "HOLSTER", but lined those two out, probably to keep the total below $30 so he could meet the "COD's require 1/3 deposit" requisite with a $10 bill. A pistol order required a WITNESS, which he did himself, said Treasury Department [1118] and FBI [1119] document experts, by scrawling "D. F. Drittal". False names are now his habit, such as the "Alek James Hidell" on ID cards that he probably created at Jaggars-Chiles-Stovall where a fellow employee had taught him the techniques he used to prepare several fake cards. [1120] Alek was Marina's pet name for him and what most Russian speakers called him because "Lee" seemed too foreign, perhaps Chinese.

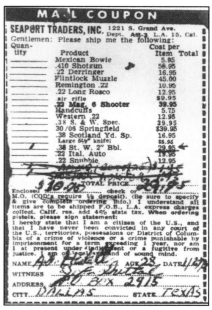

The world settled into such a peaceful lull that "The Fifty-Mile Hike" made headlines. Kennedy's self-assessed "chubby" Press Secretary, cigar-smoking *bon vivant* Pierre Salinger, described the onset: "I still shudder when I think of the Fifty-Mile Hike That Almost Was—a crisis in my personal life that White House correspondents still refer to as Salinger's Folly. It all began the first week in February 1963, when JFK ran across a letter President Theodore Roosevelt had written to the commandant of the Marine Corps in 1908, suggesting that Marine officers should hike fifty miles from time to time to prove their fitness." [1121]

JFK "sent a copy of Teddy's letter to General David M. Shoup, the Marine Corps commandant" [1122] (you know him well by now) with the suggestion that 1963's Marines should prove their fitness — which Shoup ordered and a detachment accomplished. The President eyed Pierre's twenty extra pounds behind the belt buckle and said somebody from his staff would have to prove their fitness. Salinger immediately suggested "in great shape" aide Ken O'Donnell, but Kennedy replied: "No, it should be somebody who needs the exercise— somebody who would be an inspiration to millions of other out-of-shape Americans." [1123] To make a fat story thin, Salinger failed miserably after walking only three blocks. [1124] He was excused, but the country enjoyed several weeks of 50-mile hike news that peaceful winter.

Biographer Priscilla Johnson McMillan later befriended Marina, then wrote *Marina and Lee* with her full cooperation. Her book is valuable for portraying several sensitive matters Marina shared in private with one woman, that she could not be expected to describe in public to the many men of the Warren Commission. Perhaps most disturbing:

"For Marina, the month of February 1963 was far and away the worst in all her married life. Lee had been hitting her ever since they arrived in America; in February there was a dramatic change in the style and ferocity with which he did it. No longer did he strike her once across the face with the flat of his hand. Now he hit her five or six times—and with his fists. The second he got angry, he turned pale and pressed his lips tightly together. His eyes were filled with hate. His voice dropped to a murmur and she could not understand what he was saying. When he started to strike her, his face became red and his voice grew angry and loud. He wore a look of concentration, as if Marina were the author of every slight he had ever suffered and he was bent on wiping her out, obliterating her completely. To Marina it seemed that it was not even a human being he saw in front of him. Most horrifying of all was the gleam of pleasure in his eyes." [1125]

Marina visited George and Jeanne De Mohrenschildt several times in early 1963,[1126] and they invited Lee and Marina to a small dinner party in February. Everett Glover, a chemist employed in Dallas, was at that dinner. On February 22, Glover had a gathering at his house, one of the purposes of which was to permit his friends, many of whom were studying Russian, to meet the Oswalds, who were the objects of much attention.[1127] Here occurred a meeting that may have changed American history, or at the least provided Oswald a place to hide a rifle: Marina conversed at length with another guest, "a rangy, intelligent woman with widespread interests, among them the Russian language, which she had learned to speak quite well." [1128] "Ruth Paine attended it especially to meet Marina. As a student of the Russian language, Ruth wanted to meet somebody with whom she could practice." [1129]

"Ruth Paine [1130] ... looked like the kind of woman who steered clear of meat and marched in Ban the Bomb demonstrations ... and that was pretty much who Ruth Paine was ... a woman who was New Age before New Age was cool." [1131] "Mrs. Paine had been brought up as a Quaker, and at college and afterward she had been interested in fostering better relations between Russians and Americans. ... [S]he helped arrange cultural exchanges of Russian and American artists, dancers and writers. Now, she explained to Marina, she was interested in learning Russian. [S]he suggested that they get together ... to see if some arrangement could be worked out whereby she could practice Russian with Marina." [1132] Ruth soon wrote, asking to see Marina, who responded by inviting her to visit.[1133]

It is only 9 months until November 22, after which Ruth will testify before the Warren Commission, and Gerald Ford will write a well-deserved appreciation in his book:

"A few days later Ruth Paine visited Marina and they quickly became intimates, sharing views on their common problems. Because of the importance of her knowledge of Lee Oswald's activities in the next few months, the Commission made a detailed study of her life and associations. What kind of a woman was Ruth Paine? Members of the Commission came to have a high regard for her honesty, generosity and earnestness of purpose. She was an exceptional young woman whose background bespoke a fine American tradition of idealism and aspiration. She was well educated, and prior to her marriage she had spent her time in many worthy projects—trying to help people, trying to learn more about the problems of the world and trying to improve herself. Mrs. Paine in her personal appearance before the Commission gave me the strong feeling that she was a thoroughly wholesome lady desperately trying to be cooperative and constructive." [1134]

Ruth Paine was not only a reliable witness; she was a person with the kind of mind for details that proved a boon to the work of the Commission. Her memory was supplemented by a calendar pad she happened to keep, a date book she could not have falsified if she had wanted to. She knew details with a precision that no witness could have established." [1135]

By late February, enough neighbors had complained to the Oswalds' Elsbeth Street apartment manager about the sounds of fighting and abuse that he "went to ... the owners of the building, who in turn paid a call on Lee, warning him that he and his wife would have to stop fighting or move. Lee tried to shrug it off, but the visit told him ... he had too many neighbors on Elsbeth Street, too many eyes and ears upon him. His movements were being observed. People knew he was beating his wife. What might they notice next?" [1136]

On March 2, the Oswalds moved to a $60/month upstairs apartment on Neely Street, also in the Oak Cliff district of southwest Dallas. [1137] They moved without assistance, carrying their meager belongings in their hands and in a baby stroller. [1138] Marina preferred the new apartment because it had a balcony and was, she felt, more suitable for June. [1139] This apartment will be known in history for the photos Marina will soon snap in the back yard. Here, Lee will sit out on the porch with a rifle he will soon buy, practicing, practicing. In eight months, Lee will get out of a taxi on this street, escaping from downtown where he just shot two politicians; near here he will murder a policeman. For a while after the Oswalds moved to the Neely Street apartment they got along well, [1140] but they soon began to quarrel. [1141]

Ruth Paine, 31, and Marina, 21, started to exchange visits. Mrs. Paine invited the Oswalds to her home in suburban Irving for dinner, and she took them on a picnic. These were delights because Ruth drove, which Lee could not do. When he was not present, the two women frequently discussed their respective marital problems, and Marina disclosed that she was pregnant. [1142] Marina had admired the Kennedys from when she first knew of them, and now she knows she and Jackie are sharing the discoveries, concerns and joys of the early days of pregnancy. Jackie's baby is due in September, Marina's a month later. [1143]

Now comes one of Lee's insanities, which we consider at some length because it is one of the four or five events in which he shoots someone.[1] The avowed <u>Marxist</u> decides to rid the world of an <u>anti-Communist</u>. "Oswald was familiar with the case of General Edwin Walker, [1144] an army general relieved of his command by the Kennedy administration for indoctrinating his troops with an anti-communist program of speeches and literature. After he was admonished for propagandizing his soldiers, Walker resigned from the army and retired to Dallas, where he became a leader in the ... John Birch Society." [1145] "That small organization was warning the United States about the worldwide Communist conspiracy, whose ranks, according to [its leader], included no less a figure than [Hitler conqueror and former president] Dwight D. Eisenhower. [Walker had been] making speeches claiming that he had left the Army so as not to

---

[1] #1: In the Marines in Japan, he shot himself in the elbow with a clandestine pistol, perhaps hoping to avoid deployment to the Philippines. #2: He may have shot a hated fellow Marine, but no one was ever charged with that death. #3: Now. #4: November 22 in Dallas, wounding a bystander, then Connally, then killing Kennedy. #5: Later that afternoon, executing police Officer J. D. Tippit.

collaborate in surrender of American sovereignty to the United Nations and suggesting that the United States had Communists in government." [1146]

"The general had established a significant local reputation since settling in Dallas and had been mentioned more than fifty times in the *Dallas Morning News* between July 1962 and April 1963." [1147] Lee undoubtedly read many of those fifty, for the *Morning News* was his newspaper of choice, a fact that will peak in importance when its November 20 front page will tell him that John Connally will ride through Dallas in a limousine with John Kennedy. General Walker's "exploits had also received some coverage in *The Worker,* to which Oswald now subscribed, most recently … in a story reporting Walker's call for invasion of Cuba." [1148]

Over the weekend of March 9-10, Oswald photographed the alley behind the home of Walker, and probably at about the same time he photographed the rear of the home and a nearby railroad track and right-of-way. [1149] He prepared and studied a notebook in which he outlined a plan to shoot General Walker, and he looked at bus schedules. [1150]

"Two days later, having estimated the possibilities, he comes to the conclusion that he needs a rifle, not a pistol, and so" [1151] using "a coupon clipped from the February 1963 issue of *American Rifleman* magazine" [1152] he orders a war surplus carbine [J] from Klein's Sporting Goods Company in Chicago. The rifle alone costs $12.78, but Lee chooses to have it with a four-power scope mounted for $19.95, total. Postage and handling add $1.50. He prepays the $21.45 with a U.S. Postal Money Order. He is "A. Hidell" on both order and money order.

6.5 ITALIAN CARBINE
Late military issue. Only 40" over-all. Weighs 7 lbs. Shows only slight use, test-fired and head spaced, ready for shooting. Turned-down bolt, 6-shot, clip fed, rear sight, thumb safety. **$12.78**
C20-1196 . . . .
C20-750. Carbine with brand new 4X scope—3.4" dia. (illustrated) **$19.95**
E20-751. 6.5mm Italian military ammo, 108 rds. (6-shot clip free) **$7.50**

[J] "Carbine" is a short-barrel rifle, preferable for use in close combat and on horseback (the famous Daisy BB gun is modeled on the Winchester '97 carbine). Oswald's weapon was the 40" overall length that separates one from the other, so may be correctly named either "rifle" or "carbine". The military-standard M16A2 Combat Rifle is 39.6" long. — Clancy, Tom. *Marine.*

Oswald's physical order coupon does not survive, but Klein's microfilmed it atop the envelope in which he mailed it,[1153] shown here beside the money order,[1154] which did survive.

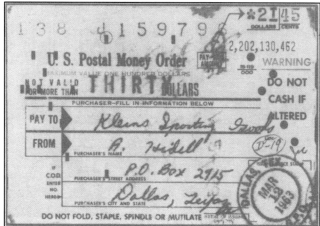

In 9½ months, FBI handwriting analysts will easily determine that all three items — coupon, envelope and money order — were handwritten by Lee Oswald. Despite the alias and numerous inventions by conspiracy theorists, these will tie the deadly rifle to him. This mail order was entirely unremarkable, but this purchase for the immediate purpose of killing General Walker will have a great impact on world history. The Mannlicher-Carcano model 91/38, its genesis, manufacture, ammunition and capabilities will be very fully described in Chapter 12 – THE RIFLE. It is sufficient here to know that it was made in 1940 for infantry use in World War II. This is not a sporting rifle for hunting animals; its purpose is to kill men. The Marine sharpshooter knows the difference, because he was trained on how to clean, load, aim, and accurately fire exactly such a weapon,[1155] to be told in Chapter 13 – THE SHOOTER.

Both guns were shipped on March 20.[1156] On March 25, the "carbine arrives some two weeks after it has been ordered, and the Smith & Wesson revolver with the sawed-off barrel, delayed for nearly two months, also comes in on the same day ..." [1157] Lee picked up the packages at the Dallas post office. For the pistol, on which he had sent only 1/3 payment, he paid the balance C.O.D.[K] The pistol will be taken from Lee after he murders Officer Tippit with it, then tries to shoot an officer who arrests him only minutes later.

"Marina was upset when she discovered the rifle. She hated guns and was annoyed that Lee was spending money on what she called 'this dangerous toy' at a time when they were scrimping and saving even on food. 'Why did you buy a gun?' she asked. 'Why don't you think of your family first?'" [1158] Lee did not reply that the purchase was for a specific purpose. He began to take the rifle by bus to the dry bed of the Trinity River for target practice, shooting toward the high banks. Oswald kept the rifle in a small storeroom at the Neely Street apartment. He spent long periods of time in the storeroom, which he told Marina she was not to enter.[1159] He told her that he intended to use the rifle for hunting.[1160] He practiced with it. She saw him leave with it once, and clean it several times.[1161] She also testified that Lee sat out on the porch at night, opening and closing the bolt, aiming at practice targets.[1162]

[K] For younger readers: Once upon a time, before credit and debit cards, we had only cash, checks and expensive government money orders. Period. Sellers had no way to know if checks were good, so they shipped orders through the post office C.O.D. = "Collect On Delivery", which the PO did.

Within the week, on Sunday, March 31, Marina was hanging diapers on the backyard clothesline when Lee came out. His shirt and trousers were black; the new pistol was stuck into his belt. He handed Marina his little camera and had her take photographs while he showed off the rifle in one hand and copies of two Communist newspapers in the other. More amused than alarmed, Marina takes three photos.[L] "Lee probably developed the photographs at work the following day ... He handed one of them to Marina and told her to keep it for the baby. On it he had written: 'For Junie from Papa.' 'Good God!' Marina was appalled. 'Why would Junie want a picture with guns?' 'To remember Papa by sometime.'" [1163] [1164] This was the first of at least three fatal hints.[M]

"Lee had not yet tried out his new weapons. As nearly as can be determined, it was on Wednesday, April 3 ... that he used his rifle for the first time." [1165] "Lee was too secretive to show his face on a rifle range ... So anomalous was he, however, that he was perfectly capable of climbing onto a crowded bus carrying a rifle poorly concealed in his raincoat." [1166] According to a careful Commission reconstruction, he "boarded [a] bus, rode a mile and a half ... to the intersection of West Commerce Street and Beckley Avenue ... and strode quickly down the levee to an uninhabited area 35 feet below called the Trinity River bottom." [1167]

"The tasks Lee had to accomplish were these. He had to get the feel of the trigger action of this particular rifle, which was new to him and more powerful than any he had used before; and he had to learn to work the bolt smoothly so as not to disturb the alignment of the barrel. He also had to adjust the sight so that all his shots landed within a fairly small radius. It was the first time he had owned a four-power sight and he had to get used to it. According to experts, learning to use a telescopic sight is easy ... and a skill that vastly enhances accuracy. It has been estimated that a man of Oswald's training and experience would be able to adjust to the new rifle and scope, 'would be capable of sighting that rifle in well, firing it,' with only ten rounds of practice." [1168] Read more in Chapter 13 – THE SHOOTER. Lee will next practice shooting on April 5, then perhaps again, before his first attempt to shoot to kill.

Biographer Priscilla McMillan learned from her subject: "Marina detested the rifle. She dreaded it and found its presence in the apartment distasteful. Terrified lest it go off, she never went near it, never touched it or moved it no matter where it might be. Compulsive housekeeper though she was, she did her cleaning in a careful circle all around it." [1169]

Lee was fired by Jaggars-Chiles-Stovall on April 6. [1170] "According to Robert Stovall, one of the founders of the company, Oswald 'was a constant source of irritation because of his lack of productive ability. . .' Stovall called his work 'inefficient [and] . . . inept.'" [1171] [N] The fact that he brought a Russian newspaper to work may also have had significance.[1172] Marina testified that Lee, who always worried about this job's security,[1173] was upset because he had liked the work.[1174] On April 8, Oswald again resorted to the Texas Employment Commission [1175] seeking employment, but their patience was probably at an end, and he was referred to no employers. Loose as usual with his dismal disregard for truth, he had lied to them that he was laid off "due to lack of work." [1176]

[L] We will see and theorists will argue about two; the third will disappear, destroyed in late November.

[M] Two others will be April 10 before the Walker shooting and November 22 before the Dallas shooting.

[N] This book's working title was *Inept* for scores of years, before I found this 50-year-old corroboration.

Lee's job problems, bad enough, were in the light of day; his nights are now sinister. Having studied bus schedules,[1177] on the evening of either April 6 or 7 he went to shoot his victim, the objective for which he had purchased the rifle he now carried. Is it realistic that a man planning to murder takes the bus to and from target practices in the Trinity River's bed, and now to carry out the murder? Yes. First, this is the "yahoo!" Wild West in the old days, and firearms are seen regularly, everywhere. And, Lee has no choice; he doesn't own a car.[O] That night he decided to postpone, and hid the weapon nearby.[1178] He "determined to act on the following Wednesday, April 10, when a nearby church was planning a meeting which, Oswald reasoned, would create a diversion that would help him escape."[1179]

On that Wednesday, Lee didn't tell Marina where he was going. He wrote a note[P] in Russian, but did not tell her that he had left it. Marina paced and worried because he was out so late, doing God knows what. About 10:00 PM, she found a key atop the note on his desk,[1180] inside the small closet where she long feared and avoided his rifle. The note in Russian, with translation, is the first item in the Warren Commission's first volume of exhibits.[1181] A better rendering is in *Marina and Lee*, because Marina helped Priscilla McMillan with that fine book:

"1. Here is the key to the post office box which is located in the main post office downtown on Ervay Street, the street where there is a drugstore where you always used to stand. The post office is four blocks from the drugstore on the same street. There you will find our mailbox. I paid for the mailbox last month so you needn't worry about it.

2. Send information about what has happened to me to the Embassy (the Soviet Embassy in Washington) and also send newspaper clippings (if there's anything about me in the papers). I think the Embassy will come quickly to your aid once they know everything.

3. I paid our rent on the second so don't worry about it.

4. I have also paid for the water and gas.

5. There may be some money from work. They will send it to our post office box. Go to the bank and they will cash it.

6. You can either throw out my clothing or give it away. *Do not keep it.* As for my personal papers (both military papers and papers from the factory), I prefer that you keep them.

7. Certain of my papers are in the small blue suitcase.

8. My address book is on the table in my study if you need it.

9. We have *friends* here and the *Red Cross* will also help you.

10. I left you as much money as I could, $60 on the second of the month, and you and Junie can live for two months on $10 a week.

11. If I am alive and taken prisoner, the city jail is at the end of the bridge we always used to cross when we went to town (the very beginning of town after the bridge)."[1182]

Marina now knows that Lee is out doing something desperate, but has no idea where he is.

Lee is bracing his new Mannlicher-Carcano on an alley fence behind General Edwin Walker's residence, looking through the telescopic sight at Walker, 40 yards away, but with the scope's 4x power it appears to be only 30 feet. Not only is Walker close, he is stationary. The deadline for 1962 Income Tax is five days away,[Q] and the general sits at his desk checking his return. The room is not bright; the desk lamp gives the only light. The small multi-paned window divided by wood muntins[R] is closed because the air-conditioning is running.[1183]

[O] And if he did own one, he has not learned to drive. Ruth will try to teach him, but he'll never learn.

[P] The second of three such forewarnings. The next will come early on the morning of November 22.

[Q] Returns were due on March 15 until Congress in 1955, pandering to procrastinators, delayed to April.

[R] Yes, that's the name. You could look it up. Even better, "Muntin" has its own article in Wikipedia!

GENERAL WALKER is the second on an Oswald notebook list of four to kill (page 547). On a decision approved by JFK, he was asked to leave the U.S. Army after describing Harry Truman and Eleanor Roosevelt as likely Communists. He defiantly resigned rather than retire, "the only US General to resign in the 20th century." [1184] The veteran of World War II and the Korean War then devoted himself to far-right causes. He ran for governor in 1962, getting the fewest votes of any candidate in that election won by John Connally. When integration was ordered at the University of Mississippi, he went to the Oxford campus to lead an attempt to block it. Two people were killed and six U.S. Marshals were shot in the ensuing riot.[S]

Lee's Communist newspaper *The Worker* has targeted the general as a threat to its beliefs. A Mississippi grand jury's decision not to press charges against Walker was Oswald's motivation for purchasing a rifle. Oswald took several photographs of the area of Walker's fancy home and developed them at work before being fired last week, April 6. [1185]

In the Marine Corps, Lee learned to shoot well, as his "Sharpshooter" qualification proves. Carefully employing his training — although it did not include aiming through a telescopic sight — he squeezes the trigger to shoot the first man he has ever attempted to murder.[T] He fires just one shot and does not wait to see the result. He runs.

At 11:30 PM, Lee is back at their apartment, to breathlessly tell the distraught Marina, "I shot Walker." She has found and read the note, and is worried sick. "Did you kill him?" "I don't know." "My God, the police will be here any minute. What did you do with the rifle?" "Buried it. Don't ask any questions." Lee turns on the radio, but there is no news. Marina lay and worried, while her husband quickly fell into a deep and night-long sleep. [1186]

Next morning, newspapers and radio tell Lee that he completely missed. He's botched the easiest non-rifle-range shot he will ever take. The bullet was deflected by the horizontal muntin separating small window panes, and missed Walker's head by a few inches.[U] Lee had such a good view of lamp-lighted Walker that he hadn't even noticed that closer wood divider.

Marina became angry and made him promise never to repeat such an act. "'Look,' Marina said, 'a rifle—that's no way to prove your ideas. If someone doesn't like what you think, does that mean he has a right to shoot *you*? Once people start doing that, no one will dare go out of doors. In Russia you used to say that there was freedom of speech in America, that everyone can say what he pleases. Okay, go to meetings. Say what you want to say *there*. Or are you afraid you have so little brains you can't make anybody listen?'" [1187]

[S] The author met, but stupidly did not recognize, a hero of this event. Murry Faulkner was the senior officer-in-charge of the sixty-five man Mississippi National Guard unit that went from the Oxford armory to the Lyceum on the University of Mississippi campus to protect federal marshals who had come to enforce integration but were faced with a bloodthirsty mob. Captain Faulkner and his local guardsmen, many undoubtedly holding anti-integration beliefs, did their duty and loyally stood their ground, sustaining numerous injuries, until 10,000 U.S. Army troops arrived. The author visited exquisite Oxford in 1994, and had coffee and played liar's poker with four local businessmen, one of whom was quiet, smiling aw-shucks Murry. I am forever ashamed that I recognized the famous name "Faulkner" because of Oxford's famed author William, but should also have known of his cousin Murry, the true American patriot. For more about Murry and his courageous stand, see Branch, Taylor. *Parting the Waters: America in the King Years, 1954-63*, page 669.

[T] Unless he was the killer of the mysteriously-dead fellow Marine, as was mentioned on page 126.

[U] The bullet is smashed and can't be identified, but when authorities learn about this attempt after the shooting in Dealey Plaza, they will conclusively match the slug's composition to Oswald's bullets.

Lee said he was sorry he had missed; shooting Walker would have been analogous to an assassination of Hitler.[1188] She kept the letter of instructions he had left, to give to authorities if he repeated his attempt, but "even after the assassination, did not turn it over to the police, Secret Service, or FBI. Only when Ruth Paine found it in a cookbook and turned it over to authorities, did Marina admit that she had had knowledge of Oswald's attempt." [1189]

Edward Jay Epstein's retrospective *The Assassination Chronicles: Inquest, Counterplot and Legend* summarized eventual resolutions of important facts about the Walker attempt:

"Marina Oswald testified to the Warren Commission that when Oswald left their house on April 10, 1963, he left her dramatic instructions in Russian about what she should do if he were arrested, killed, or had to go into hiding, and when he returned late that evening, he explained to her that he had just attempted to kill General Edwin Walker with his rifle. Her testimony is corroborated by three elements of evidence.

First, the Russian handwriting in the note has been unequivocally identified as that of Oswald by the questioned documents experts of both the Warren Commission and the House Select Committee on Assassination[s]. The note, which contains details that date it, confirms that Oswald expected to be killed, arrested, or a fugitive the week of April 10, 1963.

Second, photographs of Walker's house taken from the position where the sniper fired at Walker were found among Oswald's possessions after the Kennedy assassination. Photographic experts established that these photographs were taken with Oswald's Imperial Reflex camera. By referring to construction work in the background, the FBI was able to determine that the photographs were taken on March 9 or 10 (which was [two or three days before] Oswald ordered the Mannlicher-Carcano). [These] show Oswald had reconnoitered Walker's house.

Third, ... neutron activation analysis done in 1977 exactly matched the metallic elements found in the bullet that was recovered in Walker's home to the batch of Mannlicher-Carcano ammunition used in Oswald's rifle in the assassination of Kennedy." [1190]

Marina's biographer, Priscilla Johnson McMillan, understood Lee as well as or better than any. She "offers a salient perception: He had tried something cataclysmic — and he had not been caught. He had not even been touched. Thus by far the greatest legacy Lee carried out of the Walker attempt was the conviction that he was invulnerable, that he stood at the center of a magic circle swathed in a cloak of immunity. It was a feeling which fitted dangerously with the feeling he already had that he was special, that he had particular prerogatives. He and he alone was entitled to that which was forbidden to everybody else." [1191]

On Easter Sunday, April 14, the White House formally announces that the First Lady is pregnant. She will be the first wife of a sitting (in office) president to have a baby since Frances Folsom (Mrs. Grover) Cleveland gave birth in 1893.[1192] V

In this author's experience, a perfectly documented and entirely consistent historical record is suspect — memories are not that reliable. Thus, it is perversely comforting to find at this juncture a modicum of muddle: Marina, recovering from her shock at Lee's attempt on Walker, clearly remembers that eleven days later, on Sunday, April 21, Lee "sat in the living room and read the newspaper. It was the *Dallas Morning News*,W which had a banner headline that day: 'Nixon Calls for Decision to Force Reds Out of Cuba.'" [1193] Suddenly, Lee "put on a suit, tucked his pistol into his belt, said that Richard Nixon was coming to town, and that he was going downtown to take a look, and "he would use the pistol if the opportunity arose." [1194]

V The Clevelands named their baby Ruth, and that's how the Baby Ruth candy bar got its name.

W This is a Sunday, so he has to buy his own paper. During the week, he reads day-old papers bought by others. In six months, the *Morning News* will tell Lee where to find and shoot John Connally.

She called him into their bathroom, closed the door, held it tightly and reminded him of his promise after the Walker attempt. "He pounded on the door and threatened to beat her. Within a short time, Oswald agreed to remain in the bathroom if she would give him something to read." [1195] He sat and read for the rest of the day.

She was quite certain of all this, but the problem is that Nixon was not in Texas during that period. Marina was called back by the Warren Commission in June 1964 after she had told friends of this incident, and was subjected to questioning that fills ten pages of fine-print transcript. [1196] She was certain Lee said "Nixon". Commissioners then went down a wrong path, supposing the intended victim might be a different VP, LBJ. Asked if it could have been Johnson, she maintained several times that she had never, ever heard of the man. "He did not say 'Vice President Nixon,' he just said 'Nixon.'" [1197] The Commission left it "that the incident, as described by Marina Oswald, was of no probative value". [1198] The original G-man thought otherwise. In his life's memoir, Richard Nixon wrote that in 1964, J. Edgar "Hoover told me that Oswald's wife had disclosed that Oswald had been planning to kill me when I visited Dallas and that only with great difficulty had she managed to keep him in the house to prevent him from doing so." [1199]

There is an explanation, for which I agree completely with pathfinder [X] author James Reston, Jr., who will receive his well-deserved praise in Chapter 21 – OTHERS ON THIS TRAIL:

"Actually, Nixon was not in town at all, nor was he coming, and though Marina could not know it, Oswald did. He had said 'Nixon' for its shock value: it was Nixon's picture that was on the front page of the Dallas paper, and Nixon wasn't coming to Texas at all, and so the men of the Warren Commission dismissed the incident as having no 'probative value.'

It was *John Connolly* [sic] who was coming.

The following day the governor was scheduled to open a conference of space scientists at the Marriott Motor Inn in Dallas, and the conference, held as the American space program gloried in the success of the Mercury shots, was widely advertised. Inside that Sunday paper which Oswald had read and then so ostentatiously laid down before he went to strap on his revolver was a story on Connally's San Jacinto Bay speech the day before. Connally had been at his manly, flag-waving best. In fact, he had waved three flags—that of Texas, that of America, and the bloody shirt of anticommunism. ... [H]e said the spirit of the Texas Revolution made him stand 'just a little taller, just a little stiffer to men like Castro and Khrushchev. ... [T]he Battle of San Jacinto ... gives equal hope today, when the foot of tyranny stands but ninety miles from our shore.'

To Oswald, the sentiments expressed by Connally were no different from those expressed by General Walker or Richard Nixon. All three represented the fascist edges of the despised monolith. ... In Oswald's jangled kaleidoscope, Connally, Nixon, and Walker were interchangeable parts of the radical right." [1200] [Y]

The importance of Reston's observation is highlighted in Chapter 17 – POLITICAL PROCLIVITY, which is dedicated to that analysis. Oswald, Nixon, Connally and Walker will all be shown in their proper places on the political spectrum on page 496.

[X] *The American Heritage College Dictionary*: "pathfinder *n*. One that discovers a new course or way, esp. through or into unexplored regions." I agree, but they should have written "One who ..."

[Y] Oswald wrote all three on the "kill list" in his pocket notebook, to be described in chapter 20.

On April 24, Ruth Paine "arrived at Neely Street for a planned visit with Marina and found Lee headed for the bus station ... to seek work in New Orleans, his birthplace, where he still had family." [1201] Lee explained that he had not found employment in or around Dallas,

and Marina suggested he go to New Orleans since he had been born there.[1202] Marina later testified that the real reason behind her suggestion was that she wanted to get him out of town because of the Walker incident two weeks before.[1203] "Ruth [suggested] that Marina and Junie stay with her in Irving until Lee was ready to call for them — an arrangement that suddenly suited everyone's convenience and pride." [1204] Lee helped pack Ruth's car, and the two women moved everything to the Paine house in Irving,[1205] about midway between central Dallas and the Dallas-Fort Worth International Airport (DFW). In the photo [1206] of 2515 West Fifth Street,[1207] Irving, Ruth's soon-to-be-famous garage is on the left.

"On April 25, 1963, Oswald arrived in New Orleans with only two duffel bags, which contained some hastily packed clothes, his personal papers and the dismantled Mannlicher-Carcano rifle from which he had fired a bullet fifteen days earlier. He left everything else behind." [1208] He telephoned his aunt Lillian Murret, his mother's sister, from the New Orleans bus station. She was surprised, not knowing he had returned from "Russia". Less than a year later she clearly recounted their conversation to the Warren Commission: "[H]e said, 'I am down here trying to find a job; would you put me up for a while?' And I said, 'Well, we will be glad to, Lee,' but then I started thinking, because if he had a wife and child, I would have to make other arrangements maybe, and so I asked him, I said, 'Lee, are you alone?' and he said, 'Yes,' and I said 'Well, come right out.'" [1209] He did, and moved right in.[1210]

Lee began a search for employment on April 26 at the Louisiana Department of Labor, stating qualifications as a commercial photographer, shipping clerk, or "darkroom man." [1211] Although the employment commission made a few referrals, Oswald relied primarily upon newspaper advertisements.[1212] He spotted a classified ad seeking a "maintenance mechanic helper" [1213] and submitted an application to William B. Reily Co., which roasted, ground, canned, bagged and sold Luzianne Coffee, Standard Coffee, and other products.[1214]

"On his brief application there he may have set his own record for lies. He said he had been living at 757 French Street (the Murrets') for three years; that he had graduated from a high school that he had attended for only a few weeks; and he gave three references: his cousin John Murret, whose permission he did not ask; Sergeant Robert Hidell (a composite of his brother Robert and his own alias 'Hidell'), 'on active duty with the U.S. Marine Corps' (a fiction from beginning to end); and 'Lieutenant J. Evans, active duty U.S. Marine Corps' (the surname and first initial of a man he was to look up later that day, combined with a fictitious Marine Corps rank and identification)." [1215] Norman Mailer opined: "He understands how to give job references. At low levels of employment, who will spend time to check? Yet what a creative liar is Oswald! Every name he offers is taken from a different sector of his experience. Past, present, and future, family, Marines … are drawn upon to shape his lies. He is comfortable with a wealth of sources. If only he had been a poet instead of a liar. With it all, the false facts have a purpose. He never knows when he will be on the lam, and so he likes to leave a trail with a plethora of offshoots to befuddle future pursuers." [1216]

He began on May 10 "as a greaser for the large grinding machines." [1217] He also oiled machinery, adjusted belts, and cleaned coffee roasters [1218] at $1.50 per hour. [1219] z Aunt Lillian asked: "Well, Lee, how much does it pay?" and he said, "Well, it don't pay very much, but I will get along on it." She suggested he return to school to learn a trade, because "you are really not qualified to do anything too much." "No, I don't have to go back to school", he answered. "I don't have to learn anything. I know everything." [1220] Lee did not enjoy this work, [1221] so told his wife and Mrs. Paine that he was working in commercial photography. [1222]

He rented an apartment for $65 a month, [1223] "a shambling not-quite-wreck of a building with a waist-high iron fence surrounding an overgrown yard." [1224] Lee phoned to Irving, asking his wife to come to New Orleans. Ruth Paine testified that the invitation elated Marina: "*Papa nas liubyt*" [1225] – "Daddy loves us," she repeated again and again. "By noon the next day Marina, Ruth, and their three children were off in Ruth's station wagon on the 500-mile journey to New Orleans" [1226], arriving on May 11. [1227] Ruth told the Warren Commission about Marina's dismayed view of the apartment: "She said it is dark, and it is not very clean. ... We immediately were aware there were a lot of cockroaches." [1228]

Despite Ruth Paine's generosity and kindnesses, Lee always called her "The Pain." [1229] "Ruth ... noticed that, pleased as Lee and Marina had been to see one another at first, irritation and even anger flared up quickly between them, very often over nothing at all. ... So ferocious was their bickering that Ruth decided the presence of three extra people must be adding to the strain. She and her children left ... a day or so ahead of schedule. But the bickering went on, for it was the currency of their relationship. ... [O]rdinary conversation sounded like argument, and a real argument like a fight to the finish. What counted was the mood of the marriage, and in New Orleans, the first couple of months were hard. Marina was depressed and Lee preoccupied. They fought constantly, with little humor in their battles." [1230]

In this period, May–June 1963, Lee made three to five visits to a New Orleans lawyer, Dean Adams Andrews, Jr., about the possibility of having his Marine Corps discharge converted to honorable. [1231] Andrews testified Lee also asked if there was any problem with his citizenship. "Your presence in the United States is proof you are a citizen. Otherwise, you would be an alien with an alien registration with a green card, form 990." [1232] And, how can Marina become a citizen? "I told him to go to Immigration and get the forms. Cost him $10. All he had to do was execute them. He didn't need a lawyer. That was the end of that." [1233]

Andrews said Lee's foremost concern was the discharge: "I don't recall the dates, but briefly, it is this: ... He wanted to find out what could be done in connection with a discharge, a yellow paper discharge, so I explained to him he would have to advance the funds to transcribe whatever records they had up in the Adjutant General's office. When he brought the money, I would do the work, and we saw him three or four times subsequent to that … " [1234] "He told me he was dishonorably discharged. That's what I call a yellow sheet discharge. I told him I needed his serial number, the service he was in, the approximate time he got

---

z This $1.50, although a pittance, is progress. His previous jobs had paid $1.25 and $1.35 an hour. He never earned a salary. This small hourly wage at Reily is the highest he will ever be paid.

discharged, and, I think, $15 or $25, I forget which, and to take the service, his rate or rank, the serial number, and to write to the Adjutant General for the transcript of the proceedings that washed him out so that they could be examined and see if there was any method of reopening or reconsideration on the file. ... He said he would come back, and he came back, but I still didn't get his serial number and I still didn't get the money." [1235] Walking through downtown New Orleans in July, lawyer Andrews spotted Lee, "in front of the Maison Blanche Building giving out these kooky Castro things. ... I reminded him of the $25 he owed the office. He said he would come over there, but he never did." [1236] And that, as Marguierite regularly ended her long narratives, was the end of that.

President Kennedy's visit to Texas in November 1963 was considered for almost a year before it occurred. He had made only a few brief stops there since the 1960 campaign. [1237] During 1963, the reasons for making such a trip became more persuasive. As political leader, the President wished to resolve a factional controversy within the Democratic Party in Texas before the election of 1964. The party itself saw an opportunity to raise funds by having the President speak at a political dinner. As Chief of State, the President always welcomed the opportunity to learn, firsthand, about the problems that concerned the American people. Moreover, he looked forward to the public appearances, which he personally enjoyed. [1238]

The basic decision for the trip to Texas was made at a meeting of President Kennedy, Vice President Johnson, and Governor Connally on June 5. Kennedy had spoken earlier that day at the Air Force Academy in Colorado Springs, and had stopped in El Paso to discuss the proposed visit and other matters with the Vice President and the Governor. The three agreed that the President would come to Texas in late November 1963. [1239]

On the same day, U.S. Navy Commander Carson in The Pentagon wrote to Oswald that his request to change his undesirable discharge from the Marine Corps was still under consideration by the Navy Discharge Review Board. He is the same reserve Navy officer who had written to Lee on August 6, 1962, saying the Board had his request, and "it requires from four to six months to complete a review." [1240] In the case of Oswald, a most unusual deserter to the enemy country, it required much longer, ten months after Carson's earlier letter, nearly a year after the Board had received Lee's written request.

I explained earlier in this chapter that The Pentagon would not allow me to re-create this or other letters with the Department of Defense logo, so as was done earlier, here is the Navy Discharge Review Board's letterhead, followed by the carbon copy of their letter:

Navy Discharge Review Board letterhead in 1962: [AA] [1241]

DEPARTMENT OF THE NAVY
NAVY DISCHARGE REVIEW BOARD
WASHINGTON 25, D. C.

IN REPLY REFER TO
EXOS:QB(33)
JAP:gjc

1963 June 5: Navy Discharge Review Board to Oswald [1242]

EXOS:QB (33)
KIC:gbn

5 Jun 1963

Mr. Lee H. Oswald
2703 Mercedes Street
Fort Worth, Texas

Dear Mr. Oswald:

New address.
P.O. Box 30061
New Orleans, La

The review of your discharge from the Marine Corps has not yet been concluded. This is due, in part, to the unusual circumstances surrounding your separation. It is hoped that consideration of your case, including review of the Discharge Review Board's findings by the Secretary of the Navy, will be completed this summer.

Sincerely yours,

E. I. CARSON
Commander USNR
Secretary
Navy Discharge Review Board

[AA] Your author thinks of a similar situation from his youth to help demonstrate the reason you must do the mental juggling of putting two things together because of unnatural legal restraints. There used to be butter, only butter, until the invention (in France) of vegetable-oil-based oleomargarine — usually called simply "oleo" — now generally known as margarine. Today it is yellow, the same color as butter. But in the early 20th Century, dairy lobbies prevailed on state legislatures to forbid that coloring. So, our mothers bought sickly-looking off-white margarine that came packaged with a plastic packet of yellow-orange food coloring. Kids who had been good were allowed to knead the coloring into the oleo, to produce glop that looked somewhat like butter. The last restrictions were in dairying states Minnesota and Wisconsin in the 1960s. If you would know more, there's a fine article "Margarine" on Wikipedia.

Lee had filed a change of address notice with the Fort Worth Post Office, so the Navy's letter reached him, DC – Fort Worth – New Orleans, about June 11. He quickly mailed a Change of Address card, received at the NDRB on June 14,[1243] causing an efficient clerk to write his new address on their carbon copy of the June 5 letter, as was shown on the preceding page. Lee's COA card triply testifies to his strong interest in the matter: it bears a six-weeks-previous effective date of May 1, it includes the EXOS subject code from the letter, and proves his interest by the haste in mailing it.

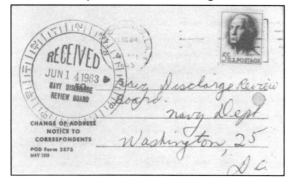 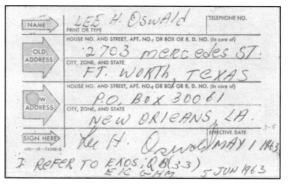

We easily imagine that Lee was not pleased with this letter, which came much later than he had been told to expect, that did not bring the hoped-for news that the U.S. Marine Corps had come to its senses and restored his discharge from "undesirable" to "honorable". But it was not unrelievedly bad. This was not just a form letter to be sent to anyone. It knew **"the unusual circumstances surrounding your separation.**" Yes, there was hope!

During this period, Oswald began to evidence thoughts of returning to the Soviet Union or going to Cuba. On June 24 he applied for a new passport.[1244] "On June 25, Lee Harvey Oswald is issued a United States passport in New Orleans, twenty-four hours after his application and one year after his return from defecting to the Soviet Union. On his passport application, he identifies his destination as the Soviet Union." [1245] "Now, he will be able to leave the United States once more, and as a political adventurer in a game of high stakes." [1246]

The US – USSR confrontation was made vivid the next day, June 26, when a million greeted President Kennedy in walled-off West Berlin.[1247] The crowds chanted "Ken-ne-DEE"

and he gave one of the most powerful and memorable speeches ever. "[T]he message was aimed as much at the Soviets as it was at Berliners, and was a clear statement of U.S. policy in the wake of the construction of the Berlin Wall. The speech is ... both a notable moment of the Cold War and a high point of the New Frontier. ... Kennedy said, 'Two thousand years ago the proudest boast was '*civis Romanus sum*' ['I am a Roman citizen']. Today, in the world of freedom, the proudest boast is '*Ich bin ein Berliner!*'

... All free men, wherever they may live, are citizens of Berlin, and, therefore, as a free man, I take pride in the words Ich bin ein Berliner!" [1248]

On July 1, Lee forced Marina to write the Russian Embassy expressing a desire to return to Russia and indicating that she would be accompanied by her husband.[1249] He directed her to explain in her letter that she wanted to return because of family problems, including the impending birth of her second child.[1250] Lee included a letter asking the Embassy to rush an entrance visa for his wife, and requesting that his visa be considered separately.[1251] Marina believed that Oswald was really planning to go only to Cuba, testifying that "his basic desire was to get to Cuba by any means, and that all the rest of it was window dressing for that purpose."[1252] She wrote to Ruth Paine that his "love" had ceased soon after Marina arrived in New Orleans.[1253]

These communications are all letters, written and put into the mail inside envelopes with postage stamps. It will be decades until long-distance telephone calls become an option, made affordable by the laying of fiber-optic cables in which each strand can carry thousands of calls. The Internet is even further away. To help with the steadily increasing mail volumes, on that same day, July 1, 1963, the US Post Office had a little figure "Mr. Zip" introduce ZIP codes,[BB] and teach us how to append them to addresses so machines could speed sorting. There was considerable grumbling that we were expected to do more work, especially when one considered that the cost of mailing a letter had recently rocketed up to 5¢!

[BB] Demonstrating the Web's unreliability, one can quickly and authoritatively learn that "ZIP" stands for "Zone Improvement Plan", "Zoning Improvement Plan" and "Zone Information Protocol". Your author, an unashamed out-of-the-closet philatelist, believes the first is correct.

On July 10, Oswald's appeal against his undesirable discharge got its formal hearing. The three-page report from the Navy Discharge Review Board to the Secretary of the Navy is clearly printed in the *Warren Commission Hearings*:[1254]

1963 July 10: Navy Discharge Review Board report to SecNav, page 1

```
REVIEW OF DISCHARGE
NAVEXOS-2409 (REV. 6-61)          DEPARTMENT OF THE NAVY
                                  NAVY DISCHARGE REVIEW BOARD
TO:  SECRETARY OF THE NAVY    JAP:gjc              DOCKET NO.  8812
                                              CHARACTER OF DISCHARGE RECEIVED
REVIEW OF THE DISCHARGE OF: OSWALD, Lee Harvey  Ex-Pfc 1653230 USMC   UNDES(UNFIT)
COUNSEL              PETITIONER PRESENT   RECORD OF PROCEEDINGS OF REVIEW MADE  DATE OF REVIEW
 NONE               [ ] YES  [X] NO      [ ] YES   [X] NO              10Jul63
                             FINDINGS
DATE OF ENTRY IN NAVAL SERVICE AGE  LENGTH OF SERVICE  Time lost: 15days  RANKS HELD     Recomputed TRAITS  GCT
 24Oct56            17/0  02Y 10M 17D          Pvt-Pfc-Pvt-Pfc         3.94  4.1      105
SUMMARY OF PETITIONER'S CLAIM: Petitioner requests recommendation for reenlistment, review of
```

case and appropriate action. He submitted a brief which essentially states that his discharge was improperly issued. Also included was pet's statement and two letters from the U.S. Embassy, Moscow. As requested by pet, his lengthy statement was read to the board. It contained his contention that the Undesirable Discharge Board found against him primarily on the grounds that he went to USSR and allegedly renounced his U.S. citizenship to become a citizen of that country. Pet denied this allegation and claimed that since he had a choice of residence as an American citizen, such action could not be judged as being fair or impartial. He further stated that he did not violate any U.S. laws by his actions and quoted in part, an American Embassy, Moscow letter which stated: "Meanwhile, your continued retention of your present Soviet passport or an extension thereof does not prejudice in any way your claim to American citizenship."

SUMMARY OF SERVICE, COMMENDATIONS, AND OFFENSES:

Enl for 3 years. No prior service claimed. Attained equiv of High School grad through USAFI; Grad 46/54 AvnFundScol, JAX and completed AC&WOperCrse, Keesler AFB.
1May57   Pro to PFC.
          MACS-1, MAG-11, 1stMAW, FMF
11Apr58   SumCM   Violate a lawful general order by having in his possession a pri-
                   vately-owned weapon that was not registered. Sent as appr: CHL
                   for 20 days and forf $25.00 per mo for two mos and red to PVT.
                   (Confinement suspended for 6 mos etc., but vacated on 27Jun58)
27Jun58   SumCM   1. Wrongfully use provoking words to a Staff NCO. (found guilty)
                   2. Assault a Staff NCO (found not guilty)
                   Sent as appr: CHL for 28 days and forf $55.00 per mo for 1 month.
          SubUnit 1, H&MS 11, MAG-11, 1stMAW
17Oct58   SRB   JAG found that injury received by pet on 27Oct57 as a result of
                   an accidental discharge of a weapon, was incurred in line of duty
                   and not result of misconduct. (Upon opening his locker, a .22
                   cal pistol fell to the floor and discharged, wounding pet in the
                   left elbow.)
          MACS-9, MWHG, 3dMAW, AirFMFPac
1Mar59   Pro to PFC
17Aug59   Pet submitted a request for dependency discharge, by reason of hardship
          on the part of his mother. Pet appeared before the Hardship/Dependency
          discharge Board who recommended that he be released from active duty for
          reason of dependency. Appr by CG, 3dMAW on 31Aug59.

                                        (SEE ATTACHED SHEET)

The first page of the **REVIEW OF DISCHARGE**, above, states "Also included was pet's statement and two letters from the U.S. Embassy, Moscow. As requested by pet, his lengthy statement was read to the board." Lee was nobody's "pet", he was the board's "petitioner". The pet's statement was the five pages attached to his petition, displayed beginning on the second page of this chapter. The easy-to-read "if he had a typewriter" text began on page 110.

1963 July 10: Navy Discharge Review Board report to SecNav, page 2

```
JAP:gjc                                          D#  8812

OSWALD, Lee Harvey       Ex-Pfc      1653230       USMC

Summary of Service, Commendations and Offenses:    (CONT'D)


11Sep59    Released from active duty (Honorable) and assigned to Ready Reserve, Class
           III, Transferred to MARTC, NAS, Glenview, Ill., for completion of 6 years
           obligated service ending 8Dec62.



MEDICAL RECORD:    Contains nothing pertinent.



           HQ, MARTC, NAS, Glenview, Ill.
29Jul60    Mobilization Planning Officer, recommended pet be discharged by reason of
           unfitness based on reliable information which indicated that pet had re-
           nounced his U.S. citizenship with the intentions of becoming a permanent
           citizen of the Union of Soviet Socialist Republics.  Pet's case was heard
           (in absentia) by the Hardship, Retention and Desirability Board who recom-
           mended discharge by reason of unfitness.  Pet was notified by certified
           mail that a board would convene to determine his fitness, and afforded him
           his rights.  The correspondence was returned unclaimed.  The findings,
           opinions and recommendations of the Board were approved by CCMART on 9Aug60,
           and forwarded to CMC for final determination.
17Aug60    CMC approved and directed discharge.
13Sep60    Discharged by HQ, MARTC, NAS, Glenview, Ill., Auth para 10277.2f, MCM.
```

Halfway down the image above is a significant misdirection. It may be inadvertent, stemming from the members of the Navy Review Board simply misunderstanding the original sequence of events. Or, like the Wizard of Oz urging Dorothy and companions: "Pay no attention to that man behind the curtain!", it may have been a deliberate attempt to shield the Commandant of the Corps and/or other Pentagon brass. That is not a compelling case, of course, because this happened four and a half months before the petitioner became famous.

As was documented in the preceding chapter MINSK, the history of changing Oswald's discharge to Undesirable certainly did not begin as stated above, on July 29, 1960 with the hardworking and efficient Mobilization Planning Officer in Illinois, Lieutenant Letscher. The process had begun well before that in October and November of 1959 when Oswald, feeling sorry for himself in Moscow, had given interviews that resulted in front-page stories back home about his defection to the enemy. Then, we know with certainty that on November 3, 1959, the Naval attaché in the Moscow Embassy wired to the Chief of Naval Operations in the Pentagon that Oswald threatened that he would tell Soviets the military secrets he had learned while operating radar in Japan near the then-secret U-2 spy plane.

Pentagon civilian officials and top brass made inquiries and decisions, culminating on March 8, 1960, with the Commandant of the Marine Corps sending a terse SPEEDLetter to the Commander of Oswald's assigned reserve unit in Glenview, Illinois, ordering that Oswald be given an Undesirable discharge for reason of being unfit. See that top-down order on page 46. Only after that Commander handed the matter to his staffer, Lt. Letscher, and the latter did his due diligence, did Letscher on "29Jul60" recommend to his boss the change of discharge — which is where the report above begins. The bottom-up recommendation is on page 56.

1963 July 10: Navy Discharge Review Board report to SecNav, page 3

```
          JAP:gjc                                    D# 8812
                                           CHARACTER OF DISCHARGE RECEIVED
REVIEW OF THE DISCHARGE OF: OSWALD, Lee Harvey  Ex-Pfc  1653230  USMC    UNDES(UNFIT)
                                   CONCLUSION
REMARKS
```

The service record of petitioner shows that he was discharged as unfit for good and
sufficient reasons. This was based on reliable information which indicated that he
had renounced his U.S. citizenship with the intentions of becoming a permanent citizen
of the Union of Soviet Socialist Republics. Further, that petitioner brought discredit to the Marine Corps through adverse newspaper publicity, which was generated
by the foregoing action, and had thereby, in the opinion of his commanding officer,
proved himself unfit for retention in the naval service.

After careful consideration of the facts presented in all available records of the
Department of the Navy and of the claims and evidence submitted, the Board finds that
the discharge was proper and equitable under standards of law and discipline applicable
at the time, or since made applicable, and that the discharge accurately reflects
petitioner's conduct and character during the period of service which was terminated
by the discharge. Not finding sufficient evidence to support a contrary conclusion,
the Board concludes that no change, correction or modification should be made in the
type or character of the discharge.

DECISION: NO CHANGE. XXXXXXXXXXXXXX

It is the decision of the Board that the character of the discharge originally issued
is proper and that no change, correction or modification be made in the Undesirable
Discharge.

            (Auth: Sec. 301, Servicemen's Readjustment Act of 1944, P.L. 346 - 78th Congress)

President   BOARD MEMBERS
                                    MEMBER
      JOHN H. CARROLL, LTCOL, USMC   LYLE W. EADS, LCDR, USN
MEMBER   MEMBER
      R. O. CARLOCK, LTCOL, USMC   VIRGIL G. BOWEN, MAJ, USMCR
                                    RECORDER CERTIFIED TO BE CORRECT
                                          J. A. POLIDORI, MAJ, USMCR
Forwarded   Reviewed and Approved JUL 19 1963

      C. W. TRAVIS, CAPT, USN   PAUL B. FAY
Director, Navy Council of Personnel Boards   Under Secretary of the Navy
REVIEW OF DISCHARGE
NAVEXOS-2409 (REV. 6-61)
```

The board decided to make no change to the Undesirable Discharge.  Their report went to
Navy Captain Travis, who as Director approved it on behalf of the Navy Council of Personnel
Boards, and forwarded it to the office of the Secretary of the Navy for the ultimate decision.
```

On July 11, 12 and 14, Ruth wrote Marina that if Lee did not wish to live with her any more, she could live at the Paines' house. Ruth had long entertained this idea. She attempted to overcome any feeling by Marina that she would be a burden by stating that Marina could help with the housework, help Ruth learn Russian, and also provide a tax advantage.[1255]

Marina replied that she had raised the subject of a separation and that it had led to arguments. She said she was happy and for a considerable period of time Lee had been good to her, which she attributed to the fact that he was anticipating their second child. Turning down the invitation, Marina said that she would take advantage of it if things became worse.[1256] Ruth said she would visit Marina in New Orleans in September, suggesting that Marina come to her house for the birth of the baby.[1257]

Marina turned twenty-two on July 17. This has been an unrelentingly sad narrative, so it's time for a bit of relieving humor, at a presidential news conference on her birthday:

> "Reporter: 'The Republican National Committee recently adopted a resolution saying you were pretty much of a failure. How do you feel about that?'
> Kennedy: 'I assume it passed unanimously.'" [1258]

Lee kept his machine-greasing job for only two months and two weeks. Reily's maintenance foreman swore an affidavit to the Warren Commission:

> "During the latter portion of his employment, I served as his immediate supervisor. As his supervisor I was aware of Oswald's performance or lack thereof of his duties. There were occasions from time to time when I was unable to locate Oswald in and about the premises and learned that he was in the habit of absenting himself from the premises without leave and visiting a service station establishment adjacent to the Reily Coffee Company known as Alba's Crescent City Garage. Furthermore, Oswald had become quite indifferent to the performance of his duties. I spoke with him from time to time about his absences and indifferences, all to no avail. Ultimately I recommended to my superiors that Oswald be discharged. My request was granted and he was discharged on July 19, 1963." [1259]

At the next-door garage, he spent many hours drinking coffee, reading gun magazines and discussing military rifles with the owner who collected and "sporterized" them.[1260] He also borrowed some of the 80 to 120 gun and National Rifle Association magazines and gun-ammunition catalogs on the garage's coffee table.[1261]

July 19 was a doubly bad day, although Lee will not know about its second setback for a week. On July 10, the Navy Discharge Review Board had recommended his undesirable discharge. Shown on the previous page, the last of three sheets has at bottom-right the space for "Reviewed and Approved" by "Secretary of the Navy" — the ultimate decision of the very long process. The magnification here shows 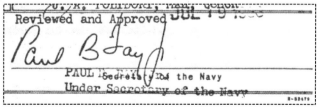 who signed for the Secretary on July 19, a sad small world coincidence.[1262]

From 1961 through 1963, whenever the President of the United States needed some fun and diversion, he frequently chose to enjoy it — walk, talk, dine, drink, joke — with a long-time buddy, Paul B. Fay Jr. They have been best friends for twenty years, since PT boat school in 1942. In Chapter 19 – THE SHOT NOT TAKEN, "Red" Fay is beside JFK in two photos and gives important testimony bearing on the assassination. It is perverse happenstance that Fay gave the final imprimatur that will result in his dear friend's death.

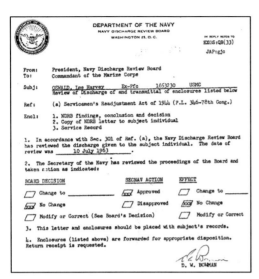

Shown here [1263] is the document that transmitted Under Secretary Fay's decision to Marine Corps Commandant Shoup. Because it specifically shows that the Secretary of the Navy (by designee) has reviewed and approved, and that the Discharge Board has notified Oswald of the decision (Encl 2.), this form will require no further action by the Marines, except to file it with Oswald's records — where all this will be dug out in only a few months for information of the Warren Commission. As you may suspect by now, and will be confirmed as 1963 and 1964 progress, the Commission will pay very little attention to Oswald's service and problems in the Marines, or to the discharge, thinking they had no essential bearing on his killing Kennedy.

Lee collected unemployment compensation weekly and, although making some slight effort to obtain another job, listed fictitious job applications on his claim forms.[1264] He soon gave up his attempt altogether and spent his days at home reading.[1265] Unemployment compensation from the State of Louisiana is not generous, but the Oswalds are thrifty, and it will suffice.

Lee has always been an avid reader, and now realizing that he really doesn't have to go to work, he spends the summer of 1963 reading books from the New Orleans Public Library. Their records show that he checked out several books a week. He is omnivorous, devouring a biography of Chairman Mao and James Bond novels. Then he turns his attention to a man he respects, John F. Kennedy. After reading William Manchester's new bestseller *Portrait of a President* (to be followed much too soon by his excellent but heartbreaking *The Death of a President*) he checks out Kennedy's *Profiles in Courage*, the 1957 Pulitzer Prize winner for biography. There in the heat, humidity, squalor and depression of their New Orleans summer, Lee reads JFK's words about great men and comes to believe in his own greatness.[1266]

"Lee began to talk about himself and his future in exalted terms ... in twenty years' time, *he* would be President or prime minister. It did not seem to matter that America has no prime minister." [1267] "[I]t appears that Lee wanted to be like Kennedy and perhaps follow in his footsteps as closely as he could. Reading Manchester's book may have reminded him that in some ways he was like Kennedy already. Both loved to read books, both loved foreign travel, both had served with the armed forces in the Pacific, both had poor handwriting and were poor spellers, both had very young children, and both had a brother named Robert." [1268] But, coincidences are not credentials! Lee lived in some parallel universe of a dreamer, never acknowledging the sad reality of his disappointing situation.

And then came a blow, if not the worst of his life, then the worst until four months from now when he will be stopped by Officer Tippit, then captured in a theatre. We have seen the documents of deliberation and decision by the board that reviews appeals of discharges from the Navy and Marine Corps. We know the result, but Lee will not learn the news until he receives the letter on the next page, sent by Registered Mail, the Post Office's [CC] most secure and accountable service. A small form announcing its arrival was placed into his

---

[CC] It was the Post Office from 1792 to 1971, when it became the semi-autonomous U.S. Postal Service.

mailbox in the New Orleans post office, probably about July 29. He then went to a counter to show identification and sign for the letter he had so long awaited, and for which he had such high hopes. We can picture Lee, probably still standing there in the post office, eagerly opening the envelope from the Pentagon to find the letter, three enclosures and a pamphlet.

1963 July 25: Navy Discharge Review Board to Oswald [1269]

DEPARTMENT OF THE NAVY
NAVY DISCHARGE REVIEW BOARD
WASHINGTON 25, D. C.

IN REPLY REFER TO
EXOS:QB(33)
JAP:gjc

Mr. Lee H. Oswald
P. O. Box 30061
New Orleans, La.

Dear Mr. Oswald:

The review of your discharge has been completed in accordance with the regulations governing the procedures of this Board. Careful consideration was given to the evidence presented in your behalf as well as that contained in your official records. The Secretary of the Navy has reviewed the proceedings of the Board.

It is the decision that no change, correction or modification is warranted in your discharge.

Sincerely yours,

D. W. BOWMAN
Captain, USN

President
Navy Discharge Review Board

Encls: Original Discharge Certificate.
Two (2) letters dated 31 Jan 1962, 13 Nov 1961.
Information on Reenlistment

NAVEXOS 1900/1 (REV. 11-62)

B22330

Oswald's pleadings since his letter to Connally have come to a dead end with a <u>form</u> letter! As shown by the letter from the *Warren Commission Hearings* on the previous page, the salutation "Dear", the two paragraphs of text, the "Sincerely yours," "President / Navy Discharge Review Board" and final line "Information on Reenlistment" were pre-printed. Lee's address, "Mr. Oswald:", "D. W. BOWMAN / Captain, USN" and the first two lines of enclosures have been typed onto a lousy form letter!

There are other insults and we can be rather certain Lee would have seen them as such. On the scanned image on the previous page, notice the four L shaped corners bracketing Lee's name and address. Those are guides for the typist to type that information in position so it will be visible through a window in the mailing envelope. As is done for bills, this saves the mailer from also addressing an envelope. Oswald knew, as do we, that anything arriving in a window envelope is either junk or bad news. We can imagine the disdain with which Lee looked at this letter, the two returned letters from the Moscow embassy he expected to prove his case, and how he crumpled and threw out the enclosure "`Information on Reenlistment`"!

On August 5, 1963, long, patient, quiet diplomacy, bargaining and mutual respect between Kennedy and his Russian counterpart, Nikita Khrushchev, paid off with the signing of the first agreement backing the superpowers away from nuclear confrontation, the treaty banning nuclear testing in the air, on land and underwater. Kennedy intended this to be the first or several strategic agreements, but never had the opportunity to add the others.

Here it is opportune to dispose, briefly, of two nonsensical undertakings by Lee during the last summer of his life. Neither has any connection to the subject of this book — his intent on November 22 — but some readers might be suspicious if they are not at least mentioned. The first, Fair Play for Cuba, is probably an attempt to establish his credibility for the second, attempting to live in Cuba. Assassination analyst Craig Zirbel observes:

> "[I]t should be noted that ... Oswald, until only a few months of his death, demonstrated no significant interest in Cuba. ... in the summer of 1963, [he] began a brief *unilateral* association with Cuba ... after this brief episode of public attention ... Oswald completely stopped his public campaign. From beginning to end this short period of frenzied pro-Castro activities lasted only 12 days (8/9/63–8/21/63). Then Oswald stopped!" [1270]

Fidel Castro had led a 1959 insurrection that replaced the corrupt Batista government of Cuba with his populism, which he then evolved into communism. New President Kennedy in early 1961 had authorized a plan he inherited from the Eisenhower administration to covertly support invasion at the Bay of Pigs. That disaster fooled no one. Castro harangued against the US and embraced the USSR. In turn, the US forbade all normal relations with Cuba. October 1962 brought the Cuban Missile Crisis, furthering fears and hatreds on both sides.

A National Fair Play for Cuba Committee in the US attempted to gain sympathy for Castro's regime. In 1963, Oswald invented a New Orleans branch of the Committee. Using the name "Lee Osborne" he paid for circulars demanding "HANDS OFF CUBA", and application forms and membership cards for the "chapter". [1271] He began on a "wharf where the USS *Wasp* was anchored. He handed out ... handbills to Navy personnel and visitors until he was unceremoniously evicted from the wharf." [1272]

On August 9, he was passing out his leaflets when three anti-Castro Cuban exiles became angry and a dispute ensued. Police arrested them all for disturbing the peace; [1273] the Cubans were released on bail; Lee spent a night in jail. He maintained he was a member of a New Orleans branch of the Fair Play for Cuba Committee which, he said, had 35 members.

He stated that he had been in touch with the president of that organization, A. J. Hidell.[1274] When Lee forced Marina to sign "A. J. Hidell" on an FPCC member card, she said, "'You have selected this name because it sounds like Fidel' and he blushed and said, 'Shut up, it is none of your business.'" [1275] He was in fact the only member of the "New Orleans branch," which had never been authorized by the National Fair Play for Cuba Committee.[1276] The Municipal Court released Lee on bail after he pleaded guilty and paid a $10 fine. All charges against the Cuban exiles were dismissed without penalty.[1277] This mug shot is only 3½ months before famous one on this book's cover.[1278]

"Marina had been worried when Lee failed to come home the night before. She knew that he was out with his leaflets and guessed that he was in trouble with the police. At least he was not with another woman. She had memories of the Walker evening, however, and so she had checked Lee's closet. The rifle, thank God, was in its place." [1279] She testified that the arrest upset Lee and that he "became less active, he cooled off a little" after it.[1280]

New Orleans television showed him and a hired helper passing out Fair Play for Cuba literature,[1281] which led a radio station to air a debate between Lee and a local opponent of Castro.[1282] Oswald defended the Castro regime and promoted Marxism, although he was put on the defensive when his defection to Russia was brought up.[1283]

"'Damn it,' he said to Marina when he returned home, 'I didn't realize they knew I'd been to Russia. You ought to have heard what they asked me! I wasn't prepared and I didn't know what to say.' Still, he was anxious to hear what he had said. He called the Murrets to let them know about the program. They were not amused. An irate Dutz said later that they had not heard the whole of the program, 'but enough.'" [1284] "Lee switched on the radio and sat in the kitchen waiting. 'Come quickly,' he called out to Marina. 'I'm about to speak now.' Marina did not understand who was saying what, but she could tell who was on what side and that Lee was claiming to be secretary of an organization. She also could tell from his voice when he was lying. "Afterwards she asked, 'Are they such fools there at the station that they actually believe you have an organization? One man is chairman, secretary, and sole member!' 'Maybe the debate will help and others will join,' Lee said. 'I doubt it,' Marina replied. Her reaction was not one of pride at hearing her husband speak, but of amusement at the way he sat, 'proud as a rooster,' listening to his own voice. 'Twenty minutes!' he said, when the program was over. 'And I spoke longer than any of them. Every minute costs a lot on radio. And I talked by far the most.'" [1285]

Oswald wrote several times to the Fair Play for Cuba Committee, telling in exaggerated terms of his activities,[1286] but getting no support or even any replies. That was explained to the Warren Commission by Vincent T. Lee, national director of FPCC until it became infamous because of Oswald's association and disbanded, ending all activities, in December 1963:

> "[Oswald wrote] that he had gone ahead and acted on his own without any authorization from the organization ... [W]hen somebody goes off like this, violating all the rules that you send him, it comes as quite a disappointment, because you have had hopes. Obviously this man was not operating in an official capacity for the organization. ... I think one of the letters mentioned how he was out somewhere all alone and that he had ... nobody working with him or through him or for him or around him or anything else. He gave me the impression that he was

completely isolated in his community, which became obvious to me from his actions which would certainly isolate him in his community. I could see very well how he would be." [1287]

Lee wrote a brief account of his pro-Castro activities, which he will take to the Cuban Embassy in Mexico, including some real whoppers: "I caused the formation of a small, active, FPCC organization of members and sympatizers where before there was none." [1288] When questioned by a New Orleans police detective after being arrested and jailed, "He said he had been associated with the FPCC since 1959; that there were thirty-five members in his FPCC chapter; that they rotated their meetings among various members' homes; and that A. J. Hidell was president of the group." [1289] His truthful wife differed: "Marina was certain that no one ever joined what she called Oswald's 'non-existing organization.'" [1290] "Marina, in fact, viewed all the activities described in the document—the 'FPCC chapter,' the demonstrations, the publicity—as mere 'window dressing' for her husband's real purpose: getting to Cuba. 'He wanted to be arrested,' she testified, 'he wanted to get into the newspapers, so that he would be known' as pro-Cuban. The FPCC operation was ... merely 'self-advertising.'" [1291]

Dr. Gerald Posner, the author of highly-recommended *Case Closed*, summarized Lee's fifteen months in the U.S.: "When he returns here, it's one failure after another. He can't hold a job, can't do anything right. He decides now he's going to go and become part of Castro's revolution, goes to New Orleans, sets up the organization to free Cuba, hands out thousands of leaflets on the streets in the summer of boiling New Orleans heat. And, guess what? He can't get one member to join his new organization. He's failed again." [1292]

On August 7, Jacqueline Kennedy went into much-too-early labor at Hyannis Port and was rushed to a nearby hospital. She had miscarried on her first pregnancy, then gave birth to stillborn Arabella. Caroline and John were born normally and healthy, although he a bit early. Patrick Bouvier Kennedy, weighing less than five pounds, took his first breath — but not well. He has hyaline membrane disease, the reason many children born so prematurely die quickly, because the lungs' air sacs have a coating that impedes gas exchange — oxygen in and carbon dioxide out. He was quickly moved to a larger more capable hospital. On the day Lee Oswald is arrested in New Orleans, Patrick, after living only thirty-nine hours, died before dawn in the oxygen chamber of a Boston hospital with his father holding his tiny hand. The President went back to comfort his wife, weeping as he told her the tragic news. She tried to comfort him, saying they still have each other, and their healthy Caroline and John. "'There's just one thing I couldn't stand—if I ever lost you . . .' Her voice had drifted off, leaving the unthinkable unspoken, and he had murmured reassuringly, 'I know, I know.'" [1293]

There is no better vantage for understanding the desperate depth to which Lee has sunk than this interview in Norman Mailer's *Oswald's Tale: An American Mystery*:

> "Marina recalls one hot night when they were sitting in their living room, and it was so hot and they were so poor. No air conditioner. It was New Orleans in summer. Husband and wife both sweating. All of a sudden, he said, 'What if we hijack a plane?' She said, 'Who is we?'
>
> 'You and me,' he told her.
>
> 'You are joking?'
>
> 'No,' he said.
>
> 'In Russia,' she said, 'it wasn't good, now America's no good— so it's Cuba.'
>
> He said, 'I am serious.'
>
> She said, 'All right, I will have to listen to you and your stupid idea.'
>
> He said, 'You don't have to kill anybody.'
>
> She repeated that as a question: 'Kill anybody?'

'You will need a gun,' he said, 'and I will have a gun, but you will not have to kill anybody. Just be there to threaten people.'

She said, 'Yes, everybody will be scared of me—a pregnant woman holding a gun, and she doesn't know how to hold it.'

He kept saying, 'Repeat after me—' That's when he tried to get her to say in English: 'Stick 'em up.' She couldn't even repeat it. She began laughing. He tried to persuade her. 'Repeat after me . . . ' but it was fiasco, just a fiasco.

She was pregnant with Rachel, and Lee was trying to teach her what she was supposed to say to passengers in English. She couldn't even pronounce the words: 'Stick 'em up.' [DD] Everybody was going to drop dead laughing. She said, 'You really are a kook. My God, you and I have nothing to eat and you are cooking up dumb things.'" [1294]

On August 28, realizing he is getting nowhere trying to gain favor by supporting Castro in Cuba, Oswald writes [EE] a letter seeking advice from the Central Committee of the Communist Party of the United States:

> "Having come back to the U.S. in 1962 and thrown myself into the struggle for progress and freedom in the United States, I would like to know weather, in your opion, I can continue to fight, handicapped as it were, by my past record, can I still, under these circumstances, compete with anti-progressive forces, above ground or weather in your opion I should always remain in the background, i.e. underground. … I feel I may have compromised the FPCC, so you see that I need the advice of trusted, long time fighters for progress. Please advise.
>
> With Ferternal Greeting
> Sincerely /signed/ Lee H. Oswald" [1295]

That day at the Lincoln Memorial on the National Mall, tens of thousands hear a minister speak about his hopes for the future, which I am not allowed to quote. [1296] Two weeks later, Ku Klux Klan members bomb a church in Birmingham, killing four little black girls and injuring another 22 adults and children who are there to hear a sermon, "The Love That Forgives".

Planning for JFK's Texas trip moves along. "The original plan called for Kennedy to spend only one day in the state, making whirlwind visits to Dallas, Fort Worth, San Antonio and Houston. In September, the White House decided to extend the trip from the afternoon of November 21 through the evening of Friday, November 22." [1297] "[I]n conjunction with the lengthened trip, Governor Connally proposed a motorcade through Dallas followed by a luncheon, and then a flight to Austin. The motorcade was to follow the traditional Dallas parade route that had been used since at least 1936." [1298]

As summer ended, Lee had been out of work for two full months, was not looking for a job, lived on unemployment compensation, sat at home reading, and had a secret plan. Ruth Paine came to New Orleans for a brief visit. It was decided that Marina would ride back with her to Irving for the birth of the baby. "Ruth … and her husband, Michael, an engineering designer … had separated temporarily, so there was sufficient space for guests." [1299] Lee and Ruth loaded the Chevrolet station wagon. [1300] "Ruth was impressed by Lee's insistence on doing every bit of packing himself. She had never seen him such a gentleman before. What she did not know was that among the items he was loading with such care into her car was, almost certainly, his rifle, dismantled, wrapped in brown paper and a blanket, and tied up in

---

[DD] You may have seen Butch Cassidy and the Sundance Kid practicing exactly these words in Spanish.

[EE] As throughout the book, we supply Lee a virtual typewriter so you don't have to read his sometimes difficult handwriting in poor Warren Commission images. The spelling we leave to him.

heavy string. Somehow he led the Paines to understand that it was 'camping equipment.'" [1301] On September 23, Marina and June rode away.[1302] Lee and Marina will never again have a home, never again live together. The rest of his life, he will be only a visitor.

Now, briefly, another of Oswald's stupidities. The first was Fair Play for Cuba. This is an attempt to get to Cuba by way of Mexico City. Marina testified that Lee had given up a plan to hijack an airplane to Cuba, which plan Marina consistently opposed, and in August told her of a new plan to go to Mexico and from there to Cuba, where he planned to stay.[1303] On September 17, he obtained a "Tourist Card" good for a journey into Mexico, stating on the application that he was employed, although in truth he was unemployed.[1304] He will now ride a bus to Mexico City because to live in the imagined paradise of Cuba, he needs a visa. The United States and Cuba have no diplomatic relations, so Mexico is the closest place to obtain that visa. To achieve his selfish dream, he abandons the USA, Marina, June, the expected baby, his mother and brothers, and his manifold disappointments.

Before she left, Lee told Marina that she should not tell anyone about his impending trip to Mexico.[1305] Marina kept this secret until after the assassination.[1306] On the previous day, Oswald's landlord had seen Mrs. Paine's car being packed and had asked Oswald, whose rent was 15 days overdue, whether he was leaving. Lee told him that Marina was leaving temporarily but that he would remain there.[1307] A neighbor testified that on the evening of September 24, he saw Oswald, carrying two pieces of luggage, hurriedly leave the apartment and board a bus.[1308] The landlord found the apartment vacant on September 25.[1309]

As Lee leaves his hometown of New Orleans for the last time, it is instructive to learn how his relatives there regarded him. His uncle Charles Ferdinand Murret,[1310] known to all as "Dutz" (he said that moniker better suited his early boxing career) gave his testimony to the Warren Commission seven months later, ending with this evaluation:

"Mr. MURRET. To tell you the truth, after he defected to Russia and went there to live and everything, I just let it go out the window. I figured, 'What's the use?' and then after he came back here and got into this radio thing about Castro, and communism, and these leaflets and all, I didn't worry myself any more about him. My main concern was keeping peace in the family and seeing that he didn't disrupt anything around there.

Mr. JENNER. In other words, you sort of gave up on him?

Mr. MURRET. I sure did, but now, Marina, I asked her how she liked America, and her face broke out in a big smile, like a fresh bloom, and she said, 'I like America.'

Mr. Jenner then thanked him for his testimony, whereupon Dutz added a final remembrance:

"Mr. MURRET. He was a hard one to get to know. You just couldn't get to know him at all, and I don't think he had much consideration for anyone, especially for his mother. ... [A]nd the thing that was so odd to me was that he seemed to always be trying to prove himself, that he was so independent. ... I just, you know, lost all interest in him after all these things happened. You just couldn't figure him out." [1311]

Oswald took with him his old passport and the new 1963 passport;[1312] his correspondence with the Communist Party and with the Soviet Embassy in Washington;[1313] newspaper clippings concerning his arrest and his activities in the Fair Play for Cuba Committee [1314] (activities which, Marina testified, he had undertaken because he thought that they would help him when he got to Cuba);[1315] and evidence that he was the "Director" of the New Orleans chapter of the Committee.[1316] He took also a written summary of important events in his life which he presumably intended to call to the attention of Cuban and Soviet officials in Mexico City to convince them to let him enter Cuba. He had included facts about his Marine service, the places where he had served, and the diplomas that he had received from military schools. He also carried notes on his stay in the Soviet Union, his interest in Communist literature, his ability to speak Russian, his organization of the New Orleans chapter of the Fair Play for Cuba Committee, his contact with police in connection with his work for the Committee, and his experience in "street agitation," as a "radio speaker and lecturer" and as a "photographer".[1317]

Lee left New Orleans by bus [1318] on September 25 — less than two months before the shooting in Dallas — transferred in Houston,[1319] crossed the border to Nuevo Laredo [1320] where he boarded another bus [1321] to Mexico City, arriving on Friday morning, September 27.[1322] He took a room at the Hotel del Comercio for $1.28 per day.[1323]

He now turned to obtaining permission to enter Cuba. Mexico required a U.S. citizen to have a Cuban visa to board a plane to Cuba.[1324] Oswald had neither a regular Cuban visitor visa, nor an intransit visa to stopover in Cuba on his way to Russia or some other country. He went immediately to the Embassy of Cuba. Senora Silvia Tirado de Duran, a Mexican citizen employed there, later made a signed statement to the Mexican police that Oswald:

> "* * * applied for a visa to Cuba in transit to Russia and based his application on his presentation of his passport in which it was recorded that he had been living in the latter country for a period of three years, his work permit from that same country written in the Russian language and letters in the same language, as well as proof of his being married to a woman of Russian nationality and being the apparent Director in the city of New Orleans of the organization called 'Fair Play for Cuba' with the desire that he should be accepted as a 'friend' of the Cuban Revolution * * *" [1325]

He also stated that he was a member of the Communist Party and displayed documents that he claimed to be evidence of his membership.[1326] He said he intended to visit in Cuba, then go on to Russia.[1327] Senora Duran filled out the appropriate Cuban application.[1328] Lee then "learned that the best way to expedite his visa was to obtain permission to visit the USSR. [He] then took off for the first of his two visits to the Soviet Embassy." [1329]

He spoke first with consular Valery Vladimirovich Kostikov.[1330] On learning Oswald's background, Kostikov passed him up to a KGB agent specializing in counterintelligence, Oleg Maximovich Nechiporenko, who wrote a 1993 book about the USSR's dealings with Oswald, cited several times throughout this book. As Lee claimed he needed a visa to Russia because the FBI was persecuting him, his "mood changed from discomfort to a state of great agitation, creating the impression of a high-strung neurotic individual." [1331] After much pleading by Lee, Nechiporenko concluded:

> "The more I learned about Oswald and the more I observed him during the course of our conversation, the less I was interested in him. I silently cursed Valery for 'transferring' him to me and decided that it was time to bring this meeting to a close. I had more important items on my agenda. I explained to Oswald that, in accordance with our rules, all matters dealing with travel to the USSR were handled by our embassies or consulates in the country in which a person lived. As far as his case was concerned, we could make an exception and give him the necessary papers to fill out, which we would then send on to Moscow, but the answer would still be sent to his permanent residence, and it would take, at the very least, four months.
>
> Oswald listened intently ... but it was clear from his gestures and the expression on his face that he was disappointed and growing increasingly annoyed. When I had finished speaking, he slowly leaned forward and, barely able to restrain himself, practically shouted in my face, 'This won't do for me! This is not my case! For me, it's all going to end in tragedy!'
>
> I shrugged my shoulders and stood up, signaling the end of our meeting. ... He departed, obviously dissatisfied with the results of our talk. He appeared to be extremely agitated. This

was how Oswald's first visit to our embassy in Mexico ended." [1332]

Oswald returned to the Cuban Embassy that same afternoon, this time bringing passport photographs. [1333] He reportedly said "the Soviets had promised him a visa." [1334] Senora Duran telephoned the Soviet Embassy to inquire about the status of that visa and was told there would be a delay of about four months. [1335] Oswald became "highly agitated and angry," particularly when he learned that he could not obtain an intransit visa to Cuba before he acquired a Russian visa. Senora Duran called Cuban consul Eusibio Azque to speak to Lee. The discussion between Oswald and Azque developed into a heated argument, which ended when Azque told Oswald that in his opinion people like him were harming the Cuban Revolution and that he would not give him a visa. [1336] Senora Duran sent the visa application to Havana. [1337] The Ministry of Foreign Affairs replied on October 15 [FF] that the visa for Cuba could be issued only after Oswald had obtained a visa for Russia. [1338] [GG]

Lee contacted the Russian and Cuban Embassies again. [1339] The Soviet Embassy was staffed by another KGB agent, Nikolai Sergeyevich Leonov, who vividly recalls:

> "When he tried to explain the reasons why he decided to return to the Soviet Union, he told again that he was under permanent observation in the United States. He felt to be persecuted, permanently, and he was scared. He was under intensive fear that something bad will happen to him. My first impression ... was that he was a little mad, a little crazy, a little out of the normal situation. That's why I tried, like a psychologist, to calm him. His hands were shaking. He was very nervous. ... Oswald became hostile when told there was no way to shorten the long application process." [1340]

It being Saturday, agent Kostikov, the first to interview Lee the previous day, arrived for the weekly volleyball match — the KGB against the military intelligence GRU! [1341] He and agent Pavel Yatskov (the embassy is well-staffed by KGB) joined the conversation, which was becoming more and more animated. Then, Kostikov says, it all plunged over a cliff:

> "Throughout his story, Oswald was extremely agitated and clearly nervous, especially when he mentioned the FBI, but he suddenly became hysterical, began to sob, and through his tears cried, 'I am afraid ... they'll kill me. Let me in!' ... [H]e stuck his right hand into the pocket of his jacket and pulled out a revolver, saying, 'See? This is what I must now carry to protect my life,' and placed the revolver on the desk where we were sitting opposite one another.
>
> I was dumbfounded and looked at Pavel, who had turned slightly pale but then quickly said to me, 'Here, give me that piece.' I took the revolver from the table and handed it to Pavel. Oswald, sobbing, wiped away his tears. He did not respond to my movements. Pavel, who had grabbed the revolver, opened the chamber, shook the bullets into his hand, and put them in a desk drawer. He then handed the revolver to me, and I put it back on the desk. Oswald continued to sob, then pulled himself together ...
>
> Valery [Kostikov] concludes: 'At this moment Oleg [Nechiporenko] literally flew into the room with his athletic bag and stopped in his tracks when he saw all of us sitting there. I looked at my watch. It was a little after ten o'clock, meaning we were already late for our volleyball game.' As he, too, joined in, Yatskov explained: 'In response to his persistent requests that we recommend that the Cubans give him a visa, as an alternative to obtaining our visa, we told him that Cuba was a sovereign nation and decided visa questions for itself.'
>
> Oswald gradually calmed down, evidently after having understood and reconciled himself to the fact that he was not about to get a quick visa. He did not take the forms we offered him.

[FF] An important day: Lee will be interviewed and hired to work at the Texas School Book Depository.
[GG] This smacks of "Catch 22", but is like a health insurance provider delaying until Medicare makes its decision, then following suit — which is a similarly-intentioned term from the game of bridge.

His state of extreme agitation had now been replaced by depression. He looked disappointed and extremely frustrated. Valery and I exchanged glances and let it be known that the subject of this conversation had been exhausted and that it was time to break it up. ... Oswald got up from his chair, and simultaneously grabbed the revolver and stuck it somewhere under his jacket, either in a pocket or in his belt. ... I bent down to get the bullets from the desk drawer. I then handed them to Oswald, who dropped them into a pocket of his jacket. We said good-bye with a nod of our heads." [1342]

"After Oswald had left, the three of us remained in the consulate and exchanged our impressions about this strange visitor. As a result of our two-day conversations with him we decided we could not take Oswald seriously. His nervousness during the conversations, his rambling and even nonsensical speech at times, his avoidance of answering specific questions, and the shifts from strong agitation to depression gave us reason to believe that his mental state was unstable or that, at the very least, he suffered from a serious nervous disorder." [1343]

Marina testified that when he returned to Texas, he was convinced that his trip had been a failure, and disappointed at having been unable to go to Cuba. [1344] A month later, in a painstakingly composed [1345] letter to the Soviet Embassy in Washington, Oswald ascribed his failure to "a gross breach of regulations" on the part of the Cuban Embassy. "Of corse," he wrote, "the Soviet Embassy was not at fault, they were, as I say unprepared." [1346]

Oswald now prepared his return to the United States. He paid $20.30 for bus tickets from Mexico City to Laredo, then on to Dallas. The travel agency recorded the reservation in the name of "H. O. Lee." [1347] Their employee testified that he probably wrote the name that way because he copied from Oswald's tourist card, which said "Lee, Harvey Oswald." [1348] When he doesn't deliberately invent false names, he accepts what others create for him.

His bus left Mexico City on October 1; he crossed into Texas, [1349] then rode a Greyhound bus directly to Dallas. [1350] "By 2:30 on the afternoon of October 3, Lee was in Dallas, only one week and one day after leaving New Orleans. He had spent perhaps $100 [HH] on the trip, but its cost to him could not be measured only in money. The real cost was the destruction of his hope. He had yearned to belong, to join a cause, to become a revolutionary, a volunteer for 'Uncle Fidel.' He had wanted to deploy his shooting skills in behalf of a tiny, embattled country that surely needed him. Instead, he was told by no less a figure than the Cuban consul that people like him were harmful to the cause of revolution. He must have suffered a grave new wound to his self-esteem." [1351] He had given up on New Orleans, Fair Play for Cuba, Mexico City, Cuba and Russia as the lifelines to save his sad sinking situation. He went back to Texas although it had been only a field fertile for frequent failures.

Lee did not contact Marina when he returned, instead going to the office of the state employment commission, where he filed an unemployment compensation claim and announced that he was again looking for work. [1352] In less than two weeks, in one of history's cruelest near-misses, this contact will engender a response one day too late to give Lee a good job that would have spared the grieving of hundreds of millions. He spent the night at the YMCA, where he registered as a serviceman in order to avoid paying the membership fee. [1353]

Friday, October 4, will be important for several events that do not appear to be related, but continue a convergence toward the shooting seven weeks later. In Dallas, Lee applied for a job as a typesetter trainee at the Padgett Printing Co. He made a favorable impression on the

---

[HH] The *Warren Report*'s "Analysis of Lee Harvey Oswald's Finances" carefully estimates his precise costs of transportation, hotel, food, entertainment and miscellaneous, for a total of $84.45.

department foreman, but this prospective employer did what all others had skipped, to their eventual regret. The plant superintendent called Jaggars-Chiles-Stovall and decided not to hire Oswald because of the unfavorable response.[1354] So, Lee needs a job and his reputation is bad.

That same day, "Governor Connally traveled to Washington to discuss the details of the visit and to ask President Kennedy what he would like to do. The President agreed that the details of events in Texas should be left largely up to the Governor." [1355] "Connally ... asked if Jackie would come along. ... [I]t seemed unlikely she would agree. ... She had declined to campaign with her husband since the 1960 primaries, and she was not scheduled to resume her activities as first lady until early 1964." [1356] But, as we will soon see, the seed has been planted for Mrs. Kennedy to make the trip, which will seat her in the limo beside her husband. As a result of Jackie's presence, the Governor will bring his wife along and similarly sit beside his Nellie. Thus, Connally will be directly in line in front of — not beside — Kennedy.

In the third and final event on that Friday, Lee telephoned Marina to tell her he was in Texas, and asked her to have Ruth pick him up in Dallas. Marina refused, and he hitchhiked out to the Paine home to stay the weekend.[1357] Marina testified that although her husband "changed for the better" and treated her better after his Mexican trip, she did not want to live with him.[1358] So, his marriage has fallen to a new nadir.

On October 7, as Lee played his small sad role in Texas, Jack Kennedy's world statesmanship and Jackie's historical sense were coupled when the President signed one of his major initiatives, a new treaty limiting nuclear testing, in the White House's Treaty Room, newly renovated through Jacqueline's leadership and dedication. The Kennedys were elegant.

On that Monday, Mrs. Paine drove Oswald to the bus station and he returned to Dallas to look for a job and a room.[1359] It's time for a bit of comic relief via a situation in which Lee is a victim, not the perpetrator. He thought the YMCA too expensive, so responded to a "FOR RENT" sign at a house in the neighborhood where he habitually rented, Oak Cliff, southwest of downtown Dallas. He obtained a room, paid $7 for the week and moved in.[1360] Almost daily, he continued his search for work. Landlady Mrs. Mary Bledsoe gave 28 fine-print pages of testimony to the Warren Commission, in which the roots of her problem with Lee became apparent. She had been "born in the country", raised in Ennis, married at 17, was uneducated and with no particular experience of the world. She recounted this Saturday conversation, five days after he'd paid for a week, when she saw him carrying out a duffelbag:[II]

"... [H]e started out with his bag and ... I thought he was going to move and ... I said, 'You are going to move?' And he said, 'No; I am just going for the weekend.' Well, I said, 'Well, I don't know.' But he said, 'And I want my room cleaned and clean sheets put on the bed.' And I said, 'Well, I will after you move because you are going to move.' He said, 'Why?' I says, 'Because I am not going to rent to you any more.' He said, 'Give me back my money, $2.' I said, 'Well, I don't have it.' So, he left Saturday morning ..." [1361]

Warren Commission counsel Joseph A. Ball thought this might be important, so asked:

"'Why did you tell him you wouldn't rent to him any more?' Mrs. Bledsoe: 'Because I didn't like him.' Mr. Ball: 'Why?' Mrs. Bledsoe: 'I didn't like his attitude. He was just kind of like this, you know, just big shot, you know, and I didn't have anything to say to him, and—but, I didn't like him. There was just something about him I didn't like or want him—just wasn't the kind of person I wanted. Just didn't want him around me.'" [1362]

With continued questioning, counsel Ball pinned down more specific reasons for the dislike:

[II] Here one word, spelled as in the *Warren Report*. There are four choices: one / two words; el / le.

Mrs. Bledsoe had a small house, four bedrooms on one floor sharing one bathroom. She had begun to rent only the previous month, so was not used to strangers in her house, in such close quarters. Worse, she expected roomers to use only their bedrooms and briefly share the bathroom — and on his first day Lee had asked to put a quart of milk into her refrigerator! Even worse, she always took a nap in the afternoon, and on several days he came home from job hunting and, no matter how quiet, he wakened her! Finally, in her opinion the worst of all: " ... [H]e talked to somebody on the phone, and talked in a foreign language.[JJ] ... I was in my room, and the telephone is over there (indicating), and I didn't like that, somebody talking in a foreign language and, so I told my girl friend, I said, 'I don't like anybody talking in a foreign language.'" [1363] Oh, the horrors!

Well, it was all too much for Mrs. Bledsoe, so poor Lee was thrown out and did not get the $2 she owed him, for the fact he'd paid $7 for seven days and was evicted after only five. Mrs. Bledsoe had more to tell the Commission, to be related in the next chapter when she testifies to what happened on her bus on November 22, a few minutes after the shooting.

Let us pause to reflect on the large ramification of this tiny event. If Mrs. Bledsoe had not taken naps, nor found milk in the refrigerator, nor heard a foreign language, she well may not have made him leave — in which case he would not flee to a rooming house on a different street after the shooting, so would not have been stopped near there by poor Officer Tippit, might have escaped or hidden a couple of days before arrest, so would not have been in the jail basement on Sunday to be shot, thus probably would have lived to testify at trial — and this book would not be necessary to state and demonstrate that his intention on the bloody Friday was to get even with John Connally. Yes, that's a long sequence of supposition, but certainly not any particular stretch of the very real probabilities.

Oswald spent the weekend of October 12-13 at Mrs. Paine's home.[1364] "According to Ruth, Oswald feared that he was losing some job opportunities because he could not drive and could only work at places reached by public transportation. That weekend, she gave him his first driving lesson. He drove three blocks to a parking lot and then around the lot, but Ruth said he was 'pretty unskilled.'" [1365] He told her he had received the last of the unemployment checks due him, and it had been smaller than the previous ones. Ruth testified that Lee was extremely discouraged because his wife was expecting a baby, he had no job prospects in sight, and he no longer had any source of income.[1366] The sad descent continues.

On Monday, October 14, Ruth drove Lee into Dallas.[1367] When he picked up his bag from Mrs. Bledsoe's roominghouse [1368], she said "Good luck" to him, but "You know, I thought to myself, 'That's good riddance.'" [1369] In the familiar Oak Cliff neighborhood he spotted "ROOM FOR RENT" on a boardinghouse at 1026 North Beckley Street, and rented a room in it for $8 per week. Manager and housekeeper Earlene Roberts testified to the Warren Commission — repeatedly moaning "to my sorrows" — that he registered and was known as O. H. Lee.[1370] She described "O. H. Lee" to the Commission: "He was just the type of person you just don't know—and I just thought he didn't like people and he would mix with nobody and he wouldn't say nothing. The only time he would ever say anything was when his rent was due ..." [1371]

Secretive as always, and perhaps to hide from the dreaded FBI, Lee "forbade Marina, who was still living with Ruth ... to tell anyone where he was living." [1372]

[JJ] Almost certainly Russian, to Marina.

Upon returning to her home in Irving, Ruth walked across the street with Marina to the most consequential kaffeeklatsch [KK] to now in the nearly fourteen billion years of this Universe. Ruth, Marina and neighbors Dorothy Roberts and Linnie Mae Randle were discussing Lee's difficulty in obtaining work. Roberts and Randle were also young mothers, and they clearly empathized with Oswald's predicament, especially since Marina's second child was about to be born. Linnie Mae Randle recalled that Buell Wesley Frazier ("I go by Wesley." [1373]), her younger brother, "had just looked for a job, and I had helped him try to find one. We listed several places that he might go to look for work. When you live in a place you know some places that someone with, you know, not very much of an education can find work." [1374] Mrs. Randle said that Wesley had applied for jobs at Manor Bakery and Texas Gypsum Company, but both involved driving a truck, so they were not practical for Lee. [1375]

"Then Mrs. Randle mentioned that her brother [age 19] [1376] had found a job [one month before] [1377] at the Texas School Book Depository, a warehouse that distributed educational books. [1378] 'I didn't know there was a job opening over there. But we said he might try over there. There might be work . . . because it was the busy season . . . .'" [1379] "Marina later urged Ruth: 'Would you please call the Texas School Depository?' 'I looked up the number in the book,' recalled Ruth, 'and dialed it, was told I would need to speak to Mr. Truly, who was at the warehouse. The phone was taken to Mr. Truly . . . and I talked with him . . .'" [1380]

Roy Truly had begun with the TSBD in 1934 and was now its superintendent. Months later, he recalled October 14: "She said, 'Mr. Truly, you don't know who I am but I have a neighbor whose brother works for you. I don't know what his name is. But he tells his sister that you are very busy. And I am just wondering if you can use another man,' or words to that effect. ... She said, 'I have a fine young man living here with his wife and baby, and his wife is expecting a baby—another baby, in a few days, and he needs work desperately.' ... And I told Mrs. Paine to send him down, and I would talk to him—that I didn't have anything in mind for him of a permanent nature, but if he was suited, we could possibly use him for a brief time. ... She told me she would tell him to come down and see me." [1381]

Lee "telephoned Ruth's home that evening to speak to Marina. [LL] Ruth got on the phone at the end of the conversation and told him about Truly, encouraging him to apply at the Texas School Book Depository as soon as possible." [1382]

The next day, Lee went to Dealey Plaza at the west end of downtown Dallas. "So he came in," Truly testified, "introduced himself to me, and I took him in my office and interviewed him. He seemed to be quiet and well mannered. I gave him an application to fill out, which he did. ... I asked him about experience that he had had, or where he had worked, and he said he had just served his term in the Marine Corps and had received an honorable discharge, and he listed some things of an office nature he had learned to do in the Marines.

"I questioned him about any past activities. I asked him if he had ever had any trouble with the police and he said, no. So thinking that he was just out of the Marines, I didn't check any further back. I didn't have anything of a permanent nature in mind for him. He looked like a nice young fellow to me ... He used the word 'sir', you know, which a lot of them don't do at this time." [1383] "Truly had two possibilities for Oswald. One position was in a storage

---

[KK] From German for "coffee" and "gossip". Thus, "ladies gathered together in small groups at one another's houses to sip coffee and talk." — http://www.kaffeeklatschseattle.com/what-is-kaffeeklatsch.html
[LL] Probably in Russian. Oh, the horrors!

warehouse some distance from Dealey Plaza. The other was as a clerk at the main Depository. Truly decided he seemed earnest enough to hire him as a clerk at the main building, to fill book orders, at $1.25 per hour." [1384] Thus, another tiny but essential step on a path to death.

Built in 1901,[1385] "The sore-eyed, tan brick structure at the corner of Houston and Elm … began as railroad offices, became a branch of the John Deere Plow Company, served later as the headquarters of a wholesaler for fancy groceries, and was converted early in the 1960's,

 to a warehouse for the Texas School Book Depository. The interior is grimy, the two freight elevators are temperamental. But if you really want a proper perspective of [Dealey Plaza] the sixth floor of the warehouse is incomparable." [1386] The building "was occupied by a private corporation, which distributed school textbooks of several publishers and leased space to representatives of the publishers. Most of the employees in the building worked for these publishers. The balance, including a 15-man warehousing crew, were employees of the Texas School Book Depository Co. itself.[1387] The photo [1388] looks from Main Street, along Houston to the Depository's front on Elm, exactly as the Kennedys and Connallys will first see it as their motorcade jogs north.

"So I told him if he would come to work on the morning of the 16th, it was the beginning of a new pay period. So he filled out his withholding slip, with the exception of the number of dependents. He asked me if he could hold that for 3 or 4 days, that he is expecting a baby momentarily. … He left, and I didn't see him any more until the morning of the 16th [the next day]. … His hours were from 8 in the morning until 4:45 in the afternoon. His lunch period was from 12 to 12:45." [1389] "Oswald was elated when he telephoned Marina that night. He told her it was good to be working with books, the work would not tire him." [1390]

The seven paragraphs above constitute a high hurdle that, to this author's considerable knowledge, no conspiracy theorist has ever cleared: All those involved — Marina, Ruth, Linnie Mae, Dorothy, Wesley and Roy — testified to the Warren Commission that the events of October 14 to 16 were precisely as stated here. These are all good, honest people, telling the truth. Lee did not get into the tall building that will overlook the motorcade in five weeks through any conspiracy! Chapter 9 will examine and reject all conspiracy theories.

This author does not know of any theorist who ever accused Roy Truly of being an assassination conspirator. Thus, any suggestion that Oswald was planted at the TSBD building overlooking Dealey Plaza must somehow circumvent Truly's even-handed choices that day. Despite no compelling need for an additional worker, he hired Oswald for temporary work because he liked his manners, influenced by Ruth's desperate plea of the family's need and the imminent birth. If Truly had decided against Oswald, or if he'd assigned him to the storage warehouse, none of us would ever have heard of Oswald or Truly, and this and thousands of assassination books would not have been printed, and forests would be thicker with more trees, and the atmosphere would contain less carbon dioxide, and our globe would be less warm.

November 22 was rooted years before — with marksman training in the Marines, the undesirable discharge, the appeal for help that Connally did not give, the purchase of a rifle to shoot General Walker, etc, etc. — and now rises into history when two ladies visit a neighbor where there is mention of a brother's new job, then an appeal by Ruth to a supervisor's good nature, and his taking on a new man for a lowly job. It's all small, random, and deadly.

Here's a similar decision, small at the time, with major consequences: In Alabama in 1955, 42-year-old Rosa Parks, tired, stopped going along with wrong, so refused to give up her seat to a white man and move to the back of a segregated bus. Her arrest resulted in protests, a 380-day bus boycott, desegregation of transportation in Montgomery, and gave the civil rights movement a shove. Rosa lived to be 92 and died in 2005. She'd have been amazed and proud to know who came to sit in her seat on that bus.[1391] Every little thing may matter!

Roy Truly remembered October 16: "He came to work the next morning. I told him what his duties were to be ... filling book orders. ... He worked with [an experienced worker], it seems to me, like only an hour or two, and then he started filling orders by himself. And from then on he worked alone." [1392] "His primary responsibility was to fill textbook orders, by finding the books in the seven-floor Depository and then bringing them to the first floor, where the orders were processed. The work atmosphere was a relaxed one, and people left Lee alone, which he liked. [When not working, he] sat by himself, reading day-old [MM] newspapers. 'He never would speak to anyone ...'" [1393]

"Lee was [assigned a specialty,] Scott, Foresman [1394] textbooks, which were located on the first and sixth [emphasis mine] floors of the building. ... The depository was an easygoing, live-and-let-live sort of place. The men mostly gathered in a small, first-floor recreation room they called the 'domino room.' There they ate sandwiches at noon, made coffee, and played dominoes. ... Most days Lee made a point of getting to work early and reading newspapers that had been left in the domino room the day before." [1395] [NN]

He would "rummage through yesterday's *Dallas Times Herald* or the current day's *Dallas News*. No one saw him buy a newspaper, but he often sat alone, running through the news items swiftly, seldom pausing to respond to a greeting." [1396] Co-worker Roy Lewis, in his oral history in Larry Sneed's excellent compilation *No More Silence*, recalled that Lee "was quiet, hardly ever talked to anybody, and kept his head in a newspaper all the time. Even when we were in the lunchroom together he'd hardly ever talk to anyone. [When teased] He just gave a little smirky smile and went on about his business reading the paper ..." [1397]

Before leaving the subject of Lee's hiring at the TSBD, there is one more cruel quirk to describe: the importance of timing. We have seen that he would not have known about the job at the Book Depository if Ruth and Marina had not gone to the kaffeeklatsch where Linnie Mae said her brother Wesley had been hired there and maybe Lee could get a job. We will now learn that if the ladies' chitchat had occurred only one day later, Lee very probably would not have taken that job— and the history of our world would be wonderfully different.

As described earlier, when Lee arrived in Dallas on October 3, he went immediately to the office of the Texas Employment Commission,[OO] applied for unemployment payments and asked help to find work. Employment interviewer Robert L. Adams of that commission

---

[MM] Nothing is unimportant! This eensy-teensy fact underpins Chapter 18 – CONNALLY WILL RIDE.
[NN] Endnote [1395] cites testimony by five workers: He didn't buy papers, he read their day-old leftovers.
[OO] 1025 Elm Street, the same as the Book Depository, the street where President Kennedy will die.

testified that on the Monday after the assassination weekend, the day both John Kennedy and Lee Oswald were buried: "I came to work, I said, 'I'll bet that boy is in my files.'" Sure enough, an "employment, application, counseling and referral card" showed he had assisted Lee three times.[1398] On October 7 and 9, with new leads for electronic sales clerk and clerk trainee jobs, he had left messages at Ruth's. Lee was interviewed but not hired for either.

On October 15, Mr. Adams phoned with a third and much better job prospect. Adams testified and signed an affidavit that he spoke with someone (the card does not show whom) at the Paines' number to give Oswald a referral for permanent employment as a ramp agent (we also know them as baggage or cargo handlers) at Trans-Texas Airways [PP] for a starting salary of $310 a month. Adams told the Warren Commission, "I learned from the person who answered the phone that Oswald was not there. [Lee was at the Texas School Book Depository being hired by Roy Truly for temporary work at $1.25 an hour.] I left a message with that person that Oswald should contact me at the Commission." [1399] Adams called again the next morning about the permanent TTA job. That October 16 was the day Lee had begun temp work at the TSBD. Adams said he "learned from the person who answered that Oswald was not there and that he had in the meantime obtained employment and was working." [1400]

Adams cancelled Oswald as a candidate for the ramp agent opportunity, and so far as we know, Lee never knew of that better job at the airport. Robert Adams opined: "Inasmuch as I did not talk with Oswald either by telephone or in person in connection with this job order, I do not know whether he was ever advised of this referral, but under the circumstances I do not see how he could have been." [1401] If Lee had known, he would have jumped at the TTA opening. His temporary TSBD job, if worked full time for a month, would pay about $217. The permanent work at Trans-Texas paid $310, 43% more! Marina testified that after Lee took the Book Depository job, he was still answering want ads because "of course, he wanted to get something better." [1402]

Timing is everything! If Ruth and Marina had gone to coffee one day later, or if Trans-Texas Airways had acted one day earlier, we would be living in a world with a happier history — probably at the price of ramp agent Lee misdirecting lots of passenger bags.

Both Oswalds were elated with the new job,[1403] although it apparently required little skill or experience [1404] and he said he still hoped to obtain a better job.[1405] He did satisfactory work at the Depository,[1406] but kept to himself and very few of his fellow employees got to know him.[1407] "But one person who engaged him in a brief conversation that first week was Buell ['Wesley'] Frazier, Linnie Mae Randle's brother. When Frazier discovered that Oswald's wife was staying at the Paines' house in Irving, he realized they were neighbors, as Frazier lived only a block from the Paines. ... Frazier recalled ... 'And he told me then . . . that he didn't have a car, you know, and so I told him . . . anytime you want to go just let me know.' So I thought he would be going home every day like most men do but he told me no, that he wouldn't go home every day and then he asked me could he ride home say like Friday afternoon on weekends and come back on Monday morning and I told him that would be just fine with me." [1408] Friday, October 18, Frazier drove him from work to the Paine house.[1409] It

_____

[PP] If you think this a short-term prospect because you never heard of Trans-Texas: Not! In 1969 it was renamed Texas International Airlines, in 1982 TIA merged with Continental Airlines, which in 2010 merged with United Airlines. Lee could have been in on the ground floor of a major success — but more likely he would have been fired after a few months for his habitual neglect of duty.

was Lee's twenty-fourth birthday; and Marina and Ruth had arranged a small celebration.[1410] "There was a birthday cake, decorations, and wine. ... Marina remembered that Lee was so touched that he had tears in his eyes. He was emotional the remainder of the evening, crying and apologizing to Marina for what he had put her through." [1411] Marina told biographer McMillan that the next evening, Saturday, "He kissed her, they made love, and Marina was exceedingly happy. It was the last time they had full intercourse." [1412]

On Sunday, October 20, he stayed with June and the Paine children while Ruth drove (Lee still does not know how to drive) Marina to Parkland Hospital where she gave birth to a daughter.[1413] When Ruth told him the news in the morning, Lee "seemed reluctant to visit the hospital." [1414] "Ruth was surprised ... until she discovered he feared that if the hospital knew he had a job, he would have to pay for Marina's stay. But Ruth had already told the hospital the previous evening that he was employed, and she assured him that his salary was so low that the maternity care was still free." [1415] Lee went to work on Monday, but that evening visited the hospital.[1416] Marina wrote:

> "Monday evening Lee visited me in the hospital. He was very happy at the birth of another daughter and even wept a little. He said that two daughters were better for each other—two sisters. He stayed with me about two hours." [1417]

"They had already talked about a name. If it was a boy, he was to be David Lee (no more 'Fidel'), and Lee had promised that in the choice of a girl's name he wouldn't interfere. But he now asked Marina what name she had put down on the baby's certificate. She had chosen 'Audrey Rachel,' 'Audrey' for Audrey Hepburn and 'Rachel' because Ruth had a niece called Rachel and Marina liked the name very much. Lee took exception to Rachel. 'It sounds too Jewish,' he said. 'Please call her Marina. Do it for me. I want our little girl to have your name.' The next day Marina simply added 'Marina' to the certificate—'Audrey Marina Rachel Oswald.' But from the outset the baby was called Rachel, and Rachel she is to this day." [1418]

TSBD supervisor Roy "Truly saw him every day. 'Good morning, Lee,' he would say. 'Good morning, sir.' Mr. Truly would ask how his new baby was, and Lee's face just broke wide open into a smile." [1419] After working a few days, he told Marina "He liked Mr. Truly a great deal and the other men were nice to him, too." [1420]

"Preparations for a presidential trip are known as 'advancing'—a lively art that demands a sturdy constitution, a flair for diplomacy, and a love for traveling under the most chaotic of circumstances. The best of the lot was Jerry Bruno, a compact little dynamo ..." [1421] "Over a month before the trip, Bruno demanded that the Texas planners' motorcade route [past the TSBD] not be taken. ... In late October, Bruno flew to Dallas to specifically meet with Connally ... In his book, *The Advanceman*, Bruno described the unusual and bitter fight that he had with Connally over the ... route. ... Connally got on the telephone to the White House and ... the White House agreed with his plans since he was in charge of the trip." [1422]

Another slim strand leading to tragedy on Elm Street strengthened that week. After the death of premature Patrick, Jacqueline Kennedy had left children and husband in the White House while she recovered in Greece for several weeks with her sister Lee Radziwill, some of it sunning on the yacht of Aristotle Onassis. Paparazzi supplied photos and tell-alls, and many disapproved. Close friends Ben and Tony (for "Antoinette") Bradlee were dinner guests at the White House on October 22, five days after Jackie's return, a month before death in Dallas. Newspaperman Ben took notes and later wrote about that intimate dinner:

"Chief topics for discussion tonight were Jackie's recent trip to Greece and a stay on Aristotle Onassis' yacht ... There had been substantial press criticism of Jackie's trip. The president had promised it to her as a way of recuperating from the hammer blow of the death of her last child, but the papers had been full of stories ..." [1423] "The president noted that what he called 'Jackie's guilt feelings' may work to his advantage. 'Maybe now you'll come with us to Texas next month,' he said with a smile. And Jackie answered: 'Sure I will, Jack.'" [1424]

"[S]he flipped open her red leather engagement book and scrawled 'Texas' across November 21 ...22 ... 23." [1425] "Jackie's decision to campaign surprised [her press secretary] Pamela Turnure. 'It was significant,' Turnure recalled, 'the first domestic trip she had ever taken with the President as President.' [QQ] Turnure wanted to know what to tell the press. 'Say I am going out with my husband on this trip and that it will be the first of many that I hope to make with him,' Jackie instructed. 'Say yes that I plan to campaign with him and that I will do anything to help my husband be elected President again.'" [1426]

At that same White House dinner on October 22, it was again proven that the world is small and inhabited by only a few surprisingly-interrelated people. Ben Bradlee journaled:

"[W]e discussed the case of the secretary of the Navy, Fred Korth, who had resigned a week ago. Korth had ostensibly quit over a disagreement with McNamara on the subject of construction of a nuclear-powered aircraft carrier ... Actually Korth had been asked to resign, after he had been caught using official Navy stationery for private business purposes ... to enrich through stock manipulation ... The president said he was convinced it was more a question of stupidity that anything else . . . more unethical than illegal." [1427]

Korth had replaced Connally as Secretary of the Navy, so he approved the final decision to not change Oswald's undesirable discharge. Also close to this story, he'd been the Fort Worth attorney representing Marguerite Oswald in her 1948 divorce from third husband Ekdahl.

On the following day, October 23, right-wing zealot resigned-General Edwin Walker made a speech in Dallas, damning the United Nations as a threat to American freedoms. The next day, observed elsewhere in the nation as UN Day, delegate to the UN Adlai Stevenson tried to speak in the same auditorium, but had to leave the podium because of booing and heckling. He was spit upon as he walked out of the auditorium through a large jeering crowd of anti-UN protestors, "armed with placards that had been stored in the home of General Walker." [1428] A matronly agitator bloodied the ambassador's bald head by striking it with her picket sign. Stevenson soon advised President Kennedy to avoid Dallas.

Lee went with Michael Paine to an October 25 meeting of the American Civil Liberties Union at Southern Methodist University. [1429] In a discussion with several people, Oswald declared that he was a Marxist, although not a Communist. He admitted that the United States was superior to the Soviet Union in the area of civil liberties and praised President Kennedy for his work in that connection. [1430] Marina and Rachel returned from hospital to the Paine home during the week, [1431] and Lee visited them in Irving the next two weekends. [1432]

"The following Monday, November 4, the Secret Service in Dallas was instructed by the White House to examine three potential luncheon sites for November 22, the date chosen for the President's Dallas visit. One site, the Women's Building at the State Fairgrounds,

---

[QQ] She was an Easterner who saw the USA as Saul Steinberg's famous 1976 *New Yorker* cover looking west from 9th Avenue. Past the Hudson River is narrow New Jersey, then a flat barren land with only a few mesas and Las Vegas before Los Angeles on the Pacific Ocean, which is only as wide as the Hudson. In fact, the First Lady had not been west of Virginia since the 1960 election!

lacked the necessary food-handling capacity, and the Market Hall was already booked for that date. That left the Trade Mart, and though it presented additional security problems, Forrest Sorrels, special agent in charge of the Dallas office, was convinced special precautions could protect the President [so he] recommended the Trade Mart be selected for the luncheon." [1433]

Since the dinner two weeks before, Jacqueline vacillated several times about going to Texas. John Connally called the White House, raising hell when she wasn't coming; she was popular and needed to be there. On November 7, it was announced that Jackie would join her husband in Texas, a trip that would include her first visit to the Johnson Ranch in Stonewall. The Johnsons made special preparations to please their guests: a hard mattress for Jack, a supply of Poland Water, and a walking horse in readiness for Jackie. There would also be swimming, a ranch tour, a demonstration of roping and herding at the barbecue grounds.

"Connally scheduled a fundraiser at the governor's mansion in Austin on Friday night, November 22, but otherwise the President's trip consisted of speeches at 'nonpartisan' events in San Antonio, Houston, Fort Worth, and Dallas. 'Kennedy wanted to come to Texas for money,' said George Christian. 'He needed support. It was his idea.'" [1434]

On Friday, November 8, as usual, Lee rode to the Paine house with Buell "Wesley" Frazier. [1435] On Saturday Ruth took him to the Texas Drivers' License Examining Station for a learner's permit, but the station was closed because it was an election day. Throughout this period, the FBI had been aware of the whereabouts of the Oswalds. FBI agent James P. Hosty visited the Paine home on November 1 and 5, and spoke with Mrs. Paine. On neither occasion was Oswald present. [1436] "Hosty's [second] visit ended as it began, on a friendly note. Marina was all smiles. She would be glad to have such a pleasant visitor any day. Hosty wrote out his name, office address, and telephone number for Ruth to give to Lee. Since Ruth was sure Lee had nothing to hide, she expected that he would go straight to the FBI himself." [1437]

Lee was immediately troubled by the FBI's interest, [1438] complaining that the agents were "trying to inhibit" his activities. [1439] He used Ruth's typewriter to type a letter to the Soviet Embassy, [1440] complaining of "tactics by the notorious FBI." [1441] "Ruth was certain that Lee was not an agent and knew nothing of interest to a foreign power. It seemed clear to her that he was 'neither bright enough nor steady enough to have been recruited' by anyone. [Take that, conspiracy theorists!] Since he had nothing to hide, she thought by far the best thing he could do was go to the FBI office ... and tell them everything they wanted to know. Only in this way would they, too, see that he had nothing to hide." [1442]

Special Agent Hosty, assigned to handle many cases, gave the Oswald investigation a low priority. He believes that Lee is simply a young man fond of communism, losing one job after another, with a troubled marriage and separated from his wife. Hosty found no need for urgency, concluding that Oswald will bumble along and maybe be worth his interest, later.

During the weekend, Ruth gave him yet another driving lesson, [1443] but Lee will die in two weeks without ever having a license. He stayed at the Paine home through Veterans Day on Monday. On that day [RR] two-year-old John Kennedy Jr. was to accompany his father to the annual wreath-laying ceremony at Arlington National Cemetery. "Mrs. Kennedy had been trying to explain to John-John [SS] what Veterans Day was all about and how he was going to get

---

[RR] It was Armistice Day when this author was younger, marking the 1918 armistice that ended WWI at the 11th hour of the 11th day of the 11th month.

[SS] Outsiders called him by this cute double name, but his parents and relatives did not. See chapter 7.

to see real soldiers with their swords when Daddy took him to the ceremony. She'd explained that Daddy was the commander in chief, and all the soldiers would be saluting him, so perhaps John should salute him, too. He'd practiced several times before anybody realized he was using his left hand. Once he got the hang of raising his right hand to his forehead, though, his arm had grown tired, and the salute was rather droopy. 'Mr. Foster will help you practice again tomorrow, John,' Mrs. Kennedy had said. 'You'll look just like the other soldiers when you salute the commander in chief.'" [1444]

Secret Service Special Agent Bob Foster practiced with John, then accompanied him to Arlington. The photo from Jerry Blaine's *The Kennedy Detail* is captioned: "John Kennedy, Jr., waits to salute his father, the Commander in Chief, at Arlington National Ceremony on Veterans Day 1963. Two weeks later, JFK is buried there." [1445] "The president walked silently toward the Tomb of the Unknown Soldier and placed the presidential wreath against it. The uniformed military color guard saluted in unison, and standing on the sidelines, Bob Foster leaned over to John-John and whispered, 'Okay. Time to salute Daddy.' His hand was still a bit curved, more like he was shading his eyes from the sun, but John-John had remembered to use his right hand. Unfortunately, his father didn't get to see it, but Foster would have John-John reenact the scene for him when they got back to the White House. The president would get a real kick out of it." [1446]

The day after the holiday, "during the noon hour, taking Ruth's advice, in a way, [Lee] went to the main FBI office at 1114 Commerce Street, not far from the depository. He walked up to the receptionist, Nanny Lee Fenner, looking 'awfully fidgety,' with what she later said was 'a wild look in his eye' and an unsealed envelope in his hand. He asked if Agent Hosty was in, and she told him Hosty was out to lunch. 'Well, get this to him,' he said, and tossed the envelope on her desk. He turned and walked back to the elevator.

"Soon afterward Hosty stopped by. 'Some nut left this for you,' Mrs. Fenner said, and handed Hosty the letter. The envelope, a 10-inch white business envelope, had one word written across it—'Hasty.' It contained a single sheet of 8 by 10 bond paper. It had no greeting, no signature, and no return address. There were only two handwritten paragraphs. One stated that Hosty had been interviewing the wife of the author without permission and the author did not like it. If you want to see me, come to me. Don't bother my wife, it said. In the next paragraph, the writer warned that if Hosty did not stop talking to his wife, he would be forced to take action against the FBI. He did not say what that action might be. Since the note was not signed, Hosty was not certain who had left it. He surmised that it might be Oswald or one other person who had been giving him trouble. Either way the complaint seemed 'innocuous,' the kind he got a good many of, and it did not appear to require action. He put it in his work box and left it." [1447]

On Wednesday the thirteenth, the Kennedys watch a pipe and drums performance by a crown jewel from Great Britain, the pipers of the Royal Highlanders Black Watch Regiment.[1448] They

"sat tightly together against the November chill as they listened from the South Portico balcony to the melancholic strains of bagpipers."[1449] Only twelve days later, the Scots will return to play their sad, wonderful music for the President's funeral.

"On Thursday, November 14, the White House gave its approval of the selection of the Trade Mart as a luncheon site. Once it was chosen, the Secret Service was directed to determine a motorcade route that would allow forty-five minutes for the President to travel from Love Field airport to the Trade Mart. That day, agents Forrest Sorrels and Winston Lawson drove over a possible route. They then met with Dallas police ..."[1450] who "reviewed the route the following day ... The *Dallas Times Herald* announced the Trade Mart selection on November 15 ..."[1451]

"Lee called Marina on Friday the fifteenth to discuss visiting for the weekend (he always first called to ask permission). She did not think it was a good idea, because Michael [Paine] was staying that weekend to celebrate his daughter's birthday, and Lee might have worn out his welcome with the three-day holiday weekend just past."[1452] Lee responded: "Well, it's a family celebration. I don't want to be in the way."[1453]

After "The Trade Mart had been selected for the luncheon ... the final leg of the routing was clear. There was no option off Main Street other than the right turn on Houston Street ... followed by a sharp left on Elm Street. The entrance to Stemmons Freeway was just a few hundred yards or so beyond that, with a right-lane merge after the underpass."[1454]

On Saturday, November 16, both Dallas dailies headline the same feature: "[T]he *Morning News* [tells] Dallas about Kennedy's motorcade down Main Street. [Lee] will read that and realize the cars will go right past the place where he's working."[1455] "[T]he *Times Herald* published the Kennedy motorcade route. It would start at Love Field and end at the Trade Mart, where he would speak to the Dallas Citizens Council and their invited guests. The nominal purpose of his speech was to salute the Graduate Research Center and congratulate Dallas on its economic progress over the last decade, but the *Times Herald* was happy to inform those who didn't already know that the real reason was pure politics."[1456]

Lee habitually reads both papers after they have been left behind by co-workers in the Depository's lunchroom or "domino room". He may know the route that Saturday or Sunday, or maybe will learn it only on Monday from second-hand newspapers. In either case, he does not take any action upon learning that the President will be driven past his workplace. This inaction will be highlighted and analyzed in Chapter 18 – CONNALLY WILL RIDE.

Lee's poor situation and the relations between the Oswalds have been sliding downhill, but have not quite hit their rock bottom. That final depth will be reached rather unexpectedly on Sunday, November 17. When Marina "saw Junie playing with the telephone dial, saying 'Papa, Papa,' she decided impulsively, 'Let's call Papa.' Marina was helpless with a telephone dial,[TT] so it was Ruth who made the call. She dialed the number Lee had given her weeks before while they were awaiting Rachel's birth, and a man answered." [1457]

"'Is Lee Oswald there?' asked Ruth.
'There is no Lee Oswald living here.'
'Is this a rooming house?'
'Yes.'
'Is this WH3-8993?'
'Yes.'

"'I thanked him and hung up,' recalled Ruth. She turned to Marina and said, 'They don't know of a Lee Oswald at that number.' Marina was startled." [1458] Here she is thousands of miles from Minsk, no income, two babies, surviving as did Blanche DuBois in Tennessee Williams' *A Streetcar Named Desire*: "I have always depended on the kindness of strangers." Poor Marina was struck a hard blow. Now she had certainty that her husband deceived her.

Marina will testify to the Warren Commission: "He telephoned me on Monday, after I had called him on Sunday, and he was not there. Or, rather, he was there, but he wasn't called to the phone because he was known by another name." [1459] Professional historian William Manchester recognized the consistent character flaw: "It was typical of Lee's ineptness that he neglected to explain that he was living ... under an assumed name." [1460] "Ruth said, 'I was in the kitchen where the phone is while Marina talked with him, she clearly was upset, and angry...' Marina asked him where he had been the previous night, and he told her he was using a different name because of the FBI, but also became angry with her for calling the rooming house. She found his alias 'unpleasant and incomprehensible.' 'After all, when will all our foolishness come to an end?' demanded Marina. 'All of these comedies. First one thing then another. And now this fictitious name.'" [1461] Marina's vivid testimony continues: "On Monday he called several times, but after I hung up on him and didn't want to talk to him he did not call again. He then arrived on Thursday." [1462]

Gerald Ford noted Lee's nadir: "It is not difficult to see that in addition to his sense of personal failure, his inability to obtain prominent recognition he felt he had the genius to deserve, his marriage was likewise a failure." [1463]

On Monday, Dallas Chief of Police Jesse Curry drove Forrest V. Sorrels of the Secret Service's Dallas office and Special Agent Winston G. Lawson of the Secret Service advance team from Washington the ten selected motorcade miles from Love Field to the Trade Mart. "Sorrels glanced up at the Dallas skyline ... and said aloud, 'Hell, we'd be sitting ducks.' The other two concurred and shrugged. There were over twenty thousand windows overlooking the route; obviously they couldn't have a man in every one. It would take an army, and would defeat the very purpose of the motorcade. Therefore no windows were inspected ..." [1464]

"The President's visit was by far the biggest story in Dallas for the entire week ... *The Dallas Morning News* had eight different stories about it on Sunday, November 17, seven more on Tuesday the 19th, three on the 20th, and eight on the 21st. ... On Friday morning, the day of the event, eleven more stories dealt with the trip ..." [1465]

[TT] I trust you know a dial to be a round plate with holes you put a finger into and turn, seven times.

Here is the first of three wonderful maps made for this book by Cartographic Concepts Inc.[1466]

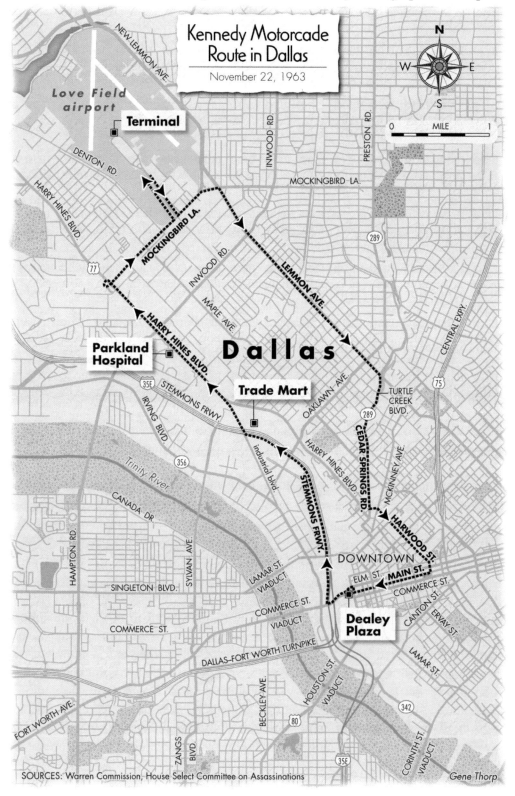

Kennedy Motorcade
Route in Dallas
November 22, 1963

SOURCES: Warren Commission, House Select Committee on Assassinations   Gene Thorp

Out of public view, there had been a "heated argument over the motorcade".[1467] For the fourth anniversary of the event, John Connally wrote an article for *Life* magazine, featured as a cover story, "Why Kennedy Went to Texas". I wanted to quote 290 of Connally's words from that article, but the syndication manager of *Life*'s owner, Time Inc., advised that their minimum fee for quoting from a magazine was $2,000 — and that I would have to pay even more because my not printing the entire article would require them to assign editors to inspect what I extracted to ensure it was true to the original. At something in the vicinity of $10 per word, that's far too rich for this retiree, so I brief the important points quoting only 10 words.

Connally wrote that he viewed Kennedy's schedule for November 22 to be overly draining, even without a motorcade in Dallas. He asked the White House planners to skip the motorcade, driving JFK directly from Love Field to the Trade Mart luncheon so he would be rested and in good spirits for that speech, and then later that day for two receptions and the trip's major speech in Austin. But, "I was overruled." [1468]

The governor despaired when the President's men not only dictated and planned the motorcade through the heart of Dallas, but published its route in the newspapers on Tuesday, "a full three days before the event." [1469] If Connally was really concerned about the route's publicity so far in advance of tragic Friday, he was to be proven incorrect, but for a perverse reason he could not have imagined. As will be the entire topic and purpose of important Chapter 18 – CONNALLY WILL RIDE, the actual threat will be the angry rejected ex-Marine who wanted to murder *him*. That man cared *not* about Kennedy, and won't learn that target Connally will be in the motorcade until he reads it from a later newspaper, on Thursday.

"Oswald did not call Marina on either Tuesday or Wednesday, the nineteenth and twentieth. The others at the rooming house noticed he sulked and did not use the phone. Oswald was simmering alone and did not want any contact with people, even his family. 'He thinks he's punishing me,' Marina told Ruth." [1470]

"That Tuesday, the *Dallas Times Herald* detailed the exact route of the presidential motorcade ... along Main Street, then turn onto Dealey Plaza, a public square that the Texas School Book Depository bordered ... then [left from] Houston Street [to] Elm Street before reaching the Stemmons Freeway." [1471] "The left turn onto Elm Street meant the cars would pass directly in front of the Depository. *The Dallas Morning News*, provided the same exacting details on both November 19 and 20." [1472] "There was no change in the motorcade route, and there was no doubt about the Elm Street crossing. Whether Oswald learned the route when first published or on the next day, when he followed his routine of reading day-old newspapers in the "domino room" of the Depository" [1473] is unknown and unimportant.

At this point, we are looking at the progression of events as they move along to a terrible Friday, November 22. Nine chapters from now the analysis of these events will begin, allowing a reasoned conclusion about what Lee Oswald intended when he fired his rifle.

There is considerable circumstantial evidence to be considered, and what I ask you to recall when we begin to balance the evidence to establish probabilities is very simply this: If Oswald had intended to shoot John F. Kennedy, he knew on Tuesday or Wednesday, November 19 or 20, all he needed to know about the traverse of that target past his building. He could have begun preparations two or three days before he was to shoot. The crucial point of important Chapter 18 – CONNALLY WILL RIDE is that he did *nothing* at all to prepare on Monday, Tuesday or Wednesday. Then it all changes as he sees the most important news article of the week, the one that will change history.

At left is the Warren Commission's display of a portion of the *Morning News* front page of Wednesday, November 20.[1474] Lee faithfully read this paper when it was left behind by his co-workers in the TSBD's domino room. Thus, he likely first saw this front page on Thursday morning, and must have focused on a short paragraph in its right-hand column:[1475]

> A security car will lead the motorcade which will travel on Mockingbird Lane, Lemmon Avenue, Turtle Creek Boulevard, Cedar Springs, Harwood, Main and Stemmons Freeway.
>
> President and Mrs. Kennedy and Gov. Connally will ride in the second car.
>
> Secret Service agents will ride in the next car and the fourth will carry Vice-President and Mrs. Johnson and Mrs. Connally.

It is difficult to believe in our security-conscious era that fifty years ago not only was the motorcade's exact route displayed in advance, but the sequence of vehicles with names of their occupants was made public. We would lose our innocence two days later, and never again would presidents ride in open cars, to be listed for assailants as if on a menu.

In fact, if you have recently been present for any ride-by of a president, you will have seen that the new norm is to have at least two, usually three, identical fancy cars or vans speeding along with U.S. and presidential flags flying — and no hint of which has the man (or woman!) him/herself behind its dark-tinted, bullet-proof windows.

The coming of President and Mrs. Kennedy in a motorcade past the Book Depository did not cause any action by Lee until he read what you see above. John Connally will be in the motorcade, riding with the Kennedys in the second car. Oswald found salvation, a remedy for the wrongs inflicted on him all his life, the redemption for his hopeless, pitiful condition. The despised-because-unhelpful Connally, "resident of Ft. Worth as I am" [1476] would be right in front of him on Friday, in the second car! And his wife won't be with him, but two cars further back. What a fine setup for Oswald to "employ all means to right this ... injustice"!

An added inducement: "On Wednesday, November 20, at about one o'clock, a small but seminal incident took place at the book depository. Warren Caster, a textbook company representative who had an office in the building, went to Roy Truly's office to show off a pair of purchases he had made during the lunch hour. Caster proudly drew from their cartons two rifles, one a Remington .22 which he had bought as a Christmas present for his son, and the other a sporterized .30-06 Mauser, which he had bought to go deer hunting. Truly picked up the Mauser and, without cocking it, lifted it to his shoulder and sighted it. He handed it back to Caster and said it was a handsome thing." [1477] "A number of men were present in Truly's office. Lee Oswald happened to be among them. Marina thinks that this could have been the decisive moment. Lee now knew the route, and he had seen guns in the building. If anyone should accuse him later of keeping a rifle there, he had a pretext. There were two rifles in the building already, so why should he be under suspicion?" [1478]

Three legs are required to support a criminal act: <u>motive</u>, <u>means</u> and <u>opportunity</u>. Lee has harbored a <u>motive</u> for twenty-one months, since February 1962 when Connally sent a two-sentence reply to Minsk, refusing to intervene and merely bucking Lee's heartfelt plea for help with the unfair discharge to an unknown bureaucrat, after which things really went downhill! Abruptly, the *Morning News* has laid out for Lee his <u>opportunity</u>: His nemesis will be in the second car below him, sitting with the President and Mrs. Kennedy.

All he needs is the <u>means</u>, and it is wrapped in a blanket in Mrs. Paine's garage, on the street where co-worker nineteen-year-old Wesley Frazier lives with sister Linnie Mae Randle. The rifle had been purchased, most probably, for Lee's attempt to assassinate General Walker. Now it can be put to a much more compelling use. Lee realizes, almost certainly early on Thursday, that he must have the rifle by noon Friday, so he must go to Irving before then.

A thorough analyst of the assassination, Gerald Posner notes: "Oswald had little time for planning, perhaps not much more than twenty-four hours. He had to decide how to slip the gun into the Depository and where to take a sniper's position. His lack of preparation is evident by the fact he only had four bullets with him, though the rifle's clip could hold six [plus one more in the chamber, ready to fire]. They were all he had left from his last practice session, and he evidently did not have time on Thursday, November 21, to buy more." [1479]

During the month Lee has worked at the TSBD, he's ridden to Irving in Wesley's car only on Friday afternoons, for the weekends. With Earl Warren presiding, Frazier answered questions from assistant counsel Joseph A. Ball of the Warren Commission:

"Mr. BALL. Now, there was the one date that Oswald came to you and asked you to drive him back to Irving, it was not a Friday, was it?

Mr. FRAZIER. No, sir; it wasn't.

Mr. BALL. It was on a Thursday.

Mr. FRAZIER. Right.

Mr. BALL. Was that the 21st of November?

Mr. FRAZIER. Yes, sir.

Mr. BALL. Well, tell us about that.

Mr. FRAZIER. Well, I say, we were standing like I said at the four-headed table ... getting the orders in and he said, 'Could I ride home with you this afternoon?' And I said, 'Sure.'

So automatically I knew it wasn't Friday, I come to think it wasn't Friday and I said, 'Why are you going homc today?' And he says, 'I am going home to get some curtain rods.' He said, 'You know, put in an apartment.' He wanted to hang up some curtains and

I said, 'Very well.' And I never thought more about it and I had some invoices in my hands for some orders and I walked on off and started filling the orders." [1480]

"Frazier, unaware that Oswald's furnished room on North Beckley was already equipped with jalousies [and curtains, as will be shown] nodded understandingly." [1481] "Later that day Lee took time to fashion a bag 26 or 27 inches long, made of the brown paper and tape that were used by the book depository employees." [1482] At quitting time, Wesley and Lee walked together, as always, the four short blocks to the parking lot. [1483] In Irving, Oswald walked "about a half block" [1484] from Wesley's sister's house to Ruth Paine's.

Future President Gerald Ford, after hearing months of testimony that illuminated the state of the Oswald marriage, pointed out: "One of the mysteries never to be solved, unless Marina in years to come recalls something she has not yet related, is whether Lee had actually made up his mind to kill when he went out to Irving or whether the decision was still hanging fire, perhaps depending on whether Marina accepted what appeared to be his peace offers and agreed to come to Dallas to live with him." [1485] In either event, Lee will learn beyond all doubt that his wife is now independent, their marriage is irremediably broken, so he will fetch the rifle hidden there, essential to "employ all means to right this gross ... injustice". [1486]

His arrival on Thursday was a surprise because he generally asked Ruth's permission before a visit. [1487] He had last talked with Marina on Monday, after the terrible weekend when she could not find him because of his phony name at the boarding house. Both women thought he had come to Irving because he felt badly about arguing with his wife about the fictitious name. [1488] Shortly after his arrival, according to Marina, she "left the bedroom and went outside to bring the children's clothes in off the line. Lee went to the garage [photo on page 134] for a few minutes, then the two of them came inside and sat on the sofa in the living room folding diapers." [1489]

Marina described their final evening to the Warren Commission, with Earl Warren again presiding and general counsel J. Lee Rankin asking the questions:

"Mr. RANKIN. Did your husband give any reason for coming home on Thursday?

Mrs. OSWALD. He said that he was lonely because he hadn't come the preceding weekend, and he wanted to make his peace with me.

Mr. RANKIN. Did you say anything to him then?

Mrs. OSWALD. He tried to talk to me but I would not answer him, and he was very upset.

Mr. RANKIN. Were you upset with him ?

Mrs. OSWALD. I was angry, of course. He was not angry—he was upset. I was angry. He tried very hard to please me. He spent quite a bit of time putting away diapers and played with the children on the street.

Mr. RANKIN. How did you indicate to him that you were angry with him?

Mrs. OSWALD. By not talking to him.

Mr. RANKIN. And how did he show that he was upset?

Mrs. OSWALD. He was upset over the fact that I would not answer him. He tried to start a conversation with me several times, but I would not answer. And he said that he didn't want me to be angry at him because this upsets him.

On that day, he suggested that we rent an apartment in Dallas. He said that he was tired of living alone and perhaps the reason for my being so angry was the fact that we were not living together. That if I want to he would rent an apartment in Dallas tomorrow—that he didn't want me to remain with Ruth any longer, but wanted me to live with him in Dallas. He repeated this not once but several times, but I refused. And he said that once again I was preferring my friends to him, and that I didn't need him.

Mr. RANKIN. What did you say to that?

Mrs. OSWALD. I said it would be better if I remained with Ruth until the holidays, he would come, and we would all meet together. That this was better because while he was living alone and I stayed with Ruth, we were spending less money.

...

Mr. RANKIN. Did this seem to make him more upset, when you suggested that he wait about getting an apartment for you to live in?

Mrs. OSWALD. Yes. He then stopped talking and sat down and watched television and then went to bed. I went to bed later. It was about 9 o'clock when he went to sleep. I went to sleep about 11:30. But it seemed to me that he was not really asleep. But I didn't talk to him." [1490]

Mailer and McMillan understand the situation: "Marina, living with Ruth, is now relatively liberated. She no longer needs him to survive." [1491] "Marina had refused his pleas that she move into Dallas with him ... He would not be looking for an apartment 'tomorrow.' He now had no need for 'curtain rods,' but earlier in the evening he had spent time in the garage." [1492]

Mrs. Paine's garage is important, and has even given its name to one of the few really fine books in the Kennedy assassination genre. [1493] As is true of most "garages" in smallish built-on-a-slab American houses, Ruth's was not used to park a car, but had long been consigned to work and storage. Lest one imagine it to be tidy with its contents easy to see, at right is a photo, [1494] rare because the door is up. The Oswalds' few possessions were on the floor at left, near the saw, lightly covered in sawdust.

"[A]bout ten o'clock ... Ruth went to the garage and painted blocks for her children for half an hour or so. Someone had been there before her, left the light on, and moved a few things around. She supposed that Lee had gone there to fetch some clothing, for the weather was turning cool and the Oswalds had their warm clothes in the garage. But Ruth did think it careless of Lee to have left the light on." [1495]

"Marina as usual was the last to bed. ... Lee was lying on his stomach with his eyes closed when she crept into bed." [1496] She "was aware that Lee was awake. She couldn't explain it; she knew. He said nothing. He did not try to touch her. She was certain that he was lying awake in the dark. It was a strange feeling. ... Sometimes, she felt that she did not know this man. In her mind, he became 'my crazy one.' She did not mean it to indicate insanity; it was synonymous with unpredictability" [1497] "She ... believed that he was so angry at her for refusing to move to Dallas right away that it was no use trying to talk to him. She thinks that he fell asleep about five o'clock in the morning." [1498] UU

President and Mrs. Kennedy had begun their Texas trip that morning, leaving the White House by helicopter and flying in Air Force One to San Antonio. Before and during the flight,

---

UU Marina is reliably quoted as telling about other activities during this night, in chapter 20.

JFK was freed from normal office business and able to do what most executives find no time for — **THINK**.[VV] We now know that he conveyed a historic decision to two companions:

James W. Douglass, for his book *JFK and the Unspeakable: Why He Died and Why It Matters*, had interviewed "Malcolm Kilduff by phone on March 7, 2002. He died on March 3, 2003, at the age of seventy-five.":[1499]

> "The man who announced President Kennedy's death to the world at Parkland Hospital on the afternoon of November 22 was Assistant Press Secretary Malcolm Kilduff. Shortly before his own death four decades later, Malcolm Kilduff told me in an interview that President Kennedy made a powerful statement to him on Vietnam just before they departed for Texas.
>
> Kilduff said he came into the Oval Office the morning of November 21 to prepare the president for a press briefing. Kilduff discovered that JFK's mind was instead on Vietnam.
>
> Kennedy said to Kilduff: 'I've just been given a list of the most recent casualties in Vietnam. We're losing too damned many people over there. It's time for us to get out. The Vietnamese aren't fighting for themselves. We're the ones who are doing the fighting.
>
> 'After I come back from Texas, that's going to change. There's no reason for us to lose another man over there. Vietnam is not worth another American life.'" [1500]

That was such an important decision, one that would have greatly changed America's focus in the 1960s from protest and violence about the war to better matters, perhaps equality, that it is excellent to have a corroborative source, an interview by historian James Reston Jr. with a trustworthy politician (there were such now-largely-extinct paragons back then) on the plane:

> "On the flight to Texas aboard Air Force One on November 21, 1963, Congressman Henry Gonzalez told of this encounter with President Kennedy that day before he was to die: 'The president started back to his compartment. Then, at the door, he turned back to Gonzalez. In the years to come, Gonzalez would keep this fleeting moment frozen in his mind, as his last direct personal touch with the deified president, but also as a fulcrum of history. "Oh, and by the way, Henry, I've already ordered all the men and all the helicopters to be out of South Vietnam by the end of the year." And he was gone.'" [1501]

There is no basis for thinking that JFK communicated that decision to LBJ, much less explain in enough detail to cause his unschooled ethnocentric nationalist vice-president to buy into the rational decision of the history-buff world-citizen President. Johnson was not at the White House, nor was he on the 707 with Kennedy. Perhaps it's because of that simple separation that the USA would tilt into more than a decade of demonstrations, confrontations and distress.

The visitors were greeted by Vice President Johnson and Governor Connally, who joined in a motorcade through San Antonio.[1502] During the afternoon, President Kennedy dedicated the U.S. Air Force School of Aerospace Medicine at Brooks AFB.[1503] They then flew to Houston where the President rode through the city in a motorcade and spoke at Rice University Stadium to a large, enthusiastic crowd.[1504] Next, a "Motorcade to Sam Houston Coliseum for a banquet in honor of Texas congressman Albert Thomas. Depart the Coliseum 9:45 P.M. Cars to airport. Fly to Fort Worth." [1505]

As everywhere during the trip, crowds showed much interest in Mrs. Kennedy. JFK asked David F. Powers, one of his "Irish Mafia", to estimate the crowd,[1506] "and he beamed when Dave gave him the reply that he wanted Jackie to hear. 'Mr. President, your crowd here today was about the same as last year's,' Dave said, 'but a hundred thousand more people came out to cheer for Jackie.' Jackie smiled, and said to her husband, 'I'm looking forward to

---

[VV] Stated in the style of the hallowed wall plaques ubiquitous in IBM's offices.

campaigning with you in 1964.'" [1507]   Shortly before midnight, the tired presidential party arrived at Carswell Air Force Base near Fort Worth,[1508] the "aw shucks" "Cowtown" cousin, thirty miles to the west of nose-in-the-air, effete, sophisticated Dallas.

Before ending this chapter, although it is painful for this author who, eleven years later was assigned to Fort Worth and came to love it and its people, there is an episode sad to relate, but key to understanding the times. Six Secret Service agents who would work the midnight shift, led by Art Godfrey,[WW] arrived in Fort Worth mid-afternoon, to check in where the Kennedys would stay. "The Hotel Texas, a historic redbrick hotel, had been elegant in its day but had long since lost its luster." [1509]   Among them was Bob Faison, "the first African-American permanently assigned to the White House Secret Service detail." [1510]   One of the six agents, Jerry Blaine, told what occurred in his book *The Kennedy Detail*:

"A short, pale-skinned young man dressed in the hotel's standard uniform stood behind the desk ... Art Godfrey walked up, rested his arm on the counter, and asked, 'Do you have some rooms ready under the name of Godfrey or the midnight shift of the Secret Service?' ... Sure enough, there were three envelopes with room keys already prepared. 'Thank you,' Godfrey said as he picked up the envelopes. The clerk, who seemed to have barely noticed the agents as they'd walked in the lobby, suddenly got a pained look in his eyes as he glanced from one agent to the next. ... 'Wait. . . I'm sorry, Mr. Godfrey,' he said as he raised his hand in protest, 'but you will have to tell the *Negro* that he will have to stay somewhere else.'

The agents stood there, not knowing what to say. Surely he must be joking. They'd never run into anything like this before. [Agent] Paul Burns stepped up to the counter and looked the young clerk dead straight in the eyes. 'Do you know who we are?' The young man flinched ever so slightly. 'Uh ... I assume you are with the Secret Service.' 'That's right,' Burns affirmed. 'Can we talk to the manager?'

The clerk returned a few minutes later with the manager of the hotel. He reiterated what the clerk had said. 'That's right, gentlemen. It is hotel policy that we do not accommodate members of the Negro race.' Burns leaned over the counter and glared at the manager. 'Well, sir, we are the Secret Service agents here to guard the President of the United States. If our agents aren't good enough to sleep in your damn beds, then we won't sleep here ... and neither will the president. We'll find somewhere else for him to stay.'

The manager read the seriousness of the threat and excused himself to make a quick telephone call. ... Bob Faison ... fortunately, seemed unaware of what was being discussed. When the manager came back, looking more than a little flustered, he said sheepishly, 'Its fine. All of you are welcome to stay.' Burns wasn't satisfied. Staring at the manager, Burns squinted his eyes with intensity and said, 'You better advise your staff and every single employee of your new policy so that we don't need to address this issue again. Is that clear?' The manager, visibly shaken, nodded and said, 'Yes, sir. You have my word. There will be no problems.'" [1511]

[WW] Not to be confused with ukulele-strumming early-days radio host Arthur Godfrey.

Your author includes that digression to remind all, and perhaps instruct the young, that the 1960s were a decade of slow and painful progress in racial relations. This remnant of discrimination was typical. Four months earlier had been the March on Washington for Jobs and Freedom that included a speech by a man who had a dream.[1512] Eighteen days later, the KKK bombing of a Birmingham, Alabama, church murdered four little black girls who were there to hear a sermon, "The Love That Forgives". There was much still to be done, but the country will waste a dozen years arguing about the US's hopeless war in Vietnam.

Some of the six Secret Service agents who would be on the midnight shift went shopping for souvenirs that afternoon. In the fine book *The Kennedy Detail* by one of those agents, Jerry Blaine, is this photo captioned: "Jerry Blaine and Art Godfrey pose in their newly purchased Western hats in front of the Hotel Texas, where JFK spends his final night." [1513]

It turns out that they had been sent to a discount-giving shop by Special Agent Mike Howard, who had a long history and good contacts in Fort Worth. Mike will be featured in Chapter 20 – OBSTRUCTION OF BEST EVIDENCE.

Your author, who made the same purchase when he arrived in Fort Worth as Branch Manager of IBM's Field Engineering Division office, points out that they got authentic Fort Worth hats — easily recognized by the inward creases on the front. Hats from Dallas and elsewhere in Texas have only the side creases. These distinctions, like cattle brands, are taken very seriously in Texas.

Agent Clint Hill noted: "There were some people standing alongside the road on the way into town, but when we pulled up to the Hotel Texas at 11:50 P.M., it was mobbed. There had to be four thousand people standing in the street and parking lot outside the hotel. ... When President and Mrs. Kennedy got out of the car, the crowd went nuts." [1514]

A reminder of the era: The Kennedys' suite "cost $106 ... but the management would not send a bill." [1515] "[T]heir three-room suite had been specially adorned with $200,000 worth of paintings and sculpture—sixteen pieces including a Monet, a Picasso, a Van Gogh, and a Prendergast—lent by local collectors.[1516] But Jack and Jackie were too exhausted to notice the thoughtfully assembled exhibit that even came with a catalogue. It was past midnight when they settled into the suite. 'You were great today,' Jack said as they embraced before heading to separate bedrooms for much-needed sleep." [1517]

Key point of this chapter:
Home in the USA after USSR disappointments, Lee went from one failure to another, then just in time stumbled upon an opportunity to "right this gross mistake or injustice".

THREE DEAD, TWO WOUNDED

1963: Friday, November 22 – Sunday, November 24

> "I thought ... that one of them motorcycles backfired, but it wasn't just a few seconds that ... I heard two more of the same type of ... sounds, and by that time people was running everywhere, and falling down and screaming, and naturally then I knew something was wrong, and so I come to the conclusion ... somebody was shooting at somebody."
> — **Lee's co-worker and ride-giver Buell Wesley Frazier** [1518]

"LEE USUALLY WOKE UP BEFORE THE ALARM RANG and shut it off so as not to disturb the children. On the morning of Friday, November 22, the alarm rang and he did not wake up. Marina was awake, and after about ten minutes she said, 'Time to get up, Alka.' 'Okay.' He rose, washed, and got dressed. Then he came over to the bed. ... 'Mama, don't get up. I'll get breakfast myself.' ... He got as far as the bedroom door, then came back and said, 'I've left some money on the bureau. Take it and buy everything you and Junie and Rachel need. Bye-bye.' Then Lee went out the door.

"'Good God,' thought Marina. 'What has happened to my husband that he has all of a sudden gotten so kind?' Then she fell back to sleep. ... He had been angry and tense in bed that night and it was nearly morning before he fell asleep. Marina supposed he was just angry at her for refusing to give in to him. Later on she wondered, what *had* he been thinking about?

"There was the odd circumstance of his telling her not to get up to fix his breakfast. There was no danger that she would—she had never done so before. Why would he tell her not to? Could it be that he did not want to run the tiniest risk of her seeing him enter the garage—and leave it? Then there was his telling her with unaccustomed gentleness to buy everything she and the children needed. He had never told her such a thing before. When she got up that morning ... she found the extraordinary sum of $170. It must have been nearly everything Lee had." [1519]

Marina did not see him leave the house, nor did Ruth Paine. When he stopped in the garage to take the package he had prepared the previous evening, they did not witness it.

Oswald walked the half-block to Wesley Frazier's house. Wesley was on the same schedule: up at 6:30, breakfast 7:00 to 7:15, out at 7:20.[1520] [A] Wesley's mother, staying with Linnie while her husband got medical attention,[1521] saw a man look in at the kitchen window. Wesley said, "'That is Lee.' ... I just turned around and looked at the clock to see what time it was and it was right around 7:21 then ... so I went in there and brushed my teeth right quick and come through there and I usually have my coat laying somewhere on the chair and picked it up and put it on and by that time my sister had my lunch ... in a sack ... over there on the washer ... right there by the door and I just walked on out and we got in the car.'" [1522] [B]

Wesley's sister Linnie Mae, "a dark, pretty woman with shoulder-length black hair",[1523] was a keen observer. Having bagged Wesley's lunch, she looked out with care because she noticed something unusual: "[Lee] was carrying a package in a sort of a heavy brown bag, heavier than a grocery bag it looked to me. It was about, if I might measure, about this long, I suppose, and he carried it in his right hand, had the top sort of folded down and had a grip like this, and the bottom, he carried it this way, you know, and it almost touched the ground as he carried it." [1524] "Mrs. Randall watched him walk toward her garage and she wiped her hands on her apron and opened the kitchen door in time to see him open the right rear door of Wes's old car and drop the bundle on the back seat." [1525]

When she testified, the Warren Commission showed Linnie the bag found on the sixth floor of the Depository, and she convincingly confirmed all important facts. The bag she saw Lee carry was the same color and the same kind of paper [1526] — check. It was 27 to 28½ inches long,[1527] the length of the rifle when disassembled into stock and action-barrel pieces – check. It was "More bulky toward the bottom [butt] than ... toward the top" [1528] — check.

Most importantly, "the top sort of folded down".[1529] Lee made the package at work on Thursday after learning (chapter 18) CONNALLY WILL RIDE. Because of hastening into action, he did not know the answers to two questions: How long was the rifle, both when assembled and ready to fire, and when the wood stock had been disassembled from the steel action and barrel? In which form, one-piece or two, would he carry it on Friday? Not knowing until he held the rifle, Lee prudently taped together a package plenty long to hold it in either form, allowing a little extra in case he recalled its length incorrectly. When he placed the disassembled rifle into the bag, he folded over the excess paper, exactly as Linnie saw, remembered, and testified about it — check. Her keen observation absolutely nailed the case!

Her brother picked up the story: "'[W]hen I got in the car I have a kind of habit of glancing over my shoulder and so at that time I noticed there was a package laying on the back seat, I didn't pay too much attention, and I said, 'What's the package, Lee?' And he said, 'Curtain rods,' and I said, 'Oh, yes, you told me you was going to bring some today.'" [1530] "Oswald's room at 1026 North Beckley ... had four small windows on one side. The landlady, Mrs. A. C. Johnson, had long ago equipped them with Venetian blinds and filmy curtains. She did not permit roomers to make changes." [1531] Wesley didn't know that.

[A] All times of day in this chapter, unless otherwise stated, are Central Standard Time, CST.

[B] If you have not already done so, please judge Wesley from this testimony, because every conceivable conspiracy theory absolutely requires that he be deeply involved, first getting Lee the job so he can be in position to shoot, then delivering him and his rifle on assassination day. It must be evident to any fair observer that Buell Wesley Frazier was an unpretentious, honest, "square" young man.

Wesley drove the 15 miles with his habitual timing: leaving a little before 7:25, arriving at the parking lot by 7:55, thus able to walk into the building a little before 8:00.[1532] Today was the fifth time Wesley had driven Lee to work. Although they meant nothing at the moment, he later testified to four unique observations: This was the first time Lee had arrived at Linnie's before Wesley was warming up the car. This was the first time Lee had a package. This was the first time Lee did not have a little sack lunch [1533] — Wesley asked and Lee said that today he'd buy from a lunch truck. Finally, most unusual [C] of all four, when they reached the Depository's parking lot on Houston Street [D] north of their work, as he and his excellent memory told the Commission:

> "Mr. FRAZIER. He got out of the car and he was wearing the jacket that has the big sleeves in them and he put the package that he had, you know, that he told me was curtain rods up under his arm, you know, and so he walked down behind the car and standing over there ... and so quick as I cut the engine off and started out of the car, shut the door just as I was starting out just like getting out of the car, he started walking off and so I followed him in.
>
> So, eventually there he kept getting a little further ahead of me and I noticed we had plenty of time to get there because it is not too far from the Depository and usually I walk around and watch them switching the trains because you have to watch where you are going if you have to cross the tracks. ... I just walked along and I just like to watch them switch the cars, so eventually he kept getting a little further ahead of me and by that time we got down there pretty close to the Depository Building there, I say, he would be as much as, I would say, roughly 50 feet in front of me but I didn't try to catch up with him because I knew I had plenty of time so I just took my time walking up there.
>
> Mr. BALL. Did you usually walk up there together.
>
> Mr. FRAZIER. Yes, sir; we did.
>
> Mr. BALL. Is this the first time that he had ever walked ahead of you?
>
> Mr. FRAZIER. Yes, sir; he did.
>
> Mr. BALL. You say he had the package under his arm when you saw him?
>
> Mr. FRAZIER. Yes, sir." [1534]

Wesley saw Lee carry his package across the loading dock in back of the building, the side away from Elm Street, and through the back door into the Depository.[1535] The Commission called Frazier back four months later, for only one question, the same question asked in three slightly different ways. The third iteration was: "Did you ever see him with a package that looked like that package any other time or at any other place?" "No, sir." [1536]

[C] Some would write "most unique", but I agree with my *American Heritage College Dictionary*: "Most grammarians regard unique as an absolute term, saying that a thing is either unique or not unique— it cannot be *very unique* or *more unique* than something else." This was "most unusual" of four.

[D] About three blocks north on the street where the Kennedy limousine will first come in sight of the Depository building, and where — the subject of Chapter 19 — Oswald will not shoot at anyone.

Lee knew the sixth floor would be unusually empty that day. "There, as in so many ways, blind chance had played into his hands. The old flooring had become oily. [Roy]

Truly, observing that books which had been stored there frequently became stained, had ordered it replaced with battleship-gray plywood. Half the floor was to be redone at a time. In preparation for the work, the rear, or northern, area had been largely cleared of cartons by doubling up in front. Thus the southern side, which would face the passing motorcade, was a crowded jungle of cartons ..." [1537] "Concealment was easy, and it was there, sometime during the morning, that Oswald built his sniper's perch ... from which the motorcade would be seen approaching dead ahead and then departing to the right front." [1538] He waited "for all the workmen to clear out ... so he could rearrange the book cartons of *Rolling Readers* ("blocks that taught children to follow lines of text" [1539]) to build his ambuscade and gun rest." [1540] "The southeast corner window, in particular, was totally shielded from view because cartons had been stacked around in a crescent." [1541] The largest contained *First Grade Think and Do*.[1542] "The beige boxes were stacked like small forts in a child's game." [1543] [1544]

Oswald's supervisor, William Shelley, who had worked for TSBD 18 years, will tell the Warren Commission that the *Think and Do* cartons are a usual large size, like many in the photo and common throughout the warehouse.[1545] But, he noted, two *Rolling Reader* cartons used to form the top of the rifle rest at the window were "unusual ... from any box on that floor ... they were little boxes". Whereas *Think and Do* were a common 22" x 18" x 20", the gun-rest boxes were only 12" x 6" x 6".[1546] Lee knew where to find what he needed.

He also assembled the rifle — carried that morning in two pieces, as proven by Linnie Mae Randle's account of the paper sack being folded over. The fold in the sack, when found, shortened it to the 27" length of the longer piece, the barrel, as will be shown in Chapter 12 – THE RIFLE. He quickly screwed the wood stock to the action and barrel. FBI Special Agent Cortlandt Cunningham, a firearms expert, told the Commission he had put it together with a screwdriver in two minutes. They challenged him to put it together right in front of them, but using a dime rather than a screwdriver. It took six minutes.[1547] Easy!

This narrative now leaves Lee alone on the sixth floor until he will shoot while all others usually in the building will be down below and out front, closer to the motorcade. He was last seen at 11:55 by one of the floor layers, Charlie Givens, who went back to retrieve his cigarettes.[1548] "When he reached the sixth floor, he saw Lee Harvey Oswald walking along the panel of windows facing Elm Street and the crowds below. There was nothing uncommon about it, except that Charlie Givens thought that, a moment ago, Lee had been on the fifth floor. It made no difference and they did not exchange greetings." [1549] "Their departure left the top stories unoccupied. In effect, the upper part of the warehouse had now met the Secret Service's definition of the classic sniper's perch—it was a deserted building." [1550]

At 7:30, as Wesley drove out of Irving and onto the Stemmons Freeway, a few miles to the west at the Hotel Texas in Fort Worth,[E] valet George Thomas wakens the President. Since before dawn, despite a steady rain, a crowd grows in the parking lot below, hoping to hear Kennedy speak from a flatbed truck. The audience is mostly men in waterproofs and stout shoes, only a few ladies with umbrellas. More than five thousand await their President.[1551]

In the first hour of his last day, John Kennedy must undergo a painful daily ritual that on this day will be partly responsible for his death. We all knew that JFK had a back problem, pleased that it was alleviated by his famous rocking chair. He, his physicians and staff wanted to project a solid healthy image. It turns out that the problem was much more serious than we realized during his election and presidency. His back was terribly injured when PT 109 was rammed, then made worse by unsuccessful surgery to fuse the lower spine, followed by infections. The poor man was in nearly-constant pain from 1944 until his death. He consulted back specialist Dr. Janet Travell beginning in 1955, then made her his White House physician.

"To alleviate the pain and to promote an image of a youthful, vigorous leader, Dr. Travell had prescribed an elaborate back brace. Members of Kennedy's inner circle had often witnessed the painful ritual that Kennedy endured in his private quarters before he ventured [into] public, when his valet ... would literally winch the canvas corset around the President's torso. Metal stays anchored the brace, and a stiff plastic pad covered the area of his sacrum. The valet would yank on the heavy straps and tighten the shoe-lace-like thongs loop by loop in a scene reminiscent of Mammy tightening Scarlett O'Hara into a corset in *Gone with the Wind*. After the corset reached maximum tightness, a six-inch wide, elasticized Ace bandage was wrapped in a figure-eight between the President's legs and then wrapped over the corset around his waist to tighten it further and keep it from slipping.

"Once in it, the president was veritably planted upright, trapped, immobilized, and almost mummified into a ramrod posture. Many would wonder how JFK could even move in such a contraption. Yet, move he did, and besides his painkillers, his corset contributed to the youthful, high-shouldered military bearing that he presented to the world. Early on the morning of November 22, the ritual took place as usual." [1552] How that brace and bandage will keep the President upright and in the line of fire will be mentioned later in this chapter, then considered at necessary length in Chapter 14 – TOO CLOSE TO CALL.

A brief digression: Any reader who has paid attention to this point knows that this author has a high regard for the *Warren Report*. Despite its hurried gestation, to be explained in chapter 8, it is a remarkably complete and accurate account of the assassination and the assassin — with only one major deficiency, as will be pointed out in chapter 21, the Warren Commission's failure to attribute to Oswald a meaningful motive for killing Kennedy. Other than that, the *Report* is reliable. To show that this author knows a contrary fact when he sees one — perhaps in the vein of "an exception proves the rule" — I here note a demonstrable but minor error in the *Report*. Relating the day's events, it states: "On the morning of November 22, President Kennedy attended a breakfast at the hotel and afterward addressed a crowd at an open parking lot." [1553] No, because he knew that Jackie would not be ready for quite a while, and because a crowd was standing outside in a drizzle, JFK went first to the damp parking lot, then afterward to the indoor breakfast. The sequence is not at all important to what's to come

---

[E] Please pardon the author for spending a little extra time here where I loved the people while I was Branch Manager of IBM's Field Engineering Division in Fort Worth, 1974 and 1975.

at midday, and is trivial in the huge work that is the *Warren Report*, but I hope my pointing out this nit may bolster the credibility of their book — and mine.[1554]

It was to be a busy day: "There'd be two speeches here at the Hotel Texas, followed by the short flight to Dallas on Air Force One; the ten-mile motorcade from Dallas's Love Field to the Trade Mart; lunch [and a speech] at the Trade Mart with a couple of thousand guests; a flight to Bergstrom Air Force Base outside Austin, where the head coach of the University of Texas Longhorns would present the president with an autographed football; another motorcade through Austin; a series of receptions; a dinner speech at the Austin fund-raising banquet; a final motorcade; and a helicopter ride to the LBJ Ranch. If today was to be anything like yesterday, President Kennedy would be exposed to half a million people. Half a million voters, in Dave Powers's eyes, but to the Secret Service they were half a million unscreened strangers, any one of whom might be a potential assassin." [1555]

"The President liked outdoor appearances because more people could see and hear him." [1556] At 8:50, Kennedy stood on the back of a flatbed truck, upbeat and triumphant. "There are no faint hearts in Fort Worth!" he lauds the applauding, approving supporters.[1557] "Standing in the drizzle, Kennedy exhorted and joked with a crowd [from which a woman] yelled, 'Where's Jackie?' He pointed to the window of their suite and said, 'Mrs. Kennedy is organizing herself. It takes her a little longer, but, of course, she looks better than we do when she does it.'" [1558] "The crowd loved this, and roared its approval." [1559] Behind the Yankee President in the photo [1560]

are the two Texans who planned the trip: Governor John Bowden Connally (Jr., but he never uses that) and Vice President Lyndon Baines Johnson.

While JFK was speaking at 9:00, in Dallas dress manufacturer Abraham Zapruder, who intended to watch the President pass a few blocks from his business, decided he should film the event, and returned home to fetch his Bell and Howell movie camera. That will turn out to be one of those seemingly inconsequential acts that will change our grasp of history.[1561] At 9:05 Richard Nixon left Dallas. This conjunction with Kennedy fed conspiracy theorists for many years and caused the unwarranted paperization [F] of many trees to print their nonsense. The truth was quite ordinary. After losing the 1960 presidential election to Kennedy, then losing a 1962 run to be governor of California ("You won't have Nixon to kick around anymore."), he was a high-priced attorney, "in Dallas to promote business" [1562] and "to attend a board meeting of the Pepsi-Cola Company, one of our firm's clients." [1563] That morning "at Love Field, the captain of American Airlines Flight 82 ... headed for Idlewild [soon JFK] Airport in New York. One of the passengers, a stewardess had told him, was Richard Nixon. Apparently the former Vice-President was not going to remain in Dallas to watch the presidential parade." [1564]

[F] A privilege of writing is being allowed to make up necessary words. Where else should they be born?

At 9:05, President Kennedy addressed a Fort Worth Chamber of Commerce breakfast in the hotel's ballroom. Jackie entered the room late, looking lovely in ... a raspberry-colored wool suit, matching pillbox hat, and white gloves.[1565] The two thousand attendees—many standing on their chairs—cheered, applauded, and whistled appreciation when she arrived. "'Two years ago,' [the President] said, 'I introduced myself in Paris by saying that I was the man who had accompanied Mrs. Kennedy to Paris. I am getting somewhat that same sensation as I travel around Texas.'"[1566] "He paused, as the entire audience laughed. Then he added, glancing at Mrs. Kennedy, 'Nobody wonders what Lyndon and I wear.'"[1567] "[H]is remarks ... sounded a somber note. 'This is a dangerous and uncertain world. 'No one expects our lives to be easy—not in this decade, not in this century.'"[1568]

The President and First Lady returned to their suite at 10:00, where they graciously phoned to thank one of the Fort Worth ladies who had loaned artwork — Monet, Picasso, Prendergast, Van Gogh and twelve others[1569] — to brighten their suite. "The President took a chance. Casually, he asked her if she was enjoying the trip. 'Oh, Jack,' she said, 'campaigning is so easy when you're President.' [JFK's political aide] Kenny O'Donnell came into the sitting room as the President said: 'How about California in two weeks?' His wife nodded happily. 'Fine,' she said. 'I'll be there.' There was nothing on the Texas trip that could lift the spirits of Mr. Kennedy more than those four words: 'Fine. I'll be there.'"[1570]

Before leaving the hotel, the President and Kenny O'Donnell talked about the risks inherent in Presidential public appearances.[1571] According to O'Donnell, JFK commented that "if anybody really wanted to shoot the President of the United States, it was not a very difficult job—all one had to do was get a high building someday with a telescopic rifle, and there was nothing anybody could do to defend against such an attempt."[1572]

The Kennedys, code named "Lancer" and "Lace" by the Secret Service, left for the day's next events, their arrival and a motorcade through Dallas. Their Fort Worth limousine, the one they had used the previous night, waited in front of the hotel. It was used to go from A to B. Another, specifically designed for motorcades, was waiting in Dallas. They could have been driven 35 miles east to begin the Dallas motorcade. Instead, they rode 7 miles west to Carswell Air Force Base where Air Force One was waiting to fly them the absurdly short distance to Love Field in Dallas. From there they would hasten about 6 miles to where crowds would line the streets, the start of the day's first motorcade.

There were multiple reasons for flying rather than going on the ground. It was thought that security from attack was better in the air. The rather new Boeing 707 had communication equipment to connect the President to the world, and medical facilities in case of emergency. Most important for this trip, "Ken O'Donnell knew that the image of the president stepping out of Air Force One, waving to an enthusiastic crowd of supporters, was a photo opportunity that couldn't be passed up. The local news stations loved this stuff. They'd have a full staff of cameramen and reporters on hand to air the arrival 'live,' and again on the evening news." [1573]

"SAM—Special Air Missions—26000 ... was the Boeing 707 that served Presidents Kennedy, Johnson and Nixon. It was the first jet-powered presidential plane." [1574] The Boeing was a beauty, unlike the plain aluminum hulls that preceded it, because "Kennedy decided the aircraft needed a distinctive look and enlisted Jackie's help on the project. She worked with the designer Raymond Loewy, who eliminated traditional military markings, put together the distinctive blue and white color scheme, the seal 'United States of America' emblazoned on both sides of the fuselage, and an American flag painted on the tail." [1575] There has been no improvement in the 50+ years since, so the same design graces President Obama's 747.

The President's limousine for motorcades, a custom-built Lincoln convertible, was already in Dallas. It traveled there in the cargo bay of an Air Force C-130 [1576] Hercules turbo-prop transport, part of the small air force accompanying Kennedy's 707. "SS100X cost the Ford Motor Company two hundred thousand dollars to build, but the Secret Service didn't have that kind of money in the budget. So Ford leased the car to the Secret Service for five hundred dollars a year." [1577] It was an important necessity for presidential security, with extra-thick steel sides, bullet-proof windows, tires that would still roll nicely even if penetrated by bullets, and an extra-powerful engine for quick getaways — all to protect the presidential party — and all superfluous if the protective top was not installed.

"Before they left Fort Worth, the Secret Service asked how JFK wanted the Lincoln prepared. There are three possible configurations [G] — a black vinyl-coated metal top; a canvas convertible top; and a clear plastic bubble top that offers protection against the rain. 'I want the bubble top,' said Jackie. 'No,' said Jack. 'If you're going out to see the people, the people ought to be able to see you.'" [1578] "His convictions were firm about this and had been restated many times. 'The people come to see me, not the Secret Service.'" [1579] "The bubble top was not bulletproof, but it might have deflected the bullets' trajectory, or the sun's reflection could have obscured [the] target." [1580]

The flight from Carswell AFB at Fort Worth to Love Field in Dallas will be short, only thirteen minutes. Colonel Jim Swindal, the Air Force pilot assigned to the Kennedys, will be in command. It isn't the journey that's important; it's the arrival's powerful image of beautiful Air Force One descending from the heavens to land and be greeted on arrival. So ...

A political legerdemain [H] was used in the flight to Dallas. At Fort Worth, as always for security reasons, the President and Vice President boarded separate jets. And as always, because being in the plane and then in the air is safer than being on the ground, Kennedy's jet departed first.[I] When JFK and Jackie came down the steps at Love Field in Dallas, waiting

---

[G] Actually, four — the one chosen, no top.

[H] A lovely French word. My favorite sonorous bon mot learned while living in France: aubergine.

[I] This is equivalent to a president almost always sitting on the right side of an automobile, an important point in Chapter 19 – THE SHOT NOT TAKEN.

there to greet them as if they hadn't seen one another for a long time were LBJ and Lady Bird. From an FBI report five days later, we learned how the trick was done:

"Mr. Gerald A. Behn, Special Agent in Charge, White House Detail, United States Secret Service, was interviewed ... and advised that during the President's visit to the State of Texas, then Vice President Johnson would always arrive at the next city to be visited ahead of the President and would join the party awaiting the President's arrival. This was accomplished by the use of two Jets; Air Force I, which carried the President; and Air Force II, carrying the Vice President. On departing from a city, Air Force I would first take off followed by Air Force II which would thereafter pass Air Force I in flight by cruising at a faster speed, thus allowing the Vice President to arrive prior to the President and be with the greeting party." [1581]

Flying to Dallas, JFK spoke with Fort Worth Congressman (to become Speaker of the House in 1987) Jim Wright, "with enthusiastic and obviously sincere appreciation of the unfeigned friendliness of the people, the demonstrative and contagious warmth of the reception [Fort Worth] had given him. 'They liked you, Mr. President,' I told him. 'I liked them,' he grinned." [1582] Descending to Dallas, Kennedy saw sunny weather. Another crowd awaited. "This trip is turning out to be terrific," he happily confides to Kenny O'Donnell. "Here we are in Dallas and it looks like everything in Texas will turn out to be fine for us!" [1583]

An overcast sky had indeed given way to bright sunshine that greeted Air Force One at Love Field at 11:40 AM. [1584] Nellie and John Connally, in the doorway below, [1585] had flown with the President from Fort Worth. [1586]

LBJ, standing at the photo's bottom-left as if he lived in Dallas, later recalled: "Mrs. Johnson and I arrived at Dallas' Love Field aboard Air Force Two at 11:35 A.M. We were greeted by the local dignitaries and immediately joined the reception line to welcome the First Family when Air Force One touched down five minutes later. [1587] There was a large, joyful crowd behind the fence, and when the Kennedys stepped out of the plane a great roar went up from thousands of throats. I remember thinking how radiant Mrs. Kennedy looked. The skies had cleared, the air was warm and the sun bright. Her pink suit and pink hat added to the beauty of the day." [1588] "[T]he Dallas mayor's wife, Dearie Cabell, handed Jackie a huge bouquet of red roses." [1589]

Standing beside LBJ to join in the greetings was Barefoot Sanders, possibly the only man in the world with that wonderful first name, whom JFK had appointed U.S. Attorney for Northern Texas. Within two hours he will be tasked with finding a judge to swear in a new president.

The Kennedys walked along a fence at the reception area greeting a large crowd of spectators that had gathered behind it.[1590] Approximately 10 minutes after the arrival at Love Field, the President and Mrs. Kennedy went to the presidential automobile to begin the motorcade.[1591]

The limousine waiting for them was almost as distinctive as their airplane. "'Midnight Blue' was the name (somewhat famous at the time) of the paint color JFK chose for his presidential car. Before and after JFK, such cars were black." [1592] The car's design and dimensions, and the positions of the four passengers in it, are critical to the thesis of this book. In Chapter 14 – TOO CLOSE TO CALL and Chapter 19 – THE SHOT NOT TAKEN there will be considerable attention to the vehicle and its seating, with measurements and illustrative photos.

If it seems there are few details of the motorcade in this chapter, that, too, is deliberate. The design of their Lincoln limousine and the geometries of the fields of fire are critically important to what happened at 12:30. There will be extensive descriptions with photos and diagrams in the two chapters dedicated to those matters. Here we simply cover the basics of the parade, Oswald's inept shooting, and the weekend's aftermath.

For now, as in Dallas that Friday, it is sufficient to note that "[T]he sun is shining and the weather is warm, with men in short sleeves and young women in light summer dresses. This is Jack's kind of day and Jack's kind of car. The only automobiles he has ever owned have been convertibles, and this is a unique Lincoln convertible ... The feature he likes best is the rear seat, which rises ten and a half inches at the flip of a switch [next to him], and there is a footrest to make him more comfortable. With the rear seat raised, he does not have to stand to be seen by a crowd." [1593] "[T]his crowd, he knew, had come to see Jackie as much as they'd come for him. He wasn't about to block their view. Still, with his height and the way the car was designed, he sat a good three or four inches higher than Governor Connally." [1594]

The specially designed 1961 Lincoln had two collapsible jump seats between the front and rear seats,[1595] inserted by adding three and a half feet to the length of the standard Continental. They were "used primarily to reward political friends who could ride with the president during motorcades." [1596] The car could be outfitted with a clear plastic bubbletop which was neither bulletproof nor bullet resistant,[1597] but because the weather is clear and the President wants no barriers between him and his people, the bubbletop is in the trunk.[1598]

At the rear on each side of the automobile were small running boards, each designed to hold a Secret Service agent, with a metallic handle for the rider to grasp.[1599] The President had frequently stated that he did not want agents to ride on these steps during a motorcade except when necessary. He had repeated this preference only a few days before, during a visit to Tampa,[1600] when he instructed the Secret Service agents: "It's excessive ... And it's giving the wrong impression to the people. Tell them to stay on the follow-up car. We've got an election coming up. The whole point is for me to be accessible to the people." [1601] One of his dedicated protectors ruefully remarked to another: "[T]he fact of the matter is, he is the Boss and those are the parameters we have to work with. He knows our focus is to protect him. But he's also not naïve. Trust me, the president knows that being a target comes with the job. ... But you don't get to be President of the United States without taking some risks." [1602]

Finally, the feature most relevant to the tragedy that will happen in Dallas this midday: "The car originally came with a privacy window between the driver and the rear of the limousine, but when the bubble top was installed, the air-conditioning couldn't cool the backseat, which made it very uncomfortable. So the privacy window was removed and a metal roll bar was installed." [1603]   Approximately 15 inches above the back of the front seat,[1604] the "roll bar ran from one side of the car to the other, above and slightly to the rear of the front seat ... [It] provided support and acted as the fastening device for the different tops." [1605] "Handgrips were cut out of the stainless steel roll bar so the president could stand and wave at the crowd while the car was moving." [1606]

Words matter, so let's settle the terminology here. The bar was not installed to do what a roll bar does: afford the occupants some protection if the vehicle rolls over. No, it was installed to give a place to hold on with a hand while standing and waving at crowds. The curator at the museum where the car eventually went on display, the Henry Ford in Dearborn, told me it is a "handrail", so I fully accept and will use that term. What the handrail caused on November 22 will be demonstrated in Chapter 19 — THE SHOT NOT TAKEN.

In the photo [1607] below as they are about to drive from Love Field are several important items. Of the two airplanes, the one at center and further away is Air Force Two, in which VP Johnson had arrived first, so he could stand on the tarmac to greet the other plane. At left and closer is Air Force One, which brought the Kennedys from Fort Worth, and in which, in a couple of hours, Johnson will be sworn in as president. The Cadillac at far left is the Secret Service backup car, "Fullback", which always drives very closely behind the president. The car at front is, of course, SS100X, the president's modified Lincoln Continental.

Most importantly, in front of the passenger compartment is the handrail, which will not be used today to steady a standing president. If you are looking for <u>Nellie</u> Connally, from this position you cannot easily identify her. She is in a jump seat on the far side of the car, her head shielded by the handrail. In half an hour, a man looking for <u>John</u> Connally, and seeing the vehicle from ahead and above, will not find him. That handrail will save the life of Governor Connally and lead to the death of President Kennedy. Read on.

President Kennedy rode on the passenger side of the rear seat with Mrs. Kennedy on his left.[1608] Governor John Connally occupied the right jump seat, Mrs. Nellie Connally the left.[1609] Driving was Special Agent William R. Greer of the Secret Service, who drove the President almost everywhere he went. On his right in the front passenger seat this day sat Roy Kellerman, the Special Agent In Charge (SAIC) for the Texas trip.[1610] His responsibilities included maintaining radio communications with the lead and followup cars, scanning the route, and getting out and standing near the President whenever the car stopped.

Secret Service arrangements for Presidential trips, which were followed in the Dallas motorcade, are designed to provide protection while permitting large numbers of people to see the President.[1611] Every effort is made to prevent unscheduled stops, although the President may, and in Dallas did, order stops in order to greet the public.[1612] When the motorcade slows or stops, agents take positions between the President and the crowd.[1613] As usual, Kennedy had given orders to minimize the obstructions between the public and himself. We will soon see in photos the close proximity of the crowds to the President, the last time this will be allowed.

The motorcade departed from Love Field at 11:50 AM. The long line of vehicles began with Dallas police motorcycles.[1614] The pilot car, manned by officers of the Dallas Police Department, preceded the main party by approximately a quarter of a mile. Its function was to alert police along the route that the motorcade was approaching and to check for signs of trouble.[1615] Next came four to six motorcycle policemen whose main purpose was to keep the crowd back.[1616]

The lead automobile, described as a "rolling command car," was an unmarked police car driven by Dallas Chief of Police Jesse Curry, occupied by local chief of the Secret Service Forrest Sorrels, Agent Winston G. "Win" Lawson from the White House detail who had "advanced" the trip, and by Dallas County Sheriff J. E. "Bill" Decker. These four scanned the crowd and the buildings along the route. Their main function was to spot problems in advance and to direct any steps necessary to meet or escape trouble.

Following normal practice, the President's limousine stayed two to five car lengths behind the lead car.[1617] "Indeed, in a city like Dallas, the Presidential chauffeur had to keep a sharp eye on the car immediately in front of him. He didn't know the route himself; he had never driven it before." [1618] Kennedy's Lincoln was flanked at its rear by four motorcycles, two on each side. They provided some cover for the President, but their main purpose was to keep back the crowd.[1619] The Secret Service and police would have preferred having two cycles close on each side of the Lincoln, but as on previous occasions, Kennedy had requested that, to the extent possible, they keep distant from and behind his car.[1620] He wanted little between himself, his wife, and the public — and he wanted to be able to stop and either hop out or let crowds approach when he perceived inviting opportunities.

The followup car, an eight-passenger Cadillac especially outfitted for the Secret Service, was code-named *Halfback* but irreverently called "the *Queen Mary* because it weighed ten thousand pounds." [1621] It followed closely behind the President's car [1622] and carried eight Secret Service agents—two in the front seat, two in the rear, and two on each of the right and left running boards.[1623] Clint Hill, head of the First Lady's Secret Service detail, was at the front of the left running board. Agents Paul Landis, Bill McIntyre and John Ready also stood on the running boards. Each agent carried a hidden .38-caliber pistol. A shotgun and automatic rifle were readily available.[1624] JFK assistants (and charter members of his Boston Irish Mafia) Dave Powers and Kenny O'Donnell sat in jump seats.[1625]

The agents in this car, under established procedure, had instructions to watch the route for signs of trouble, scanning not only the crowds but the windows and roofs of buildings, overpasses, and crossings.[1626] They were instructed to watch particularly for thrown objects, sudden actions in the crowd, and any movements toward the Presidential car.[1627] The agents in front on the running boards had directions to move immediately to positions just to the rear of the Kennedys when the President's car slowed to a walking pace or stopped, or when the press of a crowd made it impossible for the escort motorcycles to stay in position on the car's rear flanks.[1628] The two agents on the rear of the running boards were to run to the front of the President's car whenever it stopped or slowed down sufficiently for them to do so.[1629]

The remainder of the motorcade is not significant to the purpose of this book, but for completeness and very briefly, these vehicles followed: The Vice-Presidential automobile, a four-door Lincoln convertible that has been rented locally [1630] proceeded approximately two to three car lengths behind the President's followup car,[1631] a distance maintained so that spectators would normally turn their gaze from the President's automobile by the time the Vice President came into view.[1632] Riding with LBJ are Lady Bird, the troublesome liberal Texas Senator Ralph Yarborough, and more Secret Service agents. Next was the Vice-Presidential followup car, code-named Varsity, performing for the VP the same functions Presidential followup car Halfback performed for the President. Then came five cars for local dignitaries, telephone and Western Union vehicles, a White House communications car, three cars for press photographers, an official party bus for White House staff members and others, and two press buses.[1633] A Dallas police car and several motorcycles at the rear kept the motorcade together and prevented unauthorized vehicles from joining the motorcade.[1634]

"Kenny O'Donnell has worked out the route from Love Field to the Dallas Trade Mart, where the President is scheduled to speak to a large luncheon audience of leading citizens. The Secret Service felt it was too insecure to move Kennedy slowly through a crowd downtown in a city where Stevenson had recently been physically attacked, but O'Donnell would not budge. The route would not be changed. Jack has to be seen by as many people as possible ..." [1635]

As they started, JFK political advisor "Dave Powers appeared beside the Lincoln. ... He reminded Mrs. Kennedy, 'Be sure to look to your left, away from the President. Wave to the people on your side. If you both wave at the same voter, it's a waste.'" [1636]

From Love Field, the motorcade drove at speeds up to 30 miles an hour through thinly populated areas.[1637] "As the Lincoln pulls away from the airport, Jackie puts on her sunglasses. Jack tells her to take them off. 'When you're riding in a car like this, in a parade, if you have your dark glasses on, you might as well have stayed at home.'" [1638] "At the first turn off Mockingbird [Lane, the third turn of the drive], Governor Connally grabbed the metal bar [J] in front of him and raised himself up and then sat back again. He looked incredulous. Unless all the early signs were wrong, about a quarter of a million people had turned out to see Kennedy in Dallas." [1639] The President directed that the auto stop twice, the first time so he could respond to a sign asking him to shake hands.[1640] America's first Roman Catholic President also halted the motorcade to speak to a nun and her group of small children.[1641]

[J] The bar will save his life in minutes, the important subject of Chapter 19 – THE SHOT NOT TAKEN.

Soon, "they were at the head of Main Street. On the left stood Police Headquarters.[K] Duty officers stood in the windows, waving. Prisoners on the top floor strained to look down. Chief Curry made a right turn and ... Greer turned the President's car behind the Chief. For the first time, the Kennedys could see the real welcome that Dallas was tendering to its Chief of State. Except for a center lane of pavement, the entire gourd of skyscrapers was covered with people. The heads were solid for twelve blocks straight down and up the sides of the buildings. It was as though all the rest had been prelude; now the curtain had been raised and, in a flash, the big uninvited part of Dallas was ready to tender its respects." [1642]

The crowds were so dense that Special Agent Hill had to leave the left front running board of the President's followup car four times to ride on the rear of the President's limousine.[1643] Several times Special Agent John Ready came forward from the right front running board of the Presidential followup car to the right side of the President's car.[1644] Special Agent Glen A. Bennett once left his place inside the followup car to help keep the crowd away from the President's car. When a teenage boy ran toward the rear of the President's car,[1645] Ready left the running board to chase the boy back into the crowd.

"On Jackie's side of the car, she has raised the window halfway to keep her hat from blowing off or being snatched off; like British royalty, she wears white gloves to wave to the crowd. Up to two hundred fifty thousand people have turned out to greet Jack and Jackie; far more than anyone—the Kennedy advance men, the Johnson staff, the Dallas police—has anticipated. And Jackie is the reason why. There are probably twice as many people here than would have turned out for Jack alone.

"The crowd is not just huge; it surges in behind the motorcycle escort and at times brings the Lincoln almost to a halt. Jack smiles and waves languidly as the car inches its way along the middle lane, the only one that remains passable. There are a few anti-Kennedy posters and some catcalls, but the crowd in the canyon of Main Street, where skyscrapers block out the sun, applauds warmly and shouts cheerfully." [1646]

Here is a picture worth more than a thousand words. The limousine going west on Main Street encounters a bus going east. A large placard placed on the side of the bus by the Dr. Pepper Company bids "WELCOME TO BIG "D"" to the American Bottlers of Carbonated Beverages, the convention for which Richard Nixon had been in town on behalf of Pepsi-Cola, until this morning. The bus's patrons are probably surprised to be looking right down at their Governor, and right behind him the President, and — Oh my God! — Is that Jackie!? The Kennedys are looking up at the bus riders, and maybe just as surprised by this close encounter before the immense crowd waiting for them just behind the bus. What a photo! [1647] What an innocent time!

[K] Where Oswald will be a prisoner in less than two hours. Where he will die in less than two days.

After the thronged drive along Main Street, the motorcade came to the west end of downtown at the intersection of Houston Street, where Dealey Plaza begins.[1648] There, the motorcade turned right and went north on Houston Street, passing tall buildings on the right, an open park on the left, headed toward the Texas School Book Depository Building.[1649] "The large Hertz sign on top of the Depository showed 12:29 when the first car of the presidential motorcade made the turn from Main Street onto Houston ..."[1650] The crowd thinned on Houston, then abruptly along Elm Street, which curves in a southwesterly direction as it proceeds downgrade toward the Triple Underpass [L] and the Stemmons Freeway.[1651]

[L] It is known by two names: "Underpass" if you are a motorist, "Overpass" if you are a railroader.

Although the geography is indelibly burned into the memories of many oldsters, for those not then alive, here is Dealey Plaza on a wonderfully clear map prepared by Gene Thorp of Cartographic Concepts Inc for this book,[1652] then as seen from the air:[1653]

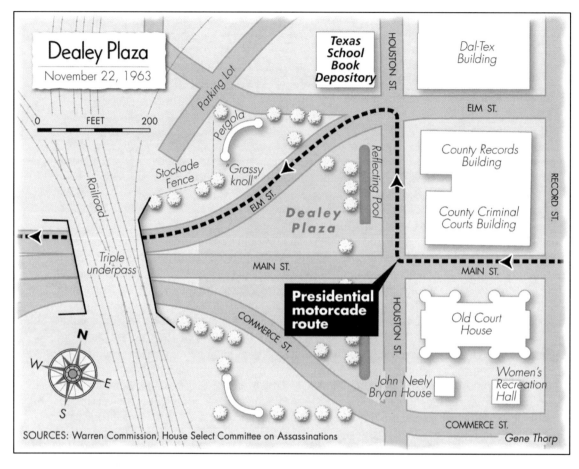

As the procession drove north on Houston Street toward Elm, a businessman standing on a concrete perch on the north side of Elm Street turned on his Bell & Howell Zoomatic camera, loaded with Kodachrome film. Abraham Zapruder wanted a souvenir of the day, and in the event recorded the most famous and useful documentation of the assassination.

There was gratification in the Presidential party about the warm reception. Evaluating  the political overtones, Kenneth O'Donnell was especially pleased because it convinced him that the average Dallas resident was like other American citizens in respecting and admiring the President.[1654] Nellie Connally wrote: "I could resist no longer and turned to the President and said, 'Mr. President, you certainly cannot say Dallas doesn't love you.' ... His eyes met mine and his smile got even wider. Dallas had surprised him. ...[T]hen I heard a loud, terrifying noise. It came from the back." [1655]   [1656]

At 12:30 PM CST, as the limousine proceeded at 11 miles per hour along Elm Street toward the Triple Underpass, shots fired from a rifle mortally wounded President Kennedy and seriously injured Governor Connally. One bullet passed through the President's neck; a subsequent bullet, which was lethal, shattered the right side of his skull. Governor Connally sustained bullet wounds in his back, the right side of his chest, right wrist, and left thigh.

The exact time of the assassination was fixed with precision by the large Hertz electric sign clock atop the Texas School Book Depository Building showing the numerals "12:30". The speed of the President's limousine was also precisely determined from the famous motion picture taken by Abraham Zapruder. His film showed that the President's automobile was moving at the exact rate of 11.2 miles per hour over a distance of approximately 136 feet immediately preceding the shot which struck the President in the head.[1657]

Mrs. Kennedy had been looking and waving to her left. After the car turned onto Elm, she heard a loud sound and a cry from Governor Connally, both to her right. "Upon turning right, she observed the President raising his hands to his throat with a puzzled expression on his face. JFK realized what had happened. 'My God, I am hit!' were his last words." [1658] To understand the three bullet hits, it is significant to note for later use that he could talk after somehow being injured by the first bullet. After the third, she cradled her mortally wounded husband and cried, "Oh, my God, they have shot my husband. I love you, Jack." [1659]

"When the first shot was fired, [Governor] Connally immediately recognized it as a rifle shot; the sound came from behind. He looked back in a reflexive motion over his right shoulder to where the sound had originated but saw only a few men, women and children standing on the grassy knoll alongside the street. There was nobody holding a gun, and the sound seemed to have come from farther away. He turned forward again and was just about to look over his left shoulder to make eye contact with President Kennedy when he felt a crippling blow to his back. [T]he adrenaline coursing through his veins threw his system into such shock that he never heard the sound of the second shot, the very shot that hit him." [1660] In his testimony before the Commission, Governor Connally was certain that he was hit by the second shot, which he stated he did not hear.[1661] Bullets left the powerful rifle at speeds much faster than the speed of sound.

Mrs. Connally looked over her right shoulder to see the President with an empty expression on his face.[1662] Roy Kellerman, in the right front seat, heard a report. Turning to his right in the direction of the noise, Kellerman saw the President's hands move up toward his neck. As he told the driver, "Let's get out of here; we are hit," Kellerman grabbed his microphone and radioed ahead to the lead car, "We are hit. Get us to the hospital immediately." [1663] The photo, taken later when the FBI recreated the shooting, looks back from Elm to the Depository.[1664]

Driver William Greer heard a noise which he took to be a backfire from one of the motorcycles flanking the Presidential car. When he heard the same noise again, Greer glanced over his shoulder and saw Governor Connally fall. At the sound of the second shot he realized that something was wrong and pressed down on the accelerator.[1665] Looking back from the front seat, Kellerman saw Governor Connally in his wife's lap.[1666]

When Mrs. Connally heard a second shot, she pulled her husband down into her lap.[1667] Observing his blood-covered chest as he was pulled into his wife's lap, Governor Connally believed himself mortally wounded. He cried out, "Oh, no, no, no. My God, they are going to kill us all." [1668] At first Mrs. Connally thought that her husband had been killed, but then she noticed an almost imperceptible movement and knew that he was still alive. She said, "It's all right. Be still." [1669] The Governor was lying with his head on his wife's lap when he heard a shot hit the President.[1670] At that point, both Governor and Mrs. Connally observed brain tissue splattered over the interior of the car.[1671] According to both Connallys, it was after this shot that Kellerman issued his emergency instructions and the car accelerated.[1672]

From the running board of the followup car, Special Agent Clint Hill, assigned to Mrs. Kennedy, was scanning the few people on the south side of Elm Street after the motorcade had

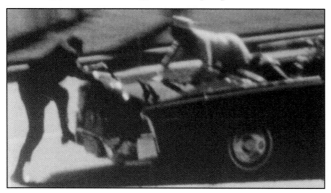

turned off Houston. He estimated that his followup car trailed the President's by only 5 feet.[1673] Hill heard a loud noise coming from his right rear. He immediately looked to his right, "and, in so doing, my eyes had to cross the Presidential limousine and I saw President Kennedy grab at himself and lurch forward and to the left." [1674] Hill ran to the President's auto.[1675] At about the time he reached it, he heard a shot that removed a portion of the President's head.[1676] M

At the instant that Hill stepped onto the left rear step of the President's automobile and grasped the handhold, the car lurched forward, causing him to lose his footing. He ran three

---

M The "official" time of death, designated by Mrs. Kennedy after Catholic last rites were administered, was 1:00 PM, but the President's head had exploded, so brain death had been at 12:31.

or four steps, regained his position and mounted the car. Between the time he originally seized the handhold and the time he mounted the car, Hill recalled:

"Mrs. Kennedy had jumped up from the seat and was, it appeared to me, reaching for something coming off the right rear bumper of the car, the right rear tail, when she noticed that I was trying to climb on the car. She turned toward me and I grabbed her and put her back in the back seat, crawled up on top of the back seat and lay there." [1677]

Dave Powers, who witnessed the scene from the followup car, believed that Mrs. Kennedy would probably have fallen off the rear end of the car and been killed if Hill had not pushed her back into the automobile. [1678] Afterward, Jacqueline Kennedy could not recall climbing out onto the trunk. [1679] Agent Hill shielded both Kennedys as the car raced at high speed to Parkland Memorial Hospital, 4 miles away. [1680] The photo [1681] is west of the Triple Underpass as the motorcycle escort reaches the onramp to Stemmons Freeway; the President's car is behind the right-hand white helmet, worn by Sergeant Steve Ellis whom we will meet in chapter 19. Within a minute, as VP Johnson, on the floor of his following car, would write

in his autobiography: "I did not realize it at the time, but we were then speeding past the Trade Mart, where 2,500 persons were waiting to greet the President of the United States. By now we were all aware that someone had been injured. But what had happened? Was it a bomb? A bullet? A firecracker exploding in front of someone's face? And who was hurt?" [1682]

Three cars behind the President was the press "pool", the few reporters whose turn it was to be close to Kennedy this day. Most reporters were in a bus back at the rear of the motorcade. In that press pool car, third behind Kennedy, "At the sound of gunfire Merriman Smith lunged for the mobile radio telephone. As the auto lurched forward, Smith crouched in the front seat, knuckles white on the phone, and barked the news to his colleague in UPI's Dallas bureau. ... The reverberations of rifle fire ... had barely stilled when the bulletin arrived in newsrooms around the world" [1683] in four minutes:

"**DALLAS, NOV. 22 (UPI)—THREE SHOTS WERE FIRED AT PRESIDENT KENNEDY'S MOTORCADE TODAY IN DOWNTOWN DALLAS JT1234PCS**" [1684]

Long before cable, three major TV networks controlled "the airwaves". CBS is showing soap opera *As the World Turns*. Just eight minutes after the shooting, newsman Walter Cronkite, [1685] "The most trusted man in America", breaks in to say that someone has fired three shots at the motorcade. Although most Americans are at work or school, and not home watching daytime television, more than 68 percent of all adults are aware of the shooting by 1:00 P.M. [1686] This author learned of the gunfire when Dewey ran in from his shipping area to my engineer's office at Colorsound at 10:45 AM in California. The more tragic news hit us within the hour.

This is the EVENTS section of the book. ANALYSIS comes next, then in EVIDENCE will be Chapter 14 – TOO CLOSE TO CALL, with a full discussion of the timing and ballistics of the three bullets. To move onward from here to the other events of the day, I briefly preview my carefully considered conviction that the sequence of shots was this:

The first shot was hurried, for the reason that Oswald could not find John Connally in the President's car where he was supposed to be, until the limo turned onto Elm Street below him. When he at last found his intended target, he fired quickly, but Connally was then shielded under a pine oak [1687] tree. The bullet missed the limo altogether, bounced off (maybe) a branch of the tree and (certainly) the pavement, then continued to the southwest. It struck a curb near the Triple Underpass, chipping off a fragment of curbstone. Stone chips then bloodied the cheek of a stalled motorist, James Tague, standing near his car at the SE end of the Triple Underpass.[N] Tague's singular story will be told in Chapter 14.

The second shot, when the limo had moved enough so Oswald could see and aim at Connally, went in a straight line toward Connally, but Kennedy was in the way. The bullet first went into his back, exited below his neck, then entered and gravely injured Connally.

The third shot hit Kennedy in the head, killing him.

From Parkland Hospital, when reporters in the motorcade got a look into the bloody limousine, "UPI flashed the news around the world:

**KENNEDY SERIOUSLY WOUNDED, PERHAPS FATALLY,
BY AN ASSASSIN'S BULLET**" [1688]

The President was immediately treated by a team of physicians who had been alerted by a police radio message from the motorcade. The doctors noted irregular breathing movements but could not detect a heartbeat. They observed the extensive wound in the President's head and a small wound approximately one-fourth inch in diameter in the lower front of his neck. In an effort to facilitate breathing, the physicians performed a tracheotomy by enlarging that throat wound and inserting a tube. "A medic came rushing out ... and asked if anybody knew the president's blood type. Every agent carried a card with the president's vital signs, and ... Roy Kellerman blurted out, 'O. R-H positive.'" [1689]

Secret Service agent Clint Hill, assigned to and standing beside Mrs. Kennedy, later wrote of using a hallway phone to call the first news to Jerry Behn in Washington, the Special Agent In Charge of the White House Detail. "[T]he operator cut into the line. 'The Attorney General wants to talk to Agent Hill.' 'Clint, what's going on down there?!'" [1690] "The interruption was so unexpected, and the Attorney General sounded so much like the President, that Clint grabbed a clipboard hook for support." [1691] "Staring at Mrs. Kennedy, I repeated, 'Shots fired during the motorcade. The president is very seriously injured. They're working on him now. Governor Connally was hit, too.' 'What do you mean seriously injured? How bad is it?' I swallowed hard, as the image of the president's head exploding replayed in my mind. The image of his lifeless body lying across Mrs. Kennedy's lap. His eyes fixed. His blood and brains all over her, all over me. *How do I tell him his brother is dead?* Looking away from Mrs. Kennedy, I closed my eyes, squeezed the phone hard, and said, 'It's as bad as it can get.'" [1692]

"[T]he Chief Executive was past saving ... [T]he entire staff of Parkland could have done nothing for him after 12:30. In fact, had he been anyone but the President of the United States, the first physician to see him would have tagged him 'DOA'—'Dead on Arrival.'" [1693] A neighborhood priest had hurried to the hospital and administered the Last Rites of the Catholic Church, including the forgiveness of sins so the soul can enter directly into Heaven.

[N] The "TWO WOUNDED" of this chapter's title are Tague and Connally. I choose to not add two soon to have their faces badly scratched in the Texas Theatre, Oswald and Patrolman Nick McDonald.

"In the hall outside [the trauma room, JFK's top assistant Ken] O'Donnell and the Secret Service and Mrs. Kennedy conferred. [Acting Press Secretary] Malcolm Kilduff was told he would have to announce the death. He wanted to know the time, the exact time. Mrs. Kennedy and O'Donnell wanted to know what time it was now. It was a minute or two before 1 P.M. The widow wanted the time of death to come after the time the priest had given her husband conditional absolution [("if you are alive")]. The heads began to nod. Dr. Malcolm Perry was called. He was asked if 1 P.M. would be all right. Yes, that would be all right. The death certificate would so state." [1694]

Kilduff tearfully made his announcement and UPI flashed it around the world:

"**FLASH**

PRESIDENT KENNEDY DEAD

JT135PCS" [1695]

Cronkite wrote that "It fell to me to make the announcement. I was doing fine ... until it was necessary to pronounce the words: 'From Dallas, Texas, the flash, apparently official. President Kennedy died at 1 p.m. Central Standard Time — some thirty-eight minutes ago [pause] . . .' The words stuck in my throat. A sob wanted to replace them.[1696] A gulp or two quashed the sob, which metamorphosed into tears forming in the corners of my eyes. I fought back the emotion and regained my professionalism, but it was touch and go there for a few seconds before I could continue ..." [1697]

The national impact of that broadcast was recalled by Allan Burns, co-creator of "The Mary Tyler Moore Show" and "Lou Grant" in his contribution to the fascinating book of show-biz recollections, *We'll Never Be Young Again*: "It was, I remember someone saying, eerily like watching Cronkite on 'You Are There', but this time the 'you' was us and the 'there' was now. I don't need to describe the expression on Walter's face when the final, awful news came; it is forever etched into our collective consciousness, like the video pictures of the hijacked jet crashing into the second tower of the World Trade Center." [1698]

Governor Connally underwent extensive surgery that afternoon in Parkland Memorial Hospital. Reconstruction of his wrist was complex; the bullet's ultimate injury to his leg was minor. Thoracic surgeons were appalled by the extent of his chest injuries — a rib shattered into sharp shards, doing injuries as close to fatal as is possible while still allowing ultimate recovery.[1699] "Throughout the operation, the Governor had lost 1,296 cc. of blood",[1700] about three pints.

Afterward, "the chief executive of the State of Texas reposed, looking like a scientific octopus. Plastic tubes ran into his body from overhead positions; others drained downward toward the floor. The fractured right wrist was suspended halfway over the bed. An oxygen mask was over his mouth ..." [1701] "The Governor could not speak with the mask on his face ... Mrs. Connally thought that this would be a good time to tell her husband some bad news. She was dwelling on it when Connally lifted the mask off with his left hand and said: 'How is the

President?' Nellie Connally said: 'He died.' The white head on the pillow nodded. 'I knew,' he said. 'I knew.' The mask snapped back on the mouth and nose." [1702]

Learning of the President's death, Vice President Johnson left the hospital under close guard and proceeded to the Presidential plane at Love Field. After Mrs. Kennedy and her husband's casket boarded the 707, Lyndon Baines Johnson was sworn in as the 36th President of the United States by an old friend, Federal District Court Judge Sarah T. Hughes. The plane took off immediately for Washington, D.C., arriving at Andrews AFB, Maryland, at 5:58 PM EST. "Part of the extensive security to meet the plane included FBI agent Francis O'Neill ... 'The casket was lowered from the plane, and then placed into the waiting ambulance,' recalls O'Neill. ... 'Bobby Kennedy and Mrs. Kennedy got into the ambulance' ... 'Kellerman got into the front seat, and Greer was the driver.'" [1703] Five hours earlier, Greer and Kellerman had those same positions in the joyful drive through Dallas.

The President's body was taken to the National Naval Medical Center, Bethesda, where it was given a complete pathological examination. The autopsy disclosed the large head wound and the wound in the front of the neck that had been enlarged by Parkland doctors when they performed the tracheotomy. Both of these were described in the autopsy report as being "presumably of exit." In addition the autopsy revealed a small wound of entry in the rear of the President's skull and another wound of entry near the base of the back of the neck. The autopsy report stated the cause of death as "Gunshot wound, head," and the bullets that struck the President were described as having been fired "from a point behind and somewhat above the level of the deceased." [1704]

We now return to Dallas at 12:30 PM CST. At the scene of the shooting, there was a bit of confusion at the outset concerning the point of origin of the shots. Dealey Plaza's acoustics were unusual, with tall hard-surface buildings reflecting sound from the north and east sides, but open space on south and west. Thus, witnesses differed in their accounts of the direction from which they believed the sound of gunfire had emanated. Within a few minutes, however, attention centered on the Depository Building as the source of the shots. [1705]

Several eyewitnesses in front of the building reported that they saw a rifle being fired from the southeast corner window on the sixth floor. One eyewitness, Howard L. Brennan, had been watching from directly across Elm Street, facing the building. He promptly told a policeman that he had seen a slender man, about 5 feet 10 inches, in his early thirties, take deliberate aim and fire a rifle in the direction of the President's car. [1706] Brennan thought he might be able to identify the man since he had noticed him in that window a few minutes before the motorcade arrived. Another witness saw the man, not so clearly, but saw the rifle fire its last two shots. [1707] At 12:34 PM, Dallas police radio mentioned the Depository Building as a possible source of the shots, and at 12:45 the police radio broadcast an accurate and detailed description of the suspected assassin, based primarily on Brennan's description. [1708]

When the shots were fired, Dallas motorcycle patrolman Marrion L. Baker was several vehicle lengths behind the President. He had turned right from Main onto Houston and was about 200 feet south of Elm Street when he heard a shot. Baker, having recently returned from a week of deer hunting, was certain the shot came from a high-powered rifle. He looked up and saw pigeons scattering in the air from their perches atop the Texas School Book Depository Building. He raced his motorcycle to the building, dismounted and pushed his way through the spectators on the entrance steps. There he encountered Roy Truly, the TSBD superintendent, who stood with his boss and intended lunch partner, Ochus V. Campbell. [1709]

Truly offered Baker his help. They entered the building and ran toward the two elevators in the rear. Finding that both were on upper floors, they ran to the stairs. Not more than two minutes had elapsed since the shooting.[1710]

Baker intended to dash to the top, but on the second floor he saw movement "through a small window in the stairwell door."[1711] It was a lunchroom; a man was walking away from him, and Baker had the impression that he was moving in a hurry. Pointing his revolver, the patrolman commanded either "Hey, you!" or "Come here"; he will later testify to both.[1712] Baker recalls:

> "[H]e started turning around toward me. He didn't have time to respond; it was momentary. He didn't have time to say anything, and I didn't have time to observe him. About that time, Mr. Truly was beside me. I asked him if this man worked for him or if he knew him, and he said, 'Yes, he works for me!' So we continued on up the stairwell to the sixth floor and to the top. Later it was learned that the man I had encountered was Lee Harvey Oswald. But at that time, the name Oswald would have meant nothing to me, especially after being told that he worked there."[1713]

Within a minute after his encounter with Baker and Truly, Oswald was seen passing the second-floor offices, walking toward the front of the building. He reached the front door just as young NBC newsman Robert MacNeil, (later of PBS's MacNeil/Lehrer Report)[O] who had jumped out of the motorcade's press bus, rushed in. MacNeil recalled:

> "I ran ... into the first building I came to that looked as though it might have a phone. It was the Texas Book Depository. As I ran up the steps and through the door, a young man in shirt sleeves was coming out. In great agitation I asked him where there was a phone. He pointed inside ... [That afternoon at the hospital] I heard on television that a young man called Oswald, arrested for the shooting, worked at the Texas Book Depository and had left by the front door immediately afterwards. Isn't that strange, I told myself. He must have been leaving just about the time I was running in."[1714]

Lee later told police that MacNeil's athletic build and good suit made him think that only one minute after being challenged by a policeman, he was confronted by a Secret Service man![1715] Oswald then hurried down the steps to Elm Street and 7 minutes later, at about 12:40 PM, boarded a bus on Elm Street seven short blocks (about four tenths of a mile) east of the Depository. The bus was westbound toward his roominghouse in Oak Cliff.

Mary Bledsoe, the landlady who had thrown Lee out six weeks before because she did not like him, especially for speaking a foreign language into her phone — Oh, the horrors! — had gone downtown to see the President. After Kennedy had passed her on Main Street, she boarded a bus and sat in her favorite seat, on the bench at right-front, where she faced the driver and saw everyone who got on or off.[1716] "And ... at Murphy ... Oswald got on. He looks like a maniac. ... and I didn't look at him. I didn't want [him] to know I even seen him, and I just looked off, and then about that time the motorman said the President had been shot ..."[1717] She testified that Oswald had passed in front of her aisle-facing seat, just a matter of a foot or two away, and "he looked so bad in his face, and his face was so distorted."[1718]

Lee stayed aboard 3 or 4 minutes, during which the bus inched ahead only two blocks because of the traffic jam created by the motorcade and his shooting, then "taking his cue from a woman who was in a hurry, asked for a transfer (which was found on him when he was arrested) and left the bus ..."[1719] as Mrs. Bledsoe watched, attentively but secretively.[1720]

[O] Keep on reading — Jim Lehrer, also in Dallas, will get to play his part, to be described in chapter 14.

We are again indebted and grateful to Gene Thorp for this excellent map, exactly the right scale to show Oswald's movements in the 80 minutes from shooting to capture: [1721]

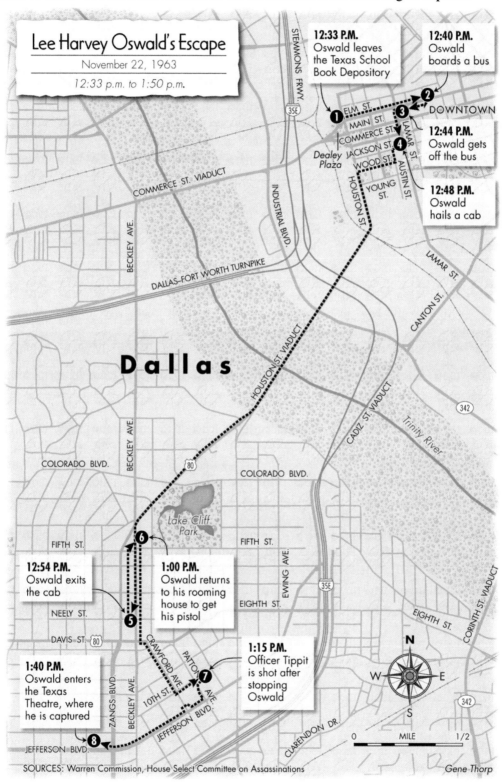

A few minutes later Lee entered a taxi four blocks away and asked the driver to take him to North Beckley Avenue, several blocks beyond his roominghouse. The trip took only six minutes. "Oswald dug into his trouser pocket and brought out a dollar bill. The meter read ninety-five cents. 'Keep the change,' he said and slammed the door." [1722] At about 1 PM Oswald's boardinghouse manager, Mrs. Earlene Roberts, had been urged by a friend to turn on the TV. She would testify to the Warren Commission: "I went and turned it on and I was trying to clear it up ... and he [known to her as O. H. Lee] come in and I just looked up and I said, 'Oh, you are in a hurry.' He never said a thing, not nothing. He went on to his room and stayed about 3 or 4 minutes ... just long enough, I guess, to go in there and get a jacket and put it on and he went out zipping it." Asked "was he running or walking?" she said: "He was walking fast—he was making tracks pretty fast." Commission counsel also asked if she ever cleaned his room — "Yes" — and concerning places he might keep a gun out of sight: "Were there any drawers or anything in there?" "Yes; there was drawers in that chifforobe [P] and he also had a vanity dresser with four drawers." But, she had never seen a gun. [1723]

Fourteen minutes later, only 45 minutes after Lee wounded two and killed one, there was another violent shooting in Dallas. The victim was Dallas Police Patrolman J.D. Tippit. He has a tenth-grade education, was a World War II paratrooper who earned a Bronze Star, is now thirty-nine years old, married with three children, a clean record during his eleven years with the force. He earns a little over $5,000 a year — equivalent to only $2.50 an hour. [1724] The letters "J.D." do not stand for anything in particular, as is common in Texas. [1725]

Tippit was alone in his patrol car at 12:45 when he was ordered by radio to proceed to the central Oak Cliff area as part of a concentration of patrol cars around the center of the city following the assassination. At 12:54 Tippit radioed that he had moved as directed and would be available for any emergency. By this time the police radio had broadcast several messages alerting officers to the suspect described by Brennan at the scene of the assassination — a slender white male, about 30 years old, 5 feet 10 inches and weighing about 165 pounds. [1726]

At 1:15 PM, Tippit was driving slowly along 10th Street in Oak Cliff (see the map to the left). Near the intersection of Patton Avenue, he pulled up alongside a walking man, who may have attracted attention by changing direction when he saw the police cruiser. [1727] The man met the radio's general description of the suspect. He walked over to Tippit's car, rested his arms on the right-hand door, and apparently exchanged words through the window. Tippit then opened his door on the left side and started to walk around the front of his car. As he reached the front wheel on the driver's side, the man on the sidewalk drew a revolver. [1728] Three nearby witnesses watched in horror as the man shot Tippit three times in the stomach and chest. The gunman began to hurry away, then stopped, walked around the car, aimed downward, and fired a fourth bullet into the temple of  the officer who was on the ground, his gun still in his holster. The stark importance of that last bullet must be emphasized and understood for its enormity: After starting to walk away, the gunman stopped, went back to where J.D. Tippit was already dying on the ground, leaned down and shot him execution-style in the head.

[P] In *To Kill a Mockingbird*, both the book and movie, Mayella asked Tom to "bust up a chifforobe".

Automobile repairman Domingo Benavides, driving a pickup truck, heard the shots and stopped near Tippit's car. He saw the gunman start toward Patton Avenue, removing empty cartridge cases from the gun as he went. Benavides rushed to Tippit's side. The patrolman was apparently dead. Benavides promptly reported the shooting to police headquarters over the radio in Tippit's car. "We've had a shooting here…it's a police officer, somebody shot him." [1729] It was now 1:16 PM. [1730]

As the gunman left the scene, he walked hurriedly to Patton Avenue and turned left, heading south. Standing on the corner of 10th and Patton was Helen Markham, who had been walking south on Patton and had seen both the killer and Tippit cross the intersection in front of her as she waited on the curb for traffic to pass. She witnessed the shooting and then saw the man with a gun in his hand walk back toward the corner and cut across the lawn of the corner house as he started south on Patton Avenue. [1731]

In the corner house, Mrs. Barbara Jeanette Davis and her sister-in-law, Mrs. Virginia Davis, heard the shots and rushed to the door in time to see the man walk across the lawn shaking a revolver, emptying it of cartridge cases. Later that day each woman found a cartridge case near the house. As the gunman turned the corner, he passed beside a taxicab parked on Patton Avenue, a few feet from 10th Street. The driver, William W. Scoggins, had seen the slaying and was now crouched behind his cab. As the gunman cut through the shrubbery on the lawn, Scoggins looked up and saw the man only 12 feet away. In his hand was a pistol and "he thought he heard Oswald muttering, 'Poor, dumb cop!' He had just taken a man's life in cold blood. This was Lee Oswald. His contempt was universal." [1732]

The gunman crossed to the west side of Patton Avenue and ran south toward Jefferson Boulevard, a main Oak Cliff thoroughfare. On the east side of Patton, between 10th Street and Jefferson, used car salesman Ted Callaway, who had heard the shooting just around the corner of his block, ran to the sidewalk. As the man with the gun rushed past, Callaway shouted "What's going on?" The man merely shrugged, ran on to Jefferson Boulevard and turned right. On the next corner was a gas station with a parking lot in the rear. The assailant ran into the lot, discarded his jacket and then continued his flight west on Jefferson. [1733]

The gunman had been seen by many witnesses who gave similar descriptions to police. At 1:28 PM, the deputy chief asked on police radio: "Is there any indication that it [murder of Tippit] has any connection with this other [murder of Kennedy] shooting?" The dispatcher replied: "Well, the descriptions on the suspect are similar and it is possible." [1734] In just under one hour, Oswald has given police two strong reasons to find him: the shooting of both the president and the governor, then the cold-blooded execution of one of their own.

In Hardy's Shoe Store farther along Jefferson, manager Johnny Calvin Brewer heard a siren after the store's radio had told of the shooting of a policeman in Oak Cliff. Brewer saw a young man who appeared to have been running, had messed-up hair and looked scared, step into the deep doorway well of his store and turn his back to the street. [1735] When a police car with siren blaring (going to a false alarm about a man running into the public library — it turned out the man worked there) made a U-turn and headed away, the man returned to the sidewalk and Brewer followed. He saw the man enter the Texas Theatre, a motion picture house 60 feet away, without buying a ticket. Brewer pointed this out to the cashier, Mrs. Julia Postal. [1736] Brewer thought this was a suspicious person because of his hiding as the police car went by, and then walking into the theatre without purchasing a ticket.

Ticket seller Julia Postal accepted his word, dialed the operator and asked for the police.[Q] At 1:45, police radio sounded the alarm: "Have information a suspect just went in [*sic*] the Texas Theatre on West Jefferson." [1737] The area was already teeming with squad cars, which quickly converged on and surrounded the small theatre. As the movie "War Is Hell" continued to play to about a dozen patrons, the house lights were turned on. Patrolman Maurice N. "Nick" McDonald and others approached a man pointed out to them by shoe salesman Brewer.[1738] McDonald ordered the man to his feet and heard him say, "Well, it's all over now." [1739] The man struck Officer McDonald's face, leaving a long scratch, while drawing a pistol from his waist. He attempted to shoot but the thumb-index-finger web of an officer's hand slowed the hammer, causing a misfire that only dented the cartridge. After a brief struggle, four officers disarmed and handcuffed the suspect, whose forehead and nose received abrasions in the scuffle. "'I didn't kill anybody!' [he] cried out, although nobody had accused him of anything." [1740]

He was taken through an angry mob on the sidewalk, and at 1:52 was bundled into a patrol car. Officers asked the suspect his name. He refused to answer. In his wallet they found no driver's license, but there were two Marine Corps "Certificate of Service" cards and two Selective Service System cards. They identified him as both Alek James Hidell and Lee Harvey Oswald. [1741]

The police car drove to Main Street, where crowds had greeted the motorcade, and dove down a ramp into the basement under Dallas Police Headquarters.[1742] Oswald stepped out of the car at the exact spot where he will be shot on Sunday morning. It is 2 PM,[1743] only 90 minutes after his shooting in Dealey Plaza, 45 minutes after his execution of the patrolman.

The police took him into the Homicide offices to investigate the shooting of Officer Tippit. There were two glass-encased interrogation rooms. As Lee was put into one, a man in the other saw him and, like Mrs. Bledsoe on the bus, knew: "Well, that is Oswald. He works for us. He is one of my boys." [1744] The man was William Hoyt Shelley,[1745] who had been brought from the TSBD, along with other employees, to get a statement as to where he was at the time of the shooting there, and what he might know about that. Shelley told the detective who had brought him in, C. W. Brown,[R] that he was Oswald's personal supervisor and was responsible for his training and work assignments.[1746] Detective Brown immediately realized that Oswald "might be the boy that was responsible for ... the President's assassination. That was my own personal opinion at that time." [1747]

Lee's lifelong lousy luck lingers. He had boarded a bus and was recognized by the lady who had rented him a room but soon threw him out because she didn't like him. He shot a patrolman in front of witnesses. He ineptly drew attention by trying to hide at a shoe store, then by going into a movie without paying. Now he is in police headquarters for a shooting in Oak Cliff and is immediately connected to the earlier shooting miles away in Dealey Plaza!

While Lee attempted to escape, executed an innocent patrolman and was captured, there have been important events at the Texas School Book Depository Building. Dallas Police Department Inspector J. Herbert Sawyer arrived at the scene shortly after hearing the first police radio messages at 12:34 PM. Officers who had been assigned to the area of Elm and

---

[Q] This is the old days, pre-9-1-1. Murder mystery movie actors barked, "Operator, get me the police!"

[R] Police work in Dallas attracted an inordinate number of men known only by their initials, common then and now in the Deep South and Texas. A civilian example from Dallas: "Who killed JR?"

Houston Streets for the motorcade were talking to witnesses and guarding the building when he arrived. Sawyer entered the Depository, conducted a quick search, and by 12:40 PM ordered that no one be permitted to leave the building.[1748]

"One Secret Service agent returned to the scene of the crime. Forrest V. Sorrels of the Dallas office ... was back in the Texas School Book Depository building within twenty-five minutes. ... [He listened to pipefitter Brennan:] 'I could see the man taking deliberate aim and saw him fire the third shot.' Brennan said that the rifle was then pulled back into the window slowly, as though the rifleman was studying the effect of the shot at his leisure. ... Sorrels began to feel a little better. He had leads. ... As he crossed the square and walked into the sheriff's office [the limousine had passed it on Houston Street while going directly toward Oswald], an officer pointed to a young couple, waiting patiently on a bench, who had also witnessed the shooting. Somewhere around was a man with pellet holes in his cheek, a man who stood in a direct line with a shot that ricocheted from the pavement beside the President's car. Mr. Sorrels began to feel encouraged. [1749]

Shortly before 1 PM, Captain J. Will Fritz, chief of the homicide and robbery bureau of the Dallas Police Department, arrived to take charge of the investigation. Searching the sixth floor, Deputy Sheriff Luke Mooney saw a pile of cartons in the southeast corner. He squeezed through the boxes and realized immediately that he had discovered the point from which the shots had been fired, soon to become infamous as "the sniper's nest". A book carton to the left of the window allowed a person sitting on it to look down while partly hidden from view of those outside. Between this carton and the half-open window were three additional cartons to make a rifle rest. The stacks of boxes, which first attracted Mooney's attention, effectively hid a person at the window from the view of anyone else on the floor.[1750]

On the floor, Mooney found three empty rifle cartridges. Dallas Police Lt. J. C. "Carl" Day, "chief of the crime scene search unit, photographed the three bullet shells in their original position." [1751] "The three empty shells were turned over to the FBI ... Ballistics tests later determined they were fired from Oswald's rifle, to the exclusion of any other gun." [1752]

Mooney's discovery intensified the search for additional evidence. At 1:22 PM, "Ten minutes after the shells were found, Deputy Sheriff Eugene Boone and Deputy Constable Seymour Weitzman were near the northwest corner of the sixth floor when they spotted the rifle, hidden between boxes only three feet from the rear stairwell." [1753] "No one touched it until Lt. Day arrived. Day could immediately estimate the chances for recovery of prints, and it was poor. 'I looked down between the boxes and saw the rifle had a well-worn leather strap. I knew there could be no fingerprints on that strap,[S] so I picked the gun up by that. The stock was pretty porous and weather-worn, so there was little chance of any prints there. Before pulling the bolt back, I satisfied myself there were no prints on the little metal lever. Then I held the gun while Captain Fritz pulled the bolt, and a live round fell out. There were no more shells in the magazine.'" [1754] Day noted that stamped on the rifle was serial number "C2766" as well as the markings "1940" "MADE ITALY" and "CAL. 6.5." The rifle was about 40 inches long, and when disassembled it could fit into a handmade paper sack that was found in the "sniper's nest" corner, within a few feet of the cartridge cases.[1755]

[S] This is 1963, decades before police looked for DNA. When O.J. Simpson was tried for murdering his wife Nicole and Ron Goldman in 1994, DNA gathering was still famously new and inexact.

While Fritz and Day were examining the rifle, TSBD superintendent Roy Truly noticed something he felt should be brought to the attention of the police. He had observed that Lee Harvey Oswald, uniquely of the 15 men who worked for him in the warehouse, was missing. "Truly called the warehouse where the job application forms were kept. He obtained Oswald's full name, an accurate physical description, and his telephone number and address at the Paines'. ... Truly told Fritz that he had a boy missing and handed him the slip of paper [with Oswald's information]. 'Thank you, Mr. Truly. We will take care of it.'" [1756]

Captain Fritz returned to police headquarters at 2:15, where Sergeant Gerald "Jerry" Hill of the Patrol Division, talking with two detectives, picks up the story: "Captain Fritz came in. He told them that he wanted them to get a search warrant and to go out to an address in Irving, and if a fellow named Lee Oswald was out there, to bring him in. I asked the Captain why he wanted him, and he said, 'Well, he was employed in the Book Depository and was there just before the shooting but had gone after the shooting and was therefore a suspect.'" [1757] "'You don't need to go out there to get him,' Jerry told the captain. 'Why?' Fritz asked, and Jerry gestured toward the interrogation room. ''Cause there the son of a bitch sits.'" [1758] The missing School Book Depository employee and the suspect who had been apprehended for killing Officer J.D. Tippit were one and the same. [1759]

That morning in Irving, while they followed President Kennedy's arrival and joyful procession through Dallas on television, Marina Oswald and Ruth Paine made plans to go out that afternoon to buy Marina a much-needed pair of shoes. [1760] Both cried and prayed when they heard that the President had been shot. "A little later, Marina was outside hanging up clothes. Ruth came to join her and told her that the reporters were saying the shots that hit the President had come from the Texas School Book Depository. At that, Marina's heart 'fell to the bottom.' [She alone knew of Lee's shooting at Walker.] 'Is there really anyone on earth but my lunatic husband crazy enough to have fired that shot?' she asked herself. Unlikely and unexplained occurrences suddenly started to drop into place: Lee's unannounced visit the night before, his shrugging and saying he knew nothing about the President's visit. Marina hid the fear that had seized her; she did not want to reveal it to Ruth." [1761]

"Marina was numb. ... When she was certain Ruth could not see her, she crept into the garage, to the place where Lee kept his rifle ... inside the heavy blanket, a green and brown wool blanket of East German make that he had bought in Russia. [T]hree weeks earlier, Marina had rolled back a corner of the blanket and spied the rifle's wooden stock. Now she found the bundle and stared at it. ... Marina did not touch the blanket, but it looked exactly as it had before. Thank God the rifle was still there, Marina thought, feeling as if a weight had been lifted from her. Yet she wondered if there was really 'a second idiot' in Dallas, anyone else crazy enough, besides her husband, even to think of such a deed." [1762]

"An hour, or a little less, after the President's death was announced, the doorbell rang. Ruth went to answer. She was greatly surprised to find six men standing on her doorstep. They were from the sheriff's office and the Dallas police, they said, and they showed their credentials. Ruth's jaw dropped. 'We have Lee Oswald in custody,' one of the policemen said. 'He is charged with shooting an officer.' It was Ruth's first clue that Lee might be linked in any way to the events of the day. The men wanted to search the house." [1763] Ruth had nothing to hide, so invited them in without a warrant and they began to search.

"Then came a question: 'Does your husband have a rifle?' 'Yes,' Marina said in Russian [to Ruth's total astonishment], [1764] and led them straight to the garage ... The blanket looked exactly as it always had, as if there were something bulky inside. As always, it was carefully tied in string. Marina shook all over, trying not to show her fright, as an officer stooped down to pick it up. It hung, limp, on either side of his arm. Ruth looked at Marina. She had gone ashen. 'So it *was* Lee,' Marina thought. *'That* is why he came last night.' For Marina it was again one of those moments when kaleidoscopic and inexplicable occurrences suddenly clicked into place. She knew now why Lee had told her to buy 'everything' she and the children needed, why he had left without kissing her goodbye." [1765]

Then there was more. "She had been half asleep when he dressed. A deputy went to her bedroom and glanced into a Russian teacup and came out of the room with Lee's wedding ring. It was of no great significance to the police, but it told the whole heartbreaking story to Marina. He had never removed his wedding ring. He had never returned it to her, even in the heat of arguments when he had beaten her with his fists. The ring in the teacup was a resignation from marriage. The end. In her heart, the young Russian pharmacist knew that, whatever the crime, 'my crazy one' was in it." [1766] "Lee had intended to do it when he left that morning. Apparently, he didn't expect to return." [1767]

About that time, "At FBI headquarters in Dallas, James Hosty heard from his superior, Gordon Shanklin, that the prime suspect in the Kennedy assassination was Lee Harvey Oswald. The name stunned him. For more than two months he had personally superintended the Oswald file. Only three weeks before, he had spoken to Oswald's wife and Ruth Paine in Irving and had learned that Oswald was working at the Texas Book Depository. Then Oswald had come to the FBI offices and, according to the receptionists who read it, left a threatening note which began: 'Let this be a warning.' ... Hosty ... claimed that it threatened ... to 'take appropriate action.'" [1768] This is a haunting echo of Oswald's written threat to Connally: "I shall employ all means to right this gross mistake or injustice ..." It would be most interesting to study the note to Hosty, but as told later in this chapter, he will destroy it in two days.

Interviewing a lying, dissembling person like Lee Oswald can be directed if he is taken by surprise, the case this day, and closely questioned based on the items in his pockets. Captain Fritz had an officer empty Lee's pockets and make a list:

1. Membership card of the Fair Play for Cuba Committee, New Orleans, Louisiana, in the name of L. H. Oswald, bearing the signature Lee H. Oswald, issued June 15, 1963, signed A. J. Hidell, chapter president.
2. Membership card of the Fair Play for Cuba Committee, 799 Broadway, New York 3, New York, ORegon 4-8295, in the name of Lee H. Oswald, bearing signature Lee H. Oswald, issued May 28, 1963, signed V. T. Lee, Executive Secretary.
3. Certificate of Service, Armed Forces of the United States Marine Corps in name of Lee Harvey Oswald, 1653230.
4. Department of Defense identification card #N4,271,617 in the name of Lee H. Oswald, reflecting service status as MCR/inact, service #1653230, bearing photograph of Lee Harvey Oswald and signed Lee H. Oswald, expiration date being December 7, 1962.
5. Dallas Public Library identification card in the name of Lee Harvey Oswald.
6. Snapshot of Lee Harvey Oswald in Marine uniform.
7. Snapshot of small baby in white cap.
8. Social Security card #433-54-3937 in name of Lee Harvey Oswald.
9. U.S. Forces, Japan, identification card in name of Lee H. Oswald, Private, SN 1653230, bearing signature of Lee H. Oswald, issued May 8, 1958.
10. Photograph of Mrs. Lee Harvey Oswald.
11. Street map of Dallas, compliments of Ga-Jo-Enkanko Hotel.

12. Selective Service System notice of classification card in name of Alek James Hidell, which bears photograph of Lee Harvey Oswald and signature "Alek J. Hidell".
13. Certificate of Service, U.S. Marine Corps, in name of Alex James Hidell.
14. Selective Service System Notice of Classification in name Lee Harvey Oswald, SSN 41-114-39-532, dated February 2, 1960.
15. Selective Service System Registration Certificate in name Lee Harvey Oswald, SSN 41-114-39-532, bearing signature Lee H. Oswald, dated October 18, 1939.
16. Slip of paper marked "Embassy USSR, 1609 Decatur St., N.W., Washington, D.C., Consular Pezhuyehko".
17. Slip of paper marked "The Worker, 23 W. 26th St., New York 10, NY"; "The Worker, Box 28 Madison Sq. Station, New York 10, NY".
18. Snub-nosed Smith and Wesson Revolver, .38. Its chambers were loaded.
19. 6 cartridges of ammunition, caliber .38. [1769]
20. $13.87. [1770]
21. The bus transfer from when he abandoned the Oak Cliff bus on Elm Street.
22. Silver color Marine Corps emblem ring.
23. Brass key marked, "P. O. Dept. Do Not Dup." to his Dallas PO Box 2915. [1771]

Three of the items are fraudulent (1, 12, 13) and two (18 & 19) are for killing. Probably most helpful in understanding what is important to the bearer are the seven (3, 4, 6, 9, 14, 15, 22) documenting his military service, which he still carries four full years after that service ended.

By ten minutes after three o'clock, "Oswald was identified by Patrolman Marrion Baker as the man he had seen in the lunchroom of the Book Depository." [1772] Agents of the FBI and the U.S. Secret Service arrived at police headquarters to participate in questioning. From 3:10 to 4:00 PM, "Homicide captain Will Fritz and FBI agents James Hosty and James Bookhout conducted the first interrogation of Oswald. His attitude, according to Bookhout, was 'very arrogant and argumentative.' Hosty said Oswald was extremely hostile." [1773]

"[O]n his return from interviewing Oswald ... Hosty was confronted at the FBI office by Special Agent in Charge J. Gordon Shanklin with the note which Oswald had left several days earlier. Shanklin, who appeared 'agitated and upset,' asked Hosty about the circumstances in which he had received the note and about his visits to Ruth Paine and Marina Oswald. On Shanklin's orders, Hosty dictated a two- to four-page memorandum setting forth all he knew about Oswald. He gave the memorandum, in duplicate, to Shanklin." [1774]

"Fritz had been trying for months to obtain a tape recorder for the homicide and robbery bureau. But he had not succeeded. As a result, the only record of Oswald's twelve hours of interrogation that weekend comes from the notes and memoranda of those who happened to be present." [1775] Lee Oswald denied having anything to do with the murders of Kennedy or Tippit. He claimed he was eating lunch at the time of the assassination, and that he then spoke with his foreman for 5 to 10 minutes before going home.

During this questioning, Ruth, Marina and her daughters, with evidence from the Paine house, were bundled into police headquarters. While they were being interviewed, "There was a commotion in the next office, and Marina looked up ... to see a stout middle-aged woman coming in ... She gave a cry and arose to hand Rachel to her paternal grandmother. Marguerite Oswald looked down at the tiny face in her arms. Tears glistened behind her glasses. The women fell into each other's arms, neither one able to communicate except by embraces and kisses. Marguerite was moaning: 'I didn't know I was a grandmother again. Nobody told me.'" [1776]

Marguerite Oswald later testified, "I was escorted into the office where Marina and Mrs. Paine was. ... And Mrs. Paine said, 'Oh, Mrs. Oswald, I am so glad to meet you. Marina has often expressed the desire to contact you, especially when the baby was being born. But Lee didn't want her to.' ... And I [Marguerite] said, 'I don't know what I am going to do. I want to stay in Dallas and be near Lee, so that I can help with this situation as much as possible.' She [Ruth] said, 'Mrs. Oswald, you are welcome in my home—if you care to sleep on the sofa.' I said, 'Thank you very much, Mrs. Paine, I will accept your offer. I will sleep on the floor in order to be near Dallas.' So we left. We went to Mrs. Paine's home. I am going to say again I did not see my son. So—I had my nurse's uniform on for 3 days."[1777]

And that's how the three women came to be in this remarkable photo by Allan Grant, taken on Saturday morning, November 23, in Ruth's kitchen in Irving. At left in her nurse's uniform is Lee's mother, Marguerite, next to a newspaper headlining Kennedy's visit. She holds month-old Rachel. Standing near her sink is the thoughtful Ruth Paine. The toddler is Oswald's older daughter, June, near her mother Marina who is folding clothes.[1778]

On Friday afternoon, Lee denied that he owned a rifle. Later, confronted with a photo "found among Oswald's possessions in the Paines' garage"[1779] showing him holding a rifle and pistol, he said it was a "composite", with his face superimposed on someone else's body.[1780] That was a lie. He had pleaded, then commanded, then posed as Marina took the photos. There is an interesting side note: We have seen two photos of him in their yard with his guns, very similar but with the rifle held on different sides. Until that night at the Paine house, only Lee and Marina knew of a third photo from that same day. Mother Marguerite told the Warren Commission what happened later that weekend to the third:

"Now, gentlemen, this is some very important facts. My daughter-in-law ... takes me into the bedroom and closes the door. She said, 'Mamma, I show you.' She opened the closet, and in the closet was a lot of books and papers. And she came out with a picture—a picture of Lee, with a gun. It said, 'To my daughter June'—written in English. ... I said, 'The police,' meaning that if the police got that, they would use that against my son, which would be a natural way to think. She says, 'You take, Mamma.' I said, 'No.' 'Yes, Mamma, you take.' I said, 'No, Marina. Put back in the book.' So she put the picture back in the book. ... So the next day, when we are at the courthouse ... She puts her shoe down, she says, 'Mamma, picture.' She had the picture folded up in her shoe." [1781]

Commission counsel Rankin questioned Marguerite closely about the photo, and had her look at COMMISSION EXHIBITS 133-A and 133-B, the two we know. To both she said "No, sir, that is not the picture." [1782] She was certain that the photo in Marina's shoe had Lee's arms extended, holding the rifle with both hands, above his head.

On Saturday as guests of LIFE magazine, Mrs. Oswald-the-mother and Mrs. Oswald-the-wife and the two baby girls moved for better protection from the press, from Mrs. Paine's home to an Executive Inn in Dallas. Marguerite continues the story at about 6 PM:

"I sensed we were alone. And there I was with a Russian girl. ... So this is where the picture comes in. ... there is an ashtray on the dressing table. And Marina comes with bits of paper, and puts them in the ashtray and strikes a match to it. And this is the picture of the gun that Marina tore up into bits of paper, and struck a match to it. Now, that didn't burn completely, because it was ... a photographic picture. So the match didn't take it completely. ... Then I took it and ... I flushed the torn bits and the half-burned thing down the commode. And nothing was said. There was nothing said." [1783]

So far as we know, Lee, Marina and Marguerite were the only three who ever saw that photo. It really doesn't matter, but is somewhat vexing because conspiracy theorists made an industry of attempting to show that the two photos we know were faked, superimposed, had shadows in wrong directions, and all sorts of objections contrary to the simple facts. Perhaps this third photo with a much different pose would have prevented all that nonsense. Oh, well.

Friday afternoon, Dallas police arrived at the boardinghouse in Oak Cliff, asking if Lee Harvey Oswald lived there. "Sometimes the Johnsons had as many as seventeen roomers, and some of the transients had rooms in the cellar." [1784] The manager, Earlene Roberts, told the Warren Commission: "I went and got the books and I said, 'No; there's no one here by that name,' and they tried to make me remember and I couldn't, and [owner] Mrs. Johnson come in in the meantime and there wasn't nobody there by that name, and Mrs. Johnson said, 'Mrs. Roberts, don't you have him?' And, I said, 'No; we don't, for here is my book and there is nobody there by that name.' We checked it back a year." [1785]

When the officers persisted, "Mrs. Johnson told me, 'Go get your keys and let them see in' ... they still had the TV on, and they was broadcasting about Kennedy. Just as I unlocked the doors Fritz' men, two of them had walked in and she come running in and said, 'Oh, Roberts, come here quick. This is this fellow Lee in this little room next to yours,' and they flashed him on television, is how us come to know ... and I said, 'Yes, that's him—that's O. H. Lee right here in this room.' And it was just a little wall between him and I." [1786]

In this photo taken by Allan Grant that afternoon,[1787] owner Gladys Johnson shows the $8-a-week "room" — "tiny, little more than a large closet—Mrs. Johnson called it her 'library' because it once did serve as her library and 'that's what it was built for,' she said" [1788] — with

"small windows ... all with venetian blinds and curtains connected to one five-and-ten-cent-store-type curtain rod." [1789] The room did not need curtain rods. And it was so small the pistol was close at hand, but had never been taken to work.

The two detectives and lieutenant waited until a search warrant arrived in the hands of Justice of the Peace David L. Johnson who had signed it, accompanied by Assistant District Attorney Bill Alexander and two more detectives.[1790] The seven then entered Lee's room.[1791] "Over the next hour and a quarter, they nearly strip the room, using the pillow cases and one of Oswald's own duffle bags to carry everything ... Only a banana peel and some uneaten fruit are left behind when they leave just after 6:00 p.m." [1792] Detective Walter Potts told the Warren Commission how he and three others piled all the stuff onto a table in Dallas Police Headquarters, then very carefully typed a two page inventory [1793] and "for the purpose of identification in court, we initialed everything we could possibly write on." [1794]

To the police, hours after the assassination-by-pistol of their fellow Officer Tippit, the most interesting item was probably "**1 brown leather holster, "38"**". To this book, the most compelling was a sheet of paper, "**Undesirable Discharge from U. S. M. C., 9-13-60**".[1795] Among the few belongings Lee kept close in his tiny room, that was important to his record of life, even if denigrating. It was later logged in by DPD Property Clerk H. W. Hill in a careful document of Oswald's properties: "**This inventory was made & invoice typed in FBI Office, Dallas Texas.**" The datum reads: "**1 Undesirable Discharge U.S.M.C., 9/13/60 Lee Harvey Oswald 1653230 #425**", the latter being a police property number.[1796] That is the last positive track I have seen of this key document. It's enough to know it existed and that Lee kept it close. The certificate is probably in a dusty box in the FBI's Dallas office, and if not there, then lost in the National Archives in Maryland. Its image survives only on a small dirty microfilm; from that and brother-in-law magic came the image on page 98.

Jumping ahead briefly to round out this episode — the next morning, Captain Fritz sends four of his detectives to again search Oswald's rooming house, as Vincent Bugliosi so charmingly tells it in his indispensable history of the weekend, *Four Days in November*:

> "to make absolutely sure that nothing was missed in yesterday's search, but Oswald's room has little to tell them. The detectives find a paperclip and a rubber band, which they confiscate, but nothing else. In fact, as Earlene Roberts points out, not only did the police clear all of Oswald's things out the day before, but they made off with a pillow case, two towels, and some washcloths belonging to the landlord." [1797]

Shortly after 4 PM, Oswald was presented, standing with three other men, in the first of three lineups before witnesses to the Tippit shooting. He was then interrogated a second time, during which Captain Fritz used information from the FBI to question Oswald about his travels to the Soviet Union and Mexico City. According to Fritz, Oswald admitted having been to the Soviet Union but denied traveling to Mexico City the previous month ... " [1798]

During the questioning on the department's third floor, more than 100 representatives of the press, radio, and television crowded into the hallway through which Oswald had to pass

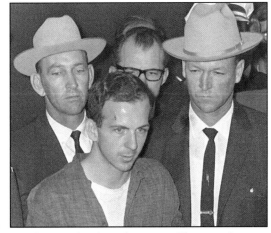

when being taken from his cell to Fritz' office. Reporters tried to interview Oswald during these shuttles. Between Friday afternoon and Sunday morning he appeared in the hallway at least 16 times. The confused conditions increased the difficulty of questioning. One detective told the Warren Commission "I realize I am not running the police department but if I had been running it wouldn't have been nobody up there; like I say, I was fed up." [1799] Asked by counsel "Would they not cooperate with your request to stand in a particular place?", he gave a fine Texas simile: "No; if you ever slopped hogs and throw down a pail of slop and saw them rush after it you would understand what that was like up there— about the same situation." [1800]   [1801]

Told on Friday that he could communicate with an attorney, Oswald made several phone calls on Saturday in an effort to procure legal representation of his own choice and discussed the matter with the president of the local bar association, who offered to obtain counsel. Oswald declined the offer saying that he would first try to obtain counsel by himself. He never did engage an attorney. [1802]

At 7:10 PM on November 22, 1963, Lee Harvey Oswald was formally advised that he had been charged with the murder of Patrolman J. D. Tippit. Several witnesses to the Tippit slaying and to the subsequent flight of the gunman had positively identified Oswald in police lineups. While definitive firearm identification evidence was not available at the time, the revolver in Oswald's possession at the time of his arrest was of a type and caliber that could have fired the shots that killed Tippit. [1803]

Friday evening, a lieutenant explains to Lee's good brother Robert "the circumstances surrounding Oswald's apprehension ... Robert realizes ... for the first time, just how strong a circumstantial case the police have against his brother for the shooting of Officer Tippit. Equally disturbing to Robert is the thought that it is difficult to explain Tippit's death unless it was an attempt to escape arrest for the assassination of the president." [1804]

Throughout Friday and Saturday, the Dallas police released many details concerning the alleged evidence against Oswald. Efforts by news representatives to reconstruct the crime and promptly report details led to erroneous and often conflicting reports. At the urgings of the newsmen, Chief of Police Curry brought Oswald to a 5-10 minute press conference in the police assembly room shortly after midnight, in the first minutes of Saturday, November 23. The room was crowded with newsmen who had arrived from all over the country. They shouted questions and flashed cameras at Oswald, who denied any involvement in anything, saying bitterly, 'I'm just the patsy.' Standing at the back during this session, unchallenged because he was well known to Dallas police as a sycophant who often brought donuts and other treats, was 52-year-old Dallas nightclub operator Jack Ruby.[1805] There is a photo of the natty dresser where his story will be told in chapter 9, on page 283.

Lee had been held for killing Officer Tippit because of that crime's many witnesses and

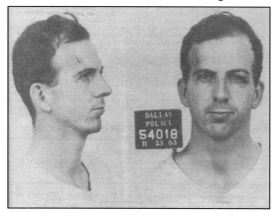

clear evidence. "At 1:35 A.M. Oswald was taken from his cell and escorted into a small room lined with file cabinets. Justice of the Peace David Johnston stood there somberly with a piece of paper in his hands. 'Is this the trial?' Oswald asked facetiously. 'No,' Judge Johnston answered. 'I have to arraign you . . . for the murder with malice of John F. Kennedy.' He read the charge [then] wrote on the bottom of the arraignment form, 'No Bond—Capital offense' and ordered Oswald remanded to the custody of the sheriff of Dallas County to await trial." [1806]

Booking photos were made,[1807] including the color photo on this book's front cover.

By 10 PM Friday, the FBI had traced the rifle found on the Depository's sixth floor to a mailorder house in Chicago. "At 4 A.M. CST, executives of Klein's Sporting Goods in Chicago, after poring over their microfilmed records for six hours, found the American Rifleman coupon with which Oswald had ordered C2766 eight months before." [1808] The rifle had been ordered by an A. Hidell for shipment to post office box 2915 in Dallas, a box rented by Oswald. Payment for the rifle was remitted by a money order signed by A. Hidell. By 6:45 PM on Saturday, the FBI was able to advise the Dallas police that, as a result of handwriting analysis of the form, money order and envelope used to purchase the rifle, it concluded that the rifle had been ordered by Lee Harvey Oswald.[1809] All doubts were resolved by his having draft cards for both Oswald and Hidell in his wallet when arrested. Dumb!

William Manchester summarized the assassin's utter ineptitude:
"The chain of circumstantial evidence was binding him ever tighter. By early Saturday morning the witnesses had identified him, his flimsy curtain rod alibi had been demolished, the FBI was checking [the] taxi manifest, and Justice Department laboratories in Washington were confirming every suspicion about the killer's fingerprints, palmprints, and the tuft of cotton shirt fibers he had left in the crevice between the metal butt plate of C2766 and the wooden stock. By daybreak the morning after the crime, conviction was an absolute certainty. The possibility of a reasonable doubt simply did not exist. It was an embarrassment of riches; the assassin of the leader of the most powerful nation on earth, everyone felt, must have displayed *some* guile. It was as though a hydrogen bomb had been accidentally launched from its silo by a bumbling technician. The more one learned about the criminal, the more the mind balked. The relationship between cause and effect was preposterous. They couldn't be balanced." [1810]

Good brother Robert Oswald, at the jail to see Lee on Saturday, is beset by Marguerite and her strange theories (*e.g.*, Lee is a secret government agent) and insatiable demands. Vincent Bugliosi nicely sums up what Robert later put into his book *Lee*:
"[T]here is something else about his mother now that gives Robert a sickening feeling. It is evident to him that his mother is not really crushed at all by the terrible charges against Lee. If anything, he senses she seems actually gratified at the attention she's receiving. She has always

had an inflated sense of her own ability and importance, a trait reflected in her son Lee. But her quarrelsome nature and limited work skills have created instead a life of obscurity. Now, she seems to instantly recognize that she will never again be treated as an ordinary, unimportant woman." [1811]

On Saturday evening, an event so obscure that you will be one of the first to learn about it:

"Lieutenant Robert E. McKinney of the Forgery Bureau appears at the office of Justice of the Peace David Johnston in Richardson, Texas, with a criminal complaint ('Affidavit' number F-155) he's prepared and signed as an affiant charging Oswald with assault with intent to murder Governor John Connally. Johnston affixes his signature to the complaint and it is officially filed at 6:15 p.m. Oswald will never be arraigned on this charge." [1812]

The Lieutenant swore he believes "that one Lee Harvey Oswald ... did ... unlawfully in and upon John B. Connally with malice aforethought did make an assault, with the intent then and there to murder the said John B. Connally." [1813] If Oswald had lived, this might have led to his being arraigned, then tried — and the truth of what he had intended might have come out, so this book would not be necessary. But, he will die within a day, the filing is not featured in any history books, so this author believes this book must be written by me and read by you.

Oswald was to be transferred from the city jail to the more secure county jail about a mile away; it had been ordered that the Sheriff hold him there for trial. The news media had been informed on Saturday night that the transfer would not take place until after 10 AM on Sunday. Many television, radio, and newspaper representatives crowded into the basement of the building shared by the jail and Dallas police department, to record the transfer. Oswald would emerge from a door in front of television cameras and proceed to the transfer vehicle. [1814]

The armored truck in which Oswald was to be transferred arrived shortly after 11 AM. Officials then decided that an unmarked police car, faster and more maneuverable, would be preferable for the short trip. [1815] In his typed 13-page "Interrogation of Lee Harvey Oswald", Captain Fritz told of a delay: "Oswald's shirt, which he was wearing at the time of arrest, had been removed and sent to the crime lab in Washington with all the other evidence for a comparison test. Oswald said he would like to have a shirt from his clothing that had been brought

to the office to wear over the T-shirt that he was wearing at the time [on this book's cover]. We selected the best-looking shirt from his things, but he said he would prefer wearing a black Ivy League type shirt, indicating that it might be a little warmer. We made this change and I asked him if he wouldn't like to wear a hat to more or less camouflage his looks in the car while being transferred as all of the people who had been viewing him had seen him bareheaded. He didn't want to do this. Then Officer J. R. Leavelle handcuffed his left hand to Oswald's right hand, then we left the office for the transfer." [1816] The tired Captain wrongly wrote of "a black Ivy League type shirt". The photo proves that the delay was because "Oswald ... insisted on wearing a black pullover sweater with jagged holes in it." [1817]

That delay of only a few minutes will cost Lee his life. "As they walked toward the ... elevator ... the plain-clothes man to whom Oswald had been manacled, said, 'If anybody shoots at you, I sure hope they are as good a shot as you are.' ... Oswald 'kind of laughed' and said, 'Nobody is going to shoot me.'" [1818] — the last words he ever spoke. At 11:21 he emerged ... flanked by detectives, took a few steps toward the car and was in the glaring light of the television cameras. The previous page's photo is the "before" of a famous pair. [1819] A man with a Colt .38 revolver suddenly darted out from an area at the front-right where newsmen had assembled. While millions watched on television, the man moved quickly and fired one shot into Oswald's abdomen. [1820] The more famous "after" photo is on page 285. "The bullet passed through Oswald's liver, spleen and aorta". [1821] He groaned with pain as he fell to the ground and lost consciousness. [1822]

Within 7 minutes, Oswald was at Parkland Memorial Hospital. Charles Jack Price, the Administrator of the Dallas County Hospital District, wrote in his statement, one of those he required of all hospital employees involved in the events: "[W]e took off for the Emergency Room. When we got down there, Dr. Charles Crenshaw [who had tried to save Kennedy] was in the corridor and said they had been alerted. He said, 'You're not going to put him in the same room the President was in, are you?' Told him I surely was glad he had thought of it and by all means, not to." [1823] Oswald was rushed into Trauma Room Two, fittingly, the same room where John Connally's life had been saved from the severe wounds Oswald had inflicted. He was then rushed upstairs into surgery, where a skilled team tried every procedure and trick they knew to save him, despite the bullet's ravages and without regard to what he'd done.

"Nellie Connally, on the hospital's second floor, became aware of what she called 'a sudden tightening of the security around us'; she asked for the reason, and a Texas Ranger said, 'Lee Harvey Oswald was just killed.' From the bed Governor Connally stared about, bewildered. This was his first day of complete consciousness—for several hours he thought it was Saturday—and the name Oswald meant nothing whatever to him." [1824] At 1:07 P.M., almost exactly two days after the 'official' time of JFK's death, Lee Harvey Oswald was pronounced to be dead. He had never regained consciousness. Strangely but fittingly appropriate to his screwed-up life, his last words had been spoken to Detective Leavelle, "Nobody is going to shoot me."

A much fuller understanding of what just happened will come in the last third of chapter 9, where the story of Jack Ruby, and why he did what he did, will be told.

There is reason to second-guess Chief Curry's insistence that Oswald be transferred at an announced time and place so newsmen and the country could watch. Despite that, there is great cause for pride in the Dallas Police Department, as later recalled in the oral testimony of Sergeant Gerald Lynn Hill who had been one of the first to search the TSBD:

"Up until Oswald was shot, we were smelling like a rose. Within a short period of time, street cops, sergeants, detectives, patrolmen, and motorcycle officers had caught the man who had killed the President of the United States, had lost an officer in the process, and had managed to do so without the FBI, Secret Service, or any of the other glory boys. Nobody could have faulted us for anything at that point ..." [1825]

A fine book proving that the best of "all news is local", *When The News Went Live*, captioned this photo:[1826] "Spectators outside the county jail cheer at the news that Oswald has been shot."

[1827] At top-right is the TSBD, and in front of it, at far right, is the oak that deflected Oswald's first bullet. That Sunday morning, this author exactly shared Nellie Connally's reaction: "When I heard that Oswald was dead, I didn't feel any sadness or sympathy. Sorry he was dead? No. But I knew that from the standpoint of history, of truth and clarity, his death was going to have unending repercussions. He died before anyone could obtain any admission, any information, from him." [1828]

The man who killed Oswald was Jack Ruby. He was instantly arrested and, minutes later, confined upstairs in the Dallas police jail. Under interrogation, he denied that his killing Oswald was in any way connected with a conspiracy involving the assassination of President Kennedy. He maintained that he had killed Oswald in a temporary fit of depression and rage over the President's death. Indicted for the murder of Oswald by the State of Texas on November 26, 1963, Ruby was found guilty on March 14, 1964, and sentenced to death.[1829] He soon died of cancer. That will be told in the next chapter, along with the SUBSEQUENT EVENTS of others in this story. His opportunity and motive for killing Oswald are told in Chapter 9 to demonstrate it was not part of a CONSPIRACY.

According to agent Hosty's sworn testimony,[1830] "Between two and four hours after Oswald's death on November 24, Shanklin summoned Hosty. Hosty recalls that Shanklin was standing in front of his desk and that he reached into a lower right-hand drawer and took out both the memorandum and Oswald's note. 'Oswald is dead now,' he said. 'There can be no trial. Here, get rid of this.' Hosty started to tear up the documents in Shanklin's presence. 'No,' Shanklin shouted. 'Get it out of here. I don't even want it in this office. Get rid of it.' Hosty then took the note and memorandum out of Shanklin's office, tore them up, and flushed them down a toilet at the FBI. A few days later, Shanklin asked Hosty whether he had destroyed Oswald's note and the memorandum and Hosty assured him that he had." [1831]

"The madness reeled beyond comprehension." [1832] In his *Memoirs*, Chief Justice of the U.S. Supreme Court Earl Warren would recall:

"About nine o'clock Saturday evening I was startled from my numbness by a call from the White House. It was Mrs. Jacqueline Kennedy, asking if I would make a short talk in the rotunda of the Capitol the following day at the ceremony for her husband as he lay in state there. I was almost speechless to hear her voice personally asking me to speak at the ceremony. I, of course, told her that I would do so. After our brief conversation, I undertook to compose something, but it was simply impossible for me to put thoughts on paper. Accordingly, I went to bed around midnight, postponing until morning the writing of the statement I must have for the ceremony at one o'clock the next afternoon. It was again difficult to write in the morning, but there could be no further delay. I was still struggling with the words at 11:20 a.m. when my daughter Dorothy came running into my study and said, 'Daddy, they just killed Oswald.' A little annoyed, I said, 'Oh, Dorothy, don't pay any attention to all those wild rumors or they will drive you to distraction.' She replied, 'But, Daddy, I saw them do it.' I rushed into her room in time to see a replay of Jack Ruby shooting President Kennedy's assassin, Lee Harvey Oswald, on her television set." [1833]

Millions watched television to see Kennedy's casket come out of the White House to go to the Capitol. Coverage abruptly transferred from the ceremonious cortege to a shadowy basement where, again and again, a man lunged at Oswald. "Never in the seven centuries of trial by jury had a crime been committed in the presence of so many spectators ... a minimum of 95 percent of the adult population was peering at television or listening to radio accounts." [1834]

"There was scarcely time to absorb the news before Jackie appeared with Caroline and John. She was dressed in black, the children in matching light blue wool coats with velvet collars and red Oxford shoes. Less than an hour after Oswald's murder, [she held] Caroline with her left hand and John with her right. For five extraordinary minutes, as the casket was put into position by pallbearers, Jackie, in bright sunlight, cut a stoical figure.

"Like her decision not to remove the bloodstained suit and stockings on her return from Dallas, the children's presence was a statement. [O]ne might have expected her not to include them in the public ceremonies. But on this occasion, she who had fought ceaselessly to protect her children's privacy wanted the world to see their loss. To a nation reeling from the murders of Kennedy and Oswald, Jackie, in her bearing, offered a much-needed image of composure and quiet courage in the face of violence, of dignity and stability against chaos." [1835]

In the Rotunda of the Capitol, Kennedy's coffin lay in the dead center, directly under the dome topped by *Statue of Freedom*, the lady who had stood there precisely one century. [1836] Heels clicked, speeches were made, Warren was eloquent, little John fidgeted and was taken away to practice his salute, Mrs. Kennedy and Caroline touched the coffin and kissed the flag, then the public filed past in solemn tribute. When agent Clint Hill went back late that night, he saw "People eight abreast in a line that stretched forty blocks. ... More than 250,000 of them [went] through the Rotunda ... and more would have, if time had permitted." [1837]

As the dreadful, unbelievable weekend ended, the gunfire toll in Dallas was complete: THREE DEAD, TWO WOUNDED. James Tague's right cheek had been bloodied, John Connally was wounded but will recover. John F. Kennedy, J.D. Tippit and Lee H. Oswald are dead.

> Key point of this chapter:
> **The factual narrative here will be dissected in following chapters**
> **to show that Lee did it, alone, and as usual for him, failed.**

— 7 —

EVENTS

MUFFLED DRUMS AND SUBSEQUENT EVENTS

1963 November 24 — The Present (2016)

THROUGH THAT TERRIBLE WEEKEND BEFORE THANKSGIVING we watched, awestruck, as history slowly marched past to the beat of muffled drums. Harry Miles Muheim, a writer who met Jack Kennedy in 1940 at Stanford University, lived in Washington, D.C. On Sunday he took his son to Constitution Avenue to witness the cortege taking JFK's body to the Capitol:

"The huge crowd stood dead silent. Only the clatter of hooves and the roll of drums could be heard. As the caisson passed before us, Mark, who had just turned nine, tugged gently at my sleeve. I bent down to listen, and he whispered: 'Is he really in the box?'

'Yes, Mark,' I said quietly. 'He's really in the box.'

'That's too bad,' said the little boy. He held tightly to my hand as we watched the caisson roll slowly up Capitol Hill." [1838]

Donald Spoto wrote: "No one who saw these images ... could ever forget them:

... the view of Jackie, her veiled head held high with consummate dignity as she led a gathering of forty world leaders, marching behind the caisson ...

... the pictures of Jack's beloved brother Bobby, holding her hand ...

... Jackie, bending down to her son, whispering that yes, now he could say good-bye to Daddy, and then—perhaps most heartbreaking of all, the next instant, when little John, [three years old that day], stepped forward and raised his hand in a salute ... [1839]

... the caisson drawn by six horses, with the flag-draped coffin atop, and behind that the riderless horse [Black Jack], with reversed boots in the stirrups, symbol of a fallen leader ...

... the one moment when Jackie's composure cracked, as she stood in the chill, waiting for the awful, final procession to begin, holding the children's hands, and when she lowered her head, her shoulders shook, and she sobbed ..." [1840]

After our shock when an unknown lurched from nowhere to kill Oswald on Sunday, the country and world needed the image above of young John on Monday. Proud and delighted with the bare-legged little man, we cried. Few have seen the wider view of that photo, shown here at right, [1841] which proves that his salute on the day he became three years old was fully as correct as the officer's.

Professor Larry J. Sabato in *The Kennedy Half-Century* perfectly recalls the emotion:

"Then it happened, the moment that no one alive at the time will ever forget. It was a child's simple gesture, and yet it brought home the true personal tragedy of November 22. As the president's flag-draped coffin was being removed from St. Matthew's Cathedral, Jackie leaned over and whispered in her son's ear. Just weeks before the assassination, the son had been taught by his father and several Secret Service agents how to salute the flag. John F. Kennedy, Jr., fatherless on his third birthday, dutifully stepped forward and pressed his tiny right hand against his forehead to say good-bye. America wept as one." [1842]

President of France Charles de Gaulle approved at the end of that long Monday, especially of Jacqueline Bouvier Kennedy: "She gave an example to the whole world of how to behave." [1843]

Legendary White House correspondent Helen Thomas, who used her well-deserved seat in the front row of the press room to be JFK's much-loved friend and worthy adversary, as the occasions demanded, fondly tells of her husband and news competitor, Douglas Cornell, dictating the Associated Press's lead story that Sunday: "The peace of eternity came in an Arlington grave today for John F. Kennedy, whose quest for enduring peace in a dangerous world was cut short by an assassin's bullet." [1844] [1845]

Of Lee's good and steady brother Robert Oswald, William Manchester wrote that "he would carry the stigma of his brother's guilt to his own grave ... The best he could do was try to carry himself like a man. He did remarkably well." [1846] Robert wrote in his memoir *Lee* of the difficult events unfolding for him that weekend: "I received a call from Parkland Hospital. Someone there asked me, 'What is to be done with your brother's body?'" [1847] Because he was assisting Marina, her two infants, the FBI and Secret Service and sheriff's deputies and police, Robert had not had quiet to think about that. Of course, his mother was no help.

Marguerite Oswald told Chief Justice Warren and his amazed commissioners that she was certain Lee was a government secret agent, therefore, "I wanted my son buried in the Arlington Cemetery." She went on, "Now, gentlemen, I didn't know that President Kennedy was going to be buried in Arlington Cemetery. All I know is that my son is an agent, and that he deserves to be buried in Arlington Cemetery." [1848] "To Robert's undisguised disgust she announced that since Lee had given his life for his country, he should be buried with full honors ... He said, 'Shut up, Mother.'" [1849] The good son knew that the only proper decision

was a simple low-key burial in a plain coffin [1850] in some local cemetery. Secret Service Special Agent Mike Howard,[A] who helped Robert in many ways all that weekend, obtained the services of a local funeral director, then arranged an elaborate password scheme, from Parkland Hospital to Dallas police to Secret Service to Robert, finally from him back to the hospital to assure that they were releasing Lee's body to the brother-approved funeral home. [1851]

[A] Mike Howard's discovery that week is the basis of Chapter 20 – OBSTRUCTION OF BEST EVIDENCE.

In *Lee: A Portrait of Lee Harvey Oswald by his Brother*, Robert continues the sad story:

"This had been settled easily and, despite the roundabout message system, had not taken much time. But from that moment on, every step was both time-consuming and disturbing. The funeral director began telephoning various cemeteries to prepare the way for me to buy a burial plot for Lee. One cemetery after another refused even to discuss the possibility of accepting Lee's body. The first cemetery the funeral director checked with at least gave a reason for the refusal ... Officer Tippit was to be buried in one of the associated cemeteries. ... The others were so vague in their comments that neither the funeral director, [nor] Mike Howard, nor I felt that they were acting out of any motive other than prejudice.

While the funeral director was kind enough to continue that search, I began telephoning various ministers in the Dallas-Fort Worth area, to request that they officiate at the burial services. I had been surprised by the earlier difficulties with the cemetery officials, but I was astonished by the reactions of the ministers I talked to. The first one, the second one, the third one, and the fourth one flatly refused even to consider my request.

One of the ministers, a prominent member of the Greater Dallas Council of Churches, listened impatiently to my request and then said sharply, 'No, we just can't do that.' 'Why not?' I asked. 'We just can't go along with what you have in mind,' he said. (All I had in mind was the simplest kind of funeral service.) And then the minister added: 'Your brother was a sinner.' I hung up. The question of who would officiate at Lee's funeral was still unsettled when I went to bed Sunday night, although the time of the funeral had been set for four o'clock Monday afternoon." [1852]

"Finally, two Lutheran ministers who seemed sympathetic appeared [on] Monday morning. One ... came back to see us. The National Council of Churches office in Dallas had asked the ministers to come out and offer to serve at the funeral service, which was now scheduled for 4 P.M. that day at the Rose Hill Cemetery. The minister did not seem at all eager to officiate, but he did say, rather reluctantly, that he would be at the cemetery at four." [1853]

"Two Rose Hill workmen were told Monday morning to dig a grave for one 'William Bobo.' The fiction didn't deceive them long; when Oswald's cheap, moleskin-covered [B] pine box arrived, it was accompanied by a hundred Fort Worth policemen, who sealed off the area to protect Marguerite, Robert, Marina and her two children. The lid was raised. Forty reporters peered over the officers' shoulders. Marina, who had been following TV and was learning about images, kissed her husband and put her ring on his finger." [1854]

Those words were in Manchester's 1967 *The Death of a President*, which was assigned Library of Congress catalog card number 67-10496. Later that year, Robert Oswald's memoir of his brother, *Lee*, LOC card number 67-29487, gave fulsome praise to Manchester's book, then contained this correction: "I do not feel that the coffin supplied by a sympathetic funeral home director can be honestly described as a 'cheap, moleskin-covered pine box.' It was a simple coffin, protected from ghouls by a metal vault, and I have since learned that the cost to the family was about the same as the amount most American families pay for a coffin and funeral service. This may seem of no great importance to others, but I know that we did what we could to pay our respects to the boy and young man we had known and loved for years before he turned to violence." [1855]

Robert now tells about the sad burial of his little brother:[1856]

"I found the long ride out to the cemetery unusually depressing because of the attitude of most of the people I had talked to in making the arrangements. Mother, Marina and the children were

---

[B] "A heavy-napped cotton twill fabric" — *American Heritage College Dictionary*

in one Secret Service car, and I was in another car driven by an officer from the Tarrant County sheriff's office. ... The Fort Worth police department and the Secret Service had set up a heavy guard at Rose Hill. I could see uniformed officers stationed every few yards along the fence that surrounded the cemetery. I suppose this should have surprised me, but I was still numb from the other experiences of the previous three days.

As soon as we passed through the gate, the driver headed directly for the chapel, which was on a low hill. I saw a number of people standing quietly at the fence line, staring at the chapel and the grave, which was at the bottom of the hill. Marina, Mother and the children went into the chapel first. I followed, accompanied by [Secret Service agents] Mike Howard and Charlie Kunkel.[C]

The chapel was completely empty. I saw no sign of any preparation for the funeral service. 'I don't understand,' I said to Mike and Charlie, and they were obviously puzzled too. They said they would try to find out what had happened. Two or three minutes later, one of them came back into the chapel, where I had been waiting. 'Well, we were a few minutes late,' he said. 'There's been some misunderstanding, and they've already carried the casket down to the grave site. We'll have a graveside service down there.'

I had taken most of the earlier disappointments about the burial arrangements without showing my feelings, but when I heard this I hit the wall with my fist and shouted, 'Damn it!' ... We drove down a curved road to the grave site. ... The Lutheran minister who had promised to be there at four had not appeared, and the Secret Service received word that he would not be coming out. The Reverend Louis Saunders, of the Fort Worth Council of Churches, had driven out to Rose Hill by himself just to see if he could be of any help to Marina and the family. When he was told that the other minister would not be there, the Reverend Mr. Saunders spoke the simple words of the burial service.

Just before the ceremony, the funeral director introduced me to the caretaker for Rose Hill. At the risk of his own job, the caretaker had agreed without hesitation to sell me the cemetery lot. The funeral director suggested to me that I could reduce the risk the caretaker had taken if I would respond to any inquiries about the lot in such a way as to leave the impression that the family had owned the plot for some time. Most people would then assume that the cemetery itself had had no choice—that it retained no control over this grave site and could not deny us the right to bury Lee there. Under the circumstances, I agreed. I make the facts public now simply to pay my respects to one of the men who behaved with warmth and compassion during a period when some Christian ministers seemed more concerned over their public image than they were with their moral obligations.

While we were sitting near the grave site, waiting for the service to begin ... I was concerned by the general intrusion of newspapermen, television correspondents, and photographers at the funeral. I motioned to Mike Howard, and when he came over I told him that I planned to have the coffin opened and would like to have all reporters and spectators moved back some distance from the grave site. He nodded, and almost immediately six or eight plainclothesmen from the Fort Worth police department formed a kind of protective semicircle between us and the crowd, insuring a certain amount of privacy.

Mother, Marina, the children and I then got up and walked toward the open coffin. After I had taken a last, long look at my brother's face, I turned to go back to the place where we had been sitting. I then noticed the semicircle of plainclothesmen standing guard, solemn and stony-faced." [1857]

[C] Mike and Charlie (a.k.a. "Chuck") are featured in Chapter 20 – OBSTRUCTION OF BEST EVIDENCE because of what they will discover this week, and Mike then described to Collin College students for years, and is at last getting a wider audience here thanks to the courtesy of James Reston, Jr.

In the photo [1858] at the grave are Marina holding June, Robert, Marguerite holding month-old Rachel, and Rev. Louis Saunders, the only minister who was willing to say a few simple words. Behind the mourners are no family, no friends; only police officers, sheriff's deputies, FBI and Secret Service agents, reporters and photographers. This is the first photo of good brother Robert in this book, so you may wish to compare with Lee, and also with his father and Lee's, Robert E. Lee Oswald, on page 3. Robert continues his narrative:

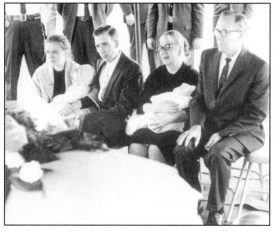

"After the brief service ended ... one of the agents asked me if I wished to stay until Lee's body was lowered. 'Yes, for a few minutes,' I said. I watched as the vault cover was put over the coffin, and then waited until the gravediggers started to lower the coffin." [1859]

Some time later I learned that several reporters who had been assigned to cover the story of Lee's burial had volunteered to serve as pallbearers and had carried Lee's body from the chapel to the grave site. Because of my preoccupation with other details, I had forgotten to ask any of my friends to serve as pallbearers. I had not had time on Saturday or Sunday to follow the news reports, and this led to another oversight. I didn't realize that I had accidentally set Lee's funeral for the same day President Kennedy was being buried in Washington and Patrolman Tippit in Dallas. If I had known, I think I would have asked that Lee's burial be delayed until Tuesday. But that week I resented deeply the criticism I heard of the timing of that stark, private burial service, with my brother being carried to his grave by strangers as the curious stared down from the cemetery fence." [1860]

"Marina was humiliated. It had been furtive and meager. That night, the lowest of her life, Marina received a telegram. She could not imagine who had sent it, unless a friend in Russia. It was from a group of American college students. Marina could hardly believe the words ...:

'We send you our heartfelt sympathy. We understand your sorrow and we share it. We are ashamed that such a thing could happen in our country. We beg you not to think ill of us. You have friends and we are with you.'

There was a long list of names at the end. It was Marina's first hint that in the long life ahead of her she did not have to be an outcast." [1861]

There was a third burial that Monday.[1862] J.D. Tippit had gone from execution to hospital to Dudley M. Hughes Funeral Home,[D] only two blocks from where he'd been killed, to his Beckley Hills Baptist Church. On Saturday and Sunday, the casket was surrounded by banks of flowers and a constant honor guard of Dallas police officers. Tippit was the first to be buried in a Memorial Court of Honor at Laurel Land Memorial Park in South Oak Cliff. On the same afternoon as the funerals of Kennedy and Oswald, seven hundred policemen were an honor guard for their fallen

---

[D] This is the firm that sent an ambulance to the shooting site to carry Tippit to hospital, where he was declared DOA. The Texas practice of being both ambulancer and mortician was validated.

brother. The Rev. Claude Tipps got it right: "He was doing his duty when he was taken by the lethal bullet of a poor, confused, misguided, ungodly assassin – as was our President." [1863]

Marie Tippit was in tears throughout the day and for long after. [1864] "The days and weeks and months that followed were just terrible," Mrs. Tippit remembered. "You keep on going because you have to. You say your prayers and  you feed your children and you read your Bible and you live one day at a time, so it gets to the point where you can live a single day without crying." [1865] Americans were even more generous to her than to Marina: "Within months, forty thousand pieces of mail containing close to $650,000 in donations are given to the Tippit family ..." [1866] In a 2013 interview she was asked to recall her contacts from Kennedys after her J.D.'s death. "Robert Kennedy called the following day. He called to express his sympathy toward me, and said if Jack had not come to Dallas, my husband would still be alive, and I agreed. And he said they were both doing their jobs. Jackie wrote a letter and sent a photo of her family. She said she had lit a flame for Jack and that it would burn forever and it would burn for my husband, too. I thought it was so thoughtful and considerate of her to do that." Fifty years after the killings, Marie Tippit, an 85-year-old great-grandmother, quietly attended a public memorial event in Dealey Plaza.

••• SUBSEQUENT EVENTS •••

Jacqueline Kennedy:
After the drums and funeral and burial, she received the dozens of visiting heads of state in the White House. After they departed, she sat Caroline and John at a tiny table and brought in a birthday cake with three candles [1867] for her son who that morning had brought the world to tears with his snappy salute to his father.

"She wanted the remains of the two children she and her husband had buried [in Massachusetts] to lie next to President Kennedy at Arlington Cemetery. Her brother-in-law Senator Ted Kennedy had made the arrangements and accompanied the two small caskets to Washington on the family plane, *Caroline*. At night on December 4 a quiet procession left the White House and headed to Arlington National Cemetery, two miles away. In stark contrast to the massive and meticulously planned public ceremony nine days earlier, this was to be an intensely private service. Completely off the record.

"President John F. Kennedy's eternal flame provided a glowing light in the darkness as Mrs. Kennedy, [Secret Service agent] Clint Hill, and a handful of relatives and close friends gathered around the grave site. The two white caskets were placed in the ground next to the remains of the father they'd never known. The twenty-minute ceremony was simple, but no less heartbreaking than all the others had been. As Clint Hill watched the tears stream down Mrs. Kennedy's face, he wondered how much longer this nightmare could go on." [1868]

"In her final days at the White House, she cleaned out the Oval Office, gave some small possessions of her husband's as gifts to the staff, oversaw the packing of their belongings [and] called for the staff to say her good-byes ... and one remarked later that 'it was so wonderful seeing her smile—to be able to smile.' She had one more official duty, an East Room ceremony for the presentation of the presidential Medal of Freedom, which she and JFK had redesigned, [by LBJ to JFK, accepted by his brother, RFK]. She slipped out before the ceremony ended, collected her children and left the White House. She wouldn't return until several years later at the invitation of Pat Nixon when her official first lady portrait was unveiled." [1869]

In the photo, "Maude Shaw bids farewell to a household staff member, followed by John Kennedy holding his flag, and Jackie Kennedy holding Caroline's hand, as they all walk through the Rose Garden and toward their car." [1870]

Mrs. Kennedy, the two children and their nanny, Maude Shaw, moved on December 6 into a redbrick townhouse in Washington D.C.'s Georgetown, loaned by family friend "Undersecretary of State Averell Harriman, who had several homes and traveled much of the time." [1871] She soon bought a house across the street which she rebuilt and where she planned to quietly raise her children. "Unfortunately, the new residence became a tourist attraction. Tour buses would actually squeeze down the narrow streets of Georgetown to pass by her house ... She was incensed. She tried to get it stopped, but couldn't. For safety and privacy, she decided to move to New York City [to] a large apartment at 1040 Fifth Avenue, across the street from Central Park." [1872]

Tragically, within five years "the deaths of Martin Luther King and Robert F. Kennedy affected Jackie profoundly. 'I don't want my children to live here anymore. If they're killing Kennedys, my kids are number-one targets. ... I want to get out of this country.' She left" [1873] and very quickly resumed an old friendship with Greek shipping tycoon Ari Onassis. They were married on his island, Skorpios, in 1968. One observer recognized it to be a perfect marriage — he wanted and got fame, she wanted and got money.

Soon after, Ari was diagnosed with myasthenia gravis, a debilitating disease of the autoimmune system, affecting the muscles, about which physicians then knew relatively little. He did not have strength to keep his eyelids raised, so they had to be taped up. Aristotle Socrates Onassis died in 1975, near Paris. He was buried at the tiny chapel on Skorpios where they had been married. Jacqueline Bouvier Kennedy Onassis and her two children moved to New York City, in or near which they would live the rest of their lives.

After six months, at the suggestion of her White House social secretary, Letitia Baldrige, Jackie went to work as an associate editor for New York publisher Viking Press. Two years later, Viking published a thriller *Shall We Tell the President?* about an attempted assassination of Ted, the only survivor of four [E] Kennedy brothers. She had no foreknowledge or connection to it, but *"The New York Times* published the first review. ... 'There is a word for such a book. The word is trash. Anybody associated with its publication should be ashamed of herself.'" [1874] Embarrassed, Jackie moved to competitor Doubleday, where she happily worked the rest of her life as an editor, to the week she died, "wearing a wig or turban to conceal her hair loss" [1875] to chemotherapy.

"In maturity she had found a romantic love with Maurice Tempelsman that lasted longer than any before it. [A friend said] 'For those of us who cared about Mrs. Onassis, it was comforting—it was terrific—to know she was with somebody who was a good, generous, and gentle man.'" [1876] [F] He held her hand to the end.

She became gravely ill with non-Hodgkin's lymphoma and its frequent companion, pneumonia. The cancer probably resulted from her 45-year smoking habit, coupled with her use of black hair dyes — we later learned that women using them have a four-times-greater risk of developing non-Hodgkin's lymphoma than women who don't. [1877] She was admitted into New York Hospital. A patient already there was stroke victim Richard Nixon, who died April 22, 1994. Nearing her end, "she discharged herself and went home to die" [1878] at the age of 64 on May 19, 1994. "The next day, John, wearing a dark suit, his eyes red from lack of sleep, went downstairs to say a few words to the hundreds of reporters, cameramen, well-wishers, and curious ... [S]lowly and without notes, he made a simple announcement ... 'Last night, at around ten-fifteen, my mother passed on ... surrounded by her friends and her family and her books and the people and things that she loved. And she did it in her own way and in her own terms, and we all feel lucky for that, and now she's in God's hands.'" [1879]

After a funeral service in New York City, the casket went "to Arlington Cemetery, where she had lit the eternal flame for her husband's memory some thirty years before. There, Jacqueline Bouvier Kennedy Onassis was buried beside John F. Kennedy and their two children, Arabella and Patrick." [1880]

Then, a leader who has perfect pitch for understanding what's important and speaking it plainly, "President Clinton eulogized the wife of the man who had served as his political inspiration: 'God gave her very great gifts and imposed upon her great burdens. She bore them all with dignity and grace and uncommon common sense. In the end, she cared more about being a good mother to her children, and the lives of Caroline and John leave no doubt that she was that, and more. May the flame she lit so long ago burn ever brighter here, and always brighter in our hearts. God bless you, friend, and farewell.'" [1881]

Caroline Kennedy:
Caroline graduated from Radcliffe, earned a law degree from Columbia, "married Edwin Schlossberg, a designer of museum interiors and exhibitions, a writer and a scholar with a Ph.D." [1882] "Grand Jackie", in her last years, doted on their children, Rose, Tatiana and Jack Schlossberg. The gracefulness of Camelot lives on: For years, we delighted to see Caroline, the embodiment of the best of both parents, elegantly introduce the Kennedy Center Honors. As this book is written, she is America's perfect, graceful ambassador to Japan. [1883]

[E] Joe, the eldest, had been killed fighting World War II in Europe.

[F] This writer is similarly comforted that Marina found Kenneth Porter, as will be told in a few pages.

John F. Kennedy, Jr.:

John Jr. graduated from Brown, earned a law degree from NYU, had difficulty with the bar exam, headlined in the *New York Post*: THE HUNK FLUNKS. He succeeded on the third attempt and worked in the district attorney's office.[1884] He then founded and edited bold political magazine *George*. A new pilot, in 1999 at age 38 he flew his small airplane into summer evening haze, then down into the water near Martha's Vineyard, killing wife Carolyn Bessette, her sister Lauren, and himself.[1885] In his eulogy, uncle Ted Kennedy made a telling point about fame for the young: "The whole world knew his name before he did."[1886]

On that, we have Ted Sorensen's reliable word that his parents called him simply "John", disliking the cute "John-John".[1887] The genesis of the double name is related by friend William Manchester in his biography of JFK and family, *One Brief Shining Moment*:

> "Young John was never 'John-John' to his parents. Here is the origin of that myth. One day the President left his Oval Office and called his son, who was playing nearby: 'John!' There was no response. Kennedy raised his voice: 'John!' This time the boy heard him, jumped up, and came on the run. A minor aide recounted the episode to a reporter, who asked: 'And what were the President's exact words?' The aide replied: 'John! John!' By the time this reached print it had become 'John-John.' Reading it, Jack caustically remarked: 'I suppose if I'd had to call him *three* times, he'd have become 'John-John-John.'"[1888]

1963:[1889] Bill Clinton (age 17, future president #42) makes earnest eye contact and shakes the hand of John Kennedy (age 46, president #35). "Clinton has named two influential moments in his life that contributed to his decision to become a public figure, both occurring in 1963. One was his visit as a Boys Nation senator to the White House to meet President John F. Kennedy. The other was listening to Martin Luther King's famous [speech I am not allowed to quote],[1890] which impressed him enough that he later memorized it."[1891]

1993:[1892] John Kennedy Jr. (age 32) makes great eye contact and shakes the hand of President Bill Clinton (age 47) at the Kennedy Library's rededication ceremony. Caroline and Jackie, seven months before her death, look on. After thirty years, the length of a generation, young John Jr. hauntingly mirrors young Bill's earnest greeting. The year of the photo above, JFK Sr. was to die by tragic accident, murdered by Oswald's ill-timed, wayward bullets. Six years after this lower photo, still-young JFK Jr. will die by accident, flying his small plane down into the great sea.

Let's end this little article about young John with a cute story about him. Historian and biographer William Manchester recounted that the son invented a name for his father:

"During their last Palm Beach vacation, John somehow picked up what he considered an outrageous insult. Crouching just out of his father's reach, he would call, 'Daddy, you are a foo-foo head!' Kennedy's jaw would sag, his eyes would bulge, he would tremble with mounting outrage and rise, crying: 'John Kennedy, how dare you call the President of the United States a foo-foo head? Wait till I get hold of you!' And the chase would be on. One evening, when ... the children were saying their good-nights, John leaned toward his father and said in a stage whisper, 'Foo-foo head!' The President froze in an attitude of total shock, and the exultant little boy darted off to bed, convinced that he had won a famous victory." [1893]

John Connally:

He fully recovered from his wounds and continued as Governor of Texas until 1969. In 1964 he went to Washington, D.C., to tell the Warren Commission about the terrible day in Dallas. We met U.S. Navy Captain Andy Kerr, legal assistant in the Secretary of the Navy's office, in Chapter 4 – MINSK, where he told of being the one who received and decided what to do with Oswald's pleading-but-threatening letter to Connally. Here, Captain Kerr tells an interesting story about Connally and that letter:

"After his testimony, he came to the Pentagon and visited me in my office. I was still the special counsel to the secretary of the navy. Although we had been in touch by telephone, this was the first time I had seen him since he had resigned from the office of secretary of the navy in 1962. He had put on a little weight, which he carried well, and was greyer at the temples. He was, if anything, even more strikingly handsome and distinguished, and had of course become more famous. His arm was still in a sling from the effects of Oswald's bullet. He had become a glamorous figure, and the women from nearby offices crowded about to catch a glimpse of him. ... [1894]

Connally and I chatted a while about old times and his experience in the Kennedy assassination. He then asked, 'Andy, remember that letter we got from Oswald from Russia? Do you suppose you could find it for me? I'd like to have it for my memorabilia. After all, the son-of-a-bitch shot me!' I told him I'd look for it and send it to him when I found it.

The letter failed to turn up, however, in a search of the files [in my] office. The Marine Corps also came up with a blank. Months passed, and ... I had almost given up when the letter was finally located in the United States Archives. I told Archivist [Robert] Bahmer [G] of Connally's request. He said that he was prevented by law from giving up the letter. 'Law? What law is that?' I asked. ... The letter, he said, had been an item of evidence before the Warren Commission. It had been discovered ...

[G] An example of government at its most professional, he became the Archivist after 30 years of service.

through a routine examination of Oswald's Marine Corps record. It turned out to be the most comprehensive example of Oswald's handwriting available to the commission. It had been used, therefore, by handwriting experts as an exemplar. The handwriting proved that Oswald had been the person who, under a false name, had purchased the rifle used to kill President Kennedy. It served the same purpose with respect to the pistol used by Oswald to kill police Officer Tippit. ...

Robert Kennedy, the archivist continued, was distressed to think that the gun used to kill his brother might end up in a private collection, with probable commercial exploitation. As attorney general, he prepared and had introduced in Congress remedial legislation. It gave the federal government the authority to seize by condemnation items of evidence in assassinations or attempts on the lives of certain high government officials. The proposed legislation was swiftly enacted into law. [The Archivist] concluded the story by telling me that the Oswald letter I was seeking had fallen under the described legislation. He had, however, a suggestion. 'I can't give you the letter, but we have the means over here to make a copy practically indistinguishable from the original. See if the governor would like that.' The copy ... was indeed a marvelous reproduction and Connally was happy to get it." [1895]

The copy in this book, although undoubtedly not such a "marvelous reproduction",[H] is on page 88. Its use as an exemplar, mentioned above, is shown at right. FBI handwriting analysts have drawn seven arrows pointing to oddities of Oswald's distinctive penmanship. [1896]

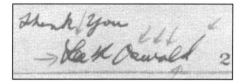

Connally finished his autobiography *In History's Shadow* shortly before his death on June 15, 1993 [1897] at the young age of 76. He wrote that he chose to let younger minds decide the large problems that land on a governor's desk, and in 1969 returned to law practice in Houston. President Nixon wanted a Democrat or two in his cabinet, and named the highly-conservative "Dino" (Democrat in name only) to be his Secretary of the Treasury. According to Theodore H. White, the gate to Richard Nixon's office and attention was zealously guarded by H. R. Haldeman, with only two allowed to reach Nixon directly on their own initiatives, John Connally and Attorney General John Mitchell. [1898] Connally resigned when palace guards Haldeman and John Ehrlichman undermined his authority.

Back at law in Texas, he headed Democrats for Nixon in 1972. [1899] Nixon began his reelection campaign in Texas with a stop at Connally's ranch. [1900] "A Southerner, a lifelong Democrat, [Connally became a] Republican because a changing instinct pulled him, as it had pulled millions of other white Southerners, away from his old moorings. ... In a time of disaster for Republicans, he boldly proclaimed himself a 'switcher' and changed parties." [1901]

Nixon wrote in his *Memoirs*: "[A]s I began preparing for the 1972 election, I also had to look ahead to 1976. I believed that John Connally was the only man in either party who clearly had the potential to be a great President. He had the necessary 'fire in the belly,' the energy to win, and the vision to lead." [1902] That was not to be.

In the depths of Nixon's Watergate crisis, Connally returned to the White House in 1973 as "Special Adviser" to the president. [1903] "On [July 29, 1974], the House Judiciary Committee voted 28-10 an article of impeachment charging Nixon violated his oath of office by abusing Presidential power. 'He has, acting personally, and through his subordinates, endeavored to' use the IRS, the FBI, and the CIA against his political adversaries, the Article stated. As chance would have it, on that same day a Federal court in downtown Washington

---

[H] Because, as told in chapter 4, either The Archives has totally misplaced the letter, or it's been stolen.

indicted John Connally—the man Nixon wanted to be his successor as President—for perjury and accepting a bribe." [1904] He was "indicted by a federal grand jury for having taken ten thousand dollars from the Associated Milk Producers, Inc., in exchange for persuading President Nixon to support a hike in milk price support" [1905] but was juried not guilty.

The taint lasted. President Ford, considering Connally to be his vice-presidential running mate in 1976, decided "his wheeler-dealer image just wouldn't fade away." [1906] Connally ran against Ronald Reagan for president in the 1980 Republican primaries, "with the dubious distinction of having spent more money in pursuit of the nomination ($11 million) than any previous candidate; and having garnered but one delegate for all his exertions, Mrs. Ada Mills of Clarksville, Arkansas." [1907] In a 1987 bust, not unusual in Texas oil cycles, he was bankrupt and allowed to keep only two hundred acres and a ranch house.[1908]

Journalist Mickey Herskowitz made a specialty of co-writing autobiographies, including those of both Connallys. In his "Co-author's Note" appendix to *In History's Shadow*, in the brief window between Connally's death and the book's printing, he added:

"In recent years, Connally suffered from pulmonary fibrosis, a rare disease that involves scarring of the lungs. His doctors emphasized that there is no known cause. The Governor had made no previous disclosure of his condition. He had one healthy lung and one that had been punctured by splinters of bone when a bullet tore through his chest and shattered part of the fifth rib. The country lost one of its most astute political minds, and Texas lost an original resource the day John Connally died, possibly from a bullet fired thirty years ago." [1909]

Nellie Connally wrote in her 2003 memoir *From Love Field*: "My gallant John died in 1993 of pulmonary fibrosis ... The doctors couldn't say for sure, but it seemed to many that the bullet fired by Lee Harvey Oswald from the same rifle that killed President John F. Kennedy thirty years before may have claimed its final victim." [1910]

Nellie Connally:

The loving, loyal wife stayed close in Parkland Hospital in 1963, first outside Trauma Room 2, then nearby as John went through five hours of surgery, and finally beside him and sleeping across the hall as he slowly recovered from his near-fatal wounds. Forty years later she wrote as fine a widow's memoir as can be, *From Love Field*, based on an excellent, exceptional task she accomplished in Austin in December 1963:

"Ten days after the President was killed and my husband was shot, and just two days after he came home—twenty pounds lighter, right arm in a cast and sling, I went off to a quiet place in the mansion with pens, pencils, and yellow pads, and wrote—what happened in that car.

I did not write it for history or for you—just for my grandchildren and all the little Connallys to come in case they had an interest (after reading in their school history books that their great-great-grandparents were in that car) in what happened on that terrible day when President John F. Kennedy was assassinated, and their grandfather almost killed. A horrible time in Texas and U.S. history.

I did not go back and add to it after so much else became known later. I just put it in the bottom drawer of an old file cabinet and let it gather dust for thirty-three years." [1911]

Her twenty-two full-length legal-pad handwritten sheets were a time capsule, magically conveying facts and emotions from one era to another. As the basis of her book, they provide a firm foundation for later historians — and this writer is grateful.

Idanell Brill "Nellie" Connally survived breast cancer, lived to greatly enjoy her grandchildren, wrote her memoir, and died at the age of 87. "At the time of her death in

2006, she was the last surviving occupant of the presidential limousine." [1912] The Kennedys had died in 1963 and 1994, her John in 1993, and the two Secret Service agents in the midnight-blue limousine's front seat in 1984 and 1985.

Lyndon Baines Johnson:

LBJ served out JFK's remaining year, then in the 1964 election soundly defeated conservative Republican Barry Goldwater with 61.3% of the votes, the highest percentage to that time in the history of the republic. He led significant progress on racial and social issues, but sank in the endless quagmire of his unpopular war in Vietnam. The Constitution's 22nd amendment allowed him to be re-elected again, so it was a shock in 1968 when he announced that he would "neither seek nor accept the nomination of my party" to run for re-election. With the antiwar movement growing, he had become a virtual prisoner in the White House and could not battle both North Vietnam and Robert Kennedy, his chief opponent who would die during that campaign. [1913] Retired to the Texas ranch, he died of a heart attack [1914] on January 22, 1973 — only two days after his presidency would have ended if he had run and been re-elected in 1968. LBJ's life was cut short, like that of a fish out of water, by being away from his natural habitat in Washington's halls of power, engaged in one-on-one finger-in-the-chest politics.[1]

Claudia "Lady Bird" Johnson:

In 1993 on Martha's Vineyard, not far from where her son will die in his plane accident, Jacqueline Kennedy Onassis entertained "Lady Bird Johnson, then eighty-one. She had been widowed for twenty years as Jackie had been for thirty. The two old friends, who had shared so much happiness and heartache over almost four decades, ate lunch under an arbor of vines. They spoke, said Mrs. Johnson later, about authors and books and their children, but not of the past. There was so much in the present to be grateful for, they both agreed." [1915] Blind and crippled by strokes, she died at home in 2007, age 94.

Lee Oswald:

He was buried in Fort Worth's Rose Hill Cemetery on the same day of drums as was Kennedy by his Eternal Flame at Arlington. That should have ended the matter, but conspiracy theorists soon erupted like the little critters in "Whack-A-Mole", determined, as Lee had put it to Connally, to "employ all means" to drive relentlessly to their frustratingly elusive goals.

Conspiracist Michael H. B. Eddowes [1916] wrote a 1975 book *Khrushchev Killed Kennedy* financed by ultra-right-wing Dallas oil billionaire H. L. Hunt,[1917] [J] later re-published as *The Oswald File*. Eddowes claimed that in the USSR, Oswald was imprisoned by the KGB who substituted one of their agents for him. The impostor married Marina, moved to Dallas, shot Kennedy, was shot by Jack Ruby and buried. Eddowes brought suit to exhume the body in Oswald's grave because it must be the Russian agent lying there. Dallas Medical Examiner Dr. Charles Petty said, "Somebody has raised the question as to who is in that grave. The easiest way to find out is to … run some tests." So they dug him up in 1981. It was Oswald.

If you would like to visit Oswald's grave, as do many thousands every year, go to the Shannon Rose Hill Cemetery's office. They probably will not give you directions to that

---

[1] In chapter 20, Special Agent Mike Howard will give his personal account of LBJ's final days.

[J] Another Texan *sans* name, known only by initials. The author has lost count of how many so far.

grave, but as was charmingly told in a 2013 story in *The New York Times*,[1918] they may deign to tell you how to find the grave of "Nick Beef", and beside it is the simple marker with only one word, "Oswald". It replaced the original, whose convoluted peregrination is told in another equally charming *New York Times* article, identified in endnote [1919].

Marina Oswald:

A few days after burying her Jack, Jacqueline Kennedy was watching the evening news on TV.

"'I have peace in my heart and hatred for no one.' ... and there was an interview with the wife [*sic*; more properly, the widow] of Lee Harvey Oswald. 'Oh, I feel so sorry for her,' Jackie said. 'She is such a nice-looking woman.'"[1920]   [1921]

Robert Oswald wrote in his memoir *Lee*: "Marina received thousands of letters from people asking whether she needed money, clothing, books, or help of any kind. Many people sent her a dollar or five or ten dollars without asking whether she needed financial aid."[1922]   Eventually, "About $70,000 reached her in this fashion."[1923]

Marina answered Warren Commission questions through 1964, with the distinction of being both their first and last witness, the only one called four times, who gave the longest testimony, transcribed onto 217 pages. Late in 1964, "Marina threw the Commission into confusion by testifying that Lee had liked the President so much, she thought it must have been Connally he was aiming at."[1924]

Here I intended to show a fine family photo of June (Oswald's first daughter), Marina's husband Kenneth, their son Mark, Marina, and Rachel (Oswald's second child). The photo is no longer available for publication. You can find it in Priscilla Johnson McMillan's 1978 paperback edition of *Marina and Lee*.

In 1965, Marina married Kenneth Jess Porter, a Texan who was very kind to her and her daughters, and together they had a son. "They were divorced in 1974, but they continue to live together as man and wife."[1925] Marina blossomed, much prettier and happier than in the bad old days when Lee beat her.

"In late 1991, Marina Oswald Porter was finally granted full citizenship ... She was planning a return to Russia. She had not been there in thirty years and much had changed. Then she added, 'Even though I was not American, I was proud of President Kennedy. He was a great leader. When I got my passport, it read, 'This person is to be shown complete respect and dignity as a citizen of the United States.'"[1926] The 2013 photo at right shows Ken, then 75, and Marina, 72.   [1927]

"'Do you know why I loved Lee?' she once said. 'I loved him because I felt he was in search of himself. I was in search of myself, too. I couldn't show him the way, but I wanted to help and give him support while he was searching.'"[1928]

Marguerite Oswald:

Good son Robert Oswald wrote knowingly in 1967 about the change in his mother when her youngest son suddenly became notorious:

> "Mother felt that now at last she was about to get the kind of attention she had sought all her life. She had an extraordinary idea of her ability and her importance. For many years she had been treated as just another woman of some minor business skill whose usefulness as an employee was limited because of her rather quarrelsome nature, and few people were even aware of her existence. But she seemed to recognize immediately that she would never again be treated as an ordinary, obscure, unimportant woman." [1929]

Hugh Aynesworth, a *The Dallas Morning News* reporter, knowingly sized her up:

> "Over the years, I also became well acquainted with Marguerite Oswald, Lee's mother. She was a very bizarre woman! She said, 'Lee Harvey, my son, even after his death has done more for his country than any other living American.' She had that inscribed on a plaque, as well. Fifty of them were made, and she sold them to reporters that came from all over the world who felt sorry for her. Marguerite probably made Lee what he became. When he got out of the service early because of an injury to her, he stayed with her only three or four days, then took off for New Orleans and got on a ship. He couldn't stand her! Anyone that was around her echoed the problem. She wanted money for everything." [1930]

In 1965, writer Jean Stafford spent several days with Marguerite. That amazing and unsettling experience is told in a book that proves treasures sometimes come in small packages, *A Mother in History*. Among the mother's gems: "Some people with a formal education are so dull that really and truly I find them stupid. All they know is what's in the books, and that's that." [1931] "I want history to be straightened out." [1932] "Oh, how I wish there was more time! I have stories and coincidences by the galore, and things that I can prove are not according to Hoyle. If we just had the time, we could write them up and become millionairesses. The first book in the series would be *One and One Make Two*." Stafford notes that "She had suggested this title in our first interview, and in the second had revised it to *One and One Don't Make Two*. Possibly they were to be in sequel, two volumes, boxed." [1933] "Why am I so concerned that the people will understand? It is natural because I am a mother in history. I am in twenty-six volumes of the Warren

> Here I wanted to show a photo of Marguerite standing at Lee's grave. The photographer's agent insisted on their exorbitant $500 minimum, so the heck with it. To see it, go on the Web to Amazon.com. In the big empty bar at top, type "a mother in history", at left click on the down-arrow and click "Books", at far right click on the magnifying glass. Click on the top item, Jean Stafford's "A Mother in History", click "See all 2 images", the first image will be the too-expensive sad photo on the cover of that book, which I highly recommend.

Report, which is all over the world, so I must defend myself and defend my son Lee." [1934] On Mother's Day 1965, Marguerite visited Lee's grave in Fort Worth, where the photo I wanted to show here [1935] was taken of "A Mother in History".

Legendary newsman Bob Schieffer wrote a wonderful retrospective of the highlights of his long career, *This Just In*, in which the first of twenty-eight stories is "Oswald's Mother". A very junior night reporter at the *Fort Worth Star-Telegram*, he went in to help out on the afternoon of the assassination:

> "I hadn't even removed my hat when I settled behind a typewriter and picked up one of the ringing phones. In all my years as a reporter, I would never again take a call like that one.
>
> A woman's voice asked if we could spare anyone to give her a ride to Dallas.
>
> 'Lady,' I said, 'this is not a taxi, and besides, the president has been shot.'
>
> 'I know,' she said. 'They think my son is the one who shot him.'

It was the mother of Lee Harvey Oswald, and she had heard on the radio of her son's arrest.

'Where do you live?' I blurted out. 'I'll be right over to get you.'" [1936]

Schieffer then talked the paper's automotive editor into driving him and Marguerite to the city jail in Dallas in a "road-test" Cadillac, and thus began his interest in the strange woman. Forty years later, he vividly remembered that ride:

"We found Mrs. Oswald on the lawn of a small home on Fort Worth's west side. She was a short, round-faced woman in enormous, black horn-rimmed glasses and a white nurse's uniform. She carried a small blue travel bag. I got into the backseat with her and Bill drove. She was distraught, but in an odd way. I would later come to believe she was mentally deranged, but for most of the trip she seemed less concerned with the death of the president and for her son than with herself. She railed about how Oswald's Russian-born wife would get sympathy while no one would 'remember the mother' and that she would probably starve. I marked it off to understandable emotional overload and I couldn't bring myself to use her self-serving remarks in the story I filed later that day. I probably should have. She would later be so brazen as to tell a reporter for *Life* magazine that 'Mama wants money,' and years later she was still saying the same things. As she had predicted, the world showed her little sympathy and she supported herself in the end by selling Oswald's clothing to souvenir hunters." [1937]

In the photo she stands on the slope of the "Grassy Knoll", with the TSBD behind.[1938] Marguerite Claverie Pic Oswald Ekdahl Oswald died of cancer on January 17, 1981 in Tarrant County, Texas. Norman Mailer wrote this elegant appreciation of her life and legacy:

"Denigrators of Marguerite Oswald will remark on how much she loved the limelight after he was gone, and it is true: His love of attention was equaled by hers—she spoke to large audiences for the first time in her life, and it was a great step forward from that sales job in New York where she was fired because of intractable body odor.

Yet, for all her latter-day notoriety, we have to recall that she died alone and full of a literal cancer to follow upon the bottomless cancer of those endless wounds within personal wounds—no, she had her life, and one would not want it, but somewhere in the bureaucratic corridors of Karmic Reassignment she is probably arguing now with one of the monitors, dissatisfied with the low station, by her lights, of her next placement. 'I gave birth to one of the most famous and important Americans who ever lived!' she will tell the clerk-angel who is recording her story.

INTERVIEWER: Do you have any family here at all?

MARGUERITE: I have no family, period. I brought three children into the world, and I have sisters, I have nieces, I have nephews, I have grandchildren, and I'm all alone. That answers that question and I don't want to hear another word about it.

There she stands with her outrageous ego and her self-deceit, her bold loneliness and cold bones, those endless humiliations that burn like sores. Yet, she is worthy of Dickens. Marguerite Oswald can stand for literary office with Micawber and Uriah Heep. No word she utters will be false to her character; her stamp will be on every phrase. Few people without a literary motive would seek her company for long, but a novelist can esteem Marguerite. She does all his work for him." [1939]

Robert Oswald:

Lee's older brother returned to work at the Acme Brick Company [K] ten days after November 22, with a Secret Service agent assigned for his protection. Characteristically, Robert did not want to be a burden and believed there was no threat, so after a week without problems, stopped the protection.[1940] In 1964 he moved to Wichita Falls,[L] a city northwest of Fort Worth and bordering on Oklahoma, as Acme's area sales manager. Some stories tend to loop without any cause or reason, which happened there when a re-trial of Jack Ruby was ordered moved from Dallas to Wichita Falls to ensure impartiality. "Unlike his mother and sister-in-law, [Robert] had talked to few persons since the assassination. He believed his brother was guilty of killing the President. ... He thought Ruby would receive a fair trial in Wichita Falls." [1941]

Despite Robert's desire to live a productive, quiet life without notoriety, echoes of his brother sometimes intrude.[M] When Lee's coffin was dug up in 1981 — see the Lee Oswald article above — the body was re-buried in a new coffin, and Robert was assured the original was destroyed. Thirty years later, he learned that it had been saved and sold at auction, with the death certificate and embalming table, for $160,000. [1942] Robert had paid $710 for Lee's coffin and funeral services, and had preserved his 1963 receipt. In 2011 he sued the funeral home and auction house for acting without his knowledge or authorization in selling something that was his property, in bad taste, and because he knew of "no case where anyone has ever bought a used coffin." [1943] After trial in 2015, the judge ruled solidly for Robert.[1944] Hooray!

The Lincoln Continental limousine:

The car was flown back to Washington for study by the FBI and Secret Service. Their work complete, the Secret Service chose to modify it, faster than building a new limo from scratch to meet their need for a secure parade vehicle. It was sent to Hess & Eisenhardt, the firm that had originally modified it from a Ford-built 1961 Lincoln Continental, and rebuilt from the ground up with heavy armor plating, bullet-resistant windows and a bulletproof permanent roof. Solid aluminum rims were also fitted inside the tires to make them flat-proof.

Originally "midnight blue" by Kennedy's choice and at his death, the car was repainted black because the blue could be too closely associated with the assassination. It remained in service for eight more years, logging 50,000 miles on the ground and over a million miles in the air, being flown to and from its destinations. It was retired in 1978 to the Henry Ford Museum in Dearborn, Michigan, where you can see it today.[1945] But, because of the permanent roof, black paint and other modifications, it does not look at all like the limousine we remember from that joyous-turned-tragic day in Dallas.

Because of the rebuilding and understandable sensitivities, the limo was not used for event reconstructions in Dallas by the Warren Commission and FBI, described and illustrated with photos in Chapters 14 – TOO CLOSE TO CALL and 19 – THE SHOT NOT TAKEN.

As this book entered its final edit in 2015, the D.C. license plates "SS100X" from the fatal day were sold in a Dallas auction to a "high-end Kennedy collector" for $100,000.[1946]

[K] Now part of Berkshire Hathaway, so Warren Buffet and this author own it, in very different amounts!

[L] The smoothest-running territory of IBM's Fort Worth office of the Field Engineering Division, of which this author had the distinct privilege of being Branch Manager in 1974-1975.

[M] This author included — I wrote repeatedly for permission to quote from his biography *Lee*, sent him $1,500, paid a Seattle attorney $7,216.48 to try through Robert's attorney, and never got a reply.

The Mannlicher-Carcano rifle:

Chapter 12 – THE RIFLE tells its story. William Manchester noted two subsequent nadirs in *The Death of a President*: "Klein's Sporting Goods revealed that 150 Mannlicher-Carcanos had been shipped to souvenir-conscious Dallasites." [1947] In 1964, Marina Oswald "went after the gun itself, arguing that since Oswald was dead it could not be held as evidence. A Denver oil man who wanted it as a souvenir sent her a $10,000 down payment ... and then sued [Attorney General Nick] Katzenbach for possession." [1948] In 1965, Congress rushed through and "President Johnson signed a bill authorizing the federal government to take ownership of the rifle that killed President Kennedy. The new legislation authorizes the attorney general to designate as federal property items of evidence collected by the Warren Commission." [1949]

The Texas School Book Depository:

Ruth Dean, a bookkeeper and cashier on the TSBD's second floor, told of November 22 in Larry Sneed's valuable *No More Silence*, then she said this: "After all this happened, the Texas School Book Depository continued to operate. In 1971, the depository bought property off of Ambassador Row and built a building and a warehouse, office space, and all of those who wanted to move to that location went to the new Depository." [1950]

"[O]n Presidents Day in 1989, a nonprofit museum ... opened at the site of the assassination. It was on the sixth floor of what used to be the Texas School Book Depository but was now the Dallas County Administration Building. The exhibits told what had happened starting with the early 1960s and the Kennedy presidency and continuing through the assassination and investigations. No theories, just history, with a lot of pictures, text, and videos." [1951] Information about that fine venue is at a great Web address: www.jfk.org

> Key point of this chapter:
> **Three Monday funerals were all sad, but diverse as could be.**
> **History dealt in very different ways with the principals.**

To end this chapter on a happy note, this gift from photographer Arthur Pollock shows many of this author's favorite people at the dedication of the JFK Library in 1993:[1952]

COMMISSION, CRITICS, REHASHES [A]

The Warren Commission, its critics, then Congress twice and a Board

> "From morning, when she rises early, until night, she is at work 'researching the case,' collating newspaper stories, studying theories of conspiracy (right-wing, left-wing, wingless, Catholic, Baptist, Jewish, Black Muslim, anarchist, fascist, federalist, masterminded by the cops, masterminded by the robbers) that have been propounded from Los Angeles to West Berlin; reading between the lines of the Warren Report and scrutinizing the errors of omission in it and those of commission, and the ambiguities and the garbles."
>
> — **Marguerite Oswald**'s day, described by Jean Stafford [1953]

"**OUT OF THE NATION'S SUSPICIONS**, out of the nation's need for facts, the Warren Commission was born." wrote Lyndon Johnson in his autobiography, *The Vantage Point*:

"There was doubt and bewilderment about what had actually happened in Dallas on November 22, 1963, and the uncertainty was compounded two days later when Lee Harvey Oswald was shot to death while in the custody of the Dallas police. A horror-stricken, outraged nation wanted the truth and no one could immediately provide it." [1954]

"[W]ith the prime suspect now dead, a blue-ribbon commission was needed to ascertain the facts. ... While I was considering what sort of investigative body to commission for this task, two facts became abundantly clear. First, this could not be an agency of the Executive branch. The commission had to be composed of men who were known to be beyond pressure and above suspicion. Second, this represented too large an issue for the Texas authorities to handle alone." [1955]

Edward Jay Epstein's book *Inquest: The Warren Commission and the Establishment of Truth* was derived from his master's thesis in government at Cornell University. It described how a national commission came to be, beginning on the day Kennedy and Oswald were buried:

"On November 25, after 'a conference with the White House,' Texas Attorney General Waggoner Carr announced that a court of inquiry would be held by the State of Texas 'to develop fully and disclose openly' the facts of the assassination. This investigation was

---

[A] "**rehash** *v* to repeat something or reuse and rework old material, making some changes but without introducing anything new" — *Encarta Dictionary*

intended to be part of a broader inquiry in which the FBI would first conduct a full investigation and report its findings to the President; then the Texas court of inquiry would examine witnesses of the assassination in public hearings; and finally a Presidential Commission would evaluate all the facts that were established and report its conclusions to the President. Waggoner Carr named two prominent Texas lawyers, Leon Jaworski [B] and Dean Robert G. Storey, as special counsel for the investigation." [1956]

"On November 26 Senator Everett M. Dirksen proposed that the Senate Judiciary Committee conduct a full investigation into the assassination. This suggestion received considerable support from both Democrats and Republicans on the floor of the Senate. The next day Congressman Charles E. Goodell proposed in the House of Representatives that a Joint Committee, composed of seven Senators and seven Representatives, conduct an inquiry into the assassination." [1957]

On November 29, "to avoid parallel investigations and to concentrate fact-finding in a body having the broadest national mandate," [1958] President Lyndon B. Johnson appointed a commission "to ascertain, evaluate, and report on" the facts of the assassination. [1959]

LBJ explained his reasoning: "The commission had to be bipartisan, and I felt that we needed a Republican chairman whose judicial ability and fairness were unquestioned. I don't believe I ever considered anyone but Chief Justice Earl Warren for chairman. I was not an intimate of the Chief Justice. We had never spent ten minutes alone together, but to me he was the personification of justice and fairness in this country." [1960]

When LBJ had settled on Earl Warren, four days after JFK's funeral, he sent Attorney General Nick Katzenbach and Solicitor General Archibald Cox to the Chief Justice to urge him to head a federal commission. Warren refused. He had, he pointed out, repeatedly spoken out against extracurricular activity by judges; he suggested they ask one of the Court's two retired justices instead. His visitors left and advised the White House of their failure. This was the kind of circumstance in which Lyndon Johnson was at his most effective. The Chief Judge hardly had time to relay his decision to two of his colleagues before his phone rang. The President wanted to see him at once. In Warren's words,

"[T]he President told me how serious the situation was. He said there had been wild rumors, and that there was the international situation to think of. ... The only way to dispel these rumors, he said, was to have an independent and responsible commission, and that there was no one to head it except the highest judicial officer in the country. I told him how I felt. He said that if the public became aroused against Castro and Khrushchev there might be war. [1961]

'You've been in uniform before,' he said, 'and if I asked you, you would put on the uniform again for your country.' I said, 'Of course.' 'This is more important than that,' he said. 'If you're putting it like that,' I said, 'I can't say no.'" [1962] So "the Chief" said "yes" and the Warren Commission was born.

[B] America came to know him well in 1974 as the dogged federal prosecutor who forced release of the White House tapes, exposing the misdeeds of President Nixon and other Watergate conspirators.

Edward Epstein continued the story:

"To complete the Commission, President Johnson chose six men who had distinguished themselves in public life and who represented important and diverse elements in the political spectrum. Two were senior Senators: Richard B. Russell, Democrat of Georgia, who had held his seat in the Senate for thirty uninterrupted years; and John Sherman Cooper, Republican of Kentucky, who had formerly served as Ambassador to India and who was generally regarded as a leading member of the liberal wing of the Republican Party. Two were leaders of the House of Representatives: Hale Boggs,[C] Democrat of Louisiana, Majority Whip of the House; and Gerald R. Ford, Republican of Michigan, chairman of the House Republican Conference. Two members were international lawyers: Allen W. Dulles, the former director of the Central Intelligence Agency; and John J. McCloy, former United States High Commissioner for Germany and former President of the World Bank.[1963]

The Commission was empowered to prescribe its own procedures and to employ such assistance as it deemed necessary. All government agencies were ordered to cooperate. There were few, if any, precedents in American history for such a Commission."[1964]

Then-Congressman and future President Gerald Ford recalled how he was talked onto the Commission: "I was resisting as strongly as I could ... I said, 'I'm sorry, Mr. President ... I've got a lot of special responsibilities. I don't have the time.' Well, you know Lyndon ... 'It's your patriotic duty, you owe it to the country,' all the lingo. I understand he did that virtually with everybody, from the chief justice on down."[1965] "'Well,' Ford said later, 'what the hell do you say? You say, 'Yes.' And I did.'"[1966]

This photo[1967] was taken on September 23, 1964, the day before the Commission presented its report to the President. Around the table are Representatives Gerald Ford and Hale Boggs, Senator Richard Russell, Chairman Earl Warren, Senator John Sherman Cooper,

---

[C] He was to be killed, with a wonderful young congressman he was helping to re-election, Nick Begich, (a friend of the author) in the 1972 disappearance of their small plane in Alaska. Many came to know and respect Hale Bogg's widow Lindy who replaced him, then their daughter Mary Martha Corinne Morrison Claiborne Boggs, better known as Cokie Roberts, awesomely good NPR political analyst. The day this footnote was written, NPR aired a commentary by Rebecca Boggs Roberts, daughter of Cokie and Steve, who spoke proudly of her two U.S. Representative grandparents.

John McCloy and Allen Dulles, and Commission General Counsel J. Lee Rankin. A flag at least as large as Old Glory and photo of a man in military cap testify that the Commission met and worked in borrowed space in the Veterans of Foreign Wars building.[1968]

"Johnson purposely chose the highly respected and politically diverse group to avoid any appearance of bias. ... Johnson, more than anybody, wanted the country to move forward and was eager to put outrageous claims of conspiracy to rest." [1969]

"After the Commission was assembled, Warren wasted no time choosing the staff members. These staffers would play a critical role in amassing, evaluating, sorting, and reviewing the voluminous amounts of evidence. Warren chose J. Lee Rankin, a former U.S. solicitor general, to act as his chief of staff. Rankin in turn played a large role in choosing the remaining staff members, clerks, stenographers, and other personnel" [1970] — thirty-two in all.

We and history are uniquely fortunate that a disarming young graduate student from Cornell, writing a thesis required to earn his master's degree — about how government functions in an unprecedented situation — received unusually candid cooperation from the commissioners, their chief counsel, and staff. Edward Jay Epstein wrote in his *Inquest*:

"[T]here were actually two separate investigations, the Commission hearings and the staff investigation.[1971] Opinions differ as to what the Commission actually did. [Assistant Counsel] Joseph Ball commented that the Commission 'had no idea of what was happening, we did all the investigating, lined up the witnesses, solved the problems and wrote the Report.' [1972] [Assistant Counsel] Wesley Liebeler, when asked what the Commission did, replied, 'In one word, Nothing.' [1973] [Assistant Counsel] Melvin Eisenberg compared the Commission to a corporation's board of directors, with Rankin as president and the staff members as the officers.[1974] [Assistant Counsel] Howard Willens reflected the consensus of the staff when he said, 'The commissioners were not in touch with the investigation at all times.' [1975] [General Counsel and director of the staff] J. Lee Rankin, on the other hand, said that some of the younger lawyers 'simply didn't understand how a government inquiry worked' and that the Commission, through its experience and collective wisdom, gave the investigation its direction and focus.[1976] In any case, there was little direct contact between the Commissioners and the staff lawyers, and to most of the lawyers 'Warren was the Commission.'" [1977]

Critic Harold Weisberg began his early (1965) book *Whitewash: The Report on the Warren Report* with "A Word About Investigations", including this appraisal of how such things are done in general, and by the Warren Commission in particular:

"The real work of the investigations is rarely performed by the members of the commission or committee. Even when actual questions are asked by the members of the investigating body only, preparation is by its staff. The members are almost invariably men already too busy. ...

It was to be expected that the President's Commission on the Assassination of President John F. Kennedy would necessarily have to lean heavily upon its staff. Almost without exception, the Commission was comprised of men already too deeply committed to public, official, and governmental activity. The most superficial examination of the volumes of testimony shows Commission members not attending hearings, or coming late because of other commitments, or leaving early to meet other responsibilities. The Chief Justice could not delegate his judicial role any more than the Congressmen and Senators could have someone else vote for them. Hence, when they had to be in more than one place at the same time, the easiest place for them *not* to be was at the Commission's hearings. Here they could and did delegate to the staff. From the very beginning the staff did almost all the work, including the interrogations. One published account of the Commission's work reports one member [Senator Richard Russell] as attending only two of 44 hearings. Members conducted a minor part of the interrogations at the hearings, leaving the bulk of such questioning to staff lawyers. Only a very small percentage of the hearings was attended by *any* members. *Most* hearings had *no* members present." [1978]

President Johnson commanded all of the federal government to do fact gathering and anything the Commission asked. The FBI and Secret Service put their most experienced people on the case. If you would know more, see "THE INVESTIGATION" in the *Warren Report*'s FOREWORD. That was followed by "COMMISSION HEARINGS", which summarized:

> "In addition to the information resulting from these investigations, the Commission has relied primarily on the facts disclosed by the sworn testimony of the principal witnesses to the assassination and related events. Beginning on February 3, 1964, the Commission and its staff has taken the testimony of 552 witnesses. Of this number, 94 appeared before members of the Commission; 395 were questioned by members of the Commission's legal staff; 61 supplied sworn affidavits; and 2 gave statements." [1979]

In their oral testimony, some witnesses were specific, responsive and succinct; Robert Oswald was a model. All witnesses were heard and treated with the respect they deserved. At the end of her first long week of testimony, Marina Oswald said to the chairman and commissioners: "I am very grateful to all of you. I didn't think among Americans I would find so many friends." To which the kindly Chief Justice responded: "You have friends here." [1980]

Other witnesses were grasshoppers, hopping about. Lee's mother, Marguerite Oswald, was indisputably the most difficult. The Chief Justice, Allen Dulles and future-President Gerald Ford sat through most of her questioning by chief counsel J. Lee Rankin. After he tried, as shown on dozens of pages of testimony, to have Marguerite explain her belief that President Kennedy had been the victim of a

> Here was to be the cover of TIME magazine of February 14, 1964, showing Marina going to testify. But the PARS agency representing TIME demanded $460 each for this cover and two others I wanted to show; $1380 was too rich for the limited print run of this book. To see the cover, large and in color, look at: http://search.time.com/results.html? N=46&Ns=p_date_range|1&Nf=p _date_range%7cBTWN+19640214+ 19640214

conspiracy between two Secret Service (or maybe they were FBI — she switched back and forth on that) agents, also involving as co-conspirators daughter-in-law Marina, Ruth Paine, a "high government official" she preferred not to name — well, Rankin gave up and tried for progress on what he hoped would be a simpler matter:

> "Mr. RANKIN. Now, as I understand she says now that she is speculating as to that being a possibility.
>
> Mrs. OSWALD. Well, now, Mr. Rankin. I have not changed my testimony, if you are implying that. I may not have put it in a position you understood. Because as I say, I certainly did not mean to imply that I had proof, because if I had proof I would not be sitting here taking all my energy and trying to show you this little by little. I would have had an affidavit and show you the proof. So if you want to call it speculation, call it speculation. I don't care what you call it. But I am not satisfied in my mind that things are according to Hoyle. And I believe that my son is innocent. And I also realize that my son could be involved. But I have no way of knowing these things unless I analyze the papers that I have, sir.
>
> Mr. RANKIN. The Commission would like to know what you base your assumption that your son was an agent on. Could you help us?
>
> Mrs. OSWALD. Would you like me to go into this story—I will start with my son's life from the very beginning.

Mr. RANKIN. Can't we get down to—

Mrs. OSWALD. No, sir, we cannot. I am sorry. This is my life. I cannot survive in this world unless I know I have my American way of life and can start from the very beginning. I have to work into this. I cannot answer these questions like in a court, yes or no. And I will not answer yes or no. I want to tell you the story. And that is the only way you can get a true picture. I am the accused mother of this man, and I have family and grandchildren, and Marina, my daughter-in-law. And I am going to do everything I can to try and prove he is innocent.

Mr. RANKIN. Well, now, Mrs. Oswald, you are not claiming before this Commission that there was anything back at the beginning, at the early childhood of your son, in which you thought he was an agent?

Mrs. OSWALD. Yes, sir—at age 16.

Mr. RANKIN. Well, why don't you start with age 16, then." [1981]

And away she went, rambling along until it became clear that she believed a Marine Corps recruiter's interest in 16-year-old Lee proved he was then being enticed into becoming a secret agent for the government.

Near the end of her three days of testimony, Marguerite Oswald said that she planned to investigate the case on her own, in parallel with what the Warren Commission would be doing. She then got into this little tiff with Earl Warren:

"Mrs. OSWALD. I am still going to try to investigate this thoroughly, because it is very important. ... Now, do you know if Lee—

The CHAIRMAN. Let's don't—we will go into those things.

Mrs. OSWALD. But if you don't know, Chief Justice Warren, how will you go into it?

The CHAIRMAN. Please don't turn this into examining the Commission. We will go into those things very thoroughly. Just go ahead with your story.

Mrs. OSWALD. Well, this is a lie, and I want to know about this lie.

The CHAIRMAN. All right, you have told us.

Mrs. OSWALD. I have not finished, sir.

The CHAIRMAN. Well, you may go ahead and tell what you want. But don't question the Commission. That is the only thing I am asking you." [1982]

Her attorney interceded at this tense point, suggesting she compose herself. She did, and her all-over-the-road testimony resumed. Soon after, she gave a shot-over-the-bow warning to Chief Justice Warren of what coming years would bring: "We have attorneys writing us. We have ministers. We have all types of people that are not satisfied with this boy being charged with the assassination of President Kennedy. And, of course, not satisfied with the way he was shot down without trial. And we are going to continue to investigate and fight this in our own way, when I leave the Commission, sir." [1983]

Epstein summarizes: "The Commission had two distinct tasks: the investigation and writing of the Report. J. Lee Rankin said, 'No one realized how long it would take to write the Report; instead of the estimated one month, it took nearly four months to complete.' [1984] ... [T]o expedite the writing ... Rankin appointed [Assistant Counsels] Norman Redlich, Alfred Goldberg, Howard Willens, and himself as a 'Re-editing Committee.' Redlich was assigned editorial responsibility for the first four chapters ... Goldberg, for the next three ... and Willens, for the eighth and final chapter." [1985] "The final draft ... was completed in mid-September. Rankin then assigned Goldberg the task of 'polishing it up.' Goldberg said that he needed six months to do a competent rewriting job, and he had less than one week. [1986] The Warren Report [was] supplemented by eighteen appendices. [1987] ... Who wrote the Report?

Although more than thirty persons had had a hand in writing it, it was written mainly by two men: Norman Redlich and Alfred Goldberg." [1988]

One of the most diligent workers, Assistant Counsel Arlen Specter, later proudly wrote: "The Warren Commission reported the truth, in as much detail and as precisely as we could. The watchword was integrity. We followed the chief justice's order, at [our] initial staff meeting, that the truth be our client." [1989] The completeness, quality and cohesion of the *Report* — fiercely challenged and always surviving for a half-century — despite monumental pressures to "get it done!", testify to the wonderful abilities and dedications of the staff. [D]

The seven appointed commissioners reviewed the staff-written report draft, to find they were divided on the paramount question of being certain about the possibility of a conspiracy. In his 1979 autobiography, *A Time to Heal*, Gerald Ford recalled:

"Warren and most of the staff had recommended that we say Oswald committed the crime. No one disagreed. Then we addressed the issue of a conspiracy and became entangled in a dispute that almost resulted in the issuance of a split report. The staff wanted us to say that there was no conspiracy, either foreign or domestic. Russell, Boggs and I thought that was too strong, so we prevailed on the other members to change the wording in a small but extremely significant way. The final report read that the commission "has found no evidence of a conspiracy." That, in my opinion, was far more accurate. When the report came out, critics charged that it was a whitewash, that we had covered up government complicity in the President's death. They make the same charges today. Nonsense! There was no complicity on the part of the CIA, FBI, Secret Service, Dallas police or any other state or federal agency. So far as foreign conspiracy is concerned, nothing I have learned in the years since then would prompt me to change any of the major conclusions we reached. I believe that the report—while not perfect— is a document of which the American people can be proud." [1990]

On September 24, 1964, all the commissioners [1991] trooped over to the White House to hand President Johnson a large, heavy blue-cover book, *Report of the President's Commission on*

the Assassination of President John F. Kennedy. Then, unimaginable dedication, accomplishment and overtime ensued at both the *New York Times* and the U.S. Government Printing Office. The *Times*, always proudly America's journal of record, printed the entire *Report* on Monday, September 28, a thick 48 pages of fine print: "this section contains the full report and parts of the 18 appendices." [1992] That was in the days before electronic scanners and computers, so all the words were keyed into Linotype hot-lead print slug machines. Just as amazingly, the federal GPO printed and the Superintendent of Documents distributed, that same Monday, the 912-page blue-cover *Report* in book form. The accompanying twenty-six *WCH* volumes, "*Hearings ...*", were published eight weeks later on

---

[D] In 30 years at IBM, this author often received imperatives to "stop tweaking" and meet deadlines. An unpublished IBM study found that personal computers cut the time to write a business letter from 20 to only 10 minutes — but writers then spent an additional 15 minutes "polishing"!

November 23, 1964 — and that's how this author received them during December, in Alaska, as a Christmas present from parents George and Mary Baker Sundborg in Washington, DC.

In his excellent biography of Earl Warren, *Chief Justice*, Ed Cray reported that the Commission had been a cost bargain. The senior counsels were paid $100 per day, junior only $75. Both received a $25-per-day expense allowance. Salaries totaled $239,000. $608,000 was paid to print the final report and its twenty-six supplementary volumes. The commission's total cost was $1.2 million.[1993]

> "The report was a best-seller. The Government Printing Office sold more than 140,000 copies of the one-volume report, and 1,500 copies of the supporting twenty-six volumes. Together, sales produced a profit of $191,400. A mass-market paperback edition sold hundreds of thousands of additional copies." [1994]

President Johnson had been a taskmaster in requiring that the *Report* be issued well before the November election. America had taken into its heart, a few years earlier, Theodore White as its historian of campaigns and elections, upon publication of his seminal *The Making of the President 1960*. In telling the events of 1964 in the sequel volume, Teddy White attested to LBJ's finely-tuned political instinct:

> "Then, overnight or over one weekend, the jump happened. In every campaign, as politicians know, there can come an unexplained quantum jump of attention when the crowds surge into the streets to cheer their candidate and give him love. It happened to Eisenhower in late September of 1952. It happened to Kennedy the first week in October of 1960. It happened to Lyndon Johnson on Monday, September 28th, 1964. His crowds, as I say, had been good and growing throughout September. But on the last weekend of September the Warren Commission issued its massive report. On Sunday afternoon the great television networks devoted hours to it; Monday-morning papers throughout the nation bannered the report, tearing open the scarcely healed wounds in the emotions of the American people, re-creating the black weekend of assassination over again. It was as if the nation hungered to see a President, real, live, healthy, in the flesh—as much as the President hungered to see them.
>
> Lyndon Johnson had read the report himself on his ranch in Texas on Saturday and Sunday, September 26th and 27th; had flown back to Washington that night; and had risen early on Monday, September 28th, to give a day to campaigning in New England.
>
> He arrived at the airfield in Providence, Rhode Island, at 9:30 A.M. on a cool fall day, and already some 3,000 people were at the airport, surging against the wire fence, girls squealing, children crying in the crush, babies held aloft ... [In] Providence (population 208,000) or Hartford, Connecticut (population 162,000), one could see in the streets of his route more people than the census gave for the entire population of the city." [1995] E

As the Commission hurried to complete its tasks, the testimonies, exhibits, photos and other documents had been jumbled without indexing into twenty-six volumes titled *"Hearings Before the President's Commission on the Assassination of President Kennedy"*. Those two shelves of books are the *sine qua non* for the serious assassination analyst. The Editors of *The New York Times*, compiling their book of important and interesting extracts, *The Witnesses*, noted:

> "[O]n Nov. 23, a year and a day after the tragedy in Dallas, the Warren Commission took a further and most extraordinary step to inform the public. It published all the evidence that the seven commissioners and their staff had seen and heard.
>
> There were 26 closely-printed volumes, 15 of testimony and 11 of exhibits, a total of more than 17,000 pages. Nothing was withheld except a few phrases omitted on the grounds of taste,

---

E In the month this chapter is written, the author and his beloved Jean were in the throng cheering the Seahawks' 43-8 (!) Super Bowl victory; 700,000 of us, more than the population of Seattle.

and those were carefully indicated ... Publication of these ... volumes disclosed the remarkable character of the Warren Commission inquiry. Historians could remember no comparably painstaking effort to obtain all the facts immediately after a great national disaster. The Commission's questions to witnesses showed that it had attempted to proceed without preconceptions: the aim was 'the truth . . . as far as it can be discovered.' Men who had served briefly with Lee Harvey Oswald in the Marines, persons who saw him on a bus to Mexico City in September, 1963—the farthest reaches of relevance were explored. And all of the material was presented to the public quietly, without salesmanship.

The scope and completeness of the 26 volumes make them essential documents for the historian and for anyone seeking to appraise for himself the validity of the Warren Commission's central conclusion—that there was no conspiracy of right or left, that the assassination was the work of one unhappy man, Lee Oswald." [1996]

Jim Bishop, author of *The Day Kennedy Was Shot*, recognized their value: "The prime source for all the years to come is *Hearings Before the President's Commission on the Assassination of President Kennedy,* volumes 1 through 26. It required two years to read and annotate the 10,400,000 words but within the maze of repetition and contradiction, there is a mass of solid evidence which, if used as a foundation, will help any author to build a book of fascinating credibility without rancor, bias, or censorship." [1997] The author of the book you hold did not attempt to read every word, but reached for those volumes thousands of times during the four years he dedicated to writing this book, and has a strong left arm to prove it.

The *Hearings* are a monument to inclusion and completeness, but certainly not to flow or simplicity. As one example, Oswald's handwritten plea to Connally, in this book on page 88, is printed three times, all in Volume XIX on page 248 (CADIGAN EXHIBIT. NO. 2 from the FBI), page 281 (CADIGAN EXHIBIT. NO. 9 from the FBI with 12 arrows added by experts pointing to handwriting exemplars) and page 713 (on page 65 of 131-page FOLSOM EXHIBIT NO. 1, Oswald's Marine Corps record). In the *Warren Report* it is typed out on page 710 to be easier to read, but with errors in transcription. In this book it is also typed out, for the same purpose, and is accurate — as if Lee had a typewriter to type in the same way he wrote.

The *Warren Report* was purposefully written and edited to be understood by citizens with ordinary education and capabilities. You, because you are reading the book you hold, are much more than that! If you have any doubts about what is about to be related, or any of the major facts in this book, then please get a copy of the *Report* and see what it says. I believe people are entitled to their own opinions, but not to their own facts — and thus I hew to clean, clear truth, which is what the Warren Commission did so well, fifty years ago.

If you prefer, in these modern days you can read the *Warren Report* online at the U.S. Archives: www.archives.gov/research/JFK/warren-commission-report You can download it as a huge .PDF file, using a link on the first page arrived at from that link.

All that having been politely said, where this author and the Warren Commission part ways is on the matter of Oswald's motive. Here we go — them first.

The *Warren Report*'s introductory *Summary and Conclusions* began with a statement of purpose: "This Commission was created ... in recognition of the right of people everywhere to full and truthful knowledge concerning these events. This report endeavors to fulfill that right and to appraise this tragedy by the light of reason and the standard of fairness. It has been prepared with a deep awareness of the Commission's responsibility to present to the American people an objective report of the facts relating to the assassination." [1998]

Next came a seventeen-page *Narrative of Events*, the solid foundation upon which this book's Events chapters 1 through 6 have been erected. Following that, the commissioners presented their *Conclusions*, which had been worked, discussed, argued and reworded until all seven agreed. "The Commission ... has reached certain conclusions based on all the available evidence. ... These conclusions represent the reasoned judgment of all members of the Commission and are presented after an investigation which has satisfied the Commission that it has ascertained the truth ..." [1999]

There were twelve *Conclusions* spread across seven pages, from "1. The shots which killed President Kennedy and wounded Governor Connally were fired from the sixth floor window at the southeast corner of the Texas School Book Depository." through "12. The Commission recognizes that the varied responsibilities of the President require that he make frequent trips to all parts of the United States and abroad." The reader can find them all in the *Warren Report*. Pertinent to the purposes of this book are three:

"4. The shots which killed President Kennedy and wounded Governor Connally were fired by Lee Harvey Oswald. This conclusion is based upon the following: *(a)* The Mannlicher-Carcano 6.5 millimeter Italian rifle from which the shots were fired was owned by and in the possession of Oswald. [to] *(g)* Oswald had attempted to kill Maj. Gen Edwin A. Walker (Resigned, U.S. Army) on April 10, 1963, thereby demonstrating his disposition to take human life." [2000]

"9. The Commission has found no evidence that either Lee Harvey Oswald or Jack Ruby was part of any conspiracy, domestic or foreign, to assassinate President Kennedy. The reasons for this conclusion are: *(a)* The Commission has found no evidence that anyone assisted Oswald in planning and carrying out the assassination. ... [to] *(h)* After careful investigation the Commission has found no credible evidence either that Ruby and Officer Tippit, who was killed by Oswald, knew each other or that Oswald and Tippit knew each other. ..." [2001]

"11. On the basis of the evidence before the Commission it concludes that Oswald acted alone. Therefore, to determine the motives for the assassination of President Kennedy, one must look to the assassin himself. Clues to Oswald's motives can be found in his family history, his education or lack of it, his acts, his writings, and the recollections of those who had close contacts with him throughout his life. The Commission has presented with this report all of the background information bearing on motivation which it could discover. Thus, others may study Lee Oswald's life and arrive at their own conclusions as to his possible motives.

"The Commission could not make any definitive determination of Oswald's motives. It has endeavored to isolate factors which contributed to his character and which might have influenced his decision to assassinate President Kennedy. These factors were:

"*(a)* His deep-rooted resentment of all authority which was expressed in a hostility toward every society in which he lived;

"*(b)* His inability to enter into meaningful relationships with people, and a continuous pattern of rejecting his environment in favor of new surroundings;

"*(c)* His urge to try to find a place in history and despair at times over failures in his various undertakings;

"*(d)* His capacity for violence as evidenced by his attempt to kill General Walker;

"*(e)* His avowed commitment to Marxism and communism, as he understood the terms and developed his own interpretation of them; this was expressed by his antagonism toward the United States, by his defection to the Soviet Union, by his failure to be reconciled with life in the United States even after his disenchantment with the Soviet Union, and by his efforts, though frustrated, to go to Cuba.

"Each of these contributed to his capacity to risk all in cruel and irresponsible actions." [2002]

This book, as you know if you read rather than skipping through, fully accepts the first two conclusions, but, differing on the matter of motive, confidently explains why he did it.

Because the purpose of this chapter is to give you a brief roundup of the many efforts to investigate and explain the assassination in Dallas, this author will say no more, but let the matter end with the commission's words on motive. More fully than they summarized above, their fifty-page chapter on that subject ended with this conclusion:

"Many factors were undoubtedly involved in Oswald's motivation for the assassination, and the Commission does not believe that it can ascribe to him any one motive or group of motives. It is apparent, however, that Oswald was moved by an overriding hostility to his environment. He does not appear to have been able to establish meaningful relationships with other people. He was perpetually discontented with the world around him. Long before the assassination he expressed his hatred for American society and acted in protest against it. Oswald's search for what he conceived to be the perfect society was doomed from the start. He sought for himself a place in history—a role as the 'great man' who would be recognized as having been in advance of his times. His commitment to Marxism and communism appears to have been another important factor in his motivation. He also had demonstrated a capacity to act decisively and without regard to the consequences when such action would further his aims of the moment. Out of these and the many other factors which may have molded the character of Lee Harvey Oswald there emerged a man capable of assassinating President Kennedy." [2003]

In simple terms, the Commission concluded about Oswald:

- He did it.
  - There was no conspiracy.
    - We don't know why he did it. [F]

Marina and Lee biographer Priscilla Johnson McMillan nicely voiced this author's only disappointment in one word: "The Commission was able to establish what happened in Dallas. But it was unable to give a clear answer to the most intriguing question of all, the question that puzzles many people even today. *Why?*" [2004]

Earl Warren died in Washington, D.C., on July 9, 1974.[2005]

••• ••• •••

[F] They correctly thought they knew why Jack Ruby had killed Lee Oswald: to spare the Kennedy family, especially widow Jacqueline, the grief of having to participate in a Dallas murder trial.

CRITICS

THE *WARREN REPORT* WAS NOT THE LAST WORD. Gerald Ford's biographer James Cannon wrote: "On the day the report was made public, James Reston [G] offered a prescient observation in *The New York Times*: 'The Warren Commission . . . has tried, as a servant of history, to discover truth. But the assassination of President Kennedy was so symbolic of human irony and tragedy, and so involved in the complicated and elemental conflicts of the age, that many vital questions remain, and the philosophers, novelists and dramatists will have to take it from here. The commission has not concluded the Kennedy mystery so much as it has opened up a whole new chapter in the Kennedy legend.'" [2006]

Warren Report dissenters wrote many hundreds of books. The first was in print before the *Warren Report*! Thomas G. Buchanan [2007] had been a journalist in Washington, D.C. In 1948, when it became known he was a member of the American Communist Party, he was the first American journalist to be fired solely for his association with that organization. [2008] As he continued to be blacklisted in the U.S., he moved to France in 1961. [2009] European interest in the shooting of Kennedy was intense in early 1964, when, as a freelancer, he wrote six articles analyzing the assassination. They were published by Paris newspaper *L'Express*.

Invited to share his theories with the Warren Commission, he was given an interview with Assistant Counsel Howard P. Willens, who asked Buchanan to write down his thoughts. He filed a document with the Commission in March 1964. His book *Who Killed Kennedy?* was an elaboration of his original articles. It was published in May 1964, [2010] six months after the November assassination and four full months before the September *Warren Report*.

Buchanan explored similarities to the murders of Negro leaders and little black girls, and also looked at length at Communism to discard it as a motive. He then presented and dismissed the idea that Oswald and Jack Ruby were both insane. Remarkably, he included a full page — to my knowledge the very first — on the possibility that Oswald was in fact gunning for Connally. He thought that unlikely, but deserves great credit for being the first to write of the possibility. His thoughts are on page 554 in Chapter 21 – OTHERS ON THIS TRAIL.

Buchanan was also the first to book-publish a JFK conspiracy theory, and he invented a dandy. With no models to build upon, he involved Oswald (named "Accomplice Three", who did not fire any shots), two unnamed gunmen "Assassin One" and "Assassin Two" who did, unnamed "Accomplice Four" and "Five" and "Six", Jack Ruby, and Officer J.D. Tippit whose real job was to kill Oswald — but that backfired when Oswald realized what was happening and fired first. The money to fund this huge undertaking came from oil barons (to prevent Kennedy from closing their tax loopholes) and from far-right conservatives (to end his arms reduction negotiations with Soviet premier Nikita Khrushchev). In Texas, both in the 1960s and still today, "far-right" and "oil barons" are not necessarily different groups.

Before publishing its *Report*, the Commission directed the FBI to investigate all of Buchanan's claims. In a 10-page report on June 3, 1964, the FBI showed that all 32 claims by Buchanan were unfounded, incorrect or immaterial. [2011] Gerald Posner put it without shading: "The FBI, which studied Buchanan's work, concluded he was responsible for 'false statements, innuendoes, incorrect journalism, misinformation, and ... false journalism,' and that his book stated as facts items 'which the Commission's investigation has disproved completely.'" [2012]

[G] This is James the father. James the son, a trailblazer to motive, will be featured in chapter 21.

While rejecting Buchanan's conspiracy creations, I admire his thoughtful insights into several matters, and in addition to Chapter 21 – Others On This Trail, have quoted him in Chapters 15 – Regarding Kennedy and 19 – The Shot Not Taken.

As a child, I learned from *Ripley's Believe It Or Not!* that if the Chinese came marching past, six-abreast, the parade would never end — Chinese were being born faster than that flow. Trying to read all JFK pro-conspiracy and anti-Commission books would be as useless as marching the citizens of China. New books seem to have appeared as rapidly as one can read.

However, I have obeyed an obligation to at least consider conspiracy books. The worst situation would be to mislead you — and waste years writing this — then learn that one of the books contains a key point disproving my central belief that Oswald did it, alone, in an attempt to wreak vengeance on Connally. So, I have read hundreds of anti-Commission books, and found precisely none that credibly point out any error in the book you hold and are reading.

For better or worse, several have influenced thoughts and beliefs of many observers, for many years or decades. I do not necessarily recommend you read any, but for a well-informed understanding of the aftermath, you may want to at least know of these:

"Harold Weisberg [was a] former journalist, investigator for the Senate Committee on Civil Liberties and analyst for the Office of Strategic Services in World War II. Incensed by the government's investigation into the assassination, he" [2013] "completed ... my first book ... in mid-February 1965." [2014] Weisberg self-published *Whitewash: The Report on the Warren Report* after the book "was offered to 63 United States book publishers ... 21 had so little interest ... they declined even to read the book." [2015] Paperback power Dell reprinted it in 1966 with cover price 95¢ and the banner "The book they tried to suppress!"

Weisberg was the first to point out discrepancies between autopsy notes, diagrams and conclusions. "[H]e argued that careful analysis of the evidence presented in the Warren Commission's report undermined the single-bullet theory and, with it, the possibility that Lee Harvey Oswald had acted alone." [2016] He has a place in my esteem for asking a good question: Why didn't Oswald take an easy shot as the motorcade came toward him on Houston Street? His words and seriously wrong answer are in Chapter 19 – The Shot Not Taken.

He wrote seven books on the subject, "each devoted to evidence in the commission report and to government documents that he uncovered using the Freedom of Information Act. ... Unlike many other critics of the investigation, Mr. Weisberg cannot accurately be called conspiracy theorist, because he did not speculate about who might have been involved in the assassination." [2017] Robert Blakey, House Special Committee on Assassinations chief counsel "who ... coauthored a Mob-did-it book *The Plot to Kill the President*" [2018] "said his 'rhetoric was so obscure, his arguments so dependent on accusation rather than logic, the effect of [his] work was to make complex issues confusing.'" [2019] Critic-of-the-critics Harrison Edward Livingstone judged, "Weisberg was never able to make clear what he believed about a conspiracy in the murder of JFK, and seems more to function as a 'watcher' of others in the case. His interference with others and protection of his turf are legendary." [2020]

Harold Weisberg's *Case Open* attempt to rebut Posner's *Case Closed* is considered in Chapter 9 – Did He Do It? As recently as 1995, Weisberg lobbed a grenade at me and others: "Defense of the Warren Report is characterized by ignorance and stupidity. The only other means of defending it is by lies." [2021] Oh well. He died at age 88 in 2002.

The first critical book to sell well was Edward Jay Epstein's *Inquest: The Warren Commission and the Establishment of Truth* published in May 1966, quoted earlier in this chapter. It had begun "as a master's thesis in government at Cornell University [to answer] a problem posed by Professor Andrew Hacker: How does a government organization function in an extraordinary situation in which there are no rules or precedents to guide it?"[2022] Epstein later rephrased the question: "[C]an the fact-finding process be insulated from considerations of anticipated consequences in a matter of political import?"[2023] He added: "The primary subject of this book is the Warren Commission, not the assassination itself."[2024] "Temperate in tone, it was a careful study of the inner workings of the Commission. Relying on fresh documents, as well as interviews with five of the commissioners and twelve members of the legal staff, Epstein charged the Commission had sought the 'political truth' rather than the factual truth about the case."[2025]

"The Chief" was displeased but stoic. When an assistant counsel on the commission sent in a complaint about Epstein's "inaccuracies and distortions", Earl Warren replied: "We can expect much writing of this kind from charlatans and lazy writers who will not take the time to analyze all the papers to determine what the facts actually are."[2026]

In 1992, Epstein looked back at his 1966 *Inquest*: "I concluded in my thesis that the Warren Commission, instead of conducting the exhaustive, no-stone-left-unturned investigation that had been represented to the public, had presided over a hasty, limited investigation that had not always been able to insulate itself from political and national security considerations. The result was that it had failed to answer the primary question of whether Oswald had acted alone or in concert with others ... *Inquest* opened up the possibility that the members of the Warren Commission, though honest, had not dug deeply enough to find the evidence of a conspiracy. As this view became the conventional wisdom, the floodgates opened to conspiracy theories."[2027] "Floodgates" is wonderfully appropriate, casting Epstein as Mickey Mouse, The Sorcerer's Apprentice in Disney's movie *Fantasia*, lazily teaching a broom to carry water, but when unable to stop it, finding he had caused a flood.

Epstein's careful, scholarly report of facts about the creation of the Commission and its workings appeals to this author, and I have quoted extensively at the beginning of this chapter. *Inquest* is excellent help for understanding the Commission, but not the assassination. Critic-of-critics Livingstone wrote: "This volume created something of a sensation in its analysis of how the Warren Commission operated. ... The book—because it was critical of the Warren Commission—became a rallying point for many of those who thought there were major flaws in the conclusions of the Commission. ... But nobody knew what Epstein thought about what really happened. In fact, he represented what was to become the fallback position of those who said, 'Well, if the Warren Report's findings of a single assassin can't be perfectly defended, we have to prepare an alternative explanation for the murder of President Kennedy.'"[2028] Harold Weisberg, looking back in 1995, called "*Inquest* a work of pseudo-scholarship based on a stupid and baseless conjecture ..."[2029] That seems overly harsh — *Inquest* is about the process of investigation, not about understanding the process's progeny.

Epstein, as did most critics, went on to write additional books. Hearing that the New Orleans District Attorney claimed to have evidence of a conspiracy to assassinate Kennedy, Epstein, the expert on the Warren Commission's investigatory methods, thought:

"a comparison of the two investigations might help to clarify some of the problems involved in forensic fact-finding, and, in April 1967, I went to New Orleans to pursue this line of inquiry.

After interviewing District Attorney [Jim] Garrison and most of the members of his staff, and examining some of the elements in his case, I realized that the means by which Garrison was attempting to establish his version of the event as the truth were drastically different from those employed by the Warren Commission. Paradoxically, the Commission, essentially an *ad hoc* body outside the judicial system, had attempted to build its case through a quasi-legal process—involving testimony, corroboration, and evaluation more or less in accordance with the customary rules of evidence—whereas Garrison, a duly constituted legal authority, was attempting to establish his case by appealing directly to public opinion." [2030]

Epstein's articles in the *New Yorker* became his second book, *Counterplot*, analyzing "The manner in which Garrison used the powers of his office and the mass media to affect public opinion ..." [2031] In the manner of an anatomist, he dissected, described and labeled Garrison as being a demagogue. Years later, a generation after the shooting in Dallas, Oliver Stone exploited ignorance to portray Garrison as a noble crusader in his truly wretched movie *JFK*, in which the part of Chief Justice Earl Warren was acted by — hold on — Jim Garrison! [2032]

Epstein's third book on the assassination, *Legend: The Secret World of Lee Harvey Oswald*, published in 1978, is an amalgam of facts about Oswald's life and half supposition about his real and possible contacts with spy agencies in the US, Russia and Cuba. In 1992, Epstein combined the three books into a Costco-sized volume of 702 pages, *The Assassination Chronicles: Inquest, Counterplot and Legend*. Reprinting each book, he added an Epilogue conveying later events. I particularly recommend this book if you believe there was any tiny smidgen of truth in the movie *JFK*. Epstein's "Epilogue V: *JFK*: The Second Coming of Jim Garrison (1992)" is one of two remedial readings that should be administered to anyone in any way favorably influenced by that vile film. (The other fine review is Patricia Lambert's more extensive *False Witness: The Real Story of Jim Garrison's Investigation and Oliver Stone's Film JFK*.) Also highly worthwhile in *Chronicles* is Epstein's "Afterword", which asks and answers seven questions, from "1. Where did the bullets come from that hit President Kennedy and Governor Connally?" through "7. Was Oswald part of a conspiracy?"

In summary, Epstein is an excellent observer-critic of the assassination investigations — and he is able to learn and politely retreat from errors of fact or thought in his early works. He eventually gets it all pretty much correct, and I admire that.

Mark Lane's *Rush to Judgment* was the first Commission-critical best seller. He wrote in an augmented 1992 edition: "This book, first published in ... 1966, became the number-one best-selling book that year in hardcover and the subsequent year in a paperback edition." [2033] "Lane, a former New York State legislator associated with some prominent left-wing causes, was an attorney who had represented Marguerite Oswald. [H] He unsuccessfully argued with the Commission that he be allowed to represent the deceased [Lee] Oswald at the hearings and thus be permitted to cross-examine the witnesses who appeared." [2034]

Denied that, he criticized the Commission with *Rush to Judgment*, which Posner terms: "an admitted brief for the defense by a skilled advocate. Using only the evidence that buttressed his arguments, he persuasively argued that the Commission's work was seriously flawed." [2035] Here is one simple example: Lane admitted that the bullets were fired by the carbine purchased under Oswald's alias "A. Hidell" and mailed to Oswald's P.O. Box 2915 in Dallas, and that people in Dealey Plaza had seen a man holding a rifle at the sixth-floor window, and that the carbine found on the sixth floor was Oswald's — but Lane then argued

---

[H] Much of Lane's legal work was noble: *pro bono* for indigents.

there was no real evidence Oswald was the shooter, because nobody had seen his face and been able to positively identify him. Lane wasn't seeking for truth, he was plumping for defense; as famously disclaimed in *Seinfeld*, "Not that there's anything wrong with that!"

Commissioner Gerald Ford, the only one of the seven to author a book, *Portrait of the Assassin*, which focused on the work and hearings, wrote: "Even Mark Lane, who harassed the work of the Commission by innuendo and inference, was given his days, not once but twice and in public hearings at his request, to talk before the Commission. His long list of questions was combined with all the others for the Commission to answer. For several hours he sat at the long table, hunched and reading from his notes, and droned out his case." [2036] "Warren Commission staff attorney Wesley Liebeler said, 'It's just incredible to listen to [Mark Lane]. He talks for five minutes, and it takes an hour to straighten out the record.'" [2037]

Biographer Bud Vestal wrote in *Jerry Ford, Up Close: An Investigative Biography*:
"Ford became an author as a result of the Warren Commission service. ... [He] said he found writing 'hard work.' The book, titled *Portrait of the Assassin*, did not sell well. People who buy books, it seemed, believed the Warren Commission report. And if Oswald had not been part of a diabolic conspiracy, the story was less interesting. When the book was published in 1965, so much was happening there were plenty of excuses to put Dallas and Oswald in the attic of the mind. It was obvious many Americans wanted to; just thinking about it hurt. Perhaps the book was premature by a generation." [2038]

In "The Great American Mystery, A Review of Mark Lane's *Rush to Judgment* in *Book Week*, August 28, 1966", Norman Mailer concluded: "*Rush to Judgment* is of course a defense attorney's brief, and it seeks to make its case as best it can, wherever it can. Those looking for comprehensive explanation of the mystery of the assassination will not find it, not here." [2039] Mailer would write his own first-rate assassination book almost a generation later.

"Walter Cronkite, in a four-part 1967 CBS documentary, concluded there were a number of examples in Lane's work of 'lifting remarks out of context to support his theories. Perhaps the most charitable explanation is that Mark Lane still considers himself a defense attorney ... [whose] duty is not to abstract truth but to his client.'" [2040]

Lane's later book *Plausible Denial* is one of a great multitude hypothecating CIA involvement in plotting and executing an assassination conspiracy. Lane "still practices law and lectures on many subjects, especially the importance of the United States Constitution (mainly the Bill of Rights and the First Amendment civil rights)." [2041]

"A rash of books appeared on the heels of Lane's success. ... Despite their differences, [they] were uniformly virulent attacks on the Warren Commission, and their advocacy often diminished their effectiveness. At their best, the critics had only exposed the Commission as incompetent, but they had not established it was wrong in its conclusions." [2042]

Some criticism from the far right is good for a laugh, if nothing else. As one example, Zad Rust began the introduction to his 1971 book about Edward Kennedy, "*Teddy Bare*":
"In the case of president Kennedy's assassination, nobody but the persons directly responsible would be able to say today who the murderers were. But there is no one in the United States or anywhere else, with a normal thinking apparatus and normal curiosity and information, who believes that the explanation of this murder offered by the Warren Commission, with its accompanying procession of strangely disappearing witnesses, is the correct one. Thinking people are, on the contrary, convinced that this Commission had no other mission than to conceal the truth, and that it was relentlessly helped in this mission by many official agencies and by *some powerful organized Force of universal scope and character*." [2043] (Italics are his.)

Rust fails badly in criticizing the Warren Commission and making a McCarthy-like charge of some vast dark "*Force*", but he at least provides lexicographical entertainment by trotting out such wonders as "comminatory", "legiferation", and "tergiversations".[2044]

Many believe in conspiracy theories; this author is not one of them. There are many Kennedy assassination conspiracy books; this is not one of them. Daniel Pipes, an editor, lecturer and specialist in the Middle East, wrote several books on the histories of conspiracies. He wisely notes that the Warren Commission's critics, by espousing conspiracy theories, cross-pollinate, feed upon and auto-fertilize themselves:

> "In the thousands of books written on the John Kennedy assassination, only a tiny proportion argue against a conspiracy. The size of [the conspiracy theory] corpus impresses some readers; 'there is so much written..., they figure some of it must be right.'[2045] The many books make it possible for conspiracy theorists to cite each others' works, thereby constructing an imposing edifice of self-referential pseudoscholarship. In the case of old topics ... they republish centuries-old books and quote them as authorities. In the case of new ones, like the John Kennedy assassination, they learnedly discuss each other's conclusions."[2046]

Critic-of-critics Harrison Livingstone pointed out a sound analysis of conspiracist interbreeding in a book cited several times in this book's Chapter 10 – PRESIDENTS, NOT PRECEDENTS: "James Clarke remarks in his book *American Assassins* that this psychological literature exhibits 'scant evidence of any primary research. Rather, the references reveal a heavy reliance on secondary sources as well as a kind of incestuous process of citing each other's work to 'document' the same questionable conclusions.'"[2047]

In 2010, retired Secret Service agent Gerald Blaine, who had done on-site advance planning for Kennedy's trip to Texas, wrote: "I would be very pleased if the results of the Warren Commission and its investigation would be accepted as the final word. However, I know that the researchers, writers, and filmmakers who continue to question those findings will never accept those as the truth. The information presented by the majority of these people is theory, not fact. They were not witnesses to the assassination; have little or no knowledge of protective procedures; did not know the dedicated agents on this assignment; and simply were not in our shoes that day in Dallas. It would be a great tragedy if history were allowed to repeat itself. We must learn from the real facts of what happened."[2048]

2012 brought *Killing Kennedy: The End of Camelot*, which quickly flew to the top of best-seller lists. I attributed that to its being a product of co-authors who had published highly successful *Killing Lincoln* the year before. The authors of both are Bill O'Reilly and Martin Dugard. I knew one as a right-wing television bombast and had never heard of the other. Expecting little, but with a self-imposed duty to look under every rock, no matter how unpromising, I purchased and read *Killing Kennedy*, and was surprised to find it well written, on point (Oswald alone shot Kennedy) and a thoroughly enjoyable easy read.

That said, I find that the book plows no new ground whatsoever, simply reassembling and rephrasing what's already been written, particularly by Manchester and McMillan. And, it goes wrong in two regards, as do most other Kennedy assassination books. First, it fails to cite a believable motive. Needing something, O'Reilly and Dugard chose envy, pronouncing that Oswald was bitter about JFK's advantages in life, and somehow, not really explained by them, that was sufficient motive to kill.[2049] Nonsense! Secondly, while vividly describing Oswald's sighting his 4-power scope on Kennedy, it fails to note the important fact that Oswald did not then fire at the approaching in-full-view Kennedy, the easy shot not taken.

I thought to quote some good writing from their book, but after repeated requests to the authors and to their publisher without courtesy of reply until far too late, "I say it's spinach!".[I]

This article about the critics has quoted some of them appraising the works of others. It will be refreshing to consider the thoughts of an upstanding ordinary man, a brick salesman in Texas, who simply used his commendable common sense. Robert Oswald, the good older brother, wrote in 1967 as rampant conspiracy theories were becoming a new fad:

> "When the first critics began expressing doubts about the Warren Commission findings, I read their words eagerly. ... My early interest in the statements, articles and books soon turned to bewilderment as the critics began making wilder and wilder charges and implying that hundreds or even thousands of people had joined in some gigantic conspiracy first to assassinate the President, then accuse an innocent man of the assassination, then murder him, and finally to cover up the conspiracy by staging a phony investigation headed by the Chief Justice of the United States and carried out by distinguished national figures of both political parties.
>
> As the tempo of the attacks increased, I was amazed that the work of several of the critics was taken seriously by anyone. These men looked for and found the minor discrepancies and apparent contradictions that do undoubtedly exist in the twenty-six volumes, and treated each of them as though it was proof of some elaborate attempt to deceive the American people." [2050]

Robert continued (and continued speaking for me): "I doubt that *Rush to Judgment* or *The Second Oswald* or *Inquest* or *Whitewash* or *Whitewash II* will be considered anything more than curiosities in the years ahead. They do appeal to those readers who find the mysterious and unknown more interesting than the factual account, however incomplete and flawed, put together by the Warren Commission." [2051]

I am pleased to give the final word on the matter to a Caltech professor who helped me learn to think hard and deep, and thus was at least partly responsible (guilty?) for the thinking that led to this book. In a 1963 letter to his wife from the Grand Hotel in Warsaw, Poland, where he was attending an international conference on gravity, Richard Feynman wrote:

> "I am not getting anything out of the meeting. I am learning nothing. Because there are no experiments this field is not an active one,[J] so few of the best men are doing work in it. The result is that there are hosts of dopes here and it is not good for my blood pressure: such inane things are said and seriously discussed that I get into arguments ... whenever anyone asks me a question or starts to tell me about his "work." The "work" is always: (1) completely un-understandable, (2) vague and indefinite, (3) something correct that is obvious and self-evident, but worked out by a long and difficult analysis, and presented as an important discovery, (4) a claim based on the stupidity of the author that some obvious and correct fact, accepted and checked for years, is, in fact, false (these are the worst: no argument will convince the idiot), (5) an attempt to do something probably impossible, but certainly of no utility, which, it is finally revealed at the end, fails, or (6) just plain wrong. There is a great deal of "activity in the field" these days, but this "activity" is mainly in showing that the previous "activity" of somebody else resulted in an error or in nothing useful or in something promising. It is like a lot of worms trying to get out of a bottle by crawling all over each other. It is not that the subject is hard; it is that the good men are occupied elsewhere. Remind me not to come to any more gravity conferences!" [2052]

●●●   ●●●   ●●●

[I] "I say it's spinach" has its own excellent Wikipedia article! Why I say that is in endnote 272.

[J] In February 2016 as this book was nearly ready for the printers, scientists confirmed Albert Einstein's 1916 prediction of gravitational waves. Dick Feynman would have loved to be alive for that!

SENATE SELECT COMMITTEE TO STUDY GOVERNMENTAL OPERATIONS WITH RESPECT TO INTELLIGENCE ACTIVITIES

BOOK V: THE INVESTIGATION OF THE ASSASSINATION OF PRESIDENT JOHN F. KENNEDY: PERFORMANCE OF THE INTELLIGENCE AGENCIES

In 1975, during the post-Watergate presidency of Gerald Ford, the U.S. Senate established a special committee to look into many reported shortcomings of U.S. intelligence agencies. Chaired by Senator Frank Church of Idaho, it became known as the Church Committee. Proceeding with unusual dispatch, it released all its findings in 1976 after minor redacting by intelligence agencies to protect national secrets. Six books of final results primarily involved foreign operations and the rights of American citizens. Although many findings and recommendations caused sensations and led to reforms and realignments of federal agencies, the inquiry into the Dallas assassination was ho-hum. [K]

A thick book #5, released in May 1976 with the approval of nine senators, but despite "nay" votes from conservative Senators John Tower and Barry Goldwater, reported what had been learned about federal agencies' performance before and after the Kennedy assassination. It is not necessary to report on the report; its own highlights excerpted below tell the story:

"I. SUMMARY AND FINDINGS

The Select Committee's investigation of alleged assassination attempts against foreign leaders raised questions of possible connections between these plots and the assassination of President John Fitzgerald Kennedy. Questions were later raised about whether the agencies adequately investigated these possible connections and whether information about these plots was provided the President's Commission on the Assassination of President Kennedy (the Warren Commission). As a result, pursuant to its general mandate to review the performance of the intelligence agencies, the Select Committee reviewed their specific performance with respect to their investigation of the assassination of the President. [L]

A. The Scope of the Committee's Investigation

The Committee did not attempt to duplicate the work of the Warren Commission. It did not review the findings and conclusions of the Warren Commission. It did not re-examine the physical evidence which the Warren Commission had. It did not review one of the principal questions facing the Commission: whether Lee Harvey Oswald was in fact the assassin of President Kennedy.

Instead, building upon the Select Committee's earlier work, and utilizing its access to the agencies and its expertise in their functions, the Committee examined the performance of the intelligence agencies in conducting their investigation of the assassination and their relationships to the Warren Commission.

...

B. Summary

In the days following the assassination of President Kennedy, nothing was more important to this country than to determine the facts of his death; no one single event has shaken the country more. Yet the evidence the Committee has developed suggests that, for different reasons, both the CIA and the FBI failed in, or avoided carrying out, certain of their responsibilities in this matter.

[K] ho-hum *adj. Informal.* Boring and dull; routine. — *American Heritage College Dictionary*
[L] Both they and I capitalize standalone word "President" when it refers to President Kennedy.

The Committee emphasizes that this Report's discussion of investigative deficiencies and the failure of American intelligence agencies to inform the Warren Commission of certain information does not lead to the conclusion that there was a conspiracy to assassinate President Kennedy.

Instead, this Report details the evidence the Committee developed concerning the investigation those agencies conducted into the President's assassination, their relationship with each other and with the Warren Commission, and the effect their own operations may have had on the course of the investigation. ...

...

C. Findings

The Committee emphasizes that it has not uncovered any evidence sufficient to justify a conclusion that there was a conspiracy to assassinate President Kennedy.

The Committee has, however, developed evidence which impeaches the process by which the intelligence agencies arrived at their own conclusions about the assassination, and by which they provided information to the Warren Commission. This evidence indicates that the investigation of the assassination was deficient and that facts which might have substantially affected the course of the investigation were not provided the Warren Commission or those individuals within the FBI and the CIA, as well as other agencies of Government, who were charged with investigating the assassination.

The Committee has found that the FBI, the agency with primary responsibility in the matter, was ordered by Director Hoover and pressured by higher government officials, to conclude its investigation quickly. The FBI conducted its investigation in an atmosphere of concern among senior Bureau officials that it would be criticized and its reputation tarnished. [M] Rather than addressing its investigation to all significant circumstances, including all possibilities of conspiracy, the FBI investigation focused narrowly on Lee Harvey Oswald.
... " 2053

In the final report, an Appendix B was titled "The FBI and the Destruction of the Oswald Note". While the committee was working in 1975, a Dallas newsman approached the FBI's top level to report that an unidentified source told him that Oswald had visited the Dallas office of the Bureau shortly before the shooting, asked to see Agent Hosty who was out, and left an angry note for him. That note was destroyed immediately after Oswald's death. An internal investigation by the FBI confirmed this "new news", but determined it had no particular evidentiary bearing on the Warren Commission's study of the assassination. Nonetheless, the years-later discovery of this secrecy within the Dallas office, and the note destroyed by Special Agent James Hosty two hours after Oswald's death on order of Special Agent-in-Charge for Dallas J. Gordon Shanklin, was a great embarrassment to the Bureau, and reinforced the Committee's basic findings.[2054]

In summary, the Church Committee found deficiencies in the work of the agencies that supplied facts and analyses to the Warren Commission, especially the FBI, but 12 years after the fact, found nothing to change the Commission's findings and the *Warren Report*.

There really wasn't any result of significance to the subject of this book, but for completeness, this topic has been included for any reader who hears of a <u>Senate</u> investigation, which is hereby laid to rest so we may proceed to the more important, lengthy — and sad — <u>House</u> investigation.

••• ••• •••

[M] Just wait until you read in chapter 20 what it appears Director J. Edgar Hoover did in this regard!

SELECT COMMITTEE ON ASSASSINATIONS
U. S. HOUSE OF REPRESENTATIVES

The many books critical of the Warren Commission created an opportunity for Congress to pretend to be working for the country's good by re-investigating the Kennedy assassination. One such book was 1977's *Betrayal* by Robert D. Morrow. Its cover says, "The man who bought the rifle [N] that killed JFK tells the story." All these are featured in the book:[2055]

- Mario Garcia Kohly, "the official de facto president-in-exile of the Cuban government";[2056]
- Anti-Castro Cuban exiles;[2057]
- A former Deputy Director of the Central Intelligence Agency;[2058]
- Other "senior people" in the CIA;[2059]
- David Ferrie, an Eastern Airlines pilot working as a CIA contract employee;[2060]
- Clay Shaw, President, New Orleans International Trade Mart and consultant to the CIA;[2061]
- Guy Banister, formerly an FBI office chief, then deputy superintendent of police in New Orleans, now a private detective and CIA operative;[2062]
- William Gemelo, an especially useful CIA contract employee because he is a Lee Harvey Oswald look-alike ("they could be twins");[2063]
- New York Congressman Adam Clayton Powell;[2064]
- Two U. S. Senators;[2065]
- Jack Ruby, in charge of the assassination operation, who hired Oswald into it;[2066]
- Officer J. D. Tippit, hired by Jack Ruby so "Lee will get shot trying to escape";[2067]
- A woman and two children posing as Marina Oswald and family;[2068]
- Four (!) Mannlicher-Carcano carbines in addition (!) to Oswald's;[2069]
- A "pristine bullet" fired from Oswald's carbine into cotton wadding;[2070]
- And, of course, Lee Harvey Oswald, a paid informer for the FBI. Brought into the conspiracy by Jack Ruby, he attempted to escape the plot but wound up becoming its patsy.[2071]

The book features one-night-stand sex at elegant hotels in Miami Beach and Madrid,[2072] torture and disembowelment,[2073] Oswald in Minsk spying on the Russians for the CIA,[2074] and even a change of the intended assassination location from Love Field to Dealey Plaza after Oswald is hired by the Texas School Book Depository.[2075] The assassination is carried out by five men in three locations firing five shots from three Mannlicher-Carcanos.[2076] One of them, the LHO look-alike, fires from the Texas School Book Depository's 6th floor [2077] while Lee Oswald, the patsy, sits on a toilet on the 2nd floor! [2078] Finally, Jack Ruby, the ubiquitous manager of the assassination operation, stops by Parkland Hospital to plant the "pristine bullet" that had been fired from Oswald's rifle,[2079] then kills Oswald so that he can't "squeal like a stuck pig to save his own skin." [2080] How's that for a nifty something-for-everyone plot?

JFK assassination conspiracy books are disturbing for many reasons. Most include just enough authentic people and events to gain a false ring of credibility, thereby diverting readers from recognizing their vacuousness. Like the storied "half-and-half" rabbit stew, made from half a rabbit and half a horse, the worst attempt to conceal their essence of nonsense pretense by seasoning with just enough good and recognizable flavoring to conceal their putrid reality.

Betrayal, manifesting all these problems and more, plunged over a moral brink into despicability when Morrow gratuitously defamed the memory of Officer Tippit by making him

---

[N] He never got the rifle. Congress thwarted him; a new law consigned it to the National Archives.

an attention-seeking supporter of Ruby's plotting. Instead of what really happened in Oak Cliff, Morrow would have us believe that a LHO look-alike shot the corrupt policeman who was a pawn, but a knowing participant, in a very big conspiracy.[2081] This is vile garbage!

In my opinion, more troubling than any of the inventions listed above is this astounding letter, a sort of imprimatur, printed at the front of the book: [2082]

THOMAS N. DOWNING
1ST DISTRICT, VIRGINIA

Congress of the United States
House of Representatives
Washington, D.C. 20515

November 4, 1976

For some time I have been concerned, as have
many Americans, about the unanswered questions regarding the assassination of President John F. Kennedy.
Along with other individuals and groups I have pressed
for the reopening of the investigation.

In the spring of 1976, Robert Morrow brought me
an advance copy of his book, "Betrayal," a fascinating
account of events leading up to that assassination,
which concludes with a remarkably plausible reconstruction of what could have happened on that dreadful day in
Dallas.

It is no exaggeration to say that the information in
this book, coupled with additional confidential material
supplied to me by Mr. Morrow, helped make the creation of
the House Select Committee on Assassinations possible.

Where the committee's investigations will lead, of
course, remains to be seen. But I am confident that investigation of the information supplied by Mr. Morrow in
"Betrayal" and the additional sources to which it will lead
the committee investigators will help to put to rest once
and for all many of the questions about the Warren Commission's investigation that have disturbed the nation for
many years.

_____
(signed by)
Thomas N. Downing, Chairman
Select Committee on Assassinations

The letter was an adumbration of absurdities to come from Downing and the House.

By the mid-1970s, growing public concern stemmed from the hundreds of books and articles suggesting conspiracies in the assassinations of both President Kennedy and Reverend Martin Luther King, Jr. Many of those nonsensical writings blamed agencies of the federal government for complicity in the killings. Those charges resonated with a public that had just been through the numbing experience of Nixon's Watergate break-in and cover-up, which gave reason to doubt the honesty of all "the Feds". Responding in 1976, Congress created the twelve-representatives House Select Committee on Assassinations (HSCA) to investigate the murders of JFK and MLK. Whom do you suppose was the powerful chairman? None other than Representative Downing, signatory to the outrageous pandering on the previous page.

The committee was special, not standing, so its authorization expired when its Congress ended. Downing retired from Congress, to be replaced as chairman by Henry Gonzalez. The House had a new Speaker in 1977, the sensible Tip O'Neill who had been hostile to the committee from its creation. Then a power struggle began between new chair Gonzalez and existing counsel Richard Sprague, a hard-liner who had ordered the staff to communicate only with him, not to any Congressmen or reporters. Gonzalez fired Sprague, but when all eleven other members of the Committee voted to keep Sprague, Gonzalez resigned.

Congressman Louis Stokes was appointed to be the third chairman in seven months, and then it was honorable for Sprague to resign. In April 1977, under the guidance of O'Neill and Stokes, the committee got a new chief counsel from Cornell University, professor of law G. Robert Blakey. Then everything became very quiet. There were no press conferences or news releases. Most of Congress and America ignored or forgot the committee.

Bob Callahan compiled a highly useful book, *Who Shot JFK?: A Guide to the Major Conspiracy Theories*, summarizing and pin-pricking dozens of them. The book is an excellent guide to the trash heap of stupid-ideas. I have entered Callahan's Connally-was-target paragraph into Chapter 21 – OTHERS ON THIS TRAIL. His sound analysis of the HSCA:

"Critics credit the Congressional Black Caucus with supplying the political muscle that finally got the new investigation off the ground. Regular closed-door meetings began in the summer of 1977. By September, 1978, the committee was prepared for public hearings on the JFK murder. On July 29, 1979, the House Select Committee on Assassinations published its final report. The primary conclusions were as follows:

The Warren Commission had been almost entirely correct in its original reconstruction of the actual assassination. The House Committee had employed a battery of scientists to examine each controversial aspect of the Warren Report, and the results of these new tests persuaded the majority of committee members that the Commission had been correct on almost each point. Lee Harvey Oswald had fired three shots at President Kennedy, and one of those bullets had passed through the President to wound Governor Connally. Arlen Specter had been correct. The 'magic bullet' theory was substantiated.

Where the Warren Commission had gone wrong—through no fault of its own, the Committee stated—was on the matter of a fourth bullet. Based on acoustical evidence which the Committee had uncovered—a microphone on one of the police escort motorcycles had been left open, producing a dictabelt recording of the actual shooting—the House Committee concluded that a second assassin had fired a fourth shot from the back of the grassy knoll. The President of the United States had in fact been killed by a conspiracy involving at least two shooters, the Select Committee announced.

The identity of this second gunman remained a mystery, however. In a carefully worded statement, the committee said that the available evidence did not 'preclude the possibility' that individual members of certain anti-Castro groups, or individual members of the Mob may have been involved. ...

What is truly fascinating is how precious little attention was paid to this Report in the public press. The *New York Times* was derisive and sly in its response. 'To the lay public,' the *Times* editorialized on January 7, 1979, 'the word [conspiracy] is [usually] freighted with dark connotations of malevolence perpetrated by enemies, foreign and political. But [in this instance] 'two maniacs instead of one' might be more like it.'" [2083] ([Brackets] by Callahan.)

The HSCA, after deciding that it heard four shots on a recording of police radio traffic, concluded there must have been a conspiracy. Two of the "shots" were too close together to have been fired by one rifle. Coupled with their acceptance of the Warren conclusion that exactly three shots were fired from the TSBD, the fourth must have come from a second assassin — a co-conspirator! — who was probably shooting from the famous "grassy knoll".

That theory was soundly (pun intended) refuted by the man with the best credentials to know: James C. Bowles, Communications Supervisor, who, according to oral history compiler Larry Sneed "is recognized as the authority on the inner workings of the radio communications of the Dallas Police Department and corresponding events at the time of the assassination." [2084] A reliable police official, Bowles later moved to the sheriff's office, then became Sheriff of Dallas County. According to his oral history, the HSCA was listening to a plastic belt on which sound was recorded by incising a groove, in the same technique as on Thomas Edison's original phonograph cylinders, and they mistook that media's inevitable snaps and pops as being gunshots! Bowles, the authority, minced no words in his denunciation:

"In the end, when the House Select Committee made its famous announcement ... 'Our clock has run out. Our committee is adjourned right on time,' they didn't determine anything: they concluded. Determination implies a bit stronger qualification of evidence. I don't use words casually if I can avoid it. They didn't determine anything other than what they decided to determine. They concluded from the processes they chose to use certain conclusions which were wholly inaccurate and unsupportable. ...

Take for example this mockery of evidence that says a fourth shot was fired from behind the fence on the grassy knoll. ... There was no other shot fired from here, or there, or somewhere else. Absolutely not! So what they've done is to let conjured evidence adulterate the purity of an ongoing investigation." [2085]

Edward Jay Epstein, who by 1992 had earned his doctorate from Harvard, agreed:

"Unfortunately, after the committee rushed to this conclusion, Dallas motorcycle policeman H. B. McClain, whose radio had been assumed to have been the source for the putative shots, stated that his radio could not possibly have made that recording. Since he had raced along with the president's limousine to the hospital, sirens shrieking full blast, his microphone could not have accounted for the eight-minute recording, which came from one spot. He was also certain his radio had been tuned to the channel for the procession, since he was listening to it attentively, whereas the tape had been made on another channel. The committee now realized, after changing its conclusions, that the very provenance of the tape was in question: No one was sure what was recorded. It could have come from any other locale in Dallas in which a police radio was opened, or have been made at a different time.

After issuing its report, the committee belatedly recommended that the problematic tape be reexamined by a panel of experts selected by the National Academy of Sciences. This panel, chaired by Professor Norman S. Ramsey of Harvard, restudied the tape and was able to prove unambiguously that, wherever the tape came from, it was made one minute after the assassination and therefore had no relevance whatsoever to the sequence of shots (or anything else). The committee's experts, it turned out, had simply analyzed the wrong tape, and the

256

committee's revised 'conspiracy' conclusion, incredibly enough, proceeded from this error. But by the time the error was revealed, in October 1982, the committee had been long dissolved, and its erroneous conspiracy conclusion had become part of popular mythology—the beginning of a trend." [2086]

Carl Oglesby enumerated the committee's negligible [O] results in *Who Killed JFK?*:

"[I]nstead of fostering a new national dedication to solving the case, the committee disbanded at the end of the 95th Congressional session and the matter was dropped. Why?

First, even though the committee's final report was undoubtedly shocking to some, Congress failed to build a political consensus for carrying the investigation further. Second, the Reagan era was about to begin and his attorney general, Ed Meese, was disinclined to renew an investigation of a 20-year-old murder of the Democratic Party's fallen hero.

Third, in 1982, the National Academy of Sciences questioned the acoustics evidence and decided that what had been interpreted as gun shots might not have been shots at all—thus casting doubt upon the key piece of evidence leading to the committee's new conclusions. The Justice Department, under Meese, was quick to reassert that the Warren Commission findings were correct—a lone assassin had killed President Kennedy." [2087]

Fifteen years earlier, the most troubling deficiency of the Warren Commission's work had been the matter of motive. As reported earlier in this chapter, they failed to describe with any semblance of conviction any motive that might have inspired Oswald to kill Kennedy.

Looking beyond their stupid last-minute conspiracy nonsense, I hoped the HSCA might at least do better than the Warren Commission in naming a motive. In the HSCA's final report on the JFK assassination (remember: they gave separate but equal — that seems to be a familiar phrase! — consideratiion to the assassination of MLK), the slightly more than three-page JFK section on "The motive" concludes thus:

"The depth and direction of Oswald's ideological commitment is, therefore, clear. Politics was the dominant force in his life right down to the last days ... Although no one specific ideological goal that Oswald might have hoped to achieve by the assassination of President Kennedy can be shown with confidence, it appeared to the committee that his dominant motivation, consistent with his known activities and beliefs, must have been a desire to take political action. It seems reasonable to conclude that the best single explanation for the assassination was his conception of political action, rooted in his twisted ideological view of himself and the world around him." [2088]

I leave it to you to decide if that's even an iota better than the Warren Commission's conclusion that he may have been angry at government, in general, so took out his frustrations and hate by shooting at the head of government of the United States.

And, knowing that Oswald was highly interested in politics, if you suspect the HSCA might be right in their "reasonable to conclude ... political action", look carefully at Chapter 17 – Political Proclivity – to see that they have it precisely, diametrically wrong.

Like wars in Afghanistan, Iraq and Syria, some affairs just never seem to end. Careful assassination researcher Vincent Bugliosi, in his chapter "The Investigations", reported:

"There was actually one further reinvestigation of the assassination, one that received virtually no attention in the media since it was conducted, without fanfare, behind the scenes. When the HSCA submitted its final report to the clerk of the House of Representatives on March 29, 1979, it made several recommendations, one of which was that the Department of Justice 'review the committee's findings' on the assassination of President Kennedy and 'report its

---

[O] Which reminds me to ask: Did you find the negligee in chapter 1?

analysis to the Judiciary Committee.' By the end of 1983, the department said it had completed 'virtually all' of its investigation, but did not issue its formal report at the time because it wanted to review 'all public comment responsive' to the National Academy of Science's review of the acoustical evidence. On March 28, 1988, the Justice Department submitted its formal report to Senator Peter W. Rodino Jr., chairman of the Committee on the Judiciary. The department's report was a rebuke to the HSCA's conclusion of conspiracy. The department said that its 'attorney and investigative personnel reviewed the entire Select Committee report as well as all relevant Federal Bureau of Investigation reports.' Before it reached its conclusion, the department said it had also asked the FBI 'to further investigate any aspect of the assassination which Departmental attorneys felt had even an arguable potential of leading to additional productive information.' The Justice Department concluded that 'no persuasive evidence can be identified to support the theory of a conspiracy' in the Kennedy assassination, and that 'no further investigation appears to be warranted ... unless new information which is sufficient to support additional investigation activity becomes available.'" [2089]

Bugliosi ended his "Investigations" chapter: "The HSCA conclusion was blatantly incorrect and unprofessional, an unfortunate, serious blemish on its otherwise excellent effort." [2090] This book's author, finding no excellence in the HSCA, thinks that was undeservedly generous.

Epstein, whom we met at the top of this chapter when he was earning his master's degree by evaluating the Warren Commission, wrote of this committee's sad legacy:

"The House Select Committee on Assassination, with its alternate conclusions, left the public thoroughly confused. According to a Gallup poll, over 80 percent of Americans doubted that the truth had come out about who killed Kennedy. So like its two predecessors—the Warren Commission, which pressured its investigators to meet a political deadline, and District Attorney Garrison, who disoriented his own investigators by making a premature and unwarranted arrest to hold the attention of the media—this investigation failed because it overreached the evidence." [2091]

What does this unfortunate incident in an early example of gross congressional ineptitude — ineptitude still being perfected as this is written — offer to this book? Not much. Because the committee was fixated on the idea of conspiracy, it gave short shrift to the question of a motive for Oswald. In 2013's *The Accidental Victim*, James Reston, Jr. summarizes: "The House Assassinations Committee took a laundry-list approach to the motive, as it acknowledged: 'Finding a possible motive for Oswald's having assassinated President Kennedy was one of the most difficult issues the Warren Commission faced.' The House Committee fell back on 'politics' as the prime driver of Oswald's action: 'It seems reasonable to conclude that the best single explanation for the assassination was his conception of political action, rooted in his twisted ideological view of himself and the world around him.'" [2092]

The HSCA's nearly meaningless namby-pamby conclusion is easily contradicted by any thoughtful consideration of the ideology and political views that are the subject of this book's Chapter 17 – POLITICAL PROCLIVITY. Any "conception of political action" by far-left Oswald would most certainly be against the right, not against JFK whose views he shared and admired.

Regarding motive, the House committee of 1979 did no better than the Warren Commission of 1964; neither stated a probable and defensible motive for Lee Oswald to want to kill President Kennedy. And that, of course, is because he had no such intent, but was gunning for Governor Connally, against whom he had a clear and understandable motive.

••• ••• •••

ASSASSINATION RECORDS REVIEW BOARD

The President John F. Kennedy Assassination Records Collection Act of 1992 [2093] directed the National Archives and Records Administration to establish the President John F. Kennedy Assassination Records Collection, to collect copies of all U.S. government records relating to the assassination. Assassination records also included those created or made available for use by, obtained by, or that otherwise came into the possession of any state or local law enforcement office that provided support or assistance or performed work in connection with a federal inquiry into the assassination.

The Act established an independent agency, the Assassination Records Review Board (ARRB) to consider and render decisions when a U.S. government office sought to postpone the disclosure of assassination records. The ARRB was not enacted to determine why or by whom the murder was committed but to collect and preserve the evidence for public scrutiny. The Board met for four years, from 1994 to 1998. When the Board was created, 98 percent of all Warren Commission documents had been released to the public. By the time the Board disbanded, all Commission documents, except income tax returns, had been released to the public. By law, all existing assassination-related documents will be made public by 2017.

The Warren Commission assistant counsel who became a Senator from Pennsylvania, Arlen Specter, wrote this evaluation while the board worked:

"We created the Assassination Review Board in 1992, to expedite disclosure of materials relevant to Kennedy's murder. I co-sponsored the legislation. The review board has transferred some ten thousand documents to the National Archives and Records Administration. The board has worked to disclose as much material as possible that may have been withheld by the FBI, CIA, or Secret Service, or any other federal agency. As I noted in a June 1997 speech on the Senate floor, 'The review board serves a vital function of removing some of the uncertainty and speculation about the contents of government files relating to President Kennedy's assassination.'" [2094]

When the Board made its final report in 1998, the Associated Press reported:

"An agency created six years ago to ferret out every available fact about the assassination of President John Kennedy says it has uncovered more than 60,000 government documents shedding some light on that tragedy but had to engage in bureaucratic battles to obtain some. ... The Assassination Records Review Board will give its report to President Clinton tomorrow [September 30, 1998] before going out of business. The report says the government 'needlessly and wastefully classified and then withheld from public access countless important records that did not require such treatment.' ... [I]ts 208-page report draws no conclusions to affirm or contradict the Warren Commission's 1964 finding that a 'perpetually discontented' Lee Harvey Oswald, acting alone, was the killer." [2095]

Despite the ARRB, a professional archive researcher hired by this author was unable to move the Archives or any other government agencies to find either the original of Oswald's letter to Connally, or Oswald's Undesirable Discharge Certificate. Only poor copies can be found.

> Key point of this chapter:
> **The Warren Commission's conclusions stand up to all criticisms.**
> **Re-investigations never found a motive for killing Kennedy.**

DID HE DO IT? WAS IT A CONSPIRACY?

YES! NO! Clearly explained and definitely proven — in books by others

> "Now the only thing I'm *sure* of is that *I* had nothing to do with the assassination. I'm not sure about anybody else. And because I am looking for the truth, everyone is under suspicion in a way. You see, I don't know who's who. I have to evaluate everybody ..."
>
> **— Marguerite Oswald**[2096]

A CONSPIRACY IS TWO OR MORE PEOPLE acting in concert to commit an unlawful act. A JFK "conspiracy theory" is any belief that denies the Warren Commission's central conclusion: Lee Harvey Oswald, acting alone, fired the bullets. Simple conspiracy theories hold that others were involved with him. More complex theories say Oswald did not shoot, but then they require convoluted dirty deeds, because to deny his involvement required others to do the shooting, then also plant the strong evidence that he did it.

This chapter considers the inextricably entwined twin questions, "Did Oswald do it?" and "Was there a conspiracy, either with him as one of the conspirators or as an innocent 'patsy'?" Finally, because of understandable disbelief about the sudden murder of Oswald, there will be a section about Jack Ruby, and how and why he did what he did.

Almost everything worth knowing about the assassination is in books and videos that will fit onto one bookshelf. One volume in that small essential collection must be historian William Manchester's 1967 bestseller, *Death of a President*. He masterfully selected the crucial facts to define the times and events, then told the story with grace. Twenty-five years later, Manchester reflected on the proliferation of conspiracy theories and wrote a letter to the editor of *The New York Times*:

"Those who desperately want to believe that President Kennedy was the victim of a conspiracy have my sympathy. I share their yearning. To employ what may seem an odd metaphor, there is an esthetic principle here. If you put six million dead Jews on one side of a scale and on the other side put the Nazi regime—the greatest gang of criminals ever to seize control of a modern state—you have a rough balance: greatest crime, greatest criminals.

But if you put the murdered President of the United States on one side of a scale and that wretched waif Oswald on the other side, it doesn't balance. You want to add something weightier to Oswald. It would invest the President's death with meaning, endowing him with martyrdom. He would have died for something.

A conspiracy would, of course, do the job nicely. Unfortunately, there is no evidence whatever that there was one." [2097]

Writing *The Kennedy Detail* many years later, retired Secret Service agent Jerry Blaine came to a similar conclusion and took it a step further:

"There was no doubt that President John F. Kennedy had stood as an icon of hope and peace and change for many Americans ... in the short tenure of his presidency, he had developed into a larger-than-life idol whose image was perpetuated by the emergence of television and a global focus on America as a result of World War II. ... So when President Kennedy was gunned down in broad daylight, the notion that one demented individual could have had the power to do such a thing seemed incomprehensible. It was too simple. There had to be a bigger explanation. And then, when Jack Ruby took it upon himself to kill the assassin who had shot down America's hopes and dreams, it was as if the world had gone mad. Nothing made sense. That kind of thing just didn't happen in America. The conspiracy theories—and that's all they were: theories, not fact—had been born out of the inability of people to cope with the simple truth." [2098]

••• ••• •••

DID HE DO IT?

or more precisely and fully

DID OSWALD FIRE THREE BULLETS AT THE LIMOUSINE?

To answer that basic question, first some testimony and conclusions from those who knew Oswald best. He had no close friends. The relatives who knew him well enough to have sound opinions on "Did he do it?" can be counted on one hand: His mother, his two brothers, his wife. That's it — we don't even need all the fingers of one hand.

Mother Marguerite, of course, as with everything she thought of or commented upon, put herself and her financial rapacity first. She denied that her dear boy could have been involved, seeing as how he was a U.S. government undercover agent, she believed probably for the CIA, who should have been given a heroic burial in Arlington National Cemetery. You have considerable opportunity to read her testimonies and probe her mind in many places throughout this book, so let us quickly pass on without reprinting here her unusual thoughts.

Oldest brother, actually half-brother — but with one deliberately hurtful exception told on page 123, that never made a difference — John Pic testified to the Warren Commission:

"Mr. JENNER. I will put it this way then: Is there anything you would like to add at the moment now that I am about to finish questioning you that you think you would like to have on the record?

Mr. PIC. If you are interested in my opinions—

Mr. JENNER. Yes, sir; anything that you want to add.

Mr. PIC. I think, I believe that Lee Oswald did the crime that he is accused of. I think that anything he may have done was aided with a little extra push from his mother in the living conditions that she presented to him." [2099]

Robert, the middle brother, the blood relative closest to and most knowledgeable about Lee, the good brother who never gave up, staying in contact even when his interest was despised, also volunteered his opinion to the Warren Commission:

> "Representative BOGGS. Have you in your own mind reached any conclusions on whether or not your brother killed President Kennedy?
>
> Mr. OSWALD. Based on the circumstantial evidence that has been reported in newspapers and over the radio and television, I would have to say that it appears that he did kill President Kennedy.
>
> Representative BOGGS. Would you, having reached that conclusion under the circumstances that you outlined a moment ago, and having known him all of his life, although not too intimately the last year of his life, would you give us any reason for why he may have done this?
>
> Mr. OSWALD. No, sir: I could not." [2100]

As Robert's exhaustive testimony (206 pages of fine print!) neared its conclusion, the presiding commissioner, former CIA Director Allen Dulles, asked him the key question: "Did he [Lee] handle the gun and shoot the shots?", to which the good brother summarized:

> "Mr. OSWALD. Sir, as I previously testified to that question, based on the circumstantial evidence that has been put forth and that I have read from the newspapers and general impression of the time that the event took place, and the subsequent following days of that event, that I would be of the opinion, purely based on these circumstantial points, that he did actually fire the rifle that killed the President of the United States and wounded the Governor of Texas, Mr. Connally." [2101]

Those were in the year 1964. A full third-of-a-century later, brother Robert was on a 1998 *Dateline NBC* TV program titled "My Brother's Keeper":

> "Interviewer Josh Mankowitz: 'Who do you think shot President Kennedy?'
>
> Robert Oswald: 'There's only one conclusion I can reach. And that was my brother, Lee — unfortunately.'
>
> JM: 'Lee Harvey Oswald, and no one else?'
>
> RO: 'That's correct.'
>
> JM: 'No co-conspirators?'
>
> RO: 'No co-conspirators. He *did* buy the rifle. He *did* buy the pistol. He *had* the general opportunity. His *palm* prints are on the rifle. If there was a conspiracy to kill the President, it was separate and apart from what Lee did.'
>
> Narrator: 'Robert has spent years studying the assassination. He actually owns all 26 volumes of the Warren Commission Report. But, the evidence which has convinced him of Lee's guilt has seemed only to fuel conspiracy theories.'" [2102]

Finally, Marina the wife, who knew Lee best of all. She had suspected him instantly in the early afternoon on that terrible Friday when Ruth Paine told her the shots had come from the building where Lee worked (page 203). She stole into Ruth's garage and "found the bundle and stared at it. ... Marina did not touch the blanket, but it looked exactly as it had before. Thank God the rifle was still there, Marina thought, feeling as if a weight had been lifted from her." [2103] Only an hour later, police arrived to ask if Lee owned a rifle. Yes, he did; she took them into the garage. An officer lifted the blanket and it fell limp, empty. She knew.

Marina's testimony to the Warren Commission through four long sessions of questions was unswerving. She was certain that he had done it. In her testimony in September 1964, where she was the Commission's final witness, she continued to be firm (page 453): "On the basis of all the available facts, I have no doubt in my mind that Lee Oswald killed President

Kennedy. At the same time, I feel in my own mind as far as I am concerned, I feel that Lee—that my husband perhaps intended to kill Governor Connally instead of President Kennedy." [2104] That eleventh-hour bombshell was not anything the commissioners wanted to hear after they were engaged in the final editing of their report, so they did nothing about it, as will be recounted in Chapter 21 – Others On This Trail.

Thus, the three realistic Oswald family members were unanimous in their reluctant but honest opinions that yes, he'd done it.

Of the three surviving passengers in the limousine, the grieving widow was not asked for her opinion — in fact, the word "Oswald" was not mentioned during her very brief and gently solicitous questioning by the commission. [2105] The other two passengers, however, had a studied opinion. In her memoir *From Love Field*, Nellie Connally relates that she and her almost-killed victim-husband John Connally researched and concluded:

> "Enough has been written about that horrible time, and the Warren Commission itself, to fill a thousand volumes. Suffice it to say that the weight of the evidence we know about convinced both John and me that Oswald—a twenty-four-year-old stock clerk who had been hired a month before to work in the Book Depository—had acted alone: a fact supported by a little investigation we conducted on our own almost ten years later.
>
> When then-President Nixon appointed my husband as secretary of the treasury in 1973, John found himself in charge of our nation's major intelligence branches.[A] With an obvious personal interest in the case and a stake in an unbiased outcome, he pored over every classified document, every memo, every report prepared on the subject. Along with his other duties, he spent months researching every scrap of evidence and found nothing to change his mind. As he said on the twentieth anniversary of the tragedy in 1983, 'Nobody in America can keep a secret that big for that long.'" [2106]

For a final opinion, there is none better than that of a man known to be scholarly, supremely well-informed and judicious. Before being elected Governor of California, then appointed Chief Justice of the Supreme Court and Chairman of the Commission, Earl Warren had been a prosecuting attorney. He could evaluate with authority. In his *Memoirs*, the final testament of a life dedicated to public service, he wrote:

> "As district attorney of a large metropolitan county for years, I personally prosecuted many murder cases and guided through my office scores of others. With that background of experience, I have no hesitation in saying that had it not been for the prominence of the victim, the case against Oswald could have been tried in two or three days with little likelihood of any but one result." [2107]

Admittedly, those are all opinions based on knowledge and evaluations of facts. If any doubt remains, perhaps you would prefer to know the facts and form your own opinion.

The book you hold was written to focus on one truth: The killing of President Kennedy was an accident, the result of habitual ineptitude by lifelong failure Lee Oswald. The fact of that jarring assertion could probably have been proven in a focused book about half this size. But, because more than a half-century has passed since the shooting in 1963 — two generations — the author added a substantial amount of supportive material, hoping to give readers the entire story, from Oswald's birth through his crime and the repeated investigations.

••• ••• •••

[A] Only partly so: The Secret Service was under the authority of Treasury, but the FBI was in the Department of Justice. CIA, DIA and others reported to other members of the cabinet.

A WINNING TRIFECTA OF PROBITY

This book is thick enough — some may say too large — without also arguing the case to prove that Oswald in fact did it, alone. Happily, there is no requirement for me to put all the facts that justify "guilty!" before you. Three others have done so, better than I could.

You already know of the first. I've said it before and say it again: The *Warren Report* is the foundation, the *Bible*, the Rosetta Stone (or your own example of an ultimately reliable source) of facts about the assassination. If you want to know more than is here, buy a used copy of the original government hardcover *Report*, or one of many available reprints. If you decide on a reprint, for efficiency and to keep your sanity while looking up items cited in this and other assassination materials, buy a book with pages numbered 1 to 888 (probably plus pages through xxiv at the front). If you can look at a *Report* before buying, see if page 669 begins: "APPENDIX XIII" "Biography of Lee Harvey Oswald". You will then have the most complete, useful and handy book of facts about the Dallas shooting and the inept shooter.

Then, if subsequent doubts about the Commission's investigation, hearings, conclusions and report concern you, save your money and avoid the hundreds of books by assassination "analysts" and critics, and buy or check out of your library *Case Closed* by Gerald Posner.

The hardcover was published in 1993, followed by a softcover ("trade") edition. It continues to sell well, readily available from many sources, including one named for a wide river in South America, also selling a Kindle edition you can download without waiting. [2108]

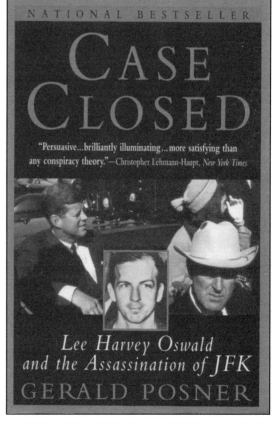

Posner began the *Preface* to his original (hardcover) book in 1993: "More than two thousand books have been written about the assassination of President John Kennedy. Most have attacked the conclusion of the government-appointed Warren Commission that a lone assassin, Lee Harvey Oswald, killed JFK. Many not only assail the Warren Report but also propose myriad suspects—including the CIA, anti-Castro Cubans, the FBI, and the mafia—for ever-expanding conspiracy theories." [2109]

After describing several of the theories, he continued: "The public has been particularly receptive to conspiracy theories in this case. Oswald's curious past, especially his defection to the Soviet Union and his apparent pro-Communist philosophy in the middle of the cold war, showed the alleged assassin was anything but ordinary. Nightclub owner Jack Ruby's killing of Oswald within forty-eight hours of the assassination raised the suspicion he had been silenced. Within days of Oswald's death, public opinion polls confirmed that two thirds of those queried doubted he acted alone." [2110]

Posner then wrote with excellence about the reasons for unease, and the fertile ground thus provided for conspiracy theorists to plant their seeds of derision or doubt. I do not quote from that here. If you believe or merely suspect that Oswald did not do it, alone, then before continuing the book in your hand — about to move on to the subjects of his ineptitude, his motive, his intent — you should read one or all three of the books so excellently researched and written to deal with "DID HE DO IT? WAS THERE A CONSPIRACY?"

The *Case Closed* hardcover sold well, in part because of heightened public interest in the assassination's thirtieth anniversary year, and because of excellent reviews. "*U.S. News and World Report* wrote about the book that 'Posner achieves the unprecedented. He sweeps away decades of polemical smoke, layer by layer, and builds an unshakable case against JFK's killer. . . . Posner now performs the historic office of correcting the mistakes and laying the questions to rest with impressive finality, bringing the total weight of evidence into focus more sharply than anyone has done before. . . . The high quotients of common sense, logic and scrupulous documentation found in *Case Closed* are niceties not often found in the field of assassination research.'" [2111]

Harold Weisberg's very early book *Whitewash: The Report on the Warren Report* was discussed in the previous chapter. As is the wont of prolific assassination theorists, he quickly wrote *Case Open: The Unanswered JFK Assassination Questions*, whose cover heralds *The Omissions, Distortions and Falsifications of Case Closed*. I have carefully read and considered his book. It is petty and vituperative: "This book is, as intended, an exposure and an indictment of Gerald Posner and his mistitled book, *Case Closed*, the most dishonest of all the many books on the assassination of President Kennedy and its investigations." [2112] Weisberg wrote of himself that he is "an unwell and partly handicapped octogenarian who has to depend on his memory and lacks meaningful access to his own materials." [2113] Yet he scorns Gerald Posner and wife Trisha for spending only three days in his basement, copying records that Weisberg had obtained by being, he claims, the imperative for the Freedom of Information Act. He repeatedly accuses Posner of incompetence for not asking for direction to important evidence among the "hundreds of thousands of pages" in the basement. *Case Open* is meant to accuse Posner of dishonesty and fraud; it brings no new evidence to the table. Weisberg wrote a full chapter, 32 pages, to blast Posner's handling of the wound to bystander James Tague by the wildly-aimed (I think first) bullet. It ends: "And this is, too, only one of the many reasons Posner and his ilk should be consigned to history's refuse heaps." [2114] That gives you a flavor of *Case Open*'s style. I advise you to do something more useful with your time.

A quality softcover of Posner's *Case Closed* came in 1994. Its *Author's Note* began:
"The response to the hardcover publication of this book surprised both me and my publisher, Random House. We were initially worried that the book might be lost in the publicity surrounding the publication of other books espousing convoluted theories. But we had underestimated the extent to which, after thirty years of virtually unchallenged conspiracy conjecture, the conclusion that Oswald acted alone in assassinating JFK had evolved, ironically, into the most controversial position. While the media's response was overwhelmingly positive, the reaction from the conspiracy community was the opposite—not simply negative, but often vitriolic. There was little effort to study my overall evidence and conclusions with anything that approached an open mind. Indeed, there was a concerted counterattack to discredit both the book and its author." [2115]

Then he described the many bitter attacks and the lesser number of inaccuracy corrections and better explanations he had put into the new softcover edition. He ended:

"There is more than enough evidence available on the record to draw conclusions about what happened in the JFK assassination. But apparently most Americans, despite the strength of the evidence, do not want to accept the notion that random acts of violence can change the course of history and that Lee Harvey Oswald could affect our lives in a way over which we have no control. It is unsettling to think that a sociopathic twenty-four-year-old loser in life, armed with a $12 rifle and consumed by his own warped motivation, ended Camelot. But for readers willing to approach this subject with an open mind, it is the only rational judgment." [2116]

Case Closed professionally takes up the conspiracy theories, one by one, shining a bright light on each, and demonstrating why, as in a famous observation, "there's no 'there' there!" But, he does miss the point regarding Oswald's motive. The related subjects of his undesirable discharge and appeal to Connally are mentioned in passing only in a footnote relating to CIA and FBI files, [2117] and in a paragraph placing the Marine Corps' rejection of his demand for review of the change of discharge within a thick stack of other bad news. [2118]

Posner lays out the simple facts of Oswald's being hired to work in the tall building that, six weeks later, would give him perfect position to shoot. Then he notes:

"Some have questioned the coincidence that Oswald obtained a job at a building that gave him a clear shot at the presidential motorcade. [New Orleans D.A.] Garrison says that Oswald was manipulated, that 'guiding hands made sure that he would be at the right place at the right time.' That argument ignores the fact that no motorcade route had even been proposed by the date Oswald was hired at the Depository. Moreover, such a theory means that [neighbor lady] Linnie Mae Randle, who suggested the Depository, and Ruth Paine, who told Oswald about it, were part of the conspiracy, as were Roy Truly and the Texas employers who rejected Oswald for jobs earlier in the week. Even Robert Stovall, Oswald's former employer, who scuttled his hiring at Padgett [earlier in the week] by a poor recommendation, would have to be part of the plot. That single incident, Oswald obtaining the job at the Book Depository, highlights two key flaws in almost every conspiracy theory—the constant interpretation of coincidence as evidence of conspiracy, and the inordinate number of people who would have had to be involved in any such plot—more than a dozen on just this issue." [2119]

Later, after very clearly showing that the plan to route the motorcade past the Texas School Book Depository had everything to do with the only possible route to turn a vehicle onto the Stemmons Freeway, and nothing to do with Oswald working there, Posner states his argument for Oswald wanting to shoot. Posner does not specifically name the target, but is obviously referring to President Kennedy. On reading in a newspaper on either Tuesday or Wednesday that the motorcade would pass right in front of him on Friday,

"[I]t is hard to overestimate the impact of that discovery. Oswald, who thought his contribution to his revolutionary cause would be the death of Walker, was suddenly faced with the possibility of having a much greater impact on history and the machinery of government. Failed in his attempts to find happiness in Russia or the U.S., rejected by the Cubans, barely able to make a living in America, frustrated in his marriage, and hounded, in his view, by the FBI, he was desperate to break out of his downward spiral. He had endured long enough the humiliations of his fellow Marines, the Russian and Cuban bureaucrats, the employers that fired him, the radio ambush in New Orleans, the refusal of V. T. Lee and other Communist leaders to acknowledge his efforts and letters. Lee Oswald always thought he was smarter and better than other people, and was angered that others failed to recognize the stature he thought he deserved. Now, by chance, he had an opportunity that he knew would only happen once in his lifetime." [2120]

That is a much better description of motive than the Warren Commission wrote, but I must strongly disagree; it is not correct. Chapter 18 – CONNALLY WILL RIDE demonstrates that upon learning that President Kennedy will ride by in front of his building, Oswald did <u>nothing</u>. And I respectfully disagree with Posner's suggestion of Oswald's motive. He did not need a complex reason to kill Kennedy, for the simple reason that he did not intend to kill Kennedy!

Otherwise, Posner's *Case Closed*, by honestly pointing out the nonsense from many "experts" and "analysts", helped this author focus on what's important. Posner fully supports my conclusion that hundreds (thousands?) of books about the assassination are useless conspiracy contrivances that may have enriched their authors' purses, but did not enrich their readers' minds. With Posner agreeing with my considered judgments, I have pulled many fatuous books from my shelves and consigned them to the listing at the back, NOT CITED.

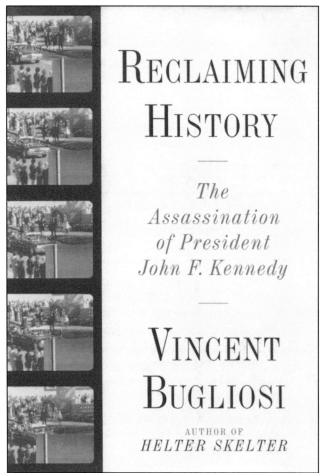

If one were to shelve *Case Closed* with other books of its size, it would fit nicely beside a desk dictionary and the *Warren Report*. To build a library of all the essential Oswald–Kennedy–Connally books, one must add several strong shelves to hold the 26 volumes of *Warren Commission Hearings* and *Reclaiming History* by Vincent Bugliosi.

The book's dust jacket is shown here,[2121] 44% of its actual dimension, so less than 20% of its awesome area. The author is introduced in a mini-biography on the inside rear flap:

"**VINCENT BUGLIOSI** received his law degree in 1964. In his career at the L.A. County District Attorney's office, he successfully prosecuted 105 out of 106 felony jury trials, including 21 murder convictions without a single loss. His most famous trial, the Charles Manson case, became the basis of his true-crime classic, *Helter Skelter,* the biggest selling true-crime book in publishing history. Two of Bugliosi's other true-crime books — *And the Sea Will Tell* and *Outrage* — also reached #1 on the *New York Times* hardcover bestseller list. No other American true-crime writer has ever had more than one book that achieved this ranking.

Bugliosi's excellence as a trial lawyer is best captured in the judgment of his peers. 'Bugliosi is as good a prosecutor as there ever was,' Alan Dershowitz says. F. Lee Bailey calls Bugliosi 'the quintessential prosecutor.' 'There is only one Vince Bugliosi. He's the best,' says Robert Tanenbaum, for years the top homicide prosecutor in the Manhattan D.A.'s office. Most telling is the comment by Gerry Spence, who squared off against Bugliosi in a twenty-one-hour televised, scriptless 'docu-trial' of Lee Harvey Oswald with the original key witnesses. After the Dallas jury returned a guilty verdict in Bugliosi's favor, Spence said, 'No other lawyer in America could have done what Vince did in this case.'" [2122]

It will become clear in the following paragraphs that *Reclaiming History* is gigantic in its size, scope and intent. Before its body pages 1 to 1612 is an Introduction on pages xi through xlvi — a fine opportunity to recall your Roman numerals — including this: "Readers might be interested to know that ... I have been working on this book for twenty-one years." [2123] The decades were rewarded by the book's publication in 2007. In the Introduction, he wrote:

> "Any reader of this book has to be struck by three things, one of which is its abnormal length. ...
> [I]f this book (including endnotes) had been printed in an average-size font and with pages of
> normal length and width, at 1,535,791 words, and with a typical book length of 400 pages, and

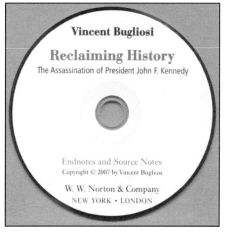

> 300 words per page, this work [including] the companion
> CD-ROM of endnotes numbering 954 pages ... would
> translate into around thirteen volumes." [2124]

Bugliosi's *Endnotes*, supplemental to the main text in the book, were put onto a disk because the book was already uncomfortably heavy. The final three pages of *Endnotes* present the only definitive, understandable explanation known to this author of the numbering and nomenclature of the 26 *Warren Commission Hearings* volumes and their contents. His CD-ROM [2125] also includes a file of *Source Notes*, 170 pages listing where he found the material he quoted or depended upon, equivalent to this book's NOTES AND SOURCES.

The title *Reclaiming History* came from Bugliosi's sound belief that true knowledge of what happened in Dallas has been confused and trashed by writers of nonsense. His ambition is that the book may allow us to reclaim the truth of our nation's history. He quotes Kennedy's larger-than-life Press Secretary on one unintended reason for that obscuration:

> "'It is the very thoroughness of the Warren Commission that has caused its problems,' the late
> Pierre Salinger noted. 'It listened patiently to everyone, no matter how credible or incredible
> the testimony. It then appended all this testimony to its report, providing an opportunity to
> anyone with a typewriter and a lot of time on his hands to write a book on the subject.'" [2126]

Bugliosi set out to research and write the ultimate — in the true sense of "final" — book about the Kennedy assassination, so sound and complete that there would never be justification for another. [2127] He hoped to demonstrate credibility so we will agree with his verdict:

> "I want to assure the readers of this book that I commenced my investigation of this case with an
> open mind. But after being exposed to the evidence, I have become satisfied beyond *all* doubt
> that Lee Harvey Oswald killed President Kennedy, and beyond all *reasonable* doubt that he
> acted alone. I am very confident that the overwhelming majority of objective readers of this
> book will end up feeling the same way." [2128]

His very long Introduction from page xi to page xlvi — let's see now, that's xxxvi pages if you're a Roman, 36 if you use Arabic numerals (invented in India!) — promises to investigate all conspiracy theories, and discredit every one of the horde. Then, he notes: [2129]

> "But the very best testament to the validity of the Warren Commission's findings is that after an
> unrelenting, close to forty-five-year effort, the Commission's fiercest critics have not been able
> to produce *any new credible evidence* that would in any way justify a different conclusion."

In the Introduction, Bugliosi states his disappointment with the more compact book I have cited and lauded on preceding pages, Gerald Posner's *Case Closed*:

"[I]t's a shame that Posner, in his book (which was written in only two years, a remarkably short period for such an immense undertaking), engaged too often in the tactics of the conspiracy theorists, because despite his omissions and distortions he managed to write an impressive work. If his book had been more comprehensive, particularly in the vast area of conspiracy, and, more importantly, had more credibility, the enormous conspiracy community would not have had the ammunition that they have used against him." [2130]

I find that to be an understandable comment from the author of such an all-encompassing book, but believe there's need for the normal-length main-facts-only book that Posner wrote.

Bugliosi's tome begins with 317-page chapter "Four Days in November", reciting the events and probable dialog from the Friday of shooting through the Monday of burials. Proud of that careful reconstruction, Bugliosi and publisher Norton packaged the chapter into its own book, also released in 2007, the softcover *Four Days in November: The Assassination of President John F. Kennedy*. Containing exactly the same material as *Reclaiming History*'s first chapter, it is an accurate, reliable recounting of those terrible days.

A one-paragraph digression: The book *Killing Kennedy* by Bill O'Reilly and Martin Dugard appeared in 2012. If you want one, suit your style by choosing between *Four Days* for authority on 512 dense pages, or *Killing Kennedy* for easier reading on 311 non-crowded pages. In 2013, O'Reilly (without historian Dugard) adapted the 2012 book into *Kennedy's Last Days* by removing much about Oswald and the assassination, then adding lots of photos and Kennedy family ephemera. An introduction to JFK, it's fine if you want to see him from birth to burial in one very easy read, but not a serious choice for knowing about his death. Perhaps its best positioning is as a photographic supplement to the *Warren Report* — although LIFE Books' *The Day Kennedy Died* is a much better choice for that purpose.

Bugliosi's "Book One — Matters of Fact: What Happened" also tells of investigations, autopsy, "magic bullet", biography, the rifle, the grassy knoll and many others, and finally a "Summary of Oswald's Guilt". Nobody's perfect. Bugliosi's 276-page biography of Oswald, equivalent to this book's chapters 1 through 5, disposes of the entire matter of the undesirable discharge, from Lee first learning of it in Minsk by a letter from his mother, to his appeal to the review board after returning to Texas, in less than one page! [2131] Worse, he uses 4/10 of that page to transcribe only a portion of the pleading-but-threatening letter to Connally (in this book on page 88). I say portion because there is an ellipsis (three dots) after "These are the basic facts of *my* case . . ." to indicate an omission — and what he omits includes the most important sentence, the precedent for shooting in Dallas: "I shall employ all means to right this gross mistake or injustice to a boni-fied U.S. citizen and ex-service man."

Somehow, he almost completely missed the Oswald – Connally connection. I surmise that happened because his life's work as a prosecutor led him to focus and write his book about the subjects of the chapter you are reading — DID HE DO IT? WAS THERE A CONSPIRACY? Mr. Bugliosi did that superbly and definitively, achieving his goal that there need be no more Kennedy assassination books. (The book you are reading, I submit, is not about that subject; it's about Lee Oswald's attempted revenge killing of John Connally.)

My "Somehow, he almost completely missed" above refers to the CD-ROM. His nearly-one-thousand pages of additional discussion in Endnotes includes one note, approximately one page if printed, beginning: "Believe it or not, there are those who actually

believe that Governor Connally was Oswald's target that fateful day, not President Kennedy."
[2132] He then briefs his belief that that is nonsense. Alas, there are twelve factual errors in that note, as you will see beginning on page 592 in Chapter 21 – OTHERS ON THIS TRAIL. I believe that if Bugliosi could have read this book and its accurate presentation of the facts, he may have changed his mind — but he died in 2015.

Reclaiming History has a full chapter "Motive". What it concludes was strongly hinted 150 pages earlier in his biography of Oswald: "On the morning of Thursday, November 21, Oswald dressed and left for work, his head roiling with the grandiose scheme that, if he dared to carry it out, would finally ensure his place in history." [2133] This presumption of what Lee was thinking is based on the assumption that his intent was to shoot Kennedy, which is the required premise of much of Bugliosi's book. More likely, I believe, is the proposition that this book's Chapter 18 – CONNALLY WILL RIDE demonstrates — that Oswald had no intention to do anything until *later* that morning, at work, when he read the previous day's discarded newspaper to learn that Governor John Connally will ride by in the motorcade.

His "Motive" chapter has an early disclaimer: "If the Warren Commission and HSCA conceded that they could not nail down for sure why Oswald killed Kennedy, I surely am not so presumptuous as to believe that I can." [2134] He then offers a gem of legal explanation, which ends with its own disclaimer, necessary for him to later give an opinion on motive:

"It should be noted that there is no such crime known as assassination, though by definition an assassination necessarily includes murder, which, next to treason, is the ultimate crime. The word *assassination* has come to mean the murder of a public official (e.g., Julius Caesar, Lincoln) or a public figure (e.g., Pancho Villa, Leon Trotsky), and hence, unlike a murder, its occurrence affects the lives of hundreds of thousands, sometimes millions of people, and often the course of public policy and events. Because of this reality, and because of the empirical evidence, we can safely say that most assassinations have, as their primary motive, the changing of history. A personal hatred of the victim by the killer, present in the majority of murders, is frequently absent or of secondary importance in assassinations. Oswald's killing of Kennedy was, of course, a classic assassination. Though we don't know his motive, the evidence is lacking that he 'hated' Kennedy." [2135]

Bugliosi approaches his own suggestion of a motive by quoting Marina: "She said her husband was 'an egomaniac who wanted to be a 'big man' but that in failing to do so he decided to show the whole world who he was by killing the president so that the whole world would know his name.'" [2136] But he needs more, so after a dozen pages of fine quotations, discussion and thought, he writes that "although Oswald may not have hated Kennedy personally, Kennedy, being the president, was the ultimate, quintessential *representative* of a society for which he had a grinding contempt. ... *And therefore, when he fired at Kennedy, in his addled mind he was firing at the United States of America*." [2137] (The emphasis italics are Bugliosi's.)

I disagree strongly with those thoughts, for the same reason that I previously disagreed with Gerald Posner's. I believe Oswald was not shooting at Kennedy, and there is no point in defining a motive for something not intended. But, to give him his due, here is Bugliosi on why Oswald would be a likely Kennedy assassin — if that's what he had intended:

"If anyone ever had the psychological profile of a presidential assassin, it was Oswald. He not only had a propensity for violence, but was emotionally and psychologically unhinged. He was a bitter, frustrated, and beaten-down loser who felt alienated from society and couldn't get along with anyone, including his wife; one who irrationally viewed himself in a historical light, having visions of grandeur and changing the world; one whose political ideology consumed his daily life, causing him to keep time to his own drummer in a lonely obsession with Marxism and Castro's Cuba; and one who hated his country and its representatives to such an extent that he defected to one of the most undesirable places on earth. If someone with not just one but all of these characteristics is not the most likely candidate to be a presidential assassin, then I would ask, Who would be? Oswald cut the mold. If he didn't, what else is missing from the equation that would add up to a likely presidential assassin?" [2138]

True, but unnecessary. It could become highly relevant by instead thinking of it as the nature of a man whose intent is to "employ all means to right this gross mistake or injustice".

Next in *Reclaiming History* comes its special strength, unique among all books. After the proof of Oswald's guilt and the fact that there were no other shooters, on the Grassy Knoll or anywhere, comes "Book Two — Delusions of Conspiracy: What Did Not Happen", nearly 500 pages that demolish every conspiracy theory known to Bugliosi. He points out that those pages — more like 1,500 if printed in normal size including their notes from the CD-ROM — are "the first anti-conspiracy *book*." [2139] No one else (except Posner) has attempted it. The final chapter is "Conclusion of No Conspiracy", its final two paragraphs strong and definitive:

> "After over forty years of the most prodigiously intensive investigation and examination of a murder case in world history, certain powerful facts exist which cannot be challenged: Not one weapon other than Oswald's Mannlicher-Carcano rifle has ever been found and linked in any way to the assassination. Not one bullet other than the three fired from Oswald's rifle has ever been found and linked to the assassination. No person other than Oswald has ever been connected by evidence, in any way, to the assassination. No evidence has ever surfaced linking Oswald to any of the major groups suggested by conspiracy theorists of being behind the assassination. And no evidence has ever been found showing that any person or group framed Oswald for the murder they committed. One would think that faced with these stubborn and immutable realities, the critics of the Warren Commission, unable to pay the piper, would finally fold their tent and go home. But instead, undaunted and unfazed, they continue to disgorge even more of what we have had from them for over forty years—wild speculation, theorizing, and shameless dissembling about the facts of the case.
>
> The purpose of this book has been twofold. One, to educate everyday Americans that Oswald killed Kennedy and acted alone, paying for his own bullets. And two, to expose, as never before, the conspiracy theorists and the abject worthlessness of all their allegations. I believe this book has achieved both of these goals." [2140]

I do, too. Hooray! The challenge now becomes simple, the outcome certain — If a reasonable reader has any doubt about Did He Do It? Was It a Conspiracy?, they may come to recognize the truth,[B] to "reclaim history" in Bugliosi's words, by reading the *Warren Report*. If that doesn't do it, then read *Case Closed*. If still not convinced, study *Reclaiming History*. (The thick book ends with "Bookends", 150 pages of miscellany, from "The Murder Trial of Jack Ruby" through an exemplary index.) If that doesn't prove the case, then perhaps the remainder of this chapter will. And if that doesn't, the problem is probably that there is not and *can not be* sufficient explanation of Oswald intending to shoot Kennedy. The remaining chapters of this book are dedicated to the proposition that he did not intend to do that, it was happenstance because he was inept. Read on, and it should all make sense!

••• ••• •••

[B] The motto of California Institute of Technology, Caltech, from which I earned a BS degree, is: "The Truth Shall Make You Free." We used to write on test bluebooks: "The truth will make you sick!"

Was It a Conspiracy?
or more fully and precisely
Did some other person(s) assist to shoot at the limousine?

The reader reaching this point in this book is almost certainly a reasonable person, open to new perspectives and unexpected truths. Probably most of the complex-minded people who believe in assassination conspiracy theories have already departed. Thus, to include a long discourse here on the evils of believing in conspiracy theories would be like "preaching to the choir". However, in the same sense that the virtuous do benefit from Sunday sermons about evil, the reader is owed a brief exposure to conspiracy theories.

There was enough unease in the year after Dallas that the *Warren Report* included Appendix XII titled "Speculations and Rumors". It began "Myths have traditionally surrounded the dramatic assassinations of history.", then in thirty-two solid pages raised and discussed matters from "The source of the shots" through "Conspiratorial relationships". Vincent Bugliosi counted the content, reporting they responded to 126 speculations.[2141]

Echoing the Commission's hint of beginning with historical precedent, the progression here will be from the general and abstract to the specific and Lee Harvey Oswald. The sad specifics about inept Oswald will begin on page 276.

An excellent exposure to the history and impact of conspiracy theories is a 1997 book by Daniel Pipes, an editor, lecturer and specialist in the Middle East, with eleven earlier books in print. The excerpts that follow are from *Conspiracy: How the Paranoid Style Flourishes and Where It Comes From*. The opening chapter, *Conspiracy Theories Everywhere*, begins:

> "Conspiracy theories—fears of nonexistent conspiracies—are flourishing in the United States. Republican, Democratic, and independent presidential candidates espouse them. Growing political institutions (the Nation of Islam, the militias) are premised on them. A majority of Americans say they believe John F. Kennedy was killed not by a lone gunman but by a conspiracy, and a majority of black Americans hold the U.S. government responsible for the spread of drugs. O. J. Simpson famously beat his criminal rap by convincing a jury of a conspiracy theory: that the Los Angeles police framed him. Two young men, their heads spinning with conspiracy theories about Washington's taking freedoms away from Americans, blew up a government building in Oklahoma City, killing 168 (including 19 children) and wounding 550." [2142]

Pipes reminds us of the difference between conspiracy and conspiracy theory:

> "[A] *conspiracy* consists of a 'combination or confederacy between two or more persons formed for the purpose of committing, by their joint efforts, some unlawful or criminal act.[2143]
>
> A *conspiracy theory* is the fear of a nonexistent conspiracy. *Conspiracy* refers to an act, *conspiracy theory* to a perception. While the first is an old term, dating to Middle English, the latter goes back only some decades.[2144]
>
> The modish conspiracy theory with the greatest allure remains the assassination of John F. Kennedy in November 1963. This most elaborated and widely believed-in conspiracy theory of recent American history stands as a monument to titillation. Yes, the event shocked Americans and left many incapable of coming to terms with its senselessness, and especially with the notion that so puny an individual as Lee Harvey Oswald could singlehandedly rupture the polity.
>
> But disproportion and belief hardly account for the enormous and enduring popularity of conspiracy theories about the Kennedy killing, all of which share the common assumption that

Oswald was a patsy who got framed. So successful have the Kennedy 'assassinologists' been that, according to opinion polls, some two-thirds of Americans in 1963 suspected a conspiracy and 56 percent of the population still do so in 1991.[2145] Almost thirty years after the 1963 assassination, polls showed three-quarters of the American population believing Oswald was part of a conspiracy and an equal number suspecting an official cover-up of the case.' [2146] " [2147]

Pipes cites several recently-in-vogue American conspiracy theories (including Vietnam-era soldiers missing in action; the Oklahoma City bombing; TWA Flight 800; UFOs at Roswell, New Mexico), then:

> "The enduring popularity of such conspiracy theories makes them highly commercial. The estimated six million people each year who visit the site of the Kennedy assassination are a significant source of revenue to Dallas. Dealey Plaza itself has become 'a conspiracy theme park, with self-anointed 'researchers' on hand every day peddling autopsy pictures.' [2148] Those wishing to experience the assassination more vividly can ride in an open Lincoln Continental convertible limousine from Love Field through Dealey Plaza, hear rifle sounds when they reach the spot where Kennedy was killed, then speed off to Parkland Memorial Hospital. Then they can visit a museum devoted to conspiracy theories about the assassination and featuring a 108-foot-long mural connecting it to many of the other famous deaths in recent American history. True devotés attend annual three-day conventions in Dallas, where seminars delve into details, and self-proclaimed witnesses sign their autographs.
>
> Beyond Dallas, the Kennedy puzzle has become a mainstay of popular culture, acquiring an iconic quality. For those who want a piece of history, artifacts are for sale, but pricey. The gun Jack Ruby used to kill Oswald has sold for $200,000. Board games, t-shirts, and bumper stickers deal with the subject. Oliver Stone's *JFK*, a conspiracy-saturated $50 million film about the president's assassination, appeared in late 1991 and caused a huge surge in conspiracism. The film was nominated for eight Academy Awards and Warner Brothers distributed a '*JFK* Study Guide' for use in high school and college history courses. It then inspired a host of other productions on the same theme, such as *In the Line of Fire* (1993), a thriller, and a November 1996 episode of *The X-Files* in which an army captain killed Kennedy on behalf of his military superiors. Two thousand books have been published on this subject in thirty years; in February 1992, no fewer than four books about the Kennedy assassination filled the American best-seller lists (listed under 'nonfiction,' though that may be a misnomer). A growing number of CD-ROMs and Internet sites deal with the issue.[2149] Such signs of unabated fascination point to the murder's becoming abstracted. It is hard to argue with Gerald Posner, the leading student of the Kennedy assassination,[C] that 'the JFK murder has, regrettably, become an entertainment business.' [2150] What began as an ugly reflection of the cold war ended as murder-mystery story and cult." [2151]

Pipes writes in his chapter *Right-Wing Nuts, Leftist Sophisticates* that conspiracy theorists of the right were the first and remain the usual suspects, but actually those of the left have now become more pervasive and more successful:

> "The Left forwards conspiracy theories that conveniently explain how two of the previous four Democratic presidents (John F. Kennedy and Jimmy Carter) left office through plots most foul. The Kennedy case is remarkable for its gumption given that the main figure, Lee Harvey Oswald, was an extreme leftist who moved to the Soviet Union, renounced his American citizenship, participated in a pro-Castro group (the Fair Play for Cuba Committee), and nearly assassinated General Edwin Walker, a well-known right-wing figure.[D] Yet attention shifted away from Oswald soon after the Kennedy murder, thanks to the work of a network of leftist

---

[C] Ten years after that was written, Vincent Bugliosi's opus proved *him* to be the new leading student.

[D] Chapter 17 – POLITICAL PROCLIVITY will explain exactly what's incompatible among those actions.

activists (e.g., Jim Garrison) and book authors both famous (Edward Jay Epstein, Mark Lane) [2152] and obscure (Thomas Buchanan, Joachim Joesten, Sylvia Meagher, Harold Weisberg). [2153]

These 'assassinologists' took two tacks. One turned Oswald into an extreme rightist ('Oswald would have been more at home with *Mein Kampf* than *Das Kapital*') [2154] and his life into an elaborate charade (Fair Play for Cuba was seen as a front for American intelligence). The other tack turned Oswald into a minor figure by focusing attention instead on a grand conspiracy in which he was but a minor cog. Oswald's politics, motives, and connections to Soviet intelligence nearly disappeared, replaced by topics that pointed to others involved in the murder. Assassination buffs raised questions about the number of guns that went off (up to sixteen), the number of shots, their trajectories, and the number of bullets that hit Kennedy. In the process, they fingered some thirty gunmen as Oswald's accomplices. This profusion of accomplices focused attention away from Oswald and onto the sponsors of this huge effort. Prominent suspects included the CIA (because Kennedy planned to shut it down), anti-Castro Cubans (due to the failure of the Bay of Pigs invasion), White Russians (angry about improved relations with the Soviet Union), the mafia (to stop Robert Kennedy's investigations into organized crime), the FBI (Hoover feared being forced out of office), the military-industrial complex (which hated the Nuclear Test-Ban Treaty), the generals (intent to stop a pullout of Vietnam), Texas oil millionaires (to end talk about canceling the oil depletion allowance), international bankers (who disliked current monetary policies), and Lyndon Johnson (who feared being dropped from the ticket in 1964). Black Americans added the idea, still alive a generation later, of the Ku Klux Klan or other white supremacists killing Kennedy because of his civil rights stance. As controversy swirled about the precise identity of the right-wing conspirators, the numbers involved steadily increased ('their meetings would have had to [be] held in Madison Square Garden'), [2155] and Oswald's role faded. Some books almost ignored his existence; others turned him into a scapegoat. Thanks to the combined efforts of leftist writers, Gerald Posner noted in 1993, 'The debate is no longer whether JFK was killed by Lee Oswald acting alone or as part of a conspiracy—it is instead, which conspiracy is correct?' [2156] " [2157]

Happily — or conversely, not — Pipes notes that while the conspiracy theorists keep busy grinding out their nonsense, most of us don't pay much attention:

"The drumbeat of contending ideas, some sane, some not, is so intense in a media-saturated culture that their messages, the columnist Charles Krauthammer explains,

'raise an eyebrow, but never a fist. A politics so trivialized is conducive to neither great decision making nor decisive leadership. But it is also nicely immunized from the worst of political pathologies. In the end, Oliver Stone—like David Duke and Louis Farrakhan and the rest of America's dealers in paranoia—is just another entertainment, another day at the movies. The shallowness of our political culture has a saving grace.' [2158] " [2159]

Because Pipes has raised the subject, and most readers will know of it, we might as well throw out some garbage right now. About JFK's death, many know only what is in Oliver Stone's 1991 movie *JFK*. Seeing Kevin Costner (as Jim Garrison) finding proof of conspiracy right in front of them on the screen, many believe there just *must* be something to it. If you have *any* belief that there is *any* reality in that movie, I urge you to read a wonderful book that speaks truth: *False Witness: The Real Story of Jim Garrison's Investigation and Oliver Stone's Film JFK* [2160] by Patricia Lambert, who had no prior opinion when she saw *JFK* and decided to find out if it was true. The book is directly on point. Lambert has done such a first-rate, truthful, well-documented job of exposing the total lie that was Jim Garrison, then the compounded lie that was Oliver Stone, I need not, and will not, say one more word about those miscreants. Read her book!

To believe that Kennedy died by the joint effort of two or more people — the definition of a conspiracy — requires complicated thoughts about unnatural acts. Consider Lee Oswald: He was a loner, a man who confided in none and trusted none. Nowhere in his adult life do we know of any situation in which he cooperated with anyone about anything! To believe that he did so on November 22, 1963, successfully, for the first time in his life, is beyond reason.

For Oswald to be part of a conspiracy, it would surely be necessary for others to think well enough of him to add him to their group. But, here's what those who knew him best told the Warren Commission: Attorney Max Clark: "I just thought he was a person that he couldn't get along with anybody or anyone. He just seemed to be a person that believed everyone else in the world was out of step but himself. ... [T]his is a guy that just was never going to be able to do anything because he couldn't get along with anybody ..." [2161] Russian immigrant leader George A. Bouhe: "I thought of him as a simpleton, but at that time I had no reason to suspect his lying." [2162] Anna Meller, one of the first emigres to meet him: "By the way, the first impression of Lee Harvey is a man absolutely sick. I mean mentally sick; you could not speak with him about anything. He's against Soviet Union; he's against United States. He made impression he did not know what he likes, really." [2163] Everett Glover, who held a soiree to introduce the Oswalds to friends, most importantly his fellow Unitarian and madrigal singer Ruth Paine, sized up the man: "Well, I came to the conclusion that he was, in the first place, obviously a fellow who was not satisfied with anything. He was not satisfied with what was in this country originally. He was not satisfied with the life in Russia. And he was not adjusting at all when he came back, so he was very maladjusted. ... In the course of fitting into a social and political group at all, he didn't adjust, didn't fit in. ... My best word to describe him, my own personal word is that he was a ne'er-do-well." [2164] Alex Kleinlerer who tried to help both Oswalds: "My overall impression of Oswald was that he was angry with the whole world and with himself to boot; that he really did not know what he wanted; that he was frustrated because he was not looked up to; and that he was dissatisfied with everything, including himself." [2165] Elena Hall, who welcomed Marina and June into her home: "He didn't appreciate nothing, never. ... He was just strange man, I guess." [2166] Her husband, who listened attentively to Oswald's words: "He is not responsible enough to have authority above him. In other words, he couldn't have anybody above him really telling him what to do. He couldn't take orders." [2167] Valentina Ray, who also hosted Marina and June while Lee looked for work and lived at the YMCA: "I thought he was rather arrogant and I did not think he was even—I did not think him too intelligent and terribly unfriendly and very much of a loner. He did not seem to care for anybody. He did not talk to anybody. You get the impression he does not like you even though you did not do anything or speak two words to him." [2168] She said her husband Frank was more harsh in his judgment: "[He] just came in huffing, puffing, said he never met anybody dumber in his life ... He considered him a complete idiot." [2169]

The man who knew him best — the only American candidate to be called Lee's friend, although he said he regretted that — was George De Mohrenschildt, who observed to the Warren Commission: "[H]e was not sophisticated you see. He was a semi-educated hillbilly. And you cannot take such a person seriously. All his opinions were crude, you see." [2170] "[A]n unstable individual, mixed-up individual, uneducated individual, without background. What government would give him any confidential work? No government would." [2171] "[K]nowing what kind of brains he had, and what kind of education, I was not interested in listening to him, because it was nothing, it was zero." [2172]

George's wife, Jeanne (pronounced *Zhon*) Eugenia Fomenko De Mohrenschildt, gave greater attention and more sympathy to Marina. She testified: "I wouldn't say they were completely starving, but they were quite miserable—quite, quite miserable, you know. Even if they were not destitute, the personality that Lee had would make anybody miserable to live with. ... He was very, very disagreeable, and disappointed." [2173] Their daughter Alexandra, sympathetic to Marina with whom she was close in age, disliked Lee: "He resented any type of authority. He expected to be the highest paid immediately, the best liked, the highest skilled. He resented any people in high places, and people of any authority ...".[2174]

One of the FBI's leading experts on criminals, their motivations and associations, John Douglas, after several pages of analysis, crisply summarizes Lee Oswald:

"Oswald's not the kind of person you'd bring into a conspiracy, even as a dupe, because you couldn't trust him. If you're an agent of some sort, you're not going to try to develop someone like Oswald. He's too unreliable, too unpredictable, too much of a flake. He's got too many personal problems, plus he's not that smart." [2175]

Jack Kennedy's astute, close advisor, Ted Sorensen, wrote this about Robert Kennedy: "His brother was gone and no investigation or revelation could bring him back. But if he had known any grounds for legitimate suspicion suggesting that others were involved in his brother's murder, it is hard to believe that he would let such a matter rest." Then, he wrote of his own conclusion: "I have read nothing that leads me to believe that any other commission proceeding in any other fashion would have produced any other names of individuals actually involved in the killing." [2176] The author of this book, after more than a half-century of reading and watching with eyes wide open, absolutely agrees.

This discussion of conspiracy, like most of this book, has admittedly been what you might expect from an engineer — carefully-examined, heavy, lengthy, unrelievedly fact-based. If you know enough truth about the murder of JFK to avoid confusion with a little fantasy, you will probably enjoy a surprisingly fine book, an artistic blend of fact and fiction: *11/22/63* by master storyteller Stephen King. After spinning out his clever tale of time travel to see and try to stop Oswald — no spoiler here! — King added a thoughtful "Afterword" about himself:

"Early in the novel, Jake Epping's friend Al puts the probability that Oswald was the lone gunman at ninety-five percent. After reading a stack of books and articles on the subject almost as tall as I am, I'd put the probability at ninety-eight percent, maybe even ninety-nine. ...

Probably the most useful source materials I read in preparation for writing this novel were *Case Closed* by Gerald Posner; *Legend*, by Edward Jay Epstein (nutty Robert Ludlum stuff, but fun); *Oswald's Tale*, by Norman Mailer; and *Mrs. Paine's Garage*, by Thomas Mallon. The latter offers a brilliant analysis of the conspiracy theorists and their need to find order in what was almost a random event. The Mailer is also remarkable. He says that he went into the project ... believing that Oswald was the victim of a conspiracy, but in the end came to believe—reluctantly—that the stodgy old Warren Commission was right: Oswald acted alone.

It is very, very difficult for a reasonable person to believe otherwise. Occam's Razor—that the simplest explanation is usually the right one." [2177]

Earl Warren was an attorney and a fully experienced prosecutor before he became Governor of California, then the nation's top jurist. He had both intellect and credentials to carefully consider all facts turned up by his Commission. Warren wrote in his *Memoirs*:

"In the assassination of President Kennedy, there are no facts upon which to hypothesize a conspiracy. They simply do not exist in any of the investigations made by the Federal Bureau of Investigation, the Secret Service, the Central Intelligence Agency, or the Departments of State, Defense, and Justice. The last was headed by the late Robert F. Kennedy, brother of our assassinated President, who certainly wanted nothing short of the truth. In addition, the authorities of the state of Texas, of the city of Dallas, and law enforcement agencies of other cities throughout the country were anxious to be helpful in every possible way. All of this was supplemented by nine months of arduous work by our own staff of outstanding lawyers independent of all of these official agencies. And none of us could find any evidence of conspiracy. Every witness who could be found was examined, and it is revealing to note at this late date—nine years after the Commission Report was filed—that not a single contrary witness has been produced with convincing evidence. Practically all the Cabinet members of President Kennedy's administration, along with Director J. Edgar Hoover of the FBI and Chief James Rowley of the Secret Service, whose duty it was to protect the life of the President, testified that to their knowledge there was no sign of any conspiracy. To say now that these people, as well as the Commission, suppressed, neglected to unearth, or overlooked evidence of a conspiracy would be an indictment of the entire government of the United States. It would mean the whole structure was absolutely corrupt from top to bottom, with not one person of high or low rank willing to come forward to expose the villainy, in spite of the fact that the entire country bitterly mourned the death of its young President and such a praiseworthy deed could make one a national hero." [2178]

Warren summarized: "The facts of the assassination itself are simple, so simple that many people believe it must be more complicated and conspiratorial to be true." [2179] He concluded:

> "I believed the Report at the time it was made and nothing has transpired to change that belief. In this respect, I wish to say that not one single witness, one document, or one artifact has been produced to provably discredit it. To our best knowledge, the facts remain precisely as reported, and, that being true, the conclusion must remain the same." [2180]

Last, having reserved this as a place of honor, Marina: Writing *Marina and Lee* in 1977, the biographer with whom Marina worked for many months, Priscilla Johnson McMillan, wrote in the book's *Epilogue*: "I have often asked Marina whether Lee might have been capable of joining with an accomplice to kill the President. Never, she says. Lee was too secretive ever to have told anyone his plans. Nor could he have acted in concert, accepted orders, or obeyed any plan by anybody else. The reason Marina gives is that Lee had no use for the opinions of anybody but himself. He had only contempt for other people. 'He was a lonely person,' she says. 'He trusted no one.' Those who knew Lee in Dallas agree with her. 'I'd have thought it was a conspiracy,' one of the Russians says, 'if only I hadn't known Lee.'" [2181]

No, there was no conspiracy — Oswald did it alone. Whenever I am tempted to doubt a dreaded reality, something I fervently hope is not true, I seek a trusted voice to provide a check — an honored source to help confirm or deny my understanding. On November 22, 1963, after Dewey ran in from the Colorsound shipping department to tell me, "The radio says Kennedy's been shot!", I needed to know the truth. I turned on the TV, and there on CBS was "the most trusted man in America". We watched as he said:

> "From Dallas, Texas, the flash, apparently official: 'President Kennedy died at 1 P.M. Central Standard Time.' Two o'clock Eastern Standard Time, some thirty-eight minutes ago." [2182]

When Walter Cronkite removed his glasses and choked up, so did I, because at that moment I knew it must be true, because he said so.

I "tuned in" [E] again as that trusted man looked back in CBS-TV's 1997 retrospective *Cronkite Remembers*. After reviewing the Kennedy assassination and many of the analyses and speculations that followed:

"There were so many questions asked about the Warren Commission Report on the assassination. We spent a lot of money, in those days, over a million dollars, to do a special investigation. And we established, to our satisfaction, that the single gunman could have fired all three shots in time, that the shadows on that little grassy knoll were not people but something else, that there were only three shots. We set out to try to prove [the] Warren Commission was wrong. All we did was prove that it was right.

I think all the evidence points to Lee Harvey Oswald as the single assassin, maybe with one accomplice, although I rather doubt that. But, this grandiose conspiracy, this Oliver Stone junk, absolute junk that that guy perpetrated on an unsuspecting generation, planted thoughts about Lyndon Johnson himself plotting the assassination, making a hero out of Garrison, the Attorney in New Orleans, who came close to being a certified nut. [All emphases were very clear in Cronkite's voice.]

Furthermore, if there had been the kind of conspiracy that that movie made out, or any of these major conspiracy theorists propound, I don't believe for one minute it could have been kept a secret for all these years. When you've got a number of conspirators, somebody usually breaks, something breaks in that story." [2183]

Like the proverbial shepherd who leaves his flock of ninety-nine sheep to look for the one who is lost, I was delighted by most of Cronkite's conclusions, but focused on his "maybe with one accomplice, although I rather doubt that." I mailed a letter to Walter Cronkite, explaining that someday I would write this book, and (in part):[2184]

... I might cite what you said on *Cronkite Remembers* in January 1997, including: "We set out to try to prove [the] Warren Commission was wrong. All we did was prove that it was right. I think all the evidence points to Lee Harvey Oswald as the single assassin, maybe with one accomplice, although I rather doubt that."

Sir, I am so in agreement that "all the evidence points to Lee Harvey Oswald as the single assassin" that I am amazed and perplexed by "**maybe with one accomplice**."

Will you please ... explain **who** might have been the one accomplice, or **what** brought you to suspect there might be one? I conclude, having read hundreds of books on the subject, that there was no accomplice. But, I have such high respect and regard for you that I cannot be 100% satisfied until I have some idea of why you said "**maybe with one accomplice**."

You understand I'm not challenging or asking you to defend. Rather, I'm simply trying to ensure that I have looked under every rock I should.

[E] Another explanation for the young: In the old days, one rotated a radio's "tuning knob" to select a station, finally wiggling it back and forth to "tune in" the clearest sound. Fancy radios had dials to show the frequency being tuned, and in the early 1950s I was a whiz at stringing complicated dial cords that connected knob shafts to frequency indicators. When television came along, we rotated a clicking "channel select" knob, then wiggled concentric "fine tuning" for the clearest picture.

Mr. Cronkite replied from Cape Cod:[2185]

> The only reason I have hedged on the single assassin judgement [*sic*] is based on the back alley shot taken at the Dallas general whose name I do not have handy. The shot maker who I believe either was positively identified as Oswald or strongly suspected to be him, apparently had an associate waiting in a car at the end of the alley. That, I seem to recall, was according to a dairy delivery man. And there were the reports that Oswald was accompanied by a friend in his visits to a shooting range outside Dallas.
>
> This is flimsy material that apparently was investigated and discarded by appropriate authorities, and my memory may be a little fuzzy on the details. But it is just enough to set off the alarms of my journalistic conscience.

I responded with thanks, and:[2186]

> My concern about your four-word phrase relative to Lee Harvey Oswald, "maybe with one accomplice," is alleviated. I remain certain that he acted alone.
>
> Yes, Oswald did fire from an alley at retired Major General Edwin A. Walker, a leader of the John Birch Society. No credible evidence supports an accomplice or a waiting car, although there may well have been, by coincidence, a non-related vehicle in or near the alley. But, I'll take another hard look at that matter.
>
> There is conflicting evidence on whether Oswald ever sighted-in his terrible little Mannlicher-Carcano at a firing range. Some shooters are sure it was he, others disagree. If, as I suspect, he did test fire the carbine and adjust its scope, and if he was accompanied, I believe it more probable than not that his friend was an innocent, and not party to a conspiracy. I'll also restudy this.
>
> Please be assured, from one who has spent years trying to know everything Oswald did and said, with the hope of understanding why he fired at the motorcade, that you are absolutely correct in your judgment that he acted alone. The world is better because of your journalistic conscience, but there are no alarms here.

No words can show the distinction between Oswald-alone and conspiracy theory more clearly than did Garry Trudeau, so this discussion concludes with his *Doonesbury* summary: [2187]

JACK RUBY

Oswald popping out of nowhere to kill Kennedy is sufficient to strain belief, although as the next chapter will show, that is the pattern of American assassinations. I am asking you to go further, to believe that not only did a nobody kill Kennedy, but that it was an accident completely typical of him — he intended to kill someone else, not our President. That's plenty to ask, so let's first simplify by dealing with another out-of-the-blue character who sprang from nowhere two days after Kennedy's death. Over the many years I've studied him, my belief has solidified that Jack Ruby should be taken at face value for who he was and what he did. Most everything worth knowing is in the *Warren Report*'s "A Biography of Jack Ruby" on pages 779–806, the source of much of the following.[2188] For a complete storytelling that brings a Damon Runyonesque character to life, read Gerald Posner's *Case Closed*, pages 350–401.

Jacob Rubenstein was born in Chicago in 1911, the sixth of nine children of Jewish immigrants from Poland. The father drank and the dysfunctional family split. Jacob attended school only through the eighth grade, then supported himself by scalping fight tickets,[2189] peddling plaster busts of FDR and punchboards whose prize was a so-called "$19 radio" that "cost him about $5 apiece."[2190] "One of his closest Chicago friends stated that Ruby's sales and promotions were 'shady' but 'legitimate.'"[2191] Jack was a plucky entrepreneur all his life. The week he shot Oswald, he was optimistically promoting a "Twist board" — two pieces of fiberboard separated by a ball bearing ring, on which one stood to twist for exercise — "$1.69 retail, hottest thing in the world."[2192]

Jacob went in and out of foster homes and trouble with the law. All his life, he was a street-smart tough guy, quick to take offense, clean, a neat dresser and popular with the ladies. He fought the draft but was "inducted into the U.S. Army Air Forces"[2193] in 1943. He trained as an aircraft mechanic at bases in the U.S. As would Oswald, "he earned a sharpshooter's rating for his firing of an M1 .30 caliber carbine."[2194] Discharged in 1946, Jack returned to Chicago to join three brothers in a small business, manufacturing and selling (Jack, naturally, was the salesman) small cedar chests, aluminum salt and pepper shakers, key chains, etc.

Family disputes in 1947 separated Jack from the business. Sister Eva had gone to Dallas where she opened the Singapore Supper Club. Jack moved to help her. He legally changed his name "because the name Rubenstein was misunderstood and too long and because he was well known as Jack L.[F] Ruby."[2195] His nickname was "Sparky" because (take your choice, according to testimonies to the Warren Commission) he waddled like comic strip horse "Sparkplug", or he was a quick thinker, or he was unpredictable and extremely volatile.[2196]

"[O]peration of nightclubs and dancehalls was his primary source of income, and his basic interest in life during the 16 years he spent in Dallas prior to shooting Lee Oswald."[2197] The *Warren Report* tells of his changing the Singapore's name to the Silver Spur Club, then managing, serially, the Bob Wills Ranch House, the Vegas Club, Hernando's Hideaway, and finally "the Sovereign Club, a private club that was apparently permitted by Texas law to sell liquor to members."[2198]

[F] He added middle name "Leon" in honor of a union official friend murdered in Chicago. Similarly, my mother's father decided David Baker was too simple, so added a middle name, "Benjamin".

Experiencing difficulty recruiting sufficient members, Ruby found himself again unable to pay the Sovereign's rent. A friend loaned him money, insisting that Ruby discontinue club  memberships, even though this would prevent the sale of liquor, and offer striptease shows as a substitute attraction. Ruby agreed, changing the Sovereign's name "to the Carousel Club. It became one of three downtown Dallas burlesque clubs and served champagne, beer, 'setups' and pizza, its only food. The Carousel generally employed four strippers,[2199] a master of ceremonies, an assistant manager, a band, three or four waitresses, and a porter or handyman. Net receipts averaged about $5,000 per month, most of which was allocated to the club's payroll. Late in 1963, Ruby began to distribute 'permanent passes' to the Carousel..." [2200] Jack gave many Carousel passes to police officers.

The Warren Commission summarized: "Although the precise nature of his relationship to members of the Dallas Police Department is not susceptible of conclusive evaluation, the evidence indicates that Ruby was keenly interested in policemen and their work. ... Ruby's police friendships were far more widespread than those of the average citizen. ... Ruby gave policemen reduced rates, declined to exact any cover charge from them, and gave them free coffee and soft drinks ... Ruby regarded several officers as personal friends, and others had worked for him. Finally, at least one policeman regularly dated, and eventually married, one of the Carousel's strippers." [2201]

The Commission's biography of Jack Ruby ended before the assassination weekend because its "desire not to interfere in the pending proceedings involving Ruby [his murder trial and appeal] necessarily limits the scope of this appendix, which does not purport to discuss the legal issues raised during Ruby's trial or his possible motive for shooting Oswald." [2202] To follow Ruby after November 22, I recommend the excellent account by Gerald Posner in *Case Closed*, from which much of the following is excerpted, unless otherwise noted.

When Oswald fired into Dealey Plaza, Jack Ruby was going about his normal routine, five blocks away in the *Dallas Morning News* office, writing his club's ads for the weekend papers. When people ran in yelling of the shooting, an advertising employee "said Ruby had a look of 'stunned disbelief,' and was 'emotionally upset.'" [2203] He decided the "classy" thing to do (important to this man with little class) was to close the Carousel out of respect for Kennedy. "After returning to the Carousel, he ordered that the club be closed for the night, and his employee Andrew Armstrong made the first phone call, to a stripper, Karen 'Little Lynn' Carlin, at 1:45 p.m., to tell her not to come in, but he was unable to reach her." [2204]

Friends and relatives testified that as the day progressed, Ruby displayed increasing emotion and depression. He had long been a regular visitor to police headquarters, usually bringing sandwiches and handing out passes to the Carousel Club, and there he was that Friday afternoon while Oswald was being questioned. In the evening he went to Temple Shearith Israel for a special memorial service and cried openly. Then he drove to Phil's Delicatessen, stocked up on kosher sandwiches and sodas, which he took to police HQ.

He was in a hallway shortly after midnight (as Saturday began), when "Oswald was brought out ... on the way to the basement assembly room for the midnight press conference. Ruby recalled that as Oswald walked past, 'I was standing about two or three feet away. I went down to the assembly room in the basement,' Ruby said. 'I felt perfectly free walking in there. No one asked me or anything.'" [2205] "One of the detectives assigned to guard Oswald was Ruby's friend A. M. Eberhardt. He noticed Ruby in the right-hand corner, with a notebook and pencil in his hand." [2206] "Ruby thought Oswald was smirking at his police guards, and in only a few minutes he was convinced that Oswald was guilty." [2207] In this view from TV, Ruby is at top-right, nattily dressed in the dark suit.[2208]

Saturday brought more tears, phone calls and mounting grief. That afternoon, radio newsman Wes Wise was in Dealey Plaza. "Ruby leaned into Wise's car window and said, his voice breaking and with tears in his eyes, 'I just hope they don't make Jackie come to Dallas for the trial. That would be terrible for that little lady.'" [2209] He may have gone again to police HQ — the evidence is conflicted — to be at the center of action. Chief Curry told the waiting reporters that Oswald would not be moved until ten the next morning, so there was no need for them to stay around.[2210]

Saturday night features a stripper-in-distress, the next link in the relentless march to death on Sunday, as told by Posner:

"By 9:30[PM] Ruby had returned to his apartment. There, he received a call from one of his strippers, Karen Bennett Carlin, whose stage name was Little Lynn. She had driven into Dallas from Fort Worth with her husband [some accounts say boyfriend] and wondered if the Carousel was going to open over the weekend, because she needed money. 'He got very angry and was very short with me,' Carlin recalled. 'He said, 'Don't you have any respect for the President? Don't you know the President is dead? ... I don't know when I will open. I don't know if I will ever open back up.'' She apologized for bothering him but still asked for part of her salary, and he promised to meet them in an hour at the Carousel. When he had not arrived by 10:30, Carlin's husband, Bruce, again telephoned the apartment, and emphasized they needed money for rent and groceries. On this occasion, Ruby spoke to the attendant at the [garage next to the Carousel] and persuaded him to lend the Carlins $5 so they could at least return to Fort Worth, and told Carlin to call him the next day about getting more money." [2211]

On Sunday morning, Bugliosi writes, "Little Lynn [2212] is [sick]— that's one of his strippers, out the whole damned weekend, probably. ... He'll probably have to send her a couple of bucks, wire it to her over in Fort Worth. She's most likely pregnant, and that salesman boyfriend of hers is out of work because his car broke down." [2213] Posner continues the story:

"Ruby did not get up until 9:00 to 9:30. ... At 10:19, while still lounging in the apartment in his underwear, he received a call from his dancer Karen Carlin (her phone record revealed the exact time). Although she sensed he 'still seemed upset,' she told him, 'I have called, Jack, to try to get some money, because the rent is due and I need some money for groceries and you told me to call.' Ruby asked how much she needed, and she said $25. He offered to go downtown and send it to her by Western Union, but told her it would 'take a little while to get dressed.' ... Ruby left the apartment a few minutes before 11:00 a.m. His route downtown took him past Dealey Plaza, where he saw the many new wreaths left overnight in memory of the President. Again, he cried. As he drove near the jail, he noticed a large crowd and assumed Oswald had already been transferred.

At the police station, if everything had gone according to plan, Oswald would have been moved to the sheriff's custody nearly an hour earlier. By 9:00 a.m., the police had cleared the basement. Guards were posted at the two driveway ramps, and at the five doorways into the garage. ... A crowd of several hundred had gathered ... in front of the jail, to watch the event. However, the transfer had undergone a series of last-second changes and delays." [2214]

The delays were each trivial, but collectively sufficient to set the stage for death: An armored vehicle was too small to hold both Oswald and guards. A larger armored van was then chosen and arrived, but it was too tall to fit down the ramp into the basement. A U.S. postal inspector arrived unexpectedly and quizzed Oswald extensively about his use of post-office boxes. That alone delayed the transfer by about half an hour. If not for all those delays — and one more to come from the prisoner himself — Ruby would have come onto the scene too late. [2215]

Any other day of the week, Jack Ruby could have gone to Western Union offices closer to his apartment, but this was Sunday and only one was open. [2216] Posner continues:

"Ruby parked across the street from the Western Union station, only one block from police headquarters, near 11:05. At Western Union, he filled out the forms for sending $25 to Karen Carlin. Then he patiently waited in line while another customer completed her business. According to the clerk, Ruby was in no hurry. It was impossible for him to know that Oswald had not been transferred, since there was no television or radio at the Western Union office. There was a public telephone, but Ruby did not use it. [Reminder: This is decades before cell phones.] When he got to the counter, the cost for sending the moneygram totaled $26.87. He handed over $30 and waited for his change while the clerk finished filling out the forms and then time-stamped the documents. Ruby's receipt was stamped 11:17. When he left Western Union, he was less than two hundred steps from the entrance to police headquarters." [2217]

The photo above [2218] shows the Western Union office, at a street corner. On the other end of the block and on the same side of the street is Dallas City Hall, which houses the Police Department. [2219] The W.U. clerk on duty that morning, Doyle E. Lane, told the Warren Commission that Jack Ruby had an ordinary transaction and was not in any hurry. The receipt at right [2220] was stamped 11:16 by a clock that had been synchronized with a master clock only minutes before, just after the master had been set at 11:00 AM by the Naval Observatory in Washington, D.C. Doyle handed Jack his change and the fresh receipt, and, there being no other customer, watched him walk to the door, go outside, turn left, and walk away at "Just ordinary gait." [2221]

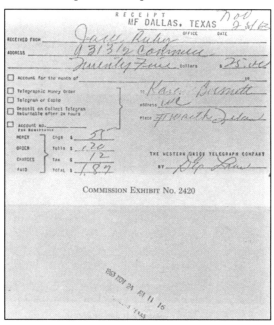

Commission Exhibit No. 2420

Meanwhile, down the block at police headquarters, Oswald decided to put on a sweater. That delay is important. Posner wrote:

"[S]ome sweaters … were brought to him, he put on a beige one, and then changed his mind and switched to a black sweater. Then he announced he was ready to leave. If Oswald had not decided at the last moment to get a sweater, he would have left the jail almost five minutes earlier, while Ruby was still inside the Western Union office.

Ruby walked the one block along Main Street and stopped near the eight-foot-wide rampway. It was guarded by policeman E. R. Vaughn. At 11:20, about fifty-five seconds before Oswald was shot, Lt. Rio Pierce drove a black car up the Main Street ramp as part of the decoy plan. … Officer Roy Vaughn stepped away from the center of the rampway, into the middle of Main Street, to stop the traffic so Pierce could safely exit.[G] Ruby slipped inside while Vaughn was distracted. He walked down the ramp and arrived at the back of a crowd of police and press only seconds before Oswald was brought past. If the car that was scheduled to move Oswald had been in its correct position at the bottom of the ramp, it would have blocked Ruby from gaining access.

Oswald was taken downstairs from the third floor to the basement. Cramped inside the garage confines were almost thirty reporters and seventy police. The glare from the bright television lights made it difficult to see. As Oswald walked into the garage, the large clock on the wall turned to 11:21" [2222]

William Manchester in *The Death of a President* takes up the story:

"In Ruby's right hip pocket was a .38 caliber revolver. He habitually carried the weapon—this was Dallas, not New York; there was no Sullivan Act—and today he was also carrying over $2,000 in cash. He had left another $1,000 in the trunk of his car, parked directly across the street from the Western Union office. His behavior was in character. He was Jack the big spender, Jack the tough; and he was about to become Jack the vindicator. [The purpose of] his trip downtown … was to wire the money to Karin. She was at home with her husband, who wasn't working steadily. Saturday should have been her payday, and she had been left in financial straits by his decision to close his clubs in mourning; Little Lynn was four months pregnant, owed rent, needed groceries, and had less than fifty cents in her purse." [2223]

Four minutes after his Western Union receipt, Jack Ruby found the villain right there in front

of him. He immediately realized this was his chance to spare Jacqueline Kennedy the grief of having to return for Oswald's trial. On the spur of the moment, as was fully characteristic of him, "Sparky" pulled out the .38 revolver he always carried.[H] He fired, yelling, "You killed my President, you rat!" [2224] This photo was snapped a split second after the one in chapter 6, where all was serene. [2225] The white car at left with Captain Fritz should have been to the right, in a position blocking Ruby, but that morning everything ran late.

[G] Detective L. D. Montgomery testified that the driver needed help from the officer guarding the ramp to drive into the street because he was <u>backing</u> up and out of the down ramp: *WCH* XIII 31.

[H] On his deathbed, he would testify: "I always carried a gun because of various altercations I had in my Club then. I carried pretty large sums of money at times." (Gertz *Moment of Madness* 488.)

In his oral history for the valuable book *No More Silence*, DPD Lieutenant Elmo L. Cunningham boiled down the importances of timing and sheer coincidence:

"An officer was supposed to go down and get his car and lead the armored car. Since no left turns were permitted in the downtown area, the officer had to drive his car up the wrong way onto the Main Street ramp, turn left and then come back onto Commerce to lead the decoy van.

One officer was stationed at the top of the Main Street ramp. When this other officer comes out the wrong way going onto Main Street, the uniformed officer then stepped into the street to stop traffic so that the car could get around him to get in front of the armored vehicle. At that point, Jack Ruby, who had just sent a telegram with money to a girl, then walked down the driveway.

The telegram was dated and stamped with a time. If you go there and walk out from the counter and down the sidewalk at a normal pace and into the City Hall basement, you won't be off five seconds from the time that Ruby made it. It was just chance. There was no way that anybody knew exactly when Oswald was coming out, not even the policemen who were waiting down there." [2226]

A detective of the Auto Theft Bureau of the Dallas Police Department's Criminal Investigation Division, Barnard S. Clardy, was one of the seventy officers stationed in the basement to protect Oswald's transfer. After the shot seen round the world, Clardy rode in the elevator with Ruby, up to the fifth floor jail He testified to the Warren Commission that Jack Ruby then said to him and other police: "If I had planned this I couldn't have had my timing better. It was one chance in a million. ... Somebody had to do it. You all couldn't." [2227]

"An ambulance [1] arrived within minutes and took Oswald to Parkland Hospital, the same trauma unit that only forty-eight hours earlier had treated President Kennedy and Governor Connally. ... The Parkland surgeons could not save him. 'It's pretty hard to imagine one bullet doing more damage than that,' says Dr. John Lattimer. 'It perforated the chest cavity, went through the diaphragm, spleen, and stomach. It cut off the main intestinal artery, and the aorta, and the body's main vein, as well as breaking up the right kidney. That wound was definitely fatal.'" [2228]

Dallas Police Captain J. W. Fritz, head of the homicide squad who had questioned Lee Oswald from the afternoon of Friday, November 22, through the morning of Sunday, November 24, turned to questioning Jack Ruby about an hour after he shot Oswald. Fritz told the Warren Commission: "I did ask him some questions and he told me that he shot him, told me that he was all torn up about the Presidential killing, that he felt terribly sorry for Mrs. Kennedy. He didn't want to see her have to come back to Dallas for a trial, and a lot of other things like that." [2229]

Special Agent In Charge Forrest Sorrels of the Secret Service was invited to join in the questioning. As recounted so nicely by Vincent Bugliosi in *Four Days in November*, he began simply and drew out emotional truth:

"'Jack—why?' Sorrels finally asks.

Ruby is longing to talk, and it all comes tumbling out.

'When this thing happened,' Ruby says, 'I was in a newspaper office placing an ad for my business. When I heard about the assassination, I canceled my ad and closed my business and have not done any business for the last three days. I have been grieving about this thing. On

---

[1] O'Neal's Funeral Home industriously operated both ambulances and hearses. They took assassinated Officer J.D. Tippit to Methodist Hospital, then to Parkland for autopsy, supplied the casket for President Kennedy, then their hearse carried him to Love Field, and now they pick up Oswald.

Friday night, I went to the synagogue and heard a eulogy on the president. I thought very highly of him.'

Tears come to Ruby's eyes. ... 'When I saw that Mrs. Kennedy was going to have to appear for a trial, I thought to myself, why should she have to go through this ordeal for this no good son of a bitch. ... I had been to the Western Union office to send a telegram. I guess I had worked myself into a state of insanity to where I had to do it. I was afraid he might not get his just punishment. Sometimes they don't, you know?'

Jack looks up at Sorrels.

'I guess I just had to show the world that a Jew has guts,' he says." [2230]

Ruby had the same immediate distaste for Oswald as did many Americans, including this author who watched TV from Friday afternoon to Monday night: "'To me,' [Jack Ruby] says, 'he had this smirky, smug, vindictive attitude. I can't explain what impression he gave me, but that is all I can . . . well, I just lost my senses.' ... He said that when Oswald killed Kennedy, 'something in my insides tore out.'" [2231]

On Monday, the day of funerals, Fritz takes matters into his own hands, very quietly ordering detectives to take Ruby down on the jail elevator used by Oswald, to arrive in the basement at a specific time. When Fritz drives in, a door is opened, Ruby dashes into the car and lies on the back floor, on his stomach. With no fuss, he is soon safe in the county jail. [2232]

Chief Justice Earl Warren and Representative Gerald R. Ford, a commission member who would become president ten years later, thought it sufficiently important to understand Jack Ruby that they went to Dallas and spent a Sunday afternoon in the interrogation room of the Dallas County Jail at Main and Houston Streets, right there on Dealey Plaza. [2233] For three hours they and commission counsel questioned Ruby, who expressed concern about their delay in coming to him. Warren said the delay was his decision, so as not to influence Ruby's trial for murder — so here they were, shortly after the trial ended.

They all got along well. At one point Ruby could not read a document. The transcript in one of the twenty-six Commission volumes says Warren offered: "If you need glasses again, try mine this time (handing glasses to Mr. Ruby). Mr. Ruby (putting on glasses). 'This is the girl...'" [2234] "Why did he kill Oswald? Ford asked. Ruby replied, according to Ford's notes, that 'he had no thought of killing Oswald until' he read a Dallas newspaper story pointing out 'that Mrs. Kennedy would have to come back to Dallas to testify at the Oswald trial.' [2235] His purpose, Ruby told Warren and Ford, was to spare Jacqueline Kennedy that burden." [2236]

Some suggest Ruby must have planned the shooting in advance, evidenced because he took his revolver downtown with him that Sunday morning. The commission wanted to know:

"Mr. RANKIN. Did you have this gun a long while that you did the shooting with?

Mr. RUBY. Yes.

Mr. RANKIN. You didn't carry it all the time?

Mr. RUBY. I did. I had it in a little bag with money constantly. I carry my money." [2237]

Warren and Ford then inspected the scene of the assassination for about two hours, including some time looking out of Oswald's window perch. [2238]

Jack Ruby's story will end quickly. He had a perfectly suitable Dallas attorney, but hired nationally famous lawyer Melvin Belli to handle his defense. Sergeant Gerald L. Hill of the Dallas police department's Patrol Division, a lifelong resident of Dallas and Fort Worth, told in his oral history of the collision of worlds resulting from that choice:

"His worst mistake, I think, was the lawyer he hired. Melvin Belli was too much for the Texas courts at that time. He was too flamboyant, too wild! He made statements which angered the jury. They couldn't get him, so they got his client and found him guilty. If he would have stayed with his original attorney, Tom Howard, I think probably public sentiment would have played a big factor in getting him off with a lighter sentence. Belli was only interested in writing a book and making money off the deal." [2239]

The two-week trial for murder went to a jury on March 14, 1964. "After about ten minutes ... they decided that Ruby was sane; after another fifteen minutes that he was guilty of murder with malice; and after a few more minutes of discussion that the verdict was death. The principal circumstance influencing their judgment, apparently, was that Ruby killed a manacled, defenseless man." [2240] An appeal granted him a new trial on the grounds that his statements to Dallas policemen immediately after the shooting should not have been allowed, and that the original court should have granted a change of venue to another jurisdiction since a fair trial was all but impossible in Dallas. In the end, it won't matter ...

Jack Ruby complained of a stomach pain for months, but Dallas jail physicians did not consider his condition serious, so treated him with Pepto-Bismol.[2241] When it became obvious Ruby was deathly ill, he was moved to Parkland Memorial Hospital, where Marina had given birth to Rachel, where Kennedy and Oswald had been certified dead, and where Connally was saved. Doctors found cancer in his liver, lungs and brain. Jack Ruby died on January 3, 1967.[2242] Dr. Earl Rose, who had tried to block removal of the body of President Kennedy in 1963 until after he had performed an autopsy,[2243] autopsied Ruby, ruling that he died of a blood clot that broke free from a leg and moved into the lungs.[2244]

Ruby family attorney Alan Adelson, in his personal memoir *The Ruby-Oswald Affair,* tells of Jack's funeral in Chicago: The rabbi, "who had known Jack, asked us to pray for the repose of his soul. 'The eyes of the world are upon us now. Jack Ruby linked himself with one of the most tragic moments in American history. He acted as a patriot, but as a misguided patriot-avenger. He would be called in scriptural idiom 'an avenger of blood' who, while his heart is hot, pursues a manslayer and overtakes him.'" [2245]

Robert Oswald related a grotesquely typical story about his own mother, Marguerite: "I learned many years ago that my mother can see conspiracies in ordinary everyday activities. Since Lee's defection, she has detected countless mysterious actions by friends, members of her family, investigators, and high officials of the U. S. Government. She was convinced just after Jack Ruby's death that Ruby was not dead. False reports about his illness were circulated deliberately, she told me, to give the government an excuse to remove him from jail. Then he was taken to a hospital, and false reports about his decline and death were issued. Another man's body was buried in Ruby's grave, she said, and Ruby himself was then freed to carry out his next assignment—perhaps another assassination." [2246]

Hugh Aynesworth, reporter for *The Dallas Morning News*, in his oral history of the assassination in *No More Silence* nicely sums up Jack Ruby's opportunity: "[H]ad it been a conspiracy, Ruby would not have slept till after 10:00 o'clock when he got a call from Little Lynn in Fort Worth. He told her, 'All right, I'll eat breakfast then go down and send you a Western Union money order,' and he did. He went down, left his dog in the car in the parking lot, and sent her the money order stamped at 11:17, went out onto Main Street and saw the crowd gathered around the ramp entrance. This was when they were pushing back the crowd to allow a police car out the Main Street ramp. He saw the crowd and obviously knew what it was about. So why did he have the gun? He always carried a gun. At that time, there was sort of an unwritten rule with the police: If you were a businessman and you carried money, you could carry a pistol." [2247]

Summarizing is simple: Shooting Oswald was the finale of a sequence of small events, each trivial but each essential. His sister Eva moved to Dallas and asked Jack to come from Chicago to help. Years later, a partner insisted he convert a private club into a striptease joint, for which Jack handed out 'passes' and did other favors for police. One of his strippers needed money to eat and pay her rent. The Western Union office, which happened to be very close to Dallas Police HQ, already had a customer on a Sunday morning. Jack was delayed, but not in any hurry. He loved crowds, saw one, walked over to see what was going on. Oswald decided to put on a sweater. A policeman backed a car up a ramp and out into the street, requiring aid from the on-guard officer to avoid a traffic accident. Without sister Eva, the partner, police acquaintances, Little Lynn, a postal inspector, the sweater choice and a backing-up car, Oswald might be alive today, almost a year younger than this author.

We should take Jack Ruby at face value — no pre-plan, no conspiracy. He did a great disservice by killing Oswald before we could understand him, for then there would be no need for this book to show that Lee Oswald acted alone and killed for his own demented reason, then Jack Ruby acted alone and killed for his own altruistic reason.

The story of Jack Ruby now concludes with a little table of major facts. There will be seventeen tables in this format in the next chapter, at the end of which will be two more about Oswald doing his shooting, after which some fact-based conclusions will be drawn.

1963: Jack Ruby shoots and kills Lee Harvey Oswald	
Weapon:	Pistol: .38-caliber (.38" diameter bullet) Colt Cobra revolver
Distance:	15 inches from left-front of Oswald's abdomen [2248]
Shots fired:	One
Killed / Hit:	Oswald died quickly of massive vascular and abdominal injuries
Assassin then:	Immediately captured, convicted, sentenced to death, died of cancer
Motive(s):	Prevent Oswald from being tried for killing President Kennedy, which Ruby feared would require Jacqueline to return and testify
Do we know beyond reasonable doubt, **whom** did the assassin intend to shoot? **Yes**	
Do we know beyond reasonable doubt, his **motive** for shooting the man he hit? **Yes**	

That's it. Yes, Oswald did it. No, there was no conspiracy. Jack Ruby just happened upon Oswald and seized his opportunity to be a mensch. A nut killed another nut. I consider those facts proven. It is time to end this chapter on whether Oswald did it, alone. On that Friday in Dallas, the total number of people trying to assassinate President Kennedy was exactly zero — and that total includes Lee Oswald! To substantiate that assertion beyond reasonable doubt, this book will soon move to its central subject — what was he trying to do?

> Key point of this chapter:
> **Lee Oswald, alone, wounded Connally and killed Kennedy.**
> **Jack Ruby, alone, on windfall opportunity, killed Oswald.**

PRESIDENTS, NOT PRECEDENTS

Other assassinations and attempts shed little light on Oswald

> "Many people in this country believe in the conspiracy theory because they are of the opinion that a crime of this magnitude could not be committed by one disoriented man. They look for an Alfred Hitchcock or Perry Mason mystery in every crime. But they overlook the history of American presidential assassinations."
>
> — **Earl Warren** [2249]

CHAPTER 18 – CONNALLY WILL RIDE begins "This is the shortest chapter in the book", then in only four pages it offers compelling evidence of Oswald's intent. That being said there, it is only fair to tell you now that this is the longest chapter, and its facts are less conclusive than those in that short chapter. You may well choose to read these two introductory pages, then skip to the two-page summary at the end, then decide if you want to know the highly interesting but non-essential histories on the 82 full pages between.

To analyze Oswald and his crime, it may be useful to sharpen our ability to understand by first looking briefly at the relevant history, just as a physician or scientist or writer begins her/his study by learning what's already known. A medical student, for example, is not required to discover on her/his own that blood circulates in the body, taught early in medical school based on William Harvey's 1628 demonstration after he revisited the discovery made by Arabian physician Ibn al-Nafis in 1242.[2250] In astronomy, engineering, law, medicine, humanities — all the arts and sciences — we stand on the shoulders of those who went before.

The history of American presidential assassinations [A] is distressingly long. At this writing, Barack Obama is president #44, the 43rd to hold the office. That disjoint is because Grover Cleveland served two non-consecutive terms,[2251] so is counted as two presidents, both #22 and #24. No president has died by accident, battle, strangulation, poison or whatever.

[A] "**assassinate** *tr.v.* To murder (a prominent person) by surprise attack, as for political reasons." – *The American Heritage College Dictionary*. The victim need not be in high office; murder is assassination when it is done because of the target's occupation or position. If you kill Julius because he kicked your cat, it's murder. If you kill him because he's Caesar, it's assassination.

But a full one-fourth of our presidents have been shot or shot-at. Starting with Lincoln, it's one of every three.[2252]

There have been four successful plus seven attempted assassinations of presidents. The four killed were Lincoln, Garfield, McKinley and Kennedy. Unsuccessful attempts were made on Jackson, Truman, (ex-president) Theodore Roosevelt, (president-elect) Franklin Roosevelt, Ford (twice), and Reagan. So far as we know, no president was assaulted for himself (per the footnote on the previous page); all were targeted because they were president.

In all but one of those eleven actions, assassins either proclaimed a reason or it was easy to discover; war opponent, enemy of the people, nationalism, fame, stalking a movie star, etc. In all but one case, we quickly and unquestionably learned the motive for the act. The one exception is the murder of John Kennedy.[2253] The point of this chapter is that the murder of JFK is singular. Of all the villains, only Lee Oswald did not have any known or realistically probable motive. And, as will be shown, we cannot reason backward from the result to his intent, because he was unique in pointing a rifle at long range at a moving target.

Studying the history of stock prices does not confer the ability to predict stock futures; knowing everything about all assassinations and attempts is no guarantee of understanding any one of them. But, as with the stock market, knowing history allows us a better ability to view any one stock in context, so similarities and differences may be highlighted and contrasted.

The history below is long enough without including many attacks that do not appear to be sincere efforts. For example, I discount a 1994 attempt to crash a small plane into Bill Clinton's White House because it's not certain what the pilot meant to do. Similar is the 2011 case of Oscar Ramiro Ortega-Hernandez, an Idahodian.[B] He drove along The Ellipse, past the south fence far from the White House, aimed an assault rifle out his Honda's passenger-side window and fired nicks into the south face of the residence while President and Mrs. Obama were in California. Such anomalies occur with some regularity, but are not included with the more serious and deliberate attacks below.

It was essential to include here the shooting of Martin Luther King, at a distance with a rifle, to compare to Oswald's similar action. So, I also include an earlier attempt to kill King, and the assassinations of Medgar Evers and Bobby Kennedy, then also the attempt on candidate George Wallace; but this chapter will not describe acts less comparable to Oswald's, such as the assaults on John Lennon, American Nazi George Lincoln Rockwell and Malcolm X.

Finally, this note of appreciation as we delve into the history of assassins in the United States: The author of this book considers himself to be an informed expert on one attempt — the shooting done by Lee Oswald. I am not a credentialed professor of American history, nor of the many attempts to kill its leaders. To give needed authority to much of this chapter, I lean heavily upon, and quote extensively from, a highly competent and well-researched book: *American Assassins: The Darker Side of Politics* by James W. Clarke. I am indebted for his extensive research, for citations of the authorities on whom he depends, and for his skill in telling his stories fully but tersely. His work allows improved understanding and comparing. If you would know more about any of what follows, I highly recommend his book.

[B] My late much-loved much-missed daughter Lynn coined this aptonym for residents of the Gem State.

1835: Richard Lawrence attempts to fire pistols at Andrew Jackson

The first six presidents of the United States were aristocrats of the landed gentry. Washington, Adams, Jefferson, Madison, Monroe and another Adams had land, money and education. In the parlance of the Twenty Tens,[C] they were of the 1%. The seventh president was one of the 99%; different in his roots, parents, poverty, outlook and politics.

Andrew and Betty Jackson, poor in Ireland, immigrated into South Carolina in 1765. To farm 200 acres, Andrew had to remove many trees. In the spring of 1767, trying to move a log too heavy for one man, he strained, collapsed and died that night. A few days later, widowed Betty Jackson gave birth to a son and named him for his father, Andrew.[D] [2254] The Revolutionary War took the boy's entire family. One brother died in battle, the other of smallpox while imprisoned, and finally mother Betty from cholera, contracted as she tended American soldiers on British prison ships.

Jackson became a lawyer in western North Carolina, which extended to the Mississippi River. When the west split off to become Tennessee, he was its first congressman, then a senator, then a judge and major-general in the state militia.[2255] He attempted to retire to The Hermitage, his plantation near Nashville, but hostilities with Britain made him a general in the U.S. Army.

Jackson earned national fame by defeating the British in the last engagement of the War of 1812, the Battle of New Orleans on January 8, 1815 — fought two weeks after the war ended. In Europe, representatives of the United States and Great Britain had agreed to peace on December 24, 1814, but news could only travel on sailing ships blown across the Atlantic Ocean.[E] [2256]

When the war ended, Jackson pivoted and led his troops against Indian tribes in the South and West, then he moved against both the Seminoles and the Spanish, and conquered Florida for the United States.[2257] The Tennessee legislature in 1822 unanimously adopted a resolution recommending to the people of the United States that they elect Jackson president.[2258]

Leading candidates for president in 1824 were John Quincy Adams, Henry Clay, William Crawford, and Andrew Jackson. Jackson received the largest vote, 43 percent,[2259] but with none having a majority, the U.S. House of Representatives, ruled by Speaker Clay, chose Adams, who then named Clay secretary of state. Outraged, Jackson set to work to create a new party, the Democrats. In 1828 he defeated Adams' re-election bid. Inaugurated in 1829, "Old Hickory"[2260] invited the ordinary people to come into the White House and celebrate.

[C] The years 2010 through 2019.

[D] He would have been "Andrew, Jr." if his father were still alive. Properly, grandfather Ignatz and father Ignatz, Jr. must be alive for a baby to be named Ignatz III. Kings, queens and ships are different, known as Henry VIII and "Queen Elizabeth II" because a few names are used repeatedly.

[E] A similar delay featured in one of Horatio Hornblower's exploits. He lied to a French enemy that Napoleon had died, suffered great remorse for months, then learned it had been true all the while.

"On the cold, gray Friday of January 30, 1835, Richard Lawrence, armed with two pistols, attempted to take the life of President Andrew Jackson. Standing on the east portico of the Capitol, Lawrence calmly waited for Jackson to emerge ... As the elderly and frail Jackson ... walked from the rotunda, Lawrence stepped from the crowd" [2261] "and from a distance of less than ten feet leveled a pistol at the president's heart and fired. The percussion cap exploded but failed to ignite the powder in the barrel. 'The explosion of the cap was so loud that many persons thought the pistol had fired,' [Senator] Thomas [Hart] Benton remembered. 'I heard it at the foot of the steps, far from the place, and a great crowd between.' The sound startled all present and froze them in their

steps. The assailant took advantage of the collective pause to raise a second pistol, aim, and squeeze the trigger. Again the cap fired, but again it failed to ignite the powder." [2262] [2263]

"Jackson by this time realized he was under mortal attack, and he charged the man with his cane. Yet others moved more quickly, and a knot of angry cabinet secretaries, military officers, and bystanders collapsed upon the man [who was then] carried away to police custody." [2264]

Jackson lived because two percussion caps failed to ignite powder, probably because of dampness.[2265] "In the course of the investigation the police tested the pistols Lawrence had aimed at the president. Each time now, the weapons fired perfectly. 'The circumstance made a deep impression upon the public feeling,' [Senator] Benton explained, 'and irresistibly carried many minds to the belief in a superintending Providence, manifested in the extraordinary case of two pistols in succession—so well loaded" [2266] "with fine glazed duelling powder and ball" [2267], "so coolly handled, and which afterwards fired with such readiness, force, and precision—missing fire, each in its turn, when levelled from eight feet at the President's heart.'" [2268] "An expert on small arms calculated that the chance of two successive misfires was one in one hundred and twenty-five thousand." [2269]

The would-be assassin, "Richard Lawrence was born in England—the date remains uncertain but probably in 1800 or 1801—and came to this country with his parents when he was about twelve years of age. The family settled in the Washington area, and Lawrence seems to have lived an uneventful and normal life as a house painter until November 1832 when he abruptly announced he was returning to England. Until that time, Richard was typically described by the relatives and acquaintances who testified at his trial as 'a remarkably fine boy . . . reserved in his manner; but industrious and of good moral habits.'" [2270]

"After a month's absence, Lawrence returned to Washington ... explaining that he had decided against the trip to England because the weather was too cold. His brother-in-law ... testified that soon after, Lawrence left once again with the intention of going to England to study landscape painting. But soon after his arrival in Philadelphia, he returned a second time, explaining that 'people' prevented him from going on to England. He added that the government also opposed his going. He complained that when he arrived in Philadelphia, he found the newspapers so full of attacks on his character and plans that he had no choice but to return to Washington until he could hire his own ship and captain for the trip." [2271]

"These incidents mark most clearly the first symptoms of Lawrence's advancing mental deterioration. At this point, he gave up his job and first expressed the delusion that was to lead to his attack on President Jackson. He explained to his perplexed sister and her husband, with whom he was living, that he had no need to work because he had large financial claims on the federal government that were now before Congress. The claims were based on his belief that he was in fact King Richard III of England [F] and, as royalty, the owner of two English estates, Tregear and Kennany that were attached to the crown." [2272]

"In this deluded state, Lawrence believed President Jackson's opposition to the establishment of a national bank would prevent him from receiving a just settlement for his claims. He reasoned that with Jackson gone, the vice-president would certainly recognize the logic of his case and permit Congress to make the proper remuneration through the national bank so that he could go on to England to settle the claim.

"While this seemed to be his primary delusion, there were also other symptoms of his worsening mental state.[2273] During the same period, Lawrence, the sober, reliable, and moral young man, suddenly became enamored with fashion. Cultivating a moustache and changing from one extravagant recently purchased costume to another three or four times a day, he would then stand mute in the doorway of his residence for hours, presumably to permit passers-by to gaze upon his sartorial splendor. Neighborhood children picked up on the fancy and addressed him as 'King Richard.' Lawrence was pleased.

"It was also at this time that he first expressed a keen and unbridled, so to speak, interest in the opposite sex. The owner of a livery stable testified that Lawrence, dressed in decidedly uncharacteristic clothing, would regularly hire two horses, one for himself and another with side-saddle for a young woman of 'loose character' with whom he would regally parade the Washington thoroughfares." [2274]

"In addition to such delusions of grandeur, the paranoia that had gripped Lawrence's senses became manifest during this period. Witnesses testified that this pleasant, mild-mannered young man suddenly became extremely suspicious and hostile. On one occasion, he threatened to kill a black maid because he claimed she was laughing at him; on another, he seized his sister by the shoulders threatening to strike her with a paperweight because he thought she had been talking about him. He was said to have struck his other sisters on numerous occasions during this period. In each instance, his conduct represented a radical departure from previous patterns of behavior. And in each, also, he acted on the basis of imagined grievances." [2275]

"Doctors and other witnesses testified to marked changes in Lawrence's physical appearance in the two years preceding his attack on the President. The effects of such changes were apparent during his trial. Dressed in a gray shooting coat, black cravat, vest, and brown pantaloons, his eyes reflected a certain strangeness as he made odd gestures or sat motionless with the demeanor of royalty. Others testified to his periodic fits of laughter and cursing, his incoherent conversations with himself, a peculiar gait that would suddenly manifest itself, and his insensitivity to cold while confined in his damp jail cell— all symptoms of severe mental impairment." [2276]

[F] Whose skeleton was found under space "R" in a car park in Leicester as this was being edited. The author had walked past that spot almost daily for two years while working for IBM in Leicester.

"At one point during the trial he rose and 'addressed himself wildly' to the court. Ranting that the United States had owed him money since 1802 when he claimed his property had been confiscated, Lawrence, suddenly calm, announced with regal contempt, 'You are under me, gentlemen.' When a deputy marshal tried to seat him, an indignant Lawrence said, 'Mr. Woodward, mind your own business or I shall treat you with severity.' Then turning slowly back to the court with head held high, he intoned with authoritative solemnity, 'It is for me, gentlemen, to pass upon you, and not you upon me.' ... then suddenly with great aplomb he sat down, seemingly lost in thought." [2277]

"In the weeks preceding his attack on the President, he would sit in his paint shop talking to himself: 'Damn him, he does not know his enemy; I will put a pistol. . . . Erect a gallows. . . . Damn General Jackson!' ... Then on the morning of the day he attacked Jackson, he was seen sitting ... in his shop, holding a book and laughing aloud to himself. Suddenly he dropped the book and left the shop chuckling, 'I'll be damned if I don't do it.'" [2278]

"Underscoring the overwhelming evidence of what would today undoubtedly be diagnosed as paranoid schizophrenia, Lawrence's family history revealed a persistent pattern of 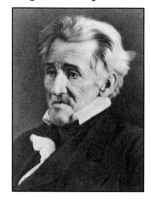 mental illness. According to testimony, Lawrence's father had been institutionalized for mental problems and an aunt had died insane.[2279] The combined evidence, bolstered by the defendant's bizarre courtroom behavior, was enough to convince the jury and even the prosecutor, our national anthem's composer Francis Scott Key, that Lawrence could not be held criminally responsible for the crime. He was subsequently acquitted, [but] to be confined in mental hospitals for the rest of his life. He died on June 13, 1861 in the Government Hospital for the Insane in Washington." [2280] [G] I have not been able to find either photo or portrait of Richard Lawrence. Here is a photo of old Andrew Jackson,[2281] who died in 1845 at The Hermitage, age 78.

"There can be little doubt that the malady which clouded Richard Lawrence's mind with the delusions, suspicions, and hostility that motivated his attempt to kill the President was genetic in origin and only circumstantially related to events of the time in the most tenuous manner." [2282] "Lawrence worked as a painter and there is speculation that exposure to the chemicals in his paints may have contributed to his derangement." [2283]

1835: Richard Lawrence attempts to fire pistols at Andrew Jackson	
Weapons:	Two cap-and-ball pistols
Distance:	8 to 10 feet
Shots fired:	One attempt with each pistol, but only the caps exploded, noisily.
Killed / Hit:	None — no projectiles were actually fired.
Assassin then:	Was captured, jailed, tried, determined to be insane, confined in mental hospitals the rest of his life.
Motive(s):	He was insane: paranoid schizophrenia.
Do we know beyond reasonable doubt, **whom** did the assassin intend to shoot? **Yes**	
Do we know beyond reasonable doubt, his **motive** for shooting the man he hit? **Yes**	

[G] Now St. Elizabeth's Hospital, longtime residence of John Hinckley, the attempted assassin who shot Ronald Reagan, whose story will be the last told of this chapter.

1865: John Wilkes Booth shoots and kills Abraham Lincoln

Abraham Lincoln's election precipitated the Civil War, then the war took his life. The election of 1860 proved the North's intentions. South Carolina left the Union before Christmas. Seven states seceded before Lincoln was inaugurated on March 4, 1861. Lincoln upheld the outgoing administration's decision to defend a fort in the harbor of Charleston, South Carolina. When Confederate forces fired on Fort Sumter, Lincoln declared a state of insurrection and called out Union troops on April 15. He will die on that date four years later. ^{H 2284}

With twice the population and industry to produce war materiel, the Union inexorably prevailed. As the war ground toward its end over 260,000 bodies,[2285] the South simply ran out of soldiers. Of 2.9 million Union enlistments, 110 thousand were killed and 211 thousand captured,[2286] leaving over 2.5 million — some of them wounded, but most able to fight. The Confederacy had about 1.3 million enlistees, of whom 94 thousand died and 462 thousand were captured, leaving only 750 thousand to fight three times as many Yankees.[I] The South's plight worsened when "Commanding General Ulysses S. Grant ended all prisoner exchanges of any kind ... because he realized that the exchanges of POWs helped ameliorate the manpower shortage in the South but did little or nothing for the Northern war effort." [2287] The Confederacy, out of men, desperately needed to force prisoner exchanges.

A 26-year-old Southerner temporarily in Washington, one of a famous family of actors, now took the stage. "It is likely that John Wilkes Booth first decided to dispose of Abraham Lincoln the day after the presidential election of 1864. The actor despised the President before that ... a passionate and violent hatred of the self-feeding type. Lincoln had to do no more than breathe to cause John Wilkes Booth to loathe him the more each day." [2288] "Lincoln's victory marked the end of any Confederate hopes for survival. ... By holding firm on the promise of emancipation and by winning an election on those grounds, Lincoln thereby guaranteed the war would end with the restoration of a Union freed from slavery." [2289] "Booth decided [to assist] the Confederacy. He would kidnap the President [to] force the North to exchange prisoners ... something the man-rich North refused to do for the man-poor South." [2290]

Booth recruited five friends to his cause. They were to be repeatedly frustrated. The conspirators detailed a plan to kidnap Lincoln from his box in Ford's Theatre on January 18, 1865, by extinguishing every light in the theater, then Booth would "lower the President over the façade of the box eleven feet to the stage, then lower himself to the stage ... [and] hustle the President offstage, out the rear door, where a covered wagon would be waiting in the alley" [2291] to convey Lincoln through Union Army battle lines and into Richmond! Sadly for

---

[H] Lincoln "is how he looked on Palm Sunday, 1865, the day General Robert E. Lee surrendered at Appomattox." (Caption from Bak, Richard. *The Day Lincoln Was Shot: An Illustrated Chronicle*) 2.

[I] "[D]eaths in Confederate prisons totaled ... a little more than 15 percent of those incarcerated. In Federal prisons ... slightly more than 12 percent. ... In comparison, those who remained on the battlefield fared much better; ... only 5 percent of the total enlistments ... were killed." (Speer xiv)

the na ve plotters, they were ready, but the President did not attend the theater that night. Thus ended the first plan, notable only for being the first-ever conspiracy against a President.

"In early February ... Booth enlisted ... Lewis Paine" [2292] to "lie in wait in the bushes at the front of the White House lawn any evening and shoot [Lincoln] as he returns from his last daily visit to the War Department. ... This is the first time on record that the thoughts of John Wilkes Booth turned from capture to kill. The soldier waited in the bushes one night and [later] told Booth that he had lost his nerve [although] he had been close enough to have strangled the President ...." [2293] Thus Booth's second plot against Lincoln ended in nothing.

At Lincoln's second inaugural on March 4 on the new west front of the Capitol, "Behind him ... were various officials and spectators. Up behind the railing of the right

buttress, looking down at the President, was the actor John Wilkes Booth,[2294] a dashing man with raven hair and a black mustache, wearing a fashionable stovepipe hat. Lincoln had seen Booth perform ... at Ford's Theater ... a week before Lincoln spoke at Gettysburg." [2295] "Booth later said, half regretfully, 'What an excellent chance I had to kill the President if I had wished, on inauguration day.'" [2296]

Lincoln held out his hand to the South "With malice toward none" while promising their defeat, "let us strive on to finish the work we are in." [2297] "To Booth, time was running out for the Confederacy. Whatever was going to be done would have to be done quickly." [2298] On March 17 the conspirators planned to capture Lincoln as he was driven to the Soldiers' Home.[2299] The kidnapping location, lonely country then, is today a busy part of Washington, near Howard University Hospital. The band waited to ambush Lincoln's carriage. "But ... the intended victim failed to put in an appearance. ... [H]e sent one of his Cabinet officials to represent him. ... When they saw not Lincoln but a stranger ... they were ... confident their plans had been discovered." [2300] There was less to it than met their eyes. "[W]hile Booth and his band waited ... the President was standing on the front steps of Booth's hotel, the National," [2301] receiving a captured rebel banner from an Indiana regiment. Thus plot three came to naught.

Booth tried again when "A notice appeared ... saying that the President and his family had reserved boxes at Ford's Theatre for [a March 29] performance of the Italian opera *Ernani*." [2302] He summoned the conspirators, but all begged off. Booth seethed and waited, resolutely hoping to capture. "Dead, the President was useless for barter. Alive, the chief conspirator reasoned, it would surely mean the release by exchange of the Confederate prisoners and possibly the recognition of the Confederacy itself, and, per consequence, the end of the war, not to mention great glory for John Wilkes Booth." [2303]

The South's capital, Richmond, fell to the Union on April 3. Confederate General Robert Edward Lee [J] surrendered to Union General Ulysses Simpson Grant on April 9. Mopping up operations would continue to the end of April, but the war was effectively over. Grant traveled to Washington, where newspapers announced that he and Mrs. Grant would be guests of the Lincolns at a Ford's Theatre performance of the comedy *Our American Cousin* on

---

[J] 74½ years later, Marguerite Oswald would name her third son "Lee" after his deceased father, Robert Edward Lee Oswald, himself named for the General, as was then popular in the South.

Good Friday, April 14. With an opportunity to strike down both the President and his General, Booth decided to act. Both John Wilkes Booth and Mary Todd Lincoln were greatly disappointed that afternoon to learn that General and Mrs. Grant (to avoid much-disliked Mary) left town and would not join the Lincolns at the theater.

With no Southern capital to receive captives, Booth decided to decapitate the North. At a final meeting, the conspirators received assignments, all to act simultaneously at 10:15 PM. Booth, alone at Ford's, would shoot Lincoln. Another would assassinate Vice President Andrew Johnson in his hotel room. Two others would go "to Seward's home and … dispatch the Secretary of State" [2304] "(who would become President in the event of the death of a succeeding Vice-President)…" [2305] The three top men of government would die the same night.

"George A. Atzerodt, a German carriage painter" [2306] walked "to kill the Vice President but his feet carried him into [a] bar and he drank and looked at the clock and drank some more." [2307] "The would-be assassin instead wander[ed] out into the streets and spen[t] this night of mayhem and murder in a local tavern, nursing his nerves and getting drunk." [2308] He "set off … to the house of his cousin [in] Maryland. He lived there quietly for five days working in the garden, but on [April 20] an informer led the soldiers to him." [2309]

Paine and David Herold rode to the house where Secretary of State William H. Seward lay in bed, his neck in a double iron brace because of a carriage accident.[2310] While Herold held the horses, Paine forced his way into the house. Stopped by Seward's son, he aimed his pistol but the gun jammed. Paine savagely smashed the son's head and neck, leaving him near death. He found the elder Seward, "so he jumped on the bed and, when he felt the helpless figure beneath him, he struck with his knife again and again." [2311] Seward's servant, William Bell, shadowed Paine from the moment he entered the house, and now chased him into the street. Herold, hearing the commotion, had deserted, galloping across the bridge to Maryland. Paine found his own horse, but without Herold to guide him, became lost in the East Capitol section. On April 17, officers "arrived at Mrs. Surratt's house to arrest her [K] … Just as they were about to go out of the door and into carriages, from the dark shadows outside stepped Paine, very dirty … He had [come] because he was desperately hungry by then, and tired—he had spent most of the hours since his attack [on Seward] hiding up in a cedar tree." [2312]

Subplots concluded, we return to the star. Booth loaded his pocket weapon,[2313] a "Deringer Percussion Pistol" [2314] commonly called a "derringer", with a wrong double "r". The six-inch-long weapon held only one .44" lead ball, but Booth had reason to be confident that would do. In a shooting gallery earlier that month, witnesses saw him expertly fire a pistol with one hand, then the other, over each shoulder, and under each arm. Every shot hit the target.[2315] "The actor loaded it carefully, and placed a percussion cap under the hammer. The derringer was ready." [2316]

The deed was described by historian Stefan Lorant: "On April 14, 1865, the actor John Wilkes Booth shot the President while Lincoln was seeing the comedy *Our American Cousin*, in Washington's Ford's Theatre. After his deed Booth leaped to the stage shouting" [2317] "Sic Semper Tyrannis" [Thus Always to Tyrants], the State motto of his home, Virginia. "When

---

[K] Her ambiguous but continual involvement — or innocence — is best told, I judge, in two books: *Murdering Mr. Lincoln* by Charles Higham and *The Assassin's Accomplice* by Kate Clifford Larson.

Virginia chose this motto ... England was that tyrant." [2318] Booth's family had regularly acted Shakespeare's Romans, so he was comfortable shouting Latin and changing the target tyrant from George III to Lincoln. "As he jumped, he caught the spur of his boot in the flag, fell and broke his leg. Also in the box are Major Henry Rathbone and his fiancée, Clara Harris...." [2319] instead of the Grants. Like Oswald's rifle in 98 years, Booth's pistol was found nearby about an hour after the shooting, on the floor of Lincoln's box. [2320]   [2321]

"Charles Leale, a young [Army] doctor ... was the first to respond. 'When I reached the President ... he was almost dead' ... Another doctor ... soon arrived, and the decision was made to remove the president from the crowded box" [2322] "to the nearest bed. Across the street, a young boarder directed that he be brought into the house of William Petersen, a German tailor who was his landlord. With blood and brain matter seeping out his wound and half his clothes cut off ... Lincoln was carried into a small bedroom ... It turned out that his six-foot, four-inch frame was too long for the bed. ... Dr. Leale directed that his body be placed diagonally ... That is how Lincoln spent the last nine hours of his life, his large, bare feet sticking out by the wall, his swelling, discolored, bleeding head propped up on two large pillows." [2323] "His devastating wound, the doctors reported with awe, 'would have killed most men instantly, or in a very few minutes. But Mr. Lincoln ... continued to struggle against the inevitable end." [2324] "At 7:22 in the morning of April 15, 1865, Lincoln breathed his last." [2325]

Booth had escaped on a horse. In Maryland he met Herold who had abandoned Paine at Seward's house. The two rode south to a farm near Bowling Green, where they were discovered by a troop of Union soldiers on the twelfth day of their flight. "Davey [Herold]

had no more fight left in him. ... [He] convinced himself, naively, that once he talked his way out of trouble the soldiers would send him home. After all, in his mind, he wasn't guilty of anything. Booth killed Lincoln, and Powell stabbed Seward. Davey just came along for the ride" [2326] so he surrendered. "Booth took his last refuge in a barn. Soldiers who found his hiding place set fire to the barn [2327] and one of them shot him" [2328] "curiously enough through his skull at almost the same spot where his own had crashed into Lincoln's head ..." [2329] or he shot himself. [2330] His last words: "Tell my mother I died for my country and did what I thought was for the best." [2331] The popular *Frank Leslie's Illustrated Newspaper* reported in the journalistic style of the times: "There was nothing very grand in his exit ... Smoked out like a rat and shot like a dog!"

As Chapter 7 told what became of the principals of 1963, here's what became of those of 1865: Lincoln's funeral train crept toward Springfield, Illinois, "fourteen days crawling westward ... through the greatest crowds that

had ever assembled in Christendom".[2332] Secretary Seward suffered severe face and chest wounds but his neck brace saved him and he recovered.[2333] George Atzerodt, David Herold, Lewis Paine and Mary Surratt (who owned a boardinghouse where the conspirators met) were tried and hanged.[2334] Mary Todd Lincoln spent a year in a mental hospital, then died in seclusion. Tad Lincoln died of tuberculosis at the age of 18. Robert Lincoln served as Secretary of War to Presidents Garfield and Arthur, and was U.S. Minister to Great Britain.

He died in 1926.[L] We will meet him, twice again, later in this chapter.

Terribly sad was the future of the Lincolns' theater guests. Major Rathbone and Clara Harris married and had three children. Anguishing over his failure to protect the President, he became mentally ill and went mad. In 1894 he attacked the children, murdering Clara as she protected them. He spent his remaining years in an asylum, where he died in 1911.[2335]

The last line of the six facts in the summary below is for the assassin's motive. Booth's is easy enough to surmise, and was confessed in his pocket diary, where wrote of Lincoln: "Our country owed all our trouble to him, and God simply made me the instrument of his punishment."[2336] Booth had a well-documented history of hating the victim he shot at a distance of inches. As will be demonstrated, Oswald had no record of disliking Kennedy, but a record of hating Connally. He shot toward both of them, in line, moving away, at distances of 177 and 265 feet.[2337] Booth couldn't miss — and Oswald did!

1865: John Wilkes Booth shoots and kills Abraham Lincoln	
Weapon:	Deringer Percussion Pistol [2338] (frequently referred to and misspelled as "derringer"), able to fire a single .38" lead ball
Distance:	Pointblank — about six inches
Shots fired:	One
Killed / Hit:	The ball penetrated through Lincoln's brain. He died 9 hours later.
Assassin then:	Jumped down to Ford's Theatre's stage, breaking his ankle, cried out "Sic Semper Tyrannis", ran to a horse, rode to Maryland and hid in a barn. A Union soldier shot him to death 12 days later.
Motive(s):	Revenge and hatred of the leader who defeated his Confederacy
Do we know beyond reasonable doubt, **whom** did the assassin intend to shoot? **Yes**	
Do we know beyond reasonable doubt, his **motive** for shooting the man he hit? **Yes**	

[L] Abraham Lincoln had four children, but only Robert survived to adulthood. He had three children. Those three had, in total, three children (Lincoln's great-grandchildren), all of whom died between 1973 and 1985. But, none of them had children. Thus, President Lincoln's family tree has died out.

1881: Charles Guiteau shoots and wounds James Garfield, who dies of infection

James Abram Garfield's "pre-presidential bio can be crammed into the following respectable sentence: The last president born in a log cabin, Garfield grew up with his widowed mother in Ohio, eked his way through college, became a ... professor who moonlighted as a preacher, married his wife, Lucretia, in 1858, fathered five children, was a Union general in the Civil War, and served the people of Ohio in the House of Representatives from 1863 to 1880." [2339]

"In 1880, the Republican Party was sharply divided into two warring factions." [2340] The Stalwarts backed ex-President U. S. Grant for a then-allowed third term. "The *Nation* defined Stalwartism as an 'indifference or hostility to civil service-reform, and a willingness to let 'the boys' have a good time with the offices.'" [2341] Opposing the patronage-as-usual Stalwarts were reformers backing Senator James G. Blaine for president. Calling themselves Half-Breeds, they included Garfield, ex-President Hayes and a young New York State legislator, Theodore Roosevelt. The Republican convention of 1880 divided equally, deadlocked between the two.

On the 34th ballot, one delegate voted for Garfield,[2342] attending only to represent Ohio.

On the next ballot, 49 more swung to him. "As the clerk began calling the roll for the thirty-sixth ballot ... Garfield was 'in much apparent emotion.' He 'protested in utmost earnestness that he had nothing to do with the movement,' and 'said he would rather be shot to death by the inch than to have furnished any just ground for such suspicion.'" [2343] Garfield had "never agreed to become even a candidate—on the contrary, having vigorously resisted it—he was suddenly the nominee." [2344] "The thirty-six ballots of 1880 stand as a record, the most ever cast to choose a Republican nominee for president ..." [2345] "[N]o Republican convention has gone more than one ballot since they needed three to nominate Thomas E. Dewey ... in 1948; no Democratic convention has since 1952 when Adlai Stevenson was chosen on the third." [2346] Garfield "was attractive as a candidate for the precise reason he's a nondescript president—his bland composure." [2347]

He was inaugurated on March 4, 1881, with rising young man Theodore Roosevelt prominent at the front of the platform. A bow to the opposition would soon figure in Garfield's death — his party's (not his) choice for vice-president was a Stalwart, "former New York customs collector Chester Alan Arthur, the most infamous spoilsman of all ..." [2348] "During the campaign, there [was] some discussion about the fact that ... Arthur would be next in line to the presidency, but the possibility of something happening to Garfield [was] so remote as to be hardly worth considering. He was in the prime of his life, the picture of health and strength, and would be president during a time of peace. Arthur would be constrained by the limits of his office, where he could do little harm. 'There is no place in which the powers of mischief will be so small as in the Vice Presidency,' [an] editor of the *Nation* [wrote]." [2349] "The Garfield administration turned out to be the second shortest in American history (only William Henry Harrison's administration was shorter, lasting only one month)." [2350]

Office seekers like those who had vexed Lincoln twenty years earlier plagued Garfield. "On March 5, Garfield's first day at work, a line began to form before he even sat down to breakfast. By the time he finished, it snaked down the front walk, out the gate, and onto

Pennsylvania Avenue." [2351] One aggressive locust "dropped by the White House every day begging to be appointed ambassador to France" [2352] despite having no qualifications. "At five feet seven inches tall, with narrow shoulders, a small, sharp face, and a threadbare jacket, Charles Guiteau was an unremarkable figure. He had failed at everything he had tried, and he had tried nearly everything, from law to ministry to even a free-love commune. He had been thrown in jail. His wife had left him. His father believed him insane, and his family had tried to have him institutionalized. In his own mind, however, Guiteau was a man of great distinction and promise, and he predicted a glorious future for himself." [2353]

"Garfield's secretary, no doubt exasperated by the persistent kook Guiteau, had pawned off Guiteau on Secretary of State James G. Blaine, explaining to Guiteau that the French ambassadorship would be decided at the State Department ... Not that Blaine suffered Guiteau for long. On May 14, having had enough of the scruffy oddball who actually believed he deserved one of the cushiest appointments in the history of diplomacy, Blaine screamed at him, 'Never speak to me again on the Paris consulship as long as you live!' Guiteau fired off a letter to the White House describing Secretary Blaine as a 'wicked man'" [2354]

For four days, as he would tell a reporter, "Guiteau's mind churned over betrayals—not just his own rude rebuff from Secretary Blaine on the Paris consulship. He worried even more for those he imagined his friends, the Stalwarts, whom Blaine and Garfield likewise had betrayed and routed. ... Then he had an epiphany: 'the idea flashed through my brain,' he remembered, '[I]f the President was out of the way everything would go better." [2355]

"Guiteau had met the president and Mrs. Garfield face-to-face and had liked them both. His plan was nothing personal; it was a political necessity—like removing hostile Indians from the plains to make way for settlers and railroads or removing the Confederates from their lines during the war. ... He—Charles Guiteau—wanted only to save the Republican Party, prevent another civil war, and respond to the dictates of God. Once the shock wore off, people would applaud him. Arthur surely would give him a presidential pardon to save him from the hangman. He would surely be grateful, since Guiteau would have made him president in the first place. Guiteau saw it all clearly." [2356]

"Charles Guiteau didn't own a gun. ... [b]ut he figured he'd need one to remove the president." [2357] "He talked a relative into lending him $15 and went to John O'Meara's gun shop ... in Washington. Two pistols in the display case caught his eye: One, a snub-nosed five-shooter with an ivory handle, cost $10; a similar model with a wood handle cost only $9. He couldn't decide, so he left. Two days later, he came back, this time leaning toward the more expensive model. After all, he thought, this gun might end up in a museum ... or the Smithsonian—the fancier handle was well worth it. When  Guiteau hesitated, O'Meara offered him the pistol for $9. Guiteau agreed; he bought it ... and several boxes of cartridges. ... The gun was a .44 caliber five-shooter English Bulldog.[2358] 'I looked at it as if it was going to bite me,' he later said. O'Meara showed Guiteau how to load the cartridges into the pistol and suggested he go outside the city limits to try shooting." [2359]

"That evening ... Guiteau walked down Seventeenth Street to ... the muddy banks of the Potomac. Finding an isolated spot, he loaded the pistol and fired off two loads of cartridges ... ten bullets altogether ... 'just to get used to the outward act of handling the weapon.' He became comfortable with it ... It fit easily in his coat pocket. A few nights later he came back to the same spot ... and shot off two more loads of cartridges. Soon he started carrying the pistol on his vigils." [2360] In a bizarre preparation a week before the shooting, he inspected the prison where he would be taken. "Just looking in through the doors and halls, he decided that, as jails went, this one was 'excellent.'" [2361] "It is the best jail in America, I understand." [2362]

His target was easily available. "Garfield, unwilling to forfeit any more of his liberty than he had already lost to political enemies and office seekers, [wrote]: 'Assassination can no more be guarded against than death by lightning, and it is best not to worry about either.'" [2363] Garfield walked freely, frequently alone, through the streets of Washington.

Guiteau began to stalk Garfield, but passed up several opportunities to kill. At church he had a clear shot but the service included "'a very stupid sermon' ... Guiteau ... shouted out, 'What think ye of Christ?' Garfield heard Guiteau's outburst and mentioned it in his diary that night ..." [2364] Next, the railroad station, but Lucretia Garfield "looked so thin and she clung so tenderly to the President's arm that I did not have the heart to fire upon him." [2365] He again took his pistol to the station to meet the arriving president, "but decided that that 'terrible hot sultry day' wasn't the right time. The next morning [he went to] catch the president on his morning horse-back ride, but Garfield hadn't gone out that day. ... [That] evening ... Garfield [walked out] on foot ... 'I was several yards behind him ... a 'splendid chance' he remembered, the president being alone." [2366] While he hesitated, Garfield entered Secretary Blaine's home. When those two emerged, he followed, but "stayed hidden in the shadows until the two men had crossed the north lawn and disappeared back within the large front door of the White House." [2367]

Guiteau had already penned an *Address to the American People*, which he placed into his pocket where it would be found after the assassination:

"I conceived of the idea of removing the President four weeks ago. Not a soul knew my purpose. I conceived the idea myself. I read the newspapers carefully, for and against the administration, and gradually the conviction settled on me that the President's removal was a political necessity, because he proved a traitor to the men who made him, and thereby imperiled the life of the Republic. ... This is not murder. It is a political necessity. It will make my friend Arthur President, and save the Republic. I have sacrificed only one. I shot the President as I would a rebel, if I saw him pulling down the American flag. I leave my justification to God and the American people." [2368]

On Friday, July 1, 1881, "it occurred to Guiteau that perhaps not everyone would accept his reasons, especially in the instant panic right after he'd taken his action. An ugly mob might gather, or the police might not understand him. So Guiteau wrote another letter that night, this one addressed to General William Tecumseh Sherman, [commander] of the [U.S.] Army:

'*To Gen. Sherman:*

I have just shot the President. I shot him several times as I wished him to go as easily as possible. His death was a political necessity. I am a lawyer, a theologian and a politician. I am a Stalwart of the Stalwarts. ... I am going to jail. Please order out your troops, and take possession of the jail at once.

Very respectfully,

Charles Guiteau'

This letter, too, he placed in an envelope, and put the envelope in his coat." [2369]

On Saturday, July 2, Garfield eagerly left the White House for a delightful week's trip to a college reunion in New England. Lucretia would join him in Philadelphia. Secretary of

State Blaine drove him in "the State Department's small two-seat carriage" [2370] to the Baltimore & Potomac Depot, on "[t]he site of the current National Museum of Art on the Washington Mall, 'B Street' being the nineteenth-century name for today's Constitution Avenue." [2371]

"After reading about the president's trip in the newspaper two days earlier [M] and deciding that this was the opportunity he had been looking for," [2372] "Charles Guiteau had awakened at 4:00 A.M. that morning ... [He] walked down Seventeenth Street to his familiar spot along the Potomac River. He practiced firing a round of cartridges from his pistol, then walked over to the railroad station. Still early, with plenty of time before the president's train was scheduled to leave," [2373] "[a]ware that he would soon be the focus of great attention, and concerned that his shoes looked a little dusty, he had them brushed and blacked" [2374] "and then found himself a quiet corner ... near the B Street entrance." [2375]

"When Garfield walked in, Guiteau was standing right behind him. ... Without a moment's hesitation, he raised the revolver he had been carrying with him for nearly a month and pointed it at Garfield's back. ... Garfield ... was just three feet away when Guiteau pulled the trigger.[2376] The bullet sliced through the president's right arm ..." [2377] "Garfield 'straightened up and threw his head back' ... 'My God! What is this?' Garfield said. Then he heard another shot ... hitting him square in the back on the right side ... He reeled sharply to the right and fell over, hitting the floor hard." [2378]

"Blaine ... saw a man holding a pistol—a small man with dark hair and a distinctive walk. He was running away. Blaine ... recognized the man—the odd little job-seeker from the State Department. For an instant, he started to chase him, but then saw the president—his friend Garfield—lying on the floor, bleeding, vomiting, barely conscious. He turned to protect him." [2379] Two police officers grabbed the assassin. "Guiteau wanted to make sure there would be no mistake. He turned to one of the officers and said: 'I did it. I will go to jail for it. I am a Stalwart and Arthur will be President.'" [2380]

[2381]

"Garfield might have survived the shooting but for what happened next. Namely, that various physicians ... searched for the bullet's location in Garfield's back by poking their grimy fingers into the wound, rooting around in the presidential innards. This despite the advances and inroads of Joseph Lister and his soon-to-be-popular theories about germs. Besides his plea of insanity, Guiteau would in fact capitalize on this medical bungling at his defense trial, arguing that the doctors killed Garfield, 'I just shot him.'" [2382]

"Garfield [was] taken to the White House ..." [2383] That afternoon, "he asked Blaine

---

[M] As Oswald also learned by reading his Dallas newspapers in the days before the motorcade, the important subject of Chapter 18 – CONNALLY WILL RIDE.

who was the man who had shot him at the train station. Blaine told him—Charles Guiteau, the office seeker. Garfield looked puzzled. 'Why did that man shoot me? I have done him no wrong. What could he have wanted to shoot me for?'" [2384] "People made obvious comparisons to Abraham Lincoln's murder just sixteen years ago—a fresh memory to most—but in some ways this was worse: Lincoln had been murdered in wartime, martyred over great issues of ending slavery and saving the Union; Garfield had been shot in a petty squabble over political patronage. What had become of our nation?" [2385]

"For weeks the President hovered between life and death.[2386] One of those at his side was War Secretary Robert Todd Lincoln, who had been at his father's bedside sixteen years

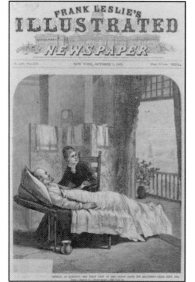

before. And twenty-five years later he would stand near the bedside of another assassinated President—McKinley." [2387] "Beginning midsummer ... Garfield's body actually had healed from the original gunshot wound ... Instead, the president now was starting to die slowly from a combination of infection, blood poisoning, and starvation." [2388] "Garfield wasted away ... He lost eighty pounds," [2389] "Plunging from 210 pounds to 130." [2390] He died on September 19.

"Garfield had lived seventy-nine days after being shot ... just forty-nine years old ..." [2391] From "his autopsy, it became immediately and painfully apparent that, far from preventing or even delaying the presidential death, his doctors very likely caused it." [2392] "Had it happened today, modern medicine certainly would have saved James Garfield's life ... with some physical therapy, [he] probably would have walked again and enjoyed a wave of popularity not unlike President Ronald Reagan a century later, after [his] March 1981 shooting by John Hinckley Jr. Even in 1881, a competent physician probably could have saved Garfield." [2393]

Guiteau proudly wrote a letter to incoming President Chester A. Arthur, taking full credit for his elevation. "The country was shocked. To kill the President so that others could get offices was more than the people could bear. The deed created revulsion against the spoils system; a cry went up for Civil Service reform. Guiteau's bullet not only killed Garfield but also ended the existence of the Stalwarts." [2394] "Arthur was mortified that Garfield's assassin claimed that he did it so Arthur could be president." [2395]

Jail guards "took [Guiteau] to be photographed; he wore a dark suit, standing collar and black cravat, and treated the event as an honor. 'I don't want to appear strained and awkward,' Guiteau told the photographer. 'If my picture is taken at all it must be a good one.'" [2396] "Before returning to his cell, he asked the photographer for a $25 royalty fee." [2397] Among all assassination *dramatis personae*, only Marguerite Oswald, 82 years later, would match his *chutzpah*.

2398

"[T]he trial ... defense raised two principal issues: insanity and causation." [2399] Guiteau's attorney "mounted a convincing insanity defense, assembling expert witnesses, including a former doctor of Guiteau's who had examined him years earlier right after Guiteau threatened his sister with an axe. Also, Guiteau's own babbling, always eccentric and frequently delusional, reads today like classic crackpot. But in 1882, the insanity defense was new and controversial; add a dead president to the mix and the country's thirst for revenge makes an insanity acquittal all the more unlikely." [2400] A "New York State ... judge had said: 'If a man has an irresistible impulse to commit murder, the law should have an irresistible impulse to hang him.'" [2401] "The situation, Guiteau insisted, was perfectly clear. 'General Garfield died from malpractice. ... The doctors who mistreated him ought to be indicted for murder ... and not me.'" [2402] "I simply shot at him." [2403]

"The trial ... ended ... after more than two months of testimony ... Less than an hour later, the jury returned with a verdict." [2404] — guilty. "Guiteau appealed, but in May, he was sentenced to hang on June 30. Guiteau was angry at the judge, the jury, the press, the American people, and, not least, President Arthur, whom Guiteau regarded as ungrateful considering that Arthur owed his pay raise and promotion to Guiteau." [2405] He wrote to the president, "I made you ... and the least you can do is to let me go." [2406] Guiteau was hanged 363 days after he shot President Garfield. Jailers dropped the trapdoor on cue when he said his "final words ... 'Glory, ready, go.'" [2407]

He left a lasting legacy: "[B]y his crime he brought about one of the most important reforms of the era: the 1883 Civil Service Act [that] placed some 86,000 federal positions under a merit system administered by an independent new Civil Service Commission. Today, the vast majority of federal employees have professional civil-service status rather than owing their jobs to politicians, a bedrock concept of modern governments around the world." [2408]

1881: Charles Guiteau shoots and wounds James Garfield, who dies of infection	
Weapon:	Pistol: 5-shot English Bulldog revolver with ivory handle, cost $9
Distance:	Three feet
Shots fired:	Two
Killed / Hit:	Garfield was severely wounded but might have recovered. Because of septic handling by doctors, he died of infection 79 days later.
Assassin then:	Was immediately taken into custody, jailed, tried, convicted, lost his appeal, and died by hanging 363 days after the shooting.
Motive(s):	Major: Change the Presidency to his faction of the Republican Party; Minor: Disappointment at not being made Ambassador to France.
Do we know beyond reasonable doubt, **whom** did the assassin intend to shoot? **Yes**	
Do we know beyond reasonable doubt, his **motive** for shooting the man he hit? **Yes**	

1901: Leon Czolgosz shoots and kills William McKinley

We may as well learn the proper pronunciations. The assassin Czolgosz is "chol'·gosh".[2409] His victim is McKinley, said the usual way except when referring to North America's highest peak, which chechakos [N] renamed for him but we true Alaskans pronounce "Denali". Really.[O]

This assassination resulted in a generation jump as dramatic as will the 1960 election of vigorous young Jack Kennedy to replace weathered Dwight Eisenhower. The last president to serve in the Civil War, William McKinley of Ohio was 18 when it began. He enlisted and served throughout, then became a lawyer and was twice elected as a Republican to the U.S. House of Representatives. While Ohio's Governor in 1892, he was nearly (and unwillingly) nominated instead of "the unpopular incumbent President, Benjamin Harrison," [2410] who was then defeated when Grover Cleveland was elected to the only non-consecutive second term in American history.

McKinley [2411] defeated William Jennings Bryan in 1896. In 1898, the Assistant Secretary of the Navy resigned at the outbreak of the Spanish-American War, "ordered himself a custom-tailored uniform from Brooks Brothers," [2412] "to lead a cavalry group of Rough Riders in Cuba. ... [H]e proved irresistible to reporters, who found in turn that the amateur naturalist, historian, and full-time politician could endlessly produce quotable copy. Moreover, with his flashing spectacles and clacking, oversized teeth, his brushy mustache and ready grin, he presented an image already so near to caricature that he endeared himself to cartoonists." [2413]

This unique American hero was Theodore Roosevelt, whose "war record made him a choice candidate for governor of New York in 1898, and he won the election that autumn. He immediately became a headache for the state Republican boss, Tom Platt ... As the governor's two-year term drew to a close ... [t]he two men were lining up for an ugly fight when the sitting Vice President ... died. This vacancy on the [1900] national ticket gave Platt the upper hand. ... The Rough Rider would ascend from the governorship to serve party and country gloriously and impotently at the President's right hand. When Platt put this case to him, Roosevelt realized he had been outmaneuvered, and he glumly accepted the job. When McKinley won re-election [a re-match against Bryan], Platt and his fellow party stalwarts believed they had finally neutered Roosevelt." [2414]

"The vice presidency was every bit as dull as Roosevelt feared. The Vice President was, on paper, a 'functionless official,' as Roosevelt wrote, 'who possesses so little real

---

[N] "chechako" (alternately cheechako): a newcomer to Alaska who has not yet been through a winter.

[O] In 1896 a prospector named it *McKinley* as political support for the then-president. The Alaska Board of Geographic Names changed the name of the mountain back to *Denali*, which is how it had been known for thousands of years. The Alaska state legislature in 1975 asked the United States Board on Geographic Names to do the same, a request blocked then and thereafter by the Ohio congressional delegation, to do honor to their fellow Buckeye, McKinley. When President Obama made the first substantive presidential visit to Alaska in 2015, he proudly announced that his Secretary of the Interior, Sally Jewell, had wisely used her executive authority to change the name back to what the native Athabascans had called it for over 10,000 years, *Denali*, "the big one". Nice!

power,' that, regrettably, 'his political weight… is almost nil.' [2415] … Roosevelt … wrote grimly, 'I have really much less influence with the President now that I am Vice-President than I had even when I was governor.'" [2416] In six months, it all changed with shocking speed.

"On August 31, [the assassin Czolgosz] arrived in Buffalo … and waited for McKinley to arrive in the city; on September 2 he purchased a .32-caliber revolver for $4.50. McKinley addressed a crowd of over fifty thousand, including Leon Czolgosz, three days later. Czolgosz planned to shoot him that day, but he found he was unable to get close enough. He then followed the president to Niagara Falls,[P] where again he could not get a clear shot. McKinley's return to the fair in Buffalo would be Czolgosz's last chance." [2417]

"At or about four o'clock in the afternoon of September 6, 1901, President William McKinley arrived [at] the Temple of Music at the Pan-American Exposition in Buffalo, New York. He walked inside and to the head of a receiving line, where he began shaking the hands of Exposition visitors." [2418] "Seven minutes into the process … McKinley took the right hand of Czolgosz, who then, with his left, fired two shots from a short-barrelled revolver concealed in a white handkerchief, which caught fire in the process. Both bullets struck their target … The first shot ricocheted off McKinley's breastbone and fell to the ground; the second entered the stomach, pierced the pancreas and one kidney and lodged in the back muscle wall." [2419] "McKinley straightened up, staggered from one potted plant to another, and collapsed, blood seeping into his pale shirt. Secret Service agents and other bystanders tackled the shooter. A fairgoer grabbed him by the throat and tried to choke him. Through this mayhem the assailant insisted stubbornly, 'I done my duty.'" [2420]

[2421]

"Robert Todd—*tod*, the German word for death—Lincoln" [2422] was "with the president, thus earning the dubious distinction of being the only man to be present at three of our nation's four presidential assassinations." [2423] He had grieved at the bedside as his father died, had been at the station to see off Garfield when he was shot, and now as president of the Pullman Palace Car Company (manufacturer of railroad cars) he was with McKinley. Lincoln died in 1926, so did not achieve the grand slam of riding in the Dallas motorcade with JFK in 1963. For a memorable insight into this history-spanning American totem, read the excellent book by Jason Emerson, *Giant in the Shadows: The Life of Robert T. Lincoln*.[2424]

"After an emergency operation at the hospital of the Exposition, the President was taken to the home of a friend. The news of McKinley's assassination reached Roosevelt that afternoon at Isle La Motte on Lake Champlain, where he was attending the annual outing of the Vermont Fish and Game League. He immediately took a special train to Buffalo, and arrived there the following day. To his relief the news was good." [2425] "Roosevelt … said of the assassin, 'If it had been I, he wouldn't have gotten away so easily. I think I'd have guzzled

---

[P] To see the larger Canadian falls, McKinley "was very careful not to walk too far across the bridge into Canada because no sitting American president had ever left the country, and he didn't want to stir up a diplomatic hullabaloo." — Vowell 212.

Q him.'" 2426 "As there seemed to be no emergency, Roosevelt left Buffalo to continue his vacation. But less than a week later, early on the morning of Friday, September 13, McKinley's condition took a severe turn for the worse ..." 2427 "By noon that day, McKinley's pulse sped up, then grew weaker. The President was in shock. Doctors administered digitalis, strychnine, and adrenaline. They plied him with camphor, coffee, and clam broth. His heart began to fail.

"Friday afternoon, a week after McKinley was shot, proved a fine day for a" 2428 "bully good tramp" 2429 "and Vice President Roosevelt put off his few official obligations and seized the moment for a swift jaunt up Mount Tahawus.R He had come to the summit and started down again when he decided to have lunch ("ox tongue" 2430) by a little lake ("Tear-in-the-Clouds" 2431), clear and blue in the heights of the Adirondacks. With sandwich in hand he surveyed a most satisfying scene—marred only by the huffing and puffing of a ranger approaching from down the slope, bearing news the Vice President could sadly guess." 2432

"[T]he message from Secretary of War Elihu Root: 'The President appears to be dying, and members of the Cabinet in Buffalo think that you should lose no time in coming.' ... As he boarded his train ... shortly before dawn [Saturday, September 14], he learned that McKinley had died. Arriving in Buffalo in the afternoon, Roosevelt joined the Cabinet members ... He then took the oath of office ... Forty-two-year-old Theodore Roosevelt was now President of the United States." 2433 He was the youngest ever to <u>hold</u> that office. Jack Kennedy at age forty-three would be the youngest ever <u>elected</u> to the presidency.

The assailant had been taken to police headquarters by "Detective sergeant James Vallely of the New York City police department, detailed to the Exposition as captain of its detective bureau ... his prisoner—a slim man, weighing about 140 pounds at a height of five foot seven or so. The detective took a couple of cigars from his coat, lit both, and gave one to the prisoner. Then, sitting comfortably as possible in a jail cell, smoking companionably ... 'Why did you shoot the President?' Vallely asked. 'I only done my duty' ... 'Are you an anarchist?' 'Yes, sir.' And the policeman asked no more; he had found out as much as he needed to know." 2434   2435

Later that Friday evening, the district attorney "led the detailed questioning. The prisoner [admitted his name was] Leon F. Czolgosz, and that he had been born in Detroit [in 1873; he was 28] 2436, had grown up in Alpena, Michigan, and had worked in various jobs throughout the industrial cities of the Great Lakes states. ... He said he had been studying anarchist teachings for seven years, and had attended anarchist meetings and speeches. ... [A]

Q A strange usage. "guzzle" in *The American Heritage College Dictionary*: "To drink greedily or habitually; To consume to excess." The word must have had a different meaning 114 years ago.

R "Tahawus", an Indian word meaning "cloud splitter", was a fine name for the highest point in New York State. "Mount" is superfluous, as it would be with the Matterhorn, Krakatoa or Denali (see the first paragraph of this article). Disrespect for First Nation names is transcontinental: Tahawus was later renamed for a governor of NY. From en.wikipedia.org "Mount Marcy" on 2012/04/02.

Buffalo lawyer who witnessed the shooting and the interrogation said later that Czolgosz gave his testimony freely, often volunteering details that went beyond the questions ... posed. 'I fully understood what I was doing when I shot the President. I realized that I was sacrificing my life. I am willing to take the consequences.' ... [The lawyer] asked Czolgosz if he would provide a signed statement ... and the prisoner agreed. ... 'I want to say to be published—'I killed President McKinley because I done my duty. I don't believe in one man having so much service and another man having none'' he dictated, and signed the statement." [2437]

"[N]obody mentions a lawyer for Czolgosz [who] had no legal counsel till the eve of trial—which came as swiftly after the President's death as the President's death had come after the shooting. No sooner did Czolgosz become an assassin that he became a defendant." [2438]

On Monday, September 9, three expert "alienists (as doctors of mental pathology were called in the late nineteenth century)" [2439] examined the shooter. "Czolgosz admitted, as he had before, having stalked and shot McKinley. ... 'I am glad I did it.' The gratified doctors took their notes, compared their opinions, and declared ... 'The most careful questioning failed to discover any hallucinations of sight or hearing. He had received no special command; he did not believe he had been specially chosen to do the deed. He always spoke of his motive for the crime as duty; he always referred to the Anarchists' belief that the killing of rulers was a duty ... He is not a case of paranoia, because he has not systematized delusions reverting to self, and because he is in exceptionally good condition and has an unbroken record of good health. He is the product of Anarchy, sane and responsible.'" [2440]

"Czolgosz was indicted on September 16, with trial set for ... the following week." [2441] That same day, "McKinley's funeral train left Buffalo. The President [Roosevelt], his cabinet, and the press were all on board in a series of special Pullman cars." [2442] No doubtlessly [S], these had been arranged by Robert Todd Lincoln. "On the ride, New York political boss Mark Hanna famously said to a newspaper publisher, 'I told William McKinley it was a mistake to nominate that wild man. I asked him if he realized what would happen if he should die. Now look, that damned cowboy is President of the United States!'" [2443] The train went to Washington where the President lay in state at the Capitol. "Geronimo himself strutted past the coffin." [2444] Finally, the train went to Canton, Ohio, McKinley's hometown, and he was buried.

The weekend immediately before the trial, two doctors hurriedly appointed for the defense "met with the prisoner both days. He appeared to them much as he had appeared to the prosecution's alienists: 'a well nourished, rather good-looking, mild-mannered young man,' who described himself as 'a laborer by occupation.' ... In short, he was sane and normal. When asked about why he had shot the President, he said simply, 'McKinley was going around the country shouting about prosperity when there was no prosperity for the poor man. I am not afraid to die. We all have to die sometime.'" [2445]

"At ten o'clock on Monday morning, September 23, 1901, in the grandly turreted and baroquely decorated City and County Hall on Franklin Square in Buffalo, Czolgosz's trial began, under paired sixteen-ton granite statues of Justice and Commerce. Despite the stately surroundings, it would be a brisk trial. Counsel for the defense would afterward be criticized

---

[S] Coined about sixty years ago, either by columnist "Hashafisti Scratchi" in CQ Magazine for Morse code-adept radio "hams", or in relentless letters to the editor of the *Daily Alaska Empire* in Juneau by a retired postmaster who always signed himself with a comma: "Albert, White".

for their work on behalf of the assassin, but in truth they mounted a daring effort to get their client acquitted on grounds of insanity. ... [T]he courtroom came to order, and the court solicited a plea from Leon Czolgosz in the murder of William McKinley. ... 'Guilty,' Czolgosz said. It was the last thing he would say in his own trial, and it would be ignored. After this small effort to claim responsibility for his crime, his fate would rest entirely in the hands of others ... 'The plea can not be accepted in this Court,' [Judge] White ruled, as the guilty plea could not be allowed in cases where capital punishment was a possibility. 'The Clerk will enter a plea of 'not guilty' and we will proceed with the trial.'" [2446]

"With that, the D.A. commenced the trial, the court drew and swore the jury, and testimony began. ... [T]he defendant's counsel ... had been asked to represent this low criminal who was fully prepared to admit his guilt, and they had absolutely no case at all, as the trial swiftly showed. There were eyewitnesses to the shooting. The prosecution had the defendant's own statement, in which he indicated sympathy with anarchists, to suggest a motive. And the only reed to which the defense could cling, the possibility of claiming insanity [was] discounted by ... the experts retained for the defense. There was little they could do, and to their credit, they did every bit of it." [2447]

"And so it went, with the eyewitnesses identifying Czolgosz as the shooter, the doctors showing that the shooting had killed the President, and the defendant's statement indicating ... that Czolgosz's 'own individual theorizing' about government, 'in connection with ... the lectures and speakers he had heard' had led him to anarchistic beliefs, and thus a political motive for murdering McKinley. He had the murder weapon, the cause of death, the confession, and the motive. It was an open-and-shut case, and in the course of an afternoon and a morning of testimony, [the prosecutor] had opened and shut it. He had left only one small opening, and when the defense rose to present its case, [the defense attorney] leapt forward to put his foot in the door. 'If your Honor please,' he said, 'the defendant has no witnesses that he will call, so that the testimony is closed at the close of the testimony of the People.' With a defendant who insisted on professing his guilt at every chance, and an expert panel of alienists who insisted he was sane, there was little point in presenting testimony." [2448]

"The trial lasted less than two days." [2449] "[E]ight measly hours." [2450] After both sides closed, "Judge White then delivered his charge to the jury, covering the elements of murder in the first and second degree, manslaughter, and, finally, legal insanity: "If he was laboring under such a defect of reason as not to know the nature and the quality of the act that he was doing or that it was wrong, it is your duty, Gentlemen of the Jury, to acquit him in this case." White several times used this phrase, direct from the M'Naghten case [2451], as a routine element of the charge, and concluded." [2452]

"At that, the jury were allowed to retire. Nobody expected them to be long. When impaneled they had all announced a prejudice toward the defendant's guilt—though each allowed 'his opinion could be removed by reasonable evidence.' They returned within twenty-five minutes with a guilty verdict. Sentencing was set for two days hence." [2453]

"On that Thursday morning, September 26, Judge White permitted Leon Czolgosz to speak briefly: 'I would like to say this much; that the crime was committed by no one else but me; no one told me to do it and I never told anybody to do it.' White, addressing the prisoner simply as 'Czolgosz,' sentenced him to death in a month, omitting even a perfunctory request for God's mercy on his soul, and ordered the prisoner removed." [2454] It was only 20 days since the shooting; 12 days after McKinley died.

One month later, on October 29, 1901, Leon Czolgosz "died by electrocution at 7:12 a.m." [2455] "When [he] came to face his end ... at Auburn State Prison, he uttered neither prayer nor imprecation, for his guards hurried him past the witnesses into the electric chair [T] while he was still trying to say his last words." [2456] "I killed the President because he was the enemy of the good people—the good working people. I am not sorry for my crime. I *am* sorry I could not see my father." [2457] "And then he did not speak again for himself, except through the hearsay testimony of witnesses to his life and death. Nor could even his remains bear witness, for after autopsy they were buried, and then—taking a measure that had been developed and tested specifically to get rid of Czolgosz's remains as quickly as possible—the jailers poured a carboy of sulfuric acid upon the body, dissolving it swiftly into the earth." [2458] Crime to capital punishment had required only 53 days — some of them used for experiments with the acid!

Historian Eric Rauchway, from whose book *Murdering McKinley* this article has greatly benefited, summarizes: "Among the presidential assassinations, William McKinley's had the most dangerously political motive. ... McKinley's assassin said plainly that he shot the President of the United States because he hated the politics of state-supported capitalism that the President and his party represented, and in so doing he echoed hosts of critics in the United States and around the world. ... [H]e wanted to strike at the American leader to prove the nation vulnerable, and to shatter its illusions of safety. He knew what he was doing, and he knew he would die if he succeeded. His reasoning was cruel, even inhuman; but however bereft of sympathy and decency his motive was, it did not lack logic." [2459]

1901: Leon Czolgosz shoots and kills William McKinley	
Weapon:	Pistol: Iver Johnson .32 revolver bought 2 days earlier for $4.50
Distance:	Less than a foot
Shots fired:	Two. "The first shot ricocheted off McKinley's breastbone and fell to the ground; the second entered the stomach, pierced the pancreas and one kidney and lodged in the back muscle wall." [2460]
Killed / Hit:	McKinley was mortally wounded. He died of "gangrenous blood poisoning" [2461] eight days later.
Assassin then:	Was immediately taken into custody, jailed, questioned about motive and sanity, tried by a jury, sentenced and electrocuted.
Motive(s):	He believed and repeatedly stated his hatred for the politics of capitalism; felt it his duty to strike a blow for common people.
Do we know beyond reasonable doubt, **whom** did the assassin intend to shoot? **Yes**	
Do we know beyond reasonable doubt, his **motive** for shooting the man he hit? **Yes**	

[T] That chair, "Old Sparky", eleven years old, was the first ever used in the U.S. — Vowell 212.

1912: John Schrank shoots and wounds Theodore Roosevelt

Theodore Roosevelt [U] had increasingly close associations with four presidential assassinations

and attempts. As a boy, he watched Lincoln's funeral in New York City on April 25, 1865. The photo [2462] at left shows the funeral procession on Broadway. Above the throngs (in the enlargement at right), "From the second-story window of their grandfather's house, on the corner of Union Square and Broadway, six-year-old Theodore Roosevelt and his brother Elliott (the father of Eleanor) are watching." [2463]

#2 was sixteen years later when 22-year-old New York State legislator Roosevelt was prominent on the platform as James A. Garfield was inaugurated in 1881, only four months before Guiteau fired the bullet that killed him. #3 was much closer, when a bullet fired into McKinley made Roosevelt president. #4 will be close-as-possible — but narrowly survived.

Theodore Roosevelt became president on the 1901 death of William McKinley, and was re-elected in 1904. "Roosevelt built the Panama Canal, earned a Nobel Prize brokering a

peace treaty between Russia and Japan, secured Moroccan independence, and sent the 'Great White Fleet' of the U.S. Navy on tour around the globe to warn the world that the United States was a power to contend with." [2464]

After almost two full terms, he favored William Howard Taft to succeed him, and Taft readily beat back old William Jennings Bryan in 1908. Four years later, disenchanted with Taft's commerce and conservation policies, Roosevelt tried to win the Republican nomination in 1912. Failing, he bolted the party and ran on the Progressive (nicknamed "Bull Moose") third-party ticket against Taft, and the Democrat nominee, Woodrow Wilson.

"On October 14, 1912, ten days after the photo at left was taken,[2465] Theodore Roosevelt walked out of the Hotel Gilpatrick in Milwaukee on his way to deliver a speech at the city's Auditorium. He climbed into his waiting car in front of the hotel. A crowd had gathered to see him, and they cheered as he took his seat. Roosevelt could not resist bouncing back up again to wave his hat

---

[U] Theodore Roosevelt did not have a middle initial, although by the age of ten months "the boy had acquired a nickname — 'Teedie' (pronounced as in T.D.)" according to Nathan Miller in *Theodore Roosevelt: A Life*, page 29. As a man he would become "Teddy" — neither inheriting a middle name or initial from his father, Theodore Roosevelt, Sr., nor passing name or initial along to his son, Theodore Roosevelt, Jr. His nickname was given to a then-new toy, told in the Wikipedia article at http://en.wikipedia.org/wiki/Teddy_bear. Now you know and can win fame in trivia contests.

... As he did so, a man stepped forward from the applauding onlookers and fired at point-blank range into Roosevelt's chest. Elbert Martin, a stenographer traveling with Roosevelt tackled the shooter and bore him to the ground. [A] politician from Milwaukee threw himself over Roosevelt and asked if he was hurt. 'He pinked me,' Roosevelt answered.

"It looked bad: there was blood on Roosevelt's shirt above his heart. But he gathered his strength, stood up, and saw Martin trying mightily to break the man's neck. 'Don't hurt him,' Roosevelt said, 'Bring him to me!' Martin obliged, handing the pistol to Roosevelt and twisting the assailant's head so Roosevelt could see into his eyes.

"After a brief glare at the man who shot him, Roosevelt sat back down and ordered the car to the Auditorium over the protests of his companions. He batted away the attentions of a doctor ... and refused all demands to see the wound. He coughed into his own hand and, seeing no blood, concluded he was well enough. 'You get me to that speech,' he ordered. 'It may be the last one I shall ever deliver, but I am going to deliver this one.' Alive to the political possibilities of even this moment, he said, 'This is my big chance, and I am going to make that speech if I die doing it.'" [2466] "On the drive to the hall, Roosevelt's aides became concerned as blood began to pool beneath the former president's feet." [2467]

"Arriving at the Milwaukee Auditorium, he allowed a doctor to determine that though the bullet had lodged in his chest, it appeared not to have pierced his heart or lungs—though nobody could be sure under such circumstances, and his entourage urged him to go to a hospital. Instead he walked out onto the stage [to address the audience of 9,000 [2468]] ... Only when he pulled his notes from his breast pocket did he finally betray surprise: the bullet had passed clean through the fifty folded-over sheets of paper before it hit him. On this occasion his loquacity had literally saved his life." [2469] An eyeglass case in Roosevelt's pocket was dented, also slowing the bullet. The photo shows heroic stenographer Elbert Martin holding the holey speech.[2470]

"Roosevelt ... to tumultuous applause ... told the audience with grim glee, 'I don't know whether you fully understand that I have just been shot or not, but it takes more than that to kill a Bull Moose.' He launched then into a heartfelt impromptu speech. 'I want to take advantage of this incident,' he said, as if being shot were simply a golden political opportunity, too good to be missed. 'I cannot speak to you insincerely within five minutes of being shot. He went on to explain that he held much the same opinion of this would-be assassin as he did of the man who shot McKinley. 'I don't know anything about who the man was who shot me tonight. ... He shot to kill. He shot the shot, the bullet went in here—I will show you.' Here he opened his vest, and the crowd let out a gasp of horror at the spill of blood on his shirt." [2471] "Shaking slightly, he began to explain why, in 1912, he was running for President yet again." [2472]

"One of his aides ... pleaded with him to stop speaking and go to the hospital. The wounded Bull Moose rounded on him ferociously. Biting off unusually clipped sentences, Roosevelt hissed, 'I am not sick at all. I am all right ... Don't you pity me. I am all right,' and then, with a flash of humor, 'I am all right and you cannot escape listening to the speech either.'" [2473]   "The audience was under his spell. ... For an hour and a half he held the platform.

At the hospital, a "surgeon commented with awe: 'It is largely due to the fact that he is a physical marvel that he was not dangerously wounded. He is one of the most powerful men I have ever seen laid on an operating table. The bullet lodged in the massive muscles of the chest instead of penetrating the lung.'" [2474]   "On determining the bullet's position in Roosevelt's body [physicians] decided that the safer course was to leave the slug where it was; Roosevelt carried it in his chest until his death in 1919." [2475]   Democrat Woodrow Wilson won the election, defeating the Republicans temporarily divided in two.

The man who "pinked" Roosevelt was John Flammang [2476] Schrank, pronounced "shrank".[2477]   A New Yorker, thirty-six, he had emigrated from Bavaria in 1885 at the age of

nine and now ran a saloon. "When he was arraigned before a Milwaukee judge, he said, 'I shot Theodore Roosevelt because he was a menace to the country. He should not have a third term. It is bad that a man should have a third term. I did not want him to have one. I shot him as a warning that men must not try to have more than two terms as President. I shot Theodore Roosevelt to kill him. I think all men trying to keep themselves in office should be killed; they become dangerous.'" [2478]

Schrank "was a mild-mannered but troubled man who was offended and obsessed with the threat, he claimed, that the Colonel's [as TR liked to be called, evoking the charge up San Juan Hill] bid for a third-term in the White House posed to the nation's democratic institutions. In Schrank's mind, breaking the two-term tradition was the first step toward dictatorship." [2479]   He added, "Let it be the right and duty of every citizen to forcibly remove a third-termer." [2480]

"So he set out to stalk the presumptive third-termer, armed with a .38-caliber pistol [2481] he bought from a dealer who was willing to ignore the licensing laws" [2482] "for fourteen dollars

... On September 21, 1912, he embarked on his pursuit of the campaigning candidate following a trail that would lead him eventually from Charleston to Augusta, Atlanta, Birmingham, Chattanooga, Nashville, Louisville, Evansville, Chicago, and Milwaukee before he finally got his chance." [2483]

"When Schrank appeared before the court, he said much what Czolgosz had: 'I am not a lunatic and never was one. I was called upon to do a duty and I have done it.' But he added one claim that saved him from prison: he said,

> 'I had a dream several years ago that Mr. McKinley appeared to me, and he told me that Mr. Roosevelt was practically his real murderer, and not this Czolgosz, or whatever his name was. Mr. Roosevelt is practically the man that has been the real murderer of President McKinley, in order to get the Presidency of the United States ... that's what I am sore about, to think that Mr. McKinley appeared to me in a dream and said, 'This is my murderer, and nobody else.''

This revelation made him certain to be declared legally insane. Under the legal doctrine of 'deific decree,' a person who received a command from God—or a reasonable equivalent—to commit murder was presumed irresponsible for his conduct. And, although it led to peculiar theological thickets, the ghost of William McKinley qualified as the equivalent of God as far as American law could determine." [2484]

"Roosevelt and his supporters despaired at this performance. As far as they could tell, Schrank was not insane at all, merely motivated by politics. As Roosevelt's doctor said, 'Schrank is not crazy ... Take that statement of his ... It is a perfectly clear and reasonable argument against a third term, and shows no mark against insanity. The only reasons for charging Schrank with insanity are that he believes in dreams ... One of the members of this very party tells me that his wife, who is a college graduate, believes in them and she is as sane a woman as I ever knew.'" [2485] "Roosevelt himself agreed:

'He was not a madman at all... I very gravely question if he has a more unsound brain than Senator La Follette or Eugene Debs [two of TR's political opponents]. He simply represents a different stratum of life and of temperament ... He had quite enough sense to avoid shooting me in any Southern State, where he would have been lynched, and he waited until he got into a State where there was no death penalty.'

"But that vision of McKinley's ghost overrode all arguments as to the assassin's rationality ... As Roosevelt's remark indicated, Schrank's insanity had nothing to do with saving his life; his decision to commit the crime in Wisconsin rather than Illinois, which imposed the death penalty, had kept him from state execution. His legal madness meant only that he would spend the rest of his days in an asylum, rather than in prison." [2486]

"Those who dealt with him ... described him as a pleasant individual who seemed perfectly normal and sane with the sole exception of his feelings towards Roosevelt. A story told of Schrank was that he had befriended the men who handled his transfer to the asylum. As they were driving to the institution, a guard remarked that the countryside they were passing through was ideal for hunting and fishing. When the guard turned to Schrank and asked him if he was a hunter, Schrank offered this reply: 'I only hunt Bull Moose.'" [2487]

"Schrank lived the remainder of his years as an inmate in the prison hospital at Waupon, Wisconsin, where he became known as 'Uncle John.' He was described as a model patient when he died at the age of sixty-seven [in] 1943. ... John Schrank never received a card or visitor in over thirty years of confinement." [2488]

Roosevelt's presidential career was 'bookended' by pistols. He ascended from vice- to president because of a gunshot to McKinley, then he was shot during his last campaign.

1912: John Schrank shoots and wounds Theodore Roosevelt	
Weapon:	Pistol: .38-caliber six-shot revolver, purchased for $14
Distance:	A very few feet
Shots fired:	One
Killed / Hit:	The bullet, slowed by papers for his speech and an eyeglass case in his coat pocket, lodged in Roosevelt's chest. He recovered.
Assassin then:	Was jailed, found insane, kept in an asylum until he died.
Motive(s):	Delusional: Believed McKinley had appeared to him in dreams and directed him to prevent Roosevelt from having a third term.
Do we know beyond reasonable doubt, **whom** did the assassin intend to shoot? **Yes**	
Do we know beyond reasonable doubt, his **motive** for shooting the man he hit? **Yes**	

1933: Giuseppe Zangara fires at Franklin Roosevelt but kills Anton Cermak

The Constitution of the United States took effect on March 4, 1789. It simply said the term of a president would be four years; thus March 4 became the date on which presidents from George Washington to Franklin Roosevelt took office. National elections [v] are held on the first Tuesday after the first Monday in November,[w] creating a four-month gap from Election Day to Inauguration Day. That delay was advantageous when travel was by horse and the fastest means of communication was a written message in a saddlebag.

The Twentieth Century brought mechanized travel and speed-of-light communication. The Twentieth Amendment to the Constitution changed Inauguration Day, beginning in 1937, to what we all know, January 20. This brief detour into constitutional law explains why the man elected in 1932 to be president, not yet inaugurated, was vacationing in February 1933. Franklin Delano Roosevelt spent the first half of the month on a yacht in the Bahamas, fishing and sunning. His legs were crippled by polio, before and during his presidency. Boats and trains gave his wheelchair wide-ranging mobility. In cities, he rode in open cars so he could remain seated while greeting crowds, being seen, and making speeches.

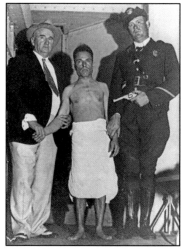

Waiting for FDR in Miami, Florida was a strange little man, only one inch above five feet as evidenced in the photo [2489] taken with two normal-size men [x] after his arrest. Master analyst of assassins James W. Clarke writes: "Not too much is known about Giuseppe Zangara. He was born in Ferruzzano in southern Italy on September 7, 1900, and lived there until ... 1923, when he sailed with his uncle ... for the United States ... Zangara's mother died when he was only two years old." [2490] When little Giuseppe was six, his father pulled him from school and forced him to work to support the family.

He was immediately beset by "the trouble" that would plague him throughout his life; he "suffered from stomach pains, which were never properly diagnosed but which he attributed to the existence of the capitalist classes. A doctor had removed his appendix, but this did not alleviate his suffering. He felt that only death could end his agony." [2491] "The malady, Zangara was convinced, was a direct result of being forced to perform hard labor carrying brick and tile as a child. Obsessed with the discomfort his stomach caused him, Zangara placed the blame on authority—to which he attributed an inextricable knot of characteristics shared by his father, wealthy capitalists, and heads of state. So closely entwined were these elements in Zangara's thinking that it was often difficult to determine to whom or to what he was referring." [2492] The day after his arrest, he was asked "What makes your belly burn?" He replied, "Because when I did tile work it hurt me there. It all spoil my machinery. My stomach—all my insides. Everything inside no good." [2493]

---

[v] Actually, we vote for "electors", who meet later and elect the president and vice president, but that's another topic, regularly used for high school debate competitions, as it was in Juneau circa 1955.

[w] This wording sets Election Day between November 2 and 8, thus avoiding "All Saints' Day" on November 1, when Catholics are obligated to attend Mass, while some recover from Halloween, which, by the way is pronounced as "hallow". There's nothing "hollow" about it!

[x] Sheriff Hardie is at left. The policeman displays (brandishes?) the pistol Zangara had fired at FDR.

This inexorable pain shaped his life. He worked as a bricklayer in New Jersey, "lived frugally and saved his money ... in almost complete isolation ... Zangara was an irritable recluse who took no part in the boisterous social life of the Italian neighborhood. He didn't smoke, drink wine, or seek the company of women. His whole life was structured around a hypochondriac's obsession with his health. ... He became a naturalized citizen on September 11, 1929 in the common pleas court in Paterson." [2494] Hoping warmth might alleviate his suffering, he traveled to Tampa, to New Orleans, through the Panama Canal to Los Angeles, to Miami, back to Panama. When nothing eased the pain, he returned to New Jersey.

"Anticipating the cold winter weather to come, he returned to Miami by bus in August 1932, where he got a cheap room ... In December, he left the hotel to avoid the higher winter rates and moved into a single room at a house ... He ate frugal fifteen cent meals at Murphy's restaurant." [2495] He tried to bolster dwindling savings by betting on horses and dogs, but lost. "Zangara was frustrated and angrier than usual. By the second week of February, with less than a hundred dollars left and a stomach that permitted no rest, Zangara decided he was going to get even. He would kill that no good capitalist Herbert Hoover in Washington. Everybody was saying Hoover was the cause of the unemployment and the soup lines. Moreover, he was convinced that it was because of men like Hoover that he had to endure the constant misery of his burning stomach. On ... February 13, Zangara ... purchased a .32 caliber pistol for eight dollars with the thought that he would take a bus to Washington to meet Mr. Hoover." [2496]

"The gun was a used, nickel-plated .32 calibre double action, top-breaking revolver with black checkered hard rubber grips." [2497] "The next morning on a walk around the docks, he happened to pick up a newspaper and read that President-elect Franklin D. Roosevelt would visit Miami the next day and ... make an evening speech at the Bayfront Park." [2498] The course of history is sometimes channeled by such mites.[Y] "Washington is cold in February, he reasoned, so why not remain in warm Miami and take out the President-elect instead. Besides, as he later observed, 'Hoover and Roosevelt—everybody the same.'" [2499]

"[O]n the evening of February 15, 1933, Vincent Astor's yacht, the *Nourmahal,* anchored ... near Bayfront Park." [2500] On his drive to a New York-bound train, Roosevelt would address a crowd in the Park. "At the southern end of the park was ... an elevated stage [above a] paved area, and it was on this pavement that Roosevelt was to speak ..." [2501] His "green Buick convertible began slowly nosing its way through the largest crowd assembled in the history of the city, estimated at 25,000.[2502] Vincent Astor, riding in the last car, commented that this was a dangerous situation. ... There was the president-elect, exposed in the rear seat of an open car that was moving at walking pace through a massive crowd. ... At least now ... the president-elect was  protected by the Secret Service. In fact, according to best estimates, the president-elect had six Secret Service operators with him, together with several dozen policemen, acting as motorcycle escort, drivers and crowd control. This contrasted with protection afforded

---

[Y] History will change terribly in 1963 when Oswald reads (chapter 18) that CONNALLY WILL RIDE.

outgoing President Herbert Hoover who, two days earlier, had attended a political dinner in New York City with an entourage of eight hundred Secret Service agents and local police." [2503] Zangara chose well in targeting Roosevelt-in-Florida as a substitute for Hoover-in-NYC.

"The president-elect's car came to a stop directly before the steps to the stage, where dignitaries were seated, among them Mayor Anton Cermak of Chicago ... All 7000 seats in front of the stage were filled, and thousands stood in the aisles and all around the seating area. It was a warm February evening. ... [A] battery of floodlights were switched on to shine on FDR's car as it stopped. All the light was concentrated on the car and the stage; the crowd stretched back into the darkness." [2504]

Zangara had arrived an hour and a half early [2505] to find a mass of people. When he tried to shove his way to the front, he was stopped "twenty-five or thirty feet from where Roosevelt was going to speak. He needed to be close to his target, because he was too small ... to see over the crowd." [2506] "At a little after 9 p.m. ... The crippled Roosevelt, speaking from his open car, gave" [2507] "a 145-word speech in less than a minute. ... He was helped down in his seat so that he could talk to the dignitaries who had left the stage to greet him.

One of them was Anton Cermak, [2508] the mayor of Chicago who came down from the stage and walked over to Roosevelt's auto to shake hands. In the previous page photo, Mayor Cermak with shiny slicked-back hair is in the lower-left corner with his back to the camera. [2509] "They had a good relationship: Cermak had helped FDR by calling the delegates to order at a critical moment during the Democratic Convention that past summer, when pandemonium had broken out on the floor among opponents of Roosevelt's nomination. Cermak had some important Chicago business to discuss with the president-elect; Roosevelt suggested they talk on the train. Cermak nodded, smiling, and walked toward the back of the car—and at the same time toward Giuseppe Zangara." [2510]

"The frustrated Zangara, unable to see his smiling and waving target, commandeered a rickety ... folding chair and from this tottering perch opened fire." [2511] With the pistol above his head, he aimed without sighting. "Five shots rang out: 'pop,' then 'pop, pop,' like a motorcycle backfiring, or the sound of firecrackers. Then 'pop, pop' again." [2512] "Five bullets tore into the flesh of as many bystanders—three head wounds, one abdominal wound and Mayor Cermak staggered against the President-elect's car as a bullet smashed into his right lung. Roosevelt miraculously escaped injury. Zangara was mobbed before being rescued by the police and hauled off to jail." [2513] "Note [the] bloodstain on [Mayor Cermak's] shirt above his belt and soiled trousers at knee where he fell." [2514]   [2515]

"The people around FDR were watching him to see how this man who was about to lead a troubled nation would react to the attempt on his life. ... Was he frightened? Nervous? Relieved that he had escaped unhurt? Was he rattled or petulant? He was none of those things. He appeared unfazed, calm, deliberate, cheerful—throughout the shooting itself as well as during its aftermath. He said and did all the right things at the right times: he stopped the car twice to pick up the wounded; he assured the crowd that he was all right; he calmly talked Cermak out of shock and he visited the victims that night and returned to the hospital the next day with flowers, cards and baskets of fruit. He had met his first test under fire, and had impressed not only his associates, but the press and the nation. It was on this note of personal courage, graciousness and self-confidence that he was to assume the reins of government seventeen days later." [2516] In New York City, "Eleanor Roosevelt remained calm ... 'I never let anything worry me. I do not believe in advising what precautions are necessary for my husband. ... As far as I am concerned, I cannot imagine living in fear of possible death. This is all I have to say on the subject.'" [2517]

Cermak lingered in the hospital while Zangara [2518] was judged sane, pleaded guilty and was convicted on four counts of assault with intent to kill. Only five days after the attack, he

was sentenced to four consecutive twenty-year terms, eighty years in total. He "expressed regret only that he had missed Roosevelt. On the stand, Zangara was at times matter-of-fact and at others defiant. Complaining of his chronic stomach problems, he said: 'I decided to kill . . . and make him [Roosevelt] suffer. I want to make it fifty-fifty since my stomach hurt I get even with capitalists by kill the President. My stomach hurt long time.'" [2519]

"When Judge E. C. Collins asked if he wanted to live, Zangara, who was still awaiting a possible second trial for murder depending upon the recovery of his victims, replied: 'I no care. I sick all time. I just think maybe cops kill me if I kill President. Somebody hit my arm when I try it.' The judge asked if he knew what he was doing when he shot at Roosevelt. Scoffing at the idea that he was insane, Zangara answered: 'Sure I know. I gonna kill President. I take picture of President in my pocket. I no want to shoot Cermak or anybody except Roosevelt. I aimed at him. I shoot at him. But somebody move my arm. They fools. They should let me kill him.' ... His defense attorney asked him if he was sorry for what he did. 'Sure,' Zangara replied, 'sorry I no kill him.'" [2520]

Mayor Cermak died on March 6, two days after Roosevelt was inaugurated to the first of his four terms. As had been the fate of President Garfield, he may have met a needless end because of too many doctors. [2521] "When Zangara was informed ... he said, 'Not my fault. Woman move my hand.'" [2522] "Zangara was immediately indicted for first degree murder ..." [2523] I would expect a charge of manslaughter for killing a bystander by accident, without intent, but lawyers know the principle that comes into play: "Transferred intent is the legal principle that *intent* can be *transferred* from one victim or tort to another. In US criminal law, transferred intent is sometimes explained by stating that 'the intent follows the bullet.' That is, the intent to kill *person A* with a bullet will apply even when the bullet kills the unintended victim, *person B*. Thus, the *intent* is *transferred* between victims." [2524]

On March 9, Zangara "entered a second remorseless guilty plea." [2525] His attorney asked, "'You would have tried to kill Mr. Hoover just as quick as Mr. Roosevelt?' 'I see Mr. Hoover, I kill him first. Make no difference. President just same bunch. All same. No make no difference who go get that job." [2526] "Circuit Judge Uly O. Thompson sentenced him to die in the electric chair at the Florida State Penitentiary ... Zangara, his dark eyes flashing, shouted back to the judge: 'You give me electric chair. I'm no afraid that chair. You're one of capitalists. You is crook man too. Put me in electric chair. I no care.'

"True to form, Zangara walked unaided to the electric chair on March 20, [1933.]" [2527] "[He] was the smallest man ever to sit in that chair; his feet did not quite reach the floor." [2528]

"Then after the shroud was placed over his head, his muffled shout was heard seconds before the first charge burned through his central nervous system: 'Go ahead. Push the button.' With not a single friend, and relatives who disavowed him, [his] unclaimed remains were buried in a ... prison grave." [2529] "[A] license plate marks his grave ..." [2530] [2531]

"From the shooting ... to the execution of Giuseppe Zangara, only five weeks had passed. It was the swiftest legal execution in America in the twentieth century." [2532]

The cause of twenty-seven years of unending pain, since little Giuseppe carried bricks as a six-year-old in Calabria, the toe of Italy's boot, was learned only after his electrocution. "An autopsy revealed that Zangara's supposed stomach problems actually had been due to" [2533] "a chronically diseased gallbladder which had adhesions ... scar tissue [to] the liver." [2534]

In *American Assassins*, James W. Clarke diagnoses: "His purpose in attacking Roosevelt and killing Cermak was not a political act in the usual sense, it was simply an expression of highly personal outrage against a society he hated: Zangara hated capitalism, and he hated American society because it was capitalistic. He could express that outrage symbolically by killing its leader. To end the miserable life that he had lived in the process was not considered a loss. Throughout his life his most common emotions were indifference and anger. ... A loveless lifetime of personal torment had destroyed other emotions: happiness, sadness, pleasure, excitement, and fear. Nothing was left except his hatred for a society that had mistreated him, and a perverse satisfaction in his own death." [2535] Clarke twins Zangara with Arthur Bremer, whom we will meet in 1972 when he shoots Governor George Wallace.

Zangara's intent to murder Roosevelt, but missing and killing Cermak by mistake, is the only precedent for Oswald's intent to murder Connally, but missing and killing Kennedy by accident. Because Cermak was simply an innocent bystander killed by inaccurately-fired bullets, this chapter has little on the life of the immigrant "born in the smokestack town of Kladno, in the hills west of Prague" [2536] who became an American and Mayor of Chicago. Zangara's wild shooting might have killed anyone — it just happened to be Cermak who was in the wrong place at the wrong time. For the same reason, this book contains little on the life of John F. Kennedy, destined to have, in the same tragic way, the same fate in thirty years.

1933: Giuseppe Zangara fires at Franklin Roosevelt but kills Anton Cermak	
Weapon:	.32-caliber revolver, used, purchased at a pawnshop for $8
Distance:	25 feet, while teetering on a folding chair to be above the crowd
Shots fired:	5 (the revolver's capacity)
Killed / Hit:	FDR was not hit. Four bystanders were injured and recovered. Chicago Mayor Cermak was shot in a lung, died 19 days later.
Assassin then:	Was quickly and easily (he was small, 105 pounds) captured, pled guilty, convicted of murder, electrocuted 33 days after shooting.
Motive(s):	Lifetime of pain and "personal outrage against society he hated" [2537] directed at America's leaders — first Hoover, then Roosevelt.
Do we know beyond reasonable doubt, **whom** did the assassin intend to shoot? **Yes**	
Do we know beyond reasonable doubt, his **motive** for shooting at that man? **Yes**	

1950: Oscar Collazo and Griselio Torresola attack the residence of Harry Truman

This incident differs from all others in this chapter in that the attackers did not come within sight of their potential victim, and may have been satisfied to "shoot up" the front of his residence to make a point. It must be included so none wonder if something is being hidden — this book is complete! Two Secret Service agents begin the narrative. In his *Protecting the President*, agent Dennis McCarthy pointed to the introduction of modern-day protection:

> "It wasn't until July 4, 1951—eighty-six years after the first Secret Service agents went to work—that the service was given the job of guarding the President permanently. Prior to that time, the duty had been reviewed annually by Congress as it considered the Treasury Department's budget ... When President Harry S Truman signed the bill, he quipped, "Well, it's wonderful to know that the work of protecting me has at last become legal." [2538]

The six previous attempts to assassinate American presidents had in common that they were at the Capitol, in a theatre, a railroad station, an exposition, outside a hotel and in a park. Strangely, none had been in or near where presidents live and work, The White House. This 1950 attack changed the pattern. The need to rethink and assign permanent responsibility for protection became evident in 1950 when Truman was the target. Secret Service agent Gerald Blaine related the event in his book *The Kennedy Detail*:

> "President and Mrs. Truman had been living in Blair House—the guesthouse that was normally used for visiting heads of state—while the White House was being renovated to include a nuclear fallout bomb shelter. Located just across Pennsylvania Avenue from the White House, Blair House at the time was a two-story brick town house that stood just about ten feet from the sidewalk.[z] A five-foot-high decorative wrought-iron fence was the only thing separating it from the heavily trafficked street. Three uniformed White House police officers guarded the exterior of the house; the small staff of Secret Service agents rotated shifts and positions throughout the interior when the president was in residence.
>
> On November 1, 1950, Agent Stewart Stout was standing post in the front hallway just inside the front door while President Truman was taking his daily afternoon nap upstairs.
>
> It was a warm, sunny day and shortly after two o'clock in the afternoon, thirty-five-year-old agent Floyd Boring had stepped outside. Floyd was ... chatting with White House police Officer Joseph Davidson, who had just rotated into position at the west-end booth. Officer Donald Birdzell was standing at the front door while Officer Leslie Coffelt took over the post at the east-end booth. People were walking along the sidewalks on both sides of the street. Suddenly Floyd Boring heard a metal click, which he immediately recognized as someone dry-firing a weapon. He turned toward the front door and saw Officer Birdzell running into the street as a slight man in a suit was slapping an automatic handgun against his hand. As Boring and Davidson drew their weapons the assailant's gun went off; the shot hit Birdzell in the kneecap just as he was pulling out his own firearm. Officer Davidson started firing double action as fast as he could while Boring, who was an excellent marksman, cocked the hammer back on his snubnose revolver and took aim at the moving target. Boring shot off a round, which went through the assailant's hat and skimmed the top of his head. Momentarily dazed, the shooter turned back toward Birdzell, who was struggling to get on his feet, and shot him again before whipping around to fire on Davidson and Boring. Boring had slipped behind a tree to take cover, and as horrified pedestrians scattered in all directions, Boring aimed again and steadily squeezed the trigger. This round likely found its mark as the gunman staggered, as he sat on the stairs to load another clip, then toppled over—out of action.

---

[z] A pair of small misstatements: The White House was being totally rebuilt inside, with a new bomb shelter at the bottom level. Blair House stood (still does) 4½ stories high above the sidewalk.

At the same time the attack on Birdzell began, a second gunman had approached from the east. He jammed his 9mm Luger into the guard booth and shot Officer Leslie Coffelt at point-blank range with a number of rounds. As Coffelt sank to the floor, the gunman turned his weapon on a plainclothes White House police officer by the name of Downs, who was just

returning to Blair House after buying groceries for the Trumans. The shots hit Officer Downs in the hip, shoulder, and neck, sending him to the ground. Then the attacker took aim at Officer Birdzell, who was kneeling, wounded, in the street. But the attacker's weapon was now empty, so as he stopped to put another clip of bullets into his weapon, he didn't

notice the mortally wounded Officer Coffelt steadying his revolver. Just before he drew his last breath, Coffelt managed to squeeze off a round that entered one ear of his assailant and went out the other, killing the man instantly. The dramatic gun battle lasted just forty seconds. [2539]

"Inside Blair House, the moment Agent Stout heard the first shots he ran to the gun cabinet and grabbed a Thompson .45-caliber submachine gun. Stout pushed in the magazine and started up the staircase to the second floor, where President Truman was in his bedroom. A house servant was yelling at Stout to go outside to help, but Stout knew he was the last line of defense for the president. He reached the second floor, pulled the activation bolt, and pointed it at the main door. If an assailant attempted to enter, he'd be dead in a second." [2540]

Reverting briefly to the opening paragraph and the forthcoming increase in protection:

"It turned out the two men were Puerto Rican nationalists and the poorly planned assassination attempt was an effort to further their cause of Puerto Rico's independence. President Truman was unscathed by the gun battle, but when SAIC James Rowley reiterated the need for more agents on the Secret Service detail, Truman finally agreed to push Congress for funding. Shortly thereafter, the number of agents went from fifteen to thirty-four." [2541]

To understand the Puerto Ricans' motivation, a brief bit of history: In 1898 the United States intervened on the side of Cubans rebelling against Spain. Spain, then the U.S., declared war on each other. Because of vastly superior naval power, the U.S. was victorious in ten weeks. It took temporary authority over Cuba, and colonial authority over the Philippine Islands, Guam and Puerto Rico. Cuba was quickly given full independence. Delayed by World War II, the Philippines gained independence in 1946. Guam became a U.S. territory. As in Alaska when this author was young, Guamanians are American citizens but their delegate in Congress has no vote and the people cannot vote for president.

Puerto Rico had been claimed for Spain by Cristoforo Colombo [AA] in 1493, and then absorbed Spanish language and customs for 400 years, a span similar to the U.S.'s from the

---

[AA] His Spanish employers called the Italian "Cristóbal Colón". You may know him by another name, one that he never heard and would not recognize even if you yelled it at him.

Pilgrims of 1620 to today. In 1898, Puerto Rico became self-ruled through a Charter of Autonomy ratified by the Spanish Cortes. Just a few months later, the United States defeated Spain in the Spanish-American War and, without cause or justification, took command of the island as part of the Treaty of Paris. President Theodore Roosevelt declared that "It is manifest destiny for a nation to own the islands which border its shores." The island then became associated with the U.S. as a commonwealth. Like the British commonwealth nations, it had some local control but was ultimately under the sufferance and rule of Washington, D.C. President Truman and Congress granted a soupçon of local control, and in 1948 Luis Munoz Mar'n became Puerto Rico's first elected governor.

Despite that measure of local autonomy, the Puerto Rican Nationalist Party wanted full independence, what Gandhi and Nehru had recently obtained for India. On October 30, 1950, Nationalists staged attacks against government offices across the island. In one of those, five men drove up to the gates in front of La Fortaleza, the governor's residence and office in San Juan, rolled down the car's windows and began firing at the two guards at the gates, and at the building's windows. Mar n's two young daughters looked out at the scene, then took cover. The governor, working in his office, was unhurt.

Most know the final scene of *Butch Cassidy and the Sundance Kid*, in which hundreds of Bolivian Army troops on rooftops above the two "Banditos Yanquis" put a memorable, thundering end to their operations. Precisely the same thing happened in San Juan. All five died in a hail of bullets, in a one-sided "fight" that lasted, at most, ten minutes.[2542]

That October 30 attack against the highest official in Puerto Rico makes no rational sense. Although brave and heroic, it was impractical by any objective evaluation. Well, precisely the same thing is going to be copycatted two days later in the United States.

Again, first a little history: The President was defended by a few men, members of the Secret Service, an arm of the Treasury Department, headquartered in the large federal office building nearest to the White House. The Special Agents (they must be good — they are all "Special"!) then and now move with the president, wherever he goes. The presidential residence and office exteriors are guarded by more stationary uniformed officers of the White House Police Force, a division of the Secret Service.[2543]

During Harry Truman's residency, the White House was found to be in great disrepair, with rot in its walls and foundations endangering the building and its residents. The building was gutted, with only the outside walls standing, to allow complete rebuilding and modernization. Harry and Bess, and frequently-visiting daughter Margaret, moved across the street into Blair House, the official quarters for important visiting guests. The police moved with them, establishing guard posts beside the sidewalk at both ends of the property.

News of the attacks in Puerto Rico made headlines in New York, and two immigrant *Nacionalistas* decided they could gain greater attention for the independence cause by making a similar attack in the U.S. The elder and leader, Oscar Collazo, had come to New York City at 17. In the Great Depression he found work only as a dishwasher, migrated back and forth to Puerto Rico where he witnessed and joined the struggle for independence. Returned to NYC, he learned a profession as expert polisher of brass frames for women's handbags, married and settled in The Bronx. Every night he spent a full hour reading and learning, especially history.

"He ... could not get over that the invasion of Puerto Rico in 1898, coming as it did after the Charter of Autonomy from Spain, was illegal, not an act of war. Therefore the American presence on the island was an occupation by force, exactly as the Germans had invaded France and Poland. The Americans weren't big brothers, helping their backward cousins into modern times, but military conquerors, there to loot, pillage, rape, and raze.

For a while in the early 1940s, the FBI took an interest in Oscar Collazo because of his Nationalist activities. A file was opened. But after a few years, based on informant information that Oscar had drifted away from the cause, the FBI decided that he was no longer worth keeping an eye on." [2544]

Griselio Torresola, eleven years younger than Oscar, immigrated to the US in 1948 from their mutual hometown, Jayuya. Only 25, he had a wife who had returned to Puerto Rico and given birth to a daughter, and now a common-law wife and son in Spanish Harlem in upper Manhattan. He had worked very briefly, was content to live cheaply on the government dole.

Collazo and Torresola were different in age, stability and education, but united in their dedication to the revolution that would free their island from hated American dominion. So, on the afternoon of October 31, they put on clean suits, shirts, ties and hats, and took a train from Penn Station to Washington, D.C., where neither had ever been. They checked into a cheap hotel near Union Station. The telephone directory in their room had what they needed, a map showing the location of the White House. [2545]

The next day was November 1, only two days after the abortive attacks in Puerto Rico including the vain shooting assault on the exterior of the governor's residence. In Washington, the two dressed carefully in suits and ties, hailed a cab and told the driver, John Gavounas, [2546] to take them to the White House where the president lived. "It was the cabdriver who says to them, No, no, he don't live there. See, they're rebuilding the White House. ... The driver then helpfully pointed across the street." [2547] The Trumans had moved into Blair House shortly after HST's re-election in 1948. Unknown to the assassins, their target had lived "across the street" for two years.

At least twice every day, Harry walked from Blair House to the White House's West Wing, to work in his Oval Office. Whenever possible he came back to have lunch with Bess and take a nap before going back to the office for a long afternoon of work. Collazo and Torresola knew nothing of this, so had no way of knowing where Truman was when they made their attack. In the event, they chose the correct building, probably by happenstance.

Looking from across Pennsylvania Avenue, they came up with a plan to attack from two directions, with less-proficient shooter Collazo giving covering fire while Torresola leapt up the stairs, through a screen door and inside to hunt for and shoot Truman. There is no need to describe the events in detail. The Secret Service account and photograph on foregoing pages convey enough to understand the abortive and deadly effort.

There is an excellent full-detail account in Stephen Hunter and John Bainbridge Jr.'s *American Gunfight: The Plot to Kill Harry Truman, and the Shoot-out That Stopped It*. They explain how the plan went wrong from the first instant because Collazo, experienced only with revolvers, was unfamiliar with his semi-automatic pistol, so put <u>on</u> its safety, making a loud click while rendering it unable to fire. Alerted, the president's defenders fired at and disabled him. Only one of Collazo's eight shots hit anyone — Officer Birdzell in the knee. At the west guardhouse, Torresola and guard Coffelt shot and killed each other. The assault lasted only 40 seconds, proceeding and ending as in the account that began three pages back.

Harry Truman immediately sent a letter to Mrs. Leslie Coffelt, wife of the slain guard, then kept all previously scheduled afternoon appointments. Given time for reflection, many authorities were puzzled by the attempt because Truman has supported the right of Puerto Rico to determine its own relationship to the United States.[2548]

One of the first civilians to arrive on the scene had just found work as a newspaper reporter. He hopped off of his streetcar that had stopped right there on Pennsylvania Avenue, got the story and phoned it in to the *Washington Post* where he was the lowest-of-the-low. It was his first story to make the front page. He was 25, and went on to have a magnificent career at the paper, to become a close friend of Jack Kennedy, and to break the news of both the Pentagon Papers and Nixon's involvement in Watergate — Benjamin C. Bradlee.

Here's the story on the nation's newspaper-of-record's front page the next day: [2549]

Evidence linked Collazo and Torresola to the Nationalist Party of Puerto Rico, but the government could not establish that their attack was part of a larger Nationalist conspiracy. Collazo was tried and sentenced to death in 1951. In 1952 President Truman commuted his sentence to life imprisonment.[2550] Acknowledging the importance of the question of Puerto Rican independence, Truman allowed a plebiscite in Puerto Rico to determine the status of its relationship to the U.S. The people voted in favor of continuing as a Free Associated State. President Jimmy Carter in 1979 commuted Collazo's sentence to the twenty-nine years served; he was released and returned to Puerto Rico, where he died in bed in 1994.[2551]

There was a similar but separate incident at the United States Capitol in 1954. Four Puerto Rican nationalists, to again highlight for Americans their struggle for independence, went to the visitors' gallery above the House of Representatives, unfurled a Puerto Rican flag and began shooting at the 240 Representatives of the 83rd Congress, who were debating an immigration bill. Thirty rounds from semi-automatic pistols wounded five Representatives, one seriously, but all recovered. The assailants were arrested, tried and convicted in federal court, and given long sentences, effectively life imprisonment. In 1978 and 1979, they were pardoned, also by President Jimmy Carter; all four returned to Puerto Rico.[2552]

The course of the American presidency may have changed because of the 1950 attack at Blair House. As would also be the entitlement of LBJ in 1968, in 1952 HST was eligible to be re-elected to a second full term but declined to run. Then-famous columnist Drew Pearson wrote at that time:

> "An unreported factor behind President Truman's decision to retire was the anguish and strain that the Truman family still feels over the attempted assassination of the President on November 1, 1950, when Secret Service Agent [*sic*] Leslie Coffelt was killed. ... [Pearson reported that the president told a congressman], 'Did you ever stop to think how you would feel if another man laid down his life for you? Well, that's the way I feel about Leslie Coffelt. It's men like him or some other good man who are really in danger in situations like that—not the President, but the men entrusted with his protection.'"[2553]

1950: Oscar Collazo and Griselio Torresola attack residence of Harry Truman	
Weapons:	Pistols, 9mm semi-automatic: OC: Walther P38. GT: Luger P08
Distances:	18" by GT at guardhouse to 30' between OC and police in street
Shots fired:	Each attacker fired all 8 bullets in his pistol, then both were shot while attempting to reload. The defenders fired a total of 15.
Killed / Hit:	Killed: Police Officer Leslie Coffelt and attacker Torresola shot and killed each other. Hit: Officers Donald Birdzell and Joe Downs, and attacker Collazo were all wounded by bullets, all recovered.
Assassins then:	Torresola dead. Collazo wounded, healed, convicted, sentenced to die, commuted to life, freed, returned to Puerto Rico, died.
Motive(s):	Draw attention in US to Puerto Rican desire for independence
Do we know beyond reasonable doubt, **whom** did the assassins intend to shoot? **Yes**	
Do we know beyond reasonable doubt, **motive** for wanting to shoot that man? **Yes**	

1958: Izola Ware Curry stabs and seriously wounds Martin Luther King Jr.

Because of a little-known attempt by a crazed woman, a sneeze or other movement could have caused the ten years 1958 to 1968 to be considerably different from what we know: a muted civil rights movement without the 1963 speech I am not able to quote,[2554] no national holiday in January and many fewer cities with MLK boulevards. Most of the information below comes from a book about the attack, *When Harlem Nearly Killed King: The 1958 Stabbing of Dr. Martin Luther King Jr.* by Hugh Pearson,[2555] from a 2014 article "The Black and White Men Who Saved Martin Luther King's Life" by Michael Daly on *The Daily Beast* website,[2556] and from the Wikipedia article "Izola Curry".[2557]

Rev. Dr. Martin Luther King, Jr. wrote his first book, *Stride Toward Freedom: The Montgomery Story* about a key event in Alabama and went on a book tour to promote it. On September 20, 1958, he was to sign books at Blumstein's department store in Harlem. A very nicely dressed woman,[2558] a "fashion plate" with large earrings and sequined spectacles, asked "Is this Martin Luther King?" "Yes, it is," he replied. Without warning, she plunged a thin razor-sharp steel letter opener into his chest with such great force that it pieced his sternum.[BB] A woman next to King knocked the attacker's fist from the handle before she could pull it out for a second stab. The would-be assassin stepped back, made no effort to flee, and shouted "I've been after him for six years! I'm glad I done it!" and obscenities about King and the NAACP.

An ivory handle protruded from King's chest, a few inches below and to the left of the knot in his tie. A woman spoke sharply: "Don't touch that knife!" King sat down in a chair. "Everything is going to be all right" he said, stony calm. The woman told him to hush, and especially, he should not sneeze! An ambulance from Harlem Hospital brought a licensed practical nurse who rightly sensed the precariousness of the situation. She and a policeman carried the chair, ever so gingerly, out to the ambulance and laid King on his back.

Rev. King had begun to make a name for himself by organizing the successful bus boycott and demonstrations in Alabama after tired seamstress Rosa Parks refused to give up her bus seat to a white man. (See President Obama in that seat on page 158.) The photo [2559] shows King and Parks in 1955, the year she stayed in her seat. It was his memoir-book about Montgomery that MLK was to sign that day in Harlem. Recognizing the national prominence of the incoming patient, the hospital phoned for its top doctors.

Harlem Hospital's chief of surgery was in a movie theater, unreachable a full half-century before cell phones would keep everyone in touch "24 / 7 / 365". He will come to the hospital after Brigitte Bardot, the sex kitten of those days, finishes baring and emoting in *La Parisienne*.

[BB] The sternum or breastbone is the long flat bony plate located in the front-center of the chest. It connects to upper rib bones via cartilage, supports the collarbone, and protects the heart.

Dr. John W. V. Cordice, Jr., the hospital's young chief of thoracic and vascular surgery, raced in from New Jersey. He had hoped to become an engineer and an aviator like Charles Lindbergh, but was told that such a career path was not open to an African-American. He followed his father into medicine, which proved to be difficult enough given the prevailing racial attitudes of the time. During World War II, Cordice got closer to his original dream as the physician for the newly-formed all-Negro fighter pilot unit, the Tuskegee Airmen.

Cordice was joined by thoracic surgeon Dr. Emil Naclerio, dressed in a tuxedo for a wedding, and expert anesthesiologist Helen Mayer. "We usually answered these kinds of emergencies together," Cordice noted. X-rays showed that King was in grave danger. The razor-sharp tip of Curry's knife was almost touching the aorta, the thick-as-your-thumb vessel taking blood from the heart to nourish the body. If the weapon's tip were even to pin-prick, the aorta could easily rip open and King would quickly die.

While the doctors prepared, detectives took Curry into the emergency room where King lay on a gurney with the blade still in his chest. Fearing that he might die of the stab wound, the police wanted to record his identification of the woman. They maneuvered her cautiously into King's view. Before he could speak, Curry cried out, "That's him! I'll report him to my lawyers!" She stood rigidly erect and haughty, proud as a queen. King, still calm and lucid though growing weaker, identified Curry before she was hustled away.

Gloved African-American hands and gloved white hands worked expertly together as the surgeons made two incisions between ribs, in the form of a cross in front of King's heart — which some took as a divine sign when it was found at his autopsy ten years later. They then inserted a rib spreader and the aorta became visible. The point of the weapon was concealed by the sternum through which it had penetrated with such surprising force. The surgeons confirmed, by exploring underneath with their fingertips, that it was exactly where the x-ray showed it to be, its potentially deadly sharpness vivid to the touch. Out of respect for their notoriously touchy boss, the two surgeons then waited for him to appear.

The Chairman of the Department of Surgery, Aubré de Lambert Maynard, a West Indian, arrived from the movie theater and attempted without success to pull the letter opener from King's chest. Cordice affixed a surgical clamp to the blade, with which Maynard then managed to pull it out. He hurriedly left the underlings to close up the incision while he announced to gathered officials and reporters that the operation had been a success. Cordice and Naclerio later stood silent at a press conference while Maynard placed himself at the center of the action. He subsequently told ever more elaborate falsehoods and presented himself ever more dramatically as the man who had saved King. Cordice and Naclerio continued their work, treating patients who were less celebrated and often unable to pay. Marguerite Cordice recalls that her father was aghast when somebody asked him if he had treated King differently than he might another patient. "What? Of course not!" he replied.

"Days later," King wrote in his autobiography, "when I was well enough to talk ... I learned the reason for the long delay that preceded surgery. [T]he razor tip of the instrument had been touching my aorta and my whole chest had to be opened to extract it. 'If you had sneezed during all those hours of waiting,' Dr. Maynard said, 'your aorta would have been punctured and you would have drowned in your own blood.'" [2560] Actually, the "whole chest" had not been opened, and further, it seems most likely that Dr. Maynard did not explain the "long delay" was because his staff knew there'd be big trouble if they proceeded while he was downtown ogling Brigitte Bardot.

While in the hospital,[2561] King said in a press release that he reaffirmed his belief in "the redemptive power of nonviolence" and issued a hopeful statement about his attacker, "I felt no ill will toward Mrs. Izola Curry and know that thoughtful people will do all in their power to see that she gets the help she apparently needs if she is to become a free and constructive member of society." King recovered after several weeks' rest.[2562]

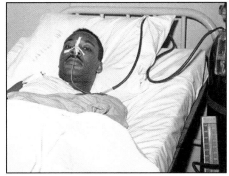

Ten years later, on the night before he died in 1968, MLK recalled the incident, and because he had not sneezed, was alive and in Memphis. He then talked of having been to the top of a mountain to see a promised land, 373 memorable words I am not legally able to quote here. The box explains this very sad situation.

In 2016, the children of Martin Luther King, Jr. and Coretta Scott King are infamously litigious in their management of the Estate of Dr. Martin Luther King, Jr. They are well known for taking legal action against any who dare to quote his words without paying whatever they ask, even to the extent that producers of the mega-budget 2014 movie "*Selma*" were unwilling to do that, and forced to paraphrase his famous speeches! The King Estate has assigned its copyright authority to "Intellectual Properties Management" of Atlanta. This book's author repeatedly asked I-P-M for permission to quote after reasonable payment, but they have not had the courtesy to send any reply. To buy that one OK, I then attempted to hire an experienced professional agent, who replied: "I am not surprised that you are having trouble with the King family and permissions. The one time I attempted to get permission to run a quote from the "I have a dream" speech, I was quoted an outrageous sum of several thousand dollars and we went another direction very quickly. That was the end of that. I truly would encourage you to give it up now or prepare to pay exorbitant sums. ... It really is not that outrageous to expect a courteous response from these people to a legitimate request." I planned to quote his irreplaceable words in several places in this book, but cannot. So, if you wish to read MLK's historic thoughts about sneezing and dreaming, please look elsewhere.

Dr. Maynard continued to claim credit for saving King until his own death in 1999 at the age of 97. Dr. Naclerio had already died in 1984, at 67. Dr. Cordice died in 2013, at 94. He had been honored in 2012 by Harlem Hospital for a long and distinguished career in which he helped save King and so many others. He said he felt as if all his training had been leading up to this recognition, as if he were just a vehicle for such accomplishments. "One of those things," the humble giant softly said.

Detectives identified the Negress attacker. Izola Ware was born to sharecroppers near Adrian, Georgia in 1916. She married James Curry; they separated after six months but she kept his name. She never remarried, never had children. As her mind began to fail with paranoia, Izola moved to New York City, working at times as a domestic. Although she was as dark black as anyone, she grew to fear the National Association for the Advancement of Colored People (NAACP), somehow believing its members to be Communists. She thought they were conspiring to keep her from getting and keeping a job. "They were making scurrilous remarks about me," she confessed. She couldn't point to any specific person, but she was sure that they were after her. From 1956 to 1958, Izola attempted to avoid NAACP persecution by seriatim moves to Cleveland, St. Louis, Charleston WV, Savannah, West Palm Beach, Lexington KY, Columbia SC, Miami, Daytona Beach, and finally back to NYC.[2563]

In the fall of 1958 she was unemployed and living out of a suitcase in a tenement. Her mind grew worse. According to biographer Hugh Pearson, "She especially detested Negro preachers. ... [I]n Curry's mind, Martin Luther King, Jr., was a young minister pimping the community for the benefit of Communists."[2564] Believing that the NAACP and King were watching her every move, the fear became unbearable and she bought a gun.[2565]

Izola Curry, like Lee Oswald with neither transportation nor funds, could not travel to assassinate, but acted when the target came to her. After she stabbed King, a police matron discovered a loaded Italian automatic pistol inside her blouse. She raved incoherently about persecution, torture and her anger at King for having undermined her Roman Catholic faith.

Arraigned for felonious assault and possession of a firearm, Izola Curry stood through a magistrate's recitation of the facts until he stated that she was alleged to have stabbed King with a knife. "No," she interrupted sharply, "It was a letter opener." Detectives sustained her correction. The instrument was a slender Japanese penknife with a gently curved blade and a handle of inlaid ivory. Like her Italian automatic, it was a stylish weapon for a stylish lady. Curry had expensive foreign tastes jarringly at odds with her low station as an itinerant maid who had drifted alone for many years since leaving a broken home and a failed marriage. Shortly after the magistrate resumed his presentation, Curry interrupted again to announce that she was accusing King of "being mixed up with the communists," adding that she had "reported the case to the FBI and it's being looked into."

She explained that she had stabbed King so that he would "listen to my problems, because I've been followed in buses and people have been making me lose my job." Basing his ruling partially on these statements, the judge ordered that Curry be taken to Bellevue Hospital for psychiatric assessment. She was diagnosed as a paranoid schizophrenic, was then found incompetent to stand trial, and was committed for an indefinite term to the Matteawan State Hospital for the Criminally Insane.[2566] "Curry disappeared permanently, leaving behind only a single deed of mysterious, unfathomable horror."[2567]

Izola was long jailed in what is now the Fishkill Correctional Facility in New York, then in a long series of institutions. After this article about her had been written, she made page 2 of many newspapers when she died in a nursing home in Queens, New York.[2568]

After the stabbing, Martin Luther King Jr. lived another 9½ years and died at age 38. Izola Ware Curry lived another 54½ years and died at age 98.

1958: Izola Ware Curry stabs and seriously wounds Martin Luther King Jr.	
Weapon:	Letter opener with long, thin, sharp steel blade and ivory handle
Distance:	In contact: pushed blade through sternum, deep into his chest
Shots fired:	None — knife attack
Killed / Hit:	None killed, King close to death if his aorta ruptured
Assassin then:	Quickly captured, identified, analyzed, found unable to help defend herself, sent to institution for criminally insane, never released.
Motive(s):	Insane: Delusional, paranoid, schizophrenic
Do we know beyond reasonable doubt, **whom** did the assassin intend to assault? Yes	
Do we know beyond reasonable doubt, her **motive** for assaulting that man? Yes	

1960: Richard Paul Pavlick stalks to car bomb President-elect John Kennedy [2569]

Newspapers ran stories about this plan to assassinate a president-elect before his inauguration, the first since Giuseppe Zangara fired at president-elect Franklin Roosevelt in 1933. But the banner headlines read "Worst Air Disaster In History Kills 132 In New York" above a story about two planes colliding over Brooklyn, killing 127 of 128 onboard plus 5 on the ground. The only surviving passenger was an 11-year-old boy. In that transitional era, one plane had propellors, the other was a jet. In another sign of those times, expansive journalism, the toll was the worst "since the Wright brothers gave wings to mankind in 1903". The second-tier headline: "Kennedy Names Republican, Brother To Cabinet".[2570] The cabinet appointees were Douglas Dillon to be Secretary of the Treasury and Bobby to be Attorney General.

A third-rank story told of Richard Paul Pavlick,[CC] 73, of Belmont, New Hampshire.[2571] Living alone, the "old crank" caused problems at town meetings and fired off enraged and belligerent letters to public figures and newspapers. He complained that the American flag was not being displayed appropriately, criticized the government and disparaged Catholics, focusing much of his anger on the Kennedy family and its wealth.[2572] His favorite subject was that Joe Kennedy had bought the presidency for his son. There's a grain of truth in that. Whereas Richard Nixon had no father and only a poor old mother, Kennedy told his friend Ben Bradlee that the election had cost his hugely rich father, Joe, $13 million.[2573] The joke at that time had father Joe saying to son Jack: "Don't spend more than you have to. I'll pay for a win, but damned if I'll pay for a landslide!"

Pavlick could do nothing to prevent Kennedy being elected, but decided to stop him from being inaugurated. The retired postal worker's history of mental problems may explain his outrage and murderous intent. He decided on an action, set about it quite deliberately — and then caused his own failure. After giving his run-down residence to a youth camp, Pavlick loaded his meager possessions into his 1950 Buick and disappeared.

He drove to the Kennedy compound at Hyannis Port, Massachusetts, next sized up the house in Georgetown, then headed south. Kennedy chose to enjoy Palm Beach's December sunshine, and that's where Pavlick chose to kill him. He purchased ten sticks of dynamite, four large cans of gasoline and blasting caps, and rigged up a simple but large car bomb — "enough to blow up a small mountain" according to a Secret Service official — in the Buick's trunk, with a detonation switch in the driver's hand. It was an early, ugly suicide bomb.

On December 11, he parked outside the Kennedy house [DD] with a simple plan: He would wait for Kennedy to come out to go to Sunday Mass,[EE] then crash into the President's car and detonate the bomb, killing both Kennedy and himself. Alas, when JFK came out that morning, he was not alone. With him were Jacqueline, Caroline and John Jr., not yet a month old. Pavlick was eager to kill Kennedy, but did not want to hurt the family, so he decided to try again another day. He went back to North Ocean Boulevard several times: in all he waited, parked in the road, for five days.[2574]

[CC] If you search for more, know that his surname is commonly misspelled without the "c" — Pavlik.

[DD] The house got its 15 minutes of fame decades later when brother Ted entertained young ladies there.

[EE] Another joke of that time: "Now that he's President, he <u>has</u> to go!"

Meanwhile, postmaster Thomas Murphy in hometown Belmont had been receiving strange postcards from Pavlick. They meant nothing until one said he would soon do something big. The postmaster laid out the cards and saw they were postmarked with dates and locations coinciding with Kennedy's travels. He called police, who contacted the Secret Service, who soon understood the man, his outbursts, and his disapproval of the election.

Recognizing that wherever Kennedy went, Pavlick was sure to follow, the Secret Service asked Palm Beach police to look out for his vehicle. On December 15, a patrolman spotted Pavlick's Buick;[2575] police surrounded the car and arrested him. This gave the first evidence — dynamite — of his plan. Pavlick told reporters he wanted to take Kennedy's life because of "the underhanded way he was elected." "Kennedy money bought the White House and the Presidency. I had the crazy idea I wanted to stop Kennedy from being President." He told Secret Service agents he had been treated at a mental hospital and asked for an exam. [2576]

"The Kennedy family remained in Florida during those final weeks of 1960. Allowed to live, they prepared for Christmas. United Press International reported that the tree in their home was donated by the West Palm Beach Optimist Club. The president-elect received, from his family ... cigars and hand-knitted socks. All seemed safe and right in their world." [2577]

Pavlick was indicted for threatening Kennedy's life, charges that were dropped in three years after JFK died in Dallas. One week after Kennedy's inauguration, the would-be assassin was committed to a mental hospital because it was clear that Pavlick lacked the ability to distinguish between right and wrong (i.e., he was legally insane). In 1966 he was released from the New Hampshire State Mental Hospital, six years after being apprehended and three years after Lee Oswald killed Kennedy. Richard Paul Pavlick died in 1975 at the age of 88 at the Veterans Administration Hospital in Manchester, New Hampshire.

Writing for *Smithsonian*, Dan Lewis offers this: "Bonus fact: If Pavlick seems old for a would-be Presidential assassin, your instincts are correct. Lee Harvey Oswald was just 24 years old, making him the youngest of all four of the men who assassinated Presidents. John Wilkes Booth was 26 when he killed Abraham Lincoln; Leon Czolgosz was 28 when he assassinated William McKinley, Charles Guiteau was 39 when he attacked James Garfield." [2578]

1960: Richard Paul Pavlick stalks to car bomb President-elect John Kennedy	
Weapon:	Suicide car bomb of dynamite
Distance:	Intended to ram and blow-up; did not because family was present
Shots fired:	None
Killed / Hit:	None
Assassin then:	Was arrested before taking action because of his postcard trail
Motive(s):	Prevent the "wrongly-elected" man from being inaugurated
Do we know beyond reasonable doubt, **whom** did the assassin intend to shoot? **Yes**	
Do we know beyond reasonable doubt, his **motive** for stalking the victim? **Yes**	

1963: Byron De La Beckwith, Jr. shoots and kills Medgar Evers

The terrible year 1963 began with struggles for equal treatment in the American South, with focus in the blackest states, Alabama and Mississippi. Authorities (there and then, they were all white) imprisoned Negro leaders, loosed truncheon-wielding police, dogs and fire hoses on marchers and demonstrators. An example readily understood is this photo [2579] on May 28 in Jackson, Mississippi, as a professor and students from Tougaloo College sat at a Woolworth's lunch counter although they were denied service. A mob of young whites poured ketchup, mustard and sugar onto them. The sit-in demonstrators silently took it, so the frustrated whites pulled them off their stools, beat them and poured salt into their wounds. On June 1, police arrested black supporters from a

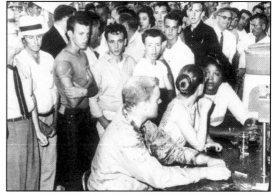

picket line outside Woolworth's. Most prominent among those arrested were long-time national leader Roy Wilkins and a younger local man, Medgar Evers, field secretary in Mississippi of the National Association for the Advancement of Colored People (NAACP).[2580]

"June 11 was a landmark in the civil rights struggle that had been raging that spring with its focus in Birmingham, Alabama. In January a governor named George Wallace had been inaugurated in Alabama with a speech promising that he 'would stand in the schoolhouse door, if necessary,' to resist court-ordered desegregation. On June 11, Wallace fulfilled his promise by standing in the doorway of the registration building of the University of Alabama at Tuscaloosa. Twice Wallace held out his hand in a 'stop' signal, and twice James Hood and Vivian Malone, two black students who were accompanied by the Deputy Attorney General of the United States, Nicholas Katzenbach, had to retreat. As the day wore on, President Kennedy, in Washington, signed an order federalizing part of the National Guard in Alabama. As guardsmen walked on the campus, Governor Wallace walked off, and the two students were allowed to register." [2581] This chapter will re-visit Wallace in 1972.

The next day, on radio and TV from the White House, President Kennedy called for a civil rights law. Most likely because of that speech, it was a night that would end in tragedy. At the Evers home, wife Myrlie and the three young children watched the speech on TV, then

waited for Medgar [2582] who was meeting with civil rights workers at a church. After Kennedy had finished, they heard their father's car and rushed for the door. Historian Taylor Branch continues the tragic story in his *Parting the Waters*:

"Evers stepped out of his Oldsmobile ... His white dress shirt made a perfect target for the killer waiting in a fragrant stand of honeysuckle across the street. One loud crack sent a bullet from a .30-06 deer rifle exploding through his back, out the front of his chest, and on through his living room window to spend itself against the

kitchen refrigerator. True to their rigorous training in civil rights preparedness, the four people inside dived to the floor like soldiers in a foxhole, but when no more shots came, they all ran outside to find him lying face-down near the door. 'Please, Daddy, please get up!' cried the children, and then everything fell away to blood-smeared, primal hysteria. ... [N]eighbors and police hoisted the mess of him onto a mattress and into a station wagon." [2583]

Evers had been mortally wounded by the bullet [FF] from a high-powered Enfield 1917 rifle. [2584] Taken to the local hospital in Jackson, he was refused entry because of his color until it was explained who he was. He died in the hospital 50 minutes later. [2585]

His body lay in an open coffin in Jackson for several days while African-American leaders worked to convince Myrlie that Medgar could still perform one more service to the cause. She finally agreed, and his body then traveled on a slow train to Washington, D.C. Evers had fought in WW II's Battle of Normandy as a U.S. Army Sergeant, so was entitled to a military burial. Taylor Branch relates:

> "Twenty-five thousand people had viewed the body in a two-day processional, and the burial service at Arlington Cemetery was the largest since that of John Foster Dulles. President Kennedy did not attend, but afterward he sent a limousine for the widow and her two older children. He gave them kind words of condolence, and for the kids there were PT-109 souvenirs plus a scoot across the bed on which Queen Elizabeth had slept." [2586]

> Here was to be a photo from the funeral of Medgar Evers, with him lying in his American-flag-draped coffin. Black Star photo service told my picture researcher: "The Estate has a minimum fee of $300 per picture." If the photo were here, the cost of every copy of this book would increase by more than $1. That photo is not important to the book's purpose, so it is not shown here. The photo is in the 1989 book *Parting the Waters: America in the King Years, 1954-63* by Taylor Branch: photo #70 in the insert section after page 688.

The assassination was quickly linked to Byron De La Beckwith. [GG] The rifle was discovered near the scene and was soon traced to him. The rifle's telescopic sight bore his fingerprints. Witnesses reported a man who looked like Beckwith, driving a car that looked like his distinctive white Plymouth Valiant with a whip antenna (to receive orders in his work as a manure dealer), asking directions to the Evers home on the night of the shooting. [2587] But he told investigators his rifle had been stolen, and two police officers said that at the time of the killing they had seen him in Greenwood, some 95 miles away.

Beckwith's father died when he was 5; his mother moved with Byron to Greenwood, Mississippi to be near family. She died when he was 12, he was raised by an uncle, served in WW II as a Marine Corps machine gunner, fighting and being wounded in the fierce battles of Guadalcanal and Tarawa. After honorable discharge, he married and settled in Greenwood, working as a salesman for most of his life, selling tobacco, fertilizer, wood stoves and a variety of other goods. [2588]

The White Citizens' Council was founded in 1954 following the Supreme Court's ruling in *Brown v. Board of Education* that school segregation was unconstitutional. Chapters across the South suppressed black activism and sustained segregation, applying pressure through boycotts, denial of loans and credit, employment termination and other means. In

---

[FF] ".30-06" is a high-power military bullet, .30-inch diameter, designed in 1906. The rifle that fired it was mass-built beginning in 1917 for American doughboys to fight the "Great War" in Europe. Thousands were sold as surplus after the war. As proven by Lee Oswald's Carcano (chapter 12), weapons designed to kill men in war also did that reliably back home in "peace" time.

[GG] Historian Branch does not even name him in his ultra-encompassing *Parting the Waters*, so in a small way I emulate that excellent example by not including a photo of the despicable assassin.

Mississippi they prevented school integration until 1964. Byron De La Beckwith, already a Ku Klux Klansman, became a member of the White Citizens' Council at its outset.

<table>
<tr><td>

Here was intended to be shown a photo of the tearful widow, Myrlie Evers, at the funeral of her murdered husband. It, too, would have cost as was described on the previous page, adding another $1.25, so it is not here. The photo is available to you in the book previously cited: photo #71 in the insert section after page 688.

</td><td>

The state twice prosecuted De La Beckwith in 1964. Mississippi had effectively disfranchised [HH] black voters since 1890, so they were thus prevented from serving on juries, whose membership was limited to voters. The jurors were all male and all white, and both trials ended with hung juries. A sign of the times in Mississippi: During the second trial, former Governor Ross Barnett interrupted the trial to shake hands with Beckwith in full view of the jury while the widow, Myrlie Evers, was testifying.

Investigation in the 1980s of the 1964 trials found that the pro-segregation Mississippi State Sovereignty Commission, tax-supported, had assisted De La Beckwith's attorneys by using state resources to investigate and cull members of the jury pool. That stimulated a new investigation and ultimately a third prosecution.

</td></tr>
</table>

A third trial, in 1994, was held before a jury of eight blacks and four whites. New evidence included testimony that he had boasted of the murder at several Ku Klux Klan rallies. Perhaps most damaging was this: He had been imprisoned for illegally carrying a bomb, probably to kill a leader of the Anti-Defamation League of B'nai B'rith. When ill in prison, he refused treatment from a black nurse's aide. A guard told of overhearing Beckwith tell the aide that "if I could get rid of an uppity" Medgar Evers, he would have no trouble dealing with the "no-account" aide. The physical evidence was essentially the same as in the 1964 trials. The 1994 jury convicted De La Beckwith of first-degree murder for killing Medgar Evers.

He appealed the verdict, but the Mississippi Supreme Court upheld his conviction. The court said the 31-year lapse between the murder and De La Beckwith's conviction did not deny him a fair trial. He was sentenced to life imprisonment without the possibility of parole for first-degree murder. He sought review in the United States Supreme Court, but was denied certiorari.[II] Suffering from heart disease, high blood pressure and other ailments, Byron De La Beckwith died in prison in 2001 at the age of 80.

1963: Byron De La Beckwith, Jr. shoots and kills Medgar Evers	
Weapon:	Rifle: Enfield, model 1917, .30-06 caliber
Distance:	About 30 feet
Shots fired:	One
Killed / Hit:	Medgar Evers, dead within an hour of major internal bleeding
Assassin then:	Was identified, tried, convicted in third trial, died in prison
Motive(s):	White man's wrath at anti-segregation leader black man
Do we know beyond reasonable doubt, **whom** did the assassin intend to shoot? **Yes**	
Do we know beyond reasonable doubt, his **motive** for shooting the man he hit? **Yes**	

[HH] "To deprive of a privilege ... or right of citizenship, esp. the right to vote." – *American Heritage*

[II] "certiorari *n.* A writ from a higher court to a lower one requesting a transcript of the proceedings of a case for review." – *Am. Heritage.* Denial means the higher court will not consider the case.

1968: James Earl Ray shoots and kills Dr. Martin Luther King, Jr.

City officials in Memphis, Tennessee, sent garbage collectors home early one rainy day in February 1968. They paid the whites for the full day, but the blacks [JJ] for only two hours. 1,300 black sanitation workers went on strike to protest this and similar inequities. In March, the Reverend Doctor Martin Luther King Jr. arrived, attempted negotiation, and when it failed, led a march. When a few participants turned violent, the nonviolent minister removed himself. Police clubbed, gassed and shot at the marchers; one black youth died and 60 were injured. King vowed to return to lead a non-violent demonstration.[2589]

He was back on April 3, planning another march. That evening, he addressed 2,000 supporters. As related earlier in this chapter, in 1958 King had been attacked by crazed Izola Curry in Harlem. She had stabbed so deeply into his chest that if he had sneezed, doctors said, his aorta would have ripped and he would have died. He spoke of his delight in not having sneezed, of death threats received upon his arrival in Memphis, and of the possibility that he might not live long enough to get to a promised land with his audience. Unfortunately, for the reason explained earlier, I can not print his eloquent words.

> A box like this on page 331 told how the children of Martin Luther King, Jr. and Coretta Scott King manage the Estate of Dr. Martin Luther King, Jr. This book's author has repeatedly asked them for permission to quote after reasonable payment, but has not had the courtesy of a reply. If you wish to read what MLK said about justice, dreaming and death, please look elsewhere.

King spent the next day planning non-violent actions. He and Ralph Abernathy stayed, as usual, in room 306 at the black-operated Lorraine Motel. Abernathy would tell the HSCA (chapter 8) in ten years: "We just felt a part of the Lorraine. ... We always stayed there, and we always stayed in that room, 306. This was the King-Abernathy suite." [2590] They and associates left their rooms and stood talking on the second floor balcony before going to dinner.[2591] At 6:01 PM the next day, a bullet

pierced Dr. King's jaw, neck, jugular vein and spine. In contrast to his near-death in Harlem in 1958, this time even the most quick-witted police and the most skillful surgeons could not have saved him. He was dead within the hour.

[JJ] An explanation especially for the younger: At that time, "Negro" was the polite term, but it quickly morphed into the disparaging "n word", so I will not use it. In recent years, "African-American" has been in vogue, but is not sufficiently precise: Immigrants from Egypt and Charlize Theron are inarguably African-Americans, but not among the people with dark skin of whom I write.

The murder rocked the nation. President Johnson appeared on television that evening, urging all Americans "to reject the blind violence that has struck Dr. King, who lived by nonviolence." Race riots broke out in most large cities. "Johnson ordered four thousand army and National Guard troops into Washington, D.C., and thousands more into cities around the country. Fires raged in the nation's capital and at one point rioters were within two blocks of the White House. The riots were contained after several days, but

clearly the nation was in turmoil."[2592] Notably, only one major city, Indianapolis, had no disorder at all because Bobby Kennedy, campaigning there for the presidency, gave a calm peace-seeking talk, as told at the beginning of the next article. Then he suspended his campaign until he and Ethel attended Dr. King's funeral in Atlanta.[2593] [2594]

On March 30, 1968 in Birmingham, Alabama, Harvey Lowmeyer finally reached a tortured decision. He had visited several gun shops, asked many questions, inspected several weapons, and even purchased a safari-grade .243 rifle, which he then decided was not sufficiently powerful for his purpose. He returned it the next day, paid a little extra, and purchased a Remington Gamemaster Model .30-06-caliber rifle, which Remington described as "the fastest hand-operated big game rifle made."[2595] He bought, and paid the dealer to mount, a premier sighting scope, a Redfield with magnification powers adjustable from 2 to 7.

He also bought boxes of Remington-Peters .30-06 Springfield high-velocity 150-grain soft-point Core-Lokt cartridges, especially designed to expand and kill anything they hit. Analyst Gerald Posner wrote that the man was now equipped to stop a charging rhinoceros at 100 yards, or to kill a man as far away as 1,500 yards — nearly a mile. Mr. Lowmeyer paid $253.59 in cash and carried his world-class killing armament out to a Ford Mustang, painted in unusual "Springtime Yellow",[2596] so pale that most observers thought it was white.

On April 3, Eric Galt stopped beside a quiet highway near Corinth, Mississippi, took his new rifle from the car's trunk, adjusted its scope to its fullest power, and practiced shooting at dozens of targets. Mr. Galt was satisfied with the rifle, and was fully confident that the scope was aimed correctly.[2597]

Mid-afternoon on April 4, John Willard rented a room in a Memphis rooming house, the derelict type known as a flophouse. He rejected the first room shown him but accepted the second that had a window with a view, paying $8.50 for a week. He then drove to purchase Bushnell binoculars with 7-power magnification, like Harvey Lowmeyer's rifle's scope, so the view through the binoculars would be the same as through the scope.[2598] When he returned to the rooming house, his parking space right in front had been taken, so he parked down the block near a fire station. Mr. Willard then spent the next 1½ hours shuttling between his upstairs room and the communal bathroom at the end of the hallway.[2599]

Shortly after 6 PM, a loud bang was heard in the building. Two tenants saw a man in a suit coming from the direction of the bathroom, which seemed to be the source of the noise, carrying something long, maybe about three feet, wrapped in a bundle. The man quickly went down stairs and out to the sidewalk. As he hurried toward his car, he saw three police squad cars ahead, parked in front of the fire station, so he dropped his bundle in an alcove and sped away.[2600] He had no way to know the police were there for a coffee and bathroom break.[2601]

As police arrived at the Lorraine, Dr. King's associates pointed toward the source of the rifle shot, across Mulberry Street at the back of a rooming house.[2602] Police arrived in front of that flophouse within minutes and found the bundle, a green bedspread wrapped around a cardboard box, inside which could be seen a gun's barrel.[2603]

The Memphis homicide squad chief inspected the new renter's room. A dresser had been moved from the window and replaced by a chair. The curtains had been opened wide, and so was the window that afforded a view of the Lorraine Motel, 200 feet away, but only if one leaned out a little. The chief easily found a much better sniping position, nearby in the bathroom at the end of the hall. To fire a rifle at the Lorraine, one had to open the window — check — push out a screen — check — and stand in the bathtub — check, with shoe scuff marks found in the tub.[2604] Outside, the blanket-wrapped bundle contained a rifle, nine extra bullets, binoculars, clothing, a newspaper article saying King was at the Lorraine, a transistor radio and an assortment of toiletries.

The FBI began its largest manhunt, assigning 3,500 agents. In one day it traced the rifle to the dealer in Birmingham, who gave a good description of Harvey Lowmeyer. A week later it traced a laundry mark on underwear in the bundle to Los Angeles, where Eric S. Galt had his clothes cleaned through March. At a low-cost housing project in Atlanta, residents reported a Mustang as being too fancy and out of place. It was registered to Eric Starvo Galt [KK] of Birmingham. Alabama's drivers' license files had his year-old application with a physical description (no photos on licenses in those days) that matched both the rifle buyer and the room renter.

In Memphis, "Galt" was found in a motel registry; a man stayed one night, checking out the morning of the shooting — proving that the man who dropped the bundle owned the Mustang. A service sticker in that car in Atlanta led to a garage in Los Angeles, then to an apartment landlady, then to a cheap hotel that Galt had left in mid-March. At his apartment, people recalled that Galt had talked about taking dance lessons. The FBI hit gold when it found the dance studio where a teacher remembered him talking about bartending school. Searching again, the FBI found that school, which had a photo of Galt's graduating class —

[KK] Your author speculates that there may have been name influence from Ernst Stavro Blofeld, novelist Ian Fleming's villainous head of SPECTRE, in the 1960s widely known as James Bond's nemesis in *From Russia With Love*, *Thunderball*, and *You Only Live Twice*.

but, alas, in the photo his eyes were closed! No problem — an FBI artist painted eyeballs onto the closed eyelids, and the Birmingham rifle dealer picked that photo out of a lineup.[2605] With only a pasticcio [LL] photo and legions of gumshoes, Lowmeyer and Galt were merging.

From a rooming house where Galt stayed briefly in Atlanta, and from the rifle, scope and binoculars in the bundle in Memphis, the FBI had a few fingerprints, not a set but if they were lucky, from the same man. Long before computers could speed through it, FBI experts hand-matched prints to file cards with ten fingerprints each from 82,000,000 people. Director J. Edgar Hoover ordered them to look first at prints of "known fugitives"; his experience suggested the killer could be an escaped convict. That narrowed the search to 53,000 cards, which primitive computers extracted from the huge file.[2606] While they were at it, early-day technical experts then selected the cards of white male fugitives with the age, height, weight and hair color shared by Galt, Lowmeyer and Willard; 2,000 cards with 20,000 fingerprints. On April 19, only fifteen days after the assassination, they found a match on the 702nd card, escaped convict James Earl Ray.[2607] He was now 40. From age 24 he was a four-time loser, mostly for robberies, who had spent twelve of the last sixteen years in prisons. While serving a twenty-year sentence in the Missouri State Penitentiary, he escaped in April 1967, then moved among the cities previously mentioned. It seemed the case had become very simple and perhaps easy, with three aliases now known to be Ray. By April 21 he topped the FBI's "Most Wanted" list and his name and photos were headlined throughout the world.

Then it all stopped. The 2½ weeks of rapid progress were followed by four weeks of nothingness. With time to cast a wider net, the FBI followed shreds of evidence hinting that Ray may have been in Mexico and Canada in 1967. In Ottawa, an RCMP task force worked through 264,000 passport applications submitted during the 12 months after Ray's escape from prison. On May 20, a constable thought the face shown at left looked like Ray's prison photos, if one removed the glasses worn by passport applicant Ramon George Sneyd.[2608] Doubt was removed when FBI handwriting experts ruled that letters *G* and *S* of Ramon *G*eorge *S*neyd and Eric *S*. *G*alt were written by the same hand.[MM] [2609]

The address on Mr. Sneyd's passport application was a Toronto rooming house. The manager recognized Ray's photo as Paul Bridgman who had arrived on April 8, four days after Rev. King's assassination. Canadian gumshoes went to work, to learn that a travel agency had sold an air ticket to Mr. Sneyd (rhymes with "paid") [2610] and he had flown to London on May 6. The FBI found letters inquiring about immigration to Rhodesia, then the world's most white-minority-dominated black-repressing country, where one might find understanding friends and shelter from extradition. Alerts were sent to authorities in Britain and Africa.[2611]

On June 8, two days after the assassination of Robert Kennedy, a man ticketed for Brussels handed his Canadian passport to a clerk at London's Heathrow Airport. All seemed to be in order until a teensy-weensy little event bookmarked the genesis of a different reality,

---

[LL] It does you good to look things up — and to become astute by learning also about the word before!
[MM] This is five years after FBI experts, perhaps the same, found that two gun orders from A. Hidell were written by the man who had sent a pleading-threatening letter from Minsk to John Connally.

to be bannered in headlines around the world next morning. The immigration officer spotted a second passport in Mr. Sneyd's pocket, asked to see it, and found it was also Canadian, for Ramon George Sneya. Sneyd explained that one, issued in Canada, had a misspelled "Sney*a*". He had obtained a replacement with the correct "Sney*d*" at a Canadian Embassy, and now that that was all cleared up, he would like to go to his plane for Belgium.

Watching all this, because things were quiet at that moment, was a Detective Sergeant who noted Sneyd's nervousness. He remembered a "Watch For and Detain" notice issued two days earlier. Mr. Ramon George Sneyd was wanted by Scotland Yard for "serious offences." The Detective Sergeant escorted the protesting Sneyd to an office where a search found a concealed .38 revolver. This was not America; tradition and strict rules required a British permit for such a weapon. Sneyd had none, explaining that he was merely passing though on his way to dangerous Africa where he might need such protection.

The Detective Sergeant knew when to escalate, and soon two investigators arrived from Scotland Yard, a Chief Inspector and a Detective Chief Superintendent.[NN] Quick as a flash, Sneyd was into London, into Cannon Row jail, and into a private cell with an armed guard. The police went off to make inquires, then returned to tell their prisoner that he would be returned to the States to face criminal charges including murder with a firearm.[2612] Lowmeyer, Galt, Willard, Bridgman and Sneyd had merged into Ray. The hunt, passed from Memphis police to U.S. G-Men to Canadian Mounties to British Bobbies, had taken sixty-five days.

Ray was extradited from London to Memphis, secretly arriving at 4 AM to thwart any copycat of Jack Ruby.[2613] A confusing multiplicity of attorneys appeared, and of course there was plenty of speculation about conspiracies, especially involving an invisible — then and forever — "Raoul" in Canada. The evidence appeared damning, and his nationally-famous chief lawyer,[OO] Percy Foreman, advised that he plead guilty rather than go to trial that might end with the death penalty.[2614] On March 10, 1969, James Earl Ray turned 41 and, hoping to avoid execution, entered a plea of guilty.[2615] Three days later he had decided that his attorneys had wrongly advised that, so he wrote a letter to the judge, asking for a hearing so he could change the plea, and change lawyers. The March 13 letter was not in the judge's hands until he returned from a vacation on March 31, and those hands were soon cold; the judge died of a heart attack while considering the letter.[2616]

Those unusual events fanned conspiracy flames, not that much was needed. The House Select Committee on Assassinations wondered about co-conspirators; its final report jumped to the same wretched conclusion as it did about Oswald's murder of Kennedy: "The committee believes, on the basis of the circumstantial evidence available to it, that there is a likelihood that James Earl Ray assassinated Dr. Martin Luther King, Jr. as a result of a conspiracy." [2617] The children of Dr. King also expressed their doubts about Ray's sole guilt.

His guilty plea sheltering him from the death penalty, Ray was sentenced to 99 years in prison, which he served at Tennessee's Brushy Mountain State Penitentiary.[2618] After eight years he scaled a 15-foot wall to make the last of his many escapes. On the third day he was found by bloodhounds on the trail of another escapee. For the rest of his life he denied guilt, claiming that at the moment Dr. King was shot, he was blocks away having a flat tire repaired

---

[NN] As Sherlock Holmes, Miss Marple, Hercule Poirot and Rumpole of the Bailey have taught us Yanks, most British police officials are amusingly dimwitted but have grand multi-worded titles.

[OO] The same mistake Jack Ruby made hiring Melvin Belli; both attorneys were puffed-up narcissists.

— "Raoul" must have fired his rifle! [2619] Ray sent petitions to courts for the trial he never had and wrote a self-serving book [2620] with help from two of the "usual suspects", a foreword by Jesse Jackson and a preface by conspiracist-attorney Mark Lane. He died at age 70 in 1998.

Having briefly exposed the facts of what he did, how he did it and how it all ended, what remains is to jump back to the beginning to answer the question of motive: Why?

James Earl Ray was born in 1928 in dirt-poor Alton, Illinois, across the Mississippi River from St. Louis, Missouri, into a family of white-trash career criminals; grandfather and father were proud of making easy money from petty crime. His middle name "Earl" was for an uncle in the Illinois state penitentiary, who would become a role model. Staying ahead of the law and the desperation of the Great Depression, the family moved upriver in Missouri, eventually settling into a rural shack in tiny Ewing. [2621]

Similar to Lee Oswald's life through age 19 in chapters 1 and 2, much of what's next will be familiar. James flunked the first grade, became a habitual truant, was 16 when he'd had enough schooling and dropped out of the 8th grade. [2622] At 17 he enlisted in the U.S. Army and found himself in Germany in post-war 1946. There he found and concentrated on a black market in cigarettes. In 1947, only 19, heavy drinking and drug use led to court martial and sentence for being drunk in quarters, with demotion from PFC to Private. He made the first of his life's many escapes, from the prison stockade, but was captured. The Army had enough of Private Ray and shipped him home to the States. [2623]

One can never be certain of the "tipping point" in an aberrant life, but what happened in December 1948 may have been formative. On the ship to the States, single soldiers rode second class whereas married soldiers and their wives were in first class. That would seem to be an agreeable choice, but the problem that haunted Ray was this: In the then-segregated Army, many of the black soldiers worked in kitchens, shopped locally, got to know the "locals" and married their German daughters. So James had to look up from second class to black men in first class doing you-know-what with their beautiful young white girls.

As if that wasn't enough to form a lifelong hatred, the one-two punch continued when the ship docked and, two days before Christmas, Ray was thrown out of the Army, only days before his hitch was scheduled to end, with a General Discharge [PP] "for ineptness and lack of adaptability to military service". [2624] In a self-serving book he later wrote in prison, *Who Killed Martin Luther King? The True Story by the Alleged Assassin*, he objected: "This was a slap in the face—if the Army had wanted, it could have let me stay a soldier another 48 hours and muster out with a standard honorable discharge." [2625] The parallels to Lee Oswald are unmistakable, perhaps significant. At the very least, po' white trash Ray had what he would think a good reason to hate both blacks and government.

Ray's first provable interest in King came on March 17, 1968. After a time in Mexico, Ray settled into Los Angeles for four months. King came to L.A. for speeches, then departed to the South. The next day, so did James Earl Ray in his Mustang. He probably listened to the radio as he went, to hear that Dr. King would be in Selma, Alabama, on March 22. Ray arrived there that same day. The next day King left and so did Ray, driving to Atlanta, the city of King's residence, Ebenezer Baptist Church and headquarters of his Southern Christian Leadership Conference. [2626] These moves clearly testify to Ray's interest in King; they are at least "shadowing" and probably "stalking".

[PP] A step better than Oswald's Undesirable, but much less than the Honorable awarded to almost all.

When MLK announced that he would join the garbage collectors' protest in Memphis, "Harvey Lowmeyer" drove west to Birmingham on March 27 where he asked many questions about hunting rifles. On March 29 he did the same in Bessemer, Alabama, then returned to Birmingham and purchased the too-weak .243 rifle as was told on page 339. On March 30 he exchanged that for a .30-06 and was ready to go shoot his game. He drove back to Atlanta, then "Eric Galt" drove to Memphis where Dr. King was expected, "John Willard" rented a room overlooking the Lorraine Motel — and you know the rest.

In this author's experience and opinion, the most useful book about the assassination of MLK is *Killing the Dream* by Gerald Posner, the much-honored author of *Case Closed*, one of the few worthwhile books about the assassination of JFK. After 332 pages about James Earl Ray and what he did, Posner closes with 3 brief pages on conspiracy (there was none) and motive. Ray was a lifelong racist who would enjoy attending a lynching, and just as content to shoot an uppity black man. Choosing the best-known campaigner for black rights added the bonus of achieving fame.[2627] And, there may have been a financial incentive; Posner writes of rewards of $50,000 and $100,000 offered by segregationists and the White Knights of the Ku Klux Klan to any hero who would murder Dr. King.[2628]

Benjamin Elijah Mayes, President of Morehouse College and longtime friend-mentor of Martin Luther King, was the final speaker, delivering the benediction at 1963's March on Washington for Jobs and Freedom where MLK spoke words I cannot quote.[2629] He had the same honor in 1968, speaking last at the burial of MLK. In part, directly to the point here:

> "Make no mistake, the American people are in part responsible. ... A century after Emancipation, and after the enactment of the Thirteenth, Fourteenth, and Fifteenth amendments, it should not have been necessary for Martin Luther King, Jr., to stage marches in Montgomery, Birmingham, and Selma, and go to jail over twenty times.
>
> The assassin heard enough condemnation of King and of Negroes to feel that he had public support. He knew that millions hated King." [2630]

In several other articles in this chapter I have depended on James W. Clarke, through his wise book *American Assassins: The Darker Side of Politics*, to help answer the "Why?" question of motive — and do so here. He makes the interesting point that racism is surely a root cause of Ray's shooting King, but with a twist. It was not necessarily that Ray killed King because he was a black man, but that he expected to get away with the killing because King was *only* a black man.[2631] Uneducated "white trash" in the old South may have known they weren't much, but they considered themselves to be more than Negroes, whom they called by the "n-word". If you would like to visualize James Earl Ray and have read or seen the movie of Harper Lee's classic *To Kill a Mockingbird*, think of Bob Ewell, the abusive father of poor Mayella.

In the 1960s there were no convictions of the killers of Medgar Evers, James Chaney, Andrew Goodman and Michael Schwerner, nor even of the dastards who blew up four little black girls in church. If there was really an offer of big money to anyone who would murder King, then James Earl Ray, a man without political interests or philosophical underpinnings, may well have considered the opportunity to be high-reward for low-risk, in the same way as he chose the many markets he robbed during his lifetime dedicated to crime-as-profession.

This assassination deserves special consideration for two physical reasons: First, it is among the very few shootings **with a rifle**. It is the only other attempt, with Oswald's, on a prominent person **at a distance**. As I have said, there are strong parallels between Oswald and Ray, best set forth in the most useful book about Ray's life, *The Strange Case of James Earl*

Ray: The Man Who Murdered Martin Luther King by Clay Blair, Jr., where it is noted that on November 22, 1963, James Earl Ray was, his habitual situation, in the Missouri State Penitentiary because of his usual crime, armed robbery of markets:[2632]

> "Did James Earl Ray identify with Lee Harvey Oswald? If he were so inclined, there was much to be found in common. Both were about the same age. They were not unalike in physical appearance. Both were slight of stature, moody, reticent, loners. Both were awkward in the presence of women. Both had emerged from shattered homes. Both had trouble in school. Both had been disciplined by court-martial in the military—drummed out of elite corps. Both were—in different styles—rebels against society. Both had bottled up untold rage and resentment. Both had turned to unspeakable violence to vent these emotions.
>
> But Lee Harvey Oswald had an edge. Even in death, he had achieved status and recognition—enormous status. The world would not soon forget Oswald. He had struck down an incredibly popular president. His picture could be found in almost any magazine. His life, his family, had been probed in microscopic detail. The deed had generated a whole industry of books. A special presidential commission, headed by the Chief Justice, had investigated the murder, published volumes of testimony. Oswald would become a historical figure, ranking beside John Wilkes Booth, Abraham Lincoln's assassin. Oswald's had been truly a big lick. Had Oswald's deed planted a seed in Ray's mind?"[2633]

The foregoing quotation may leave the impression that Oswald (A) deliberately killed Kennedy (B) to become famous. While stipulating that those two thoughts are what most Americans believed then in the 1960s, and for all the fifty-plus years since, your author disagrees with both. The valid points above are that the two misfits were considerably similar, and Ray may well have recognized and yearned for fame similar to that achieved by Oswald.

A key point — important to consider as you compare Ray with Oswald — is that to kill a stationary man at a distance of 207 feet, Ray carefully aimed through a tested 7-power scope on a rifle that rested on a windowsill. Oswald hurriedly aimed his misaligned 4-power scope and two shots hit within a moving-away car at distances of 177 and 265 feet. The would-be assassins shared many characteristics, but when it was time to kill, Ray had all the advantages and deftly murdered his intended victim with one bullet. Oswald failed with three shots.

1968: James Earl Ray shoots and kills Dr. Martin Luther King, Jr.	
Weapon:	Rifle: .30-06 with 2-to-7-power scope
Distance:	205 feet (says Blair) or 207 feet (says Posner)
Shots fired:	One precise shot through MLK's jaw, neck, jugular, spine.
Killed / Hit:	King, taken to hospital, was beyond saving, dead in an hour.
Assassin then:	Wrapped the rifle, left bundle and drove away, captured, pleaded guilty to avoid death penalty, died in prison 30 years later.
Motive(s):	Racism: disrespect of the nation's leading black leader; Seizing an opportunity to amount to something and gain fame; And possibly the hope of earning large financial rewards.
Do we know beyond reasonable doubt, **whom** did the assassin intend to shoot? **Yes**	
Do we know beyond reasonable doubt, his **motive** for shooting the man he hit? **Yes**	

1968: Sirhan Bishara Sirhan shoots and kills Robert F. Kennedy

On the night Dr. King died, a good friend was to make a presidential campaign speech. Instead, he spoke "from the back of a truck to a large group of Indianapolis blacks. His face was in anguish, and a cold wind was blowing, as he told them Martin Luther King had been murdered." [2634] "Most of the audience had not heard the news. They gasped in horror as [he] delivered it. The night was very cold, and [MLK's friend] stood hunched in a black overcoat, his face gaunt, speaking extemporaneously from the depths of his despair:

"In this difficult day, in this difficult time for the United States, it is perhaps well to ask what kind of a nation we are and what direction we want to move in. For those of you who are black ... you can be filled with bitterness, with hatred, and a desire for revenge. We can move in that direction as a country, in great polarization—black people amongst black, white people amongst white, filled with hatred toward one another. Or we can make an effort, as Martin Luther King did, to understand and to comprehend, and to replace that stain of bloodshed that has spread across our land, with an effort to understand with compassion and love. ... Let us dedicate ourselves to that, and say a prayer for our country and for our people." [2635]

"The Indianapolis police chief had warned him not to go into that black ghetto that night as the bearer of such news." [2636] "On the night of April 4, Indianapolis was one of the few major American cities that did not erupt in flames." [2637] In two months and two days, King's friend would die; his assassin already had a gun and was practicing.

Robert "Bobby" "RFK" was the younger brother of John "Jack" "JFK", murdered 4½ years before. Lyndon Johnson replaced JFK, then won a record victory over Barry Goldwater in 1964. Eligible to run for another four-year term in 1968, he was expected to do exactly that. Biographer Dick Schaap wrote in 1967: "Bobby Kennedy may once have dreamed of running for President in 1968, but he realizes now that this is impossible, barring the death of Lyndon Johnson or, equally unlikely, a decision by Johnson not to seek a second full term." [2638] Then, against overwhelming odds, plucky brave Bobby obeyed his strong convictions on March 16, 1968, with this public announcement: [2639]

"I am announcing today my candidacy for the Presidency of the United States.

I do not run for the Presidency merely to oppose any man, but to propose new policies. I run because I am convinced that this country is on a perilous course and because I have such strong feelings about what must be done that I am obliged to do all I can. ...

My decision reflects no personal animosity or disrespect toward President Johnson. He served President Kennedy with the utmost loyalty and was extremely kind to me and members of my family in the difficult months which followed the events of November 1963. ... I have deep sympathy for the burdens he carries today. But the issue is not personal; it is our profound differences over where we are heading.

I do not lightly dismiss the dangers and difficulties of challenging an incumbent President; but these are not ordinary times and this is not an ordinary election. At stake is not simply the leadership of our party or even our country—it is our right to moral leadership on this planet."

Fifteen days later, President Johnson astonished us all by withdrawing from the race.[2640] Kennedy's competition was reduced to Senator Eugene McCarthy of Minnesota, popular with liberals and the young; and Vice President Hubert Humphrey, a solid centrist but tainted by his association with LBJ and Vietnam. Having entered months behind his competitors, Kennedy campaigned with vigor.[QQ] "McCarthy ... defeated Kennedy in Oregon, the first time a Kennedy had ever lost an election," [2641] but then Kennedy "kept winning ... in Indiana, in the

---

[QQ] Which he pronounced in the Bostonian language, "vigah".

District of Columbia, in Nebraska ..." [2642]   Late in May, a writer asked "'You know, don't you, that somebody's going to try to kill you?' Kennedy looked up slowly. 'That's the chance I have to take. You've just got to give yourself to the people and trust them. From then on, either luck is with you or it isn't. I'm pretty sure there'll be an attempt on my life sooner or later. Not so much for political reasons. ... Plain nuttiness, that's all." [2643]   RFK spared his family from campaigning, but took his pal Freckles.[2644]

"Robert Kennedy might have been alive today if Israel had not become a major factor [in] Presidential campaigns." [2645]   In a TV debate with McCarthy on June 1, he "wooed the Jewish vote by endorsing more arms for Israel ... That day, an olive-skinned, bushy-haired Palestinian-American ... bought a box of ammunition for his .22-caliber pistol." [2646]

On June 4, RFK won the grand prize, California's Democratic presidential primary, and a highly satisfying victory over Hubert Humphrey in South Dakota, HHH's birthplace.[2647] He was on track to win the nomination, then to defeat expected opponent Richard Nixon.

At midnight with Ethel at his side, two months pregnant with their eleventh child, he spoke to supporters in a ballroom of the Ambassador Hotel in Los Angeles.[RR]   "Bobby's deep-set blue eyes sparkled. He smiled broadly." [2648]   "Kennedy jokingly thanked ... his dog, Freckles [above], 'and I'm not doing this in the order of importance, but I also want to thank my wife, Ethel.' Laughter all round." [2649]   A few minutes later, "So, my thanks to all of you, and now it's on to Chicago, and let's win there!" [2650]   At 12:15 AM Wednesday, June 5, to avoid the enthusiastic crowd, they hurried out through a hotel pantry, a long narrow hallway. A man jumped out from behind a dish trolley. "His eyes were narrowed in concentration, and he seemed to have 'a sick smile on his face.' 'Kennedy, you son of a bitch!'" [2651]   He "pulled a revolver ... and from three or four inches away shot into Kennedy's head just behind his right ear." [2652]   Reacting to that first shot, Kennedy twisted and was wounded twice more, behind his right armpit. Two bullets penetrated into his back and neck, but did not hit any vital organs.

RFK had been championed, and was accompanied that evening, by world-class athletes including 287-pound [2653] tackle Roosevelt Grier of the Los Angeles Rams, superbly conditioned all-around athlete Rafer Johnson, and famous author and attempter of many sports George Plimpton. The three of them, plus hotel employees and two Kennedy aides, were having difficulty holding the little man with the pistol. He kept on firing into the crowd, using all eight bullets in his revolver, hitting five persons besides Kennedy, before he was eventually pinned against a serving counter.[2654]   This was before major presidential candidates had protection by the U.S. Secret Service. In fact, that protection was put into effect the next day by quick action from President Johnson and Congress.   (Photo) [2655]

[RR] The hotel, famous for its large lawn and palm trees bordering Wilshire Boulevard, closed to the public in 1989. It then starred as a movie location in *"Pretty Woman"* and *"Forrest Gump"*.

Kennedy was taken to a nearby hospital, then moved to higher-capability Good Samaritan Hospital. Doctors attempted hours of delicate brain surgery while Mrs. Martin Luther King Jr., Mrs. Jacqueline Kennedy and many members of the Kennedy family arrived, some from Europe. More than a day later, at 2 A.M. on Thursday, Press Secretary Frank Mankiewicz read from a yellow pad, "Senator Robert Francis Kennedy died at 1:44 A.M. today, June 6, 1968. ... He was forty-two years old." RFK's campaign and Democrats' chances had ended. The "assassin's bullet killed hope and ushered in the Nixon years." [2656]

You may recall at the hospital in 1963 a considerable tussle between JFK's party who wanted to get his body out of Dallas, and Texans who demanded a local autopsy. With time to plan while RFK lingered for 25½ hours, his party agreed to a local autopsy, "performed ... by Dr. Thomas Noguchi [who] had previously officiated in the autopsy of Marilyn Monroe." [2657] He wrote, "The cause of death is ascribed by me as a gunshot wound of the right mastoid penetrating the brain." [2658] Also, "A gunpowder tattoo ... around the fatal entry wound on the edge of Kennedy's right ear ... indicate[s] that ... the muzzle distance was very, very close." [2659] This Kennedy, as had his older brother, died of a bullet into the brain. Very unlike Oswald's shot from hundreds of feet, Sirhan's pistol nearly touched Bobby's head as he fired.

President Johnson sent a presidential jet, an identical twin of 1963's "Air Force One". Jacqueline Kennedy would not board until assured this was not the plane that had carried her dead husband from Dallas to Washington. The 707 flew to RFK's adopted New York. The coffin went from La Guardia Airport to St. Patrick's Cathedral in midtown Manhattan, where thousands were waiting on line,[SS] and in two days 151,000 passed through the cathedral.[2660] "At times ... the line of people outside the church stretched to a mile and a half; some waited seven hours to enter." [2661] 600 of Bobby's friends stood turns as an honor guard.

After mass on Saturday, "the casket was ... put aboard a special train. ... Great crowds of people lined the railroad tracks and waited for hours in the hot sunshine to watch the train pass." [2662] [2663] A slow cortege took Robert Kennedy from Union Station, with a pause in front of his Department of Justice, past the gaze of Abraham Lincoln in his memorial, across the Potomac to Arlington National Cemetery. Bobby Kennedy was buried near his brother Jack. On that day there was also some good news: James Earl Ray,  assassin of the Rev. Dr. Martin Luther King, Jr., was arrested in London.

To know the assassin — the purpose of this article — we must go back three days to the pantry of the Ambassador Hotel. Five others had been hit by five other bullets; they all recovered. Officers of the Los Angeles Police Department arrested the assassin. LAPD Chief Daryl Gates promised a careful and thorough investigation to avoid an onslaught of conspiracy theories. Predictably, he was not successful. Theorists were enamored of a mysterious missing "woman in a polka-dot dress", "too many bullet holes", the assassin's claim that he was framed or turned into a robot, and RFK's many enemies including Cubans, Teamsters and the Mafia. Does this all sound familiar? Twenty years later, when the cry of "Conspiracy!"

[SS] People in the East queue "on" line, but in the West we do the same "in" line.

had begun to subside, the LAPD managed to throw figurative gasoline on the embers by destroying the investigation files in a space-saving cleanup.

The assassin was Sirhan Bishara Sirhan,[2664] "outside ... a small, brown man. On the  inside he is aloof and lonely; sensitive and touchy to the point of being prickly..." [2665] He was a Palestinian, born in 1944 in Jerusalem. His parents and their seven children became refugees during Israel's bloody creation in 1947. He saw the horrors of the Arab-Israeli War, including the death of his brother with whom he was playing, run over by a Zionist truck. It was too painful. "In 1957, the family immigrated to the United States ... their entry made possible by the sponsorship of a church in Pasadena. ... [When] Sirhan's father later returned to Jordan alone",[2666] "his absence also added a sense of abandonment to the feelings of isolation the family already was experiencing in a totally new and alien environment." [2667]

"A major element in all their difficulties was the fact that they had come to the United States reluctantly, and only as a last resort. Their true home was Palestine, and they had been forced to leave. Thus they were resistant to American acculturation and continued to speak Arabic, listen to Arabic music, read Arabic newspapers, and observe Arabic customs, all in the hope that someday they could return to their homeland." [2668]

"[I]t was with intense anger and humiliation that Sirhan read, listened to, and watched reports on Israel's invasion of the Sinai on June 5, 1967. His political hero was Egyptian President Nasser, but Nasser's forces were defeated with shocking swiftness by the Israeli army and air force. Israeli units gained total control of the Sinai in only three days. Then in three more days, they turned toward the Jordanian frontier to capture the Old City of Jerusalem (where Sirhan had spent part of his childhood) and the strategically important Golan Heights. The brief but devastating engagement that ended on June 10 became known as the Six Day War. For Arabs throughout the world it was their most humiliating defeat. For Palestinian Arabs such as Sirhan, it meant that prospects of ever regaining their homeland were now more remote than they had ever been." [2669]

"[T]wo major concerns seemed to weigh on Sirhan's mind: his disappointment with life in the United States and the realization that his dream of ever returning to Jordan was quickly fading. ... With such events paramount in Sirhan's thoughts, there is little doubt that he read in the Arab papers that the *New York Times* reported on January 9 and 10, 1968, Senator Kennedy's proposed sale of fifty Phantom jet bombers to Israel. Sirhan was enraged when he learned of the proposal. He had been an admirer of President Kennedy and thought of him as a reasonable person who had attempted to understand the Arab position. He had had similar hopes for his younger brother. Now his disappointment was profound." [2670] Senator Kennedy "regularly made well-publicized appearances in synagogues, and photographs often appeared of him wearing a yarmulke when he addressed Jewish audiences." [2671] "Already on record supporting the sale of more bombers to Israel, Kennedy's election, in Sirhan's view, would signal the beginning of the end for the Palestinian Arabs struggling to survive on the Israeli border. Kennedy had to be stopped." [2672]

Police found notebooks in which Sirhan had repeatedly written "RFK must die." [TT] "On May 18, 1968, Sirhan wrote in his notebook: ... 'Robert F. Kennedy must be assassinated before 5 June 68.' Why June 5, 1968? It was the first anniversary of the humiliating Six Day War. It also just happened to be the day after the California presidential primary, which was central to the Senator's presidential aspirations. As Sirhan later explained ... 'June 5 stood out for me, sir, more than my own birth date. I felt Robert Kennedy was coinciding his own appeal for votes with the anniversary of the Six Day War.'" [2673]

"[O]n Saturday, June 1, he ... purchased two boxes of .22 caliber hollow-point high velocity ammunition and drove to a pistol range [to practice]. The next day ... after again practicing ... he went to a Kennedy campaign rally at the Ambassador Hotel in Los Angeles. Sirhan's stalk continued in the lobbies and banquet rooms of the Ambassador but without success. Time was growing short. Sirhan was committed to the June 5 deadline he had programmed himself to meet. On Monday, June 3, the day before the primary, Kennedy was scheduled to speak in San Diego ... Sirhan made the two-hour trip to San Diego in his battered 1956 De Soto and then returned that evening to Pasadena—once more without success." [2674] And then it was the day for primary elections.

On election day, he was at a gun range about eleven thirty. He signed in, paid the admission fee, set up his target and practiced until 5 PM when the range closed for the day. The shooter next to him "fired Sirhan's gun.[2675] ... It was a cheap .22 with black plastic grips and a short barrel. [The shooter] asked Sirhan why he was firing high-velocity Mini-Mags for target shooting. Sirhan shrugged. 'They're supposed to be the best brand.'" [2676] [UU] "During the five to six hours he was on the range Sirhan fired seven or eight hundred rounds." [2677]

At trial, his attorneys did not contest the facts, but based his defense on diminished capacity. In *American Assassins: The Darker Side of Politics*, James W. Clarke writes:

> "Sirhan ... is hardly the mentally unbalanced paranoid schizophrenic that his defense attorneys and psychiatrists attempted to portray. Sirhan's trial stands out as the longest, most detailed defense of an assassin based on psychiatric evidence. Only the trial of the psychotic Charles Guiteau nearly a century before and Arthur Bremer's trial three years later compare in terms of the sheer volume of psychiatric (or alienist) testimony. Thus, the Sirhan trial provides an excellent illustration of the attempts by attorneys and psychiatrists to deny the rationality of a politically inspired murder on the basis of the (California) doctrine of 'diminished capacity' ... which holds that a person cannot be convicted of first degree murder if he or she were unable, for whatever reason—alcohol, drugs, or mental impairment—to premeditate the act in a rational manner. In other words, anything that diminishes a person's mental capacity lessens the actual responsibility for the crime committed." [2678]

After almost seventeen hours of deliberation, the jury reached its verdict:

> "We, the jury in the above entitled action, find the Defendant Sirhan Bishara Sirhan guilty of Murder, in violation of Section 187, Penal Code, a felony, as charged in Count 1 of the Indictment. We further find it to be Murder in the first degree. This 17th day of April, 1969."

[TT] Lee Oswald similarly wrote in his notebook featured in chapter 20, "I WILL KILL JOHN CONNALLY"
[UU] Hollow-point bullets have only one purpose: to kill. They mushroom and shatter on entering flesh.

Sirhan stared straight ahead during guilty verdicts on all six counts.[2679] "On April 23, the jury voted that Sirhan should be put to death in California's gas chamber ... Senator Edward Kennedy sent ... a moving, five-page, hand-written letter, saying, in part, 'My brother was a man of love and sentiment and compassion. He would not have wanted his death to be a cause for taking of another life.' [Nonetheless, the judge] sentenced Sirhan to death." [2680]

California's Supreme Court ruled in 1972 that capital punishment violated the state constitution's prohibition against cruel or unusual punishment, so his sentence was commuted to life in prison.[2681] Sirhan has parole hearings every five years. In 2011, after 42 years in prison, at his 14th parole hearing ... "parole was denied on the grounds that Sirhan still does not understand the full ramifications of his crime." [2682] And, of course there has to be a conspiracy theory: "On November 26, 2011, Sirhan's defense teams filed new court papers for a new trial, saying that 'expert analysis of recently uncovered evidence shows two guns were fired in the assassination and that Sirhan's revolver was not the gun that shot Kennedy.'" [2683]

Analyst and author James W. Clarke in *American Assassins* sums up:

"In the final analysis, what we see in Sirhan is a coldly calculating and remorseless assassin who killed for political reasons—reasons that were difficult for many to grasp or accept in 1968 and 1969. But now with the increased awareness of the intensity of Arab and Islamic feelings and values in the Middle East, Sirhan's motives, no matter how objectionable and deplorable, cannot be dismissed as irrational. His values and political perspective are shared by millions of other Arabs. Sirhan's crime ... was no different than the atrocities of numerous Palestinian terrorists who continue to bomb and assassinate in attempts to reach their political objectives. He is no more irrational than the Black September terrorists who murdered the Israeli athletes at the 1972 Munich Olympics, or the two Zionist assassins who killed Lord Moyne in 1944, or the Zionists who participated in the Deir Yassin massacre in 1948.[VV] Sirhan was mad or irrational only to the extent that war and intense nationalism are mad or irrational." [2684]

Clarke wrote that analysis several years before four airplanes were commandeered and crashed on 9/11 in 2001. You might choose to go back and re-read that paragraph, because now we have even greater need to understand.

1968: Sirhan Bishara Sirhan shoots and kills Robert F. Kennedy	
Weapon:	Pistol: .22 Iver-Johnson Cadet revolver with hollow-point bullets
Distance:	An inch or two from Kennedy's right ear, leaving a powder burn
Shots fired:	All eight that were in the pistol: three hit Kennedy; five hit others
Killed / Hit:	Kennedy died of one bullet into the brain. Two bullets did not hit vital organs. Five people nearby were wounded but recovered.
Assassin then:	Convicted, sentenced to death, later reduced to life imprisonment
Motive(s):	A Palestinian, he was angry at RFK's support of Israel
Do we know beyond reasonable doubt, **whom** did the assassin intend to shoot? **Yes**	
Do we know beyond reasonable doubt, his **motive** for shooting the man he hit? **Yes**	

[VV] "250 old men, women, and children were massacred by Zionist attackers on April 10, 1948. For Arabs, Deir Yassin remains a symbol of Zionist brutality as immoral and evil as the atrocities the Zionists themselves had fled in Europe." — James W. Clarke in *American Assassins*.

1972: Arthur Bremer shoots and paralyzes George Wallace

George Wallace, elected Governor of Alabama in 1962, became a national figure as he fought against integration of the races. You may picture him standing in the doorway to bar black students from the University of Alabama. You are probably familiar with the worst of the Alabama confrontations, including Selma's fire hoses, beatings and snarling police dogs; and the bomb blast that killed four small girls in their church in Birmingham. Wallace is shown here meeting in 1965 with President Lyndon Johnson, who urged him to defuse the ugly racial crisis.[2685]

When Richard Nixon ran for re-election in 1972,[WW] his Democrat opponents were liberal, intellectual, pro-civil-rights senators Hubert Humphrey and George McGovern. Wallace saw an opening for a "populist", a plain-speaking man of the common people, so he entered a few primaries and did well in the South and Midwest. With primaries coming in Maryland and Michigan, "he felt confident that ... he would enter the [Democrats'] convention with 300 to 400 delegates—perhaps enough to block a first- or second-ballot nomination of his remaining chief rivals, McGovern and Humphrey. Then, he felt, he would have a chance to broker the convention or—it was not beyond possibility, he thought—even get the nomination himself. At the least ... he could force the ... party to move to the right." [2686]

On January 13, 1972, a young man shunned by his first girlfriend and ordered by her mother to leave the girl alone, that same day went to a gun store. "Arthur Herman Bremer, an introspective, hypersensitive, 21-year-old psychopath from Milwaukee, shopped carefully before selecting the revolver with which he initially intended to kill President Richard M. Nixon, before changing his target to George Wallace. He rejected buying one of the cheap handguns popularly known as Saturday Night Specials. ... He appreciated the difficulties of getting past the walls of Secret Service agents that surround a candidate. If he could do it, he wanted no malfunctions. His life was one big malfunction as it was, but when it came to assassination, he needed quality weapons to be successful. Above all, he burned to be successful.

"So he purchased two high-quality handguns: a 9 mm Browning automatic with a fourteen-shot clip and [for $90 [2687]] a revolver of comparable power, a blunt, ugly little stopper named Undercover II, manufactured by the Charter Arms Company [that] holds five .38-caliber cartridges, the same size used by most police departments. It is extremely accurate and can be fired as fast as the trigger is pulled. Most importantly, it is so small that with its one and seven-eighths inch barrel ... it can easily be concealed in a man's hand. It is, as the name implies, designed for undercover police work. Bremer carried it in his ... jacket pocket." [2688]

On March 2, Arthur Bremer began writing "on the blue-lined pages ... of an ordinary school composition book. 'Now I start my diary of my personal plot to kill by pistol either Richard Nixon or George Wallace,' the first sentence read. 'I entend [*sic*] to shoot one or the other while he attends a champagne'—meaning campaign—'rally for the Wisconsin Presidential Preference Primary.' ... Bremer buried [the diary] on April 3. It was a 148-page chronicle, replete with every misspelling imaginable, of the author's descent into his own lower mind."

[WW] The election when burglary on Nixon's behalf made "Watergate" something more than a building.

[2689] The diary ... was unearthed in 1980 and reunited with the "second part, some 114 pages ... found in Bremer's car after the Wallace shooting. It was subsequently published under the title, *Diary of an Assassin*," [2690] "the inspiration for Martin Scorsese's 1976 film *Taxi Driver*, which later inspired John Hinckley to attempt to kill President Ronald Reagan." [2691]

The diary "ended with Bremer at last finding his real place in the world, his true being. He was an assassin. No, that wasn't quite right. He coined the word 'assassinator' because 'assassin' was such a pedestrian term. He was an assassinator. Even though he couldn't spell either word, he found his identity as an assassin and this identity gave him strength, purpose, and, deadliest of all, persistence." [2692]

"On April 4, [he] took a plane to New York to investigate the feasibility of flying or driving from there to Ottawa [to shoot Nixon]. Fear of failure haunted him more and more, along with tortured sexual drives. It was as if time, as well as money and sanity, were running out. Everything was threatening to fly apart. The time when he had to kill was imminent. ... He brought his guns along in a small carry-on bag [XX] and strolled off the plane without them. In the men's room he heard himself paged over a loudspeaker. One of the flight attendants found the bag and returned it to him. Unopened. With a smile." [2693] Captured by big city temptations, he frittered away his money, returned to Milwaukee, then drove to do his killing.

"He arrived in Ottawa on April 16, just before Nixon's state visit, and stalked the president through battalions of security police and phalanxes of war protesters. ... On three occasions, Nixon's limousine went right past the waiting assassinator but he did not have time for a clear shot. ... Then it was over. The few days in Ottawa had produced nothing. After Nixon's departure, Bremer began to slip into a primal rage. ... [He] returned to Milwaukee in a depression. ... [By] May 4 ... he gave up on Nixon. 'I've decided Wallace will have the honor of—what would you call it? ... He went to the library and checked out Sirhan Sirhan's *R.F.K. Must Die!* and [Aziz] Shihab's *Sirhan*." [2694]

Bremer then moved with Wallace as he campaigned in Michigan. He put himself into what he thought would be good positions in Dearborn, then Cadillac, finally Kalamazoo — and in each was not able to get a clear close shot. "Bremer spent the weekend gentling his failing [Rambler Rebel] automobile to Maryland, to the rallies at Wheaton and Laurel. Car, money, and mind were nearly depleted. His smile was frozen." [2695]

"While campaigning in Michigan early in May, [Wallace told a reporter] that he was not especially concerned about hecklers from college campuses. 'Hell,' he said, 'I don't mind the kids. They're just young and full of spit and vinegar. They ain't the ones I fear. The ones that scare me are the ones you don't notice. . . I can just see a little guy out there that nobody's paying attention to. He reaches into his pocket and out comes the little gun, like that Sirhan guy that got Kennedy.'" [2696]

George and Cornelia [YY] Wallace flew to Maryland on May 15. The "first rally was at a park in Wheaton ... a boisterous, restless crowd of three thousand ... Standing close to the stage ... Bremer ... applauded Wallace loudly and often and asked a Secret Service agent if he could induce the governor to come down and shake hands. ... But the governor, after curtailing his speech by about fifteen minutes, was hustled directly to his car; his security people prevailed on him to forgo working the crowd because of the hecklers' number and temper.

[XX] Yes, before 9/11 there were no inspections, no concerns, except for possible hijacking to Cuba.

[YY] His first wife Lurleen, standing-in for term-limited George, had died while Governor in 1968.

"The Wallace caravan ... before heading to the Laurel Shopping Center, stopped at a Howard Johnson restaurant for a lunch break. The unpleasantness in Wheaton had not dulled Wallace's appetite; his bill of fare included a hamburger steak doused in ketchup, mashed potatoes, boiled carrots, apple pie, milk, and iced tea. While Wallace was eating heartily, Bremer drove [to Laurel] and found a place close to the stage, just as he had in Wheaton." [2697]

CBS cameraman Laurens W. Pierce "saw a familiar figure standing close to the platform. He had noticed the young man at previous rallies. He was about five feet six inches tall, not quite Wallace's height, with close-cropped white-reddish hair. Typically, the man was wearing a red and white striped shirt, a dark tie, charcoal jacket with large Wallace buttons above the lapels, dark pants, and clip-on sunglasses. A chilling smile was the most arresting thing about him. It was a strange, inward kind of knowing smile, almost a smirk." [2698]

"The Governor was worried about attempts on his life. ... As a precaution [he] often wore a bullet-proof vest. That afternoon, the heat and humidity were particularly oppressive, especially on the asphalt parking area where he was to speak, and the Governor decided he would forego the vest." [2699]

When Wallace "finished his fifty-minute discourse on the evils of big government, the federal courts, the national media, social planners, bureaucrats, and pseudo-intellectual college professors, he drew thunderous applause. He descended from the stage, signed some autographs, and turned toward the blue station wagon that had carried him and Cornelia to the rally. But many in the crowd implored him to approach the rope barrier so they could shake his hand. Wallace, never needing much encouragement to plunge into a crowd, handed his suit coat to an aide and moved to the folks. He grabbed the hand[s of a man and his] mother ... and greeted [a couple]. At that point, Bremer pushed between the [couple] and started firing a .38-caliber revolver." [2700]

"It takes less than a thousandth of a second for a bullet to be fired. The hammer strikes a soft metal cap containing primer, a pinhead of shock-sensitive explosive material. The explosion of the primer sets the nitrocellulose in the gunpowder on fire. The burning powder releases water and an immense volume of carbon dioxide that builds up pressure and pops the bullet out of its casing like a cork from a champagne bottle. Rifling, spiral grooves inside the barrel, sets the bullet spinning, usually one revolution every sixteen inches. This gives it directional stability and prevents it from tumbling through the air. It also makes the bullet burrow into its target like an electric drill. In the approximately three feet between Bremer and Wallace, each bullet spun about two and one-quarter times before screwing itself, at the speed of 750 feet per second, into Wallace's body." [2701] "He emptied all five shots into Wallace before [two men] wrestled him to the ground and started beating and kicking him. Wallace fell on his back, with his arms flung out to either side." [2702]

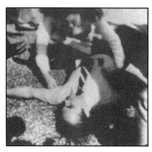

"For Cornelia, all motion stopped. Her thoughts were clear and oddly analytical. ... She turned and saw Wallace flat on his back, his left arm flung out ... a spreading red stain above his waist on the right side. ... She had a chance to save him before another gunman finished him off on the ground. To do that, she decided to die. As slowly as everything was moving for her, it took only six seconds after the shooting for Cornelia to reach Wallace. She flung herself on him, trying to cover his body with hers." [2703] [2704]

"[P]olicemen had grabbed Bremer from the mob and stuffed him, bruised and bleeding, into the back of a squad car. ... Fights broke out between Wallace supporters and hecklers. Some people screamed and others wept. Amid the mayhem, it was only belatedly that someone noticed three others down: Secret Service Agent Nicholas Zarvos, with a throat wound; Dora Thompson, a local Wallace volunteer, with a bullet in her right leg; and Alabama State Trooper E. C. Dothard, with a slight stomach wound." [2705] "Wallace was hit four times and maybe five times [by five shots], which means that each of the bullets that hit him had to go through him and hit someone else." [2706]   [2707]

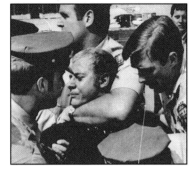

"At the hospital, a team of surgeons [worked] on Wallace [m]ore than five hours ... He had been struck twice in the right arm and once in the left shoulder blade. One bullet had crashed into his abdomen, perforating the stomach and large intestine; enough of Wallace's undigested lunch had splattered into his body cavities to cause several serious infections. But the real problem was that a fifth slug had penetrated the spinal canal and had severed a bundle of nerves carrying impulses from the lower body to the brain. Wallace would never walk again. He would never have control over his bladder or bowel functions. He would no longer be sexually active. And what would prove to be most psychologically debilitating of all, he would never have another day without grinding, insistent pain—pain that neither drugs nor acupuncture nor sophisticated neurological surgery would eradicate. ... Cornelia ... apparently ... knew, because when Wallace's campaign manager arrived at the hospital [she] greeted him by saying, 'Well, Charlie, it looks like we've got another FDR candidate on our hands.'" [2708]

"[A]lmost immediately, President Nixon granted Secret Service protection to additional candidates, as well as to Senator Ted Kennedy, even though he was not a candidate for president." [2709]

"Bremer was sentenced to ... jail; Wallace got life, imprisoned in his own body. But the day after the shooting, Wallace's already impressive campaign was crowned with an exceptional double victory. In Maryland, Wallace took 39 percent of the vote to Humphrey's 27 percent; McGovern was third with 22 percent. In Michigan, Wallace attracted 51 percent of the total vote. McGovern finished second with 27 percent, and Humphrey drew a disappointing 16 percent ... By day's end, Wallace, of all the Democratic candidates, was by far the popular choice among the voters. Overall, he had amassed more than 3,300,000 votes—700,000 more than Humphrey and over a million more than McGovern." [2710]

"On the night of Tuesday, July 11, George Wallace reached the pinnacle of his political career. Two Secret Service agents and an Alabama state trooper lifted the governor in his gleaming, chrome wheelchair to the [Democratic national] convention platform. ... For the next nine minutes, despite fierce pain, he spoke in a strong voice, summarizing his views on how to make the Democratic party 'become what it used to be—the party of the average working man.'" [2711] "Wallace was nominated for president on July 12 and received nearly four hundred first-ballot votes. ... The day after making his speech, Wallace was rushed back to Birmingham for emergency operations to clean out his internal infections. As he slowly recovered in Alabama, national politics went on without him for the first time in a decade." [2712]

"As a result, the unlikely George McGovern was able to win the ... presidential nomination, setting the stage for the 1972 Democratic equivalent of the Republican debacle of

1964. ... Nixon was swept into a second term in a major political landslide. His impressive victory [led to] a fatal arrogance that would ... lead to Nixon's political destruction." [2713]

Wallace's "assailant turned out to be an emotionally stunted, impenetrably twisted man who had set out to kill President Nixon but, when he could not catch up to him, considered shooting McGovern, and finally switched his target to Wallace. 'I have to kill somebody,' he confided to his diary. 'I am one sick assassin.' An hour after the shooting, Secret Service agents, without a search warrant, entered Bremer's cluttered Milwaukee apartment and found Wallace campaign buttons, Black Panther literature, an old high school theme [notebook] in which Bremer fantasized that his father had married Donna Reed, and a scribbled note about masturbation; incredibly, no one objected when several reporters entered the apartment and, in some cases, made off with some of Bremer's possessions. The Prince Georges County police officers who searched Bremer's car parked at the shopping center found, among other things, two books about the assassination of Robert Kennedy." [2714]

"Within two minutes of the shooting, the presidential aide H. R. Haldeman had been notified and had relayed the information to Nixon. About the same time, Assistant FBI Director W. Mark Felt [ZZ] called another of Nixon's aides, Charles Colson, to inform him that his boss, Acting Attorney General Richard Kleindienst, had instructed the FBI to establish its jurisdiction by moving agents to every investigative locale, including Bremer's apartment. Felt told Colson that his agents would not enter the apartment until they obtained a search warrant. Colson rushed to the president's office, and the two men quickly hatched a bizarre plot that far surpassed in its base criminality anything of which Nixon subsequently was accused in the Watergate-inspired articles of impeachment: Colson operative E. Howard Hunt, a retired CIA agent, would break into Bremer's apartment and plant pro-McGovern literature there. Authorities and the media would be convinced that the attempted assassination was rooted in left-wing Democratic politics. Colson prepared the ground by phoning Felt to pass along 'rumors' that he and Nixon supposedly had heard that Bremer 'had ties with [Ted] Kennedy or McGovern political operatives [and] that obviously there could be a conspiracy.' Within an hour, Hunt's bags were packed, and he had made a plane reservation. But the FBI had moved too quickly; before Hunt departed, agents had obtained their warrant and had sealed off Bremer's apartment. Nixon upbraided Colson for not having slowed down the FBI; he later complained that the agency's sudden competence had resulted in a lost opportunity to damage his likely opponent in the fall." [2715] [AAA]

[ZZ] As "Deep Throat", Felt will soon guide Watergate reporters Bob Woodward and Carl Bernstein.

[AAA] Author Stephan Lesher, whose *George Wallace: American Populist* is the source of much of this material, wrote an endnote: "To me, the heart-stopping aspect ... is that it unequivocally brands Nixon as the reprehensible crook he claimed not to be. Nixon had been forced out of office because of his role in covering up the break-in at Democratic party headquarters; there is no evidence that he ordered the break-in or even knew about it in advance. But a month before the Watergate break-in, the president ordered his subordinates to enter the apartment of the man who had just shot a presidential candidate, plant phony evidence, possibly affect the outcome of the nominating and electoral processes, and perhaps skew the conclusions that investigators might reach concerning the safety of all future campaigners. The episode brands Nixon as a morally bankrupt felon who made it clear that any act, regardless of its illegality, would be condoned and protected if it served the president's ambitions." — Lesher endnote 148 on pages 565-566.

Arthur Bremer went on trial July 31, 1972, in a Maryland court. "He was charged with four counts of attempted murder, assault with intent to murder, assault and battery, and carrying and using a handgun. ... Bremer entered a plea of not guilty by reason of insanity." [2716] "Judge Ralph Powers was about to leave on holiday and decided that the case would not be allowed to delay his plans." [2717] "The trial moved swiftly under Powers's firm guidance. On August 4, the jury convicted Bremer on all counts. Asked if he had a statement to make, Bremer arose and said, 'Well, [the prosecutor] mentioned he would like society to be protected from someone like me. Looking back on my life, I would have liked it if society had protected me from myself.' ... Powers sentenced him to sixty-three years in state prison. ... The following month a three-judge panel ... reduced Bremer's sentence to fifty-three years." [2718]

What had been the assassinator's motive? The savvy author of *American Assassins*, James W. Clarke, concluded:

> "Is it possible that Bremer was merely a publicity-seeking weirdo desiring, as the stereotype of assassins suggests, a moment in the limelight? Although Bremer seemingly looked forward to the publicity that his act was calculated to generate, his primary purpose was to insult or outrage society in the most perverse manner possible—and publicity was important only to achieve that end. Bremer wanted to show his contempt for a society he did not fit into and therefore hated. ... Here is a man who has committed a calculating, premeditated, and horrible act for no reason other than he felt like it." [2719]

In the photo at right, "On his last day as governor in January 1987, Wallace gazed at a bust of Lurleen in the capitol rotunda." [2720] She was there not for being his wife, but for being governor when term limits had prevented his continuing to hold the office. "In 1992, when asked to comment on the 20th anniversary of his attempted assassination, Wallace replied, 'I've had twenty years of pain.'" [2721] "In August 1995, Wallace wrote a [highly religious 'Dear Arthur' ... 'born-again' ... 'you can go to heaven like I am going to heaven' [2722]] letter expressing forgiveness to Bremer, but Bremer never replied." [2723] George Corley Wallace Jr. died in Montgomery in 1998, at the age of 79. Arthur Herman Bremer served thirty-five and a half years, and in 2007 was released on parole that will continue to 2025. [2724]

1972: Arthur Bremer shoots and paralyzes George Wallace	
Weapon:	.38-caliber Undercover II 5-shot revolver from Charter Arms Co.
Distance:	3 feet
Shots fired:	5 (the revolver's capacity)
Killed / Hit:	None killed. Wallace was hit with four or five bullets, paralyzed and in pain his remaining 26 years. Three people behind him were wounded once each; all recovered.
Assassin then:	Was wrestled to ground, beaten and kicked, saved by police, tried for murder and assault, convicted, imprisoned, paroled.
Motive(s):	A psychopathic frustrated lover and loser, determined to get even by assassinating Nixon, but having to settle for Wallace.
Do we know beyond reasonable doubt, **whom** did the assassin intend to shoot? **Yes**	
Do we know beyond reasonable doubt, his **motive** for shooting the man he hit? **Yes**	

1974: Samuel Byck attempts to hijack a jetliner to crash into Richard Nixon

This incident was news to me; if ever I knew, I forgot about it. That was apparently what the authorities intended: "Byck's failed assassination attempt and subsequent death ... faded into relative obscurity. While the news media reported on Byck's actions, they did not disclose the reason why Byck attempted to hijack the plane for fear that it might inspire copycat crimes. As a result [his] plot remained relatively unknown, except among members of the United States Secret Service and of analogous security organizations in friendly countries." [2725]

While consulting *American Assassins: The Darker Side of Politics* by James W. Clarke, I found the story of this man who tried to hijack a passenger airplane to crash into The White House, for the purpose of killing President Nixon and his staff to put an end to the then-hot Watergate affair. I am uncertain how to pronounce would-be assassin Byck's name. Sources differ, but considering their reliabilities, I have come to believe it is probably "Bike". [2726]

Clarke relates the incident: "A little after 7 a.m. on February 22, 1974, sleepy-eyed passengers shuffled into a line waiting at Gate C at Baltimore-Washington International Airport to board Delta Flight 523 for Atlanta. It was a cold, gray drizzling Baltimore morning. A jowly heavy-set man walked up behind the security guard and, suddenly drawing a .22 caliber pistol from beneath his dark raincoat, fired two shots. One of the shots tore through the officer's back, severing the main aorta, killing him instantly. As shocked passengers recoiled in terror, the man, with the lumbering agility and swiftness of a bear, leaped over the security chain, ran down the boarding ramp, and boarded the [DC-9] [2727] plane.

"Confronting the crew in the cockpit, the perspiring and panting assailant fired a warning shot and ordered: 'Fly this plane out of here.' Then, following a second command to close the door, the flight attendants seized the opportunity to leave the plane. A shot was fired as they fled.

"Turning again to the pilot and co-pilot, the man repeated his command to 'take off.' The pilot responded that he could not do anything until the wheel blocks were removed. Enraged, the man fired a shot that struck the co-pilot in the stomach, screaming 'The next one will be in the head.' He then grabbed a passenger and shoved her toward the control panel ordering her: 'Help this man fly this plane.' Just then shots were heard from outside the plane. Pushing the passenger back toward her seat, the man whirled and fired two shots hitting the already wounded co-pilot above the left eye and the pilot in the shoulder. ... The pilot lost consciousness.

"Turning again toward the ... cabin, the gunman reloaded his pistol and then seized another passenger by the hair and dragged her forward to the entrance of the cockpit where he again shot the wounded pilot and dying co-pilot as they slumped over the controls." [2728]

Outside, "Police officers attempted to shoot out the tires of the aircraft in order to prevent it from taking off. However, the .38 caliber bullets fired from the Smith & Wesson revolvers issued to the officers at that time period failed to penetrate the tires of the aircraft and instead ricocheted off, some hitting the wing of the aircraft. [A] police officer on the jetway stormed the plane and fired four shots through the aircraft door at Byck with a .357 Magnum revolver taken from the deceased [airport security guard]. Two of the shots penetrated the thick window of the aircraft door" [2729] "splattering glass throughout the cabin and cutting the panic-stricken hostage on the thigh. Moved by her pleas for mercy, the man released his grip instructing her to return to her seat. As she moved away from him, two more shots were fired through the broken window, striking the would-be hijacker in the lower chest and stomach. Clutching his chest with both hands, he staggered and dropped to the floor. Then reaching for his pistol, he rested the barrel against his right temple and squeezed the trigger. Authorities later found a briefcase gasoline bomb [made out of two one-gallon jugs of gasoline and an igniter] [2730] under his body.

"Who was this man who had killed two innocent victims and critically wounded a third before taking his own life? Where did he so desperately want to take the plane? What would be worth the carnage inflicted on that gray ... morning? Who was Samuel Joseph Byck?" [2731] For the full story, read Clarke's fine book. Here, in summary, the life of a loser:

- Born in 1930 to poor Jewish parents in South Philadelphia. [2732]
- Did not graduate from high school. [2733]
- U.S. Army 1954-1956, firearm-trained. [2734]
- Married, four children, forced by wife to separate in 1971, [2735] divorced in 1973. [2736]
- Outshone by his two successful younger brothers. [2737]
- Failed in one job and business venture after another.
- Rejected by SBA for a loan to open a tire business in a school bus.
- Treated as both in- and out-patient for anxiety and depression.
- Diagnosed as having a 'manic-depressive illness.'
- Believed he, like many, was a victim of "the system" and government in particular. [2738]
- Condemned the SBA and Nixon administration for corruption and oppression. [2739]
- Questioned by the Secret Service for saying someone ought to kill President Nixon. [2740]
- Arrested twice for protesting in front of the White House without a permit. [2741]
- Dressed in a Santa suit for another protest. [2742] He was 70 pounds overweight. [2743]
- Plastered his old Buick with 'Impeach Nixon' stickers. [2744] [BBB]
- Fearing scrutiny if he bought a firearm, stole a .22 caliber revolver from a friend. [2745]

Returning to Clarke: "Byck read about other assassins (he had photocopied a chronology of assassinations from the pages of the *Report to the National Commission on the Causes and Prevention of Violence*) and was intent upon making his own death and the President's, in his words, a 'smashing success.' The plan that evolved was, indeed, spectacular. Rather than using the ... firearms of past assassins, Byck planned to destroy not only the President but to incinerate a good portion of his entire administration by crashing a commercial jetliner directly into the White House. Byck [2746] explained his bizarre plan ... on tape the day before:

'I will try to get the plane aloft and fly it towards the target area, which will be Washington, D.C., the capitol of the most powerful wealthiest nation of the world. ... By guise, threats or trickery, I hope to force the pilot to buzz the White House—I mean, sort of dive towards the White House. When the plane is in this position, I will shoot the pilot and then in the last few minutes try to steer the plane

---

[BBB] For the 1960 election, this author, 21, obtained three NIXON LODGE bumper stickers, craftily cut and rearranged to NIX ON NIXON   DODGE LODGE and was then regularly stopped by police.

into the target, which is the White House. ... Whoever dies ... will be directly attributable to the Watergate scandals.'" [2747]

"Although most of the last tapes he made [CCC] contain only oblique references to his personal problems, it is clear that such problems propelled him toward his tragic end. On his birthday [January 30], he claimed that he had been a good father and stated resentfully that his ex-wife and children were partially responsible for his actions. Five days later, he acknowledged that he had no reason to live now that his family had deserted him." [2748] To end it all with a blow against the government he so hated, he went to the airport.

Clarke analyzes:

"It seems reasonable to suggest that if Samuel Byck had had other options in his personal life, he would not have chosen to die as he did. ... He simply had nothing to live for. So in death he tried to establish his personal value—the respect he had lost—through an elaborate political rationalization of his attempt to kill an unpopular and corrupt president. And in so doing, in a manner similar to Lee Oswald, he hoped to place the burden of guilt on the real causes of his misery—an unloving wife and children and ... mother.

"In this context, it seems clear that his displaced anger toward the Small Business Administration, other government agencies, and the President were merely symptomatic, rather than causal, factors in his attempt on the President's life. This is not to suggest that his political resentments were irrational: they were widely shared by many Americans during this period. But like Oswald, the extreme intensity of these resentments can only be understood in the context of Samuel Byck's peculiarly personal problems as the neurotic and compensatory act of a ... would-be assassin." [2749]

Your author agrees that Oswald's resentment was causative in his shooting to kill; but it was not directed at a president — his extreme intensity was directed at Connally. Read on.

"Byck is ... one of the (failed) assassins portrayed in Stephen Sondheim's and John Weidman's 1991 musical *Assassins*. His role in the musical is built largely around the tapes sent to ... famous public figures, which he 'records' during two scene-length monologues, the first addressed to [Leonard] Bernstein and the second to Nixon himself. A movie based on his story, *The Assassination of Richard Nixon,* was released in 2004. ... The History Channel also ran a special on Byck entitled *The Plot to Kill Nixon*." [2750] Both are available on DVDs — but I haven't looked at them. In Byck's case, the reality is more than sufficiently like fiction.

1972: Samuel Byck attempts to hijack a jetliner to crash into Richard Nixon	
Weapon:	Hijacked a DC-9 jetliner to crash into The White House
Distance:	Point-blank at airport guard, a few feet at pilot and co-pilot
Shots fired:	Ten (he reloaded), the final shot from his .22 pistol held to his head
Killed / Hit:	Killed airport guard and co-pilot, gravely wounded the pilot
Assassin then:	Shot-at by police with fierce .357, killed himself with his puny .22
Motive(s):	Desperation of a lifelong loser, rationalized as anti-government
Do we know beyond reasonable doubt, **whom** did the assassin intend to kill? **Yes**	
Do we know beyond reasonable doubt, his **motive** for targeting that person? **Yes**	

[CCC] Hear 6½ edited minutes of his many tapes at www.youtube.com/watch?v=VHAWUby7V-A

1975: Lynette Fromme points a pistol at Gerald Ford

Jerry Ford, president for only two years and five months, was the target of two independent assassination attempts within two weeks, both in California, both by women.

In his autobiography, Ford recalled September 5, 1975: "[I]n Sacramento, I left the [h]otel and walked across the capitol grounds toward the office of Governor Jerry Brown. ... The weather that morning was clear; the sun was shining brightly, and there were several rows of people standing behind a rope that lined the sidewalk to my left. They were applauding and saying nice things; I was in a good mood, so I started shaking hands. That's when I spotted a

'Squeaky' Fromme After Capture

woman wearing a bright red dress. She was in the second or third row, moving right along with me as if she wanted to shake my hand. When I slowed down, I noticed immediately that she thrust her hand under the arms of the other spectators. I reached down to shake it—and looked into the barrel of a .45 caliber pistol pointed directly at me. I ducked." [2751]

See endnote 2752 (at back in NOTES AND SOURCES) to read why I cannot show you the TIME magazine cover of the same lady, same week.

[2752]

The Colt automatic had been in a leg holster under the woman's blood-red nun's robe. Secret Service agents grabbed the gun and captured her. For an assault, the law imposed only a fine and imprisonment for "not more than ten years, or both." [2753] But she became the first person prosecuted under a federal law, enacted after the murder of John Kennedy, that "punished by imprisonment for any term of years or for life" an attempt to kill the President. She was charged with attempted murder, tried and convicted within three months of the incident, and sentenced to life in prison. She spent 34 years in federal prisons, broken only by a two-day escape, before being released on parole.

She is "Squeaky" Fromme. Much of what follows comes from a superb biography by Jess Bravin: *Squeaky: The Life and Times of Lynette Alice Fromme*. Before looking into her strange life and times, let's get her surname right. It's pronounced with two syllables, as in "a gift **from me** to you", as she insisted to her trial judge. [2754] Not wanting to hurt people's feelings, she acquiesced [2755] to incorrect one-syllable pronunciations that rhymed with "roam" and "prom" — but it's really "from-me." [2756] Because that name was mispronounced at her arraignment, the narrow-minded judge decided she had to be tried as "Froam"! [2757] It really didn't matter — in the event, she refused to attend most of her trial.

Lynette Alice Fromme, born in 1948 in Santa Monica, [2758] grew up in Los Angeles' beach suburbs. Her father dominated and abused Lynne [2759] — certainly physically, [2760] perhaps incestuously. [2761] She increasingly disconnected from her high school class of 1966. She smoked, drank, overdosed on barbiturates, slit her wrists, [2762] turned-on and dropped out. An early "flower child," she drifted in and out of her parents' home, finally left in 1967 when her father "argued over some kind of definition from the dictionary, that's how dumb it was," she later said. "His way or no way. I said, 'yes, but,' and he said, 'yes, but nothing.'" [2763]

As she would testify four years later in the famous "Helter Skelter" murder trial, "I was in Venice [California], sitting down on a curb crying, when a man walked up and said, 'Your father kicked you out of the house, did he?'" [2764] The man told her, "Up in the Haight,

I'm called the Gardener. I tend to all the flower children." [2765] "'I grabbed my books,' Lynne later wrote, 'running to catch up with him. I didn't know why—I didn't care—and I never left.' The Gardener, of course, was Charles Manson." [2766]

"Manson [2767] was thirty-two years old. Over seventeen of those years—more than half his life—had been spent in institutions." [2768] His most recent release had been in March 1967, although "he begged the authorities to let him remain in prison. Prison had become his home,

SO VENTURA CAL
47623
22 APR 1968

he told them. He didn't think he could adjust to the world outside." [2769] Charlie already had one woman in his '48 Chevy, so Lyn Fromme became the third member of the Manson Family, which grew to 14 women and 6 men living in a "group marriage commune." [2770] in those blissful days of being against the war in Vietnam and in favor of lots and lots of sex.

Lyn "was thin, red-headed, covered with freckles. Though nineteen, she looked much younger." [2771] The Family sometimes stayed at the Spahn Movie Ranch in the San Fernando Valley. Manson assigned her to care for owner George Spahn, eighty years old and largely blind. "She had him in the palm of her hand. She cleaned for him, cooked for him, balanced his checkbook, made love with him." [2772] Lyn

"would sit with him for hours, listening to country music on the radio, letting him slide his hand up her skirt. When he pinched her, she would loose a cute little shriek, and George would chuckle. He named her for that sound: 'Squeaky.'" [2773]

On two terrible days in 1969, Family members descended into Los Angeles to murder pregnant actress Sharon Tate and four others one night, then the LaBianca couple the next. The Tate-LaBianca murders became known as "Helter Skelter", the name of a popular song by The Beatles. Manson and several others were arrested and tried. Prosecutor Vincent Bugliosi explained to the jury "that one of Manson's principal motives for these seven savage murders was to ignite Helter Skelter; in other words, start the black-white revolution ... ultimately leading to a civil war ... which Manson predicted ... the black man [would win, but] once they destroyed the entire white race, would be unable to handle the reins of power ... and would therefore have to turn over the reins to those white people who had escaped Helter Skelter; i.e., Charles Manson and his Family." [2774]

Squeaky was not involved in the murders, so ran the Family in Charlie's absence. She came to public notice as one of the girls keeping vigil on the sidewalk near the courthouse. [2775] Three of the defendants, plus Squeaky and others on the curb, then created a memorable image after they "lit matches, heated bobby pins red-hot, then burned X marks on their foreheads, after which they ripped open the burnt flesh with needles, to create more prominent scars." [2776]

During the trial, "Richard Nixon commented at a press conference that ... in the case of Manson, 'here is a man who was guilty, directly or indirectly, of eight murders without reason.' ... The jury had been sequestered ... [an] attorney brought a copy of the *Los Angeles Times* into court." [2777] "Manson suddenly stood and, turning toward the jury box, held up a copy … A bailiff grabbed it but not before Manson had shown the jury the huge black headline: MANSON GUILTY, NIXON DECLARES. After an extensive voir dire, all eighteen [jurors and alternates] stated under oath that they had not been influenced by the headline and that they would consider only the evidence presented to them in court. As [a juror] put it, he'd listened to every bit of the testimony; Nixon hadn't; "I don't believe Mr. Nixon knows *anything* about it." [2778] "Lyn focused on Nixon's statement. She would not forgive him." [2779]

All the defendants were convicted and sentenced to death. When the California State Supreme Court abolished the death penalty in 1972, their sentences were commuted to life imprisonment. Prosecutor Bugliosi wrote in his best seller *Helter Skelter*, "there is little left of the Manson Family now, though little Squeaky, chief cheerleader of the Manson cause, is still keeping the faith. Although undisputed leader of the Family while Charlie is in absentia, and presumably involved in the planning of their activities, and though arrested more than a dozen times on charges ranging from robbery to murder, she has only been convicted a few times, and always on minor charges." [2780] That was 1974, before she became *really* famous.

Several Manson women moved to Sacramento in 1973, to be close to Charlie, then in Folsom prison near that city. Lyn and the others formed the Order of the Rainbow [2781] in the apartment they rented close to the state capitol campus, and wore long nuns' habit-like robes, but bright red. "Lyn appeared at news bureaus around Sacramento to deliver fearsome press releases attributed to Manson, along with baskets of fresh-baked cookies for the reporters. 'We're waiting for our Lord and there's only one thing to do before He comes off the cross and that's clean up the earth,' Lyn explained. 'We're nuns now. … Our red robes are an example of the new morality…. They're red with the sacrifice, the blood of the sacrifice.'" [2782] They invented "The International People's Court of Retribution" [2783], lived on welfare,[2784] and spent their days writing press releases and letters to polluters.

A news release in July 1975 "was titled 'Manson is Mad at Nixson'—with the parallel spelling intended. It blamed former President Nixon for the conviction of the Tate-LaBianca defendants because of his comment during the trial that Manson was guilty. Along with various other indictments of society, the release pronounced: 'If Nixon's reality wearing a Ford face continues to run this country against the law, your homes will be bloodier than the Tate-LaBianca homes and My Lai [DDD] put together.'" [2785] "Lyn displayed some of the photos she had clipped from newspapers and magazines. 'These are people we find very offensive,' she said. She held a picture of Nixon, and one of Ford toasting a foreign dignitary. Ford was doing a terrible job, Lyn said, and 'he will have to pay for what he's doing. Nixon's karma is getting back at him. Ford is picking up in Nixon's footsteps, and he is just as bad.'" [2786]

From a friend, Lyn borrowed a Colt .45 semi-automatic pistol.[2787] Then, "[A]fter days, weeks, years and years of rejection … No one … would hear her message. She recalled what she had been told, in so many ways, so many times: 'We're not interested in you and your goddamn trees. President Ford is coming to town.' If that's what everybody was interested in, she would be, too. She would do something with President Ford. That would get everybody's attention. The gun was just to get President Ford to notice, Lyn said." [2788]

"Secret Service agent Larry Buendorf had seen the gun and quickly threw the woman to the ground before the pistol could fire …" [2789] "Unbelievably, she did not know to cock the pistol first, and the gun did not fire." [2790] "The entire assault lasted a split second. Other

---

[DDD] A wanton massacre of an entire innocent village in Vietnam by American soldiers.

agents hurried Ford to safety inside the state Capitol, where, after briefly composing himself, he continued on to the governor's office." [2791] "The incident may have lasted only a fraction of a second, but its aftermath would be of longer duration. For many Americans, the sudden prospect of losing Ford crystallized their affection for the nation's leader, even though he had not received a single vote for president." [2792]

Lyn was jailed in Sacramento, where trial would be held in the Federal court. (Coincidences continue: "More than twenty years after Lyn's conviction, [the] courthouse became the setting for the trial of another extremist charged with ecologically motivated terrorist acts: that of Theodore J. Kaczynski, the alleged Unabomber." [2793] And even more: "'This is not a 'Who done it,' but a 'Why he done it,'' said Paul Rothstein, a constitutional-law expert and professor at Georgetown University law school. 'That's what the fight's going to be about — his inner emotions and his mental state.'" [2794]) Preparing for Squeaky's trial, the Federal Public Defender's investigator asked her: "'If I were a reporter and I had a camera here and I were to ask you, 'Why?' what would you say?' Lyn answered right away: 'For the trees,' she said. [He] seemed puzzled, so Lyn elaborated. The trees were ancient, she said, many had existed since before Jesus was born." [2795] Logging of stately old-growth trees then underway in Redwood National Park had devastated Lyn.[2796]

A jailer quoted Lyn: "Well, you know, when people around you treat you like a child and pay no attention to the things you say, you have to do something." [2797] She also said "she had had no intention of harming the president, but rather of raising the nation's consciousness about the issues that really mattered ... The authorities' heavy reaction to the pistol incident seemed to surprise her. 'What are they mad about? The gun didn't go off.'" [2798]

The trial began with Lyn representing herself, and ended with her not even attending because of what she perceived as gagging by the judge. In her absence, the public defender did his best. There was conflicting testimony on three key points:

First, was the pistol loaded? Well, it depended on how you looked at it. There were bullets in the clip, but there was no bullet in the firing chamber. So, Lyn could not fire by pulling the trigger — she would first have to pull back the slide to chamber a bullet. She may or may not have known that. If she knew it, she may or may not have had sufficient strength to do it.

Second, had she pulled the trigger? Some witnesses heard a click, some didn't. Ford ("the man that was looking right down the barrel of the gun" [2799]) did not hear a click.[2800] Neither did the Secret Service agent who grabbed her wrist.[2801] [2802]

Third, what did she mean by what she said immediately after the incident? Was it innocent: "Don't worry, it didn't go off."? Or was it incriminating: "Damn, it didn't go off!"? [2803] There was considerable debate about the tone of Squeaky's voice, thought to be an indicator of her intent.

The trial was quick. The U.S. Attorney laid out the straightforward case that she had aimed the pistol, which contained bullets, and was thus guilty. A first, the defense's leadoff witness was President Ford, testifying by videotape, the first president to use that medium.

The jury (hurrying to get home for turkey?) took only two days to reach a verdict the night before Thanksgiving. When she heard "Guilty", Lyn screamed "You animals!" [2804] She "was the first woman in history convicted of attempted assassination of a president." [2805] "[T]he day Lyn was convicted of attempting to assassinate him, President Ford announced that the United States would forswear conducting any assassinations of its own. ... [T]he president said he had 'issued specific instructions to U.S. intelligence agencies that under no circumstances shall any agencies participate or plan any assassination of foreign leaders.'" [2806]

Sentencing was a week before Christmas. Squeaky's defense attorney said: "The only thing I have to say, Your Honor, is that I feel that had Miss Fromme wanted to kill the President, he would be dead. And that she did want to draw attention to her ecological issues." [2807] In a 120-page letter to the judge, "Lyn had written that before leaving her apartment, she had put a cartridge into the Colt .45's firing chamber and then ejected it, leaving the chamber empty. 'I ejected that one and saw it fall to the floor,' the letter said. She wrote that she had no intention of killing the president." The judge responded before imposing sentence: "Now, unfortunately, your version of what happened on that day comes too late," said the judge. "Unfortunately, having been afforded the opportunity to testify and having refused it, your explanation of the incident, even if it's to be believed ... is now wasted. It is of no help whatsoever for any legal purpose insofar as this case is concerned." [2808]

To Lyn, it was as always. She probably "recalled what she had been told, in so many ways, so many times: 'We're not interested in you and your goddamn trees.'" [2809] The judge then said: "being unable to find any reason or justification for imposing a sentence of less severity than the maximum provided by Congress for the commission of the crime with which you've been convicted, ... it is the sentence of this court that you be imprisoned for the term of your natural life in the custody of the Attorney General of the United States." [2810]

Lyn went into a women's prison in Alderson, West Virginia, to serve a life sentence. She "escaped in 1987 and was recaptured two days later about two miles from the prison." [2811] "Lynette 'Squeaky' Fromme was released from federal prison in 2009 after serving time for the attempted assassination of President Ford." [2812] She now lives in Marcy, New York.[2813]

1975: Lynette Fromme points a pistol at Gerald Ford	
Weapon:	Pistol: .45-caliber Colt automatic
Distance:	Handshaking distance — a couple of feet
Shots fired:	None (four bullets were in pistol's clip, but none in firing chamber)
Killed / Hit:	None
Assassin then:	Convicted of attempted assassination, sentenced to life in prison
Motive(s):	Major: Draw attention to need to save environment, especially trees; Minor: Anger at Nixon for helping to convict Charles Manson
Do we know beyond reasonable doubt, **whom** did the assassin intend to shoot? **Yes**	
Do we know beyond reasonable doubt, her **motive** for threatening to shoot him? **Yes**	

1975: Sara Jane Moore fires a pistol at Gerald Ford

Only two weeks after idealistic Lyn Fromme dressed in bright red robes and an attention-demanding tall witch's hat to point a pistol at President Ford and maybe — but probably not — pull a trigger that could not fire because she had not loaded a bullet into the firing chamber, there was another inconsiderate but considerably better-considered attempt to shoot him.

Uniquely, the intended victim lived to tell about the two attempts, from his perspective, so we have another interesting advantage of reading in his autobiography:

"Squeaky Fromme, I thought, was an aberration. There had been misfits and kooks in every society since the beginning of time. I didn't think California harbored a larger number of these people than any other part of the country, so I wasn't overly concerned about my personal safety when I returned to the state on September 19 ... to San Francisco ... [O]n September 22 [I] attended a luncheon of the World Affairs Council of Northern California. [2814]

Shortly before three-thirty that afternoon, I stepped out of the hotel entrance and walked toward the armored Lincoln Continental that would whisk me to the airport. Groups of people stood on both sides of the entrance and there was an even larger crowd of three thousand or more across the street in Union Square. Dick Keiser, the head of the Secret Service detail, had advised me not to cross the street and shake hands in the crowd. I waved once or twice as I walked toward the car. Bang! I recognized the sound of a shot, and I froze. There was a hushed silence for a split second. Then pandemonium broke out. [The photo below is captioned by the Gerald R. Ford Presidential Library: "President Ford winces at the sound of the gun ... ".] [2815]

Agents ... forced me down behind the car. Then they opened the door and pushed me

inside. [Chief of Staff Don] Rumsfeld and the agents piled in on top of me; somebody shouted, "Go," and the car took off. I don't think anyone ever drove to the airport faster than we did that afternoon, but I wasn't worried about setting a new speed record. What did bother me after we had traveled several blocks was that the agents were still on top of me in the back of the car, and they were heavy as hell. 'Hey,' I said finally, 'will you guys get off? You're going to smother me.'

During the long flight back to the capital, Secret Service agents gave me a report on the incident. My assailant this time had been a forty-five-year-old matron named Sara Jane Moore, who had ties to radical groups in the San Francisco Bay area. Her weapon had been a .38 caliber revolver which she had fired from a distance of about forty feet. The slug passed a few feet to my left, hit the front of the hotel, then ricocheted off to the right. An alert bystander, Olive [sic] Sipple, noticed the gun in her hand and reached out to deflect her aim. ...

I was determined not to let the second near miss intimidate me, and when we returned to the White House later that night, I told reporters: 'I don't think any person as President ought to cower in the face of a limited number of people who want to take the law into their own hands. The American people want a dialogue between them and their President and their other public officials. And if we can't have that opportunity of talking with one another, seeing one another, shaking hands with one another, something has gone wrong in our society. I think it's important that we as a people don't capitulate to the wrong element, an infinitesimal number of people who want to destroy everything that's best about America.'" [2816]

The scene of the shooting is clearly engraved in this author's memory. Ford had walked down the front steps of the St. Francis Hotel to Post Street. On our wedding day at year-end 1966, my lovely young bride Jean and I flew from Oregon to San Francisco. We had reservations at the St. Francis, but on walking into that same main entrance to check in, I was told that they had no record of us, and were completely full. I appealed to the manager on duty, pointing out the beautiful lady standing nearby "to whom I've been married only a few hours, who thinks I'm wonderful, and is she now to believe that I'm incompetent?"

The manager asked for a few minutes, then returned to say, "We have a room for you, but will probably need to move you to another after a day or two. Will that be all right?" Of course it was — anything would do for the first night of our honeymoon — so we registered and were conducted up to the second floor, to a room directly above the main entrance, and found ourselves in The Governor's Suite! It consisted of four large rooms, with a balcony for speech-making above the main entrance on Post Street, across from Union Square, the hub of San Francisco. Out the balcony's door, we overlooked the sidewalk across Post Street from which a bullet would fly in nine years — and that's all I'll say about the honeymoon.

On September 22, 1975, a crowd of about 3,000 stood across from the St. Francis. Much of the preceding article was indebted to Jess Bravin's spot-on biography *Squeaky: The Life and Times of Lynette Alice Fromme*. While at it, he added a few insightful pages about a lady in that crowd, Sara Jane "Sally" Moore, including:

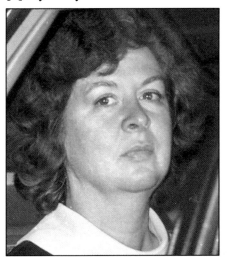

"[F]orty-five-year-old Moore [2817] had worked as an FBI informant, and become a peripheral figure in Bay Area radical movements. ... a frumpy Middle American mom [EEE] more than a revolutionary soldier. Indeed, even though she managed to insinuate herself into circles friendly to the Symbionese Liberation Army, [FFF] her most militant act seemed to be volunteering as a bookkeeper for People in Need, a food-for-the-poor program established by the SLA.

Moore seemed to enjoy the attention she received through her contacts with different sides of social tumult—the radicals, the government, and the press. All three groups, however, had grown tired of Moore ... "flaky" ... her urgent phone calls increasingly went unanswered." [2818]

"Moore had been evaluated by the Secret Service earlier in 1975, but agents decided that she posed no danger to the President. She had been picked up by police on an illegal handgun charge the day before the Ford incident, but was released. The police confiscated her .44 caliber revolver and 113 rounds of ammunition." [2819] "Inspector Jack O'Shea ... warned federal agents that she 'could be another Squeaky.'" [2820]

[EEE] Her five marriages had all ended; three of her four children had been adopted by her parents.
[FFF] Explaining the SLA is beyond the scope of this fat book. There is a fine article in Wikipedia.

"Two Secret Service men went to question her, but found no grounds for an arrest. Moore, meanwhile, was not daunted; she bought herself another pistol. On September 22, Moore took her .38 caliber revolver and mingled amid the crowd outside the St. Francis. Her presence went unnoted by security agents, their gaze instead drawn by protesters hoisting placards with such messages as RELEASE PATTY HEARST, ARREST GERALD FORD! The Secret Service detail persuaded Ford to skip shaking hands with the crowd and instead to head to his limousine.

Sally Moore managed to get a shot off at the president when he emerged from the hotel, but a bystander, Oliver Sipple, deflected her aim. She missed Ford by five feet, with the ricocheting bullet striking a cab driver in the groin. Said Moore upon her arrest: 'I'm no Squeaky Fromme.' ...

Like Lyn, Moore at first claimed she had no intention of killing the president. 'It was kind of an ultimate protest against the system,' she said days after her arrest. 'I did not want to kill somebody, but there comes a point when the only way you can make a statement is to pick up a gun.'" [2821]

"After her arrest, Moore insisted that she had a purpose: to unite the Bay Area's radical community, to 'forge some kind of unity between the rage that led to the formation of the SLA combined with the theoreticians.'

Nearly a year later ... Moore spoke ... in an interview with *Playboy* magazine.[2822] 'Since I was arrested, I've been in four different jails. In each of them, people have asked me, 'What were you trying to do when you fired the shot?' I always say, 'I was trying to kill him.' That's good for a minute or two of dead silence, because everybody expects I'm going to be struck dead on the spot. But then—whether the women are black or white, old or young, in for assault and battery, possession of marijuana or whatever—every one of them says, with really intense emotion, 'I wish you *had* killed the motherfucker.'

Moore seemed particularly angry at one individual for interfering with her goal. Listing all the hitches on her road to assassinate the president, Moore complained that 'good old Squeaky Fromme did her thing. If it hadn't been for *that* incident, Ford would probably have crossed the street to shake hands and I would have had a better chance.'" [2823]

On the sidewalk stood Oliver Wellington "Billy" Sipple, 33, a decorated Marine Corps PFC seriously wounded by shrapnel in Vietnam. He noticed that the woman beside him was aiming a .38-caliber revolver. Instinctively, Sipple lunged at the woman just as her finger squeezed

the trigger. The gun fired, but Sipple's grab deflected her aim and caused the bullet to miss. It ricocheted off the hotel's stone facade and hit taxi driver John Ludwig in the groin, did not penetrate, but left him in pain. Asked if he needed anything, Ludwig said he'd like to meet the president. Told that Ford's schedule would not allow that, Ludwig said "Hell with Ford!", so the FBI soon arrived to interrogate him as a possible threat. He eventually received a White House letter expressing regret for his injury. Still miffed, he sold the letter for $100. [2824] In the photo,[2825] Billy at left reaches behind the be-striped lady in front. Sara's face is just to the right of the pole. A black arrow near the right margin points up at her nose.

Billy Sipple, the hero, fared badly. An early member of San Francisco's growing gay community, he had not told his family of his orientation. From his friends, newsmen learned and wrote of that. In Detroit, his hometown, parents and brothers were harassed and ridiculed — and disowned him. Only after many years was there a prickly reconciliation. His brother George said: "[Our parents] accepted it. That was all. They didn't like it, but they still accepted. He was welcomed. Only thing was: Don't bring a lot of your friends." [2826] Sipple drank heavily, was treated at VA hospitals for "shell shock" before PTSD was a name, gained weight to 300 pounds, and died at age 47 of pneumonia. His family collected his effects from San Francisco, including a prized framed letter from his apartment wall: "I want you to know how much I appreciated your selfless actions last Monday ... Jerry Ford." [2827]

Moore was sentenced to federal prison to serve a life term. She escaped in 1979 but was recaptured in one day.[2828] Investigative journalist Geri Spieler befriended her and wrote *Taking Aim at the President: The Remarkable Story of the Woman Who Shot at Gerald Ford*. One of the oldest inmates in the country, Sara said of Gerald Ford: "People kept saying he would have to die before I could be released, and I did not want my release from prison to be dependent on somebody, on something happening to somebody else, so I wanted him to live to be 100." [2829] He came close, dying at 93 in December 2006.[GGG]

Sara Moore benefited from "a federal law that makes parole mandatory for inmates who have served at least 30 years of a life sentence and have maintained a satisfactory disciplinary record." [2830] She was released on December 31, 2007. In 2009 [2831] on NBC-TV's *Today* program, the grandmotherly lady reflected on her escape from prison thirty years earlier: "If I knew that I was going to be captured several hours later, I would have stopped at the local bar just to get a drink and a burger." [2832]

1975: Sara Jane Moore fires a pistol at Gerald Ford	
Weapon:	Pistol: .38 caliber revolver
Distance:	40 feet (measured curb-to-curb across that normal street) [2833]
Shots fired:	One, because the man next to her deflected the aim
Killed / Hit:	None killed, one bystander hurt by ricocheting bullet
Assassin then:	Captured, pleaded guilty, sentenced to prison for life, released on parole after 32 years in 2007 at age 77.
Motive(s):	She said "to unite the Bay Area's radical community"
Do we know beyond reasonable doubt, **whom** did the assassin intend to shoot? **Yes**	
Do we know beyond reasonable doubt, her **motive** for attempting to shoot him? **Yes**	

[GGG] The author's father, George Sundborg, also born in 1913, had known Ford while working in the U.S. Senate, and was considerably pleased to outlive him. Dad died in 2009, almost 96.

1981: John Hinckley, Jr. fires a pistol, wounding Ronald Reagan and three others

On the 70th day of his presidency, March 30, 1981, Ronald Reagan performed one of a president's bread-and-butter duties, a speech to a convention at Washington's Hilton Hotel.[2834] Afterward, he walked across a sidewalk to his limousine, past a group of onlookers standing behind the inevitable cameramen. In the small crowd, a man called out, "President Reagan!", then fired six pistol shots in three seconds. A Secret Service agent quickly dove onto the lone gunman, as other agents pushed Reagan into the limousine.[2835]

In 1963, some confusion about the number of bullets Lee Oswald fired resulted from John Connally's delayed reaction to the bullet that so severely wounded him. In 1981, delayed reaction was again a factor, and this time it caused more than confusion — it was nearly fatal. President Reagan was face-down on the floor between the seats, with Secret Service Agent Jerry Parr (at front-right in the photo) lying on top of him. Because Reagan appeared to be uninjured, Parr directed the driver to go to the White House. The president felt a pain in his chest, which he and the agent attributed to his being pressed down onto the transmission hump. The agent got off, the president sat up — the pain was still there.

Reagan later described "the most paralyzing pain . . . as if someone had hit you with a hammer. ... I thought that maybe [Parr's] gun or something, when he had come down on me, had broken a rib. But when I sat up on the seat and the pain wouldn't go away and suddenly I found that I was coughing up blood, we both decided that maybe I had broken a rib and punctured a lung."[2836] "[M]y handkerchief was sopped with blood and [Parr] handed me his. Suddenly, I realized I could barely breathe. No matter how hard I tried, I couldn't get enough air. I was frightened and started to panic a little. I just was not able to inhale enough air."[2837]

Almost to the White House, the agent told the driver to speed to George Washington University Hospital.[2838] There was no stretcher at the emergency entrance, so agents helped the president walk in, but his "eyes rolled upward, and his head went back, his knees buckled and he started to collapse."[2839] Reagan's pallor and the location of his pain were classic symptoms of a heart attack, but when his shirt came off, a doctor found a small wound under the left armpit.[2840] Only then, almost fifteen minutes after the bullets flew, did they discover that he had been shot. One bullet had struck the limousine, flattened, then penetrated into Reagan's chest. It collapsed his left lung and rested there, within an inch of his heart and aorta.[2841]

Although in pain and coughing blood, the seasoned actor was able to get off a couple of good ones. When wife Nancy rushed into the emergency room, "Ronnie" lifted up the oxygen mask to say: "Honey, I forgot to duck."[2842] Later, about to be anesthetized for surgery, he looked around at the doctors: "Please tell me you're all Republicans!"[2843] In the recovery room he used a famous W. C. Fields line: "All in all, I'd rather be in Philadelphia."[2844] Americans who had recently given him a great victory in part because he had boldly confronted President Carter with "There you go again!" knew this strong man would be OK.

Surgeons found and sewed shut the rip in his lung that was hemorrhaging blood into the pleura. An on-the-table X-ray finally spotted the bullet, flattened into the size and shape of a dime when it hit the limousine before bouncing into the lung. Reagan had lost a full half of his body's blood.[2845] By any standards, it was a close call. He fully recovered, served eight years as president, retired to his California ranch and died at 93 of Alzheimer's disease.

The photo below shows all four who will be wounded in the next three seconds.[2846] At left in the white coat is Secret Service Agent Jerry Parr, who will not be wounded and will shove Reagan into the limousine at right, then lie on top of him. In front of his chin is James Brady, who will be most severely and lastingly injured. Reagan is happily waving to the small crowd at rear which includes the assassin. Nearest that group, looking at the camera, is uniformed Officer Thomas Delahanty. At right in the light suit is Agent Tim McCarthy.

Two of the six bullets missed, one was in Reagan, three others were wounded. Officer Delahanty of the Washington police was shot in the neck. At Washington Hospital Center, surgeons did their best to repair the damage, but that bullet had ricocheted off his spinal cord, causing permanent nerve damage to his left arm. Delahanty will be cited for heroism for his valiant effort to protect the President, but will ultimately have to retire from the Washington police force due to his disability.[2847]

Secret Service Agent McCarthy proved the rumor that agents will "take a bullet" to save the person they protect. He opened the limousine door for the president. After Agent Parr shoved Regan into the vehicle, McCarthy, above in the light suit, turned toward the shots, spread his arms and legs to safeguard the president, and was hit. Surgeons at GWU Hospital successfully removed a bullet from his abdomen, he fully recovered, was honored for his bravery and had a long career with the Secret Service and then Illinois police.[2848]

White House Press Secretary James Brady, who received the first bullet because he was then between the shooter and his target, was severely wounded and would never fully recover. Out of loyalty, Reagan insisted he keep the title of press secretary. Deputy Press Secretary Larry Speakes took over Brady's duties, but remained "deputy" for his entire tenure.[2849]

James Brady survived the bullet wound to his head but, partially paralyzed, spent most of his life in a wheelchair. He and valiant wife Sarah led the Brady Campaign to Prevent Gun Violence. "'I wouldn't be here in this damn wheelchair if we had common-sense legislation,' Mr. Brady said in 2011." Jim and Sarah were primarily responsible for Congress passing the Brady Handgun Violence Prevention Act, requiring background checks and waiting periods for many gun buyers. Jim Brady, only 73, died as this was being written in 2014.[2850] The medical examiner in Northern Virginia ruled his death to be a homicide, allowing prosecutors to now charge the shooter with murder,[2851] but (the first update in 2015) they decided to not do so.[2852]

The would-be assassin was John Warnock Hinckley Jr.[2853] It won't take long to tell his

story; he was insane. A normal youngster, in high school he began to withdraw and isolate himself. Leaving home for college, he attended Texas Tech only sporadically for seven years, never had a friend or girlfriend, did not graduate. He went to Hollywood and Nashville to try without success to write and sell songs, invented an imaginary girlfriend, never had a lasting job, sponged from this parents, sat alone in apartments and became obese.

In 1976, Hinckley became fixated on the movie *Taxi Driver*, which he watched fifteen times as he patterned himself on the lead character by dressing, eating and drinking like Travis Bickle, who thinks he can win a young lady by assassinating the presidential candidate for whom she is campaigning. When that was thwarted, he became obsessed with a child prostitute, played by then-13-year-old Jodie Foster. Bickle rescues the girl by murdering her pimp. Hinckley bought, then practiced with, the same guns as Bickle.

Jodie Foster was 17 in 1980, a student at Yale University. Hinckley took a room in New Haven, frequented the campus, spoke with Foster by phone, slipped poems and messages under her door.[2854] She rebuffed him. Emulating movie taxi driver Bickle's plan to impress, Hinckley began to stalk President Jimmy Carter on the campaign trail. After Reagan became president in 1981, Hinckley moved to D.C. He wrote a last letter to Jodie Foster in March:

> "Over the past seven months I've left you dozens of poems, letters and love messages in the faint hope that you could develop an interest in me. Although we talked on the phone a couple of times I never had the nerve to simply approach you and introduce myself. ... The reason I'm going ahead with this attempt now is because I cannot wait any longer to impress you."[2855]
> "I would abandon this idea of getting Reagan in a second if I could only win your heart and live out the rest of my life with you."[2856]

In 1982 a jury found Hinckley not guilty by reason of insanity in the shootings of President Reagan and three others, a verdict that caused widespread dismay. That use of the insanity defense changed American law; in 1984 Congress made use of the insanity plea more difficult by switching the burden of proof from prosecution to defense. Concomitantly, many states tightened their rules governing release of prisoners institutionalized after being found not guilty by reason of insanity.

John Hinckley was institutionalized in St. Elizabeth's Hospital in D.C., where the first attempted assassin in this chapter, Richard Lawrence, had been confined for life, almost a century and a half earlier. Testifying that it is indeed a small world, or that birds of a feather really do flock together, when Hinckley first asked for a pass to spend a day off-campus from St. Elizabeth's, officials found letters he had written to Lynette Fromme, who had clicked a pistol near President Ford to gain attention to the plight of redwood forests.[2857] He occasionally pops up in the news as he asks for parole or some other freedom. In recent years he has been allowed brief trips out, from which he reliably returns.

Describing pistols and Arthur Bremer's attempt on presidential candidate George Wallace eight years earlier, Thomas S. Healey opined:

> "Hinckley shot Reagan and his press secretary, James Brady, with a small-bore pistol [.22"]. Had Hinckley used a weapon with the throw weight of Bremer's [.38"], Reagan likely would have become the third president to be assassinated in this century, after William McKinley in 1901 and John F. Kennedy in 1963. Brady, permanently disabled with a head wound, would not have survived either." [2858]

Daniel Pipes, the expert critic of conspiracy theories, quoted in the preceding chapter, offers an interesting testimony to the inevitable prevalence of coincidences:

> "John W. Hinckley, Jr.'s, attempted assassination of Ronald Reagan in 1981 prompted little speculation, though the videotape of the shooting incident has unexplained flashes of light, and presidential guards initially looked the wrong way for the gun—possible indications of more than one assassin. More interesting yet, Hinckley's father was reported to be a friend of Vice President George Bush, who would have been the direct beneficiary of Reagan's death. Most remarkable, John Hinckley's brother Scott was scheduled to have dinner with Bush's son Neil on the very evening of the shooting. Yet these connections cast no suspicions on the vice president. The silence surrounding the RFK and Reagan episodes points to the exceptional, and possibly manufactured, nature of the speculation surrounding the JFK assassination." [2859]

An interesting insight on Hinckley came from Dallas Police Homicide Detective Gus Rose, who attended and commented on two days of interrogations of Lee Oswald:

> "To me, he seemed like a real radical nut. I've talked to all kinds of people and worked hundreds of murder cases; some of them are just as rational as we are today. But he was just a radical nut. When I saw interviews with John Hinckley after he shot Reagan, it was so reminiscent of the way Oswald acted during some of his interviews. I'm convinced that they were two of a kind." [2860]

Finally, recent "coming out" news items: At the 2013 Golden Globes award ceremony, Jodie Foster made a nice little speech during which she expressed gratitude to her former partner Cydney Bernard, female, with whom she has two sons. The 2014 news is that Jodie Foster has married her girlfriend, photographer and actress Alexandra Hedison, who was previously the three-year girlfriend of Ellen DeGeneres. Hinckley's motive for using violence upon President Reagan was attempting to impress and attract the romantic favor of Foster. It now appears probable that he had been barking up the wrong tree.

1981: John Hinckley, Jr. wounds Ronald Reagan and three others	
Weapon:	Pistol: .22-caliber Rohm RG-14 revolver
Distance:	About 20 feet
Shots fired:	All six that were in the pistol, in three seconds
Killed / Hit:	None were killed, but Reagan and White House Press Secretary Jim Brady were very seriously wounded. A policeman and a Secret Service agent were also wounded; both fully recovered.
Assassin then:	Not guilty by reason of insanity, committed to mental hospital
Motive(s):	Impress movie actress Jodie Foster
Do we know beyond reasonable doubt, **whom** did the assassin intend to shoot? **Yes**	
Do we know beyond reasonable doubt, his **motive** for shooting the man he hit? **Yes**	

1963: Lee Harvey Oswald shoots President Kennedy and Governor Connally

This book is about this crime, so very little need be said here. More will come later. First, a few items not bearing on the principal thrust of this book may be of interest. Oswald's inept failure to escape after the shooting is not unusual. Of all who attacked presidents, only John Wilkes Booth had made plans to escape; he knew to jump down from Lincoln's box to the stage and had a horse waiting for him in the alley behind Ford's Theatre. That's it. No other assassin or would-be had any escape plan. In this regard, Oswald was entirely typical.

Booth was unusual in another way. Of all attacks on presidents, his on Lincoln was one of only two that involved a conspiracy — a concerted action by two or more to commit a criminal act. The other was 1950's two-man shoot-'em-up on the sidewalk outside Blair House while Harry Truman napped upstairs. As Earl Warren wisely pointed out in the box atop this chapter, conspiracies are not a usual element of American assassinations.

Pistols are very much the favored weapons of choice when Americans go gunning. Of all the attacks chronicled here, De La Beckwith used his redneck rifle because that's what he habitually carried; James Earl Ray and Lee Harvey Oswald fired rifles because they both lurked in distant waits. All others got up close and fired pistols.

Kennedy was wounded much more severely than Lincoln, Garfield and McKinley. After being shot, Lincoln lived nine hours, McKinley eight days, Garfield 79 days; but JFK was brain dead immediately, officially declared dead in half an hour. The principal reason for that speed: the power of a rifle bullet, also proven by the quick deaths of Evers and King.

Oswald did the reverse of one precedent: When Giuseppe Zangara shot at President-elect Franklin Roosevelt, he accidentally killed the Mayor of Chicago, standing nearby.

Every preceding article in this chapter ended with a box of facts. This will, too, but here two are displayed to show very different conclusions about motive, depending on which man was Oswald's target. To make sense of the summary boxes there are two key considerations, only briefly mentioned here and to be fully developed in following chapters:

Lee Oswald set himself a much more difficult task than any of the seventeen assassins already described in this chapter, by choosing a distant target (only Ray also did this) that was moving (MLK was not). None made attempts on victims moving faster than a walk. Booth's pistol was inches from Lincoln when he fired; Czolgosz was shaking McKinley's hand when he fired into him; Guiteau was three feet from Garfield.[2861] Oswald was singularly distant.

Those physical comparisons are more objective and probably less controversial than the bottom-line in both tables: Motive. For an authority I call on hard-working JFK analyst Sylvia Meagher, who did what the Warren Commission did not, compiling a complete index to their 26 volumes. She then wrote a book pointing out the differences between the facts displayed in those supplement books and the conclusions in the *Warren Report*. On motive:

> "Attempts on the lives of American Presidents have been made by political conspirators, anarchists, or individuals judged to be insane—manifestly demented and requiring institutionalization. ...
>
> The assassination of President Kennedy is the first which appears to have a 'motiveless' motive. The Warren Commission has concluded that Oswald was guilty but has not made a definite determination of his reasons. The Report throws out various suggestions—that his Marxist beliefs were a contributing factor, that personal failure had embittered him, that he was developing a persecution syndrome, and other halfhearted offerings—without committing the Warren Commission to a conclusive finding which it might have to defend." [2862]

"The complete absence of any motive was a main factor in the doubt of Oswald's guilt that flourished all over the world after the assassination. The Warren Commission has not resolved this problem despite its microscopic research into Oswald's life." [2863]

"But he was without a personal or political motive for assassinating the President, and he was not irrational, disturbed, or psychotic. If he had no sane reason for killing Kennedy, and if he was not insane, how are we to understand his alleged crime?" [2864]

An excellent question! Answering it factually and fully is the purpose of this book.

In the manner that summarized the seventeen preceding assassinations and attempts, here are two tables of facts — the first with the conventional assumption that Oswald aimed to kill President John F. Kennedy; the second with the thesis of this book that his intent was to kill Governor John B. Connally. In each, note well the two bottom lines!

1963: Lee Harvey Oswald shoots with intent to kill President John F. Kennedy	
Weapon:	Rifle: 6.5mm Mannlicher-Carcano carbine with 4-power sight
Distance:	177 feet at shot that wounded, 265 feet at third shot that killed
Shots fired:	Three: (1) Missed; (2) Wounded both; (3) Killed Kennedy
Killed / Hit:	Kennedy wounded, then shot dead. Connally wounded, recovered.
Assassin then:	Fled the scene, killed policeman Tippit, was captured, questioned, killed by Jack Ruby two days later.
Motive:	See chapter 15: None known; he was a Kennedy fan.
Do we know beyond reasonable doubt, **whom** did the assassin intend to shoot? **No**	
Do we know beyond reasonable doubt, his **motive** if he wanted to kill Kennedy? **No**	

— or —

1963: Lee Harvey Oswald shoots with intent to kill Governor John B. Connally	
Weapon:	Rifle: 6.5mm Mannlicher-Carcano carbine with 4-power sight
Distance:	177 feet at second shot, the one that severely wounded Connally
Shots fired:	Three: (1) Missed; (2) Wounded both; (3) Missed Connally
Killed / Hit:	Connally wounded, recovered. Kennedy accidentally shot dead.
Assassin then:	Fled the scene, killed policeman Tippit, was captured, questioned, killed by Jack Ruby two days later.
Motive:	See chapter 16: Revenge for refusal to help with the objective of his last two years of life, overturning his undesirable discharge.
Do we know beyond reasonable doubt, **whom** did the assassin intend to shoot? **No**	
Do we know beyond reasonable doubt, his **motive** if he wanted to kill Connally? **Yes**	

Key points of this chapter:
Comparing Oswald to other assassinations and attempts:
 Only two (the other against MLK) used rifles at distance;
 Only one, Oswald, attempted to shoot a moving victim;
 Only one, Oswald, had no motive – if he shot at Kennedy;
 but a clear motive, <u>like all others</u>, if he shot at Connally.

FAILURE

Oswald's significant successes and failings do not balance.

> "All the news mediums said he was such a failure in life. A failure in life?" she cried out in stunned disbelief. "He was twenty-four years old when he was murdered! ... Lee Harvey a failure? I am smiling. ... I find this a very intelligent boy, and I think he's coming out in history as a very fine person."
> — **Marguerite Oswald** [2865]

THE FIRST SIX CHAPTERS PRESENTED THE ESSENTIALS of Lee Oswald's life with his MOTHER, as a MARINE, in MOSCOW and MINSK, then home as a MISFIT, finally as one of THREE DEAD. This chapter's purpose is to gain perspective, evaluating his life in its entirety to answer a simple but telling question: When he fired at the limousine, was he more likely to succeed in hitting his target — or to fail by accidentally killing an unintended person?

This path to understanding aggregates the significant successes and failings of his life to reveal the big picture. The facts are the trees; the objective is to see the shape and dimensions of his entire life, the forest. About Oswald, as President Clinton said at the funeral of Richard M. Nixon: "Oh, yes, he knew great controversy amid defeat as well as victory. He made mistakes; and, they, like his accomplishments, are part of his life and record. ... [M]ay the day of judging President Nixon on anything less than his entire life and career come to a close." [2866]

Lee Oswald did not become an inept [A] failure at the stroke of 12:30 PM on November 22, 1963. As to all of us, life dealt Lee cards both good and bad. For him, the bad cards began with his father's death two months before he was born. His mother remarried but soon divorced. His brothers were sent to orphanages, so he was alone with a twisted mother and no father figure. Those were bad but not his fault, and not what this chapter considers. This is about character, the nature of the man, as judged from the choices he deliberately made.

Lee lived 24 years, one month and six days. These are his most significant successes and failures. All were told in the chapters named in the headings below. These are the natures of, and results from, his decisions, from infancy to death:

[A] "awkward or clumsy; incompetent" – *The American Heritage Dictionary, Second College Edition*.

Significant Successes

MOTHER

When Lee was about age 2, his aunt Lil thought him "a good looking, friendly child" —

In school and through all his life, an avid reader —

A neighbor thought Lee, about 10, was an intelligent child, who picked things up easily —

At 16, Lee worked in a shoe store and wrote that he had been a "retail shoesaleman" —

Spent the next year reading and memorizing brother Robert's *Marine Corps Manual* —

At age 17, he was accepted as an enlistee in the U.S. Marine Corps, just like his big brother Robert.

Significant Failings

but a neighbor who gave him daycare differed: "a bad, unmanageable child who threw his toy gun at her".

A neighbor saw Lee, about age 8, chase brother John with a knife and throw it at him.

but a terrible speller. Several analysts have speculated that he may have been dyslexic.

His 4th grade teacher described a lonely boy, quiet and shy, who did not easily form friendships.

but also "a bad kid," who was "quick to anger" and "mean when he was angry, just ornery."

Almost 13, Lee threatened John's wife Marge with a pocket knife during a quarrel about watching TV.

John observed that Lee "became hostile and thereafter remained indifferent to me and never again was I able to communicate with him in any way."

By 7th grade in New York City, Lee became a habitual truant, which will continue through all schooling.

An attendance officer alleged Lee was "excessively absent from school," had refused to register at or attend school, and was "beyond the control of his mother insofar as school attendance is concerned."

At age 13, a court remanded him to confinement for psychiatric observation.

The diagnosis was "personality pattern disturbance with schizoid features, passive-aggressive tendencies."

8th grade teachers: "[H]e refused to salute the flag, did little work, and seemed to spend most of his time sailing paper planes around the room."

Teachers also reported: "quick-tempered, constantly losing control, getting into battles with others."

In 9th grade, responding to the question whether he had "any close friends in this school" he wrote "no".

Friends of Mrs. Oswald thought he was demanding and insolent toward her; she had no control over him.

but his employer said they had tried to train him as a salesman without success and he had in fact been a stockboy. Lifelong pattern of aggrandizing begins.

In 10th grade, wrote false note over mother's name to school that they were moving, then dropped out.

Mother fraudulently tried to help him enlist in Marines a year before the minimum age: he was rejected.

alone, while he did not attend high school. He will have no further schooling except in the Marines.

MARINE

Scored significantly above the Marine Corps average in reading and vocabulary —
but significantly below their average in arithmetic and pattern analysis.

Trained on rifle, scored well as a "sharpshooter".

In training, was promoted to private, first class (PFC), his highest Marine position —
despite ranking poorly, 46th of 54 students. Courts martial will soon demote him back to private.

Derided as "Ozzie Rabbit", later "Oswaldskovich".

In Japan, learned about the secret U-2 spy plane —
later tried to tell the Soviets, but they did not trust him.

Dropped his against-orders personal pistol, shot himself in the arm, found guilty at court martial, reduced in rank to private, 20-day sentence suspended.

Passed test of eligibility for the rank of corporal —
but never promoted because of another court martial.

Argued and poured a drink on his sergeant, again guilty at court martial, old suspended sentence now to be served plus the new: 48 hard days in the brig.

Returned to the US where others complained that he was the reason for their unit's failed inspections.

Tried to impress Marine officers as being worldly and politically wise, but fooled few, alienated many.

Taught himself fully serviceable Russian.

Promoted back to the rank of private, first class.

Complained even more than most low-level Marines.

Argued back when given any order by any officer.

Just before discharge, scored as a rifle "marksman".

Obtained an honorable discharge from the U.S. Marine Corps, early, exactly as he wanted it —
not for completion of his agreed term of service, but by trumping up the excuse of his mother's minor nose injury — just as he had learned from her examples.

Acknowledged by signing a form that he was aware of obligation to now serve 3 years in Marine Reserve.

Acquired his first U.S. passport —
falsely stating it was to attend colleges in Europe.

MOSCOW

Signed at Fort Worth Selective Service his commitment to assignment for next three years in the Reserves.

Despite his need-to-care excuse to the Marines, spent only two days with his mother, gave her $100 and rushed to New Orleans, then sailed for Moscow.

Told English customs officials he would remain there a week, then go to Switzerland for college, but that afternoon flew to Helsinki, Finland.

In Helsinki, obtained a visa to Russia —
for a tourist visit limited to six days.

In Moscow, was given a sympathetic Intourist guide —
who helped him write a petition for Soviet citizenship.

MVD and KGB suspected he was an American spy.

KGB sent a "reporter" to make an assessment. Lee gave him an interview, never published.

KGB concluded they cannot use him as their spy.

On the evening his visa expires, is ordered to depart. His life plan is shattered. Shocked, he attempted (or at least made a showy attempt at) suicide.

Found by guide and taken to hospital, wrist stitched.

He was still in Russia after his visa had expired —
He decided on action, went to the American Embassy

Next day: "I relize I am in the Insanity ward."
but hospital concluded he slit wrist to avoid forced exit.
and demanded that his US citizenship be revoked.
Claimed he had offered US military secrets to Soviets.
Embassy wired Washington, noting his offering secrets
    to Soviet intelligence. FBI, CIA and Chief of
    Naval Operations thought of the top-secret U-2.
CNO learned and wired Moscow that Oswald is under
    obligation to Reserve service through Dec. 1962.
Commandant of Marines learned one of his men is so
    low as to tell US secrets in the enemy's capital.
Waiting in hotel, gave interviews to two young, pretty
    American reporters. Printed in US, their stories
    will come to attention of the Marines, and thereby
    induce change of his discharge from "honorable".
Nov. 1, 1959 newspaper told mother where son went.
Fort Worth newspaper made call to Lee in Moscow;
    when he heard mother was on line, he hung up.
Probably to impress Soviets, Lee sent two written
    demands that US Embassy revoke his citizenship.

Consul replies he can do that by appearing in person —

but he did not go to sign the prepared documents.
Wrote brother Robert: "America is the country I hate."

In mid-November is told he can remain in USSR —
January 1960: He is still in Moscow hotel when John
    Kennedy begins his campaign to become President.

while KGB decides that to do with this strange man.

Soviets deny citizenship; give him a Document for
    Stateless Persons, dispatch him to isolated Minsk.

Begins to receive regular, generous money subsidy
    from the Soviet "Red Cross" —

which is in reality a front for the MVD, the Ministry of
    Internal Affairs.
As ordered to do, takes a train from Moscow to Minsk.

MINSK

No talent: assigned to menial metal work in a factory.

Was given a "Russian dream" apartment by river.

March 1960: Unknown to him, Marine Commandant
    orders his discharge from reserve as undesirable.
A suspect: 'under constant surveillance' by the KGB.
April: Marine Corps writes him in Texas re discharge.
June: Unknown to him, Marguerite, who doesn't know
    his whereabouts, begins objections to Marines.
Lee is disappointed in Soviet life, especially the food.
September: Discharged by USMC as undesirable, in
    part for reason he did not answer correspondence.
    He still knows nothing of this long process.
Increasingly critical of life and work in USSR.

In Minsk, made two friends —

2/3 of the only three friends of his entire adult life.
February 1961: Wrote US Embassy in Moscow: wants
    his passport, states his intent to return to US.
MVD, continually intercepting and reading all his mail,
    stopped his generous payments after that letter.

Married a lovely, kind girl, Marina —

after first-love Ella rejected his proposal.

Lied to Marina that his mother, Marguerite, was dead.

May: Wrote "In spite of fact I married Marina to hurt Ella I found myself in love with Marina."

Marina is pregnant —

when he surprised her with desire to return to the US.

Asked Embassy "for full guarantees that I shall not, under any circumstances, be persecuted for any act pertaining to my case" upon return to the US.

Had to admit to Marina that his mother was not dead.

Lied to Marina that scar on left elbow from accidental discharge of against-regulations personal pistol in Japan was a wound from action in Indonesia.

Refused to explain suicide(?) scar on his left wrist.

Went to Moscow Embassy — Saturday, it was closed.

Lied, saying he had never sought Soviet citizenship.

Complained to Sen. Tower of being illegally detained in USSR. Clerk took State Dept advice, ignored.

Plant director reported to KGB that "... performance was unsatisfactory ... does not display the initiative ... over-sensitive ... careless in his work".

KGB decided "he was a gray, mediocre personality."

Got passports from US, exit permission from USSR —

both of them happy to get him out of the Soviet Union.

Got exit travel loan from US Embassy in Moscow —

after being denied loan from International Red Cross.

January 1962: Letter from mother told him for the first time of "dishonorable discharge" by the Marines.

Wrote pleading-threatening letter to John Connally.

Baby girl born, June, whom he loved.

Angered by brush-off letter from Connally.

Secretary of the Navy sent his letter to the Marines, recommended no action; now having his address, USMC wrote him, fully explaining their actions.

Oswald appealed to USMC for reversal or a hearing.

USMC wrote Oswald that his only possible appeal is to the US Navy Discharge Review Board.

Marina's MVD uncle prophesized: "Alik is unhappy everywhere. Maybe he'll go back and not like it there and then he'll want to come back here."

Sailed across the Atlantic to New York in some style on Holland-America Line's *SS Maasdam* —

where Lee was ashamed of Marina's cheap dresses and didn't allow her to be seen in public.

In New York, lied without necessity about money to get free hotel room; also lied that he had been a Marine guard at the US Embassy in Moscow.

MISFIT

At Love Field in Dallas: "What, no photographers?"

Mailed his appeal to Navy Discharge Review Board —

neither understanding nor addressing USMC's many reasons for making the discharge "undesirable".

FBI agents, assigned to contact and evaluate him, found Lee to be "tense ... arrogant ... insolent".

Lived with brother Robert, then with his mother —
Hired by Louv-R-Pak, lucky that employer did not
    check his fraudulent account of history —

Began to pay back State Department and Robert loans.
FBI closed his file as "unworthy" —

but couldn't stand her, so moved to a cheap apartment.
on which he lied that he had been "machinist and sheet
    metal worker" in the Marines, had "honourable"
    discharge. Was paid low wage of $1.25/hour.

after he lied about what he offered the Soviet Union.
Angry when Russian immigrants "adopt" Marina.
Constant arguments; began to hit, then beat Marina.
One Russian émigré helper said Oswald was "all anti,
    anti- the Soviet Union, anti- the United States, anti-
    society in general and anti- us."
Discouraged Marina from learning English so he could
    better control her and her contacts.
Abandoned Louv-R-Pak job, went to live in Dallas Y.

Hired by graphic arts company because this employer
    did not check with previous, Louv-R-Pak —
Talked Marina into move from Ft. Worth to Dallas —

but lied about discharge. Paid better, $1.35/hour.
    Learned to use photo equipment to make fake IDs.
into a "pigsty" she immediately hated. They fought.
Marina fled from him, moved in with Russian friends.

Begged Marina to move back, she did —

Russians "give up", end their support of her and June.
In his entire life, his only friends have been Alexander
    Ziger and Pavel Golovachev in Minsk; and maybe
    now George De Mohrenschildt in Dallas, although
    the new "friend" liked to toy with Lee the way a
    cat likes to play with a mouse before killing it.

Had Thanksgiving at brother Robert's —

where Lee saw brother John Pic for the first time in 10
    years; they will never again see each other.
Robert will also lose contact, will not see Lee until he
    is in the Dallas jail, exactly one year later.

Completed repayment of $425 to State, $200 to Robert.

Using fake name "A. J. Hidell", mail-ordered a pistol.
Took pleasure in hitting Marina many times, with fists.
Had to move when neighbors complained of fights.

Despite battering her, impregnated Marina.

Decided to kill far-right zealot, resigned Gen. Walker,
    so ordered a powerful rifle with telescopic sight.
Posed for famous backyard photos with rifle and pistol.
Fired by Jaggars-Chiles-Stovall for being inefficient,
    inept, unproductive and irritating.
Employment Commission stopped finding him jobs.
Fired the rifle at Walker but missed. Marina quickly
    learned of this but kept mum. After 11/22, Ruth
    Paine found out and immediately told authorities.
Talked of going to shoot ex-president Nixon; it is more
    likely that the intended victim was John Connally.
Unsuccessful in Fort Worth, then Dallas, decided to try
    for work in his birthplace, New Orleans.

Packed to take Marina with him to New Orleans —

but Marina instead chose safety in Ruth Paine's home
    in Irving, near Dallas. Lee took the bus, alone.

Hired to grease machines at Reily Coffee Co., his third
    hiring when employer did not check his references.

Paid his best wage, $1.50/hour, he spent much time at
    adjacent garage reading about and discussing guns.

Aunt Lil suggested he return to school to learn a trade, because "you are really not qualified to do anything too much." "No, I don't have to go back to school. ... I don't have to learn anything. I know everything."

Phoned Marina to come join him in N.O., she did —

into small dark apartment with cockroaches, where they immediately became angry and resumed fighting. Ruth quickly fled in dismay — and her '55 Chevy.

Lee made 3-5 visits to a lawyer, about having what he said was a "dishonorable" discharge converted to honorable —

but told he must pay a fee of $15 to $25, did not show up again or follow through.

Got a new passport, for "travel to Soviet Union".

Marina wrote Ruth that Lee's "love" had ceased. Ruth invited Marina to live with her, more permanently.

July 19, 1963: At Reily Company, he had failed to lubricate, made false entries in logs to cover-up machine breakdowns. Was found out and fired after two months because of inattention to duties.

Also July 19: JFK's close PT-boat buddy, Red Fay, Under-Secretary of Navy, approves the Discharge Board decision to leave "undesirable" unchanged.

Lee did not look for a job, stayed at home, reading.

Lee bragged to Marina that "in twenty years' time, *he* would be President or prime minister."

Received a form letter: discharge will not be changed.

Invented Fair Play for Cuba Committee N.O. chapter.

Handing out leaflets, got into fight with anti-Castro Cuban exiles, jailed overnight, guilty of disturbing the peace, $10 fine. "Even though they started the fight, *they* were released and *I* was fined." [2867]

On radio, debated a Castro opponent, lost credibility because the station knew he had lived in Russia.

To very pregnant Marina: "What if we hijack a plane?"

Sought advice from Communist Party but got no reply.

Ruth came for a visit, saw big problems, took pregnant Marina and little June back to Texas with her.

Lee loaded his blanket-wrapped rifle into Ruth's car.

Lee and Marina will never again have a home or live together. He will be only an occasional visitor.

Swearing Marina to secrecy, left New Orleans, went alone to Mexico City in an attempt to get to Cuba.

Sneaked out of New Orleans apartment in the evening to avoid paying his overdue rent.

Unsuccessful at the Cuban embassy, went to Soviets.

Interviewed by KGB agent at USSR embassy, became agitated. Hoping for immediate visa, he was told to mail an application, wait at least four months.

Again to Cuban embassy, said Soviets promised a visa. Cuban call to Soviets learned it was a lie. Got into heated argument with consul who refused all help.

Returned to US on bus from Mexico City to Dallas —

Back to Soviet embassy, became agitated and pulled out a pistol(!) KGB agents snatched from him. They concluded he swings from depressed to unstable.

giving up after sad failures: New Orleans, Fair Play for Cuba, unemployment, separation, Cuba, Russia.

Did not contact Marina, took room at the YMCA.

Not hired when (at last!) a job interviewer phoned his previous employer and got an earful!

Hitchhiked to Ruth's home to be with Marina —

but she does not want to live with him.

The Y too expensive, paid $7 a week rent for a room, offends landlady, is told to leave after 5 days, does not get $2 refund. She will identify him on 11/22.

Ruth gave him driving lesson to help job prospects —
Rented a tiny room with curtains in Oak Cliff —

but found him to be "pretty unskilled".

under false name "O. H. Lee".

Sent to, but not hired for, two entry jobs as a clerk.

At kaffeeklatsch with neighbor, Ruth and Marina learn lady's brother was hired at the Texas School Book Depository, and said there might be an opening!

Ruth phoned TSBD, made a plea for Lee, then quickly urged him. He went, was interviewed and hired by Roy Truly, the fourth time hired when the new employer did not check his true history —

but was paid only $1.25/hour – less than previous jobs.

TSBD job paid about $217/month —

but by only one day he didn't learn of Trans-Texas Air opening for $310/month, 43% more than at TSBD.

Found free newspapers at work, bought by others —

but read in solitude, said nothing, only smirked.

Met co-worker Buell "Wesley" Frazier who lived one block from Ruth's house, had a car, offered rides.

Celebrated his 24th birthday with Ruth and Marina —

amid his tears and regrets for brutal treatment of wife.

Fathered two daughters, the second of them Rachel —

born in a hospital he avoided because he could not pay.

Took more driving lessons from Ruth Paine —

but he never became competent, never had a license.

FBI agent was ready to shelve the Oswald file —

but Lee was incensed at FBI visits to Ruth and Marina, went to FBI office, left a threatening note.

Nov. 15: Marina asked Lee not to visit that weekend, having worn out his welcome the previous week.

Nov. 17: Marina missed Lee, had Ruth phone him —

to be told no Lee Oswald lives at his rooming house.

Lee phoned, Marina learned he uses name O. H. Lee. She finds that 'unpleasant and incomprehensible', so thereafter always quickly hangs up on him.

Nov. 18: Lee read, probably this Monday, the route that Kennedy will take in front of the TSBD —

but does nothing until Nov. 20 paper, read on Nov. 21, says Connally will ride — he springs into action!

Nov. 20: Lee saw Roy Truly admire a .30-06 Mauser rifle brought into the TSBD by a book rep —

and, according to Marina, probably right then learned a pretext for bringing his rifle into the building.

He never again tried to call Marina, but by surprise …

Nov. 21: Rode to Irving to "pick up curtain rods" —

but really to retrieve the rifle, hidden in Ruth's garage.

Apologized to Marina, begged that they live together —

but she refused to even speak to him.

Did not turn off the garage light after taking the rifle, so Ruth Paine deduces he's been there.

Went to bed at 9:00 PM —

Marina joined him in bed, sensed he is awake but they do not speak, ever again, except next morning …

THREE DEAD, TWO WOUNDED

Friday, November 22: "Time to get up, Alka" Marina says after Lee sleeps through the alarm.

Linnie Mae Randall saw him, without precedent, carry a heavy brown package, put it into Wesley's car. She will later accurately describe it as exactly the correct size and shape to contain the rifle.

"Curtain rods", Lee lied when Wes asked about the package; but his room has curtains on four rods.

When Wes parked near the TSBD, Lee hurried away, quickly and alone, to and into the building.

Built a wall of book cartons and a gun rest; hidden from others, then assembled the rifle and waited.

Seen in the window, looking down Houston Street to see the approaching motorcade.

Easily saw Kennedy, but is unable to spot his intended victim, hidden by both windshield and handrail.

Seen in the window taking aim with his rifle. Howard Brennan will give police an excellent description.

Fired three times: wounded a distant standing driver; wounded Kennedy and Connally; killed Kennedy.

He was the first person questioned by the first officer who entered the Texas School Book Depository.

Left the TSBD unnoticed except by a young newsman, not-yet-famous Robert MacNeil —

whose athletic build and good suit made Lee think he was a Secret Service agent.

Walked east on Elm, boarded a bus to Oak Cliff —

and was recognized by former landlady sitting at front.

Because of what he had done, the bus moved only short distance until it's jammed in traffic. He got off.

Found and took a taxi to Oak Cliff —

where his 5¢ tip helped to make him memorable.

An accurate description was broadcast to police units at 12:45 PM, only 15 minutes after the shooting.

Based on Brennan's good description, he was stopped by Officer J. D. Tippit at 1:15 PM.

Several eyewitnesses saw him fire four pistol bullets to execute Tippit, heard him say "Poor dumb cop".

Seen by a large trail of witnesses as he hurried away.

Drew attention of a shoe store manager by sheltering from a passing police car.

Lost opportunity to hide in movie theater by sneaking in without paying, drawing attention of the shoe man, who told the ticket seller, who called police.

15 officers arrived to find fewer than 15 in the theatre — not a great hiding place.

He was pointed out, then gave himself away, standing and hitting an officer; "Well, it's all over now."

His pistol was taken away, he's handcuffed and placed under arrest, barely 35 minutes after killing Tippit.

Wallet had Marine Corps and Selective Service cards for Alek James Hidell and Lee Harvey Oswald.

He arrived into Dallas headquarters at 2:00 PM, only 90 minutes after he fired the shots in Dealey Plaza.

In Homicide office, recognized by TSBD supervisor.

Three cartridge shells were quickly found on 6th floor.

Deputy sheriff soon found the poorly concealed rifle.

Only one employee of the TSBD building was missing; Roy Truly notices, told police it's Lee Oswald.

Head of detectives Captain Fritz ordered his officers to Irving to search for Oswald, is told: "Captain, we can save you a trip. There the s.o.b. sits."

Police at Ruth's home learn from Marina that Lee has a rifle, go to garage, see that it is gone from blanket.

Marina now understands why Lee this morning left her $170 and his wedding ring.

Marguerite finds she has new grandchild, Rachel — only when she met Marina at police headquarters, then learned that Lee forbade telling her of the birth.

Lee denied having a rifle. Confronted with backyard photo of him holding it, he said photo is faked.

His use of name "O. H. Lee" at boardinghouse slowed police, but then landlady recognized him on TV.

Offered right to counsel, Lee made futile phone calls to a left-wing attorney in New York.

Identified by witnesses; charged with murdering Tippit.

Nov. 23, 1:35 AM: Arraigned for murder of Kennedy.

Police easily tied him to rifle, ordered by "A. Hidell", same name as on false cards in his wallet.

On Sunday morning, police were all ready to transfer him to the safer County jail — but he wanted to wear a sweater. If he had not decided that at the last moment, he would have left the jail while Jack Ruby was still doing his business inside the Western Union office.

After his last words "Nobody is going to shoot me.", escorted by innumerable police in the Dallas Police Headquarters building, he was shot.

In Parkland Hospital where John Kennedy and John Connally were treated, he was declared dead.

Hoped to become famous — but instead became infamous.

Subsequent insults told in Chapter 7, including a burial with no service, friends or pallbearers, then exhumation to be sure who was buried, are not Oswald's fault and should not be counted among the failings of his actions.

The forest above has trees of many sizes, from saplings to giants. Although they have different importances, simply counting may help to show if there is balance. 59 of them semi-balance, coupling a success with a negating failing. In addition, there were **16 successes**, events good for him, some of his doing, some by others — far outnumbered by **155 failings**.

I can think of no other person, living or dead, real or fictive, whose life was so characterized by bad luck and disappointments — except for poor Joe Btfsplk in Li'l Abner, who has his own article in Wikipedia, complete with the hovering rain cloud that follows him.

In November 1991, Marina Oswald Porter told Dr. Cyril Wecht, a pathologist who had extensively studied the Kennedy case: "Lee was a lousy husband, a lousy father, a lousy person. He first told me he had no mother, that she had died. Then one day out of the blue, his mother showed up. I could never figure him out. I was not and am not an enigma. Lee was the enigma. ... On one hand, Lee was a brilliant manipulative person. But at other times, he was as dumb an idiot as a person can be." [2868]

Ruth Paine was asked by the Warren Commission if Lee had any friends — "None that I know of" — and from Allen Dulles: "You mentioned that Lee did not receive any calls at your house. Did he make any telephone calls?", to which Ruth's response tells volumes about the man: "I heard him call what he said was the 'Time.' You know, he dialed, listened and hung up, and then he told us what time it was. That is all his social contact." [2869]

Jim Bishop in *The Day Kennedy Was Shot* assessed why the FBI never showed much interest in the returned defector: "He never worked as anything but a laborer or minor flunky. The only thing he ever learned in a job was, while working for a photo-copying service, to superimpose photographs and to fake military service cards and I.D. cards." [2870]

Chief Justice of the United States Supreme Court Earl Warren, whom Lyndon Johnson commandeered to head the *President's Commission on the Assassination of President Kennedy*, wrote in his autobiography: "Lee Harvey Oswald had been a misfit all his life." [2871] "He was a complete malcontent. ... I have written this much about Oswald's background simply to show that he was a total failure in everything he undertook; that he was incapable of working or living satisfactorily with anyone. Although of reasonable intelligence, he had no skills, and had a disposition and orientation that would not enable him to plan, counsel with or take orders from anyone." [2872] "Lee Oswald [was] a disoriented, willful and violence-prone young man ... a failure in everything he undertook, alienated from the rest of the world wherever he might be, with almost no friends or funds". [2873]

This author cannot say it better, so will say no more.

It's time to close this chapter with a question to you about this unfortunately low-quality but authentic photo. [2874] While Oswald's unit was deployed on Corregidor in 1958, John Wayne was in the vicinity to film "The Barbarian and the Geisha". He dropped in to greet the troops and have a meal. While "The Duke" sits at table, eating and chatting with the Marines, who is that downcast radar specialist we see in the back, wearing a tee shirt and assigned to KP duty because of getting crosswise with his sergeant? If you can't guess, it may be beneficial to reconsider the meaning of this chapter.

> Key point of this chapter:
> **Judging from his life history, was Lee Oswald likely to succeed in committing the crime of the century? Certainly not!**

THE RIFLE

Characteristics and capabilities of Oswald's rifle and bullets

---

Old joke:
World's Greatest War Surplus Bargain!
Italian Army Rifle
Never fired! Dropped only once!
— **George Sundborg**[2875]

YOU HOLD IN YOUR HANDS ONE OF TWO BOOKS essential to understand the killing in Dallas. The other — I've said it before and I'll say it again — is the *Report of the President's Commission on the Assassination of President John F. Kennedy*, better known as the *Warren Report*. The Warren Commission, charged with finding and disseminating the important facts, gave their *Report* completeness, detail and authority. If you do not have a copy, then witness here the solid foundations the *Warren Report* built, judging from its description of the weapon with which Lee Oswald wounded and killed:

"The Rifle

"The rifle found on the sixth floor of the Texas School Book Depository shortly after the assassination was a bolt-action, clip-fed, military rifle, 40.2 inches long and 8 pounds in weight.[2876] Inscribed on the rifle were various markings, including the words 'CAL. 6.5', 'MADE ITALY', 'TERNI', and 'ROCCA'; the numerals '1940' and '40'; the serial number C2766; the letters 'R-E', 'PG', and 'TNI'; the figure of a crown; and several other barely decipherable letters and numbers.[2877] The rifle bore a very inexpensive Japanese four-power sight, stamped '4 x 18 COATED', 'ORDNANCE OPTICS INC.', 'HOLLYWOOD CALIFORNIA', and 'MADE IN JAPAN'[2878] and a sling consisting of two leather straps, one of which had a broad patch, which apparently had been inserted on the rifle and cut to length.[2879] The sling was not a standard rifle sling, but appeared to be a musical instrument strap or a sling from a carrying case or camera bag.[2880] A basic purpose of a rifle sling is to enable the rifleman to steady his grip, by wrapping the arm into the sling in a prescribed manner. The sling on the rifle was too short to use in the normal way, but might have served to provide some additional steadiness.[2881]

"The rifle was identified as a 6.5-millimeter Mannlicher-Carcano Italian military rifle, Model 91/38.[2882] This identification was initially made by comparing the rifle with standard reference works and by the markings inscribed on the rifle.[2883] The caliber was independently determined by chambering a Mannlicher-Carcano 6.5 millimeter cartridge in the rifle for fit, and by making a sulfur cast of the inside of the rifle's barrel which was measured with a micrometer.[2884] (The caliber of a weapon is the diameter of the interior of the barrel, measured between opposite lands. The caliber of American weapons is expressed in inches; thus a .30-caliber weapon has a barrel which is thirty one-hundredths or three-tenths of an inch in diameter. The caliber of continental European weapons is measured in millimeters. A 6.5-millimeter caliber weapon corresponds to an American .257-caliber weapon, that is, its barrel diameter is about one-fourth inch.) [2885] The identification was later confirmed by a communication from SIFAR, the Italian Armed Forces Intelligence Service. This communication also explained the markings on the rifle, as follows: 'CAL. 6.5' refers to the rifle's caliber; 'MADE ITALY' refers to its origin, and was inscribed at the request of the American importer prior to shipment; 'TERNI' means that the rifle was manufactured and tested by the Terni Army Plant of Terni, Italy; the number 'C2766' is the serial number of the rifle, and the rifle in question is the only one of its type bearing that serial number; the numerals '1940' and '40' refer to the year of manufacture; and the other figures, numbers, and letters are principally inspector's, designer's, or manufacturer's marks.[2886]

"The Model 91/38 rifle was one of the 1891 series of Italian military rifles, incorporating features designed by Ritter von Mannlicher and M. [Salvatore] Carcano. The series originally consisted of 6.5-millimeter caliber rifles, but Model 38 of the series, designed shortly before World War II, was a 7.35-millimeter caliber. Early in World War II, however, the Italian Government, which encountered an ammunition supply problem, began producing many of these rifles as 6.5-millimeter caliber rifles, known as the 6.5-millimeter Model 91/38.[2887] The 91/38 has been imported into this country as surplus military equipment, has been advertised quite widely, and is now fairly common in this country.[2888] [A]

"Like most bolt-action military rifles, the 91/38 is operated by turning up the bolt handle, drawing the bolt to the rear, pushing the bolt forward, turning down the bolt handle, and pulling the trigger. Bringing the bolt forward and turning down the bolt handle compresses the spring which drives the firing pin, and locks the bolt into place. When the trigger is pulled, the cocked spring drives the firing pin forward and the cartridge is fired. The face of the bolt bears a lip, called the extractor, around a portion of its circumference. As the bolt is pushed forward, this lip grasps the rim of the cartridge. As the bolt is pulled back, the extractor brings the empty cartridge case with it, and as the cartridge case is being brought back, it strikes a projection in the ejection port called the ejector, which throws it out of the rifle. Meanwhile, a leaf spring beneath the clip has raised the next cartridge into loading position. When the bolt is brought forward, it pushes the fresh cartridge into the chamber. The trigger is pulled, the cartridge is fired, the bolt handle is brought up, the bolt is brought back, and the entire cycle starts again. As long as there is ammunition in the clip, one need only work the bolt and pull the trigger to fire the rifle.[2889]

"The clip itself is inserted into the rifle by drawing back the bolt, and pushing the clip in from the top. The clip holds one to six cartridges.[2890] If six cartridges are inserted into the clip and an additional cartridge is inserted into the chamber, up to seven bullets can be fired before reloading.[2891] When the rifle was found in the Texas School Book Depository Building it contained a clip [2892] which bore the letters 'SMI' (the manufacturer's markings) and the number '952' (possibly a part number or the manufacturer's code number).[2893] The rifle probably was sold without a clip; however, the clip is commonly available.[2894]

[A] *The Gun: A "Biography" of the Gun That Killed John F. Kennedy* by Henry S. Bloomgarden is a charming book tracing 91/38s through invention, manufacture, use, import and sale, with the full life story of C2766. The book is hard to find, but you who read this are smart and resourceful!

"Rifle Cartridge and Cartridge Cases

"When the rifle was found, one cartridge was in the chamber.[2895] The cartridge was a 6.5-millimeter Mannlicher-Carcano cartridge, manufactured by the Western Cartridge Co., at East Alton, Ill. This type of cartridge is loaded with a full metal-jacketed, military type of bullet, weighing 160-161 grains. The bullet has parallel sides and a round nose. It is just under 1.2 inches long, and just over one-fourth inch in diameter.[2896] Its velocity is approximately 2,165 feet per second.[2897] The cartridge is very dependable; in tests runs by the FBI and the Infantry Weapons Evaluation Branch of the U.S. Army, the C2766 rifle was fired with this Western Cartridge Co. ammunition over 100 times, with no misfires. (In contrast, some of the other ammunition available on the market for this rifle is undesirable or of very poor quality).[2898] The cartridge is readily available for purchase from mail-order houses, as well as a few gunshops; some 2 million rounds have been placed on sale in the United States.[2899]

"The presence of the cartridge in the chamber did not necessarily mean that the assassin considered firing another bullet, since he may have reloaded [B] merely by reflex.[2900]

"Apart from the cartridge in the rifle, three expended cartridge cases were found in the southeast portion of the sixth floor of the Texas School Book Depository Building, lying between the south wall and a high stack of boxes which ran parallel to the wall.[2901] The cartridge cases were a short distance to the west of the southeast corner window in that wall.[2902] Based on a comparison with test cartridge cases fired from the C2766 rifle, the three cartridge cases were identified as having been fired from the C2766 rifle.[2903] (See Commission Exhibit No. 558, p. 556.) A test was run to determine if the cartridge-case-ejection pattern of the rifle was consistent with the assumption that the assassin had fired from the southeast window.[2904] In this test, 11 cartridges were fired from the rifle while it was depressed 45° downward, and 8 cartridges were fired from the rifle while it was held horizontally. The elevation of the ejected cartridge cases above the level of the ejection port, and the points on the floor at which the ejection cartridge cases initially landed, were then plotted. The results of these tests are illustrated by the diagrams, Commission Exhibits Nos. 546 and 547. Briefly, Commission Exhibit No. 547 shows that with the weapon depressed at a 45° angle, the cartridge cases did not rise more than 2 inches above the ejection port; with the weapon held horizontally, they did not rise more than 12 inches above the ejection port.[2905] Commission Exhibit No. 546 shows that if a circle was drawn around the initial landing points of the cartridge cases which were ejected in the test while the rifle was held depressed at 45°, the center of the circle would be located 86 inches and 80° to the right of the rifle's line of sight; if a circle was drawn around the initial landing points of the cartridge cases ejected while the rifle was held horizontally, the center of the circle would be 80 inches and 90° to the right of the line of sight. In other words, the cartridge cases were ejected to the right of and at roughly a right angle to the rifle.[2906] The cartridge cases showed considerable ricochet after their initial landing, bouncing from 8 inches to 15 feet.[2907] The location of the cases was therefore consistent with the southeast window having been used by the assassin, since if the assassin fired from that window the ejected cartridge cases would have hit the pile of boxes at his back and ricocheted between the boxes and the wall until they came to rest to the west of the window.[2908]

"The Rifle Bullets

"In addition to the three cartridge cases found in the Texas School Book Depository Building, a nearly whole bullet was found on Governor Connally's stretcher and two bullet fragments were found in the front of the President's car.[2909] The stretcher bullet weighed 158.6 grains, or several grains less than the average Western Cartridge Co. 6.5-millimeter

---

[B] "reloaded" is misleading, perhaps making one think of putting more cartridges into the rifle. The meaning is the re-cycle movement of the bolt as described near the bottom of the previous page.

Mannlicher-Carcano bullet.[2910] It was slightly flattened, but otherwise unmutilated.[2911] The two bullet fragments weighed 44.6 and 21.0 grains, respectively.[2912] The heavier fragment was a portion of a bullet's nose area, as shown by its rounded contour and the character of the markings it bore.[2913] The lighter fragment consisted of [a] bullet's base portion, as shown by its shape and by the presence of a cannelure.[2914] [C] The two fragments were both mutilated, and it was not possible to determine from the fragments themselves whether they comprised the base and nose of one bullet or of two separate bullets.[2915] [D] However, each had sufficient unmutilated area to provide the basis of an identification.[2916] Based on a comparison with test bullets fired from the C2766 rifle, the stretcher bullet and both bullet fragments were identified [2917] as having been fired from the C2766 rifle." [2918]

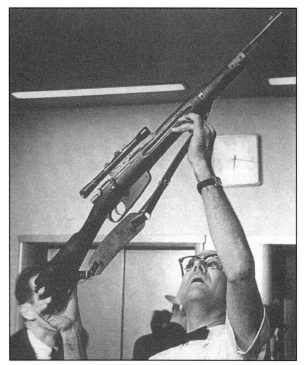

Police Lieutenant Day carries the assassination rifle above newsmen in DPD headquarters.[2919]

Police carry Oswald's makeshift rifle bag out of the School Book Depository.[2920]

"Immediately after the assassination President Johnson ordered the FBI to conduct a full investigation into the tragedy and report its findings to him. ... On December 9 the FBI submitted to the Commission a summary report of its investigation to date ... entitled *Investigation of Assassination of President John F. Kennedy, November 22, 1963*." [2921] This FBI report was neither released to the public nor placed into the *Warren Report* or its 26

[C] "Cannelure" is "a groove around a bullet into which the edge of the cartridge case is crimped" — *Merriam-Webster Unabridged Dictionary*.

[D] The two pieces came from a bullet's tip and a bullet's base and did not overlap, so FBI expert Robert Frazier suggested it was likely, but not proven, that they came from one bullet. They had been found on the front seat floor of the limousine. Both were stained, probably with blood. It is most likely they had shattered from the final bullet, the one that exploded President Kennedy's brain.

volumes of hearings and exhibits. Fortunately, it was given by a Commission lawyer, 28 years later, to assassination researcher Edward Jay Epstein.[2922] It included these facts about the rifle, many of them in the *Warren Report* and recapped in this book's Chapter 5 – MISFIT, but it may be helpful to see them all together here:

Rifle Ordered by Oswald
    FBI investigation determined that this rifle was part of a shipment of surplus Italian military weapons purchased for resale in the United States by Klein's Sporting Goods, Chicago, Illinois. The company's records disclose that the rifle, identified by serial number C 2766, was shipped, with rifle scope mounted, on March 20, 1963, by parcel post to A. Hidell, Post Office Box 2915, Dallas, Texas. … The gun was ordered by airmail and the envelope was postmarked March 12, 1963, at Dallas. Payment was made by U. S. Postal Money Order 2,202,130,462 in the amount of $21.45, issued at Dallas, Texas, March 12, 1963, payable to Klein's Sporting Goods. It was signed by A. Hidell, Post Office Box 2915, Dallas, Texas. Post Office Box 2915 had been rented on October 9, 1962, through an application signed by Lee H. Oswald and was relinquished on May 14, 1963. The FBI Laboratory conducted handwriting examinations based on known handwriting specimens of Oswald's from a 1963 passport application … and from a letter dated January 30, 1961,[E] which he sent to John B. Connally, now the Governor of Texas, formerly Secretary of the Navy.[F]
    The FBI Laboratory examination of the handwriting on the envelope addressed to Klein's Sporting Goods, in which the rifle order was contained, determined that the envelope was addressed by Oswald. …
    The examination by the FBI Laboratory of the hand printing appearing on the above order form for the rifle determined that it was prepared by Oswald. …
    The handwriting on the money order issued in payment for the rifle was determined by the FBI Laboratory to have been prepared by Oswald. …
    It was determined by the FBI Laboratory examination that the handwriting on the application for Post Office Box 2915 was prepared by Oswald. …
    It should be noted that the above rifle was sent to Oswald, using the alias A. J. Hidell, at Post Office Box 2915 in Dallas, on the same date that the revolver previously referred to as having killed Officer Tippit was shipped to him from Los Angeles.

Tests of Rifle
    By actual tests it has been demonstrated by the FBI that a skilled person can fire three accurately aimed shots with this weapon in five seconds." [2923]

[E] That is the date Oswald wrote on the letter, but it was January 30, 1962 — he forgot the year change.

[F] Oswald's "I shall employ all means …" letter was used as a known handwriting exemplar (photo on page 225), but apparently its threat was not recognized as the key to understanding his motive.

Savvy assassination analyst Gerald Posner in his valuable *Case Closed* revealed how some just-plain-nutty theories originated: "Seymour Weitzman and Luke Mooney, two Dallas policemen, thought at first glance that the rifle was a 7.65 bolt-action Mauser. Although the officers quickly admitted their mistake, that initial misidentification led to speculation that a different gun was found on the sixth floor and that Oswald's Carcano was later swapped in for the murder weapon. There are considerable similarities between a bolt-action Mauser and a Carcano. Firearms experts say they are easy to confuse without a proper exam.[2924] Yet Mark Lane devoted an entire chapter trying to portray a simple mistake as evidence of conspiracy.[2925] Robert Sam Anson wrote that the scope was set for a left-handed person[2926]. There is no such thing as a left-handed scope, and tests determined that the very slight misalignment of Oswald's scope may actually have aimed the rifle slightly toward Kennedy if the scope was centered on Connally.[2927] Sylvia Meagher charged that the Carcano had a 'hair trigger,' which would have hurt Oswald's marksmanship.[2928] But the Carcano required three pounds of pull, whereas a hair trigger requires less than sixteen ounces.[2929] "[2930]

Assassination analysts Bob Callahan, then Edward Jay Epstein reported: "On the morning of November 27, 1963, FBI Agent Robert Frazier [G] found himself on a local firing range with the rifle that had allegedly killed President Kennedy in his hands. His assignment that morning was simple, though the most important of his career: test the rifle to see if Oswald could have actually made those shots. During the course of the morning Frazier and two other FBI agents, Charles Killion and Courtland Cunningham, all tested the gun for accuracy. Each agent ..."[2931] "fired three shots at a target fifteen yards away. All the shots were high and to the right of the aiming point ... "[2932] "The final FBI tests were held at [an FBI range at its training facility at] Quantico,[H] Virginia, on March 16, 1964. Frazier fired three series of shots at a target a hundred yards away. ... [A]ll his shots were about five inches high and about five inches to the right of the aiming point.[2933] Frazier [testified] that the inaccuracy was due to an uncorrectable mechanical deficiency in the telescopic sights."[2934]

The problem was that some internal roughness or tightness inside the sight prevented the crosshair ring from moving while adjustment screws were turned. Frazier later found that firing a few rounds jarred the sight enough to cause the adjustment to become correct.[2935]

Any reasonable doubt about the sighting and accuracy of Oswald's weapon — not one like it, but the actual weapon itself — should be answered by the testimony of FBI firearms expert Robert A. Frazier, who established his credentials in part by saying that in the field of "firearms comparisons—I have made in the neighborhood of 50,000 to 60,000."[2936] He was questioned by Commission member Hale Boggs and assistant counsel Melvin Aron Eisenberg:

"Representative BOGGS. There is no reason to believe that this weapon is not accurate, is there?

Mr. FRAZIER. It is a very accurate weapon. The targets we fired show that.

Representative BOGGS. That was the point I was trying to establish.

Mr. FRAZIER. This Exhibit 549 [2937] is a target fired, showing that the weapon will, even under rapid-fire conditions, group closely—that is, one shot with the next.

...

Mr. EISENBERG. Mr. Frazier, turning back to the scope, if the elevation cross-hair was defective at the time of the assassination, in the same manner it is now, and no

---

[G] Not known to be related to either Lee's ride-giver, Buell Wesley Frazier, or the Dallas Police Captain in charge of the radio patrol platoon on November 22, William Bennett Frazier.

[H] Where we met FBI trainee Clarice Starling in the memorable movie "*Silence of the Lambs*".

compensation was made for this defect, how would this have interacted with the amount of lead which needed to be given to the target?

Mr. FRAZIER. Well, may I say this first. I do not consider the crosshair as being defective, but only the adjusting mechanism does not have enough tolerance to bring the crosshair to the point of impact of the bullet. As to how that would affect the lead—the gun, when we first received it in the laboratory and fired these first targets, shot high and slightly to the right.

If you were shooting at a moving target from a high elevation, relatively high elevation, moving away from you, it would be necessary for you to shoot over that object in order for the bullet to strike your intended target, because the object during the flight of the bullet would move a certain distance.

The fact that the crosshairs are set high would actually compensate for any lead which had to be taken. So that if you aimed with this weapon as it actually was received at the laboratory, it would be necessary to take no lead whatsoever in order to hit the intended object. The scope would accomplish the lead for you.

I might also say that it also shot slightly to the right, which would tend to cause you to miss your target slightly to the right." [2938]

Chapter 14 – TOO CLOSE TO CALL will describe and illustrate in the requisite full detail how Lee fired downward at the limousine. As seen through his sight it was moving up and to a lesser degree, to the right. If the scope had been misaligned then as it was when it was fired by the experts including Frazier, then the misalignment would help Oswald hit his target.

But, as Chapter 14 should nail down beyond argument, if Oswald tried to hit Connally, that's the target he would concentrate on, and he'd probably not see — but would by accident hit and possibly kill – Kennedy. The two were too close together as the bullets fly for there to be any actionable difference in aiming point, and as that chapter's title implies, the actual result of his shooting does not help in figuring out his intent — it's simply TOO CLOSE TO CALL.

The Warren Commission wanted such an important matter as the rifle to be subject to a second opinion, so had the United States Army Ballistic Research Laboratory conduct its own independent tests. Ronald Simmons, Chief of the Infantry Weapons Evaluation Branch of that laboratory, testified to their findings. [2939] Overall, this expert related, they had found that Oswald's cheap surplus Mannlicher-Carcano was as accurate as the present-day (*i.e.*, 1964) U.S. military rifle, the M-14. Bullets fired at a 100-yards target dispersed — made a group of holes — only an inch across. When Army experts found that the sight was not accurately aimed, rather than change its adjustments and thereby interfere with its evidentiary value, they added three thin metal shims to the sight so it was aimed accurately. [2940] Thus the Army fired with accurate sights. No one knows with certainty whether Oswald aimed at the limousine through the rifle's scope or with its open sights. In the Marines where he had been trained, the open sights were for relatively close combat, and scopes were for the few sharpshooters firing at particularly distant targets. Probably, he used the slightly inaccurate telescope.

With the independent testimonies of Frazier and Simmons, the *Warren Report* in its Chapter IV "THE ASSASSIN" rightly suggested that the defective scope was actually an advantage for the sniper. The advantage was "leading": Seen from Oswald's window when he fired, the limousine was moving up and to the right — so an inaccurate sight sending bullets in precisely that up-and-right direction freed Oswald from having to make much adjustment himself. In addition, and probably much more importantly, when one considers the probability that Oswald was aiming at Connally, who had fallen down and to his left after being badly wounded by the second bullet, then the defect of the cheap sight becomes truly important. Oswald's following Connally down-and-left with a rifle misaimed high-and-right sent the third bullet into Kennedy, now higher and to the right of Connally because of being constrained by his Ace bandage and back-bracing corset, to be explained in chapter 14.

COMMISSION EXHIBIT 1303 [2941] shows the rifle, its butt at 0 on the tape measure. Overall, it is exactly 40.2" long when assembled and ready to fire, as shown.[2942]

COMMISSION EXHIBIT 1304–Continued [2943] shows the rifle disassembled to be shorter. The bottom piece, the stock, is 34.8" in length; the action, barrel and scope only 28.9".

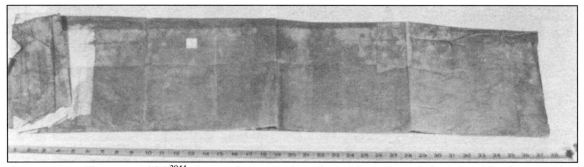

COMMISSION EXHIBIT 1304 [2944] shows the paper bag Oswald made to bring the rifle from Ruth's garage, discarded on the 6th floor. Somehow the Warren Commission cropped off its left end at 0 on the tape measure. It is 37½" long, more than enough for the 34.8" disassembled rifle.

Because Oswald's extensive Marine training — to be described in the next chapter — had been on rifles with open sights, the Commission very properly wanted to know the effect of having a telescopic sight on the assassination rifle. It called possibly the world's greatest expert on precisely that. Master Sergeant James A. Zahm, in the Corps for 18 years, was in charge of the Marksmanship Training Unit Armory in the Weapons Training Battalion, Marine Corps Training School, Quantico, Virginia.

Assistant counsel Arlen Specter first qualified the witness to be an expert — easy, as he had been engaged in competitive shooting since 1952 and became a distinguished rifleman in 1953.[1] In 1964 he was the noncommissioned officer in charge of the Marines' long-range team, for whom use of scopes was central. His testimony about a scope like Oswald's:

"Mr. SPECTER. Can you characterize the increased efficiency of a marksman in using a four-power scope as opposed to using only the iron sights?

Sergeant ZAHM. Well, with the iron sights you have more room for error [including] when you are concentrating on your sights, your targets tend to become blurred because of the close focus of your eye in alining[J] the sights.

Now this as opposed to telescope of a four-power nature it is a natural characteristic of a telescope when you are looking for your target, it is a natural thing to center your target in the view of your telescope, and in the center view of your telescope is the aiming crosshairs. This is only one point.

If you get this one point, the crosshairs in the proper relationship to your target, this is an aid in locating, finding your target, because you are using the scope in the sense as binoculars. Once you have found your target, your sights are already alined, and then through good trigger manipulation the shot should be well on the target.

Mr. SPECTER. With respect to rapid-fire shooting, how does the telescopic sight on a four-power scope work out?

Sergeant ZAHM. Four-power being a reasonably low-power scope, it has a fairly broad field of view. By this we mean it covers a reasonable amount of area out at about 100 yards, about I think probably around 30 feet or so. Using the scope, rapidly working a bolt and using the scope to relocate your target quickly and at the same time when you locate that target you identify it and the crosshairs are in close relationship to the point you want to shoot at, it just takes a minor move in aiming to bring the crosshairs to bear, and then it is a quick squeeze.

Mr. SPECTER. Would you characterize it as easy, difficult, or how would you characterize it to use a scope, a four-power scope in rapid fire?

Sergeant ZAHM. A real aid, an extreme aid.

…

Mr. SPECTER. Would it be very difficult for a man with Oswald's capabilities as a marksman to use a rifle with a four-power scope?

Sergeant ZAHM. No; I feel that the instruction that he had received qualifies him on the basic fundamentals of marksmanship. There are just a few refinements in the operation of the bolt rifle and the scope through a minimum amount of experimenting would make him as proficient with the bolt and the scope as it did with the weapons he received instruction on, and if not it would improve his proficiency actually through the use of the telescope. I feel that this would be an advantage.

Mr. SPECTER. How many shots in your opinion would a man like Oswald have to take in order to be able to operate a rifle with a four-power scope, based on the training he had received in the Marine Corps?

---

[1] Fast: one to two years. It is generally accepted that becoming truly proficient at any non-trivial endeavor requires approximately 10,000 hours of work or practice, five full-time years.

[J] The *Warren Commission Hearings* spelled without the usual "g", so that's how it is spelled here.

Sergeant ZAHM. Based on that training, his basic knowledge in sight manipulation and trigger squeeze and what not, I would say that he would be capable of sighting that rifle in well, firing it, with 10 rounds.

...

Mr. SPECTER. Would the use of a four-power scope be a real advantage to a marksman of Mr. Oswald's capabilities or of a slight advantage, or how would you characterize the advantage that he would obtain, if any, from the use of such a scope?

Sergeant ZAHM. I consider it a real advantage, particularly at the range of 100 yards,[K] in identifying your target. It allows you to see your target clearly, and it is still of a minimum amount of power that it doesn't exaggerate your own body movements. It just is an aid in seeing in the fact that you only have the one element, the crosshair, in relation to the target as opposed to iron sights with alining the sights and then alining them on the target. It is a real aid." [2945]

Specter then asked Sgt. Zahm several hypothetical questions about the exact situation, angles and distances of aiming at the moving-away limousine, all of which resulted in Zahm opining the shots were easy for an ex-Marine with Oswald's training and his scope-equipped rifle.[2946]

The FBI gave the Commission a 20-page report titled: "Possible target practice in the vicinity of Love Field, Dallas, Texas." [2947] In addition to interviewing Marina and tracing bus routes Oswald might have taken to practice areas, the FBI investigated the availability of 6.5mm Mannlicher-Carcano carbines and ammunition in the Dallas area. Both the carbines and ammunition were readily available. One experienced gun dealer they interviewed about that also gave a working professional's opinion of Oswald's carbine and its scope: [2948]

> On March 12, 1964, Mr. John H. Brinegar, owner, The Gun Shop, 11448 Harry Hines Blvd., telephone CH 7-2600, Dallas, Texas, advised he has been a gunsmith for the past 30 years. He stated at the end of World War II, "GI's" began bringing Italian Carcano 6.5 rifles back to the United States. He advised that subsequently New York gun dealers began importing this rifle from Italy by "boat loads" and, as a consequence, this rifle has had wide distribution.
>
> Mr. Brinegar stated this rifle was a very cheap rifle and could have been purchased for $3.00 each in lots of 25. Mr. Brinegar advised that likewise 6.5 ammunition manufactured by the Western Cartridge Company also had wide distribution throughout the United States and could be purchased through any number of wholesale dealers.
>
> Mr. Brinegar advised that in his personal opinion the scope of the rifle used by Lee Harvey Oswald would have been mounted by the factory.[L] He explained that in mounting the scope the bolt would have to be altered. This expense plus the expense of drilling the necessary holes for the scope mounting would amount to not less than $15.00 [M] and it would be impractical to spend this amount on a $3.00 gun.

[K] Oswald's target distance was 60, then 90, yards when he fired his wounding, then killing, shots.
[L] It wasn't; the scope was mounted by Klein's in Chicago, the mail-order dealer that sold to Oswald.
[M] If done only one at a time, not in a high-volume operation such as Klein's.

In 1992, Edward Jay Epstein combined his earlier writings into one thick volume, *The Assassination Chronicles: Inquest, Counterplot and Legend*. He added a final "Afterword: The State of the Evidence, the Evidence of the State (1992)". Assessing all evidence, some of which he had once challenged, he concluded that there were three shots, all came from high on the southeast corner of the Texas School Book Depository building, two of the shots had done all the wounding and killing, and they had been fired through a capable weapon:

> "Although questions can be raised about the general accuracy of the Mannlicher-Carcano rifle found in the depository, there can be no doubt that the particular weapon can be fired with deadly accuracy at a target a hundred yards away—the distance from the depository to the president's car.[N] After the assassination three different FBI agents fired this exact rifle and scored bull's-eyes two of three times." [2949]

The bullets fired by Oswald each had a solid lead core surrounded by a full copper jacket, a metal covering designed to keep the bullet intact as it entered a target, thereby increasing its penetration. Analyst Gerald Posner footnoted in *Case Closed*: "Mandated by the Geneva Convention of 1922, the purpose of enclosing bullets with full metal jackets was to reduce combat fatalities. The bullets were designed to pass through bodies and, if no major organs were struck, only to wound the victim. Before metal jackets, bullets often detoured inside the body. That the 6.5mm Carcano ammunition was designed to do exactly what it did on the President and the Governor is often ignored. Dr. John Lattimer and Dr. John Nichols created experiments to test the bullet's toughness. Nichols shot a 6.5mm slug through four feet of ponderosa pine boards, and Lattimer put one through two feet of elm wood. Both bullets appeared undamaged (Lattimer, *Kennedy and Lincoln*, p. 272). Moreover, ballistics expert Larry Sturdivan pointed out that another attribute of the Carcano bullet is that it is 'one of the most stable bullets we have ever done experimentation with' (HSCA Vol. I, p. 386)." [2950]

Robert Frazier, the FBI's foremost firearms expert, testified to the Warren Commission that he had fired bullets from two different lots of ammunition in a special apparatus at the Naval Research Laboratory in Washington, DC. Averaging the results for all the bullets fired, the speed of a bullet leaving the rifle, its muzzle velocity, was 2,165 feet per second. [2951]

The Commission wanted to understand the reliability of Oswald's ammunition, so assistant counsel Melvin Aron Eisenberg asked FBI expert Frazier:

> "Mr. EISENBERG. Mr. Frazier, can you give an estimate of the total number of bullets fired in the various tests made with this rifle?
>
> Mr. FRAZIER. Approximately 60 rounds.
>
> Mr. EISENBERG. And were all of these rounds 6.5 mm. Western Mannlicher-Carcano ammunition?
>
> Mr. FRAZIER. Yes, sir.
>
> Mr. EISENBERG. Did you have any misfires?
>
> Mr. FRAZIER. No, sir.
>
> Mr. EISENBERG. Did you find the ammunition dependable?
>
> Mr. FRAZIER. Very dependable.
>
> Mr. EISENBERG. Can you think of any reason why someone might think this is an undependable type of ammunition?
>
> Mr. FRAZIER. No, sir; The Western Cartridge Co. has always manufactured, in my experience, very dependable ammunition." [2952]

[N] See the first footnote on the previous page — the actual distances were 60 and 90 yards.

Doubters and theorists like to point out that the Warren Commission's conclusion depends on one shooter, Oswald, having shot three times in 5.6 seconds or less — and then crow that the Commission shot itself in the foot with this requirement, because it was impossible for Oswald to have done that — because, they yelled, nobody can do it!

I simply recommend to any reader who believes in that mistaken proposition that he or she read pages 117 and 193-195 of the *Warren Report*. That should be convincing, but if not, then an excellent analysis is available in Gerald Posner's *Case Closed*. He does a fine job of assessing the rifle's capabilities compared to all parameters of the actualities in Dallas. With particular regard to the time necessary to fire the three shots:

> "The first issue is the timing. In 1964, the FBI's test-firing of Oswald's Carcano determined that a minimum of 2.25 to 2.3 seconds was necessary between shots to operate the bolt and re-aim. Since the first bullet was already in the rifle's chamber and ready to fire, that meant Oswald had to operate the bolt action twice (just as Harold Norman heard on the fifth floor). According to the Warren Commission, the fastest he could have fired all three shots was 4.5 seconds. However, that minimum time is now out of date. CBS reconstructed the shooting for a 1975 documentary. Eleven volunteer marksmen took turns firing clips of three bullets at a moving target. None of them had dry practice runs with the Carcano's bolt action, as Oswald had had almost daily while in New Orleans. Yet the times ranged from 4.1 seconds, almost half a second faster than what the Warren Commission thought was possible, to slightly more than 6 seconds, with the average being 5.6 seconds, and two out of three hits on the target. Based on its 1977 reconstruction tests, the House Select Committee lowered the time between shots on the Carcano to 1.66 seconds, with the shooter hitting all the targets. This reduced the time necessary for three effective shots to 3.3 seconds." [2953]

If that is not enough, then carefully view the TV program *Real History: The Secret KGB JFK Assassination Files*. Produced by Associated Television International, it was broadcast on The Learning Channel in 2000, and is readily and inexpensively available on DVD. Midway through the 2-hour program, after interviewing Russian ballistics experts and showing their re-creation confirming the Warren Commission's basic conclusions, we watch as a man practices with a Carcano,[o] then take shots at three targets. ... [W]e clearly see that — unhurried — the third shot follows the first by 5.33 seconds, then in a second set of shots, 4.79 seconds.

If that video is not available, here is strong testimony by FBI firearms expert Robert A. Frazier, questioned by Warren Commission assistant counsel Melvin Aron Eisenberg:

> "Mr. EISENBERG. How much practice had you had with the rifle [P] before the last series of four targets were shot by you?
>
> Mr. FRAZIER. I had fired it possibly 20 rounds, 15 to 20 rounds, and in addition had operated the bolt repeatedly.
>
> Mr. EISENBERG. Does practice with this weapon—or would practice with this weapon—materially shorten the time is which three shots could be accurately fired?
>
> Mr. FRAZIER. Yes, sir; very definitely.
>
> Mr. EISENBERG. Would practice without actually firing the weapon be helpful—that is, a dry-run practice?
>
> Mr. FRAZIER. That would be most helpful, particularly in a bolt-action weapon, where it is necessary to shift your hand from the trigger area to the bolt, operate the bolt, and go back to the trigger after closing the bolt." [2954]

---

[o] Not Oswald's rifle, but essentially identical.

[P] Frazier and other American experts used Oswald's actual murder-weapon rifle.

In Chapter 5 – MISFIT, Marina told how Lee, in addition to going out to either rifle ranges, or more likely, open spaces to fire bullets, would frequently sit out on their porch and dry-fire the rifle. That is why Eisenberg asked. Frazier said that what Lee did "would be most helpful".

The Commission also called two firearms experts from the Marine Corps. First to testify was Major Eugene D. Anderson, assistant head of the Marksmanship Branch at Marine Corps Headquarters in Washington, DC. He had been in the Corps 26 years and had achieved the highest possible rank as a rifleman, "distinguished rifle shot". Most of his testimony, about Oswald's training and scores, will be in the next chapter – THE SHOOTER. Evidence about Oswald's ability to get off three fast shots could go into either chapter. Being primarily determined by the mechanical operation of the rifle, it is here – THE RIFLE. At the end of his testimony, assistant counsel Arlen Specter asked one question and got one important answer:

> "Mr. SPECTER. Major Anderson, assume if you will that there were three shots fired by the assassin with a Mannlicher-Carcano rifle in a time span of 4.8 to 5.6 seconds. Would that speed of firing be within the capabilities of Mr. Oswald based upon the information as to his marksmanship ability from the Marine Corps records?
> Major ANDERSON. Yes, sir; it would." [2955]

The next witness was Master Sergeant James A. Zahm, whose testimony about the advantages of having a 4-power scope on the rifle has been reported above. As with Major Anderson, at the end of questioning Zahm, counsel Specter asked one question to obtain one answer:

> "Mr. SPECTER. Assuming that there were three shots fired in a range of 4.8 to 5.6 seconds, would that speed of firing at that range indicated in the prior questions [177 to 265 feet] [2956] be within Mr. Oswald's capabilities as a marksman?
> Sergeant ZAHM. Yes." [2957]

Brother Robert Oswald hoped that evidence would exonerate Lee, but as a realist, accepted facts. He was interviewed on *Dateline NBC* in a 1998 TV segment, "My Brother's Keeper":

> Narrator: "There was one question Robert tried to answer on his own. Could Lee, only an adequate shot in the Marines, have fired quickly and accurately enough to kill the President — three shots during the longest six seconds in American history? Twice, following the assassination, Robert timed himself firing three shots with a rifle similar to the mail-order rifle Lee was accused of using. We asked him to demonstrate for us what he'd done."
> Interviewer Josh Mankowitz (looking at his watch): "Ready?" Robert Oswald (his rifle loaded and cocked): "Ready." JM: "Go." RO: "Fire ... fire ... fire." JM: "Four and a half seconds." (Careful timing shows this is accurate.) RO: "What's the question?" JM: "I guess, can you do it in less than six? I guess the answer is ..." RO: "Yes." [2958]

Before turning to the conclusions that experts and the Commission drew about the rifle, I acknowledge that there is very little mention of Oswald's pistol in this chapter. The short-barrel .38 revolver was ugly, inaccurate at distance, but powerful and deadly at close range. Its purchase, before that of the rifle, was described in Chapter 5. It was shown in Chapter 6 when used to execute Officer Tippit. Facts about the pistol are incontrovertible, even for the most dedicated conspiracy theorists. This chapter largely ignores the pistol to focus like a 4-power scope on the rifle, because this is the book that says: "Hold on a minute! Maybe what you thought you knew about the Kennedy assassination should be reconsidered with an open mind, because from the result — Kennedy died, Connally was only wounded — you cannot know what Oswald intended." And that, of course, concerns the rifle.

If you want more about the pistol, I very highly recommend the truly excellent book *With Malice: Lee Harvey Oswald and the Murder of Officer J.D. Tippit* by Dale K. Myers. It was carefully researched and written to detail (863 large pages!) the murder of the patrolman, not the President, so contains facts about everything related to the pistol, gunman and events in Oak Cliff in the sad hour of 1:00 to 2:00 that dreadful afternoon.

If you are so fortunate as to have access to the rare 26 volumes of *Hearings Before the President's Commission on the Assassination of President Kennedy*, look into Volume III, on pages 451 to 482, then 487 to 492, to read the testimony of FBI firearms expert Cortlandt Cunningham, assigned to be the specialist on studying, understanding and testing Oswald's pistol. There is no equivalent reliable information anywhere else. Two interesting facts from that testimony will be noted below, beginning near the bottom of the next page.

Most of the testimony in this chapter was about the rifle, to the Warren Commission by the FBI's leading — but not their only — firearms expert:

"Mr. EISENBERG. Mr. Frazier, did any other firearms experts in the FBI laboratory examine the three cartridge cases, the bullet, and the two bullet fragments which you have testified as to today?

Mr. FRAZIER. Yes, all of the actual firearms comparisons were also made by Charles Killion and Cortlandt Cunningham. These examinations were made separately, that is, they made their examination individually and separately from mine, and there was no association between their examination and mine until both were finished.

Mr. EISENBERG. Did the three of you come to the conclusions which you have given us today as your own conclusions?

Mr. FRAZIER. Yes, sir.

Mr. EISENBERG. Did anyone in the FBI laboratory who examined the evidence come to a different conclusion as to any of the evidence you have discussed today?

Mr. FRAZIER. No, sir." [2959]

In that first very long session with the Commission, expert Frazier was questioned in great detail about his certainty that all three cartridge cases found on the 6th floor had been fired and ejected by Oswald's rifle, and that all bullets (including CE 399, the "pristine bullet" from Connally's stretcher in Parkland Hospital) had been fired from Oswald's rifle, to the exclusion of all other rifles. Frazier was certain of those findings. But, when asked about the bullet that had narrowly missed General Walker by smashing into a window frame, Frazier had to follow FBI policy. He testified to markings on that badly-smashed bullet that corresponded to, and likely had been caused by Oswald's rifle, but it was too deformed to be certain. Those questions and answers occupy 24 fine-print pages in the *Warren Commission Hearings*.

FBI identifications dealt not in probabilities; only "yes" and "no", or "did" and "did not". Perhaps that is why the Commission summoned an expert with national reputation for an independent view. Joseph D. Nicol, Superintendent of the Bureau of Criminal Identification and Investigation for the State of Illinois was given all the bullets, fragments and cartridge cases discussed in this chapter. When his tests were complete, he testified:

"Mr. EISENBERG. Now, Mr. Nicol, we had testimony from a Mr. Frazier yesterday of the FBI Firearms Section, and he testified that the FBI does not make probable identifications, but merely positive or negative identifications.

Mr. NICOL. I am aware of their position. This is not, I am sure, arrived at without careful consideration. However, to say that because one does not find sufficient marks for identification that it is a negative, I think is going overboard in the other direction. And for purposes of probative value, for whatever it might be worth, in the absence of very definite negative evidence, I think it is permissible to say that in an exhibit such as [the bullet that had missed Walker] there is enough on it to say that it could have come, and even perhaps a little stronger, to say that it probably came from this, without going so far as to say to the exclusion of all other guns. This I could not do." [2960]

The Commission called FBI agent Robert Frazier back weeks later. In a long testimony, he brought the clothing worn by Kennedy and Connally to relate what he had learned from the bullet holes and nicks; then he described his close examination of the limousine in the wee hours of November 23; and the bullet fragments he found on the carpet below the left jump seat (where Nellie had cradled wounded John); and described an injury to the inside of the windshield glass from a reduced-speed bullet fragment; and a dent in the chrome strip above the windshield, also from a slowed fragment. [2961] In July, he submitted an affidavit that he had reviewed the testimony of Cortlandt Cunningham, that he had conducted independent tests similar to those done by Cunningham, and "reached the same conclusions". [2962]

To ensure agreement of all experts from all viewpoints, FBI Agent Cunningham also submitted an affidavit that he had reviewed Frazier's tests and testimony, and "on the basis of these independent examinations, I reached the same conclusions reached by Mr. Frazier." [2963] Cunningham brought the disassembled assassination rifle [Q] to the Commission to show how he could assemble it, using a screwdriver, in 2 minutes. He was probably a bit surprised when the attorney conducting the session, Joseph A. Ball, offhandedly asked if it was necessary to have a screwdriver. [R] Cunningham replied: "Any object that would fit the slots on the five screws that retain the stock to the action." Ball rejoined: "Could you do it with a 10-cent piece?" "Yes, sir." And Ball asked him to please do so. Because one of the five screws was clumsy to reach with the dime, it took 6 minutes to assemble the rifle, ready to fire. [2964]

Firearms expert Frazier had specialized his tests, and then given his testimony, on Oswald's rifle. In a similar manner, Cunningham had specialized on the pistol Oswald had used to ambush and injure, then execute, Officer Tippit. His testimony about the pistol occupied 44 small-print pages in the *Warren Commission Hearings*. [2965] There, this author learned two interesting new facts: As discussed elsewhere, Oswald's pistol had started life with a barrel 5" long, but for sales appeal and "concealment", 2¾" had been cut off. That greatly reduced the weapon's accuracy at long range — absolutely no effect at short range — not necessarily because the bullets travel a shorter distance down the barrel, but because the rear and front sights must be much closer together, so cannot be aimed as accurately at the target "due to the shorter sight radius." [2966] The second new fact, about which the Commission questioned Cunningham at length, was about paraffin tests to determine whether a suspect has fired a weapon. The Dallas Police Department had done such tests on Oswald's two hands and cheek. Cunningham testified, explained and even demonstrated with his own hands, that such tests are generally useless. Sometimes people fire weapons and do not acquire any residue; other times some can pick up residue without doing any firing. [2967]

To put the last nail into the structure, FBI Special Agent and firearms expert Charles L. Killion also stated by affidavit that he had reviewed the tests and testimonies of Cunningham and Frazier, and agreed with both of his fellow experts in all regards. [2968]

[Q] Two photos of the rifle on page 396 may be helpful to understanding this material.

[R] I have never heard that a screwdriver was or was not found in the TSBD, nor whether anyone looked for one, and it probably doesn't matter. There were probably handyman's tools somewhere there.

Having that evidence and those professional opinions, it's time to state briefly, in their own words, what the Commission members concluded about Oswald's rifle. First, there was this exchange among two Commissioners, Representative Hale Boggs and John J. McCloy (former President of the World Bank and High Commissioner for post-war Germany, and current coordinator of U.S. disarmament activities), and FBI firearms expert Robert Frazier:

"Representative BOGGS. This is a military weapon, is it not?

Mr. FRAZIER. Yes, sir.

Mr. MCCLOY. That is designed to kill a human being.

Representative BOGGS. Exactly." [2969]

And this between counsel Melvin Eisenberg and the expert witness:

"Mr. EISENBERG. Now, based upon the characteristics of Exhibit 139 [THE RIFLE], and the ammunition it employs, and based upon your experience with the weapon, would you consider it to have been a good choice for the commission of a crime such as the assassination?

Mr. FRAZIER. Yes, sir; I would.

Mr. EISENBERG. Can you explain that?

Mr. FRAZIER. Yes. Any rifle, regardless of its caliber, would be a good choice if it would shoot accurately.

Mr. EISENBERG. And did you find this shot accurately?

Mr. FRAZIER. Yes, sir." [2970]

Depending on your age, you may or may not know that for decades most of us considered CBS radio and television anchor Walter Cronkite to be "the most trusted man in America." When there were conflicting reports, we would tune to CBS to see what "Uncle Walter" [S] thought, being a man with keen instincts, Midwest fairness and no axe to grind. He was so respected and trusted that almost all historians regard Lyndon Johnson's downfall because of his dreadful war in Vietnam to have begun the night Walter Cronkite returned from that country and told us he had grave doubts about all the positive stories we had heard.

In retirement, Cronkite wrote a memoir, *A Reporter's Life*, in which he told of the CBS News tests of what Oswald was supposed to have done in Dallas, including this about the rifle:

"The larger conclusion depended on many minor conclusions based on what many felt was skimpy or downright doubtful evidence. At CBS News we set out to examine each of the questions of evidence that bothered us all. ... We built a firing range duplicating the view Oswald had from his perch in the [TSBD] window, complete with the various obstructions to his vision as the Kennedy car passed along the street below. From that position experts fired a rifle identical to the one Oswald had allegedly used, and proved to many doubters that it could indeed have been fired three times while Oswald had the President in his sights." [2971]

I hope and trust you will find that conclusion equally as applicable and on-point if the target Oswald had in his sights was not the President, but was the Governor.

[S] What our children called him because he spent several minutes with us most evenings through the magic of a home-built Heathkit color TV.

That's what this author thinks you should know about the rifle. As in most important matters, an independent second opinion may be valuable, so this is what analyst Gus Russo wrote in his book *Live by the Sword: The Secret War Against Castro and the Death of JFK*:

"[T]he bolt-action 6.5 mm Mannlicher-Carcano rifle Oswald owned has been widely maligned as too inferior to be used in the assassination. The truth is that this weapon is so powerful—and accurate—at the range of the Kennedy murder that it should be among the last choices for a weapon someone would want pointed at them from that distance. At the turn-of-the-twentieth-century, for example, the Mannlicher-Carcano was the weapon of choice for those competing in 1,000-yard shooting contests!" "The rifle has been further ridiculed because of its bolt-action mechanism, which obviously impedes the ability to fire off multiple shots in rapid succession—presumably necessary under the circumstances. This criticism, however, ignores the fact that the knob on the end of the bolt is not there for either aesthetic reasons or comfort. This practical addition allows the well-practiced shooter minimal hand movement when cycling from the trigger to the bolt—essentially rotating the trigger hand in one plane past the knob, with no extraneous movement. This is easier demonstrated than described. Someone skilled in the weapon's use could recycle the weapon in under two seconds, much less than was actually needed in the Kennedy case. ... Marina Oswald was disturbed by Lee's repeated dry-firing speed drills on their New Orleans front porch." "Oswald's ammunition was similarly deadly. The Mannlicher-Carcano bullets are full-metal jacketed, hyper-velocity (2,700 fps—feet per second), and heavy-loaded (160 grains—twice the amount of today's bullets of the same caliber). In addition, they are extremely long projectiles, giving them (especially in combination with the gain twist rifle barrel) increased stability. HSCA ballistics expert Larry Sturdivan testified that the Mannlicher-Carcano bullet is 'one of the most stable bullets we have ever done experimentation with.'" [2972]

If you want even more, including color photos and recent mostly-accurate information, see an excellent article with useful Web links at http://en.wikipedia.org/wiki/JFK_assassination_rifle

Key point of this chapter:
Lee's surplus rifle with 4-power sight was designed, and fully adequate, to kill at the distance he intended.

THE SHOOTER

Oswald's ability to aim, fire, hit and kill with THE RIFLE

> "My rifle and myself are the defenders of my country. We are the masters of our enemy. We are the saviors of my life."
> — **U.S.M.C. Creed on Oswald's** *Scorebook* [2973]

THE UNITED STATES MARINE CORPS TRAINS ALL, lowest recruit to Commandant, to be so adept at shooting that the enemy's guy will be the one killed. That is the basic idea of how to prevail in combat. The Marines trained Lee to be that good, and here is a photo:[2974] [A]

[A] Some assassination conspiracy theorists, including his mother Marguerite (in Jean Stafford's *A Mother in History*, page 58), suggested that he aimed "left-handed", requiring a different adjustment of the rifle's sight. Here is proof of his being trained to aim and fire in a normal right-handed manner.

The Warren Commission asked the Marine Corps to supply information "relative to Marksmanship capabilities of Lee Harvey Oswald." From Marine Corps HQ in the Pentagon came a 2½-page letter "By direction of the Commandant of the Marine Corps" from Lieutenant Colonel A. G. Folsom, Jr., head of the Records Branch of the Personnel Department. Note two signs of the times in the photo images below and on the two pages following: Atop the first page, the zone x'ed out and ZIP code added; on page two, the fine art of typing into neat columns without benefit of a computer or word processor.

1964 June 8: USMC Lt. Col. Folsom to WC General Counsel Rankin [2975]

Anderson Exhibit No. 1

DEPARTMENT OF THE NAVY
HEADQUARTERS UNITED STATES MARINE CORPS
WASHINGTON XX D. C. 20380

DG–bmt
8 Jun 1964

Mr. J. Lee Rankin
General Counsel
President's Commission on the
    Assassination of President Kennedy
200 Maryland Avenue NE
Washington, D. C. 20002

Dear Mr. Rankin:

This is in reply to your letter of 2 June 1964 relative to marksmanship capabilities of Lee Harvey OSWALD, former Private First Class, 1653230, U. S. Marine Corps. In view of the lapse of time since Mr. Oswald was separated from the Marine Corps, it would be impossible to ascertain precisely the number of hours in which he participated in weapons marksmanship practice or how many rounds of ammunition he fired. In addition, the service records of the Marine Corps are designed only to show what formalized marksmanship practice and marksmanship qualification courses a Marine has fired. As you will note from Mr. Oswald's service record book, a copy of which I believe the Commission has in its custody, the form marked NAVMC 118(6)-PD (Rev. 7-54) shows Mr. Oswald's weapons firing record.

During the time Oswald fired at the Weapons Training Battalion, Marine Corps Recruit Depot, he was attached to the Second Recruit Training Battalion, Marine Corps Recruit Depot, San Diego, California. At the time he completed familiarization firing at the range at the Naval Air Station, Atsugi, Japan, he was attached to Marine Air Control Squadron 1, Marine Aircraft Group 11, 1st Marine Aircraft Wing. At the times he fired the range at the Marine Corps Air Facility, Santa Ana, and Marine Corps Air Station, El Toro, California, he was attached to Marine Air Control Squadron 9, Marine Wing Headquarters Group, 3d Marine Aircraft Wing.

The information provided to the right of the final qualification column is not contained in his service records but is based upon regulations in effect at the time. In addition, under course "A" you will notice the entry of 212MM. This final qualification score being designated as MM (marksman) is in error and should have read SS (sharpshooter).

Page 2 of 3

DG–bmt
8 Jun 1964

RANGE	DATE	COURSE	WEAPON	FINAL QUAL	AUTHORIZED AMMO ALLOW	PERIOD
WpnsTrng Bn MCRD	21Dec56	#"A"	M-1	212MM	400 rds	2 wks
WpnsTrng Bn MCRD	17Dec56	FAM	BAR	None	75 Rds	
WpnsTrng Bn MCRD	11Dec56	FAM	Pistol	None	100 rds	
NAS Atsugi Jap	2May58	FAM	12Guage RIOT GUN	None	10 rds	
NAS Atsugi Jap	7May58	FAM	.45 Pistol	None	100 rds	
MCAF Santa Ana Calif	9Mar59	FAM	12 Guage RIOT GUN	None	10 rds	
MCAS El Toro Calif	6May59	*"B"	M-1	191MM	200 rds	

For Course "A", as shown above, qualification scores were as follows:

EXPERT –220; SHARPSHOOTER –210; MARKSMAN –190

For the Course marked "B", the qualification is:

EXPERT –225; SHARPSHOOTER –215; MARKSMAN –190

Regarding a comparison of the Marine Corps' requirements with those of the other services, it is believed that the requirements of the other services can be best obtained by you directly from those services. Enclosed, however, are copies of Marine Corps regulations describing the several marksmanship courses. These were effective at the time Oswald was on active duty in the Marine Corps.

The Marine Corps considers that any reasonable application of the instructions given to Marines should permit them to become qualified at least as a marksman. To become qualified as a sharpshooter, the Marine Corps is of the opinion that

2

In case you didn't read the last two sentences of first (previous) page of the Colonel's letter: The entry on the first line above under "**FINAL QUAL**" is in error with its "**212MM**" meaning Marksman. The score 212 rated Oswald better, as a Sharpshooter.

```
                                              DG—bmt
                                            8 Jun 1964

most Marines with a reasonable amount of adaptability to
weapons firing can become so qualified.  Consequently, a low
marksman qualification indicates a rather poor "shot" and a
sharpshooter qualification indicates a fairly good "shot".
I trust the foregoing will serve the purpose of your inquiry.


                        A. G. FOLSOM, JR.
                 Lieutenant Colonel U. S. Marine Corps
                Head, Records Branch, Personnel Department
           By direction of the Commandant of the Marine Corps

Encl:
(1) Copies of MARCOR Regs
     describing marksmanship courses
```

Lieutenant Colonel Allison G. Folsom, Jr., U.S.M.C., had appeared earlier before a Warren Commission staffer to deliver a complete copy of Oswald's service record.[2976] It was unusually large, 131 pages, because of his two courts martial, many documents relating to his mother's supposed injury and resultant "need" for him to be discharged early — and the top-level decision to discharge him from the Marine Reserve as "undesirable" when it became known that he was in Moscow, badmouthing the USA. Folsom's testimony, eight pages, was primarily to explain typing errors and abbreviations in Oswald's record.[2977]

Commission staff attorney John Hart Ely was about to wrap up his Q&A session with Folsom, the final matter being Oswald's "U.S. Marine Corps Scorebook for use with the U.S. Rifle, Caliber 30 M-1", when he ventured for the first time to ask the colonel for an opinion:

"Mr. ELY. I just wonder, after having looked through the whole scorebook, if we could fairly say that all that it proves is that at this stage of his career he was not a particularly outstanding shot.

Colonel FOLSOM. No, no, he was not. His scorebook indicates—as a matter of fact—that he did well at one or two ranges in order to achieve the two points over the minimum score for sharpshooter.

Mr. ELY. In other words, he had a good day the day he fired for qualification?

Colonel FOLSOM. I would say so.

Mr. ELY. Well, Colonel, as far as I can see, that is all the testimony that we need from you with regard to these records." [2978]

So here we have direct testimony on the point that was later reaffirmed in Colonel Folsom's letter above and on the two previous pages: Lee THE SHOOTER had some good days, some not so good. That variability will be a significant consideration, later in this chapter.

With all due respect to the colonel in charge of Marine Corps personnel records, the full Commission wanted to hear directly from a firearms expert, so three months later took testimony from Major Eugene D. Anderson of the Marksmanship Branch at Marine Corps Headquarters. Twenty-six years in the Corps, the major had achieved the ultimate rifleman qualification, "distinguished rifle shot". His opinion about Oswald's ability to quickly fire three shots was in the previous chapter, as it related most directly to THE RIFLE. His more important testimony here, about Oswald's training and correct interpretation of his scores when shooting a rifle, resulted in many pages of dialogue with assistant counsel Arlen Specter:

"Mr. SPECTER. Would you outline the marksmanship training, if any, which a Marine recruit receives in the normal course of Marine training?

Major ANDERSON. He goes through a very intensive 3 weeks' training period." [2979]

To make it brief, Anderson described the first week: familiarization with the .30 caliber [B] M-1 rifle, including care and cleaning, sighting, aiming, manipulation of the trigger. The second week included firing a small-bore .22 rifle to begin the use of live ammunition, then to a rifle range to sight-in the .30 M-1 rifle, firing a few rounds to carefully adjust the sights. The third week involved extensive firing with intensive coaching, culminating in firing 50 rounds for a qualification score. Every weapon, training event and firing is carefully documented into one or more "standard record scorebooks", the basis of the next questions:

"Mr. SPECTER. Would your presumption be that L. H. Oswald, whose test score you have before you, would have received the training such as that which you have just described?

Major ANDERSON. Absolutely. He fired every day according to this. ...

Mr. SPECTER. And the basis for your statement on that would be your conclusion based on the fact that L. H. Oswald had undergone a test where he completed these documents under the category of 'US Marine Corps Scorebook for US Rifle Caliber .30 M-1 and US Carbine Caliber .30 M-1-A1?'

Major ANDERSON. Yes, sir; this document shows by dates and days as indicated that he fired daily and sighted in his rifle as prescribed.

Mr. SPECTER. Of course, you didn't know Mr. Oswald personally?

Major ANDERSON. I never knew him whatsoever.

Mr. SPECTER. So that your conclusion as to his training is based upon the inference which arises from the document which I have presented to you. That is to say, you know that if a man has one of those scorebooks, that he must have received that training?

Major ANDERSON. Absolutely. He received this in full." [2980]

Assistant Counsel Specter, the staff lawyer specialized in the mechanics of firing, trajectories and hits, then referred the major to the letter from Colonel Folsom on preceding pages, asking many questions (those not printed here are indicated by ...) about Oswald's training record and the results of his basic-training qualification score, shot four days before Christmas 1956:

"Mr. SPECTER. And what was his final qualification there?

Major ANDERSON. 212.

Mr. SPECTER. And what rating is that equivalent to, or within what range of rating is that score?

Major ANDERSON. That should have been a sharpshooter.

Mr. SPECTER. And what was the authorized ammunition allowance?

Major ANDERSON. 400 rounds for recruit firing.

Mr. SPECTER. And during what period was that?

Major ANDERSON. That was to be fired within a 2-week period.

Mr. SPECTER. Did he have exposure on another course for M-1 firing at a later date?

Major ANDERSON. The record shows that 6 May 1959 he fired the B course.

...

Mr. SPECTER. What are the differences between the A and B courses, Major Anderson ?

Major ANDERSON. The A course is fired at 200, 300, and 500 yards. The B course is exactly the same course as far as targets, number of rounds and positions are concerned, but it is fired entirely at 200 yards. [C]

[B] Somewhat larger diameter than the 6.5 mm assassination rifle, which is equivalent to .257 caliber.
[C] Oswald's longest shot in Dallas, the third, which killed Kennedy, was a distance of 88 yards.

...

Mr. SPECTER. And what weapon was used at that time?

Major ANDERSON. The M-l rifle.

Mr. SPECTER. And what score was obtained on that occasion?

Major ANDERSON. 191 for marksman.

Mr. SPECTER. And what was the authorized ammunition allowance?

Major ANDERSON. 200 rounds.

Mr. SPECTER. Would there be any reason why the scores might differ from 212 to 191, based on the layout of the courses or any of the conditions surrounding those tests ...?

Major ANDERSON. Yes; the day the 212 was fired appears to be according to the record book to have been an ideal day under firing conditions.

...

Major ANDERSON. [W]hen he fired that he had just completed a very intensive preliminary training period. He had the services of an experienced highly trained coach. He had high motivation. He had presumably a good to excellent rifle and good ammunition. We have nothing here to show under what conditions the B course was fired. It might well have been a bad day for firing the rifle—windy, rainy, dark. There is little probability that he had a good, expert coach, and he probably didn't have as high a motivation because he was no longer in recruit training and under the care of the drill instructor. There is some possibility that the rifle he was firing might not have been as good a rifle as the rifle that he was firing in his A course firing, because [he] may well have carried this rifle for quite some time, and it got banged around in normal usage." [2981]

Or — more probably the reason Oswald didn't shoot well in May 1959 was that by then he was back in California, had decided that the Marine Corps — indeed, the entire United States — was not for him. He was ready to use a fake excuse to get out early and go to happiness in Russia. He had a short-timer's don't-care attitude.

Future United States Senator from Pennsylvania Arlen Specter then asked the Marine Corps' ultimate authority on firearm training and marksmanship rating:

"Mr. SPECTER. Based on what you see of Mr. Oswald's marksmanship capabilities from the Marine Corps records which you have before you, Major Anderson, how would you characterize him as a marksman?

Major ANDERSON. I would say that as compared to other Marines receiving the same type of training, that Oswald was a good shot, somewhat better than or equal to—better than the average let us say. As compared to a civilian who had not received this intensive training, he would be considered as a good to excellent shot." [2982]

Turning from the Marines in 1956 and 1959 to Dallas in 1963, Assistant Counsel Specter then propounded a very lengthy — because of being very explicit — question, showing the witness the reenactment photos in chapter 14 that were taken through the Carcano's actual 4-power scope, about Oswald's ability to make the shot that wounded both Kennedy and Connally, "with that bullet striking at a distance from 176.9 feet to a distance of 190.8 feet":

"Mr. SPECTER. Now assuming those factors to be true for purposes of this next question, how would you characterize the difficulty of a shot at that range, which would strike the President in the lower portion of his neck at a spot indicated by a white mark on the back of the stand-in [in] the photograph marked 'Re-enactment'? My question, then, is how would you characterize the difficulty or ease of that shot for a marksman with Mr. Oswald's capabilities?

Major ANDERSON. In my opinion this is not a particularly difficult shot, and that Oswald had full capabilities to make this shot." [2983]

Moving to the greater-distance final shot, the deadly one that blew out the President's brain, Specter next carefully asked another highly-detailed hypothetical question, but "at a distance from rifle in window to the President of 265.3 feet":

> "Mr. SPECTER. ... I ask you again for an opinion as to the ease or difficulty of that shot, taking into consideration the capabilities of Mr. Oswald as a marksman, evidenced by the Marine Corps documents on him.
>
> Major ANDERSON. I consider it to be not a particularly difficult shot at this short range, and that Oswald had full capabilities to make such a shot." [2984]

Master Sergeant James Zahm, in charge of the Marksmanship Training Unit Armory in the Weapons Training Battalion of the Marine Corps Training School at Quantico, Virginia, was introduced in the previous chapter when he gave extensive expert testimony on the advantages of having a scope on THE RIFLE — in general and to Oswald in particular. Because of this witness's years of experience in rifle training, assistant counsel Arlen Specter asked Zahm:

> "Mr. SPECTER. Based on the tests of Mr. Oswald shown by those documents [his USMC firearm training and scoring books], how would you characterize his ability as a marksman?
>
> "Sergeant ZAHM. I would say in the Marine Corps he is a good shot, slightly above average, and as compared to the average male of his age throughout the civilian, throughout the United States, that he is an excellent shot." [2985]

It is worth reflecting at this point, as we consider Marine Corps marksmanship ratings, that the US Marines train their personnel to be, objectively, as good as any in the world. The Marines also use psychology to boost subjective feelings of competence. When soldiers go into battle, every service wants its men to believe they are better than those they face and shoot, so they have the courage to do the facing and shooting. In part, the Marines do this with categories that could be named by advertising agencies on Madison Avenue, from the required-minimum "Marksman" through middling "Sharpshooter" to highest "Expert Rifleman." [D] In his two measured qualifications, eager recruit Lee scored in the middle group, then shortly before his discharge from active duty, slightly above the required minimum.

The Warren Commission also heard about Oswald's rifle shooting from Ex-Marine Nelson Delgado, who had served with him. Delgado has been quoted in Chapters 2 – MARINE about Lee arguing against all orders, and in 3 – MOSCOW about what happened to teammates after his defection to Russia. His testimony below is not about Lee's first year as a "gung ho" recruit, but his third, returned from Japan and mentally preparing for an early discharge:

> "Mr. LIEBELER. You were about to tell us ... about the rifle practice that you engaged in. Would you tell us about that in as much detail as you can remember?
>
> Mr. DELGADO. We went out to the field, to the rifle range ...
>
> ...
>
> Mr. LIEBELER. Did you fire with Oswald?
>
> Mr. DELGADO. Right; I was in the same line. By that I mean we were on line together, the same time, but not firing at the same position, but at the same time, and I remember seeing his [target]. It was a pretty big joke, because he got a lot of 'Maggie's drawers,' you know, a lot of misses, but he didn't give a darn.
>
> Mr. LIEBELER. Missed the target completely?
>
> Mr. DELGADO. He just qualified, that's it. He wasn't as enthusiastic as the rest of us. We all loved—liked, you know, going to the range.
>
> ...

[D] There's also seldom-achieved-by-mere-mortals "Distinguished", earned by Anderson and Zahm.

Mr. LIEBELER. You told the FBI that in your opinion Oswald was not a good rifle shot; is that correct?

Mr. DELGADO. Yes.

Mr. LIEBELER. And that he did not show any unusual interest in his rifle, and in fact appeared less interested in weapons than the average marine?

Mr. DELGADO. Yes. He was mostly a thinker, a reader. He read quite a bit." [2986]

If Private Oswald was disappointed in his final qualification score of 191, this author suggests that was not because the score was low, but that it was a wasted point above the 190 minimum required of all Corpsmen. What Lee wanted most of all in 1959 was a quick exit from the Marines so he could go to Russia; thus he didn't want the Marines to want to keep him. There was no selfish image polishing involved. He had no glimmer of an idea — but he would have loved it! — that you and I would be thinking of his 191 more than half-a-century later!

Much of the expert testimony and most of the professional opinions in the previous chapter, THE RIFLE, were given by FBI firearms expert Robert A. Frazier. After he firmly established that he considered Oswald's rifle "a good choice for the commission of a crime such as the assassination", the Commission member chairing that session of testimony, Representative Hale Boggs of Louisiana, took advantage of the years of experience with rifles sitting in front of him, and this colloquy ensued:

"Representative BOGGS. Would you consider the shots difficult shots—talking about the shots from the sixth-floor window to the head of the President and to Governor Connally?

Mr. FRAZIER. No, sir; I would not under the circumstances—a relatively slow-moving target, and very short distance, and a telescopic sight.

Representative BOGGS. You are not answering that as an expert.

Mr. FRAZIER. From my own experience in shooting over the years, when you shoot at 175 feet or 260 feet, which is less than a hundred yards, with a telescopic sight, you should not have any difficulty in hitting your target.

Representative BOGGS. Putting my question another way, you would not have to be an expert marksman to accomplish this objective?

Mr. FRAZIER. I would say no, you certainly would not. ... I would say you would have to be very familiar with the weapon to fire it rapidly, and do this—hit this target at those ranges. But the marksmanship is accomplished by the telescopic sight. I mean it requires no training at all to shoot a weapon with a telescopic sight once you know that you must put the crosshairs on the target and that is all that is necessary." [2987]

Mother Marguerite brought to the Warren Commission his *U.S. Marine Corps Scorebook* [2988] that "was left in his sea bag, when he came home from the Marine Corps." [2989] Lee had used it to record hundreds of practice shots with his .30 caliber M1 rifle. It demonstrates the Corps' technique for improving marksmanship: fire-score-learn-repeat, over and over, from several positions, at targets of various shapes and sizes, at differing distances, with carefully judged cross-winds. The inside front cover proudly printed an inspiring exhortation from the Commandant: "EVERY MARINE may be proud of the reputation the Marine Corps has established and maintained over the past fifty years as a Corps of outstanding marksmen. Now, you have the opportunity to uphold this splendid tradition. This score book will aid you in the accomplishment of your mission." [2990] After 80 pages of diagrams, tutorials and target-scoring record forms, the back cover displayed: "MY RIFLE The creed of a United States Marine", which ended "Before God I swear this creed. My rifle and myself are the defenders of my country. We are the masters of our enemy. We are the saviors of my life." [2991]

The proudest accomplishment of Oswald's entire life, being an honorable US Marine, was destroyed by the change of his discharge status. It is reasonable to expect that he felt what decades later came to be known as "dissed", needed to defend his honor, so turned to what he had learned and practiced, the splendid tradition of outstanding marksmen. Private Oswald's *Scorebook*, sold by his avaricious mother, will feature in evidence that follows.

In *The Death of a President*, William Manchester expertly applied his own comparable experience to assess Oswald's challenge that noontime in Dallas:

> "A subsequent controversy developed over whether or not the shots fired from the warehouse on November 22 had been difficult ones, and echoes of the dispute are heard today [this was written in 1967]. Here the author must appear briefly as an expert witness. This writer has carefully examined the site in Dallas and once qualified as an Expert Rifleman on the U.S. Marine Corps range at Parris Island, S.C., firing the M-l rifle, as Oswald did, from 500, 300, and 200 yards. From the sixth floor in the Book Depository, Oswald would look down on a slowly drifting target less than ninety yards away, and his scope brought it within twenty-two yards. At that distance, with his training, he could scarcely have missed." [2992]

Assassination analyst Gus Russo, in his conspiracy-theory book, *Live by the Sword: The Secret War Against Castro and the Death of JFK*, offered a few — not enough — fact-based analyses, including this, what one should expect from Marine-trained Oswald:

> "One of the earliest criticisms of the Warren Commission's 'Oswald alone' conclusion was based on the official Marine reports of Oswald's marksmanship. The Marine scale starts with 'marksman' (the lowest qualifying score), moves upward to 'sharpshooter,' and ends at 'expert' (the top score). On Oswald's last test with the Marines, he qualified with the score of marksman. This rating is misleading for two reasons:
>
> 1. Oswald's scores were hampered by the fact that they were averaged between sitting and standing positions. When in a sitting position, bracing the rifle for steadiness (as was clearly done in the JFK killing),[E] Oswald often scored as a sharpshooter. Dr. John Lattimer, a former World War II wound ballistics specialist for the Army, purchased Oswald's original rifle scorebook from his days with the Marine Corps. The book reveals that in two rapid-fire tests at 200 yards, Oswald scored a 48 and 49 (out of 50). For these tests, Oswald used the .30 caliber M-l Garand, which is much heavier, and with a stronger recoil, than the light-weight .257 caliber (6.5 mm) Mannlicher-Carcano used to kill Kennedy. In addition, the M-l was not equipped with a scope, as was the Carcano. And whereas JFK was less than a hundred yards away, the Marine tests were conducted at distances ranging from 200 to 500 yards.
>
> 2. A Marine marksman or sharpshooter is anything but a bad shot, as some critics have implied. [Russo then cited the expert testimonies, quoted above, of Major Anderson and Master Sergeant Zahm.] Among the numerous marksmen and current Marine trainers I consulted, there is total unanimity on this point. Using expressions such as 'shooting fish in a barrel' and 'virtually point blank,' the experts call the Kennedy shooting a simple feat for a former Marine marksman." [2993]

Marina, as told in Chapter 5 – MISFIT, had been greatly troubled by Lee's rifle. She feared it even when she was home alone and it was high on a shelf in his closet, giving it both great attention and a wide berth.[F] In a detailed interview on the specific subject of Oswald's use of the rifle, she was quite certain that in the sixteen days from the time it arrived by mail order

---

[E] Your author does not necessarily concur on this, believing Oswald may have been kneeling to get the fullest benefit of the gun rest he had built of cartons by the window. It really doesn't matter.

[F] "*idiom:* Ample space or distance to avoid an unwanted consequence." – *American Heritage College Dictionary*

(March 25, 1963) to his firing at General Walker (April 10), "Oswald cleaned his rifle on about four or five occasions", plus "at least one time after the General Walker incident and before their trip to New Orleans."[2994] It would be natural for a trained rifleman to clean his newly-received rifle, but cleaning it five or six times would be pointless unless he did as the Marines train, cleaning and oiling the bore and action <u>after</u> <u>firing</u> to prevent rust and other deterioration. Accordingly, it's likely he practiced firing it on several occasions.

She was uncertain how many times he had taken the rifle out of their home to practice with it, but testified in vivid detail to the time when he wrapped it in an overcoat, then she pushed little June in the carriage and waited with him until he boarded a bus with a sign she had learned to read, "LOVE FIELD" — she was certain of that because he had told her it meant the "field of love" — to practice shooting.[2995]

The Commission had the FBI re-interview Marina and take her to re-create the walk to their bus stop. The result was a 20-page report titled **"Possible target practice in the vicinity of Love Field, Dallas, Texas."**[2996] The FBI was probably accurate in focusing the search for Lee's practice area: "Marina was asked if she knew if Oswald ever practiced at a target range or public place. She said she did not know he had so practiced and doubted if he had because of his secretive nature."[2997] With that high probability, knowing the man, FBI agents then interviewed a scheduler for Dallas Transit Company,[2998] learning that the "LOVE FIELD" bus had a stop close to a bank of the Trinity River that flows through Dallas.

Like most rivers in parched but frequently storm-hit Texas, the Trinity's water usually runs in a narrow channel, centered in a wide flood plain between dirt levees 35 feet high. FBI agents noted: "This area of Trinity river bottom could be used for rifle firing with either of the levees as an abutment."[2999] In other words, the isolated, undeveloped, flat, dry bottom made a fine rifle range and the high banks were good bullet stops. Two gun shop owners and dozens who lived adjacent to the river were interviewed and confirmed that they and many strangers used the floodplain bottom for test firing and target practice with rifles and pistols.[3000]

Lee could have, but did not, purchase ammunition from Klein's on his mail order for the rifle: "E20-7051. 6.5mm Italian military ammo, 108 rds. (6-shot clip free) $7.50" In all likelihood, when he should have been greasing coffee machines in New Orleans but sat in the next-door garage reading gun magazines and discussing rifles, he had learned that such old ammunition was considered to be undependable and subject to misfires. He must have bought his US-made, reliable Western Cartridge 6.5 mm military-jacket ammunition in Dallas.

The FBI did extensive interviewing and phoning throughout north-central Texas to find all possible sources of the bullets Lee fired at the limousine. They located a grand total of two dealers, one of whom bought his small stash from the other. The primary dealer was Johnny Brinegar, owner of The Gun Shop, whose estimation of the Mannlicher-Carcano was given in the previous chapter. He had purchased a case, 1000 rounds, packaged as 50 boxes of 20.[3001]

So, how much practice firing did Lee do? Probably 15 shots, if he was his usual tight self and bought only one box of 20. He fired one bullet at Walker. Because he had to act in haste when he read that CONNALLY WILL RIDE (chapter 18), he did not have opportunity to fill the rifle to capacity, so took it to the TSBD on November 22 with only the 4 cartridges that had been in it while in Ruth's garage. He fired 3 at the limousine and left one in the rifle. If the supposition of one box of 20 is correct, 15 practice shots were adequate for a man who had fired hundreds of larger bullets in his Marine training. If the supposition of one box is wrong, then he would have fired 35 or 55 or more in practice — but that's unlikely for this tightwad.

Further, as was told in Chapter 5 – MISFIT, Marina said that on many dark evenings, Lee sat out on their porch or balcony, depending on which rental they were living in, and repeatedly pulled the bolt and dry-fired the Carcano, over and over. The logical conclusion from these facts is that Lee had lots of practice with the assassination rifle. For a man with his first-class training and his easy close shot at the limo, it was certainly enough.

Lee carried the rifle with him on April 24 when he, alone, took a bus to New Orleans. I know of no testimony or other hint that he fired it while there. When Ruth fetched Marina and June from the marital strife of New Orleans on September 23, Lee quietly placed the wrapped rifle into the car and it went to Irving, Texas, where it was laid with other Oswald family possessions on the floor of Mrs. Paine's not-yet-famous garage. Lee was separated from it for two months, from then until the evening of November 21, except for possible dry-firing practices in Ruth's garage during his weekend visits to her home. Nobody knows. But, as you will see in Chapter 20 – OBSTRUCTION OF BEST EVIDENCE, Marina told her Secret Service guards that Lee had dry-fired at Ruth Paine's TV set on that November 21 evening before he blasted three real bullets into Dealey Plaza.

Norman Mailer, in his nicely-researched and beautifully-written *Oswald's Tale*, took up the possible arguments for and against the "magic bullet" that passed through two men. In the same vein, he then wrote this sound analysis of the capability of THE SHOOTER:

"It is the same with Oswald's marksmanship. He is judged by various people, depending on the needs of the ax they grind, to be a poor rifleman, a fair one, a good one, or virtually an expert. Much the same has been stated about the difficulty of the shot itself. It has been estimated to be everything from as easy as Sergeant Zahm has testified to nearly impossible.

Such a debate is, however, moot. A rifleman can fire with accuracy one day and be far off target on another. Why should we ascribe any more consistency to a man with a gun (in the equivalent of combat conditions) than we would expect from a professional basketball player whose accuracy often varies dramatically from night to night?

Moreover, we are dealing with Oswald. We have seen him become hysterical on one occasion and, on another, be the coolest man in the room. If we have come through the turnings of this book without comprehending that the distance between his best and worst performance is enacted over a wide spectrum, then we have not gained much. The point is that Oswald, at his best, was certainly capable of hitting a moving target at eighty-eight yards on two out of three shots over five and a half seconds even if in Russia he could not drop a rabbit with a shotgun from ten feet away." [3002]

Another aspect of Lee's ability to hit his target on November 22 must be mentioned. He had been trained, evaluated, then later practiced, firing at targets that just sat there, allowing him to take as much time as he needed to squeeze off his first shot. Chapter 19 will illustrate and discuss why he did not fire THE SHOT NOT TAKEN as the limousine drove toward him along Houston Street. When he first, at last, saw his intended victim, the Lincoln was passing him and going under the shelter of a tree. He had to sight as best he could through its largely opaque branches, then hurriedly pull the trigger as the car emerged into his view.

The distance was short, the target was moving slowly, only 11 miles an hour. If he had been prepared for the situation it would have been an easy shot, but so far as we know, it was not the type of shot he had ever fired, except perhaps during some hunting forays in Texas or Byelorussia. He was never in combat; the Marines did not train a radar operator for quick firing. So, added to Oswald's lifelong (Chapter 11 – FAILURE as a reminder) history of erratic behavior and unintended outcomes, 12:30 PM that Friday brought the novel challenge of a receding target going into hiding, then coming out into view.

Two transcending truths are learned in this chapter, and they may at first appear to be antithetical.[G] The first is that Oswald had long familiarity with rifles and shooting, had been very well trained by what was likely the world's best organization for such training, and was an excellent shot by all normal civilian standards. With THE RIFLE designed for exactly his purpose, THE SHOOTER was entirely capable of hitting and killing at the short range from his window to the slow limousine.

But, a second theme has been noticed, judged and testified to under oath: Sometimes he was very good with a rifle, and on other occasions was lousy. His qualification tests in the Marines display a large difference between the good "sharpshooter" score in boot camp and his low "marksman" score during the summer before he left the Corps. From the testimony of a friend and Quonset-hut bunkmate, that latter qualification firing was in a period when he simply didn't care. As Mailer pointed out above, those who habitually give challenges their best efforts usually do well and sometimes achieve superlative results — Wilt Chamberlain had an excellent average of 50 points in NBA games, but once scored 100 [H] [3003] — but at other times have a bad day and are really quite undistinguished.

It's not a matter of "on one hand... on the other...", it's simply that when the subject is Lee Harvey Oswald, well, as Fats Waller famously mused, "One never knows, do one?" Sometimes he tried, sometimes he didn't; and even when he tried, he usually failed.

The man who probably knew more than any other about Lee's ability with rifles was brother Robert, who had taught him to shoot and hunted with him. When Robert Oswald testified, Warren Commission counsel Jenner questioned him closely about Lee's ability with firearms. Robert's knowledge included an afternoon in September 1959 after Lee had left the Marine Corps, while he was secretly on his way to Russia. The two went out to hunt rabbits and squirrels on an in-law's farm. When asked: "Did he exhibit any proficiency in the use of that .22 caliber gun (a bolt-action rifle) on that occasion?", Robert (ex-Marine and experienced hunter) answered: "I would say an average amount." [3004] Robert then related that after his brother Lee's return from Minsk:

"Mr. OSWALD. [W]e talked about hunting over there, and he said that he had only been hunting a half dozen times, and so forth, and that he had only used a shotgun, and a couple of times he did shoot a duck.

Mr. JENNER. It was all shotgun shooting, no rifle shooting?

Mr. OSWALD. No rifle shooting, sir. That is all they were allowed to have, the shotgun." [3005]

In his fraternal memoir *Lee*, Robert wrote eight pages [3006] expressing surprise that Lee had such unexpected success in assassinating Kennedy. Here is an example: "The contrast between Lee's failure to kill General Walker and his tragic success on November 22 cannot be accounted for unless we assume that he spent a considerable amount of time practicing with the Mannlicher-Carcano during the intervening months, growing accustomed to the weapon and its telescopic sight." [3007] But there is no evidence that Lee spent any considerable time practicing with the rifle after Walker in April and before Kennedy in November. He was in New Orleans

---

[G] "diametrically opposed" — *American Heritage College Dictionary*
[H] Playing for the Philadelphia Warriors against the New York Knicks on March 2, 1962. The final score was 169–147. The total 316 points and his 100 are records that stand to this (2016) day.

and Mexico, and when all that failed, he lived in rooming houses in Dallas while the rifle lay hidden, probably untouched and unpracticed-with, in Mrs. Paine's garage.

Robert concludes: "I find it easier to believe that Lee spent some time practicing with the Mannlicher-Carcano between April and November than to accept the Commission's conclusion that the rifle was stored away during most of that time—particularly for several weeks before the assassination. Without a considerable amount of practice with that weapon, I do not understand how Lee could have fired it with an accuracy that some of the best riflemen in the United States found it difficult to match." [3008]

There is no good answer to Robert's well-founded doubt — if one assumes that Lee had such great success by intentionally killing Kennedy. But, the answer becomes quite simple when one knows that Lee's aim was to kill Connally. His world's-best training allowed his second hurried bullet to wound Kennedy on its path to the target, Connally. Badly-wounded Connally then toppled to the left. Kennedy remained upright because of being less badly wounded, and because his tight corset and elastic wrap did not allow him the same body bend that put Connally pretty much out of sight. Thus, Oswald's third bullet, meant for Connally, destroyed Kennedy's brain.

Those last sentences jumped ahead. The position of one man in the path to the other is the topic of the next chapter, TOO CLOSE TO CALL, and the clearest evidence that Oswald intended to aim at Connally is the subject of Chapter 19 – THE SHOT NOT TAKEN.

There is no call for surprise at Oswald's sharpshooting success. He had great training but no success. He accidentally killed the wrong man.

Key point of this chapter:
Oswald was well trained and fully capable of killing with his rifle, but his shooting — like everything with him — was erratic.

TOO CLOSE TO CALL

Oswald's shots do not identify his intended target

> "[T]he highest duty of the ... writer is to remain true to
> himself and to let the chips fall where they may."
> — **President Kennedy**, a month before his death [3009]

THE PRECEDING CHAPTERS have set out the essential facts to bring all readers, regardless of age or personal knowledge of the assassination, to a shared understanding. You now know enough about the events of that terrible weekend to have a well-reasoned conviction that Lee Oswald fired his rifle from the sixth floor window of the Texas School Book Depository, wounding Governor Connally and killing President Kennedy. I trust you believe that truth, beyond all reasonable doubt, because it is a simple physical fact. This and the next six chapters of EVIDENCE go beyond "What happened?" to "What did he intend?"

We begin simply by counting the bullets — three — moving on to demonstrate that one missed to wound a bystander, then attempt to determine where the other two were aimed.

In June 1964, the Warren Commission took testimony from Jacqueline Kennedy. Chief Justice Earl Warren and her brother-in-law, Attorney General Robert Kennedy, attended while the commission's chief counsel, J. Lee Rankin, asked questions. These questions and answers brought out her experience before the third (fatal to the brain) bullet:

"Mrs. KENNEDY. And then—do you want me to tell you what happened?

Mr. RANKIN. Yes; if you would, please.

Mrs. KENNEDY. You know, there is always noise in a motorcade and there are always motorcycles besides us, a lot of them backfiring. So I was looking to the left. I guess there was a noise, but it didn't seem like any different noise really because there is so much noise, motorcycles and things. But then suddenly Governor Connally was yelling, 'Oh, no, no, no.'

Mr. RANKIN. Did he turn toward you?

Mrs. KENNEDY. No; I was looking this way, to the left, and I heard these terrible noises. You know. And my husband never made any sound. So I turned to the right. And all I remember is seeing my husband, he had this sort of quizzical look on his face, and his hand was up, it must have been his left hand." [3010]

She then mentioned the terrible third shot, after which Rankin returned to the first shot of which she had been aware (which was probably Oswald's second shot because his first bullet, fired in haste, was almost certainly the one that missed altogether):

"Mr. RANKIN. Do you have any recollection of whether there were one or more shots?

Mrs. KENNEDY. Well, there must have been two because the one that made me turn around was Governor Connally yelling. And it used to confuse me because first I remembered there were three and I used to think my husband didn't make any sound when he was shot. And Governor Connally screamed. And then I read the other day, that it was the same shot that hit them both. But I used to think if I only had been looking to the right I would have seen the first shot hit him, then I could have pulled him down, and then the second shot would not have hit him. But I heard Governor Connally yelling and that made me turn around, and as I turned to the right my husband was doing this [indicating with hand at neck]. He was receiving a bullet. And those are the only two I remember. [pause] And I read there was a third shot. But I don't know. [pause] Just those two." [3011]

Sufficient physical evidence and testimony from many witnesses establish with certainty that Oswald fired three bullets. A majority of bystanders, and two men on the floor a few feet directly below him, agreed they had heard three shots, and that's the number of fired cartridge shells found on the 6th floor. One of the three, I think the first, missed badly and maybe was deflected by a branch of the pine oak tree between Oswald and the limousine, ricocheted from the pavement of Elm Street — or did both: nicked the branch, then the pavement.

Forty years after the bullets, four newsmen from KRLD, CBS's Dallas radio and TV affiliate, looked back and compiled all their local knowledge into a wonderful compact book, *When The News Went Live*. They wrote of 1963: "We did not know then that the first of the three shots had ricocheted off an oak limb and hit a Main Street curb." [3012] On the page 190 map, the tree is the one standing alone, close to the northwest curb of Elm Street.

Under major heading "**THE SHOT THAT MISSED**", the *Warren Report* analyzed:

"From the initial findings that *(a)* one shot passed through the President's neck and then most probably passed through the Governor's body, *(b)* a subsequent shot penetrated the President's head, *(c)* no other shot struck any part of the automobile, and *(d)* three shots were fired, it follows that one shot probably missed the car and its occupants. The evidence is inconclusive as to whether it was the first, second, or third shot which missed.

If the first shot missed, the assassin perhaps missed in an effort to fire a hurried shot before the President passed under the oak tree, or possibly he fired as the President passed under the tree and the tree obstructed his view. The bullet might have struck a portion of the tree and been completely deflected. ...

Some support for the contention that the first shot missed is found in the statement of Secret Service Agent Glen A. Bennett, stationed in the right rear seat of the President's followup car, who heard a sound like a firecracker as the motorcade proceeded down Elm Street. At that moment, Agent Bennett stated:

'I looked at the back of the President. I heard another firecracker noise [the second] and saw that shot hit the President about four inches down from the right shoulder. A second shot [this is now the actual third shot, but only the second shot he saw hit] followed immediately and hit the right rear high of the President's head.' [3013]

Substantial weight may be given Bennett's observations. Although his formal statement was dated November 23, 1963, his notes indicate that he recorded what he saw and heard at 5:30 p.m., November 22, 1963, on the airplane en route back to Washington, prior to the autopsy, when it was not yet known that the President had been hit in the back." [3014]

The Commission correctly assigns substantial weight to a statement written by a trained Secret Service agent, within hours, before his observation could be influenced by other evidence.

Young auto salesman James Tague had been driving east on Commerce Street, going downtown to take his fiancée to lunch,[3015] and was almost through the Triple Underpass when he found traffic totally blocked. His white car stopped half under, half out of the south-most of the three underpass openings. Waiting for traffic to move, he got out to watch the motorcade a block away. Two deputy sheriffs and a policeman were in his vicinity.[3016]

Jim Tague is important to our being certain of what happened to Oswald's errant shot, very probably the first of three fired. Here are two views of the same photo to show why.

The first [3017] was taken seconds after the presidential limousine had raced away toward

the hospital. It shows a family on the grass between the Depository and Elm Street, hoping for safety from killing bullets such as those they had just observed. A motorcycle at left and two photographers race to the southwest, where the limo had gone. Importantly for us, low in the background is a line of eastbound cars stalled on Commerce Street because of the motorcade.

At the far right of the photo, at the right end of the black rectangular opening where Commerce Street runs through the underpass, you will see a white car just emerging, and can barely discern a man standing by its rear bumper. He is Jim Tague, and here is an extreme blowup [3018] of that innocent bystander, at the far right of the photo above. He has been wounded but does not yet realize it. The far (south) curb of Main Street, just toward us from him, is where a bullet ricocheted and blasted small fragments from the curb to bloody him on cheek and jaw.

A TSBD bookkeeper on the Elm Street curb, while hearing the first bang, "saw a shot or something hit the pavement ... you could see the sparks from it ... toward the middle of the lane" [3019] behind the President's car. "A jacketed bullet, striking the pavement at 1,904 feet per second ... was deflected slightly upward, headed diagonally across Dealey Plaza, hit a curb and broke the shell into fragments, and the spent grains peppered James Tague on the cheek." [3020] The bullet had hit and left a scar on the top of the south curb of Main Street [A] slightly east of the Triple Underpass. Tague heard a "loud firecracker" [3021], then two more. "I recall that something had stinged me, and then the deputy sheriff looked up and said, 'You have blood

---

[A] North-to-south, the east-west streets are Elm (westbound), Main (two-way), Commerce (eastbound).

there on your cheek.'" [3022]   "[H]e did have a slight cut on his right cheek." [3023]   In his oral history for the valuable book *No More Silence*, Jim Tague continues his important story:

"So I reached up and felt a couple of drops of blood. That was the first time that I recalled that there'd been something that had stung me, much like a sweat bee sting. So he [Deputy Sheriff Buddy Walthers] said, 'Let's go back over to where you were standing.' Before we could cross Main Street we saw the mark on the curb from across the street. It appeared that a shot had hit the curb right at my feet. I don't know the exact measurements but it was on the rounded edge of the curb on the south edge of Main Street about ten to twelve feet out from the Triple Underpass." [3024]

That afternoon Jim Tague went into the bedlam of the Dallas Police Department to give a statement about his wounding by fragments of pavement when the stray bullet hit a curb in front of him in the previous photos. A homicide detective had a photograph [3025] taken to document the red skin wounds on his right cheek and jaw. Against his fair clean-shaven skin, they are red and evident in the original color photo, still visible but much less distinct in grayscale at right.

DPD Accident Investigator J. W. Foster (another Texan with initials rather than names) had been assigned to keep the top of the Triple Overpass clear. He was an eyewitness in front of the Lincoln during the shooting: "At that time, all I could tell about the shots was that they all sounded about the same, and they came from back toward Elm and Houston Streets. None of them came from the grassy knoll." [3026] After the limousine had sped away below him:

"I ... walked on down to the south side of Elm. The plaza had been freshly mowed the day before, thus I noticed this clump of sod that was laying there and was trying to find out what caused that clump of grass to be there. That's when I found where the bullet had struck the concrete skirt by the manhole cover and knocked that clump of grass up.

Buddy Walthers, one of the sheriff's deputies, came up and talked to me about it, and we discussed the direction from which the bullet had come. It struck the skirt near the manhole cover and then hit this person who had stood by the column over on Commerce Street. He came by and had a cut on his face where the bullet had struck the column. You could see about where the bullet had come from by checking the angle where it scraped across the concrete and the column where it struck the pedestrian. It appeared to have come from the northeast, approximately from the book store area, but we were never able to find the slug." [3027]

"Deputy Sheriff Eddy R. 'Buddy' Walthers filed an investigative report on the Tague bullet with the Dallas County Sheriff's Department. Walthers had [two newsmen] take photographs of the point of impact on the curbstone where Tague was standing when he was hit in the face by either a piece of cement or a bullet fragment. ... At the insistence of Walthers and a Dallas motorcycle police officer, Tague reported his minor wound to the Homicide Section of the Dallas Police Department that same day." [3028]   "Tague was photographed with blood running down his cheek ..." [3029] Wounded witness Jim Tague now has a close encounter — but he won't realize that — with the man who wounded him:

"[W]hile I was in [Homicide detective] Gus Rose's office giving him a statement, there was a commotion to our right as Oswald was brought in. Matter of fact, they put him in the office next to the one we were in. Mr. Rose told me, 'That's the guy that shot the policeman over in

Oak Cliff.' I said, 'I didn't know there'd been a policeman shot.' He responded, 'Yeah, killed him!' That was the extent of the conversation. There was no connection to the President." [3030]

"The Dallas FBI case officer for the JFK assassination, Robert P. Gemberling, included a section on the Tague bullet in a ... report ... 'Information to the Effect One Bullet Fired During Assassination Went Wild, Crashed into Curb, and Struck Jim Tague.'" [3031] Then, in a report to the Warren Commission, Director J. Edgar Hoover said the FBI had "determined from a microscopic study that the lead object that struck the curb was moving in a general direction away from the Texas School Book Depository Building." [3032] But, probably innocently as they hurried to write their *Report*, the Commission did nothing with these facts.

Jim Moore, sound author [B] of *Conspiracy of One: The Definitive Book on the Kennedy Assassination*, deftly follows that errant bullet in this account with which I fully agree:

"I believe that Oswald did shoot through the break in the foliage. I believe that this first, hurried shot missed. Casual readers might call this unimportant. If the bullet didn't hit anything, why bother? I didn't say it didn't hit anything. I merely said it missed both the President and the Governor.

The first shot struck the Elm Street roadway near the right rear of the limousine. Bounding low beneath the auto, it ranged diagonally across Dealey Plaza and struck the south Main Street curbway. The impact knocked pieces of concrete into the face of spectator James Tague, who reported the incident to police.

I believe that President Kennedy shared Tague's experience. Doubtless the bullet hitting the concrete only a few feet from the President showered President Kennedy with bits of concrete and possibly metal fragments. Since the bullet struck to the right rear of the limousine, it's likely no one else was affected by the missed shot.

Five eyewitnesses saw either the bullet strike the pavement or its aftermath. ... Mrs. Virgie Baker was standing on the north curb of Elm Street as the shots were fired. She told [the Commission] that she saw something hit the pavement in the middle lane, behind the Presidential automobile. ... Mr. and Mrs. Jack Franzen were standing a few feet down Elm Street from Mrs. Baker. Both noticed small fragments flying about inside the President's car immediately following the first shot. Postal Inspector Harry Holmes saw the bullet strike the roadway through binoculars from his office across the Plaza. And Royce Skelton, atop the triple overpass, saw pieces of concrete fly up at the rear of the limousine.

Oswald, then, missed his first shot ... Perhaps the bullet was deflected at first by a tree branch. The slug struck the concrete behind and to the right side of the Presidential automobile. ... President Kennedy, of course, heard the sound of the first shot. Pelted or forcibly struck by bits of concrete and metal, he lived the next two seconds in a daze. His right arm, which had been waving to the Elm Street crowd, froze in place. By the time he emerged from behind the road sign and back into Zapruder's view, his hands were rising to cover his face. Critics and investigators alike have universally assumed that as the President reappears in the Zapruder film, he is reacting to a bullet wound. I submit that he is reacting instead to a gunshot, one which missed but was nonetheless felt.

By frame 230 of the Zapruder film, Governor Connally is facing straight ahead as he prepares to turn to his right. Connally has heard the sound of a rifle shot, and is making the turn to see if he could spot the President in the corner of his vision. Nearly two-and-a-half seconds have elapsed since the first shot, long enough for Lee Harvey Oswald to work the Carcano bolt and draw a fresh bead with the Italian rifle. A third of a second later, Kennedy and Connally are hit." [3033]

[B] His deliberate A-B-C style reminds me of myself; as Martha Stewart says, "That's a good thing."

Jim Tague will soon play a vital role in correcting errors so that history correctly records what actually happened. As he tells it in his *No More Silence* oral history:

"Immediately after the assassination there was talk about three shots which was the same number I heard and that all three had hit Kennedy and Connally. All three shots were accounted for. Well, I knew that our great government, the FBI, the Secret Service, they're smart and they were going to find out the truth about what really happened. They'd dig in and be coming around to me to find out about this one shot which had missed and hit the curb near me. ...

Into the spring of the next year, the papers were saying that the Warren Commission was wrapping up its findings about three shots: two that hit Kennedy, and one that hit Connally. I was distressed and concerned about my credibility. Whenever I mentioned this thing, I was told, 'You're crazy!'

One day I was talking to a man I knew in the service department at my place of business and mentioned, 'You know, the photographer of *The Dallas Morning News* took the picture; there was a deputy sheriff who was there also and he brought some other police officers; I gave a statement to the Dallas Police Department and another to the FBI and this is wrong!' So he went to a news reporter who worked for the *Dallas Times Herald*, and since the *Times Herald* was only five to ten minutes away, it wasn't an hour till a young reporter named Jim Lehrer of the later MacNeil-Lehrer Report [C] called and said he'd like to talk to me. ...

So it wasn't long after that that all of a sudden it was learned that the Warren Commission was going to be reconvened. At that time, I was called for the first time to give my testimony to ... the Warren Commission. Of course I got the testimony of the photographer, Buddy Walthers, and other people who corroborated that there had been a shot which had missed. Lo and behold, all of a sudden the newspapers came out with a new theory that two shots hit in the car and one of the bullets went completely through Kennedy, the one that also did all the damage to Connally. Since all of this had become a personal thing to me, I felt vindicated." [3034]

James Tague is in history with a minor abrasion but an important role; his wound and his dogged determination to correct a mistaken belief proved that only two bullets did all the damage to the politicians in the limo on Elm Street. We leave him with the happy outcome that the fiancée he was going to take to lunch — but he canceled their date to make his report to the police — became his wife, as he proudly told the Warren Commission. [3035]

To any reader with an open mind, the foregoing should have established that one of the three bullets, almost certainly the first, did not hit the Lincoln or its passengers. Thus, our search to know Oswald's intent is simplified to two of his shots, very probably the last two.

It is not important that this book prove precisely when the three bullets were fired, or what became of each. For what it may be worth, this author has been studying this subject for fifty-two years and believes: Oswald waited until he at last found Connally in the limousine; that was while it was turning hard-left below him; he fired his first shot in great haste as the limousine disappeared under the damnable oak tree; that first hurried shot missed altogether, to spray Kennedy's cheek and cause Tague's small injury; the second shot "hit Kennedy in the back, exited the front of his neck, pierced Governor Connally's body, exited his chest, shattered the radius bone of his [right] wrist, and superficially wounded his thigh"; [3036] the third shot blew apart Kennedy's head, killing him.

The Warren Commission heard testimony, received depositions and reports, made tests, researched, argued, then carefully stated twelve conclusions. This is the third:

[C] We met Jim Lehrer's latter-day partner Robert MacNeil back in chapter 6 when he rushed into the Depository and asked the fleeing Lee Oswald where he might find a phone. It's a small world.

"Although it is not necessary to any essential findings of the Commission to determine just which shot hit Governor Connally, there is very persuasive evidence from the experts to indicate that the same bullet which pierced the President's throat also caused Governor Connally's wounds. However, Governor Connally's testimony and certain other factors have given rise to some difference of opinion as to this probability but there is no question in the mind of any member of the Commission that all the shots which caused the President's and Governor Connally's wounds were fired from the sixth floor window of the Texas School Book Depository." [3037]

That wishy-washy conclusion was necessary to obtain the unanimity that Chief Justice Warren believed essential to earn public trust in his commission's work. One commissioner was the problem, the holdout against stating the obvious conclusion that one bullet wounded two men. The naysayer was Senator Richard B. Russell of Georgia, a power in the Senate because he'd been there since 1933. Russell had been a problem on the commission since day one. He had not wanted to be a commissioner, attended very few hearings and meetings, but without understanding the Commission's workings and findings, objected to much. This is as good a place as any to include his doubts; and to get to them, we go by way of LBJ.

In November 1964, five days after being handed the *Warren Report*, President Johnson spoke on a recorded phone with FBI Director J. Edgar Hoover, as analyzed in Max Holland's *The Kennedy Assassination Tapes*. The two briefly discussed the possibility, despite the *Report*'s conclusion, of multiple gunmen — hence "they" in the president's question:

"Johnson: How'd it happen they hit Connally if [he was] two feet ahead of him?
Hoover: Connally turned . . . Connally turned to the president when the first shot was fired, and I think in that turning, it was where he got hit.
Johnson: [I]f he hadn't turned, he probably wouldn't [have] got hit.
Hoover: I think that's very likely." [3038]

No! That's absolutely wrong. Their supposition that Connally could have avoided a bullet aimed at Kennedy cannot stand, as astute author-editor Holland explained in this footnote:

"Connally did hear the first shot (which missed), and it prompted him to turn around to see if the president had been hit. Nonetheless, the act of turning did not put Connally in the line of fire; *any* missile that passed through the president was likely to hit the governor. If anything, as suggested earlier, turning might have saved Connally's life because the missile that did hit him thereby missed his heart and arteries." [3039]

Holland summarizes, I believe entirely correctly: "If John Connally had not looked back over his right shoulder after hearing the first shot, to see if the president was hurt, he probably would have been shot through the heart. By turning, he saved himself in all likelihood." [3040]

Holland also noted a meeting between President Johnson and Chief Justice Earl Warren in 1967, more than three years after Dallas. As a result of their talk in the Oval Office:

"[T]he president may even come to understand, for the first time, that John Connally's dissent from the single bullet theory is specious, seemingly plausible but in fact impossible." [3041]

Holland then offers a reasonable suggestion for the later insistence by both Connallys that the governor was hit by his own bullet, not one that had first passed through Kennedy:

"The Commission staff has concluded that one of the three missiles missed entirely, and that another hit both President Kennedy and Governor Connally in that order. This conclusion is at odds with the direct testimonies of the governor and Mrs. Connally, both of whom adamantly maintain that the governor was hit by his own missile, not one that hit the president first. This unshakable belief is traceable to the anger Mrs. Connally felt at Parkland Hospital, when she perceived that her wounded but alive husband was being ignored at the expense of an already-dead president." [3042]

One more LBJ conversation may be of passing interest: Putting together the fact of Jim Tague's bloodied cheek and John Connally's reaction to hearing that first shot argues strongly for #1 being heard by Connally and wounding Tague, #2 wounding Kennedy and Connally, and #3 killing Kennedy. Any who dispute that logical conclusion may take some comfort from President LBJ's discussion with recalcitrant Senator Richard Russell about the Commission's wrestling with the bullet sequence question:

> "Russell: I was the only fella [commissioner] there that even . . . *practically*, that suggested any change whatever in what the staff had got up. This *staff* business always scares me. I like to put my *own* views down. But we got you a pretty good report.
> Johnson: Well, what difference does it make which bullet got Connally?
> Russell: Well, it don't *make* much difference. ..." [3043]

The American Bar Association held a mock trial in 1992 to try the evidence for and against Oswald. In a courtroom-like setting, testimony was elicited from experts who had opportunity to study 28 years of evidence and opinions. One witness was Dr. Robert Luis Piziali of Failure Analysis Associates, an expert in recreating events and analyzing injuries. [3044]

Trustworthy assassination analyst Gerald Posner wrote: "Failure Analysis used a technique called 'reverse projection' to answer the questions. First it created a full-sized model of the presidential limousine. Then a camera was placed in relation to where Zapruder was standing, and the lens was set to the same focal length, so the view of the car was identical to that afforded in the film. Using the Zapruder film, the images of Kennedy and Connally were sketched into the car, and then people who were the exact height and weight of the two men were placed into the seats in the positions shown on the film. Failure Analysis achieved precision on the placement ... Then the wounds on the President and Governor were measured and extended into the animation.

"At that point the computer was ready to answer two questions. The first was whether one bullet could cause all the wounds, and the answer was yes." [3045] "The second question resolved by the ... re-creation is where the sniper would have to be located for the single bullet to have the correct trajectory. Utilizing the information on the wounds and the location of the men and the car, the computer worked backward to provide a 'cone' within which the sniper had to be. 'In this case,' says Dr. Piziali, 'the cone is almost centered on the sixth floor of the Texas School Book Depository. The shot could only have come from within that cone.'" [3046]

After lengthy examination about the testimonies, observations and documentations of witnesses, reconstructions, surveyors, autopsists and others, and about his own conclusions from all the evidence, Dr. Piziali was asked to sum up the conclusions. He replied: "I believe the evidence shows that there were 3 shots fired from the southeast corner, 6th floor window of the TSBD. The first bullet is not accurately accounted for, we simply have an approximation of when it was fired. The second bullet was fired more than 3 seconds after the first bullet. It wounded both the President and the Governor. The third bullet was fired 5 seconds later, hit the President in the head and killed him. The bullets found were fired from the same gun, the Mannlicher Carcano owned by Lee Harvey Oswald." [3047] Expert witness Dr. Piziali stuck to his testimony and the conclusion just given, throughout a vigorous cross-examination that fills seven pages of print. [3048] A jury at the ABA convention split, with 7 voting to convict Oswald and 5 to acquit.

Jim Bishop noted in *The Day Kennedy Was Shot* that when Oswald chose his window and set up his stacks of boxes to hide from any who entered the floor, "He would have an open, commanding view everywhere except as the motorcade passed the broad tree below. The only open space in the tree was furnished by the 'V' of two main branches." [3049] If you have followed the life of Lee Oswald in the preceding chapters, or only the summary list in Chapter 11 – FAILURE, you should be able to predict where he hurriedly fired his first shot — yes, right into the V of those oak branches.

Bishop's *The Day Kennedy Was Shot* has an Epilogue with his discoveries and thoughts five years after the assassination, after he read and considered the "evidence" and arguments presented in the tsunami of books after the *Warren Report*. He offered this sound logic:

> "A good case can be made out for any theory about the three shots. ... The best procedure is to work backwards. The vast majority of witnesses agree that they heard three shots. Zapruder's film proves that the third shot blew the top off of John Kennedy's head. This leaves two for accounting. Governor John Connally, who remained alert and conscious through the ghastly scene, is a hunter. He heard a rifle shot and swung toward his right, then toward the left to look at the President. Mr. Kennedy was lifting both hands upward. A second shot rang out, and the President grasped the throat area and began to fall toward his left. At the same time, the Governor felt as though someone had slammed him in the back. This would indicate that the second shot hit Mr. Kennedy, furrowed between the strap muscles of the neck, nicked his tie, emerged pristine, having hit no bone, punctured Connally's rib cage, and emerged exactly where the films show Connally's right wrist to be—coming up toward his chest. It hit the wrist, fractured it, and was spent in a shallow furrow on the left thigh and remained there until it fell off [onto] a stretcher.
>
> If there is a mystery—and I don't think there is—it lies in the first shot. A direct line from Oswald's window, down to the position of SS-100-X, and straight to the underpass at Commerce, will show that this is the one which hit the pavement on the right side of the car, sending up a shower of gravel from the pavement. A woman on the curb opposite the car was hit by a 'spray'. President Kennedy's seat in the car was elevated three feet higher than the Connally jump seats.[D] Undoubtedly Kennedy heard the first shot; undoubtedly he felt the spray of concrete and realized that someone had taken a shot at him. The bullet is believed to have tumbled upward off the pavement, nicked a curb, and sprayed the face of James Thomas Tague standing beside his car at the underpass—on a straight line from that sixth-floor window." [3050]

Except for the error in stating the relative heights of the seats, Bishop's analysis is soundly reasoned and correct, firmly buttressed by testimony of Secret Service Special Agent in Charge of the Dallas trip Roy Kellerman, riding in the limousine's front-right seat. He testified: "... there is a report like a firecracker, pop. And I turned my head to the right because whatever this noise was I was sure that it came from the right and perhaps into the rear, and as I turned my head ... I heard a voice from the back seat and I firmly believe it was the President's, 'My God, I am hit'". [3051] Warren Commission members and counsel pressed SAIC Kellerman on the matter for several minutes, until it was resolved:

> "Mr. KELLERMAN. Why I am so positive, gentlemen, that it was his voice—there is only one man in that back seat that was from Boston, and the accents carried very clearly.
>
> Mr. SPECTER. Well, had you become familiar with the President's voice prior to that day?
>
> Mr. KELLERMAN. Yes; very much so.
>
> Mr. SPECTER. And what was the basis for your becoming familiar with his voice prior to that day?
>
> Mr. KELLERMAN. I had been with him for 3 years.

[D] "three feet" is wrong, likely a misprint. Kennedy's seat was about three <u>inches</u> above Connally's.

Mr. SPECTER. And had you talked with him on a very frequent basis during the course of that association?

Mr. KELLERMAN. He was a very free man to talk to; yes. He knew most all the men, most everybody who worked in the White House as well as everywhere, and he would call you.

Mr. SPECTER. And from your experience would you say that you could recognize the voice?

Mr. KELLERMAN. Very much, sir; I would." [3052]

There is a good reason for belaboring that point: The bullet that went through Kennedy's neck and flew on to wound Connally caused sufficient damage to Kennedy's throat and larynx that he could not have cried out after that shot, especially loudly enough to be heard from the back of the open limo to the front seat. So, following Jim Bishop's "reasoning backward" example above: The third bullet blew up Kennedy's head. The second injured him (and Connally) so badly that he could not speak clearly with a Boston accent. Thus, it had to have been the first bullet that both caused and allowed Kennedy to say "I am hit". The sound conclusion is that Kennedy's face was sprayed when the first errant shot hit curb or pavement nearest him.

We also have Governor Connally's testimony, carefully considered and given many times, that he had heard the first shot, reacted to it, and believed he was not hit by that bullet. His wife Nellie corroborated that sequence, as was mentioned earlier.

Dallas Deputy Sheriff Jack Faulkner of the county's Criminal Investigation Division (long before CIDs became a mainstay of TV), stood on the sidewalk and watched the President pass by the corner of Main and Houston. An experienced law enforcement officer, he did better than the many who simply "heard three shots", period: "I heard three very distinct shots. I'll never forget the sequence: there was a pause between number one and number two, then number two and three were rapid." [3053]

Only one scenario meets all the physical requirements: There were three shots. The first missed the limo altogether and shattered, sending a spray that hit only President Kennedy sitting at the right-rear and not the other five in the limo, then continued to the southwest, to slightly but definitely injure Jim Tague. The second bullet went through Kennedy's neck, then Connally's chest and wrist and into his leg. The third bullet killed Kennedy.

Let us carefully and precisely consider the facts and converge what they mean. Two of Oswald's bullets hit people sitting in the limo. He was a trained and experienced shooter. There were no other cars or targets close by. Therefore, we may confidently know without doubt that he must have intended to shoot one of the six people in that car.

We may quickly eliminate two because there is no rational reason for thinking Oswald had ever heard of either. In the front seat of this motorcade car, a customized 1961 Lincoln Convertible designated "SS100X" by the Secret Service, were two of its agents. On the left, as almost always, the driver was William R. "Bill" Greer.[E] On the right-front passenger seat was "Roy H. Kellerman, Assistant Special Agent in Charge of the White House Detail, who was the Secret Service official responsible for the entire Texas journey." [3054] "Bill Greer and Roy Kellerman were two of the most loyal, diligent, and conscientious men on the White House Detail".[3055] They lived and worked in the nation's capital, and were in Dallas only this one midday, for the sole purpose of taking the Kennedys from Love Field to the Trade Mart,

---

[E] He will drive JFK later on November 22, taking the body to the plane in Dallas, then to autopsy near Washington D.C., then in the darkest hours of the next morning, home to The White House. Greer will make another very important appearance in this book, in Chapter 19 – THE SHOT NOT TAKEN.

then back to the plane. Period. Neither was wearing a uniform or doing anything whatever to attract Oswald's attention. They were not his targets.

This photo [3056] shows the Lincoln moving west toward Dealey Plaza. Directly behind driver Greer is Nellie Connally, wife of Texas Governor John Connally, on the left jump seat. Seated behind her, on the left side of the full-width bench-type rear seat, is Jackie Kennedy.   Not even among the most demented assassination writings have I ever seen any suggestion that Oswald intended to harm either of the wives. We may confidently rule them out as his targets.

Just as we narrowed three bullets to the two of interest, here six in the car are reduced to two possible targets for Oswald: President Kennedy on the right side of the rear seat, and, in front of him on the right jump seat, Governor Connally. As he aimed and fired, Oswald must have intended to kill one or the other. There's no other possibility. But, which?

The natural belief, then and now, is that the target was the more important, the one who was hit by two bullets, the one who died — President Kennedy. But all we may be certain of from physical evidence is that Oswald intended to kill either Kennedy or Connally.

This chapter focuses on trajectories of the two bullets that hit Kennedy and Connally as they sat in the Lincoln. It will clearly show that only an inch or two, one way or the other, would have caused the bullets to hit differently, and likely kill the other man. Seeing how the two sat, to understand the simple geometry involved, is essential. So, ahem, "Let us begin" [F] with this photo [3057] of the Lincoln at Love Field, minutes before Air Force One arrived.

[F] JFK's inaugural address.

The Lincoln had been stretched three feet to provide more space for graceful entry and exit, and especially to add two jump seats, "allowing the president to accommodate guests without having them obscure the crowds' view of him on the slightly higher backseat." [3058] In the previous photo, they have not yet been folded down for sitting. At the front of this passenger area, slightly behind and well above the back of the front seat, stands a tall stainless steel handrail, extending across the car's width. With four equally-spaced slots in its top surface, it is used by politicians to brace themselves when they stand in parades, their shoes touching the jump seats. Photos of that usage are in Chapter 19 – THE SHOT NOT TAKEN, where the supreme importance of the handrail on November 22 will be made evident.

Notice that the rear bench-type seat goes all the way from side to side, but the jump seats are set in about a half-foot from the doors, which are unusually thick and protrude into the interior a few inches. We will soon see President Kennedy at the far right of his bench seat, and Governor Connally sitting in the only position possible for him, squarely on his jump seat. Thus Connally will be aligned several inches to the left of Kennedy

Alongside the back seat in the car's sidewall is a panel with a radio, a reading light and an important switch. There is an identical panel on the right side, where the President always sits. "The feature [Kennedy] likes best is the rear seat, which rises ten and a half inches at the flip of a switch, and there is a footrest to make him more comfortable. With the rear seat elevated, he does not have to stand to be seen by a crowd." [3059]

The photo [3060] below, as they begin the drive into Dallas, shows the relative positions of the two possible targets. The back seat has been raised a few inches and Kennedy is somewhat higher than Connally. The height difference is more apparent if one looks across at the two similar-height wives, Jackie's head clearly higher than Nellie's. Kennedy is closer to the right side than Connally, as stated above in describing the previous photo.

This is a preview of the fact that the Kennedys are high and easily seen from any angle, whereas, especially viewed from the front, the Connallys are down in the handrail's shadow. That will be discussed and diagrammed in Chapter 19 – THE SHOT NOT TAKEN.

It is obvious, beyond doubt, that John Connally's jump seat is in front of, and about three inches lower than, the President's seat. It is therefore not a surprise — it's a necessity! — that a bullet from the rear that passes through Kennedy must then enter Connally's back.

Some have derisively called the copper-jacketed lead slug that wounded both men the "magic bullet". Yes, it did a lot of damage without deforming much, as it was designed to do. See Chapter 12 – THE RIFLE. If you are seriously concerned about that, now is a good time to take chapter 9's recommendation: Read *Case Closed* if you have a few days or *Reclaiming History* if you can spare a few weeks. You will not understand what follows in this chapter until you first accept the straight-through wounding of Kennedy and Connally by one bullet.

The third bullet, because Connally's abrupt reaction after the second shot wounded him badly by entering his body three times — and with a quick life-saving pull-down from Nellie — hit the only head visible where Connally's had been, Kennedy's, and killed him.

The point is that the two were so much in line that nobody can persuasively prove anything about Oswald's intention from the facts of what actually eventuated. You need not take this engineer-author's word for it. Here's a more expert description:

FBI Special Agent James Hosty was the man in the Dallas office who had Oswald's file — along with a few dozen other cases — before the shooting, but did not meet Lee until three hours after the killings. Like this author, after retirement he wrote the one book that was in him: *Assignment: Oswald*. He ended it with a Postscript conveying his thoughts and conclusions on the assassination — culminating in the firm belief that Oswald "did it", alone. This excerpt presents the professional analysis of a trained and experienced FBI man:

"People also confront me with the 'magic bullet' problem. I am no forensic scientist, but I think I can give a fair summary on why there is no magic to that bullet. ... Kennedy and Connally were not sitting in perfect, straight-back postures in a line. Kennedy's seat was slightly higher than Connally's and a few inches off to the right side. When the second shot was fired, the Zapruder film indicates Kennedy was leaning forward, perhaps in reaction to hearing the off-target first shot.[G] Connally is twisting around in his seat to look behind him, also apparently reacting to the first shot. He is holding his hand down on his thigh.

The two men are in this position when the second shot is fired. The bullet goes into the back of Kennedy's neck at an angle and exits at the front through the knot of his tie. The threads of this tie were examined; they were blown outward, consistent with an exit wound. The bullet ... now begins to tumble in the airspace between Kennedy's neck and Connally's back. This tumbling is consistent with ballistic studies of bullets that enter and then exit without striking any bone, as was the case with Kennedy. The tumbling bullet then enters Connally's upper back sideways, not front or back first. Connally's back wound is oblong, consistent with a sideways entry, not a normal entry wound. The bullet, now traveling through Connally's body, smashes sideways into one of his ribs. Deflected off the bone, the bullet's direction changes slightly and exits Connally's body a little lower, just below the nipple. The bullet, now traveling more slowly because of its impact with the rib and having traversed two bodies, continues its downward path; it has just enough speed to strike Connally's wrist, damaging the wrist bones. The slowed bullet now ricochets off Connally's wrist bone, penetrates his pant leg and barely embeds itself in the flesh of his thigh.

When Connally was placed on a stretcher at Parkland Hospital, his trousers were removed, he was placed on a second stretcher and urgently wheeled into emergency surgery. During the

---

[G] More than that, as argued earlier, this author believes he'd just been blasted on the right side of his face by granules of concrete thrown up by the fired-in-haste errant first bullet.

frenzied efforts to save Connally's life, medical personnel did not notice the bullet fall out of Connally's leg and onto the first stretcher. A short time later, a hospital attendant discovered this bullet and gave it to an FBI agent, who gave it to a Secret Service agent. ... [T]he bullet did not zig and zag; its path is easily understood when carefully examined. Again, it is important to remember that Kennedy was leaning forward and Connally had turned to look behind him.

People also take issue with the bullet's condition, which they describe as pristine. First, one should remember that no two bullets change condition in exactly the same way when fired into an object. Second, the bullet is *not* pristine; it is partially flattened on one side, consistent with the bullet hitting Connally's rib sideways when it was traveling at its highest speed. Prior to that, the bullet had only traveled through soft flesh. After striking the rib, it rapidly began to lose its velocity, so that when it hit its next hard object, Connally's wrist, it was traveling much more slowly, preventing any further damage to the bullet. There is also one inescapable bit of evidence many ignore: the traces of lead recovered from Connally's wrist conclusively match the so-called stretcher bullet. The bullet was copper-jacketed with a lead core. The core was exposed on the rear end only; a small amount of it was squeezed out like toothpaste from a tube and left in Connally's wrist." [3061]

When the wounding bullet passed through both of them, the two men reacted differently. John Connally did as would most of us; he slumped down and to his open side, toward the center of the car and his wife Nellie. He thus became less visible, more protected from the next shot. John Kennedy, after that same bullet penetrated his neck, acted much differently. He simply sat there, upright, with a puzzled look and hands rising, probably to his face stung by fragments from the wayward (probably first) shot, and then also to his neck injury from the wounding (probably second) shot. He did not slump, and thus was still highly visible and in essentially the same position for the arrival of the fatal (definitely third) bullet. The President kept this bolt-upright posture because he had no choice — his body was imprisoned.

Kennedy suffered from "osteoporosis that severely weakened his lumbar spine—worsened by injuries on the Harvard football field and in the navy—and that led to three difficult operations." [3062] We all knew of his rocking chair; many had heard that he wore a back brace. On this day he is also wearing a second brace, a rigid corset, required since two months before. There are two similar accounts of the immobilizing accident. Investigative reporter Seymour Hersh in his 1997 bestseller *The Dark Side of Camelot*:

"Kennedy may have paid the ultimate price ... for his sexual excesses and compulsiveness. He severely tore a back muscle while frolicking poolside with one of his sexual partners during a West Coast trip in the last week of September 1963. The pain was so intense that the White House medical staff prescribed a stiff canvas shoulder-to-groin brace that locked his body in a rigid upright position. It was far more constraining than his usual back brace, which he also continued to wear. The two braces were meant to keep him as comfortable as possible during the strenuous days of campaigning, including that day in Dallas.

Those braces also made it impossible for the president to bend in reflex when he was struck in the neck by the bullet fired by Lee Harvey Oswald. Oswald's first successful shot was not necessarily fatal, but the president remained erect — and an excellent target for the second, fatal blow to the head. Kennedy's extra brace, which is now in the possession of the National Archives in Washington, was not mentioned in the public autopsy report, nor was the injury that had led to his need for it." [3063]

Hersh cited his source: "Hugh Sidey, *Time* magazine's White House correspondent, recalled in an interview for this book, a woman acquaintance of Sidey's 'came to me and told me how Kennedy tried to put the make on her at the pool. She wrenched away and [the President] fell into the pool, hurting his back.'" [3064] Hersh had the laudable integrity to add a footnote with a slightly different version of the injury:

"In a column published in *Time* magazine on May 18, 1987, Sidey gave a slightly different version, moving the scene of the action from a pool to a bedroom. 'One insider,' he wrote, 'claimed that Kennedy reinjured his weakened back during a bedroom tussle at a party in Bing Crosby's Palm Springs, Calif., house, which the President was using in September, 1963, thus forcing him to return to a rigid back brace. That brace held him erect in the limousine two months later in Dallas after the first gunshot struck him. The [next] shot killed the still upright President.' Sidey wrote the column after Senator Gary Hart of Colorado, a Democratic candidate, was forced to withdraw from the 1988 presidential campaign upon being publicly linked to a woman who was not his wife. Sidey's account attracted little attention." [3065]

Here are the back brace and body corset in photos. At left is the brace Kennedy had worn for years, shown in Sally Bedell Smith's book *Grace and Power* with caption: "Earl E. T. Smith ... a close friend of Jack's ... is seen standing on the patio of Joe Kennedy's home in Palm Beach with JFK, who is wearing his special brace— visible only in private—to ease his back pain." [3066]

Now we must mentally add to Kennedy on November 22, over that brace but under his elegant suit, the long "stiff canvas shoulder-to-groin brace that locked his body in a rigid upright position." None have recognized the importance of that medical garment, which will be called "the corset" here to differentiate it from "the brace", nearly so acutely as my fellow-believer and pathfinder, James Reston, Jr. He ends his excellent 2013 book *The Accidental Victim* with these final two pages:

"On February 11, 2013 I traveled out to the National Archives in College Park, Maryland ... It had been a struggle to get the Archives to agree to let me see the corset that the president was wearing on November 22, 1963. One had to have a good scholarly reason as to why looking at the picture of it was not enough, for, appropriately, the Archives was intent to resist the voyeurism that sometimes surrounds the Kennedy assassination. My reason was that I need to see the actual brace to evaluate the stiffness of the plastic disc in the back of the brace that covered the president's sacrum and further bolted him upright in his seat on that day.

Two archivists brought the artifact to the antiseptic viewing room in a pristine wooden box. [3067] Opening it carefully, as if they felt the weight of history, and then putting on white gloves, they lifted the tan corset out and laid it on the table. I asked them to measure it and put my wide palms over my own midsection to imagine how complete the grip of the thing was. And then they spread out the wide Ace bandage that had been wrapped over the corset. If in developing my theory about the psychological importance of Oswald's military discharge I was channeling my own military service and remembering how much I valued my own honorable discharge, now I was referencing my experience as a pretty good, but often injured college athlete and the many times I had used an Ace bandage to hold my bruised and battered body together. It was almost beyond imagining how tight that corset and Ace bandage ensemble must have felt, as the president went out in public. I wondered how he stood it. One of the archivists pulled out the plastic disc from its envelope in the back of the brace. I did not want to touch it.

In past projects I had felt before the detritus of history. I had handled the transcript of Galileo's interrogation by the Inquisition. I had watched a North Carolina prison director snake the tubes of a lethal injection apparatus between his fingers as we talked about a female prisoner he was about to execute. I had walked the walls of crusader castles when I was writing about the Third Crusade of Richard the Lionheart and Saladin....and waded through the tall grass around the pavilion of Jonestown, littered with toys and baby bottles.

But there was something different about this 'damned girdle' as the late Senator Yarborough had called it in our conversation 25 years ago. This is as close as I ever want to get again to the quintessence of tragedy.

THE END" [3068]

James Altgens, a Dallas photographer for the Associated Press, stationed himself in Dealey Plaza with the thought of getting a good photo of the Kennedys in their limousine as it entered that tranquil nearly-empty space, with the wall of tall buildings of downtown Dallas as backdrop. Standing on the south curb of Elm Street as the Lincoln approached, when he heard the first shot he snapped a photo that became famous as the best of the scene between the first and second bullets, with Secret Service agents looking back toward Oswald's window.

In his oral history of the day, Altgens realized that: "[S]ince Jack Kennedy had a back brace on, it made good sense to me, as I learned later, that he didn't fall over when he was shot the first time because the brace would have held him in place in that seat. So the brace really did him a disservice; it held him up as a target so he could be shot again and again." [3069]

After the bullet (almost certainly the second) had passed through his neck and sped on to gravely injure John Connally, Jack Kennedy leans only slightly toward his wife on his left, but is still very much upright. Jackie is puzzled, so she lovingly takes hold of his face and tries to look into his eyes to learn what's wrong. Abraham Zapruder's film and several photos show that he just sat there while she leaned over to him, until their faces were only inches apart. James Reston made the critical observation: "Without the corset, the force of the first bullet, traveling at a speed of 2,000 feet a second, would surely have driven the president's body forward, making him writhe in pain like Connally, and probably down onto the seat of his limousine, beyond the view of Oswald's cross hairs for a second shot." [H] [3070]

After that bullet went through both, life-or-death will be determined by what happens before the next arrives in 2.5 seconds. There's no time for thought and action, only enough for involuntary reaction, ballistics and physics. The President's back brace, made more rigid this morning by wrapping it and his thighs in Ace bandages, holds his body erect. If not for that, the next (last) bullet would very possibly have hit Connally. But the governor slumps down; the President can't, so the third bullet explodes Kennedy's steady in-the-open brain.

I trust that, thus far, this chapter has firmly established what Oswald's bullets caused. Now it is appropriate to move to the crux of the matter; to see what Oswald saw, because that will be the essential basis for our understanding — or lack — of what he intended.

"There were at least three official reenactments of the assassination, involving various combinations of FBI, Secret Service, and Dallas Police Department personnel ..." [3071] The December 1963 reenactment by the Secret Service will be described and shown in Chapter 19 – The Shot Not Taken because its photos began when the limousine turned into Dealey Plaza and drove toward the School Book Depository, before Oswald began shooting.

[H] Reston means the second shot that hit. Because the first missed, it will be the third shot Oswald fired.

Here we look at the third and final reenactment, staged for the specific purpose of determining whether one bullet could have wounded both Kennedy and Connally. The alignment of the two will show you what Oswald saw as he aimed. This reenactment was the creation of Arlen Specter, a dogged young Assistant Counsel for the Warren Commission who would go on to a famous career as a District Attorney, then U.S. Senator.[1] Edward Epstein in his book *Inquest* describes how Specter did it:

> "In May [1964], Specter proposed that the Commission conduct a reconstruction of the assassination based on the [Zapruder] film in order to determine whether Connally and Kennedy were hit by the same bullet.[3072] Specter said that the Commissioners initially opposed a reconstruction, 'because they felt it would look bad at this late date to show that the basic facts were not known.'[3073] [General Counsel] Rankin ... gave a different reason; he said that the Commission was reluctant to permit a reconstruction for fear that 'an overenthusiastic lawyer' might 'make the facts fit the hypothesis.' Thus the Commission agreed to the reconstruction ... on the condition that it would be supervised personally by Rankin."[3074]

> On May 23, 1964, Rankin, [Assistant Counsel Norman] Redlich, and Specter went to Dallas to conduct the reconstruction. The ... sequence of events of the assassination was meticulously reconstructed. An open limousine, with stand-ins for Kennedy and Connally,

> simulated the movements of the Presidential limousine on the day of the assassination. The limousine was slowly pushed until its position coincided exactly with the position of the limousine shown in the film of the assassination; at each point a photograph was taken from the 'sniper's nest' in the Texas Book Depository through the telescopic sight of the murder rifle. In this manner, each film frame was correlated with the assassin's line of sight, and the trajectory was measured. Through this reconstruction it was possible to determine the assassin's view and the trajectory on each of the three shots."[3075]

The *Warren Report* photo [3076] above shows how the wonderful pairs of "RIFLE SCOPE" photos and enlargements about to be shown here were taken from Oswald's window, through his actual scope mounted on his actual carbine. You will see here exactly what he saw then.

The photo at left [3077] shows two exactly correct-height FBI agents sitting in a Cadillac limousine, in precise positions for Kennedy and Connally. David Lifton writes: "A car similar to the Presidential limousine was used, two FBI agents acted as models for Kennedy and Connally,[J] and the clothing of each was marked with chalk where the bullet allegedly entered.

---

[1] Arlen Specter was a unique politician who switched parties — both ways! Elected to be Philadelphia District Attorney as a Democrat, he changed to Republican to free himself from the local party machine. Nearing the end of 30 years in the U.S. Senate, he switched back to Democrat in an attempt to improve his chances of re-election, but that failed. He died in 2012 at age 82.

[J] Arlen Specter's typed agenda for the reconstruction required: "We should have a 6-foot, 2-inch man available to simulate Governor Connally. Governor Connally's clothing should be taken to be worn by the man sitting in his position." — Appendix of H. E. Livingstone's *Killing Kennedy*, page 389, displaying a May 12, 1964 memo released by the Assassination Records Review Board.

"In addition, a camera rigged to take a picture through the telescopic sight of the rifle provided a view [down] from the sniper's nest. ... After correcting for the slope of Elm Street, the Report came up with its monument to accuracy: 17 degrees, 43 minutes, 30 seconds." [3078] In the photo at left,[3079] taken after the drive, Arlen Specter, the Warren Commission's specialist on ballistics, holds a rod showing the angle at which one bullet from Oswald's perch was able to wound both, as had been carefully measured by the surveyor's instrument in the background.

Critic Harrison Edward Livingstone in *Killing the Truth* objects: "One problem was that they used a Cadillac limousine rather than the Lincoln that Kennedy and Connally rode in, and the placement of the seats and the distances between them might not have been the same." [3080] The Lincoln was not available for the test. It had been driven by Ford Motors to customizing firm Hess and Eisenhardt to be fully rebuilt. At right is a photo of what Specter and the FBI were re-creating; the Lincoln limo as it departed Love Field to begin the motorcade.[3081]

Placement of the FBI actors above is substantially the same as positions of the actual victims.

An important difference is that the Lincoln driven in Dallas could be open as it was on November 22, or capped with a full metal top, or its passengers visible through a clear plastic bubble top. When not in use, the tops rode inside the unusually large trunk. When one was selected for use, its front edge had to be clamped to the Lincoln's framework. What is importantly missing from the re-creation photos is prominent in the "real" photo above at right, more vivid in the two large photos on earlier pages: the Lincoln's cross-bar roof support (also used as, and in this book called, the "handrail") that will hide Connally from Oswald's sight as the limousine rolls north on Houston Street toward the Book Depository. The light-haired agent at top is fully open to view from the front; Connally was not. That fact will be the foundation of Chapter 19 – THE SHOT NOT TAKEN.

Despite the different limo, the purpose of the May 1964 reconstruction was achieved, demonstrating that the theory jointly developed by Assistant Counsel Arlen Specter and Commissioner Gerald Ford was viable — one bullet from the sixth-floor window could indeed have wounded and passed through President Kennedy, then traveled on in a straight line to also wound Governor Connally.[K] Serendipitously, the Commission's reenactment photos now allow us to see what Oswald saw and fired at, so we may understand that the result does not prove his intent — it will be shown to be TOO CLOSE TO CALL.

[K] The worst of the conspiracy theories show the bullet doing a mid-air zig-zag. Balderdash!

The Commission took photos of the limo and stand-ins at many spots along Elm Street. Each photo through Oswald's scope from his window was then printed in an exhibit with two

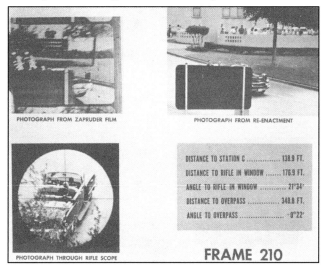

other photos: The frame [L] from Abraham Zapruder's film at top-left, and a new photo taken from Zapruder's position on the day of the reconstruction at top-right, to show that the limousine was properly positioned. By using Zapruder's film, the two men were precisely positioned and postured for each photo. Two of those Commission Exhibits are important to this book. The first, above at left,[3082] is when the Commission concluded, considering all evidence, the wounding bullet passed through Kennedy, then through Connally. Above at right is an enlargement of the exhibit's bottom-left "PHOTOGRAPH THROUGH RIFLE SCOPE".[3083]

Here is the second Commission Exhibit of importance.[3084] The limousine has moved further down Elm Street to where Zapruder frame 313 shows with certainty the terrible instant

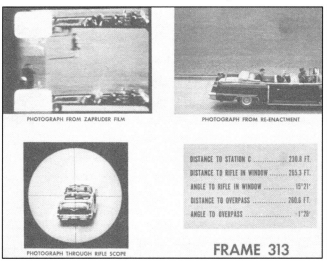

when the third and last bullet blew off part of Kennedy's head. The film was in Kodachrome color, the explosion of brain matter was a soft pink; one can never put that cloud out of mind.

[L] Zapruder frames are numbered from the first (#1) to last (#486) he photographed in 26½ seconds.

We see in these photos almost exactly what Oswald saw as he fired his shots that hit — the "magic bullet" that wounded both, then the final bullet that killed Kennedy. If you are in a normal reading position, holding this book at a comfortable distance, the small photos at bottom-left inside each montage pretty much depict the size and appearance of Oswald's naked-eye views. The enlargements are what you would experience looking with one eye through the rifle's scope — hauntingly like what Oswald saw as he pulled the trigger.

There are several important points. First, look at the two scope enlargements and see in both that as Oswald looked through that scope, the vehicle and its passengers are moving upward and, to a lesser degree, to the right. In other words, if he held the rifle steady, he would see the limo move from the crosshairs into the upper-right quadrant of the scope's field. When one fires a high-velocity weapon at a target moving directly toward or directly away from the shooter, aim directly at the target and the bullet will fly to that spot. But, when firing at a target that is moving across the field of view, one should make allowance for the fact that the target will be in a different position when the bullet arrives to it.

That is the situation here. If ex-Marine Oswald's training kicked in, he should have put the scope's crosshairs on his target, then raised up a little, and to the right a little less, before pulling the trigger. That "leading" would put the bullet right on target, if everything else (the scope's alignment with the barrel, the limo's constant speed) is correct. By careful analysis of the Zapruder film, the Commission established that while the wounding and killing shots were fired,[3085] "the speed of the President's automobile is computed at an average speed of 11.2 miles per hour."[3086] That is 16.43 feet per second.[M] The Carcano's muzzle velocity when firing Oswald's 6.5-mm Western Cartridge Co. bullets was 2,165 feet/second.[3087]

For the frame 210 shot that wounded both men, the time for the bullet to travel 176.9 feet (see the FRAME 210 panel above) was 0.0817 second, during which the target was driven forward 1.3422 feet, which is 16 inches. Using simple geometry and the 17°43'30" angle of the bullet[N] (stated on page 438 to the right of the photo of Arlen Specter illustrating it), during the bullet's flight the target would move "up" 5 inches[O] and "to the right" 2 inches. If Oswald had both ingrained instinct and time to recall and use his Marine training, he should have aimed 5" high and 2" to the right of what he wanted to hit.

For the frame 313 bullet that blew apart the President's brain, the results are similar. The bullet's travel was 50% farther. From several lines of evidence, we know the driver slowed the limo after hearing the earlier shots, so perhaps it traveled 35% slower than during the frame 210 shot. Because it was farther away, the angle was less (11°30'30" instead of 17°43'30"), coincidentally 35% smaller. These differences rather closely offset one another, so for the frame 313 shot, Oswald should have adjusted about the same; 5" up and 2" right.

[M] On precision: Of a man 6 feet tall, it is literally and precisely correct to say he is 1.8288 meters tall, because "The international foot [was] defined in 1959 as exactly equal to 0.3048 meter." (*The World Almanac and Book of Facts 2009*). But, the 5-digit number "1.8288" implies an accuracy not necessarily supported by the original single-digit "6 feet". To avoid losing precision while concatenating measurements, it is best to work with fullest-practical accuracy (thus the 16.43 derived above from less-precise 11.2), then express the final result with an expression that will honestly convey to the audience how much precision we believe is truly present in the result.

[N] The 21°34´ in FRAME 210 is before subtracting the path of the limo on Elm Street's downhill slope.

[O] Computation with the stated measurements yields 5.147953 inches. We thus simply say "5", but neither 4 nor 6, so the reader understands our confidence in the overall accuracy of the result.

As was mentioned in Chapter 12 – THE RIFLE, that is close to what his scope's misalignment did "automagically".

Here's the important point: All of the actual photos at frame 313 show an overriding difference from the calm situation at frame 210. By the time the killing bullet arrives in frame 313 — and remember that's the Zapruder frame in which the terrible pink cloud blows up from Kennedy's head — Connally has been hit and has screamed. The film clearly shows that his Nellie has pulled him toward her, left, down and nearly out of sight. Kennedy is held rigidly by his corset, so is leaning a much lesser amount toward Jacqueline on his left. Of the two possible targets, the President remains much more exposed.

The two reenactment photos are in a Cadillac with a soft top that is stored inside a white cover on top of the forward edge of the trunk. As you can see in the large clear photos earlier in this chapter, the actual Lincoln Continental limousine used on the fatal day had no similar bulky ridge. Thus, even more so than is shown in the re-creation photos, after the wounding (second) bullet, Kennedy remained high in the open.

In his autobiography, Arlen Specter, the Warren Commission's assistant counsel and expert on ballistics and trajectories, wrote about the path of the second bullet: "Then there was Connally, sitting right in the line of fire, directly in front of Kennedy ..." [3088] He assumed that Oswald was aiming at Kennedy, thus the purpose of his statement was to explain how Connally came to be wounded. I hope this book is now establishing the much greater probability that Oswald was aiming at Connally. Accordingly, Specter might well say today, if I may put words into his mouth: "Then there was Kennedy, sitting right in the line of fire, directly in the path to Connally."

In this author's experience and judgment, the current ultimate authority on the bullets, ballistics, positions, paths, sounds and wounds is a 2005 book, *The JFK Myths: A Scientific Investigation of the Kennedy Assassination* by Larry M. Sturdivan. He is a professional wound ballistics researcher, whose *curriculum vitae* suggests that timing is indeed everything:

> "On November 22, 1963 (the day of the assassination), he received and accepted a job offer involving wound ballistics from the Aberdeen Proving Ground in Maryland. The next spring he would observe ballistic tests conducted at the Biophysics Laboratory of Edgewood Arsenal in support of the Warren Commission's investigation." [3089]

Vincent Bugliosi in his *Reclaiming History* is the ultimate researcher to Oswald's guilt and the absence of conspiracy; Sturdivan is the equivalent expert on proof of where the three bullets originated and went. Gifted at explaining, he has gone to great lengths to find 69 photos and other figures to illustrate his fine book, which is very highly recommended if you would like to know more about the ballistics, all consistent with what we are about to see and measure.

Here comes some math and geometry, so I will move cautiously, explaining every step as clearly as I know how. There will be footnotes and endnotes to help. To begin, next is a much higher definition print my photo researcher found at the National Archives, of a photo shown previously that was scanned from one of the Warren Commission *Hearings* books. [3090] Arlen Specter stands beside the limousine driven for the FRAME 210 and FRAME 313 exhibits on page 439. The photo carefully reconstructs the positions and postures of Kennedy (left) and Connally (right) at the moment the wounding bullet passed through them. The FBI agents are the same as shown previously, chosen to have the correct heights. For simplicity, I will now call them "Kennedy" (back seat, dark hair) and "Connally" (jump seat, light hair).

During the re-creation drive, a surveyor's transit was used to measure the very precise angle described earlier. Afterward, in the photo above taken in a garage, the transit is on the far side of the limo, and next to it is a surveyor's cord aligned at the precise angle the transit measured of the second bullet, the one that went through both Kennedy and Connally. Arlen Specter holds a stiff rod, slightly toward us but as close as possible to the path of that bullet. The photo shows that his rod is parallel to the accurate cord.

Jim Tague's determined effort was convincing that one bullet, almost certainly the first of the three, had caused his wound. Thus, all effects in the limousine must have come from two bullets, of which the last killed Kennedy; so the wounding of both men must have been from one bullet. The re-creation was done to ascertain whether or not that was possible.

All photographs and measurements in this chapter testify with one voice: Yes! The men are so well aligned that if any bullet was intended for Kennedy, it must have necessarily continued on that path to also hit Connally. Saying that same truth another way, almost all bullets Oswald could fire at Connally, head or torso, must first hit Kennedy.

Before looking closer, it is helpful to know that, on average, an adult man's head measures approximately 9 inches in height, from the bottom of the chin to the top of a hairless crown. For our purposes, that is a sufficiently accurate measurement to apply to the next image.

Above is an enlarged area from the previous photo. Although Oswald had to fire off his shots very rapidly — Chapter 19 - THE SHOT NOT TAKEN is devoted to explaining why — it is most likely that he would have wanted to put his bullets into the middle of a head. A parallel white path is added above to show the difference between the heads of Kennedy and of Connally. Using the scale of 9" for full head height, the difference is seen to be about 4 inches. On page 439, through the FRAME 210 scope, the difference looks more like 8 inches.

Averaging those together, the difference in aim to a point on one man, or to the same point on the other, is now known to be close to 6 inches. The "DISTANCE TO RIFLE IN WINDOW" (see FRAME 210 on page 439) is 176.9 feet.[P] 6 inches divided by 176.9 feet = 0.5 ÷ 176.9 = 0.00283,[Q] the sine [R] of the angular difference. Arcsine (the angle whose sine is) 0.00283 = 0.162 arc degrees, which is 9.717 arc minutes, which may be expressed more meaningfully as 9 minutes 43 seconds of angle — slightly less than 1/6 of one degree.

What this means is that if Oswald aimed at one specific feature on one of the men — the center of the head, the right earlobe, the heart — it doesn't matter — then shifted his aim to that same spot on the other, he would have swung the rifle just less than one-sixth of a degree.

[P] This is the Commission estimate of the distance to Kennedy's back, the measure that interested them. For the angle we are about to calculate, it serves just as well for the distance to Connally.

[Q] The calculator says 0.0028264556246467. Similarly, for the angle calculated in the next sentence, the calculator reads 0.161944158 degrees. If you read the earlier note about precision, you will know why the two measurements used here don't deserve more digits in the stated result.

[R] "for a given angle in a right triangle, a trigonometric function equal to the length of the side opposite the angle divided by the hypotenuse" — *Encarta Dictionary* The same result would have come from instead using the tangent function; at such small angles, they are essentially the same.

Conversely, and more importantly for what we are considering, if he intended to aim at some body part on one of the men, he would have accidentally hit the same body part on the other by either misaiming or inadvertently moving the rifle less than one-sixth of a degree.

How much is that? Consider the Earth's Moon, which you can see most nights, except if you live here in Seattle (a local joke). In the sensible metric system,[S] the Moon has a mean diameter of 3,474 km,[3091] although its apparent size varies a little because of a somewhat eccentric orbit. The Moon's center averages 384,405 km from the Earth's center. The radius of the Earth is 6,378 km. Seen from the Earth, the Moon subtends[T] an optical angle of arcsine (3474 ÷ (384405 - 6378)) = arcsine 0.00919 = 0.527 arc degrees = 31.6 arc minutes.[3092] Said simply, we see the Moon as half a degree wide.

The math is done! Here's one way to appreciate the difference in aiming at Kennedy as opposed to aiming at Connally for Oswald's second shot, the one that passed through both of them: Take a rifle — if you don't have one, use a yardstick — outside at night when the Moon is anywhere between half and full. Aim at one edge of the Moon, then move your aim 1/3 of the way across toward the other illuminated edge — which is the same as 2/3 of the way from the edge to the center, if you find that easier to eyeball — and that's the difference for Oswald to aim at one potential victim instead of at the other.

Now much more meaningfully, do this: Aim your rifle or yardstick at a star or planet anywhere in the general vicinity of the Moon, say "Bang", then in 3 seconds, shift your aim to the Moon, to 1/3 of the distance from one edge to the other, say "Bang" again, but be careful to not let your aim move another 1/3 of the Moon's width, because if that happens, you will have shot the wrong man!

That would have been Oswald's view and challenge if he used the Carcano's open sights, as several analysts believe he did for speed in sighting and using his Marine training. But he may have aimed through the 4-power scope — this author believes he did, based on the evidence that the scope was in place when a deputy sheriff found the hastily-hidden rifle. If you have a rifle with 4-power scope, then by all means use that. You have the same objective, to quickly re-aim from some star or similar object to a point 1/3 of the way across the Moon from an edge, and hold that aim steady while pulling the trigger.

In daytime, or when the Moon is less than half, or if you live in Seattle, or prefer to visualize Oswald's challenge indoors, stand a penny on end, leaning slightly back against something, so you can see Lincoln's head. Measure 22 feet from it,[U] put your toes there, aim your yardstick — be very careful if you do this indoors with a rifle! — at something else in the room, quickly pull an imaginary trigger, then in 3 seconds or less re-aim at one edge of the penny and again pull the imaginary trigger — but don't let your aim move near the other edge of that penny, or you will have accidentally shot the wrong man!

[S] If you can't stand this, multiply kilometers by 0.6 to get miles; but please don't do anything to the angles measured in degrees and minutes and seconds because the ancient Babylonians (who lived beside today's war-torn Tigris and Euphrates Rivers) revered 60 and 360. Now you know.

[T] "*Mathematics* To be opposite to and delimit: *The side of a triangle subtends the opposite angle.*" — *American Heritage College Dictionary*

[U] The US penny's diameter is precisely 0.750". For a penny to subtend the same 9.717 arc minute angle as there was for Oswald between Connally and Kennedy, it must be this distance from your "rifle". Check: 0.750" ÷ (22' x 12"/foot) = 0.00284, which is essentially the same challenge as the 0.00283 Oswald faced.

Oswald had to do all this, and before the next shot also lift the knob on the Carcano's bolt handle, pull back the bolt to eject the used shell, push the knob forward then down to seat a new cartridge, then aim and steady while he pulled the trigger — all in 3 seconds. Yes, he was trained, and many other riflemen have shown it can be done. But, now you know that not only were those manipulations necessary, but the aim to the target was quite narrow and demanded precision — not a strong suit for inept Lee — or the wrong man would be shot.

Before we leave the subject of "too close", here is "how close" in the opinion of the ultimate expert on this subject, George Thomas Shires, the surgeon who led the team that repaired Connally's wounds. Saturday, the day after the shooting, when it appeared that Governor Connally would survive, *The New York Times* reported:

> "Dr. Tom Shires, chief of surgeons at the University of Texas Southwestern Medical School, said the governor probably would have been killed, if he had not turned. 'After consulting with Mrs. Connally and others on the scene,' Dr. Shires said, 'the consensus is that the governor was quite fortunate that he turned to see what happened to the president. If he had not turned to his right, there is a good chance he probably would have been shot through the heart. As it was, the bullet caused a tangential wound.'" [3093]

Compared to the above-described six-inch external difference between Kennedy and Connally, what the doctors saw was only an inch or two inside Connally separating the terrible but survivable bullet path from a deadly path of destruction through the heart or aorta. If the shot had been different by that inch or two, Connally would have died and the headlines might well have asked — then, that very day! — **WHO WAS THE TARGET?**

Finally, about the testimonies in the previous chapter – THE SHOOTER – that the shots Oswald made were well within his capability. Those evaluations were made on the supposition — the only supposition anyone had in 1964 — that the intended target was Kennedy, who sat high in the back seat, considerably higher and more visible than in the two re-creation photos shown earlier in this chapter for Zapruder frames 210 and 313, done in a different car with its folded convertible top, on top of the trunk, masking much of the President's back.

Oswald had somewhat easy shots at Kennedy, but only difficult shots at Connally, largely concealed past the President's head and body. Shots at Kennedy would probably hit him, but if into soft tissue, then with every opportunity for the bullets to go on into Connally. Shots at Connally must almost certainly first hit Kennedy. You now know, well beyond any reasonable doubt, that after-the-fact results of shots at either the President or the governor could not possibly identify which man was Oswald's intended victim.

This chapter has presented detailed discussions of the three shots Oswald made, with full discussion of their possibilities and probabilities. There is no reason to write more about what these twenty-five pages have shown. The summary in the box below should suffice.

Key point of this chapter:
The men were so in line and overlapped that bullets intended for one hit the other. Which was the target? It is TOO CLOSE TO CALL. To know Oswald's intent, we must look at other evidence.

REGARDING KENNEDY

What Oswald stated and conveyed about John Kennedy

> "What moved some misguided wretch to do this horrible deed may never be known to us ..."
> — **Chief Justice Earl Warren**
> Eulogy, November 24, 1963 [3094]

> "One of the deepest mysteries at the outset of the hearings was *why* would Lee Oswald want to kill a President?"
> — **Representative Gerald Ford**
> Member, Warren Commission [3095]

THIS BOOK'S FACTS AND ANALYSES are presented to answer the basic question: What was Oswald attempting to do? If you have followed the logical progression thus far, you should now agree that Oswald, acting alone, tried to murder either John Kennedy or John Connally. Following chapters will consider Oswald's politics, then look at physical evidence: When did Oswald take his first deliberate action toward assassination? Why then? Why didn't Oswald fire while the limousine was approaching? Why did he wait until it was going away?

This chapter and the next are devoted to testimonial evidence. Lee Harvey Oswald spoke his mind, quite freely, about many subjects. Highly interested in politics, he habitually talked about politicians. This chapter presents the testimony of every person who said she or he heard Oswald say anything regarding John F. Kennedy. The next chapter will do the same about John B. Connally. The reason for many sources is that any one or a few may be wrong — Oswald lied, for example, when he denied killing Kennedy or Tippit, we know better with certainty — but the aggregate weight of years of unguarded opinions becomes significant.

I made a careful search of the *Warren Report*, all of its accompanying 26 volumes, and several hundred books and other media listed in sections REFERENCES CITED and NOT CITED. Every quotation here is documented to its source in the section NOTES AND SOURCES.

The sequence below is first those who knew Oswald best — himself, his wife, mother, brother — followed by all others who heard his opinions, in alphabetic order. If a person is quoted on multiple occasions, those are in date order. Here is every instance known to me of Lee Harvey Oswald ever having said or conveyed anything about John Fitzgerald Kennedy:

Lee Oswald during interrogations in Dallas Police Headquarters on November 22–24, 1963

The Last Words of Lee Harvey Oswald is a highly useful and reliable compilation by assassination researcher Mae Brussell,[3096] documenting the quotations below. Sadly, there was neither a tape recorder nor a stenographer at Captain Fritz's questioning sessions, so Brussell's multi-sourced quotes are the most authoritative we will ever have:

Friday 11/22:

> **"I didn't shoot President John F. Kennedy or Officer J. D. Tippit."**
>
> **"John Kennedy had a nice family."**
>
> **"My wife and I like the Presidential family. They are interesting people."** [3097]

Saturday 11/23:

> **"I didn't shoot John Kennedy. I didn't even know Governor John Connally had been shot."**
>
> **"I had nothing personal against John Kennedy."**
>
> **"Nothing irritated me about the President."** [3098]

Sunday 11/24:

> **"American people will soon forget the President was shot, but I didn't shoot him."**
>
> **"Since the President was killed, someone else would take his place, perhaps Vice-President Johnson. His views about Cuba would probably be largely the same as those of President Kennedy."**
>
> **"I did not kill President Kennedy or Officer Tippit. If you want me to cop out to hitting or pleading guilty to hitting a cop in the mouth when I was arrested, yeah, I plead guilty to that. But I do deny shooting both the President and Tippit."** [3099]

Marina Oswald before the shooting, reported by Jim Bishop in *The Day Kennedy Was Shot*

While watching TV of JFK in Dallas on November 22, "Mrs. Oswald felt excited about this because, as she said, her husband was a chronic critic of all things American, but he had read several favorable articles about Kennedy, aloud and translated them in his pidgin Russian. ... [She] recalled that, when speaking about the President of the United States, her husband had once observed that eliminating him would do no good, because the American system was so devised that the man who took his place would continue the same political policy." [3100]

Every quotation will be followed by its important sentence(s):

"[H]e had read several favorable articles about Kennedy, aloud and translated them in his pidgin Russian." "[O]bserved that eliminating [the President] would do no good"

Marina Oswald after the shooting, reported by Ruth Paine to the Warren Commission

Marina's best friend volunteered what happened the evening of the terrible day, November 22:

> "Mrs. PAINE. After we had returned from the police station ... had dinner, had talked for a little while in the living room, seen and sent home two Life reporters, and then were preparing for bed. And she and I talked a little bit, standing in the kitchen. She said ... in a spirit of confusion and with a stunned quality, I would say, to her voice and her manner. She said to me all the information she had or most of it that she had about the Kennedy family came to her through translation from Lee ... if Lee read in the paper something about the Kennedys, or if there was something in Time Magazine about them, he would translate to Marina, that is, put into Russian what was said in this news media, and, therefore, inform

her. And she thought that if he had had negative feelings about Kennedy, that this would have come along with the translation from Lee. But there was no such indication of dislike from Lee to her.

Mr. JENNER [assistant counsel]. It has impressed you to the point at which you wish to relate it here. Why is that? You were relating it to what—to her groping as to why her husband committed this act?

Mrs. PAINE. Her wondering whether he could have, but not in a defensive way, but in this stunned way that I am trying to describe. ...

Mr. JENNER. That is, is it your concept that she was ruminating—how could he have said these things or called her attention to these things with respect to President Kennedy, and still have assassinated him?

Mrs. PAINE. Yes." [3101]

"[I]f he had had negative feelings about Kennedy ... this would have come along with the translation from Lee. But there was no such indication of dislike" "[H]ow could he have said these things or called her attention to these things with respect to President Kennedy, and still have assassinated him?"

Marina Oswald after the shooting, reported by Jim Bishop in *The Day Kennedy Was Shot*

On November 22, perhaps the same incident reported differently, but more likely later, just before taking a shower and setting her hair, "She wandered around the living room ... asking aloud what Lee could have 'against' President Kennedy. Nothing. That was the strange thing. He had read articles to her, translating into Russian as the avalanche of phrases and sentences tripped from the mind in English to the tongue in Russian, and she knew that he always injected his opinions. Marina tried to remember his rendition of these articles about John F. Kennedy. He had said nothing critical about the man. If he felt no hatred for the man, then he could not have killed him. The motive, the pressure, the compulsion were not present." [3102]

"He had said nothing critical about the man. If he felt no hatred for the man, then he could not have killed him. The motive, the pressure, the compulsion were not present."

Marina Oswald in November 24 interview tape-recorded by Secret Service agents

On the day that her husband died, Marina was taken into protective custody by agents of the Secret Service — protective for the same reason as when Oswald killed Kennedy, no one knew if it was part of a larger plot. Now, the shocking shooting by Jack Ruby might be part of a larger scheme to kill Marina and her children. They treated her gently, with courtesy, much differently from her brusque handling by the FBI, as told in the next item. Because President Johnson specifically commissioned the FBI to be the primary gatherer-of-facts for the Warren Commission, almost all FBI interviews are of record in the *Warren Report* and its addenda, and the few interviews by others, such as the Secret Service in this case, are obscure.

In research for his moralistic book about the underpinnings and consequences of the Kennedy assassination, *JFK and the Unspeakable: Why He Died and Why It Matters*, James W. Douglass found the transcript of that interview:

"Marina Oswald had said, from the weekend of the assassination onward, that her husband had only a positive attitude toward President Kennedy. In an initial, tape-recorded interview by the Secret Service on Sunday evening, November 24, 1963, she was asked through an interpreter, Peter Paul Gregory, 'what Lee's feelings were for President Kennedy.' She answered: 'This is the truth. Lee never spoke bad about President Kennedy.' It was for this reason that Marina Oswald was certain her husband 'would not have been shooting at President Kennedy … Lee had nothing against President Kennedy.' She was asked again through the interpreter how she knew that. 'She said this, that Lee expressed to her that Kennedy was a good President.'" [3103]

"Marina … said … her husband had only a positive attitude toward President Kennedy." "This is the truth. Lee never spoke bad about President Kennedy." "Lee had nothing against President Kennedy." "Lee expressed … that Kennedy was a good President."

Marina Oswald in November 27 interview by FBI Special Agent James Hosty

On November 27, 1963, Marina was secluded at the Inn of the Six Flags in Arlington, midway between Dallas and Fort Worth. The Dallas FBI office sent the agent who had held the Oswald case file to interview her. Hosty (more quotes from him are below under his name) wrote that when the interpreter introduced him, "Marina … recognized me immediately. Her expression went cold and her spine went rigid. [An interpreter told him] 'She said she already knows you because you have been out to her home before the assassination.'" [3104] Lee had taught her to mistrust the FBI, and she felt bullied by FBI agents on and after November 22. The interview went downhill quickly, but at least provided this within Hosty's FBI report:

> "Marina Oswald then stated she was tired of answering questions. When told that the Government only wanted the facts, she stated she had the same facts as everyone else and no other. Marina Oswald was then asked if she ever had any conversations with her husband about former President John F. Kennedy. Marina Oswald stated 'No.' She was then asked if her husband, Lee Oswald, ever indicated in any way that he intended to kill former President Kennedy. She stated 'No, I feel he did not do it because he never spoke against President Kennedy at any time.' When asked if he had ever said anything against Texas Governor John Connally, she stated she could not recall any statements that Lee Oswald made against Texas Governor John Connally. When asked if Lee Oswald could have had a grudge against Texas Governor Connally, she stated she did not know. Marina Oswald then stated 'I swear before God that Lee Oswald did not intend to kill President Kennedy.' When asked if she believed in God, Marina Oswald stated she has believed in God since the death of her mother. When asked if she was a Christian, she said 'Yes.'" [3105]

"[Marina] was then asked if … Lee … ever indicated in any way that he intended to kill former President Kennedy. She stated 'No, I feel he did not do it because he never spoke against President Kennedy at any time.'" "Marina … then stated 'I swear before God that Lee Oswald did not intend to kill President Kennedy.'"

Marina Oswald in November 30 interview by two other FBI agents

Three days later, eight days after the shooting, Marina was interviewed by two FBI agents she had not previously met, one of whom was Anatole A. Boguslav, a Russian speaker. This interview went much better than Hosty's, above. Marina told them of her excitement about Kennedy coming to Dallas, then branched into what they reported thus:

> "Mrs. Oswald said she liked President Kennedy and Jackie Kennedy because both of them appeared, in their photographs, to be very sympathetic people. She said that she would often have Oswald read the captions under photographs of President Kennedy and Jackie. She said she admired them both. She stated she has asked Oswald on one occasion what kind of a President Mr. Kennedy was and he had replied that Kennedy was a good President. She said Oswald never gave any indication whatsoever that he intended any harm to the President.

She said she feels intuitively that if Oswald was trying to kill the President, that one shot would have been enough; and she feels, therefore, that he might have been aiming at the other person (Governor Connally). She said Oswald never mentioned any possible plans that he might have about assassinating the President. She said she cannot understand this thing." [3106]

"Oswald ... replied that Kennedy was a good President." "Oswald never gave any indication whatsoever that he intended any harm to the President."

Marina Oswald in testimony to the Warren Commission, #1 of 7

In February 1964, Marina Oswald was called to be the Warren Commission's first witness. On the second day, general counsel J. Lee Rankin asked: "Did he ever say anything about President Kennedy?", to which she responded: "No. At least—I was always interested in President Kennedy and had asked him many times to translate articles in a newspaper or magazine for me, and he always had something good to say. He translated it, but never did comment on it. At least in Lee's behavior—from Lee's behavior I cannot conclude that he was against the President, and therefore the thing is incomprehensible to me." [3107]

"[H]e always had something good to say." "At least ... from Lee's behavior I cannot conclude that he was against the President, and therefore the thing is incomprehensible to me."

Marina Oswald in testimony to the Warren Commission, #2 of 7

Later in her February 1964 testimony, Marina was again asked to give her impression of Lee's attitude toward Kennedy. She replied: "[W]hen I found out that Lee had shot at the President, for me this was surprising. And I didn't believe it. I didn't believe for a long time that Lee had done that. That he had wanted to kill Kennedy—because perhaps Walker was there again, perhaps he wanted to kill him." [3108] In her final testimony, seven months later, she volunteered: "When the assassination of President Kennedy took place, I was asking people whether ... General Walker was with President Kennedy. It perhaps was a silly question, but I thought that he—" [3109] and then a Senator interrupted.

"I didn't believe for a long time that Lee had [shot at the President]. That he had wanted to kill Kennedy ..."

Marina Oswald in testimony to the Warren Commission, #3 of 7

On the last of her first sessions, the long days of testimony in February 1964, when counsel had finished his prepared questions, the commissioners were invited ask theirs. Representative and House Majority Whip Hale Boggs of Louisiana initiated this colloquy:

"Representative BOGGS. During the weeks and months prior to the assassination ... did you ever at any time hear your late husband express any hostility towards President Kennedy?

Mrs. OSWALD. No.

Representative BOGGS. What motive would you ascribe to your husband in killing President Kennedy?

Mrs. OSWALD. As I saw the documents that were being read to me, I came to the conclusion that he wanted in any—by any means, good or bad, to get into history. But now that I have heard a part of the translation of some of the documents, I think that there was some political foundation to it, a foundation of which I am not aware.

Representative BOGGS. By that, do you mean that your husband acted in concert with someone else?

Mrs. OSWALD. No, only alone.

Representative BOGGS. You are convinced that his action was his action alone, that he was influenced by no one else?

Mrs. OSWALD. Yes, I am convinced. ... No one knows the truth, no one can read someone else's thoughts, as I could not read Lee's thoughts. But that is only my opinion." [3110]

"'[D]id ... your late husband express any hostility towards President Kennedy?' 'No.'"

Marina Oswald in testimony to the Warren Commission, #4 of 7

Called back in June 1964, Marina was questioned this time by commissioner Allen W. Dulles, retired Director of Central Intelligence:

"Mr. DULLES. I am just asking questions. Will you say here that he never did make any statement against President Kennedy?

Mrs. OSWALD. Never.

Mr. DULLES. Did he ever make any statement about him of any kind?

Mrs. OSWALD. He used to read and translate articles from the newspaper about Kennedy to me and from magazines, favorable articles about Kennedy. He never commented on them and he never discussed them in any way but because of his translations and his reading to me he always had a favorable feeling about President Kennedy because he always read these favorably inclined articles to me. He never said that these articles never were true, that he was a bad President or anything like that." [3111]

"[H]e always had a favorable feeling about President Kennedy because he always read these favorably inclined articles to me."

Marina Oswald in testimony to the Warren Commission, #5 of 7

This author read all of Marina's testimony, hundreds of pages, and thought he had noted all instances of her being questioned about Lee's attitude toward JFK, but apparently I missed one. In his book *Portrait of the Assassin*, commissioner Gerald Ford reported this colloquy:

"Question. Did your husband make any comments about President Kennedy on that evening, of the twenty-first [of November, the night before the shooting]?

Mrs. OSWALD. No.

Question. Had your husband at any time that you can recall said anything against President Kennedy?

Mrs. OSWALD. I don't remember any—ever having said that. I don't know. He never told me that.

Question. So apparently he didn't indicate any approval or disapproval, as far as he was concerned, of President Kennedy?

Mrs. OSWALD. Yes, that is correct. The President is the President. In my opinion, he never wanted to overthrow him. At least he never showed me that. He never indicated that he didn't want that President." [3112]

"'Had your husband at any time that you can recall said anything against President Kennedy?' 'I don't remember any— He never told me that.'" "'[H]e didn't indicate any approval or disapproval ... of President Kennedy?' '[T]hat is correct. ... He never indicated that he didn't want that President.'"

Marina Oswald in testimony to the Warren Commission, #6 of 7

In September 1964, Marina Oswald testified a final time to the Warren Commission, largely for the benefit of commissioners who had not been present during her previous appearances, including Senator John Sherman Cooper of Kentucky:

"Senator COOPER. [Y]ou testified that many times or a number of times he read you articles about President Kennedy?

Mrs. OSWALD. Yes.

Senator COOPER. And said at one time, discussing President Kennedy's father, that he had made his money through wine and he had a great deal of money, and that enabled him to educate his sons and to give them a start. I want you to remember and tell the Commission if he did ever express any hatred or dislike for President Kennedy. You have several times—not changed—but you have told the Commission things you did not tell them when first asked. Now, if he did speak to you about President Kennedy, we think you should tell the Commission.

Mrs. OSWALD. I don't think he ever expressed hatred toward President Kennedy, but perhaps he expressed jealousy, not only jealousy, but envy, but perhaps he envied, because he said, 'Whoever has money has it easy.' That was his general attitude. It was not a direct quotation.

Representative [Hale] BOGGS [of Louisiana]. Pursuing this—I asked you that very question in Washington back in February, and the answer was 'No.' I asked you whether or not your husband ever expressed hostility toward President Kennedy—is your answer still 'No'?

Mrs. OSWALD. My answer is 'No.' He never expressed himself anything against President Kennedy, anything detrimental toward him. What I told them generally before, I am repeating now too." [3113]

"He never expressed himself anything against President Kennedy, anything detrimental toward him."

Marina Oswald in testimony to the Warren Commission, #7 of 7

A few minutes later, their *Report* almost written and to be published in only three weeks, the commissioners asked a final few clean-up, clear-up questions. With no question or preamble, Marina exploded this eleventh-hour grenade: "I feel in my own mind that Lee did not have President Kennedy as a prime target when he assassinated him." Representative Hale Boggs asked, "Well, who was it?" Marina: "I think it was Connally. That's my personal opinion that he perhaps was shooting at Governor Connally, the Governor of Texas." [3114] Several more questions followed to be certain of what she was saying — two translators were being used. Her testimony became completely clear when Marina very carefully said: "On the basis of all the available facts, I have no doubt in my mind that Lee Oswald killed President Kennedy. At the same time, I feel in my own mind as far as I am concerned, I feel that Lee—that my husband perhaps intended to kill Governor Connally instead of President Kennedy." [3115]

Senator Richard Russell, chairing the session, was perturbed by this testimony, not contained in Marina's previous sessions. He became an inquisitor, adversely confrontational in asking several questions about Oswald's views on Connally. Marina maintained that Oswald had reason to dislike Connally. Without being asked at this time about the President, she volunteered: "[B]ut actually, I didn't think that he had any idea concerning President Kennedy." [3116] This is the end of what she said to the Commission regarding Kennedy. Her testimony about Lee's view of Connally is in Chapter 16 – REGARDING CONNALLY. All the relevant testimony from this important commission session is printed in full in Chapter 21 – OTHERS ON THIS TRAIL.

"I didn't think that he had any idea concerning President Kennedy."

<u>Marina Oswald</u> in 1977 through biographer Priscilla Johnson McMillan in *Marina and Lee*

"In the summer of 1963 both Lee and Marina, like so many others in America, had special feelings about the Kennedys. The names of the President and his wife were a staple item of their household conversation. ... As for the President, Lee said that he was Roman Catholic, one of a large family of brothers and sisters, a Democrat, and that his father was a millionaire who made money in the whiskey business. 'His papa bought him the presidency,' Lee remarked, and to Marina's surprise she failed to detect resentment in the way he said it. 'Money paves the way to everything here,' Lee added, and she thought she did hear resentment in that remark—not against the President but against capitalism. Lastly, he told her that in spite of his father's help, Kennedy was equipped to be President and deserved it." [3117]

"Marina got the impression that her husband liked and approved of the President and believed that for the United States in 1963, John F. Kennedy was the best President the country could hope to have. His only reservation seemed to be that socialism was a better system. Lee did say that some critics blamed Kennedy for 'losing' Cuba. He added, however, that Kennedy would like to pursue a better, more gentle policy toward Cuba but was not free to do as he wished. A President, he explained, had to reckon with the opinions of others." [3118]

"Kennedy was equipped to be President and deserved it." "[Lee] liked and approved of the President and believed that for the United States in 1963, John F. Kennedy was the best President the country could hope to have."

<u>Marina Oswald</u>, reported by Priscilla Johnson McMillan in 1977 biography *Marina and Lee*

In the *Epilogue* of her biography of the two Oswalds, McMillan noted after spending months working with Marina: "She, too, has been alone for years with the question, Why? Why did Lee do it? For the overwhelming fact, the fact she mentions again and again, was that Lee liked President Kennedy. He frequently said that for the United States at this moment of its history, Kennedy was the best possible leader, just as Khrushchev was for Russia. Whenever Marina pointed out how handsome the President was, Lee agreed with her. And when she mentioned how beautiful Mrs. Kennedy was, he agreed again. He agreed, moreover, without the special edge of reserve that told her he was thinking something else. And when the Kennedys' baby died in the summer of 1963, he had been as upset as she." [3119]

"[T]he overwhelming fact ... she mentions again and again, was that Lee liked President Kennedy. He frequently said that for the United States at this moment of its history, Kennedy was the best possible leader"

<u>Marina Oswald Porter</u>, quoted by Priscilla Johnson McMillan in *Marina and Lee*

On the last page of her 23-page *Epilogue* after 558 pages of biography, McMillan writes: "Marina is still puzzled as to why her husband killed the President. 'But he liked Kennedy!' she protests to this day." [3120]

"But he liked Kennedy!"

Marina Oswald Porter in her statement added to 1978 paperback edition of *Marina and Lee*

Priscilla Johnson McMillan obtained full cooperation from Marina, now Mrs. Kenneth Porter, while writing the biography *Marina and Lee*, published in hardcover in 1977. As was then usual, a Bantam paperback edition appeared in 1978, with an introductory "Statement" by Marina.[3121] It included:

"I believe that Lee acted alone in this murder and shot the President, ironically, a man whom he respected and admired."

Marina Porter in August 1978 deposition to the House Select Committee on Assassinations

The latter part of Chapter 8 – COMMISSION, CRITICS, REHASHES tells the sad story of the U.S. House of Representatives Select Committee on Assassinations. Marina was questioned in Washington on August 9, 1978, by counsel James Wolf. When he introduced her as "Marina Oswald Porter", her attorney asserted that "Mrs. Porter's name now is Mrs. Kenneth Porter or Mrs. Marina Porter." On the sixty-third page of her transcribed testimony:

> "Q [Mr. WOLF]. When he [Lee] came on Thursday night, the night prior to the assassination … Did he discuss President Kennedy that evening, his visit to Dallas?
>
> A [Mrs. PORTER]. I tried to discuss it with him. I was very enthusiastic about it, over it, and I tried to get as much information from him as I could and he refused to talk about it.
>
> Q. Was that unusual?
>
> A. Judging right now, yes.
>
> Q. Did he usually want to discuss President Kennedy?
>
> A. Yes.
>
> Q. What would his usual comments about President Kennedy be?
>
> A. Well, my impression was that he liked him very well.
>
> Q. Did he mention Governor Connally that night?
>
> A. No.
>
> …
>
> Q. Lee's attitude toward President Kennedy was certainly different than his attitude toward General Walker, am I correct?
>
> A. Yes.
>
> Q. Had you had any prior indication of any dislike for President Kennedy on his behalf?
>
> A. No; that is what is so strange about the whole event." [3122]

"'What would his usual comments about President Kennedy be?' '[M]y impression was that he liked him very well.'" "'Lee's attitude toward President Kennedy was certainly different than his attitude toward General Walker, am I correct?' 'Yes.'" "'Had you had any prior indication of any dislike for President Kennedy on his behalf?' 'No; that is what is so strange about the whole event.'"

Marina Porter in September 1978 testimony to the House Select Committee on Assassinations

Marina was then questioned in Washington for 1½ days on September 13 and 14, 1978, by Representatives and committee attorneys. All testimony pertaining to Lee's views on Kennedy is transcribed below. In the fourteen years since appearing before the Warren Commission, Marina had learned good English and had no need for translators. The first questions on our subject were asked by James E. McDonald, staff counsel for the committee:

"Q [Mr. MCDONALD]. Can you recall Oswald expressing at this time, soon after your marriage but … prior to your return to the United States, do you recall him expressing any views about the United States and its political system, either pro or con, for or against—

A [Mrs. PORTER]. No.

Q. [continuing]. And specifically regarding John Kennedy?

A.   What I learned about John Kennedy it was only through Lee practically, and he always spoke very complimentary about the President. He was very happy when John Kennedy was elected.

Q. And you are saying while you were still in the Soviet Union he was very complimentary about John Kennedy?

A.   Yes, it seemed like he was talking about how young and attractive the President of the United States is.

Q. Can you recall during this time when he ever expressed any contrary views about Kennedy?

A. Never." [3123]

Marina's next questioning that elicited testimony about Lee's view of Kennedy came from U.S. Representative Lunsford Richardson "Rich" Preyer of North Carolina, who had been a state and U.S. District Court judge, and was thus skilled at asking good questions:

"Q [Mr. PREYER]. Did Lee ever talk about United States politics after you were married, that is, did he talk about officials of the United States, such as the President or the Secretary of State or, did he talk about policies of the U.S. Government?

A [Mrs. PORTER].   If he did, he wasn't talking to me about it, because I wasn't really interested in his political view or anybody's political view.

Q. Specifically did he ever talk about President Kennedy?

A. Whatever he said about President Kennedy, it was only good, always." [3124]

Counsel McDonald returned and asked Marina about Lee's "friendship" with White Russian count and immigrant George De Mohrenschildt, who "on the day he agreed to an interview with the [HSCA] was found dead of a gunshot to the mouth, an apparent suicide.": [3125]

"Q [Mr. MCDONALD]. Did Lee and DeMohrenschildt ever talk politics in your presence?

A [Mrs. PORTER]. They probably have.

Q. Can you recall any such conversations?

A. No.

Q.   Can you recall in your presence whether George DeMohrenschildt and Lee ever spoke about President Kennedy?

A. If I say right now that, yes, I do, they probably talked about, and then you ask me about the details which I cannot remember, but, yes, the name John Kennedy was mentioned in their conversation.

Q. Can you recall in what context? In other words, were they speaking favorably of Kennedy?

A.   I think so. Well, I recall that George DeMohrenschildt told me once that when he was younger, I mean he knew Jackie Kennedy before she was married to John Kennedy when she was a young lady and spoke very nicely about her.

Q. And how about Lee's views at the time? Do you recall whether they were ever engaged in argument?

A. I do not recall ever hearing Lee talking badly about John Kennedy or Kennedy family." [3126]

Representative Preyer returned to ask another question:

"Q [Mr. PREYER]. We have asked you at various times what he said about President Kennedy or his family and other political figures. At this time in New Orleans did he have anything to say about President Kennedy or his family?

A [Mrs. PORTER]. During the New Orleans period Mrs. Kennedy was expecting a child and Lee told me about that. He was quite concerned about her health and he informed me that

456

she has a few miscarriages before and he was hoping nothing would happen to this baby. I think he said the baby died." [3127]

The committee's chairman, Representative Louis Stokes of Ohio, had presided throughout her testimony, and now asked Marina questions beginning with Lee's attitude toward Kennedy, then moved to Connally, to be shown in Chapter 16 – REGARDING CONNALLY. Here is the portion REGARDING KENNEDY:

> "Q [Chairman STOKES]. Mrs. Porter, throughout your testimony here today you have indicated that Lee Harvey Oswald always spoke of liking President Kennedy; is that correct?
>
> A [Mrs. PORTER]. That is true, sir.
>
> Q. You never heard him speak of him in a hostile manner?
>
> A. No.
>
> Q. Then is it consistent, in your opinion, then, that a man who spoke of President Kennedy as he did also was accused of having killed the President?
>
> A. That is very hard for me to comprehend." [3128]

Chairman Stokes then asked about Lee's animus toward Connally, to be picked up from this point in Chapter 16 – REGARDING CONNALLY.

"[H]e always spoke very complimentary about the President." "He was very happy when John Kennedy was elected." "Whatever he said about President Kennedy, it was only good, always." "'[W]ere [Lee and friend] speaking favorably of Kennedy?' 'I think so.'" "I do not recall ever hearing Lee talking badly about John Kennedy or Kennedy family." "He was quite concerned about [Mrs. Kennedy's] health and ... he was hoping nothing would happen to this baby." "'Lee ... always spoke of liking President Kennedy; is that correct?' 'That is true, sir.'" "'You never heard [Lee] speak of [Kennedy] in a hostile manner?' 'No.'"

Marina Oswald Porter in 1991 interview by Harrison Edward Livingstone

Warren Commission critic Livingstone reports a telephone interview with Marina in his 1992 book *High Treason 2: The Great Cover-Up: The Assassination of President John F. Kennedy*. He had sent her his earlier book *High Treason*. In May 1991 she phoned him, saying it was easier for her to speak English than to write it. He noted: "Marina has led a quiet life since the assassination, being a housewife, and raising two intelligent daughters. She was fortunate in finding a husband, a prosperous businessman, who takes good care of her and protects her. Meanwhile, she reads what she can on the assassination and gradually fills in some of the blanks in her understanding of what happened during those terrible days in 1963 ..." He then reports this to-the-point conversation:

> "[Livingstone:] 'So in your mind you didn't feel that he was capable of shooting at the President?'
>
> [Marina:] 'For twenty-five years I tried to find out the reason. I digged into everything, including my conscience. I tried to find the reason why would he do such a thing, and I could not. So after I made my speculations maybe because of communism or this and that. Because it didn't make any logical explanation to me why John Kennedy, because he adored that man. That I would never ever believe.'
>
> [Livingstone:] 'You say he adored John Kennedy?'
>
> [Marina:] 'Oh, yes.'" [3129]

"'[H]e adored that man.' 'You say he adored John Kennedy?' 'Oh, yes.'"

Marina Porter in 1991 conversation with Cyril Wecht, M.D.

In November 1991, as reported in Chapter 11 – FAILURE, Marina Porter talked by telephone with Dr. Cyril Wecht, a pathologist who had extensively studied the Kennedy case.

She said: **"The Lee I knew really loved JFK."** [3130]

Marguerite Oswald (the mother) in testimony to the Warren Commission

As her outrageously disconnected and self-serving testimony neared an end, the chief counsel ticked down a list of questions, including this:

"Mr. RANKIN. Did you ever hear your son say anything for or against President Kennedy?
Mrs. OSWALD. While Marina and Lee were in my home that month, and I had a television—
Mr. RANKIN. About what time was that?
Mrs. OSWALD. This was July, 1962—when they stayed the month with me. Yes, they were delighted with President Kennedy, both.
Mr. RANKIN. What did they say about him?
Mrs. OSWALD. Nothing political — just 'Like President Kennedy.' He was telling Marina about President Kennedy. 'I like President Kennedy' — 'I like, too.'" [3131]

"[T]hey were delighted with President Kennedy"   "He was telling Marina ... 'I like President Kennedy'"

Robert Oswald (the brother) in testimony to the Warren Commission

The next-older brother, the only family member who had stayed in touch with Lee, was questioned by the former Director of Central Intelligence, Allen Dulles:

"Mr. DULLES. This question of mine covers the whole period of your relationship with your brother. Do you recall during that entire period, up to November 22, that your brother made any comments with regard to President Kennedy of a derogatory nature or character or of any other character? Did he ever discuss the President with you during the whole period? Of course, he was only President for the last 3 years.
Mr. OSWALD. No, sir; I do not recall at any time that he ever mentioned President Kennedy's name or referred to him in any way, either pro or con." [3132]

Robert Oswald recalling 1963 in his 1967 book *Lee*

The older brother received a phone call at his Acme Brick Company office on the afternoon of the shooting, asking him to come to the FBI office in Dallas. There, he was first asked if he wanted an attorney ("No") and was his brother's name Harvey Lee Oswald or Lee Harvey Oswald? Then, the first substantive question: "Have you ever heard Lee express any hostility toward the President?" He answered simply: "No, I haven't." [3133]

Samuel B. Ballen in testimony to the Warren Commission   (We now go in alphabetic order.)

Ballen, a Dallas businessman, was called before the Warren Commission because in 1962 he had interviewed Oswald, at the request of his "close friend" George De Mohrenschildt, to see if he could give the recently-arrived unemployed man a job in any of his companies. He spent two full hours with Lee whom he liked at the outset, but then judged to be a "hardheaded", "negative", "sarcastic" "rugged individualist" unfit for teamwork, so had no interest in hiring or helping him. Obviously, Ballen was a skilled and attentive interviewer. Because what is set forth below is his subjective judgment, rather than an objective conveyance of Oswald's words, here first is a portion of his testimony that buttresses Mr. Ballen's credibility: On November 22, learning that Oswald had been arrested, immediately "I told my wife that if you lined up 50 individuals, the one person who would stand out as being suspicious or strange would be Lee Harvey Oswald." [3134] So, he's a good judge! During his testimony in March 1964:

"Mr. LIEBELER. Did he ever demonstrate or indicate to you any particular hostility toward any official of the U.S. Government?

Mr. BALLEN. None whatsoever; none whatsoever. My own subjective reaction is, that the sum total of these 2 hours that I spent with him, I just can't see his having any venom towards President Kennedy.

Mr. LIEBELER. Did President Kennedy come up in any way during the course of your discussion?

Mr. BALLEN. No; it did not. The sum total of his reaction, limited as it was that I got from this individual, is that this man would have—this is subjective, I can put no concrete support in there, but I would have thought that this is an individual who felt warmly towards President Kennedy.

Mr. LIEBELER. You drew that inference simply as a general impression based on the 2 hours that you spent conversing with him ?

Mr. BALLEN. That's correct.

Mr. LIEBELER. Could you—and you can't pinpoint anything specifically that led you to that conclusion?

Mr. BALLEN. No, sir.

Mr. LIEBELER. Did you have any discussion, or was the name of Governor Connally mentioned?

Mr. BALLEN. No; it was not." [3135] [A]

"I just can't see his having any venom towards President Kennedy." "I would have thought that this is an individual who felt warmly towards President Kennedy."

FBI Special Agent James Bookhout in testimony to the Warren Commission

Special Agent Bookhout of the Dallas office had been with the FBI 22 years. On leave on November 22, he stood along Main Street to watch the motorcade, but because of the crowd could not see the President. Hearing sirens, he learned from a man with a transistor radio that shots had been fired, so he walked toward the office and was sent to the police homicide and robbery bureau to be liaison between FBI and DPD. When Oswald was brought in, he joined FBI agent Hosty (below) in listening. Excerpts on the subject at hand:

"Mr. STERN. Was he asked whether he had shot the President, or Officer Tippit?

Mr. BOOKHOUT. Yes; he was asked that, and denied shooting either one of them, or knowing anything about it.

...

Mr. STERN. When he was asked about involvement in the assassination of President Kennedy, or the shooting of Officer Tippit, how would you describe his denials?

Mr. BOOKHOUT. Well, I don't know exactly how to describe it, but as I recall, he spoke very loudly. In other words, he was—he gave an emphatic denial, that is about all I can recall on it." [3136]

[A] The last question and answer are displayed to show how witnesses get into the "Other witnesses" listings below and in the next chapter, REGARDING CONNALLY, if they are asked and say "No".

Bookhout also testified about Oswald's responses to questions the next day, Saturday:

"Mr. STERN. In your report before this interview you mentioned that he again denied shooting President Kennedy, and apparently said that he didn't know until then that Governor Connally had been shot?

Mr. BOOKHOUT. That's correct. That was his statement, that he denied shooting President John F. Kennedy on November 22, 1963, and commented that he did not know that Governor John Connally had been shot.

Mr. STERN. Did you form any impression about whether he was genuinely surprised? Did he look genuinely surprised to you, or how did you feel about that? I am just asking for your impression. If you don't have one, say so.

Mr. BOOKHOUT. No; I have no impression on that. I arrived at no conclusion." [3137]

"[H]e ... denied shooting either one of them, or knowing anything about it." "[A]sked about involvement in the assassination of President Kennedy, or the shooting of Officer Tippit ... he gave an emphatic denial" "[H]e denied shooting President John F. Kennedy on November 22, 1963, and commented that he did not know that Governor John Connally had been shot."

Thomas G. Buchanan in his book *Who Killed Kennedy?*

"No personal affront had been inflicted on Lee Oswald by the President himself, or by the office that he represented. The United States had given him the money that he asked for, to return from Russia and to bring his wife and family back with him; it had given him a passport to go back there, if it pleased him; nothing Oswald had requested of the government had been denied him." [3138]

"No personal affront had been inflicted on Lee Oswald by the President himself ... nothing Oswald had requested of the government had been denied him."

George Sergei De Mohrenschildt in 1964 testimony to the Warren Commission

This man strode through life, as my mother would say, "full of himself!" One of the D-FW Russian emigres aptly cast him: "Actually, he should have lived 300 or 400 years ago and been an explorer or pirate or something like that", [3139] but he was a petroleum geologist and engineer. Among the many called before the Commission, George was especially important for two reasons. One lady reported that Marina said that both De Mohrenschildts, George and his fourth (was it third? — there is confusion) wife Jeanne were "our best friends in Dallas." [3140] During his testimony, when told that Marina "said Lee liked you", he replied "I am sorry that he did, but, obviously he did. ... He did not have any friends, you see. Maybe he identified me not as a Russian, because I have not much Russian blood in me anyway. Maybe he identified me as some sort of an internationalist, American. I am trying to think of other friends that he had. I cannot recall, myself, a friend of his, actually. I could not say that. He could be my son in age,  you see. He is just a kid for me, with whom I played around. Sometimes I was curious to see what went on in his head. But I certainly would not call myself a friend of his." [3141] [3142]

James Reston, Jr. sized up the two: "The relationship between de Mohrenshildt [*sic*] and Oswald became a sick one as de Mohrenshildt acted out the role of the overbearing surrogate father who secretly despises and ridicules his adopted son. But Oswald had at last found someone to listen to his half-baked opinions and to joust with him." [3143]

Asked if he knew anything about "Lee possibly inflicting some harm on Vice President Nixon", he responded:

> Mr. DE MOHRENSCHILDT. It doesn't ring a bell at all. But what I wanted to underline, that was always amazing to me, that as far as I am concerned he was an admirer of President Kennedy.
>
> Mr. JENNER. I was going to ask you about that. Tell me the discussions you had in that connection. Did you have some discussions with him?
>
> Mr. DE MOHRENSCHILDT. Just occasional sentences, you know. I think once I mentioned to him that I met Mrs. Kennedy when she was a child you know, she was a very strong-willed child, very intelligent and very attractive child you see, and a very attractive family, and I thought that Kennedy was doing a very good job with regard to the racial problem, you know. We never discussed anything else. And he also agreed with me, 'Yes, yes, yes; I think it is an excellent President, young, full of energy, full of good ideas.'" [3144]

After the assassination, he wrote a note of sympathy to long-time acquaintance Mrs. Janet Lee Auchincloss, mother of Jacqueline Kennedy. A revealing part was: "Both my wife and I tried to help poor Marina, who could not speak any English, was mistreated by her husband. She and the baby were malnourished and sickly." [3145] During testimony, he was asked to explain a remark in the note: "Somehow, I still have a lingering doubt, notwithstanding all the evidence, of Oswald's guilt." He explained: "Unless the man is guilty, I will not be his judge—unless he is proven to be guilty by the court, I will not be his judge, and there will be always a doubt in my mind, and throughout my testimony I explained sufficiently why I have those doubts. And mainly because he did not have any permanent animosity for President Kennedy. That is why I have the doubts." [3146]

"I think it is an excellent President, young, full of energy, full of good ideas." "[H]e did not have any permanent animosity for President Kennedy."

George De Mohrenschildt in a manuscript he wrote shortly before his 1977 suicide

If someone has to play the part of "friend of Oswald in America", we must assign that role to George De Mohrenschildt — there are no other candidates. The characterization is not without controversy. Harrison E. Livingstone spoke of "DeMohrenschildt, the fabled Russian count and Texas oilman long connected to intelligence operations who befriended and respected Oswald." [3147] On the contrary, James Reston, Jr. disagreed:

> "After the assassination, George De Mohrenschildt, who despised Oswald, was the best witness on the question of what moved— and did not move—Oswald. De Mohrenschildt was overcome with guilt for his trifling with Oswald, and in 1977 he committed suicide after proclaiming that he was a moral conspirator in the assassination of Kennedy." [3148]

I agree with Reston's evaluation. George believed he had a superior intellect, and enjoyed leading-on and toying with Oswald. When asked to testify by the House Select Committee on Assassinations, De Mohrenschildt put a pistol into his mouth and blew out his brain. Deprived of his much-wanted testimony, the committee was compensated by discovering and printing a 246-page manuscript typed by De Mohrenschildt. Although a draft containing some errors and misspellings, it stands absolutely without peer as a first-hand study and analysis of Oswald. Here are George De Mohrenschildt's observations of what Lee thought of President Kennedy:

"[W]hen I was in the hot water because of my friendship with Lee, a friend of mine testified: 'George always liked stray dogs and stray people.' Many people considered Lee a miserable misfit, an insult to the American way of life, and completely disregarded him." [3149]

"Fortunately I remember well so much of what he said. I remember distinctly that one of those evenings together we talked of John F. Kennedy. Lee liked him and certainly did not include him among those despicable politicians he mentioned before. I showed him [the] President's picture on the cover of Time Magazine and Lee said 'how handsome he looks, what open and sincere features he has and how different he looks from the other ratty politicos.'

"I don't remember exactly the words but Lee spoke most kindly of the gradual improvement of the racial relations in the United States, attributing this improvement to the President. Like most young people he was attracted by the Kennedy's personality but he also knew that JFK's father was a rascal who made money off whisky and being bullish on the stock-market which is betting against this country's economy." [3150]

"One of the reasons we agree with Mrs. Marguerite Oswald that her son was probably innocent of Kennedy's assassination - and we insisted on this during the Warren Committee [sic] interviews (although it was never brought up publicly) - was the following: Lee actually admired President Kennedy in his own reserved way. One day we discussed with Lee Kennedy's efforts to bring peace to the world and to end the cold war. 'Great, great!' exclaimed Lee. "If he succeeds, he will be the greatest president in the history of this country.'" [3151]

George and Lee loved to tell each other jokes, mostly about the rigors of life under the Soviet bureaucracy, but sometimes about America, such as: "Kennedy had a terrible nightmare. He wakes up Jacquie: 'Honey, what a terrible thing, I dreamed I was spending my own money, not government's.' Again we laughed, but without resentment, we both likes [sic] President Kennedy. So I finished my foolish jokes by this one: 'John Kennedy runs to his mother at night. 'Mama! Mama! Help! Bobby tries to run MY country.'' I think it was at that time that I told Lee that I had known Jacqueline Kennedy as a young girl, as well as her mother, father and all her relatives and how charming the whole family was." [3152]

"Very tired by our testimonies, we were invited after our ordeal to the luxurious house of Jacqueline Kennedy's mother and her step-father, Mr. Hugh Auchincloss ... in Georgetown. ... Eventually, we had to talk sadly about the assassination. Allan Dulles was there also and he asked me a few astute questions about Lee. One of them was, I remember, did Lee have a reason of hating President Kennedy? However, when I answered that he was rather an admirer of the dead President, everyone took my answer with a grain of salt. Again the overwhelming opinion was that Lee was the sole assassin.

"Finally both Jeanne [Mrs. De Mohrenschildt] and Janet (Mrs. Auchincloss) got very emotional, embraced each other and cried together, one over the loss of her son-in-law, another over the loss of a great president she admired so much. ... [W]e were still in the Auchincloss' luxurious mansion, about ready to leave. 'Incidentally,' said Mrs. Auchincloss coldly, 'my daughter Jacqueline never wants to see you again because you were close to her husband's assassin.' 'It's her privilege,' I answered." [3153]

"Lee Harvey Oswald might have been sometimes violent, like almost anyone amongst us, he might kill a person he hated, he might have been violent to a racist or a pseudo-racist, to someone who might want to hurt him and his family. But to assassinate the President he rather admired, just for the glory of it, is entirely foreign to his personality." [3154]

"Let us hope that this book, poorly written and disjointed, but sincere, will help to clear up our relationship with our dear, dead friend Lee." [3155] Thus ended the dead man's manuscript.

"Lee liked him and certainly did not include him among ... despicable politicians ..." "Lee said 'how handsome [Kennedy] looks, what open and sincere features he has and how different he looks from the other ratty politicos.'" "Lee spoke most kindly of the gradual improvement of the racial relations in the United States, attributing this improvement to the President." "Like most young people he was attracted by ... Kennedy's personality ..." "Lee actually admired President Kennedy in his own reserved way." "One day we discussed ... Kennedy's efforts to bring peace to the world and to end the cold war. 'Great! Great!' exclaimed Lee. 'If he succeeds, he'll be the greatest President in the history of this country.'" "[W]e both likes [sic] President Kennedy." "[H]e was rather an admirer of the dead President" "[T]o assassinate the President he rather admired, just for the glory of it, is entirely foreign to his personality."

Jeanne De Mohrenschildt in testimony to the Warren Commission

George's wife (pronounced Zhon) had been born in Manchuria to Russian parents. She was quickly interested in, and very kind to, the young Oswalds when they arrived in Texas. Having spent considerable time with them, Jeanne offered this reasoned assessment:

"Mrs. DE MOHRENSCHILDT. [I]t seems to be that everything went wrong for Lee, starting with his childhood, you know, and no matter what he did it was always a failure. So anything that seems to be President Kennedy touched was turning into gold, he was so successful in his marriage. You know he was such a wonderful President and he had health and public office, everything, you know, so it could be that in the bottom of Lee's heart was some antagonism, you know.

Mr. JENNER. Did you have that impression of the man?

Mrs. DE MOHRENSCHILDT. No, never at all.

Mr. JENNER. Did you have any impression that he was envious at any time?

Mrs. DE MOHRENSCHILDT. No, and in fact that is what doesn't make any sense, because I don't think he ever said anything against, and whatever the President was doing, Kennedy was doing, Lee was completely exactly with the same ideas, exactly. If he would shoot Walker that would be understandable, even if he would be shooting at Connally that is understandable, too." [3156]

...

"[H]e is completely in accord with President Kennedy's policy on the subject [of equality of rights]. That is why it doesn't make exactly sense. He has no reason whatsoever, to our knowledge [to be opposed to Kennedy]." [3157]

She was one of the first to recognize the incongruity of Oswald acting badly to his political soul mate Kennedy, thus suggesting the shooting would be much more understandable if the target had been General Walker (not present on November 22) or Governor Connally (sitting directly in line with President Kennedy).

"I don't think he ever said anything against, and whatever ... President ... Kennedy was doing, Lee was completely exactly with the same ideas, exactly." "[C]ompletely in accord with President Kennedy's policy" "[I]t doesn't make exactly sense. He has no reason whatsoever"

Captain J. W. "Will" Fritz in Dallas Police Headquarters on November 22–24, 1963

Fritz, "chief of the homicide and robbery bureau of the Dallas Police Department" [3158], was the "primary interrogator while Oswald was in police custody".[3159] "Fritz, who died in 1984, told the Warren Commission in 1964 he made no notes during the interrogation".[3160] However, "prior to testifying before the Commission, [Fritz and others] had prepared memoranda setting forth their recollections of the questioning of Oswald and his responses." [3161] On page 9 of 13 in his typed memo, Fritz wrote, "I asked him what he thought of President Kennedy and his family, and he said he didn't have any views on the President. He said, 'I like the President's family very well. I have my own view about national policies.'" [3162]

Unfortunately for learning the prisoner's motive, there is no record of anyone asking Oswald on November 22-24 what he thought of Connally. Commissioner Allen Dulles asked Fritz: "Did he say anything about Governor Connally?" to which the unfortunate answer was: "No, sir; I don't think I questioned him about the Governor at that time. I might have asked him at one time. I remember telling him at one time he shot the Governor." [3163] Dulles asked again in a different way — the same technique Fritz described to the Commission as an effective tool in questioning a reticent person: "Did he express any animosity against anyone, the President or the Governor or Walker or anybody?" to which Fritz responded: "No, sir; he did not." [3164]

In 1997 "Five pages of Fritz's notes were released ... by the Assassination Records Review Board. The notes were discovered among some of Fritz's belongings, which were donated to the board. ... The notes are only the second set of original, handwritten notes taken on the interrogation that have surfaced in 34 years. Earlier [in 1997], the board released notes made by former FBI agent James Hosty Jr., (below) who also questioned Oswald." [3165] Fritz's notes included these words: "Didn't own rifle ... to Marines says got usual medals ... Says nothing against Pres. ... denies shooting Pres. ... does not want to talk further." [3166]

"[H]e said he didn't have any views on the President." "I like the President's family very well. I have my own view about national politics." "Says nothing against Pres."

Detective L. C. Graves of Dallas in testimony to the Warren Commission

Graves worked on Captain Fritz's homicide squad. On the Sunday that Oswald will die, November 24, he and detective James Leavelle (below) brought the prisoner down from his fourth floor jail cell to Captain Fritz's third floor office. Graves left the office, returning when it was almost time to transfer Oswald to the county jail. He told the Warren Commission "Well, I walked in and [heard] Oswald say that— 'Well, people will soon forget that the President was shot.'" [3167] Counsel asked: "Was he asked ... whether or not he did it?" to which Graves answered: "Oh, yes; he was asked, but of course—He said no, he didn't shoot him." [3168] As they began to walk to the elevator, Lee wanted something over his tee-shirt. Graves had a shirt ready, but Lee insisted on a black sweater — causing the delay that leads to his death.[3169] Graves then held Oswald's left arm as they moved down and toward the car. In the famous photos (see pages 211 and 285), Jack Ruby kills Oswald by reaching in front of Graves (black suit, black hat), who then wrestled away the pistol after the one fatal shot.

"Well, people will soon forget that the President was shot." "He said no, he didn't shoot him."

Paul Roderick Gregory in testimony to the Warren Commission

As told in Chapter 5 – MISFIT, shortly after arriving in Fort Worth, Lee went to Peter Paul Gregory, a petroleum engineer born in Siberia, to get a recommendation as a translator. Peter then took his college-student son Paul to meet the Oswalds, and Paul went to their home about eight times for Russian lessons from Marina. He also drove them on Thanksgiving 1962 from Robert Oswald's home to the Fort Worth bus station. Paul was close to the couple in age, and in conversation learned much about Lee and his opinions, including this:

> "Mr. GREGORY. He always expressed a great admiration for Khrushchev. He seemed to think he was quite a brilliant man. ... And while we were on Khrushchev, whenever he would speak about Khrushchev, Kennedy would naturally come into mind, and he expressed admiration of Kennedy. Both he and Marina would say, 'Nice young man.' I never heard him say anything derogatory about Kennedy. He seemed to admire the man, because I remember they had a copy of Life magazine which was always in their living room, and it had Kennedy's picture on it, or I believe Kennedy or someone else, and he always expressed what I would interpret as admiration for Kennedy.
>
> Mr. LIEBELER. Can you recall any specific details concerning his remarks about Kennedy or the conversation that you had with him concerning Kennedy?
>
> Mr. GREGORY. No; just that one time, as I can remember in their apartment that we did look at this picture of Kennedy, and Marina said, 'He looks like a nice young man.' And Lee said something, yes, he is a good leader, or something, as I remember, was a positive remark about Kennedy.
>
> Mr. LIEBELER. He never expressed any adverse feelings or made any adverse remarks about President Kennedy in your presence?
>
> Mr. GREGORY. No." [3170]
>
> ...
>
> "Mr. LIEBELER. Did Oswald ever indicate to you that the world situation was not due to the people in the world, but was caused by the leaders in the various countries?
>
> Mr. GREGORY. I think so. Once or twice he made that exact statement, and I can't remember if it was Marina or Lee. That is the exact words.
>
> Mr. LIEBELER. Was that translated into any animosity against the leaders of the two countries, either Khrushchev or Kennedy?
>
> Mr. GREGORY. I could not say. I would not think so, because of what I have already said about the fact that Lee had expressed admiration of Khrushchev and had expressed that positive feeling toward Kennedy." [3171]

Forty-nine years later, shortly before the fiftieth anniversary of the assassination, among a frenzy of articles, books and movies, a piece by Paul Gregory appeared in the November 10, 2013, Sunday Magazine of *The New York Times* under the title "This Close to a Killer". Now the Cullen professor of economics at the University of Houston and a research fellow at the Hoover Institution at Stanford, he wrote of that first apartment on Elsbeth Street:

> "The Oswald living room was extraordinarily bare; there was a shabby sofa and chair and a worn coffee table where a copy of Time magazine featuring John F. Kennedy as its Man of the Year was prominently displayed. (The issue, which would curiously remain in the same place during all my visits, was dated Jan. 5, five months before the Oswalds' arrival in the U.S.) We sat there uncomfortably for some 20 to 30 minutes until Lee burst in the door, dressed in his customary simple slacks, a plaid shirt with open collar and sleeves rolled up to the elbows, carrying a stack of weighty books from the Fort Worth public library. The conversation segued to the Time cover; Marina ventured that the president appeared to be a nice man and that the

first lady, at least from the pictures she had seen, appeared quite glamorous. She also said that she seemed to be a good mother. Lee, in his curt way, agreed." [3172]

The magazine always on the table has morphed from the LIFE of Paul's Warren Commission testimony to TIME in his present memory, but he is reaffirming the brunt of his testimony, that Lee had not expressed any negativism about Kennedy.

"He seemed to admire the man" "[H]e always expressed what I would interpret as admiration for Kennedy" "Lee said … yes, he is a good leader … a positive remark about Kennedy" "[E]xpressed that positive feeling toward Kennedy" "Marina ventured that the president appeared to be a nice man … Lee, in his curt way, agreed."

FBI Agents James Hosty and James Bookhout of Dallas in report on November 23, 1963

These two from the Dallas FBI office listened to Captain Fritz's first questioning of Oswald on Friday afternoon, November 22. Their report, typed and signed the next day, contained this: "Oswald frantically denied shooting Dallas police officer Tippett [*sic*] or shooting President John F. Kennedy." [3173] When Hosty testified to the Warren Commission in May 1964, he was asked about "frantically" and said the word should have been "emphatically". [3174] He was then asked repeatedly, and affirmed every time, that both he and agent Bookhout had proofread and approved the report, and both somehow missed the wrong word. Bookhout, when he testified, said that report was primarily Hosty's, he had not paid particular attention, and now that he thought of it, "frantically would probably describe it". [3175] Corrected with Hosty's preference:

"Oswald emphatically denied shooting … Tippit or shooting President John F. Kennedy."

FBI Agent James Hosty in 1964 testimony to the Warren Commission

One of forty-plus agents in the FBI's Dallas office, Hosty became famous because he had been assigned to investigate and track Oswald before the shooting because of his defection to Russia, his return with a Russian wife, his Fair Play for Cuba activity in New Orleans, his visit to the Russian embassy in Mexico City, his correspondence with the Russian embassy in Washington, and his subscriptions to communist newspapers. Because he was responsible for Oswald's case, Hosty listened to the questioning on November 22. His testimony included:

> "Captain Fritz asked him if he always carried a pistol when he went to the movie, and he said he carried it because he felt like it. He admitted that he did have a pistol on him at the time of his arrest, in this theatre, in the Oak Cliff area of Dallas. He further admitted that he had resisted arrest and had received a bump and a cut as a result of his resisting of arrest. He then denied that he had killed Officer Tippit or President Kennedy." [3176]

"He then denied that he had killed Officer Tippit or President Kennedy."

James Hosty in his 1996 book *Assignment: Oswald*

Hosty's FBI report on November 23 (above, two up) was dictated on a very busy day and not carefully proofread. His testimony six months later to the Warren Commission (immediately above) was verbatim, without benefit of editing. Therefore, I believe the truest report of Captain Fritz's questioning of Oswald on November 22, three hours after the shooting, is presented in the book Hosty wrote with the assistance of his son, because he then had both his report and the Commission's 26 volumes for unhurried reference: "Fritz leaned in toward Oswald. 'Lee, did you shoot the president?' 'No. I emphatically deny that.' Oswald's jugular was popping out. 'What about that officer in Oak Cliff. Did you shoot him?' 'No. I deny that, too,' Oswald said just as earnestly." [3177]

"'Lee, did you shoot the president?' 'No. I emphatically deny that.'"

"Frank" Krystinik in testimony to the Warren Commission

Raymond Francis "Frank" Krystinik, a co-worker with Michael Paine at Bell Helicopter, was called by the Warren Commission because he spoke with Oswald at the ACLU meeting mentioned earlier. They compared civil liberties in the Soviet Union to those in the USA:

> "Mr. KRYSTINIK. I said, what do you think about the movement in the South in reference to Mr. Kennedy? And he said he thinks that Kennedy is doing a real fine job, a real good job, I have forgotten.
>
> Mr. LIEBELER. So far as civil rights were concerned?
>
> Mr. KRYSTINIK. Yes, sir. That was the only comment that was made in reference to President Kennedy." [3178]
>
> ...
>
> "Mr. LIEBELER. And the impression you received of his attitude toward President Kennedy was one of approval and one of favor?
>
> Mr. KRYSTINIK. I would say yes. I don't know about President Kennedy in general, how he felt, but in reference to the civil rights issue, the impression I had was that he was favorably impressed by Mr. Kennedy." [3179]

"[H]e thinks that Kennedy is doing a real fine job, a real good job ... in reference to the civil rights issue."

Detective James R. Leavelle of Dallas Police in testimony to the Warren Commission

Leavelle was on the homicide squad of the Dallas Police Department. On November 24, he accompanied Oswald to Captain Fritz's office and stayed while various federal officials asked questions, shortly before departure down the elevator to the basement for transfer to the county jail. Called before the Warren Commission, he testified that Secret Service inspector Thomas J. Kelley asked "whether or not [Oswald] thought the attitude of the U.S. Government toward Cuba would be changed since the President had been assassinated." Oswald said "he felt like when the head of any government died or was killed, whatever, there was always a second in command who would take over and he said in this particular instance it would be Johnson. He said 'So far as I know, Johnson's views and President Kennedy's views are the same', so he would see no particular difference in the attitude of the U.S. Government toward Cuba." [3180]

He also recalled "that the captain asked him about the shooting of the President, and the shooting of the officer [and] he denied shooting either one." [3181] Minutes after the detective heard that statement, they moved Oswald toward greater safety in the county jail. To prevent his escape, Lee's right wrist was handcuffed to Leavelle's left [3182] — so in the photos showing Jack Ruby shooting Oswald (pages 211 and 285), Leavelle is the officer in the light-color suit and matching cowboy hat.

"'So far as I know, Johnson's views and ... Kennedy's views are the same', so he would see no particular difference in the attitude of the U.S. Government toward Cuba."
"[T]he captain asked him about the shooting of the President, and the shooting of the officer [and] he denied shooting either one."

Harrison Edward Livingstone in *Killing the Truth: Deceit and Deception in the JFK Case*
In his 1993 book, knowledgeable critic Livingstone says:
"Oswald, it is now known, thought very highly of Kennedy." [3183]

Harrison Edward Livingstone in 1995 book *Killing Kennedy: And the Hoax of the Century*
Livingstone wrote many assassination books. In his 1995 *Killing Kennedy: And the Hoax of the Century*, he included a fifty-three page chapter meant to discredit Gerald Posner's excellent *Case Closed*, which I review and recommend in Chapter 9: DID HE DO IT? Livingstone's try at badmouthing Posner fell far short, and wasted a lot of trees. But, he made an interestingly wrong argument. It's instructive to examine what such a long-term dedicated critic of other assassination writers said in an attempt to throw a rock at Posner:

> "The evidence is well established that Oswald thought highly of Kennedy and bore no grudge against him. It is not rational, therefore, that he would have participated in a plot to kill him, or killed him on his own. Had Oswald shot Kennedy, he would have been glad to see him dead, and this would have been immediately apparent. It wasn't. Posner's failure to deal with the subject of Oswald's admiration for Kennedy is one of many serious flaws in his book." [3184]

Carefully stated point-by-point, Livingstone's argument is: Posner wrote *Case Closed* to argue that Oswald succeeded with his intent to kill Kennedy. After Oswald in fact accomplished what he intended, he should have been glad. But, it was apparent he did not show anything resembling gladness. Therefore, it must be true that Oswald was not an assassin or conspirator — and that really had to be the case anyway, because it "is well established that Oswald thought highly of Kennedy and bore no grudge against him" — and Posner failed to explain that serious discrepancy.

The error in Livingstone's assault is simple: Posner's purpose was specifically to show that Oswald, alone, did the shooting, and *Case Closed* nicely proved that. As do most people, whether assassination experts or not, Livingstone assumes that if Oswald killed Kennedy, that must have been what he intended. And, because there are at least two lines of evidence (Oswald's regard for JFK, his lack of gladness after killing JFK) that argue against Oswald being either a sole assassin or one of several in a conspiracy, then Oswald must not have had any reason to kill Kennedy — and thus must be either a not-guilty innocent or a "patsy".

I think it only fair to have put before you one far-off-the-mark shot, as some critics take at others. Enough! Or, as Italians say with their much more expressive word: Basta!
"The evidence is well established that Oswald thought highly of Kennedy and bore no grudge against him."

Lieutenant Francis L. Martello of New Orleans in testimony to the Warren Commission
Oswald was arrested and jailed in August 1963 for a disturbance as he handed out "Fair Play For Cuba" leaflets. Lieutenant Martello of the New Orleans Police Department took an interest because of a previous assignment in the Intelligence Division, and questioned Oswald to determine whether other agencies should be notified. (No.) On the day after Oswald killed Kennedy, the FBI had Martello write a memorandum. As he had tried to understand where Oswald's loyalty lay, "I asked him what he thought about President John F. Kennedy and Nikita Khrushchev. He said he thought they got along well together. I then asked him if he

had to place allegiance or make a decision between Russia or America, which he would choose and he said 'I would place my allegiance at the foot of democracy.'" [3185]

Commission assistant counsel Wesley Liebeler questioned Martello to expand on his memorandum. Twelve fine-print pages of Q&A included:

"Mr. LIEBELER. Now, your memorandum also indicates that you asked Oswald what he thought about President Kennedy and Premier Khrushchev, and the memorandum also indicates that Oswald said that he thought they got along very well together. What was his attitude when he made that remark? Tell us as much as you can remember of the background of that aspect of your conversation.

Mr. MARTELLO. The reason I asked that question was again to get his feelings on where his loyalty would rest between America and Russia, and it was just another way of asking the same question. He gave me the impression that he seemed to favor President Kennedy more than he did Khrushchev in his statement. This is unusual, and I couldn't quite understand his reason for this reaction, as all of his thoughts seemed to go into the direction of the Socialist or Russian way of life, but he showed in his manner of speaking that he liked the President, the impression I got, or, if he didn't like him, of the two he disliked, he disliked the President the least. He is a very peculiar type of an individual, which is typical of quite a few of the many demonstrators that I have handled during the period of 2 years while in the Intelligence Division. They seemed to be trying to find themselves or something. I am not expert in the field or anything, not trying to go out of my bounds, but quite a few of them, after lengthy interviews you find that they have some peculiarities about their thinking that does not follow logically with their movements or their action.

Mr. LIEBELER. And this attitude that Oswald demonstrated toward the President is an example of that sort of thing? Is that correct?

Mr. MARTELLO. That is correct, sir.

Mr. LIEBELER. It didn't seem to fit in with the rest of his statements?

Mr. MARTELLO. Didn't seem to fit in.

Mr. LIEBELER. Do you remember any more specifically or in any more detail just what the conversation concerning Kennedy was?

Mr. MARTELLO. It would only be vaguely at this time, but it was in the general areas of leadership of the President in comparison to the leadership of Khrushchev, how each was leading the various countries, and again an analogy or comparison of the two forms of government, which one he thought was running it the best, but we didn't go into this at any great length.

Mr. LIEBELER. Well, your recollection is quite clear that, in spite of the fact that Oswald demonstrated a general inclination to favor the Soviet Union and its institutions, he did in spite of that indicate a preference for President Kennedy as opposed to Premier Khrushchev?

Mr. MARTELLO. That is correct, sir.

Mr. LIEBELER. And that he in no way demonstrated any animosity or ill feelings toward President Kennedy?

Mr. MARTELLO. No, sir; he did not." [3186]

"[H]e seemed to favor President Kennedy more than he did Khrushchev." "[H]e liked the President ... or, if he didn't like him, of the two he disliked, he disliked the President the least." "'[H]e in no way demonstrated any animosity or ill feelings toward President Kennedy?' 'No, sir; he did not.'"

Priscilla Johnson McMillan in biography *Marina and Lee*

Writing with Marina's full cooperation, McMillan gained perhaps the best post-assassination understanding of Lee of all writers. Judging Marina's account of the couple's last summer together, in New Orleans, she summarized "it appears that Lee wanted to be like Kennedy and perhaps follow in his footsteps as closely as he could. Reading Manchester's book [*Portrait of a President*] may have reminded him that in some ways he was like Kennedy already." [3187]

"[I]t appears that Lee wanted to be like Kennedy and perhaps follow in his footsteps as closely as he could."

Detective Leslie Dell Montgomery of Dallas Police in testimony to the Warren Commission

Along with Graves and Leavelle (above) Montgomery of the homicide squad was assigned on November 24 to accompany Oswald and other officers to the elevator, to the basement, and to the car for transfer to the county jail. Commission counsel asked about his wait in Captain Fritz's office: "Do you remember about what Oswald said and what was said to Oswald during that period?" He responded: "I remember they asked him why he shot the President, and, of course, he said he didn't do it." [3188] Oh, how I wish that were accurate, and that Oswald had answered, because Montgomery says they asked *"why"*, which would be a unique inquiry into motive. But, no others report a "why" question, and in any case, Oswald did not reply with anything substantive. In photos of Jack Ruby shooting Oswald, Montgomery is directly behind Oswald, in the dark suit and light cowboy hat.

"[T]hey asked him why he shot the President, and, of course, he said he didn't do it."

Lillian Claverie Murret in testimony to the Warren Commission

In April 1964, Marguerite's sister, Lee's New Orleans aunt, testified before the Commission. Assistant counsel Albert Jenner questioned her for a long day, and at the end:

"Mr. JENNER. Did Lee ever speak of President John Fitzgerald Kennedy or Mrs. Jacqueline Kennedy?

Mrs. MURRET. He said one time that he thought Mrs. Jacqueline Kennedy was a very fine person, and that he admired her for going around with her husband, and so forth, but he never spoke about that again, or never said anything about it. In fact, I think he said he liked him.

Mr. JENNER. Liked President Kennedy?

Mrs. MURRET. Yes." [3189]

"'In fact, I think he said he liked him.' 'Liked President Kennedy?' 'Yes.'"

Marilyn Dorothea Murret in testimony to the Warren Commission

On the same day as her mother (above), Lee's eleven-years-older cousin, a science teacher, testified before Commission assistant counsel Wesley Liebeler, who elicited this:

"Mr. LIEBELER. [H]ad you ever discussed politics with [Lee] at all?

Miss MURRET. He never mentioned anything of any political significance at all, never.

Mr. LIEBELER. Never said anything about President Kennedy?

Miss MURRET. No, sir.

Mr. LIEBELER. Or Governor Connally?

Miss MURRET. No; but I can't remember whether it was—if that was before or if it was on that program, where he said something complimentary about Kennedy, but he never mentioned anyone else.

Mr. LIEBELER. What program are you referring to?

Miss MURRET. That might have been when they showed when he was interviewed after the Fair Play for Cuba, because it was after the assassination that they reran that.

Mr. LIEBELER. That was a television program?

Miss MURRET. Yes; television.

Mr. LIEBELER. And you say that you saw it after the assassination?

Miss MURRET. Yes.

Mr. LIEBELER. And you don't recall, but you think the man said something complimentary about Kennedy on that?

Miss MURRET. Yes.

Mr. LIEBELER. And other than that you never heard him speak of President Kennedy?

Miss MURRET. No." [3190]

"[H]e said something complimentary about Kennedy, but he never mentioned anyone else." "'[Lee] said something complimentary about Kennedy on [TV]?' 'Yes.'"

Carl Oglesby in his book *Who Killed JFK?*

"Oswald's alleged 'capacity for violence' does not explain why he would kill two men as politically diverse as JFK and Walker. Marina testified that Oswald praised JFK but called [Major General Edwin] Walker [at whom Oswald shot on April 10, 1963] a 'fascist,' 'compared [him] to Adolf Hitler' and remarked that 'if someone had killed Hitler in time it would have saved many lives.'" [3191]

"Marina testified that Oswald praised JFK but called [General Edwin] Walker a 'fascist'"

Michael Paine in testimony to the Warren Commission

Michael, the husband separated from Ruth Paine, testified to the Warren Commission on three occasions. During his first appearance in March 1964, he was questioned three times about Oswald's attitude toward President Kennedy:

"Mr. DULLES. Did he ever mention the President in this or any other conversation?

Mr. PAINE. He mentioned the President only once that I can remember specifically; at the ACLU meeting I think.

Mr. DULLES. At the which?

Mr. PAINE. At the ACLU meeting I took him to. He had mentioned, he thought President Kennedy was doing quite a good job in civil rights, which was high praise coming from Lee." [3192]

...

"Mr. LIEBELER. Did he ever indicate to you any specific hostility toward President Kennedy?

Mr. PAINE. I think at this ACLU meeting he mentioned this specifically that he thought Kennedy had done a good job in civil rights. That was it—generally my impression was that he liked—he didn't like anybody, but he disliked Kennedy least ..." [3193]

...

"Mr. DULLES. In the light of subsequent information and developments, and the information which is publicly available, have you reached ... any conclusions as to whether or not Lee Harvey Oswald was the assassin of the President?

Mr. PAINE. When the police first asked me did I think he had done it, my dubiousness in my mind arose from not seeing how this could fit, how this could help his cause, and I didn't think he was irrational." [3194]

Although he did not understand a reason, Paine then opined that Lee had done the shooting.

"[H]e thought President Kennedy was doing quite a good job in civil rights, which was high praise coming from Lee." "[G]enerally my impression was that ... he didn't like anybody, but he disliked Kennedy least."

Ruth Paine in November 1963 newspaper interviews

Days after the shooting, Marina's good friend and protector, with whom she and her children lived, and where Lee stayed most weekends, was quoted in two newspaper interviews. Ruth Paine said: "Marina ... felt very favorably toward the President and his family. Most of what she learned of American news was provided by Lee, who translated from newspapers and news magazines. Marina said he never transferred any negative feelings toward President Kennedy." [3195] "As far as I know Oswald had never been critical of Kennedy. He had been critical of General [Edwin] Walker, but I never heard him say anything against the President. In fact, it was my impression that he respected him." [3196]

"Marina said he never transferred any negative feelings toward President Kennedy." "Oswald had never been critical of Kennedy." "I never heard him say anything against the President. In fact, it was my impression that he respected him."

Warren Commission Members and Counsel

Most testimony sessions were attended by only one or two commissioners, but in June 1964 for questioning of Secret Service Chief Rowley there was a large and prominent turnout, including Earl Warren, Allen Dulles, Senator John Sherman Cooper, Representatives Hale Boggs and Gerald Ford, and Chief Counsel J. Lee Rankin. Reflecting on Rowley's conclusion that Oswald's letter to Connally should have been recognized as a threat, the members then had this discussion summarizing Oswald's regard for President Kennedy:

"Representative BOGGS. This fellow [Oswald] was interviewed by the FBI several times—he was interviewed in New Orleans when he allegedly had his Fair Play Committee. ... Mrs. Paine was interviewed about him shortly before the visit of the President, after he had gone to work at the Texas School Book Depository. I agree that there had been no indication of a threat on the President's life. But, obviously he was a person in the FBI files who was under some degree of surveillance. It would seem to me strange that the FBI did not transmit this information to the Secret Service.

Mr. ROWLEY. The FBI, Mr. Congressman, are concerned with internal security. ... Their concern was talking to him in this vein, in the course of which there was no indication that he bore any malice toward anyone, and particularly to the President of the United States. ...

...

Representative BOGGS. And if I remember correctly, there has never been—we have had no testimony from anyone that Oswald ever threatened the President of the United States. Is that correct?

Mr. RANKIN. That is correct." [3197]

"'[W]e have had no testimony from anyone that Oswald ever threatened the President of the United States. Is that correct?' 'That is correct.'"

Craig I. Zirbel in his book *The Texas Connection*

In Chapter 21 – OTHERS ON THIS TRAIL, nearly four pages will quote from, then dismiss, the arguments in a portion of Zirbel's book that lays out and rejects several assassination theories. However, as usual in this life in which almost nothing is purely black or white, with shades of gray being the rule, there is some saving merit. In *The Texas Connection* I found that limited to two excerpts:

> "If Oswald in fact shot President Kennedy, then he obviously changed his mind about Kennedy's leadership qualities some time within weeks of the assassination. This is because it was conceded by all (even the Warren Commission) that Oswald greatly admired Kennedy. By most standards Oswald would have been more likely to vote for Kennedy than shoot him." [3198]

The last thirteen words are a gem, nicely encapsulating much of this chapter of this book: **"Oswald would have been more likely to vote for Kennedy than shoot him."**

> "Oswald repeatedly denied that he killed President Kennedy. He affirmatively stated that he did not have any personal animosity against the President or his family. It was also his opinion that John Kennedy would be recognized as one of America's greatest leaders. For these reasons, Oswald's motive has always remained a mystery. Even Warren Commission member Gerald Ford recognized the troublesome concept of Oswald killing Kennedy without a motive and voiced concern about it. ... If one believes that Oswald was in any way telling the truth when he made these statements, then his statements alone are proof that a conspiracy existed. Further, if it is believed that a person does not ordinarily commit a murder without a motive, then Oswald's lack of one implicitly proves the existence of a conspiracy involving others who were participants with a motive." [3199]

The latter excerpt demonstrates the complications along the path to explaining Oswald if one assumes or believes he meant to shoot Kennedy. The failure to find any motive for killing Kennedy should, in a more reflective world, have caused critics to back up and re-think: What was the motive, who was the target? But, in this case as with most others, a wrong assumption then required highly complex explanations — by Zirbel that Oswald was in a conspiracy, but because he had no motive it was not he, but his fellow conspirators, who meant to assassinate the President. These are the worthwhile observations in the two excerpts:

"[I]t was conceded by all (even the Warren Commission) that Oswald greatly admired Kennedy." "By most standards Oswald would have been more likely to vote for Kennedy than shoot him." "Oswald repeatedly denied that he killed President Kennedy." "Oswald affirmatively stated that he did not have any personal animosity against the President or his family." "It was also his opinion that John Kennedy would be recognized as one of America's greatest leaders."

Other witnesses before the Warren Commission

Many witnesses interviewed by the Commission were asked if they had, at any time, heard or heard of Lee Oswald, at any time, saying anything about President Kennedy. These witnesses testified that he had never said anything about Kennedy in their presence, and if asked, that they had never heard that he had said anything about Kennedy to any other persons: Adrian Thomas Alba;[3200] Max E. Clark;[3201] Declan P. Ford;[3202] Katherine Katrina Evstratova "Katya" (Mrs. Declan) Ford;[3203] Alexandra De Mohrenschildt Taylor Gibson;[3204] Everett D. Glover;[3205] Elena A. Hall;[3206] John Raymond Hall;[3207] Ilya A. Mamantov;[3208] Anna N. Meller;[3209] Ruth Hyde (Mrs. Michael) Paine;[3210] Gary E. Taylor.[3211]

Commission member Gerald Ford, in his book *Portrait of the Assassin*, described the nature of the testimony of the first witness in the group above, which fits all twelve: "Alba's impressions of Lee Harvey Oswald agreed with dozens of other witnesses in most every respect. ... He was never known to have said a critical word about President Kennedy." [3212]

•••

On the preceding 27 pages, 52 articles displayed contexts for 109 quotations, listed at the end of each. To make sense of all that, the quotations are now collected together, then duplicates will be discarded. The remaining significant ones will then be judged for inclination, all with the purpose that at the end of the next chapter we can very fairly decide whether it was more likely that Oswald would aim at one man in the limousine rather than the other. Codes after the quotations below will be explained and used after this list of all the quotations.

All of Oswald REGARDING KENNEDY, in the order in which the quotations appeared above:

"I didn't shoot President John F. Kennedy or Officer J. D. Tippit." {O}

"John Kennedy had a nice family." {O}

"My wife and I like the Presidential family. They are interesting people." {O}

"I didn't shoot John Kennedy. I didn't even know Governor John Connally had been shot." {O}

"I had nothing personal against John Kennedy." {O}

"Nothing irritated me about the President." {O}

"American people will soon forget the President was shot, but I didn't shoot him." {O}

"Since the President was killed, someone else would take his place, perhaps Vice-President Johnson. His views about Cuba would probably be largely the same as those of President Kennedy." {O}

"I did not kill President Kennedy or Officer Tippit. If you want me to cop out to hitting or pleading guilty to hitting a cop in the mouth when I was arrested, yeah, I plead guilty to that. But I do deny shooting both the President and Tippit." {O}

"He had read several favorable articles about Kennedy, aloud and translated them in his pidgin Russian." {O}

"Observed that eliminating the President would do no good" {O}

"If he had had negative feelings about Kennedy this would have come along with the translation from Lee. But there was no such indication of dislike" {O}

"How could he have said these things or called her attention to these things with respect to President Kennedy, and still have assassinated him?" {O}

"He had said nothing critical about the man. If he felt no hatred for the man, then he could not have killed him. The motive, the pressure, the compulsion were not present." {O}

"Marina said her husband had only a positive attitude toward President Kennedy." {O}

"This is the truth. Lee never spoke bad about President Kennedy." {O}

"Lee had nothing against President Kennedy." {O}

"Lee expressed that Kennedy was a good President." {D}

"Marina was then asked if Lee ever indicated in any way that he intended to kill former President Kennedy. She stated 'No, I feel he did not do it because he never spoke against President Kennedy at any time.'" {O}

"Marina then stated 'I swear before God that Lee Oswald did not intend to kill President Kennedy.'" {O}

"Oswald replied that Kennedy was a good President." {D}

"Oswald never gave any indication whatsoever that he intended any harm to the President." {O}

"He always had something good to say." {O}

"At least from Lee's behavior I cannot conclude that he was against the President, and therefore the thing is incomprehensible to me." {O}

"I didn't believe for a long time that Lee had shot at the President. That he had wanted to kill Kennedy" {O}

"'Did your late husband express any hostility towards President Kennedy?' 'No.'" {O}

"He always had a favorable feeling about President Kennedy because he always read these favorably inclined articles to me." {D}

"'Had your husband at any time that you can recall said anything against President Kennedy? 'I don't remember any— He never told me that.'" {D}

"'He didn't indicate any approval or disapproval of President Kennedy?' 'That is correct. He never indicated that he didn't want that President.'" {O}

"He never expressed himself anything against President Kennedy, anything detrimental toward him." {D}

"I didn't think that he had any idea concerning President Kennedy." {D}

"Kennedy was equipped to be President and deserved it." {O}

"Lee liked and approved of the President and believed that for the United States in 1963, John F. Kennedy was the best President the country could hope to have." {O}

"The overwhelming fact she mentions again and again, was that Lee liked President Kennedy. He frequently said that for the United States at this moment of its history, Kennedy was the best possible leader" {O}

"But he liked Kennedy!" {D}

"I believe that Lee acted alone in this murder and shot the President, ironically, a man whom he respected and admired." {O}

"'What would his usual comments about President Kennedy be?' 'My impression was that he liked him very well.'" {O}

"'Lee's attitude toward President Kennedy was certainly different than his attitude toward General Walker, am I correct?' 'Yes.'" {O}

"'Had you had any prior indication of any dislike for President Kennedy on his behalf?' 'No; that is what is so strange about the whole event.'" {D}

"He always spoke very complimentary about the President." {O}

"He was very happy when John Kennedy was elected." {O}

"Whatever he said about President Kennedy, it was only good, always." {O}

"'Were Lee and friend speaking favorably of Kennedy?' 'I think so.'" {O}

"I do not recall ever hearing Lee talking badly about John Kennedy or Kennedy family." {D}

"He was quite concerned about Mrs. Kennedy's health and he was hoping nothing would happen to this baby." {O}

"'Lee always spoke of liking President Kennedy; is that correct?' 'That is true, sir.'" {D}

"'You never heard Lee speak of Kennedy in a hostile manner?' 'No.'" {D}

"'He adored that man.' 'You say he adored John Kennedy?' 'Oh, yes.'" {O}

"The Lee I knew really loved JFK." {O}

"They were delighted with President Kennedy" {O}

"He was telling Marina ... 'I like President Kennedy'" {O}

"I just can't see his having any venom towards President Kennedy." {O}

"I would have thought that this is an individual who felt warmly towards President Kennedy." {O}

"He denied shooting either one of them, or knowing anything about it." {D}

"Asked about involvement in the assassination of President Kennedy, or the shooting of Officer Tippit he gave an emphatic denial" {W}

"He denied shooting President John F. Kennedy on November 22, 1963, and commented that he did not know that Governor John Connally had been shot." {W}

"No personal affront had been inflicted on Lee Oswald by the President himself ... nothing Oswald had requested of the government had been denied him." {O}

"I think it is an excellent President, young, full of energy, full of good ideas." {O}

"He did not have any permanent animosity for President Kennedy." {O}

"Lee liked him and certainly did not include him among despicable politicians " {O}

"Lee said 'how handsome Kennedy looks, what open and sincere features he has and how different he looks from the other ratty politicos.'" {O}

"Lee spoke most kindly of the gradual improvement of the racial relations in the United States, attributing this improvement to the President." {O}

"Like most young people he was attracted by Kennedy's personality " {O}

"Lee actually admired President Kennedy in his own reserved way." {D}

"One day we discussed Kennedy's efforts to bring peace to the world and to end the cold war. 'Great! Great!' exclaimed Lee. 'If he succeeds, he'll be the greatest President in the history of this country.'" {O}

"We both liked President Kennedy." {D}

"He was rather an admirer of the dead President " {O}

"To assassinate the President he rather admired, just for the glory of it, is entirely foreign to his personality." {O}

"I don't think he ever said anything against, and whatever President Kennedy was doing, Lee was completely exactly with the same ideas, exactly." {O}

"Completely in accord with President Kennedy's policy" {D}

"It doesn't make exactly sense. He has no reason whatsoever" {O}

"He said he didn't have any views on the President." {W}

"I like the President's family very well. I have my own view about national politics." {W}

"Says nothing against Pres." {W}

"Well, people will soon forget that the President was shot." {W}

"He said no, he didn't shoot him." {W}

"He seemed to admire the man" {D}

"He always expressed what I would interpret as admiration for Kennedy" {O}

"Lee said ... yes, he is a good leader ... a positive remark about Kennedy" {O}

"Expressed that positive feeling toward Kennedy" {D}

"Marina ventured that the president appeared to be a nice man ... Lee, in his curt way, agreed." {O}

"Oswald emphatically denied shooting Tippit or shooting President John F. Kennedy." {W}

"He then denied that he had killed Officer Tippit or President Kennedy." {D}

"'Lee, did you shoot the president?' 'No. I emphatically deny that.'" {W}

"He thinks that Kennedy is doing a real fine job, a real good job ... in reference to the civil rights issue." {O}

"'So far as I know, Johnson's views and Kennedy's views are the same', so he would see no particular difference in the attitude of the U.S. Government toward Cuba." {W}

"The captain asked him about the shooting of the President and the shooting of the officer and he denied shooting either one." {W}

"Oswald, it is now known, thought very highly of Kennedy." {O}

"The evidence is well established that Oswald thought highly of Kennedy and bore no grudge against him." {O}

"He seemed to favor President Kennedy more than he did Khrushchev." {O}

"He liked the President ... or, if he didn't like him, of the two he disliked, he disliked the President the least." {D}

"'He in no way demonstrated any animosity or ill feelings toward President Kennedy?' 'No, sir; he did not.'" {O}

"It appears that Lee wanted to be like Kennedy and perhaps follow in his footsteps as closely as he could." {O}

"They asked him why he shot the President, and, of course, he said he didn't do it." {W}

"'In fact, I think he said he liked him.' 'Liked President Kennedy?' 'Yes.'" {O}

"He said something complimentary about Kennedy, but he never mentioned anyone else." {O}

"'Lee said something complimentary about Kennedy on TV?' 'Yes.'" {D}

"Marina testified that Oswald praised JFK but called [General Edwin] Walker a 'fascist'" {O}

"He thought President Kennedy was doing quite a good job in civil rights, which was high praise coming from Lee." {O}

"Generally my impression was that he didn't like anybody, but he disliked Kennedy least." {O}

"Marina said he never transferred any negative feelings toward President Kennedy." {O}

"Oswald had never been critical of Kennedy." {D}

"I never heard him say anything against the President. In fact, it was my impression that he respected him." {O}

"'We have had no testimony from anyone that Oswald ever threatened the President of the United States. Is that correct?' 'That is correct.'" {O}

"It was conceded by all (even the Warren Commission) that Oswald greatly admired Kennedy." {O}

"By most standards Oswald would have been more likely to vote for Kennedy than shoot him." {O}

"Oswald repeatedly denied that he killed President Kennedy." {W}

"Oswald affirmatively stated that he did not have any personal animosity against the President or his family." {D}

"It was also his opinion that John Kennedy would be recognized as one of America's greatest leaders." {D}

Winnowing is now required to obtain a more accurate picture of Oswald's feelings, from which we may then discern a motive for shooting Kennedy — or a lack of such motive. To illustrate the reason for winnowing, consider one crime observed from two positions: by two people in a car, and from a different vantage by twenty-four people on a bus. If the two testified that they saw "A" but the twenty-four told of a different "B", should we disregard "A" because there are twelve times as many opinions and testimonies for "B"? No. Then, if one of the car riders told a broadcast audience what he saw, should we discredit "B" because now there may be thousands who heard "A"? Again, no. Either view may be correct, and we need to assess each different view for the credibility it deserves — no more, no less.

To obtain an unbiased flavor of what we are told, the "echoes" must be weeded out. After each statement on the long list above is a code; there are three:

{O} indicates Original testimony or opinion about Lee's regard for Kennedy.

{W} is a Witness's statement that he or she heard an {O} Original statement.

{D} indicates a Duplicate (repeated, even in different words) of an {O} or a {W}.

Many of the 23 {D} duplicates are of Marina's repeated testimony, where she was asked similar questions over and over, and answered similarly. Many of the 13 {W} codes are assigned to statements such as "They asked him why he shot the President, and, of course, he said he didn't do it." An {O} was assigned to the Original "I didn't shoot President John F. Kennedy or Officer J. D. Tippit." statement by Oswald, so it should not be counted twice.

To give a fairly-weighted sense of what Oswald said or conveyed, the 36 {W} and {D} statements are removed from the 109; this new list contains only the 73 {O} Originals in the same sequence as in the four pages above, which is the same as in the articles in this chapter. The arrows after the statements below will be explained and used after the list is complete.

Original statements by or about Oswald REGARDING KENNEDY, in the same order as above:

"I didn't shoot President John F. Kennedy or Officer J. D. Tippit." ⇔

"John Kennedy had a nice family." ⇧

"My wife and I like the Presidential family. They are interesting people." ⇧

"I didn't shoot John Kennedy. I didn't even know Governor John Connally had been shot." ⇔

"I had nothing personal against John Kennedy." ⇔

"Nothing irritated me about the President." ⇔

"American people will soon forget the President was shot, but I didn't shoot him." ⇔

"Since the President was killed, someone else would take his place, perhaps Vice-President Johnson. His views about Cuba would probably be largely the same as those of President Kennedy." ⇔

"I did not kill President Kennedy or Officer Tippit. If you want me to cop out to hitting or pleading guilty to hitting a cop in the mouth when I was arrested, yeah, I plead guilty to that. But I do deny shooting both the President and Tippit." ⇔

"He had read several favorable articles about Kennedy, aloud and translated them in his pidgin Russian." ⇧

"Observed that eliminating the President would do no good" ⇔

"If he had had negative feelings about Kennedy this would have come along with the translation from Lee. But there was no such indication of dislike" ⇔

"How could he have said these things or called her attention to these things with respect to President Kennedy, and still have assassinated him?" ⇧

"He had said nothing critical about the man. If he felt no hatred for the man, then he could not have killed him. The motive, the pressure, the compulsion were not present." ⇔

"Marina said her husband had only a positive attitude toward President Kennedy." ⇧

"This is the truth. Lee never spoke bad about President Kennedy." ⇔

"Lee had nothing against President Kennedy." ⇔

"Marina was then asked if Lee ever indicated in any way that he intended to kill former President Kennedy. She stated 'No, I feel he did not do it because he never spoke against President Kennedy at any time.'" ⇔

"Marina then stated 'I swear before God that Lee Oswald did not intend to kill President Kennedy.'" ⇔

"Oswald never gave any indication whatsoever that he intended any harm to the President." ⇔

"He always had something good to say." ⇧

"At least from Lee's behavior I cannot conclude that he was against the President, and therefore the thing is incomprehensible to me." ⇔

"I didn't believe for a long time that Lee had shot at the President. That he had wanted to kill Kennedy" ⇔

"'Did your late husband express any hostility towards President Kennedy?' 'No.'" ⇔

"'He didn't indicate any approval or disapproval of President Kennedy?' 'That is correct. He never indicated that he didn't want that President.'" ⇔

"Kennedy was equipped to be President and deserved it." ⇧

"Lee liked and approved of the President and believed that for the United States in 1963, John F. Kennedy was the best President the country could hope to have." ⇧

"The overwhelming fact she mentions again and again, was that Lee liked President Kennedy. He frequently said that for the United States at this moment of its history, Kennedy was the best possible leader" ⇧

"I believe that Lee acted alone in this murder and shot the President, ironically, a man whom he respected and admired." ⇧

"'What would his usual comments about President Kennedy be?' 'My impression was that he liked him very well.'" ⇧

"'Lee's attitude toward President Kennedy was certainly different than his attitude toward General Walker, am I correct?' 'Yes.'" ⇧

"He always spoke very complimentary about the President." ⇧

"He was very happy when John Kennedy was elected." ⇧

"Whatever he said about President Kennedy, it was only good, always." ⇧

"'Were Lee and friend speaking favorably of Kennedy?' 'I think so.'" ⇧

"He was quite concerned about Mrs. Kennedy's health and he was hoping nothing would happen to this baby." ⇧

"'He adored that man.' 'You say he adored John Kennedy?' 'Oh, yes.'" ⇧

"The Lee I knew really loved JFK." ⇧

"They were delighted with President Kennedy" ⇧

"He was telling Marina ... 'I like President Kennedy'" ⇧

"I just can't see his having any venom towards President Kennedy." ⇔

"I would have thought that this is an individual who felt warmly towards President Kennedy." ⇧

"No personal affront had been inflicted on Lee Oswald by the President himself ... nothing Oswald had requested of the government had been denied him." ⇔

"I think it is an excellent President, young, full of energy, full of good ideas." ⇧

"He did not have any permanent animosity for President Kennedy." ⇔

"Lee liked him and certainly did not include him among despicable politicians " ⇧

"Lee said 'how handsome Kennedy looks, what open and sincere features he has and how different he looks from the other ratty politicos.'" ⇧

"Lee spoke most kindly of the gradual improvement of the racial relations in the United States, attributing this improvement to the President." ⇧

"Like most young people he was attracted by Kennedy's personality " ⇧

"One day we discussed Kennedy's efforts to bring peace to the world and to end the cold war. 'Great! Great!' exclaimed Lee. 'If he succeeds, he'll be the greatest President in the history of this country.'" ⇧

"He was rather an admirer of the dead President " ⇧

"To assassinate the President he rather admired, just for the glory of it, is entirely foreign to his personality." ⇔

"I don't think he ever said anything against, and whatever President Kennedy was doing, Lee was completely exactly with the same ideas, exactly." ⇧

"It doesn't make exactly sense. He has no reason whatsoever" ⇔

"He always expressed what I would interpret as admiration for Kennedy" ⇧

"Lee said ... yes, he is a good leader ... a positive remark about Kennedy" ⇧

"Marina ventured that the president appeared to be a nice man ... Lee, in his curt way, agreed." ⇧

"He thinks that Kennedy is doing a real fine job, a real good job ... in reference to the civil rights issue." ⇧

"Oswald, it is now known, thought very highly of Kennedy." ⇧

"The evidence is well established that Oswald thought highly of Kennedy and bore no grudge against him." ⇧

"He seemed to favor President Kennedy more than he did Khrushchev." ⇧

"'He in no way demonstrated any animosity or ill feelings toward President Kennedy?' 'No, sir; he did not.'" ⇔

"It appears that Lee wanted to be like Kennedy and perhaps follow in his footsteps as closely as he could." ⇧

"'In fact, I think he said he liked him.' 'Liked President Kennedy?' 'Yes.'" ⇧

"He said something complimentary about Kennedy, but he never mentioned anyone else." ⇧

"Marina testified that Oswald praised JFK but called [General Edwin] Walker a 'fascist'" ⇧

"He thought President Kennedy was doing quite a good job in civil rights, which was high praise coming from Lee." ⇧

"Generally my impression was that he didn't like anybody, but he disliked Kennedy least." ⇩

"Marina said he never transferred any negative feelings toward President Kennedy." ⇔

"I never heard him say anything against the President. In fact, it was my impression that he respected him." ⇧

"'We have had no testimony from anyone that Oswald ever threatened the President of the United States. Is that correct?' 'That is correct.'" ⇔

"It was conceded by all (even the Warren Commission) that Oswald greatly admired Kennedy." ⇧

"By most standards Oswald would have been more likely to vote for Kennedy than shoot him." ⇧

With judgment as even-handed as possible, I have attached an arrow to each statement above. Most of the 27 with ⇔ are of the nature "said nothing against" or "had no reason to shoot". Although those most certainly tend to negate any inclination to murder Kennedy, they do not convey an opinion, either positive or negative, so are judged and labeled as neutral. Not helpful to learning Oswald's motive, those statements are not considered any further.

That leaves 46 that are clearly positive or negative. There is only one of the latter, Michael Paine's judgment: "Generally my impression was that he didn't like anybody, but he disliked Kennedy least." Although less negative toward the President than toward the billions of other humans, it has been given a ⇩ arrow, which has the ancillary benefit of keeping the opinions from being unanimous, which might furnish some tiny reason for suspicion.

There are 45 original, unduplicated statements that express or judge a positive regard by Oswald for Kennedy, each given an ⇧ arrow.

In visual form, here is the pattern of all favorable and unfavorable opinions ever known to be stated by or attributed to Oswald:

Kennedy
⇧ ⇧ ⇧ ⇧
⇧ ⇧ ⇧ ⇧
⇧ ⇧ ⇧ ⇧
⇧ ⇧ ⇧ ⇧
⇧ ⇧ ⇧ ⇧
⇧ ⇧ ⇧ ⇧ ⇧
⇧ ⇧ ⇧ ⇧ ⇧
⇧ ⇧ ⇧ ⇧ ⇧
⇧ ⇧ ⇧ ⇧ ⇧
⇧ ⇧ ⇧ ⇧ ⇧
⇩

We are not voting here, so the imbalance of 45 to 1, by itself, is not proof of anything. Judgment will be reserved until it becomes clear how Oswald felt about the only other possible target in the limousine at which he shot — and that is the subject of the next chapter.

> Key point of this chapter:
> **Relatives, friends and others testify to Oswald's comments regarding Kennedy: 45 positive, 1 slightly negative.**

— 16 —

EVIDENCE

REGARDING CONNALLY

What Oswald stated and conveyed about John Connally

> "I received an honorable discharge and then those bastards in the Navy changed it into an undesirable discharge. And Connally signed this undesirable discharge." [A]
>
> — **Lee Oswald** [3213]

LEE OSWALD ALSO SPOKE ABOUT JOHN CONNALLY. Almost all of us say more about our country's president than we do about our state's governor, and that was also true of him. Although witnesses testified to many fewer comments about Connally than about Kennedy, there are certainly enough in this chapter to give a reliable picture of the ex-Marine's opinion of the ex-Navy man. [B] In the same sequence as was used in the REGARDING KENNEDY chapter — Oswald, then his family, then others in alphabetic sequence — here are all his known comments REGARDING CONNALLY:

<u>Lee Oswald</u> in his letter from Minsk to John Connally on January 30, 1962
The pleading, threatening letter on page 88 caught this author's attention in 1964, giving birth to this book more than 50 years later. The letter also inspired Oswald analyst Edward Jay Epstein to have it professionally studied by handwriting expert Thea Stein Lewinson. [3214] Her opinion was summarized in Epstein's *Legend: The Secret World of Lee Harvey Oswald*:

> "The handwriting analysis of this letter to Connally indicates that it was spontaneously written. Oswald apparently was under great pressure to do something about his discharge and felt himself in a difficult predicament. Further, stresses in the handwriting suggest that he was venting considerable anger toward Connally." [3215]

"[S]tresses in the handwriting suggest that [Oswald] was venting considerable anger toward Connally."

[A] No, Connally did not sign the discharge, but what truly matters is that Lee believed he did.

[B] Connally served with distinction in World War II, directing aviation from carriers in the Pacific. Back in Texas, we went into radio, finance and politics. He attached himself to Lyndon Johnson, and that's how he became Secretary of the Navy, which put him into Oswald's sights.

Lee Oswald in Dallas Police Headquarters on November 23, 1963

During an interrogation by Dallas Police Captain J. W. "Will" Fritz in his office on Saturday, as was reported in the previous chapter because Oswald was also talking about Kennedy:

"I didn't shoot John Kennedy. I didn't even know Governor John Connally had been shot." [3216]

Marina Oswald in testimony to the Warren Commission regarding Connally, #1 of 2

During Marina's first testimony to the Warren Commission in February 1964:

"Mr. RANKIN. Do you recall anything being said by your husband at any time about Governor Connally?

Mrs. OSWALD. Well, while we were still in Russia, and Connally at that time was Secretary of the Navy, Lee wrote him a letter in which he asked Connally to help him obtain a good character reference because at the end of his Army service he had a good characteristic—honorable discharge—but that it had been changed after it became known he had gone to Russia.

Mr. RANKIN. Had it been changed to undesirable discharge, as you understand it?

Mrs. OSWALD. Yes. Then we received a letter from Connally in which he said that he had turned the matter over to the responsible authorities. That was all in Russia. But here it seems he had written again to that organization with a request to review. But he said from time to time that these are bureaucrats, and he was dissatisfied." [3217]

"[W]e received a letter from Connally ... [Lee said] these are bureaucrats, and he was dissatisfied."

Marina Oswald in testimony to the Warren Commission regarding Connally, #2 of 2

The previous chapter introduced Marina's final testimony to the Warren Commission when she abruptly volunteered: "On the basis of all the available facts, I have no doubt in my mind that Lee Oswald killed President Kennedy. At the same time, I feel in my own mind as far as I am concerned, I feel that Lee—that my husband perhaps intended to kill Governor Connally instead of President Kennedy."[3218] Her entire testimony relevant to the Kennedy-or-Connally question is in Chapter 21 – OTHERS ON THIS TRAIL, because she was way out front in that regard. There were several questions to elicit Lee Oswald's views regarding John Connally:

"Senator [Richard] RUSSELL [Jr. of Georgia]. You've testified before us before that Lee told you he was coming back to Texas—if he was back in Texas, he would vote for Connally for Governor. Why do you think he would shoot him?

Mrs. OSWALD. I feel that the reason that he had Connally in his mind was on account of his discharge from the Marines and various letters they exchanged between the Marine Corps and the Governor's office, but actually, I didn't think that he had any idea concerning President Kennedy.

Representative [Hale] BOGGS [of Louisiana]. Well, now, my next question is—did he ever express any hostility to Governor Connally?

Mrs. OSWALD. He never expressed that to me—his displeasure or hatred of Connally, but I feel that there could have been some connection, due to the fact that Lee was dishonorably discharged from the Corps, and there was an exchange of letters between the Governor's Office and Lee. That's my personal opinion." [3219] C

C Actually, the letter to Lee was from Connally at his campaign office, before he was elected governor.

Commissioner Russell, greatly troubled by the suggestion that her husband had aimed at the Governor, so must have killed the President by mistake, next asked these questions:

"Senator RUSSELL. I am concerned about this testimony, Mrs. Oswald, about your believing now that Lee was shooting at Connally and not at the President, because you did not tell us that before. ... Did you not further testify that Lee said in discussing the gubernatorial election in Texas that if he were here and voting, that he would vote for Mr. Connally?

Mrs. OSWALD. Yes.

Senator RUSSELL. Now, do you think he would shoot and kill a man that he would vote for, for the Governor of his state?

Mrs. OSWALD. The only reason is—I am trying to analyze, myself, there was a reason—more reason to dislike Connally as a man than he had for Kennedy.

Senator RUSSELL. Well, she testified before that he had spoken, as far as Lee spoke favorably of anyone, that he had spoken favorably of both Kennedy and of Governor Connally.

Mrs. OSWALD. He also told me that he was also favorable toward Connally, while they were in Russia. There is a possibility that he changed his mind, but he never told her that.[D]

Senator RUSSELL. Well, I think that's about as speculative as the answers I've read here. He might have changed his mind, but he didn't tell her anything about it, as she testified—that discussing politics in Texas, that he said that if he were here when they had the election, that he would vote for John Connally for Governor, and that was after he got the letter about the Marine Corps. ... I want to know what Connally had done to Lee since he got back from Russia that would cause him to change his mind, to shoot him?

Mrs. OSWALD. I do not know, but there is a possibility that Lee became hateful of Connally because the matter of this dishonorable[E] discharge was dragging so long."[3220]

Senator Russell then became pedantic, edging into hostile, grilling poor Marina on her lack of knowledge about Connally resigning as Secretary of the Navy to run for Governor, on the chain of command from the President to the Marine Corps, about Oswald reading books about Kennedy, Hitler and others, and finally "Do you know whether or not Lee knew Connally personally or did he know that he was going to be in this motorcade at all?" "I did not know ... I don't know".[F] [3221] That is what she said to the Commission regarding Oswald and Connally. All relevant testimony from this commission session is in Chapter 21 – OTHERS ON THIS TRAIL. It is important to know that the *Warren Report* did not mention Marina's belief that Lee had a motive to aim at Connally, which she pointed out to the commissioners, and which they chose to ignore — probably because of great pressure from President Johnson to finish up. At the time of this testimony, the *Report* was almost certainly written, circulated, revised and nearly ready for the printer. "Timing is everything", and they were out of time.[G]

"[T]here was ... more reason to dislike Connally ... than ... Kennedy." "'Did you ... testify that Lee said ... that if he were here ... he would vote for Mr. Connally?' 'He ... was ... favorable toward Connally while ... in Russia. There is a possibility that he changed his mind" "[T]here is a possibility that Lee became hateful of Connally because the matter of this dishonorable discharge was dragging so long."

[D] The third-person pronouns "they" and "her" were spoken by her Russian-English interpreter.

[E] Lee's hardship discharge had been changed to "undesirable", but many called it "dishonorable".

[F] In fact, Lee did not know Connally personally; he did know Connally would be in the motorcade.

[G] Your author adds this footnote on the last day of 2015: Writing this book was complete on April 22, 2015, except for wonderful chapter 20, added when I learned what Mike Howard had seen. Then it required nine months with two agents to obtain and buy permissions to use photos and quotations.

Marina Porter in 1978 testimony to the House Select Committee on Assassinations

Described in chapter 15 was all pertinent testimony by Marina to the HSCA on Lee's attitude REGARDING KENNEDY. The last questioning there, about the incomprehensible contradiction if he intended to shoot the President he so consistently admired, came from committee chairman Louis Stokes, who continued his inquiry with this REGARDING CONNALLY:

"Q [Chairman STOKES]. Now, have you on occasions indicated that you thought perhaps he was not shooting at President Kennedy but was trying to hit someone else?

A [Mrs. PORTER]. It was my aloud speculation which doesn't have any foundation for it because it was very hard for me to even think about a person who could like someone can do such a thing to him. The reason I mentioned Mr. Connally, I mentioned his name only because Lee was corresponding at one time in his life with Governor Connally.

Q. Can you tell us a little bit more about that? What had he in effect said about Governor Connally?

A. Not very much. I just learned from him when we were in Russia that he did write Governor Connally for some legal matter. I think about his coming back to the United States or have something to do with the service, I do not recall what it was.

But then he received a letter from Governor Connally. Lee pointed out the envelope with, instead of a stamp, it was Mr. Connally's picture on it [see it on page 93] and he explained to me that is how people who want to be elected, it is a form of advertisement before an election or something like that.

Q. Did this have something to do with the type of a discharge that he had which he was dissatisfied with?

A. Well, at the time I thought it was just a matter of getting entrance visa or permission to enter United States again. That is what I thought at the time. Anyway, I heard the name in the Soviet Union, Mr. Connally. I thought maybe he was angry somehow at that man.

Q. I am sorry?

A. I thought maybe for some reason he was angry at that man.

Q. In expressing that anger, do you recall what he said?

A. No, I did not say that he was expressing anger. Immaturely [sic] [H] I tried to make some kind of logical explanation for why all this happened. It was hard for me to believe that he really was aiming at Mr. Kennedy.

Q. Were there several occasions in which he expressed himself regarding Governor Connally?

A. I don't remember right now.

Q. Can you recall having given testimony to someone regarding his attitude toward Governor Connally?

A. I had so many testimonies, I do not recall that. I don't remember.

Q. So at this time you have no recollection of that?

A. No." [3222]

Chairman Stokes did nothing with her suggestion that Connally might have been the target. He had as little interest in steering his committee's work in that direction as had the Warren Commissioners fourteen years before.

In his 2013 book *The Accidental Victim*, James Reston, Jr., as is his great talent, accurately and succinctly noted the origin of Marina's suggestion that the target was Connally:

"In 1978, Marina Oswald testified before the House Assassinations Committee. Almost offhandedly, assigning no particular significance to it herself and finding that the politicians of

---

[H] "Immaturely [sic]" is in the HSCA's published transcript. "[sic]" means they recognized an error but printed what she probably did not say, without correction. I think she most likely said "Naturally".

the House were no more interested than the Warren Commission had been, she told of how Connally's brush-off letter in February 1962 was the origin of the grudge, and of how it had arrived at their Minsk apartment in the big, white envelope whose front flaunted the large smiling face of John Connally, advertising his candidacy for governor of Texas." [3223]

"I heard the name in the Soviet Union, Mr. Connally. ... I thought maybe for some reason he was angry at that man."

Marguerite Oswald in testimony to the Warren Commission

After questioning the elder Mrs. Oswald about her knowledge of Lee's letter to John Connally — she learned about it after the assassination — commission general consul J. Lee Rankin asked: "Did you ever hear your son say anything against Governor Connally?" Marguerite answered — briefly, for once — "No, sir." [3224]

Robert Oswald in testimony to the Warren Commission

Commission member Allen Dulles and assistant counsel Albert Jenner, after asking brother Robert whether Lee had ever expressed an opinion about Kennedy ("No"), asked the same about John Connally. After pointing out that he had already testified about Lee's saying that he had written to Connally, thinking he was the Secretary of the Navy, for help with changing his discharge, Robert replied: "I do not recall any further discussion on that subject. And he did not indicate to me the pro or con of any antipathy toward Mr. Connally." [3225]

Robert Oswald recalling 1963 in his 1967 book *Lee*

On the afternoon of the shooting, at the Dallas FBI office he was asked: "Have you ever heard Lee express any hostility toward the President?" "No." The next question, probably within the first two minutes of the interview, was right on target: "We have a report that your brother was angry at Governor Connally because of some trouble over his discharge when Connally was Secretary of the Navy." "I told the agent that I had never heard Lee express any hostility toward Connally. I knew that Lee had addressed a letter to Connally protesting the reclassification of his discharge after his defection to Russia. But then Lee had received a letter informing him that Connally was no longer Secretary of the Navy, and had read that answer in my presence. He had said nothing at all to me that day that indicated he held Connally personally responsible for his dishonorable discharge from the Marines." [3226]

FBI Agent James Bookhout of Dallas in testimony to the Warren Commission

Special Agent Bookhout, with the FBI 22 years, told the Warren Commission about joining agent Hosty on Saturday, November 23, to listen to Oswald's responses to questions:

> "Mr. STERN. In your report before this interview you mentioned that he again denied shooting President Kennedy, and apparently said that he didn't know until then that Governor Connally had been shot?
>
> Mr. BOOKHOUT. That's correct. That was his statement, that he denied shooting President John F. Kennedy on November 22, 1963, and commented that he did not know that Governor John Connally had been shot.
>
> Mr. STERN. Did you form any impression about whether he was genuinely surprised? Did he look genuinely surprised to you, or how did you feel about that? I am just asking for your impression. If you don't have one, say so.

Mr. BOOKHOUT. No; I have no impression on that. I arrived at no conclusion." [3227]

"[H]e denied shooting President John F. Kennedy on November 22, 1963, and commented that he did not know that Governor John Connally had been shot."

George Bouhe in testimony to the Warren Commission

This elder and leader of the Fort Worth-Dallas Russian-speaking émigré community, in his testimony to the Commission was one of the first to suggest that Oswald may have had hostility toward Governor Connally because of Connally's refusal to help him with the discharge status. Bouhe volunteered this as his own analysis, not based on anything specific that Oswald had said. Because it is not direct testimony about an Oswald utterance, it does not bear witness in this chapter, but is recounted in Chapter 21 – OTHERS ON THIS TRAIL.

George De Mohrenschildt in a manuscript before his 1977 suicide

In the previous chapter REGARDING KENNEDY, under the same heading, are all of the George De Mohrenschildt manuscript words recording what Lee had said about President Kennedy. He also wrote of occasions on which they had spoken about John Connally:

"One day as George and Lee discussed the shortcomings of both the US and USSR, Lee said: 'Look at the politicians here, most of them. They want to be praised publicly of their honesty and good will. Connelly [sic], the governor of Texas, for example. In reality they will do all the degrading actions and yet try to appear in a good light.' This was the first time he mentioned his loathing for Governor Connally. What caused it, we shall show later." [3228]

"One of those evenings Lee spoke for the first time of his discharge from the Marine Corps. 'I received an honorable discharge and then those bastards, in the Navy, changed it into an undesirable discharge, just because I went to Russia and threw my passport in the face of the American consul.'
  'Didn't they do it because you lied? You were supposed to go back to the States to help making a living for your mother. . .' 'Oh, hell, that was just a crooked excuse,' he said sullenly. 'And Connally signed this undesirable discharge. . .'" [3229]

"'Say, Lee, it's in Japan that you got your discharge from the marine corps?' Lee did not like to elaborate on this touchy subject. 'I had to work to support my mother.' But it developed later, as we all know, that he did not go back to USA to support his mother but changed his mind and instead went to Russia. ... Later on Lee's honorable discharge was changed to undesirable discharge and he hated to talk about it, considered it unfair to him. This explains his hatred of Connelly [sic] who was Secretary of the Navy at the time of the change of Lee's discharge." [3230]

James Reston, Jr., in his pioneering book *The Accidental Victim*, correctly analyzed the two entries from De Mohrenschildt's manuscript:

"In 1978 the House Assassinations Committee discovered a manuscript de Mohrenschildt was writing to work out his metaphysical responsibility. In it the émigré spoke of Oswald's admiration for Kennedy and his hatred for John Connally.[3231] ... As he related Oswald's warm feeling toward Kennedy, he spoke equally of Oswald's torment over the unfairness of his military discharge downgrade. It explained Oswald's '*hatred of John Connally*,' the emigre wrote (emphasis mine)." [3232] ("mine" means Reston.)

"Lee said: '[T]he politicians ... want to be praised publicly [for] their honesty and good will. Connally ... for example. In reality they will do all the degrading actions and yet try to appear in a good light.' This was the first time he mentioned his loathing for

Governor Connally." " 'I received an honorable discharge and then those bastards in the Navy changed it into an undesirable discharge ... And Connally signed this undesirable discharge.' " "Lee's honorable discharge ... changed to undesirable ... explains his hatred of Connally who was Secretary of the Navy at the time of this change" "Oswald's torment over the unfairness of his military discharge downgrade ... explained Oswald's hatred of John Connally."

Alexandra De Mohrenschildt Taylor Gibson in testimony to the Warren Commission

The American-born daughter of Russian émigrés George and Jeanne, close to Marina in age, was asked by her parents to help the Oswalds and did so on several occasions. She was a keen observer and an accurate judge of character, one of the few to describe with believable detail Marina's bad teeth, lazy habits and unsavory penchant for arguing with Lee. As James Reston, Jr. points out: "Alexandra was a good witness, for in the fall of 1962, she had been married to an engineer with liberal politics named Gary Taylor and had listened as Oswald and Taylor engaged in political discussion." [3233] Associate Counsel Albert E. Jenner, Jr. questioned this credible witness at considerable length, including:

"Mr. JENNER. Was President Kennedy ever mentioned in the course of the discussions between your husband and Lee?

Mrs. GIBSON. Never, never. ... No, he was never mentioned. Now, the only person ever mentioned pertaining to that was the Governor of Texas. ... It was the Governor of Texas who was mentioned mostly.

Mr. JENNER. Tell us about that.

Mrs. GIBSON. First you are going to have to tell me who the Governor was.

Mr. JENNER. Connally.

Mrs. GIBSON. Connally. Wasn't that the one that—

Mr. JENNER. That had been Secretary of the Navy.

Mrs. GIBSON. That had been Secretary of the Navy, was it? Well, for some reason Lee just didn't like him. I don't know why, but he didn't like him.

Mr. JENNER. Would this refresh your recollection, that the subject of Governor Connally arose in connection with something about Lee's discharge from the Marines?

Mrs. GIBSON. I don't recall. I just know Lee never spoke too much about why he left the Marines or anything like that. I don't know. Maybe it was a dishonorable discharge, I don't know. All I know is that it was something he didn't talk about. And there was a reason why he did not like Connally.

Mr. JENNER. Whatever the reason was, he didn't articulate the reason particularly?

Mrs. GIBSON. No; he just didn't like him.

Mr. JENNER. But you have the definite impression he had an aversion to Governor Connally?

Mrs. GIBSON. Yes; but he never ever said a word about Kennedy.

Mr. JENNER. Did you answer?

Mrs. GIBSON. Yes; I did; yes.

Mr. JENNER. Your answer is yes?

Mrs. GIBSON. Yes.

Mr. JENNER. That he did have a definite aversion?

Mrs. GIBSON. Yes.

Mr. JENNER. To Governor Connally as a person?

Mrs. GIBSON. Yes.

Mr. JENNER. And did he speak of that reasonably frequently in these discussions?

Mrs. GIBSON. No; not really, no. He didn't bring it up frequently.

Mr. JENNER.　But he was definite and affirmative about it, was he?

Mrs. GIBSON.　Yes;　he didn't like him." [3234]

"[F]or some reason Lee just didn't like [Governor Connally].　I don't know why, but he didn't like him."　"Maybe it was a dishonorable discharge, I don't know.　All I know is that it was something he didn't talk about.　And there was a reason why he did not like Connally."　"'[Y]ou have the definite impression he had an aversion to Governor Connally?'　'Yes; but he never ever said a word about Kennedy.'"　"'He didn't bring it up frequently.'　'But he was definite and affirmative about it, was he?'　'Yes;　he didn't like [Governor Connally].'"

Chief of U.S. Secret Service James Rowley in testimony to the Warren Commission

Former Director of Central Intelligence Allen Dulles questioned the long-time head of the agency that protects presidents about whether Oswald's letter to Connally was threatening, whether Oswald should have been known to his agency, and whether he would be highlighted under new rules adopted after Dallas.　Chief Rowley stated intelligently and forcefully:

> "Now, Oswald wrote to the Governor intimating that he would use whatever means was necessary to obtain the change of his undesirable, or as he called it, dishonorable discharge. All legal means had been used in his case, where the Navy Review Board had examined it and came to a decision.　And this is an example of what we were trying to include in [warning] of this type of individual. ... [T]he first interest of this type was the letter to Governor Connally as Secretary of the Navy, in which he said he would use whatever means he could to correct that discharge, inferring, of course, that he would apply illegal means if he could." [3235]

Unfortunately, the new threat assessment procedures and that professional opinion came in June 1964, too late to save lives in November 1963.

"Oswald wrote ... the letter to Governor Connally as Secretary of the Navy, in which he said he would use whatever means he could to correct that discharge, inferring, of course, that he would apply illegal means if he could."

Other witnesses before the Warren Commission

Many witnesses interviewed by the Commission were asked if they ever heard of Lee Oswald saying anything about John Connally, either to them or to others.　Because of their closeness to Lee, and because they testified to the Commission about his comments REGARDING KENNEDY, the "I never heard him say anything about Connally" statements of mother Marguerite and brother Robert (twice) are included as articles above.

In addition, these fourteen witnesses testified that he had never said anything about Connally in their presence, nor had they ever heard that he had said anything to any other persons:　Samuel B. Ballen;[3236]　Max E. Clark;[3237]　Jeanne Eugenia Fomenko (Mrs. George) De Mohrenschildt;[3238]　Declan P. Ford;[3239]　Katherine Katrina Evstratova "Katya" (Mrs. Declan) Ford;[3240]　J. W. "Will" Fritz;[3241]　Paul Roderick Gregory;[3242]　Elena A. Hall;[3243]　John Raymond Hall;[3244]　Anna N. Meller;[3245]　Marilyn Dorothea Murret;[3246]　Michael R. Paine;[3247]　Ruth Hyde (Mrs. Michael) Paine;[3248]　Gary E. Taylor.[3249]

All of Oswald REGARDING CONNALLY, in the order in which the quotations appeared above:

"Stresses in the handwriting suggest that Oswald was venting considerable anger toward Connally." {O}

"I didn't shoot John Kennedy. I didn't even know Governor John Connally had been shot." {O}

"We received a letter from Connally. Lee said these are bureaucrats, and he was dissatisfied." {O}

"There was more reason to dislike Connally than Kennedy." {O}

"'Did you testify that Lee said that if he were here he would vote for Mr. Connally?' 'He was favorable toward Connally while in Russia. There is a possibility that he changed his mind'" {O}

"There is a possibility that Lee became hateful of Connally because the matter of this dishonorable discharge was dragging so long." {O}

"I heard the name in the Soviet Union, Mr. Connally. I thought maybe for some reason he was angry at that man." {O}

"He denied shooting President John F. Kennedy on November 22, 1963, and commented that he did not know that Governor John Connally had been shot." {W}

"Lee said: 'The politicians want to be praised publicly for their honesty and good will. Connally, for example. In reality they will do all the degrading actions and yet try to appear in a good light.' This was the first time he mentioned his loathing for Governor Connally." {O}

"I received an honorable discharge and then those bastards in the Navy changed it into an undesirable discharge. And Connally signed this undesirable discharge." {O}

"Lee's honorable discharge changed to undesirable explains his hatred of Connally who was Secretary of the Navy at the time of this change." {W}

"Oswald's torment over the unfairness of his military discharge downgrade explained Oswald's hatred of John Connally." {D}

"For some reason Lee just didn't like Governor Connally. I don't know why, but he didn't like him." {O}

"Maybe it was a dishonorable discharge, I don't know. All I know is that it was something he didn't talk about. And there was a reason why he did not like Connally." {O}

"'You have the definite impression he had an aversion to Governor Connally?' 'Yes; but he never ever said a word about Kennedy.'" {D}

"'He didn't bring it up frequently.' 'But he was definite and affirmative about it, was he?' 'Yes; he didn't like Governor Connally.'" {D}

"Oswald wrote the letter to Governor Connally as Secretary of the Navy, in which he said he would use whatever means he could to correct that discharge, inferring, of course, that he would apply illegal means if he could. " {O}

As was done with statements about Kennedy in the preceding chapter, the 17 above about Connally are now winnowed to give a better, fairly-weighted sense of what Oswald said or conveyed. From the 17 statements, 2 {W} Witness and 3 {D} Duplicate statements are removed; the final list on the next page contains only the 12 {O} Originals:

Original statements by or about Oswald REGARDING CONNALLY, in same order as above:

"Stresses in the handwriting suggest that Oswald was venting considerable anger toward Connally." ⇩

"I didn't shoot John Kennedy. I didn't even know Governor John Connally had been shot." ⇔

"We received a letter from Connally. Lee said these are bureaucrats, and he was dissatisfied." ⇩

"There was more reason to dislike Connally than Kennedy." ⇩

"'Did you testify that Lee said that if he were here he would vote for Mr. Connally?' 'He was favorable toward Connally while in Russia. There is a possibility that he changed his mind'" ⇧

"There is a possibility that Lee became hateful of Connally because the matter of this dishonorable discharge was dragging so long." ⇩

"I heard the name in the Soviet Union, Mr. Connally. I thought maybe for some reason he was angry at that man." ⇩

"Lee said: 'The politicians want to be praised publicly for their honesty and good will. Connally, for example. In reality they will do all the degrading actions and yet try to appear in a good light.' This was the first time he mentioned his loathing for Governor Connally." ⇩

"I received an honorable discharge and then those bastards in the Navy changed it into an undesirable discharge. And Connally signed this undesirable discharge." ⇩

"For some reason Lee just didn't like Governor Connally. I don't know why, but he didn't like him." ⇩

"Maybe it was a dishonorable discharge, I don't know. All I know is that it was something he didn't talk about. And there was a reason why he did not like Connally." ⇩

"Oswald wrote the letter to Governor Connally as Secretary of the Navy, in which he said he would use whatever means he could to correct that discharge, inferring, of course, that he would apply illegal means if he could." ⇩

Employing the same even-handed treatment as REGARDING KENNEDY in the preceding chapter, those 12 statements have been judged and arrows attached. One with ⇔ is the same "I didn't shoot …" as in the Kennedy chapter; it does not convey a regard, so is removed. Marina's recall "He was favorable toward Connally while in Russia. There is a possibility that he changed his mind" is at least positive at one time, so gets a thumbs-up ⇧. Some, including members of the Warren Commission, thought that significant, but it is not when one considers its timing. It was uttered in Minsk, when Lee had hope that this discharge would be returned to honorable. He mailed his appeal for that only after returning to Texas, and learned of its ultimate flat denial in mid-1963. Thus, he had no specific reason in Minsk to hate Connally for refusing to help until the process ended with the detested "undesirable" intact. Then, and only then, did he have good reason to dislike Connally, "a resident of Ft. Worth as I am."

The other ten merit and receive ⇩ arrows. Bringing forward the visual presentation at the end of preceding chapter REGARDING KENNEDY, and joining to it the original statements from this chapter REGARDING CONNALLY, here is the pattern of all favorable and unfavorable opinions ever known to be stated by or attributed to Oswald regarding the two possible targets in the limousine on Elm Street:

	Kennedy	Connally
	⇧ ⇧ ⇧ ⇧	
	⇧ ⇧ ⇧ ⇧	
	⇧ ⇧ ⇧ ⇧	
Positive = Favorable	⇧ ⇧ ⇧ ⇧	
	⇧ ⇧ ⇧ ⇧	
	⇧ ⇧ ⇧ ⇧ ⇧	
	⇧ ⇧ ⇧ ⇧ ⇧	
	⇧ ⇧ ⇧ ⇧ ⇧	
	⇧ ⇧ ⇧ ⇧ ⇧	
	⇧ ⇧ ⇧ ⇧ ⇧	⇧
	⇩	⇩
		⇩
		⇩
		⇩
Negative = Unfavorable		⇩
		⇩
		⇩
		⇩
		⇩
		⇩

The process of these two chapters has reached its goal. The stark difference above brightly illuminates that he thought very differently about the two — he liked Kennedy and disliked Connally. Does this prove motive? No, but it is strong evidence from a dead man who did not live to answer questions, and did not leave an explanation of why he did what he did. If there were to be a trial of Lee Oswald, the display above, in which every one of those fifty-seven arrows can be traced back to its root, would be highly persuasive to a jury.

For any who think Oswald must have intended to kill Kennedy because that's what he did, this should erect a very large STOP-AND-THINK sign.[1] The simple physical evidence of Chapter 14 – TOO CLOSE TO CALL demonstrated that killing versus wounding could just as easily have gone the other way — one absolutely cannot reason back to the intent. If you think it most likely that Oswald aimed at Kennedy, please explain why the man who thought as these two chapters clearly demonstrated would do that. Why would he disregard his strong dislike for Connally to instead harm Kennedy, whom he so clearly liked? If you can answer that, you will be, so far as this long-observing author knows, the first to do so, ever!

> Key point of this chapter:
> **Relatives, friends and others testify to Oswald's comments regarding Connally: 1 perhaps positive, 10 negative.**
> **The contrast to Kennedy: 45 - 1 is dramatic and important.**

---

[1] Wherever this author worked at IBM, yes, we really did have THINK signs on our office walls.

POLITICAL PROCLIVITY [A]

Oswald probably obeyed his natural predilection

> "History is a relentless master. It has no present, only the past rushing into the future. To try to hold fast is to be swept aside."
> — **John F. Kennedy** [3250]

THERE IS ANOTHER STRONG DEMONSTRATION OF PROBABILITY that deserves to be considered because it illustrates a telling relationship among the trio of interest: Oswald, Kennedy and Connally. This chapter is a brief explanation and exhibition of what the spectrum of political positions may add to our understanding of the killer's intent.

Lee Oswald was always interested in politics, from his childhood in New York City where he received his first political handout on a sidewalk, until he died. He regularly read newspapers and considered himself to be politically astute. And he was, in his immature way. He could probably define the "political spectrum" and place parties and politicians on it.

Most have heard of that spectrum but may benefit from a brief refresher from the increasingly comprehensive and accurate online Wikipedia:[B] "The terms Right and Left refer to political affiliations which originated early in the French Revolutionary era of 1789–1799, and referred originally to the seating arrangements in the various legislative bodies of France. The aristocracy sat on the right of the Speaker (traditionally the seat of honor) and the commoners sat on the Left.[C] ... According to the simplest left–right axis, communism and socialism are usually regarded internationally as being on the left, opposite fascism and conservatism on the right." [3251]

[A] "A natural propensity or inclination, predisposition." – *The American Heritage College Dictionary*

[B] A small request: If you use Wikipedia, please join in contributing to its financial support. Thank you!

[C] Our Congress is backward; as seen by the Vice President in the Senate and the Speaker in the House, the more-aristocratic Republicans are on the left, the commoner Democrats are to her-or-his right. This may have been done for reasons similar to switching the diagonal stripes on American neckties from the British / to our \. Our rebellious colonial forefathers proudly took the leaning in heraldry that had long been reserved for bastards. Now you know.

It is generally agreed that in the United States, the political array progresses thus: [D]

Communist	Socialist	Liberal	Progressive	Democrat	Moderate	Republican	Conservative	Tea Party [E]	John Bircher	Fascist

In parliamentary democracies, the larger European countries being prime examples, where a majority of all the members in a legislative body must agree on one leader for the government, coalitions are regularly developed among relatively similar parties and politicians. There you will hear of "liberal democrats", "Christian conservatives", etc.

Birds of a feather flock together. It is human nature to like, live and associate with those most like us; and on the contrary to be suspicious of or hostile to, and accordingly to distance ourselves from, those who think and act in opposition. Because of that reality, we now look at Lee Oswald and where he fit into the world of the 1960s, because that may tell us much about the probability of what he intended in Dallas. Placed on the left-to-right spectrum displayed above, after considerable thought and fact-checking with authorities this author respects, these are the principal players worthy of our consideration in the early 1960s:

Khrushchev	Castro	Oswald	Kennedy	Johnson	Nixon	Connally	Walker

You may disagree about the placement of one or another by one position — perhaps thinking that Oswald really belongs to the left between Nikita Khrushchev and Fidel Castro — and that's just fine. But I do not believe that anyone above can plausibly be moved by more than one position. Their philosophies are well-enough known to require these relative positions.

Most important to this discussion — in truth, the reason for it — is the considerable difference between Kennedy and Connally, validated by the citizens of Texas as Lyndon Johnson explained the purposes of the fatal trip in his autobiography: "A Texas poll, taken a few weeks before his trip, showed that only 38 per cent of the people approved of what he was doing as President. The same poll showed Governor Connally with an 81 per cent approval. The fact is that [conservative] Governor Connally was more in tune with the prevailing [conservative] political thinking in Texas." [3252] In political approval, the difference between 38% and 81% is not a valley, it's the Grand Canyon!

President Kennedy, inured to the need for getting along with opposing political figures, had to calm his less-political wife. In 1964 she would tell historian Arthur Schlesinger:

"[T]he day before Jack died in Texas, I said to him, 'I just can't stand Governor Connally. I can't stand his soft mouth.' He was so pleased with himself and he'd spend all our times in the car telling Jack, I guess, how far he'd run ahead of him in Texas. So, I'd say, 'What's he

---

[D] Libertarian, an amalgam of being socially liberal while also fiscally conservative, is more a personal philosophy than political position, thus somewhat of a different dimension, so is not included here.

[E] If some of these names are gone and forgotten by the time you read this — I say good riddance!

trying to tell you? It seems so rude what he's saying to you all the time.' ... and then when I said that I hated Connally, Jack was so sweet. He sort of rubbed my back—it was as we were going to bed—and said, 'You mustn't say that, you mustn't say that.' He said, 'If you start to say or think that you hate someone, then the next day you'll act as if you hated him,' and then, 'We've come down here to Texas to heal everything up and you'll make it all impossible.' ...

During the Dallas motorcade, in the last words they spoke, Connally, a conservative Democrat, told the President of a soon-to-be-published poll that showed him running ahead of JFK in Texas in 1964. Kennedy replied, 'That doesn't surprise me.'" [3253]

Looking at the eight men (no women — this was 50+ years ago, back in the dark ages) in their political positions on the previous page, let us consider some realities and probabilities.

We know with absolute certainty that Oswald, earlier in 1963, shot with intent to kill Edwin Walker. Two years before, General Walker got himself into trouble by espousing John Birch Society beliefs to his troops. After investigation, Kennedy OKed removing him from the list of those promotable to a higher level, bringing his career to an end. Walker then resigned, to devote himself to extreme right wing political activity. Lee told Marina he had shot at Walker. That unsuccessful (what else? — that's the norm with Lee) attempt had this pattern:

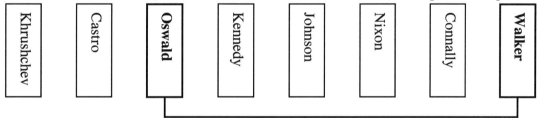

A month before the Dallas tragedy, a newspaper quoted Walker: "Kennedy is a liability to the free world.", and a Texas Democratic National Committeeman warned: "A man who would make that kind of statement is capable of doing harm to the President." [3254] Marina told the Warren Commission that when she asked why he had tried to kill Walker, Lee "said that this was a very bad man, that he was a fascist, that he was the leader of a fascist organization ..." [3255] He added that if someone had killed Adolf Hitler in time it would have saved many lives.

Fifteen years after Oswald's 1963 shots at Walker (in April) and the Kennedy/Connally limousine (in November), the House Select Committee on Investigations, which I discussed and disrespected (today, simply "dissed") in Chapter 8 – REHASHES, very slightly redeemed its incompetence with this observation in its final report's section "The motive":

"In the city of Dallas, no one figure so epitomized anticommunism as General Walker. Considering the various activities to which Oswald devoted his time, his efforts and his very existence, General Walker could be readily seen as 'an ultimate enemy.' It is known that Oswald was willing to risk death for his beliefs, so it is certainly not unreasonable to find that he might attempt to kill Walker, a man who was intensely opposed to his ideology." [3256]

Yes, with Adolf Hitler dead, Edwin Walker was Oswald's "ultimate enemy".

Skilled and thoughtful analyst Vincent Bugliosi saw the situation and resultant problem clearly: "[A]lthough his trying to kill General Walker made some sense in that it was the Far Left (Oswald) shooting at the Far Right (Walker), why would someone on the political left like Oswald shoot at someone in the middle, or if anything, left of center, like Kennedy?" [3257]

The pattern illustrated in the political spectrum above is classic: murderous dislike for an enemy, or at least one greatly disliked, at a position far removed from one's self.

Knowing that, is it more likely that Lee aimed at Kennedy, a liberal much like himself:

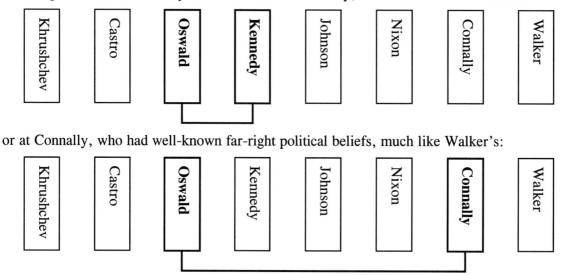

or at Connally, who had well-known far-right political beliefs, much like Walker's:

The pattern on the previous page shows the one verified attempt to murder. Of the two here, which is the similar pattern for Oswald? Certainly it is the lower, for him to intend harm to right-wing conservative Connally, with views similar to Walker's, very distant from himself on the left. The stark contrast between these two charts, assessed from a political viewpoint, affords solid reason to think Oswald's intended victim was more likely Connally, not Kennedy.

Two women who knew him best, plus two analysts and his only friend, have put words into testimony and writing to explain the probabilities displayed above:

Marina was asked in her first 1964 testimony before the Warren Commission for her impression of Lee's attitude toward Kennedy. She replied: "[W]hen I found out that Lee had shot at the President, for me this was surprising. And I didn't believe it. I didn't believe for a long time that Lee had done that. That he had wanted to kill Kennedy—because perhaps Walker was there again, perhaps he wanted to kill him." [3258] [F]

In her final testimony, she volunteered: "When the assassination of President Kennedy took place, I was asking people whether ... General Walker was with President Kennedy. It perhaps was a silly question, but I thought that he—" [3259] and then a Senator interrupted.

No, Walker was not there again, in the limousine with President Kennedy as it passed the Texas School Book Depository. But sitting directly in front of Kennedy, in a straight line for bullets from the 6th floor window, was a man whose rightist beliefs approached those of General Walker.

After Marina, Mrs. Jeanne De Mohrenschildt probably knew Lee better than any other woman, because of the extensive time she spent with the couple. During her 1964 testimony to the Warren Commission, George's wife was asked:

"Mr. JENNER. Did you have any impression that [Lee Oswald] was envious [of President Kennedy] at any time?

Mrs. DE MOHRENSCHILDT. No, and in fact that is what doesn't make any sense, because I don't think he ever said anything against, and whatever the President was doing, Kennedy

---

[F] Credit must be given for voicing this, only months after the shooting, that perhaps Oswald was aiming at an understandably hated person and hit Kennedy by accident. She was (still is) a smart cookie!

was doing, Lee was completely exactly with the same ideas, exactly. If he would shoot Walker that would be understandable, even if he would be shooting at Connally that is understandable, too." [3260]

As always when any witness volunteered an idea that might have led the Commission to Lee's actual motive and intent, and thus to the truth, no further questions were asked about why it would be so understandable that the Lee who shot at Walker would also shoot at Connally. If only a commissioner or counsel had pursued that line, the Warren Commission might have understood Oswald's motive in 1964, and this book would not be necessary 50+ years later!

In 1978, Marina (formerly Oswald) Porter was questioned by counsel James Wolf of the U.S. House of Representatives Select Committee on Assassinations:

> "Q [Mr. WOLF]. Lee's attitude toward President Kennedy was certainly different than his attitude toward General Walker, am I correct?
> A [Mrs. PORTER]. Yes.
> Q. Had you had any prior indication of any dislike for President Kennedy on his behalf?
> A. No; that is what is so strange about the whole event." [3261]

Sadly, fifteen years after the shooting in Dallas, this new committee did not think seriously about Marina's affirmation that Lee's attitudes toward Walker and Kennedy were certainly different, so it would be strange for the man who shot at one to shoot at the other.

Assassination analyst Carl Oglesby's book *Who Killed JFK?* highlighted the meaning of the displays above: "Oswald's alleged 'capacity for violence' does not explain why he would kill two men as politically diverse as JFK and Walker. Marina testified that Oswald praised JFK but called Walker a 'fascist,' 'compared [him] to Adolf Hitler' and remarked that 'if someone had killed Hitler in time it would have saved many lives.'" [3262]

Finally, it is interesting to look at this subject in a mirror. The women quoted above had in common the thought that if the Lee they knew had fired, it should have been at someone on the far-right conservative-to-fascist wing. The same incongruity was expressed in a fine little 1964 book by Warren Leslie, a Dallas newspaper reporter turned business executive, who continued to write books and articles. *Dallas Public and Private* is a serious work by a life-long Dallasite, explaining the city's traditions, institutions, leaders and culture. Writing of the immediate aftermath of November 22, he reported:

> "The first thought in the minds of the scores of people I've seen since the assassination was that it must have been done by a member of the right wing. Many of the local rightists themselves thought so. I watched the color go completely from a man's face at the Imperial Club when the murder was announced. Politically, he stands well to the right of Goldwater. At that moment, he was convinced that one of his colleagues had committed murder." [3263]

The point made before this was that if Oswald fired, it should be at a rightist. Now we have the mirror-image opinion, from Leslie, that whoever fired at Kennedy should have been "a member of the right wing." Yes, any way one looks at the shooting while paying heed to the politics involved in wounding and murdering politicians by politically-oriented assassins, there is absolutely no sense, no reasonableness in thinking it was Oswald of the left-of-center shooting at Kennedy of the left-near-center. None.

Marina testified that after Lee told her of his attempt to kill General Edwin Walker: "I told him that he had no right to kill people in peacetime, he had no right to take their life because not everybody has the same ideas as he has. People cannot be all alike. He said that this was a very bad man, that he was a fascist, that he was the leader of a fascist organization, and when I said that even though all of that might be true, just the same he had no right to take his life, he said if someone had killed Hitler in time it would have saved many lives." [3264]

George De Mohrenschildt, Lee's only "friend" in the U.S., typed a manuscript after the shooting in Dallas, discovered and re-printed by the HSCA after his suicide. Excerpts have been included in chapters 15 and 16 relating Oswald's statements about Kennedy and Connally. In addition, De Mohrenschildt, a person knowledgeable about and interested in politics, wrote of Lee's position, and potential targets, in terms of the political spectrum:

> "Lee gave George a print of one of the famous photos, taken by Marina in the back yard, of him proudly showing his rifle, pistol, and two Communist publications. George wrote of "The ... picture of Lee with the rifle and Marina's inscription" [3265] "in Russian. In translation it reads 'This is the hunter of fascists! Ha! Ha! Ha!'" [3266] "would indicate that he might have been considering hunting fascists - and in his mind General Walker was one - but certainly not our president Kennedy." [3267]

> "Think on the inscription on the picture we had ... How could a hunter of the fascists be the assassin of a young and liberal President? Would Lee address this photograph so endearingly to me, knowing well how much I liked John F. Kennedy, had he intended to assassinate him? Would his wife call him, even sneeringly, 'the fascists' hunter' if her husband was preparing to assassinate the most liberal President America ever had?" [3268]

This has been a simple chapter making a simple point. Let's leave it at this: If anyone chooses to argue that Oswald intended to kill Kennedy, will he or she please explain why Lee would do that despite their similar politics, instead of aiming at the equally-available Connally, a politician with beliefs vastly different from his, over there on the right wing close to General Walker, at whom we are certain beyond all doubt that Oswald fired with intent to kill?

It may well be argued that this is all ancillary. Oswald's prime motive for shooting at Connally was not political leanings, but because of the terrible injustice Lee believed had been done to him with Connally's assistance. But, hating his victim's politics undoubtedly helped!

Key point of this chapter:
Far-left-wing Lee Oswald was more likely to intend to murder right-wing Connally than fellow left-of-center Kennedy.

CONNALLY WILL RIDE

When Oswald sprang into action, and what he could not do, are revealing

> "No one will ever know what passed through Oswald's mind during the week before November 22, 1963."
> — The *Warren Report* [3269]

THIS IS THE SHORTEST CHAPTER in the book. What's here was reported, but not analyzed, in Chapter 5 – MISFIT. It is revealing and argues with great strength and clarity about Oswald's intent, so deserves its own dedicated chapter. As experienced prosecutor Vincent Bugliosi wrote, "I never take a chance on assuming a jury is going to see something important without my help. So many things in life are only obvious once they are pointed out." [3270]

Three key questions, the subject of this chapter, are: When did Lee Oswald take his first overt action toward shooting someone in the limousine on Friday, November 22, 1963? What does that tell us? Were there other actions he should have taken, but did not have time? The answers to those three are quite definite and unambiguous; they point with precision.

In chapter 5 it was shown on page 164 that on Friday, November 15, a week before the shooting, the *Dallas Times Herald* announced that President Kennedy would attend a lunch event on November 22 at the Dallas Trade Mart, adjacent to the northbound Stemmons Freeway. Any thoughtful person could predict that the President would fly into Dallas, almost certainly landing at Love Field. Then, there would most probably be some motorcade through downtown, and that would almost certainly be on the main street of Dallas, Main Street. To display the Kennedys to as many voters as possible, and thus to avoid driving past the Trade Mart twice (on a drive to downtown, then back again to it) the motorcade must proceed along Main Street in an east-to-west direction. These are all probabilities, not certainties, but all are very high probabilities. Anyone could predict and win bets on all of them. [3271]

To drive from Main Street to the Stemmons Freeway, and thence on to the Trade Mart, the only path — without unnecessarily demolishing a road divider before the Triple Underpass, never considered — would be to turn north onto Houston, then west onto Elm to get to the Stemmons — and thus pass directly in front of the Texas School Book Depository. From westbound Main Street to northbound Stemmons there were no other reasonable possibilities.

Everything in the two preceding paragraphs was "Elementary, my dear Watson!" [A] to anyone familiar with the area as early as Friday, November 15. Lee could have recognized the availability of Kennedy-as-target that Friday. If, as usual, he read newspapers only when left behind by his TSBD workmates, he would have known no later than Monday, November 18.

On Saturday, November 16, both Dallas papers (page 164) confirmed the plans, with the *Times Herald* eliminating any need for conjecture: "The Trade Mart is on Stemmons Freeway and the presidential party apparently will loop through the downtown area, probably on Main Street, en route from Dallas Love Field." [3272] With no need to bet on probabilities, Oswald could, no later than Monday, be quite certain of Kennedy-as-target riding past him.

"The President's visit was by far the biggest story ... *The Dallas Morning News* had eight different stories about it on Sunday, November 17 ..." [3273] On Tuesday, November 19, the *Dallas Morning News* reported the President's motorcade would travel "Main to Houston, Houston to Elm, Elm under the Triple Underpass to Stemmons Freeway, and on to the Trade Mart." [3274] That same day, November 19, the afternoon newspaper, the *Dallas Times Herald*, reported: "The motorcade will then pass through downtown ... west on Main, turning back to Elm at Houston and then out Stemmons Freeway to the Trade Mart." [3275] It was definite in either, confirmed by being in both, that Kennedy would ride by in front of the Depository.

Lee habitually read both of the newspapers because they had different political leanings. It's almost certain that he did that, read both, but we don't know when. It may have been as early as the day they were published, Tuesday, or as late as the following morning, Wednesday. We will never know, there is no way to find out — and it does not matter.

On either Tuesday or Wednesday, November 19 or 20, Oswald would know with certainty that President Kennedy would ride in front of his building on Friday. The key point is that like "the dog in the night" (to be explained in chapter 19), he did nothing — this is very important and worth repeating — *he did nothing on Tuesday or Wednesday*.

A security car will lead the motorcade which will travel on Mockingbird Lane, Lemmon Avenue, Turtle Creek Boulevard, Cedar Springs, Harwood, Main and Stemmons Freeway.

President and Mrs. Kennedy and Gov. Connally will ride in the second car.

Secret Service agents will ride in the next car and the fourth will carry Vice-President and Mrs. Johnson and Mrs. Connally.

On Wednesday, November 20, 1963, the *Dallas Morning News* printed on its front page an article that will change history. A clipping of the full article was displayed on page 168. Shown here on the left is a close-up of the column that must have caught Lee's full attention, then galvanized him into immediate action — very importantly, the first overt action he takes that will allow him to fire at the limousine on Friday. [3276]

"President and Mrs. Kennedy and Gov. Connally will ride in the second car." is the first mention that John Connally will ride in the motorcade. Not only does it put him into some vehicle, but it explicitly says he will ride with the Kennedys in the second car, which will pass in front of the Book Depository.

[A] Although it's regularly attributed to him, Sherlock Holmes never said that. He said "elementary" and he also said "my dear Watson", but never together. As with many other footnotes, now you know!

A brief digression: It is usual in human events that forecasts do not eventuate precisely as planned, and that will be true of the article above. The second paragraph predicts three passengers in the car behind the leading security car: two Kennedys and the Governor. Then the third paragraph says that Nellie Connally will be in the fourth car, two vehicles behind, riding with Lyndon and Lady Bird Johnson.

On Friday, for fence-mending party unity important to the President, U.S. Senator Ralph Yarborough will be arm-twisted into riding in the Vice President's car. Perhaps that won't leave room for Mrs. Connally, or maybe someone with good sensibilities realizes that novice campaigner Mrs. Kennedy will benefit from being with another politician's wife, or simply to bring better balance, Nellie and John Connally will ride together, directly in front of Jacqueline and John Kennedy. That is not quite what news articles prepared Lee to expect on Friday, and may help explain why there will be (next chapter) The Shot Not Taken.

The supremely important fact completely missed by the Warren Commission, and then by most observers, is this: For days, knowing that **Kennedy** will be right in front of him, **Oswald did nothing**. In stark contrast, immediately upon learning that **Connally** will ride by in front of him, **Oswald sprang into action**.

He most likely read the Wednesday newspaper in the TSBD domino room at 10:00 AM on Thursday, November 21. If you question this supremely important timing, please re-read the testimony of five co-workers on page 158, all listed in the endnote there. Lee recognized the opportunity to get justice or revenge — he would probably feel them to be one and the same — and quickly had the thought and took the action described in full on page 169; that is, before noon he went to his ride-giver, Wesley Frazier who was "standing ... at the four-headed table ... and he said, 'Could I ride home with you this afternoon?'" [3277] Good guy Wes agreed, and Lee could now fetch his man-killing rifle from Ruth Paine's garage in Irving.

That important timing is not the only important evidence. There are two clinchers: Chapter 12 – The Rifle stated that the rifle could be loaded with seven cartridges — and before going into action, it certainly should be. But Lee fired three and one was left unfired: four! So, he carried to certainly the most important act of his life a rifle missing three potentially-essential rounds. Why? There is only one logical answer: The four cartridges were what had remained from his last practice session. Because there were only a few dealers, and Lee could not drive, he had no opportunity to buy more and have a firearm ready for anything. If he had known of his chance at Connally one day earlier, he could easily have bused to buy bullets for a full load — and also taken a second important action:

I was delighted to read Thomas Mallon's portrait-in-words of Ruth Hyde Paine, the solid woman who befriended and sheltered Marina and also helped Lee, in his sensitive book *Mrs. Paine's Garage: and the Murder of John F. Kennedy*. Apropos of absolutely nothing in his main text, Mallon inserted this perceptive footnote:

> "Ruth still believes that Oswald may not have decided to shoot the President until Thursday, the 21st, during his workday at the Book Depository. Had he taken the decision earlier, he would likely have carried his pistol to work that day, knowing he couldn't return to his rooming house that night—not while he was depending on a ride out to Irving with Linnie Mae Randle's brother to pick up the more-important rifle." [3278]

Yes! Here is yet another supremely important "didn't do" that is very strong evidence, and I am much comforted to learn that another person, Ruth whom I greatly admire, also noticed it.

It's probably clearest to explain this point by walking it backward: Immediately after firing three rifle shots at the Kennedy-Connally limousine, what did Lee set out to accomplish? He did not attempt to flee from Dallas, such as to a Greyhound or Trailways bus station or to the railway depot — perhaps to flee to Mexico City to be able to prove, this time, to the Cuban embassy his new credential as an assassin of Castro's enemy. No, rather than trying to escape, he hastened to his rented room, specifically to get his .38 revolver. Why? That was to be very decisively demonstrated within minutes when he shot, then with a fourth bullet executed, poor Officer Tippit who stopped him. His purpose was to have the pistol to avoid capture.

It should be apparent that even Lee, who did not usually think things through with logic, would have *first armed himself with the pistol before firing the rifle*, to best protect himself as he fled from the TSBD to wherever in the world he planned to go. If he had thought, on any day through Wednesday, November 20, of firing his rifle at the motorcade on Friday, November 22, then he could have easily armed himself with the pistol — by going as usual on the Wednesday evening bus to his rented room, returning to the TSBD with the pistol on Thursday morning and easily concealing it in any of hundreds of crannies among book cartons, then on Thursday evening going with Wes to Irving to pick up the rifle.

But — *he did not* — and to this author that is clinching proof, added to his hurried trip on Thursday to Irving for the more essential rifle, that *he did not know* of his opportunity to accomplish his true intent *until Thursday* morning, when he read in the front-page Wednesday news article that CONNALLY WILL RIDE!

Ruth Hyde Paine, an intelligent, curious, solid thinker, noted that "Had he taken the decision earlier, he would likely have carried his pistol to work that [Thurs]day, knowing he couldn't return to his rooming house that night" because making the decision on Thursday, he could go to either his room or Mrs. Paine's garage, but *not both*, so he was forced to choose the latter because the killing shots he intended for Friday absolutely required the rifle.

These are three compelling facts, not opinions, not probabilities — *facts*. First, Lee did nothing for several days after knowing that President Kennedy would ride past him, but hastened into action as soon as he learned that Connally would be in the car. Second, to go to Paines' for the rifle, he could not also go to a dealer to buy cartridges to fill the rifle. Third, he hurried from the TSBD to his pistol after firing the rifle, only because he did not know he was going to need the rifle until it was too late for him to retrieve both rifle and revolver.

This chapter has presented physical evidence in the form of indisputable timing that Oswald did nothing when he knew that Kennedy would pass by, but that he took immediate action to enable shooting as soon as he learned that CONNALLY WILL RIDE right in front of him. Then, to get his absolutely essential rifle, he did not have time to buy cartridges to fill it, nor could he have the pistol he certainly wanted for his escape.

Key points of this chapter:

Oswald showed no interest and did nothing when he knew that Kennedy would ride by his building, but sprang into action when he read Connally would be in the car. He had only a chance to get the rifle. Not buying bullets to fill it, and not having his pistol, make a case that Connally was the target.

THE SHOT NOT TAKEN

Strong evidence that Oswald's intent was to shoot Connally

> "We came west on Main Street to Houston Street and took a right, facing right into that building. The building with the window was looking right at us as we came up to Elm Street."
> — **Stavis "Steve" Ellis**,[A] sergeant of motorcycle escort [3279]

PRESIDENT KENNEDY WAS SITTING, AS ALWAYS, on the passenger (right) side of the back seat as the limousine entered Dealey Plaza and turned toward Lee Oswald. Why "**AS ALWAYS**"? Because that's where all Presidents sit, and where Kennedy had dependably seated himself since exactly two days after his inauguration.

We are fortunate to know and share the precise moment when the new President learned where to sit. Two days into his presidency, on January 22, 1961, Kennedy invited his newly-appointed Under Secretary of the Navy, Paul Fay, to go to Sunday Mass with him. The two had become great friends when they trained together in 1942 at PT boat school, became captains of the small but fast plywood boats, then in tandem battled the Japanese navy in the South Pacific. Fay was a red-headed Irishman, full of camaraderie and fun, a close companion for Kennedy's last 21 years. Who could be a better choice for the important Navy post than the best Navy wartime buddy? In the 1943 photo [3280] of PT officers in the Solomon Islands, Kennedy is front and center. Fay has his usual big smile at right — and on the next page.

[A] The quote is from *No More Silence*, where a footnote illuminates how we Americans got our names: "The name Stavis has been a curiosity to a number of researchers, including the author. Sergeant Ellis's father was a Greek immigrant who entered Ellis Island at the age of thirteen. His surname, Heliopoulis, was eventually changed to Ellis either as a shortened version of Heliopoulis or for Ellis Island itself. Stavis is the Anglicized derivation of the Greek 'Stavros,' while 'Steve,' as Ellis is known to his friends, is the Americanized version of Stavis." — Sneed, Larry A., page 142.

In his loving memoir of good friend JFK, *The Pleasure of His Company*, "Red" Fay described learning where to sit in a presidential car:

"Sunday morning at 10:30 I was at the White House, waiting for the President at the south entrance ... About 10:50 he came striding in with that very special gait of his. When he got to the car, I stood aside so the President could enter. He seated himself behind the driver, and I jumped into the seat on his right. As we left the White House grounds by the west gate, a gathering of a hundred or so cheered as we passed through. Strangely enough, most of them seemed to be peering in on my side of the car and those who didn't spot the President next to me seemed a little perplexed. Being a friendly soul, I happily waved back.

'I hope this strong display of affection for the new Under Secretary of the Navy is in recognition of his lovable image and doesn't in any way reflect an early waning of support for the new President,' the President said.

Bill Greer, the Secret Service man who was driving,[B] volunteered: 'Mr. President, if you will excuse my overhearing you, I believe the rather bewildered look on the faces of some of the people we have passed is caused by the way you and Mr. Fay are seated. It is customary for the President to sit on the side away from the driver, so he can get in and out of the limousine fastest.'

That was the last time I ever made that mistake." [3281]

Two years later, this photo in *The Pleasure of His Company* proves that the two old Navy skippers had learned where to sit. *"The Under Secretary of the Navy with friend, feeling very grand. Palm Beach, Easter, 1963."* [3282] Seven months later, President Kennedy will be sitting in the same position as his limousine rounds a corner in Dallas and drives into destiny.

Kennedy always rode on the passenger side. This author knows of no photos of him sitting elsewhere. If you want to see a president on the driver's side, go to the movies, where they sit on whichever side suits the scene. The only opportunities to see real presidents on the driver's side is on one-way streets or driveways where they must use a left curb, as was the case in 1981 when Ronald Reagan was shot (Chapter 10) in a clockwise hotel driveway.

Donald Rumsfeld was Secretary of Defense from 1975 to 1977, then 2001 to 2006 — both the youngest and the oldest to hold that office. He earned a place in books of famous quotations with this famous remark: "Now what is the message there? The message is that there are no 'knowns.' There are things we know that we know. [The author suggests an example: our name.] There are known unknowns. That is to say there are things that we now know we don't know. [Example: The date we will die.] But there are also unknown unknowns. There are things we do not know we don't know." [3283] [Example from my Caltech geology education in the 1950s: Maps show that South America could fit snugly into Africa, which was smugly scorned as a mere coincidence — before we knew that continents drift!]

Rumsfeld wrapped-up: "So when we do the best we can and we pull all this information together, and we then say 'well that's basically what we see as the situation,' that is really only the known knowns and the known unknowns. And each year, we discover a few more of those unknown unknowns." [3284] Some poorly-educated and less-thoughtful people tried to ridicule his observation, largely because it "sounds funny". Maybe — but it is profound.

[B] Two years and ten months later, agent Greer will drive Kennedy through Dallas.

To those three categories, this author humbly adds a fourth, apropos to the matter under discussion, which may be called "unknown knowns".[c] There are things we know but we don't know that we know them. The relevant example here is that Americans, without knowing that they know it, know that a president sits on the passenger side of a limousine. To see him (and by the time you read this, it may well be her) on the driver's side would be as foreign as seeing a bride and her bridesmaids on the right side of a church. The bride and her party will be on the left — a known known — and a President in a car will be on the right, although you probably didn't know you knew that until it was pointed out here — an unknown known.

The point is simple: If the target had been Kennedy, then Oswald knew to look for him exactly where he was. As the limousine approached on Houston Street, Kennedy should be in the back seat, on its right side — to Oswald's left as he looked head-on — and there he was!

But the target — the underpinning of this book — was Governor John B. Connally. Both Dallas newspapers said he would ride in the President's car, but where would he sit? The evidence of the past 24 hours proved that was impossible to know in advance. On Thursday the two Kennedys flew from the White House to San Antonio, were met by Governor and Mrs. Connally, then rode into downtown in the fatal no-top Lincoln. JBC sat in the left (driver side) jump seat. Nellie sat behind him as seen here [3285] on the rear seat, with Jackie to her right in the middle, but then moved to the right jump seat, to the right of JBC, directly in front of JFK, who remained in his "always" seat, the right-rear.

Later that Thursday, riding to dedicate the Aerospace Medical Division, Connally sat at the left of the rear seat with the President to his right — only the two of them on the seat. Jackie was in the left jump seat ahead of JBC, and Nellie was in the right jump seat in front of JFK. Then, going to Air Force One, Connally moved again, to the left jump seat, with Nellie in the other and Jackie on the left of the rear seat with JFK on the right, as always. John Connally was moving around all that Thursday, [3286] and there's another twist coming.

On Friday morning in Fort Worth, they rode to Air Force One in a standard Lincoln with one passenger seat, no jump seats. Nellie rode in another car. John Connally sat on the seat's left, Jackie in the middle and Kennedy, as always, on the right.[3287] If Oswald had some preconception of where to find Connally as the Lincoln drove toward him on Houston Street in Dallas later that midday, this is probably where he would expect to find him — on the same seat as Jack and Jackie. But he will not be there.

---

[c] This passage was written more than three years before the 2014 release of a documentary movie about Rumsfeld titled "The Unknown Known".

A hero in Dallas was Secret Service agent Clint Hill, assigned to protect Jackie. Standing on the left running board of the follow-up car, he would have preferred to be on the left step on the back of the presidential limo, but JFK ordered no barrier between himself and the people. On hearing the first shot, Hill made a split-second decision and memorable dash, barely managing to hop onto the Lincoln's step, then crawled across to Jackie who was out on the trunk trying to retrieve a chunk of brain. He lay above her and the President, ready to take a bullet if there were to be another, all the way to the hospital. Clint Hill was haunted for years by "What if?" fixations and dreams: "What if I'd been riding on the rear of the limousine? I might have shielded the President. What if I'd reacted a half-second faster? I might have taken that third bullet, so it would not have blown apart Kennedy's head."

In 1990, Hill returned to Dealey Plaza for the first time. As told in the book *The Kennedy Detail* by Secret Service agent Jerry Blaine with assistance from Hill and many other agents: "For nearly two hours, Clint walked around the area and went over the sight lines, the angles." [3288] Then he went up into the Sixth Floor Museum. "His chest tightened as he walked toward the lair that Oswald had built of book boxes—reconstructed as it had been found the day of the assassination. Clint looked out the window and saw the clear view to the street, saw how close it was. He shook his head. ... After walking the streets below and now seeing the clear view that Oswald had, Clint realized that even if he had been on the back of the president's limousine, Oswald could have hit the president as the car approached the intersection of Houston and Elm." [3289] Yes, that would been easy, THE SHOT NOT TAKEN.

Before narrowing our focus, here is the big picture in four views from Oswald's sixth-floor window, just as Clint Hill saw them, photographed by Harrison Edward Livingstone for his book *Killing the Truth: Deceit and Deception in the JFK Case*: [3290]

1. Looking SSE down Houston Street, to corner where limo will arrive from left.

2. Looking down onto the intersection of Houston (ahead) and Elm (at right).

3. Looking SSW over oak trees that line the north (near) side of Elm Street.

4. Looking WSW down Elm Street, where two bullets hit victims in the limousine.

Having set the scene as Oswald saw it while waiting at his window, it is now time to watch the Lincoln limousine and its victims enter into photo 1 and exit through photo 4.

In Chapter 14 – TOO CLOSE TO CALL, we saw what Oswald saw when he fired at either Kennedy or Connally in the limousine moving away from him, in the area of photo 4 above. Those views came from a special-purpose reenactment in May 1964 to learn if the "magic bullet" theory could be correct — could one bullet have wounded both men? (Answer: Yes, in fact there was no way to avoid that because they were inline as the bullet arrived.)

For the limited purpose of the 1964 inquiry, it had to correspond precisely with frames of the Zapruder film, so its photos began only when the limousine made the 120-degree left turn from Houston Street onto Elm Street, because Zapruder started his camera when he, on the famous "grassy knoll" beside Elm, could first see the car. The important November 22 non-event occurred (or did not occur — it depends on how you regard it) before those photos.

Now we benefit from an earlier reenactment of the limousine's drive through Dealey Plaza. On December 5, 1963, two weeks after the shooting, the Secret Service moved a white convertible along the path of the limousine in which Kennedy had been murdered. The vehicle stopped every 25 feet as they took two simultaneous photos to show the views from Oswald's sixth-floor window, both plain eyesight and through his rifle's telescopic sight. There were 25 photo pairs altogether, showing the target limousine as it moved a total distance of 600 feet.

This car was shorter, with no jump seats and only four occupants, two in front and two in back. That was thought sufficient, months before anybody thought of one bullet wounding both men, so the purpose was only to show the views Oswald would have had of Kennedy. Of course, as always, there was no thought that the target was anyone other than the President. Thus, in the photos through the telescopic sight, the head of the JFK double is dead center.

The photo at left [3291] from the December 1963 reconstruction series is what the Secret Service wanted to know, precisely what Oswald saw when he fired the non-fatal bullet that wounded Kennedy and Connally.[D] On the left are memorial flowers and wreaths. There are several times as many hidden by the trees on the right, shown in the photo [3292] below

with the vehicle in exactly the same position, looking from where Abraham Zapruder had stood to make his movie thirteen days earlier. As at Kensington Palace in 1996 for Princess Diana and at Ground Zero after 9/11/2001, flowers help share loss and show respect — or as this author realized at the Seattle Center fountain after 9/11, they may not be much, but at least they are something we can do.

As was done earlier in this book to place photos and their explanations in good sequence, this page has room below to illustrate the graciousness of America's much-loved 35th President:

Dallas Police Sergeant Stavis "Steve" Ellis, in his contribution to the oral histories of those close to the assassination, spoke the quotation that tops this chapter. Here he is in his motorcycle patrolman's uniform, being greeted by the President at Love Field on that Friday morning in Dallas, immediately before they both rode into history.[3293]

[D] Compare with the Frame 210 PHOTOGRAPH THROUGH RIFLE SCOPE in chapter 14.

Happily for this writer and this chapter, the Secret Service began that series of photos when the vehicle left Main Street, where huge crowds had greeted the Kennedys thirteen days earlier, and turned right onto Houston, giving Oswald his first view of the Kennedy-Connally

limo, which he knew from the newspapers would be the second, behind the lead car. Before considering the set of re-creation photos, first look at four actual pictures taken by two amateur photographers. These were not included in the 26 Warren Commission books of exhibits. On November 24, 1967, *LIFE* magazine's cover featured John Connally and these headlines: "A CONTRIBUTION TO HISTORY   Governor Connally sets the record straight on the fateful visit WHY KENNEDY WENT TO TEXAS   Together with unpublished pictures by nine bystanders   LAST SECONDS OF THE MOTORCADE".   The first two [3294] were taken by real-estate man Phil Willis,

standing on the northwest corner of Main and Houston. In the first, above-right, the limousine comes to the end of dense crowds on both sides of Main Street and reaches Houston Street, with the Secret Service backup car close behind. In the second by the same man at the same spot, the limo begins to go north on Houston, directly toward Oswald. The two Kennedys are clearly visible, their heads several inches higher than those of the Connallys, who are more difficult to find on either side of the small vertical window behind the driver.

To understand what came next, it would be ideal to see exactly what Oswald saw that day from his overlook, the sixth-floor window nearest Houston Street. No such image exists, nor can it ever be accurately re-created, because, among other reasons, the Lincoln limousine was a highly-customized one-of-a-kind. After the killing it was returned to the customizing firm to be torn apart and rebuilt with a powerful engine, heavy armor plating and a permanent welded-on bulletproof steel roof. No, we can never see what he saw that day. But, with no thanks to either the FBI or the Warren Commission, we can come moderately close.

Others employed in the Texas School Book Depository watched from several of the 84 windows that faced onto Elm Street. Four were ladies working for the Scott, Foresman Co., by coincidence publisher of the books that Lee Oswald most frequently picked. They clustered in an open window on the fourth floor, the sixth window from the Houston Street (east) end. [3295] With Victoria "Vickie" Adams, Dorothy May Garner and Sandra Styles who simply watched, was 57-year-old clerk Elsie Dorman. "As the motorcade passed, Dorman sat on the floor and took photographs of the parade with her husband's movie camera. At the sound of the shots she became excited and didn't take any more movies." [3296]

In March 1964, the FBI collected for the Warren Commission statements from all 73 still-alive persons who were at work in the TSBD on the fatal day. Elsie's included this:

"On November 22, 1963 I went to a window near my desk to view and photograph the Presidential Motorcade as it passed along Houston and Elm Streets. I was using my husband's camera and was not too familiar with its operation. As the Motorcade turned on to Houston Street from Main Street, I started taking photographs. I was seated on the floor with the camera in the window. The window was raised. I continued taking photographs but as the Motorcade turned from Houston Street on to Elm Street I became excited and did not get any more photographs.

I was at this window attempting to photograph the Motorcade when I heard a noise like gunshots. I did not see Lee Harvey Oswald at that time. I do not know Lee Harvey Oswald and have no recollection of having seen him.   I do not recall seeing any strangers in the building on the morning of November 22, 1963." [3297]

An unusual failure by both the FBI and Commission was that they took no action prompted by her testimony, given in immediate questioning and the written statement above, that she was "taking photographs". Neither asked to see the "photographs". They did not ask "what kind?", so missed learning about her movie, which helpfully augmented, from a different vantage, the famous film by Abraham Zapruder.[3298] It was left to *LIFE* magazine to find Elsie. In their issue of November 24, 1967, which featured Governor Connally's cover article about JFK's visit to Texas, was an "EDITORS' NOTE Finding Pictures of a Moment in History".

Managing Editor George P. Hunt described *LIFE*'s efforts to find and display 23 previously unpublished photographs taken by amateurs on the fatal Friday. During the summer of 1967, *LIFE* had learned that a lady employed by publisher Scott, Foresman Co. on the fourth floor of the Texas School Book Depository had been at a window facing Elm Street and taken a movie of the motorcade. Probably because of shock upon realizing what she had filmed, "she had kept it in a closet and never showed it to anyone." [3299]

Michael Benson reports in *Encyclopedia of the JFK Assassination* that, probably as a result of *LIFE*'s pioneering work, "Assassination researcher Richard Sprague visited Mrs. Dorman in 1967 and watched her movie.   ... [S]he did film right through the shooting sequence, however, she aimed high in her excitement and filmed 'mostly trees.' Mrs. Dorman died in 1983." [3300]

Elsie's movie was grainy, poorly focused, and she jiggled the camera a lot. But it's all we have, so is priceless. Here are two revealing frames, a blob defect on the right one: [3301]

Relative to Elsie's pictures, it is significant to know that Lee had a much better view than they suggest, for four reasons. First, no amateur movie film in those days could capture the high definition we see with our eyes. Second, what you see here are scans made for me by the Sixth Floor Museum, in dots. These scans at 72 dots-per-inch are not as fine and detailed as was Elsie's film, which itself was a poor capture of reality. Third, because this book is printed in black-and-white, Elsie's color frames have been converted to grayscale ("a range of shades of gray without apparent color")[3302], in this case 64 shades of gray. On the film and in reality, the Kennedys are much more quickly recognizable than seen here. JFK's auburn hair and her bright pink jacket and pillbox hat shone — although Mrs. Kennedy's clothes do not bear on Oswald's ability to identify, because he had no way to know what she would wear that day.

Fourth and most important, if we were in the car and looking at the TSBD, Lee would be almost directly ahead and high, whereas Elsie was quite far to the left and much lower. His windowsill was 61 feet above the sidewalk; hers was 40 feet. She was sitting on the floor; he was standing at that time (testimony in a paragraph below). Adding the difference between eye levels of standing versus sitting, he was approximately 24 feet higher.[3303] Her window was 28 feet to the left (west) of his. Thus, contrasted to her pictures showing the car off to the left, he saw it almost straight ahead, and thus — most importantly as the rest of this chapter will elucidate — he could see the Kennedys better from his higher vantage.

In his monumental *Reclaiming History*, Vincent Bugliosi describes the view of three TSBD workers on the fifth floor, directly below Oswald: "The view is terrific, since from their perch they can see south to the corner of Houston and Main and beyond, as well as all the way west down the curving sweep of Elm to the Triple Underpass ..."[3304] Lee's view, from ten feet above them, was even better.

Now that we know what Oswald could see when he looked along Houston Street from his perch, let us have definite testimony that he had, in fact, looked at what is shown in Elsie's pictures. "A few minutes earlier [shortly before the motorcade entered Dealey Plaza], Mrs. Carolyn Walther, who worked as a cutter in a dress factory, walked to a point opposite the School Book Depository with Mrs. Pearl Springer to watch the parade. Mrs. Walther saw a man at the end window of the fourth or fifth floor.[E] Both his hands were on the ledge and in his right hand he held a rifle, pointed downward. The stranger was staring across Houston, toward the edge of Main, where the parade was expected momentarily."[3305]

Knowing that he was looking for the approaching motorcade, you will best understand Oswald's opportunity, and what he did or did not do with it, by having a sense of the speed of the target, and from that, knowing the amount of time he had to fire:

Testifying to the Warren Commission, Secret Service agent Bill Greer, who had driven President Kennedy his entire term, three years to now, everywhere in the world, and who was more familiar with limousine SX-100 than anyone, estimated that he had driven the one block on Houston Street at a speed between 12 and 15 m.p.h.[3306] When he made the 120-degree turn from Houston onto Elm, he thought his speed may have been between 9 and 11 m.p.h. After completing the turn onto Elm, we know with great exactness from the Zapruder film that when the bullets were fired, the limo was going 11 m.p.h., which is 16.13 feet per second. From the Zapruder film, the FBI and Commission determined that the time between a bullet hitting Kennedy's neck and the one that exploded his head was confined to the range of 4.8 to 5.6

[E] The TSBD front design changed as the eye went up, making many think the sixth floor was the fifth.

seconds, and that between the two hits the limousine traveled 85 feet. $85 \div 16.13 = 5.27$ seconds, which is nearly the mid-point of the possible range. All measurements fit and cross-check with accuracy, so it appears we know movement facts with considerable precision.

The limo slowed somewhat in turning right 90° from Main onto Houston, then sped up, then slowed again as it turned left 120° onto Elm. Considering all that, it seems most probable that the average speed of the limousine on Houston Street, in the one block from where it made the right turn from Main Street and first came into Oswald's view, until it came below him as it turned onto Elm, was 12 miles per hour, which is 17.6 feet per second. That really doesn't matter much because the bearing, the angle from Oswald to the limousine, was not wavering, but only very slowly moving slightly to his left until the turn onto Elm. And, his bullets had a velocity more than 100 times that of the approaching limo. Aiming and hitting would be easy!

In years of looking I have not found a video of the car's entire drive on Houston Street that day. Nonetheless, it is possible to be quite precise about the timing of its progress. The Secret Service staged a re-creation [F] for their documentary film *Assassination of President John F. Kennedy*.[3307] To aid the filming, the Dallas Police Department assigned the two motorcycle officers who had been next to the rear bumper of Kennedy's limousine. The film's narrator says: "The two motorcycle policemen are the two men who were in the same relative position to the president's car at the time of the assassination. They assisted in determining the approximate speed of the president's car during the filming of these scenes." [3308]

The documentary film shows the drive five times (one in slow-speed), from different viewpoints. The four at normal speed have similar timings. These are the durations of seven portions of the limousine's drive, as seen from the sniper's nest, each to the nearest second:[3309]

8   Duration in seconds from when Kennedy becomes visible as the limo going W on Main Street emerges from behind the Dallas County Jail and Courthouse, until the limo completes its 90° right turn onto Houston Street and is on the street's centerline;

13   Limousine drives N near the centerline of Houston, almost directly toward Oswald;

10   Duration of 120° left turn from Houston, until the limousine goes WSW on Elm Street, Looking down, Oswald can first see Connally at about the midpoint of this turn;

5   On Elm Street until the passengers begin to be hidden by oak tree branches;

3   Duration that mid-car passenger compartment is hidden from Oswald by the oak tree; He probably fired the first shot just as the limo went under the tree, approximately 9 seconds after he first saw Connally;

2   After passengers are again visible until the shot that wounds Kennedy and Connally;

<u>5</u>   Time from wounding shot to the third and final shot that explodes Kennedy's head.

46   Total time, in seconds, from first appearance of Kennedy until the shot into his head.

As noted earlier, the Secret Service's reenactment in December 1963 gave us photos beginning when the limousine turned from Main onto Houston. Please note as you look at these that the Secret Service used a white Cadillac with no jump seats, not the actual Lincoln Continental. Because of design differences, the passengers in the Cadillac are slightly higher above the ground and more exposed than those in the Lincoln had been on the fatal day two weeks earlier — especially Governor and Mrs. Connally in the low jump seats.

[F] Yes, this is the third re-creation. I'd happily trade them all for one with right-sized stand-ins seated in the actual Lincoln Continental!

The first [3310] shows how Oswald saw the Lincoln as it began to drive directly toward him. The re-creation vehicle is in the position shown in the photos on pages 511 and 530.

Here is a later photo [3311] in that reenactment series, showing what Oswald could see below him, approximately 20 seconds after the previous photo, as the limo turned 120 degrees left onto Elm Street to drive west to the Triple Underpass:

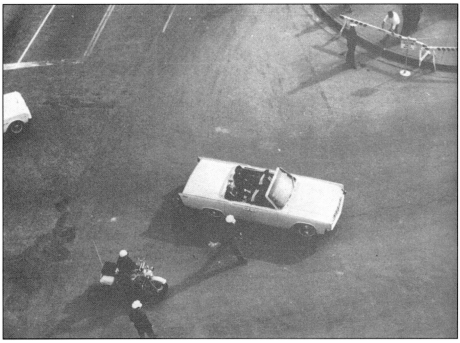

Why didn't Oswald take an easy shot — one would do the job — as the limo approached him? The reason is obvious and the most compelling circumstantial evidence in this book. To aid understanding, consider one situation in detail: the middle example [3312] of the Secret Service's series, with the limo midway between coming into sight from Main and turned onto Elm:

We do not know when Oswald looked with unaided eyes to find his target or when he used the four-power scope on his carbine to enlarge and put cross-hairs on the target. Here is what he could have seen while aiming his rifle, in a photo [3313] taken at the same spot as the one above, with the camera looking through the actual telescope on Oswald's rifle (page 437):

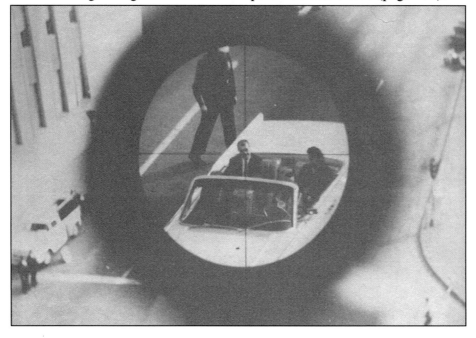

If President Kennedy had been the target, he would have been shot as accurately and killed as easily as the reenactor in the photo above.

While this easy shot is in mind, here is a photo of the TSBD, taken on the day of the assassination, from Houston Street. The two previous photos are from Oswald's position, toward the limo. This is what occupants of the limo would have seen if they had looked up toward Oswald.[3314] The arrow points to his window.

The undeniable fact is that Oswald did not shoot as the limousine approached. He waited until it had passed, then opened fire. Given that fact, let us apply logic to analyzing whether Oswald's delay argues for or against a specific occupant of the limousine being his intended victim. As discussed in Chapter 14 – TOO CLOSE TO CALL, there is no reason to imagine that Oswald meant to murder either of the two men in the front seat, or either of the wives. Let us proceed to consider what Oswald could or would have done if his target were Kennedy, then if it was Connally.

If Oswald had intended to assassinate Kennedy, he would have had two significant advantages over the case of Connally-as-victim. First, everyone in Dallas knew that the motorcade was in honor of Kennedy, and thus he would have a prominent place in it. Oswald would have expected exactly what turned out to be true — JFK would be in the usual position of honor in a motorcade, seated in the first big limousine. As the car behind the police lead auto turned the corner from Main onto Houston and came toward Oswald's position, he immediately saw that it was a long limousine flying flags, and he could easily spot the familiar face of JFK. If there were any doubt, he would also immediately recognize Jackie Kennedy, in her bright pink outfit, next to the President. Locating Kennedy-as-victim would have been completed within seconds of the turn onto Houston Street.

Oswald's ability to shoot Kennedy would begin immediately after that identification. If Kennedy were the target, it would have been easy and quick. Kennedy was in the back seat of the limousine, in a direct line of sight from the Depository's sixth floor, wholly unprotected from the moment his face was recognizable. We will soon look at a photo on page 530 showing that Oswald could see Kennedy from the moment the car entered Houston Street.

Kennedy, from coming into Oswald's view until being obscured by the oak tree on Elm Street, was visible for about 36 seconds (see the timings on page 514). Of that, the drive on Houston Street, directly toward Oswald, took about 20 seconds. After a generous 5 seconds to recognize Kennedy, Oswald had 15 seconds to fire at an easy target — don't take my word for it, look back two photos — if the President had been the target.

Oswald did not shoot during those 15 seconds, and there must be a reason for his delay. No one can find that reason in evaluating Kennedy as the intended victim. Many others have preceded me in noting that lack of action. Chapter 21 – OTHERS ON THIS TRAIL will pay due respect to those who have thought of the possibility that Oswald's intent was to assassinate John Connally. This chapter, about the meaning of THE SHOT NOT TAKEN at Kennedy, is the appropriate place to recognize eleven who have commented or written about that incongruous lack of action. As you will see, most grasp entirely erroneous straws in attempting to explain — but they deserve some mention. At least they noticed that the "why not?" question existed.

FBI Director J. Edgar Hoover testified before the Warren Commission in 1964. After discharging the primary reason for his appearance — swearing under oath that Oswald had not been an agent of the FBI — Hoover wandered on his own leash,[G] without being asked, through many other topics. As will be quoted in Chapter 21 – OTHERS ON THIS TRAIL (page 555), he briefly speculated that perhaps Oswald was really gunning for Connally instead of Kennedy, mused about the autopsy and the speed of the limo, then revealed his complete ignorance of the layout of Dealey Plaza with this:

> "Now, some people have raised the question: Why didn't he shoot the President as the car came toward the storehouse where he was working? The reason for that is, I think, the fact there were some trees between his window on the sixth floor and the cars as they turned and went through the park. So he waited until the car got out from under the trees, and the limbs, and then he had a perfectly clear view of the occupants of the car, and I think he took aim ..." [3315]

Hoover set out on a worthwhile path, but left it by badly misplacing the one overarching tree. That obscuring oak had nothing to do with "Why didn't he shoot ... as the car came toward" him. It was much farther along the motorcade route, west on Elm Street. Look at the photos on pages 508 and 515 for a reminder of the treeless, fully-open shots Oswald did not take.

In those days, nobody dared to correct or contradict the original G-man. Critic Harold Weisberg observed: "Unimpeded by the incontrovertible and obviously contrary fact, Hoover supplied his own answer ...",[3316] and off wandered J. Edgar to deny the possibility that Oswald had been recruited as an agent by the Soviets, then to discuss life in Minsk, then mother Marguerite's mental instability. In TV fiction on *The West Wing*, presidential assistant Sam Seaborn would ruefully say, "We came *this* close to curing cancer!" In reality we may have

---

[G] The British say "lead", which seems more appropriate for one taking oneself for a random walk.

come *this* close to understanding Oswald's crime, less than half a year after he committed it, but lost that opportunity because of one wandering mind.

Pioneer conspiracy theorist Thomas G. Buchanan (Chapter 8) supposed a large crew of conspirators, of whom two were to fire rifles at Kennedy. His "Assassin One" was ahead of the limo, behind the "Grassy Knoll" fence. While Oswald was elsewhere in the Depository, "Assassin Two" was in the sixth-floor far-right window we know so well. Both were to fire simultaneously, when Kennedy became a target from both positions. What did not happen next is illuminating. "So Assassins One and Two were waiting. ... And, at last, the presidential car came into view, turned right from Main Street into Houston and was coming straight toward the sixth-floor window of the Texas School Book Depository. If Assassin Two, the man who had been hiding in the stockroom, had been all alone, now was the moment that he would have chosen for his first shot—now, before the car had turned the corner and begun receding. But the moment passed, and Kennedy drove on toward the ambush that [Buchanan says] was waiting." [3317]

Buchanan correctly judged that a shooter's preferred field of fire would be toward Kennedy as he grew larger in the sight as he approached the TSBD, sitting in plain view, high up in the car, with no trees or traffic signs obstructing the shot. So, Buchanan's gunman in the window from which Oswald (in the real world) shot, waited only because he had been ordered to hold fire until Kennedy was nearing the Grassy Knoll. The clear, easy, obvious shot was not taken by "Assassin Two" for that reason — and Buchanan deserves credit for noting and (wrongly) explaining the failure to take the easy shot from Oswald's window.

Harold Weisberg was another early to notice the incongruity and ask obvious questions in his 1965 book criticizing the Commission, *Whitewash*: "One glaring omission deserves a final comment. The Commission was reconstructing the crime [for the photos on preceding pages], ostensibly to find out what happened, not to prove that Oswald alone committed it. When the motorcade turned toward the Depository Building on Houston Street, for several hundred feet there was a completely unobstructed view of it from the sixth-floor window. The police photographs and the forgotten Secret Service reconstruction of 1963 also show this. There was not a twig between the window and the President. [Take that, J. Edgar Hoover!] There were no curves in that street, no tricky shooting angles. If all the shots came from this window, and the assassin was as cool and collected as the Report represents, why did he not shoot at the easiest and by far the best target? Why did he wait until his target was so difficult that the country's best shots could not duplicate his feat?" [3318]

In his book's *Conclusion*, Weisberg asked 35 "Why?" questions pointing out Warren Commission discrepancies and omissions. One was: "Why did the Report not address itself to the unreasonableness of an assassin in the sixth-floor window waiting for a very difficult shot at the President without need when he had such an excellent target and for a longer time as the motorcade approached the building?" [3319] Weisberg then tripped and fell, answering his question by asserting it proved that Oswald was not at the window and did no shooting. The absence of easy shooting at the approaching Kennedy meant, to Weisberg, that the assassins (plural, he thinks) were elsewhere, maybe at the Grassy Knoll. Watching Weisberg propound the truly fundamental question that could have led to enlightenment, then answer it with an agonizingly wrong answer, is as sad as seeing a marathon's leader "hit the wall" at mile 25.

As you know by now, I have little respect for assassination conspiracy books. Of the hundreds I have read, the one I dislike least,[H] because it is much like this book you hold in its detail, photos, carefully explained reasoning and documentation, is Josiah Thompson's *Six Seconds in Dallas: A Micro-Study of the Kennedy Assassination*, published in 1967.

Noting many discrepancies in witness testimonies and autopsy findings, he decided the most reasonable scenario had three gunmen firing four bullets. His first and third shots came from Oswald's window, from "the gunman", who may or may not have been Lee Oswald. The second bullet was fired from the roof of the County Records Building on the east side of Houston Street. The fatal fourth came, he believes, from the "Grassy Knoll". Reconstructing the sixth-floor gunman's view and lack of action, Thompson wrote:

"[T]he roar of the crowd up the street signaled the approach of the motorcade [and] drew the attention of the gunman in the sixth-floor window. Looking down on the knoll, he may have been trying to catch a glimpse of his confederate. But the trees shielded the corner of the stockade fence from his view. A rustle in the crowd drew his attention back to Houston Street. An unmarked white Ford—the pilot car—had made its right turn and now was coming straight toward him. A phalanx of motorcycles followed and then the dark blue presidential Lincoln. Looking down he could see the President smiling at Mrs. Connally. His grip tightened on the rifle. This was the perfect shot—as the President approached the Depository. Had he been a lone assassin, this would have been the time to shoot; he would have fired while the car was still on Houston Street. But he was not alone, and must hold his fire until the guns of his two confederates could bear on the limousine. If he fired now (perfect though the shot might be for him), the Lincoln might stop, turn sharply, and escape the trap. As Bill Greer eased the 4-ton limousine around the 120-degree turn onto Elm Street, the gunman above shifted into firing position. The victim had entered the trap." [3320]

As with horseshoes, one of the few games in which "close" counts, Thompson deserves points for noticing the opportunity for an easy shot on Houston Street. And he gets a bonus for illustrating those words with the two reenactment photos I chose for page 516. Finally, he gets another point for how he captioned those photos, "The shot not fired ...", almost the title of this chapter. As was earlier critic Buchanan, Thompson is enthralled with the idea of a complicated conspiracy, so misses the simple explanation — Oswald didn't take a "perfect shot" at Kennedy because that easy target was not his intended victim.

In his best-selling book *The Day Kennedy Was Shot*, Jim Bishop visualized Oswald's view, noted the inexplicable delay in firing, and ended pessimistically:

"The car glided noiselessly across Houston. In the sixth floor window, the mediocre marksman could have had Mr. Kennedy in his sights and probably did. From Oswald's perch, the President of the United States was coming directly toward him. He could fix Kennedy in the crosshairs so that, at four hundred feet, the victim appeared to be one hundred feet away. There was one shell in the chamber; there were three more in the clip below, ready to jump to duty. Oswald could have fired all four into the face of the President at this moment. The target moved neither right nor left as Greer came down the middle. It just grew larger in the sights, the tan, smiling face growing bigger in the telescopic lens with each fifth of a second. Why not fire now? No one knows. No one will ever know.." [3321]

This author believes that is not the case. You, faithful reader, will know, reading in this chapter the first fact-based comprehensive answer to "Why not fire now?".

[H] In Chapter 15 – REGARDING KENNEDY, the only opinion I could characterize as somewhat negative toward the President was that Oswald "didn't like anybody, but he disliked Kennedy least".

One reasonable reason for Oswald's not firing as the limousine drove up Houston Street toward him was articulated by James Reston, Jr. in an endnote in his 1989 biography of John Connally, *The Lone Star*. By then, Reston had already realized that the intended target must have been Connally, and before the book came out, had written that in a *TIME* magazine cover article. Both the magazine and his book are featured in Chapter 21 – OTHERS ON THIS TRAIL. In the biography, he gave an explanation of Oswald not taking the easy shot with these words — and notice that this theory would apply regardless of which man was the target:

> "As for Oswald not shooting when the vehicle approached the building, this projects the discussion into the speculative realm of the criminal mind. For instance, Oswald may have felt he had a better chance of getting away if he fired when the vehicle was already past his sniper's nest than when it was approaching. Also, psychologists speak of a 'motor program' that takes place in the mind of a person in a high state of excitement and anxiety, especially a life-and-death situation. Oswald was in such a state. In a 'motor program,' the person cannot be asked to make precise, intelligent judgments about fine points of reason and logic. It may be less important what Oswald was feeling and doing in the split seconds before he pulled the trigger than what was in his mind two [1] days before the assassination when he settled upon his intention." [3322]

Reston is a pathfinder, honored by this author for being on the right track, but a difference between us is that he has not written of the physical reason that Oswald could not fire as the limo came toward him. I think we need not explore "the speculative realm of the criminal mind". The more likely reason is much simpler: Oswald could not see his intended victim!

Marguerite's biographer, the gifted Jean Stafford, wrote of studying Dealey Plaza

> "as I had the other two times I had been over this same ground, that the distance between the sixth-floor window of the Texas Book Depository and the place where the car, slowing for a turn, had been, seemed to be much less than it had appeared in photographs. I was struck, moreover, by the fact that between the window and the target there was no obstruction of any kind to challenge aim or deflect the attention, no eave or overhang or tree. The drop shot, from a steadied rifle, was fired on a day of surpassing clarity; the marksmanship of the gunner did not have to be remarkable." [3323]

Quite similarly, Dr. Cyril Wecht in his 1993 book *Cause of Death* reflected on his visit

> "to the sixth floor of the Texas School Book Depository. The Dallas Historical Society has done a wonderful job of refurbishing the floor into a place where tourists and history buffs can relive that day in 1963. As I stared out the window of the sixth floor, the exact spot where Oswald supposedly stood, I looked out over Houston and Elm streets. Why did Oswald not shoot the president as the motorcade proceeded down [J] Houston Street? The view was much clearer and straight on. Why did he wait until the president's car had traveled so far down Elm Street that his sight would have been sporadically blocked by tree branches? If Oswald had indeed been the lone gunman, why did he wait and seriously compromise his neurotic plan?" [3324]

Sadly, the doctor began with the preconceived notion of a multi-gunman conspiracy, so he mistakenly believed the only reason Oswald waited was so the other guns would also bear on Kennedy as the Lincoln rolled away from him on Elm Street. But there was no conspiracy, as the many elapsed years and topics in Chapter 9 prove. If only Wecht had impartially considered the wait, he might have solved the puzzle long before this book.

---

[1] This is off point: Oswald read of his target on Thursday, then quickly asked for a ride to his rifle, the foundation of Chapter 18 – CONNALLY WILL RIDE. He had nothing in mind two days before.
[J] "down" is mysterious. The street is level, the car drove north, neither of which calls for "down".

Also in 1993, a conspiracy theorist who earned a deserved reputation as the master of all assassination-related photographs, Robert J. Groden, released a large-format photo book: *The Killing of a President: The Complete Photographic Record of the JFK Assassination, the Conspiracy, and the Cover-Up*. Adjacent to the photo of the Lincoln turning from Main onto Houston, which was shown on page 191 and will be again on page 529, he wrote:

> "The President's car approached the intersection [of Houston and Elm] and provided a perfect vantage point for unobstructed firing on the President from the sixth floor of the School Book Depository. Why did the sniper—or snipers—wait until the car had passed the Depository?" [3325]

In 239 pages he does not answer that question, probably because he's busy illustrating how several gunmen fired five bullets that hit both Kennedy and Connally [3326] plus another three to five co-conspirators who completely missed the limousine and its occupants! [3327] Although the great majority of witnesses in Dealey Plaza heard three shots, he explains eight to ten.

1993 was a big year for conspiracy books. Prolific critic and theorist Harrison Edward Livingstone released his third book about the assassination, *Killing the Truth: Deceit and Deception in the JFK Case* that year. He noticed the shot not taken:

> "Dr. Roger McCarthy, an engineer who studies wounds and accidents, testified at the American Bar Association mock trial of Lee Harvey Oswald in the summer of 1992 ... that it would have been irrational for a sniper to shoot at the target going away from him ... when he could have shot at the car as it approached him as it came down [K] Houston Street." [3328]

On a mock trial stand, Dr. McCarthy was asked if he had reached any overall conclusions from examination of the evidence. Yes he had, "the first being that the evidence shows that the best shots from the TSBD were passed up in favor of difficult shots from that location, which were easy shots from the grassy knoll." [3329] The questioning attorney showed an animation of the limo's drive, then: "I want to ask you please to explain what, if anything, is shown in this animation which leads to your conclusion that the best shots from that location in the Depository were, in fact passed up if someone was there." [3330] McCarthy testified:

> "Well, there's 2 reasons. First of all, this is an assassination attempt and an ambush. And you can see that now every vital organ of the President is exposed to the shooter in the Depository and at the closest point [as the limo was below Oswald's window, turning from Houston onto Elm] in that shot he's got a shot of 86 ft. That's not even the length of this room. With a high powered rifle and a 4 power scope! Now, that is a high probability shot. And if you're in the business of committing a heinous crime, like an assassination, you would shoot the target as it was coming towards you because, first of all, if you miss, every subsequent shot gets better if it is coming your direction, unless he can turn and escape. One of the big drawbacks of a President and presidential motorcade is there's no escape to the rear. There's other cars, there's vans, and there's people along the side. It is easy to figure out the path of the motorcade, there's people along the route the whole line. The car cannot veer off the path of the motorcade unless it wishes to run down people.
>
> Therefore, if you take your shot when he's coming towards you down the street, first of all you get a closer shot than the ones that were ultimately taken. Secondly, the quarry to escape the target of the ambush—that is the person you're shooting at—if they wish to escape they have to come over you and that's the ideal ambush target 'cause every shot becomes a higher probability in the attempt to escape." [3331]

The attorney then asked: "Now, Dr., do you have an opinion, based upon your analysis of why a shooter located in the 6th floor window of that building would pass up what you believe

---

[K] Another "down" without apparent reason. There will be more, but with no comment thereupon.

are the best shots coming down Houston Street in favor of shots as the President is moving away down Elm Street?" [3332] McCarthy had indeed thought about it:

> "Well, the only rational reason that I can think of for giving away those shots which are much much easier to make, would be the same argument I advanced before about the ambush dynamics. Only this time you would have to have an assistant who was going to gain better shots as a result of the target escaping if you missed. And, of course, the assistant wouldn't have to take shots if you hit.
>
> So you would be in a situation where you would start the shooting sequence at the earliest that your second—your assistant—could acquire the target; start your shooting sequence from the 6th floor, then you would drive the target into the 2nd shooter who would get progressively better shots as yours got progressively worse." [3333]

In summary, this witness was expert in the field of shootings. He had been paid to take time to examine and understand all the evidence that had emerged during the 28 years since the assassination. His expert opinion was that Oswald could have made easy shots that would have killed President Kennedy. But he did not take those shots, waiting until he had only difficult shots at the departing limousine. Therefore, this expert concludes, the only logical explanation is that there was a conspiracy, and one or more shooters positioned down by the grassy knoll were going to take their easy shots as the limousine passed in front of them.

This expert witness had come to the same conclusion as several analysts cited earlier: Assuming that Oswald intended to shoot Kennedy, the only explanation for not firing while he was an easy target, drawing nearer, was that Oswald was only one of several shooters in a conspiracy, so he waited until the President had moved along Elm Street to a point where the shooter(s) at the Grassy Knoll or elsewhere could also aim at Kennedy. But that explanation does not make any sense unless one believes there was a conspiracy, and I hope chapter 9 and the books it cites convinced you of this very simple truth — Lee Oswald acted all my himself.

Two years later, 1995, in his fourth assassination book, *Killing Kennedy: and the Hoax of the Century*, the same Livingstone makes the same argument for himself instead of quoting a mock trial witness. He used a chapter "The Official Story" to argue that what we were fed by the Commission and others is provably false. He wrote:

> "For a gunman to wait while the limousine carrying Kennedy came toward him for a full block all the way down Houston Street, watching it turn the corner just below him when he could have dropped a brick or a grenade on the car, then to wait until the car went well down Elm Street before taking deadly aim at this much more difficult target is preposterous. This is what the official story would have us believe. The alleged trajectories from the window never happened. The gunman was across the street in another building, and they [the Commission] made up the angles and distances." [3334]

Toward the end of that same book, Livingstone rephrases and extends that argument:

> "As I have said throughout my previous books, and as has been noted by a few other writers, it is totally irrational for anyone not to have fired at the car as it approached the Texas School Book Depository along Houston Street, and instead wait for it to turn the last corner, disappear beneath a big tree, and then begin firing at it as it goes away from the Depository. The reason the car was not fired upon until it had passed by the building was that it was driving into an ambush facing it on both sides of the bridge. Someone began firing from low down and behind when they had a clear shot at the car along the center lane of Elm Street, and that helped ensure the car went forward into the primary shooters." [3335]

And off goes Warren Commission critic Livingstone to demonstrate that Oswald's easy shots were not taken because he didn't shoot. Shots, he says, came from a gunman who fired from behind, not in the Texas School Book Depository Building but to its east, in the Dal-Tex Building. Livingstone believes there were others, elsewhere, at least one firing a pistol from where he stood hiding behind a storm drain under the Elm Street sidewalk! [3336]

In summary of the above, Livingstone believes that if Oswald had been a shooter, he would have fired as the limousine approached and not waited for a much more distant and difficult target as it rolled away. Thus, he attempts to use the obvious shot not taken to prove falsification by official investigators, incompetence by the Commission, and misleading arguments by Posner in *Case Closed*, in which they all showed that Oswald was certainly the shooter. If Livingstone had sat quietly, thought through his statements and opened himself to their true meaning — that Oswald indeed fired, but was trying to kill John Connally, so he waited until he could see Connally — well, he could have written this book! — and I would have done something different with my fifty years of thinking and four years of writing.

Also in 1995, a conspiracy theorist cited above, Robert J. Groden, released his second large-format photo book, *The Search for Lee Harvey Oswald: A Comprehensive Photographic Record*. In his earlier *The Killing of a President* he had wondered why Oswald didn't take the easy shot as Kennedy approached. Now, the master of assassination photographs shows one taken from Oswald's position with caption: "The view from the sixth-floor window of the Texas School Book Depository. The perfect shot for a lone assassin would have been from this direction as the car approached. Why wasn't it fired from here?" [3337] In 1993, Groden had asked the same question but gave no answer. Here, he does:

"Had there been only one assassin, whether or not it was Lee, the perfect shot would have been when the limousine was on Houston Street, heading north toward the book depository. The view was totally unobstructed. As the car was approaching the shooter, the target would have been getting larger in the rifle scope. The car and the target were moving slowly to make the turn onto Elm Street moments later. The rifle would not have to project out of the window, risking disclosure of the gunman. Finally, the sun would not be glaring into the eyes of the gunman.

Instead we are told the lone assassin chose to shoot just after the car had disappeared behind a live oak tree and had begun to speed up, making the target smaller and smaller. He waited until the bright Texas sun was glaring and reflecting directly into his eyes. He waited for the possibility that Secret Service agents might jump onto the running boards on the rear of the car, thus blocking the view from the window.

The only reason for the assassin to wait was that there was at least one other assassin waiting on the grassy knoll to the right front of the motorcade and probably another elsewhere within Dealey Plaza; probably there were two or more other assassins. The best way to assure success would be to catch the president in a crossfire. This is exactly what happened." [3338]

Groden's analysis could be plausible — if Kennedy had been the target. Unfortunately, he, like most analysts, created complex conspiracy theories to explain the failure to shoot, for the reason that he did not think of or explore the fact that Oswald was gunning for Connally.

Those eleven wrote or testified about the importance of THE SHOT NOT TAKEN. Hoover wrongly imagined that non-existent trees were in the way. Buchanan, Thompson, Wecht, McCarthy and Groden believed Oswald was in a conspiracy and had to hold fire until Kennedy could also be targeted by other gunmen. Weisberg and Livingstone posited that no gunman was at the TSBD window and all the shots came from the Grassy Knoll ahead (Weisberg) or the Dal-Tex Building behind (Livingstone). Reston says the answer may lie in the "speculative realm of the criminal mind". Bishop and Stafford recognized that the shot was very easy, even for a gunman without remarkable marksmanship, but did not suggest a reason for no shooting at Houston Street.

For five chapters and now most of a sixth, we have begun to choose Oswald's likely target by considering, then rejecting, the probability that it was the President. Now consider the only other logical possibility, that Oswald intended to kill John Connally.

When the limousine rounded the corner onto Houston Street and headed for him, Oswald could not see Connally because the Governor was in a jump seat, just behind the front seat of the car. Mrs. Connally, Nellie, was in the other jump seat, on the driver's side of the Continental. John Connally, seated low in the middle of the car, was protected from Oswald's line of fire until the limousine arrived at Elm Street by the bulletproof glass windshield, by the upturned visors above that windshield, by being in the shadow of unusually-tall agent Roy Kellerman in the front seat, and most importantly, by a unique metal bar.

The cause of THE SHOT NOT TAKEN is simple and obvious, once explained. We will begin by understanding how the limousine was built, then look at more photos. The Warren Commission questioned Roy Kellerman, the Secret Service agent in the front-right seat on the drive through Dallas. Especially useful is this testimony:

"Mr. SPECTER. Will you describe what, if anything, is present between the front seat and the rear seat area?

Mr. KELLERMAN. Yes, sir. This metal partition that is erected in back of the driver, between the driver and the passengers in the rear seat, is a metal framework that goes over the car. It has four holes in it. These holes are utilized by the President for parades. As an example, say it was used in Washington where you had an official visitor, and in using one of the streets here as your parade route, he and his guest would stand in this car where the people could view them a little better than sitting in the rear seat.

Mr. SPECTER. Where is that metal bar positioned with respect to the front seat?

Mr. KELLERMAN. It is positioned over the front seat; the top of this bar would be 4 or 5 inches over my head.

Mr. SPECTER. Is it directly over the back portion of the front seat?

Mr. KELLERMAN. Yes, sir. Directly over the front seat.[L]

Mr. SPECTER. And you describe it as 4 or 5 inches over your head. Can you give us an estimate of the distance above the top of the front seat?

Mr. KELLERMAN. Oh, I am guessing in the neighborhood of 15, 18 inches.

Mr. SPECTER. What is the width of that metal bar?

Mr. KELLERMAN. The bar, 4 to 6 inches, I would say." [3339]

That metal bar is key to understanding why Oswald did not fire as the limousine drove almost directly toward his perch. The Lincoln Continental had been built by Ford Motor Co. in 1961, then shipped to Rossmoyne, Ohio, a suburb of Cincinnati, for customization by the Hess & Eisenhardt company, world-class specialists in custom autos.

"Hess & Eisenhardt had a hand in both designing and customizing JFK's massive Lincoln X-100 presidential limousine, which was built for the Secret Service by the Ford Motor Co and Hess & Eisenhardt. The legendary coach was built by cutting a standard convertible in half and stretching it by 33" between the front and rear axles. The unitized vehicle's rocker panels, cowl and cross-members were reinforced with 1/4" and 1/2" sheet steel and two new cross-members were added to make the vehicle as rigid as possible.

[L] No, as coming photos show, the bar's front edge is slightly behind the back of the front seat.

Hess & Eisenhardt divided the passenger compartment in two with a disappearing glass divider behind the chauffeur's blue leather bench seat. A removable stainless-steel roll-bar was placed above the divider that allowed the president to steady himself if he wished to stand during a parade or public appearance. A pair of jump seats were installed in the rear compartment as was a hydraulic rear bench seat that could be raised by 10 1/2" allowing better visibility of the president, even while seated. A blue leather interior with matching Mouton carpeting and gold-embroidered lap robes incorporating the Presidential Seal were fitted as well." [3340]

The purpose of the high stainless steel bar with four handhold slots was demonstrated in many photos from Kennedy's presidency. It allowed him to stand with the local VIPs and wave to crowds, as is shown in Germany in the photo at left,[3341] and in Costa Rica at the right.[3342]

Various sources call that piece the "crossbar", "frame", "framework", "handhold", "metal bar", "railing" and "roll-bar". The Lincoln was built by Ford and is now in the Henry Ford Museum in Dearborn, so I appealed there for an unequivocal decision. The Curator of Transportation, the nomenclator, wrote me that it's a "handrail". So it will be hereinafter.

Because no photos were taken on November 22 from Oswald's lair, we must work up to knowing what he could see by considering other photos from that day. The first, below,[3343] shows the limousine earlier in its drive. This photo only hints at the difficulty anyone out in front would have trying to see Governor Connally.

Roy Kellerman, the Secret Service agent in charge of the Dallas stop, is in the front seat, directly in front of Connally. "At six feet, four inches, Kellerman was a full three inches taller than President Kennedy" [3344] Connally was tall, standing about the same height

as Kennedy, but his low-slung jump seat lowered his head well below Kellerman's. When a person ahead looked into the front of the Lincoln, they could see agents Kellerman and Greer, but not John and Nellie Connally.

Now we should see, clearly, the impediments in addition to Kellerman that are ahead of Connally. Next is a well-known photo [3345] on Main Street before the turn onto Houston and toward Oswald. Note well, from the front, the tall, reflective, tinted windshield, the tipped-up sun visors atop it, and finally the handrail. Keep all those in mind as the limousine drives on.

The photo above is familiar, featured on the covers of Stephen King's best-seller *11/22/63*, The Newseum's *President Kennedy Has Been Shot* and Bill O'Reilly's *Kennedy's Last Days*. Kennedys sit high and clear; Connallys are more difficult to find, but visible from the side.

The one and only photo [3346] I have ever found taken from a higher vantage, more ahead of the limousine, is shown below. Whom do you see? President and Mrs. Kennedy, very clearly. Whom do you not see at first look, until I suggest you look again because he's right there, but largely hidden by the handrail? Governor Connally! He wore his Texas hat during the early part of the motorcade, but had it off along Main Street and into Dealey Plaza. Hat or no hat, he's very hard to see from in front of the limousine — the view Oswald had.

The photo [3347] below is a Polaroid [M] taken by bystander Jack A. Weaver as the limousine turns from Main onto Houston Street. Weaver gave his photo to the FBI for analysis, so we are able to witness the last half minute of sanity. JFK is adjusting his hair exactly where the bullet will hit. Ahead on the left is the Texas School Book Depository where the partially-open window, far right on the next-to-top floor, reveals boxes. This is the sniper's nest. We have testimony that Oswald was looking directly toward here at this moment. I believe he is in the right-half of his right-end window in this photo, but hidden in the Sun's bright midday glare.

Importantly, see how high and visible the Kennedys sit, and see how, at this very moment, Oswald from his high perch will easily and quickly see and identify them, but will not readily see or recognize John Connally, sitting much lower in the lee of a side window — and within seconds, the windshield, upturned visors, Agent Kellerman, and the handrail.

In May 1964, County Surveyor Robert H. West made a careful survey of Dealey Plaza to facilitate analysis of the shooting.[3348] Measurements are in feet. Oswald's windowsill is at altitude (above sea level) 490.9', the sidewalk in front of TSBD at 430.2'. The windowsill is 1' above the sixth floor. Oswald was almost 5'9" tall, so his eyes were about 4'4" above the windowsill. The sidewalk is 6" above the street. From Main to Elm, Houston Street is level. The limousine's handrail was 4'6" above the pavement. Thus, Oswald's eyes were $4.3+(490.9-430.2)+0.5-4.5=61.0'$ above the handrail as the limousine drove toward him.

[M] Miraculous in the 1960s, Polaroid film was loaded with chemicals that developed a photo in a minute!

That same detailed survey map allows measuring precise horizontal distances from Oswald to the limousine. As it straightened from its turn from Main onto Houston, just on the north side of the Main Street crosswalk, as shown in the upper photo on page 515, the limousine's handrail was 283.1' from him. After the limousine neared him but had not yet begun its turn onto Elm Street, shown in both photos on page 516, it was a distance of 154.3'.

Thus, the downward angle of Oswald's view into the limousine's passenger space at the farthest position is arctan [N] $(61.0 \div 283.1) = $ arctan $0.216 = 12.2°$. When the limousine was in the closer position, the angle was arctan $(61.0 \div 154.3) = $ arctan $0.395 = 21.6°$. In other words, when he looked down into the limousine, re-created for the Warren Commission with the carefully positioned but dissimilar white vehicle in the photos on page 516, he (and you looking at those photos) are looking down at an angle of 21.6°. By comparison, Oswald's last two shots that wounded and killed on Elm Street, were at a similar downward angle of 24°.

Now those rather accurate sightline angles may be applied to a photograph of the actual limousine, taken precisely when Oswald first saw it, as it turned onto Houston Street. This is the photo, previously used in Chapter 6 just before Nellie said the last words Jack ever heard, showing what people at street level saw as the limousine turned onto Houston Street:[3349]

For any who may wish to know the dimensions of the Lincoln, including its three rows of

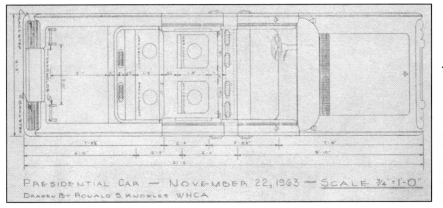

seats, the windshield and the handrail with four slots for hands, just ahead of the jump seats, this diagram was carefully drawn by the White House after the tragic day. The two Kennedys sat farther apart than the two circles drawn on the back seat.[3350]

[N] arctan means "the angle whose tangent is"; tangent means "the vertical (the length of the far side) divided by the horizontal (the distance to that far side)".

On this page the same photo is shown twice, with dark areas showing the portions of the vehicle and occupants that Oswald could not see at all clearly from his vantage, looking downward into the Lincoln from above its front. For any speculating that Oswald might see Connally through the tinted windshield, please consider that 6' 4" agent Kellerman was sitting directly in front of the shorter governor, who was in a much lower seat. You will see this in many photos in this chapter. There could be many images like those below, showing what was blocked from the assassin's view as the car drove toward him. These two should suffice.

The first shows what Oswald could see and not see at a downward angle 12.2° into the car as it began to drive toward him on Houston Street. This photo corresponds to the first reenactment position on page 515. The Connallys are both hidden behind the windshield, its upturned visors, and tall agents Kellerman and Greer. Over the top of the handrail, Oswald can immediately see the heads and faces of both Kennedys:

Below, the second image shows what Oswald could see and not see looking into the car at a downward angle of 21.6°, as the Lincoln neared the end of its one-block drive toward him on Houston Street. This is when the limo is ready to turn left onto Elm Street, the reenactment position shown in natural view and through his rifle's scope on page 516. The Kennedys are now fully visible, but John Connally (on the far side of Nellie) is still hidden by the handrail:

Putting it all together, the realistic situation is that almost the entire drive along Houston Street toward Oswald was required before Connally's head emerged from behind obstructions, and for the assassin to recognize him. There was no adequate time for Oswald to then aim and fire, because to do so after finding Connally would have had him firing almost vertically down into the top of Connally's head, an angle where the human body is smallest. Worse, because his window was only partially raised and had a brick sill projecting outside, the rifle may not have been able to aim down at such a steep angle. Lee then hurried to get off his first shot, the one that was wild and injured Jim Tague, fired in haste as the limousine went under the shelter of the branches and leaves of the oak tree on the curb of Elm Street.

The handrail is the most important element that contributed to saving the life of John Connally, but within seconds the delay it cost will take, by accident, the life of John Kennedy.

When the Warren Commission ended its hearings, it called Secretary of the Treasury C. Douglas Dillon, who had authority over the Secret Service, to preview its findings relative to protecting presidents. Commissioner John J. McCloy, former President of the World Bank and then-current coordinator of U.S. disarmament activities, offered this about the handrail:

> "We had some testimony here in connection with the assassination where it was developed that the access within the car to the body of the President became very important. In the car in which the President was assassinated there was a bar behind the front seat making it very difficult if not impossible for the Secret Service man who was operating from the front seat to get to the body of the President, and we were strongly of the view that cars that should be hereafter designed should have freedom of access. Either the man should be in the jump seat or there should be means by which you could get, the Secret Service man could get to the body of the President in case of a threat of an attack, and I think it is likely we will mention that in the report. But it seemed to me this is something to bear in mind in connection with the design of a new armored car." [3351]

The matter was moot — our presidents would never again ride in open-top vehicles. There would be no more standing in parades, no necessity for handrails.

With photos and words, this chapter has documented these facts:
- As the motorcade entered into Dealey Plaza, Oswald was looking at that exact point.
- He was able to immediately see and easily recognize President Kennedy.
- There were no trees or other obstructions to an easy shot as Kennedy approached.
- That was an advantageous shot because, if missed, the target would be larger for the next.
- Oswald did not fire at Kennedy during the 20 seconds while he had a clear line of fire.
- Governor Connally was hidden from Oswald's sight from the moment the limousine came into view until it was close to being directly below him.
- Shortly after the limousine turned onto Elm Street, it was sheltered by an oak tree.
- He fired very quickly after being able to see Connally, although that was a difficult shot, attempted through the branches of that tree between him and the receding vehicle.

To explain the significance of Oswald's *not* shooting as the limousine approached him, when he had his clearest line of fire at Kennedy, I enlist the help of Sir Arthur Conan Doyle. In his story of *Silver Blaze*, Sherlock Holmes investigates the death of that racehorse's trainer, John Straker. The official investigator is Inspector Gregory, "a man who was rapidly making his name in the English detective service," [3352] according to Holmes' friend and chronicler, Dr. John Watson. In Holmes' more reserved opinion, Gregory "is an extremely competent officer. Were he but gifted with imagination he might rise to great heights in his profession." [3353]

After they had walked side-by-side, with both seeing and hearing the same evidence, Sherlock Holmes has deduced how Straker died, but the inspector (as is usually true of officials in Holmes stories) is still completely in the dark. Gregory is, however, bright enough to ask:

"'Is there any point to which you would wish to draw my attention?'

'To the curious incident of the dog in the night-time.'

'The dog did nothing in the night-time.'

'That was the curious incident,' remarked Sherlock Holmes." [3354]

Holmes then explains the solution. To throw a race and profit handsomely from betting against his horse, the favorite, trainer Straker had taken Silver Blaze from the stable in the middle of the night, with the intent of making him slightly lame by cutting a leg tendon. The horse, alarmed, had killed Straker with a kick to the head. Holmes explained to mystified inspector Gregory, "I had grasped the significance of the silence of the dog, for one true inference invariably suggests others. ... [A] dog was kept in the stables, and yet, though someone had been in and fetched out a horse, he had not barked enough to arouse the two lads in the loft. Obviously the midnight visitor was someone whom the dog knew well." [3355]

I seriously submit to your careful consideration that there exists only one logical explanation for the fact that Oswald did not take the easy shot as the limousine drove slowly toward him through level open space, growing closer and larger every second. He saw President Kennedy, but *he could not see his target*.

In 1964 it was difficult, at first, for many, including several members of the Warren Commission, to accept "the Single-Bullet Theory" developed by staff lawyer Arlen Specter. In his autobiography *Passion for Truth* written 36 years later, Senator Specter wrote of that unanticipated but essential and true interpretation: "It began as a theory, but when a theory is established by the facts, it deserves to be called a conclusion." [3356] The same is true here — Oswald's intent is very clearly established by the facts of **THE SHOT NOT TAKEN**.

Key point of this chapter:

If Oswald had been gunning for Kennedy, he would have taken easy shots at him, in plain sight as the limousine approached. The fact that he did not fire then is very strong evidence that his target was the man then concealed from view, John Connally.

OBSTRUCTION OF BEST EVIDENCE [A]

Momentous news: Conclusive evidence was removed from Oswald's notebook

> "The past actually happened, but history
> is only what someone wrote down."
> — A. Whitney Brown [3357]

YOU HAVE PROBABLY FOUND SEVERAL SURPRISING DISCOVERIES in this book, especially in EVIDENCE chapters 14 through 19. Until now, maybe only a few dozen people have wondered why Oswald had not fully loaded his rifle in preparation for the most important act of his life — why only 4 cartridges in a rifle designed for 7? Hundreds might have thought about the fact that he had not taken an easy and deadly shot at President Kennedy as he sat there in totally unobstructed sight, growing larger and easier as the limousine drove <u>toward</u> the TSBD. Why had Lee waited to fire until the car was driving <u>away</u>, sheltered by a tree and getting smaller? Why had he passed up many easy opportunities to bring his pistol to the site of his murderous attempt, to have it for his getaway? He slept beside it in his little rented room, and on any morning from Monday through Thursday could have brought it on his bus ride to the TSBD. Why was he forced to rush by bus, taxi and on foot, to arm with the pistol as his paramount imperative immediately <u>after</u> shooting the rifle?

Those and many other facts presented to this point are strong circumstantial evidence, and there's nothing second-rate about circumstantial evidence, as prosecutor Vincent Bugliosi will attest on page 612. It's like a rope or cable, with every settled fact adding a strand to the total strength of the evidence. And so I expected for fifty years to consign it to your judgment, ending the presentation of evidence at this point, all circumstantial, believing that it was sufficient for you to reach a considered verdict: Much more likely than not, Oswald intended to obtain revenge on Connally, but ineptly managed to shoot and kill our President by accident. That's where I have expected to rest the case — until a huge surprise at almost the last minute.

I strove to present all important facts that illuminate Oswald's intent, hoping to write what trailblazer James Reston, Jr. predicted might "end up being the last word on this matter."

[A] *The American Heritage College Dictionary* defines **obstruction of justice**: "The criminal offense, under common law and according to the statutes of many jurisdictions, of obstructing the administration and due process of law." Wikipedia has a fine article: "**Best evidence rule**".

Until mid-2015, I thought I had everything of importance. But, as a Caltech-trained engineer with respect for scientific humility, I anticipated that there would later appear matters I'd not known of, and would dearly wish I had. Well, very handily, that has already happened!

After his *The Accidental Victim* was published in 2013, I told Reston about my ambition to write this larger, more comprehensive book. He graciously encouraged me to persevere. On several occasions I have asked his guidance and judgment, which he has given unsparingly. In June 2015 he sent a message containing a wonderful bombshell: [3358]

"Dear Pierre,

After *The Accidental Victim* was published, the son of Officer Tippit was in touch with me. A policeman himself, he was very eager to talk and subscribes entirely to our theory about Connally. Most importantly, his certainty comes from discussions he had with a Secret Service officer, Mike Howard, who was [on duty in Dallas] that day. And so I was in touch with Howard, and if you don't know about this already, I strongly urge you to be in touch with him yourself. [A]fter the assassination ... he found ... a small green notebook, and in it, he discovered a page where, according to Howard, Oswald wrote that there were four people he wanted to kill: General Walker and Richard Nixon were two ... I can't remember one of them ... but John Connally was the most prominent name of them all. According to my discussion with Howard, through Connally's name LHO drew a dagger with blood dripping from it.

But then, according to Howard, after he turned the notebook over to the FBI for transportation to Washington, somehow that page was ripped out of the notebook and presumably destroyed. Howard surmises that ... J. Edgar Hoover had ordered its destruction. (Remember LHO's threatening letter to the FBI weeks before the assassination was also destroyed on orders from Washington.) ... Howard believes [Hoover] would have wanted the page destroyed ... because it showed the FBI's incompetence.

I made the effort to go to the National Archives to look at the green notebook. There is indeed evidence that a page was torn out.

For decades Mike Howard has been telling audiences that Connally was the target. But his audiences were small; his story ignored; and publicity about him and his evidence was confined to small audiences in Texas. I think Howard's story should be in your book. Good luck, J.R."

I contacted Mike Howard through the SAIL (Seniors Active in Learning) program at Collin College, whose faculty roster identifies: "**Mike Howard** is a retired Secret Service Agent who served [under] four presidents. He shares recollections and insights gained from being part of the family at the White House and in their private homes." Here's a photo from the SAIL program Web page, showing Mike teaching his course on the Kennedy assassination. [3359]

He is James M. Howard, retired Special Agent of the U.S. Secret Service. [3360] "Mike" lives on a ranch somewhere in Texas, [B] balancing that with being a part-time armed bailiff in a municipal court armed with a pistol on his belt, "been doing that since 1951", even more happy to not use it.

[B] Mike has appeared on the NBC-TV national talk show "A Closer Look", hosted by Faith Daniels.
He now enjoys retirement and privacy. Credible news agencies wishing to interview him are asked to contact the author (information on page ii) who will relay requests to Mike for his consideration.

Mike is now 84, very sharp; age has brought him appreciations for (in alphabetic order) God, his Martha, politeness, religion, respect, service and truth.

He was a police officer in Saginaw, Texas, for seven years before joining the Secret Service in Dallas in 1961. The Dallas office was small; two years later as this story begins in 1963 it was only Special Agent in Charge Forrest Sorrels and three Special Agents.[C] Although a year younger, senior to Mike by two years was Charles Kunkel, who had been a motorcycle officer in Arlington, Texas, midway between Dallas and Fort Worth.

Mike remembers clearly, as if a week ago, the dramatic and shattering week beginning on Thursday, November 21. His experience in Saginaw made him the Service's specialist in Fort Worth matters — the two cites abut. Before the Kennedy-Johnson-Connally party arrived, Mike was in Fort Worth, advancing their overnight stay there. With Special Agents Bill Duncan and Ned Hall, he checked and posted guards for Hotel Texas suites and facilities. Mike was present when the hotel tried to bar Special Agent Bob Faison, who happened to be Negro, as told with sadness by your ex-Fort Worthian author near the end of chapter 5.

Mike and others met Air Force One at Carswell Air Force Base and provided what security they could on an almost-midnight drive through darkness and rain to the Hotel Texas.

The President and Jacqueline were so impressed by the thousands standing in heavy rain to wave that they rolled down their car's windows and waved back. Kennedys and agents were soaking wet when they arrived at the hotel. In the photo,[3361] Mike is full-face, midway between Connally and Jackie. He shares a final memory of that night. He was called to the front desk where U.S. Senator Yarborough had been told they did not have a room reservation for him and the hotel was entirely full. Mike gave the senator his room; he slept 1½ hours on the couch in another agent's room. Such is the glorious life of a tired, wet government agent!

Early on the morning of our nation's worst Friday, Mike was the "point man" who escorted the President (with many "dignitaries") as he strode from the hotel, across the street to climb up onto a flatbed truck, to give a gracious "thank you" talk and explain that Jackie was still putting herself together, but it would be worth the wait, as she would look much better than anyone else. Here's Mike in his tan London Fog raincoat, leading and guarding his President. After Kennedy's talk, then the Chamber of Commerce breakfast, Mike and the visitors drove out to Air Force One. When it passed the "point of no return" enroute to Dallas, Agents Bill, Mike and Ned returned to the hotel and swept the Kennedy suite, carefully removing communications devices and picking up all left-behind and used items.

[C] They and FBI field agents are "Special" because they are trained and authorized to perform both of the quite-different functions of investigation (brain) and of enforcement (brawn).

They did this with a practiced left-hand search; upon entering a room, the agent put his left hand on the adjacent wall, walking and touching walls while looking for items, until he was back at the starting point, then into the center of the room for a similar clockwise walk.[D]

The rooms had modern color (!) TV receivers, which were on during their sweep. When an agent heard "Shots were fired in Dallas ...", they immediately raced down and out. Standing at the front entrance was Tarrant County Sheriff Lon Evans and his official car. Three Secret Service agents and a deputy sheriff jumped in, and Evans sped 120 miles an hour. Mike was one of the first to have a new wonder, a two-way radio. When it said JFK had been shot and taken to Parkland Memorial Hospital, they went directly there. Mike says the crowd and frenzy outside the emergency entrance was overwhelming — and dangerous.

In those early moments when it was not known if the Russians were invading or what, Mike and many other lawmen stood guard outside JFK's trauma room. After death was pronounced and JFK put into a casket, Mike went along to Love Field. There were two rolling stairways at Air Force One. The JFK casket and party went up the stairs near the tail, where seats had been removed to make room. The Johnson entourage was at the front of the Boeing 707. Mike and all other Secret Service agents, not yet knowing the source of the killing bullets, urged that the new president and his jet get away immediately to the relative safety of the skies, enroute to the capital. But LBJ steadfastly insisted that he must be sworn in, and sent for an old friend to conduct the ceremony. Being as helpful as possible in the difficult circumstance, Mike took up a guarding position on the platform at the top of the front steps. From years in courts, he recognized and greeted Judge Sarah T. Hughes when she climbed the steps to administer the oath of office to LBJ. So Mike was on guard duty very close by, but not in the famous photos of LBJ being sworn in.

With AF1 about to depart (at last!), an agent on the tarmac waved Mike down to him to relay an order to go immediately to the Fort Worth Police Department. Mike hurried 30 miles to "Where the West Begins". FW police wanted his help "interviewing" (the polite phrase) a cocky young man, about 21, who had refused to tell them anything. Shortly after the shooting in Dealey Plaza, he was driving away from Dallas on the fast toll road, the Dallas-Fort Worth Turnpike, when he stopped to fill at an Enco service station. In those days, gas stations gave service. As the attendant cleaned windows, he noticed two long firearms on the back seat. The station's radio was blaring the news from Dallas, causing the young driver to laugh, "Somebody killed that Catholic president!" As he drove away, the observant attendant phoned authorities, with the result that a half-dozen police cruisers were waiting when the armed man stopped to pay his exit toll[E] at the turnpike's Fort Worth end.

With all-points bulletins out for a young man with a rifle and Oswald not yet captured, he was of great interest, but told the FW police, "None of your business." Mike asked to have a few minutes with him. When alone, Mike reached toward his pistol, saying they didn't have time for this silence nonsense, and maybe it would just be easiest if he blew the man's head off to save everyone a little time and trouble. Confronted with a stone face and imminent death, the young man made haste to explain that he was from Ranger, Texas, west of Fort Worth,

---

[D] The author does this in galleries, parties, Costco warehouses, etc. Without having to think about where to go, it reliably takes one to all corners, missing nothing, with the facile right hand free.

[E] The DFW Turnpike was partly government, partly private. Opened in 1957, the tolls paid it off in 1977. It is now an unrecognized part of Interstate 30, a fate similar to that of hallowed Route 66.

half way out to Abilene. He'd driven into Dallas the day before to pick up his father's repaired rifle, and had bought himself a shotgun. Then he decided to enjoy the pleasures of Big D, so found a young lady who passed the night with him in the downtown Union Hotel.

On Friday they watched JFK's motorcade pass, he gave her some money, they parted and he headed for Ranger — and you know the rest. He was in tears of fear as he ended his story. At Mike's suggestion, the FW PD kept him overnight until Saturday, when he drove off to Ranger, sadder, wiser, and with a story to tell. Mike's old friend Tom Carter, FBI Resident Agent in Fort Worth, asked as they were leaving, "Would you really have shot him?" Mike honestly replied, "I was with the President this morning, and he was a good guy, and now he's dead and I'm some upset! But, no, I would not have shot him."

Having firmly settled that matter, Mike drove his blue 1963 Ford Police Interceptor — "It drove like a truck!" — to Dallas, where he encountered the mob in Dallas Police HQ. Saturday, the Secret Service's Inspector Tom Kelley arrived from Washington. He and Mike escorted Robert Oswald, the older brother, to the jail to have his last-ever talk with Lee.

Rumors of lynch mobs having been heard, an order came from Washington that the Secret Service take the Oswald family into protective custody for their own safety. Mike and his partner Charles Kunkel ("Charlie" to most, "Chuck" to Mike) now displayed the detective talents that, coupled with their protective abilities, gave them the deserved title of Special Agents. They learned that LIFE magazine writers and photographers had taken the four Oswald ladies (ages 56, 22, 1¾ years, 1 month) from their downtown Friday-night hotel to some secret location, in anticipation of getting exclusive photos and stories.

Mike recalls — as is usual with him, as if it happened last week — that he and Chuck Kunkel got an assistant manager with a passkey to let them into the hotel room just vacated by the Oswalds. Carefully searching, Mike thought it looked as if someone might have written on a notepad beside the bed. He recalls that in those days, hotels did not supply ballpoint pens, but instead put out stubby little pencils. Two years before, during his training, he had learned how to lightly shade a sheet of paper gray, to reveal (in white) any impressions in it from writing on a page that had been above it. Mike did that, for the first and last time in his long career, and was astounded and delighted to see the words "Executive Inn"!

He and Chuck hurried to the Dallas Executive Inn, where they learned that two rooms had been taken, one for men and another for two women with babies. Although still exhausted from their very short sleeps in Fort Worth, the two kept watch through the night from the Inn's parking lot. On Sunday morning, Mike remained on lookout at the Executive Inn while Chuck drove to Arlington (halfway to Fort Worth), returning with Russian translator Peter Paul Gregory [F] and Robert Oswald, picked up at a Howard Johnson restaurant, and two detectives borrowed from the Arlington Police Department, where Chuck had been a motorcycle cop, so knew the department well.

Then, as Mike puts it, "We kidnapped the women" from the LIFE contingent, hurrying them toward a better hideaway, a new addition built onto the Inn of the Six Flags in Arlington, which Chuck knew from his previous police work. There were two cars. Mike drove the first, Chuck beside him, the four Oswald women on the back seat. The second had the two detectives, plus Robert Oswald and Peter Gregory.

[F] The man who had tested Lee to be a translator. Marina then tutored his son, Paul, and earned $35!

Marina will soon tell Mike that she was terrified at this moment. In the Soviet Union, citizens knew well that if someone had killed Nikita Khrushchev, the assassin's family would be scooped up and "disappeared" for the rest of their lives into a prison camp in Siberia. She was quite certain that she and her little babies were being driven toward some American equivalent of the Gulag. Conversely and happily, when she soon learned that the two Secret Service Special Agents were nice gentlemen ordered by President Johnson to protect her and her girls, she rebounded and bonded tightly to them, always admiring their concern for her.[G]

Marina asked to stop at Ruth Paine's house to pick up clothes and much-needed diapers for soaking-wet Rachel.[H] Fate intervened when Mike's police radio brought word that Lee had just been shot. To avoid expected media at Ruth's in Irving, Chuck made a fast decision and diverted the two cars to the home of that city's chief of police, whom he knew. Marguerite and Marina and the little girls were warmly welcomed, and given coffee and snacks.

Also thinking fast, Mike had Marina phone Ruth Paine to list the things she needed. Mike and one of the borrowed detectives stayed with the Oswalds at the chief's home, while Chuck and the other detective drove to Ruth's, soon returning with the desired items, including clothes, money and diapers — and the small treasure that is the central purpose of this chapter. Mike recalls vividly that he was on the chief's front lawn when Chuck pulled up and, busy with mothers and babies, quickly handed him a small bluish-green notebook.

As Marina changed Rachel's diaper, they heard that Lee had died at Parkland Hospital. Marguerite and Marina both insisted on going immediately to verify that it was really Lee and that he was really dead. Against the Secret Service agents' best judgment for their safety, that's what they did. Here they arrive at the hospital. Marina (June hidden) is followed by Marguerite carrying Rachel. Mike is at right in sunglasses. Behind him are two local detectives he and Chuck had borrowed.

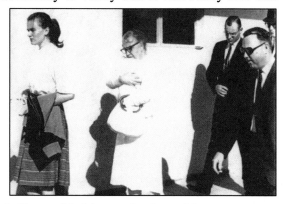

When they were taken to Lee's body, Mike says Marina was as cool as a cucumber, perhaps from her training as a pharmacist, as she lifted his closed eyelids, looked into his dead eyes, then lowered the lids. Mike then drove the ladies and babies to the Inn. Newsmen were following close behind, so he radioed back to the second car, which then stopped and held the media until Mike was out of sight to the west, so effectively that reporters never found the new hideaway. Just in case, Arlington police helpfully stationed a young officer with an automatic military rifle to guard the approaches to their new building, not yet in use by other guests.[I]

[G] Mike has hundreds of stories that would fill a really interesting book. Here's one: When Marina was later beset by a conspiracy theorist, as told in chapter 7, to dig up Lee's grave to see if it contained a Soviet agent, she asked Mike for his advice ("Do what you want.") and support. When the coffin was opened, she reached in and removed from among the bones the wedding ring she had placed on Lee's finger at the burial, calmly telling Mike that proved the remains were those of her "Alik".

[H] This is years before Pampers were in common use. Diapers were cloth, usually laundered at home.

[I] Mike loves to tell how, later that week, two FBI agents did not wait at an agreed meeting point, and when walking toward the room were surprised and forced to lie face down with the automatic rifle hovering over their heads until they were identified by the Secret Service!

Mike says the next days, Sunday to Wednesday, with Marina, her toddler Junie and baby Rachel, and Robert and Marguerite Oswald were memorable; he pictures them as if last week. One memory: He and Chuck Kunkel took turns sleeping on a couch. One night, Marina shook him awake, saying in great alarm, "Mama! Knife! Mama! Knife!" Mike motioned Marina to "Show me", and she took him into the bedroom where Marguerite slept. Marina pointed under Marguerite's pillow. Mike reached in very quietly and came out with a 1917 U.S. Army bayonet, the kind that was mounted on Springfield '03 rifles for close-up combat in World War I trenches. Marguerite had been driven to her home for clothes and other necessities, and Mike believes she spirited that long, sharp man-killing blade into the Inn of the Six Flags in a sewing bag, the only container of sufficient length. He hid the bayonet

under cushions on his couch and went back to snoozing. Other Marguerite encounters were memorable but best not put into print!

Monday was highly stressful for all, Oswalds and agents alike, when they attended a very trying burial. Fuller information about the day, in Robert's sad words, are in chapter 7, where you will have read that he gratefully used gracious Mike Howard as his only "gofer", assistant and confidant. Mike stood near to the family to be protective, and very close to Robert to be helpful, and here he is with them at the sad little graveside ceremony.

All these years, Mike has saved the document he helped prepare while helping Robert plan the simple funeral service. Here it is, with no soloist, organist, escorts or boutonnieres:

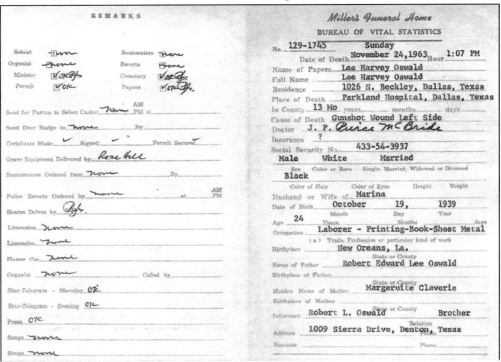

Special Agent Mike Howard had known Marguerite Oswald for only a day, but was beginning to recognize her ambitions as a world-class would-be manager of perceptions. Although she had other clothes available, she insisted on going to the burial still clad in the white nurse's dress she had been wearing since her son did his killing. Mike and others recognized that she was both presenting herself as a nurse, which she was not (well, unlicensed "practical nurse" at best) and making a big deal of displaying her pretended privations including not being able to change clothes under the pressing circumstances.

Robert later told the Warren Commission that all of the Secret Service agents were courteous gentlemen, but matters with Marguerite reached a slow boil on "approximately Wednesday, November 27 ... between Mr. [Charles] Kunkel and my mother ... at which time my mother stated to him to the best of my remembrance, that 'Please, sir, don't say anything to me at all.' And Mr. Kunkel's reply was—and he was irritated—that he would not unless he had to, and for her not to please say anything to him. And that was the end of that." [3362]

Mike emphasizes that the assigned role of the Secret Service that week was to protect. President Johnson assigned the FBI to do interviewing and fact-gathering, but previous contacts between Marina (and Lee, but he's dead) and the FBI had been so tense and unsatisfactory that she refused to talk with them, especially when she saw pushy agent James Hosty. So she couldn't be branded uncooperative, Mike encouraged Marina to answer a few questions from a new FBI man she had never met. Then, Mike and Chuck pitched in to take extensive statements. Here they are, doing that. Mike is at left with the tape recorder, his nicely polished shoe on the coffee table. On the couch, friendly translator Peter Gregory sits at left, Marina is in the center, and Chuck Kunkel on the right holds the recorder's microphone.

One tantalizing matter that came up during their time with Marina has never been reported; at least it's not in this author's memory from the hundreds of books he's read in the last half-century. In her testimonies to the Warren Commission and her work with Priscilla Johnson McMillan for the wonderful and indispensable book *Marina and Lee*, Marina said that Lee had gone to bed first on Thursday, their last night together, and that when she got into bed, she was quite sure that he was still awake, but silent. In fifty years, I have not suspected that anything else happened that night.

Mike Howard testifies that during their days at the Inn of the Six Flags, Marina told of a much more interesting and compelling sequel. She said after the house was quiet with Ruth gone to her bedroom, Lee left their bed, went out of the bedroom and closed the door. Marina was close to, but not asleep at the time. She quietly arose, she said, opened the door only a crack, and there was Lee at the dining room table with the rifle that he must have brought in from the garage. She watched as he disassembled and reassembled it. Then, as she had seen many times during the past months, he repeatedly dry fired it, going through all the motions necessary to fire bullets, but with no cartridges in the rifle. She said that he didn't simply fire, but carefully aimed and pretend-fired at the Paine's TV set. This is compelling testimony because it is contemporary. A lot has happened, but what Marina told the agents had happened within the last six days — very fresh in her mind and probably told with absolute accuracy.

History, close-up, is usually a bit messy, "like nailing Jell-O to the wall", especially if revealed after half a century, and veracity is vouched for by a pinch or two of gray to soften the black and white. This author is satisfied that the statements above are factual. Leaving further investigation to historians, it's now time to move to the main point of this chapter.

Quietly sequestered with Robert and the women, Mike and Chuck had time to inspect Lee's little blue-green pocket notebook, the kind designed to contain both notes and addresses. It was very interesting. For starters, it was obviously of Russian manufacture; the thumb-index tabs were not A, B, C, but strange characters from the Cyrillic alphabet. Lee had purchased the book during his early lonely days in Moscow and began filling it with notes and thoughts. He had drawn a map of central Moscow and entered the names of his Intourist guides and of the U.S. press's "preety" ladies who interviewed him, all described back in Chapter 3 – Moscow.

Before diving inside the notebook, the reader deserves to know how it had gone from Lee Oswald to Mike Howard. On bloody Friday, it was not on Lee when he was arrested at the Texas Theatre. Swarms of police staked out both Lee's boardinghouse and Ruth Paine's house where Marina and babies lived, and where most Oswald possessions were stored, many in the soon-famous garage. Police carefully took all items of interest from Lee, his room, and Ruth's, then carefully inventoried everything — and the notebook was not among them!

It turns out this is a faint echo of April 10, 1963, when Lee left their apartment to shoot General Edwin Walker. He had written, in Russian, names, addresses and information Marina would need if he did not return. He did return after narrowly missing Walker, and in excitement forgot that piece of paper. Marina secretly kept it, not knowing what he might do next, thinking it could be important. Accepting Ruth's genuine hospitality, she moved into the Paine home, where she was eager to learn American cooking and became engrossed in Ruth's shelf of cookbooks. And she hid Lee's pre-Walker paper in one of them, as told on page 132.

Police searched thoroughly on November 22, taking just about all of the Oswald's possessions. Understandably, they ignored Ruth's shelf of cookbooks,[J] where there was a greater treasure.

On Thursday, November 21, Lee had come with neither precedent nor warning to fetch his rifle from Ruth's garage, for his evil purpose the next day. Mike Howard learned during the next week — from whom he can't recall — Marina told someone that on Thursday evening she had seen Lee put something up on Ruth's cookbook shelf, and she recognized what it was. On Friday after he went to work with his bag of "curtain rods", she looked on the shelf, found his greenish notebook, and left it there. Marina was highly familiar with the book, having first seen it in Minsk, always carried by her new husband.

That's entirely possible, but for two reasons this author wishes to offer one other possibility. The first reason is because Mike is uncertain of the information's path to him. The second is that Ruth Paine will, sometime in the next few months, find tucked into one of her cookbooks the piece of paper hidden there by Marina, the instructions Lee had written and left behind when he went out to shoot General Walker. Marina had saved that, rightly expecting that at some future time it might be valuable. Given those facts, it seems improbable to your author that Marina would hide something from Lee among the cookbooks, and that Lee would then also choose the same hiding place for his notebook. It could be, but does not ring loudly the bell of probability. It really won't matter, but here's my alternate:

We know with certainty that when Marina rose on Friday morning, she found on the dresser Lee's wedding ring and something he had never ever given her, a large pile of money, $170! These unprecedented leavings are circumstantial evidence of great strength that he intended to do something far out of the ordinary that day. Because we know that Marina, not Lee, had already used the cookbooks to hide a secret, your author "puts the case"[K] that Lee may have left the notebook beside the bed, with the ring and money. On finding it, Marina had hidden it on the cookbook shelf. It doesn't matter; when Marina phoned Ruth on Sunday with her list of needs, she asked for the notebook from the shelf — and that's how what had been missed by police and FBI came to Mike Howard's hands.

I have asked Mike whether he is the only person alive in 2015 who saw the notebook that week. He recalls that in addition to those mentioned above, the Secret Service sent in two Special Agents to help out. Leon Gopadze, so fluent in translating between Russian and English that he did just that when Marina testified to the Warren Commission, came from San Francisco. Gary Seal arrived from either Florida or New Orleans (Mike is always frank when he's unsure), to help Marina move from the Inn to a home where she was next sheltered. Mike expects that Gopadze must have passed away, and has no idea whether Seal ever saw the notebook before it was ordered to Washington, or whether he is still living. Two other possible witnesses will be named on the third following page.

During their secret, quiet confinement in the Inn, when there were no other duties to perform, Chuck and Mike studied the little book and remarked on its interesting contents. So you can see what they saw, the next two pages show Warren Commission *Hearings* pages on which are printed photos of eight notebook pages. Below the photos, the Commission supplied translations of several Russian-language entries.

[J] In chapter 5 is a large photo of Ruth's kitchen on Saturday morning, November 23. If you know to look above Ruth, there are the high shelves of cookbooks, the notebook then hidden among them.

[K] "Now, Pip," said Mr. Jaggers, "put this case ..." in Charles Dickens' great book *Great Expectations*.

COMMISSION EXHIBIT 18: Oswald's notebook, pages 12 – 15:[3363]

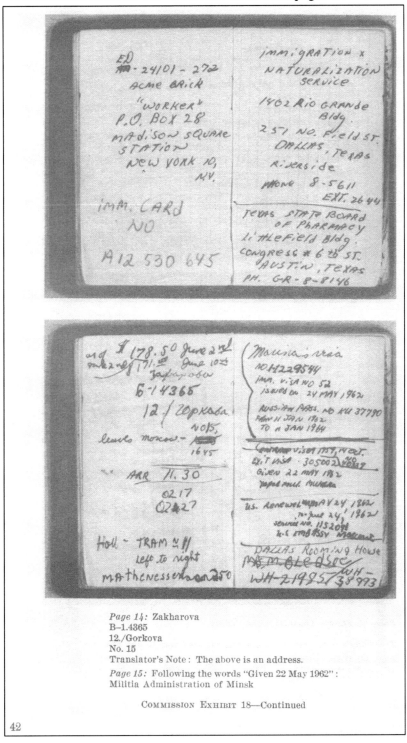

Page 14: Zakharova
B–1.4365
12./Gorkova
No. 15
Translator's Note: The above is an address.
Page 15: Following the words "Given 22 May 1962":
Militia Administration of Minsk

COMMISSION EXHIBIT 18—Continued

42

The page at top-left, #12 in the notebook, begins with phone number and extension of brother Robert at "ACME BRICK".[3364] Page #15 at bottom-right ends "DALLAS ROOMING HOUSE" and, crossed out, "MRS. M. BLEDSOE", the landlady who threw him out for speaking Russian!

Commission Exhibit 18: Oswald's notebook, pages 16 – 21[3365]:

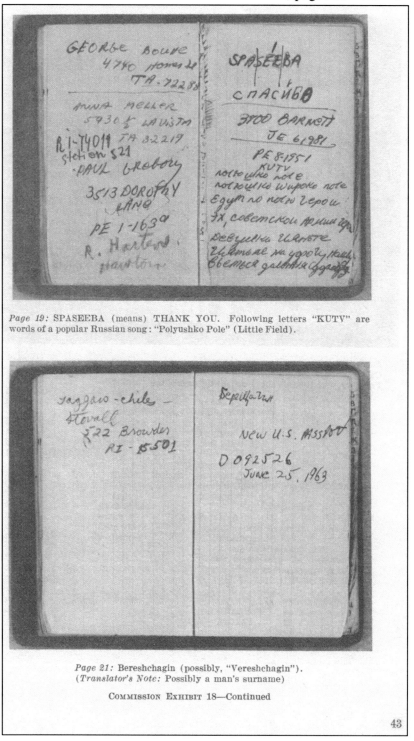

Page 19: SPASEEBA (means) THANK YOU. Following letters "KUTV" are words of a popular Russian song: "Polyushko Pole" (Little Field).

Page 21: Bereshchagin (possibly, "Vereshchagin").
(*Translator's Note:* Possibly a man's surname)

Commission Exhibit 18—Continued

43

The page at top-left, #16 in the notebook, begins "GEORGE BOUHE", leader of Dallas Russian émigrés, and names Paul, the son of translator Peter Gregory. Page #21 at the bottom-right records the number and date of Oswald's "NEW U.S. PASSPORT" obtained in New Orleans.

On November 27, President Johnson informed his executive branch and all government agencies, federal, state and local, that he had designated the FBI to consolidate facts for the investigation of the Dallas assassination.[L] He instructed them to send all relevant information and evidence to FBI headquarters in Washington. From Secret Service headquarters in the nation's capital, Inspector Thomas Kelley sent the order to all field offices, and so it came to the little hideaway in the Inn of the Six Flags.

That day, Mike Howard remembers, Chuck Kunkel drove to their Secret Service office in Dallas to hand in all they had. There were "two and a half"[M] large reels of recorded tape with Chuck and Mike interviews of Marina, Marguerite and Robert Oswald. There was Marguerite's trove of news clippings about her son's defection. And, there was Lee Oswald's pocket notebook. That's the last they ever saw of it.

Mike had (still has) great respect for the professionalism of those with whom he served. He believes that the agents in the Dallas office carefully inventoried and packed the evidence, including the notebook, with whatever else was there. He expects that Special Agents Bob Stewart, by far their best typist, and John Joe Howlett, their principal investigator, handled the material, and could (if alive, Mike doesn't know) testify to it. The Special Agent in Charge of Dallas, Forrest Sorrels, immediately sent it to Washington, DC, to the attention of the Secret Service's Inspector, Thomas J. Kelley, who then may have personally taken it to the nearby FBI Building, handing the notebook to either Director J. Edgar Hoover or to a very-high-level designated assistant. And that, as Marguerite Oswald was wont to say, was that.

When life returned to normal — well, a sadly subdued normal in a shocked USA — Mike went to a new and interesting assignment. With LBJ now President, his immediate family members needed protection. Mike went off to Austin, to be a member of the Secret Service team assigned to guard daughter Lynda Bird Johnson at the University of Texas. A gentleman, he does not tell any stories of that time, but I think of the famous song sung by a romantically-frustrated out-on-a-date president's daughter in the 1962 Broadway musical "*Mr. President*": "The Secret Service – makes me nervous – when I start to pant — and I can't!"

Almost a year later, the *Warren Report* was published, with its sound conclusions that Oswald had indeed "done it", and he'd done it all alone, and the Commission was sorry to say that they could not specify his motive, but perhaps it might have been a general dislike of government and officials. Then at the end of 1964 the Commission threw together and printed its 26 fat volumes of *Hearings*, containing transcripts of testimonies and depositions, but much more voluminously, thousands of documents, photos and other interesting exhibits.

Filling many fascinating pages are transcripts of the interviews taped at the Inn of the Six Flags, and photos of Marguerite's clippings, most from the *Fort Worth Star-Telegram*. Their appearance in the *Hearings* attests that the evidence from the Inn had arrived safely at FBI headquarters.

One set of those 26 books made it to the Secret Service, where Special Agent Charles Kunkel looked at the pages shown earlier in this chapter and exclaimed, according to Mike, "Well, how do you like that!".

[L] "assassination" because that is the usual usage until now, although this book shows that Oswald was attempting to kill Connally for what he had done or not done (murder), and certainly not for being Governor of Texas (assassination) — and that the death of Kennedy was an accidental homicide.

[M] Mike Howard is always careful and precise. It was neither 2 nor 3 — it was 2½ recorded reels.

Here's what Chuck Kunkel saw, and quickly called to the attention of his friend and companion caretaker of the Oswalds at the Inn of the Six Flags, Mike Howard:

COMMISSION EXHIBIT 18: Oswald's notebook, pages 16 – 19[3366]:

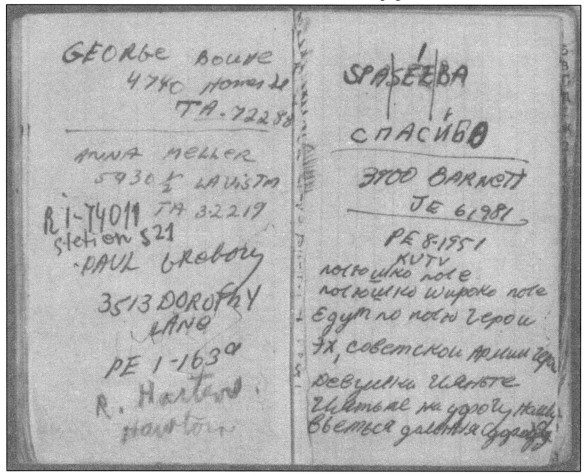

There was a page missing! While that fact may be obvious if you know it and are looking to find it, it's not at all obvious if you didn't know and were not watching for it. Right? Well, did you notice the missing sheet, two pages ago in this book? Did you notice that the two pages side-by-side at top are numbered 16 and 19? Very few have ever noticed that, including this author who has owned and looked through those Texas-size books of Warren Commission *Hearings* for more than a half-century!

Chuck Kunkel was looking for that specific page because he and Mike had been greatly amazed at what Lee had written. Mike recalls the words vividly — not a hint of hesitation when you ask him. He can't quite remember if this was written all on one side, or maybe on two sides of one sheet, but these are very definitely the words that were on the torn-out paper:

[other notes about other matters]

I WILL KILL [here is a bloody
JOHN CONNALLY dagger]

GENERAL WALKER

I WILL KILL JAMES HOSTY

THE VICE PRESIDENT

[other notes about other matters]

That page with those four entries was in the notebook when Chuck drove it to Dallas so it would go to FBI HQ. Mike says he and Chuck recognized this to be a "kill list". They understood that rightist-conservative Connally fit well with a far-right fascist such as Walker. They knew FBI agent James Hosty, but at that moment had no idea why he was on the list. You know from Chapter 5 – MISFIT that Hosty repeatedly interviewed Marina while Lee was at work, arousing Lee's anger (jealousy?) to the point of leaving a nasty note for Hosty at the FBI office; a note soon destroyed by order of SAIC Shanklin, hours after Oswald's death.

Mike and Chuck puzzled about what Oswald might have had against LBJ. Then a light went on when they realized it didn't say "Johnson", it said "The Vice President", undoubtedly meaning none other than the (also conservative) vice president of the United States at the time Oswald defected to the USSR, Richard Nixon! Now all the pieces fit!

When the notebook appeared in the Warren Commission *Hearings*, as you have seen, the sheet was missing. Chuck Kunkel, looking for it, quickly realized it was gone and told Mike. A two-page sheet having disappeared is corroborated by a staffer, either FBI or Warren Commission, who had noticed the small edge remnant of the missing sheet, so numbered the two top pages, as was printed in the Commission's captions three pages ago, 16 and 19.

When was the missing sheet removed? What happened to it? Mike Howard and James Reston, Jr. and this author are one in believing that FBI Director J. Edgar Hoover ordered that page removed and destroyed — probably burned in FBI HQ in DC and the ashes flushed down a toilet — the same as Hosty did in Dallas to destroy evidence of Oswald's anger at him.

Hoover, a highly defensive and political animal, would have wanted "**JAMES HOSTY**", a Special Agent of his agency, hidden from public view to avoid embarrassing questions about any possible FBI involvement with Oswald, something about which assassination conspiracy theorists asked anyway for many years, even without that piece of hard evidence.

Some may speculate that President Lyndon Johnson might have wanted "I WILL KILL JOHN CONNALLY" to vanish, to avoid embarrassing his protégé with a bright political future. Johnson and Hoover had lived across a street from one another in Washington, were friends and confidants, so close that Johnson gave Hoover one of his famous Beagle dogs (not the famed LBJ, "Little Beagle Johnson"), and had named another "J. Edgar Beagle". Did Hoover show the notebook to LBJ and get his approval — adding another chip to Hoover's much-loved pile of IOU credits — before destroying the page? Probably not, and we may never know. My estimation: If Hoover told LBJ of the page that could prove troublesome to both of them, the wise politician could have quietly replied to the G-man, "Do whatever you need to."

Mike Howard became very close to the Johnson family when he went with them to their retirement on the ranch by the Pedernales River. Mike and Lyndon were fond of each other, which made the assignment stressful for Mike as the recent leader of the free world declined in bodily health. LBJ's mind was always good, and when Mike would caution him to "take it easy", Johnson replied, "Mike, it doesn't matter. No man in my family lives past 65."

Sure enough, LBJ died on January 22, 1973, at the age of 64, exactly two days after a second full term, if he had run, which would have ended on January 20. Mike has a fine insight. President Nixon had phoned LBJ the previous week to tell him that the decision was made and the White House would order the end of operations in Vietnam. LBJ was gratified and lived long enough to hear that announcement, then quietly and contentedly died in peace.

Chuck Kunkel, the first agent to handle the incriminating notebook, who could testify to its kill list, and who first realized that the page had been removed while the book was with the FBI, died a few years ago in his back yard while practicing with his putter.

This very important chapter is based on Mike's testimony in meaningful interviews with the author. He and I are certain that Kennedy was killed by accident, Connally was the intended victim, although innocent of any transgression except in Oswald's twisted mind. We both perceive the tragedy as being the child of two villains, Lee and his mother. Although Marguerite did not raise Lee to shoot people, the way she raised him inculcated the self-importance and anger that led him to shoot. Mike is semi-retired on his ranch in Texas where he loves Martha, married 64 years, enjoys having cat Sarah Palin on his lap, and rides his 15-year-old Appaloosa. Here's a 2015 photo of Mike and Tequilla.

> Key points of this chapter:
> **Secret Service Special Agent (retired) Mike Howard has been telling small classes for years that Oswald's intent was to kill Connally, and the proof had been in his pocket notebook. At last, Mike and what he knows have a wider audience.**

OTHERS ON THIS TRAIL

You hold the only comprehensive book; others have had the idea

> "I'm delighted to know that another author has taken up the argument. It looks like your book will end up being the last word on this matter. Best wishes."
> — **James Reston, Jr.** [3367]

OTHERS HAVE HAD THE SAME THOUGHT, that Oswald aimed at Connally and killed Kennedy by accident, then said or wrote that as the most probable explanation of the shooting. I was early in thinking and accepting, but am late in writing. It is only fair to note those who already expressed the belief, from 1963 through 2015; that's the purpose of this chapter.

What has been laid before you in Chapters 14 – TOO CLOSE TO CALL through 19 – THE SHOT NOT TAKEN is a theory about intent. Chapter 20 told about a page of solid unassailable proof, but it was removed from his notebook and destroyed. Because Oswald is dead, there is not now and never will be any way to prove intent beyond all possible doubt. The Big Bang, evolution and man-caused global warming are theories accepted by most who have sufficient education, who have studied and thought about them. But, logical as they are, there are vocal dissenters. The theory that Lee Oswald intended to murder John Connally is less important than, for example, the rise of oceans. But it possesses enough gravitas that some have argued against it. Included below in chronological order are both those who agree and the gainsayers. As some deer must have once said to an antelope, "Hark! I heard a discouraging word!"

1963 (November 30): **Marina Oswald** in interview by the FBI

Eight days after the shooting, in the week Lee was buried, Marina was interviewed by two FBI agents, one them Russian-speaking Anatole A. Boguslav, so we may have confidence in their understanding. Marina told of her excitement about the Kennedys coming to Dallas because she and Lee admired them. The agents then typed into their report dated December 1, 1963:

> "She said Oswald never gave any indication whatsoever that he intended any harm to the President. She said she feels intuitively that if Oswald was trying to kill the President, that one shot would have been enough; and that she feels, therefore, that he might have been aiming at the other person (Governor Connally). She said Oswald never mentioned any possible plans that he might have about assassinating the President. She said she cannot understand this thing." [3368]

The FBI was ordered by President Lyndon Johnson to be the chief gatherer of facts for the Warren Commission, and did so with great energy. That bureau report of December 1, 1963, was one of the first documents in the hands of the commissioners and their staff. But, despite the strong and broad pointer she gave in the interview above, absolutely nothing was done to investigate or even consider the possibility that Oswald had aimed at Connally. I can think of two possible excuses. First, the thought that our dashing young President might have been killed only as an accidental victim was too outrageous to be seriously considered by the FBI. Second is a simple organizational principle: President Johnson had created the *Commission on the Assassination of President Kennedy*, and <u>not</u> the *Commission on the Attempted Assassination of Governor Connally and Resulting Accidental Death of President Kennedy*. Even if the Feds thought of pursuing Marina's suggestion — well, that wasn't their charter!

Despite this author's considerable admiration for the Warren Commission, for its speed and thoroughness in assembling most of the facts that have ever become known relevant to the assassination, it is a great blemish that they did nothing with her very early suggestion above. The staff had that report, with Marina's delineation of a motive that made sense, two full months before the commissioners began taking testimony — and did not follow its lead.

When the Commission had organized and staffed itself, Lee's widow was the first witness called to testify — for four long days, two sessions a day, February 3 through 6, 1964. The transcript of that first testimony requires 126 pages of fine print that begins Volume I of 26 volumes of *Hearings Before the President's Commission on the Assassination of President Kennedy*, abbreviated *WCH* in this book's NOTES. She was called again in June and July to clear up new matters that had arisen from other witnesses. Finally, as will be reported below, she was called a fourth time in September 1964 as the Commission's last witness.

During her appearances, end-bracketing the Commission's hundreds of sessions of testimony and accumulation of thousands of documents, Marina was never, ever, asked even one question about Connally-as-target. As set forth below at "<u>1964 (September 6)</u>", she again made the suggestion in her final testimony, then was ungraciously batted down by the bellicose chairman of that session, Senator Richard Russell.

<u>1964 (January 30): David W. Belin</u>, assistant counsel of the Warren Commission
Savvy assassination historian James Reston, Jr., whose writings will be featured later in this chapter, noted another early opportunity for the Commission to find truth: "[T]here was apparently some consideration in the Warren Commission of the possibility that Connally was, indeed, Oswald's real target. On January 30, 1964, Warren Commission assistant counsel, David W. Belin, wrote a memo to chief counsel J. Lee Rankin, entitled "Oswald's knowledge that Connally would be in the presidential car and his intended target." Many years later, Belin would say that the Commission rejected the possibility on the 'common sense' grounds that if Connally was the target, Oswald would have fired as the presidential limousine approached the Book Depository rather than when it had already passed the building, and that Oswald had numerous other opportunities to kill Connally as the governor made public appearances around the state." Reston then reasons: "As for Oswald not shooting when the vehicle approached the building, this projects the discussion into the speculative realm of the criminal mind. For instance, Oswald may have felt he had a better chance of getting away if he fired after the vehicle was already past his sniper's nest than when it was approaching. ... It may be less important what Oswald was feeling and doing in the split seconds before he pulled

the trigger than what was in his mind two days before the assassination when he settled upon his intention." [3369]

The two "common sense" explanations by Belin will be echoed by many gainsayers, as you will see in the following pages, and both are wrong. The explanations above by Reston have merit — I do not disagree with them — but to my mind they are not as compelling as these next two paragraphs:

Oswald did not fire as the limousine approached the Book Depository for the simple reason that he could not find his target, hidden in the shelter of the windshield and handrail. The fact that he did not fire until he saw Connally, the basis of Chapter 19 – THE SHOT NOT TAKEN, is strong evidence that he did not shoot Kennedy when that was easy because his intent was to shoot Connally, which Oswald did as soon as he could aim at him.

The second, that Oswald had many other opportunities "around the state" might be true of normal assassins who could go to the victim, but not for Lee Oswald who had no car, did not know how to drive, and did not have money to hire taxis, private jets or whatever in which he could take his rifle to the governor without arousing suspicions. After his final rejection by the Navy Discharge Review Board and return from Louisiana, he in fact *shot the first time* Governor Connally came near him.

1964 (March 23): **George Bouhe** in testimony to the Warren Commission

This good man, an elder and social leader of the Dallas-Fort Worth Russian-speaking émigré community, in his testimony to the Commission was one of the first to suggest that Lee Oswald may have had hostility toward Governor Connally. During his questioning by Assistant Counsel Wesley J. Liebeler:

"Mr. LIEBELER. Did he ever express any hostilities toward any individual in the Government?

Mr. BOUHE. Never heard. And I must emphasize again that to talk politics with a man like that, I would find totally hopeless and useless. I never did it. But if anybody asked me, did he have any hostility against anybody in the Government, which I didn't hear myself, I would say Governor Connally.

Mr. LIEBELER. Why do you say that?

Mr. BOUHE. Because, where, I can't find the paper, but when he was in Minsk, he wrote a letter. I have it some place, but I don't know where, in the paper here.

Mr. LIEBELER. Let me ask you this, Mr. Bouhe. Did Oswald tell you that he wrote a letter to Governor Connally?

Mr. BOUHE. No, sir.

Mr. LIEBELER. You learned that only after reading it in the paper?

Mr. BOUHE. Absolutely. No correspondence. We didn't discuss. I would say my conversations with Oswald were at rock bottom minimum.

Mr. LIEBELER. Did you have any feeling before the assassination that he had any hostility toward any individual in the Government?

Mr. BOUHE. You mean as of the end of December, 1962?

Mr. LIEBELER. Yes.

Mr. BOUHE. I did not hear him say anything like that. But in reading this press news after the assassination, it clearly describes there the letter which he wrote from Minsk to Governor Connally, who was at the time Secretary of the Navy, and told him that he wants to correct the injustice being done an ex-serviceman and citizen, and I almost see the period 'as soon as possible.' Connally passed it to the Marine Corps, according to the paper, which did nothing about it. And then I think it was the Newsweek magazine story which said, quoting

Oswald, 'Well, I will leave nothing undone to correct this injustice.' That is what I know from the press. To me, I would say that it looks like a threat.

Mr. LIEBELER. But you don't have any knowledge of Oswald's displeasure with Governor Connally?

Mr. BOUHE. Absolutely not.

Mr. LIEBELER. If he had any prior to the assassination?

Mr. BOUHE. No, sir." [3370]

Liebeler went on to ask about Marina's ability with English and other subjects, so this early opportunity was lost, for the Commission to follow Bouhe's rational thought to its logical conclusion, to point the Commission to something it never found — a motive for the shooting.

1964 (April 21): **Gov. John Bowden Connally, Jr.** in testimony to the Warren Commission

With his right arm still healing in a sling, Governor Connally traveled to Washington to testify. He and his evidence would be important, so most commissioners were present. After eleven pages of transcript about the reasons and plans for Kennedy's trip to Texas, followed by Connally's memory of the three shots, his wounds and recovery, this transpired:

"Representative BOGGS. I wonder if I might ask a question?

The CHAIRMAN. Go right ahead.

Representative BOGGS. This is a little bit off the subject, but it is pretty well established that the Governor was shot and he has recovered. Do you have any reason to believe there was any conspiracy afoot for somebody to assassinate you?

Governor CONNALLY. None whatever.

Representative BOGGS. Had you ever received any threat from Lee Harvey Oswald of any kind?

Governor CONNALLY. No.

Representative BOGGS. Did you know him?

Governor CONNALLY. No.

Representative BOGGS. Had you ever seen him?

Governor CONNALLY. No.

Representative BOGGS. Have you ever had any belief of, subsequent to the assassination of President Kennedy and your own injury, that there was a conspiracy here of any kind?

Governor CONNALLY. None whatever.

Representative BOGGS. What is your theory about what happened?

Governor CONNALLY. Well, it is pure theory based on nothing more than what information is available to everyone, and probably less is available to me, certainly less than is available to you here on this Commission.

But I think you had an individual here with a completely warped, demented mind who, for whatever reason, wanted to do two things: First, to vent his anger, his hate, against many people and many things in a dramatic fashion that would carve for him, in however infamous a fashion, a niche in the history books of this country. And I think he deliberately set out to do just what he did, and that is the only thing that I can think of.

You ask me my theory, and that is my theory, and certainly not substantiated by any facts.

Representative BOGGS. Going on again, Governor, and again using the word 'theory,' do you have any reason to believe that there was any connection between Oswald and Ruby?

Governor CONNALLY. I have no reason to believe that there was; no, Congressman. By the same token, if you ask me do I have any reason not to believe it, I would have to answer the same, I don't know.

Representative BOGGS. Yes.

Governor CONNALLY.   I just don't have any knowledge or any information about the background of either, and I am just not in a position to say.

Mr. DULLES. You recall your correspondence with Oswald in connection with Marine matters, when he thought you were still Secretary of the Navy?

Governor CONNALLY. After this was all over, I do, Mr. Dulles. As I recall, he wrote me a letter asking that his dishonorable discharge be corrected. But at the time he wrote the letter, if he had any reason about it at all, or shortly thereafter, he would have recognized that I had resigned as Secretary of the Navy a month before I got the letter, so it would really take a peculiar mind, it seems to me, to harbor any grudge as a result of that when I had resigned as Secretary prior to the receipt of the letter.

Mr. DULLES. I think I can say without violating any confidence, that there is nothing in the record to indicate that there was—in fact, Marina, the wife, testified, in fact, to the contrary. There was no animus against you on the part of Oswald, as you—

Governor CONNALLY. I have wondered, of course, in my own mind as to whether or not there could have conceivably been anything, and the only—I suppose like any person at that particular moment, I represented authority to him. Perhaps he was in a rebellious spirit enough to where I was as much a target as anyone else. But that is the only conceivable basis on which I can assume that he was deliberately trying to hit me.

Representative BOGGS. You have no doubt about the fact that he was deliberately trying to hit you?

Governor CONNALLY. Yes, I do; I do have doubt, Congressman. I am not at all sure he was shooting at me. I think I could with some logic argue either way. The logic in favor of him, of the position that he was shooting at me, is simply borne out by the fact that the man fired three shots, and he hit each of the three times he fired. He obviously was a pretty good marksman, so you have to assume to some extent at least that he was hitting what he was shooting at.

   On the other hand, I think I could argue with equal logic that obviously his prime target, and I think really his sole target, was President Kennedy. His first shot, at least to him, he could not have but known the effect that it might have on the President. His second shot showed that he had clearly missed the President, and his result to him, as the result of the first shot, the President slumped and changed his position in the back seat just enough to expose my back. I haven't seen all of the various positions, but again I think from where he was shooting I was in the direct line of fire immediately in front of the President, so any movement on the part of the President would expose me." [3371]

Recovering in hospitals and at home, John Connally had had lots of time to think, and he had considered the possibility that Oswald might have been aiming for either of them. He was wrong that "he hit each of the three times he fired" — the first shot had missed the car, hit the street with a visible spark and blast of fragments on JFK's right, then flew on to wound Jim Tague. And, JFK could not slump — Connally did. Most important is his careful judgment: "I am not at all sure he was shooting at me. I think I could with some logic argue either way." He is one of very few, only six months after Oswald killed Kennedy, to realize that. As was always the case, the Commission was not interested and did not pursue that possibility.

1964 (April 24): **Jeanne De Mohrenschildt** in testimony to the Warren Commission

Three days after Connally, one month after Bouhe, the wife of Oswald's "friend" George testified. It was then well known that Lee had shot at General Edwin Walker. When asked if Oswald might have been jealous of, or opposed to Kennedy, she gave this insight:

"Mrs. DE MOHRENSCHILDT. [I]n fact that is what doesn't make any sense, because I don't think he ever said anything against, and whatever ... President ... Kennedy was doing, Lee was completely exactly with the same ideas, exactly. If he would shoot Walker that would be understandable, even if he would be shooting at Connally that is understandable, too." [3372]

She pointed to the incongruity if Oswald had aimed at Kennedy; the shooting would be more rational if his target had been General Walker (who was not in the limo) or Governor Connally (who was, sitting directly in line with President Kennedy). See chapter 17's spectrum.

1964 (May): Thomas G. Buchanan in *Who Killed Kennedy?*

Expatriate American freelance journalist Thomas G. Buchanan wrote a series of articles published by *l'Express* of Paris to bring the public's attention to the questions he believed needed to be raised about the conflicting information and official statements that were being reported in the American media. Many Europeans agreed with his take on the matter when trying to make sense of the incomprehensible assassination of the young American President they so greatly admired. As told in Chapter 8 – COMMISSION, CRITICS, REHASHES, Buchanan then augmented those articles into a slim book, *Who Killed Kennedy?*, published a full four months before the speedy *Warren Report*. While considering the possibility that Oswald killed because of insanity, Buchanan wrote this very long paragraph — to my studied knowledge the first in-print footprint (yes, there's something amiss in that metaphor!) on this trail:

"It must be assumed, if there is any merit in the thesis that the murderer of Kennedy was 'crazy,' that he was a paranoid who thought that he was being personally persecuted; that, like [assassin of President Garfield] Guiteau, he had nursed some private grievance until it had come to be obsessive, and he felt the only way in which he could avenge the wrong that had been done him was to fire the murder weapon. But since Oswald is the only suspect who has been officially accused, acceptance of this thesis would imply that Kennedy was not the target— that the shots were fired, instead, at Texas Governor John Connally. There has not ever been the slightest indication of a private injury which Oswald felt that he had suffered at the hands of Kennedy himself. Police at Dallas charged, however, that Lee Oswald once had sent a letter threatening the life of Connally, who had been Secretary of the Navy in September, 1959, when Oswald was released from active duty at his own request in order to support his mother. When he subsequently tried to swear allegiance to the Soviet Union, he was given a discharge from the Marine reserves as 'undesirable,' as might have been expected.[A] The reports first issued were that Oswald had thereafter menaced Connally, feeling his military service had been honorable—as, indeed, it had [B]—and that his subsequent political decision had no relevance to the performance of his duty while he was in uniform. But when the contents of the letter Oswald wrote in early 1962 to Connally were known, the 'threats of violence' turned out to be no more specific than the phrase, 'I shall employ all means to right this gross mistake or injustice to a bona fide U.S. citizen and ex-serviceman'— hardly the basis for belief that he was planning to assassinate him. A deranged man who was brooding over his rejection by his former military service would have made some effort, on returning to the United States, to rejoin it; but there is no record that he ever tried to do so. Connally, moreover, played no role in the Marines' decision; he replied to Oswald's letter that the matter was no longer in his jurisdiction, and that it had been referred to his successor. Any feeling of hostility that Oswald might have had would thus, presumably, have been diverted to the man who ultimately had rejected his request, or to the officer who signed his discharge in the first place. If, by some

---

[A] This was written during the Cold War when all patriotic Americans were expected to be anti-Soviet.

[B] Well, no, actually he was a lousy serviceman with a bad record as outlined in Chapter 2 - MARINE.

insane illogic, Connally had been in fact the target, is it likely that the murderer would choose the day when Kennedy was riding in the car beside him, with a huge armed escort; or that, firing three shots, he would hit the wrong man twice?" [3373]

To which I respond:

- Mr. Buchanan, you deserve credit for being far ahead of most in even considering the possibility of Connally-as-target.
- You were absolutely correct that Oswald had no complaint whatever against Kennedy.
- Connally was not Secretary of the Navy in 1959; he was appointed to that office in 1961 by newly-elected Kennedy. It's important to be correct, especially on easy facts.
- Oswald was so disappointed with life in the USSR that he soon realized having been a Marine had been his life's acme.
- An unhappy malingerer in the Marines, Oswald would not consider rejoining; and if he did, he was sufficiently realistic to realize that the Corps would not want him.
- Isolated in Minsk, he knew only what his mother had written him about the discharge, and had no information on which officer(s) or department(s) had made the change to "undesirable".
- "[T]he officer who signed his discharge in the first place" had given him an honorable discharge, as proven on the wallet-size discharge card he carried every day from 1959 through November 22, 1963.
- Probably to a large extent, Oswald felt hostility toward Connally because the appeal was for help from a fellow Texan "resident of Ft. Worth as I am."
- Connally's terse reply in a campaign envelope with his smiling face framed in a large star was grotesquely memorable, stamping a vivid personal image onto his brusque rejection of Oswald's plea.
- It is naïve to expect that Oswald would think logically. That was never his manner.
- He shot at Connally the first chance he had — and Kennedy just happened to be sitting there.
- Firing three shots of which the first missed entirely to wound a bystander over a block away, then hitting his target only once and a wrong man twice, is entirely typical of inept Oswald.

1964 (May 14): **J. Edgar Hoover** in testimony to the Warren Commission

The FBI's first-and-only Director testified before Chairman Earl Warren, four commissioners, staff and several observers. He was called to lend gravitas to the Bureau's assertion of only limited contacts with Oswald, and to state that Oswald had not been an agent or in any way connected to the Bureau. He did so, then rambled through other topics, guided only by the wanderings of his mind in which one thing branched into several others. He was second only to Marguerite Oswald in this characteristic. Midway through his testimony, he opined that it would have been better for all if the Embassy in Moscow had allowed the defector to formally renounce his U.S. citizenship. Then the original G-man continued with this disjointed stream:

"I haven't the slightest doubt that he was a dedicated Communist. There has been some question raised which cannot be resolved, because Oswald is dead, as to whether he was trying to kill the President or trying to kill the Governor. He had had some correspondence with the Governor as to the form of his discharge from the Marine Corps. It was not a dishonorable discharge, but a discharge less than honorable after he defected. Governor Connally had left the Navy Department, and was back in Texas as Governor. Oswald may have had his anger or his animosity against the Governor, but no one can say definitely—that is mere speculation, no one can tell that, because the gun and the sighting of the gun was directed at the car. Now, first, it was thought that the President had been shot through the throat that is what the doctors at the Parkland Hospital felt when he was brought in ...” [3374]

and away he went into autopsies, etc. Then he introduced the worthwhile mystery of Oswald not firing as the limo approached, as related in Chapter 19 – THE SHOT NOT TAKEN. What the respected Director said here, plus what followed about the delay in firing, might have led the Commission and the country to understand Oswald’s true target, right then in 1964, but Hoover’s mind wandered off track and the golden opportunity was left behind in the ditch.

1964 (September 6): **Marina Oswald** in testimony to the Warren Commission

As reported above in this chapter’s first article, she had been the first witness to testify before the Commission. When almost all of the *Warren Report* had been written, only three weeks before it would be published, she was called again a fourth time, to be the final witness. After commissioners’ prepared questions to clear up other matters, this ensued when she was given an open invitation to say anything that had not been covered in her many days of testimony:

“Senator [John Sherman] COOPER [of Kentucky]. Just one other question—is there any other fact about this subject, which you have been asked by the Commission or by anyone else that you have knowledge of that you have not told us about it? Any fact that would bear on this inquiry?

Mrs. OSWALD. I would be glad to, but I don’t know of any.

Representative [Hale] BOGGS [of Louisiana]. May I just ask one or two questions? [He asked three questions: When did Marina last see, hear from or communicate with Marguerite? Answers: Months ago. ‘She tried to get in touch with me.’] And you refused to see her?

Mrs. OSWALD. Yes. I think that she may have been bad influence with the children—improper influence with the children. I feel that—I hardly believe—that Lee Oswald really tried to kill President Kennedy. I feel in my own mind that Lee did not have President Kennedy as a prime target when he assassinated him.

Representative BOGGS. Well, who was it?

Mrs. OSWALD. I think it was Connally. That’s my personal opinion that he perhaps was shooting at Governor Connally, the Governor of Texas.

Senator [Richard] RUSSELL [Jr. of Georgia]. You’ve testified before us before that Lee told you he was coming back to Texas—if he was back in Texas, he would vote for Connally for Governor. Why do you think he would shoot him?

Mrs. OSWALD. I feel that the reason that he had Connally in his mind was on account of his discharge from the Marines and various letters they exchanged between the Marine Corps and the Governor’s office, but actually, I didn’t think that he had any idea concerning President Kennedy.

Representative BOGGS. Well, now, my next question is—did he ever express any hostility to Governor Connally?

Mrs. OSWALD. He never expressed that to me—his displeasure or hatred of Connally, but I feel that there could have been some connection, due to the fact that Lee was dishonorably discharged from the Corps, and there was an exchange of letters between the Governor’s Office and Lee. That’s my personal opinion.

Representative BOGGS. Just a minute. Excuse me, Senator. I asked you in February, Mrs. Oswald, I said, ‘What motive would you ascribe to your husband in killing President Kennedy?’ And, you said, ‘As I saw the documents that were being read to me, I came to the conclusion that he wanted by any means, good or bad to get into history, and now that I've read a part of the translation of some of the documents, I think that there was some political foundation to it, a foundation of which I am not aware.' And then you go on and you express no doubt in your mind that he intended to kill President Kennedy.

Mrs. OSWALD. Did I say that, this last time in Dallas? The last time in Dallas, apparently there was some misunderstanding on the part of my answers to the Commission, because I was told by Mr. [William] McKenzie [her attorney [C]] that it wasn't reported accurately. The record should read that on the basis of the documents that I have read, I have no doubt—that I had available to me to read—I had no doubt that he did—

Mr. [Leon I.] GOPADZE [interpreter]. That he could kill him—

Mr. [Peter P. or Paul D. — the Commission's introduction to this testimony mysteriously says both [3375]] GREGORY [interpreter]. Could or have wanted to—could have wanted to—

Mr. GOPADZE. He could kill—she doesn't say 'want'—he could have killed him.

Representative BOGGS. Let's straighten this out because this is very important.

Mrs. OSWALD. Okay.

Representative BOGGS. I'll read it to you, 'I gather that you have reached the conclusion in your own mind that your husband killed President Kennedy?' You replied, 'Regretfully— yes.' Now, do you have any reason to change that?

Mrs. OSWALD. That's correct. I have no doubt that he did kill the President.

Representative BOGGS. Now, the other answer as I read it was: 'On the basis of documents that you had seen presented at the Commission hearings'—isn't that right?

Mrs. OSWALD. The word 'documents' is wrong—the facts presented—that's what I mean.

Representative BOGGS. Again we get back to the question of motive. You said again today that you are convinced that Lee Oswald killed President Kennedy. You said something additionally today, though, and that is that you feel that it was his intention not to kill President Kennedy, but to kill Governor Connally. Now, am I correct in saying that she had not said this previously? [D]

Mr. [J. Lee] RANKIN [general counsel]. Ask her that.

Representative BOGGS. Let's get an answer. I think this answer is quite important.

Mrs. OSWALD. On the basis of all the available facts, I have no doubt in my mind that Lee Oswald killed President Kennedy. At the same time, I feel in my own mind as far as I am concerned, I feel that Lee—that my husband perhaps intended to kill Governor Connally instead of President Kennedy.

Representative BOGGS. Now, let me ask you one other question: Assuming that this is correct, would you feel that there would be any less guilt in killing Governor Connally than in killing the President?

Mrs. OSWALD. I am not trying to vindicate or justify or excuse Lee as my husband. Even if he killed one of his neighbors, still it wouldn't make much difference—it wouldn't make any difference—a killing is a killing. I am sorry." [3376]

Questioning shifted to her age (22), was she a Communist (no) and had she been expelled from the Komsomol youth movement when she married an American (yes). Then the most senior commissioner present, presiding at the session, troubled by her eleventh-hour declaration that

---

[C] "It really is a small world. McKenzie was the attorney who represented Marina Oswald after the assassination. McKenzie's office-mate was Pete White, who represented Jack Ruby before the assassination." — Michael Benson, *Encyclopedia of the JFK Assassination* 143.

[D] No, you are not correct. She said that in November 1963, the month of the assassination, as related in an FBI report given to the Commission nine months ago! See the first entry in this chapter.

the President had been killed accidentally while Oswald aimed at the Governor, reverted to the subject. You will see him becoming belligerent and belittling, but Marina will hold her own:[E]

"Senator RUSSELL. I am concerned about this testimony, Mrs. Oswald, about your believing now that Lee was shooting at Connally and not at the President, because you did not tell us that before.

Mrs. OSWALD. At that time I didn't think so, but the more I mull over it in my own mind trying to get it in my own mind what made him do what he did, the more I think that he was shooting at Connally rather than President Kennedy.

Senator RUSSELL. Now, did you not testify before that Lee wrote a letter to Connally when he was Secretary of the Navy about the nature of his Marine discharge?

Mrs. OSWALD. Yes.

Senator RUSSELL. And that when he got a letter back, that you asked him what it was?

Mrs. OSWALD. Yes.

Senator RUSSELL. And he said, 'Well, it's just some Bureaucrat's statement'?

Mrs. OSWALD. Yes. Yes.

Senator RUSSELL. Did you not further testify that Lee said in discussing the gubernatorial election in Texas that if he were here and voting, that he would vote for Mr. Connally?

Mrs. OSWALD. Yes.

Senator RUSSELL. Now, do you think he would shoot and kill a man that he would vote for, for the Governor of his state?

Mrs. OSWALD. The only reason is—I am trying to analyze, myself, there was a reason—more reason to dislike Connally as a man than he had for Kennedy.

Senator RUSSELL. Well, she testified before that he had spoken, as far as Lee spoke favorably of anyone, that he had spoken favorably of both Kennedy and of Governor Connally.

Mrs. OSWALD. He also told me that he was also favorable toward Connally, while [we] were in Russia. There is a possibility that he changed his mind, but he never told [me] that.

Senator RUSSELL. Well, I think that's about as speculative as the answers I've read here. He might have changed his mind, but he didn't tell her anything about it, as she testified—that discussing politics in Texas, that he said that if he were here when they had the election, that he would vote for John Connally for Governor, and that was after he got the letter about the Marine Corps.

Mrs. OSWALD. That happened in Russia when he received some kind of pamphlet with a picture of Connally,[F] a separate time, at which time he remarked that when he returned, if and when he returned to Texas he would vote for Connally.

Senator RUSSELL. That's right—that's exactly right, but yet now you say that he was his prime target. I want to know what Connally had done to Lee since he got back from Russia that would cause him to change his mind, to shoot him?

Mrs. OSWALD. I do not know, but there is a possibility that Lee became hateful of Connally because the matter of this dishonorable discharge was dragging so long.

Senator RUSSELL. Yes; but Connally had left the Navy, where he had anything to do with the discharge, before he got the pamphlet about his being a candidate for Governor?

Mrs. OSWALD. I am not sure when that particular thing happened, whether Mr. Connally was the Secretary of the Navy or what he was doing.

[E] The author and his wife Jean have helped two Russian families to assimilate and thrive in America. From knowing and admiring our Redinas and Vishniakovs, we better understand plucky Marina's intelligence and spirit, and her good command of English after being in the USA only two years.

[F] If Lee received a "pamphlet" "a separate time", he may have been on the campaign's mail list.

Senator RUSSELL. Well, it's a matter of common knowledge that he ran for Governor after he resigned as Secretary of the Navy.

Mrs. OSWALD. I don't know.

Senator RUSSELL. Did you not know that when Mr. Connally was running for Governor of Texas, he was no longer Secretary of the Navy and had nothing to do with the Marine Corps?

Mrs. OSWALD. Yes, I knew—I knew that he was not the Secretary of the Navy any more because Lee told me that Connally stated in the letter to Lee that he was no longer Secretary of Navy and hence he couldn't do anything for him, and that Connally referred the petition to the proper authorities.

Senator RUSSELL. Mrs. Oswald, didn't Lee read about government a great deal? Didn't Lee read about civic affairs and about government a great deal?

Mrs. OSWALD. He read books about Kennedy, about Hitler, about others.

Senator RUSSELL. Haven't you been in this country long enough to know that the President is Commander and [sic] Chief of the Army and Navy and he's even head of the Secretary of the Navy. He can order him to do anything he wants to? [So, who's testifying here?]

Mrs. OSWALD. I didn't pay any attention to it or I didn't know it or wasn't told.

Senator RUSSELL. Do you have any facts on which you base your opinion now that Lee Oswald was shooting and was intending to kill Connally rather than President Kennedy?

Mrs. OSWALD. I have no facts whatsoever. I simply express an opinion which perhaps is not logical at all, but I am sorry if I mixed everybody up.

Senator RUSSELL. You haven't mixed anybody up, except I think that you have your evidence terribly confused.

Mrs. OSWALD. No; I have no facts whatsover [sic]. I'm sorry I told them that.

Senator RUSSELL. Do you know whether or not Lee knew Connally personally or did he know that he was going to be in this motorcade at all?

Mrs. OSWALD. No; I did not know whether Lee knew or ever contacted the Governor personally, and I don't know whether Lee knew that the Governor would be in the motorcade.[G]

Senator RUSSELL. But Lee did take his gun into town that day, and so far as you know, I believe you said that was the first day he had carried it into town?

Mrs. OSWALD. I do not personally know that Lee took the rifle that morning or the night before. Apparently the Commission has witnesses or information to that effect, but of my own knowledge, I don't know.

Senator RUSSELL. Did you not testify that you thought this was Lee's rifle that was shown you as the one that shot Connally and the President?

Mrs. OSWALD. Yes; I testified that that was the rifle.

Mr. GOPADZE [a translator]. No—I'm sorry. As far as she knows about the arms, the rifle which was shown to her looked like the one he had.

Mr. GREGORY [the other translator]. Yes; that's right.

Senator RUSSELL. That's all I asked her. That's just exactly what I asked her.

Mr. GREGORY. Yes; that's correct.

Senator RUSSELL. In discussing the motorcade, did he say anything about Connally would be riding with the President ?

Mrs. OSWALD. No; he did not." [3377]

[G] Oswald did not know Connally personally. He did read that Connally would be in the motorcade, and upon learning that fact, he jumped into action, the point of Chapter 18 – CONNALLY WILL RIDE.

The questioning turned to Oswald's shooting at General Walker, then on to other subjects, and finally ended at 8 PM, and that was the end of all testimony taken by the Warren Commission.

Marina's unanticipated suggestion was a problem. For months the commissioners and Chief Counsel Rankin had been urging the fourteen assistant counsels and staff to push ahead writing the *Report*. The original work plan had been to complete the *Report* in June. Now three months late, there was absolutely no appetite to revisit or revise, especially on such a central matter as Oswald's target. Lyndon Johnson, a man used to getting his way, and now only an unelected President, wanted the damn thing done before the election that would bestow *imprimatur* by actually electing him to that office.

The first outside expert to analyze the Commission, Edward Jay Epstein, reported the internal dissent evident two days after Marina's bombshell: "By September, however, most of the lawyers were extremely reluctant to make changes in their chapters. One lawyer, concerned about this attitude, wrote: 'Eight months' work of the Commission and staff is in serious danger of being nullified because of the present impatience to publish. . . . Staff members are becoming increasingly unwilling to discuss change or refinement, which would cause a printing delay.'" [3378] "Time pressure thus affected the writing of the Report as it had affected the investigation." [3379] Marina's interview by the FBI way back in 1963, or J. Edgar Hoover's testimony in May, or this testimony in September could have nudged the investigation onto a path to understanding Oswald's intent — but now it was too late. Her suggestion was acknowledged by a brief entry in the *Warren Report*, the next item.

1964 (September 24): The Warren Commission in the *Warren Report*

The *Warren Report* presents only the facts and conclusions the commissioners and their staff thought most important to put into the one-volume book, buttressed by their ruminations and opinions on what many of those facts mean. Within a fifty-page chapter "Lee Harvey Oswald: Background and Possible Motives", the *Report* briefly nods to the idea that Oswald may have intended to shoot Connally rather than Kennedy:

"Oswald ... continued to be concerned about his undesirable discharge. It is clear that he thought he had been unjustly treated. Probably his complaint was due to the fact that his discharge was not related to anything he had done while on active duty and also because he had not received any notice of the original discharge proceedings, since his whereabouts were not known. He continued his efforts to reverse the discharge by petitioning the Navy Discharge Review Board, which finally declined to modify the discharge and so advised him in a letter dated July 25, 1963.

Governor Connally's connection with the discharge, although indirect, caused the Commission to consider whether he might have been Oswald's real target. In that connection, it should be noted that Marina Oswald testified on September 6, 1964, that she thought her husband 'was shooting at Connally rather than President Kennedy.' In support of her conclusion Mrs. Oswald noted her husband's undesirable discharge and that she could not think of any reason why Oswald would want to kill President Kennedy. It should be noted, however, that at the time Oswald fired the shots at the Presidential limousine the Governor occupied the seat in front of the President, and it would have been almost impossible for Oswald to have hit the Governor without hitting the President first. Oswald could have shot the Governor as the car approached the Depository or as it was making the turn onto Elm Street. Once it had started down Elm Street toward the Triple Underpass, however, the President almost completely blocked Oswald's view of the Governor prior to the time the first shot struck the

President. Furthermore, Oswald would have had other and more favorable opportunities to strike at the Governor than on this occasion when, as a member of the President's party, he had more protection than usual. It would appear, therefore, that to the extent Oswald's undesirable discharge affected his motivation, it was more in terms of a general hostility against the government and its representatives rather than a grudge against any particular person." [3380]

To which I respond:

- The first one and one-third paragraphs above are entirely correct and on-target.
- Yes, "the Governor occupied the seat in front of the President, and it would have been almost impossible for Oswald to have hit the Governor without hitting the President first." That succinctly states the truth of Chapter 14 – TOO CLOSE TO CALL.
- "Oswald could have shot the Governor as the car approached the Depository or as it was making the turn onto Elm Street." is the primary defect in the arguments above. No, the truth of the matter, precisely the opposite of that, is in Chapter 19 – THE SHOT NOT TAKEN. As the limo approached on Houston Street, Kennedy was quickly and highly visible and available as a target, but Oswald did not fire because he was looking for Connally — who was hidden by several obstructions above and in front of his head.
- "Once it had started down Elm Street toward the Triple Underpass, however, the President almost completely blocked Oswald's view of the Governor prior to the time the first shot struck the President." This restates the TOO CLOSE TO CALL point above. Having found Connally as the limo passed below him, Oswald took the first possible shots at his target, and despite his skill as a rifleman, Kennedy was too much in the bullets' paths to the intended victim, Connally.
- The argument that "Oswald would have had other and more favorable opportunities to strike at the Governor than on this occasion when, as a member of the President's party, he had more protection than usual." is appealing, and would make sense for most assassins, but not for Lee Oswald who had no car, who could not drive if he borrowed, rented or stole one, and who moved by walking or taking a bus — neither a good choice taking a rifle to murder! Also, he and Connally were seldom in the same city.
- After the insulting form-letter rejection of his final appeal, Lee waited less than four months for Connally to come to him. When he read in the paper on Thursday that his target would be right in front of him the next day, then and only then did he find his opportunity to "employ all means to right this gross mistake or injustice" as he had threatened Connally from Minsk twenty-two months before.
- Connally's protection might have been unfavorable, but he was slowly passing close by, sitting in a car with no roof, and none of the guards were looking up at Lee's window.
- Oswald's motivation stemmed from the correct statement above in the first paragraph quoted from the *Report*. He never showed "a general hostility against the government and its representatives". The evidence in Chapter 15 – REGARDING KENNEDY explains why he did not take a shot at Kennedy. Chapter 16 – REGARDING CONNALLY strongly argues that he certainly had "a grudge against [a] particular person", so he held his fire until his first opportunity to shoot Connally, at which time Kennedy, entirely by accident, sat squarely in the paths of the bullets.

1964-1966: **James P. Matthews** and **Ernest Schwork**, editors, *The Complete Kennedy Saga!*
This large-format soft-cover is subtitled *Four Books in One!* As best I can decipher, after the

assassination a magazine publisher in Hollywood put out several *LIFE* magazine-size specials, then reprinted them in this. It has no date, but shows Ted Kennedy being carried from an air crash and Bob Kennedy running for U.S. Senate in New York, both events of late 1964. This large scrapbook compiles miscellany including lots of photos, *Congressional Record* pages, some *Warren Report*, etc. Among the ephemera it prints two full-page images of the letter from Oswald-in-Minsk to Connally-in-Fort-Worth. Adjacent to one is this (in full):

> "Was this the motive behind Lee Oswald's assassination of President Kennedy and the shooting of Texas Gov. John Connally? While living in Russia in 1961, Oswald petulantly demanded that Connally, then Secretary of the Navy, reverse the dishonorable discharge he received after leaving the Marines and traveling to the Soviet Union. Was Governor Connally the true target for killing by Oswald?" [3381]

In one sentence among those five lines there are four errors:

- Oswald lived in Byelorussia, a Soviet state near to but different from Russia.
- The letter was dated 1961, but that was Lee's mistake: He wrote it in 1962.
- Connally had resigned from being SecNav before the letter was written.
- The discharge was not dishonorable, although that's what Lee thought and wrote.

Regardless, this compact item deserves a place here — it was early to ask the right question.

1965: Gerald R. Ford & John R. Styles in *Portrait of the Assassin*

In his book rephrasing and assessing the testimony, Representative Ford, the commissioner to be President in nine years, raised and dismissed the possibility of Lee gunning for Connally:

> "Lee had learned from his correspondence with his mother that the Marine Corps had given him a discharge that was other than honorable. He did not seem to be certain that it was a 'dishonorable discharge,' as he sometimes referred to it, when in reality it was an 'undesirable discharge.' This action had been taken after his denunciation of the United States and his declaration that he intended to spend the rest of his life in the USSR.
>
> Although much was made of this after the fateful events in Dallas, and although he had written a letter of protest to Texas Governor John Connally, who had served as Secretary of the Navy, it would appear that Lee's reaction to this action has been generally misunderstood. In searching for a motive for Lee's murder of President Kennedy and his wounding of Governor Connally, speculation naturally developed that he was seeking revenge for a grievous personal injury. Nowhere do his reactions appear to have been violent to his Marine Corps discharge. His comments on this subject to his mother and brother are calm, collected, even in some respects indifferent.
>
> ... Even after Lee had returned to the United States he did little or nothing to argue his military status. A routine review turned down his appeal for reconsideration, but he did not seem to brood about it. To be relieved of reserve duty and any sense of responsibility for future military service appeared to be a fair settlement to him. Certainly this so-called 'grievance' had nothing to do with the shooting in Dallas. The Commission's ballistic research indicates there was 'persuasive evidence' that the bullet which struck Governor Connally was a total accident. Had a Secret Service man or Vice President Johnson been riding in that 'jumper' seat he might have been the one to be hit." [3382]

To which I respond:

- It is not true that "much was made of this" reaction by Lee to the change of discharge. If there had been any attention to the possibility that Oswald shot at Connally to avenge his refusal to help "right this gross ... injustice", the Commission and public would probably have known the true motive for the shooting in 1964 — and this book would not be necessary 52 years later. When Marina Oswald (twice), George Bouhe, Jeanne De Mohrenschildt and J. Edgar Hoover suggested in clear testimony that Lee may have been aiming for Connally, the commissioners and staff simply didn't want to hear that, and did nothing. No, not "much was made of this" — in fact, nothing was made of it.

- His second argument is that Lee's reactions to the change of discharge were not violent, were even indifferent, and that he did not pursue the matter. Because the election year of 1964 kept Ford quite busy as a congressman and chairman of the House Republican Conference, he did not have time to understand or evaluate all evidence received by the Commission, nor in this author's opinion did he possess the intellectual capacity and curiosity to assimilate and consider disparate topics. In this book you have seen the same evidence that was available to Ford, but you have seen the letters and documents back and forth between Oswald and the Marines and Navy in sequence — and Gerald Ford did not. He was totally inaccurate in stating that Oswald was indifferent and did not pursue the matter — hundreds of pages in this book show otherwise. It is true that Lee's reaction to the discharge was not violent — until the first time he got the chance he had been waiting for, on Friday, November 22, 1963!

- Ford's third point is vacuous. He says Oswald's "grievance had nothing to do with the shooting"; "the bullet which [sic] struck ... Connally was a total accident"; anyone "riding in [Connally's] seat might have been the one hit." If one begins with the belief that Oswald was gunning for Kennedy, then Ford's statement that a person in the jump seat, no matter whom, would stand a good chance of being hit, is true. Chapter 14 – TOO CLOSE TO CALL, looked at the physical and geometric evidence to prove precisely that. The man on the back seat and the man on the jump seat were in line. From the wounding and killing, you cannot draw a conclusion. Because of that, Ford cannot answer the basic question: Which was Oswald's target? He began with an unsound argument, then backed into an illogical conclusion devoid of foundation.

1970: **Albert H. Newman** in *The Assassination of John F. Kennedy: The Reasons Why*

Many other books noted here are, in my humble opinion, useless. This elegantly-produced 635-page volume is a dichotomy. The author was careful, reasoned well, and presented his thoughts and conclusions with commendable clarity. His major thrust was to supply what the Warren Commission did not — a motive for Oswald — which he attributed to hatred of well-known opponents of Fidel Castro (his key examples are General Edwin Walker, Richard Nixon and John Kennedy). Newman also supplied a singular explanation of Lee's going to his boarding house for the pistol: Having shot at Kennedy, and not yet knowing the outcome but realistic enough to know that he would be identified and arrested, he wanted a doubly-good outcome, so was on his way, now armed with the pistol, to assassinate General Walker whom he had narrowly missed a few months before! It's typical of Oswald's lifetime of misses that Walker was not at his home, site of Lee's earlier attempt, but was that day in Louisiana![3383]

I am impressed with the depth of thought that went into that idea, characteristic of the scholarly thought and analysis throughout — but what is inexplicable is how diametrically wrong Newman is in many of this conclusions. He claims to have gone through the 26 volumes of *Warren Commission Hearings*, but somehow missed the wounded James Tague, so came up with an irrelevant, unsupported idea of what became of the third shot.

Newman gets credit and a place in this chapter for having noted Oswald's letter to John Connally that pleaded for fellow-Texan assistance with his discharge status. Then, he writes:

> "The coincidence of the letter to Connally and the latter's wounding in the presidential assassination has led some to speculate that Oswald was really gunning for the governor. Answering this speculation, the Commission cogently pointed out that had this been the case, Oswald would have fired when the presidential limousine was still on Houston Street rather than after the turn onto Elm, since Connally, seated on the jump seat in front of the President, would have been exposed to direct fire then rather than afterward." [3384]

To which I respond: No, no, no! He simply echoes the Commission's failure to comprehend, cited three pages earlier under "1964 (September 24)". Chapter 19 – THE SHOT NOT TAKEN demonstrates in words, photos and logic that the Commission, and now Mr. Newman by depending on their statement, are turning simple but non-obvious facts on their heads. If Lee had wanted to kill Kennedy, he most probably would have fired an easy can't-miss shot or two as the limousine drove toward him on Houston Street. If he wanted to kill Connally, the one and only time during the limo's roll through Dealey Plaza that he could not accomplish that was while it drove on Houston Street, when Connally was hidden from Oswald's view. The wait until Elm Street argues that Connally was the target.

1973: **Ann Fears Crawford** and **Jack Keever** in *John B. Connally: Portrait in Power*

Crawford and Keever do not take up the possibility of Connally-as-target in the body of their biography. However, in one footnote below a summary of the Commission's conclusions:

> "The Warren Commission noted that Oswald had written Connally when he was secretary of the navy. The government had switched Oswald's honorable discharge to a dishonorable discharge after he defected to Russia, and Oswald was trying to get this reversed. He stated he would 'employ all means to right this gross mistake or injustice.' On January 30, 1962, Connally, who had already resigned to run for governor, advised Oswald he was forwarding his letter to his successor. Oswald's wife said in Russia 'he spoke well' of Connally. 'Lee said when he would return to the United States he would vote for him' for governor." [3385]

When small simple facts are wrong, can we trust important conclusions? The government did not switch the discharge to "dishonorable", but to "undesirable". This is not a shade of difference — there's even a level in between: bad conduct — but an entirely different matter, akin to the difference between murder and manslaughter. And, Connally did not advise on January 30. That's when Oswald wrote in Minsk. It was received by Connally's campaign office in February, and Connally "advised Oswald he was forwarding his letter" in a cold, terse two-sentence reply dated February 23. Facts matter, at least as hallmarks of correctness.

Crawford and Keever rest their case upon two quotations from Marina. The quotes are accurate, but dated — they related what Lee said in Minsk, before the Oswalds returned to the USA, and long before Lee received the Navy Discharge Review Board's rejection in a form letter of July 25, 1963. If one understands the man profiled in chapters 1 through 5, then summarized in 11 – FAILURE, there should be no surprise that he would not have damned John Connally while in Minsk, while he had bright hope "to right this gross mistake or injustice to a boni-fied U.S. citizen and ex-service man." Only after writing his many letters and receiving the humiliating form-letter rejection of his final appeal would Lee focus his disappointment and wrath upon the "fellow resident of Fort Worth" to whom he had entrusted his plea. Marina, who lived through the appeal process, did not see a conflict. One month into 1962, her husband was merely miffed with disappointment but hopeful of a good outcome. In mid-1963, he learned there would not be a desired outcome. Before the end of that year, his anger had boiled into rage for revenge on the smiling politician who had not helped him.

It's only a footnote in their large book, so these authors get a "D" for facts, another "D" for evaluation, but a "B" for doing what many did not — at least noticing the possibility.

1974: Charles Ashman in *Connally: The Adventures of Big Bad John*

In his biography of Connally eleven years after Dallas, investigative biographer Ashman briefly recounts the reasons and planning for Kennedy's trip to Texas, telling in a half-dozen pages Connally's part in the parade and shooting on November 22. Then:

> "At first there was speculation as to whether Connally, rather than Kennedy, was the intended victim of the assassination. In the course of the Warren Commission's investigation, it was discovered that Lee Oswald had written a letter to John Connally on January 30, 1962. While Oswald was still a member of the U.S. Marine Corps Reserve, he went to live in Russia. At the American Embassy in Moscow, he announced that he meant to become a Soviet citizen and swore out an affidavit that said: 'I affirm that my allegiance is to the Soviet Socialist Republic.' The Marine Corps got news of Oswald's action, convened a special board and gave him an 'undesirable' discharge. Enraged, he wrote a letter to Connally as Secretary of the Navy, promising to 'employ all means to right this gross mistake or injustice to a bona fide U.S. citizen and ex-serviceman.' Connally sent Oswald's letter to his successor, Fred Korth, and the matter went no further. Oswald evidently hadn't realized that Connally had stepped down from his post as Secretary of the Navy a few weeks before he received the letter.
>
> The Warren Commission was also told that Oswald had visited Governor Connally's Austin office in 1963.[H] According to the published Report, however, this information was never substantiated from state visitors' records. Connally himself denied having any knowledge of such a visit.
>
> If Connally had been Oswald's target, shots would probably have been fired when the limousine was still on Houston Street, where the Governor would have been exposed to direct fire. It is also significant that, when Oswald was told after his arrest that Connally had been shot, his reaction was, as described by one policeman, that of 'genuine concern and surprise.'
>
> In his testimony before the Warren Commission, the Governor said he felt that the bullets were not intended for him and that there had been no conspiracy of any kind. His theory of what happened was that '... you had an individual here with a completely warped, demented mind who, for whatever reason, wanted to do two things. First, to vent his anger, his hate, against many people and many things in a dramatic fashion that would carve for him, in however infamous a fashion, a niche in the history books of this country. And I think he deliberately set out to do just what he did, and that is the only thing that I can think of.'" [3386]

First giving Ashman deserved credit for considering Connally-as-target, one must resolutely reject his analysis in the third quoted paragraph. His dismissal because "shots would probably have been fired when the limousine was still on Houston Street, where the Governor would have been exposed to direct fire" is exactly backward. As discussed in this book's Chapter 19 – THE SHOT NOT TAKEN, a thinking person will realize that Oswald would have fired at Kennedy, if that's what he truly wanted to do, as the limousine advanced up Houston Street toward him, because Kennedy was quickly recognized, clearly in view all that time, and was a wonderfully steady target. Only the scenario of Oswald looking for Connally who was hidden

---

[H] This author would be delighted to agree because that would strengthen the case for Lee's interest in Connally, but the purported visit's date does not fit with Oswald's known whereabouts.

deep within the Lincoln by its handrail, then seeing and identifying him too late to shoot from ahead, accounts for the shots not being fired while the limousine was on Houston Street.

The "significant" fact that Oswald showed "genuine concern and surprise" when told that Connally had been shot is just as well argued from the opposite side: Oswald had known since his arrest that he had killed Kennedy and Officer Tippit because that's what he was being interrogated about and charged with. When he first heard that he had succeeded in shooting his intended victim, he registered surprise, and probably felt delight! But, when he learned that Connally was only wounded and would survive, he naturally showed concern, not because Connally had been hit, but for the reason that he was not dead!

1987: Captain Andy Kerr in his *A Journey Amongst the Good and the Great*

Kerr's autobiography about his life in and after the U.S. Navy highlights his years as special counsel to the Secretary of the Navy, nicely positioned to share his unique insights into the Oswald-Connally connection. Kerr was quoted in chapter 4 on how John Connally came to be the SecNav instead of Franklin D. Roosevelt, Jr., then on how the letter from Oswald in Minsk to Connally in Fort Worth was received, how he researched the situation and made the decision to do nothing to help. Chapter 7 told of his unsuccessful effort in 1964 to obtain that letter for Governor Connally. About the shooting, he reasoned wisely and wrote well:

> "On 22 November 1963, while riding beside President Kennedy in a motorcade in Dallas, John Connally, then governor of Texas, was shot through his arm and lung by Lee Harvey Oswald. President Kennedy was shot and killed in the same incident. The history books say it slightly differently—that Connally was wounded during Oswald's assassination of President Kennedy. The assumption is always that Oswald was shooting at Kennedy and that Connally was hit by accident or as a secondary target of opportunity. Could it not, however, have been the other way around? In spite of all of the investigations, including that of the Warren Commission, and the continuing fascination with and theories about the event, no one has yet come up with a credible motive for the shooting of Kennedy by Oswald. Against this, we know for a fact that Oswald once asked Connally for help in what may have been a *cri de coeur*.[1] He was turned down flat. What greater motivation does a psychopath need?" [3387] "We shall never know if [Connally's] wounds at the hands of Oswald were ... due to a stroke of bad luck, i.e., riding next to an assassinee. On the other hand, on that fateful day, it may have been Kennedy who was unluckily riding next to the wrong person!" [3388]

1988: James Reston, Jr. in *TIME* magazine

We come now to a Renaissance man — researcher, writer, teacher — who has done more than any other to explore and write about Connally-as-target. His father was distinguished newspaperman James "Scotty" Reston, longtime Washington Bureau Chief and briefly Editor of *The New York Times*. On the afternoon of assassination, Scotty "filed a story, not always quite seeing the keys on my typewriter: 'America wept tonight, not alone for its dead young president, but for itself. The grief was general, for somehow the worst in the nation had prevailed over the best. The indictment extended beyond the assassin, for something in the nation itself, some strain of madness and violence, had destroyed the highest symbol of law and order.'" [3389] Of all reflections on the assassination known to this author, that was among the finest. As you will see, the apple will fall not far from the tree.

---

[1] "An impassioned outcry, as of entreaty or protest." — *The American Heritage College Dictionary*

Reston *pater* introduces James Jr.: "our second son ... my namesake but fortunately he had his mother's smile and style ... checked into the University of North Carolina, and later taught in the English department there for a while. He spent his junior year at ... Oxford, where he fell in love with soccer and the English language. I tried to persuade him ... that newspaper reporting was a lifetime educational process, but he rejected all suggestions that he join the *Times* and chose instead the reckless adventure of writing books." [3390]

From this point on in this book, "Reston" will refer to James Jr., who "has written for *The New Yorker*, *Esquire*, *Vanity Fair*, *Time*, *Rolling Stone*, and many other publications." [3391] His many books, plays and television documentaries demonstrate a wide-ranging curiosity, adaptability, competence and productivity. They include *To Defend, To Destroy: A Novel*, 1971; *Our Father Who Art in Hell: The Life and Death of Rev. Jim Jones*, 1981; *Sherman's March and Vietnam*, 1985; *Collision at Home Plate: The Lives of Pete Rose and Bart Giamatti*, 1991; *The Last Apocalypse: Europe at the Year 1000 A.D.*, 1999; *Fragile Innocence: A Father's Memoir of His Daughter's Courageous Journey*, 2006;[3392] *The Accidental Victim* (later in this chapter at 2013); and probably in print before you read this, *The Terrorist's Wife*.[3393] "With his enormous energy and curiosity, he pursued a wide range of interests, from the natural sciences to philosophy to rhetoric. ... 'In leisure as in work I teach what I know, and learn what I do not know,' he would say later." James Reston, Jr. wrote that about Gerbert of Aurillac, but it's a perceptive description of himself.[3394]

I know Reston as a trailblazer. After the Universities of North Carolina and Oxford, he was an assistant to U.S. Secretary of the Interior Stewart Udall, an intelligence officer in the U.S. Army, lecturer in Creative Writing at the University of North Carolina, a fellow at the American Academy in Rome, a scholar in residence at the Library of Congress, and is now a Senior Scholar at the Woodrow Wilson International Center for Scholars in Washington, DC. The *TIME* magazine issue of November 28, 1988, 25 years after November 22, 1963, ran three articles offering new insights on what happened in Dallas. The cover showed a rifle scope's crosshairs on Connally, with headline "J.F.K.'S ASSASSINATION: WHO WAS THE REAL TARGET?" and caption "Twenty-five years later, a new book argues Oswald was actually out to get John Connally". The boxed sidebar above explains why you can't see that cover here.

> Here was to be the cover of TIME, showing the limo and its occupants during the shooting, with a rifle scope's crosshairs on Connally. But the agency representing TIME demanded $460 each for this cover and two others I wanted to show. $1380 was too rich for the limited print run of this book. To see the cover large and in color, look at: http://search.time.com/results.html?N=46&Ns=p_date_range|1&Nf=p_date_range%7cBTWN+19881128+19881128

Toward the end of this chapter you will see Reston's 2013 book dedicated to the subject, *The Accidental Victim*. He and I have corresponded, he has helped and encouraged, and was nice enough to include in one of his emailed notes the good wish I am proud to display in the box at the top of this chapter.

Reston's cover story in *TIME*, "Was Connally the Real Target?", was the first widely disseminated exposition of the reality of what Oswald intended, and of his tragic ineptitude. It compactly told in 7 pages what I have documented at length in the 214 pages of this book's first six chapters. What Reston originally wrote for his 1989 book, and honed with skill after it ran in *TIME*, we will reprint from the biography that begins on the next page. There you will experience the considerable grace and style Reston commands so fluently.

Three weeks after Reston's article, *TIME* printed four letters from readers. In those days, *TIME* proudly stated that it selected letters representative of the views of all who wrote. Until shortly before this book's publication, those letters were here, but I finally had to remove them when Time Inc's Syndication Manager ruled that "none of the letters printed in any of our magazines are available for license." [3395] I cannot show them here without *TIME*'s permission, but there's an easy work-around. You can read them on the WorldWideWeb at http://content.time.com/time/subscriber/vault/1988/12/19881219/6/1550.jpg

Reston's reasoned words apparently did not convince. Two of the four readers called it "mere conjecture" and "nonsense"! [J] Another said it didn't matter; whoever was the target, JFK was dead. And — the French would term this *obligatoire* — the fourth charged that both the Warren Commission and Reston had ignored clear evidence of conspiracy. *Sacrebleu!* [K]

1989: James Reston, Jr. in *The Lone Star: The Life of John Connally*

The *TIME* article was extracted from Reston's forthcoming biography, *The Great Expectations of John Connally*. When released the next year, the title had morphed to *The Lone Star: The Life of John Connally*,[3396] a thumping thick biography, chronicling and assessing the life of an interesting, fallible man. The shooting and wounding in Dallas is only a movement in this Reston symphony, but an important one because it interested him in learning what the Warren Commission could not find, Oswald's motive. Reston blazed the trail of a true pathfinder while writing the story of Connally's life.

His thoughtful chapter "The Assassin" is a fine reduction that would make a French chef proud, only 24 of the 700 pages. There is little about Oswald that you haven't seen in this book, but Reston includes an extensive consideration of politics, fully understandable knowing that he was raised in Washington, D.C. where his father represented *The New York Times*, followed by his own work for Stuart Udall. If you would like a full history and analysis of the Texas trip, who made what decision, and which politician sat next to whom on Air Force One, then read this fine biography. I reprint here, in full, the chapter about Oswald for the purpose of giving my book's readers an account with the same result as mine, but from a very different viewpoint. You should find his historian's gentle lyricism a nice change from my engineer's rat-a-tat-tat of facts, facts, facts.

[J] Your author hopes the much more complete set of facts in this book will be more convincing, but fears his Dad was correct, as quoted in the PREFACE: "Nobody wants to hear that!"

[K] Which my *Larousse* charmingly translates as "zounds" and "hell's bells".

"The Assassin

"FROM THE BEGINNING of his victorious 1962 campaign through his accession to the governorship in January 1963 and his first bold speeches as the state's chief executive, John Connally epitomized the big man of Texas. He stood in his elegant boots with the wealthy over the poor, the business executive over the working man, white over black and Hispanic, the glamorous over the commonplace. In short, he symbolized Texas royalty over Texas peasantry. He was a taunting, polarizing figure, engendering feelings of intense loyalty and utter contempt, even hate. His first term as governor began in a decisive year of change in America, when political passions were overheated, though they had not yet reached the boiling point, and where hate mail and threats on lives were common. America was in the throes of a racial revolution.

The same year Connally returned to Texas for his political race, another Texan, in many ways his very antithesis, also returned after an extended absence. Lee H. Oswald, as he signed himself, was a small, wiry, homely loner, twenty-four years of age. Like Connally, he, too, considered Fort Worth to be his home, and he had left it with a splash that had made front-page headlines in the *Star Telegram* every bit as large as those used a year later when President Kennedy appointed Fort Worth oilman John Connally secretary of the navy: **FORT WORTH MAN TO BECOME A RED TO WRITE A BOOK? . . . FORT WORTH DEFECTOR CONFIRMS RED BELIEFS . . . MY VALUES DIFFERENT, DEFECTOR TOLD MOTHER . . . TURNCOAT HANGS UP ON MOTHER**. The details were lurid and shocking. Oswald had dropped out of high school after his freshman year to join the Marine Corps, the service of just a few good men. His three-year hitch in the corps began with an average qualification as a sharpshooter, proceeded through electronics and radar training, and had concluded with a tour in Atsugi, Japan, on a base from which U-2 aircraft took off for Russia.

Then, reported the Fort Worth paper, the turncoat had read *Das Kapital* as he defended freedom in Japan, had saved all his money—$1,600—to travel to the Soviet Union, and in his last months in the service had thought of nothing but defection. Later, while he languished in the sumptuous Metropole Hotel in Moscow awaiting final word on his citizenship application, he had submitted to an interview by UPI. Why had he defected? He gave three reasons: racial discrimination, the treatment of the underdog, and the hate in his native land.

Lee Harvey Oswald's facade was flamboyant and petulant, but his adventure in Russia began with the pathos of a Dostoevsky tale. He had taken a ship from New Orleans to Great Britain, and then had flown to Helsinki, a point from which he knew the entry into Russia would somehow be easier. Arriving on Soviet soil early in October, he brashly approached his Intourist agent, a stolid woman named Rimma, and blurted out that he wished to apply for Soviet citizenship. In the days that followed, the sympathetic Rimma took him through the necessary gates, helping him with his letter to the Supreme Soviet and, on his twentieth birthday, October 18, 1959, sweetly presenting him with a copy of Dostoevski's *The Idiot*. Three days later, however, Oswald's colossal effort of will was imperiled. In his diary he described his response.

October 21: Meeting with single official. Balding, stout, black suit, fairly good English, askes what do I want. I say Sovite citizenship. He tells me 'USSR only great in literature and wants me to go back home.' I am stunned. I reiterate. He says he shall check and let me know weather my visa will be extend. (It exipiers today).

Eve. 6.00. Recive word from police official. I must leave country tonight at 8 P.M. as visa expirs. I am shocked!! My dreams! I retire to my room. I have $100 left. I have waited for 2 year to be accepted. My fondes dreams are shattered because of a petty offial. because of bad planning, I planned to much! 7.00 P.M. I decide to end it. Soak rist in cold water to numb the pain Than slash my left wrist. Than plaung wrist into bath tub of hot water. I think 'when Rimma comes at 8 to find me dead, it will be a great shock. Somewhere a violin plays, as I watch my life whirl away. I think to myself, 'how easy to die' and 'a sweet death' (to violins) about 8.00. Rimma finds my unconscious (bathtub water a rich, red color) She screams (I remember that . . . Poor Rimma stays by my side as interrpator far into the night. I tell her to go home (my mood is bad) but she stays. She is my friend. She has a strong will. Only at this moment, I notice she is preety.

Upon his release from the hospital a week later, Oswald again confronted the daunting face of Soviet bureaucracy, but this time the strange American was taken more seriously. His passport did not seem to be enough for them, so Oswald presented his most prized possession, a laminated card which displayed his honorable discharge from the Marine Corps. Throughout all that transpired after his discharge, Oswald defined himself through his Marine Corps service. The corps had shaped him. It proved his importance. He flaunted it now with the hope that the Soviets would see how big a catch he was. Delay was inevitable. Three days later, as he clattered around his hotel room at the Metropole, he was tormented with anxiety and loneliness, writing, "Oct 30: I have been in hotel three days. It seems like three years. I must have some sort of showdown!"

The next day he slipped out of the hotel and took a cab to the American embassy. There he presented himself to a wry and experienced professional named Richard Snyder. Snyder found him to be a well-dressed, intelligent, and very determined twenty-year-old. Oswald got right to the point. Slapping his passport down on the desk, he demanded the right to renounce his American citizenship. By no means was Snyder unprepared for the situation. Snyder had processed a renunciation of American citizenship for another American named Petrulli, who had applied for Soviet citizenship some weeks earlier. But a month later the Soviets had decided that they did not want Petrulli, who turned out to be a mental case, and Snyder had to do a good deal of fudging to reassert American authority and to annul the renunciation. With Oswald, he was determined to stall as long as he could—although he knew he could not do so forever, for Oswald was fully within his rights. If Oswald was in command of his senses, which he certainly appeared to be, the action was, Snyder cautioned him, permanent and irrevocable.

Snyder tried to draw Oswald out, asking him a number of soft questions and stressing the enormous import of what the young man proposed to do. At one point Snyder asked him his reasons.

"I am a Marxist!" Oswald replied histrionically, as if that covered all bases.

"Well, then," replied the comfortable Mr. Snyder, "you're going to be very lonesome in the Soviet Union." Oswald was not amused.

Oswald's speech was aggressive and strident, and he would not be deterred. Finally, Snyder seized upon the bureaucrat's final pretext: the embassy was technically closed that afternoon and for the weekend. The applicant would have to come back in a few days. Oswald stormed out.

Instead of returning the following business week, Oswald wrote the embassy an outraged letter, charging that the consul had denied him his legal right to renounce and that his application for citizenship was now pending before the Supreme Soviet. In a final flourish, which the American consul later recalled to be distinctly "Oswaldish" in its comical pomposity and sonorousness, Oswald wrote, "In the event of [the acceptance of my application to the Supreme Soviet], I shall request my government to lodge a formal protest regarding this incident."

In his interview with Snyder, Oswald had made one threat that could not be ignored. He promised to turn over to the Soviets all the military secrets he had learned in the marines. As a radar operator with a secret clearance, he had access to information about the radar and radio frequencies of all squadrons, all tactical call signs, the relative strength of squadrons, the number and type of aircraft in each, the names of commanding officers, and the authentication code for entering and exiting the Air Defense Identification Zone, as well as radio frequencies and the range of radar both for his squadron and squadrons contiguous to his own. Immediately, Snyder alerted the naval attaché in the embassy, who wired the Navy Department in Washington. As a result, codes, aircraft call signs, and radio and radar frequencies in the scope of Oswald's knowledge were changed. Certain things, however, could not be changed, such as the frequency range of the new height-finding radar, just introduced at enormous cost into the Marine Corps air defense system. In its displeasure, the Navy Department initiated an action against Oswald which would four years later devastate him and for which he would come to blame John Connally.

As he moped around the Metropole Hotel, Oswald's sole link to America and to his past was his older brother, Robert. Robert Oswald had reached Lee by telegram in early November, calling his decision to defect a mistake. On November 26 Lee replied angrily in a long letter, full of cant. "See the segregation. See the unemployed and what automation is. Remember how you were laid off at Convair. . . . I will ask you a question, Robert: what do you support the American government for? What is the ideal you put forward? Do not say 'freedom' because freedom is a word used by all peoples through all of time. Ask me, and I will tell you I fight for communism." Toward the end of this harangue, he declared the importance of ideology over blood. He had four parting shots: "1. In the event of war I would kill any American who put on a uniform in defense of the American government—any American. 2. In my own mind, I have no attachments of any kind to the U.S. 3. I want to—and I shall—live a normal, happy, and peaceful life here in the Soviet Union *for the rest of my life*. 4. My mother and you are *not* objects of affection, but only examples of workers in the U.S. You should not try to remember me in any way I used to be. . . . I am not all bitterness or hate. I come here only to find freedom. . . . In truth," he said in closing, "I feel I am at last with my own people."

After this farewell from the grandstand, Oswald receded into the proletariat. If he expected to be fussed over, to be made a hero in the Soviet state, he was disappointed. The KGB took no interest in him. He was never questioned about his military service in Japan, nor about new American radars or about U-2 aircraft. He was considered "not very bright" and the local authorities in Minsk, where he was sent to work in a radio factory, were requested to keep an eye on him, lest he turn out to be some sort of "sleeper agent."

Oswald's dream for a "normal, happy, and peaceful life" in Russia was realized for the first nine months of his expatriation. He found the work in the factory easy. His fellow workers treated him warmly, especially as he began to acquire the language. If he was not accorded a hero's status, he was, nevertheless, given special treatment. Assigned an apartment with a splendid view overlooking the Svisloch River, he raked in 1,400 rubles a month, twice the salary of other workers on his level. Seven hundred rubles was a supplement, "to help out," from a mysterious branch of the Red Cross, and Oswald would crow in his diary that this income was the equivalent to that of the director of the radio factory. "It is a Russian's dream," he wrote blissfully in March. The summer brought rapturous walks in the deep pine forests of Byelorussia. He had joined a hunting club at the factory, and with a shotgun on his shoulder (for private ownership of rifles and pistols was forbidden in the Soviet Union) he ventured into the rural regions around Minsk. These trips made a deep impression. The peasants he met and in whose homes he sometimes stayed overnight were frequently close to starvation. Often, out of sympathy, he would leave what game he had shot. He was also fascinated by the radio speakers in peasants' huts, which kept up a constant patter of exhortation day and night and which could not be turned off. At this early stage, however, he merely took note of these exotic aspects of the totalitarian state. Other images cut deeper. In the fall he rhapsodized about the golds and reds of the landscape. "Plums, peaches, apricots and cherries abound in the last Fall weeks," he wrote in his diary. "I am a healthy, brown color and stuffed with fresh fruit."

With the approach of his first Russian winter, Oswald, like the hero of *The Idiot*, developed a melancholy and then a dread of the cold and the darkness. He began to take more notice of the trappings of the Communist state around him. "I am increasingly aware of the presence of Lebizen, the shop party secretary, fat, fortyish, and jovial on the outside. He is a no-nonsense party regular." He began to resent compulsory attendance at boring factory meetings, where the factory doors were locked and no one ever voted No to a formal proposal. He was horrified at the poor quality and the cost of simple necessities like clothes and shoes. While the slogans and exhortations of the state cluttered his mind, the dreary routine of the worker's life began to undercut his operatic dream.

The turning point for Oswald was not political but emotional. In early January, he fell hopelessly in love with a comrade at the factory named Ella, who after a dalliance spurned him. To his diary, he declared that he was "misarable," and a few weeks later he wrote, "I am starting to reconsider my desire about staying. The work is drab. The money I get has no where to be spent. No nightclubs or bowling allys. No place of recreation acept the trade dances. I have had enough." On February 1 he wrote to Richard Snyder that he wanted to go home.

Oswald's overture at this point was exploratory. Ambivalence rather than total disaffection marked his psychology, and he was moving toward negative perceptions of both political systems.

His life took another turn in March when, at a "boring" trade union dance, he met a stubborn blonde pharmacist with a French hairdo named Marina (who had lived the first six years of her life near the Arctic Circle in Murmansk and Archangel). In contrast to Ella, who had snickered at the awkwardness of his marriage proposal, Marina accepted his attentions and in April the two were married. In his diary he declared, "In spite of fact I married Marina to hurt Ella, I found myself in love with Marina."*

     * [Reston's footnote:] This line above all others was to wound Marina
      when the diary was published several months after Oswald's death.

Marriage did not change his desire to get out of the Soviet Union, however, and in July 1961 the Oswalds applied for an exit visa, hoping to return to America. The change in Oswald's attitude toward his adopted state was evident in a letter he wrote to Robert just after he returned from a talk with Snyder about going home. "The Russians can be crule and very crude at times. They gave a cross examination to my wife on the first day we came from Moscow. They knew everything, because they spy and read the mails. But we shall continue to try and get out. We shall not retreat. As for your package, we never received it. I suppose they swiped that to, the bastards."

Now that Oswald had asked to go home, the cruelty of the Russians took another form. His "Red Cross" allotment of 700 rubles a month abruptly stopped. Oswald finally saw it for what it was: he had been a paid stooge. He had never told anyone of his supplement and only when he was on his way home to Texas was he able to write about it, and then only to himself. The important thing is the lesson he drew from it.

> Whene I frist went to Russia in the winter of 1959 my funds were very limited. So after a certain time, after the Russians had assured themselfs that I was really the naive american who believed in communism, they arranged for me to recive a certain amount of money every month. OK. it came technically through the Red Cross as finical help to a Roos polical immigrate but it was arranged by the M.V.D. I told myself it was simply because I was hungry and there was several inches of snow on the ground in Moscow at that time, but it really was *payment* for my denuciation of the U.S. in Moscow and a clear promise that for as long as I lived in the USSR life would be very good. I didn't realize all this, of course for almost two years.
>
> As soon as I became completely disgusted with the Sovit Union and started negotiations with the American Embassy in Moscow for my return to the U.S. my "Red Cross" allotment was cut off.
>
> I have never mentioned the fact of these monthly payments to anyone. I do so in order to stat that I shall never sell myself intentionly or unintentionly to anyone again.

Soon enough the American government displayed an equivalent cruelty toward him. Lee Harvey Oswald had achieved one significant thing in his life. He had joined the U.S. Marine Corps, and, despite the dislike of his mates and two courts-martial (for possessing an illegal weapon and for fighting), and despite loudly proclaiming himself to be a Marxist and gaining the barracks nickname of "Oswaldskovich," he had made it through. His reward after three years was an honorable discharge. In his billfold he carried the laminated proof of his achievement as if it were an executive gold card. It was a credential he would need, and need desperately, when he returned to America.

In January 1963 [L] Oswald was attempting to control his excitement over the imminent birth of his first child and the prospect of returning to the United States. On January 5 he wrote to Robert, "I really do not trust these people, so I shall wait untill I'm in the U.S. before I become overjoyed." Two weeks later the blow struck. He received a letter from his mother, Marguerite: the Marine Corps had changed his discharge from honorable to dishonorable. In fact, Marguerite Oswald conveyed the news as more

---

[L] This says 1963, whereas Oswald wrote the year date "1961", but it was truly January 1962.

catastrophic than it really was. The downgrading had actually stopped one notch [M] short of "dishonorable," at "undesirable," but that was bad enough. Anything less than an honorable military discharge is a curse in America, especially for a working man, and Oswald knew it instinctively. The news was fresh only to Lee Harvey Oswald. The action had been taken a year and a half before he learned of it. For two years his mother had not known where her son was or even if he were dead or alive, but she had labored bravely with letters to the Defense Department and the State Department, to Sam Rayburn and Congressman Jim Wright of Fort Worth, to overturn the Marine Corps decision or at least to obtain a fair hearing. In her anguish during his long silence, Marguerite had seized upon the comforting notion that her son had been hypnotized and drugged by the Russians before he was carted off to the evil empire. To Mrs. Oswald, Lee's name had been "dishonored" more by the Marine Corps action than by her son's apparent defection. In one letter to the navy she said she hoped the corps "would do something about this awful thing of a dishonorable discharge, because I have grandchildren. . . . My whole family has served in the service, and Lee served the service for three years. I want his name cleared."

Lee Harvey Oswald was crushed at the news. That he would care at all is noteworthy. Why should a true convert to Communism, one so desperate for political action, one so ready to take up arms against America—in short, the person who was described by the Warren Commission—have a moment of anxiety over what the fascist United States and its most dangerous military force did in his buried military records? The true believer would be amused. But Oswald did care. He cared deeply. At bottom, his military service gave meaning to his life, and it was the *only* thing that did.

He immediately wrote letters to complain of the injustice, and he had a valid case. His discharge had been changed for actions he took not in the Marine Corps but as a private citizen afterwards. It had been changed without a fair hearing, upon the basis of rumors that were largely unsubstantiated and upon statements like his threat to turn over military secrets that were made at a moment of high stress (and which in fact he never carried out). Perhaps more important than the emotional impact were the practical consequences. As he prepared to go home, Oswald knew intuitively that his road in America would be far rougher now.

On January 31, 1962,[N] he wrote to the secretary of the navy. In his schoolboy scrawl, full of his usual misspellings and awkward constructions, now made more awkward by the syntax of the Russian language, he pleaded his case grandly. He began with a reference to the common bond he shared with Secretary Connally. He wished to call the secretary's attention to a case "about which you may have personal knowledge since you are a resident of Fort Worth as am I." The Fort Worth papers, he wrote Connally, had blown his case into "another turncoat sensation" when, in fact, he had come to Russia to reside "for a short time, much in the same way E. Hemingway resided in Paris."

"I have and allways had the full sanction of the U.S. Embassy, Moscow, USSR," he lied, and now that he was returning to the United States, "I shall employ all means to right this gross mistake or injustice to a boni-fied U.S. citizen and ex-serviceman." He asked Connally personally to "repair the damage done to me and my family."

On the same day he wrote to Robert, who was also then living in Fort Worth, for he feared that his letter to Connally would not make it through the Russian censors. He asked Robert to be in touch with Connally independently to see how this injustice might be rectified.

Connally, of course, had resigned as secretary of the navy the previous December, six weeks earlier. What the ex-serviceman got from the ex-navy secretary a month later—on February 23—was the old bureaucratic brush-off. Connally's response was perfunctory. He promised to pass the problem on to his successor. Thus, at the beginning of this painful personal matter, Oswald had been spurned by a fellow Texan, and he resented it. Connally represented the U.S. government, and his perfunctory response fortified Oswald's bitterness against the country and now against an individual.

[M] Actually, it was two notches: Between "undesirable" and "dishonorable" there was "bad conduct".

[N] Close: It was one day earlier than this when Oswald wrote "January 30, 1961" atop his letter.

Connally's brush-off was followed by a cascade of subsequent slights by naval and Marine Corps functionaries. A letter from the Navy Department told Oswald that the department contemplated no change in the discharge. On March 22 Oswald appealed for further review. The department replied that it had no authority and sent yet another form, referring Oswald to the Navy Discharge Review Board. Oswald filled out the form in Minsk, but he did not mail it until he landed in America. This last appeal, before he gave up, carried the tone of moral outrage: "You have no legal or even moral right to reverse my honorable discharge." It, too, led nowhere. It was a classic case of a powerless nonentity mired in an endless, hopeless battle with an aloof, faceless military establishment, except that Oswald could now associate one face with his distress.

Finally, in late May 1962, the Oswalds got out of Russia. They made their way to Rotterdam, where on June 4 they boarded the *Maasdam*, a Holland America Line ship, bound for New York. Aboard ship, Oswald fell into a reflective mood, and on sheets of Holland America Line stationery, he wrote his thoughts:

> I wonder what would happen if somebody was to stand up and say he was utterly opposed not only to governments, but to the people, too the entire land and the complete foundations of his socially [society]. Too a person knowing both systems and their factional accessories, their can be no mediation between the systems as they exist today That person must be opposed to their basic foundations and representatives, and yet, it is imature to take the attitude which say 'a curse on both your houses.' In history, there are many such examples of the members of the new order rooted in the idealestical tradition of the old. As history has shown time again, the state remains and grows, whereas true democracy can be practiced only at the local level. While the centralized state, administrative, political, and or supervisual remains, their can be no real democracy, only a loose confederation of communities at a national level without any centralized state what so ever. The mass of survivors, however, will not beblong too any of these groups. They will not be fanatical enough to join extremest groups and will be too disillusioned too support either the communits or capitalist parties in their respective countries, after the atomic catorahf [catastrophe]. They shall seek an alternative to those systems which have brought true mysery. . . . They would deem it neccary to oppose the old systems but support at the same time their cherished trations.
> I intend to put forward just such an allturnative.

The Oswalds arrived in Fort Worth only a few weeks before John Connally won the intense and highly publicized Democratic primary for the gubernatorial nomination. They had no money and almost no possessions, but they did have a six-month-old baby. Lee had virtually no qualifications for employment. Worse than that, the Fort Worth paper had reported the return of the turncoat. Marina spoke no English, and her husband seemed determined to keep it that way. Their isolation and hopelessness might have been even more miserable but for the help of the White Russian émigré community in the Dallas-Fort Worth area. Small but tightly knit and supportive, this community comprised about fifty people who had gravitated to Texas, most of them after the Second World War. Generally they were already expatriates, having arrived in America from such places as Iran and Turkey, to which they had fled from Russia. As a rule, they were fervently anticommunist, just as they were possessed by an enduring fascination for what was going on in Communist Russia. The community had a titular leader, a kind and energetic gentleman in his late fifties named George Bouhe, who had fled Russia across a river into Finland in 1923. Bouhe took an immediate interest in the Oswalds and helped them get settled by providing them with a little cash here and there, ten or twenty dollars, bringing them groceries, and helping Marina find a dentist and a pediatrician. For his pains, he got only insults from Oswald, for Bouhe's charity smacked of the kind of help he was determined never again to accept. Bouhe persisted nonetheless, mainly out of concern for Marina, who seemed to him to be a "lost soul." To Bouhe, Oswald himself was a simpleton and a boor and, soon enough, a wife abuser. Moreover, from the comparative speed and ease with which the Oswalds had exited Russia, Bouhe came to suspect Oswald of some continuing clandestine relationship with the Soviet state. Still, he persevered because, as a matter of belief, he felt that Communism breeds among the down and out, and he hoped that a greater degree of comfort might assuage Lee Oswald's bitterness.

Part of Bouhe's sympathy and charity went to helping Oswald find work, and here Oswald ran immediately into the problem of his tainted military discharge. He was competing for the lowest rank of employment among the unskilled. "When he went to the Texas Employment Commission in Fort Worth to ask for a job, and they said what can you do—nothing," Bouhe later told the Warren Commission. "Where did you work last—Minsk—. He couldn't progress. He couldn't get any place." Inevitably, it came back to the discharge, for he could fudge his last place of work. "When he was applying for a job, we picked up some application blanks someplace, and you have to say about your military service. And where it says 'Discharged,' I'd ask how? And he would say, 'Put down *honorable*.' "

"That was the extent of your discussion?" counsel of the Warren Commission asked.

"Right. He would freeze up like a clam."

Even though it was easy enough for any prospective employer to check his discharge claim, lying about his marine record worked initially. Oswald's first job, which he got a month after his arrival, was at a Fort Worth welding company as a sheet-metal worker. On his application, he cited sheet-metal work in the Marine Corps as a qualification.

Bouhe confined his role with Oswald to that of an informal social worker. To discuss politics with such an ingrate as Oswald was less than pointless, and Bouhe avoided it studiously. But the old White Russian had noticed Oswald's fixation with his military discharge, had seen how it made Oswald clam up, and how his lying about it launched him into a state of high anxiety. After the assassination, after he read of John Connally's bureaucratic slight, and knowing that Oswald was especially tormented by the bad discharge at the very time when Connally was about to be promoted to the pinnacle of Texas government, Bouhe put the pieces together: "If anybody asked me, did Oswald have any hostility towards anybody in government, I would say Governor Connally."

In early October 1962, a month before election day, Oswald quit his job. He quit on the very day that the candidate Connally came to Dallas to give speeches to a women's group and to the country club set. Apparently he hated the hard, hot, dirtiness of welding. Ironically, the company was sorry to see him go. "I imagine if he had pursued that trade, he might have come out to be a pretty good sheet-metal man," his supervisor told the Warren Commission.

Precisely as this event took place, Marina and the baby took up residence in the home of Alexandra de Mohrenshildt,[O] who was the daughter of another Russian émigré in Dallas, a flamboyant loudmouth named George de Mohrenshildt, who toyed with Oswald in uneven intellectual games and was to exert a very negative influence on him. Thus, Lee Oswald was observed by Alexandra de Mohrenshildt at the very time when he had again put himself on the job market, and she was to see a good deal of Oswald in the ensuing months.

A year and a half later, Alexandra de Mohrenshildt came before the Warren Commission. With this witness, as with others who had known Oswald personally after his repatriation, the commission probed Oswald's comparative attitude toward his eventual victims, looking for some insight that might explain his motive to murder.[P] Alexandra was a good witness, for in the fall of 1962 she had been married to an engineer with liberal politics named Gary Taylor, and she had listened as Oswald and Taylor engaged in political discussion.

"Was President Kennedy ever mentioned in the course of the discussions between your husband and Lee?" counsel asked.

"Never, never," Alexandra replied. "It was the governor of Texas who was mentioned mostly."

"Tell us about that."

"First you are going to have to tell me who the governor was."

"Connally."

[O] The Warren Commission put a "c" in there — de Mohrenschildt — and so does your author.

[P] This is generous of Mr. Reston, Jr. The author of this book has never believed that the Commission seriously looked for anything beyond his motive to murder <u>Kennedy</u> — and thus they found none!

"Connally—wasn't that the one that—"

"That had been secretary of the navy."

"That had been secretary of the navy, was it? Well, for some reason, Lee just didn't like him. I don't know why, but he didn't like him."

"Would it refresh your recollection, that the subject of Governor Connally arose in connection with something about Lee's discharge from the marines?" counsel prodded.

"I don't recall. Lee never spoke too much about why he left the marines or anything like that. I don't know. Maybe it was the dishonorable discharge. I don't know. All I know is that it was something he didn't talk about. And there was a reason why he did not like Connally."

"Whatever the reason was, he didn't articulate the reason particularly?"

"No, he just didn't like him."

"But you have the definite impression he had an aversion to Governor Connally?"

"Yes, but he never ever said a word about Kennedy."

"But he did have a definite aversion to Governor Connally as a person?"

"Yes."

"Did he speak of that reasonably frequently in those discussions?"

"No, not really, no. He didn't bring it up frequently."

"But he was definite and affirmative about it, was he?"

"Yes, he didn't like him."

In October, when Alexandra de Mohrenshildt came to know Oswald, and John Connally was in Dallas arguing for the continuation of the poll tax, Oswald had an experience that was becoming routine. The clerk at the Texas Employment Commission identified a good job opening in the photography department of a printing concern in Dallas called Jaggars-Chiles-Stovall. Before Oswald went over for his interview, the company had asked the employment commission clerk about Oswald's last place of employment and was told that he had recently been discharged from the marines. When Oswald entered the Jaggars office he made a good impression. He was presentably dressed and well mannered. Almost immediately the subject of his military career came up, as the potential employer asked about his last place of work.

"The marines," Oswald said brashly.

"Oh, yes—yes," the employer said. "Honorably discharged, of course," he added as a half-question, thinking he was being amusing.

"Oh, yes," Oswald replied with technical truthfulness.

Oswald was again seized with the emotion of rage. Was this going to come up every time? His anxiety that his lies might be found out was intense. Later, the Jaggars-Chiles-Stovall man, John G. Graef, told the Warren Commission that it never occurred to him to check up on whether the applicant was telling the truth about the discharge, though it would have been perfectly easy to do so.

Oswald was to work six months at the Jaggars outfit. But his efficiency began to deteriorate in three months. He did not get along with the other employees, strange loner that he was. His behavior was unpredictable, his attitude unpleasant. Working in the close quarters of a photographic laboratory gave him claustrophobia, and this increased his churlishness. Early in 1963, as his work at Jaggars declined, his thoughts drifted back to Russia, and his memory blocked out the overwhelming negative feelings he had had upon his departure. He began to talk to Marina about reentering the Soviet Union. Wherever he was—Russia with its spies and its drab, boring existence, America with its capitalist moguls and its exploitation— was wrong for him. The system, whatever it was, was to blame. When the actual dismissal took place, in early April, Oswald brought it upon himself by flaunting a Soviet publication at work, once again turning failure into something noble: political martyrdom. On the day that he was fired, Oswald remarked that he hated capitalist exploitation and that the Jaggars firm had reaped a lot more from his labor than they had paid him in wages.

He had seen the end coming. Weeks before his dismissal he had secretly used the Jaggars facilities after hours to forge a new Marine Corps discharge and draft classification document in the name of Alik

James Hidell, the name under which he ordered his first weapon, a .39 caliber Smith and Wesson revolver, by mail, as well as his second, a high-powered Italian carbine called a Mannlicher-Carcano.

Three days into his first week of unemployment, on April 10, Lee Harvey Oswald became an assassin. He made an attempt on the life of General Edwin Walker, the reactionary symbol of Dallas, the darling of the Birchers, the one-time candidate for governor of Texas against John Connally. Oswald missed Walker's head by about an inch. He had become a very dangerous man, and in choosing Walker as a target of his murderous frustrations he was turning upon a pure figure of the far right.

Only one person, Marina Oswald, knew about the attempt on General Walker. Her husband had confessed his action to her. In her narrow, isolated world, unable to speak or read English, she knew nothing of American political figures, with the exception of the Kennedys. General Walker might have been a kitchen appliance for all she knew. But when Lee Oswald confided in her, she understood his capability to kill for political reasons, and she was horrified. She saw what form his frustrations and failures were now taking and she, above anyone, appreciated his violent tendencies; she knew the dangerous flash points. Two weeks later, with Oswald still out of work and raging around their dingy apartment, she acted.

On Sunday, April 21, the headline in the *Dallas News* read, NIXON CALLS FOR DECISION TO FORCE REDS OUT OF CUBA. It reported a strident speech which former Vice President Richard Nixon had made the previous day in Washington, excoriating Kennedy for being "defensive" on Castro, demanding a "command decision" to remove the Soviets and calling for a redefinition of the manifest destiny of the Monroe Doctrine into a doctrine of liberation. Oswald laid the paper down and withdrew into an adjacent room. When he reemerged he was dressed in a tie and white shirt. His pistol was shoved into his best gray pants.

"Where are you going?" Marina demanded.

"Nixon is coming to town. I want to go have a look."

"I know what your 'looks' mean," she said coldly, and then, thinking quickly, she inveigled him into following her into the bathroom. Once he was inside, she slipped out and slammed the door, and held it with all her strength. For several minutes he pushed and she held and they shouted at one another, and Marina wept in terror. She pleaded with him not to go, to promise her he would never again go for one of his "looks," and at last, emotionally spent, he agreed and she let him out. In the days after this episode, later known as the "Nixon incident," Oswald became as docile and torporous [Q] as a coral snake. Later, the Warren Commission dismissed this event as insignificant.

Actually, Nixon was not in town at all, nor was he coming, and though Marina could not know it, Oswald did. He had said "Nixon" for its shock value: it was Nixon's picture that was on the front page of the Dallas paper, and Nixon wasn't coming to Texas at all, and so the men of the Warren Commission dismissed the incident as having no "probative value."

It was *John Connally* who was coming.

The following day the governor was scheduled to open a conference of space scientists at the Marriott Motor Inn in Dallas, and the conference, held as the American space program gloried in the success of the Mercury shots, was widely advertised. Inside that Sunday paper which Oswald had read and then so ostentatiously laid down before he went to strap on his revolver was a story on Connally's San Jacinto Bay speech the day before. Connally had been at his manly, flag-waving best. In fact, he had waved three flags—that of Texas, that of America, and the bloody shirt of anticommunism. Before the soaring monument on the San Jacinto battlefield south of Houston, he said the spirit of the Texas Revolution made him stand "just a little taller, just a little stiffer to men like Castro and Khrushchev." His speech was full of death imagery. Connally had read from a letter written by the commander of the Alamo, Colonel William B. Travis, a letter well known to Texas schoolchildren: "The enemy has demanded a surrender—I answered the demand with a cannon shot, and our flag still waves proudly from the walls. Victory or Death!" He quoted another letter, this from a fourteen-year-old boy at the tragic

---

[Q] Neither my fully-trusted *American Heritage College Dictionary* nor any found online, including the venerable *Oxford English Dictionary*, list this fine word, more languorous than the usual "torpid".

massacre at Goliad, that other place sacred to Texans: "They are going to shoot us in the back. Let us turn our faces and die like men." As for the Battle of San Jacinto, it had imparted "renewed hope in 1836 to all people who were under the foot of tyranny or who were threatened by tyranny. It gives equal hope today, when the foot of tyranny stands but ninety miles from our shore."

To Oswald, the sentiments expressed by Connally were no different from those expressed by General Walker or Richard Nixon. All three represented the fascist edges of the despised monolith. In the first line of his grammatically tortured essay, written aboard ship on his return from Russia to the United States, he had wondered about capitalist and even "fasist" elements in America who "allways profess patriotism toward the land and the people, if not the government, although their movements must surely lead to the bitter destruction of all and everything. . . . In these vieled, formless patriotic gestures, their is the obvious 'axe being ground' by the invested interests of the sponsors of there [R] expensive undertaking." In Oswald's jangled kaleidoscope, Connally, Nixon, and Walker were interchangeable parts of the radical right.[S] During this time, Marina Oswald had taken a picture of Oswald, with his revolver on his hip and his rifle coddled in his right arm and held skyward. Turning her fear into mockery, which was her best and only tool to control him, Marina had scrawled across the picture: "Hunter for fascists. . . . Ha. . . . ha. . . . ha." It was the laughter of terror and despair.

Connally was bad blood for Oswald. On October 5, 1962, six months earlier, Connally had swung into Dallas for two highly publicized campaign speeches, and Oswald on the same day was laid off at the welding company. Now Connally turned up in Dallas, exactly two weeks after he lost his job at Jaggars-Chiles-Stovall, and he was having no luck in finding another job. In Oswald's deck of fantasies, paranoias, and delusions, Connally seemed to be the deadly queen of spades. When the queen's face turned up, bad things happened.

If in April Oswald became a hunter of figures on the right, it is hard to imagine President John F. Kennedy becoming a quarry. The political topics which engaged Oswald's passion and his rage now were civil rights, disarmament with the Soviet Union, and Cuba. Upon the first two, Kennedy acted as Oswald would have approved in the year preceding November 22, 1963, and upon the third, Cuba, Kennedy had become a voice of moderation.[T]

In October 1962, when Oswald lost his first job, Kennedy was dealing with the riots at Ole Miss, and with the lurid archsegregationist Ross Barnett. Meanwhile, Oswald's first target, General Walker, who had gone to Ole Miss, was arrested by Kennedy's federal troops for inciting to riot, and upon his release was welcomed back triumphantly to Dallas.

In the spring of 1963, after Oswald took off for New Orleans to find work, Kennedy was grappling with the massive resistance of George Wallace and the police dogs of Bull Connor in Birmingham and was sending in federal troops to protect the blacks there. On June 10, Kennedy gave his famous speech on disarmament at American University. In it, the president was generous about the Russian people, expressing sentiments with which Oswald could agree: "No government or social system is so evil that its people must be considered as lacking in virtue," Kennedy said. "As Americans we find Communism profoundly repugnant as a negation of personal freedom and dignity. But we must still hail the Russian people for their many achievements—in science and space, in economic and industrial growth, in culture and in acts of courage."

At American University, Kennedy took the occasion to announce the opening of high-level talks between Britain, the United States, and the Soviet Union on a limited nuclear test ban treaty. Throughout the summer, the hopeful possibility of an accord dominated the news. On July 20, a draft agreement was concluded, the first effort to bring nuclear weapons under international control in the eighteen years of the nuclear age.

In late July, both Connally and Oswald also made significant and revealing public appearances. On July 19, Connally traveled to Miami for the national governors' conference, and he went with all the high-

---

[R] In one sentence he erroneously substitutes <u>both</u> "their" and "there" for the other. Is this dyslexia?

[S] Which is why I wrote Chapter 17 – POLITICAL PROCLIVITY. These peas are not in Oswald's pod.

[T] Why did I include this long piece by Reston? Because he is an educated, observant, fluent historian!

flown, defiant rhetoric of Colonel Travis at the Alamo. In this case, however, the crumbling walls were the Southern laws of segregation, which were under frontal attack from Kennedy and the civil rights leaders. Of the public accommodation sections of Kennedy's integration plan, Connally said, "They would be laws which in my judgment would strike at the very foundation of one of our most cherished freedoms: the right to own and manage private property." The governor sweetened his speech with praise of moderation and voluntary desegregation, with talk of education and economic opportunity as the solution to racism, with sympathy for the hard-pressed national leadership. But he got himself and his state foursquare in the Southern camp, making the difference between himself and George Wallace and Ross Barnett only a matter of degree, of tone, of emphasis. Interestingly, Lyndon Johnson, who came from the same Texas soil, had now made the leap ahead of his region. Admittedly, it was easier for Johnson—he was a national rather than a regional figure now—and he was supposed to toe the administration's line. But Johnson's words went farther than mere fealty to the boss. In his opening address to the governors' conference, he opened a gap between himself and his constituency in the audience: "Our foremost challenge is to face and dispose of the problem of human rights which has burdened and compromised our society for a hundred years: the problem of inequality of our Negro citizens."

On July 27, a few days after the conference, Lee Harvey Oswald also made a speech. From New Orleans he ventured to Mobile, Alabama, a town whose hardened Dixie attitude toward race was made all the more impenetrable by its romance with Confederate chivalry, and whose powers and leading lights no doubt subscribed to the view their Governor Wallace had expressed to the U.S. Senate Commerce Committee only a few days earlier: that the civil rights movement was led by Communists and directed from Moscow. Oswald had a cousin who was studying to be a Jesuit priest at Spring Hill College. He had invited Oswald to speak to the Jesuit scholastics about his experiences in Russia. This was unquestionably the most dignified moment in the wretched life of Lee Harvey Oswald. He was to be part of a lecture series which included pastors from other faiths as well as other personages who had something significant to say, and he could be sure that the earnest novitiates would treat him with respect and openness. He made a good impression. The audience, including senior priests, found him articulate, engaging, and informative, if somewhat nervous and humorless. Their expectation that they would derive a clearer view of life in the Soviet Union from this recent resident than from official reports seems to have been fulfilled. He engaged their interest immediately with a personal narrative of his time in the Minsk factory and then expressed his central belief: he disliked capitalism because of its exploitation of the poor. He had been disillusioned by Russian Communism because of the gap between Marxist theory and Soviet reality. "Capitalism doesn't work. Communism doesn't work. In the middle is socialism and that doesn't work either," he said.

If Oswald was a crackpot, the scholastics did not perceive it. They took him seriously, plying him with questions afterwards, and Oswald, far from cowed, answered adroitly, succinctly, and without petulance.

"What impressed you most about Russia?," someone asked.

"The care that the state provides everyone," he replied. "If a man gets sick, no matter what his status is, how poor he is, the state will take care of him. . . . If the Negroes in the United States knew it was so good in Russia, they'd want to go there."

That was as abrasive as Oswald got. In the decisive summer of 1963 in Alabama, only a few weeks after Medgar Evers had been assassinated in neighboring Mississippi, and a few weeks before the Birmingham bombing where four small girls were killed, the remark was scarcely revolutionary, but it showed something about Oswald's political passions: the black man and the little man were those with whom he identified. The country was already preparing for the great march on Washington in a few weeks, when Martin Luther King, Jr., would speak of his dream. Southern governors, including Connally, warned of disruptions the march might bring. Kennedy, on the other hand, told a press conference in July that he hoped leaders in government, in business, and in labor would do something about the fundamental problem that had led to the demonstration. To Oswald, Kennedy might, within the limits of the American system, have seemed something of a hero.

Marina Oswald was to say later that her husband never uttered a harsh or angry word against Kennedy; if he had any negative emotion, it was envy. In the year before the assassination, Oswald avidly read William Manchester's flattering biography of Kennedy, *Portrait of a President*, and Kennedy's *Profiles in Courage*. He had become fascinated by the lives of great men, and to Marina he predicted that he would be "prime minister" of America in twenty years. In the spring and summer of 1963, Marina Oswald was pregnant again, as was Mrs. Kennedy, and Marina followed the course of Mrs. Kennedy's term keenly. In April 1963 the Oswalds watched a televised report of the Kennedys in Palm Beach together to see if Mrs. Kennedy was showing signs of her pregnancy. While later testimony suggested Lee Oswald harbored a mild resentment of the Kennedys' wealth, he told Marina that JFK was qualified to be president and deserved to be president. By the summer, Marina would flip through magazines looking for pictures of Kennedy, and when she found one would demand of Lee that he translate the accompanying article, which he did.

The one man who had a revealing political relationship with Oswald was the pompous, supercilious émigré George de Mohrenshildt. Born in Byelorussia, a man twice Oswald's age, a dandy who luxuriated in his manly good looks and physical strength, de Mohrenshildt seemed to be attracted to a relationship with Oswald largely for reasons of self-amusement. To de Mohrenshildt, Oswald was a bauble, who was the most fun when he was confused by de Mohrenshildt's brilliant arguments and awed by the émigré's elegant worldliness. Moreover, de Mohrenshildt fancied himself to be an old-world aristocrat, and he traded shamelessly on the fact that in the high society of New York in the late 1930s he had known Black Jack Bouvier and his six-year-old daughter, Jacqueline. He also fancied himself to be a forward-looking liberal, although when he left Dallas in the spring of 1963, having seen quite a bit of Lee Oswald in the previous six months, he left to take a job with Papa Doc Duvalier in Haiti. The relationship between de Mohrenshildt and Oswald became a sick one as de Mohrenshildt acted out the role of the overbearing surrogate father who secretly despises and ridicules his adopted son. But Oswald had at last found someone to listen to his half-baked opinions and to joust with him.

After the assassination de Mohrenshildt was the best witness on the question of what moved—and did not move—Lee Harvey Oswald, both politically and emotionally. Before the Warren Commission he was defensive and unhelpful, fearful of the consequences for his professional life of his friendship with the assassin, but as time went on de Mohrenshildt was overcome with guilt and remorse for his trifling with Oswald, and in 1977 he committed suicide after proclaiming that he was a moral conspirator in the assassination of Kennedy. In 1978 the House Assassinations Committee discovered a manuscript which de Mohrenshildt was writing to work out his metaphysical responsibility before he took his life. In it the émigré spoke of both Oswald's admiration for Kennedy and his hatred for John Connally. The extent of Oswald's dissatisfaction with the president is contained in his reaction to the lame jokes that de Mohrenshildt would tell him. Had Lee heard the one about what Kennedy said to the businessmen? "The economic situation is so good that if I weren't your president, I would invest in the stock market right now," says the president. "So would we," reply the businessmen, "—if you weren't our president." Oswald laughed heartily. Even better, he liked the one de Mohrenshildt told about Kennedy's terrible nightmare: the president sits bolt upright one night in bed, turns to his wife, and says, "Jackie, honey, I just dreamt that I was spending *my own money* and not the government's." Oswald laughed heartily at that as well, "but without resentment," de Mohrenshildt reported.

"Lee actually admired President Kennedy in his own reserved way," the memoir continues. "One day we discussed Kennedy's efforts to bring peace to the world and to end the cold war. 'Great! Great!' exclaimed Lee. 'If he succeeds, he'll be the greatest president in the history of this country.' Kennedy's efforts to alleviate and to end segregation were also admired by Lee, who was sincerely and profoundly committed to a complete integration of the blacks and saw in it the future of the United States." As he spoke of these warm sentiments toward Kennedy, he spoke equally of Oswald's torment over the unfairness of his military discharge downgrade. It explained Oswald's "hatred of John Connally," de Mohrenshildt wrote.

In all the literature that has been generated by the assassination of John F. Kennedy nowhere can there be found a single reference to any personal animosity that Oswald felt toward the president.[U] Indeed, the reverse is true. To believe that John F. Kennedy, as the liberal president of the United States and the humane leader of the free world, was Oswald's prime target, as the Warren Commission did, one must believe that between the attack on Walker in April and the killing of Kennedy in November, Oswald's pathology of violence broadened into a cosmology of direct violent action against the highest authority, and that somehow he had worked this all out in his head. The logic of the Warren Commission was that from April to November, Oswald moved from ire against right-wing figures to hatred of all figures of authority generally, regardless of whether they were benign toward the concerns that moved Oswald: civil liberties, regard for the working man, accommodation with the Soviet Union.

The night before his own speech in Mobile, Oswald had listened approvingly with Marina as the president announced the nuclear test ban treaty. Even on the subject of Cuba, which in New Orleans Oswald had taken up as the latest cause to draw attention to himself, the assassin gave Kennedy the benefit of the doubt. To Marina he remarked that Kennedy was inclined toward a softer attitude regarding Cuba than many on the American political scene.

In the few months before Kennedy went to Dallas in November, his statements on Castro were boilerplate. In Florida on November 18, only four days before his death, his rhetoric about Castro was far from inflammatory. The administration's efforts "to isolate the virus of Communism" had met with success, Kennedy thought, and Castro, once a formidable symbol of revolution in the hemisphere, had faded. Kennedy even berated those stale naysayers who continued to complain about Castro and blamed all the hemisphere's problems on Communism or on right-wing generals. "The harsh facts of poverty and social justice will not yield easily to promises or good will," the president said.

Even if one accepts Oswald's concern for Cuba as sincere and deeply felt, is it conceivable that Kennedy's statements on Cuba in the latter part of 1963 could have become the motive for assassination? The Warren Commission thought so. Its members never considered the difference between benign and violent political action, for that moved the question from the familiar turf of politics to the unfamiliar area of emotion and psychology. They were unconcerned to untwist Oswald's "twisted ideological view." By simply labeling it *twisted*, they abrogated their responsibility to explain it.

At issue is Oswald's will to murder, whether, at its core, it was emotional or intellectual. Toward Connally, he seemed to have a simple grudge, a grudge which engaged his emotions and his anger and which was consistent, probably as a secondary consideration, with his overall political instincts. The members of the Warren Commission and later the House Committee on Assassinations may have been reluctant to attempt to untangle Oswald's psychology, but Marina, who knew him best, offered important testimony on that subject.

She testified three times before the Warren Commission. Each time, in greater and more convincing detail, she revealed important episodes she had either forgotten or repressed, as well as providing more convincing explanations of her husband's state of mind. In her first appearance, as the commission's very first witness only six weeks after the assassination, she regretfully acknowledged that she now accepted her husband as the president's murderer. Why had he done it? For good reasons or bad, she replied, her husband wanted to become a memorable figure of history. The commission seized upon this as a simple, comprehensible, and salable motive, and never let go of it. Of Connally, she testified that her husband had promised to vote for him for governor if he had a chance. In her second appearance, in June 1964, she suddenly remembered the "Nixon incident," with her husband shouting at her through the bathroom door, "You always get in my way!" but the commission promptly dismissed the entire matter as insubstantial. Her third appearance took place in Dallas only three weeks before the Warren Commission Report was released, when its conclusions were already set in stone. It was no time to reopen a Pandora's box of motives, but as she was questioned by Congressman Hale Boggs of Louisiana, she said, seemingly out of thin air, "I feel in my own mind that Lee did not have President Kennedy as a prime target when he assassinated him."

[U] In Chapter 15 – REGARDING KENNEDY, the author had difficulty finding even one tiny semi-negative.

"Well, who was it?" Boggs asked, almost languorously.

"I think it was Connally," she replied. "That's my personal opinion—that he perhaps was shooting at Governor Connally, the governor of Texas."

This was not what they wanted to hear, and Senator Richard Russell jumped on her. "You've testified before us before that Lee told you, if he was back in Texas, he would vote for Connally for governor. Why do you think he would shoot him?"

"I feel that the reason that he had Connally in his mind was on account of his discharge from the marines and various letters they exchanged between the Marine Corps and the governor's office, but actually, I didn't think that he had any idea concerning President Kennedy."

"Well, did he ever express any hostility towards Governor Connally?" Boggs asked.

"He never expressed that to me—his displeasure or hatred of Connally," she said, holding her ground, for he seems to have expressed so little of a political nature to her. "I feel that there could have been some connection, due to the fact that Lee was dishonorably discharged from the corps. That's my personal opinion."

Instead of pursuing this new and highly significant tack or calmly attempting to elicit more from her, Boggs and Russell proceeded to browbeat the widow with the inconsistency of this with her prior testimony, and they quickly left the subject altogether. No reference to it whatever appears in their final report because, of course, the final report was already written.

It would be fourteen years before an additional, decisive detail was added to this thorny question of motive. In 1978, Marina Oswald testified before the House Assassinations Committee. Almost offhandedly, assigning no particular significance to it herself and finding that the politicians of the House were no more interested than the Warren Commission had been, she told of how Connally's brush-off letter in February 1962, the origin of the grudge, had arrived at their Minsk apartment in a big, white envelope whose front flaunted the large, smiling face of John Connally, advertising his candidacy for governor of Texas." [3397]

Later in *The Lone Star*, Reston stated the reality that had caused me to name this book *Tragic Truth*: "[T]he Warren Commission [was not] inclined to take seriously the notion that Governor Connally had been Oswald's target. For the country to have lost its president in the greatest crime of the century, when the chief of state might have been an incidental or accidental target, was an irony too grotesque to contemplate." [3398] If Reston didn't already have it lurking in mind, that last sentence may have suggested the title of his 2013 book, the first dedicated to the subject of Connally-as-target, *The Accidental Victim* — to be discussed later in this chapter.

One would think Reston's next book, *Collision at Home Plate: The Lives of Pete Rose and Bart Giamatti*, published in 1991, would be a complete change of pace for the author, but not so. He tells of digging out information on Pete Rose: "Supplementing this body of work was a drawer full of newspaper and magazine references at the Cincinnati Public Library, equal in size to the entries for John F. Kennedy. Soon the trial records of Rose's associates and the voluminous Dowd Report to Commissioner A. Bartlett Giamatti (and its nine attendant volumes) would be added to the published record. The process began to feel very much like the experience with my previous biography, of John Connally, in researching the Warren commission files and poring through the trials of Watergate figures." [3399] The author of the book you hold can associate with Reston's reflection. We both plowed through the *Warren Report* and its twenty-six attendant volumes, and many of the hundreds (thousands? — it feels so) of books on the Kennedy assassination.

1991: **Malcolm Kilduff** interviewed in *High Treason 2*

Harrison Edward Livingstone, critic of the Warren Commission and self-appointed chief critic of the other critics, wrote several books about the assassination. *High Treason 2: The Great Cover-Up*, published in 1992, relates a number of interviews by Livingstone of people who were present at, or he thought relevant to, the 1963 assassination. Here are the pertinent sections of one interview:

> "On April 17, 1991, I spoke to Malcolm Kilduff, a very interesting man who was with Kennedy when he died. ... He had worked for the State Department in Washington in public affairs and traveled a lot with Secretary of State Dean Rusk before working for Kennedy. ... He filled in for Pierre Salinger as press secretary on the fatal trip, and had the unhappy job of telling the assembled reporters that the President had died and what had happened at the hospital. ..." [3400]
>
> "Kilduff went with LBJ to the White House and stayed on until 1965." [3401]

Kilduff clearly recalled his immediate reaction to the shots, and as a lifelong newspaperman, reported it a quarter-century later as if he were interviewing himself:

> "I'm sitting in the right front seat [of the press pool car], three cars back. So I immediately turn around and I look up. What am I looking at? I am looking at the window of the School Book Depository. Why am I looking at that? Because to me that is where the shots are coming from." [3402]

Livingstone then prints four-pages about his own personal interests (bullets, entry and exit wounds, the supposedly mismanaged autopsy) before relating this interchange, in which his opening statement below is because he believes that Oswald-in-the-window was not the killer:

> "[Livingstone:] I told Kilduff that the killer would have shot at the car as it came toward the window rather than when it was going away from it. ...
>
> [Kilduff:] 'No, he wouldn't have. He had the windshield in the way.[V] ... I would have waited until it turned left, because I would have—of course, you have to get into the theory also that he wasn't really after Kennedy, too, that he was actually after Connally because of his bad discharge from the Marine Corps, and Connally had been Secretary of the Navy—'
>
> [Livingstone:] 'But he could always shoot at Connally!'[W]
>
> [Kilduff:] 'Yeah, but this would have been more dramatic, but that I don't want to get into it because it is obfuscating what you and I are talking about now. My own deep-seated belief is that he was actually after Connally. I've been saying that for years. And I've talked to John Connally about it. And John feels the same way.[X] He had reason to shoot Connally, and he didn't have a motive to shoot Kennedy.'" [3403]

Livingstone prints two more pages of interview about powder burns, gloves and Tippit, then:

> "[Kilduff:] 'If there is anything I have been sure of in my life, it's three shots, and if there is anything else I am sure of, it's that they came from the School Book Depository where I was looking. I could see that window where the shots were coming from up there.'" [3404]

Then the conclusion of Livingstone's interview of Kilduff:

> "[Livingstone:] 'So, you don't think there was any plot?'
>
> [Kilduff:] 'No. I think everyone wants to find more of a reason for having lost a president than just the simple act of a maniac. Of a man who was avenging his less-than-honorable discharge from the Marine Corps, and that he was after Connally. And I totally realize the question that comes up, well, why doesn't he pick a better place and a better time? Well,

---

[V] Yes! This is highly perceptive. The windshield and handrail obscured Connally, but not Kennedy.

[W] No! Oswald could not drive, could not take a rifle onto a bus without incurring suspicion, Connally lived and worked far away in Austin, Oswald moved to New Orleans, etc, etc.

[X] This is a surprise. I can find no record of John Connally ever expressing this view on the record.

he wanted to do what was the most dramatic. Well, that was a bad rifle. And there are many witnesses to this, that he had that rifle bench-tested well and that that rifle fell to the left and down,[Y] which would account for that first shot. So he was aiming at Connally, and of course the motorcade sped up there a little bit, as there were very few people there in Dealey Plaza. And going down that little incline there, no matter how little it sped up, that bullet aimed at Connally would have naturally gone into Kennedy, who was sitting right behind Connally. You can see how it would have happened if you can accept the theory that the shots were coming from the sixth floor of the School Book Depository. That to me is what simplifies it. Not that I am looking for simplicity.[Z] I am merely trying to make sense out of something that so many have tried to complicate.'" [3405]

Mac Kilduff was an original and one of the most highly dedicated New Frontiersmen. This author thinks it highly significant that the man who was in tears as he made the official announcement of JFK's death was later able to bear the great pain of realizing that Kennedy was not even the target, but only an innocent victim, in the wrong place at the wrong time.

1992: Craig I. Zirbel in *The Texas Connection*

A conspiracy theory sailing close to the edge of libel and sedition laws, this book tries to make a case that Lyndon Johnson masterminded Kennedy's assassination! Zirbel did considerable research, although his endnotes [3406] are woefully inadequate, especially because they do not cite any sources for his more outrageous claims. His arguments are beguiling — fully rounded, all encompassing and internally consistent. But they are reasonable only to a true believer who has already made a blind leap of faith. Zirbel's theory requires one to believe:

- Lyndon Baines Johnson wanted more than anything to be President.[3407] When Kennedy won the nomination, LBJ forced himself onto the ticket as the Vice-Presidential candidate.[3408] This is a wretched *Genesis*. LBJ personally preferred to continue as Senator from Texas and Majority Leader of the U.S. Senate. To the consternation of his advisers,[3409] Kennedy offered the Vice-Presidency because "Lyndon Johnson was, in his opinion, the next best qualified man to be President." [3410] After much hesitation, and to the great consternation of *his* advisers, Johnson accepted. Most believe Johnson ran because, as Lady Bird said, "the party needed Johnson on the ticket if they were going to carry anything in the South or Midwest" [3411] with the noble goal of defeating Richard Nixon.

- V.P. LBJ recognized that his earliest chance at the Presidency, assuming JFK lived out the usual two terms, would be in 1968. Worse, he feared that Kennedy would force him to resign in disgrace because of scandals, or would drop him from the 1964 ticket.[3412] But, in 1968 LBJ would be 60 years old. At age 47 he had suffered a massive heart attack. His father had died of heart disease at age 60; his uncle died of a heart attack at age 57.[3413]

- He devised a game plan that would make him President in his fifties, with a chance to serve out his term.[3414] [AA] LBJ got protégé John Connally to join an assassination conspiracy. To lure Kennedy to a death trap, Connally helped Johnson convince the victim that he must visit Texas before the 1964 campaign.[3415] Connally then presented the idea of a motorcade

---

[Y] In fact, the rifle was quite good and only very slightly misaimed; see Chapter 12 – THE RIFLE.

[Z] Seek simplicity! This is a perfect illustration of applying Occam's Razor to discern truth.

[AA] In fact, LBJ died at the age of 64 on January 22, 1973 — only two days after his allowed second full term as President would have ended. His final four years were in retirement on his ranch.

through Dallas.[3416] He beat down White House and Secret Service opposition to have it take the slow and dangerous path past the Texas School Book Depository.[3417]

- With the motorcade route agreed, the conspirators recruited Lee Harvey Oswald.[3418] "Three probable factors motivated Oswald to agree to act for Johnson: a promise to change his discharge status (he desperately wanted to right a wrong) ...".[3419] The conspirators placed Oswald in a job in the Book Depository "when a job opening did not exist".[3420] [BB]

- Oswald "the patsy"[3421] was not informed of any conspiracy. He was told to fire a single shot — not at Kennedy, but just into his general vicinity — to warn JFK and his Secret Service that the President's security was inadequate.[3422] Two or three hired assassins then killed Kennedy.[3423] Two days later, co-conspirator Jack Ruby silenced Oswald.[3424]

As is true of hundreds of assassination conspiracy books, *The Texas Connection* is ill-founded and lacks any substantive evidence. Its focal theory is appalling. That said, Zirbel must be given credit where it is due. He not only found the Connally-was-the-target theory, he also thought about it, briefly explained it, and then argued against and rejected it. Several chapters of his book describe what he terms "seven basic theories relating to the assassination", from "The Lone Assassin" through "The Vietnam Assassination" and "The CIA Assassination" to "The Assassination of Governor Connally".[3425] Here, in full as it appears in *The Texas Connection*, is that seventh assassination theory Zirbel describes and rejects:

"GOVERNOR CONNALLY AS THE INTENDED TARGET THEORY

"Another assassination theory has recently developed which does not necessarily involve a conspiracy. The theory made the cover of *Time* magazine and is part of a book written by James Reston, Jr. entitled *The Lone Star: The Life of John Connally*. Reston's theory is that Oswald had no intention to kill President Kennedy, rather Governor John Connally was his target. The initial basis for Reston's claim is that before the murder Oswald undeniably had contacts [CC] with Connally. From this foundation, the theory proceeds to the conclusion that Oswald blamed Connally as the Secretary of the Navy for his military discharge status downgrade. To the theory's credit, it is true that Oswald had communicated with Connally (when he was the Ex-Secretary of the Navy) in hopes that Connally would get the military to reverse its decision. It was also true that Oswald was upset with his military downgrade after his discharge. Combining these facts with evidence of Oswald's repeated positive statements about President Kennedy ('JFK deserved to be President . . . He will be the greatest President in history'), the conclusion drawn by Reston is that Connally was the intended target and Oswald missed and accidentally killed Kennedy.

Both facts and common sense reveal that any theory that Governor John Connally was the actual assassination target is a fantasy. Regardless whether Oswald was shooting at Kennedy or Connally, as an ex-marine he choose [*sic*] the wrong weapon. He could not have hit either man with the cheap Mannlicher-Carcano rifle. Further, an attempt to kill Governor Connally at that time and location made no sense at all. Why would anyone who wanted to kill Connally wait until he was in a Presidential motorcade? As the governor of Texas, Connally, as most governors on all but the assassination day, had only limited security protection. Before November 22, 1963, Oswald had the opportunity to kill Governor Connally at almost any time before he was within Presidential security. Connally had his permanent residence in Oswald's home town of Fort Worth, Texas, and Oswald could have killed him there any time. Lastly, if one compares the

---

[BB] Zirbel ignores surpassingly honest testimony that Lee learned of the job from Ruth Paine, who heard of a possible opening from neighbor Linnie Mae Randle, whose brother was recently hired there.

[CC] "contacts" (plural) is overblown. There was only one "contact", their letters from and to Minsk.

location of Governor Connally, when he was shot, to the alleged sniper post (6th floor Book Depository) it becomes clear that the theory is meritless. This is because the theory is premised upon Oswald passing up all clear shots at Governor Connally in order to shoot through President Kennedy in an attempt to strike his target.

Reston's theory, premised on the belief that Oswald chose the worst possible day to try to kill the governor, missed and killed Kennedy by mistake, is simply not believable." [3426]

Zirbel follows a logical progression. His first paragraph is an accurate summary of the theory. His last rushes to unjustifiable judgment. All the meat is in the second paragraph. Evaluated objectively, one of his three objections cuts neither way, making it neither more nor less likely that Oswald's target was Connally. The other two, on balance, actually argue that Oswald intended to murder Connally, not Kennedy!

ZIRBEL OBJECTION #1: "Regardless whether Oswald was shooting at Kennedy or Connally, as an ex-marine he choose [*sic*] the wrong weapon. He could not have hit either man with the cheap Mannlicher-Carcano rifle."

A clear-thinking would-be assassin with sufficient money might well have chosen a newer, more expensive weapon for such an important purpose. Zirbel needs to get around the problem of the cheap Mannlicher-Carcano and its cheap sight, because if Oswald were part of a conspiracy, the others would have insisted on his having a more modern rifle. Zirbel ducks: Oswald did not aim at anyone; he could have used any firearm to fire off a warning shot that was not intended to kill, but only to convey the message that security should be better. [3427]

We who believe that Oswald aimed at a target may choose either of two theories. Until now, most have assumed that the lifelong screw-up fired an old rifle with a lousy sight at Kennedy and miraculously did what he intended, killing him. I believed that for a year, until 1964 when I found Oswald's letter to Connally and began the long trek to writing this book.

I believe the only logical theory (more credibility, less miracle): Lee Oswald fired as quickly as he could when his hated target, John Connally, came into view. He came close. The second bullet penetrated Kennedy's neck, then seriously wounded Governor Connally. The third shot, fired in a hurry as the limo moved further away and Connally crumpled down onto Nellie's lap, exploded the rigidly-erect President's brain.

CONCLUSION #1: There was nothing wrong with THE RIFLE; see chapter 12. It was Oswald and a necessary hurry, not the rifle, that hit both men and killed the wrong one.

ZIRBEL OBJECTION #2: "Further, an attempt to kill Governor Connally at that time and location made no sense at all. Why would anyone who wanted to kill Connally wait until he was in a Presidential motorcade? As the governor of Texas, Connally, as most governors on all but the assassination day, had only limited security protection. Before November 22, 1963, Oswald had the opportunity to kill Governor Connally at almost any time before he was within Presidential security. Connally had his permanent residence in Oswald's home town of Fort Worth, Texas, and Oswald could have killed him there any time."

Zirbel is mistaken or sadly misleading in saying that "Connally had his permanent residence in Oswald's home town of Fort Worth, Texas, and Oswald could have killed him there any time." Presidents, governors, senators, representatives, legislators, servicemen and college students all have both "temporary" (where they work) and "permanent" (where they consider home and are registered to vote) addresses. A more precise term for "permanent" is "official". To say "Oswald could have killed him there any time" is specious. One might as well say that Oswald could have killed Kennedy "at almost any time" by lurking around JFK's permanent address at 122 Bowdoin Street in Boston, Massachusetts.[3428] It just isn't so.

Oswald's ability to shoot anyone existed for precisely 242 days, from arrival of his mail-ordered carbine and pistol on March 25, 1963 [3429] until he fired both on November 22, 1963. During that entire time, Governor Connally lived in the Governor's Mansion on Lavaca Street in Austin, the Texas capital. Just as Oswald lived in Dallas, near his work, so did Connally live in Austin, near his work. The distance between the two was 195 miles.

Oswald did not own or have use of a car. Even if he borrowed or rented, he did not know how to drive. To travel to assassinate, he could not use public transportation, for even in gun-totin' Texas in the 1960s, the Mannlicher-Carcano would draw unwanted attention. He couldn't even hitch a ride with the rifle. The one time he did it, with Wesley Frazier on the fateful day, the driver asked about his long bundle and Lee had to lie about curtain rods.

Oswald could not travel to his target. Whether he wanted to shoot Connally, Kennedy, Chairman Mao or Groucho Marx, the target had to travel to him, like a duck in a shooting gallery, to present itself in front of his rifle. November 22 was LHO's first chance, equally, at either Connally or Kennedy. It cuts neither way that this was the day he fired.

CONCLUSION #2: The assassination day was Oswald's first opportunity to kill either Kennedy or Connally, so we learn nothing bearing on his motive. It's equal.

ZIRBEL OBJECTION #3: "Lastly, if one compares the location of Governor Connally, when he was shot, to the alleged sniper post (6th floor Book Depository) it becomes clear that the theory is meritless. This is because the theory is premised upon Oswald passing up all clear shots at Governor Connally in order to shoot through President Kennedy in an attempt to strike his target."

It is correct that Connally became a difficult target after the limousine rolled past the TSBD and down the slope of Elm Street, with its rear toward the assassin, because Kennedy in the elevated back seat obstructed the view of Connally in front of him. Therefore, the objection argues that because he waited, Oswald must not have intended to murder Connally.

Nonetheless, Zirbel's argument is precisely diametrically wrong, probably because he had no particular reason to study and understand the Lincoln's windshield, raised visors and handrail that hid Connally from Oswald's search as the car rolled toward him. There were absolutely no "clear shots" until Connally became visible, when the target was turning and retreating, with Kennedy obscuring the intended victim. If this book had been written before 1992, Zirbel might have heeded the facts in important Chapter 19 – THE SHOT NOT TAKEN.

Before leaving Zirbel, I note a perplexing inconsistency: Later in his book, he uses the same "passing up all clear shots" objection to argue that Oswald could not have been aiming at Kennedy! He said: "... Oswald, as an assassin allegedly bent on killing Kennedy, passed up opportunities to kill Kennedy when he had a clear shot. Instead he waited to shoot Kennedy until after his limousine emerged, without warning, from a blocking tree. This does not make sense. Lee Harvey Oswald's best target zone to kill Kennedy was when the limousine slowly turned onto Elm Street and passed directly in front of him. The target was traveling at its slowest point [*sic*], the target was at its closest point, the target was in clear view and was not blocked by anything. However, at the location where Kennedy was actually shot, his position was much more difficult for Oswald to hit (as opposed to all other prior areas) from the Book Depository ...".[3430]

Close but no cigar! He is precisely correct and wise to note that Oswald's best shot at Kennedy was as the limo approached. But, when Zirbel wrote "This does not make sense.", he should have sat and thought, and might have stumbled onto the reason — and the truth.

CONCLUSION #3: Oswald's wait to fire argues forcefully, as in Chapter 19 – THE SHOT NOT TAKEN, that his intended target was not Kennedy — it was Connally.

1993: **John Connally** in his autobiography *In History's Shadow: An American Odyssey*

In the *TIME* article and biography of Connally referenced above, James Reston, Jr. expressed his entirely correct understanding of what had happened in Dallas. Five years later, John Connally co-wrote his autobiography, where he didn't think much of that idea:

"Of course, one of the subplots to the assassination was the Wrong Target theory; namely, that Oswald really intended to kill John Connally. According to this scenario, he believed that I ignored a letter he had written to me, as Secretary of the Navy, in which he demanded that I rescind the dishonorable discharge he received from the Marine Corps after his defection to the Soviet Union. He wanted an honorable discharge and the restoration of his rights.

By the time Oswald wrote me, I had left Washington and was running for governor of Texas. The letter was never forwarded to me, and today it is in the archives of the U.S. Navy. I have never read it.

While the theory did not originate with her, it was Oswald's wife, Marina, who gave it currency. As the first witness to testify before the Warren Commission, she had been the source of the photographs, had disclosed the botched attempt to kill General Walker, and had revealed Oswald's preoccupation with President Kennedy.

Then, questioned for the third time, in Dallas in September of 1964, she announced that she had changed her mind, and now felt the President was not the prime target. 'I think it was Connally,' she said, a conclusion that led Senator Russell Long to mutter, 'Baffling.'

I do not entirely disregard the possibility that the second shot was a mistake: when Kennedy's body slumped, the bullet barely missed him and drilled me instead. But I have a conviction—less than evidence, more than a belief—that Lee Harvey Oswald wanted to kill both of us, the two men in the car who represented authority to him." [3431]

That is really, seriously arrant nonsense, but must be discredited, bit by bit, lest anyone think there may be some tiny grain of truth in there, someplace:

- "[T]he dishonorable discharge he received ..." quotes Lee Oswald, who likely got the wrong word from his mother. The discharge was "undesirable", not nearly as bad.
- "The letter was never forwarded to me" proves a profound lack of understanding of the situation. Connally must think the letter went to Washington while he was in Texas, campaigning for the governorship. *Au contraire*! Oswald, isolated in Minsk (that's why the Russians sent him there, to be "out in the sticks"), thought Connally was still Secretary of the Navy, but did not have an address for his Washington, D.C. office. So, he mailed it to Connally in their shared-hometown. The letter did not need any forwarding — it was mailed directly to John Connally in Fort Worth, TX.
- "[I]t is in the archives of the U.S. Navy" is wrong, as Connally well knew in 1964. The John Connally article in Chapter 7 – MUFFLED DRUMS AND SUBSEQUENT EVENTS tells of his asking for the letter, learning that it was confined by law in the U.S. Archives, and happily accepting a "marvelous copy" from Captain Andy Kerr.
- "I have never read it." This is proven wrong by the paragraph above, and — my belief that I can't prove — probably doubly wrong. All photos of the letter show, written in

its top margin: "Refer to SecNav". My estimation is that when the letter arrived in the Fort Worth campaign HQ, the only old salt there who would know to write the six letters "SecNav" was ex-Navy officer and ex-SecNav John Bowden Connally.

- "Marina ... had revealed Oswald's preoccupation with President Kennedy." This turns truth on its head. Oswald had no preoccupation with Kennedy except approval, respect and admiration to which Marina (and a multitude) repeatedly testified. See chapter 15.
- "[S]he announced that she had changed her mind, and now felt the President was not the prime target." No, absolutely not! In no way did Marina say that she had changed her mind, because she did not, and did not have to. See the first article in this chapter, her FBI statement five days after Lee's burial, when the very first opinion she ever expressed was that her husband probably meant to kill Connally.
- "[A] conclusion that led Senator Russell Long to mutter, 'Baffling.'". This is all becoming quite sad and troubling. Russell Billiu Long was a U.S. Senator from Louisiana. This author worked for him in 1959 during summer and Christmas college breaks, typing constituent addresses into an ancient labeling system. A rosy-cheeked cheery gentleman of the South, he was not on the Warren Commission. It was Senator Richard Brevard Russell, Jr. of Georgia, a member of the Commission and chair of that final session, who bullied poor Marina and dismissed as "Baffling" her unwelcome but honest testimony as the Commission was hurrying to completion.
- "[W]hen Kennedy's body slumped, the bullet barely missed him and drilled me instead." It surpasses belief that Connally so badly mangled a non-judgmental fact of physical evidence. Kennedy did not slump because he could not. See Chapter 14 – TOO CLOSE TO CALL, for the highly-significant role of Kennedy's tight back-supporting corset and Ace bandage that kept him bolt upright, and in the line of fire when Oswald tried again to hit Connally with his third shot. Kennedy's head was in the trajectory. Even if JFK had not been imprisoned by the corset, Oswald's first bullet missed, then the second went through Kennedy's neck "and drilled me" (Connally). Kennedy had neither cause, ability nor time to slump before the shot that went through his neck and on to terribly wound Connally.
- "I have a conviction ... that ... Oswald wanted to kill both of us, the two men in the car who represented authority to him." Every man has a right to his opinion, but I dismiss this as simple expansion of the Warren Commission's inane and unsupported stretch for a motive for shooting Kennedy — hatred of authority. He's saying: "Me too!" to the Commission's grasp to pull some weak semblance of motive out of plain air.
- Connally's book, written in the final months of his life as he "suffered from pulmonary fibrosis",[3432] did not get the professional, critical checking it deserved. There are many errors. One easily-seen and -described will suffice: A full-page photo of the ill-fated limo, taken from its left side with Nellie and Jackie closest to the camera, is captioned: "... in this clip from the famed Zapruder film ...".[3433] No, any who paid the slightest attention know that Zapruder filmed from the right, the side of John and Jack.

It must be the case that much or most of the book was written by his co-author Mickey Herskowitz, with little input, revision or approval from Connally, who certainly knew better — if he had time or ability to think — about most of these errors.

1993: Bob Callahan in *Who Shot JFK? A Guide to the Major Conspiracy Theories*

The book is a gallery of the major conspiracy theories at the 30-years-after anniversary. There is little of value in that rubbish heap, although his synopsis of the House Select Committee on Assassinations is worthy, and is quoted in chapter 8. Callahan deserves partial credit and an incomplete grade for this brief but accurate stand-alone mention of Connally-as-target:

> "Well, what about Oswald's motive? Research suggested that if anything, Oswald had a stronger motive for taking a shot at Texas Governor John Connally, who, as former head of the Navy department, had denied Oswald an honorable discharge from military service. Most of those testifying to Oswald's character claimed he deeply admired President Kennedy. Concerning motive, it would have been easier to make the case that Oswald was aiming at Connally on Nov. 22, 1963." [3434]

As do many who think of the possibility that Oswald targeted Connally, Callahan then loses the path while criticizing the Warren Commission's list of five factors that may have added up to a motive: "[O]ne Commission lawyer complained to a colleague that the list read like a series of cliches from a TV soap opera. ... [T]he Commission had launched this small exercise into psychopathology without the advantage of having even one professional psychologist on its staff. It had been left to amateur shrinks such as Gerald Ford and Allen Dulles to plumb the depths of Lee Harvey Oswald's mind." [3435] Yes, the Commission was wrong in being satisfied with a very weak case for a wrong motive — but Callahan also missed by not following to a logical conclusion his thought that Connally may have been the target.

1998: Stewart Galanor in *Cover-Up*

Your author is reminded that Oswald was said (chapter 15, page 471) to dislike everyone, but of all men, perhaps he disliked Kennedy the least. I dislike all assassination conspiracy books, but of them all, perhaps dislike this the least. Galanor is an author of textbooks, multimedia consultant and technical writer. In 176 photo-filled tersely-worded pages, he presents many major objections to the *Warren Report*. He never mentions Connally-as-target, but in discussing the missed shot, probably the first of the three, he writes:

> "If the assassination were an easy shot, why did the first shot, the easiest of the shots, miss? Anyone familiar with Dealey Plaza must wonder, if Oswald were the lone assassin, why he did not shoot when the President was in clear view as the limousine rode towards him on Houston Street, or when the limousine slowly made a 120 degree turn at the corner, or when it rode over 100 feet down Elm Street before it passed beneath the oak tree." [3436]

A reasonable man, Galanor takes this important non-act to be further evidence that Oswald was not the only one firing at JFK, but was allowing accomplices on the Grassy Knoll to join in.

1999: Richard Belzer in *UFOs, JFK, and Elvis: Conspiracies You Don't Have To Be Crazy To Believe*

According to the hype on his book's dust jacket: "The Betz was a popular stand-up comedian, a pioneering morning radio host, and an actor in every show business medium from off-Broadway to major Hollywood movies" [3437] and TV. One of Belzer's six "Surreal Motives" is:

> "*The OOPS Theory.* This theory is based on the idea that Oswald was really shooting at Connally but missed. Although Oswald had even less reason to kill the Texas governor than he did to assassinate the president, this was an idea suggested by a hypnotized Marina Oswald. 'You are getting sleepy.' What a nightmare." [3438]

Belzer must have spent too much time on UFOs and Elvis to understand Oswald's reason to kill the governor. His is the only hallucinatory reference to a "hypnotized" Marina. Garbage!

1999: **William Rubinstein** in article "Oswald Shoots JFK: But Who is the Real Target?"

Professor William D. Rubinstein reminds me of James Reston, Jr. Born in the US in 1946 and educated at Swarthmore College and Johns Hopkins University, he then worked at universities in England and Australia before his current position as Professor of Modern History at the University of Wales, Aberystwyth. Like Reston, his wide-ranging curiosity has resulted in a diverse library of at least sixteen books including *Genocide: A History* and *Men of Property: The Very Wealthy in Britain Since the Industrial Revolution*. According to his Wikipedia biography, "Rubinstein also researches unconventional history, and topics discussed by amateur historians but ignored by academics." [3439]

Pursuing that avocation, at the end of the 20th Century this professional historian looked into the assassination in Dallas and was dismayed:

> "That no academic historian has ever examined Kennedy's assassination is a reproach to the historical profession. The training of academic historians in assessing evidence could hardly have been put to better or more important use, and this is one case in which academic historians should have left the ivory tower." [3440]

His brief history of the assassination and its investigation by "amateurs" from the Warren Commission, then its many critics, through the House Select Committee on Assassinations to 1992's Assassination Records Review Board, appeared as a 4,000-word article in the October 1999 issue of the British journal *History Today*. The professor's focus was the inevitable confusion and loss of belief engendered by so many untrained amateurs publishing analyses of the assassination and criticizing the Warren Commission. After 3,000+ words of that, this:

> "What is the true explanation of what happened and why? Buried in the first volume of the Warren Report (p.314) [DD] is a remarkable suggestion, which has received no publicity then or since, but which might just represent the truth of the assassination. This is the possibility that Oswald's real target was not Kennedy but John Connally. There is a surprising amount of circumstantial evidence to support this possibility. Oswald apparently held a grudge against Connally, who had (as Secretary of the Navy) signed a letter to Oswald stating that his dishonourable discharge from the Marine reserves would not be reviewed. For the 'hunter of fascists', Connally was a plausible target: a right-wing Democrat who subsequently joined the Republican Party. Significantly, when Marina Oswald heard the news of the assassination, she thought that her husband 'was shooting at Connally rather than Kennedy'. It would have been easy for Oswald to have aimed at Connally, hesitated for a fraction of a second, and shot the President, sitting two feet behind him in the moving car. This intriguing suggestion has been totally ignored by all Warren critics, since, if Connally was the target, there was plainly no conspiracy. This theory should certainly be studied more closely." [3441]

Some applause, and little comment, is required. Living in Wales and probably depending on British sources, he was apparently unaware of James Reston's 1988 *TIME* article or Connally

---

[DD] His citation is mystifying. The *Warren Report* is only one volume, and in the official book printed by the Government Printing Office, the Connally-may-be-target suggestion is on pages 387-388, as was reported in the ninth article in this chapter, at "1964 (September 24)". The first volume of the *Warren Commission Hearings* on its page 314 records the testimony of Lee's brother Robert, saying that Lee in fact killed Kennedy, with nary a mention of Connally-as-target.

biography in 1989. The discharge was not "dishonourable" (the British spelling, which Lee Oswald faithfully used for no discernible reason), but lesser "undesirable". Connally signed not a letter stating that the classification would not be reviewed, but a two-sentence note saying he was no longer the Secretary of the Navy, and was forwarding the letter to his replacement. There was no need for Oswald to hesitate between aiming at Connally and Kennedy — they were very much in a line, Kennedy blocking the bullets' only path to Connally.

With those exceptions, the professor's thoughts and article were "spot on" ("right on" is the equivalent American phrase). For my money, James Reston, Jr., is a good and reliable historian; perhaps if Rubinstein had read either his *TIME* article or *The Lone Star*, he would not have written his plea for professional historians to search for the truth, because it seems Reston had already found and spotlighted it!

2003: Nellie Connally in *From Love Field: Our Final Hours with President John F. Kennedy*

After writing of husband John's use of his position as Secretary of the Treasury to thoroughly investigate Oswald and any possibility of a conspiracy (page 264), Mrs. Connally wrote:

> "More chilling to us personally was the fact that Oswald's dishonorable discharge papers had been signed by none other than Kennedy's then-secretary of the Navy, John Connally. We learned Oswald had written letters protesting that decision, but if his anger had been directed at John, it was misplaced. At the time of Oswald's discharge, my husband was back in Texas, busily campaigning to be its next governor. ... [B]ut the idea that John might have been a target still sends chills up and down my spine." [3442]

The loyal wife is slightly off-course: Changing Oswald's discharge status from "honorable" to "undesirable" had been directed by the Commandant of Marines in 1960, while Eisenhower was still president and long before Connally became SecNav. Oswald's appeal to the Navy Discharge Review Board was approved in 1963 by Assistant Secretary of the Navy Paul B. "Red" Fay, Jr., JFK's buddy and fellow PT boat skipper, long after Connally had resigned and been elected Governor of Texas. But, in true naval tradition, the captain is accountable for everything done by anyone in his command, so Nellie may have thought John responsible, although the discharge actions bracketed, coming before and after his term. She also wrote that the two of them studied the assassination and concluded Oswald did it — alone.

2007: Vincent Bugliosi in *Reclaiming History: The Assassination of President John F. Kennedy*

Bugliosi's book was introduced and described on page 268. The product of twenty-one years of work, it is the monumental ultimate authority on DID HE DO IT? WAS IT A CONSPIRACY? — the twinned subjects of my chapter 9. To keep his book's size manageable, the less-important items worth including but not printing were consigned to a file of Endnotes on a CD-ROM included with the book. One of those notes reads:

> "Believe it or not, there are those who actually believe that Governor Connally was Oswald's target that fateful day, not President Kennedy. But obviously, with Oswald's dreams of grandeur and his immersion in the fortunes of Marxism on a national and international scale, a state governor would be small potatoes to him. When Governor Connally was asked, within days after the assassination, about the speculation that Oswald had been after him that day, he scoffed at the suggestion. "I'm sure," he said, "that Oswald—as deranged and hateful as he may have been—never wanted to assassinate me. If he wanted, he could have done so

countless times in Dallas and elsewhere in Texas. I had been campaigning all over Texas . . . for 11 months this year riding in parades, horseback, open cars, on street corners, with no security whatever. I could have been easy prey for anyone. Stories to the effect that Oswald was out to get me are, in my opinion, simply not true" (HSCA Record 180-10116-10050, CBS interview of Connally at his bedside at Parkland Hospital, most likely on the Wednesday or Thursday following the assassination, p.1; *Parade Magazine*, September 18, 1991, p.2). Additionally, the argument that Oswald may have hated Connally, blaming him for his "undesirable" discharge from the Marine Corps Reserve, has no merit. Although Oswald wrote Connally, then secretary of the navy, in 1962, seeking to have his undesirable discharge changed to honorary, he received a letter back saying that Connally was no longer secretary of the navy and that his request would be turned over to Connally's successor. Oswald's brother Robert, who was present when Oswald received the letter, said his brother "said nothing at all to me that day that indicated he held Connally personally responsible" for his undesirable discharge, nor did he indicate any hostility toward Connally at any time thereafter (Oswald with Land and Land, *Lee*, pp.19, 139–140; 1 H 450, WCT Robert Edward Lee Oswald). Marina herself told the Warren Commission that her husband had never expressed any hostility toward Connally and indeed had told her he intended to vote for him for governor (5 H 607). (Connally's successor, Fred Korth, ultimately sent Oswald a letter rejecting his request.)

It was Marina herself who is believed to have given birth to the notion that maybe her husband had been out to kill Connally, not Kennedy. In her last appearance before the Warren Commission on September 6, 1964, after testifying that "I have no doubt in my mind that Lee Oswald killed President Kennedy," she added that "at the same time . . . I feel that Lee, that my husband perhaps intended to kill Governor Connally instead of President Kennedy" (5 H 608). But of course, if Connally had been Oswald's target, why would he shoot at Connally at a moment in time when most of Connally's body was being shielded by Kennedy's body, requiring him to shoot through Kennedy's body to reach Connally? His best shot at Connally would have been when the presidential limousine was proceeding northbound on Houston. Even Marina later acknowledged she was wrong about her Connally opinion when some Secret Service agents pointed out to her that by the time of the fatal head shot to Kennedy, Kennedy had already been wounded and was leaning toward his wife, his body no longer in alignment with Connally's body. So at the time of the head shot, Oswald could only have been aiming at Kennedy, not Connally. (McMillan, *Marina and Lee*, p.571)." [3443]

Although I greatly admire his book, as was surely evident in chapter 9, I must disagree with twelve (!) key points in this endnote. Vincent Bugliosi is a fine thinker, certainly able to discern truth by assembling and pondering facts. The problem is that many of the "facts" in these two paragraphs are, ahem, in fact nonfactual, irrelevant or just plain wrong:

- "a state governor would be small potatoes to him" assumes that Oswald's motive was to disrupt government, the motive Bugliosi settled on (see my page 271). No, Oswald's motive was personal, to avenge what he thought was a grievous injustice, for which he'd appealed to Connally for help and been rudely denied in two sentences. Lee's hatred was entirely personal, nothing to do with being a governor.
- Connally's scoff at the suggestion of Oswald gunning for him was understandable — that's what we all thought after he shot and killed our President.
- "I had been campaigning all over Texas . . . for 11 months this year", if Connally said it in late November 1963, may have been the aftereffect of his severe injuries or the anesthetics of surgeries. It was wrong by an entire year. He campaigned from December 1961 to November 5, 1962, was elected on November 6, 1962, then inaugurated on January 15, 1963. There was nothing for him to campaign for in 1963.

- "he could have done so countless times in Dallas and elsewhere in Texas" is wrong on two counts. Oswald had spent much of 1963 in New Orleans — in case Connally in the quote above really meant 1963 instead of a campaign year. And, as was pointed out previously in this chapter, Lee had no way to get himself and his rifle to the places where Connally might have "been easy prey". He had no car, didn't even know how to drive, and wasn't about to conspicuously carry the rifle in taxis or buses to get to places where his target was appearing and campaigning. When you really think about real facts, Connally riding past the TSBD was Lee's <u>first</u> opportunity to shoot him.
- "Oswald wrote Connally, then secretary of the navy, in 1962" is incorrect. Oswald in isolated Minsk did not know when he wrote on January 30, 1962, that Connally had resigned 41 days earlier, December 20, 1961, to return to Texas and run for governor. It's trivial, but facts are facts, and Connally was never Secretary of the Navy in 1962.
- Bugliosi's assertion "the argument that Oswald may have hated Connally, blaming him for his 'undesirable' discharge ... has no merit." is speculation, misaimed. Oswald may or may not have blamed Connally for the discharge. He had pleaded for help from that specific man "since you are a resident of Ft. Worth as I am." (page 88) Although Connally, busy running to be governor, acted properly by forwarding the letter to the new Secretary of the Navy, Lee would have seen that as what James Reston terms "a classic bureaucratic brush-off". Self-aggrandizing Lee had learned from his mother to take all minor rejections as major insults, never to be forgiven or forgotten. Worse, Lee saved the envelope (page 93) that brought the rejection, with Connally's large smiling face to remind him, all the rest of his life, who it was that refused him.
- "brother Robert, who was present when Oswald received the letter" is a mystery with no foundation, because Connally's rejection was mailed to Minsk, Byelorussia (see the envelope on page 93) from which Lee had written. Robert was never in that country.
- Recollections and opinions of Robert and Marina about Lee's regard for John Connally have been presented in full in Chapter 16 – REGARDING CONNALLY, to which you are directed to get the full flavor of what they testified, said and wrote — highly negative.
- "Connally's successor, Fred Korth, ultimately sent Oswald a letter rejecting his request" is wrong, probably a result of not looking at the complex letters and forms that then went back and forth. Korth, in fact, never sent anything to Oswald. As told in my MINSK chapter, Lee then heard from lower and lower levels in the Marine Corps, until his final appeal to the Naval Discharge Review Board was rejected, with the result sent to sensitive-to-insult Oswald in a typed-in form letter from a lowly Captain in a service in which Oswald had not served, the U.S. Navy. This final blow came in late July 1963, and he shot Connally at his first opportunity, less than four months later.
- And now we must double back to Bugliosi quoting Connally saying that Oswald had all of 1963 to shoot him. Well, no. Lee had hope, and thus no reason to take revenge, until he received the rejection in July 1963. But he was in New Orleans, then Mexico. He did not return to Texas (John B. Connally, Governor) until October 3, 1963!
- "His best shot at Connally would have been when the presidential limousine was proceeding northbound on Houston." is flat wrong, a common misperception. This book devotes one of its most important chapters, 19 – THE SHOT NOT TAKEN, to why Oswald did not fire while the limousine approached him in a clear field of fire, for the simple reason that he could not see his target! He saw the Kennedys, but not Connally.

- Finally, Bugliosi's objection on the basis that Oswald might have aimed at Connally for the last shot and thus not hit Kennedy in the head, is a relaxed conjecture of leisurely hindsight. Lee was certainly in a panic from not having seen Connally until the limo turned virtually below him, then firing a first wild shot as his victim became shielded under a tree. Witnesses who were skilled professionals said the sequence of the three shots was "bang   bang bang". The final shot was immediately after the second that had accurately hit Connally — although going through Kennedy's soft tissue on the way — as quickly as the bolt-action rifle could be recycled. Expecting great accuracy from Oswald is simply too much. He did the best he could under the unanticipated circumstance of having to fire at a limo driving away from him, with the intended victim "leaning toward his wife" Nellie but still somewhat in line past the innocent victim, who was to a much lesser degree "leaning toward his wife" Jacqueline.

I continue to be a huge fan of Vincent Bugliosi, greatly appreciating the monumental work he did to research and write *Reclaiming History*. But, on this one endnote in the middle of the large file of such additional material on the CD-ROM, I must part company, attributing our disparity to the fact that he was embroiled in an immense task, writing thousands of pages to definitively prove four simple little words: "Oswald did it, alone." Mr. Bugliosi died before I could send him a copy of this book. I suspect he would have accepted the high probability that Oswald's motive was retribution against the unhelpful Connally, and his criminal intent was to assassinate the despised Connally.

2013: James Reston, Jr. in *The Accidental Victim: JFK, Lee Harvey Oswald, and the Real Target in Dallas*

Chapter 9 recommended two books full of compelling evidence that Oswald did it, alone. *Case Closed* by Gerald Posner was likened to the best-selling *Merriam-Webster's Collegiate Dictionary*.[EE] By contrast, for those wanting <u>all</u> the facts, more like *Webster's Third New International Dictionary, Unabridged* [FF], I recommended Vincent Bugliosi's encyclopedic achievement *Reclaiming History*. But, neither delved into the important matter of motive.

To read solid evidence that Oswald's intent was to kill Connally, and in failing to do that, he killed Kennedy by accident, there are only two books as of early 2016. You hold the big, fat equivalent of *Webster's International Dictionary*. In similar comparison, any who want a smaller easy-to-read book [GG] will be greatly pleased with and well served by Reston's *The Accidental Victim*, the fifteenth book (as I count them) from a professional historian and writer. It appeared two months before the fiftieth anniversary of the assassination, so was quite probably hurried to benefit from heightened interest late in 2013. It is based on Reston's two earlier writings on the subject (previous articles in this chapter), but shows signs of a rapid preparation after the author had spent many years thinking about other subjects. To nail facts correctly, a re-dip into the pool, even by an expert, is no substitute for a long period of total immersion, even by a first-timer.

[EE] Eleventh edition has 225,000 definitions on 1,664 pages, $17.10 from an e-retailer named for a wide river.

[FF] Third edition has 472,000 entries on 2,662 pages, weighs 12.5 pounds, $78.19 from the same vendor.

[GG] 203 pages, about 250 words/page. The book you hold is 774 pages, more than 500 words/page.

The book was released with several small errors of fact. I have documented them to Mr. Reston, so the e-book available from ZolaBooks.com has probably been corrected. The hardcover [3444] by Zola Books and Assembly! Press for the History Book Club had and may still have the errors, unless/until a second edition. That said, they are nits that will not evidence

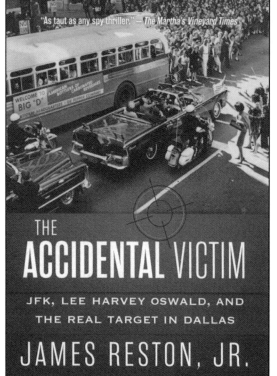

themselves to most readers, and their existence should not dissuade you from reading a book that is "right on" ("spot on" if you're British) in its reasoning, and will proudly stand the test of time as the first book (at least that this author knows of) fully dedicated to correctly explaining what really happened in Dallas.

One error may confuse highly perceptive readers. When Lee Oswald sat down in Minsk to write a letter to John Connally that combined pleading with threatening, he made a mistake common to many of us. The calendar had just flipped after 12 months of 1961, to January 1962, but atop his letter (page 88) he wrote "January 30, 1961". That date was carried over into the book, with a concomitant comment on Connally's "delay" in answering until February 1962. In reality, especially from the heat of a spiritied campaign for governor, Connally sent an exemplary, speedy reply.

As with bouillabaisse, creators will differ on how much of what ingredients to use. Reston pretty much left out, and my book leans heavily, on the physical evidence and facts in chapters 14 through 19. Where he writes elegant persuasive rhetoric, your present author, an engineer, tromps along measuring and aligning and bracing and strengthening.[HH] For example, Reston argues that Oswald had personal psychological reasons for disliking Connally; I agree, cite that very briefly, then compile a complete chapter 16 by consulting hundreds of sources to document everything he was ever known to have said REGARDING CONNALLY.

As was described at the beginning of Chapter 20 – OBSTRUCTION OF BEST EVIDENCE, my *Tragic Truth* was destined to construct its case with circumstantial evidence — very strong, yes, but circumstantial. Then came the wondrous tip from Reston, telling me of strong factual evidence that had come to light after his book was published. He shared his news, urged me to follow up and use it, and the story of Mike Howard and the Kill List in Oswald's notebook was added here. I am immensely grateful for that tip, and all who read this book should know and appreciate James Reston and his continuing dedication to shining a bright light on facts.

In summary, I embrace Reston and what he wrote, recognizing Oswald's disdain for Connally, and explaining how that caused the misfit to kill the President without any intention of doing so. *The Accidental Victim* is a significant milestone on the path to truth.

HH Some say left-brained engineers (such as Dilbert and I) think belt and suspenders, together, are the way to hold up trousers. We don't take that as an insult, but as a compliment to our preparedness!

•••

There have been twenty-seven articles in this chapter. Some participants, observers or analysts saw that the most likely reason for the shooting was that Oswald had good reason (in his mind, and that's what matters) to vent his anger, and perhaps also his frustration with a life and marriage that were both on the rocks, by taking revenge on Connally. But some argued against that, and some were neutral. There may be more who have spoken or written on the topic, but I think none of great import. I have watched this field (while hoping somebody would write this book) for a half-century, and should know.

Before ending this review, I state my admiration for all of them, both the ayes and the nays, for having their eyes wide open to see what most have not even noticed. Almost no Americans or interested world citizens paused to consider that in this case, as in many, one should not blindly conclude that what was done is what was meant. All those cited here at least recognized the need to think — about what Oswald intended. Some got it very badly wrong, usually as these articles have shown, because they didn't have their facts correct.

You probably noticed that many wrongly concluded that if Connally was the intended victim, Oswald would have shot him as the limousine approached on Houston Street, because Connally was sitting in open air, between Oswald's perch in the TSBD and President Kennedy on the back seat. But the naysayers did not think of the unique combination of the visors-up tinted windshield, the unusually tall agent in the front passenger seat, and the opaque overhead handrail. In conjunction, those hid the real target sitting low in a jump seat. That would have made a great difference in many opinions stated in this chapter — if only they'd known.

All of these viewpoints were tossed into our pool of common knowledge, and in the opinion of this watcher, have caused nary a ripple. I had great hopes for Reston's 1988 article and 1989 book, then for his 2013 book. Unfortunately, they passed with little notice.

As will be noted in the next (and final) chapter, A TRAGIC REALITY, it was not at all necessary that Kennedy be present in the limo for there to be rifle fire at Elm Street. All that was required was a motorcade with John Connally sitting in an open car in line with a crowd-attracting celebrity. Oswald would have fired at his intended target, Connally, and missing to the same degree, would have shot John Wayne, Groucho Marx, Kermit the Frog, Queen Elizabeth or Prince Philip (in that case, depending on which sat inline with Connally).

Nothing about Connally-as-target has lodged in the American consciousness, so I try again with the book you hold, hoping that a rather complete all-angles-considered approach may push the sad truth across a tipping point. Perhaps this encyclopedic treatment is what has been needed. Maybe the EVIDENCE chapters 14 through 20 will cause some to see unassailable logic that cannot be matched by the old thought that Oswald must have wanted to kill Kennedy because that's what he did. The tragic reality is disturbing and repugnant, but it is the truth.

Key point of this chapter:
**Several participants and analysts have thought of
   Connally-as-target, but only James Reston Jr.
   has published. Hoping for greater acceptance,
   your author wrote a fully comprehensive book.**

A TRAGIC REALITY

Based on solid evidence, the truth is undeniable and heartbreaking

"Motivation, as any psychiatrist will tell us, is always difficult to assess."
         — **Senator John F. Kennedy**,
         Profiles in Courage, 1955 [3445]

"It has been said that the only thing we learn from history is that we do not learn. But surely we can learn if we have the will to do so. Surely there is a lesson to be learned from this tragic event."
         — **Chief Justice Earl Warren**, at JFK's memorial
         in the Capitol Rotunda, November 24, 1963 [3446]

THE FACTS OF THE KILLING IN DALLAS are clear, and have been since hours after the event. Everyone is entitled to an opinion, but not to his or her own facts. This book has presented *the* facts underlying the accidental death of President Kennedy, perhaps in more detail than required, but the author is an engineer who enjoyed a long, rewarding career at IBM believing that belt-plus-suspenders, then doublecheck before moving, is the prudent path to success.

What's new in this book, never before pulled together so one can see the confluence of events, are the many actions and documents underpinning the worst thing that ever happened to Lee Oswald, the change of his honorable discharge from active duty in the U.S. Marine Corps into an undesirable discharge from its Reserve. Most of that was in the 26 books of *Hearings* released by the Warren Commission in 1964 to support its *Report*. This book's significant "new news" is in the surprising revelation about his notebook in chapter 20 – OBSTRUCTION OF BEST EVIDENCE. This book's purpose is now accomplished, presenting all important material so that we can at last understand *why* Oswald fired his rifle as he did on November 22, 1963.

The physical facts of the shooting in Dallas are entirely forthright. Dallas sheriff's deputy Jack Faulkner, an experienced criminologist and later Captain of the Sheriff's CID, said in his oral history: "I think that I have as good a picture of the assassination as anybody, especially since I was involved in the investigation. Personally, I think the whole thing was quite simple." [3447] In fact, Deputy Faulkner had it figured out before 2 PM on the fatal day, less than 90 minutes after the shooting, shortly after he left the TSBD's sixth floor:

"[T]here must have been 75 to 100 officers on that floor; I didn't feel that there was anything else to find. ... [A]t about 1:30 I left and walked over to ... the sheriff's office and ran into Charlie Brown, who was an FBI agent. He was listening to the radios and said, 'Jack, I think they've got him! They arrested a man in the Texas Theater that killed a Dallas police officer, and he worked at the Texas School Book Depository.' I said, 'Well, it looks like that closes the case,' and I still think it did." [3448]

Dallas Police Captain W.R. "Pinky" Westbrook, in charge of Personnel and Internal Affairs, assisted on the tragic Friday by hurrying to the scene of the Tippit shooting, then to the Texas Theater for the capture of Oswald, and back to headquarters to help with the mob of newsmen. From a small remove, he understood the upshot of Homicide Dept. Captain Fritz's afternoon:

"[A]s far as the investigation was concerned, by 6:00 o'clock that evening, Fritz made the statement that the investigation was closed. He was criticized for that. Later, investigations were conducted by the FBI, the Secret Service, the attorney general's office, and other agencies, plus the Warren Commission. After all that, there was not one relevant piece of evidence which proved Oswald guilty or not guilty that Fritz didn't have by 6:00 o'clock that evening." [3449]

This book has presented facts explaining what happened in Dallas that day, through Chapter 19 – THE SHOT NOT TAKEN and Chapter 20 – OBSTRUCTION OF BEST EVIDENCE. Chapter 21 – OTHERS ON THIS TRAIL gave credit where it's due. I may have been one of the first to understand Oswald's motive, late in 1964, a year after the tragedy, and after fifty years am the second to write a book about that; the first to document all aspects in a full-length presentation. Now that the factual foundation is complete, this last chapter pulls it all together.

This book's focus is the mind of Lee Harvey Oswald, attempting to learn *why* he did what he did. About that mind, we will never be able to know more than we can surmise from the known facts. Because of Jack Ruby's misguided would-be-heroic act, Lee died only two days after firing his own shots. During those few hours, he did not have an attorney, did not receive any medical or psychological exam. Thus, we cannot learn from direct observation whether or not he had physical or neurological defects that could help explain his actions.

In all probability, if he had lived and stood trial, he would have wanted to mount a defense based on righting a grievous wrong, but his attorneys would have talked him into the only viable course, defending or pleading guilty due to temporary insanity. Then, we would have had the benefit of neurologic and psychiatric examinations, and would have learned whether there was any defect in his thinking apparatus, or whether the problem was what had been loaded into it. Personally, I am certain that it was the latter.

Chapter 1 – MOTHER expressed my statement that there were two villains, the one who fired the bullets, but also his mother Marguerite, the only long-term formative influence on him during his entire life. The woman must be described with words such as petty, narcissist, suspicious, unforgiving — and worse. That chapter ended with a list denoting the character Lee had acquired by the time he left home at seventeen to join the Marines, and it is truly a terrible list. This book used the phrase "the apple does not fall far from the tree" to applaud the excellent thinking and writings of James Reston, Jr. The phrase is also useful to note that son Lee went into the world with the unnaturally negative and sick attitudes he learned from his only parent, Marguerite Oswald.

••• THE SIMPLE FACTS OF WHAT HAPPENED •••

Fifty years of careful and objective study of the EVENTS in chapters 1–6, subjected to the ANALYSIS and EVIDENCE in chapters 9–20, allow me to assert beyond all reasonable doubt that this is exactly what happened during Lee's short adult life, and on that dreadful Friday:

- In three years as a Marine, Oswald learned almost nothing except a few military secrets, which he later informed the US Embassy in Moscow he would tell to the Soviet Union, America's enemy in those depths of the Cold War.

- He delighted in arguing with and demeaning officers. He was twice convicted at courts martial, and forced to stand at attention in the brig for 48 days. He was a lousy Marine and the Corps was pleased to grant his request for early release. That substandard service was the greatest accomplishment of his life. He thereafter always carried with pride the wallet card certifying that he had "honorably served on active duty"; it was in his pocket when he was arrested in Dallas four years later.

- Upon receiving an early discharge from active duty on the fraudulent grounds of helping his mother, he raced to Moscow, expecting a glorious welcome and fine life in Marxism. Instead, he was received with great suspicion. After he avoided expulsion with a show of suicide, the Soviets decided it might be a tiny victory to keep him, but where he could do no harm, so he was sent to unimportant Minsk to shape metal in a factory.

- Isolated, he learned from his mother in 1962 that the Marines instigated and completed a process in 1960 to throw him out of the Corps because of "unfitness", with an undesirable discharge, the middle of five grades. Either Marguerite or Lee mistakenly said it was the worst, dishonorable, and that's how Lee thereafter always thought of it and described it.

- The day he received that terrible news, he wrote an appeal to John Connally *"since you are a resident of Ft. Worth as I am."* He thought Connally was Secretary of the Navy, having no way to know in isolated Minsk that he'd resigned to run for governor of Texas. His letter contained the direct threat *"I shall employ all means to right this gross mistake or injustice to a boni-fied U.S. citizen and ex-service man."*

- He received only a two-sentence reply, coldly offering no sympathy but merely sending his appeal to the new SecNav. The campaign envelope with that brush-off featured a large grinning image of Connally's face. Marina said Lee was infuriated, and we may be certain he carried that hateful personified image the rest of his short life.

- His mother, seeking news of Lee in the USSR, had gone to Washington, asked for a personal meeting with President Kennedy on his sixth day in office, and was mollified by a meeting at the State Department with the top experts on Russia. Lee, inheriting her demands for undue respect and attention, wrote to the Navy Secretary but received letters from ever-lower ranks of officers, finally from a mere Lieutenant.

- Realizing his mistake in defecting into a bleak life in Byelorussia without honor or rewards, he returned to the US, accompanied by the only positive results of his 2¾ years there, a lovely wife and new daughter. Expecting media attention at home, he found that he was a forgotten non-entity, impoverished, forced to accept help from his good brother and to work at low-paying entry-level jobs — when hired after lying about his not-honorable discharge.

- On his fourth day in the US, he mailed his lengthy final appeal to the Discharge Review Board of a military branch where he had not even served, the Navy. Only six weeks later he asked for a progress report, and was told to be patient.

- Eighteen months after learning of the bad discharge, thirteen months after mailing his final appeal, he received a form letter with typing in the blanks, denying his appeal. There was no possible recourse, he was stuck forever with the Undesirable Discharge. We know it was important to him because he had the despicable, denigrating certificate in his tiny rented room on the day he was arrested for killing a police officer.
- With no particular skills, he was hired for a series of entry-level jobs, always falsely stating he had served honorably in the Marines. Marina was warmly welcomed into a Russian émigré community, but her friends learned to dislike Lee for his terrible attitudes, then had specific reason to despise him when it became apparent to all that he was taking out his frustrations by ever-worse beatings of Marina. She moved in with a series of friends and he began the new normal of their marriage, living alone in cheap rooming houses.
- Oswald embarked upon desperate quests. He mail-ordered a small pistol, then a powerful military rifle. Only 16 days after the rifle arrived, he fired at ultra-right General Edwin Walker, missing by about an inch. Encouraged by Marina to get out of Dallas, he moved to New Orleans, was fired for inattention to a menial job and was arrested for street brawling in favor of Fidel Castro. Marina left him alone, returning to Texas to live with a truly good soul, Ruth Paine. The Oswalds never again lived together.
- Then his ultimate stupidity and rejections came when he bused to Mexico City and appealed to Cuban and Russian embassies for visas to enter their countries. He was seen as a loose cannon — literally when pulling out a pistol while desperate with the Russians! — and sent packing. He retreated to Dallas, not even promptly informing Marina.
- He got his final job through a happenstance neighborhood ladies chat, $1.25/hour as a temporary order puller at the Texas School Book Depository, five weeks before it was announced that President Kennedy would ride by directly in front of that building.
- He asked to visit Marina at Ruth's the weekend before the shooting, but was told to stay away. His marriage hit its ultimate low when his wife learned she could not even phone him because he was living under a false name at his rooming house.
- On Monday, November 18, it was evident to all that Kennedy's motorcade must pass by the front of the Depository. That was then featured in both Dallas newspapers on Tuesday, November 19. Lee Oswald read newspapers brought into the TSBD, then discarded by his co-workers. On a day between Monday and Wednesday he knew with absolute certainty that President Kennedy would be in front of his building, and *did nothing*.
- The Wednesday papers announced that Governor John Connally would ride in JFK's car. Lee read that on Thursday morning and *sprang into action*. Having no car and not knowing how to drive, he had only one evening to go to the rooming house for his pistol, or go to a gun shop to buy a full fill of bullets for the rifle, or get the rifle. That he could do only one of the three is strong evidence that he learned of his target on that Thursday.
- He asked a co-worker for a ride to Ruth's house that evening, where Marina lived and the rifle was hidden in the garage. This was to be his first-ever non-weekend trip there. During the afternoon he estimated his rifle's size and made a paper bag to conceal it.
- That evening, his arrival was a surprise to Marina and Ruth. He attempted to cozy up to Marina, begging her to move to an apartment with him, but was coldly and firmly rejected. He went to bed alone, after which Ruth found the garage light on and knew he must have been in there for some reason. Marina said nothing on getting into bed or upon seeing him get up to practice dry firing the rifle, aiming at Ruth's TV set.

- On Friday, November 22, 1963 — an ordinary date that will burn into national memory a few hours later — he put a long paper bag into the car, then hurried it into the Depository.
- During the morning, on the sixth floor where he was the primary worker because of the book orders he specialized in filling, he arranged tall stacks of book cartons to create a shield, to keep any who arrived on the floor from seeing the front corner window that best overlooked both Houston and Elm Streets.
- He declined to join co-workers who left to watch the motorcade pass, staying alone on the sixth floor, between his wall of cartons and the great view from his chosen window.
- He and his rifle were seen by people waiting to see the President, but were not perceived as alarming. One woman clearly saw him looking directly down the one-block length of Houston Street as JFK's car turned onto it and drove toward him.
- For a long 21 seconds, the limousine approached nearer and nearer with Kennedy sitting high and unprotected, an easy shot getting better by the second. *Oswald did nothing*. Seeing the geometry of the car and his from-the-front view blocked by a tinted windshield with upturned visors, a tall agent, and especially by the unique handrail just behind the front seat, one can understand the reason Oswald did nothing; he was unable to find the target he was looking for — John Connally — low and out of sight in a jump seat.
- When the Lincoln arrived below Lee and turned 120° left onto Elm, he was first able to see Connally, but could not shoot then because the target was too nearly straight down; he could not fire because of his only-partly-open window and its protruding ledge.
- As soon as the car was in position to be sighted with the rifle, probably through the 4-power scope, possibly with its open sights — we don't know which — he fired three rapid shots.
- The first shot went through the branches of an oak tree hiding the car. It may have been deflected, or perhaps simply missed because of his haste to fire while he could not see his target through the leaves. The bullet hit Elm Street's pavement behind Kennedy, sending up grains that blasted the side of his face. The heavy slug then continued its flight to the southwest until it hit a curb near the Triple Underpass, sending up another blast, concrete particles, wounding bystander Jim Tague on cheek and chin.
- The second shot, fired when Kennedy and Connally were in a direct line with the bullet's path, went through Kennedy's neck, then through Connally's chest and wrist, finally stopping in his thigh. He almost died, and if an inch different, he would have.
- The third shot, fired after Connally had been pulled down to the left by his Nellie, but as Kennedy continued to sit strangely bolt upright, blew off the top-right of Kennedy's head in a memorably ugly pink cloud of blood and brain.
- Oswald hurried across the sixth floor to the stairway in the opposite corner, hiding the rifle in a prepared crevasse between stacks of cartons. He went down stairs to the second floor, was stopped by the first police officer into the building, but was quickly identified as an employee by the superintendent and was free to go.
- He hastened out the front door, down the steps, walked left along Elm Street and boarded a bus headed for his rooming house. When the trip became hopeless because of traffic jammed in the area of the shooting, he walked to a taxi and rode to his rooming house, hurried to his room, put his revolver into his belt and hurried out. Note well his haste to the pistol. He could not do that before the shooting for the important reason that he didn't know he would need it until he read on Thursday that Connally would be in front of him on Friday.

- An excellent description having been broadcast on police radio, he was stopped by patrol Officer J.D. Tippit, whom he wounded, then executed with a bullet fired into the brain.
- Observed by many witnesses as he hurried away, he attracted the attention of a shoe store clerk who saw him duck into a movie theatre without paying. A phone call brought police to surround the theatre. Identified by the shoe salesman, Oswald was arrested with a brief struggle. He was downtown in Dallas Police HQ at 2 PM, only 90 minutes after he killed Kennedy, 45 minutes after he killed Tippit.

••• OSWALD'S ANGER MAY HAVE BEEN EVEN WORSE •••

Oswald in Minsk wrote to his Senator from Texas (page 75), "... I beseech you , Senator Tower , to rise the question ..." of why the Soviets had not granted him an exit visa. There is a question this author must "rise" before closing the book.

I know as fact that Lee Oswald blamed John Connally for not using his authority as Secretary of the Navy, or even as recently-resigned ex-Secretary, to command or influence the Marine Corps to expunge the hated undesirable discharge and return his status to honorable. Although Connally's decision to not get involved is understandable, testimony in Chapter 16 – REGARDING CONNALLY from several who knew Oswald amply demonstrates that Lee's hatred stemmed from Connally's not taking the action for which he had pleaded.

Here's what I have never known: In his isolation in Minsk, carefully selected by cautious Soviet authorities because it was an out-of-touch backwater, did Oswald believe that Connally had played a part in the original decision to issue the undesirable discharge?

The first evidence of that decision was the 8 March 1960 SpeedLetter from the Marine Commandant to Oswald's reserve command (page 46) to discharge him for being "unfit", which required "undesirable" status. With Lee in Minsk knowing nothing about the process, the letters were sent, the hearings were held, the board met, the decision was made — while Dwight D. Eisenhower was President and William B. Franke, risen through the Pentagon bureaucracy, was the Secretary of the Navy until John Kennedy became President. Connally replaced Franke in 1961, so he played no role in the 1960 discharge downgrade.

The question is, did Lee Oswald know that? Connally's bright wife Nellie didn't know it! In her life memoir, she wrote that her husband had, indeed, signed the "dishonorable" discharge! See page 592. No! It was not dishonorable — though Lee always said it was — and Connally did not sign it. Definitive written testimony from an educated man, George De Mohrenschildt, said that Lee complained to him that "Connally signed this undesirable discharge" (page 488). We can never probe that to be absolutely certain whether Oswald truly believed that Connally was largely responsible for the discharge. De Mohrenschildt killed himself shortly after writing his memorandum about Lee's complaint, and Oswald himself was quickly silenced by Jack Ruby, the impetuous executioner.

Could Oswald's enmity have been not only because Connally refused to help reverse the discharge, but also because Lee believed, like Nellie, that John Connally had in fact played a role by signing it in the first place, then refused Oswald's appeal to do the honorable thing and correct his "mistake or injustice"? It's a strong possibility, but we will never know.

••• ••• •••

••• Best evidence, written by Oswald in his notebook •••

The facts and analyses on the preceding five pages are circumstantial, reasoning from events and their timings to discern what they must mean, in the manner of the master of deduction, Sherlock Holmes: If the dog did not bark, then whoever came into the stable must have been well-known to him; If Oswald did not have his pistol, then he must not have known of a need for it until it was too late to fetch both the must-have rifle and the should-have pistol.

Chapter 20 – Obstruction of Best Evidence reveals strong direct evidence of what Oswald intended. The FBI gathered evidence for the Warren Commission, which then printed

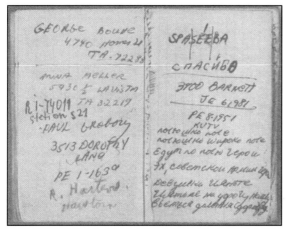

important items in its 26 volumes of *Hearings*. Here, reduced, is the 13th of 52 photos of Oswald's notebook,[3450] first displayed on this book's page 544 then full-page-width on 546.

Chapter 20 is the product of testimony by a good, honest, sharp-minded Special Agent retired from the Secret Service, Mike Howard. He told what Oswald printed in the notebook, on a page that was then torn from the book after it left his possession in Texas and before it was photographed in D.C. Considering what he and fellow agent Charles Kunkel saw on the page before it went missing, Mike and this author and others suspect FBI Director J. Edgar Hoover had the page removed.

Mike and Chuck had several days to study the notebook at the Inn of the Six Flags, with this list reconstructed through Mike's vivid memory of exact words and sequence.[3451]

They realized (page 547) that THE VICE PRESIDENT was former V.P. Nixon. Then all the pieces fit: Oswald shot at Walker (131) and Connally (192), had attempted to go shoot Nixon (132), and had written a note threatening Hosty (163). As they sent the notebook to the FBI's HQ in Washington, they looked forward to seeing the evaluation of this page's clear and stark "kill list" of conservatives and enemies. Both were surprised when the Warren *Report* said nothing about it, and then shocked when the *Hearings* showed the image above, after this page had been removed — neither noticed nor investigated by the Warren Commission.

Mike has lectured about this for years,

[other notes about other matters]

I WILL KILL [here is a bloody
JOHN CONNALLY dagger]

GENERAL WALKER

I WILL KILL JAMES HOSTY

THE VICE PRESIDENT

[other notes about other matters]

and now, here in this book, as James Reston, Jr. assesses, "Mike Howard's decisive evidence will go up in lights. It's been a 50 year quest on his part."[3452]

••• ••• •••

The tragedy explained here was a nearly unbelievable blow, arriving without any warning on the weekend before Thanksgiving 1963. The world slowed, as if in a nightmare, while history was made. For this author, then 24, the most memorable image was the brave widow, a child on each hand, following her dead husband up the stairway into the Capitol as we cried.[3453]

••• Difficult Questions if he Intended to Shoot Kennedy •••

For more than a half-century the general belief has been that Lee Harvey Oswald must have intended to shoot and kill President John Fitzgerald Kennedy, because, of course, that is what he accomplished. There has been no compelling reason to think otherwise — except among those few who have wondered about the absence of motive.

The Warren Commission, of which this author has always thought very highly, answered all questions except the important one of intent: *why?* They attributed Oswald's action to perhaps a general dislike of government. But if that had been the case, why would he take it out on Kennedy, a man whom he had told so many people he greatly admired?

That's only one of at least a dozen disparities. Now that this book has presented many heretofore unnoted or unexamined facts that testify politically, psychologically or physically about Oswald's intent and motive, these are the more salient questions anyone must now answer — all of them! — in order to assert that his intent was to shoot Kennedy:

- First, consider the physical geometry shown in Chapter 14 – TOO CLOSE TO CALL, and acknowledge that it is logically impermissible in this case to reason backward from result to intent. Connally was severely wounded and nearly died, Kennedy died quickly — but the result could easily have been the other way. Who died was determined by the difference between aiming at the top instead of the bottom of a moving, receding penny, 22 feet away, as calculated on page 444. Please, begin your reasoned approach by acknowledging that Oswald's intent cannot be deduced except by evaluating evidence other than the result.

- Before the shooting in November, the April attempt to kill ultra-right-wing retired General Edwin Walker in Dallas was unsolved. Then Marina Oswald told authorities that Lee had done it, handing them facts that demonstrated his guilt, confirmed by analysis of the slug that had missed by only an inch because of an unseen muntin, a divider of window panes. Analyst Carl Oglesby in *Who Killed JFK?* pointed out the incongruity in Lee's attempt to shoot Walker: "Oswald's alleged 'capacity for violence' does not explain why he would kill two men as politically diverse as JFK and Walker. Marina testified that Oswald praised JFK but called Walker a 'fascist', 'compared [him] to Adolf Hitler' and remarked that 'if someone had killed Hitler in time it would have saved many lives.'" [3454] Admitting that Oswald was interested and somewhat astute in his knowledge of politics, and considering the spectrum of beliefs shown in Chapter 17 – POLITICAL PROCLIVITY, how can one explain that a man who had attempted to kill Walker, his natural enemy, would then also attempt to murder Kennedy, his greatly-admired natural ally?

- As do many of us, Lee Oswald commented frequently on the character and actions of the President of the United States. Chapter 15 – REGARDING KENNEDY cites 109 quotations of Oswald saying something about JFK. After removing 36 duplicates because more than one person heard the same thing, and another 27 that are essentially neutral, there are 46 that express some opinion. One was judged to be at least somewhat negative. Forty-five were clearly favorable, positive. Why would Oswald shoot Kennedy, whom he had regularly evaluated and given an amazingly good 45-to-1 ratio of favorability?

- Most of us talk with some regularity about our president, but much less frequently about our governor. Chapter 16 – REGARDING CONNALLY assembled all 17 pieces of testimony from those who heard Oswald say anything about Connally. Then 5 were eliminated as duplicates, 1 was neutral, leaving 11 with thumbs-up or thumbs-down.

One, testified by Marina, was favorable <u>before</u> Oswald learned of the undesirable discharge, and was later rebuffed when he asked Connally to help "right this gross mistake or injustice". Ten of the eleven opinions were definitely unfavorable. After a man quickly fires at two in-line people in a moving car, how can one believe he did not mean to kill the one disliked by a 10-to-1 ratio?

- The Sherlock Holmes story of *Silver Blaze*, featuring the dog who revealingly did nothing in the night, underscores the importance of unusual non-happenings — strong evidence that may be deduced from noting things that did not happen, or whose delays testify strongly. Any who wish to argue that it was Oswald's intent to shoot Kennedy will find a great task in answering the next four questions, all of the *"why didn't he?"* persuasion:

- Chapter 18 – CONNALLY WILL RIDE argues with force that Lee Oswald must have had a strong desire to take vengeance on John Connally, evidenced by the exceptionally clear fact that he leapt into action only upon reading in the newspaper, on Thursday morning, November 21, 1963, that Governor Connally would be in the motorcade, sitting in the presidential limousine with the Kennedys. Now those facts much be explained by any who would like us to believe that the target was Kennedy. The first of three related questions is very simple to ask, and difficult to answer: Knowing sometime between Saturday, November 16 and Wednesday, November 20, that Kennedy would ride in front of his workplace, why didn't Lee Oswald get a ride from Wes Frazier to Irving, to fetch his rifle from Ruth Paine's garage on Monday, Tuesday or Wednesday?

- Well, there might be an answer to that question, along the lines that Lee did not want to take a chance of anyone finding the rifle in some hiding place in the Book Depository, so it was more prudent to not bring it until the day it was needed. Okay, that's an answer that may work. But, if that was his choice, then there must be answered the question of the rifle that was not fully loaded — which sounds like the title of a Sherlock Holmes adventure. As documented in Chapter 12 – THE RIFLE, his Mannlicher-Carcano was an Italian Carcano rifle with a German Mannlicher-designed mechanism. It was intended to hold six bullets in the automatic-feed clip, plus one seated in the chamber, ready to fire before the six in the clip fed up to the chamber; it was designed for seven cartridges. Ammunition for the rifle was stocked by dealers in Dallas. The question that needs to be answered if Kennedy was the target: Knowing that Kennedy was coming, and the rifle was about to be used for the most important purpose imaginable, why did Oswald take it to the Depository holding only four cartridges? Why did he not, in preparation for an ultimate act of assassinating a president, on Monday or Tuesday or Wednesday evening, buy a box of cartridges and load the rifle to its capacity as he had undoubtedly been trained by the Marines, to be ready for any unforeseen eventuality? Why a rifle only 4/7 loaded with ammunition?

- There are probably no good answers to the two preceding questions, but it gets worse — here comes a tougher one. As soon as he had fired and hidden his rifle, what was Oswald's immediate imperative and action? It was to rush to his rented room in Oak Cliff to grab his pistol. He did nothing else there, tucked the revolver into his belt and hurried past the boardinghouse manager to the street. Nobody knows what he planned to do next — perhaps it was simply to get away from the area ASAP — but it is resoundingly certain because of his rush to the boardinghouse that he considered the pistol to be essential to whatever he had in mind. So, if you would argue that Kennedy was the intended target, then answer this: Perhaps reserving Thursday evening to pick up the rifle in Irving, and knowing on Monday or Tuesday or Wednesday that Kennedy would ride by on Friday, why, oh why, as he bused <u>every day</u> to/from his room in the boardinghouse, didn't Lee bring the pistol back to the TSBD, so he'd have it there to use in his getaway? That, as we used to say in the old days of radio quiz programs, is "The Sixty-Four Dollar Question"!

- If those three *"why didn't"* questions aren't enough, Chapter 19 – THE SHOT NOT TAKEN was dedicated to one more. In this author's opinion after a half-century of considertion, this is both the most significant and the easiest to ask. Anyone who believes that Oswald's intent was to shoot Kennedy must answer: Why, when the limo was coming almost directly toward him, with a steady azimuth and absolutely no obstructions, no problems with sun angle, no other difficulties, and was getting larger and easier by the second — why didn't Lee take the easy shot or shots at Kennedy who sat high and unprotected? Why didn't he fire when the Lincoln had absolutely no path for escape after the first crack of a bullet — where the car could not turn around or dive into non-existent cover? Why did he wait to fire until Kennedy was moving away, under the canopy of a sheltering oak, getting smaller by the second? Why did he wait until the limousine could make an escape by accelerating straight ahead, or turning left or right onto empty grass? Putting all those into one question: Why THE SHOT NOT TAKEN?

- Then there's the question that was first asked, to my knowledge, by Norman Mailer in his excellent study *Oswald's Tale: An American Mystery*. Chapter 11 – FAILURE, a proud product of the engineer-author of this book, listed the most significant events in Lee's life. Of those 171, 16 were successes and 155 were failings. Why, as Mailer asked, should one believe that a hopeless failure through all his life would, at the moment of ultimate challenge, the assassination of a president surrounded by his best-in-the-history-of-the-world protection, be successful? *Why?*

- Finally, to end this set of questions that must be answered by any who advocate that Lee Oswald meant to shoot President Kennedy, consider the revelation by retired Secret Service Special Agent Mike Howard of the incriminating direct evidence, the "kill list" Lee had printed into his pocket notebook. With that list beginning "I WILL KILL JOHN CONNALLY" and its writer putting a bullet through Connally that came within an inch of killing him, how can anyone believe that his target was someone else in that limousine?

••• ••• •••

The official statement in Dallas by acting presidential press secretary Mac Kilduff came only one hour after the shooting: "President John F. Kennedy died at approximately 1:00 o'clock, Central Standard Time, today, here in Dallas. He died of a gunshot wound in the brain. I have no other details regarding the assassination of the President." [3455] And so we first heard it and have consistently thought of it until now — the assassination of President Kennedy.

Kennedy's close friend Ben Bradlee observed that, like wisdom and good whiskey, knowing truth takes time: "Journalism is just the first rough draft of history, the late Philip Graham once said to emphasize the reality that journalists never could know the whole truth right away. The whole truth takes too long to emerge, and it consists of too many strands for a single journalist to catch in the single sitting that daily journalism demands." [3456]

In *The Making of the President 1960*, the first in his best-selling quadrennial series, Theodore H. White explained the historian's need for time. He had been present in the hotel suites when John Kennedy chose Lyndon Johnson to run for the Vice-Presidency, and had full access to the "principals, emissaries, intermediaries".[3457] The problem was not any lack of testimony, but quite the opposite, too many disparate stories told by those who were there. Within months of the event he wrote: "What can be reconstructed now out of the contemporary recall of those present must be seen as a fog-shrouded range of facts in which occasionally one peak or another appears at a given hour of the day, but whose connection to the next peak of facts is obscured by the clouds in between. History is always best written generations after the event, when cloud, fact and memory have all fused into what can be accepted as truth, whether it be so or not." [3458]

James Reston, *New York Times*man father of James Jr. frequently quoted in this book, wrote in his autobiography *Deadline: A Memoir*: "When President Kennedy was murdered in 1963, it was at first suspected that this was part of a Communist conspiracy ... ".[3459] Yes, so most of us started at "Oswald-the-Communist shot Kennedy." When we learned that he was a silly pretend-Marxist misfit, we moved along to "Oswald-the-misfit shot Kennedy." We were smugly content, having corrected our original misperception. Thereby complacent, until now we have not moved a final step to the reality, "Oswald-the-inept shot Kennedy by mistake."

In the search to understand the murder of John F. Kennedy, getting even simple facts to lie down and be documented has proven difficult and time consuming. Forests have been cut down for paper to print innumerable theories, most with outlandish conspiracies. But none except the simplest — Oswald did it, alone — have risen to the level of beyond-any-doubt. And that one conclusion — Oswald did it, alone — has not been widely accepted and believed, I judge, primarily because it does not answer the simple question, "Why?". There being no evidence of any motive for Oswald to assassinate Kennedy, thinking people knew something was wrong, so have stopped short of belief, have not found peace, continued to wonder.

Your author is contrite that it has taken fifty-one years since he first thought to lay out his evidence, analyses and conclusion. From 1964 to now, I expected either of two opposite circumstances: New evidence would emerge to argue that my basic thesis was incorrect or unsupportable — or the opposite: Someone else would come to the same conclusion and write a definitive book. Neither has happened, so in 2016, this at last is a full presentation of what I believe to be the ugly truth of what happened on November 22, 1963.

Coming to the understanding that Oswald killed Kennedy by mistake may be intellectually satisfying — knowing a truth — but it is also equally emotionally disturbing — recognizing that the truth is a tragedy.

The other researcher who wrote a book like this, James Reston, Jr., whose title *The Accidental Victim: JFK, Lee Harvey Oswald, and the Real Target in Dallas* foretold that it demonstrates that the intended victim was Connally, not Kennedy, wrapped up with this simple but profound observation: "Few now seem willing to countenance the truth that the key to the greatest crime of 20th-century American history can be found in the loose wires and weak connections in the confused mind of a pathetic American outcast." [3460]

Among all reflections on John Fitzgerald Kennedy's death, the most deservedly famous was written 25 years later by William Manchester, author of *Death of a President*:
"[I]f you put the murdered President of the United States on one side of a scale and that wretched waif Oswald on the other side, it doesn't balance. You want to add something

weightier to Oswald. It would invest the President's death with meaning, endowing him with martyrdom. He would have died for something." [3461]

That was quoted more fully in chapter 9, beginning discussion of the need by many to include a conspiracy to help balance things. Now that the solid facts of the matter have been presented, we have come to the inescapable conclusion that Lee Oswald did it, alone, and that through his usual ineptness, he only wounded his target, but killed the President he revered. Manchester was correct in noting that JFK should have died for something with more meaning. It is now our tragedy to know a more ugly truth: he died for <u>less</u> than what we've believed!

Prosecutor Vincent Bugliosi judged correctly that Oswald's shooting of President Kennedy is the most important murder in the entire history of our country. [3462] Jacqueline Kennedy prophetically voiced the killing's most central and tragic point, telling William Manchester in an interview for his book *The Death of a President*: "What was so terrible was the thought that it had been an accident, a freak, that an inch or two here, a moment or two there would have reversed history." [3463]

Others who wrote about the Kennedy assassination went into detail about the planning, reasons and politics for JFK's visit to Dallas, which I find completely unnecessary. All that was necessary was to put Connally into an open vehicle, sitting directly in line with some other person sufficiently important to have a motorcade in Dallas. Kennedy, himself, was not important. In his place could have been John Wayne, Groucho Marx, or Queen Elizabeth II. If it played out as on that Friday in 1963, Oswald would fire at, and wound, the Governor — and kill an actor, comedian, or royalty. Then the misguided would spend years investigating why Oswald so hated pretend-cowboys, cigar-smoking wise guys, or British royalty.

Albert Einstein explained some complicated things, in part because he relied on his guiding maxim: "Everything should be made as simple as possible, but not simpler!" [3464] For the shooting in Dallas, there are only two alternative explanations from which to choose:

(1) Oswald intended to shoot **Kennedy**, so:
    (a) Although he very much liked Kennedy, he decided to kill him;
    (b) When the motorcade route for Kennedy was published, he did nothing;
    (c) Two days later, on Thursday, he asked for a ride to retrieve the rifle, but because
        of that unnecessary delay, did not fully load the rifle and did not get his pistol;
    (d) As the car drove toward him and he had a clear shot at Kennedy, he did nothing;
    (e) Only after the car turned, passed and the shot became difficult, he began to fire.

(2) Oswald intended to shoot **Connally**, so:
    (a) When the motorcade route for Kennedy was published, he did nothing;
    (b) As soon as he read that Connally would be in the car, he immediately asked for a
        ride to get the rifle, but had no time to fully load it, or to fetch his pistol;
    (c) When the car drove up Houston, where he could not see Connally, he did nothing;
    (d) As soon as the car turned and he saw Connally, he aimed and fired.

Which of those explanations is complex and artificial, and which is simple and natural?

••• ••• •••

As noted several times, we lost direct ability to absolutely prove why Oswald did what he did because he died before he could reveal what was in his mind, and before his guilt could be determined by our gold standard, trial by jury. Nevertheless, it is quite possible to become certain of his intent by understanding the overwhelming circumstantial evidence we have.

There's nothing wrong with that. Please consider this explanation given to the jury by prosecutor Vincent Bugliosi in the famous *Helter Skelter* double-murder case:

> "Circumstantial evidence is not ... like a chain. You could have a chain spanning the Atlantic Ocean from Nova Scotia to Bordeaux, France, consisting of millions of links, and with one weak link that chain is broken. Circumstantial evidence, to the contrary, is like a rope. And each fact is a strand of that rope. And as the prosecution piles one fact upon another we add strands and we add strength to that rope. If one strand breaks — and I'm not conceding for a moment that any strand has broken in this case — but if one strand does break, the rope is not broken. The strength of the rope is barely diminished. Why? Because there are so many *other* strands of almost steel-like strength that the rope is still more than strong enough to bind these ... defendants to justice. That's what circumstantial evidence is all about." [3465]

And thanks to Secret Service Special Agent Mike Howard, we now also have direct evidence that, added to the circumstantial, most assuredly nails the case beyond any possible doubt.

Robert Oswald says he believes his younger brother Lee acted alone in killing President John F. Kennedy in 1963, but he still doesn't know why. In his book *Lee*, Robert analyzes:

> "The fact that there was no understandable political motivation behind the assassination may be one reason so many critics have been unable to accept the central conclusion of the Warren Commission—that there was one assassin, and that his name was Lee Harvey Oswald." [3466]

> "While I am ready at any time to be convinced that the Warren Commission was wrong, I have not yet read or heard or seen any evidence that has shaken my conviction that Lee and Lee alone fired the shots that wounded Governor Connally and killed the President of the United States." [3467]

> "When the report appeared in September, I realized that the Commission had failed completely in its search for the answer to the question, Why? ... After offering a few generalizations that could apply to many people who have never committed any serious crime, the Commission confessed: 'the Commission does not believe that it can ascribe to him any one motive or group of motives.'" [3468]

In her introduction to the 1977 paperback edition of Priscilla Johnson McMillan's bestselling biography *Marina and Lee*, Marina wrote: "When I visited Lee for the last time in that jail in Dallas, I saw fear in his eyes which he tried to cover up with bravado. But I also saw that he was carrying a burden of regret heavier than he or anyone could bear." [3469] This statement is stronger evidence than we might obtain from any other source. Marina is the only person who both knew Lee so well and also interacted with him during the few hours he lived after the shooting. We must accept as factual her observation of his heavy burden of regret. It is not important to decipher whether that was regret for killing Kennedy when he had no desire to do so, or regret for failing to kill Connally when that was his intent. Either way, his regret argues that Oswald failed, and only accomplished his usual, the opposite of what he had intended.

The President I miss was lovingly summed up by the woman closest to him for twelve years — much longer than his marriage to Jacqueline — Evelyn Lincoln, his personal secretary in both the Senate and the White House. She was in Dallas that morning of November 22, and in her memoir wrote this remembrance of her last sight of him leaving Love Field:

"I looked over to the President's car, which had started to move. There [he was], his right hand in the air, waving at the people as he drove by. I can still see that scene — the President waving as he passed that vast and friendly crowd of people. And I'll always remember him that way because that's the way he really was: a handsome, young, energetic President who had grace and intellect, a man who loved every inch of his country, especially its people." [3470]

It is important to say to those not then alive that it mattered greatly that President Kennedy was murdered before he served his full term — more likely two terms totaling eight years. There are many significant reasons why the too-early death of that specific man made a difference.

To many in my generation, Kennedy was a natural leader because we understood and embraced his goals when, 43, he replaced Eisenhower, a 70-year-old complacent conservative grandfather figure. When JFK and his "new generation of leadership, born in this century" [3471] died, so did the affiliation, interest and dreams of many young people. The outpouring of grief begun that dreadful weekend in 1963 foreshadowed and morphosed into the intense turmoil of the next ten years, the famously riotous, combative 60s, never equaled.

If he had not died, America probably would have avoided most of the Vietnam disaster, deadly there and divisive at home. The AP wrote: "Seven weeks before President Kennedy was assassinated on Nov. 22, 1963, American military leaders were planning a withdrawal of U.S. forces from South Vietnam ... 'All planning will be directed towards preparing RVN (Republic of Vietnam) forces for the withdrawal of all U.S. special assistance units and personnel by the end of calendar year 1965'" [3472] This was to be a monumentally important policy shift that did not happen because Oswald murdered Kennedy.

In the Oval Office on October 2, 1963, 51 days before his death, General Maxwell Taylor and Secretary of Defense Robert McNamara presented to President Kennedy what they had learned during their just-completed Vietnam trip. [3473]

The week after that meeting, Kennedy approved plans to withdraw 1,000 military personnel by the end of 1963, and to train Vietnamese so that by the end of 1965, functions performed by U.S. military could be carried out by them. That done, it was thought possible to withdraw the bulk of U.S. personnel. The U.S. was to be out of Vietnam in 1965.

The President's decision was recorded by his National Security Advisor: [3474]

```
                    THE WHITE HOUSE
                      WASHINGTON


TOP SECRET - EYES ONLY                 October 11, 1963




NATIONAL SECURITY ACTION MEMORANDUM NO. 263

TO:        Secretary of State
           Secretary of Defense
           Chairman of the Joint Chiefs of Staff

SUBJECT:  South Vietnam

At a meeting on October 5, 1963, the President considered the
recommendations contained in the report of Secretary McNamara
and General Taylor on their mission to South Vietnam.

The President approved the military recommendations contained
in Section I B (1-3) of the report, but directed that no formal
announcement be made of the implementation of plans to with-
draw 1,000 U.S. miltitary personnel by the end of 1963.

After discussion of the remaining recommendations of the report,
the President approved an instruction to Ambassador Lodge which
is set forth in State Department telegram No. 534 to Saigon.


                              McGeorge Bundy



Copy furnished:
    Director of Central Intelligence
    Administrator, Agency for International Development


                                    cc:
                                       Mr. Bundy ✓
                                       Mr. Forrestal
                                       Mr. Johnson
                    TOP SECRET - EYES ONLY  NSC Files
```

Six weeks later, idealist-realist Kennedy died. Political Lyndon Johnson, with little sense of history or world view, did not consent to lose or withdraw from a war without victory, so he chose to escalate and throw in ever more troops. No-nonsense President Gerald Ford pulled us out ten years later. 58,300 Americans died in Vietnam,[3475] plus more at home in the killing by the National Guard at Kent State University and many other confrontations. In tragic reality, all were victims of Oswald's inept killing of the wrong man.

That is what I have learned and think you should know about Lee Harvey Oswald — what he intended, what he did, and why we and our world are different because the hate-filled, inept, would-be assassin of John Connally accidentally killed our President with a near miss. That is our tragic truth.

©1963 MAULDIN
Chicago Sun-Times   3476

REFERENCES CITED

> "I'll write a book and the title of it will be *One and One Make Two* or *This and That*. Oh, I could write three books or five books! I could write books and *books* on what I know and what I have researched."
> — **Marguerite Oswald** [3477]

BOOKS ABOUT OSWALD and the assassination of John Kennedy could fill a large bookstore. Some opine there are thousands, but one critic, years ago, huffily said there were only 660! Many were not useful to this author, so are listed in the next appendix, **NOT CITED**. Below are the 253 specific sources used for references. Books printed in other versions may have content and pagination different from those listed here. (hc) is a hardcover, (sc) a full-size soft-cover "trade press" book, and (pb) is a smaller paperback, also known as a "pocketbook".

Government Reports

Report of the President's Commission on the Assassination of President John F. Kennedy and 26 accompanying volumes of Hearings and Exhibits. Washington, D.C.: U.S. Government Printing Office, 1964 (hc). The **NOTES** in this book use two reference abbreviations:

WR The single-volume report, popularly known as the ***Warren Report***, published in dark-blue hardcover on September 27, 1964. Because an interested reader can readily obtain this volume, I cite both the *Report* and the accompanying volumes when materials are in both. There may be differences, because the *Report* was simplified and condensed. For example, this book's citation "*WR* 710, typed from *WCH* XIX 713" directs you to page 710 of the *Warren Report* for a typed version of Oswald's letter to Connally, and to page 713 in volume XIX of the accompanying volumes for the handwritten original. Without this double referencing, if seeking the photo of his letter, you would begin your search at the last line of the typed version on *Warren Report* page 710: "Moscow, USSR.[766]" The *Report's* page 864 has "NOTES TO PAGES 702-711", where one finds "766. Folsom DE 1, p. 65." This is a reference to page 65 of Deposition Exhibit number 1 from USMC Lt. Col. Allison G. Folsom. I hope to save you from "Yes, but where's that?" with the simpler and doubled references in this book's **NOTES**.

The one-volume ***Warren Report*** has been condensed, expanded, annotated and reprinted in many forms. The original can be found in many used bookstores. Exact reprints of the GPO volume with its pagination (page numbering) recently in print include those by Barnes & Noble Books (hc) and by St. Martin's Press (hc and sc).

WCH *Hearings Before the President's Commission on the Assassination of President Kennedy* is the title of all 26 volumes (numbered I through XXVI) published soon after the *Warren Report*, on November 23, 1964. They are much more than "hearings". Norman Mailer reflected in 1995: "For two generations of Americans, the Warren Commission's twenty-six volumes of Hearings and Exhibits have become a species of Talmudic text ... To the novelists and historians who may be writing on this subject a hundred years from now, the twenty-six volumes will also be a Comstock Lode ...".[3478] To guide the reader through the thick set, these abbreviations are used in my **NOTES**:

Testimony by witnesses before the Commission or its staff is printed in Volumes I through XV. The presentation of testimony is generally "in the order in which it was taken".[3479] An alphabetic index of testifying witnesses is in Volume XV on pages 753 - 801. I recommend you read the Foreword in Volume I (on pages v and vi) to know how testimony was taken and what is dependable.

Oswald's letter to Connally (trail begun on the previous page) was brought to the Commission by Marine Lt. Col. Allison G. Folsom. His testimony is on pages 303 to 311 of Volume VIII, so would be cited in this book's **NOTES** as *WCH* VIII 303-311.

Commission Exhibits. "Exhibits introduced in connection with the testimony before the Commission in numerical order" begin in Volumes XVI through XVIII. The exhibits in those 3 volumes are numbered CE 1 (Lee's note for Marina on the evening he went to shoot Walker) through CE 1053-F (Secret Service budget requests). Then there are "Other exhibits introduced before the Commission in numerical order" in Volumes XXII through XXVI. These range from CE 1054 (photos of three men who were in a lineup with Oswald) through CE 3154 (descriptions of CEs 1054 - 3154, the Commission's last-minute attempt at an index). An index in Volume XV on pages 801 - 813, in numeric sequence by Commission Exhibit Number, shows where to look in Volumes I through XV for testimony about each exhibit.

Deposition Exhibits. "Exhibits introduced in connection with sworn depositions and affidavits, grouped alphabetically by name of witness" are in Volumes XIX through XXI. An index in Volume XV on pages 813 - 826, alphabetic by name of the witness who introduced an exhibit, shows where in Volumes I through XV they handed-in or testified about each exhibit.

Deposition Exhibits are where we see Oswald's handwritten letter to Connally, the 65th piece of paper deposited by Marine Colonel Folsom, so the Commission's caption under the letter is "FOLSOM EXHIBIT NO. 1 — Continued (p. 65)". Its location is cited in this book's **NOTES** as "*WR* 710 (the typed version in the *Warren Report*), typed from *WCH* XIX 713".

HSCA *Final Report of the Select Committee on Assassinations, U.S. House of Representatives, Ninety-fifth Congress, Second Session: Summary of Findings and Recommendations*. House Report 95-1828. Washington, D.C.: U.S. Government Printing Office, 1979. The government-printed report is essentially impossible to find at any price. If you require the report in book form, find a fat paperback whose cover shows a 1979 price of $3.95, but now sells for about ten times that: *The Final Assassinations Report: Report of the Select Committee on Assassinations, U.S. House*

of Representatives. Foreword by Tom Wicker. Introduction by G. Robert Blakey. New York: Bantam Books, 1979 (pb). Because that little book contains extraneous matter and uses different pagination (page numbering) than the government report, I suggest you will have it much easier if you consult the original report on this Web site:
http://history-matters.com/archive/jfk/hsca/report/html/HSCA_Report_0001a.htm
which is the source of the report text included in this book. Page numbers in this book's endnotes are those printed on the report's pages, which, unfortunately, differ from the index ("click to go to page") numbering on the Web site.

HSCAH ***Hearings before the Select Committee on Assassinations of the U.S. House of Representatives, Ninety-Fifth Congress, Second Session.*** The committee set up two subcommittees, one on John F. Kennedy, the other on Martin Luther King, Jr. The Kennedy subcommittee published twelve volumes of Hearings and Appendices about its investigation, printed in Washington, D.C. by the U.S. Government Printing Office in 1979. Like the printed report, these volumes are essentially impossible to find in any printed form, but are free on this Web site that has better print capabilities than others:
http://www.aarclibrary.org/publib/contents/hsca/contents_hsca_vols.htm
The first five volumes, numbered I through V, transcribe the hearings and testimony.

HSCAHA ***Appendix to Hearings before the Select Committee on Assassinations of the U.S. House of Representatives, Ninety-Fifth Congress, Second Session.*** The subcommittee on Kennedy also published seven volumes of Appendices, numbered VI through XII, available from the same Web site as the hearings, above.

Official Congressional Directory for the use of the United States Congress, 89th Congress, 1st Session, beginning January 4, 1965. (Referred to in notes as ***Congressional Directory***.) Washington: United States Government Printing Office, 1965 (hc).

SSCIA ***Final Report of the Select Committee to Study Governmental Operations with respect to Intelligence Activities, United States Senate, Ninety-Fourth Congress, Second Session: Book V: The Investigation of the Assassination of President John F. Kennedy: Performance of the Intelligence Agencies***. Washington, D.C.: U.S. Government Printing Office, 1976. The source of the report text included in my book is Web site http://www.intelligence.senate.gov/pdfs94th/94755_V.pdf Page numbers in my book's endnotes are those printed on the report's pages, which differ slightly from the index ("click to go to page") numbering on the Web site.

Books

Abrams, Herbert L. ***The President has been Shot: Confusion, Disability, and the 25th Amendment in the Aftermath of the Attempted Assassination of Ronald Reagan***. New York: W. W. Norton, 1992 (hc).

Ackerman, Kenneth D. ***Dark Horse: The Surprise Election and Political Murder of President James A. Garfield***. New York: Carroll & Graf, 2003 (hc).

Adelson, Alan. ***The Ruby-Oswald Affair***. Seattle: Romar Books, 1988 (hc).

American Heritage, The Editors of. *RFK: His Life and Death*. Narrative by Jay Jacobs. With an eyewitness account of The Last Thirty-six Hours by Kristi N. Witker. New York: Dell, 1968 (pb).

Anthony, Carl Sferrazza. *The Kennedy White House: Family Life and Pictures, 1961–1963*. New York: Touchstone, 2001 (hc).

Ashman, Charles. *Connally: The Adventures of Big Bad John*. New York: William Morrow, 1974 (hc).

Associated Press. *The Torch is Passed*. New York: The Associated Press, 1963 (hc).

Bak, Richard. *The Day Lincoln Was Shot: An Illustrated Chronicle*. Foreword by William Hanchett. Dallas: Taylor Publishing, 1998 (sc).

Baker, Judyth Vary. *Me & Lee: How I Came to Know, Love and Lose Lee Harvey Oswald*. Foreword by Edward T. Haslam. Afterword by Jim Marrs. Walterville, OR: Trine Day LLC, 2010 (hc).

Ballard, Robert D., with Michael Hamilton Morgan. *Collision with History: The Search for John F. Kennedy's PT 109*. Washington, D.C.: National Geographic, 2002 (hc).

Belzer, Richard. *UFOs, JFK, and Elvis: Conspiracies You Don't Have To Be Crazy To Believe*. New York: Ballantine Books, 1999 (hc).

Benson, Michael. *Encyclopedia of the JFK Assassination*. New York: Checkmark Books, 2002 (sc).

Benson, Michael. *Who's Who in the JFK Assassination: An A-to-Z Encyclopedia*. New York: Citadel Press, 1993 (sc).

Beran, Michael Knox. *The Last Patrician: Bobby Kennedy and the End of American Aristocracy*. New York: St. Martin's Press, 1998 (hc).

Beschloss, Michael R., editor. *Taking Charge: The Johnson White House Tapes, 1963-1964*. New York: Touchstone, 1998 (sc).

Bishop, Jim. *The Day Kennedy Was Shot*. New York: Funk & Wagnalls, 1968 (hc).

Bishop, Jim. *The Day Lincoln Was Shot*. New York: Gramercy Books, no date (hc).

Blaine, Gerald, with Lisa McCubbin. *The Kennedy Detail: JFK's Secret Service Agents Break Their Silence*. New York: Gallery Books, 2010 (hc).

Blair, Clay, Jr. *The Strange Case of James Earl Ray: The Man Who Murdered Martin Luther King*. New York: Bantam Books, 1969 (pb).

Bloomgarden, Henry S. *The Gun: A "Biography" of the Gun That Killed John F. Kennedy*. New York: Grossman, 1975 (hc).

Bradlee, Benjamin C. *Conversations with Kennedy.* New York: W. W. Norton, 1975 (hc).

Branch, Taylor. *Parting the Waters: America in the King Years, 1954-63.* New York: Simon & Schuster, 1989 (hc).

Brands, H. W. *Andrew Jackson: His Life and Times.* New York: Doubleday, 2005 (hc).

Bravin, Jess. *Squeaky: The Life and Times of Lynette Alice Fromme.* New York: St. Martin's Press, 1997 (hc).

Brussell, Mae, compiler. *The Last Words of Lee Harvey Oswald.* On pages 47-52 in Wallechinsky, David, and Irving Wallace. *The People's Almanac #2.* New York: Bantam Books, 1978 (pb).

Buchanan, Thomas G. *Who Killed Kennedy?* New York: G. P. Putnam's Sons, 1964 (hc).

Bugliosi, Vincent. *Four Days in November: The Assassination of President John F. Kennedy.* New York: W. W. Norton, 2007 (sc).

Bugliosi, Vincent. *Outrage: The Five Reasons Why O.J. Simpson Got Away with Murder.* New York: Island Books, 1997 (pb).

Bugliosi, Vincent. *Reclaiming History: The Assassination of President John F. Kennedy.* New York: W. W. Norton, 2007 (hc) including a CD-ROM containing its Endnotes and Source Notes.

Bugliosi, Vincent, with Curt Gentry. *Helter Skelter: The True Story of the Manson Murders.* New York: Bantam Books, 1975 (pb).

Callahan, Bob. *Who Shot JFK?: A Guide to the Major Conspiracy Theories.* New York: Fireside Books, 1993 (pb).

Canal, John A. *Silencing the Lone Assassin.* St. Paul, MN: Paragon House, 2000 (hc).

Cannon, James. *Time and Chance: Gerald Ford's Appointment with History.* New York: HarperCollins, 1994 (hc).

Carman, Harry James, Harold Coffin Syrett, and Bernard W. Wishy. *A History of the American People.* Vol. II. New York: Knopf, 1961 (hc).

Clancy, Tom. *Marine: A Guided Tour of a Marine Expeditionary Unit.* New York: Berkley Books, 1996 (sc).

Clark, Champ, and the Editors of Time-Life Books. *The Assassination: Death of the President.* Alexandria, VA: Time-Life Books, 1987 (hc).

Clarke, James W. *American Assassins: The Darker Side of Politics.* Princeton: Princeton University Press, 1982 (sc).

Cole, Donald B. *The Presidency of Andrew Jackson*. Lawrence, KS: University Press of Kansas, 1993 (hc).

Connally, John, with Mickey Herskowitz. *In History's Shadow: An American Odyssey*. New York: Hyperion, 1993 (hc).

Connally, Nellie, with Mickey Herskowitz. *From Love Field: Our Final Hours with President John F. Kennedy*. New York: RuggedLand, 2003 (hc).

Crawford, Ann Fears, and Jack Keever. *John B. Connally: Portrait in Power*. Austin: Jenkins Publishing Co., 1973 (hc).

Cray, Ed. *Chief Justice: A Biography of Earl Warren*. New York: Simon and Schuster, 1997 (hc).

Cronkite, Walter. *A Reporter's Life*. New York: Alfred A. Knopf, 1996 (hc).

Dallek, Robert. *An Unfinished Life: John F. Kennedy: 1917 - 1963*. Boston: Little, Brown, 2003 (hc).

Daniel, Clifton, editor in chief. *20th Century Day by Day*. Introduction by Arthur M. Schlesinger, Jr. American edition 2000. London: Dorling Kindersley Limited, 2000 (hc).

Douglas, John, and Mark Olshaker. *The Anatomy of Motive: The FBI's Legendary Mindhunter Explores the Key to Understanding and Catching Violent Criminals*. New York: Lisa Drew/Scribner, 1999 (hc).

Douglass, James W. *JFK and the Unspeakable: Why He Died and Why It Matters*. Maryknoll, NY: Orbis Books, 2008 (hc).

Doyle, Sir Arthur Conan. *The Complete Sherlock Holmes*. Garden City, NY: Doubleday & Company, 1930 (hc).

Emerson, Jason. *Giant in the Shadows: The Life of Robert T. Lincoln*. Carbondale and Edwardsville, IL: Southern Illinois University Press, 2012 (hc).

Epstein, Edward Jay. *The Assassination Chronicles: Inquest, Counterplot and Legend*. New York: Carroll & Graf, 1992 (sc).

Epstein, Edward Jay. *Counterplot*. New York: Viking Press, 1969 (hc).

Epstein, Edward Jay. *Inquest: The Warren Commission and the Establishment of Truth*. Introduction by Richard H. Rovere. New York: Viking Press, 1966 (hc) and New York: Bantam Books, 1966 (pb) for its "Special Appendix" not in the hc.

Epstein, Edward Jay. *Legend: The Secret World of Lee Harvey Oswald*. New York: Reader's Digest Press / McGraw-Hill, 1978 (hc).

Fay, Paul B., Jr. *The Pleasure of His Company*. New York: Harper & Row, 1966 (hc) There are two versions. Page references here are to the "FIRST EDITION", which has its photos printed on glossy paper.

Fetherling, George. Research associate: Christopher Martin. *The Book of Assassins: A Biographical Dictionary from Ancient Times to the Present*. New York: John Wiley & Sons, 2001 (hc).

Feynman, Richard P., as told to Ralph Leighton. *What Do You Care What Other People Think? Further Adventures of a Curious Character*. New York: Bantam, 1989 (pb).

The Final Assassinations Report: See HSCA in Government Publications at the top.

Ford, Gerald R. *A Time to Heal: The Autobiography of Gerald R. Ford*. New York: Harper & Row, 1979 (hc).
Ford, Gerald R., and John R. Stiles. *Portrait of the Assassin*. New York: Simon and Schuster, 1965 (hc).

Fries, Chuck, and Irv Wilson with Spencer Green. *We'll Never Be Young Again: Remembering the Last Days of John F. Kennedy*. Los Angeles: Tallfellow Press, 2003 (hc).

Gaines, Ann Graham. *Andrew Jackson: Our Seventh President*. Mankato, MN: The Child's World, 2009 (hc).

Galanor, Stewart. *Cover-Up*. New York: Kestrel Books, 1998 (hc).

Garner, Joe. *We Interrupt This Broadcast: The Events That Stopped Our Lives – from the Hindenburg Explosion to the Death of John F. Kennedy Jr*. Foreword by Walter Cronkite. "Updated second edition" including two audio CDs. Naperville, IL: Sourcebooks, 2000 (hc).

Garrison, Jim. *On the Trail of the Assassins*. New York: Warner Books, 1988 (pb).

Gertz, Elmer. *Moment of Madness: The People vs. Jack Ruby*. Preface by Jon R. Waltz. Chicago: Follett Publishing, 1968 (hc).

Goodwin, Doris Kearns. *Team of Rivals: The Political Genius of Abraham Lincoln*. New York: Simon & Schuster Paperbacks, 2006 (sc).

Groden, Robert J. *The Killing of a President: The Complete Photographic Record of the JFK Assassination, the Conspiracy, and the Cover-Up*. Foreword by Oliver Stone. New York: Viking Studio, 1994 (sc).
Groden, Robert J. *The Search for Lee Harvey Oswald: A Comprehensive Photographic Record*. Introduction by Cyril H. Wecht. New York: Penguin Studio, 1995 (hc).

Hampton, Wilborn. *Kennedy Assassinated! The World Mourns: A Reporter's Story*. New York: Scholastic Inc., 1997 (pb).

Hartogs, Renatus, and Lucy Freeman. *The Two Assassins*. New York: Thomas Y. Crowell, 1965 (hc).

Healey, Thomas S. *The Two Deaths of George Wallace: The Question of Forgiveness*. Montgomery, AL: Black Belt Press, 1996 (hc).

Hecht, Jamey. *Limousine, Midnight Blue: Fifty Frames from the Zapruder Film*. Los Angeles: Red Hen Press, 2009 (sc).

Hersh, Seymour M. *The Dark Side of Camelot*. Boston: Back Bay Books, 1998 (sc).

Heymann, C. David. *RFK: A Candid Biography of Robert F. Kennedy*. New York: Dutton / Penguin Group, 1998 (hc).

Higham, Charles. *Murdering Mr. Lincoln: A New Detection of the 19th Century's Most Famous Crime*. Beverly Hills, CA: New Millennium Press, 2004 (hc).

Hill, Clint, with Lisa McCubbin. *Mrs. Kennedy and Me*. New York: Gallery Books, 2012 (hc).

Hirsch, Phil, editor. *The Kennedy War Heroes*. New York: Pyramid Books, 1962 (pb).

Holland, Max. *The Kennedy Assassination Tapes*. New York: Alfred A. Knopf, 2004 (hc).

Hosty, James P., Jr., with Thomas C. Hosty. *Assignment: Oswald*. New York: Arcade Publishing, 1996 (hc).

Howe, Randy. *Flags of the Fifty States: Their Colorful Histories and Significance*. Second Edition. Guilford, CT: Lyons Press, 2010 (hc).

HSCA   Abbreviation in NOTES for *Final Report of the Select Committee on Assassinations, U.S. House of Representatives ... Summary of Findings and Recommendations* listed and described in Government Publications at the top.

HSCAH   Abbreviation in NOTES for *Hearings before the Select Committee on Assassinations of the U.S. House of Representatives*. See Government Publications at the top.

HSCAHA   Abbreviation in NOTES for *Appendix to Hearings before the Select Committee on Assassinations of the U.S. House of Representatives*. See Government Publications at top.

Huffaker, Bob, Bill Mercer, George Phenix, and Wes Wise. *When The News Went Live: Dallas 1963*. Foreword by Dan Rather. Lanham, MD: Taylor Trade Publishing, 2004 (hc).

Hunter, Stephen, and John Bainbridge, Jr. *American Gunfight: The Plot to Kill Harry Truman, and the Shoot-out That Stopped It*. New York: Simon & Schuster, 2005 (hc).

Hurt, Henry. *Reasonable Doubt: An Investigation into the Assassination of John F. Kennedy*. New York: Henry Holt and Company, 1987 (sc).

James, Ann. *The Kennedy Scandals & Tragedies*. Lincolnwood, IL: Publications International, 1991 (sc).

James, Marquis. *The Life of Andrew Jackson*. Garden City, NY: Garden City Publishing, 1940 (hc).

Jansen, Godfrey. *Why Robert Kennedy Was Killed: The Story of Two Victims*. Foreword by Abdeen Jabara. New York: The Third Press of Joseph Okpaku Publishing Co., 1970 (hc).

Johnson, Lyndon Baines. *The Vantage Point: Perspectives of the Presidency 1963–1969*. New York: Holt, Rinehart, Winston, 1971 (hc).

Jovich, John B., editor. *Reflections on JFK's Assassination: 250 Famous Americans Remember November 22, 1963*. (no place given): Woodbine House, 1988 (sc).

Kaiser, David. *The Road to Dallas: The Assassination of John F. Kennedy*. Cambridge, MA: Belknap Press of Harvard University Press, 2008 (hc).

Kaiser, Robert Blair. *R.F.K. Must Die! A History of the Robert Kennedy Assassination and Its Aftermath*. New York: Grove Press, 1970 (pb).

Kantor, Seth. *The Ruby Cover-Up*. New York: Zebra Books, 1978 (pb).

Kaplan, John, and Jon R. Waltz. *The Trial of Jack Ruby*. New York: Macmillan, 1965 (hc).

Kennedy, John F. *Profiles in Courage*. Memorial Edition with forward by Robert F. Kennedy. New York: Harper & Row, 1964 (pb).

Kennedy, Robert F. *Thirteen Days: A Memoir of the Cuban Missile Crisis*. Introductions by Robert S. McNamara and Harold Macmillan. New York: Signet Books, 1969 (pb).
Kennedy, Robert F. *To Seek a Newer World*. New York: Bantam Books, 1968 (pb).

Kenney, Charles. *John F. Kennedy: The Presidential Portfolio: History as told through the collection of the John F. Kennedy Library and Museum*. Introduction by Michael Beschloss. Includes audio CD of phone and dictation. New York: PublicAffairs, 2000 (hc).

Keogh, Pamela Clarke. *Jackie Style*. Introduction by Valentino. New York: HarperCollins, 2001 (hc).

Kerr, Andy. *A Journey Amongst the Good and the Great*. Annapolis, MD: Naval Institute Press, 1987 (hc).

Khrushchev, Nikita. *Khrushchev Remembers: The Last Testament*. Translated and edited by Strobe Talbott. Foreword by Edward Crankshaw. Introduction by Jerrold L. Schechter. Boston: Little, Brown & Co., 1974 (hc).

King, Stephen. *11/22/63: A Novel*. New York: Scribner, 2011 (hc).

Klaber, William, and Philip H. Melanson. *Shadow Play: The Untold Story of the Robert F. Kennedy Assassination*. New York: St. Martin's Paperbacks, 1998 (pb).

Koch, Thilo. *Fighters for a New World*. New York: G.P. Putnam's Sons, 1969 (hc).

Kunhardt, Dorothy Meserve, and Philip B. Kunhardt, Jr. *Twenty Days: A Narrative in Text and Pictures of the Assassination of Abraham Lincoln and the Twenty Days and Nights that followed – The Nation in Mourning, the Long Trip Home to Springfield*. Foreword by Bruce Catton. Secaucus NJ: Castle Books, 1993 (hc).

Kunhardt, Philip B., Jr., editor. *LIFE in Camelot: The Kennedy Years*. Boston: Little, Brown, 1988 (hc).

Lambert, Patricia. *False Witness: The Real Story of Jim Garrison's Investigation and Oliver Stone's Film JFK*. New York: M. Evans and Company, 1998 (hc).

Lane, Mark. *Plausible Denial: Was the CIA Involved in the Assassination of JFK?* New York: Thunder's Mouth Press, 1992 (sc).

Lane, Mark. *Rush to Judgment*. Augmented edition with author's added "Lastword" and "Fact or Fiction: *JFK*". New York: Thunder's Mouth Press, 1992 (sc).

Larson, Kate Clifford. *The Assassin's Accomplice: Mary Surratt and the Plot to Kill Abraham Lincoln*. New York: Basic Books, 2008 (hc).

Lasky, Victor. *J.F.K.: The Man and the Myth*. New York: Macmillan, 1963 (hc).

Leamer, Laurence. *The Kennedy Men: 1901-1963: The Laws of the Father*. New York: HarperCollins, 2001 (hc).

Leaming, Barbara. *Mrs. Kennedy: The Missing History of the Kennedy Years*. New York: Simon & Schuster, 2002 (sc).

Lesher, Stephan. *George Wallace: American Populist*. Reading, MA: Addison-Wesley, 1993 (hc).

Leslie, Warren. *Dallas Public and Private*. New York: Avon Books, 1964 (pb).

Lewis, Lloyd. *The Assassination of Lincoln: History and Myth*. Introduction by Mark E. Neely, Jr. Previously published under the title of *Myths after Lincoln*. New York: MJF Books, no date but 1994 or later (hc).

Life Books, The Editors of. *The Day Kennedy Died: 50 Years Later LIFE Remembers the Man and the Moment*. New York: Life Books, 2013 (hc).

Lifton, David S. *Best Evidence: Disguise and Deception in the Assassination of John F. Kennedy*. New York: Macmillan, 1980 (hc).

Lincoln, Evelyn. *My Twelve Years with John F. Kennedy*. New York: Bantam Books, 1966 (pb).

Livingstone, Harrison Edward. *High Treason 2: The Great Cover-Up: The Assassination of President John F. Kennedy*. New York: Carroll & Graf, 1992 (hc).

Livingstone, Harrison Edward. *Killing Kennedy: And the Hoax of the Century*. New York: Carroll & Graf, 1995 (hc).

Livingstone, Harrison Edward. *Killing the Truth: Deceit and Deception in the JFK Case*. New York: Carroll & Graf, 1993 (hc).

Livingstone, Harrison Edward, and Robert J. Groden. *High Treason: The Assassination of JFK & the Case for Conspiracy*. With author's preface to the 1998 edition and 160 pages of addendum. New York: Carroll & Graf, 1998 (sc).

Lorant, Stefan. *The Glorious Burden: The American Presidency.* New York: Harper & Row, 1968 (hc).

Mailer, Norman. *Oswald's Tale: An American Mystery*. New York: Random House, 1995 (hc).

Mailer, Norman. *The Time of Our Time*. New York: Random House, 1998 (hc).

Mallon, Thomas. *Mrs. Paine's Garage: and the Murder of John F. Kennedy*. New York: Pantheon Books, 2002 (hc).

Manchester, William. *The Death of a President*. New York: Harper & Row, 1967 (hc).

Manchester, William. *One Brief Shining Moment*. Boston: Little, Brown & Company, 1983 (hc).

Marsico, Katie. *Andrew Jackson*. Tarrytown, NY: Marshall Cavendish Benchmark, 2011.

Marvin, Richard. *The Kennedy Curse*. New York: Belmont Books, no date given (pb).

Matthews, James P., and Ernest Schwork, editors. *The Complete Kennedy Saga! Four Books In One!* Los Angeles: Associated Professional Services, no date: about 1965 (sc).

McCarthy, Dennis V. N., with Philip W. Smith. *Protecting the President: The Inside Story of a Secret Service Agent*. New York: Dell Publishing, 1987 (pb).

McKnight, Gerald D. *Breach of Trust: How the Warren Commission Failed the Nation and Why*. Lawrence, KS: University Press of Kansas, 2005 (hc).

McMillan, Priscilla Johnson. *Marina and Lee*. New York: Harper & Row, 1977 (hc). (The 1978 Bantam Books pb has the same text, but its 16-page photo section is different.)

Meacham, Jon. *American Lion: Andrew Jackson in the White House*. New York: Random House, 2008 (hc).

Meagher, Sylvia. *Accessories After The Fact: The Warren Commission, The Authorities, and The Report*. Preface by Senator Richard S. Schweiker. Introduction by Peter Dale Scott. New York: Vintage Books, 1992 (sc).

Meagher, Sylvia. *Subject Index to the Warren Report and Hearings & Exhibits*. New York: Scarecrow Press, 1966 (hc).

Millard, Candice. *Destiny of the Republic: A Tale of Madness, Medicine, and the Murder of a President*. New York: Doubleday, 2011 (hc).

Moldea, Dan E. *The Killing of Robert F. Kennedy: An Investigation of Motive, Means, and Opportunity*. New York: W. W. Norton, 1995 (hc).

Moore, Jim. *Conspiracy of One: The Definitive Book on the Kennedy Assassination*. Introduction by Carl A. Henry. Rev. ed. Fort Worth: The Summit Group, 1991 (sc).

Morrow, Robert D. *Betrayal*. New York: Warner Books, 1976 (pb).

Myers, Dale K. *With Malice: Lee Harvey Oswald and the Murder of Officer J.D. Tippit*. Second Edition. Milford, MI: Oak Cliff Press, 2013 (hc). This expanded blue-cover edition has 863 pages, with augmented information on Tippit and his family, compared to the first edition of 1998 that had a red cover and 702 pages.

Nechiporenko, Oleg M. *Passport to Assassination: The Never-Before-Told Story of Lee Harvey Oswald by the KGB Colonel Who Knew Him*. Trans. from Russian by Todd P. Bludeau. New York: Birch Lane, 1993 (hc).

Nelson, Scott Reynolds. *A Nation of Deadbeats: An Uncommon History of America's Financial Disasters*. New York: Alfred A. Knopf, 2012 (hc).

Newman, Albert H. *The Assassination of John F. Kennedy: The Reasons Why*. New York: Clarkson N. Potter, 1970 (hc).

Newman, John. *Oswald and the CIA*. New York: Carroll & Graf, 1995 (hc).

Newseum, The, with Cathy Trost and Susan Bennett. *President Kennedy Has Been Shot*. Includes CD of radio and television broadcasts, narrated by Dan Rather. Naperville, IL: Sourcebooks, 2003 (hc).

New York Times. *Page One: Major Events 1900-1997 as Presented in The New York Times*. New York: Galahad Books, 1997 (hc).

New York Times. *The Witnesses: The Highlights of Hearings before the Warren Commission on the Assassination of President Kennedy*. Introduction by Anthony Lewis. New York: Bantam Books, 1964 (pb). (Edited selections from the Warren Commission Hearings. This is worth finding even if you can access the 26 volumes. It compiles the most important testimony and exhibits, and best of all, is presented in a logical sequence.)

Nixon, Richard M. *RN: The Memoirs of Richard Nixon*. New York: Grosset & Dunlap, 1978 (hc).

Oates, Stephen B. *With Malice Toward None: A Biography of Abraham Lincoln*. New York: HarperCollins Perennial, 2011 (sc).

O'Donnell, Kenneth P., and David F. Powers with Joe McCarthy. *Johnny, We Hardly Knew Ye*. New York: Pocket Books, 1973 (pb).

Oglesby, Carl. *Who Killed JFK?* Berkeley: Odonian Press, 1992 (pb).

Onassis, Jacqueline Kennedy. *Jacqueline Kennedy: Historic Conversations on Life with John F. Kennedy*. Interviews with Arthur M. Schlesinger, Jr., 1964. Foreword by Caroline Kennedy. Introduction and Annotations by Michael Beschloss. New York: Hyperion, 2011 (hc with 8 CDs of recordings of conversations).

O'Reilly, Bill. *Kennedy's Last Days: The Assassination That Defined a Generation*. New York: Henry Holt and Company, 2013 (hc).

O'Reilly, Bill, and Martin Dugard. *Killing Kennedy: The End of Camelot*. New York: Henry Holt and Company, 2012 (hc).

O'Sullivan, Shane. *Who Killed Bobby? The Unsolved Murder of Robert F. Kennedy*. New York: Sterling Publishing, 2008 (hc).

Oswald, Robert L., with Myrick and Barbara Land. *Lee: A Portrait of Lee Harvey Oswald by His Brother*. New York: Coward-McCann, 1967 (hc).

Pearson, Hugh. *When Harlem Nearly Killed King: The 1958 Stabbing of Dr. Martin Luther King, Jr*. New York: Seven Stories Press, 2002 (hc).

Perret, Geoffrey. *Jack: A Life Like No Other*. New York: Random House, 2001 (hc).

Picchi, Blaise. *The Five Weeks of Giuseppe Zangara: The Man Who Would Assassinate FDR*. Chicago, IL: Academy Chicago Publishers, 1998 (hc).

Pinsker, Matthew. *Lincoln's Sanctuary: Abraham Lincoln and the Soldiers' Home*. New York: Oxford University Press, 2003 (hc).

Pipes, Daniel. *Conspiracy: How the Paranoid Style Flourishes and Where It Comes From*. New York: Free Press, 1997 (hc).

Posner, Gerald. *Case Closed: Lee Harvey Oswald and the Assassination of JFK*. Revised edition with author's note. New York: Anchor Books, 1994 (sc).

Posner, Gerald. *Killing the Dream: James Earl Ray and the Assassination of Martin Luther King, Jr*. New York: Random House, 1998 (hc).

Prouty, L. Fletcher. *JFK: The CIA, Vietnam, and the Plot to Assassinate John F. Kennedy*. Introduction by Oliver Stone. New York: Citadel Press, 1996 (pb).

Rattenbury, Richard, and Thomas E. Hall. *Sights West: Selections from the Winchester Museum Collection* (revised edition). Cody, Wyoming: Buffalo Bill Historical Center, 1981 (sc).

Rauchway, Eric. *Murdering McKinley: The Making of Theodore Roosevelt's America*. New York: Hill and Wang, 2003 (hc).

Ray, James Earl. *Who Killed Martin Luther King? The True Story by the Alleged Assassin*. Foreword by Jesse Jackson. Preface by Mark Lane. New York: Marlowe & Company, 1997 (sc).

Reston, James. *Deadline: A Memoir*. New York: Random House, 1991 (hc).

Reston, James, Jr. *The Accidental Victim: JFK, Lee Harvey Oswald, and the Real Target in Dallas*. New York: Jointly printed by Zola Books and Assembly! Press, 2013 in "Exclusive History Book Club Edition". Also available from www.zolabooks.com as an e-book in an .epub file readable by Adobe Digital Editions.

Reston, James, Jr. *The Terrorist's Wife*. Expected to be published in 2016.

Reston, James, Jr. *Collision at Home Plate: The Lives of Pete Rose and Bart Giamatti*. New York: Edward Burlingame Books, 1991 (hc).

Reston, James, Jr. *The Last Apocalypse: Europe at the Year 1000 A.D.* New York: Anchor Books, 1999 (pb).

Reston, James, Jr. *The Lone Star: The Life of John Connally*. New York: Harper & Row, 1989 (hc).

Roper, Professor Jon. *The Complete Illustrated Guide to the Presidents of America*. Wigston, Leicestershire, UK: Lorenz Books (Anness Publishing Ltd.), 2013 (hc).

Russo, Gus. *Live by the Sword: The Secret War Against Castro and the Death of JFK*. Baltimore: Bancroft Press, 1998 (hc).

Rust, Zad. *Teddy Bare: The Last of the Kennedy Clan*. Belmont, Massachusetts: Western Islands, 1971 (sc).

Sabato, Larry J. *The Kennedy Half-Century: The Presidency, Assassination, and Lasting Legacy of John F. Kennedy*. New York: Bloomsbury, 2013 (hc).

Sagan, Carl. *Contact*. New York: Pocket Books, 1986 (pb).

Salinger, Pierre. *P.S., A Memoir*. New York: St. Martin's Griffin, 1995 (pb).
Salinger, Pierre. *With Kennedy*. New York: Avon Books, 1967 (pb).

Schaap, Dick. *R. F. K*. Picture Editor: Michael O'Keefe. New York: Signet Books, 1967 (pb).

Schieffer, Bob. *This Just In: What I Couldn't Tell You On TV*. New York: Berkley Books, 2004 (sc).

Schlesinger, Arthur, Jr. *Kennedy or Nixon: Does it make any difference?* New York: Macmillan, 1960 (hc).
Schlesinger, Arthur M., Jr. *A Thousand Days: John F. Kennedy in the White House*. Boston: Houghton Mifflin, 1965 (hc).

Semple, Robert B., Jr., editor. *Four Days in November: The Original Coverage of the John F. Kennedy Assassination by the Staff of The New York Times*. Introduction by Tom Wicker. New York: St. Martin's Press, 2003 (hc).

Shesol, Jeff. *Mutual Contempt: Lyndon Johnson, Robert Kennedy, and the Feud That Defined a Decade*. New York: W. W. Norton, 1997 (pb).

Shvets, Yuri B. *Washington Station: My Life as a KGB Spy in America*. Trans. from Russian by Eugene Ostrovsky. New York: Simon & Schuster, 1994 (hc).

Smith, Sally Bedell. *Grace and Power: The Private World of the Kennedy White House*. New York: Random House, 2004 (hc).

Smith, Walter H. B. *The Book of Rifles*, 3rd edition. Harrisburg, PA: Stackpole, 1963 (hc).
Smith, Walter H. B. *Mannlicher Rifles and Pistols*. Harrisburg, PA: The Military Service Publishing Co., 1947 (hc).
Smith, Walter H. B. *Small Arms of the World*, 6th ed. Harrisburg: Stackpole, 1960 (hc).

Sneed, Larry A. *No More Silence: An Oral History of the Assassination of President Kennedy*. Denton, TX: University of North Texas Press, 1998 (sc).

Sorensen, Theodore C. *Kennedy*. New York: Harper & Row, 1965 (hc).
Sorensen, Theodore C. *The Kennedy Legacy*. New York: Macmillan, 1969 (hc).

Spada, James. *Jackie: Her Life in Pictures*. New York: St. Martin's Press, 2000 (hc).

Specter, Arlen, with Charles Robbins. *Passion for Truth: From Finding JFK's Single Bullet to Questioning Anita Hill to Impeaching Clinton*. New York: HarperCollins, 2000 (hc).

Speer, Lonnie R. *Portals to Hell: Military Prisons of the Civil War*. Mechanicsburg, PA: Stackpole Books, 1997 (hc).

Spieler, Geri. *Taking Aim at the President: The Remarkable Story of the Woman Who Shot at Gerald Ford*. Basingstoke, Hampshire, England: Palgrave-Macmillan, 2008 (hc).

Spignesi, Stephen. *J.F.K. Jr*. Secaucus, NJ: Citadel Press / Carol Group, 1999 (pb).

Spoto, Donald. *Jacqueline Bouvier Kennedy Onassis: A Life*. New York: St. Martin's Press, 2000 (hc).

Stafford, Jean. *A Mother in History*. New York: Pharos Books, 1992 (sc).

Sturdivan, Larry M. *The JFK Myths: A Scientific Investigation of the Kennedy Assassination*. St. Paul, MN: Paragon House, 2005 (sc).

Sullivan, Robert, editor. *The Most Notorious Crimes in American History*. New York: Life Books, 2007 (large hc).

Swanson, James L. *End of Days: The Assassination of John F. Kennedy*. New York: William Morrow, 2013 (hc).

Swanson, James L. *Manhunt: The Twelve-Day Chase for Lincoln's Killer*. New York: HarperCollins, 2006 (hc).

Swanson, James L., and Daniel R. Weinberg. *Lincoln's Assassins: Their Trial and Execution*. Santa Fe, NM: Arena Editions, 2001 (hc).

Thomas, Evan. *Robert Kennedy: His Life*. New York: Simon & Schuster, 2000 (hc).

Thomas, Helen. *Front Row at the White House: My Life and Times*. New York: Lisa Drew/Scribner, 1999 (hc).

Thomas, Helen. *Thanks for the Memories, Mr. President: Wit and Wisdom from the Front Row at the White House*. New York: Lisa Drew/Scribner, 2002 (hc).

Thompson, Josiah. *Six Seconds in Dallas: A Micro-Study of the Kennedy Assassination*. New York: Bernard Geis Associates, 1967 (hc); With 1976 preface by the author: New York: Berkley Medallion, 1976 (pb).

Thornley, Kerry. *Oswald*. Chicago: New Classics House, 1965 (pb).

Time-Life Books, The Editors of. *Assassination: True Crime*. Richmond, VA: Time-Life Books, 1994 (hc).

Time-Life Books, The Editors of. *Turbulent Years: The 60s*. Richmond, VA: Time-Life Books, 1998 (hc).

United Press International: Klagsbrun, Francine, and David C. Whitney, editors. *Assassination: Robert F. Kennedy – 1925-1968*. New York: Cowles, 1968 (hc).

United Press International and American Heritage Magazine. *Four Days: The Historical Record of the Death of President Kennedy*. New York: American Heritage Publishing, 1964 (hc).

Vestal, Bud. *Jerry Ford, Up Close: An Investigative Biography*. New York: Coward, McCann and Geoghegan, 1974 (hc).

Vowell, Sarah. *Assassination Vacation*. New York: Simon & Schuster, 2005 (sc).

Warren, Earl. *The Memoirs of Earl Warren*. New York: Doubleday & Company, 1977 (hc).

Watney, Hedda Lyons. *Jackie O*. Fourth Edition. New York: Tudor Publishing, 1990 (pb).

WCH   Abbreviation in **NOTES** for *Hearings Before the President's Commission on the Assassination of President Kennedy* (the *"Warren Commission Hearings"*), the twenty-six volumes described under Government Publications at the top.

Wecht, Cyril, with Mark Curriden and Benjamin Wecht. *Cause of Death*. New York: Dutton, 1993 (hc).

Weisberg, Harold. *Case Open: The Unanswered JFK Assassination Questions*. (The cover says *The Omissions, Distortions and Falsifications of Case Closed*.) New York: Carroll & Graf, 1994 (pb).

Weisberg, Harold. *Never Again! The Government Conspiracy in the JFK Assassination*. New York: Carroll & Graf, 1995 (sc).

Weisberg, Harold. *Photographic Whitewash: Suppressed Kennedy Assassination Pictures*. Frederick, MD: Harold Weisberg (self published), 1976 (sc).

Weisberg, Harold. *Whitewash: The Report on the Warren Report*. New York: Dell Publishing, 1966 (pb).

White, Theodore H. *America in Search of Itself: The Making of the President 1956-1980*. New York: Warner Books, 1983 (sc).

White, Theodore H. *Breach of Faith: The Fall of Richard Nixon*. New York: Dell Publishing, 1976 (pb).

White, Theodore H. *The Making of the President*
1960. New York: Atheneum, 1961 (hc);
1964. New York: Atheneum, 1965 (hc);
1972. New York: Bantam Books, 1973 (pb).

Wilson, Francis. *John Wilkes Booth: Fact and Fiction of Lincoln's Assassination*. Boston: Houghton Mifflin, 1929 (hc).

Winik, Jay. *April 1865: The Month That Saved America*. New York: HarperCollins, 2001 (hc).

Wofford, Harris. *Of Kennedys and Kings: Making Sense of the Sixties*. With added Foreword by Bill Moyers. Pittsburgh, PA: Univ. of Pittsburgh Press, 1992 (sc).

Wolff, Perry. *A Tour of the White House with Mrs. John F. Kennedy*. New York: Dell Publishing, 1963 (pb).

WR Abbreviation in NOTES for *Report of the President's Commission on the Assassination of President John F. Kennedy* (the *"Warren Report"*) under Government Publications, at top.

Zirbel, Craig I. *The Texas Connection*. New York: Warner Books, 1992 (pb).

Periodicals and Primary Printed Sources

AP is an abbreviation for Associated Press; UPI is for United Press International.

LIFE magazine *and TIME* magazine

The New York Times (National edition unless stated otherwise.)

The Seattle Times (Final edition unless stated otherwise.)

Radio, Television, Films, VHS, DVD and CD-ROM recordings

DVD: *The Day Kennedy Died*. Written and directed by Leslie Woodhead. Narrated by Kevin Spacey. Produced by Finestripe Productions and SNI/SI Networks L.L.C. for Smithsonian Channel and ITV, 2013.

DVD: *JFK: The Final Hours*. National Geographic Channel, 2013.

TV: *Dateline NBC*. Interview of Robert Oswald by Josh Mankowitz in segment titled "My Brother's Keeper", broadcast by NBC-TV on 14 June 1998.

TV: *The Day Lincoln Was Shot*. TNT Original. Script by Tim Metcalf and John Gray, adapted from Jim Bishop's book, broadcast by TNT on 12 Apr. 1998.

TV: *Real History: The Secret KGB JFK Assassination Files*, hosted by Roger Moore, presented by Associated Television International, The Learning Channel, 03 March 2000.

Internet, World Wide Web and Other Sources

Each is specifically defined in section NOTES AND SOURCES that follows the next, NOT CITED.

NOT CITED

> "I said, 'You know, Lee, I am getting ready — I was getting ready to write a book on your so-called defection.' He said, 'Mother, you are not going to write a book.' I said, 'Lee, don't tell me what to do. I cannot write the book now, because, Honey, you are alive and back. But don't tell me what to do.'"
>
> — **Marguerite Oswald** [3480]

THE PREVIOUS SECTION, REFERENCES CITED, lists 253 sources for all NOTES AND SOURCES. In addition to the works listed there, I have read, watched and listened to hundreds of others. Some are excellent for their intended purposes; many have helped shape my understanding, but contain nothing specific to the matter at hand. Others, especially those hawking conspiracy theories, are wastes of time and trees. I list them all below for any who may ask, "But did you consider the startling revelations in ... ?". Yes! — I read, considered, loved some, disliked others, and have not cited these 199 as sources or foundations for this book:

Adler, Bill, editor. *The Kennedy Wit*. New York: Citadel Press, 1964 (hc).

Adler, Bill, editor. *More Kennedy Wit*. New York: Bantam Books, 1965 (pb).

Andersen, Christopher. *The Day John Died*. New York: William Morrow, 2000 (hc); New York: Avon Books, 2001 (sc).

Andersen, Christopher. *Jackie After Jack: Portrait of the Lady*. New York: Warner Books, 1999 (hc).

Andrew, Christopher, and Vasili Mitrokhin. *The Sword and the Shield: The Mitrokhin Archive and the Secret History of the KGB*. New York: Basic Books, 1999 (hc).

Baldrige, Letitia. *In The Kennedy Style: Magical Evenings in the Kennedy White House*. Menus and recipes by White House Chef René Verdon. New York: Doubleday, 1998 (hc).

Baldrige, Letitia. *A Lady, First: My Life in the Kennedy White House and the American Embassies of Paris and Rome*. New York: Viking, 2001 (hc).

Balsiger, David, and Charles E. Sellier, Jr. *The Lincoln Conspiracy*. Los Angeles: Schick Sunn Classic Books, 1977 (pb).

Bartlett, W.B. *The Assassins: The Story of Medieval Islam's Secret Sect*. Thrupp, Stroud, Gloucestershire, England: Sutton Publishing, 2001 (hc).

Bishop, Jim. *A Day in the Life of President Kennedy*. New York: Bantam Books, 1964 (pb).

Blakey, G. Robert, and Richard N. Billings. *The Plot to Kill the President*. New York: Times Books, 1981 (hc); republished as *Fatal Hour: The Assassination of President Kennedy by Organized Crime*. New York: Berkley Books, 1992 (pb).

Block, Herbert. *Straight Herblock*. New York: Simon and Schuster, 1964 (hc).

Blundell, Nigel. *Fact or Fiction? Unsolved Crimes*. London: Sunburst Books, 1995 (hc).

Bradlee, Benjamin C. *A Good Life: Newspapering and Other Adventures*. New York: Touchstone, 1996 (sc).
Bradlee, Benjamin. *That Special Grace*. Philadelphia: J.B.Lippincott, 1964 (hc).

Brown, Walt. *The People v. Lee Harvey Oswald*. New York: Carroll & Graf, 1992 (sc).
Brown, Walt. *Treachery in Dallas*. New York: Carroll & Graf, 1995 (hc).

Burns, James MacGregor. *John Kennedy: A Political Profile*. New York: Avon Books, 1960 (pb).

Burns, Robert P. *A Theory of the Trial*. Princeton, NJ: Princeton University Press, 1999 (hc).

Carr, William H. A. *JFK: The Life and Death of a President*. New York: Lancer Books, 1964 (pb).

Cornwell, Gary. *Real Answers: The True Story told by Gary Cornwell, Deputy Chief Counsel for the U.S. House of Representatives Select Committee on Assassinations, in charge of the investigation of the John F. Kennedy Assassination*. Spicewood, TX: Paleface Press, 1998 (hc).

Craig, John R., and Philip A. Rogers. *The Man on the Grassy Knoll*. New York: Avon Books, 1992 (pb).

Crenshaw, Charles A., with Jens Hansen and J. Gary Shaw. *JFK: Conspiracy of Silence*. Introduction by John H. Davis. New York: Signet, 1992 (pb).

Cyriax, Oliver. *Crime: An Encyclopedia*. North Pomfret, VT: Trafalgar Square, 1996 (sc).

Dallas, Rita, with Jeanira Ratcliffe. *The Kennedy Case*. New York: Popular Library, 1973 (pb).

Damore, Leo. *The Cape Cod Years of John Fitzgerald Kennedy*. New York: Four Walls Eight Windows, 1993 (sc).

Davis, John H. *The Bouviers: Portrait of an American Family*. New York: Avon Books, 1970 (pb).
Davis, John H. *The Kennedy Contract: The Mafia Plot to Assassinate the President*. New York: HarperPaperbacks, 1993 (pb).
Davis, John H. *Mafia Kingfish: Carlos Marcello and the Assassination of John F. Kennedy*. New York: Signet, 1989 (pb).

Davison, Jean. *Oswald's Game*. Foreword by Norman Mailer. New York: W. W. Norton, 1983 (hc).

DeGregorio, William A. *The Complete Book of U.S. Presidents*. Fifth Edition. New York: Gramercy Books, 2001 (hc).

DeLillo, Don. *Libra*. New York: Penguin Books, 1989 (pb).

de Toledano, Ralph. *R.F.K.: The Man Who Would Be President*. New York: Signet, 1968 (pb).

DiEugenio, James. *Destiny Betrayed: JFK, Cuba, and the Garrison Case*. Introduction by Zachary Sklar. New York: Sheridan Square Press, 1992 (hc).

Donovan, Robert J. *The Assassins*. New York: Popular Library, 1964 (pb).
Donovan, Robert J. *PT 109: John F. Kennedy in World War II*. Introductory letter by President Kennedy. New York: Crest, 1961 (pb).

Douglas, John, and Mark Olshaker. *The Cases That Haunt Us: From Jack the Ripper to JonBenet Ramsey, the FBI's Legendary Mindhunter Sheds Light on the Mysteries That Won't Go Away*. New York: Lisa Drew/Scribner, 2000 (hc).

Duffy, James P., and Vincent L. Ricci. *The Assassination of John F. Kennedy: A Complete Book of Facts*. New York: Thunder's Mouth Press, 1992 (sc).

Duffy, James R. *Conspiracy: Who Killed JFK?* Introduction by Alfonse M. D'Amato. New York: S.P.I. Books, 1992 (pb).

Evans, Peter. *Nemesis: The True Story: Aristotle Onassis, Jackie O, and the Love Triangle That Brought Down the Kennedys*. New York: ReganBooks of HarperCollins, 2004 (hc).

Fairlie, Henry. *The Kennedy Promise: The Politics of Expectation*. Garden City, NY: Doubleday, 1973 (hc).

Fetzer, James H., editor. *Assassination Science: Experts Speak Out on the Death of JFK*. Chicago: Catfeet Press, 1998 (pb).

Fetzer, James H., editor. *The Great Zapruder Film Hoax: Deceit and Deception in the Death of JFK*. Chicago: Catfeet Press, 2003 (sc).

Fetzer, James H., editor. *Murder in Dealey Plaza: What We Know Now That We Didn't Know Then About the Death of JFK*. Chicago: Catfeet Press, 2000 (sc).

Fleming, Glenn B. *The Two Faces of Lee Harvey Oswald: A Tale of Deception, Betrayal and Murder*. Manchester, England, U.K.: Empire Publications, 2003 (sc).

Fonzi, Gaeton. *The Last Investigation*. New York: Thunder's Mouth Press, 1993 (hc).

Fox, Sylvan. *The Unanswered Questions About President Kennedy's Assassination*. New York: Award Books, 1965 (pb).

Frewin, Anthony. *Sixty-Three Closure*. New York: Four Walls Eight Windows / No Exit Press, 2000 (sc).

Fuhrman, Mark. *Murder in Brentwood*. Foreword by Vincent Bugliosi. Washington, D.C.: Regnery Publishing, 1997 (hc).

Furiati, Claudia. *ZR Rifle: The Plot to Kill Kennedy and Castro*. Translated from Portuguese by Maxine Shaw. Melbourne, Australia: Ocean Press, 1994 (pb).

Garbutt, Paul. *Assassin! From Abraham Lincoln to Rajiv Gandhi*. Shepperton, Surrey, England: Ian Allan Ltd, 1992 (sc).

Giancana, Sam and Chuck. *Double Cross: The Explosive, Inside Story of the Mobster Who Controlled America*. New York: Warner Books, 1992 (hc).

Goodwin, Doris Kearns. *The Fitzgeralds and the Kennedys: An American Saga*. New York: Touchstone, 2001 (sc).

Grimwood, Ken. *Replay*. New York: Ace Books, 1992 (pb).

Groden, Robert J., and Harrison Edward Livingstone. *High Treason: The Assassination of President John F. Kennedy: What Really Happened*. With an article by Col. Fletcher Prouty. New York: Conservatory Press, 1989 (hc). Reprinted as *High Treason: The Assassination of President John F. Kennedy and the New Evidence of Conspiracy*. New York: Berkley Books, 1990 (pb). For a 1998 version, see Livingstone and Groden, below.

Halberstam, David. *The Best and the Brightest*. New York: Random House, 1969 (hc).

Hancock, Larry. *Someone Would Have Talked: Documented! The Assassination of President John F. Kennedy and the Conspiracy to Mislead History*. Southlake, TX: JFK Lancer Productions & Publications, 2006 (hc).

Harrington, William. *Columbo: The Grassy Knoll*. New York: Tom Doherty Associates, 1993 (hc).

Heller, Deane and David. *Jacqueline Kennedy: The Complete Story of America's Glamorous First Lady*. Derby, CT: Monarch, 1961 (pb).

Hepburn, James. *Farewell America: The Plot to Kill JFK*. Originally published in French as *L'Amerique Brule* (America Is Burning), possibly written by French intelligence agents. Introduction by Will Turner. Roseville, CA: Penmarin Books, 2002 (sc).

Herold, David E. 1844-1865, defendant. (as cataloged by the Library of Congress). *The Assassination of President Lincoln and The Trial of the Conspirators: The Courtroom Testimony as Originally Compiled by Benn Pitman, Recorder to the Commission*. Facsimile Edition with introduction by Philip Van Doren Stern. Westport, CT: Greenwood Press, 1974 (hc).

Heymann, C. David. *A Woman Named Jackie*. New York: Carol Communications, 1989 (hc).

"Hidell, Al, and Joan d'Arc", compilers. *The Conspiracy Reader: From the Deaths of JFK and John Lennon to Government-Sponsored Alien Cover-Ups*. Secaucus, NJ: Citadel Press, 1999 (pb).

Hinckle, Warren, and William H. Turner. *Deadly Secrets: The CIA-Mafia War Against Castro and the Assassination of J.F.K.*. New York: Thunder's Mouth Press, 1992 (hc).

Holloway, Diane. *The Mind of Oswald*. Victoria, BC: Trafford Publishing (on demand), 2000 (sc).

James, Richard. *Why President Kennedy & Brother Robert Died: An Assassination Theory*. (no place given): 1st Books Library, 2002 (sc).

James, Rosemary, and Jack Wardian. *Plot or Politics? The Garrison Case and Its Cast*. New Orleans: Pelican Publishing House, 1967 (sc).

Johnson, Haynes, with Manuel Artime, Jose Perez San Roman, Erneido Oliva and Enrique Ruiz-Williams. *The Bay of Pigs: The Leaders' Story of Brigade 2506*. New York: Dell Publishing, 1964 (pb).

"Jones, John Paul", editor. *Dr. Mudd and the Lincoln Assassination: The Case Reopened*. Conshohocken, PA: Combined Books, 1995 (hc).

Kalugin, Oleg, with Fen Montaigne. *The First Directorate: My 32 Years in Intelligence and Espionage Against the West*. New York: St. Martin's Press, 1994 (hc).

Kennedy, John F. *A Nation of Immigrants*. Introduction by Robert F. Kennedy. New York: Harper & Row, 1964 (pb).

Kennedy, John F. *The Strategy of Peace*. Edited and with introduction by Allan Nevins. New York: Harper, 1960 (pb).

Kennedy, John F. *To Turn the Tide*. Edited by John W. Gardner. Foreword by Carl Sandburg. New York: Popular Library, 1962 (pb).

Kennedy, John F. *Why England Slept*. Foreword by Henry R. Luce. Garden City, NY: Dolphin, 1962 (pb).

Kessler, Ronald. *The Sins of the Father: Joseph P. Kennedy and the Dynasty He Founded*. New York: Warner Books, 1996 (hc).

Kirkwood, James. *American Grotesque: An Account of the Clay Shaw–Jim Garrison Kennedy Assassination Trial in the City of New Orleans*. New York: HarperPerennial, 1992 (sc).

Klein, Edward. *Just Jackie: Her Private Years*. New York: Ballantine Books, 1998 (pb).

Klein, Edward. *The Kennedy Curse: Why America's First Family has been Haunted by Tragedy for 150 Years*. New York: St. Martin's Press, 2003 (hc).

Kurland, Michael. *How to Try a Murder: The Handbook for Armchair Lawyers*. New York: Macmillan, 1997 (sc).

Ladowsky, Ellen. *Jacqueline Kennedy Onassis*. New York: Literary Express, 1998 (hc).

La Fontaine, Ray, and Mary La Fontaine. *Oswald Talked: The New Evidence in the JFK Assassination*. Gretna, LA: Pelican, 1996 (hc).

Lamb, Brian. *Booknotes: Stories from American History*. New York: PublicAffairs, 2001 (hc).

Lane, Mark, and Dick Gregory. *Murder in Memphis: The FBI and the Assassination of Martin Luther King*. New York: Thunder's Mouth Press, 1993 (sc).

Law, William Matson, with Allan Eaglesham. *In the Eye of History: Bethesda Hospital Medical Evidence in the JFK Assassination*. Southlake, TX: JFK Lancer Productions & Publications, Second Edition, 2005 (sc).

Lawrence, Lincoln. *Were We Controlled?* New Hyde Park, NY: University Books, 1967 (hc).

Lawrence, Lincoln, and Kenn Thomas. *Mind Control, Oswald & JFK: Were We Controlled?* Kempton, IL: Adventures Unlimited Press, 1997 (pb).

Lewis, Bernard. *The Assassins: A Radical Sect in Islam*. New York: Oxford University Press, 1987 (sc).

Loken, John. *Oswald's Trigger Films: The Manchurian Candidate, We Were Strangers, Suddenly?* Ann Arbor, MI: Falcon Books, 2000 (sc).

Mahoney, Richard D. *Sons & Brothers: The Days of Jack and Bobby Kennedy*. New York: Arcade Publishing, 1999 (pb).

Maier, Thomas. *The Kennedys: America's Emerald Kings*. New York: Basic Books, 2003 (hc).

Manchester, William. *Portrait of a President: John F. Kennedy in Profile*. Revised edition with a new introduction and epilogue. Boston: Little, Brown, 1967 (hc).

Marrs, Jim. *Crossfire: The Plot that Killed Kennedy*. New York: Carroll & Graf, 1989 (sc).

Matthews, Jim, publisher. *Four Dark Days in History: November 22, 23, 24, 25 1963*. Los Angeles: Special Publications Inc, 1963 (large magazine format).

May, Ernest R., and Philip D. Zelikow. *The Kennedy Tapes: Inside the White House During the Cuban Missile Crisis*. Cambridge, MA: Belknap Press of Harvard University Press, 1997 (hc).

McClellan, Barr. *Blood, Money & Power: How LBJ Killed JFK*. New York: Hannover House, 2003 (hc).

McDonald, Hugh C., as told to Geoffrey Bocca. *Appointment In Dallas: The Final Solution to the Assassination of John F. Kennedy*. New York: The Hugh McDonald Publishing Corp., 1975 (pb).

Meagher, Sylvia, and Gary Owens. *Master Index to the JFK Assassination Investigations*. Metuchen, NJ: Scarecrow Press, 1980.

Melanson, Philip H. *The Martin Luther King Assassination: New Revelations on the Conspiracy and Cover-Up, 1968-1991*. Foreword by Noah W. Griffin. New York: Shapolsky, 1991 (sc).

Melanson, Philip H. *The MURKIN Conspiracy: An Investigation into the Assassination of Dr. Martin Luther King, Jr*. New York: Praeger Publishers, 1989 (hc).

Melanson, Philip H. *The Robert F. Kennedy Assassination: New Revelations on the Conspiracy and Cover-Up, 1968-1991*. Foreword by Anthony Summers. Introduction by John H. Davis. New York: Shapolsky, 1991 (hc).

Mellen, Joan. *A Farewell to Justice: Jim Garrison, JFK's Assassination, and the Case That Should Have Changed History*. Dulles, VA: Potomac Books, 2007 (sc).

Menninger, Bonar. *Mortal Error: The Shot that Killed JFK*. New York: St. Martin's Press, 1992 (hc).

Miller, Nathan. *Theodore Roosevelt: A Life*. New York: William Morrow, 1992 (hc).

Miller, Tom. *Jack Ruby's Kitchen Sink: Offbeat Travels through America's Southwest*. Foreword by Pete Hamill. Washington, DC: Adventure Press (National Geographic Society), 2001 (sc).

Miller, William "Fishbait", as told to Frances Spatz Leighton. *Fishbait: The Memoirs of the Congressional Doorkeeper*. New York: Warner Books, 1978 (pb).

Moore, Steve, compiler. *The Fortean Times Book of Inept Crime*. Illustrated by Geoff Coupland. London: John Brown, 1996 (pb).

Moran, Edward. *America in the 1960's*. (Boxed booklet and 4 audio CD's) New Rochelle, NY: GAA Corporation, 1999.

Morris, W. R., and R. B. Cutler. *alias Oswald*. Collector's Edition. Manchester, MA: GKG Partners, 1985 (hc).

Morrow, Robert D. *First Hand Knowledge: How I Participated in the CIA-Mafia Murder of President Kennedy*. Introduction by John H. Davis. New York: S.P.I. Books [Shapolsky], 1992 (hc).

Netzley, Patricia D. *The Assassination of President John F. Kennedy*. New York: New Discovery Books, 1994 (hc).

Neustadt, Richard E. *Presidential Power: The Politics of Leadership from FDR to Carter*. New York: Macmillan, 1980 (sc).

North, Mark. *Act of Treason: The Role of J. Edgar Hoover in the Assassination of President Kennedy*. New York: Carroll & Graf, 1991 (sc).

Oglesby, Carl. *The JFK Assassination: The Facts and the Theories*. Preface by Norman Mailer. New York: Signet, 1992 (pb).

O'Leary, Brad, and L. E. Seymour. *Triangle of Death: The Shocking Truth About the Role of South Vietnam and the French Mafia in the Assassination of JFK*. Nashville: WND Books, 2003 (hc).

Pell, Derek. *Assassination Rhapsody*. Introduction by Harold Jaffe. Brooklyn: Autonomedia, 1989 (pb).

Pepper, William F. *Orders to Kill: The Truth Behind the Murder of Martin Luther King*. New York: Carroll & Graf, 1995 (hc).

Pietrusza, David. *1920: The Year of the Six Presidents*. New York: Carroll & Graf, 2007 (hc).

Piper, Michael Collins. *Final Judgment: The Missing Link in the JFK Assassination Conspiracy*. Washington, DC: Wolfe Press, 1995 (pb).

Popkin, Richard H. *The Second Oswald: A Startling Alternative to the Single Assassin Theory of the Warren Commission Report*. Introduction by Murray Kempton. New York: Avon Library / New York Review of Books, 1966 (pb).

Popular Library. *A Concise Compendium of the Warren Commission Report on the Assassination of John F. Kennedy*. Introduction by Robert J. Donovan. New York: Popular Library, 1994 (pb).

Pottker, Jan. *Janet and Jackie: The Story of a Mother and Her Daughter, Jacqueline Kennedy Onassis*. New York: St. Martin's Press, 2001 (hc).

Pradt, Mary A., compiler. *You Must Remember This: 1961*. New York: Warner Treasures, 1995 (hc).

Radziwill, Lee. *Happy Times*. New York: Assouline Publishing, 2000 (hc).

Ramsay, Robin. *Who Shot JFK?* Harpenden, Hertfordshire, Great Britain: Pocket Essentials, 2002 (pb).

Reader's Digest Association. *Great Mysteries of the 20th Century*. Pleasantville, NY: Reader's Digest Association, 1999 (hc).

Reedy, George E. *The Twilight of the Presidency*. New York: Mentor Books, 1971 (pb).

Rees-Jones, Trevor, with Moira Johnston. *The Bodyguard's Story: Diana, the Crash, and the Sole Survivor*. New York: Warner Books, 2000 (hc).

Reeves, Richard. *President Kennedy: Profile of Power*. New York: Simon & Schuster, 1993 (hc).

Rehnquist, William H. *Grand Inquests: The Historic Impeachments of Justice Samuel Chase and President Andrew Johnson*. New York: Quill, 1993, 1999 (pb).

Renehan, Edward J., Jr. *The Kennedys at War, 1937–1945*. New York: Doubleday, 2002 (hc).

Roberts, Craig. *Kill Zone: A Sniper Looks at Dealey Plaza*. Tulsa: Typhoon Press (subsequently named Consolidated Press), 1994 (sc).

Russell, Dick. *The Man Who Knew Too Much*. Foreword by Carl Oglesby. New York: Carroll & Graf, 1992 (pb).

Russell, Dick. *On the Trail of the JFK Assassins: A Groundbreaking Look at America's Most Infamous Conspiracy*. New York: Skyhorse Publishing, 2008 (sc).

Saferstein, Richard. *Criminalistics: An Introduction to Forensic Science*. Second Ed. Englewood Cliffs, NJ: Prentice-Hall, 1981 (hc).

Sauvage, Léo. *The Oswald Affair: An Examination of the Contradictions and Omissions of the Warren Report*. Trans. from French by Charles Gaulkin. Cleveland: World Publishing Company, 1966 (hc).

Scheim, David E. *Contract on America: The Mafia Murder of President John F. Kennedy*. Introduction by John H. Davis. New York: Zebra Books, 1989 (pb).

Scott, Peter Dale. *Deep Politics and the Death of JFK*. Berkeley: University of California Press, 1996 (sc).

Shapiro, Stanley. *A Time to Remember*. New York: Signet, 1988 (pb).

Shaw, Mark. *The John F. Kennedys: A Family Album*. New York: Farrar, Straus, 1964 (hc).

Shaw, Maud. *White House Nannie: My Years with Caroline and John Kennedy, Jr.* New York: Signet, 1966 (pb).

Shenon, Philip. *A Cruel and Shocking Act: The Secret History of the Kennedy Assassination.* New York: Henry Holt, 2013 (hc).

Shermer, Michael. *Why People Believe Weird Things: Pseudoscience, Superstition, and Other Confusions of Our Time.* Foreword by Stephen Jay Gould. New York: W. H. Freeman, 1997 (sc).

Smith, Matthew. *JFK: Say Goodbye to America: The Sensational and Untold Story behind the Assassination of John F. Kennedy.* Foreword by Jim Marrs. Edinburgh: Mainstream Publishing, 2004 (sc).

Smith, Matthew. *JFK: The Second Plot.* Edinburgh: Mainstream Publishing, 2002 (sc).

Strauss, Steven D. *The Complete Idiot's Guide to The Kennedys.* Indianapolis: Macmillan alpha books, 2000 (sc).

Summers, Anthony. *Conspiracy.* With four page "Update" by the author. New York: Paragon House, 1991 (sc).

Summers, Anthony. *Not In Your Lifetime.* "Updated edition" of *Conspiracy*, with postscript by John Newman. New York: Marlowe & Co., 1998 (sc).

Tanenbaum, Robert K. *Corruption of Blood.* New York: Dutton, 1995 (hc).

Thompson, Robert E. *The Trial of Lee Harvey Oswald.* (Based on a teleplay) New York: Ace Books, 1977 (pb).

Toobin, Jeffrey. *The Run of His Life: The People v. O. J. Simpson.* New York: Random House, 1996 (hc).

Tregaskis, Richard. *John F. Kennedy: War Hero.* New York: Dell Publishing, 1962 (pb).

Van Buren, Abigail. *Where were you when President Kennedy was shot? Memories and Tributes to a Slain President as Told to Dear Abby.* Foreword by Pierre Salinger. Kansas City, MO: Andrews and McMeel, 1993 (pb).

Vankin, Jonathan. *Conspiracies, Cover-Ups and Crimes: Political Manipulation and Mind Control in America.* New York: Paragon House, 1991 (hc).

Vold, George B., and Thomas J. Bernard. *Theoretical Criminology.* Third Edition. New York: Oxford University Press, 1986 (hc).

von Post, Gunilla, with Carl Johnes. *Love, Jack.* New York: Crown Publishers, 1997 (hc).

Weberman, Alan J. and Michael Canfield. *Coup D'Etat in America: The CIA and the Assassination of John F. Kennedy.* Foreword by Henry B. Gonzalez. San Francisco: Quick American Archives, 1992 (sc).

Weichmann, Louis J. (chief witness). (As cataloged by editor Floyd E. Risvold.) *A True History of the Assassination of Abraham Lincoln and of the Conspiracy of 1865.* New York: Knopf, 1975 (hc).

Weisberg, Harold. *Martin Luther King: The Assassination.* Postscript by James Earl Ray. New York: Carroll & Graf, 1971 (sc).

West Publishing Company. *Federal Criminal Code and Rules, 1996 Edition.* St. Paul, MN: West Publishing, 1996 (sc).

Whalen, Richard J. *The Founding Father: The Story of Joseph P. Kennedy*. New York: Signet Books, 1966 (pb).

Whipple, Chandler. *Lt. John F. Kennedy — Expendable!* New York: Envoy, 1962 (pb).

White, Nancy Bean. *Meet John F. Kennedy*. New York: Random House Step-Up Books, 1965 (hc).

White, Theodore H. *The Making of the President–1968*. New York: Pocket Books, 1970 (pb).

Willis, Garry, and Ovid Demaris. *Jack Ruby*. New York: Da Capo Press, 1994 (pb).

Wilson, Colin, editor. *The Mammoth Book of the History of Murder*. New York: Carroll & Graf, 2000 (sc).

Wilson, Colin, and Damon and Rowan Wilson. *World Famous Murders*. London: Robinson Publishing, 1993 (sc).

Wilson, Kirk. *Unsolved: Great True Crimes of the 20th Century*. New York: Carroll & Graf, 1991 (sc).

Wise, David, and Thomas B. Ross. *The U-2 Affair*. New York: Random House, 1992 (hc).

Woerden, Henk van. *The Assassin: A Story of Race and Rage in the Land of Apartheid*. Translated by Dan Jacobson. First American Edition. New York: Henry Holt, 2001 (hc).

Wood, James Playsted, and the Editors of Country Beautiful Magazine. *The Life and Words of John F. Kennedy*. New York: Scholastic Book Services, 1965 (sc).

The World Almanac of U.S. Politics: 1995-97 Edition. Mahwah, NJ: World Almanac Books, 1995 (sc).

Wrone, David R. *The Zapruder Film: Reframing JFK's Assassination*. Lawrence, KS: University Press of Kansas, 2003 (hc).

Zelizer, Barbie. *Covering the Body: The Kennedy Assassination, the Media, and the Shaping of Collective Memory*. Chicago: University of Chicago Press, 1992 (sc).

Zerby, Chuck. *The Devil's Details: A History of Footnotes*. Montpelier, VT: Invisible Cities Press, 2002 (hc).

Radio, Television, Films, VHS, DVD and CD-ROM recordings

CD-ROM: *Investigation of the Assassination of President John F. Kennedy by the U.S. House of Representatives, 95th Congress*. Dallas: L. M. P. Systems, 1993.

CD-ROM: *JFK Assassination: A Visual Investigation*. Redmond, Washington: Medio Multimedia, 1993.

DVD: *American Assassin: Lee Harvey Oswald Behind the Iron Curtain*. Robert Bayne, producer/director. South San Francisco, CA: InSight Films by CAV Distributing Corporation, no date given.

DVD: *Assassination & Aftermath: The Death of JFK and the Warren Report*. 20th Century with Mike Wallace on CBS TV network, 1994. DVD from The History Channel.

DVD: *Image of an Assassination: A New Look at the Zapruder Film*. Produced and directed by H.D. Motyl. MPI Home Video, 1998.

DVD: *JFK*. (the movie) Directed by Oliver Stone. Based on the books *On the Trail of the Assassins* by Jim Garrison and *Crossfire: The Plot that Killed Kennedy* by Jim Marrs. Warner Bros., 1991. "Director's cut" film on DVD.

DVD: *JFK: 3 Shots that Changed America*. The History Channel, 2009.

DVD: *JFK: 50 Years: A Commemorative Collection*. Topics Entertainment, 2013.

DVD: *JFK: The Lost Bullet*. National Geographic Channel, 2011.

DVD: *JFK: A New World Order*. "Cine-O-Matic Inc. for exclusive distribution by Mill Creek Entertainment", 2013. The black-and-white United States Secret Service documentary film *Assassination of President John F. Kennedy* is the second feature on "Bonus Disc". "Photographed in cooperation with Eddie Barker - Director of News, Jim Underwood - Newsman, Henk Dewit - Photographer, KRLD-TV. Directed by Special Agents John Joe Howlett and Talmadge Bailey. Narrated by Jim Underwood."

DVD: *The Lost JFK Tapes: The Assassination*. National Geographic Channel, 2009.

DVD: *The Men Who Killed Kennedy: The Definitive Account of American History's Most Controversial Mystery*. Produced and directed by Nigel Turner on The History Channel, 1988-1995. Six programs in two-DVD set from The History Channel.

DVD: *November 22nd and The Warren Report: The 1964 CBS News Report on The John F. Kennedy Assassination*. Issued by PRS, distributed by Kunaki, LLC. 2010.

DVD: *Unsolved History: JFK: Beyond the Magic Bullet*. Discovery Channel, 2003.

DVD: *Unsolved History: JFK Conspiracy*. Discovery Channel, 2003.

DVD: *Unsolved History: JFK, Death in Dealey Plaza*. Discovery Channel, 2003.

Radio: Schorr, Daniel (NPR Senior News Analyst). News analysis on National Public Radio's Weekend Edition – Sunday, 12 May 2002.

TV: *Cronkite Remembers*. Walter Cronkite on CBS-TV News Special Presentation. 26 Jan. 1997.

TV: *Failed Assassinations* on *History's Mysteries presented by Arthur Kent*. The History Channel. 03 Jan. 2000.

TV: *JFK: A Personal Story*. Interview of UPI White House Bureau Chief Helen Thomas by Jack Perkins. A&E Biography Special: Arts and Entertainment Network. 06 April 1997.

TV: *Oprah*. Interview of Marina Oswald Porter by Oprah Winfrey. NBC. 22 Nov. 1996.

TV: *A Question of Conspiracy* on *History's Mysteries presented by Arthur Kent*. The History Channel. 22 May 2000.

TV: *The Times of Harvey Milk*. Dir. Robert Epstein. Prod. Richard Schmiechen. Black Sands Productions, 1984.

VHS pre-recorded tape: *Conspiracy? Jack Ruby*. A&E TV network, 1996. VHS videotape by A&E Television Networks purchased from The History Channel.

VHS pre-recorded tape: *JFK: The End of Camelot*. Directed by Steve Ruggi. Edited by Paul Carlin. Discovery Channel Video, 1996.

NOTES AND SOURCES

> "You got to get twenty-seven outs to win.
> You could look it up."
> — **Casey Stengel** [3481]

THROUGHOUT THIS BOOK, REFERENCE MARKS such as [314] appear after significant content. This is the section to which those marks point, with one or more sources for every item with a reference mark. When multiple sources exist, especially for obscure or controversial facts, several sources may be given. When a fact is in the *Warren Report*, that is the first reference because readers can easily find that indispensable book or a reprint with the same pagination. The *Warren Report* cites sources for most facts, noted here with "which cites" and its sources.

In the notes below for each chapter, a source is identified in full on first appearance, after which only an abbreviation or an author's last name (and a word or two from a book title, if she/he wrote several) is used for others from that source. When there are more basic or original sources, they are also shown, with the most dependable (in this author's opinion) listed first. If in doubt about any source, clarification probably awaits in the earlier section REFERENCES CITED on pages 617–634. You may find more than you want to know here, but you should find anything you seek.

These abbreviations are used in the notes:

AP: Associated Press

CD: Commission Document, 1-1555, not printed in *WCH*, as explained on page 113.

CE: Commission Exhibit, 1-3154, printed in the 26 books of *WCH*.

DMN: *Dallas Morning News*

HSCA: Select Committee on Assassinations, U.S. House of Representatives
(*HSCA*, *WCH* and *WR* are listed atop REFERENCES CITED, Government Publications)

NYT: *The New York Times*

ST: *The Seattle Times*

UPI: United Press International

WCH: *Warren Commission Hearings*, titled in full: *Hearings Before the President's Commission on the Assassination of President Kennedy* – the 26 volumes

WP: *Washington Post*

WR: *Warren Report*, titled in full: *Report of the President's Commission on the Assassination of President John F. Kennedy*

PREFACE

[1] On a sign outside the Essex Unitarian Church in Kensington, London, England, which identifies Emerson as "American Unitarian Essayist and Poet (1803 - 1882)".

[2] The set's price was found in a book by The New York Times. *The Witnesses: The Highlights of Hearings before the Warren Commission on the Assassination of President Kennedy*, Introduction by Anthony Lewis on page vii.

[3] The handwritten letter is shown on page 88, then accurately transcribed as if typewritten, for easier reading, on page 89.

[4] *Report of the President's Commission on the Assassination of President Kennedy* (popularly known as the *Warren Report*) page 463; hereinafter expressed in the form *WR 463*. If you would like to have your own copy, see the INDEX entry "Warren Commission : *Report* : How to buy a useful copy".

[5] *Hearings Before the President's Commission on the Assassination of President Kennedy*, Volume V, page 450; hereinafter expressed in the form *WCH V 450*.

[6] *WR 462*.

[7] *WR 463*.

[8] *WR 387*, which cites "5 H 605 (Marina Oswald)", which means book 5 of the *Hearings* on page 605. In this book's terminology that would be *WCH V 605 (Marina Oswald)*.

[9] Quoted as fair use (for brevity) from David Gates speaking at Northwest Bookfest, "Bookfest review" in *The Seattle Times* 15 Nov. 1999, page C2.

[10] Quoted briefly as fair use from Mailer, Norman. *The Time of Our Time* 867, an excerpt from his *Pieces and Pontifications* (1982).

[11] Quoted with kind permission from Wilson, Francis. *John Wilkes Booth: Fact and Fiction of Lincoln's Assassination*, page x. Copyright notice supplied by publisher: "Excerpts from JOHN WILKES BOOTH: Fact and Fiction of Lincoln's Assassination by Francis Wilson (Boston: Houghton Mifflin Harcourt, 1929)".

[12] Quoted with kind permission from Schlesinger, Arthur, Jr. *Kennedy or Nixon: Does it make any difference?* vii.

[13] Etched into a glass panel outside The Laurie B. Oki Scene Gallery, The Seattle Center, Seattle WA.

READER'S GUIDE

[14] Phil Chernofsky, creator of *And Every Single One Was Someone*, said the seven Harry Potter volumes totaled 1.1 million words, as quoted in "The Holocaust told in 1 word, 6 million times" in *The Seattle Times* 26 Jan. 2014: A5.

— 1 — MOTHER

[15] TESTIMONY OF MRS. LILLIAN MURRET in *Hearings Before the President's Commission on the Assassination of President Kennedy*, volume VIII, page 98. Additional testimony will hereinafter be expressed as *WCH VIII 98 (Lillian Murret)*.

[16] Transcribed by the author from an interview of Robert Oswald by Josh Mankowitz in a segment titled "My Brother's Keeper" on *Dateline NBC*, broadcast by NBC-TV on June 14, 1998. After a protracted process, I obtained permission to include this material from NBC News Archives LLC at a price of $250, for a total of 269 words in this and a three other quotes. I am responsible for the accuracy of the transcription. As required by my license agreement with NBCUniversal Archives, I acknowledge that NBC is the sole owner of the text, including all copyright and other exclusive rights in it.

[17] Quoted with kind permission after payment, from Manchester, William. *The Death of a President*, page 91. Permission acknowledgement: "Reprinted with permission of Don Congdon Associates, Inc. © 1967, renewed 1995 by William Manchester."

[18] Quoted with permission from Mailer, Norman. *Oswald's Tale: An American Mystery* 789.

[19] TESTIMONY OF MRS. MARGUERITE OSWALD on *WCH I 182*.

[20] Photo imported from http://oswald-photos.blogspot.com/2012/09/marguerite-claverie-oswald-1907-1981.html The author and his professional picture researcher have spent considerable time doing due diligence, but are unable to identify the original source. If there is a copyright holder, please see CREDITS AND PERMISSIONS on page ii.

[21] *Report of the President's Commission on the Assassination of President John F. Kennedy*, best known as the *Warren Report*, page 669, which will hereinafter be expressed in the form *WR 669*. The reference itself cites "Allison G. Folsom, Jr., DE (DEPOSITION EXHIBIT) 1, p. 98; see CE (COMMISSION EXHIBIT) 2205, p. 569."

[22] *WR 669*, which cites "*WCH I 252 (Marguerite Oswald); WCH VIII 92 (Lillian Murret)*."

[23] *WR 669*, which cites "*WCH I 252-253 (Marguerite Oswald); WCH VIII 95-96 (L. Murret)*."

[24] *WR 669*, which cites "*WCH I 252 (Marguerite Oswald)*."

[25] *WR 669*, which cites "*WCH VIII 98 (L. Murret)*."

[26] *WR 669*, which cites "*WCH VIII 97 (L. Murret)*."

[27] *WR 669*, which cites "*WCH I 252 (Marguerite Oswald)*."

[28] *WR 669*, which cites "*WCH I 252-253 (Marguerite Oswald); see WCH VIII 93 (L. Murret)*."

[29] Quoted with permission after payment, from Stafford, Jean. *A Mother in History* 26.

[30] *WR 669*, which cites "*WCH VIII 197-198 (Edward John Pic Jr.); see WCH VIII 92-93 (L. Murret)*. Mrs. Murret described Pic at that time as 'a person who did not talk unless you spoke to him'; *WCH VIII 93*."

[31] *WR 669*, which cites "John Pic DE 1."

[32] *WR* 669, which cites "*WCH* I 253 (Marguerite Oswald); see *WCH* VIII 95, 99 (L. Murret)."

[33] *WR* 669, which cites "*WCH* VIII 95, 99 (L. Murret), 162-168 (Marilyn Dorothea Murret); *WCH* XI 5 (J. Pic) compare *WCH* VIII 46 (Myrtle Evans). For Mrs. Oswald's testimony to the same effect before the Commission, see *WCH* I 253."

[34] *WCH* VIII 93 (Lillian Murret).

[35] TESTIMONY OF EDWARD JOHN PIC, JR. on *WCH* VIII 196.

[36] *WCH* VIII 198 (Edward John Pic, Jr.).

[37] *WR* 669, which cites "*WCH* XI 2 (J. Pic); CE 2208; see *WCH* VIII 198 (E. Pic)."

[38] *WR* 669, which suggests "Compare *WCH* VIII 199 (E. Pic) with *WCH* I 253 (Marguerite Oswald); compare *WCH* VIII 47 (M. Evans)."

[39] AFFIDAVIT OF EDWARD JOHN PIC, JR. on *WCH* XI 82.

[40] *WR* 669, which cites "*WCH* VIII 104 (L. Murret); *WCH* XI 5 (J. Pic); see *WCH* I 253 (Marguerite Oswald)."

[41] *WCH* VIII 104 (Lillian Murret).

[42] *WR* 669, which cites "*WCH* I 253 (Marguerite Oswald)."

[43] *WR* 669, which cites "CE 1958, 1959."

[44] *WR* 669, which cites "CE 2000; *WCH* I 253 (Marguerite Oswald); *WCH* VIII 104 (L. Murret)."

[45] *WR* 669, which cites "*WCH* I 253 (Marguerite Oswald)."

[46] *WR* 669, which cites "CE 2208; *WCH* I 267 (Robert Edward Lee Oswald)."

[47] *WR* 669, which cites "CE 2197, p. 79."

[48] *WR* 669, which cites "*WCH* XI 12 (J. Pic); see *WCH* VIII 105 (L. Murret); see generally CE 2198, pp. 65-67, 69."

[49] Photo imported from http://2.bp.blogspot.com/-Nb99zTqaExc/UGD-3mmIp7I/AAAAAAAAAGk/yuWZwQAJfHc/s1600/1937+with+signature.jpg   The author and his professional picture researcher have spent considerable time doing due diligence, but are unable to identify the original source. If there is a copyright holder, please see CREDITS AND PERMISSIONS on page ii.

[50] *WCH* VIII 106 (Lillian Murret).

[51] *WR* 670, which cites "CE 2211, p. 618-1; see *WCH* I 225 (Marguerite Oswald), 268 (R. Oswald); *WCH* VIII 47 (M. Evans)."

[52] *WR* 670, which cites "*WCH* I 225 (Marguerite Oswald); Folsom DE 1, p. 123."

[53] *WR* 670, which cites "*WCH* I 225 (Marguerite Oswald)."

[54] Quoted with permission after payment, from Ford, Gerald R., and John R. Stiles. *Portrait of the Assassin* 309.

[55] *WR* 670, which cites "See *WCH* VIII 47 (M. Evans), 106 (L. Murret)."

[56] *WR* 670, which cites "CE 2200."

[57] Epstein, Edward Jay. *Legend: The Secret World of Lee Harvey Oswald* 56.

[58] *WR* 670, which cites "*WCH* I 270 (R. Oswald); *WCH* XI 7, 8-9, 11 (J. Pic); compare *WCH* VIII 107 (L. Murret)."

[59] *WR* 670, which cites "*WCH* I 270 (R. Oswald); *WCH* XI 7 (J. Pic); but see *WCH* XI 17 (J. Pic)."

[60] *WR* 670, which cites "*WCH* XI 9 (J. Pic); compare *WCH* VIII 107 (L. Murret)."

[61] TESTIMONY OF JOHN EDWARD PIC on *WCH* XI 7, 9.

[62] *WR* 670, which cites "See CE 2199, 2203."

[63] The photo is scanned and cropped from COMMISSION EXHIBIT 283 on *WCH* XVI 803. Coming from that US Federal government source, it is in the public domain.

[64] TESTIMONY OF ROBERT OSWALD on *WCH* I 304.

[65] *WR* 670, which cites "*WCH* VIII 40 (Viola Peterman)."

[66] *WR* 670, which cites "CE 2197."

[67] *WR* 670, which cites "*WCH* XI 11 (J. Pic)."

[68] Quoted from Oswald, Robert L., with Myrick and Barbara Land. *Lee: A Portrait of Lee Harvey Oswald by His Brother* 32. The 1967 copyright notice in the book is to those three co-authors. Publisher Coward-McCann no longer exists in 2015. Through a long series of mergers and acquisitions, its successor is Penguin Random House, which my copyright agent contacted, learning they do not have either copyright or any information on the authors. To obtain permission to quote from this essential biography, the author attempted without success to locate Mr. Oswald. My copyright agent tried to find the Land couple, learning that he has died and she moved to an unknown location. As a source this book is unique, unequaled by any other, so I retained the services of McCormack Intellectual Property Law in Seattle, where experienced copyright attorney Lauren A. Kingston located the Texas attorney who recently represented Mr. Oswald in his successful suit of a funeral home that wrongly sold Lee's original, decomposed coffin, for which Robert had paid and still has the receipt. Lauren sent a letter requesting permission on 8/06/2015, but no reply; again on 8/19/15 enclosing a personal letter of explanation and appeal from me to Robert, again no reply. On 9/26/15 I wrote another letter to Robert and enclosed my check 3276 for $1,500 to his attorney's trust account, a very generous amount considering what other authors and publishers have charged for quotes. That was sent by Lauren to Oswald's attorney, with a letter saying her client (me) wanted to pay, and pointing out that regardless of what they may do with my check, based on our previous attempts "your failure to respond is taken as an agreement that your client grants permission for use of portions of his book "Lee" and will not object to my client's use of the excerpts in his upcoming book." Again there was no reply, so

on 11/17/15 I personally sent a letter and "no strings" gift check 3300 for $1,500 to "Robert or Vada Oswald, or their heirs, trustees or administrators", saying I would like to pay for his insights, even if he would not reply to me. I marked the check "For: Freewill gift, appreciating *Lee*". My attorney advised that I make no further efforts, "to avoid any type of harassment claim, however farfetched that may be." As this book is completed in February 2016, neither check has been cashed, nor has there ever been any reply. Chasing this one source, I have paid more than $7,400 to my copyright agent and attorney for their attempts to contact Oswald so I could pay the generous $1,500 and obtain a reply. I hereby claim the right to quote after performing due diligence, augmented by my attorney's estoppel notice to Robert Oswald's attorney. Please see <u>CREDITS AND PERMISSIONS</u> on page ii. For more about Marguerite's notion shop, see also *WR* 670, which cites "*WCH* VIII 43 (Peterman); *WCH* XI 11, 12 (J. Pic); see *WCH* VIII 48 (M. Evans)."

[69] *WR* 670, which cites "*WCH* XI 12 (J. Pic)."

[70] *WR* 670, which cites "CE 2197, p. 80."

[71] *WR* 670, which cites "Pic DE 5. The record contains also a separate application for the admission of Robert, dated Jan. 3, 1942; J. Pic DE 3."

[72] *WCH* XI 12 (John Pic).

[73] *WR* 670, which cites "J. Pic DE 2, p. 3; see *WCH* I 272 (R. Oswald)."

[74] *WR* 670, which cites "J. Pic DE 2, p. 4."

[75] *WR* 670, which cites "CE 2201, p. 63; see *WCH* VIII 35-36 (Anne Boudreaux)."

[76] *WR* 670, which cites "J. Pic DE 2, p. 1; *WCH* VIII 46, 51 (M. Evans); *WCH* XI 18 (J. Pic)."

[77] *WR* 670, which cites "*WCH* VIII 106-107 (L. Murret)."

[78] *WR* 670-671, which cites "*WCH* VIII 36-37 (Boudreaux); see CE 2204."

[79] *WR* 671, which cites "*WCH* VIII 37 (Boudreaux)."

[80] Quoted from Oswald, Robert 33. This source was described in endnote [68].

[81] *WR* 671, which cites "*WCH* VIII 36 (Boudreaux)."

[82] *WR* 671, which cites "J. Pic DE 2, p. 1; *WCH* XI 13, 14 (J. Pic)."

[83] *WR* 671, which cites "See J. Pic DE 2, p. 2."

[84] *WR* 671, which cites "See *WCH* VIII 112-113 (L. Murret)."

[85] Leahy, Michael (*Arkansas Democrat-Gazette*). "Still haunted by a brother's legacy" *Philadelphia Inquirer* 1997 Nov. 21: A22.

[86] *WR* 671, which cites "J. Pic DE 2, pp. 1, 4."

[87] *WR* 671, which cites "*WCH* XI 15 (J. Pic)."

[88] *WCH* XI 17 (John Pic).

[89] *WR* 671, which cites "*WCH* XI 17, 20 (J. Pic); see *WCH* I 271 (R. Oswald); compare *WCH* I 273 (R. Oswald)."

[90] *WR* 671, which cites "*WCH* XI 20 (J. Pic); see *WCH* I 271 (R. Oswald); *WCH* VIII 108-109 (L. Murret)."

[91] *WR* 671, which cites "*WCH* I 254 (Marguerite Oswald); *WCH* I 272, 273 (R. Oswald); *WCH* XI 18, 20-21 (J. Pic)."

[92] *WR* 671, which cites "For descriptions of Ekdahl, see *WCH* I 250 (Marguerite Oswald), 274 (R. Oswald); *WCH* VIII 66-67 (Julian Evans), 110-111 (L. Murret); *WCH* XI 21-22 (J. Pic). Marguerite testified that she was working at a hosiery shop when she met Ekdahl; *WCH* I 255; compare CE 2213, p. 27; but compare *WCH* XI 18 (J. Pic)."

[93] *WR* 671, which cites "*WCH* I 255 (Marguerite Oswald); see *WCH* XI 21 (J. Pic)."

[94] *WR* 671, which cites "Pic DE 2-A."

[95] *WR* 671, which cites "*WCH* I 255 (Marguerite Oswald)."

[96] *WR* 671, which cites "*WCH* I 255 (Marguerite Oswald). The home's rules did not permit children with two living parents to remain there; see *WCH* XI 21 (J. Pic); compare *WCH* VIII 107 (L. Murret)."

[97] *WR* 671, which cites "*WCH* I 255 (Marguerite Oswald)."

[98] *WR* 671, which cites "*WCH* I 255 (Marguerite Oswald); *WCH* VIII 50 (M. Evans), 110 (L. Murret)."

[99] *WR* 671, which cites "*WCH* I 255 (Marguerite Oswald)."

[100] *WR* 671, which advises "See p. 670, endnote 50."

[101] *WR* 671, which cites "CE 1963, p. 543; *WCH* I 255 (Marguerite Oswald); see J. Pic DE 4, p. 1."

[102] *WR* 671, which cites "*WCH* I 269 (R. Oswald); *WCH* VIII 49-50 (M. Evans); *WCH* XI 22, 23 (J. Pic)."

[103] *WR* 671-672, which cites "J. Pic DE 2, p. 4; *WCH* I 272, 273 (R. Oswald); *WCH* XI 21, 22 (J. Pic)."

[104] *WR* 672, which cites "*WCH* I 255 (Marguerite Oswald); see *WCH* I 275 (R. Oswald); *WCH* XI 22 (J. Pic). Robert believed, apparently incorrectly, that Ekdahl was already living in Dallas when the family moved there; *WCH* I 274 (R. Oswald)."

[105] *WR* 672, which cites "See *WCH* I 250, 251 (Marguerite Oswald); *WCH* VIII 113 (L. Murret)."

[106] *WR* 672, which cites "J. Pic DE 4."

[107] *WR* 672, which cites "CE 2211, p. 618-1; *WCH* XI 23 (J. Pic)."

[108] *WR* 672, which cites "*WCH* XI 23 (J. Pic)."

[109] Lee's aunt Lillian Murret, while testifying, was asked by a WC counsel if she had any pictures of the family. She replied: "I have her picture with Mr. Ekdahl when they were married." The counsel asked: "I wonder if you would give that to your husband and let him bring that in the morning when he comes in?" Dutz Murret brought it in, and it went into *WCH* XX 639 as MURRET EXHIBIT NO. 1, and thus we see the happy couple in this photo scanned from there. Coming from

that U.S. Federal government source, it is in the public domain.

[110] *WR* 672, which cites "*WCH* I 281 (R. Oswald); *WCH* XI 27 (J. Pic); see *WCH* XI 21, 24."

[111] *WR* 672, which cites "*WCH* XI 27."

[112] *WR* 672, which cites "*WCH* I 275 (R. Oswald); *WCH* XI 23-24 (J. Pic); see *WCH* I 255 (Marguerite Oswald)."

[113] *WR* 672, which cites "*WCH* I 277 (R. Oswald); *WCH* XI 23-30 (J. Pic)."

[114] *WR* 672, which cites "*WCH* VIII 45, 49 (M. Evans)."

[115] *WR* 672, which cites "*WCH* VIII 50-51 (M. Evans)."

[116] *WR* 672, which cites "CE 2218; *WCH* XI 25 (J. Pic). Robert testified that his recollection is that the family did not move to Benbrook until after Christmas 1945, which he and John spent with school friends because the Ekdahls (and Lee) were in Boston. *WCH* I 278 (R. Oswald)."

[117] *WR* 672, which cites "CE 1874, pp. 5-6."

[118] Quoted from Oswald, Robert 37-38. This source was described in endnote [68].

[119] *WR* 672, which cites "See *WCH* XI 24-25 (J. Pic)."

[120] *WR* 672, which cites "*WCH* I 251 (Marguerite Oswald); *WCH* VIII 111 (L. Murret); compare *WCH* VIII 50-51 (M. Evans)."

[121] *WR* 672, which cites "*WCH* I 251 (Marguerite Oswald); see *WCH* XI 73 (J. Pic)."

[122] *WR* 672, which cites "*WCH* I 251 (Marguerite Oswald); *WCH* XI 25-26 (J. Pic)."

[123] *WCH* I 312 (Robert Oswald).

[124] *WCH* I 313 (Robert Oswald).

[125] *WR* 673, which cites "CE 1413, p. 18."

[126] *WR* 673, which cites "CE 1413, p. 18."

[127] *WR* 673, which cites "*WCH* XI 26 (J. Pic); CE 2206; see *WCH* I 251 (Marguerite Oswald); CE 2211, p. 618-6."

[128] *WR* 673, which cites "CE 2211, p. 618-6."

[129] *WR* 673, which cites "CE 2211, p. 618-5."

[130] *WR* 673, which cites "*WCH* XI 27 (J. Pic); compare *WCH* I 251 (Marguerite Oswald)."

[131] Quoted from Oswald, Robert 38. This source was described in endnote [68].

[132] *WR* 673, which cites "*WCH* I 250 (Marguerite Oswald)."

[133] *WCH* I 250-251 (Marguerite Oswald). *WR* 673 cites "*WCH* XI 27-28 (J. Pic); see *WCH* VIII 112 (L. Murret)."

[134] *WR* 673, which cites "See CE 1960-A, p. 1; *WCH* XI 28 (J. Pic); compare *WCH* I 251 (Marguerite Oswald); for one explanation of Mrs. Oswald's conduct, see *WCH* VIII 112 (L. Murret)."

[135] *WR* 673, which cites "CE 1960-A, p. 3."

[136] *WR* 673, which cites "CE 1960-A."

[137] *WR* 673, which cites "CE 1960-A, pp. 1-4."

[138] *WR* 673, which cites "CE 1960-B; see *WCH* I 251-252 (Marguerite Oswald)."

[139] *WCH* XI 29 (John Pic); *WR* 673, which advises "see *WCH* I 252 (Marguerite Oswald)."

[140] *WR* 673, which cites "CE 1960-C, p. 2."

[141] *WR* 673-674, which cites "CE 1960-C, pp. 3-5."

[142] Quoted from Oswald, Robert 39. This source was described in endnote [68].

[143] *WCH* XI 28 (John Pic); *WR* 674, which cites "CE 1963, p. 544; CE 2212."

[144] Quoted from Oswald, Robert 40. This source was described in endnote [68].

[145] *WR* 674, which cites "CE 2211, p. 618-5."

[146] *WR* 674, which cites "CE 1874, p. 6; CE 2219; see *WCH* I 279 (R. Oswald); *WCH* XI 29 (J. Pic)."

[147] *WR* 674, which cites "*WCH* XI 29 (J. Pic)."

[148] Quoted with permission after payment, from King, Stephen. *11/22/63: A Novel*, page 467. Copyright notice supplied by publisher: "Reprinted with the permission of Scribner, a Division of Simon & Schuster, Inc., from 11/22/63 by Stephen King. Copyright © 2011 by Stephen King. All rights reserved."

[149] *WR* 674, which cites "*WCH* XI 30-31 (J. Pic)."

[150] Quoted with permission from McMillan, Priscilla Johnson. *Marina and Lee*, page 203. The essential source to knowing the Oswalds was published by Harper & Row in 1977, copyright © Priscilla Johnson McMillan. With exceptions of only the *Warren Report* and *Hearings*, I have relied on it more than any other source, using 113 direct quotations of which this is the first. Gracious permission to quote was given by Devin R. Wilkie, Permissions and Rights at Steerforth Press.

[151] CE 1874, p. 7 on *WCH* XXIII 680.

[152] Quoted with permission from McMillan 204. Permission statement is in endnote [150].

[153] *WR* 674, which cites "CE 1874, pp. 6-7."

[154] *WR* 674, which cites "*WCH* XI 30 (J. Pic)."

[155] *WR* 674, which cites "CE 1873-D; *WCH* I 292 (R. Oswald); *WCH* VIII 85 (Hiram Conway); *WCH* XI 30 (J. Pic)."

[156] *WR* 674, which cites "*WCH* XI 30 (J. Pic)."

[157] *WR* 674, which cites "*WCH* XI 30 (J. Pic)."

[158] *WR* 674, which cites "CE 1873-D."

[159] *WR* 674, which cites "CE 1873-D."

[160] *WR* 674, which cites "CE 1873-E, -F, -G; Robert Oswald testified that Ridglea West was newly built, which probably explains the transfer; *WCH* I 297."

[161] *WR* 674, which cites "CE 1873-D; see CE 1873-E, -F, -G."

[162] *WR* 674-675, which cites "CE 1873-D."

[163] *WR* 675, which cites "See p. 687, infra, but see p. 733 infra." ("Infra" means "below" or "beneath".)

[164] *WR* 675, which cites "CE 1873-D."

[165] *WR* 675, which cites "CE 2220, p. 241."

[166] *WR* 675, which cites "*WCH* I 297, 298 (R. Oswald) (insurance agent); *WCH* XI 31, 32 (J. Pic) (department stores); CE 2213, pp. 25-26 (assistant store manager, Lerner Shops; department store sales representative, Literary Guild)."

[167] *WR* 675, which cites "*WCH* VIII 119 (L. Murret); *WCH* XI 31 (J. Pic); see *WCH* VIII 163 (M. Murret)."

[168] *WR* 675, which cites "*WCH* I 281 (R. Oswald); *WCH* XI 31, 34, 40, 80 (J. Pic)."

[169] *WR* 675, which cites "*WCH* VIII 86 (Conway); *WCH* VIII 89-90 (Conway)."

[170] *WCH* XI 32 (John Pic).

[171] Quoted from Oswald, Robert 42. This source was described in endnote [68].

[172] *WCH* XI 32 (John Pic).

[173] *WR* 675, which cites "*WCH* XI 32-33 (J. Pic)."

[174] *WCH* XI 34 (John Pic), *WR* 675.

[175] Oswald, Robert 45.

[176] Quoted from Oswald, Robert 40-41. This source was described in endnote [68].

[177] *WCH* XI 75 (John Pic).

[178] *WR* 675, which cites "*WCH* I 297-298 (R. Oswald)."

[179] *WR* 675, which cites "*WCH* I 298-299 (R. Oswald)."

[180] *WCH* I 363 (Robert Oswald).

[181] *WR* 675, which cites "*WCH* I 225-226 (Marguerite Oswald); *WCH* XI 36-37 (J. Pic)."

[182] *WR* 676, which cites "*WCH* I 226 (Marguerite Oswald); *WCH* XI 37-39 (J. Pic)."

[183] *WR* 676, which cites "*WCH* XI 38 (J. Pic)."

[184] *WR* 676, which cites "*WCH* XI 38-39 (J. Pic)."

[185] *WR* 676, which cites "Marguerite and John gave different accounts of the origins of the quarrel. Compare *WCH* I 226-227 (Marguerite Oswald) with *WCH* XI 38-39 (J. Pic)."

[186] COMMISSION EXHIBIT NO. 1382 is an FBI report dated "12/10/63", shown on *WCH* XXII 687.

[187] *WCH* I 226-227 (Marguerite Oswald).

[188] *WCH* XI 81 (John Pic).

[189] *WCH* XI 40-41 (John Pic).

[190] Quoted with permission from McMillan 206. Permission statement is in endnote [150].

[191] *WR* 676, which cites "*WCH* I 227 (Marguerite Oswald); CE 1384; CE 2205, p. 570; CE 2222."

[192] *WR* 676, which cites "CE 2213, pp. 25, 28; John Carro DE 1, p. 1."

[193] *WR* 676, which cites "CE 1384."

[194] *WR* 676, which cites "CE 1384."

[195] *WR* 676, which cites "CE 1384."

[196] *WR* 676, which cites "CE 1384."

[197] This photo is held by the National Archives and Records Administration, so is in the public domain.

[198] *WR* 676, which cites "CE 1384, 2224, p. 4."

[199] *WR* 676, which cites "CE 1384; compare CE 2224, p. 4."

[200] *WR* 676, which cites "CE 2225."

[201] *WR* 676, which cites "CE 1384, 2226."

[202] *WR* 676, which cites "CE 2226, p. 7."

[203] *WR* 677, which cites "*WCH* XI 42, 43-44, (J. Pic)."

[204] *WR* 677, which cites "Carro DE 1, p. 1. Concerning this and subsequent truancy proceedings, see generally *WCH* VIII 202-214 (Carro)."

[205] *WR* 677, which cites "Carro DE 1, p. 1."

[206] *WR* 677, which cites "CE 1384."

[207] Epstein *Legend* 59.

[208] *WR* 677, which cites "Carro DE 1, p. 1; see *WCH* I 227 (Marguerite Oswald)."

[209] *WR* 677, which cites "Youth House is described by members of its staff at the time Lee was sent there at *WCH* VIII 215-218 (Dr. Renatus Hartogs), 225-226 (Evelyn Grace Strickman Siegel)."

[210] *WR* 380, which cites "Hartogs DEPOSITION EXHIBIT 1, p. 2."

[211] Quoted with permission after payment, from Warren, Earl. *The Memoirs of Earl Warren*, page 364. Copyright notice supplied by publisher: "Excerpt(s) from THE MEMOIRS OF EARL WARREN by Earl Warren, copyright © 1977 by Nina E. Warren, as Executrix of the Estate of Earl Warren. Used by permission of Doubleday, an imprint of the Knopf Doubleday Publishing Group, a division of Penguin Random House LLC. All rights reserved. Any third party use of

this material, outside of this publication, is prohibited. Interested parties must apply directly to Penguin Random House LLC for permission."

[212] Quoted with permission from Hartogs, Renatus, and Lucy Freeman. *The Two Assassins* xiii.

[213] *WR* 677, which cites "Hartogs DE 1, p. 2. Dr. Hartogs' recommendations are discussed more fully in *WR* chapter VII, pp. 379-380."

[214] *WR* 677, which cites "Carro DE 1, p. 5."

[215] *WR* 677, which cites "CE 2224, p. 7; Carro DE 1, p. 5 ; see CE 2213, p. 18."

[216] *WR* 678, which cites "CE 1384."

[217] Quoted with permission after payment, through the great courtesy of Edward Jay Epstein, from his *Legend* 60.

[218] *WCH* XI 44 (John Pic).

[219] *WR* 678, which cites "CE 1384."

[220] *WR* 678, which cites "Carro DE 1, p. 5."

[221] *WR* 678, which cites "Carro DE 1, p. 6."

[222] *WR* 678, which cites "Carro DE 1, p. 6."

[223] *WR* 678, which cites "Carro DE 1, p. 6."

[224] *WR* 678, which cites "CE 1384."

[225] *WR* 678, which cites "Carro DE 1, pp. 6-7."

[226] *WR* 678, which cites "CE 2223, p. 4."

[227] *WR* 678-679, which cites "CE 2223, p. 4."

[228] *WR* 679, which cites "Carro DE 1, p. 7 ; CE 2223, p. 5."

[229] *WR* 679, which cites "See CE 2223, p. 5."

[230] Albert E. Jenner, Jr., assistant counsel of the Warren Commission, while taking testimony from Mrs. Lillian Murret on 1964 Apr. 6, *WCH* VIII 123.

[231] *WR* 679, which cites "CE 2223, p. 5."; see Carro DE 1, p. 7."

[232] *WR* 679, which cites "Carro DE 1, p. 8."

[233] *WR* 679, which cites "*WCH* I 231 (Marguerite Oswald); *WCH* VIII 122-123 (L. Murret). The address was later changed to 809 French Street; *WCH* VIII 122 (L. Murret)."

[234] *WR* 679, which cites "CE 1413, pp. 12, 14."

[235] *WR* 679, which cites "CE 1413 3-5, p. 14."

[236] *WR* 679, which cites "CE 1413 6-8, 13, 14."

[237] Photo is COMMISSION EXHIBITS 284-285 on *WCH* XVI 804-805, held by the National Archives and Records Administration, so it is in the public domain. *Life* magazine says it was a "ninth-grade English class rehearsing Casey at the Bat."

[238] *WR* 679, which cites "CE 1413 9-10 ; see *WR* chapter VII, p. 383."

[239] *WR* 679, which cites "See *WCH* VIII 6-7, 12-13 (Edward Voebel), 63, 65 (M. Evans), 71 (J. Evans), 131 (L. Murret), 159-160 (M. Murret); CE 2233, 2235, 2236."

[240] *WR* 679, which cites "*WCH* I 198 (Marguerite Oswald); *WCH* VIII 70-71 (J. Evans); compare *WCH* VIII 18 (Wulf). Edward Voebel, who thought Lee was not a "great reader," didn't see him read anything except "comic books and the normal things that kids read"; *WCH* VIII 12 (Voebel)."

[241] *WR* 679, which cites "*WCH* VIII 2-3, 5 (Voebel), 22-25 (Bennierita Smith), 124 (L. Murret), 159-160 (M. Murret); compare CE 2232, 2234."

[242] *WR* 679, which cites "*WCH* VIII 55-57 (M. Evans), 70 (J. Evans); compare *WCH* VIII 10-11 (Voebel)."

[243] *WR* 679, which cites "CE 2201, p. 63; CE 2238, p. 2."

[244] *WR* 679, which cites "CE 2238, p. 2."

[245] *WR* 679-680, which cites "CE 2238, p. 2; see *WCH* I 198 (Marguerite Oswald); CE 1413, p. 9."

[246] *WR* 680, which cites "CE 1413, p. 9."

[247] *WR* 680, which cites "CE 2238, p. 2."

[248] *WR* 680, which cites "*WCH* VIII 53-54, 56-57 (M. Evans); see *WCH* VIII 123 (L. Murret)."

[249] *WR* 680, which cites "See *WCH* VIII 56-57 (M. Evans)."

[250] *WR* 680, which cites "*WCH* I 197 (Marguerite Oswald); see *WCH* VIII 57 (M. Evans), 123 (L. Murret), 158-159 (M. Murret); CE 2231."

[251] *WR* 680, which cites "*WCH* I 310-311 (R. Oswald)."

[252] *WR* 680, which cites "CE 1413, p. 15; see CE 1873-1, -J."

[253] CE 199 on *WCH* XVI 579; duplicated as CE 1413, p. 11 on *WCH* XXII 814.

[254] *WR* 680, which cites "CE 1413, p. 15; see CE 1873-H."

[255] *WCH* I 375 (Robert Oswald).

[256] Mailer *Oswald's Tale* 377.

[257] *WR* 680, which cites "*WCH* I 196-198 (Marguerite Oswald); *WCH* VIII 130-131 (L. Murret)."

[258] *WR* 680, which cites "*WCH* XI 32 (J. Pic)."

[259] *WCH* I 198, 200 (Marguerite Oswald).

260 *WR* 680, which cites "CE 1386, p. 251; CE 2227, 2228, 2229, 2230, 2237; see *WCH* I 198-199, 224 (Marguerite Oswald)."

261 *WR* 680-681, which cites "Folsom DE 1, p. 7."

262 *WR* 681, which cites "*WCH* I 199 (Marguerite Oswald)."

263 *WR* 681, which cites "CE 1873-J, -K."

264 *WR* 681, which cites "CE 1873-J, -K."

265 *WR* 681, which cites "CE 2240, p. 2."

266 *WR* 681, which cites "CE 2240, p. 2-3."

267 Quoted from Oswald, Robert 79. This source was described in endnote 68.

268 Quoted with permission from Baker, Judyth Vary. *Me & Lee: How I Came to Know, Love and Lose Lee Harvey Oswald*, page 135.

269 *WCH* XI 3-4 (John Pic).

270 *WCH* XI 77-78 (John Pic).

271 Quoted as fair use from Leahy, Michael (*Arkansas Democrat-Gazette*), "Still haunted by a brother's legacy", *Philadelphia Inquirer* 1997 21 Nov.: A22. Most of the words are from Robert Oswald, to whom this author appealed and offered, and finally had his copyright attorney file an estoppel notice, as recounted in endnote 68.

272 O'Reilly, Bill, and Martin Dugard. *Killing Kennedy: The End of Camelot* 14. This is the first citation of that book, thus the appropriate place to explain why I never directly quote from it. My copyright agent applied on my behalf to literally hundreds of authors and publishers (whichever held each copyright) for permissions to quote from their works. He was successful in almost every case, evidenced by well over a thousand of these endnotes beginning "Quoted with permission" or "Quoted with permission after payment". Obeying the O'Reilly-Dugard book's publisher's instructions, in June 2015 he mailed via USPS an 8-page on-paper request to the Permissions Dept. of Henry Holt and Company. After two months and no reply, he sent multiple Internet requests, again to that publisher, and also to co-author O'Reilly and to O'Reilly's legal department. He never received the courtesy of any response from any. With this book written and ready to publish, the author took over to carefully retrace and augment his paths. I sent requests by Internet, always offering to pay whatever fee they asked, to six possible contacts, politely asking each for the courtesy of a reply or re-direction: Bill O'Reilly, Martin Dugard, the duplicate contact addresses specified by the book's publisher (permissions@hholt.com) and (rights@hholt.com), the Director of Permissions (by her name) for Henry Holt & Company, and Macmillan, the capstone of their publishing group, publisher of my father's books, *Opportunity in Alaska* in 1945 and *Hail* Columbia in 1954. None had the simple courtesy to reply, so as the young child said to a doting mother at the dinner table in a *New Yorker* cartoon caption by E. B. White, "I say it's spinach, and I say to hell with it." I refuse to beg and do not quote from that book. *** Update two months later in January 2016: The Director of Permissions for Henry Holt & Company sent an email: "... we are unable to grant permission rights for the book ...". After seven wasted months, that's that. Spinach!

273 *WCH* XI 12 (John Pic).

274 Transcribed by the author from an interview of Robert Oswald by Josh Mankowitz in a segment titled "My Brother's Keeper" on *Dateline NBC*, broadcast by NBC-TV on June 14, 1998, and quoted here with permission after payment. The NBC license agreement is described in endnote 16.

275 Quoted with permission from McMillan 212. Permission statement is in endnote 150.

276 *WCH* VIII 98 (Lillian Murret).

277 Testimony of Marilyn Dorothea Murret on *WCH* VIII 164.

278 Quoted from Oswald, Robert 48. This source was described in endnote 68.

279 *WCH* I 311 (Robert Oswald).

280 Quoted with permission from McMillan 208. Permission statement is in endnote 150.

281 Quoted with permission after payment, from Bishop, Jim. *The Day Kennedy Was Shot* 9.

282 Testimony of Mrs. Lee Harvey Oswald on *WCH* I 5.

283 Testimony of Peter Paul Gregory on *WCH* II 345.

284 Quoted with permission from McMillan 211. Permission statement is in endnote 150.

— 2 — Marine

285 Testimony of John Edward Pic on page 45 of volume XI (11) of the *Hearings before the President's Commission on the Assassination of President Kennedy*. Hereinafter this would be cited in the form: *WCH* XI 45 (John Pic).

286 Photo is included in CE 287 on *WCH* XVI 807. Robert Oswald's biography *Lee*, in caption for photo 9 in photo section after page 96, dates it to April, 1959. The photo from the U.S. Marine Corps was taken by a federal government employee in the performance of official duty, so is in the public domain.

287 *Report of the President's Commission on the Assassination of President John F. Kennedy*, better known as the *Warren Report*, page 681, hereinafter *WR* 681, which cites "Folsom DE 1, p. 3. The abbreviations used on the official record to designate Lee's units and duty stations are explained in CE 1961, pp. 3-5." DE is abbreviation of Deposition Exhibit; CE is for Commission Exhibit.

288 *WR* 681, which cites "Folsom DE 1, p. 1; see *WCH* VIII 304 (Folsom)."

289 *WR* 681, which cites "Folsom DE 1, p. 7; see *WCH* VIII 307-308 (Folsom)."

[290] *WR* 681, which cites "Folsom DE 1, p. 7."

[291] *WR* 681, which cites "See CE 239; *WCH* VIII 310-311 (Folsom)."

[292] *WR* 681, which cites "Folsom DE 1, p. 6; see *WCH* VIII 311 (Folsom); see generally *WCH* XI 104 (Kerry Wendell Thornley)." Further explained in testimony on *WCH* VIII 306-307 (Folsom).

[293] *WR* 682, which cites "Folsom DE 1, p. 6."

[294] Oswald, Robert L., with Myrick and Barbara Land. *Lee: A Portrait of Lee Harvey Oswald by His Brother* 84; *WCH* VIII 305 (Folsom)." This source was described in endnote [68].

[295] *WR* 682, which cites "Folsom DE 1, p. 3."

[296] *WR* 682, which cites "CE 1962, p. 3."

[297] *WR* 682, which cites "CE 1962, p. 4."

[298] *WR* 682, which cites "Folsom DE 1, p. 3."

[299] *WR* 682, which cites "Folsom DE 1, p. 3."

[300] *WR* 682, which cites "CE 1961, pp. 1-2."

[301] *WR* 682, which cites "See CE 1961, pp. 2-3."

[302] *WR* 682, which cites "Folsom DE 1, p. 10."

[303] *WR* 682, which cites "Folsom DE 1, p. 118."

[304] *WR* 682, which cites "Folsom DE 1, p. 120."

[305] *WR* 682, which cites "Folsom DE 1, p. 3."

[306] *WR* 682, which cites "Folsom DE 1, p. 3; see *WCH* VIII 305 (Folsom); compare *WCH* VIII 268 (Daniel Patrick Powers)."

[307] *WR* 682, which cites "CE 1961, p. 2; see *WCH* VIII 269 (Powers)."

[308] *WR* 682, which cites "Folsom DE 1, p. 119; *WCH* VIII 267-268 (Powers)."

[309] *WR* 682, which cites "*WCH* VIII 268 (Powers)."

[310] *WR* 682, which cites "*WCH* VIII 270 (Powers)."

[311] *WR* 682-683, which cites "*WCH* VIII 277-278, 279 (Powers); see generally *WCH* VIII 269-271."

[312] *WR* 683, which cites "Folsom DE 1, p. 116."

[313] *WR* 683, which cites "Folsom DE 1, p. 7."

[314] *WR* 683, which cites "Folsom DE 1, p. 3."

[315] *WR* 683, which cites "Folsom DE 1, p. 3."

[316] This photo was purchased to show here, with credit: Donald Uhrbrock / The LIFE Images Collection / Getty Images.

[317] *WR* 683, which cites "Folsom DE 1, p. 13."

[318] *WR* 683, which cites "Folsom DE 1, p. 13."

[319] *WR* 683, which cites "Folsom DE 1, p. 3 ; CE 1961, p. 4."

[320] *WR* 683, which cites "*WCH* VIII 278-279 (Powers)."

[321] *WR* 683, which cites "*WCH* VIII 279 (Powers)."

[322] *WR* 683, which cites "*WCH* VIII 279 (Powers)."

[323] Photo by U.S. Air Force is in the public domain.

[324] Epstein, Edward Jay. *Legend: The Secret World of Lee Harvey Oswald* 54-55.

[325] Quoted with permission from Newman, John. *Oswald and the CIA* 30.

[326] *WR* 683, which cites "Folsom DE 1, p. 111."

[327] *WR* 683, which cites "*WCH* VIII 320 (Paul Edward Murphy)."

[328] *WR* 683, which cites "Folsom DE 1, p. 3 ; CE 1961, p. 4."

[329] Folsom Exhibit No. 1–Continued (pp. 111-112).

[330] Folsom Exhibit No. 1–Continued (p. 59).

[331] *WR* 683, which cites "Folsom DE 1, p. 8."

[332] Epstein *Legend* 73.

[333] *WR* 683-684, which cites "CE 1961, p. 4."

[334] *WR* 684, which cites "*WCH* VIII 279-280 (Powers)."

[335] *WR* 684, which cites "Folsom DE 1, p. 5."

[336] *WR* 684, which cites "Folsom DE 1, p. 3."

[337] Photo is included in CE 289 on *WCH* XVI 809. It is held by the National Archives and Records Administration, so is in the public domain.

[338] Quoted with permission from McMillan, Priscilla Johnson. *Marina and Lee*, pages 77-78. Permission statement is in endnote [150].

[339] *WR* 684, which cites "Folsom DE 1. p. 9."

[340] Epstein *Legend* 78.

[341] *WR* 684, which cites "Folsom DE 1. p. 32; see *WCH* VIII 322 (Mack Osborne); *WCH* XI 84, 85 (Thornley)."

[342] *WR* 684, which cites "Folsom DE 1. p. 9."

[343] *WR* 684, which cites "Folsom DE 1. p. 8; see *WCH* VIII 308 (Folsom)."

[344] *WR* 684, which cites "Folsom DE 1, p. 3."

[345] Epstein *Legend* 79.

[346] *WR* 684, which cites "Folsom DE 1. p. 10."

[347] Quoted from Oswald, Robert 88. This source was described in endnote [68]. The denial was further explained in testimony on *WCH* VIII 309 (Folsom).

[348] *WR* 684, which cites "Folsom DE 1. p. 3."

[349] *WR* 684, which cites "CE 1961, p. 5."

[350] *WR* 684, which cites "Folsom DE 1, p. 3."

[351] *WR* 684, which cites "Folsom DE 1, p. 3."

[352] *WR* 684, which cites "*WCH* VIII 317 (Peter Francis Connor), 318 (John Rene Heindel), 320 (Murphy)."

[353] *WR* 684, which cites "*WCH* VIII 320 (Murphy); compare *WCH* VIII 285 (Powers)."

[354] *WR* 684, which cites "Folsom DE 1, p. 13; CE 1961, p. 5."

[355] *WR* 684, which cites "Folsom DE 1, p. 36."

[356] *WR* 684, which cites "Folsom DE 1, p. 3; CE 1961, p. 5."

[357] *WR* 684, which cites "*WCH* VIII 290 (John E. Donovan); see generally *WCH* VIII 231-232 (Delgado)."

[358] *WR* 684-685, which cites "*WCH* VIII 297-298 (Donovan); but see CE 1961, p. 3."

[359] *WR* 685, which cites "*WCH* VIII 291, 292 (Donovan)."

[360] *WR* 685, which cites "*WCH* VIII 298-299 (Donovan)."

[361] *WR* 685, which cites "See *WCH* VIII 233-234, 258, 262 (Delgado), 316 (Botelho), 318 (Allen D. Graf), 319 (David Christie Murray, Jr.), 320 (Murphy), 321-322 (Osborne), 323 (Richard Dennis Call); *WCH* XI 85, 89-91, 100-101 (Thornley)."

[362] *WR* 685, which cites "*WCH* VIII 233 (Delgado); see *WCH* VIII 291 (Donovan)."

[363] *WR* 685, which cites "See *WCH* VIII 245 (Delgado), 297 (Donovan), 316 (Botelho), 319 (Murray), 321 (Henry J. Roussel, Jr.); *WCH* XI 92 (Thornley); but see *WCH* VIII 320 (Murphy)."

[364] *WR* 685, which cites "*WCH* VIII 317 (Donald Camarata),. 322 (Osborne), 323 (Call)."

[365] *WR* 685, which cites "*WCH* VIII 265 (Delgado), 292-293, 297 (Donovan); *WCH* XI 106-107 (Thornley); but see *WCH* VIII 322 (Call)."

[366] Quoted with permission from McMillan 78. Permission statement is in endnote [150].

[367] *WR* 685, which cites "*WCH* VIII 244 (Delgado), 292 (Donovan), 315 (Botelho), 316 (Camarata), 319 (Murray), 320 (Murphy), 321 (Roussel), 321 (Osborne), 322 (Call), 323 (Erwin Lewis); *WCH* XI 87 (Thornley)."

[368] Epstein *Legend* 86.

[369] Epstein *Legend* 79.

[370] Quoted with permission after payment, from Epstein *Legend* 87.

[371] *WR* 685, which cites "*WCH* VIII 242 (Delgado), 292 (Donovan), 315 (Botelho), 317 (Camarata), *WCH* XI 87-88 (Thornley); compare *WCH* VIII 320 (Murphy)."

[372] *WR* 685, which cites "Folsom DE 1, p. 7; see *WCH* VIII 307."

[373] *WR* 686, which cites "*WCH* VIII 315 (Botelho), 323 (Call); but see *WCH* VIII 257-258 (Delgado)."

[374] *WR* 686, which cites "*WCH* VIII 316 (Camarata)."

[375] *WR* 686, which cites "*WCH* VIII 316 (Camarata); see *WCH* VIII 321 (Roussel)."

[376] *WR* 686, which cites "*WCH* VIII 319 (Murray)."

[377] *WR* 686, which cites "*WCH* VIII 315 (Botelho)."

[378] *WR* 686, which cites "*WCH* VIII 257-258 (Delgado), 321 (Roussel)."

[379] Quoted with permission from McMillan 79. Permission statement is in endnote [150].

[380] *WR* 686, which cites "*WCH* VIII 317 (Camarata), 317 (Connor), 318 (Graf), 321 (Roussel), 322 (Osborne), 322-323 (Call)."

[381] *WR* 686, which cites "*WCH* VIII 290 (Donovan)."

[382] *WR* 686, which cites "*WCH* VIII 297 (Donovan)."

[383] *WR* 686, which cites "*WCH* VIII 292 (Donovan)."

[384] *WR* 686, which cites "*WCH* VIII 295 (Donovan)."

[385] *WR* 686, which cites "*WCH* VIII 293 (Donovan)."

[386] *WR* 686, which cites "*WCH* VIII 293 (Donovan)."

[387] *WR* 686, which cites "*WCH* VIII 292 (Donovan)."

[388] *WR* 686, which cites "*WCH* XI 87 (Thornley)."

[389] *WR* 686, which cites "*WCH* XI 87 (Thornley)."

[390] *WR* 686-687, which cites "*WCH* XI 98 (Thornley)."

[391] *WR* 687, which cites "*WCH* VIII 232-233, 241, 246-248 (Delgado)."

[392] *WR* 687, which cites "*WCH* VIII 233 (Delgado)."

[393] *WR* 687, which cites "See *WCH* VIII 240-241, 243-244, 255 (Delgado)."

[394] *WR* 687, which cites "*WCH* VIII 240 (Delgado)."

[395] TESTIMONY OF NELSON DELGADO on *WCH* VIII 230.

[396] *WCH* VIII 234 (Delgado).

[397] *WR* 687, which cites "*WCH* VIII 244, 254 (Delgado); *WCH* XI 90 (Thornley); see *WCH* XI 105 ('something . . . by Dostoievsky')."

[398] *WR* 687, which cites "*WCH* VIII 300 (Donovan), 316 (Botelho), 319 (Murray), 320 (Murphy), 322 (Osborne), 322-323 (Call)."

[399] *WR* 687, which cites "*WCH* VIII 323 (Call)."

[400] *WR* 687, which cites "*WCH* VIII 251 (Delgado), 295 (Donovan)."

[401] *WR* 687, which cites "*WCH* VIII 295-296 (Donovan)."

[402] *WR* 687, which cites "Folsom DE 1, p. 3."

[403] *WR* 687, which cites "Folsom DE 1, p. 105."

[404] *WR* 687, which cites "Folsom DE 1, p. 106; see *WCH* VIII 309 (Folsom)."

[405] *WR* 688, which cites "CE 228, p. 1."

[406] *WR* 688, which cites "CE 228, p. 1; see CE 228, p. 3."

[407] *WR* 688, which cites "CE 228, p. 2."

[408] *WR* 688, which cites "CE 228, p. 2."

[409] *WR* 688, which cites "CE 228, p. 2."

[410] *WR* 688, which cites "CE 228, p. 2."

[411] *WR* 688, which cites "See CE 229, 232."

[412] *WR* 688, which cites "CE 234."

[413] Anderson Exhibit No. 1 on *WCH* XIX 16-18.

[414] Quoted in Oswald, Robert 93. This source was described in endnote [68].

[415] Folsom Exhibit No. 1–Continued (p. 89) on *WCH* XIX 732.

[416] CE 201 (two pages) on *WCH* XVI 581-582. The transcription in this book is more accurate than the one in the *WCH*.

[417] Testimony of Mrs. Marguerite Oswald on *WCH* I 204, referring to CE 201, above.

[418] *WR* 688, which cites "Folsom DE 1, p. 84."

[419] *WR* 688, which cites "Folsom DE 1, pp. 86-91; compare CE 2241."

[420] Quoted with permission from McMillan 80. Permission statement is in endnote [150].

[421] Folsom Exhibit No. 1–Continued (pp. 100-101) on *WCH* XIX 740-741.

[422] Folsom Exhibit No. 1–Continued (p. 94) on *WCH* XIX 735.

[423] Testimony of Robert Edward Lee Oswald *WCH* I 361.

[424] *WCH* I 366 (Robert Oswald). Allen W. Dulles had been the Director of Central Intelligence.

[425] Quoted from Oswald, Robert 94. This source was described in endnote [68].

[426] *WCH* I 367 (Robert Oswald).

[427] *WCH* I 360 (Robert Oswald).

[428] *WCH* I 364 (Robert Oswald).

[429] Folsom Exhibit No. 1–Continued (p. 79) on *WCH* XIX 725.

[430] Folsom Exhibit No. 1–Continued (p. 80) on *WCH* XIX 726.

[431] Hirsch, Phil, editor. *The Kennedy War Heroes* 158.

[432] Quoted as fair use (for brevity) from article "Shoup of Tarawa" by W. Douglas Lansford, printed in Hirsch (above) 140-141.

[433] Photo by U.S. Marine Corps is in the public domain.

[434] Quoted as fair use from http://www.arlingtoncemetery.net/shoup.htm on 2012/04/30.

[435] Quoted with permission from Sorensen, Theodore C. *The Kennedy Legacy* 88.

[436] *WR* 688, which cites "Folsom DE 1, pp. 79-80."

[437] Folsom Exhibit No. 1–Continued, pp. 10, 78.

[438] *WR* 687, which cites "Folsom DE 1, p. 3."

[439] CE 1114 on *WCH* XXII 77-78.

[440] *WR* 746: "Issuance of Passport in 1959" in Appendix XV.

[441] CE 1114, page 2, on *WCH* XXII 78.

[442] *WR* 689, which cites "CE 946."

[443] Folsom Exhibit No. 1–Continued (p. 28) on *WCH* XIX 679. Less-clear copies are on *WCH* XIX 676 and 734.

[444] Photo of DD Form 217 MC is Cadigan Exhibit No. 21 on *WCH* XIX 294. The photo (and perhaps the card itself) is held by the National Archives and Records Administration, so is in the public domain. The card is item 3 on the property list, CE 1148 on *WCH* XXII 178.

[445] Photo of DD Form 1173 is held by the National Archives and Records Administration, catalogued as "FBI Exhibit number B1", not a number used by the Warren Commission. The card is item 4 on property list, CE 1148 on *WCH* XXII 178.

[446] Folsom Exhibit No. 1–Continued (p. 29) on *WCH* XIX 680.

[447] Folsom Exhibit No. 1–Continued (p. 77) on *WCH* XIX 724.

[448] *WCH* XI 80 (John Pic).

[449] Folsom Exhibit No. 1–Continued (pp. 4, 28) on *WCH* XIX 659 and 679.

— 3 — MOSCOW

[450] Lee Oswald letter from Moscow to Robert Oswald dated "Nov 26. 1959", COMMISSION EXHIBIT No. 295 pages 7-8, on pages 821 and 822 of *Warren Commission Hearings* volume 16. References hereinafter employ abbreviations, so this would be: CE 295 on *WCH* XVI 821-822.

[451] *Warren Report* page 689, hereinafter *WR* 689, which cites "*WCH* I 201-202 (Marguerite Oswald); CE 1135, p. 172."

[452] Oswald, Robert L., with Myrick and Barbara Land. *Lee: A Portrait of Lee Harvey Oswald by His Brother* 95. This source was described in endnote [68]. See also TESTIMONY OF MRS. LILLIAN MURRET on *WCH* VIII 118.

[453] TESTIMONY OF ROBERT EDWARD LEE OSWALD on *WCH* I 329, hereinafter shortened to: *WCH* I 329 (Robert Oswald).

[454] Quoted from Oswald, Robert 95. This source was described in endnote [68].

[455] *WCH* I 359 (Robert Oswald).

[456] This was scanned from photo 10 in the photo insert after page 96 in Robert Oswald's *Lee*, with caption: "The last time I saw Lee before he went to Russia was in September, 1959, the day I took this picture of him holding Cathy in front of our home in Fort Worth." This source was described in endnote [68].

[457] *WR* 689, which cites "CE 1135, p. 172."

[458] CE 1944 on *WCH* XXIII 743.

[459] *WR* 689, which cites "*WCH* I 201-202, 212 (Marguerite Oswald); CE 1396, p. 6."

[460] *WR* 689, which cites "*WCH* I 201-202, 212 (Marguerite Oswald); CE 1396, p. 6."

[461] TESTIMONY OF MRS. MARGUERITE OSWALD on *WCH* I 212.

[462] *WCH* I 203 (Marguerite Oswald).

[463] *WCH* VIII 119 (Lillian Murret).

[464] *WR* 689, which cites "CE 2673, 2665, p. 305."

[465] *WR* 689, which cites "CE 2712."

[466] *WCH* I 201 (Marguerite Oswald).

[467] *WR* 689-690, which cites "CE 200."

[468] *WR* 689, which cites "CE 2665, p. 305."

[469] *WR* 690, which cites "CE 2665, p. 305; see CE 2674."

[470] *WR* 690, which cites "CE 2675, p. 2."

[471] *WR* 690, which cites "CE 2675, pp. 2-3; *WCH* XI 116 (George B. Church, Jr.), 117 (Mrs. George B. Church, Jr.)."

[472] *WR* 690, which cites "CE 2711, p. 39; CE 946, p. 7; CE 2676, p. 1."

[473] There is no cause for uncertainty about these dates: Oswald's passport is shown on *WCH* XVIII 162.

[474] *WR* 690, which cites "CE 2676, pp. 1, 3."

[475] *WR* 690, which cites "CE 2677. Oswald could have arrived at 5:05 p.m., flying via Copenhagen, or at 5:35 p.m., via Stockholm. See Official Airline Guide, North American Edition, October 1959, p. C-721. But he would have been too late to visit the Russian consulate that day. See CE 2714."

[476] *WR* 690, which cites "CE 946, p. 9."

[477] *WR* 690, which cites "CE 946, p. 8; CE 24, entry of Oct. 16, 1959; CE 985, document No. 1A."

[478] Scanned from Oswald's *Historic Diary*, displayed as COMMISSION EXHIBIT (CE) 24 on *WCH* XVI 94-105. Coming from that US Federal government source, it is in the public domain.

[479] *WR* 691, which cites "CE 18; see, for example, pp. 3, 7, 22, 23, 27, 29, 31, 35, 61, 81; see also CE 827; *WCH* I 30, 104 (Marina Oswald)."

[480] *WR* 690, which cites "CE 24, entry of Oct. 16, 1959."

[481] *WR* 691, which cites "CE 24, entry of Oct. 16, 1959."

[482] *WR* 691, which cites "CE 24, entry of Oct. 17, 1959."

[483] *WR* 690-691, which cites "CE 3124."

[484] *WR* 691, which cites "CE 24, entry of Oct. 16, 1959."

[485] Quoted with permission from Shvets, Yuri B. *Washington Station: My Life as a KGB Spy in America* 197. Copyright notice supplied by publisher: "Reprinted with the permission of Simon & Schuster, Inc. from WASHINGTON STATION by Yuri B. Shvets. Copyright © 1994 Yuri B. Shvets."

[486] Quoted with permission from Shvets 26. Copyright notice is immediately above in endnote [485].

[487] Photo is CE 2963 on *WCH* XXVI 444. It is held by the National Archives and Records Administration, so is in the public domain.

[488] *WR* 691, which cites "CE 24, entry of Oct. 17, 1959."

[489] *WR* 691, which cites "CE 24, entry of Oct. 18, 1959."

[490] CE 1399 on *WCH* XXII 738.

[491] *WR* 691, which cites "*WCH* V 617 (Marina Oswald); CE 935, 827, 1438, 2760; compare CE 25, pp. 1B-2B."

[492] *WR* 691, which cites "*WCH* V 274 (Richard Edward Snyder)."

[493] *WR* 691.

[494] Transcribed as fair use (for brevity) from TV: *Real History: The Secret KGB JFK Assassination Files*, broadcast on The Learning Channel on 03 March 2000.

[495] Quoted with permission after payment from Nechiporenko, Oleg M. *Passport to Assassination: The Never-Before-Told Story of Lee Harvey Oswald by the KGB Colonel Who Knew Him* 34. Copyright notice supplied by publisher: "Copyright © 1993 by Oleg M. Nechiporenko. All rights reserved. Reprinted by arrangement with Kensington Publishing Corp. www.kensingtonbooks.com". I paid their required $300 not for the quotes, but because the photo of Oswald's Identity Document for Stateless Persons displayed on page 43 is not available from any other source, so I had to meet their price.

[496] *WR* 691, which cites "CE 24, entry of Oct. 20, 1959."

[497] Extract from CE 24 pages 1-2 on *WCH* XVI 94-95, with spelling as used in the Commission's transcription.

[498] *WR* 692, which cites "CE 24, entry of Oct. 23, 1959."

[499] *WR* 692, which cites "CE 985, documents 1C-1—1C-4."

[500] *WR* 692, which cites "CE 985, document 1C-3, p. 10."

[501] *WR* 692, which cites "CE 985, document 1C-3, p. 10."

[502] *WR* 692, which cites "CE 24, entry of Oct. 23, 1950."

[503] *WR* 692, which cites "CE 24, entry of Oct. 23-26, 1959."

[504] *WCH* I 341-342 (Robert Oswald), quoting from his diary for Jan. 19, 1964 in CE 323, page 27, on *WCH* XVI 915.

[505] *WR* 692, which cites "CE 985, document 1C-2, pp. 1, 8-9."

[506] *WR* 692, which cites "CE 24, entry of Oct. 28, 1959."

[507] *WR* 692.

[508] *WR* 692-693, which cites "CE 24, entry of Oct. 28, 1959."

[509] *WR* 693, which cites "CE 24, entries of Oct. 29-31, 1959."

[510] Manchester, William. *The Death of a President* 30.

[511] *WR* 693, which cites "CE 24, 912, 913 pp. 264, 263, 261."

[512] *WR* 693, which cites "See CE 908, p. 1; CE 909, p. 1; *WCH* V 260-261 (Snyder)."

[513] *WR* 693, which cites "See generally *WCH* V 262-265, 269-270, 287-291 (Snyder); 300-304, 322-324 (John A. McVickar); CE 908, 909, 910."

[514] Quoted with permission after payment, from Epstein, Edward Jay. *Legend: The Secret World of Lee Harvey Oswald* 94.

[515] Quoted from Oswald, Robert 104. This source was described in endnote [68]. See also *WCH* V 264 (Snyder).

[516] Quoted with permission from Newman, John 1.

[517] TESTIMONY OF RICHARD EDWARD SNYDER on *WCH* V 271-272.

[518] *WCH* V 290 (Snyder).

[519] Quoted with permission from McMillan, Priscilla Johnson. *Marina and Lee*, page 82. Permission statement for this source is in endnote [150].

[520] *WR* 693, which cites "*WCH* V 269 (Snyder); see CE 101, 941."

[521] CE 257 on *WCH* XVI 719; duplicated as CE 913 on *WCH* XVIII 109.

[522] Quoted from Oswald, Robert 104. This source was described in endnote [68].

[523] Quoted with permission from Newman, John 439, showing the *Department of State* incoming telegram to Washington from Moscow.

[524] *Historic Diary* page 4, CE 24 on *WCH* XVI 97.

[525] Quoted with permission from Newman, John 7.

[526] *WCH* V 291 (Snyder).

[527] Newman, John 8.

[528] Quoted from Oswald, Robert 98. This source was described in endnote [68].

[529] Quoted from Oswald, Robert 72. This source was described in endnote [68].

[530] Quoted from Oswald, Robert 105. This source was described in endnote [68].

[531] CE 270 on *WCH* XVI 721-748.

[532] The newspaper story shown was scanned and cropped from a photo in John Newman's *Oswald and the CIA*, page 440. That photo shows his source in handwriting: "CD 692 Wash. Post 11-1-59" and rubber stamp "Document Number 591-252A for FOIA Review on JUN 1976". FOIA means Freedom of Information Act.

[533] Excerpt from COMMISSION EXHIBIT 270—Continued. These paragraphs are on *WCH* XVI 727-728

[534] Quoted with permission from Kantor, Seth. *The Ruby Cover-Up* 95. See also CE 24 entry of Nov. 1. 1959; CE 2672; P. Johnson DE 5, p. 15; *WCH* I 323 (Robert Oswald); TESTIMONY OF PRISCILLA MARY POST JOHNSON on *WCH* XI 458.

[535] *WR* 694, which cites "CE 2715, p. 61; CE 2684; *WCH* I 322 (R. Oswald)."

[536] *WR* 694, which cites "CE 2715, p. 61."

[537] *WR* 694, which cites "CE 2715; *WCH* I 323 (R. Oswald)."

[538] Quoted with permission from Lane, Mark. *Plausible Denial: Was the CIA Involved in the Assassination of JFK?*, on the fifth (un-numbered) page in his Preface. Mr. Lane very kindly granted permission in a personal email to the author on 2016/02/03, saying "I grant you permission as requested in your letter. You, of course, are correct that it would be fair use, but I appreciate that you contacted me. I wish you the very best with your book Tragic Truth and I would very much enjoy reading your work when you are finished." A copy will be inscribed and mailed to him, with my great thanks.

[539] Quoted with permission after payment, from Epstein *Legend* 96.

[540] Quoted with permission from Newman, John 28.

[541] Quoted with permission from Newman, John 444, showing Naval Message (a secure form of telegram) to Moscow from Washington.

[542] CE 918 on *WCH* XVIII 116.

[543] Quoted with permission from Newman, John 33.

[544] Quoted with permission from Newman, John 43-44, which cites "John Donovan, quoted in 'Oswald in Russia: Did He Tell Our Military Secrets?' *New York Journal American*, December 2, 1963. See also NARA FBI New York Field Office file 105-38431, and NARA JFK RIF 124-10160-10438."

[545] Quoted with permission from Newman, John 44, which cites "John Donovan, quoted in 'Oswald Was a Troublemaker' *Washington Evening Star*, December 2, 1963. See also NARA JFK records, NIS, box 1."

[546] Quoted with permission after payment, from Epstein *Legend* 103.

[547] CE 912 on *WCH* XVIII 108; *WCH* V 267-269 (Snyder).

[548] *WCH* V 280 (Snyder).

[549] CE 919 on *WCH* XVIII 117.

[550] CE 920 (two pages) on *WCH* XVIII 118-119.

[551] Testimony of Frances G. Knight on *WCH* V 374.

[552] *WR* 694, which cites "CE 24, entry of Nov. 2-15, 1959."

[553] CE 294 on *WCH* XVI 814, read to the Commission by Robert's attorney on *WCH* I 321.

[554] *WR* 695, which cites "CE 24, entry of Nov. 16, 1959."

[555] *WR* 695, which cites "CE 24, entry of Jan. 4, 1960; CE 985, documents 1A, 2A."

[556] *WR* 695, which cites "CE 942, 943, 2683, p. 29; *WCH* V 302 (McVickar)."

[557] *WR* 695, which cites "See Fort Worth Star Telegram, Nov. 15, 1959, 'Fort Worth Defector Confirms Red Beliefs'; CE 24, entry of Nov. 15, 1959; CE 1385; see also CE 1438."

[558] *WR* 695, which cites "CE 1385, p. 2."

[559] CE 1385, pp. 1-12 on *WCH* XXII 701-710.

[560] *WR* 695-696, which cites "CE 1385, pp. 1-12."

[561] *WR* 696, which cites "CE 2717; CE 24, entry for Nov. 15, 1959."

[562] *WR* 696, which cites "CE 1385, p. 16."

[563] Scanned from CE 2716 on *WCH* XXVI 90. The newspaper is identified in *WR* 863, note 543, as "Fort Worth Star Telegram, Nov. 15, 1959".

[564] *Historic Diary* page 4, CE 24 on *WCH* XVI 97.

[565] *WR* 696, which cites "CE 24, entry of Nov. 16, 1959."

[566] *WR* 696, which cites "CE 24, entry of Nov. 16, 1959."

[567] *WR* 696, which cites "*WCH* XI 446-447 (P. Johnson)."

[568] *WR* 696, which cites "The interview is described in P. Johnson DE 1, 5, 6; *WCH* XI 444-460. Oswald told Aline Mosby that he had read the Communist Manifesto. CE 1385, p. 6."

[569] Quoted with permission after payment, from Epstein *Legend* 100.

[570] *WR* 696, which cites "P. Johnson DE 1, p. 6."

[571] *WR* 696, which cites "*WCH* XI 447, 459 (P. Johnson); CE 911."

[572] Quoted with permission from McMillan (name of Priscilla Johnson after marriage), *Marina and Lee*, page 84. Permission statement is in endnote [150].

[573] *Historic Diary* page 5, CE 24 on *WCH* XVI 98.

[574] *WR* 696-697, which cites "CE 24, entries of Nov. 17-Dec. 30, Dec. 31, 1959; *WCH* V 616 (Marina Oswald)."

[575] CE 295 on *WCH* XVI 815-823.

[576] CE 297 on *WCH* XVI 825.

[577] *WR* 697, which cites "CE 202, 206; *WCH* I 204 (Marguerite Oswald)."

[578] Quoted with permission after payment from Nechiporenko 39. Copyright notice is in endnote [495].

[579] Quoted with permission after payment from Nechiporenko 40. Copyright notice is in endnote [495].

[580] Quoted with permission after payment from Nechiporenko 40-41. Copyright notice is in endnote [495].

[581] Quoted with permission after payment from Nechiporenko 125-126. Copyright notice is in endnote [495].

[582] Photo scanned with permission after payment ($300, more than $1 for each copy of this book the author intends to buy) from Nechiporenko, fifth photo in insert section after 48. Copyright notice is in endnote [495]. About the document, see *WR* 697, which cites "CE 24, entry of Jan. 4, 1960; compare CE 985, documents 1A, 2A, 3A (1); CE 935."

[583] Quoted with permission after payment from Nechiporenko, caption on fifth photo in insert section after 48. Copyright notice is in endnote [495].

[584] *WR* 697, which cites "CE 24, entry of Jan. 4, 1960."

[585] *WR* 697, which states "In 1963, the population of Minsk was about 650,000."

[586] *WR* 697, which cites "CE 24, entry of Jan. 4, 1960."

[587] Epstein *Legend* 108 and his endnote 8 on 296.

[588] *WR* 697, which cites "CE 24, entry of Jan. 4-5, 1960; *WCH* V 292-293 (Snyder)."

[589] *WR* 697, which cites "CE 24, entries of Jan. 5 and 7, 1960."

— 4 — Minsk

[590] Quoted with permission after payment, from Warren, Earl. *The Memoirs of Earl Warren* 364. Copyright notice is in endnote [211].

[591] Testimony of Richard Edward Snyder on *WCH* V 294. *WCH* is the 26-volume *Warren Commission Hearings*. *WCH* V 294 means the reference is to page 294 in volume V.

[592] *WR* 697, which cites "CE 24, entry of Jan. 7, 1960." *WR* is *Warren Report*. CE means Commission Exhibit.

[593] *WR* 697, which cites "CE 24, entry of Oct. 18, 1960."

[594] *WR* 697, which cites "CE 24, entry of Jan. 8, 1960."

[595] *WR* 698, which cites "*WCH* V 590 (Marina Oswald); *WCH* VIII 347, 350 (Max Clark); *WCH* IX 81 (Taylor), 147 (Paul Gregory); see P. Johnson DE 1, pp. 1, 6; P. Johnson DE 5, p. 7; CE 1385, p. 16."

[596] *WR* 697, which cites "CE 1108."

[597] *WR* 697, which cites "CE 92, p. 3; see CE 2669."

[598] *WR* 697, which cites "CE 1128, p. 1; CE 1109, p. 2."

[599] *WR* 697, which cites "*WCH* V 616 (Marina Oswald); see *WCH* VIII 360 (George A. Bouhe); 9 H 145 (Paul Roderick Gregory); 9 H 79-80 (Gary E. Taylor); 2 H 339 (Peter Paul Gregory); CE 2669."

[600] *WR* 697-698, which cites "CE 1108."

[601] *WR* 698, which cites "CE 92, pp. 8-9."

[602] *WR* 698, which cites "*WCH* VIII 360 (Bouhe) (900 rubles), 385 (Anna N. Meller) (800 rubles); *WCH* V 407-408 (Marina Oswald) (800 rubles); CE 1401, p. 271 (800-900 rubles); CE 1110 (700-850 rubles); CE 1128; CE 24, entry of Jan. 13, 1960 (700 rubles); *WCH* II 339 (Peter Gregory) (800 rubles); *WCH* VIII 348 (Clark) (800-900 rubles)."

[603] *WR* 698, which cites "CE 2720; see CE 1401, p. 271."

[604] *WR* 698, which cites "*WCH* I 95 (Marina Oswald); CE 1401, p. 275."

[605] CE 24, entry of Jan. 13, 1960, on *WCH* XVI 99.

[606] *WR* 698, which cites "*WCH* I 92-93 (Marina Oswald); CE 1401, p. 275."

[607] *WR* 698, which cites "CE 24, entry of Mar. 16, 1960; compare *WCH* I 92 (Marina Oswald)."

[608] *WR* 698, which cites "CE 24, entry of Mar. 16, 1960; see also *WCH* I 92 (Marina Oswald)."

[609] *WR* 698, which cites "See *WCH* I 93 (Marina Oswald)."

[610] *WR* 698, which cites "CE 2721; CE 25, pp. 1B-2B."

[611] *WR* 698, which cites "CE 24, entries Jan. 7 to Mar. 17, 1960; see CE 93, p. 4 (erroneously referring to 'Roza Agafonava')."

[612] CE 24, entry of Jan. 13, 1960, on *WCH* XVI 99.

[613] Testimony of Allison G. Folsom, Lt. Col., USMC on *WCH* VIII 304.

[614] Folsom Exhibit No. 1—Continued (p. 72) on *WCH* XIX 719 shows the original, typed on a "NAVAL SPEED LETTER" form, filed in Oswald's Marine Corps service record book.

[615] Paragraph 13266 on page 13-53 of "Marine Corps Personnel Manual" "MARCORPERMAN" updated from 13 Sep 1961 through 4 Apr 1967, on Page 547 of 990 of http://www.hqmc.marines.mil/Portals/61/Docs/FOIA/MCPM[1].pdf accessed on 2014/12/24. Although somewhat more recent and with a different paragraph number, USMC HQ said, in reply to my FOIA request, that this was the renumbered equivalent of paragraph 10277 in effect on 8 Mar 1960.

[616] Page 10-28 of "Marine Corps Manual | 1949 | Volume I | Personnel and General Administration" accessed at http://onlinebooks.library.upenn.edu/webbin/book/ then searching and selecting "Marine Corps manual, 1949".

[617] *WR* 698, which cites "CE 24, entry of June-July 1960."

[618] *WR* 698, which cites "*WCH* I 91 (Marina Oswald); CE 993, p. 5."

[619] *WR* 698-699, which cites "*WCH* I 96 (Marina Oswald); *WCH* II 396-397 (M. Paine); *WCH* V 405-406 (Marina Oswald); *WCH* VIII 362 (Bouhe); CE 2678, pp. 13-14; CE 2679."

[620] Quoted with permission from Mailer, Norman. *Oswald's Tale: An American Mystery* 115-116.

[621] Quoted from Oswald, Robert L., with Myrick and Barbara Land. *Lee: A Portrait of Lee Harvey Oswald by His Brother* 110. This source was described in endnote [68].

[622] *WR* 699, which cites "CE 2759; CE 24, entry of Jan. 1, 1961."

[623] Quoted with permission from Wecht, Cyril *Cause of Death* 58. Copyright notice supplied by publisher: "From CAUSE OF DEATH by Cyril Wecht, copyright © 1993 by Dr. Cyril H. Wecht, M.D., J.D. Used by permission of Dutton, an imprint of Penguin Publishing Group, a division of Penguin Random House LLC."

[624] CE 204 shows two photos of this letter: On *WCH* XVI 585 it is not on letterhead and is not signed; On *WCH* XVI 590 it is on letterhead and is signed. Folsom Exhibit No. 1 also shows two photos of it: *WCH* XIX 675 is a carbon copy, not on letterhead; *WCH* XIX 715 is a carbon copy, not on letterhead, stamped at the bottom "CERTIFIED TO BE A TRUE COPY" with signature "M G Letscher" to the right of normal position, and also showing a receipt for Certified Mail form on which Marguerite has signed "Lee H Oswald" on the "SIGNATURE OR NAME OF ADDRESSEE" line and signed her own name under "SIGNATURE OF ADDRESSEE'S AGENT". Both are from Oswald's service record book. The re-created letters include the Marine Corps logo, obtained from http://www.defense.gov/multimedia/web_graphics/, and considered to be fair use after due diligence in requesting permission from The Corps, which made no response to repeated requests.

[625] CE 204 page 7 on *WCH* XVI 591.

[626] CE 204 page 8 on *WCH* XVI 592.

[627] Quoted with permission after payment, from Epstein, Edward Jay. *Legend: The Secret World of Lee Harvey Oswald* 125-126.

[628] Epstein *Legend* 126.

[629] CE 204 page 8 on *WCH* XVI 592, which begins "[A letter included in Commission Exhibit 204 was too illegible to be reproduced. The contents of this letter are as follows.]", then displays, set in type, the words of her letter. CE 205 on *WCH* XVI 593 is a typed page with the same information, its source not identified, ending "(Mrs. Oswald confirms reading of letter as correct)".

[630] CE 204 shows two photos of this letter: *WCH* XVI 586 is on letterhead but not signed; *WCH* XVI 589 is on letterhead and signed. FOLSOM EXHIBIT NO. 1—Continued (p. 21) on *WCH* XIX 674 is a carbon copy, not on letterhead, from Oswald's service records.

[631] FOLSOM EXHIBIT NO. 1 shows three photos of this letter: Continued (p. 20) on *WCH* XIX 673 is a carbon copy, not on letterhead; Continued (p. 68) on *WCH* XIX 716 is the original of the letter, signed on letterhead. Below it on *WCH* XIX 716 is FOLSOM EXHIBIT NO. 1—Continued (p. 69), the envelope which carried the letter to "Lee H. OSWALD; 3613 Hurley; Fort Worth, Texas" by Certified Mail, "RETURN RECEIPT REQUESTED; DELIVER TO ADDRESSEE ONLY". It was "Returned to Writer" with "REASON CHECKED Unclaimed". FOLSOM EXHIBIT NO. 1—Continued (p. 71) on *WCH* XIX 718 is on letterhead but not signed. Someone has circled Oswald's serial number and drawn a line down to a scrawled word (probably "File") with an initial and two check marks. Newly typed in the bottom-left corner is "Copy to: CMC (Code DK)" which means a copy was sent to the Commandant of the Marine Corps. The original letter with its round-trip envelope, and the two copies, were all in Oswald's service record book.

[632] Khrushchev, Nikita. *Khrushchev Remembers: The Last Testament* 449.

[633] *WR* 699, which cites "CE 24, entry of May 1, 1960."

[634] *WR* 699, which cites "CE 24, entry of June-July 1960."

[635] Lasky, Victor. *J.F.K.: The Man and the Myth* 375.

[636] Quoted with permission after payment, from Stafford, Jean. *A Mother in History* 65.

[637] Photo scanned from CE 2607 on *WCH* XXV 882. Coming from that US Federal government source, it is in the public domain.

[638] FOLSOM EXHIBIT NO. 1–Continued (pp. 55, 54) on *WCH* XIX 703, 702. A less-clear copy is on *WCH* XIX 672-673(top).

[639] FOLSOM EXHIBIT NO. 1–Continued (p. 52) on *WCH* XIX 701 (top).

[640] FOLSOM EXHIBIT NO. 1–Continued (p. 52) on *WCH* XIX 701 (bottom).

[641] FOLSOM EXHIBIT NO. 1–Continued (p. 53) on *WCH* XIX 702 (top).

[642] FOLSOM EXHIBIT NO. 1–Continued (p. 51) on *WCH* XIX 700.

[643] Image scanned from FOLSOM EXHIBIT NO. 1–Continued (p. 50) on *WCH* XIX 699. Coming from that US Federal government source, it is in the public domain.

[644] Image scanned from FOLSOM EXHIBIT NO. 1–Continued (p. 48) on *WCH* XIX 697. Coming from that US Federal government source, it is in the public domain. Shown here is the upper half of the document; the lower half contains irrelevant material and blank spaces, so was cropped out to reduce space here.
The same document with much worse clarity is FOLSOM EXHIBIT NO. 1–Continued (p. 16) on *WCH* XIX 670.

[645] FOLSOM EXHIBIT NO. 1–Continued (p. 15) on *WCH* XIX 669 (bottom).

[646] Image scanned from FOLSOM EXHIBIT NO. 1–Continued (p. 10) on *WCH* XIX 665. Coming from that US Federal government source, it is in the public domain. This is a crop of the bottom of the last column.

[647] Image scanned from FOLSOM EXHIBIT NO. 1–Continued (p. 4) on *WCH* XIX 659. Coming from that US Federal government source, it is in the public domain. This is a crop of the top of the form; the remainder of it is blank.

[648] *WCH* VIII 303 (Folsom). He used the "Jr." when stating his name, but the Warren Commission generally did not do that.

[649] *WCH* VIII 305 (Folsom).

[650] FOLSOM EXHIBIT NO. 1–Continued (p. 14) on *WCH* XIX 669 (top).

[651] FOLSOM EXHIBIT NO. 1–Continued (p. 10) on *WCH* XIX 665.

[652] *WR* 689, which cites "CE 2016, p. 11-13."

[653] Quoted as fair use (for brevity) from Khrushchev 473.

[654] *WR* 699, which cites "CE 24, entry of Aug.-Sept. 1960."

[655] *WR* 700, which cites "*WCH* IX 80 (Taylor); *WCH* V 590 (Marina Oswald)."

[656] *WR* 700, which cites "*WCH* V 590 (Marina Oswald); see *WCH* VIII 348 (Clark)."

[657] *WR* 700, which cites "*WCH* XI 142 (Gibson); *WCH* VIII 60 (M. Evans); *WCH* V 590 (Marina Oswald)."

[658] *WR* 700, which cites "*WCH* IX 145, 151 (Paul Gregory)."

[659] *WR* 700, which cites "*WCH* IX 145, 154, 156 (Paul Gregory)."

[660] *WR* 700, which cites "CE 92, p. 5."

[661] *WR* 700, which cites "CE 92, p. 5."

[662] TESTIMONY OF PAUL RODERICK GREGORY on *WCH* IX 145.

[663] *WR* 700, which cites "CE 92, p. 6-7."

[664] *WR* 700, which cites "CE 92, pp. 7-8."

[665] *WR* 700, which cites "CE 92, p. 12."

[666] McMillan, Priscilla Johnson. *Marina and Lee* 112-113.

[667] Quoted with permission from McMillan 116-117. Permission statement is in endnote [150].

[668] Quoted with permission from McMillan 167-168. Permission statement is in endnote [150].

[669] *WR* 699, which cites "CE 24, entries of Jan. 1, Jan 2, 1961."

[670] *WR* 699, which cites "CE 24, entry of Jan. 3, 1961."

[671] *WR* 701, which cites "CE 985, documents 3A (l)-(2); compare CE 24, entry of Jan. 4, 1961."

[672] *WR* 701, which cites "CE 24, entry of Jan. 4, 1961."

[673] Quoted with permission after payment, from Leamer, Laurence. *The Kennedy Men: 1901-1963: The Laws of the Father* 482, which cites for the call "White House, telephone memorandum, January 26, 1961, in the John F. Kennedy Presidential Library"; and for Mrs. Oswald being in Washington *Atlanta Constitution*, December 7, 1963".

[674] TESTIMONY OF MRS. MARGUERITE OSWALD on *WCH* I 205. I am not making this up!

[675] *WCH* I 205 (Marguerite Oswald).

[676] Referred to but not shown in *WCH*. A photocopy from the CIA is in Newman, John. *Oswald and the CIA* 473.

[677] Quoted with permission from Newman, John 473.

[678] *WCH* I 210 (Marguerite Oswald).

[679] *WCH* I 210 (Marguerite Oswald).

[680] *WCH* I 206-207 (Marguerite Oswald).

[681] Quoted with permission after payment, from Stafford, Jean. *A Mother in History* 66.

[682] Transcribed as fair use (for brevity) from *Real History: The Secret KGB JFK Assassination Files*, The Learning Channel on 03 March 2000.

[683] Transcribed as fair use (for brevity) from *Real History: The Secret KGB JFK Assassination Files*.

[684] *WR* 701, which cites "*WCH* V 277 (Snyder)."

[685] Quoted with permission after payment, from Epstein *Legend* 128.

[686] *WR* 701, which cites "*WCH* V 276-277 (Snyder); CE 931."

[687] *WR* 701, which cites "CE 933, 1084."

[688] *WR* 701, which cites "CE 2666."

[689] Quoted with permission after payment, from Epstein *Legend* 130.

[690] *WR* 701, which cites "CE 940."

[691] *WR* 701, which cites "*WCH* V 278 (Snyder); CE 1403, p. 727."

[692] *WR* 701, which cites "CE 25, pp. 1B-2B; see *WCH* V 407-408 (Marina Oswald)."

[693] *WR* 701, which cites "CE 940, 1085."

[694] *WR* 701, which cites "CE 970, 971; *WCH* V 352-354 (Bernice Waterman)."

[695] *WR* 702, which cites "CE 24, entry of Mar. 17, 1961. Marina thought that the date was Mar. 4. *WCH* I 90 (Marina Oswald); CE 994, p. 1."

[696] "COMMISSION EXHIBIT 24—Continued" on *WCH* XVI 102.

[697] *WR* 702, which states "This and the succeeding paragraphs about Marina's life before she met Oswald are based primarily on CE 1401, pp. 256-261. Additional sources are indicated where appropriate."

[698] *WR* 702, which cites "See also *WCH* I 84 (Marina Oswald)."

[699] McMillan 17.

[700] *WR* 702, which cites "See *WCH* I 84-85 (Marina Oswald)."

[701] *WR* 702, which states "Marina is unclear about her age at the time of this move; compare *WCH* I 84 (Marina Oswald) ('approximately five'), with CE 1401, p. 256 ('about seven')." In McMillan's *Marina and Lee*, written with Marina's full cooperation, on page 21 she is almost six.

[702] Quoted with permission from McMillan 28-29. Permission statement is in endnote [150].

[703] *WR* 702, which cites "CE 49."

[704] *WR* 702, which cites "*WCH* I 84 (Marina Oswald)."

[705] Quoted with permission from McMillan 40. Permission statement is in endnote [150].

[706] *WR* 702, which cites "*WCH* I 87 (Marina Oswald); CE 49."

[707] Quoted with permission from McMillan 40. Permission statement is in endnote [150].

[708] Quoted with permission from McMillan 40. Permission statement is in endnote [150].

[709] *WR* 702-703, which cites "*WCH* I 85 (Marina Oswald)."

[710] *WR* 703, which cites "*WCH* I 85 (Marina Oswald)."

[711] Quoted with permission from McMillan 48. Permission statement is in endnote [150].

[712] Quoted with permission from McMillan 48-49. Permission statement is in endnote [150].

[713] Quoted with permission from McMillan 53. Permission statement is in endnote [150].

[714] McMillan 64-65.

[715] *WR* 703, which advises "See CE 51, 57."

[716] *WR* 703, which cites "*WCH* I 89 (Marina Oswald)."

[717] *WR* 703, which cites "*WCH* I 89 (Marina Oswald)."

[718] Quoted with permission from McMillan 66-67. Permission statement is in endnote [150].

[719] Newman, John 476 shows a photocopy released by the CIA under a FOIA request.

[720] *WR* 703, which cites "*WCH* I 87-89 (Marina Oswald)."

[721] Quoted with permission from McMillan 70. Permission statement is in endnote [150].

[722] *WR* 703, which cites "*WCH* I 88, 89 (Marina Oswald)."

[723] *WCH* I 91 (Marina Oswald); CE 994, p. 5; CE 1401, pp. 261, 267-268; CE 993, p. 7.

[724] CE 1401 (page 261) on *WCH* XXII 745.

[725] CE 1789 (page 2) on *WCH* XXIII 402.

[726] *WCH* I 91 (Marina Oswald); CE 985, document 1C-1, p. 1; CE 1401, pp. 268-269.

[727] *WR* 703, which cites "CE 1401, p. 270; compare CE 994, p. 9."

[728] Quoted with permission from McMillan 97. Permission statement is in endnote [150].

[729] Quoted as fair use (for brevity) from "Today in History" in *The Seattle Times* on April 17, 2013, p. A2.

[730] Quoted with permission after payment, from Epstein *Legend* 136.

[731] Quoted with permission from McMillan 98-99. Permission statement is in endnote [150].

[732] *WR* 704, which cites "CE 1401, p. 269; but see *WCH* II 302 (K. Ford)."

[733] Quoted with permission from McMillan 103. Permission statement is in endnote [150].

[734] *WR* 704, which cites "CE 1111; CE 24, entry of Apr. 31 [sic], 1961."

[735] Quoted with permission from McMillan 99. Permission statement is in endnote [150].

[736] Quoted with permission from McMillan 107-108. Permission statement is in endnote [150].

[737] *WR* 704, which cites "CE 24, entry of Apr. 31 [sic], 1961."

[738] Photo scanned and slightly cropped from CE 314-A on *WCH* XVI 869. Coming from that US Federal government source, it is in the public domain.

[739] *WR* 704, which cites "CE 1401, p. 274."

[740] *WR* 704, which cites "CE 24, entry of May 1, 1961."

[741] *WR* 704, which cites "CE 24, entry of May 1961."

[742] *WR* 704, which cites "CE 24, entry of June 1961."

[743] *WCH* I 207 (Marguerite Oswald).

[744] *WCH* I 208 (Marguerite Oswald).

[745] *WR* 704, which cites "CE 24, entry of June 1961."

[746] O'Reilly, Bill, and Martin Dugard. *Killing Kennedy: The End of Camelot*, page 62 — cited but not quoted. The author's statement about that source is in endnote [272].

[747] Photo scanned from CE 2595 on *WCH* XXV 876. From that US Federal government source, it is in the public domain.

[748] *WR* 704-705, which cites "CE 252."

[749] Quoted with permission after payment, from Epstein *Legend* 131.

[750] *WR* 705, which cites "CE 1401, p. 277; CE 1403, p. 725."

[751] *WR* 705, which cites "CE 1401, pp. 274-276."

[752] *WR* 705, which cites "CE 1401, p. 274."

[753] *WR* 705, which cites "CE 1401, p. 276; CE 993, p. 12."

[754] *WR* 705, which cites "CE 1401, p. 277."

[755] *WR* 705, which cites "CE 298."

[756] *WR* 705, which cites "CE 299."

[757] Quoted with permission after payment, from Hill, Clint, with Lisa McCubbin. *Mrs. Kennedy and Me* 71-72. Copyright notice supplied by publisher: "Reprinted with the permission of Gallery Books, a division of Simon & Schuster, Inc. from MRS. KENNEDY AND ME: AN INTIMATE MEMOIR by Clint Hill and [sic] Lisa McCubbin. Copyright © 2012 by Clint Hill and Lisa McCubbin. All rights reserved."

[758] *WR* 705, which cites "CE 180."

[759] Quoted with permission from McMillan 155. Permission statement is in endnote [150].

[760] *WR* 705, which cites "CE 1403, p. 727."

[761] Quoted from Oswald, Robert 111. This source was described in endnote [68].

[762] *WR* 705, which cites "CE 24, entry of July 8, 1961; CE 24, entry of July 1961."

[763] *WR* 705-706, which advises "See *WR* appendix XV, p. 754."

[764] *WR* 706, which cites "CE 24, entry of July 9, 1961; see *WCH* I 96-97 (Marina Oswald); CE 1401, p. 280."

[765] *WR* 706, which cites "CE 1401, p. 290; CE 1403, p. 726."

[766] *WR* 706, which cites "CE 935."

[767] *WR* 706, which cites "CE 24, entries of Oct. 16, 1959, through Jan. 4, 1960; CE 908."

[768] *WR* 706, which cites "CE 1385, p. 4; P. Johnson DE 1, pp. 3, 6, 14; P. Johnson DE 2, pp. 1-2; *WCH* XI 456 (P. Johnson); CE 985, document 1C-2, p. 6."

[769] *WR* 706, which cites "CE 1109, 1110, 1128."

[770] Quoted with permission from McMillan 143. Permission statement is in endnote [150].

[771] Quoted with permission from Newman, John 248.

[772] *WR* 706, which cites "CE 909, 935, p. 2."

[773] CE 935 page 3 on *WCH* XVIII 139.

[774] *WR* 706, which cites "CE 946, pp. 2-3; *WCH* V 284 (Snyder)."

[775] *WR* 706, which cites "CE 935, p. 2."

[776] *WR* 706, which cites "CE 938."

[777] *WR* 706, which cites "*WCH* V 284 (Snyder); CE 946, p. 6."

[778] Quoted with permission after payment, from Epstein *Legend* 142.

[779] *WR* 706, which cites "*WCH* V 319 (McVickar)."

[780] *WR* 706, which cites "*WCH* V 319 (McVickar); CE 1401, pp. 278-279."

[781] *WR* 706, which cites "CE 944; *WCH* V 304-306, 318-319 (McVickar); CE 959."

[782] Quoted with permission from McMillan 131. Permission statement is in endnote [150].

[783] *WR* 706, which cites "CE 24, entry of July 14, 1961; CE 301."

[784] *WR* 706-707, which cites "CE 301."

[785] Quoted from Oswald, Robert 112-113. This source was described in endnote [68].

[786] Quoted from Oswald, Robert 112. This source was described in endnote [68].

[787] *WR* 707, which cites "*WCH* I 90, 97 (Marina Oswald); but see CE 1401, p. 276."

[788] *WR* 707, which cites "*WCH* I 97 (Marina Oswald)."

[789] Quoted from Oswald, Robert 112. This source was described in endnote [68].

[790] *WR* 707, which cites "*WCH* I 97 (Marina Oswald); *WCH* V 591-592 (Marina Oswald)."

[791] *WR* 707, which cites "*WCH* IX 147 (Paul Gregory); see also CE 301; CE 24, entry of July 15-Aug. 20, 1961."

[792] *WR* 707, which cites "CE 935, p. 1; CE 985, documents 1B, 2B, 3B, 4B; see CE 1401, pp. 277-278, 280."

[793] *WR* 707, which cites "CE 24, entry of July 16-Aug. 20, 1961."

[794] *WR* 707, which cites "CE 24, entry of Aug. 21-Sept. 1, 1961."

[795] Douglass, James W. *JFK and the Unspeakable: Why He Died and Why It Matters* xxii.

[796] Douglass xxii.

[797] *WR* 707, which cites "CE 24, entry of Sept.-Oct. 18, 1961."

[798] *WR* 707, which cites "CE 1122, pp. 2-3."

[799] *WR* 707-708, which cites "CE 1122, pp. 2-3."

[800] *WR* 708, which cites "*WCH* I 97 (Marina Oswald)."

[801] *WR* 708.

[802] Quoted with permission from McMillan 158. Permission statement is in endnote [150].

[803] *WR* 708, which cites "CE 1087."

[804] *WR* 708, which cites "*WCH* V 591, 618 (Marina Oswald)."

[805] *WR* 708, which cites "CE 1403, p. 745; *WCH* V 592 (Marina Oswald)."

[806] *WR* 708, which cites "*WCH* V 591-592, 604-605, 617-619 (Marina Oswald)."

[807] *WR* 708, which cites "CE 253."

[808] CE 1076 on *WCH* XXII 25.

[809] *WR* 708-709, which cites "CE 1076."

[810] CE 1058 page 4 on *WCH* XXII 6 (right).

[811] Photo scanned and cropped from CE 2623 on *WCH* XXV 890. Coming from that US Federal government source, it is in the public domain. Photo is in the National Archives.

[812] CE 1058 page 5 on *WCH* XXII 7 shows a carbon copy, so dark as to be almost unreadable; CE 1058 page 6, also on *WCH* XXII 7, shows a re-typed "true copy" of the letter, legible but not quite accurate.

[813] CE 1058 page 7 on *WCH* XXII 8.

[814] CE 1058 page 8 on *WCH* XXII 8.

[815] Photo scanned and slightly cropped from CE 2627 on *WCH* XXV 892. Coming from that US Federal government source, it is in the public domain.

[816] CE 1058 page 3 on *WCH* XXII 6.

[817] Photo scanned from CE 2625 on *WCH* XXV 891. Coming from that US Federal government source, it is in the public domain.

[818] CE 1058 pages 1-2 on *WCH* XXII 5.

[819] CE 985–Continued on *WCH* XVIII 433.

[820] Quoted with permission from Nechiporenko, Oleg M. *Passport to Assassination: The Never-Before-Told Story of Lee Harvey Oswald by the KGB Colonel Who Knew Him* 53. Copyright notice is in endnote [495].

[821] Quoted with permission from Nechiporenko 61-62. Copyright notice is in endnote [495].

[822] Quoted with permission from McMillan 168. Permission statement is in endnote [150].

[823] TESTIMONY OF MRS. DOROTHY GRAVITIS on *WCH* IX 135.

[824] *WR* 709, which cites "CE 24, entry of Dec. 25, 1961; *WCH* V 592, 598, 604-605 (Marina Oswald); see also CE 1403, p. 725."

[825] *WR* 709, which cites "CE 1401, p. 267."

[826] *WR* 709, which cites "CE 189."

[827] *WR* 709, which cites "CE 2731; compare CE 2660."

[828] *WR* 709, which cites "CE 2680, pp. 7-8."

[829] *WR* 709, which cites "CE 2680, pp. 3-4."

[830] CE 246 on *WCH* XVI 688-689.

[831] *WR* 709, which cites "CE 1078."

[832] *WR* 709, which cites "CE 256."

[833] *WR* 709, which cites "CE 1079."

[834] *WR* 709, which cites "CE 2692."

[835] *WR* 709, which cites "CE 247."

[836] *WR* 709-710, which cites "CE 247."

[837] *WR* 710, which cites "CE 190."

[838] *WR* 710, which cites "CE 1080, p. 2; CE 1101."

[839] *WR* 710, which cites "CE 314."

[840] *WR* 710, which cites "Folsom DE 1, p. 10; see *WR* p. 689."

[841] FBI transcript of tape recording on November 25, 1963 is CE 270. Quotations are excerpted from *WCH* XVI 734-737.

[842] TESTIMONY OF ROBERT EDWARD LEE OSWALD on *WCH* I 317.

[843] *WCH* I 323 (Robert Oswald).

[844] Wolff, Perry. *A Tour of the White House with Mrs. John F. Kennedy* 6, 235-248.

[845] Image scanned from CE 18 on *WCH* XVI 39. Coming from that US Federal government source, it is in the public domain.

[846] This photo was purchased to show here, with credit: Thomas D. McAvoy / The LIFE Images Collection / Getty Images.

[847] Quoted with permission from Zirbel, Craig I. *The Texas Connection* 141-142.

[848] Photo taken by the DOD Signal Corps was purchased from the LBJ Presidential Library in Austin, Texas.

[849] Quoted with permission from O'Donnell, Kenneth P., and David F. Powers with Joe McCarthy. *Johnny, We Hardly Knew Ye*, page 274.

[850] Quoted with permission from Kerr, Andy. *A Journey Amongst the Good and the Great* 93.

[851] Quoted with permission from Schlesinger, Arthur M., Jr. *A Thousand Days: John F. Kennedy in the White House* 153-154.

[852] Fay, Paul B., Jr. *The Pleasure of His Company* 197.

[853] Image scanned from the handwritten original, FOLSOM EXHIBIT NO. 1—Continued (page 65) on *WCH* XIX 713. Coming from that US Federal government source, it is in the public domain. The Warren Commission retyped from this into its *Report* on page 710, but with errors. The careful transcription in this book accurately reflects Oswald's handwriting.

[854] Image scanned by Gina McNeely of Gina McNeely Picture Research (www.ginamcneely.com) at the National Archives and Records Administration in College Park, MD on 2014/12/30, then converted to grayscale. After days of searching, Archives JFK material experts Gene Morris and James Mathis concluded the original letter could not be found, and came up with this, the best image known to them, contained in the FBI "Key Person File | Lee Harvey Oswald | Box 31".

[855] This is the preceding image from the National Archives, cropped to the edges of the original letter, then improved to more probably resemble the original letter. My brother-in-law David Muerdter used Corel PaintShop Pro for Moiré correction to smooth the dot pattern, then reduced background darkness, and finally applied a contrast curve to improve readability.

[856] *WCH* I 180 (Marguerite Oswald).

[857] Quoted with permission after payment, from Epstein *Legend* 148.

[858] Epstein *Legend* 306.

[859] Quoted with permission after payment, from Epstein *Legend* 307 in note 9.

[860] CE 314 on *WCH* XVI 865 (first page); 314—Continued on 866-867 (second and third pages).

[861] CE 314—Continued on *WCH* XVI 868 (both front and back of the envelope).

[862] TESTIMONY OF JAMES J. ROWLEY on *WCH* V 468.

[863] *WR* 710-711.

[864] CE 1081 on *WCH* XXII 28.

[865] *WR* 711, which cites "CE 222."

[866] *WR* 711, which cites "CE 192."

[867] *WR* 711, which cites "CE 1082, 1102."

[868] *WR* 711, which cites "CE 193."

[869] *WR* 711, which cites "CE 24, entry of Feb. 15, 1962; CE 993, pp. 15-16; CE 1112."

[870] *WR* 711, which cites "CE 994, p. 16."

[871] CE 315 on *WCH* XVI 870-873 (three pages and front of the envelope). Not shown here are Lee's instructions at the bottom on how to use a zone number within Minsk.

[872] *WR* 711, which cites "CE 994, p. 1; but see CE 60, 61, 64."

[873] *WR* 711, which cites "CE 24, entry of Feb. 23, 1962."

[874] *WR* 711, which cites "CE 59, 61."

[875] *WR* 711, which cites "CE 24, entry of Feb. 23, 1961."

[876] This image was scanned from Reston, James, Jr. *The Accidental Victim: JFK, Lee Harvey Oswald, and the Real Target in Dallas* on page 22 of the printed book. Reston, the "Trailblazer", has generously given permission to show it here.

[877] Quoted with the gracious permission of James Reston, Jr., author and copyright owner of *The Accidental Victim* 22-23.

[878] Quoted with the gracious permission of James Reston, Jr., author and copyright owner (the copyright has reverted to him from the book's publisher) of *The Lone Star: The Life of John Connally* 236.

[879] A carbon copy of the letter from Oswald's service record file is FOLSOM EXHIBIT NO. 1—Continued (page 63) on *WCH* XIX 711. Another copy, its source not stated, stamped as received at the Navy Department on FEB 27 1962, is CE 2663 on *WCH* XXVI 19.

[880] Quoted with permission from Kerr 122.

[881] Quoted with permission from Kerr 1-3.

[882] *WR* 711, which cites "CE 316."

[883] *WR* 711, which cites "CE 195."

[884] *WR* 711, which cites "CE 316."

[885] *WR* 711, which cites "CE 1093, 2682."

[886] *WR* 711, which cites "CE 1086."

[887] *WR* 711, which cites "CE 1095."

[888] Quoted with permission from McMillan 179. Permission statement is in endnote [150].

[889] *WR* 711, which cites "CE 249, 1103."

[890] CE 24 page 12, entry of Mar. 24, 1962, on *WCH* XVI 105; CE 22 on *WCH* XVI 80."

[891] *WR* 711, which cites "CE 249, 1083, 1088, 2687, 2088."

[892] Photo is CE 2622 on *WCH* XXV 889 with caption "From left, Marina, June and Lee Harvey Oswald in Minsk." Coming from that US Federal government source, it is in the public domain.

[893] TESTIMONY OF JOHN EDWARD PIC on *WCH* XI 78.

[894] FOLSOM EXHIBIT No. 1—Continued (p. 62) on *WCH* XIX 710.

[895] Two carbon copies of this letter appear in the *Warren Commission Hearings*. The carbon retained in Oswald's personnel file is "Folsom Exhibit No. 1—Continued (p. 61)" on *WCH* XIX 709. "FILE / 1653230 / JV" is hand-printed at the bottom-right. 1653230 was Oswald's military serial number. The second carbon copy is the fifth sheet of paper in "COMMISSION EXHIBIT 2686—Continued" on *WCH* XXVI 47. At the bottom of the page is typed: "Blind Copy to: CNO (OP-921E)". This copy was one of many items relating to Oswald in the files of the Chief of Naval Operations.

[896] "1 Undesirable Discharge USMC 9/13/60 Lee Harvey Oswald 1653230 #425" on Police Department, City of Dallas, "Property Clerk's Invoice or Receipt" pre-numbered form No. 11196 shown on COMMISSION EXHIBIT No. 2003, page 282, on *WCH* XXIV 342 (left).

[897] My great thanks to professional researcher Gina B. McNeely of Gina McNeely Picture Research, www.ginamcneely.com, who first persevered at the Archives on behalf of this book to find the good image displayed earlier of Oswald's letter to Connally. After considerable searching there for the discharge certificate, she convinced this author that it was unknown to archivists and probably never in the National Archives. She and archivists pointed to CE 2077 on *WCH* XXIV 512, a report by FBI agents in Dallas that they had inventoried all items from Oswald's rented room and Ruth Paine's house. They then sent to FBI HQ "items pertinent to the investigation" including a box of Feenamints, a Spanish dictionary and several shirts (!); but "those items not believed pertinent to the investigation at this time ... are being retained in the Dallas Office." Apparently they ruled the Undesirable Discharge certificate as "not believed pertinent". It may still molder in some carton or file in Dallas, or be long gone into a landfill or recyclable paper digester. Oh, well, as the memorable Saturday-morning TV cartoon character Yosemite Sam used to say, "Ratzafrass!".

[898] The clean image here was produced from the paid-for image from the Dallas Municipal Archives by brother-in-law David Muerdter's expert use of Corel PaintShop Pro on an image cropped by the author. Dave increased the contrast for easier readability, and removed dirty spots and scratches from the image purchased from Dallas (endnote [900] below).

[899] Searching with Bing, the author imported this image from http://texashistory.unt.edu/ark:/67531/metapth339674/m1/1/ on the website of the University of North Texas. The low-resolution pinkish thumbnail, imported on 2014/10/01 then converted to grayscale, was taken at an angle with ghostly hands holding down the document, then multiply scratched.

[900] Hoping to obtain a better image, researcher Gina McNeely contacted the City Archivist, Dallas Municipal Archives, City Secretary's Office, City of Dallas, who emailed on 2015/01/12: "we do not possess the original. ... We would be happy to provide you a scan of our copy at whatever dimensions you specify." The author paid the required fee, and after a full month the City Archivist sent four versions of the microfilm photo referred to in endnote [898] above. The Dallas "copy" was a print from the old microfilm, but with the advantage of much higher resolution than the preceding thumbnail. I paid for the right to use this image, the first of many purchased for use in this book. And, as required, I gratefully state: "Courtesy Dallas Municipal Archives, City of Dallas". When the book is printed, I will send one to comply with another requirement: "The Municipal Archives requires a complimentary copy of any product reproducing Archives images." The Dallas City Archivist emailed to the author on 2015/02/03: "We scanned directly off the paper copy we've had since 1964 in the Dallas Police Department – a photocopy from an enlargement of a microfilm frame. For the Warren Commission investigation, DPD flew any requested documents to the FBI, who filmed it and returned about 95% of originals, by my estimation. If there's a way I can find the microfilm roll the image is on, it is possible we can scan from

that. It would be at least one generation closer to the original." That was not requested after my esteemed brother-in-law Dave Muerdter performed his magic.

901 FOLSOM EXHIBIT No. 1—Continued (p. 45) and (p. 46) on *WCH* XIX 695. The envelope, postmarked in Minsk on 21 March, a day before the letter's date (!?) is FOLSOM EXHIBIT No. 1—Continued (p. 47) on *WCH* XIX 696. The letter also appears typed-out by the FBI in CE 823 pages 6-7 on *WCH* XVII 723-724, in which the typist has converted Oswald's "Undiserable" to "Undiresable"(!).

902 FOLSOM EXHIBIT No. 1—Continued (p. 46) (left half, upside-down) on *WCH* XIX 695.

903 FOLSOM EXHIBIT No. 1—Continued (p. 43) on *WCH* XIX 693.

904 Photograph at left courtesy of the Oregon State University's Special Collections & Archives Research Center. In the Ava Helen and Linus Pauling Papers, 1873-2013, it is photo 1962i.12. OSU's statement of Fair Use allows its inclusion here for "comment ... scholarship, and research". Thank you. As also with Caltech, "Go Beavers!".

905 Photograph at right was imported from profiles.nlm.nih.gov. The U.S. National Library of Medicine, a division of the National Institutes of Health, says its material is in the public domain.

906 Quoted with very kind permission without charging a fee, from Thomas, Helen. *Thanks for the Memories, Mr. President: Wit and Wisdom from the Front Row at the White House*, page 25.

907 Quoted with permission after payment, from Thomas, Helen. *Front Row at the White House: My Life and Times*, page 59. Copyright notice supplied by publisher: "Reprinted with the permission of Scribner, a Division of Simon & Schuster, Inc., from FRONT ROW AT THE WHITE HOUSE by Helen Thomas. Copyright © 1999 by Helen Thomas. All rights reserved."

908 *WR* 712, which cites "CE 1313."

909 *WR* 712, which cites "CE 985, document 9A; CE 1108, 1314."

910 *WR* 712, which cites "CE 1108, 1109, 1128, p. 3."

911 *WR* 712, which cites "CE 1401, p. 275; *WCH* I 93 (Marina Oswald); see also *WCH* V 590 (Marina Oswald)."

912 *WR* 712, which cites "CE 985, document 8A."

913 Quoted with permission from Heymann, C. David. *RFK: A Candid Biography of Robert F. Kennedy* 304. Copyright notice supplied by publisher: "From RFK: A CANDID BIOGRAPHY [*sic*] by C. David Heymann, copyright © 1998 by C. David Heymann. Used by permission of Dutton, an imprint of Penguin Publishing Group, a division of Penguin Random House LLC."

914 Quoted with permission after payment, from Hill with McCubbin 154. Copyright notice is in endnote [757].

915 *WR* 712, which cites "CE 946, p. 11."

916 *WR* 712, which cites "*WCH* V 604, 617-618 (Marina Oswald); CE 2722."

917 Quoted with permission from McMillan 185-186. Permission statement is in endnote [150].

918 Photo on left is scanned from CE 2628 on *WCH* XXV 892. Photo on right is scanned from CE 2629 on *WCH* XXV 893. Coming from that US Federal government source, both are in the public domain.

919 Epstein *Legend*, page 150 and page 308 note 16.

920 *WR* 712, which cites "CE 946, pp. 11, 15; see CE 1401, p. 280."

921 O'Reilly and Dugard 86.

922 *WR* 712, which cites "CE 2654. 2662, 2690, 2704."

923 The passport is CE 946—Continued on *WCH* XVIII 160-171. The renewal and admitting stamps are on the passport's page 15, shown on *WCH* XVIII 167.

924 *WR* 712, which cites "CE 2656."

925 *WR* 712, which cites "CE 34."

926 *WR* 712, which cites "CE 1098. After his return to the United States, Oswald repaid the loan in full. See *WR* appendix XV, p. 773."

927 *WR* 712, which cites "CE 1099, 1401, p. 280."

928 *WR* 712, which cites "CE 57."

929 O'Reilly and Dugard 86-87.

930 *WR* 712, which cites "CE 29. 946, 1099."

931 *WR* 712, which cites "*WCH* I 101 (Marina Oswald)."

932 O'Reilly and Dugard 87.

933 Quoted with permission from McMillan 192. Permission statement is in endnote [150].

934 Quoted with permission from Newman, John, page 579: chapter 14 note 96.

935 O'Reilly and Dugard 87.

936 Image scanned from CE 227 on *WCH* XVI 620. Coming from that US Federal government source, it is in the public domain.

937 *WR* 713, which cites "CE 946, p. 15."

938 Quoted with permission from McMillan 216-217. Permission statement is in endnote [150].

939 *WR* 713, which cites "CE 2655."

940 *WR* 713, which cites "CE 2213, pp. 19-20; CE 2657."

941 *WR* 713, which cites "CE 2655, 2657."

942 Quoted with permission from McMillan 217. Permission statement is in endnote [150].

[943] *WR* 713, which cites "CE 2213, pp. 18-24."

[944] *WR* 713, which cites "CE 2213, pp. 18-24; CE 2657."

[945] *WR* 713, which cites "CE 2213, p. 24."

— 5 — MISFIT

[946] Quoted with permission after payment, from Warren, Earl. *The Memoirs of Earl Warren* 364, 365. Copyright notice is in endnote [211].

[947] Quoted with permission after payment, from Warren 365. Copyright notice is in endnote [211].

[948] *Report of the President's Commission on the Assassination of President Kennedy* (popularly known as the *Warren Report*) Appendix XIII "Biography of Lee Harvey Oswald" page 713, hereinafter expressed in the form *WR* 713, which cites COMMISSION EXHIBIT (hereinafter CE) 2692, which is displayed in one of the 26 *WCH* volumes (see *Hearings* below).

[949] *WR* 713, which cites *WCH* I 372 (Robert Oswald).

[950] *WR* 714, which cites *WCH* I 330-331 (Robert Oswald).

[951] *Hearings Before the President's Commission on the Assassination of President Kennedy*, Volume I, page 331; hereinafter expressed in the form *WCH* I 331 (Robert Oswald); see also *WCH* I 464 (Robert Oswald).

[952] *WR* 714, which cites CE 2189, p. 1; *WCH* I 312, 331 (Robert Oswald); *WCH* I 4 (Marina Oswald).

[953] *WR* 714, which cites *WCH* I 312 (Robert Oswald).

[954] TESTIMONY OF ROBERT EDWARD LEE OSWALD on *WCH* I 385-386; hereinafter in form *WCH* I 385-386 (Robert Oswald).

[955] CE 780 on *WCH* XVII 658.

[956] Image scanned from CE 2661 (p. 1) on *WCH* XXVI 14 (bottom). Coming from that US Federal government source, it and next six are in the public domain. Larger but darker copies of this and next six are in CE 780 on *WCH* XVII 651-657.

[957] Image scanned from CE 2661 (p. 8) on *WCH* XXVI 17 (top).

[958] Image scanned from CE 2661 (p. 2) on *WCH* XXVI 14 (top).

[959] Image scanned from CE 2661 (p. 3) on *WCH* XXVI 15 (bottom).

[960] Image scanned from CE 2661 (p. 4) on *WCH* XXVI 15 (top).

[961] Image scanned from CE 2661 (p. 5) on *WCH* XXVI 16 (bottom).

[962] Image scanned from CE 2661 (p. 6) on *WCH* XXVI 16 (top).

[963] Transcription of CE 2661 (p. 2) on *WCH* XXVI 14 (top).

[964] Transcription of CE 2661 (pages 3-6) on *WCH* XXVI 15-16.

[965] *WR* 714, which cites *WCH* II 337-338 (Peter Gregory); CE 384.

[966] *WR* 714, which cites *WCH* II 338 (Peter Gregory); CE 384.

[967] *WR* 715, which cites *WCH* II 339-340 (Peter Gregory); *WCH* IX 143 (Paul Gregory).

[968] Quoted with permission from McMillan, Priscilla Johnson. *Marina and Lee*, page 224. Permission statement for this source is in endnote [150].

[969] Quoted with permission from McMillan 240. Permission statement is in endnote [150].

[970] *WR* 715, which cites CE 823, p. 11; *WCH* I 315 (Robert Oswald); *WCH* IV 415 (Fain).

[971] *WR* 715, which cites *WCH* IV 418 (Fain).

[972] *WR* 715, which cites CE 823, p. 13.

[973] TESTIMONY OF RUTH HYDE PAINE (RESUMED) on *WCH* III 117.

[974] Epstein, Edward Jay. *Legend: The Secret World of Lee Harvey Oswald*, page 202.

[975] The papers and issue dates were identified for the Commission by the FBI: CE 1406 on *WCH* XXII 789.

[976] Quoted with permission from Newman, John. *Oswald and the CIA* 273.

[977] Quoted as fair use (for brevity) from http://www.aarclibrary.org/publib/contents/wc/contents_wcdocs.htm on 2013/06/18.

[978] Quoted with permission from Newman, John 585: note 71 to chapter 15.

[979] Quoted with permission after payment, from Hill, Clint, with Lisa McCubbin. *Mrs. Kennedy and Me* 154, for which the copyright notice is in endnote [757].

[980] *WR* 715, which cites *WCH* I 133 (Marguerite Oswald); CE 1943; CE 2189, p. 2; *WCH* I 4 (Marina Oswald); *WCH* I 312 (Robert Oswald).

[981] *WR* 715, which cites *WCH* I 133 (Marguerite Oswald).

[982] *WR* 715, which cites CE 2189, p. 2; *WCH* I 133-135 (Marguerite Oswald).

[983] Quoted with permission after payment, from Epstein *Legend* 165.

[984] *WR* 715, which cites *WCH* I 5 (Marina Oswald).

[985] *WCH* I 315 (Robert Oswald).

[986] Quoted with permission after payment, from King, Stephen. *11/22/63: A Novel* 468. Copyright notice is in endnote [148]. His title says "a novel", but King's actual facts are more reliable than those of many who call themselves "historians".

[987] *WR* 715, which cites *WCH* IV 419 (Fain); CE 2189, pp. 2-3, 18; *WCH* I 4-5 (Marina Oswald); *WCH* I 134-135 (Marguerite Oswald); *WCH* X 230 (Chester Allen Riggs, Jr.).

[988] Quoted from Oswald, Robert L., with Myrick and Barbara Land. *Lee: A Portrait of Lee Harvey Oswald by His Brother*, page 122. This source was described in endnote [68].

[989] Quoted with permission after payment, from Epstein *Legend* 166.

[990] Quoted with permission from McMillan 227. Permission statement is in endnote [150].

[991] *WR* 715, which cites Graves Deposition Exhibit (hereinafter DE) 1; CE 1943; CE 2189, p. 12; *WCH* X 161-163 (Tommy Bargas).

[992] *WR* 715, which cites CE 1943. CE 1943 is a negative image, the positive is CE 2189 on *WCH* XXIV 885.

[993] CE 2189 on *WCH* XXIV 885.

[994] *WR* 715, which cites Graves DE 1.

[995] Quoted with permission after payment, from King, Stephen. *11/22/63: A Novel* 374. Copyright notice is in endnote [148].

[996] *WR* 715, which cites *WCH* X 165 (Bargas).

[997] *WR* 715, which cites *WCH* I 5 (Marina Oswald).

[998] Quoted with permission from Kaiser, David. *The Road to Dallas: The Assassination of John F. Kennedy*, page 178. Permission notice provided by Harvard University Press: "The Road to Dallas: the Assassination of John F. Kennedy by David Kaiser, Copyright © 2008 by David Kaiser."

[999] *WR* 716, which cites *WCH* I 136 (Marguerite Oswald).

[1000] *WR* 716, which cites *WCH* I 6 (Marina Oswald); *WCH* II 300 (K. Ford).

[1001] *WR* 716, which cites *WCH* IX 226 (George De Mohrenschildt); see *WCH* IX 77 (Taylor), 308 (J. De Mohrenschildt).

[1002] *WR* 716, which cites *WCH* XI 119 (Alexander Kleinlerer); *WCH* VIII 384 (Meller), 393 (Elena A. Hall); *WCH* II 341 (Peter Gregory); *WCH* IX 225-226 (G. De Mohrenschildt); compare *WCH* V 419 (Marina Oswald).

[1003] CE 780 on *WCH* XVII 660 displays both the hard-to-read letter and its envelope.

[1004] Email reply from "Adrien F CIV OSD PA Creecy-Starks (US)" to the author on August 26, 2015.

[1005] The letterhead was scanned and cropped from a document shown later in this chapter, from Folsom Exhibit No. 1—Continued (p. 38) on *WCH* XIX 688. Coming from that US Federal government source, it is in the public domain.

[1006] Image scanned from CE 1089 on *WCH* XXII 37. Coming from that US Federal government source, it is in the public domain. The handwritten date was probably added at the Warren Commission to assist in numbering and exhibiting items in chronologic order. A fuzzier copy is CE 780 on *WCH* XVII 659.

[1007] Quoted with permission from Kaiser, David 177, which cites *WCH* XVII 728-740. Permission notice is in endnote [998].

[1008] *WR* 716, which cites CE 824, pp. 4-6; *WCH* IV 419-424 (Fain).

[1009] Quoted with permission after payment, from Epstein *Legend* 164.

[1010] *WR* 716, which cites *WCH* I 20 (Marina Oswald).

[1011] Quoted with permission from McMillan, page 233, which cites "Testimony of John W. Fain, Vol. 4, p. 423." Permission statement for McMillan is in endnote [150].

[1012] Quoted with permission from Newman, John 271, which cites "Clarence Kelley, *Kelley: The Story of an FBI Director*, p. 261."

[1013] Quoted with permission after payment, from Ford, Gerald R., and John R. Stiles. *Portrait of the Assassin* 123-124.

[1014] *WR* 716, which cites *WCH* VIII 357-358 (Bouhe), 452-455 (Igor Vladimir Voshinin); see generally *WCH* IX 4-12 (Paul M. Raigorodsky); *WCH* VIII 354-355 (Clark); *WCH* IX 305-306 (J. De Mohrenschildt).

[1015] *WR* 716, which cites *WCH* VIII 358-359 (Bouhe), *WCH* II 341 (Peter Gregory).

[1016] *WR* 717, which cites *WCH* IX 168, 217, 224-226, 281 (G. De Mohrenschildt); *WCH* I 7 (Marina Oswald).

[1017] Quoted with permission from McMillan 243-244. Permission statement is in endnote [150].

[1018] Testimony of Elena A. Hall on *WCH* VIII 395.

[1019] *WCH* VIII 398 (Elena A. Hall).

[1020] O'Reilly, Bill, and Martin Dugard. *Killing Kennedy: The End of Camelot* 103 — cited but not quoted. The author's statement about that source is in endnote [272].

[1021] *WR* 717, which cites *WCH* IX 236 (G. De Mohrenschildt); see *WCH* VIII 359, 371-372 (Bouhe).

[1022] *WR* 717, which cites *WCH* VIII 371-373 (Bouhe), 383-385 (Meller), 393-395 (E. Hall), 422-423 (Valentina Kay); *WCH* XI 119 (Kleinlerer); *WCH* IX 307, 324-325 (J. De Mohrenschildt); *WCH* I 7 (Marina Oswald); *WCH* IX 231 (G. De Mohrenschildt).

[1023] *WR* 717, which cites *WCH* IX 309, 311 (J. De Mohrenschildt); *WCH* VIII 366, 372 (Bouhe), 382, 384 (Meller), 394 (E. Hall).

[1024] *WR* 717, which cites *WCH* VIII 384 (Meller); see also *WCH* VIII 394 (E. Hall).

[1025] *WR* 717, which cites *WCH* IX 309 (J. De Mohrenschildt); *WCH* II 300 (K. Ford).

[1026] Testimony of Mrs. Marguerite Oswald on *WCH* I 135.

[1027] *WR* 717, which cites *WCH* VIII 445 (Mrs. Voshinin), 376 (Bouhe).

[1028] *WR* 717, which cites *WCH* XI 123 (Kleinlerer).

[1029] Quoted with permission from McMillan, page 249, which cites "Conversation with Anna N. Meller, August 1964." Permission statement for McMillan is in endnote [150].

[1030] *WR* 717, which cites *WCH* II 308 (K. Ford); *WCH* VIII 374 (Bouhe), 381 (Meller).

[1031] *WR* 717, which cites *WCH* XI 123 (Kleinlerer).

[1032] *WR* 718, which cites *WCH* VIII 345-346 (Clark), 364-365 (Bouhe).

[1033] McMillan 249.

[1034] *WR* 718, which cites *WCH* I 140 (Marguerite Oswald); *WCH* VIII 365 (Bouhe), 383 (Meller).

1035 McMillan 234.

1036 *WR* 718, which cites *WCH* I 140 (Marguerite Oswald); *WCH* VIII 365 (Bouhe).

1037 *WR* 718, which cites *WCH* VIII 395-396 (E. Hall), 365 (Bouhe); see *WCH* II 300 (K. Ford).

1038 *WR* 718, which cites CE 994, p. 25; *WCH* I 10, 32, 34 (Marina Oswald); *WCH* XI 296 (Marina Oswald).

1039 Quoted with permission after payment, from Posner, Gerald. *Case Closed: Lee Harvey Oswald and the Assassination of JFK* (revised with author's note, 1994 softcover), page 82. Copyright notice supplied by publisher: "Excerpt(s) from CASE CLOSED: LEE HARVEY OSWALD AND THE ASSASSINATION OF JFK by Gerald L. Posner, copyright © 1993 by Gerald L. Posner. Used by permission of Random House, an imprint and division of Penguin Random House LLC. All rights reserved. Any third party use of this material, outside of this publication, is prohibited. Interested parties must apply directly to Penguin Random House LLC for permission."

1040 Quoted with permission from McMillan 236. Permission statement is in endnote [150].

1041 *WCH* I 139-141 (Marguerite Oswald).

1042 *WR* 717, which cites *WCH* IX 77 (Taylor); *WCH* VIII 366 (Bouhe), 407 (John Hall); *WCH* I 137-138 (Marguerite Oswald).

1043 *WR* 717, which cites *WCH* VIII 366 (Bouhe); *WCH* IX 230 (G. De Mohrenschildt); see *WCH* I 6 (Marina Oswald).

1044 *WR* 718, which cites Helen Cunningham DE 1-A; *WCH* X 120 (Cunningham). See also *WCH* I 138 (Marguerite Oswald).

1045 Quoted with permission after payment, from King, Stephen 501. Copyright notice is in endnote [148].

1046 Quoted with permission after payment, from Stafford, Jean. *A Mother in History* 57. See also *WCH* I 141 (Marguerite Oswald).

1047 *WR* 716, which cites *WCH* I 141 (Marguerite Oswald).

1048 *WR* 718, which cites CE 820-A; see *WCH* X 166 (Bargas).

1049 *WR* 719, which cites CE 792; *WCH* VII 295 (Harry D. Holmes); CE 1152.

1050 *WR* 719, which cites *WCH* X 281-282 (Richard Leroy Hulen), 290 (Colin Barnhorst).

1051 *WR* 718, which cites *WCH* I 7-8, 31 (Marina Oswald); *WCH* VIII 394-395 (E. Hall); *WCH* IX 324 (J. De Mohrenschildt).

1052 *WR* 718, which cites *WCH* VIII 407 (J. Hall).

1053 *WR* 718, which cites *WCH* VIII 388 (Meller), 366 (Bouhe); *WCH* X 119 (Cunningham).

1054 *WR* 719, which cites *WCH* X 120-130 (Cunningham); Cunningham DE 1, 1-A, 2, 2-A, 4; *WCH* XI 477-478 (Cunningham); *WCH* X 144-146 (Donald E. Brooks); 150 (Irving Statman).

1055 *WR* 719, which cites *WCH* XI 477 (Cunningham); Cunningham DE 4; *WCH* X 175-177 (John G. Graef).

1056 TESTIMONY OF JOHN G. GRAEF on *WCH* X 178.

1057 *WR* 719, which cites *WCH* X 181 (Graef), 172 (Robert Stovall); CE 1144, p. 13.

1058 Quoted with permission from Kaiser, David 178. Permission notice is in endnote [998].

1059 Quoted with permission from Kaiser, David 179. Permission notice is in endnote [998].

1060 *WR* 719, which cites *WCH* I 8 (Marina Oswald).

1061 For a sense of the crisis of public concern, see Garner, Joe. *We Interrupt This Broadcast: The Events That Stopped Our Lives – from the Hindenburg Explosion to the Death of John F. Kennedy Jr.*, page 45, and for what that publication does best, listen to its enclosed compact disc 1, track 14.

1062 Quoted with permission after payment, from Hill with McCubbin 193. Copyright notice is in endnote [757].

1063 Quoted with permission from Kennedy, Robert F. *Thirteen Days: A Memoir of the Cuban Missile Crisis* 36-37.

1064 Quoted with permission from the Introduction to Kennedy, Robert *Thirteen Days*. The Dean Rusk quotation is in the Introduction by Harold Macmillan. Different views, each excellent, are in Sorensen, Theodore. *Kennedy* 667-718 and Nixon, Richard M. *RN* 244.

1065 Quoted with permission after payment, from Sorensen, Theodore C. *Kennedy* 380; see also Manchester, William. *One Brief Shining Moment* 247.

1066 Quoted with permission from Kaiser, David 179, which notes "On this period see Epstein, *Legend*, pp. 469-79, and *Warren Report*, pp. 714-22." Permission notice for Kaiser is in endnote [998].

1067 DOBBS EXHIBIT NO. 9 on *WCH* XIX 576.

1068 DOBBS EXHIBIT NO. 11 on *WCH* XIX 578.

1069 *WR* 720, which cites *WCH* X 237-238 (Mrs. Tobias); CE 1160, p. 2; see also *WCH* I 8 (Marina Oswald).

1070 *WR* 720, which cites *WCH* IX 89-91 (Taylor); *WCH* XI 470 (Taylor), 120-121 (Kleinlerer), 139-140 (Gibson); *WCH* I 8 (Marina Oswald).

1071 Quoted with permission after payment, from King, Stephen 529. Copyright notice is in endnote [148].

1072 TESTIMONY OF MRS. DONALD (ALEXANDRA DE MOHRENSCHILDT TAYLOR) GIBSON on *WCH* XI 140-141.

1073 Quoted with permission from McMillan 262. Permission statement is in endnote [150].

1074 Quoted with permission from Kaiser, David 179. Permission notice is in endnote [998].

1075 AFFIDAVIT OF ALEXANDER KLEINLERER on *WCH* XI 120.

1076 *WR* 720, which cites *WCH* XI 120 (Kleinlerer).

1077 *WR* 720, which cites *WCH* IX 244 (G. De Mohrenschildt), 313 (J. De Mohrenschildt); *WCH* I 35 (Marina Oswald).

1078 *WR* 720, which cites *WCH* V 415 (Marina Oswald); CE 994, p. 26; *WCH* X 242-243 (Mrs. Tobias), 258 (M. F. Tobias).

[1079] *WR* 720, which cites *WCH* II 309-310 (K. Ford); *WCH* VIII 375-376 (Bouhe), 382 (Meller); see *WCH* IX 226 (G. De Mohrenschildt); CE 994, p. 22.

[1080] Quoted with permission from McMillan 307. Permission statement is in endnote [150].

[1081] *WR* 720, which cites *WCH* I 32-33 (Marina Oswald).

[1082] Quoted with permission from McMillan 308. Permission statement is in endnote [150].

[1083] Quoted with permission after payment, from King, Stephen 476. Copyright notice is in endnote [148].

[1084] *WR* 720, which cites *WCH* IX 232-233 (G. De Mohrenschildt), 310 (J. De Mohrenschildt); *WCH* VIII 386 (Meller); *WCH* X 245-246 (Mrs. Tobias); *WCH* I 11 (Marina Oswald); *WCH* V 416 (Marina Oswald); *WCH* XI 296 (Marina Oswald); CE 1817.

[1085] *WR* 720, which cites *WCH* VIII 388 (Meller).

[1086] *WR* 720, which cites *WCH* I 11 (Marina Oswald); *WCH* XI 297 (Marina Oswald).

[1087] *WR* 720, which cites *WCH* I 11-12 (Marina Oswald), compare *WCH* XI 297-298 (Marina Oswald).

[1088] *WR* 721, which cites *WCH* I 11-12 (Marina Oswald); *WCH* II 299-300 (K. Ford); *WCH* VIII 388 (Meller), 365 (Bouhe); *WCH* XI 296 (Marina Oswald).

[1089] *WR* 721, which cites *WCH* II 299 (K. Ford); but see CE 994, p. 27.

[1090] *WR* 721, which cites *WCH* II 299 (K. Ford).

[1091] *WR* 721, which cites *WCH* VIII 416 (V. Ray); *WCH* II 304 (K. Ford), 325 (D. Ford); *WCH* I 11-12 (Marina Oswald).

[1092] *WR* 721, which cites CE 994, p. 27-28.

[1093] *WR* 721, which cites *WCH* XI 299 (Marina Oswald).

[1094] *WR* 721, which cites *WCH* II 304 (K. Ford), 325 (D. Ford); *WCH* VIII 416 (V. Ray); see *WCH* I 11 (Marina Oswald).

[1095] *WR* 721, which cites *WCH* VIII 372 (Bouhe); *WCH* IX 238, 266 (G. De Mohrenschildt); *WCH* I 35 (Marina Oswald).

[1096] *WR* 721, which cites *WCH* IX 238, 266 (G. De Mohrenschildt).

[1097] *WR* 721, which cites *WCH* II 318 (K. Ford).

[1098] *WR* 721, which cites *WCH* XI 299 (Marina Oswald).

[1099] Quoted from Oswald, Robert 130. This source was described in endnote [68].

[1100] *WR* 721, which cites *WCH* I 386-389 (Robert Oswald); CE 320; *WCH* XI 52-60 (J. Pic).

[1101] Quoted as fair use (for brevity) from Leahy, Michael (Arkansas Democrat-Gazette), "Still haunted by a brother's legacy" printed in the *Philadelphia Inquirer* 21 Nov. 1997: A22.

[1102] Photo scanned from Oswald, Robert; photo 11 in the insert after page 96. The quotation is from the caption below that photo. The book does not state credits or sources for any of its photos, most of which appear to be family "snapshots" taken or owned by Robert Oswald. This source was described in endnote [68].

[1103] TESTIMONY OF JOHN EDWARD PIC on *WCH* XI 52.

[1104] *WCH* XI 79 (John Pic).

[1105] Quoted with permission from Newman, John 271.

[1106] *WCH* XI 59 (John Pic).

[1107] Quoted with permission from McMillan, page 290, which cites "Testimony of John Edward Pic, Vol. 11, p. 59." (Which is the same reference as in the endnote immediately above, but in her fuller style.) Permission statement for McMillan is in endnote [150].

[1108] *WCH* I 389-391 (Robert Oswald). Robert had saved and presented the letter (CE 322) and postcard (CE 324).

[1109] *WCH* I 392 (Robert Oswald).

[1110] *WCH* XI 63 (John Pic).

[1111] *WR* 722, which cites CE 986, p. 2748-A.

[1112] *WR* 722, which cites CE 93, p. 3: 1147; *WCH* VIII 370-371 (Bouhe).

[1113] *WR* 722, which cites CE 1172.

[1114] *WR* 722, which cites *WCH* I 5 (Marina Oswald); CE 2642; *WCH* VIII 371 (Bouhe); see *WCH* VIII 382 (Meller); *WCH* IX 150 (Paul Gregory).

[1115] *WR* 722, which cites *WCH* I 5 (Marina Oswald); *WCH* V 392-393, 416 (Marina Oswald); CE 1404, p. 456; CE 2652.

[1116] Quoted with permission after payment, from Epstein *Legend* 203.

[1117] Image scanned from CE 790 on *WCH* XVII 678. From that US Federal government source, it is in the public domain.

[1118] TESTIMONY OF ALWYN COLE on *WCH* IV 361, 375.

[1119] TESTIMONY OF JAMES C. CADIGAN on *WCH* VII 424.

[1120] *WR* 723, which cites *WR* chapter IV, p. 121; *WR* appendix X, pp. 571-577; *WCH* X 198-199, 201 (Ofstein).

[1121] Quoted with permission after payment, from Salinger, Pierre. *With Kennedy* 301; an amplified version is in Salinger's *P.S., A Memoir* 127-133.

[1122] Quoted with permission after payment, from Salinger *With Kennedy* 301.

[1123] Quoted with permission after payment, from Salinger *With Kennedy* 302.

[1124] Salinger *With Kennedy* 303.

[1125] Quoted with permission from McMillan 317. Permission statement is in endnote [150].

[1126] *WR* 722, which cites *WCH* IX 256 (G. De Mohrenschildt).

[1127] *WR* 722, which cites *WCH* X 19-29 (Everett D. Glover); *WCH* II 435-444 (R. Paine).

[1128] Quoted with permission from Garrison, Jim. *On the Trail of the Assassins* 71.

[1129] Quoted with permission from Douglass, James W. *JFK and the Unspeakable: Why He Died and Why It Matters* 168, which cites *WCH* IX 257.

[1130] Photo purchased from AP and slightly cropped. ©The Associated Press.

[1131] Quoted with permission after payment, from King, Stephen 544. Copyright notice is in endnote [148].

[1132] Quoted with permission after payment, from Epstein *Legend* 207. See also *WCH* II 435-444 (R. Paine); *WCH* II 385-386 (M. Paine); *WCH* I 35-36 (Marina Oswald).

[1133] *WR* 723, which cites *WCH* I 36 (Marina Oswald); *WCH* II 443-445 (R. Paine); CE 404.

[1134] Quoted with permission after payment, from Ford and Stiles *Portrait* 180-181.

[1135] Quoted with permission after payment, from Ford and Stiles *Portrait* 276.

[1136] Quoted with permission from McMillan 329. Permission statement is in endnote [150].

[1137] *WR* 723, which cites *WCH* XI 155-156 (M. Waldo George); see CE 1133, 1134, 1167, pp. 465-467.

[1138] *WR* 723, which cites *WCH* X 241 (Mrs. Tobias), 258-259 (M. F. Tobias).

[1139] *WR* 723, which cites *WCH* I 10 (Marina Oswald); see *WCH* IX 94 (Taylor).

[1140] *WR* 724, which cites *WCH* I 10 (Marina Oswald).

[1141] *WR* 724, which cites *WCH* XI 155-156 (George); *WCH* II 470, 472 (R. Paine).

[1142] *WR* 723, which cites *WCH* II 445-457 (R. Paine).

[1143] O'Reilly and Dugard 143-144.

[1144] Photo from the U.S. Army is in the public domain.

[1145] Quoted with permission from Douglass 332, which cites "Donald Janson and Bernard Eismann, *The Far Right* (New York: McGraw-Hill, 1963), pp. 174-76."

[1146] Quoted with permission from Kaiser, David 182. Permission notice is in endnote [998].

[1147] Quoted with permission from Kaiser, David 183. Permission notice is in endnote [998].

[1148] Quoted with permission from Kaiser, David 183. Permission notice is in endnote [998].

[1149] *WR* 724, which cites *WR* chapter IV, pp. 184-185.

[1150] *WR* 724, which cites *WCH* I 17-18, 38 (Marina Oswald).

[1151] Quoted with permission from Mailer, Norman. *Oswald's Tale: An American Mystery* 498.

[1152] *WR* 119. Image of Klein's full-page advertisement in the February 1963 *American Rifleman* magazine was imported from http://www.classroomhelp.com/lessons/Presidents/Kennedy_Assasination/Oswald.html, which below its image of the ad states: "Source: http://mcadams.posc.mu.edu/kleins.jpg via Wikipedia, Public Domain." The smaller image is of another (specific and clearer) Klein's ad for the Carcano. The author's Web search indicates that Klein's is no longer in business.

[1153] Image scanned from CE 785 on *WCH* XVII 675. Coming from that US Federal government source, it is in the public domain. The same is also shown but darker on *WCH* XVII 635.

[1154] Image scanned from CE 788 on *WCH* XVII 677. Coming from that US Federal government source, it is in the public domain. For a clear color photo of the Money Order, see Life Books, The Editors of. *The Day Kennedy Died: 50 Years Later LIFE Remembers the Man and the Moment* 159.

[1155] O'Reilly and Dugard 152-153.

[1156] *WR* 723, which cites *WCH* VII 365 (William J. Waldman), 376-377 (Heinz W. Michaelis).

[1157] Quoted with permission from Mailer *Oswald's Tale* 500.

[1158] Quoted with permission from McMillan 339. Permission statement is in endnote [150].

[1159] *WR* 723, which cites *WCH* V 396 (Marina Oswald).

[1160] *WR* 724, which cites *WCH* I 13 (Marina Oswald).

[1161] *WR* 724, which cites *WCH* I 14-15, 93-94 (Marina Oswald); *WCH* V 396-398 (Marina Oswald); CE 1156, p. 442; CE 2694.

[1162] Testimony of Mrs. Lee Harvey Oswald (resumed) on *WCH* I 65.

[1163] Quoted with permission from McMillan 341. Permission statement is in endnote [150].

[1164] This photo is CE 134 on *WR* 126, an enlargement cropped from CE 133-A, shown with CE 133-B on the same page. Coming from that US Federal government source, it is in the public domain. The photo is held by the National Archives and Records Administration.

[1165] Quoted with permission from McMillan 347. Permission statement is in endnote [150].

[1166] Quoted with permission from McMillan 348. Permission statement is in endnote [150].

[1167] Quoted with permission from McMillan, page 347, which cites "Exhibit No. 2694, Vol. 26, pp. 58-62." Permission statement for McMillan is in endnote [150].

[1168] Quoted with permission from McMillan, page 347, which cites "Warren Commission Report, p. 192; Testimony of Sergeant James A. Zahm, Vol. 11, p. 308." His testimony is at length in Chapter 13 – The Shooter. Permission statement for McMillan is in endnote [150].

[1169] Quoted with permission from McMillan 349. Permission statement is in endnote [150].

[1170] *WR* 724, which cites *WCH* X 187-189 (Graef), 198-199, 204-205 (Ofstein), 172-173 (Stovall); *WCH* XI 479 (Theodore F. Gangl).

[1171] Quoted with permission after payment, from Posner *Case Closed* 109, which cites for irritation "Testimony of Robert Stovall, WC Vol. X, p. 172."; and for inefficient and inept "p. 173." Copyright notice is in endnote [1039].

[1172] *WR* 724, which cites *WCH* X 189 (Graef); *WCH* XI 479 (Gangl); Gangl DE 1.

[1173] *WR* 724, which cites *WCH* VIII 409 (John Hall).

[1174] *WR* 724, which cites *WCH* I 18 (Marina Oswald); *WCH* II 517 (R. Paine).

[1175] *WR* 724, which cites Cunningham DE 1-A; *WCH* XI 478 (Cunningham).

[1176] *WR* 724, which cites John W. Burcham DE 1.

[1177] *WR* 724, which cites *WCH* I 17-18, 38 (Marina Oswald).

[1178] *WR* 724.

[1179] *WR* 724, which cites *WCH* I 16-17 (Marina Oswald).

[1180] McMillan 352.

[1181] Commission Exhibit 1 on *WCH* XVI 1-2.

[1182] Quoted with permission from McMillan 352-353. Permission statement is in endnote [150].

[1183] O'Reilly and Dugard 157.

[1184] https://en.wikipedia.org/wiki/Edwin_Walker accessed on 2015/12/23.

[1185] O'Reilly and Dugard 158.

[1186] Quoted with permission from McMillan 353. Permission statement is in endnote [150].

[1187] Quoted with permission from McMillan 359. Permission statement is in endnote [150].

[1188] *WR* 724, which cites *WCH* I 16-18 (Marina Oswald).

[1189] Quoted with permission after payment, from Epstein *Legend* 213.

[1190] Quoted with permission after payment, through the great courtesy of Edward Jay Epstein, from his *The Assassination Chronicles: Inquest, Counterplot and Legend* 590-591.

[1191] Quoted with permission from Mailer *Oswald's Tale* 517, which cites McMillan *Marina and Lee* 374.

[1192] O'Reilly and Dugard 161.

[1193] Quoted with permission from McMillan 368. Permission statement is in endnote [150].

[1194] *WR* 188, which cites *WCH* V 392 (Marina Oswald).

[1195] Quoted with permission after payment, from Bishop, Jim. *The Day Kennedy Was Shot*, page 322. Subsequent references will be in form Bishop *Kennedy* 322.

[1196] *WCH* V 387-400 (Marina Oswald)..

[1197] *WCH* V 605 (Marina Oswald).

[1198] *WR* 187-189, which cites *WCH* V 389-390 (Marina Oswald).

[1199] Quoted with permission from Nixon, Richard M. *RN: The Memoirs of Richard Nixon* 252.

[1200] Quoted with the gracious permission of James Reston, Jr., author and copyright owner of *The Lone Star: The Life of John Connally* 228-229, which cites *Dallas Morning News*, April 21, 1963.

[1201] Quoted with permission from Mallon, Thomas. *Mrs. Paine's Garage: and the Murder of John F. Kennedy* 31.

[1202] *WR* 725, which cites *WCH* II 457-458 (R. Paine); *WCH* I 18 (Marina Oswald).

[1203] *WR* 725, which cites *WCH* I 18-19 (Marina Oswald).

[1204] Quoted with permission from Mallon 32.

[1205] *WR* 725, which cites *WCH* II 459 (R. Paine); *WCH* I 19 (Marina Oswald).

[1206] This photo, imported from http://thetraveltrolley.com/, then converted to grayscale and slightly cropped, is very similar to CE 431 on *WCH* XVII 159, at the National Archives, but is more clear. The author's experienced, professional picture researcher has performed due diligence in an extensive search for both the original source and any copyright owner of this specific image, without success, so it is printed as fair use. Please see Credits and Permissions on page ii.

[1207] King, Stephen 545.

[1208] Quoted with permission after payment, from Epstein *Legend* 215.

[1209] Testimony of Mrs. Lillian Murret on *WCH* III 133.

[1210] *WR* 725, which cites *WCH* VIII 133-134 (Lillian Murret), 164 (Marilyn Murret).

[1211] *WR* 725, which cites *WCH* XI 474-476 (John Rachal); Rachal DE 1.

[1212] *WR* 725, which cites Rachal DE 1; Rachal DE 2; *WCH* VIII 135 (L. Murret); CE 1893, 1946, 1951; Bobb Hunley DE 3.

[1213] Quoted with permission from Baker, Judyth Vary. *Me & Lee: How I Came to Know, Love and Lose Lee Harvey Oswald*, page 222.

[1214] Baker 267*n* (which means the footnote on page 267).

[1215] Quoted with permission from McMillan, page 388, which cites "Exhibit No. 1144, Vol. 22, p. 162."; in this book's format: CE 1144 on *WCH* XXII 162. Permission statement for McMillan is in endnote [150].

[1216] Quoted with permission from Mailer *Oswald's Tale* 537.

[1217] Quoted with permission from Mailer *Oswald's Tale* 536.

[1218] Baker 267*n*.

[1219] *WR* 726, which cites *WCH* X 214-219 (Charles Joseph LeBlanc); *WCH* XI 473-474 (Barbe).

[1220] *WCH* VIII 136 (Lillian Murret).

[1221] *WR* 726, which cites *WCH* VIII 137 (L. Murret).

[1222] *WR* 726, which cites *WCH* II 517 (R. Paine).

[1223] *WR* 726, which cites *WCH* VIII 58 (M. Evans), 72-73 (J. Evans), 186 (Charles Murret); *WCH* X 265-266 (Mrs. Jesse Garner).

[1224] Quoted with permission after payment, from King, Stephen 288. Copyright notice is in endnote [148].

[1225] Thanks to brother-in-law and Russian language expert G. Larry Penrose for correcting this transliteration.

[1226] Quoted with permission from McMillan 395. Permission statement is in endnote [150].

[1227] *WR* 726, which cites *WCH* II 468-469, 475-477, 484-485 (R. Paine); *WCH* VIII 139-141 (L. Murret), 186 (C. Murret); *WCH* I 19 (Marina Oswald).

[1228] Testimony of Ruth Hyde Paine on *WCH* II 471.

[1229] Quoted with permission from Baker 292.

[1230] Quoted with permission from McMillan 397. Permission statement is in endnote [150].

[1231] Epstein, Edward Jay. *Counterplot* 15.

[1232] Testimony of Dean Adams Andrews, Jr. on *WCH* XI 327

[1233] *WCH* XI 327 (Andrews).

[1234] *WCH* XI 326 (Andrews).

[1235] *WCH* XI 336-337 (Andrews).

[1236] *WCH* XI 328 (Andrews).

[1237] *WR* 28, which cites *WCH* IV 130 (Gov. John B. Connally, Jr.); *WCH* VII 441 (Kenneth O'Donnell).

[1238] *WR* 28, which cites *WCH* VII 441-443 (Kenneth O'Donnell).

[1239] *WR* 28, which cites *WCH* VII 475 (Clifton C. Carter).

[1240] CE 1089 on *WCH* XXII 37, reproduced and re-created earlier in this chapter.

[1241] The letterhead was scanned and cropped from a document shown later in this chapter, from Folsom Exhibit No. 1—Continued (p. 38) on *WCH* XIX 688. Coming from that US Federal government source, it is in the public domain.

[1242] Image scanned from CE 1091 on *WCH* XXII 38, a carbon copy, not on letterhead and not signed. Coming from that US Federal government source, it is in the public domain.

[1243] Images of address and reverse sides scanned from CE 780 on *WCH* XVII 658. Coming from that US Federal government source, these are in the public domain.

[1244] *WR* 727, which cites CE 1969.

[1245] Quoted with permission from Douglass xxvi.

[1246] Quoted with permission from Mailer *Oswald's Tale* 558.

[1247] Photo, lightly cropped, is from the National Archives and Records Administration, in the public domain.

[1248] Quoted from http://en.wikipedia.org/wiki/Ich_bin_ein_Berliner (Four words in a foreign language with its own Wikipedia article!) This author imports only fair use materials from Wikipedia, and hopes readers will join in generously supporting this most excellent wonder of modern life: https://donate.wikimedia.org/ "Wikimedia Foundation is a non-profit charity (tax ID number 20-0049703) established in the United States under IRS Code Section 501(c)(3), and, for that reason, donations from persons or entities located in the United States may benefit from tax deductible status."

[1249] *WR* 727, which cites *WCH* I 10, 68 (Marina Oswald); *WCH* II 448 (R. Paine); CE 408.

[1250] *WR* 727, which cites CE 12.

[1251] *WR* 727, which cites CE 13.

[1252] *WR* 727, which cites *WCH* I 44, 47 (Marina Oswald).

[1253] *WR* 727, which cites CE 408.

[1254] Images of three pages scanned from Folsom Exhibit No. 1—Continued (pages 40-42) on *WCH* XIX 690-692, where the pages are printed in reversed sequence. Coming from that US Federal government source, they are in the public domain. CE 2016 is a small dark copy on *WCH* XXIV 431-432.

[1255] *WR* 728, which cites *WCH* II 449, 491-496 (R. Paine); CE 410, 411, 412.

[1256] *WR* 728, which cites CE 415.

[1257] *WR* 728, which cites CE 416.

[1258] Quoted with permission from Fries, Chuck, and Irv Wilson with Spencer Green. *We'll Never Be Young Again: Remembering the Last Days of John F. Kennedy*, page 77, which cites "(from press conference, July 17, 1963)".

[1259] Affidavit of Emmett Charles Barbe, Jr. on *WCH* XI 473-474.

[1260] *WR* 726, which cites *WCH* X 214-219 (LeBlanc), 220-229 (Adrian Alba).

[1261] Testimony of Adrian Thomas Alba on *WCH* X 219-229.

[1262] Image is an enlargement of a portion of Folsom Exhibit No. 1—Continued (p. 40) on *WCH* XIX 690. Coming from that US Federal government source, it is in the public domain.

[1263] Image scanned from Folsom Exhibit No. 1—Continued (page 38) on *WCH* XIX 688. Coming from that US Federal government source, it is in the public domain. It is the top of this letter that was scanned and cropped to show the NDRB letterhead above carbon copies, twice, earlier in this chapter.

[1264] *WR* 727, which cites Burcham DE 1; Rachal DE 1; Hunley DE 2, 5; CE 421, 1911.

[1265] *WR* 727, which cites CE 1781, p. 550. CE 1781, p. 550.

[1266] O'Reilly and Dugard 185-186.

[1267] Quoted with permission from McMillan 424. Permission statement is in endnote [150].

[1268] Quoted with permission from McMillan 426. Permission statement is in endnote [150].

[1269] Image scanned from FOLSOM EXHIBIT NO. 1—Continued (p. 39) on *WCH* XIX 689. Coming from that US Federal government source, it is in the public domain. Another copy is CE 1092 on *WCH* XXII 39.

[1270] Quoted with permission from Zirbel, Craig I. *The Texas Connection* 52-53.

[1271] *WR* 728, which cites Lee DE 2, 4; CE 1410, 1411, 1413, pp. 28-31; CE 2542, 2543, 2544. 2545.

[1272] Quoted with permission after payment, from Epstein *Legend* 220.

[1273] *WR* 728, which cites *WCH* X 37-38 (Bringuier); CE 1413, pp. 19-27.

[1274] *WR* 728, which cites CE 826, pp. 5-10; *WCH* X 53-57 (Francis L. Martello).

[1275] *WCH* V 401 (Marina Oswald).

[1276] *WR* 729, which cites *WCH* X 90 (Vincent T. Lee); *WCH* I 64-65 (Marina Oswald); *WCH* V 402-403 (Marina Oswald).

[1277] *WR* 729, which cites CE 1413, pp. 19, 21, 34; Lee DE 6; *WCH* X 38-39 (Bringuier).

[1278] Photo "Oswaldneworleans" by New Orleans Police Department - New Orleans Police Department photographic records. Imported from Wikipedia: http://en.wikipedia.org/wiki/File:Oswaldneworleans.jpg#/media/File:Oswaldneworleans.jpg as fair use. There are no other similar photographs taken at the time, so this photograph can be reasonably described as "unique" and "irreplaceable".

[1279] Quoted with permission from McMillan 433. Permission statement is in endnote [150].

[1280] *WR* 729, which cites *WCH* I 24 (Marina Oswald).

[1281] *WR* 729, which cites *WCH* X 39-41 (Bringuier), 64-66 (Charles Hall Steele, Jr.); Garner DE 1; Prank Pizzo DE 453A, 453B; Bringuier DE 1, 2.

[1282] *WR* 729, which cites *WCH* XI 158-169 (William Kirk Stuckey); *WCH* X 42-4,3 (Bringuier).

[1283] *WR* 729, which cites *WCH* XI 169-171 (Stuckey); Stuckey DE 3; Bringuier DE 3, 4.

[1284] Quoted with permission from McMillan, page 441, which cites "Testimony of Charles F. Murret, Vol. 8, p. 187." Permission statement for McMillan is in endnote [150].

[1285] Quoted with permission from McMillan 441-442. Permission statement is in endnote [150].

[1286] *WR* 729, which cites Lee DE 1, 2, 4, 5, 6, 7

[1287] TESTIMONY OF VINCENT T. LEE on *WCH* X 90-94.

[1288] CE 93 on *WCH* XVI 341.

[1289] Quoted with permission after payment, through the great courtesy of Edward Jay Epstein, from his *Counterplot* 22, which cites "Hearings, Vol. X, p. 54.", which in this book's style is TESTIMONY OF FRANCIS L. MARTELLO on *WCH* X 54.

[1290] Quoted with permission after payment, from Epstein *Counterplot* 20, which cites "Hearings, Vol. I, p. 64.", equivalent to TESTIMONY OF MRS. LEE HARVEY OSWALD on *WCH* I 64.

[1291] Quoted with permission after payment, from Epstein *Counterplot* 24, which cites "Report, p. 412." and "Hearings, Vol. I, p. 24.", equivalent to *WR* 412 and TESTIMONY OF MRS. LEE HARVEY OSWALD on *WCH* I 24.

[1292] Transcribed as fair use (for brevity) from TV: *Real History: The Secret KGB JFK Assassination Files*, broadcast on The Learning Channel on 03 March 2000.

[1293] Quoted with permission after payment, from Manchester, William. *The Death of a President* 8. Permission acknowledgement is in endnote [17].

[1294] Quoted with permission from Mailer *Oswald's Tale* 596-597.

[1295] CE 1145 pp. 11-12 on *WCH* XXII 168.

[1296] A box on page 333 explains why prudent writers may not quote any words spoken by Dr. Martin Luther King, Jr.

[1297] Quoted with kind permission from Ashman, Charles. *Connally: The Adventures of Big Bad John* 26.

[1298] Quoted with permission from Zirbel 162.

[1299] Quoted with permission from Garrison 71-72.

[1300] *WR* 730, which cites *WCH* I 26 (Marina Oswald); *WCH* III 9 (R. Paine).

[1301] Quoted with permission from McMillan, page 462, which cites "Testimony of Michael R. Paine, Vol. 2, pp. 414-418, and Vol. 9, pp. 436-444." For the unloading into the garage and Ruth's ignorance of the blanket's content, see Mallon *Mrs. Paine's Garage* 40. Permission statement for McMillan is in endnote [150].

[1302] *WR* 730, which cites CE 2124, p. 383; CE 2125, pp. 475, 477-478; CE 2479; compare *WCH* X 276-277 (Jesse J. Garner).

[1303] *WR* 730, which cites *WCH* I 22-23, 37, 46-47 (Marina Oswald); CE 1404, pp. 451-453.

[1304] *WR* 730, which cites CE 2481, 2478; appendix XIV, p. 745.

[1305] *WR* 730, which cites *WCH* I 37, 45 (Marina Oswald).

[1306] *WR* 730, which cites *WCH* I 23 (Marina Oswald); CE 1156, p. 444.

[1307] *WR* 730, which cites *WCH* X 276 (Jesse J. Garner), 274 (Mrs. Jesse Garner).

[1308] *WR* 730, which cites *WCH* XI 460-464 (Eric Rogers).

[1309] *WR* 730, which cites *WCH* X 276 (Jesse J. Garner).

[1310] TESTIMONY OF JOHN M. MURRET on *WCH* VIII 189.

[1311] TESTIMONY OF CHARLES MURRET on *WCH* VIII 187-188.

[1312] *WR* 730, which cites CE 1969; CE 946; *WCH* XI 217 (Pamela Mumford); CE 2121, p. 39.

[1313] *WR* 730, which cites CE 93, 986, 2121, p. 39; CE 2564.

[1314] *WR* 730, which cites *WCH* I 25 (Marina Oswald); CE 2121, p. 39; CE 93.

[1315] *WR* 730, which cites *WCH* I 24-25 (Marina Oswald).

[1316] *WR* 731, which cites CE 2121, p. 39.

[1317] *WR* 731, which cites CE 93.

[1318] *WR* 731, which cites *WCH* I 27 (Marina Oswald).

[1319] *WR* 731, which cites *WCH* XI 179-180 (Estelle Twiford), 179 (Horace E. Twiford); CE 2533; CE 2961 2962.

[1320] *WR* 732, which cites *WCH* XI 214 (McFarland); CE 1143, p. 4; CE 2191, pp. 5-7; CE 2534.

[1321] *WR* 733, which cites CE 2193, pp. 1-2; CE 2123, 2566, pp. 2-3.

[1322] *WR* 733, which cites CE 2463, pp. 10-12; CE 2566, p. 2.

[1323] *WR* 733, which cites CE 2121, pp. 47, 54; CE 2120, 3073, p. 7.

[1324] *WR* 734, which cites CE 2568.

[1325] *WR* 734, which cites CE 2121, p. 39; CE 3073, p. 7.

[1326] *WR* 734, which cites CE 2564; see CE 93.

[1327] *WR* 734, which cites CE 2445, p. 2.

[1328] *WR* 734, which cites CE 2121, p. 39.

[1329] Quoted with permission from Mailer *Oswald's Tale* 634.

[1330] *WR* 734, which cites CE 2764

[1331] Quoted with permission from Nechiporenko, Oleg M. *Passport to Assassination: The Never-Before-Told Story of Lee Harvey Oswald by the KGB Colonel Who Knew Him* 69. Copyright notice is in endnote [495].

[1332] Quoted with permission from Nechiporenko 70-71. Copyright notice is in endnote [495].

[1333] *WR* 734, which cites CE 2121, p. 39; CE 2449.

[1334] Quoted with permission from Mailer *Oswald's Tale* 636.

[1335] *WR* 734, which cites CE 2121, p. 39.

[1336] *WR* 735, which cites CE 2121, pp. 39-40; CE 2120; compare CE 2445.

[1337] *WR* 735, which cites CE 2121, p. 39.

[1338] *WR* 735, which cites CE 2445, p. 3; CE 2121, p. 40; CE 2564, p. 303.

[1339] *WR* 735, which cites "Confidential information", probably meaning it came from CIA observation or a secret source.

[1340] Transcribed as fair use (for brevity) from TV: *Real History: The Secret KGB JFK Assassination Files*.

[1341] Nechiporenko 75. (I don't have to invent anything when the facts are this good!)

[1342] Quoted with permission from Nechiporenko 75-79. Copyright notice is in endnote [495].

[1343] Quoted with permission from Nechiporenko 81. Copyright notice is in endnote [495].

[1344] *WR* 735, which cites *WCH* I 27-28, 50 (Marina Oswald); CE 1156, p. 445.

[1345] *WR* 735, which cites *WCH* III 13-18, 51-52 (R. Paine); *WCH* IX 395 (R. Paine).

[1346] *WR* 735, which cites CE 15.

[1347] *WR* 736, which cites CE 2530, 2531, 2537, 2536, 2458, 2121, pp. 64-69; CE 1166, pp. 2-3; CE 2469, pp. 1-2; CE 2538, 2532, p. 5; CE 2638, 3073, pp. 2, 3.

[1348] *WR* 736, which cites CE 2639, 2539, p. 1.

[1349] *WR* 736, which cites

[1350] *WR* 736, which cites CE 2121, pp. 8, 60, 72-78; CE 2129, pp. 2, 6; CE 2130, 2459, 2460, 2535, pp. 10-11; CE 2577.

[1351] Quoted with permission from McMillan 470. Permission statement is in endnote [150].

[1352] *WR* 737, which cites Burcham DE 1; Cunningham DE 1-A; *WCH* XI 478 (Cunningham).

[1353] *WR* 737, which cites Hulen DE 7, 11; *WCH* X 281-283 (Hulen), 285-290 (Barnhorst); *WCH* I 27 (Marina Oswald).

[1354] *WR* 737, which cites *WCH* XI 479 (Gangl); Gangl DE 1.

[1355] Quoted with permission from Ashman, Charles. *Connally: The Adventures of Big Bad John* 26.

[1356] Quoted with permission after payment from Smith, Sally Bedell. *Grace and Power: The Private World of the Kennedy White House* 423. Copyright notice supplied by publisher: "Excerpt(s) from GRACE AND POWER: THE PRIVATE WORLD OF THE KENNEDY WHITE HOUSE by Sally Bedell Smith, copyright © 2004 by Sally Bedell Smith. Used by permission of Random House, an imprint of Penguin Random House LLC. All rights reserved. Any third party use of this material, outside of this publication, is prohibited. Interested parties must apply directly to Penguin Random House LLC for permission."

[1357] *WR* 737, which cites *WCH* III 26-31. 33 (R. Paine); *WCH* I 27-28, 50 (Marina Oswald).

[1358] *WR* 737, which cites *WCH* I 28, 50 (Marina Oswald).

[1359] *WR* 737, which cites *WCH* III 30-31 (R. Paine).

[1360] *WR* 737, which cites *WCH* III 31 (R. Paine); *WCH* VI 401-402 (Mary E. Bledsoe).

[1361] Testimony of Mary E. Bledsoe on *WCH* VI 405-406.

[1362] *WCH* VI 406 (Bledsoe).

[1363] *WCH* VI 406 (Bledsoe).

[1364] *WR* 737, which cites *WCH* III 12, 32, 35 (R. Paine).

[1365] Quoted with permission after payment, from Posner *Case Closed* 200. Copyright notice is in endnote [1039].

[1366] *WR* 737, which cites *WCH* III 5, 33-34 (R. Paine).

[1367] *WR* 737, which cites *WCH* III 32 (R. Paine); *WCH* IX 428-429 (R. Paine).

[1368] *WR* 737, which cites *WCH* VI 407 (Bledsoe).

[1369] *WCH* VI 407 (Bledsoe).

[1370] Testimony of Mrs. Earlene Roberts on *WCH* VI 436.

[1371] *WCH* VI 436-438 (Roberts).

[1372] Quoted with permission after payment, from Epstein *Legend* 239.

[1373] Testimony of Buell Wesley Frazier, *WCH* II 211.

[1374] Quoted with permission after payment, from Posner *Case Closed* 200, which cites "Testimony of Linnie Mae Randle, WC Vol. II, p. 246." Copyright notice is in endnote [1039].

[1375] Posner *Case Closed* 200, which cites "Testimony of Ruth Paine, WC Vol. IX, p. 393."

[1376] *WCH* II 211 (Frazier).

[1377] *WCH* II 212 (Frazier).

[1378] Posner *Case Closed* 200, which cites "Testimony of Ruth Paine, WC Vol. III, p. 34.

[1379] Quoted with permission after payment, from Posner *Case Closed* 200, which cites "Testimony of Linnie Mae Randle, WC Vol. II, p. 247." Copyright notice is in endnote [1039].

[1380] Quoted with permission after payment, from Posner *Case Closed* 200. Copyright notice is in endnote [1039].

[1381] Testimony of Roy Sansom Truly, *WCH* III 213.

[1382] Quoted with permission after payment, from Posner *Case Closed* 201, which cites "Testimony of Ruth Paine, WC Vol. III, p. 34-35." Copyright notice is in endnote [1039].

[1383] *WCH* III 213-214 (Roy Truly).

[1384] Quoted with permission after payment, from Posner *Case Closed* 202, which cites "Gerald R. Ford and John R. Stiles, *Portrait of the Assassin* ... p. 282." Copyright notice is in endnote [1039].

[1385] Connally, Nellie, with Mickey Herskowitz. *From Love Field: Our Final Hours with President John F. Kennedy* 06.

[1386] Quoted with permission after payment, from Manchester *Death* 51. This form with a key word from the book's title is used because more than one book by the author is cited in these notes. Permission acknowledgement is in endnote [17].

[1387] *WR* 4-5.

[1388] This photo was purchased to show here, with credit: Roger Viollet / Getty Images. Of hundreds of very similar photos available, I chose to pay for this because it was taken on November 23, 1963; the street is almost clear; and a length of Houston Street, up which the limousine had driven the previous day, is in the foreground.

[1389] *WCH* III 214 (Roy Truly).

[1390] Quoted with permission after payment, from Posner *Case Closed* 202. Copyright notice is in endnote [1039].

[1391] Photo of President Obama imported from WhiteHouse.gov is courtesy of The White House, in public domain.

[1392] *WCH* III 214 (Roy Truly).

[1393] Quoted with permission after payment, from Posner *Case Closed* 202. The final quote is from co-worker Bonnie Ray Williams. Copyright notice is in endnote [1039].

[1394] The format "Scott, Foresman" is taken from the testimony of Oswald's supervisor, William H. Shelley, who had worked at the TSBD since 1945 — 18 years — and should know. See *WCH* VI 339.

[1395] Quoted with permission from McMillan, page 480, which cites "Testimony of Bonnie Ray Williams, Vol. 3, p. 164; Testimony of Daniel Arce, Vol. 6, p. 364; Testimony of Roy Sansom Truly, Vol. 3, p. 218; Testimony of Billy Lovelady, Vol. 6, p. 337; and Testimony of Charles Douglas Givens, Vol. 6, p. 352." Permission statement for McMillan is in endnote [150].

[1396] Quoted with permission after payment, from Bishop *Kennedy* 57.

[1397] Quoted with permission from oral history of Roy E. Lewis, Eyewitness, in Sneed, Larry A. *No More Silence: An Oral History of the Assassination of President Kennedy* 85-86.

[1398] Testimony of R. L. Adams, April 1, 1964, *WCH* X 138.

[1399] Affidavit of Robert L. Adams, August 4, 1964, *WCH* XI 481.

[1400] *WCH* XI 481 (Robert L. Adams); *WCH* IX 389 (Ruth Paine).

[1401] *WCH* XI 481 (Robert L. Adams).

[1402] *WCH* I 68 (Marina Oswald).

[1403] *WR* 738, which cites *WCH* III 37 (R. Paine); CE 994, p. 38.

[1404] *WR* 738, which cites *WCH* III 214-216 (Truly).

[1405] *WR* 738, which cites *WCH* I 68 (Marina Oswald).

[1406] *WR* 738, which cites *WCH* III 214-216 (Truly); *WCH* VI 328 (William H. Shelley).

[1407] *WR* 738, which cites *WCH* III 217-218 (Truly); *WCH* VI 375 (Jack E. Dougherty), 394 (Geneva L. Hine), 382-383 (Eddie Piper); *WCH* II 219 (Buell W. Frazier).

[1408] Quoted with permission after payment, from Posner *Case Closed* 202-203, which cites "Testimony of Wesley Buell Frazier, WC Vol. II, p. 216." Copyright notice is in endnote [1039].

[1409] *WR* 738, which cites *WCH* II 217 (Buell W. Frazier).

[1410] *WR* 738, which cites *WCH* III 40 (R. Paine); *WCH* I 52 (Marina Oswald); CE 994, p. 40.

[1411] Quoted with permission after payment, from Posner *Case Closed* 203, which cites "McMillan, *Marina and Lee*, p. 475." Copyright notice is in endnote [1039].

[1412] Quoted with permission from McMillan 476. Permission statement is in endnote [150].

[1413] *WR* 738, which cites *WCH* III 39 (R. Paine); *WCH* I 54 (Marina Oswald).

[1414] Quoted with permission from Mailer *Oswald's Tale* 652, which cites McMillan 477.

[1415] Quoted with permission after payment, from Posner *Case Closed* 203, which cites "Testimony of Ruth Paine, WC Vol. III, p. 40." Copyright notice is in endnote [1039].

[1416] *WR* 738, which cites *WCH* III 39-40 (R. Paine); CE 994, p. 40.

[1417] *WR* 738, which cites CE 994, p. 40.

[1418] Quoted with permission from McMillan 477-478. Permission statement is in endnote [150].

[1419] Quoted with permission from McMillan, page 480, which cites "Testimony of Roy Sansom Truly, Vol. 3, pp. 216-218." Permission statement for McMillan is in endnote [150].

[1420] Quoted with permission from McMillan 474. Permission statement is in endnote [150].

[1421] Quoted with permission after payment, from Salinger *With Kennedy* 211-212.

[1422] Quoted with permission from Zirbel 162-163.

[1423] Quoted with permission from Bradlee, Benjamin C. *Conversations with Kennedy* 215, 218-219.

[1424] Quoted with permission from Bradlee 219-220.

[1425] Quoted with permission after payment, from Manchester *Death* 9. Permission acknowledgement is in endnote [17].

[1426] Quoted with permission after payment from Smith, Sally Bedell 423. Copyright notice is in endnote [1356].

[1427] Quoted with permission from Bradlee 220-221.

[1428] Quoted with permission from McMillan 514. Permission statement is in endnote [150].

[1429] *WR* 738, which cites *WCH* I 55 (Marina Oswald); *WCH* II 407-408 (M. Paine); *WCH* IX 462-468 (Raymond F. Krystinik).

[1430] *WR* 739, which cites *WCH* IX 462-468 (Raymond F. Krystinik); *WCH* II 407-412 (M. Paine).

[1431] *WR* 739, which cites *WCH* I 54-55 (Marina Oswald); *WCH* III 40-41 (R. Paine).

[1432] *WR* 739, which cites *WCH* III 41 (R. Paine).

[1433] Quoted with permission after payment, from Posner *Case Closed* 209, which cites for instruction "Testimony of Forrest Sorrels, WC Vol. VII, p. 334." and for rejecting two sites "WR, p. 31." and for accepting Trade Mart "Testimony of Forrest Sorrels, WC Vol. VII, p. 335." Copyright notice is in endnote [1039].

[1434] Quoted with permission after payment from Smith, Sally Bedell. 424. Copyright notice is in endnote [1356].

[1435] *WR* 740, which cites *WCH* II 217 (Frazier).

[1436] *WR* 739, which cites *WCH* IV 449-154 (James A. Hosty); *WCH* I 48. 56-57 (Marina Oswald); *WCH* III 92, 96-104 (R. Paine).

[1437] Quoted with permission from McMillan 496. Permission statement is in endnote [150].

[1438] *WR* 739, which cites *WCH* III 101-102 (R. Paine); *WCH* I 57 (Marina Oswald).

[1439] *WR* 739, which cites *WCH* III 102 (R. Paine).

[1440] *WR* 739, which cites CE 15.

[1441] Quoted with permission from Mailer *Oswald's Tale* 659, which cites CE 103 on *WCH* XVI 443-444 and *WCH* III 14 (Ruth Paine).

[1442] Quoted with permission from McMillan 496-497. Permission statement is in endnote [150].

[1443] *WR* 740, which cites *WCH* II 514 (R. Paine); *WCH* III 41 (R. Paine); *WCH* XI 153-154 (R. Paine); *WCH* I 62 (Marina Oswald).

[1444] Quoted with permission after payment of $350, from Blaine, Gerald, with Lisa McCubbin. *The Kennedy Detail: JFK's Secret Service Agents Break Their Silence* 72. Copyright notice supplied by publisher: "Reprinted with the permission of Gallery Books, a division of Simon & Schuster, Inc. from THE KENNEDY DETAIL: JFK'S SECRET SERVICE AGENTS BREAK THEIR SILENCE by Gerald Blaine, with Lisa McCubbin. Copyright © 2010 by Gerald S. Blaine and Lisa McCubbin. All rights reserved."

[1445] The photo, taken by Cecil Stoughton, an official White House photographer, was purchased from AV Archives at the John F. Kennedy Presidential Library and Museum, Boston. The original displays truly glorious Fall leaf colors.

[1446] Quoted with permission after payment, from Blaine with McCubbin 72. Copyright notice is in endnote [1444].

[1447] Quoted with permission from McMillan 506-507. Permission statement is in endnote [150].

[1448] Bugliosi, Vincent. *Four Days in November: The Assassination of President John F. Kennedy*, page 220; reprinted from Bugliosi, Vincent. *Reclaiming History: The Assassination of President John F. Kennedy*, page 139.

[1449] Photo purchased from AV Archives at the John F. Kennedy Presidential Library and Museum, Boston.

[1450] Quoted with permission after payment, from Posner *Case Closed* 217, which cites for the decision "Secret Service memo to Commission of July 10, 1964, concerning Trade Mat decision (CD 1251), CE 1360, WC Vol. XXII, p. 613."; and for the forty-five-minute request "Testimony of Winston Lawson, WC Vol. IV, p. 325." Copyright notice is in endnote [1039].

[1451] Quoted with permission after payment, from Posner *Case Closed* 217, which cites for review of route "Statement of Special Agent Winston Lawson concerning his official duties from November 4 to ... 22, 1963, in preparation for President Kennedy's trip to Dallas, CE 769, WC Vol. XVII, p. 3." Copyright notice is in endnote [1039].

[1452] Quoted with permission after payment, from Posner *Case Closed* 217, which cites "Interview with Marina Oswald, August 21, 1992; Testimony of Marina Oswald, WC Vol. I, p. 54." Copyright notice is in endnote [1039].

[1453] Quoted with permission from McMillan 513. Permission statement is in endnote [150].

[1454] Quoted with permission after payment, from Blaine with McCubbin 98. Copyright notice is in endnote [1444].

[1455] Quoted with permission after payment, from King, Stephen 650. Copyright notice is in endnote [148].

[1456] Quoted with permission after payment, from King, Stephen 681. Copyright notice is in endnote [148].

[1457] Quoted with permission from McMillan 515. Permission statement is in endnote [150].

[1458] Quoted with permission after payment, from Posner *Case Closed* 217-218, which cites "Interview with Ruth Paine, April 18, 1992; Testimony of Ruth Paine, WC Vol. III, p. 44." Copyright notice is in endnote [1039].

[1459] *WCH* I 65 (Marina Oswald).

[1460] Quoted with permission after payment, from Manchester *Death* 102. Permission acknowledgement is in endnote [17].

[1461] Quoted with permission after payment, from Posner *Case Closed* 218, which cites for Marina's anger "Testimony of Ruth Paine, WC Vol. III, p. 45."; and for Lee's anger "Testimony of Marina Oswald, WC Vol. I, pp. 53-54, 63-66; Testimony of Ruth Paine, WC Vol. III, p. 45."; and for Marina regarding alias "Testimony of Marina Oswald, WC Vol. I, p. 66" and "p. 63." Copyright notice is in endnote [1039].

[1462] *WCH* I 65 (Marina Oswald).

[1463] Quoted with permission after payment, from Ford and Stiles *Portrait* 259.

[1464] Quoted with permission after payment, from Manchester *Death* 32-33. Permission acknowledgement is in endnote [17].

[1465] Quoted with permission from Kaiser, David 357. Permission notice is in endnote [998].

[1466] This map, *Kennedy Motorcade Route in Dallas*, was specially prepared by its creator for this book, in return for a modest fee paid. Credit: "Maps ©2012 by Gene Thorp, Cartographic Concepts Incorporated, www.mapmanusa.com."

[1467] Quoted as fair use (for brevity: 5 words) from a headline in *Life* magazine, November 24, 1967, page 100B.

[1468] Quoted as fair use (for brevity: 3 words) from Connally, John. "Why Kennedy Went to Texas", *Life* magazine, November 24, 1967, page 100B.

[1469] Quoted as fair use (for brevity: 7 words) from Connally, John. "Why Kennedy Went to Texas", *Life* magazine, November 24, 1967, page 100B.

[1470] Quoted with permission after payment, from Posner *Case Closed* 218, which cites "Testimony of Ruth Paine, WC Vol. III, p. 46." Copyright notice is in endnote [1039].

[1471] Quoted with permission after payment, from Posner *Case Closed* 218-219, which cites "'Yarborough Gets JFK Table Spot,' *Dallas Times Herald*, November 19, 1963 (CD 320), CE 1362, p. 614." Copyright notice is in endnote [1039].

[1472] Quoted with permission after payment, from Posner *Case Closed* 219, which cites "'Yarborough Seating Pondered,' *Dallas Morning News*, November 19, 1963 (CD 320), CE 1363, WC Vol. XXII, p. 615; 'Yarborough Invited to Travel with JFK,' *Dallas Morning News*, November 20, 1963 (CD 320), CE 1364, WC Vol. XXII, p. 616." Copyright notice is in endnote [1039].

[1473] Quoted with permission after payment, from Posner *Case Closed* 219. Copyright notice is in endnote [1039].

[1474] Image scanned from CE 1364 on *WCH* XXII 616. Coming from that US Federal government source, it is in the public domain.

[1475] Image is an enlargement, cropped from CE 1364 on *WCH* XXII 616. Coming from that US Federal government source, it is in the public domain.

[1476] Oswald's letter to John Connally from Minsk on January 30, 1962, shown in chapter 4.

[1477] Quoted with permission from McMillan, page 519, which cites "Testimony of Roy S. Truly, Vol. 7, pp. 381-382; Testimony of Warren Caster, Vol. 7, pp. 387-388." Permission statement for McMillan is in endnote [150].

[1478] Quoted with permission from McMillan, page 519, with endnote on 628: "After the assassination, this is precisely what Oswald said about the discovery of his rifle in the Book Depository Building." Permission statement is in endnote [150].

[1479] Quoted with permission after payment, from Posner *Case Closed* 262. Copyright notice is in endnote [1039].

[1480] TESTIMONY OF BUELL WESLEY FRAZIER on *WCH* II 222.

[1481] Quoted with permission after payment, from Manchester *Death* 94. Permission acknowledgement is in endnote [17].

[1482] Quoted with permission from McMillan 520. Permission statement is in endnote [150].

[1483] *WCH* II 223 (Frazier).

[1484] *WCH* II 224 (Frazier).

[1485] Quoted with permission after payment, from Ford and Stiles *Portrait* 317.

[1486] Oswald's letter from Minsk to Connally, shown in Chapter 4 – MINSK.

[1487] *WR* 740, which cites *WCH* II 508 (R. Paine); *WCH* III 46, 56-57 (R. Paine); *WCH* IX 414 (R. Paine); *WCH* I 65 (Marina Oswald).

[1488] *WR* 740, which cites *WCH* II 508 (R. Paine); *WCH* III 46 (R. Paine); *WCH* I 64-65 (Marina Oswald).

[1489] Quoted with permission from McMillan 521. Permission statement is in endnote [150].

[1490] *WCH* I 65-66 (Marina Oswald). Corroborating testimony by Ruth Paine is at *WCH* III 46-49, 56-60 and *WCH* IX 418.

[1491] Quoted with permission from Mailer *Oswald's Tale* 665.

[1492] Quoted with permission from McMillan 523. Permission statement is in endnote [150].

[1493] Mallon, Thomas. *Mrs. Paine's Garage: and the Murder of John F. Kennedy.*

[1494] This photo was displayed (and written upon?) by the Warren Commission as CE 429 on *WCH* XVII 157. This better image is from the National Archives and Records Administration at College Park, MD.

[1495] Quoted with permission from McMillan 524. Permission statement is in endnote [150].

[1496] Quoted with permission from McMillan 524. Permission statement is in endnote [150].

[1497] Quoted with permission after payment, from Bishop *Kennedy* 534-535.

[1498] Quoted with permission from McMillan 524. Permission statement is in endnote [150].

[1499] Quoted with permission from Douglass endnotes 526 and 527 on page 463.

[1500] Quoted with permission from Douglass 304.

[1501] Quoted with the gracious permission of James Reston, Jr., author and copyright owner of *The Accidental Victim: JFK, Lee Harvey Oswald, and the Real Target in Dallas* 111, which cites "Henry B. Gonzalez, interview with author."

[1502] *WR* 42, which cites "4 H 130 ([John] Connally); 7 H 444-445 (O'Donnell)." The seating in the car during this motorcade is revealing, and will be discussed further in chapter 19. For a photo, see Life Books, The Editors of. *The Day Kennedy Died: 50 Years Later LIFE Remembers the Man and the Moment* 40.

[1503] *WR* 42, which cites "7 H 445 (O'Donnell)."

[1504] *WR* 42, which cites "7 H 472 (David F. Powers)."

[1505] Quoted with permission after payment, from Hill with McCubbin 271. Copyright notice is in endnote [757]. See *WR* 42, which cites "4 H 130 ([John] Connally); 7 H 445 (O'Donnell)."

[1506] *WR* 42, which cites "7 H 472 (David F. Powers)."

[1507] Quoted with permission from O'Donnell, Kenneth P., and David F. Powers with Joe McCarthy. *Johnny, We Hardly Knew Ye* 23. Ted Sorensen reports the same interchange with different words in his biography *Kennedy* — but he wasn't present.

[1508] *WR* 42, which cites "4 H 130 ([John] Connally); 7 H 445 (O'Donnell)."

[1509] Quoted with permission after payment, from Blaine with McCubbin 175. Copyright notice is in endnote [1444].

[1510] Quoted with permission after payment, from Blaine with McCubbin 163-164. Copyright notice is in endnote [1444].

[1511] Quoted with permission after payment, from Blaine with McCubbin 165-166. Copyright notice is in endnote [1444].

[1512] A box on page 333 explains why prudent writers may not quote any words spoken by Dr. Martin Luther King, Jr.

[1513] Photo was taken by Cecil Stoughton, an official White House photographer, and is in the collection of the John F. Kennedy Presidential Library and Museum, Boston".

[1514] Quoted with permission after payment, from Hill with McCubbin 280. Copyright notice is in endnote [757].

[1515] Quoted with permission after payment, from Bishop *Kennedy* 7.

[1516] The only photo known to this author of some of the world-class art pieces hanging on walls of their plain hotel suite is in Life Books, The Editors of. *The Day Kennedy Died: 50 Years Later LIFE Remembers the Man and the Moment* 44.

[1517] Quoted with permission after payment from Smith, Sally Bedell 438. Copyright notice is in endnote [1356].

— 6 — THREE DEAD, TWO WOUNDED

[1518] TESTIMONY OF BUELL WESLEY FRAZIER, *Hearings Before the President's Commission on the Assassination of President Kennedy*, Volume II, page 234; hereinafter expressed as *WCH* II 234 (Frazier). The first three ellipses (...) in this quotation are omissions of him saying "you know", up with which in this work of his life this author shall not put.

[1519] Quoted with permission from McMillan, Priscilla Johnson. *Marina and Lee*, pages 524-525. Permission statement is in endnote [150].

[1520] *WCH* II 224 (Frazier).

[1521] *WCH* II 211 (Frazier).

[1522] *WCH* II in sequence 225, 226, 225 (Frazier).

[1523] Quoted with permission after payment, from Bishop, Jim. *The Day Kennedy Was Shot* 33. Subsequent references will be in form Bishop *Kennedy* 33.

[1524] TESTIMONY OF LINNIE MAE RANDLE on *WCH* II 248.

[1525] Quoted with permission after payment, from Bishop *Kennedy* 33.

[1526] *WCH* II 249 (Randle).

[1527] *WCH* II 250 (Randle).

[1528] *WCH* II 251 (Randle).

[1529] *WCH* II 248 (Randle).

[1530] *WCH* II 226 (Frazier).

[1531] Quoted with permission after payment, from Bishop *Kennedy* 35.

[1532] *WCH* II 213 (Frazier).

[1533] *WCH* II 220 (Frazier).

[1534] *WCH* II 228 (Frazier).

[1535] *WCH* II 229 (Frazier).

[1536] *WCH* VII 531 Frazier).

[1537] Quoted with permission after payment, from Manchester, William. *The Death of a President* 115. Permission acknowledgement is in endnote [17].

[1538] Quoted with permission after payment, from Manchester *Death* 115. This form with a key word from the book's title is used because more than one book by the author is cited in these notes. Permission acknowledgement is in endnote [17].

[1539] Quoted with permission from Specter, Arlen, with Charles Robbins. *Passion for Truth: From Finding JFK's Single Bullet to Questioning Anita Hill to Impeaching Clinton*, page 108.

[1540] Quoted with permission after payment, from Ford, Gerald R., and John R. Stiles. *Portrait of the Assassin* 326. See also Testimony of William H. Shelley on *WCH* VII 391-392. Photos of the arranged cartons are in Studebaker Exhibit A - J on *WCH* XXI 643-649.

[1541] Quoted with permission from McMillan, page 529, which cites "Exhibit No. 723, shown in Warren Commission Report, p. 80, and in Vol. 17, p. 504." Permission statement for McMillan is in endnote [150].

[1542] Bishop *Kennedy* 128.

[1543] Quoted with permission after payment, from Bishop *Kennedy* 161.

[1544] Photo is Commission Exhibit No. 723 on *Warren Report* page 80, with caption: "Shield of cartons around sixth floor southeast corner window." Coming from that US Federal government source, it is in the public domain. Subsequent references to Commission Exhibit will use the abbreviation CE.

[1545] Testimony of William H. Shelley, *WCH* VII 392.

[1546] *WCH* VII 391-392 (Shelley).

[1547] Testimony of Cortlandt Cunningham, *WCH* II 251-253.

[1548] McMillan 529, which cites "Testimony of Charles Douglas Givens, Vol. 6, pp. 349-350."

[1549] Quoted with permission after payment, from Bishop *Kennedy* 127.

[1550] Quoted with permission after payment, from Manchester *Death* 133. Permission acknowledgement is in endnote [17].

[1551] Manchester *Death* 106.

[1552] Quoted with the gracious permission of James Reston, Jr., author and copyright owner of *The Accidental Victim: JFK, Lee Harvey Oswald, and the Real Target in Dallas* 123-125.

[1553] *Report of the President's Commission on the Assassination of President Kennedy* (popularly known as the *Warren Report*) page 42; hereinafter expressed as *WR* 42; which cites "2 H 63-64 (Kellerman); 7 H 459 (Lawrence F. O'Brien)." In the form used in this book, that first citation would be "*WCH* II 63-64 (Kellerman)".

[1554] A useful and generally reliable timeline is available at http://karws.gso.uri.edu/Marsh/Jfk-conspiracy/time.htm

[1555] Quoted with permission after payment, from Blaine, Gerald, with Lisa McCubbin. *The Kennedy Detail: JFK's Secret Service Agents Break Their Silence* 182. Copyright notice is in endnote [1444].

[1556] *WR* 42, which cites "7 H 443-444 (O'Donnell)."

[1557] Manchester *Death* 114.

[1558] Quoted with permission after payment from Smith, Sally Bedell *Grace and Power: The Private World of the Kennedy White House* 438. Copyright notice is in endnote [1356].

[1559] Quoted with permission from Johnson, Lyndon Baines. *The Vantage Point: Perspectives of the Presidency 1963–1969*, page 1. Credit line supplied by publisher: "Excerpts from the book THE VANTAGE POINT: Perspectives of the Presidency by Lyndon Baines Johnson. Copyright © 1971 by HEC Public Affairs Foundation. Reprinted by the gracious permission of Henry Holt and Company, LLC. All rights reserved."

[1560] Photo was purchased to show here: William Allen, photographer, *Dallas Times Herald* Collection / The Sixth Floor Museum at Dealey Plaza.

[1561] The most complete and dependable reporting on Abraham Zapruder, showing the man, his position on the grassy knoll and every frame of his historic film is in Life Books, The Editors of. *The Day Kennedy Died: 50 Years Later LIFE Remembers the Man and the Moment* 80-95. LIFE bought his film, and is its ultimate restorer and authority.

[1562] Quoted with permission after payment, from Bishop *Kennedy* 27.

[1563] Quoted with permission from Nixon, Richard M. *RN: The Memoirs of Richard Nixon* 252.

[1564] Quoted with permission after payment, from Bishop *Kennedy* 67.

[1565] Photo by Ferd Kaufman was purchased from AP and cropped. ©The Associated Press.

[1566] Quoted with permission after payment, from Bishop *Kennedy* 79.

[1567] Quoted with permission after payment, from Hill, Clint, with Lisa McCubbin. *Mrs. Kennedy and Me* 284, for which the copyright notice is in endnote [757].

[1568] Quoted with permission after payment from Smith, Sally Bedell 438-439. Copyright notice is in endnote [1356].

[1569] Manchester *Death* 120.

[1570] Quoted with permission after payment, from Bishop *Kennedy* 83.

[1571] *WR* 42, which cites "7 H 456 (O'Donnell)."

[1572] *WR* 42, which cites "7 H 456 (O'Donnell)."

[1573] Quoted with permission after payment, from Blaine with McCubbin 189. Copyright notice is in endnote [1444].

[1574] Quoted with permission after payment, from Thomas, Helen. *Front Row at the White House: My Life and Times*, page 165, for which the copyright notice is in endnote [907].

[1575] Quoted with permission after payment, from Thomas, Helen. *Front Row* 166-167. This form with key words from the title is used because more than one book by this author is cited in these notes. Copyright notice is in endnote [907].

[1576] O'Reilly and Dugard 257.

[1577] Quoted with permission after payment, from Blaine with McCubbin 80. Copyright notice is in endnote [1444].

[1578] Quoted with permission after payment, from Perret, Geoffrey. *Jack: A Life Like No Other*, page 397, which cites "Klein, *All Too Human*, 344; Pam Turnure/Nancy Tuckerman Oral History, John F. Kennedy Library". Copyright notice supplied by Perret's publisher: "Excerpt(s) from JACK: A LIFE LIKE NO OTHER by Geoffrey Perret, copyright © 2001 by Geoffrey Perret. Used by permission of Random House, an imprint and division of Penguin Random House LLC. All rights reserved. Any third party use of this material, outside of this publication, is prohibited. Interested parties must apply directly to Penguin Random House LLC for permission."

[1579] Quoted with permission after payment, from Bishop *Kennedy* 27.

[1580] Quoted with permission after payment, from Posner, Gerald. *Case Closed: Lee Harvey Oswald and the Assassination of JFK* 262n (which means the footnote on page 262). Copyright notice is in endnote [1039].

[1581] FBI file # BA 89-30, report of interview by Special Agents James W. Sibert & Francis X. O'Neill Jr., conducted and dictated 11/27/63, typed 11/29/63. This report, in neither *WR* nor *WCH*, "released by The National Archives too late to appear in the hardcover edition of *Inquest*" by Mark Lane, is on page 171 of the Oct. 1966 Bantam paperback *Inquest*. As the work product of federal government employees in the normal discharge of their duties, it is in the public domain.

[1582] Quoted with permission from Jovich, John B., editor. *Reflections on JFK's Assassination: 250 Famous Americans Remember November 22, 1963* 42.

[1583] O'Reilly and Dugard 257.

[1584] *WR* 42, which cites "4 H 349 (Lawson); 2 H 67 (Kellerman)."

[1585] Photo was purchased to show here: *Dallas Times Herald* Collection / The Sixth Floor Museum at Dealey Plaza.

[1586] *WR* 42, which cites "5 H 561 (Pres. Lyndon B. Johnson); 4 H 130 ([John] Connally); CE 2526."

[1587] *WR* 43, which cites "5 E 560 (Johnson); 7 H 474 (Clifton C. Carter); 2 H 146 (Rufus W. Youngblood)."

[1588] Quoted with permission from Johnson 4. Copyright and permission notice is in endnote [1559].

[1589] Quoted with permission after payment, from Blaine with McCubbin 199. Copyright notice is in endnote [1444].

[1590] *WR* 43, which cites "7 H 461 (O'Brien); 2 H 67 (Kellerman); 4 H 339, 350 (Lawson)."

[1591] *WR* 43, which cites "5 H 561 (Johnson); 2 H 115 (Greer)."

[1592] Quoted with permission from Hecht, Jamey. *Limousine, Midnight Blue: Fifty Frames from the Zapruder Film* 69.

[1593] Quoted with permission after payment, from Perret 397-398. Copyright notice is in endnote [1578].

[1594] Quoted with permission after payment, from Blaine with McCubbin 201-202. Copyright notice is in endnote [1444].

[1595] *WR* 43, which cites "CE 344, 345, 346."

[1596] Quoted with permission after payment, from Blaine with McCubbin 80. Copyright notice is in endnote [1444].

[1597] *WR* 43, which cites "2 H 65 (Kellerman); 2 H 114 (Greer)."

[1598] *WR* 45, which cites "2 H 67 (Kellerman)."

[1599] *WR* 45, which cites "CE 345."

[1600] *WR* 45, which cites "2 H 136-137 (Hill); CE 1025."

[1601] Quoted with permission after payment, from Blaine with McCubbin 149. Copyright notice is in endnote [1444].

[1602] Quoted with permission after payment, from Blaine with McCubbin 150. Copyright notice is in endnote [1444].

[1603] Quoted with permission after payment, from Blaine with McCubbin 79. Copyright notice is in endnote [1444].

[1604] *WR* 45, which cites "2 H 64-65 (Kellerman)."

[1605] Quoted with permission after payment, from Hill with McCubbin 276. Copyright notice is in endnote [757]. See also *WR* 45, which cites "2 H 64-65 (Kellerman)."

[1606] Quoted with permission after payment, from Blaine with McCubbin 80. Copyright notice is in endnote [1444].

[1607] Photo was purchased to show here: Tom C. Dillard Collection, *The Dallas Morning News* / The Sixth Floor Museum at Dealey Plaza.

[1608] *WR* 45, which cites "4 H 130-131 ([John] Connally); 2 H 68 (Kellerman); 2 H 115 (Greer)."

[1609] *WR* 45, which cites "2 H 115 (Greer)."

[1610] Blaine with McCubbin 162; *WR* 45, which cites "2 H 115 (Greer)."

[1611] *WR* 43, which advises "See 4 H 335-336 (Lawson)."

[1612] *WR* 43, which cites "4 H 132 ([John] Connally); 2 H 135 (Clinton J. Hill); 2 H 70 (Kellerman); 4 H 326, 351 (Lawson)."

[1613] *WR* 43, which cites "2 H 135-136 (Hill); 4 H 351 (Lawson)."

[1614] *WR* 43, which cites "CE 768, p. 5."

[1615] *WR* 43, which cites "2 H 67 (Kellerman); 4 H 327 (Lawson)."

[1616] *WR* 43, which cites "CE 768, p. 5; 2 H 67 (Kellerman)."

[1617] *WR* 43, which cites "2 H 68 (Kellerman); 4 H 327-328 (Lawson); 2 H 116 (Greer)."

[1618] Quoted with permission after payment, from Manchester *Death* 36. Permission acknowledgement is in endnote [17].

[1619] *WR* 45, which cites "2 H 70 (Kellerman)."

[1620] *WR* 45, which cites "4 H 338-339 (Lawson)."

[1621] Quoted with permission after payment, from McCarthy, Dennis V. N., with Philip W. Smith. *Protecting the President: The Inside Story of a Secret Service Agent*, page 188.

[1622] *WR* 45, which cites "2 H 135 (Hill)."

[1623] *WR* 45, which cites "2 H 134 (Hill)."

[1624] *WR* 45, which cites "2 H 134-135 (Hill)."

[1625] *WR* 45, which cites "7 H 446 (O'Donnell); 7 H 473 (Powers)."

[1626] *WR* 45, which cites "4 H 327, 329 (Lawson)."

[1627] *WR* 45, which cites "4 H 327, 329 (Lawson); 7 H 342 (Sorrels)."

[1628] *WR* 45, which cites "4 H 327 (Lawson); 2 H 135-136 (Hill)."

[1629] *WR* 45, which cites "2 H 136 (Hill)."

[1630] O'Reilly and Dugard 259.

[1631] *WR* 45-46, which cites "2 H 147 (Youngblood)."

[1632] *WR* 46, which cites "2 H 148 (Youngblood)."

[1633] *WR* 46, which cites "CE 767, attachment 3; CE 1126."

[1634] *WR* 46, which cites "2 H 70 (Kellerman); 4 H 336 (Lawson)."

[1635] Quoted with permission after payment, from Perret 398, which cites "Helen O'Donnell, *A Common Good* (New York: 1998), 332." Copyright notice for Perret is in endnote [1578].

[1636] Quoted with permission after payment, from Manchester *Death* 131. Permission acknowledgement is in endnote [17].

[1637] *WR* 46, which cites "4 H 130-131 ([John] Connally); 2 H 67, 70 (Kellerman); 2 H 115 (Greer)."

[1638] Quoted with permission after payment, from Perret 398, which cites "Klein, *All Too Human*, 344; Jacqueline Kennedy interview, Theodore White Papers, John F. Kennedy Library." Copyright notice for Perret is in endnote [1578].

[1639] Quoted with permission after payment, from Bishop *Kennedy* 135.

[1640] *WR* 46, which cites "4 H 132 ([John] Connally); 2 H 135 (Hill); 2 H 70 (Kellerman)."

[1641] *WR* 46, which cites "4 H 132 ([John] Connally)."

[1642] Quoted with permission after payment, from Bishop *Kennedy*, pages 159-160. See also *WCH* IV 131 (John Connally); *WCH* VII 447 (O'Donnell); *WCH* VII 473 (Powers).

[1643] *WR* 46, 48, which cites "2 H 135-136 (Hill); CE 398; CE 1024, statement of Clinton J. Hill, p. 2."

[1644] *WR* 48, which cites "2 H 135 (Hill)."

[1645] *WR* 48, which cites "2 H 71 (Kellerman)."

[1646] Quoted with permission after payment, from Perret 398. Copyright notice is in endnote [1578].

[1647] Photo purchased from AP, shown full-size without cropping. ©The Associated Press.

[1648] *WR* 48, which cites "CE 876; 2 H 71 (Kellerman)."

[1649] *WR* 48, which cites "CE 878; 2 H 71-72 (Kellerman)."

[1650] Quoted with permission after payment, from Posner *Case Closed* 231. Copyright notice is in endnote [1039].

[1651] *WR* 48, which cites "5 H 561 (Johnson); 4 H 132 ([John] Connally)."

[1652] This map, *Dealey Plaza*, was specially prepared by its creator for this book in return for a very modest fee asked and paid. Credit: "Maps ©2012 by Gene Thorp, Cartographic Concepts Incorporated, www.mapmanusa.com."

[1653] Aerial photo with names is held by the National Archives and Records Administration, so is in the public domain.

[1654] *WR* 48, which cites "7 H 447 (O'Donnell); 7 H 468 (O'Brien); 7 H 473 (Powers)."

[1655] Quoted with permission from Connally, Nellie, with Mickey Herskowitz. *From Love Field: Our Final Hours with President John F. Kennedy*, page 07 and her manuscript's page 7 on page 163, typed on page 145. See also "4 H 147 (Mrs. John B. Connally. Jr.); 4 H 131 ([John] Connally)."

[1656] Photo by Jim Altgens was purchased from the AP, then slightly cropped. ©The Associated Press.

[1657] *WR* 49, which cites "5 H 160-161 (Lyndal L. Shaneyfelt)."

[1658] Quoted with permission from Sabato 217.

[1659] *WR* 49, which cites "5 H 179-180 (Mrs. John F. Kennedy)."

[1660] Quoted with permission after payment, from Blaine with McCubbin 214, for which the copyright notice is in endnote [1444]. See also John Connally's recollection at *WCH* IV 132-133.

[1661] *WR* 49, which cites "4 H 135-136 ([John] Connally)."

[1662] *WR* 50, which cites "4 H 147 (Mrs. Connally)."

[1663] *WR* 50, which cites "2 H 73-74 (Kellerman)."

[1664] Photo scanned from CE 740 on *WCH* XVII 513 (top). Coming from that US Federal government source, it is in the public domain.

[1665] *WR* 50, which cites "2 H 117 (Greer)."

[1666] *WR* 50, which cites "2 H 74-77 (Kellerman)."

[1667] *WR* 50, which cites "4 H 147 (Mrs. Connally)."

[1668] *WR* 50, which cites "4 H 133 ([John] Connally)."

[1669] *WR* 50, which cites "4 H 147 (Mrs. Connally)."

[1670] *WR* 50, which cites "4 H 133 ([John] Connally)."

[1671] *WR* 50, which cites "4 H 133 ([John] Connally); 4 H 147 (Mrs. Connally)."

[1672] *WR* 50, which cites "4 H 147 (Mrs. Connally); 4 H 133 ([John] Connally)."

[1673] *WR* 50, which cites "2 H 138 (Hill)."

[1674] *WR* 50-51, which cites "2 H 138 (Hill)."

1675 This image is frame 371 of Abraham Zapruder's movie, purchased to show here: Zapruder Film © 1967 (Renewed 1995) / The Sixth Floor Museum at Dealey Plaza.

1676 *WR* 51, which cites "2 H 138-139 (Hill)."

1677 *WR* 51, which cites "2 H 138-139 (Hill)."

1678 *WR* 51, which cites "7 H 473 (Powers)."

1679 *WR* 51, which cites "5 H 180 (Mrs. Kennedy)."

1680 *WR* 4.

1681 This photo was originally noticed by the author and imported from the Amazon.com listing for Vincent Bugliosi's *Four Days in November: The Assassination of President John F. Kennedy*, a fine book in which this photo does not appear. The author's experienced professional picture researcher, who found or examined almost all the 275 images in this book, learned from a researcher at The Sixth Floor Museum at Dealey Plaza that the photographer was Mel McIntire, for whom they have no contact information. Subsequent searches via Bing and Google confirm that, and show this photo many times, but with only scant information that McIntire is a member of LinkedIn. The author, also enrolled on LinkedIn, made three attempts to contact Mel McIntire, without reply. I conclude that he is deceased or incommunicative. Having done due diligence, I claim the right to show the photo as fair use. Please see CREDITS AND PERMISSIONS on page ii.

1682 Quoted with permission from Johnson 8-9. Copyright and permission notice is in endnote [1559].

1683 Quoted with permission after payment, from Thomas, Helen. *Front Row* 68. Copyright notice is in endnote [907].

1684 Quoted with permission after payment, from Bishop *Kennedy* 192.

1685 To hear Cronkite's reporting, see Garner, Joe. *We Interrupt This Broadcast: The Events That Stopped Our Lives – from the Hindenburg Explosion to the Death of John F. Kennedy Jr.*, page 52, and listen to its enclosed compact disc 1 track 15.

1686 Manchester *Death* 189, which cites a University of Chicago study.

1687 Manchester *Death* 150, 154. In *The Day Kennedy Was Shot*, page 172, Jim Bishop calls it a "piney oak".

1688 Quoted with permission after payment, from Thomas, Helen. *Front Row* 69. Copyright notice is in endnote [907].

1689 Quoted with permission after payment, from Blaine with McCubbin 226. Copyright notice is in endnote [1444].

1690 Quoted with permission after payment, from Hill with McCubbin 295. Copyright notice is in endnote [757].

1691 Quoted with permission after payment, from Manchester *Death* 177. Permission acknowledgement is in endnote [17].

1692 Quoted with permission after payment, from Hill with McCubbin 295-296. Copyright notice is in endnote [757].

1693 Quoted with permission after payment, from Manchester *Death* 169. Permission acknowledgement is in endnote [17].

1694 Quoted with permission after payment, from Bishop *Kennedy* 232.

1695 Quoted with permission after payment, from Bishop *Kennedy* 267.

1696 This photo was purchased to show here, with credit: CBS Photo Archive / Getty Images. ©CBS Worldwide Inc.

1697 Quoted with permission from Cronkite, Walter. *A Reporter's Life* 305.

1698 Quoted with permission from Fries, Chuck, and Irv Wilson with Spencer Green. *We'll Never Be Young Again: Remembering the Last Days of John F. Kennedy* 178.

1699 *WR* 4.

1700 Quoted with permission after payment, from Bishop *Kennedy* 376.

1701 Quoted with permission after payment, from Bishop *Kennedy* 375.

1702 Quoted with permission after payment, from Bishop *Kennedy* 376.

1703 Quoted with permission after payment, from Posner *Case Closed* 298, which cites his "Interview with Francis O'Neill, November 5, 1992." Copyright notice is in endnote [1039].

1704 *WR* 4.

1705 *WR* 4.

1706 Manchester *Death* 157. Brennan's typed and sworn VOLUNTARY STATEMENT to the Sheriff's Department is page 17 of DECKER EXHIBIT NO. 5323 on *WCH* XIX 470; also reproduced in New York Times *The Witnesses* on Exhibit page 51.

1707 The VOLUNTARY STATEMENT of Amos Lee Euins is page 21 of DECKER EXHIBIT NO. 5323 on *WCH* XIX 474; It is also reproduced in New York Times. *The Witnesses* on Exhibit page 52.

1708 *WR* 5.

1709 Bishop *Kennedy* 156. Ochus is mentioned here by virtue of his wonderful name.

1710 *WR* 5.

1711 Quoted with permission from Sabato 11.

1712 Quoted with permissions from both the oral history of Marrion L. Baker, Solo Motorcycle Officer, in Sneed, Larry A. *No More Silence: An Oral History of the Assassination of President Kennedy* 124; and from Manchester *Death* 279, for which the permission acknowledgement is in endnote [17].

1713 Quoted with permission from Marrion L. Baker in Sneed 124-125.

1714 Quoted with permission from Jovich 29,31. Vincent Bugliosi in his *Reclaiming History: The Assassination of President John F. Kennedy*, page 260, and its reprint *Four Days in November: The Assassination of President John F. Kennedy*, page 417, does not mention MacNeil, but writes in a footnote that the man may have been WFAA radio newsman Pierce Allman. MacNeil's account is also in Newseum *President Kennedy Has Been Shot*, page 35. In *The Day Kennedy Died: 50 Years Later LIFE Remembers the Man and the Moment* by The Editors of Life Books, MacNeil himself wrote almost two full pages in 2013, where he says "it doesn't matter much."

[1715] Manchester *Death* 279; http://en.wikipedia.org/wiki/Robert_MacNeil

[1716] TESTIMONY OF MARY E. BLEDSOE, *WCH* VI 408.

[1717] *WCH* VI 409 (Bledsoe).

[1718] *WCH* VI 409 (Bledsoe).

[1719] Quoted with permission from Kaiser, David. *The Road to Dallas: The Assassination of John F. Kennedy* 366-367. Permission notice is in endnote [998].

[1720] *WR* 6.

[1721] This map, *Lee Harvey Oswald's Escape*, was specially prepared by its creator for this book, in return for a modest fee paid. Credit: "Maps ©2012 by Gene Thorp, Cartographic Concepts Incorporated, www.mapmanusa.com."

[1722] Quoted with permission after payment, from Bishop *Kennedy* 218. See also McMillan 533, which cites "Warren Commission Report, pp. 161-162."

[1723] TESTIMONY OF MRS. EARLENE ROBERTS, *WCH* VI 438-440.

[1724] O'Reilly and Dugard 280.

[1725] Myers, Dale K. *With Malice: Lee Harvey Oswald and the Murder of Officer J.D. Tippit*, Second Edition, 38, which cites "author's interviews of Tippit family members, 1998-2004" and specific confirmation by brother Wayne Tippit in 1996; See also http://en.wikipedia.org/wiki/J._D._Tippit, which cites "Dale K. Myers, 'Biography: A Boy Named J.D.'"

[1726] *WR* 6.

[1727] Myers 114-115.

[1728] *WR* 6-7. The photo of Oswald's snub-nose revolver was scanned from CE 143 on *WCH* XVI 513. Coming from that US Federal government source, it is in the public domain.

[1729] Quoted with permission, as stated in Oglesby, Carl. *Who Killed JFK?* 17.

[1730] *WR* 7.

[1731] *WR* 7.

[1732] *WR* 7; Ford and Stiles *Portrait* 289.

[1733] *WR* 7.

[1734] Tape recording of Dallas police radio, transcribed in CE 1974 page 181 on *WCH* XXIII 922.

[1735] Kaiser, David 369; Myers 197-198.

[1736] *WR* 7-8.

[1737] *WR* 8.

[1738] *WR* 8.

[1739] Report of Patrolman #1178 M.N. McDonald, WARREN COMMISSION DOCUMENT 87.

[1740] Quoted with permission from Connally, Nellie 56.

[1741] Epstein *Legend* 244; Myers 308-309.

[1742] Bishop *Kennedy* 284.

[1743] *WR* 8.

[1744] TESTIMONY OF C. W. BROWN on *WCH* VII 248.

[1745] *WCH* VI 327 (Shelley).

[1746] *WCH* VII 248 (C. W. Brown).

[1747] *WCH* VII 248 (C. W. Brown).

[1748] *WR* 8.

[1749] Bishop *Kennedy* 250-252.

[1750] *WR* 8.

[1751] Quoted with permission after payment, from Posner *Case Closed*, page 268, which cites "Testimony of Carl Day, WC Vol. IV, p. 250." Copyright notice is in endnote [1039].

[1752] Quoted with permission after payment, from Posner *Case Closed* 269, which cites "Testimony of Robert Frazier, WC Vol. III, pp. 414-28; testimony of Joseph Nicol, WC Vol. III, pp. 505-7; CE 558, WC Vol. XVII, p. 556." Copyright notice is in endnote [1039].

[1753] Quoted with permission after payment, from Posner *Case Closed* 269-270, which cites "Testimony of Will Fritz, WC Vol. IV, p. 206; testimony of Luke Mooney, WC Vol. III, p. 293." Copyright notice is in endnote [1039].

[1754] Quoted with permission after payment, from Posner *Case Closed* 270, which cites his "Interview with Carl Day." Copyright notice is in endnote [1039].

[1755] *WR* 9.

[1756] Quoted with permission from McMillan, page 534, which cites "Testimony of Roy S. Truly, Vol. 3, p. 230." Permission statement for McMillan is in endnote [150].

[1757] Quoted with permission from the oral history of Gerald L. Hill, Patrol Division, in Sneed 299.

[1758] Quoted with permission from Huffaker, Bob, Bill Mercer, George Phenix, and Wes Wise. *When The News Went Live: Dallas 1963*, page 31. See also Sabato 19, which cites "William E. Scott, *November 22, 1963: A Reference Guide to the JFK Assassination* (Lanham, MD: University Press of America, 1999) 25."

[1759] *WR* 9.

[1760] TESTIMONY OF RUTH HYDE PAINE on *WCH* IX 343.

[1761] Quoted with permission from McMillan, page 538, which cites "Testimony of Ruth Hyde Paine, Vol. 9, pp. 432-433.";
see also Bugliosi *Reclaiming History* 64-65, citing "1 H 67, 74, WCT Marina N. Oswald; CE 2003, 24 H 219; 9 H 432–433, WCT Ruth Hyde Paine; McMillan, *Marina and Lee*, p. 538."; reprinted as Bugliosi *Four Days* 101, with same citations. Permission statement for McMillan is in endnote [150].

[1762] Quoted with permission from McMillan 538. Permission statement is in endnote [150].

[1763] Quoted with permission from McMillan 539. Permission statement is in endnote [150].

[1764] Mallon, Thomas. *Mrs. Paine's Garage: and the Murder of John F. Kennedy*, page 57.

[1765] Quoted with permission from McMillan, pages 539-540, which cites "Testimony of Ruth Hyde Paine, Vol. 3, p. 79." Permission statement for McMillan is in endnote [150].

[1766] Quoted with permission after payment, from Bishop *Kennedy* 361.

[1767] Quoted with permission after payment, from Bugliosi *Four Days in November*, page 286, citing "McMillan, *Marina and Lee*, p. 544; 1 H 72-73, WCT Marina N. Oswald.". *Four Days in November* was reprinted from Bugliosi *Reclaiming History*, page 179, with the same citations. For *Four Days*, the copyright notice supplied by publisher: "From FOUR DAYS IN NOVEMBER: THE ASSASSINATION OF PRESIDENT JOHN F. KENNEDY by Vincent Bugliosi. Copyright © 2007 by Vincent Bugliosi. Used by permission of W. W. Norton & Company, Inc."

[1768] Quoted with permission after payment, from Epstein *Legend* 244 and its *Chapter XV* endnote 2 on 327.

[1769] Items 1-17 are in FBI report of 11/25/63 citing photographs and identifications supplied to the Bureau by Captain Fritz on 11/24/63, CE 1986 on *WCH* XIV 17. The list with 18-19 added, plus several mistakes, is on Bishop *Kennedy* 291-292.

[1770] Two FBI Special Agents laboriously compiled a description of the nine bills, listing for each its denomination, type, serial number and series. They also listed the values of the seven coins, including a half-dollar. Both are in CE 1149 on *WCH* XXII 179. It is left as an exercise for the reader to figure out the necessary denominations of nine bills and seven coins so they total $13.87.

[1771] CE 1148 on *WCH* XXII 178.

[1772] Quoted with permission from Oglesby *Who Killed JFK?* 19.

[1773] Quoted with permission from Oglesby 19.

[1774] Quoted with permission from McMillan, endnote 22 on page 625, which cites testimony to the U.S. House of Representatives Judiciary Committee's Subcommittee on Civil and Constitutional Rights (Hearings on FBI Oversight, Serial No. 2, Part 3), Hosty on pages 124-175 and Shanklin on 59-129. Permission statement is in endnote [150].

[1775] Quoted with permission from McMillan, page 549, which cites "Warren Commission Report, p. 200." Permission statement for McMillan is in endnote [150].

[1776] Quoted with permission after payment, from Bishop *Kennedy* 492.

[1777] TESTIMONY OF MRS. MARGUERITE OSWALD on *WCH* I 143-144.

[1778] This photo ©1963 Allan Grant/LIFE Magazine was purchased from and is shown with the kind permission of Karin Grant.

[1779] Quoted with permission after payment, from Epstein *Legend* 246-247.

[1780] *WR* 16.

[1781] *WCH* I 146 (Marguerite Oswald).

[1782] *WCH* I 147-148 (Marguerite Oswald).

[1783] *WCH* I 152 (Marguerite Oswald).

[1784] Quoted with permission after payment, from Bishop *Kennedy* 311.

[1785] *WCH* VI 438 (Roberts).

[1786] *WCH* VI 441 (Roberts).

[1787] This photo ©1963 Allan Grant/LIFE Magazine was donated by and is shown with the kind permission of Karin Grant.

[1788] Quoted with permission after payment, from Bugliosi *Reclaiming History: The Assassination of President John F. Kennedy*, pages 765-766. Copyright notice supplied by publisher: "From RECLAIMING HISTORY: THE ASSASSINATION OF PRESIDENT JOHN F. KENNEDY by Vincent Bugliosi. Copyright © 2007 by Vincent Bugliosi. Used by permission of W. W. Norton & Company, Inc."

[1789] Quoted with permission after payment, from Bugliosi *Four Days* 194n (the footnote on page 194); which was reprinted from Bugliosi *Reclaiming* 123n. Copyright notice is in endnote [1767].

[1790] TESTIMONY OF WALTER EUGENE POTTS on *WCH* VII 198; POTTS EXHIBIT B, page 2 marked 231, on *WCH* XXI 144.

[1791] "Report of Officer's Duties" by F. M. Turner on page marked 251 in COMMISSION EXHIBIT NO. 2003 on *WCH* XXIV 327.

[1792] Quoted with permission after payment, from Bugliosi *Four Days* 216; which was reprinted from Bugliosi *Reclaiming* 136. Copyright notice is in endnote [1767].

[1793] *WCH* VII 198-199 (Potts).

[1794] *WCH* VII 199 (Potts).

[1795] POTTS EXHIBIT A-1 on *WCH* XXI 141 and A-2 on *WCH* XXI 142.

[1796] "Police Department | City of Dallas | Property Clerk's Invoice or Receipt | No. 11196", November 26, 1963, on page marked 282 in COMMISSION EXHIBIT NO. 2003 on *WCH* XXIV 342. My symbol | means to move down to a new line.

[1797] Quoted with permission after payment, from Bugliosi *Four Days* 353, citing "Sims Exhibit A, 21 H 517; CE 2003, 24 H 288; CE 2003, 24 H 348; 7 H 439, WCT Earlene Roberts; 7 H 134, WCT Elmer L. Boyd; 7 H 177, WCT Richard M. Sims."; which was reprinted from Bugliosi *Reclaiming* 221, with the same citations. Copyright notice for *Four* Days is in endnote [1767]. How's that for documenting the confiscation of a paperclip and rubber band!?

[1798] Quoted with permission from Oglesby 19.

[1799] TESTIMONY OF JAMES R. LEAVELLE on *WCH* VII 269.

[1800] *WCH* VII 268 (Leavelle).

[1801] Photo purchased from AP, then tightly cropped. ©The Associated Press.

[1802] *WR* 16.

[1803] *WR* 16.

[1804] Quoted with permission after payment, from Bugliosi *Four Days* 265-266, citing "Oswald with Land and Land, *Lee*, p. 25"; which was reprinted from Bugliosi *Reclaiming* 167, with the same citation. Copyright notice is in endnote [1767].

[1805] *WR* 17.

[1806] Quoted with permission after payment, from Epstein *Legend* 247-248.

[1807] This booking photo pair is scanned from LEWIS (AUDREY L.) EXHIBIT NO. 1 on *WCH* XX 533. Coming from that US Federal government source, it is in the public domain. The photo pair is now in the National Archives.

[1808] Quoted with permission after payment, from Manchester *Death* 456. Permission acknowledgement is in endnote [17].

[1809] *WR* 16.

[1810] Quoted with permission after payment, from Manchester *Death* 457-458. Permission acknowledgement is in endnote [17].

[1811] Quoted with permission after payment, from Bugliosi *Four Days* 247-248, citing "Oswald with Land and Land, *Lee*, pp. 22-23"; which was reprinted from Bugliosi *Reclaiming* 156, with the same citation. Copyright notice is in endnote [1767].

[1812] Quoted with permission after payment, from Bugliosi *Four Days* 374, citing "15 H 508, WCT David L. Johnston; Johnston Exhibit No. 5 [*sic*: should say Johnston Exhibit No. 1], 20 H 315; Affidavit in Johnston Exhibit No. 5, 20 H 323" and "Johnston Exhibit No. 1, 20 H 315." Copyright notice is in endnote [1767].

[1813] JOHNSTON EXHIBIT NO. 5 on *WCH* XX 323.

[1814] *WR* 17.

[1815] *WR* 17.

[1816] COMMISSION EXHIBIT NO. 2003, pages marked I138D and I138E on *WCH* XXIV 270.

[1817] Quoted with permission from McMillan, page 555, which is probably based upon, but does not cite, the officer who helped him: *WCH* XIII 5 (L. C. Graves). Permission statement is in endnote [150].

[1818] Quoted with permission after payment, from Manchester *Death* 520. Permission acknowledgement is in endnote [17].

[1819] This photo is PAPPAS EXHIBIT NO. 1 on *WCH* XXI 19, a publication of the Federal government from which it was scanned. It was taken by *Dallas Morning News* photographer Jack Beers. The author's experienced professional picture researcher used considerable effort doing due diligence to obtain permission to use, or to buy, but never had any response from the archive of the *Dallas Morning News*. Even the knowledgeable Sixth Floor Museum in Dallas is unable to provide contact information. After those efforts, I claim fair use. Please see CREDITS AND PERMISSIONS on page ii.

[1820] For amazing reports of the shooting, interrupting the events in Washington, see Garner, Joe. *We Interrupt This Broadcast: The Events That Stopped Our Lives – from the Hindenburg Explosion to the Death of John F. Kennedy Jr.*, pages 56-57, and listen to its enclosed compact disc 1 track 16.

[1821] Quoted with permission after payment, from Manchester *Death* 524. Permission acknowledgement is in endnote [17].

[1822] *WR* 17.

[1823] PRICE EXHIBIT NO. 34 on *WCH* XXI 265.

[1824] Quoted with permission after payment, from Manchester *Death* 519-520. Permission acknowledgement is in endnote [17].

[1825] Quoted with permission from oral testimony of Gerald L. Hill, Patrol Division, Dallas Police Department, in Sneed 304.

[1826] Photo purchased to show here: *Dallas Times Herald* Collection / The Sixth Floor Museum at Dealey Plaza.

[1827] Huffaker, Bob, Bill Mercer, George Phenix, and Wes Wise. *When The News Went Live: Dallas 1963* page 124.

[1828] Quoted with permission from Connally, Nellie 88.

[1829] *WR* 17-18.

[1830] Quoted with permission after payment, from Epstein *Legend* 252.

[1831] Quoted with permission from McMillan, endnote 22 on page 625, which cites testimony to the U.S. House of Representatives Judiciary Committee's Subcommittee on Civil and Constitutional Rights (Hearings on FBI Oversight, Serial No. 2, Part 3), Hosty on pages 124-175 and Shanklin on 59-129. Permission statement is in endnote [150].

[1832] Quoted with permission after payment, from Cray, Ed. *Chief Justice: A Biography of Earl Warren* 413. Copyright notice supplied by publisher: "Reprinted with the permission of Simon & Schuster, Inc. from CHIEF JUSTICE: A BIOGRAPHY OF EARL WARREN by Ed Cray. Copyright © 1997 by Ed Cray. All rights reserved."

[1833] Quoted with permission after payment, from Warren, Earl. *The Memoirs of Earl Warren* 352-353. Copyright notice is in endnote [211].

[1834] Quoted with permission after payment, from Manchester *Death* 526, 530. Permission acknowledgement is in endnote [17].

[1835] Quoted with permission from Leaming, Barbara. *Mrs. Kennedy: The Missing History of the Kennedy Years* 349.

[1836] http://en.wikipedia.org/wiki/Statue_of_Freedom

[1837] Quoted with permission after payment, from Hill, Clint, with Lisa McCubbin. *Mrs. Kennedy and Me* 316, 317, for which the copyright notice is in endnote [757].

— 7 — Muffled Drums and Subsequent Events

[1838] Quoted with permission from Fries, Chuck, and Irv Wilson with Spencer Green. *We'll Never Be Young Again: Remembering the Last Days of John F. Kennedy*, page 88.

[1839] Photo cropped very tightly from the photo of endnote [1841], which was purchased from Corbis: © Bettmann / Corbis.

[1840] Quoted with permission from Spoto, Donald. *Jacqueline Bouvier Kennedy Onassis: A Life* 203-204.

[1841] Photo purchased and cropped medium from Corbis: © Bettmann / Corbis; one of the more expensive in this book.

[1842] Quoted with permission from Sabato, Larry J. *The Kennedy Half-Century: The Presidency, Assassination, and Lasting Legacy of John F. Kennedy* 32.

[1843] Quoted with permission after payment, from Manchester, William. *The Death of a President* 611. Permission acknowledgement is in endnote [17].

[1844] Quoted with permission after payment, from Thomas, Helen. *Front Row at the White House: My Life and Times*, page 229, for which the copyright notice is in endnote [907].

[1845] Photo was imported from the Amazon.com listing for Vincent Bugliosi's book *Four Days in November: The Assassination of President John F. Kennedy* — but the image is not in that book. The Amazon.com site says this photo was "Uploaded by David Von Pein". The author and his experienced picture researcher spent considerable time trying to identify the photographer and copyright holder, if any, without success, so after due diligence, I display it as fair use. Please see Credits and Permissions on page ii.

[1846] Quoted with permission after payment, from Manchester *Death* 529. This form with a key word from the book's title is used because more than one book by the author is cited in these notes. Permission acknowledgement is in endnote [17].

[1847] Quoted from Oswald, Robert L., with Myrick and Barbara Land. *Lee: A Portrait of Lee Harvey Oswald by His Brother* 156. This source was described in endnote [68].

[1848] Testimony of Mrs. Marguerite Oswald on *WCH* I 169.

[1849] Quoted with permission after payment, from Manchester *Death* 529. Permission acknowledgement is in endnote [17].

[1850] Photo purchased from Corbis, then tightly cropped: © Corbis.

[1851] Oswald, Robert 157.

[1852] Quoted from Oswald, Robert 158-159. This source was described in endnote [68].

[1853] Quoted from Oswald, Robert 160. This source was described in endnote [68].

[1854] Quoted with permission after payment, from Manchester *Death* 568. Permission acknowledgement is in endnote [17].

[1855] Quoted from Oswald, Robert 222. This source was described in endnote [68].

[1856] A brief account of the burial, with excellent photos as their magazine does them so well, is in Life Books, The Editors of. *The Day Kennedy Died: 50 Years Later LIFE Remembers the Man and the Moment* 136-137.

[1857] Quoted from Oswald, Robert 161-164. This source was described in endnote [68].

[1858] Photo purchased from Corbis: © Bettmann / Corbis. Fourteen lesser-quality photos of the burial, looking in all directions from the not-used chapel to the coffin, are Commission Exhibits 165-179 on *WCH* XVI 522-529.

[1859] Quoted from Oswald, Robert 164. This source was described in endnote [68].

[1860] Quoted from Oswald, Robert 165. This source was described in endnote [68].

[1861] Quoted with permission from McMillan, Priscilla Johnson. *Marina and Lee* 558. Permission statement is in endnote [150].

[1862] Photo purchased from the Fort Worth Star-Telegram Collection, Special Collections Division, the University of Texas at Arlington Libraries, Arlington, Texas.

[1863] Myers, Dale K. *With Malice: Lee Harvey Oswald and the Murder of Officer J.D. Tippit*, Second Edition, page 35, which cites "Dallas Morning News, 11-26-63, Sec. 1, p. 1, *Heroic Patrolman Lauded at Rites* by Kent Biffle".

[1864] Photo purchased from AP and shown full size without cropping. ©The Associated Press.

[1865] Myers 36, which cites "Granberry, Michael, 'Pain Lingers for Tippit's Widow,' *Dallas Morning News*, November 20, 2003".

[1866] Quoted with permission after payment, from Bugliosi, Vincent. *Four Days in November: The Assassination of President John F. Kennedy* 506; which was reprinted from Bugliosi, Vincent. *Reclaiming History: The Assassination of President John F. Kennedy* 315. Copyright notice is in endnote [1767].

[1867] Watney, Hedda Lyons. *Jackie O*, fourth edition, 211.

[1868] Quoted with permission after payment, from Blaine, Gerald, with Lisa McCubbin. *The Kennedy Detail: JFK's Secret Service Agents Break Their Silence* 311. Copyright notice is in endnote [1444].

[1869] Quoted with permission after payment, from Thomas, Helen. *Front Row* 249. This form with key words from the title is used because more than one book by this author is cited in these notes. Copyright notice is in endnote [907].

[1870] Photo purchased from AV Archives at the John F. Kennedy Presidential Library and Museum, Boston. The caption is quoted with permission from Anthony, Carl Sferrazza. *The Kennedy White House: Family Life and Pictures, 1961-1963*, page 287. Copyright notice supplied by publisher: "Reprinted with permission of Touchstone, a division of Simon & Schuster, Inc. from THE KENNEDY WHITE HOUSE by Carl Sferrazza Anthony. Copyright © 2001 by Carl Sferrazza Anthony. All Rights reserved."

[1871] Quoted with permission from Spoto 209.

[1872] Quoted with permission after payment, from Blaine with McCubbin 333. Copyright notice is in endnote [1444].

[1873] Quoted with permission from Keogh, Pamela Clarke. *Jackie Style* 163.

[1874] Quoted with permission from Spoto 281.

[1875] Quoted with permission from Spada, James. *Jackie: Her Life in Pictures* 168.

[1876] Quoted with permission from Spada 161.

[1877] Andersen, Christopher. *Jackie After Jack: Portrait of the Lady* 476.

[1878] Quoted with permission from Keogh 241.

[1879] Quoted with permission from Keogh 241.

[1880] Quoted with permission from Keogh 243.

[1881] Quoted with permission from Spada 169.

[1882] Quoted with permission from Spoto 301.

[1883] A brief account of Caroline's life to 2013, with three excellent photos, is in Life Books, The Editors of. *The Day Kennedy Died: 50 Years Later LIFE Remembers the Man and the Moment* 176-177.

[1884] Spada 162.

[1885] A brief account of John's later life, with four encompassing photos, is in Life Books, The Editors of. *The Day Kennedy Died: 50 Years Later LIFE Remembers the Man and the Moment* 178-179.

[1886] Quoted with permission from Spignesi, Stephen. *J.F.K. Jr.* 149.

[1887] Sorensen, Theodore C. *Kennedy* 375.

[1888] Quoted with permission from Manchester, William. *One Brief Shining Moment* 252.

[1889] Photo purchased from Corbis, then moderately cropped: ©Arnie Sachs/CNP/Corbis.

[1890] A box on page 333 explains why prudent writers may not quote any words spoken by Dr. Martin Luther King, Jr.

[1891] Quoted as fair use (for brevity) from http://en.wikipedia.org/wiki/Bill_Clinton on 2012/06/13.

[1892] Photo shown with the gracious permission of photographer Arthur Pollack / *The Boston Herald*.

[1893] Quoted with permission from Manchester *Moment* 258. This form with a key word from the book's title is used because more than one book by the author is cited in these notes.

[1894] Photo showing Connally with Johnson on the same trip to Washington is an Official Presidential Portrait taken by Yoichi R. Okamoto, and is shown by courtesy of the LBJ Presidential Library Collection.

[1895] Quoted with permission from Kerr, Andy. *A Journey Amongst the Good and the Great* 23-25.

[1896] Image cropped from signature area that was scanned from Cadigan Exhibit No. 9 on *WCH* XIX 281. Coming from that US Federal government source, it is in the public domain.

[1897] "Today in History", *The Seattle Times* 16 June 1999, page A4.

[1898] White, Theodore H. *The Making of the President 1972* 294.

[1899] Connally, John, with Mickey Herskowitz. *In History's Shadow: An American Odyssey* 231-269.

[1900] White *The Making of the President 1972* 408.

[1901] Quoted with kind permission from White, Theodore H. *America in Search of Itself: The Making of the President 1956-1980* 235. See also Cannon, James. *Time and Chance: Gerald Ford's Appointment with History* 172.

[1902] Quoted with permission from Nixon, Richard M. *RN: The Memoirs of Richard Nixon* 674.

[1903] White, Theodore H. *Breach of Faith: The Fall of Richard Nixon* 310-311.

[1904] Quoted with permission from Cannon 285.

[1905] Quoted with permission from White *America in Search of Itself* 236-237.

[1906] Quoted with permission from Ford, Gerald R. *A Time to Heal: The Autobiography of Gerald R. Ford* 402.

[1907] Quoted with permission from White *America in Search of Itself* 237.

[1908] Connally, John 307.

[1909] Quoted with permission from Connally, John 367.

[1910] Quoted with permission from Connally, Nellie, with Mickey Herskowitz. *From Love Field: Our Final Hours with President John F. Kennedy* 133, 135.

[1911] Quoted with permission from Connally, Nellie 115-116.

[1912] Quoted as fair use (for brevity) from http://en.wikipedia.org/wiki/Nellie_Connally on 2013/09/18.

[1913] Blaine with McCubbin 371.

[1914] Cronkite, Walter. *A Reporter's Life* 365.

[1915] Quoted with permission from Spoto 304.

[1916] http://en.wikipedia.org/wiki/Michael_Eddowes, consulted on 2013/08/22.

[1917] Benson, Michael. *Who's Who in the JFK Assassination: An A-to-Z Encyclopedia*, page 124.

[1918] http://www.nytimes.com/2013/08/10/us/mystery-from-the-grave-beside-oswalds-solved.html

[1919] http://www.nytimes.com/2012/04/11/us/a-dispute-over-lee-harvey-oswalds-tombstone.html

[1920] Quoted with permission from Spoto 207.

[1921] This photo with June and Rachel was purchased to show here: Tom. C. Dillard Collection, *The Dallas Morning News* / The Sixth Floor Museum at Dealey Plaza.

[1922] Quoted from Oswald, Robert 173. This source was described in endnote [68].

[1923] Quoted with permission from McMillan, page 561. There is a more complete account in Mallon, Thomas. *Mrs. Paine's Garage: and the Murder of John F. Kennedy*, pages 76-86. Permission statement for McMillan is in endnote [150].

[1924] Quoted with permission from McMillan 571. Permission statement is in endnote [150].

[1925] Quoted with permission from McMillan 568. Permission statement is in endnote [150].

[1926] Quoted with permission from Wecht, Cyril *Cause of Death* 57-58. Copyright notice is in endnote [623].

[1927] This photo was purchased from Corbis, converted to grayscale and moderately cropped. ©SDFL/Splash News/Corbis. The photo, reportedly taken at a Walmart in Texas, is one of the most expensive purchased to show in this book.

[1928] Quoted with permission from McMillan 446. Permission statement is in endnote [150].

[1929] Quoted from Oswald, Robert 23. This source was described in endnote [68].

[1930] Quoted with permission from Sneed, Larry A. *No More Silence: An Oral History of the Assassination of President Kennedy* 33.

[1931] Quoted with permission after payment, from Stafford, Jean. *A Mother in History*, page 92.

[1932] Quoted with permission after payment, from Stafford 103.

[1933] Quoted with permission after payment, from Stafford 94.

[1934] Quoted with permission after payment, from Stafford 25.

[1935] The photo I wanted to show is on the cover of Stafford, Jean. *A Mother in History* (the Bantam paperback edition), which credits "Photo by Carl Fischer, Courtesy of McCall's Magazine".

[1936] Quoted with permission from Schieffer, Bob. *This Just In: What I Couldn't Tell You On TV*, page 5. Copyright notice supplied by publisher: "From THIS JUST IN by Bob Schieffer, copyright © 2003 by Bob Schieffer. Used by permission of G. P. Putnam's Sons, an imprint of Penguin Publishing Group, a division of Penguin Random House LLC."

[1937] Quoted with permission from Schieffer 6. Copyright notice is in endnote [1936].

[1938] Photo was purchased to show here: Bill Winfrey Collection, *The Dallas Morning News* / The Sixth Floor Museum at Dealey Plaza.

[1939] Quoted with permission from Mailer, Norman. *Oswald's Tale: An American Mystery* 790, which credits in endnote on page xxxv: "Unpublished interview of Marguerite Oswald by Lawrence Schiller, 1976."

[1940] Oswald, Robert 173-174.

[1941] Quoted with permission from Gertz, Elmer. *Moment of Madness: The People vs. Jack Ruby*, page 468.

[1942] http://www.examiner.com/article/lee-harvey-oswald-s-brother-from-wichita-falls-sues-over-sale-of-casket

[1943] "In a Texas Court, a Fight for Lee Harvey Oswald's Coffin" by David Montgomery, *The New York Times*, Dec. 11, 2014, on the Web at http://www.nytimes.com/2014/12/12/us/in-a-texas-court-a-fight-for-lee-harvey-oswalds-coffin.html?_r=0

[1944] http://www.nytimes.com/2015/01/31/us/oswalds-coffin-belongs-to-his-brother-not-funeral-home-a-judge-rules.html

[1945] http://en.wikipedia.org/wiki/SS-100-X   See also http://en.wikipedia.org/wiki/The_Henry_Ford#Henry_Ford_Museum

[1946] *The Seattle Times* "Odds & Ends" 2015/11/08, page A2.

[1947] Quoted with permission after payment, from Manchester *Death* 634. Permission acknowledgement is in endnote [17].

[1948] Quoted with permission after payment, from Manchester *Death* 635. Permission acknowledgement is in endnote [17].

[1949] Quoted with permission after payment, from Stafford 121.

[1950] Quoted with permission from Sneed 72.

[1951] Quoted with permission after payment, from Blaine with McCubbin 392. Copyright notice is in endnote [1444].

[1952] This photo is shown with the gracious permission of photographer Arthur Pollack / *The Boston Herald*. In the front row, then-President Bill Clinton is surrounded by Kennedys, from left: Ethel, Ted, Jackie, John Jr., Caroline. Behind them are spouses, friends and some of the next generation of Kennedys.

— 8 — COMMISSION, CRITICS, REHASHES

[1953] Quoted with permission after payment, from Stafford, Jean. *A Mother in History* 5-6.

[1954] Quoted with permission from Johnson, Lyndon Baines. *The Vantage Point: Perspectives of the Presidency 1963–1969* pages 18-19. Copyright and permission notice is in endnote [1559].

[1955] Quoted with permission from Johnson 26. Copyright and permission notice is in endnote [1559].

[1956] Quoted with permission after payment, through the great courtesy of Edward Jay Epstein, from his *Inquest: The Warren Commission and the Establishment of Truth* (hc) 4, which cites "*Texas Supplemental Report on the Assassination of President John F. Kennedy and the Serious Wounding of Governor John B. Connally*, pp. 1, 8, 20, Austin, Texas, 1964".

[1957] Quoted with permission after payment, from Epstein *Inquest* 4-5.

[1958] *Warren Report* (hereinafter *WR*) on its front-material page x.

[1959] "EXECUTIVE ORDER NO. 11130" on *WR* 471.

[1960] Quoted with permission from Johnson 26. Copyright and permission notice is in endnote [1559].

[1961] The author has not found a photo taken at the time LBJ jawboned Earl Warren into chairing his commission, so this photo from 1968 will have to do. Purchased from the Lyndon B. Johnson Presidential Library, it is image B561-11, which credits White House photographer Mike Geissinger.

[1962] Quoted with permission after payment, from Manchester, William. *The Death of a President*, page 630, for which the permission acknowledgement is in endnote [17]. A fuller personal account is in Cray, Ed. *Chief Justice: A Biography of Earl Warren* 414-417.

[1963] In his autobiography *The Vantage Point* on page 27, Lyndon Johnson wrote "I appointed the two men Bobby Kennedy asked me to put on it—Allen Dulles and John McCloy—immediately."

[1964] Quoted with permission after payment, from Epstein *Inquest* 5.

[1965] Quoted with permission from Specter, Arlen, with Charles Robbins. *Passion for Truth: From Finding JFK's Single Bullet to Questioning Anita Hill to Impeaching Clinton* 54, which credits Specter's interview of Ford.

[1966] Quoted with permission from Cannon, James. *Time and Chance: Gerald Ford's Appointment with History* 76.

[1967] Photo is held by the National Archives and Records Administration, so is in the public domain. Great thanks for finding many images to Britney N. Crawford, Archivist, Special Emphasis Program Manager (SEPM), Special Access and FOIA Branch (RD-F) at NARA in College Park, MD.

[1968] Warren, Earl. *The Memoirs of Earl Warren* 361. Copyright notice is in endnote [211].

[1969] Quoted with permission after payment, from Blaine, Gerald, with Lisa McCubbin *The Kennedy Detail: JFK's Secret Service Agents Break Their Silence* 306. Copyright notice is in endnote [1444].

[1970] Quoted with permission from Hosty, James P., Jr., with Thomas C. Hosty. *Assignment: Oswald* 138.

[1971] Quoted with permission after payment, from Epstein *Inquest* 22, which cites "Interviews with Goldberg, Willens, Ford, Liebeler, Eisenberg."

[1972] Quoted with permission after payment, from Epstein *Inquest* 22, which cites "Ball Interview."

[1973] Quoted with permission after payment, from Epstein *Inquest* 22, which cites "Liebeler Interview."

[1974] Quoted with permission after payment, from Epstein *Inquest* 22, which cites "Eisenberg Interview I."

[1975] Quoted with permission after payment, from Epstein *Inquest* 22, which cites "Willens Interview."

[1976] Quoted with permission after payment, from Epstein *Inquest* 22, which cites "Rankin Interviews I and II."

[1977] Quoted with permission after payment, from Epstein *Inquest* 22, which cites "Liebeler Interview."

[1978] Quoted with permission from Weisberg, Harold. *Whitewash: The Report on the Warren Report* 25-27.

[1979] *WR* page xiii.

[1980] Testimony of Mrs. Lee Harvey [Marina] Oswald on *WCH* I 125.

[1981] Testimony of Mrs. Marguerite Oswald on *WCH* I 195.

[1982] *WCH* I 219 (Marguerite Oswald).

[1983] *WCH* I 236-237 (Marguerite Oswald).

[1984] Quoted with permission after payment, from Epstein *Inquest* 129, which cites "Rankin Interview I."

[1985] Quoted with permission after payment, from Epstein *Inquest* 129, which cites "Rankin Interview II."

[1986] Quoted with permission after payment, from Epstein *Inquest* 132, which cites "Goldberg Interview."

[1987] Quoted with permission after payment, from Epstein *Inquest* 132, which cites in part: "Appendix XIII, the longest appendix (72 pages), is a biography of Lee Harvey Oswald, and was written by Lloyd L. Weinreb, then a Department of Justice lawyer temporarily working with the commission."

[1988] Quoted with permission after payment, from Epstein *Inquest* 132.

[1989] Quoted with permission from Specter 122.

[1990] Quoted with permission from Ford, Gerald R. *A Time to Heal: The Autobiography of Gerald R. Ford* 76.

[1991] In the photo, left-to-right: McCloy, Rankin, Russell, Ford (who will occupy this oval office in ten years), Warren, Johnson, Dulles, Cooper, Boggs. The photo taken by official White House photographer Cecil Stoughton is in, and shown through the courtesy of, the Lyndon Baines Johnson Presidential Library Collection. The author straightened, converted to grayscale and cropped.

[1992] Quoted as fair use (for brevity) from *The New York Times*, Monday, September 28, 1964, page 1 A, "The Warren Commission's Report" "Note to Readers".

[1993] Cray 419.

[1994] Quoted with permission after payment, from Cray 428. Copyright notice is in endnote [1832].

[1995] Quoted with kind permission, without fee, from White, Theodore H. *The Making of the President 1964* 383-384.

[1996] Quoted with permission from the Introduction by Anthony Lewis on pages vii-viii in *The Witnesses: The Highlights of Hearings before the Warren Commission on the Assassination of President Kennedy*, Selected and Edited by *The New York Times*, copyright © 1964 by The New York Times Company. This permission was graciously given by Kymberli Wilner, Content Licensing Manager, The New York Times, the final permission needed for this book. Hooray!

[1997] Quoted with permission after payment, from Bishop, Jim. *The Day Kennedy Was Shot* xvi.

[1998] *WR* 1.

[1999] *WR* 18.

[2000] *WR* 19-20.

[2001] *WR* 21-22.

[2002] *WR* 22-23.

[2003] *WR* 423-424.

[2004] Quoted with permission from McMillan, Priscilla Johnson. *Marina and Lee* 6. Permission statement is in endnote [150].

[2005] "Today in History" *The Seattle Times* 09 July 2003: A12.

[2006] Quoted with permission from Cannon 77, which cites "James Reston [Sr.], NYT, September 28, 1964."

[2007] Thomas G. Buchanan died in 1988. The author gives thanks to his daughter, Marian Buchanan, who on behalf of herself and her siblings, his heirs, made valuable suggestions that corrected and augmented his references throughout this book.

[2008] http://thomasgbuchanan.com/1948-the-media-report-on-the-first-case-of-a-blacklisted-journalist/

[2009] http://thomasgbuchanan.com/biography/

[2010] Buchanan's book was first published in London by Secker & Warburg. A revised and expanded edition was published in the U.S. by G. P. Putnam's Sons in November 1964. For the benefit of this book's readers, most expected to be Americans, the citations in chapters 9, 15, 19 and 21 will reference the American hardcover by Putnam.

[2011] COMMISSION EXHIBIT 2585 on *WCH* XXV 857-862; reproduced in New York Times. *The Witnesses*, Exhibit pages 58-64.

[2012] Quoted with permission after payment, from Posner, Gerald. *Case Closed: Lee Harvey Oswald and the Assassination of JFK* 412, which cites "Testimony of Alan Belmont, WC Vol. V, p. 30." Copyright notice is in endnote [1039].

[2013] Quoted as fair use (for brevity) from *The New York Times*: http://www.nytimes.com/2002/03/04/us/harold-weisberg-88-critic-of-inquiry-in-kennedy-death.html

[2014] Quoted with permission from Weisberg *Never Again!* xii.

[2015] Quoted with permission from Weisberg *Whitewash* 9.

[2016] Quoted as fair use (for brevity) from *The New York Times*: http://www.nytimes.com/2002/03/04/us/harold-weisberg-88-critic-of-inquiry-in-kennedy-death.html

[2017] Quoted as fair use (for brevity) from *The New York Times*: http://www.nytimes.com/2002/03/04/us/harold-weisberg-88-critic-of-inquiry-in-kennedy-death.html

[2018] Quoted as fair use from Livingstone, Harrison Edward. *Killing the Truth: Deceit and Deception in the JFK Case* 321. Prolific critic and writer Livingstone is said to have become ill and more difficult than usual in 2013. In 2014 he moved into a convalescent home, in which he died in February 2015. Radio host Bob Oliver, who in the apparent absence of family had helped him move, wrote: "He was under conservatorship monitored by Carl Powers [of the] Monterey County [CA] Public Guardian Office." (http://vincepalamara.com/2015/06/05/harry-livingstone-rip-more-information-on-his-last-yearsdays-and-passing/) From helpful Lauren at publisher Perseus Books (subsidiary.rights@perseusbooks.com), my copyright agent Corey Dong learned that his book copyrights had reverted to him; she advised we contact attorney Steven J. Andre in Carmel, CA, for matters related to Livingstone's estate, if any. My agent conveyed to Andre by phone my request for permission to quote, then repeated it in an email message; Andre has not replied. Having done due diligence through my exemplarily excellent agent, I claim the right of fair use under the copyright law. Please see my CREDITS AND PERMISSIONS on page ii.

[2019] Quoted with permission after payment, from Posner *Case Closed* 412, which cites "Robert Blakey, *Fatal Hour* [re-title of re-publication of *The Plot to Kill the President*] p. 44." Copyright notice is in endnote [1039].

[2020] Quoted as fair use from Livingstone *Killing the Truth* xxii. A statement about this source is in endnote [2018].

[2021] Quoted with permission from Weisberg *Never Again!* 323.

[2022] Quoted with permission after payment, from Epstein *Inquest* xviii.

[2023] Quoted with permission after payment, from Epstein, Edward Jay. *Counterplot* 5.

[2024] Quoted with permission after payment, from Epstein *Inquest* xv.

[2025] Quoted with permission after payment, from Posner *Case Closed* 414. Copyright notice is in endnote [1039].

[2026] Quoted with permission after payment, from Warren *Memoirs*, editor's note on 363. There are editor's notes throughout that autobiography because Earl Warren died before the book was in final form for printing, so the editor, in order to not change any of Warren's words, inserted notes where necessary. Copyright notice is in endnote [211].

[2027] Quoted with permission after payment, from Epstein, Edward Jay. *The Assassination Chronicles: Inquest, Counterplot and Legend* (hereinafter *Chronicles*) 13-14.

[2028] Quoted from Livingstone *Killing the Truth* xxii-xxiii. A statement about this source is in endnote [2018].

[2029] Quoted with permission from Weisberg *Never Again!* xliii.

[2030] Quoted with permission after payment, from Epstein *Counterplot* 6.

[2031] Quoted with permission after payment, from Epstein *Counterplot* 7.

[2032] Epstein *Chronicles* 291.

[2033] Quoted with gracious permission from Lane, Mark. *Rush to Judgment* page vii, from his "Lastword" in 1992 edition. Permission statement from Mr. Lane is in endnote [538].

[2034] Quoted with permission after payment, from Posner *Case Closed* 412. Copyright notice is in endnote [1039].

[2035] Quoted with permission after payment, from Posner *Case Closed* 412-413. Copyright notice is in endnote [1039].

[2036] Quoted with permission after payment, from Ford, Gerald R., and John R. Stiles. *Portrait of the Assassin* 440.

[2037] Quoted with permission after payment, from Posner *Case Closed* 413n (which means the note on his page 413). Copyright notice is in endnote [1039].

[2038] Quoted with permission after payment, from Vestal, Bud. *Jerry Ford, Up Close: An Investigative Biography* 121-122.

[2039] Quoted as fair use (for brevity: 41 words) from *Book Week*, August 28, 1966.

[2040] Quoted with permission after payment, from Posner *Case Closed* 412-413, which cites "'The Warren Report,' CBS News, Part IV, June 28, 1967." Copyright notice is in endnote [1039].

[2041] Quoted as fair use (for brevity) from http://en.wikipedia.org/wiki/Mark_Lane_(author)#Later_career on 2012/08/06.

[2042] Quoted with permission after payment, from Posner *Case Closed* 413-414. Copyright notice is in endnote [1039].

[2043] Quoted with kind permission of The John Birch Society from Rust, Zad. *Teddy Bare: The Last of the Kennedy Clan* ix.

[2044] Found in Rust on pages 52, 159, 151.

[2045] Quoted with permission after payment, from Pipes, Daniel. *Conspiracy: How the Paranoid Style Flourishes and Where It Comes From*, note to page 34 on page 209: "Bill Alexander, the ex-assistant district attorney of Dallas, discussing the Kennedy assassination. Quoted also, with permission after payment, from Gerald Posner, *Case Closed … 467.*" Copyright notice is in endnote [1039].

[2046] Quoted with permission after payment, from Pipes 34.

[2047] Quoted from Livingstone, Harrison Edward. *Killing Kennedy: And the Hoax of the Century* 294n. A statement about this source is in endnote [2018].

[2048] Quoted with permission after payment, from Blaine with McCubbin, page xvii. Copyright notice is in endnote [1444].

[2049] O'Reilly, Bill, and Martin Dugard. *Killing Kennedy: The End of Camelot* 248 — cited but not quoted. The author's statement about that source is in endnote [272].

[2050] Quoted from Oswald, Robert L., with Myrick and Barbara Land. *Lee: A Portrait of Lee Harvey Oswald by His Brother* 220. This source was described in endnote [68].

[2051] Quoted from Oswald, Robert 221. This source was described in endnote [68].

[2052] Quoted with permission from Feynman, Richard P., as told to Ralph Leighton. *What Do You Care What Other People Think? Further Adventures of a Curious Character*, pages 91-92.

[2053] *Final Report of the Select Committee to Study Governmental Operations with respect to Intelligence Activities, United States Senate, Ninety-Fourth Congress, Second Session: Book V: The Investigation of the Assassination of President John F. Kennedy: Performance of the Intelligence Agencies* 1, 2, 6. This report is next cited as *SSCIA*.

[2054] *SSCIA* 95-97.

[2055] Morrow, Robert D. *Betrayal*.

[2056] Quoted with permission from Morrow 11, 16, 239.

[2057] Morrow 11, 16.

[2058] Morrow 14, 17, 97-109.

[2059] Quoted with permission from Morrow 18.

[2060] Morrow 19, 21, 77, 105.

[2061] Morrow 76, 104.

[2062] Morrow 102, 104.

[2063] Quoted with permission from Morrow 103, 106, 115.

[2064] Morrow 53, 55-61.

[2065] Morrow 78, 95.

[2066] Morrow 76, 115, 118, 172.

[2067] Quoted with permission from Morrow 193-194, 227, 283.

[2068] Morrow 179-183.

[2069] Morrow 126.

[2070] Morrow 165.

[2071] Morrow 118, 125, 169, 198.

[2072] Morrow 63, 87.

[2073] Morrow 71.

[2074] Morrow 89.

[2075] Morrow 169, 171, 173-174.

[2076] Morrow 213-217.

[2077] Morrow 216.

[2078] Morrow 218.

[2079] Morrow 231.

[2080] Quoted with permission from Morrow 233.

[2081] Morrow 227.

[2082] The Congressman's letter is printed on Morrow 8.

[2083] Quoted with permission from Callahan, Bob. *Who Shot JFK?: A Guide to the Major Conspiracy Theories* 116-117.

[2084] Quoted with permission from Sneed, Larry A. *No More Silence: An Oral History of the Assassination of President Kennedy* 169.

[2085] Quoted with permission from oral history of James C. Bowles, Communications Supervisor, in Sneed 175.

[2086] Quoted with permission after payment, from Epstein *Chronicles* 23-24.

[2087] Quoted with permission from Oglesby, Carl. *Who Killed JFK?* 24-25.

[2088] *The Final Assassinations Report: Report of the Select Committee on Assassinations, U.S. House of Representatives*. Bantam Books, 1979 paperback 62.

[2089] Quoted with permission after payment, from Bugliosi, Vincent. *Reclaiming History: The Assassination of President John F. Kennedy* 379. Copyright notice is in endnote [1788].

[2090] Quoted with permission after payment, from Bugliosi *Reclaiming History* 381. Copyright notice is in endnote [1788].

[2091] Quoted with permission after payment, from Epstein *Chronicles* 24.

[2092] Quoted with the gracious permission of James Reston, Jr., author and copyright owner of *The Accidental Victim: JFK, Lee Harvey Oswald, and the Real Target in Dallas*, page 53.

[2093] Most of the first two paragraphs is based on information in, but not quoted from, Wikipedia, as retrieved on 2014/09/10: http://en.wikipedia.org/wiki/President_John_F._Kennedy_Assassination_Records_Collection_Act_of_1992

[2094] Quoted with permission from Specter 122.

[2095] Quoted as fair use (for brevity) from Feinsilber, Mike (*AP*). "Six-year review of JFK slaying ends" *The Seattle Times* 29 Sep. 1998: A4.

— 9 — DID HE DO IT? WAS IT A CONSPIRACY?

[2096] Quoted with permission after payment, from Stafford, Jean. *A Mother in History* 49-50.

[2097] Quoted with permission after payment, from Posner, Gerald. *Case Closed: Lee Harvey Oswald and the Assassination of JFK*, revised edition of 1994 (sc), page 469, which cites "Letter to the Editor of *The New York Times*, by William Manchester, February 5, 1992." Copyright notice is in endnote [1039]. When only one book by an author is cited in this book's NOTES, second and later citations will show only the author's surname. If two or more books by an author are cited anywhere in these NOTES, as is the case with Posner, second and later citations will show the specific book's title, in full or shortened, after the author's surname.

[2098] Quoted with permission after payment, from Blaine, Gerald, with Lisa McCubbin. *The Kennedy Detail: JFK's Secret Service Agents Break Their Silence*, pages 363-364. Copyright notice is in endnote [1444].

[2099] TESTIMONY OF JOHN EDWARD PIC on *WCH* XI 80. Hereinafter, a second reference will be in form *WCH* XI 80 (John Pic).

[2100] TESTIMONY OF ROBERT EDWARD LEE OSWALD on *WCH* I 314.

[2101] *WCH* I 448 (Robert Oswald).

[2102] Transcribed by the author from an interview of Robert Oswald by Josh Mankowitz in a segment titled "My Brother's Keeper" on *Dateline NBC*, broadcast by NBC-TV on June 14, 1998, and quoted here with permission after payment. The NBC license agreement is described in endnote [16].

[2103] Quoted with permission from McMillan, Priscilla Johnson. *Marina and Lee* 538. Permission statement is in endnote [150].

[2104] TESTIMONY OF MRS. LEE HARVEY OSWALD on *WCH* V 608.

[2105] TESTIMONY OF MRS. JOHN F. KENNEDY on *WCH* V 178-181.

[2106] Quoted with permission from Connally, Nellie, with Mickey Herskowitz. *From Love Field: Our Final Hours with President John F. Kennedy* 121-122.

[2107] Quoted with permission after payment, from Warren, Earl. *The Memoirs of Earl Warren* 367. Copyright notice is in endnote [211].

[2108] The author scanned this image of his purchased paperback's cover. This is half size; the book is 6" wide, this is 3".

[2109] Quoted with permission after payment, from Posner *Case Closed*, author's note on page xvii. Copyright notice is in endnote [1039].

[2110] Quoted with permission after payment, from Posner *Case Closed* xvii. Copyright notice is in endnote [1039].

[2111] Quoted as fair use from Livingstone, Harrison Edward. *Killing Kennedy: And the Hoax of the Century* 284-285, which cites "*U.S. News and World Report*, August 30, 1993, p. 62." A statement about Livingstone is in endnote [2018].

[2112] Quoted with permission from Weisberg, Harold. *Case Open: The Unanswered JFK Assassination Questions* 171.

[2113] Quoted with permission from Weisberg *Case Open* 167.

[2114] Quoted with permission from Weisberg *Case Open* 166.

[2115] Quoted with permission after payment, from Posner *Case Closed* xiii. Copyright notice is in endnote [1039].

[2116] Quoted with permission after payment, from Posner *Case Closed* xvi. Copyright notice is in endnote [1039].

[2117] Posner *Case Closed* 52.

[2118] Posner *Case Closed* 135.

[2119] Quoted with permission after payment, from Posner *Case Closed* footnote on 202. Copyright notice is in endnote [1039].

[2120] Quoted with permission after payment, from Posner *Case Closed* 219-220. Copyright notice is in endnote [1039].

[2121] Scanned image of the author's purchased hardcover book's dust jacket, half size. The book is 7.1" wide, this is 3.55".

[2122] Quoted with permission after payment, from Bugliosi, Vincent. *Reclaiming History: The Assassination of President John F. Kennedy*, text on inside rear flap of dust jacket. Copyright notice is in endnote [1788].

[2123] Quoted with permission after payment, from Bugliosi *Reclaiming History* xlv. Copyright notice is in endnote [1788].

[2124] Quoted with permission after payment, from Bugliosi *Reclaiming History* xliv including its footnote, and xlv. Copyright notice is in endnote [1788].

[2125] Scanned image of the CD-ROM in a pocket inside the back cover of the author's purchased Bugliosi *Reclaiming History*, half size. The source image is 4.9" square, this is 2.45".

[2126] Quoted with permission after payment, from Bugliosi *Reclaiming History* xxxv, which cites "Roberts [Charles], *Truth about the Assassination*, p. 9." Copyright notice is in endnote [1/88].

[2127] The author of *Tragic Truth* experienced a fine reflection of Bugliosi's completeness when the widow of a photographer whose work I purchased and included asked why I was writing a book, since *Reclaiming History* really said all that could be said. I replied that I fully agreed he had nailed the questions "Did he?" and "Alone?", but had ignored "Why?".

[2128] Quoted with permission after payment, from Bugliosi *Reclaiming History* xliv. Copyright notice is in endnote [1788].

[2129] Quoted with permission after payment, from Bugliosi *Reclaiming History* xli. Copyright notice is in endnote [1788].

[2130] Quoted with permission after payment, from Bugliosi *Reclaiming History* xxxviii. Copyright notice is in endnote [1788].

[2131] Bugliosi *Reclaiming History* 627-628.

[2132] Quoted with permission after payment, from Bugliosi *Reclaiming History* The endnote to "Governor Connally's reaction" on page 475 of the printed book is on pages 321-322 of the file Endnotes.pdf on the CD-ROM enclosed in a pocket inside the book's back cover. Copyright notice is in endnote [1788].

[2133] Quoted with permission after payment, from Bugliosi *Reclaiming History* 785. Copyright notice is in endnote [1788].

[2134] Quoted with permission after payment, from Bugliosi *Reclaiming History* 936. Copyright notice is in endnote [1788].

[2135] Quoted with permission after payment, from Bugliosi *Reclaiming History* 937n. Copyright notice is in endnote [1788].

[2136] Quoted with permission after payment, from Bugliosi *Reclaiming History* 938, citing "CE 1787, 23 H 399, Secret Service interview of Marina Oswald on December 3, 1963." Copyright notice is in endnote [1788].

[2137] Quoted with permission after payment, from Bugliosi *Reclaiming History* 948-949. Copyright notice is in endnote [1788].

[2138] Quoted with permission after payment, from Bugliosi *Reclaiming History* 949. Copyright notice is in endnote [1788].

[2139] Quoted with permission after payment, from Bugliosi *Reclaiming History* 974. Copyright notice is in endnote [1788].

[2140] Quoted with permission after payment, from Bugliosi *Reclaiming History* 1461. Copyright notice is in endnote [1788].

[2141] Bugliosi *Reclaiming History* xxxi.

[2142] Quoted with permission after payment, from Pipes, Daniel. *Conspiracy: How the Paranoid Style Flourishes and Where It Comes From*, page 1.

[2143] Quoted with permission after payment, from Pipes 20, with note on 207: "Henry Campbell Black, *Black's Law Dictionary*, 4th ed. (St. Paul, Minn.: West Publishing, 1951), p. 382."

[2144] Quoted with permission after payment, from Pipes 21, with note on 207: "The German term *Verschworungsmythos* ('myth of conspiracy') serves better than the English *conspiracy theory*, for it more directly points to the imaginary content.

[2145] Quoted with permission after payment, from Pipes note to 15 on 206: "*The Washington Post*, 19 May 1991."

[2146] Quoted with permission after payment, from Pipes note to 15 on 206: "*Time*, 13 January 1992, reports 73 percent believing in a conspiracy and 72 percent suspecting an official cover-up; *The New York Times*, 4 February 1992, reports 77 percent and 75 percent, respectively."

[2147] Quoted with permission after payment, from Pipes 14-15.

[2148] Quoted with permission after payment, from Pipes note to 16 on 206: "*The New York Times Magazine, 17 November 1996.*"

[2149] Quoted with permission after payment, from Pipes, who lists Internet discussion groups and World Wide Web sites in his Appendix C, including this on page 200: "John F. Kennedy assassination: alt.conspiracy.jfk. Many sites provide old documentation; this one monitors current thinking."

[2150] Quoted with permission after payment, from Pipes note to page 17 on page 206: "Posner, *Case Closed*, p. xi".

[2151] Quoted with permission after payment, from Pipes 16-17.

[2152] Quoted with permission after payment, from Pipes note to 167 on 231: "Edward Jay Epstein, *Inquest...*; Mark Lane, *Rush to Judgment...*"

[2153] Quoted with permission after payment, from Pipes note to 167 on 232: "Thomas C. Buchanan, *Who Killed Kennedy?...*; Joachim Joesten, *Oswald: Assassin or Fall Guy?...*; Sylvia Meagher, *Accessories after the Fact: The Warren Commission, the Authorities, and the Report...*; and Harold Weisberg, *Whitewash, the Report on the Warren Report...*"

[2154] Quoted with permission after payment, from Pipes note to 167 on 232: "Jim Garrison, quoted in Gerald Posner, *Case Closed... 443.*"

[2155] Quoted with permission after payment, from Pipes note to 167 on 232: "Steven E. Ambrose, 'Writers on the Grassy Knoll: A Reader's Guide,' *The New York Times Book Review*, 2 February 1992."

[2156] Quoted with permission after payment, from Pipes note to 168 on 232: "Posner, *Case Closed*, p. x."

[2157] Quoted with permission after payment, from Pipes 166-168.

[2158] Quoted with permission after payment, from Pipes note to 183 on 234: "Charles Krauthammer, ''JFK': A Lie, But Harmless,' *The Washington Post*, 10 January 1992."

[2159] Quoted with permission after payment, from Pipes 183.

[2160] Lambert, Patricia. *False Witness: The Real Story of Jim Garrison's Investigation and Oliver Stone's Film JFK.*

[2161] TESTIMONY OF MAX E. CLARK on *WCH* VIII 354-355.

[2162] TESTIMONY OF GEORGE A. BOUHE on *WCH* VIII 362.

[2163] TESTIMONY OF ANNA N. MELLER on *WCH* VIII 381.

[2164] TESTIMONY OF EVERETT D. GLOVER on *WCH* X 23.

[2165] AFFIDAVIT OF ALEXANDER KLEINLERER on *WCH* XI 122-123.

[2166] TESTIMONY OF ELENA A. HALL on *WCH* VIII 394.

[2167] TESTIMONY OF JOHN RAYMOND HALL on *WCH* VIII 414.

2168 TESTIMONY OF MRS. FRANK H. RAY (VALENTINA) on *WCH* VIII 422.

2169 *WCH* VIII 418 (Valentina Ray), quoting her husband Frank Ray.

2170 TESTIMONY OF GEORGE S. DE MOHRENSCHILDT on *WCH* IX 236.

2171 *WCH* IX 237 (George S. De Mohrenschildt).

2172 *WCH* IX 242 (George S. De Mohrenschildt).

2173 TESTIMONY OF JEANNE DE MOHRENSCHILDT on *WCH* IX 308-309.

2174 TESTIMONY OF MRS. DONALD (ALEXANDRA DE MOHRENSCHILDT TAYLOR) GIBSON on *WCH* XI 128.

2175 Quoted with permission after payment of $75 (for 58 words), from Douglas, John, and Mark Olshaker. *The Anatomy of Motive: The FBI's Legendary Mindhunter Explores the Key to Understanding and Catching Violent Criminals* 249. Copyright notice supplied by publisher: "Reprinted with the permission of Scribner, a Division of Simon & Schuster, Inc., from THE ANATOMY OF MOTIVE by John Douglas with [*sic*] Mark Olshaker. Copyright © 1999 by Mindhunter, Inc. All rights reserved."

2176 Quoted with permission from Sorensen, Theodore C. *The Kennedy Legacy* 100.

2177 Quoted with permission after payment, from King, Stephen. *11/22/63: A Novel* 845. Copyright notice is in endnote [148].

2178 Quoted with permission after payment, from Warren, pages 366-367. Copyright notice is in endnote [211].

2179 Quoted with permission after payment, from Warren 362. Copyright notice is in endnote [211].

2180 Quoted with permission after payment, from Warren 366. Copyright notice is in endnote [211].

2181 Quoted with permission from McMillan 567. Permission statement is in endnote [150].

2182 Transcribed from *Cronkite Remembers*, a CBS News Special Presentation television broadcast on January 26, 1997, and printed here with the gracious permission (without charging me a fee!) of CBS News.

2183 Transcribed from *Cronkite Remembers*, as above, and printed courtesy of CBS News.

2184 The author's letter to Walter Cronkite, 04 Dec. 1997.

2185 Cronkite, Walter. Reply to the author, 21 July 1998.

2186 The author's reply to Walter Cronkite, 30 July 1998.

2187 This strip was in newspapers on 11 Dec. 1993. This book's image was purchased and is reprinted with the permission of UNIVERSAL UCLICK. DOONESBURY © 1993 G. B. Trudeau. All rights reserved.

2188 Unless otherwise noted, information in this section is from the *Warren Report* Appendix XVI: "A Biography of Jack Ruby" on *WR* pages 779-806.

2189 TESTIMONY OF HYMAN RUBENSTEIN [Jack's oldest brother] on *WCH* XV 10.

2190 Same as previous note; also see *WCH* XV 25.

2191 *WR* 788, which cites *CE* 1241, an FBI report on *WCH* XXII 351.

2192 Quoted with permission from Adelson, Alan. *The Ruby-Oswald Affair*, as shown in advertisement on 9th page of photo insert section; also see *WCH* XV 25.

2193 *WR* 790.

2194 *WR* 790.

2195 *WR* 793-794, which cites *CE* 1182, an FBI report on *WCH* XXII 296.

2196 *WR* 786, 789, and *WCH* XV 28 (Hyman Rubenstein).

2197 *WR* 794.

2198 *WR* 795.

2199 Photo of Ruby and two entertainers was obtained from the National Archives and Records Administration, so is in the public domain. If you carefully study the young lady on the right and look ahead one page, you will know who she is.

2200 *WR* 795.

2201 *WR* 800-801.

2202 Introduction to "A Biography of Jack Ruby" on *WR* 779.

2203 Posner *Case Closed* 368-371.

2204 Quoted with permission after payment, from Bugliosi, Vincent. *Four Days in November: The Assassination of President John F. Kennedy* 274, citing "CE 2303, 25 H 245; 13 H 333, WCT Andrew Armstrong Jr."; which was reprinted from Bugliosi, Vincent. *Reclaiming History: The Assassination of President John F. Kennedy* 172, with same citations. Copyright notice is in endnote [1767].

2205 TESTIMONY OF MR. JACK RUBY on *WCH* V 189.

2206 Quoted with permission after payment, from Posner *Case Closed* 378, which cites "Testimony of A. M. Eberhardt, *WCH* Vol. XIII, p. 189; testimony of Arthur William Watherwax, *WCH* Vol. XV, p. 568." Copyright notice is in endnote [1039].

2207 Quoted with permission after payment, from Posner *Case Closed* 378, which cites "Testimony of Jack Ruby, *WCH* Vol. V, p. 189." Copyright notice is in endnote [1039].

2208 Photo was obtained from the National Archives and Records Administration, so is in the public domain.

2209 Quoted with permission from Douglass, James W. *JFK and the Unspeakable: Why He Died and Why It Matters* 295.

2210 Adelson, page 7.

2211 Quoted with permission after payment, from Posner *Case Closed* 387 388. Copyright notice is in endnote [1039].

2212 Photo of Karen 'Little Lynn' Bennett Carlin is in the National Archives and Records Administration, so is public domain.

[2213] Quoted with permission after payment, from Bugliosi *Four Days* 9, citing "Hall (C. Ray) Exhibit No. 3, 20 H 47" and "13 H 204, WCT Bruce Ray Carlin; 13 H 206, 210, WCT Karen Bennett Carlin."; which was reprinted from Bugliosi *Reclaiming History* 8, with the same citations. Copyright notice for *Four Days* is in endnote [1767].

[2214] Quoted with permission after payment, from Posner *Case Closed* 391. Copyright notice is in endnote [1039].

[2215] Also noted by author James Reston, Jr., in his featured article "Was Connally the Real Target?" in *TIME* magazine, 28 Nov. 1988, page 44.

[2216] Adelson 11.

[2217] Quoted with permission after payment, from Posner *Case Closed* 392-393. Copyright notice is in endnote [1039].

[2218] Photo is in the collection of the National Archives and Records Administration, so is in the public domain.

[2219] Bugliosi *Four Days* 425, which was reprinted from Bugliosi *Reclaiming History* 265.

[2220] Images scanned from CE 2420 (front) and 2421 (time-stamped back) on *WCH* XXV 523. Coming from that US Federal government source, this pair in the public domain.

[2221] Testimony of Doyle E. Lane on *WCH* XIII 221-226.

[2222] Quoted with permission after payment, from Posner *Case Closed* 393-394. Copyright notice is in endnote [1039].

[2223] Quoted with permission after payment, from Manchester, William. *The Death of a President* 522-523, for which the permission acknowledgement is in endnote [17].

[2224] Quoted with permission after payment, from Posner *Case Closed* 395. Copyright notice is in endnote [1039].

[2225] Robert Jackson, photographer for the *Dallas Times Herald*, won a Pulitzer Prize for this famous photo. For a reasonable price and a copy of this book, he graciously sold this author the right to show his photo — very much appreciated!

[2226] Quoted with permission from the oral history of Lieutenant Elmo L. Cunningham in Sneed, Larry A. *No More Silence: An Oral History of the Assassination of President Kennedy* 280.

[2227] Testimony of Barnard S. Clardy on *WCH* XII 412-413.

[2228] Quoted with permission after payment, from Posner *Case Closed* 395-396. Copyright notice is in endnote [1039].

[2229] Testimony of J. W. Fritz on *WCH* IV 243.

[2230] Quoted with permission after payment, from Bugliosi *Four Days* 455-456, citing "Dean Exhibit No. 5010, 19 H 440" and "13 H 67-68, WCT Forrest V. Sorrels"; which was reprinted from Bugliosi *Reclaiming History* 284. For more on Ruby's statement, see also Sabato, Larry J. *The Kennedy Half-Century: The Presidency, Assassination, and Lasting Legacy of John F. Kennedy* 29. Copyright notice for *Four Days* is in endnote [1767].

[2231] Quoted with permission after payment, from Bugliosi *Four Days* 505, citing "Hall (C. Ray) Exhibit No. 3, 20 H 57"; which was reprinted from Bugliosi *Reclaiming History* 315. Copyright notice is in endnote [1767].

[2232] Bugliosi *Four Days* 499, which was reprinted from Bugliosi *Reclaiming History* 311. Copyright notice is in endnote [1767].

[2233] Testimony of Mr. Jack Ruby, *WCH* V 181-213.

[2234] *WCH* V 192 (Jack Ruby).

[2235] *WCH* V 199 (Jack Ruby).

[2236] Quoted with permission from Cannon, James. *Time and Chance: Gerald Ford's Appointment with History* 76-77.

[2237] *WCH* V 207-208 (Jack Ruby).

[2238] Epstein, Edward. *Inquest* (hc) 25, which cites "*N.Y. Times*, June 8, 1964, p. 21:4."

[2239] Quoted with permission from oral history of Sergeant Gerald L. Hill in Sneed 301-302.

[2240] Quoted with permission from Gertz, Elmer. *Moment of Madness: The People vs. Jack Ruby* 66, which credits for trial information: "Kaplan, John, and Jon R. Waltz. *The Trial of Jack Ruby*."

[2241] Posner *Case Closed* 401.

[2242] Posner *Case Closed* 401.

[2243] Manchester *Death* 634. This form with a key word from the book's title is used because more than one book by the author is cited in these notes.

[2244] Adelson 37.

[2245] Quoted with permission from Adelson 6.

[2246] Quoted from Oswald, Robert L., with Myrick and Barbara Land. *Lee: A Portrait of Lee Harvey Oswald by His Brother* 216-217. This source was described in endnote [68].

[2247] Quoted with permission from Sneed, Larry A. *No More Silence: An Oral History of the Assassination of President Kennedy* 29-30.

[2248] Graves (L.C.) Exhibit No. 5003-B, FBI report of Dallas Homicide Detective's statement on 11/24/63, on *WCH* XX 23.

— 10 — Presidents, Not Precedents

[2249] Quoted with permission after payment, from Warren, Earl. *The Memoirs of Earl Warren* 363. Copyright notice is in endnote [211].

[2250] http://en.wikipedia.org/wiki/Circulatory_system accessed on 2014/12/29.

[2251] Roper, Professor Jon. *The Complete Illustrated Guide to the Presidents of America*, page 121.

[2252] Vincent Bugliosi in *Reclaiming History: The Assassination of President John F. Kennedy*, pages 117-118, part of which was reprinted as *Four Days in November: The Assassination of President John F. Kennedy* 186-187, compacts most of this chapter's meat into one massive two-page-bottom footnote meatloaf, ending with this fact.

[2253] Zirbel, Craig I. *The Texas Connection* 32.

1835: LAWRENCE – JACKSON

[2254] Gaines, Ann Graham. *Andrew Jackson: Our Seventh President* 5-6.

[2255] Marsico, Katie. *Andrew Jackson* 31-32.

[2256] Gaines 17-18.

[2257] Meacham, Jon. *American Lion: Andrew Jackson in the White House* 35-36.

[2258] James, Marquis. *The Life of Andrew Jackson* 352.

[2259] Gaines 23.

[2260] Portrait (before photography) is from the Library of Congress, in the public domain.

[2261] Quoted with permission from Clarke, James W. *American Assassins: The Darker Side of Politics* 195, which cites "'Trial of Richard Lawrence,' in *Assassination and Insanity: Guiteau's Case Examined and Compared with Analogous Cases from the Earlier to the Present Times,* ed. William R. Smith (Washington, D.C., 1881), pp. 26-80. See also United States v. Richard Lawrence (March 1835), Circuit Court, District of Columbia, Case No. 15, 577; *Niles Register,* vol. 48, 1836; and *Criminal Appearances* 119 (March 1835), United States District Court of the District of Columbia, Record Group 21, National Archives."

[2262] Quoted with permission after payment, from Brands, H. W. *Andrew Jackson: His Life and Times*, pages 503-504. Copyright notice supplied by publisher: "Excerpt(s) from ANDREW JACKSON: HIS LIFE AND TIMES by H.W. Brands, copyright © 2005 by H.W. Brands. Used by permission of Doubleday, an imprint of the Knopf Doubleday Publishing Group, a division of Penguin Random House LLC. All rights reserved. Any third party use of this material, outside of this publication, is prohibited. Interested parties must apply directly to Penguin Random House LLC for permission."

[2263] The drawing, shown on Wikipedia, is in the collection of the Library of Congress, thus is in the public domain.

[2264] Quoted with permission after payment, from Brands 504. Copyright notice is in endnote [2262].

[2265] Cole, Donald B. *The Presidency of Andrew Jackson*, page 221.

[2266] Quoted with permission after payment, from Brands 505. Copyright notice is in endnote [2262].

[2267] Quoted as fair use after due diligence from James, Marquis *The Life of Andrew Jackson*, page 685. The author's copyright agent has tried without success to find either a copyright database entry or the book's publisher, Garden City Publishing. Having performed due diligence, the author claims the right to use this and a following quote, both very short, as fair use. If any valid copyright holder arises, please see CREDITS AND PERMISSIONS on page ii.

[2268] Quoted with permission after payment, from Brands 505. Copyright notice is in endnote [2262].

[2269] Quoted after due diligence from James, Marquis 685. See the citation in endnote [2267] above.

[2270] Quoted with permission from Clarke 195, which cites Smith, ed. (above) 'Trial of Richard Lawrence,' in *Assassination and Insanity: Guiteau's Case Examined and Compared with Analogous Cases from the Earlier to the Present* Times 33.

[2271] Quoted with permission from Clarke 196, which cites "Smith, ed., 'Trial,' pp. 30-31."

[2272] Quoted with permission from Clarke 196, which cites "Smith, ed., 'Trial,' p. 31."

[2273] Quoted with permission from Clarke 196, which cites "Smith, ed., 'Trial,' p. 30."

[2274] Quoted with permission from Clarke 196, which cites "Smith, ed., 'Trial,' p. 35."

[2275] Quoted with permission from Clarke 197, which cites "Smith, ed., 'Trial,' p. 31."

[2276] Quoted with permission from Clarke 197, which cites "Smith, ed., 'Trial,' pp. 32, 34, 38."

[2277] Quoted with permission from Clarke 197, which cites "Smith, ed., 'Trial,' p. 30."

[2278] Quoted with permission from Clarke 197-198, which cites "Smith, ed., 'Trial,' p. 32."

[2279] Quoted with permission from Clarke 198, which cites "Carlton Jackson, 'Another Time, Another Place—The Attempted Assassination of President Andrew Jackson,' *Tennessee Historical Quarterly* 26 (Summer 1967): 188."

[2280] Quoted with permission from Clarke 198.

[2281] Photo in the Library of Congress is in the public domain.

[2282] Quoted with permission from Clarke 198.

[2283] Quoted as fair use (for brevity) from http://en.wikipedia.org/wiki/Richard_Lawrence_(failed_assassin) on 2012/10/06.

1865: BOOTH – LINCOLN

[2284] The famous "cracked plate" photo is preserved in the Library of Congress, so is in the public domain.

[2285] Speer, Lonnie. *Portals to Hell: Military Prisons of the Civil War*. Battle deaths were 204,000 (Speer's note 8 on page 342) and "56,000 prisoners of war died in confinement" (page xiv).

[2286] Speer. Enlistments and captured are in note 5 on page 341; deaths are in note 8 on page 342.

[2287] Quoted 38 words as fair use from Carman, Syrett, and Wishy. *A History of the American People*. Vol. II 57.

[2288] Quoted with permission after payment, from Bishop, Jim. *The Day Lincoln Was Shot* (hereinafter *Lincoln*) 62.

[2289] Quoted with permission from Pinsker, Matthew. *Lincoln's Sanctuary: Abraham Lincoln and the Soldiers' Home* 181-182.

[2290] Quoted with permission after payment, from Bishop *Lincoln* 64-65.

[2291] Quoted with permission after payment, from Bishop *Lincoln* 76.

[2292] Quoted with permission after payment, from Bishop *Lincoln* 77-78.

[2293] Quoted with permission after payment, from Bishop *Lincoln* 80.

[2294] Photo, moderately cropped, is from the National Archives and Records Administration, so is in the public domain.

[2295] Quoted with permission after payment, from Oates, Stephen B. *With Malice Toward None: A Biography of Abraham Lincoln*, page 410.

[2296] Quoted with permission after payment, from Kunhardt, Dorothy Meserve, and Philip B. Kunhardt, Jr. *Twenty Days: A Narrative in Text and Pictures of the Assassination of Abraham Lincoln and the Twenty Days and Nights that followed – The Nation in Mourning, the Long Trip Home to Springfield*, page 35. Copyright notice supplied by publisher: "Brief excerpts from pp. 35, 189, 190 from TWENTY DAYS by DOROTHY MESERVE KUNHARDT and PHILIP B. KUNHARDT, JR. Copyright © 1965 by Dorothy Meserve Kunhardt and Philip B. Kunhardt, Jr.; renewed © 1993 by Philip B. Kunhardt, Jr. Reprinted by permission of HarperCollins Publishers."

[2297] Quoted with permission after payment, from Oates 411.

[2298] Quoted with permission after payment, from Bishop *Lincoln* 82.

[2299] Wilson, Francis. *John Wilkes Booth: Fact and Fiction of Lincoln's Assassination*, page 25.

[2300] Quoted with permission from Wilson 27. Copyright notice is in endnote [11].

[2301] Quoted with permission after payment, from Bishop *Lincoln* 90.

[2302] Quoted with permission after payment, from Bishop *Lincoln* 90-91.

[2303] Quoted with permission from Wilson 30. Copyright notice is in endnote [11].

[2304] Quoted with permission after payment, from Bishop *Lincoln* 192.

[2305] Quoted with permission from Clarke, James W. *American Assassins: The Darker Side of Politics*, page 34.

[2306] Quoted with permission after payment, from Kunhardt *Twenty Days* 190. Copyright notice is in endnote [2296].

[2307] Quoted with permission after payment, from Bishop *Lincoln* 205-206.

[2308] Quoted as fair use (for brevity: 27 words) from Winik, Jay. *April 1865: The Month That Saved America* 226. Please see CREDITS AND PERMISSIONS on page ii.

[2309] Quoted with permission after payment, from Kunhardt *Twenty Days* 190. Copyright notice is in endnote [2296].

[2310] Bishop *Lincoln* 17-18.

[2311] Quoted with permission after payment, from Bishop *Lincoln* 222.

[2312] Quoted with permission after payment, from Kunhardt *Twenty Days* 189. Copyright notice is in endnote [2296].

[2313] Photo from the Library of Congress, which credits "Photo by Carol M. Highsmith", a living photographer who has donated all her photos to the LOC, cropped to maximize our view of the Deringer, is in the public domain.

[2314] Bishop *Lincoln* 185.

[2315] Clark, Champ, and the Editors of Time-Life Books. *The Assassination: Death of the President*, page 65. I wanted to quote verbatim from this elegant source, but my copyright agent and I did not receive any reply to our requests for permission.

[2316] Quoted with permission after payment, from Bishop *Lincoln* 185.

[2317] Quoted with permission after payment, from Lorant, Stefan. *The Glorious Burden*, page 278, caption for similar woodcut from *Harper's Weekly*, April 29, 1865.

[2318] Quoted with permission from Howe, Randy. *Flags of the Fifty States: Their Colorful Histories and Significance*, page 38.

[2319] Quoted with permission after payment, from Lorant 278.

[2320] Bishop *Lincoln* 236.

[2321] This contemporary drawing, slightly cropped, from the Library of Congress, is in the public domain.

[2322] Quoted with permission after payment of $150, an unusually large amount for two very brief quotations, from Goodwin, Doris Kearns. *Team of Rivals: The Political Genius of Abraham Lincoln* 739. Copyright notice supplied by publisher: "Reprinted with the permission of Simon & Schuster, Inc. from TEAM OF RIVALS: THE POLITICAL GENIUS OF ABRAHAM LINCOLN by Doris Kearns Goodwin. Copyright © 2005 by Blithedale Productions, Inc.. All rights reserved."

[2323] This small quotation relates a historical fact. The author and his copyright agent could not find a way to contact the original author or publisher. Because it is both fact and brief, it is shown as fair use from Bak, Richard. *The Day Lincoln Was Shot: An Illustrated Chronicle*, page 97.

[2324] Quoted with permission after payment, from Goodwin 741. Copyright notice is in endnote [2322].

[2325] Quoted with permission after payment, from Lorant 279, which credits *Harper's Weekly*, May 6, 1865.

[2326] Quoted with permission from Swanson, James L. *Manhunt: The Twelve-Day Chase for Lincoln's Killer* 323.

[2327] Drawing from the Library of Congress, slightly cropped, is in the public domain. Its bottom margin holds the caption: "Capture of Harrold and the Shooting of Booth in the Barn of Garaths Farm by a detachment of the 16th New York Cavalry under the Order of Col Baker".

[2328] Quoted with permission after payment, from Lorant 282, which credits *Harper's Weekly*, May 13, 1865.

[2329] Quoted with kind permission from Lewis, Lloyd. *The Assassination of Lincoln: History and Myth*, page 187.

[2330] Time-Life Books, The Editors of. *Assassination: True Crime* 52.

[2331] Quoted with permission from Wilson 8. Copyright notice is in endnote [11].

[2332] Quoted with permission from Lewis 129.

[2333] Television movie: *The Day Lincoln Was Shot* on TNT, 12 Apr. 1998.

[2334] Photo scanned with permission from Swanson, James L., and Daniel R. Weinberg. *Lincoln's Assassins: Their Trial and Execution*, figure 192 on page 110, which credits "Courtesy of Christie's". It has been slightly cropped to fit this book.

[2335] Henry Rathbone's experience at the Lincoln Assassination and his murder of Clara is described in the biography *Worst Seat in the House: Henry Rathbone's Front Row View of the Lincoln Assassination* by Caleb Stephens.

[2336] Clark, Champ, and the Editors of Time-Life Books. *The Assassination: Death of the President*, page 138.

[2337] Warren, Earl. *The Memoirs of Earl Warren* 368-369. Copyright notice is in endnote [211]. The distances are corrected an iota to match the exhibits and conclusions in the *Warren Report*.

[2338] Rattenbury and Hall 32.

1881: GUITEAU – GARFIELD

[2339] Quoted with permission after payment, from Vowell, Sarah. *Assassination Vacation* 125. Copyright notice supplied by publisher: "Reprinted with the permission of Simon & Schuster, Inc. from ASSASSINATION VACATION by Sarah Vowell. Copyright © 2005 Sarah Vowell."

[2340] Quoted with permission after payment, from Millard, Candice. *Destiny of the Republic* 30. Copyright notice supplied by publisher: "Excerpt(s) from DESTINY OF THE REPUBLIC: A TALE OF MADNESS, MEDICINE AND THE MURDER OF A PRESIDENT by Candice Millard, copyright © 2011 by Candice Millard. Used by permission of Doubleday, an imprint of the Knopf Doubleday Publishing Group, a division of Penguin Random House LLC. All rights reserved. Any third party use of this material, outside of this publication, is prohibited. Interested parties must apply directly to Penguin Random House LLC for permission."

[2341] Quoted with permission after payment, from Lorant, Stefan. *The Glorious Burden*, page 345.

[2342] Photo of James A. Garfield, cropped, from Library of Congress.

[2343] Quoted with permission from Ackerman, Kenneth. *Dark Horse* 112, which cites Warner Bateman to John Sherman, June 12, 1880. Sherman Papers, Library of Congress.

[2344] Quoted with permission after payment, from Millard 45. Copyright notice is in endnote [2340].

[2345] Quoted with permission from Ackerman 116.

[2346] Quoted with permission from Ackerman footnote 9 on page 94.

[2347] Quoted with permission after payment, from Vowell 131-132. Copyright notice is in endnote [2339].

[2348] Quoted with permission after payment, from Vowell 132. Copyright notice is in endnote [2339].

[2349] Quoted with permission after payment, from Millard, page 167, which cites Reeves, Thomas C. *Gentleman Boss: The Life and Times of Chester Alan Arthur*, page 241. Copyright notice for Millard is in endnote [2340].

[2350] Quoted with permission after payment, from Lorant 363.

[2351] Quoted with permission after payment, from Millard 88. Copyright notice is in endnote [2340].

[2352] Quoted with permission after payment, from Vowell 167. Copyright notice is in endnote [2339].

[2353] Quoted with permission after payment, from Millard 1. Copyright notice is in endnote [2340].

[2354] Quoted with permission after payment, from Vowell 167-168. Copyright notice is in endnote [2339].

[2355] Quoted with permission from Ackerman 345-346, which cites *New York Herald*, Oct. 6, 1881.

[2356] Quoted with permission from Ackerman 347, which cites Guiteau testimony, *Report of the Proceedings in the Case of the United States v. Charles J. Guiteau, Tried in the Supreme Court of the District of Columbia, Holding a Criminal Term, and Beginning November 14, 1881* (hereafter *United States v. Guiteau*), p. 587.

[2357] Quoted with permission from Ackerman 354, which cites Guiteau testimony, *United States v. Guiteau*, p. 636.

[2358] Guiteau's pistol has been lost. This photo of a .44 English Bulldog revolver, but without his fancy ivory handle, was purchased from Corbis and very lightly cropped: © Corbis.

[2359] Quoted with permission from Ackerman 355, which cites Guiteau testimony, *United States v. Guiteau*, p. 637.

[2360] Quoted with permission from Ackerman 355, which cites Guiteau testimony, *United States v. Guiteau*, p. 637.

[2361] Quoted with permission from Ackerman 365, which cites Kingsbury, Robert. *The Assassination of James A. Garfield*, p. 9.

[2362] Quoted with permission after payment, from Millard 118, which cites *United States v. Guiteau*, 701. Copyright notice is in endnote [2340].

[2363] Quoted with permission after payment, from Millard 90, which cites Sherman, John. *Recollections of Forty Years in the House, Senate and Cabinet*, 789. Copyright notice for Millard is in endnote [2340].

[2364] Quoted with permission after payment, from Millard 119, which cites Garfield, James A. *The Diary of James A. Garfield*, 4 vols. Edited by Harry James Brown and Frederick D. Williams, June 12, 1881, 4:609. Copyright notice for Millard is in endnote [2340].

[2365] Quoted with permission from Ackerman 357, which cites *New York Herald*, Oct. 6, 1881.

[2366] Quoted with permission from Ackerman 372, which cites *New York Herald*, Oct. 6, 1881; Guiteau testimony, *United States v. Guiteau*, pp. 692-93.

[2367] Quoted with permission from Ackerman 373-374, which cites Guiteau testimony, *United States v. Guiteau*, p. 694.

[2368] Quoted with permission after payment, from Vowell 169-170. Copyright notice is in endnote [2339].

[2369] Quoted with permission from Ackerman 375, which cites *New York Times*, July 3, 1881.

[2370] Quoted with permission from Ackerman 376.

[2371] Quoted with permission from Ackerman footnote 3 on 376.

[2372] Quoted with permission after payment, from Millard 127, which cites "Riggs House is Demolished," *Bryan Times*, July 18, 1911. Copyright notice is in endnote [2340].

[2373] Quoted with permission from Ackerman 377, which cites *New York Herald*, Oct. 6, 1881.

[2374] Quoted with permission after payment, from Millard 129. Copyright notice is in endnote [2340].

[2375] Quoted with permission from Ackerman 377, which cites *New York Herald*, Oct. 6, 1881.

[2376] Drawing, slightly cropped, signed by "W. J. Mathews" from the Library of Congress.

[2377] Quoted with permission after payment, from Millard 131-132, which cites Clark, James C. *The Murder of James A. Garfield: The President's Last Days and the Trial and Execution of His Assassin*, 58. Copyright notice is in endnote [2340].

[2378] Quoted with permission from Ackerman 378, which cites *New York Herald*, Oct. 6, 1881; Blaine testimony, *United States v. Guiteau*, p. 121.

[2379] Quoted with permission from Ackerman 378, which cites Blaine testimony, *United States v. Guiteau*, p. 121.

[2380] Quoted with permission from Ackerman 379, which cites Metropolitan Police Officer Patrick Kearney testimony, *United States v. Guiteau*, p. 187; Rosenberg, Charles E. *The Trial of the Assassin Guiteau: Psychiatry and the Law in the Gilded Age*, pp. 2-3. See also *New York Times* and other newspapers, July 3, 1881.

[2381] Drawing, slightly cropped, credited to "Arthur Berghaus and Charles Upham, July 1881" from the Library of Congress.

[2382] Quoted with permission after payment, from Vowell 160. Copyright notice is in endnote [2339].

[2383] Quoted with permission after payment, from Lorant 361.

[2384] Quoted with permission from Ackerman 392, which cites "*Washington Evening Star*, July 2, 1881; *Chicago Tribune*, July 3, 1881; *Boston Globe*, July 4, 1881; Reeves, Thomas C. *Gentleman Boss: The Life and Times of Chester Alan Arthur*, p. 239. Note slight variations in the wording; I've [Ackerman] used all three versions."

[2385] Quoted with permission from Ackerman 394.

[2386] Cover of magazine dated October 1, 1881, showing Lucretia Arthur caring for her husband, attributed at bottom "From a Sketch by a Staff Artist", from the Library of Congress.

[2387] Quoted with permission after payment, from Lorant 361.

[2388] Quoted with permission from Ackerman 420.

[2389] Quoted with permission after payment, from Vowell 125. Copyright notice is in endnote [2339].

[2390] Quoted with permission after payment, from Millard 217. Copyright notice is in endnote [2340].

[2391] Quoted with permission from Ackerman 427.

[2392] Quoted with permission after payment, from Millard 253. Copyright notice is in endnote [2340].

[2393] Quoted with permission from Ackerman 439.

[2394] Quoted with permission after payment, from Lorant 364.

[2395] Quoted with permission after payment, from Vowell 171. Copyright notice is in endnote [2339].

[2396] Quoted with permission from Ackerman 406, which cites *Chicago Tribune*, July 5, 1881.

[2397] Quoted with permission after payment, from Millard 185, which cites Clark [see Millard 131-132 above], 65. Copyright notice is in endnote [2340].

[2398] Photo is shown through the courtesy of Heritage Auctions, Dallas, cropped from an oval.

[2399] Quoted with permission from Ackerman 444, which cites Guiteau, *United States v. Guiteau*, p. 1160.

[2400] Quoted with permission after payment, from Vowell 175. Copyright notice is in endnote [2339].

[2401] Quoted with permission from Ackerman 408, which cites Rosenberg [see Ackerman 379 above], pp. 54-55, 103.

[2402] Quoted with permission after payment, from Millard 239, which cites Clark [see Millard 131-132 above], 122-23. Copyright notice is in endnote [2340].

[2403] Quoted with permission from Ackerman 444.

[2404] Quoted with permission after payment, from Millard 241. Copyright notice is in endnote [2340].

[2405] Quoted with permission after payment, from Vowell 175-176. Copyright notice is in endnote [2339].

[2406] Quoted with permission after payment, from Millard 242, which cites Rosenberg [see Ackerman 379 above], 233-34. Copyright notice is in endnote [2340].

[2407] Quoted with permission from Fetherling, George. *The Book of Assassins: A Biographical Dictionary from Ancient Times to the Present*, page 175.

[2408] Quoted with permission from Ackerman 446.

1901: CZOLGOSZ – MCKINLEY

[2409] Quoted with permission after payment, from Rauchway, Eric. *Murdering McKinley: The Making of Theodore Roosevelt's America*, from his footnote on page 18. Copyright notice supplied by publisher: "Excerpts from MURDERING MCKINLEY: THE MAKING OF THEODORE ROOSEVELT'S AMERICA by Eric Rauchway. Copyright © 2003 by Eric Rauchway. Reprinted by permission of Hill and Wang, a division of Farrar, Straus and Giroux, LLC."

[2410] Quoted with permission after payment, from Rauchway 34. Copyright notice is in endnote [2409].

[2411] Photo from the Library of Congress, tightly cropped, is in the public domain.

[2412] Quoted with permission after payment, from Vowell, Sarah. *Assassination Vacation*, page 200. Copyright notice is in endnote [2339].

[2413] Quoted with permission after payment, from Rauchway 9-10. Copyright notice is in endnote [2409].

[2414] Quoted with permission after payment, from Rauchway 10. Copyright notice is in endnote [2409].

[2415] Quoted with permission after payment, from Rauchway 10, which cites Theodore Roosevelt, *American Ideals, The Strenuous Life, Realizable Ideals*, National edition, 13:138, 142. Copyright notice for Rauchway is in endnote [2340].

[2416] Quoted with permission after payment, from Rauchway 10, which cites Theodore Roosevelt to Edward Bellamy and Maria Storer, April 17, 1901, *The Letters of Theodore Roosevelt*, ed. Elting E. Morison et al, 3:57. Copyright notice for Rauchway is in endnote [2409].

[2417] Quoted with permission from Fetherling, George. *The Book of Assassins: A Biographical Dictionary from Ancient Times to the Present* 111.

[2418] Quoted with permission after payment, from Rauchway 3. Copyright notice is in endnote [2409].

[2419] Quoted with permission from Fetherling 110-111.

[2420] Quoted with permission after payment, from Rauchway 3. Copyright notice is in endnote [2409].

[2421] Drawing from the Library of Congress, cropped here to the central third, is in the public domain.

[2422] Quoted with permission after payment, from Vowell 233. Copyright notice is in endnote [2339].

[2423] Quoted with permission after payment, from Millard, Candice. *Destiny of the Republic* 249. Copyright notice is in endnote [2340].

[2424] Emerson, Jason. *Giant in the Shadows: The Life of Robert T. Lincoln*.

[2425] Quoted with permission after payment, from Lorant, Stefan. *The Glorious Burden* 474.

[2426] Quoted with permission after payment, from Vowell 230. Copyright notice is in endnote [2339].

[2427] Quoted with permission after payment, from Lorant, Stefan. *The Glorious Burden* 474.

[2428] Quoted with permission after payment, from Rauchway 27. Copyright notice is in endnote [2409].

[2429] Quoted with permission after payment, from Vowell 223. Copyright notice is in endnote [2339].

[2430] Quoted with permission after payment, from Vowell 226. Copyright notice is in endnote [2339].

[2431] Quoted with permission after payment, from Vowell 226. Copyright notice is in endnote [2339].

[2432] Quoted with permission after payment, from Rauchway 27-28. Copyright notice is in endnote [2409].

[2433] Quoted with permission after payment, from Lorant 475.

[2434] Quoted with permission after payment, from Rauchway 16-17. Copyright notice is in endnote [2409].

[2435] Photo is cropped from the left-hand of four portraits in a montage titled "Leon Czolgosz, who shot President McKinley. The above pictures are snap-shots of the assassin taken just after his arrest." purchased from the Library of Congress.

[2436] Fetherling 110.

[2437] Quoted with permission after payment, from Rauchway 19, which cites testimony of James Quackenbush, transcript of Supreme Court, Erie County, *The People of the State of New York* against *Leon F. Czolgosz*, p. 65. Copyright notice is in endnote [2409].

[2438] Quoted with permission after payment, from Rauchway 30. Copyright notice is in endnote [2409].

[2439] Quoted with permission after payment, from Rauchway 20. Copyright notice is in endnote [2409].

[2440] Quoted with permission after payment, from Rauchway 26-27, which took the doctors' declaration from scrapbook of Lloyd Vernon Briggs, Crerar Manuscript no. 80, University of Chicago Special Collections, p. 81. Copyright notice is in endnote [2409].

[2441] Quoted with permission after payment, from Rauchway 39. Copyright notice is in endnote [2409].

[2442] Quoted with permission after payment, from Rauchway 38. Copyright notice is in endnote [2409].

[2443] Quoted with permission after payment, from Rauchway 38. Copyright notice is in endnote [2409].

[2444] Quoted with permission after payment, from Vowell 233. Copyright notice is in endnote [2339].

[2445] Quoted with permission after payment, from Rauchway 42, which cites one of the doctors: "Carlos F. MacDonald, with Edward Anthony Spitzka, "The Trial, Execution, Autopsy and Mental Status of Leon F. Czolgosz, alias Fred Nieman, the Assassin of President McKinley," *American Journal of Insanity* 58:3 (January 1902), 369-404, esp. 384-85." Copyright notice is in endnote [2409].

[2446] Quoted with permission after payment, from Rauchway 43-44. Copyright notice is in endnote [2409].

[2447] Quoted with permission after payment, from Rauchway 45. Copyright notice is in endnote [2409].

[2448] Quoted with permission after payment, from Rauchway 47. Copyright notice is in endnote [2409].

[2449] Quoted with permission from Fetherling 112.

[2450] Quoted with permission after payment, from Vowell 215. Copyright notice is in endnote [2339].

[2451] The definition of insanity from an 1843 English court, by now universally applied in English-speaking courts.

[2452] Quoted with permission after payment, from Rauchway 50. Copyright notice is in endnote [2409].

[2453] Quoted with permission after payment, from Rauchway 51-52, which cites MacDonald and Spitzka [see Rauchway 42 above], 373. Copyright notice is in endnote [2409].

[2454] Quoted with permission after payment, from Rauchway 52, which cites trial transcript [see Rauchway 19 above], p. 135. Copyright notice is in endnote [2409].

[2455] Quoted with permission from Fetherling 112.

[2456] Quoted with permission after payment, from Rauchway 53. Copyright notice is in endnote [2409].

[2457] Quoted with permission from Clarke, James. *American Assassins: The Darker Side of Politics* 39, which cites MacDonald [with Spitzka, see Rauchway 42 above], 375; and Walter Channing, "The Mental State of Czolgosz, the Assassin of President McKinley," *The American Journal of Insanity* 59 (October 1902): 274..

[2458] Quoted with permission after payment, from Rauchway 53, which cites the burial with acid: Charles Hamilton Hughes, "Medical Aspects of the Czolgosz Case," *Alienist and Neurologist* 23 (January 1903), 40-52, esp. 42. Copyright notice is in endnote [2409].

[2459] Quoted with permission after payment, from Rauchway, Preface, pages ix-x. Copyright notice is in endnote [2409].

[2460] Quoted with permission from Fetherling 111.

[2461] Quoted with permission from Fetherling 111.

1912: SCHRANK – T. ROOSEVELT

[2462] Photo from the Theodore Roosevelt Birthplace Historic Site, a National Park Service property, is in the public domain.

[2463] Caption quoted with permission after payment, from Lorant 280. The photo at right is an enlargement of the upper-left corner of the photo at left, credited above.

[2464] Quoted with permission after payment, from Vowell, Sarah. *Assassination Vacation*, page 234. Copyright notice is in endnote [2339].

[2465] Photo from the Library of Congress with "10/4/12" written on it, closely cropped, is in the public domain.

[2466] Quoted with permission after payment, from Rauchway, Eric. *Murdering McKinley: The Making of Theodore Roosevelt's America* 183-184, which cites Oscar King Davis, *Released for Publication: Some Inside Political History of Theodore Roosevelt and His Times, 1898-1918*, 375-78. Copyright notice for Rauchway is in endnote [2409].

[2467] Quoted with permission from Fetherling, George. *The Book of Assassins* 330.

[2468] Clarke, James. *American Assassins: The Darker Side of Politics* 215.

[2469] Quoted with permission after payment, from Rauchway 184. Copyright notice is in endnote [2409].

[2470] This photo of TR's speech manuscript torn by bullet hole was scanned by the author from Lorant 527, which credits the "Theodore Roosevelt Association". As such, at my researcher's suggestion, it is shown as fair use.

[2471] Quoted with permission after payment, from Rauchway 191-192. Copyright notice is in endnote [2409].

[2472] Quoted with permission after payment, from Rauchway 184. Copyright notice is in endnote [2409].

[2473] Quoted with permission after payment, from Rauchway 192. Copyright notice is in endnote [2409].

[2474] Quoted with permission after payment, from Lorant 532.

[2475] Quoted with permission from Fetherling 330.

[2476] en.wikipedia.org/wiki/John_F._Schrank on 2012/04/17. I date Wikipedia references because that source benefits from continual edits and updates. Dates are year/month/day, because "April 17, 2012" would be like "tens, ones, hundreds".

[2477] Photo from the Library of Congress is in the public domain.

[2478] Quoted with permission after payment, from Rauchway 196, which cites "Sanity Board Named to Examine Schrank," *New York Times*, November 13, 1912, p. 9. Copyright notice is in endnote [2409].

[2479] Quoted with permission from Clarke 216.

[2480] Quoted with permission after payment, from Lorant 527.

[2481] Photo from the Library of Congress, tightly cropped, is in the public domain.

[2482] Quoted with permission after payment, from Rauchway 196-197. Copyright notice is in endnote [2409].

[2483] Quoted with permission from Clarke 219, which cites Oliver E. Remy et al., *The Attempted Assassination of Ex-President Theodore Roosevelt*, p. 202.

[2484] Quoted with permission after payment, from Rauchway 197, which cites "Full Text of Assassin's Confession," *New York Times*, November 23, 1912, p. 11. Copyright notice is in endnote [2409].

[2485] Quoted with permission after payment, from Rauchway 197-198, which cites "Do Not Believe Schrank Is Insane," *New York Times*, October 20, 1912, p. 2. Copyright notice is in endnote [2409].

[2486] Quoted with permission after payment, from Rauchway 198, which cites TR to John St. Loe Strachey, December 6, 1912, *The Letters of Theodore Roosevelt*, ed. Elting E. Morison et al, 8 vols, 7:676-77. Copyright notice is in endnote [2409].

[2487] Quoted with permission from Fetherling 331.

[2488] Quoted with permission from Clarke 221.

1933: ZANGARA – PRESIDENT FRANKLIN ROOSEVELT – MAYOR ANTON CERMAK

[2489] Photo from the State Archives of Florida, lightly cropped, purchased from FloridaMemoryStore@dos.myflorida.com.

[2490] Quoted with permission from Clarke, James W. *American Assassins: The Darker Side of Politics* 167, 168.

[2491] Quoted with permission from Fetherling, George. *The Book of Assassins: A Biographical Dictionary from Ancient Times to the Present* 383.

[2492] Quoted with permission from Clarke 168.

[2493] Quoted with permission from Clarke 169.

[2494] Quoted with permission from Clarke 169-170.

[2495] Quoted with permission from Clarke 170.

[2496] Quoted with permission from Clarke 171.

[2497] Quoted with permission from Picchi, Blaise. *The Five Weeks of Giuseppe Zangara: The Man Who Would Assassinate FDR* 55.

[2498] Quoted with permission from Clarke 171, which cites: "Giuseppe Zangara, 'Sworn Statement of Joseph Zangara,' Miami, Dade County, Florida, February 16, 1933, p. 10-11."

[2499] Quoted with permission from Clarke 171, which cites "'Sworn Statement' [full citation above], p. 9."

[2500] Quoted with permission from Picchi 1.

[2501] Quoted with permission from Picchi 8.

[2502] Photo purchased from, and shown courtesy of, the Franklin D. Roosevelt Presidential Library and Museum, Hyde Park.

[2503] Quoted with permission from Picchi 10.

[2504] Quoted with permission from Picchi 11.

[2505] Picchi 14-15.

[2506] Quoted with permission from Picchi 12.

[2507] Quoted with permission from Clarke 171.

[2508] Photo from the Library of Congress is in the public domain.

[2509] Picchi 98, caption for the same photo.

[2510] Quoted with permission from Picchi 14.

[2511] Quoted with permission from Clarke 171-172.

[2512] Quoted with permission from Picchi 15.

[2513] Quoted with permission from Clarke 172.

[2514] Quoted with permission from Picchi 99, caption for the same photo as displayed to the right.

[2515] Photo from the State Archives of Florida, tightly cropped, purchased from FloridaMemoryStore@dos.myflorida.com.

[2516] Quoted with permission from Picchi 26.

[2517] Quoted with permission from Picchi 38.

[2518] Photo from the State Archives of Florida, moderately cropped, purchased from FloridaMemoryStore@dos.myflorida.com.

[2519] Quoted with permission from Clarke 172, which cites "*Newark Evening News*, February 20, 1933, 1 and 3."

[2520] Quoted with permission from Clarke 172, which cites "*Newark Evening News*, February 20, 1933, 3."

[2521] Picchi 131-138, 146-147.

[2522] Quoted with permission from Picchi 138.

[2523] Quoted with permission from Clarke 172.

[2524] Quoted as fair use from http://en.wikipedia.org/wiki/Transferred_intent on 2012/09/29, which cites "http://www.lexisnexis.com/lawschool/study/outlines/html/torts/torts01.htm".

[2525] Quoted with permission from Clarke 172.

[2526] Quoted with permission from Picchi 150.

[2527] Quoted with permission from Clarke 172-173, which cites "*Newark Evening News*, March 10, 1933, 1."

[2528] Quoted with permission from Picchi 190.

[2529] Quoted with permission from Clarke 173.

[2530] Quoted with permission from Picchi 196.

[2531] Photo of the front page of the *Fitchburg* (MA) *Sentinel* was imported from RareNewspapers.com, and is used with the gracious permission of Timothy Hughes Rare & Early Newspapers.

[2532] Quoted with permission from Picchi xi.

[2533] Quoted with permission from Fetherling 383.

[2534] Quoted with permission from Picchi 194.

[2535] Quoted with permission from Clarke 174.

[2536] Quoted with permission from Nelson, Scott Reynolds. *A Nation of Deadbeats: An Uncommon History of America's Financial Disasters*, page 159.

[2537] Quoted with permission from Clarke 174.

1950: COLLAZO AND TORRESOLA – TRUMAN

[2538] Quoted with permission after payment, from McCarthy, Dennis V. N., with Philip W. Smith. *Protecting the President: The Inside Story of a Secret Service Agent*, page 141.

[2539] Photo purchased from Corbis and moderately cropped: © Bettmann/ Corbis.

[2540] Quoted with permission after payment, from Blaine, Gerald, with Lisa McCubbin. *The Kennedy Detail: JFK's Secret Service Agents Break Their Silence*, pages 34-36. Copyright notice is in endnote [1444].

[2541] Quoted with permission after payment, from Blaine with McCubbin 36. Copyright notice is in endnote [1444].

[2542] Hunter, Stephen, and John Bainbridge, Jr. *American Gunfight: The Plot to Kill Harry Truman, and the Shoot-out That Stopped It*, page 33, quoting *The New York Times*, which had quoted an eyewitness.

[2543] Hunter and Bainbridge 66 and 76.

[2544] Quoted with permission after payment, from Hunter and Bainbridge 127. Copyright notice supplied by publisher: "Reprinted with the permission of Simon & Schuster, Inc. from AMERICAN GUNFIGHT: THE PLOT TO KILL HARRY TRUMAN--AND THE SHOOT-OUT THAT STOPPED IT by Stephen Hunter and John Bainbridge. Copyright © 2005 by Stephen Hunter and John Bainbridge, Jr.. All rights reserved."

[2545] Hunter and Bainbridge 49.

[2546] Hunter and Bainbridge 289.

[2547] Quoted with permission after payment, from Hunter and Bainbridge, pages 87-88. Copyright notice is in endnote [2544].

[2548] Daniel, Clifton, editor in chief. *20th Century Day by Day* 690. (The book's editor-in-chief married Margaret Truman in 1956, thereby becoming Harry Truman's son-in-law.)

[2549] Scanned and cropped to highlight this story, from compendium book by The New York Times. *Page One: Major Events 1900-1997 as Presented in The New York Times*, in which the pages are not numbered, but sequenced by date. The right to show this page was purchased for a surprisingly high price from the *NYT*'s agent PARS International Corp., which requires this credit notice: "From The New York Times, November 2, 1950 © 1950 The New York Times. All rights reserved. Used by permission and protected by the Copyright Laws of the United States. The printing, copying, redistribution, or retransmission of this Content without express written permission is prohibited."

[2550] Matthews, James P., and Ernest Schwork, editors. *The Complete Kennedy Saga! Four Books In One!*, page 83 in third "book" titled *Highlights of the Warren Report*.

[2551] http://en.wikipedia.org/wiki/Truman_assassination_attempt, accessed on 2014/11/18. See also Hunter and Bainbridge, page 323.

[2552] http://en.wikipedia.org/wiki/United_States_Capitol_shooting_incident_(1954), accessed on 2014/11/13.

[2553] Quoted with permission after payment, from Hunter and Bainbridge, page 266: "Washington Merry-Go-Round" by Drew Pearson in the *Washington Post*, April 13, 1952. Copyright notice is in endnote [2544].

[2554] **1958: CURRY – KING**

A box on page 333 explains why prudent writers may not quote any words spoken by Dr. Martin Luther King, Jr.

[2555] Pearson, Hugh. *When Harlem Nearly Killed King: The 1958 Stabbing of Dr. Martin Luther King, Jr.*

[2556] Daly, Michael. "The Black and White Men Who Saved Martin Luther King's Life", *The Daily Beast*, 20 January 2014, on the Web at http://www.thedailybeast.com/articles/2014/01/19/the-black-and-white-men-who-saved-martin-luther-king-s-life.html

[2557] http://en.wikipedia.org/wiki/Izola_Curry on 2014/04/29

[2558] Photo purchased from Corbis and moderately cropped: © Bettmann / Corbis.

[2559] This photo, imported and cropped from http://en.wikipedia.org/wiki/Rosa_Parks on 2014/04/29, is in Record Group 306 PSD, photos obtained by the U.S. Information Agency over the years, in the National Archives at College Park, MD, where it is marked on back "Ebony Publications". The author's experienced professional picture researcher has made repeated attempts to obtain authorization to use, or to buy, from Ebony Publications / Magazine, but they have never responded. After that due diligence, copyright law allows it to be printed here. Please see CREDITS AND PERMISSIONS on page ii.

[2560] Quoted with permission from Pearson, who cites "King's misstatement of facts regarding surgery: *The Autobiography of Martin Luther King, Jr.*, edited by Clayborne Carson, (Warner Books, 1998), pp. 117-120."

[2561] Photo by John Lent was purchased from AP and moderately cropped. ©The Associated Press.

[2562] Fetherling, George. *The Book of Assassins: A Biographical Dictionary from Ancient Times to the Present* 109.

[2563] Pearson 49.

[2564] Quoted with permission from Pearson 50.

[2565] http://laurenscountyafricanamericanhistory.blogspot.com/2010/01/izola-ware-curry.html on 2014/04/30.

[2566] Pearson cites "Curry's fate after the stabbing: *The Daily News*, September 21, 1958; *The New York Herald Tribune*, September 21, 1958; *Amsterdam News*, September 27, 1958, October 4, 1958, October 11, 1958."

[2567] Quoted with permission after payment, from Branch, Taylor. *Parting the Waters: America in the King Years, 1954-63*, pages 243-245. Copyright notice supplied by publisher: "Reprinted with the permission of Simon & Schuster, Inc. from PARTING THE WATERS: AMERICA IN THE KING YEARS, 1954-1963 by Taylor Branch. Copyright © 1988 by Taylor Branch. All rights reserved."

[2568] Margalit Fox of *The New York Times*, "Would-be King assassin in 1958, cited in his last speech, dies at 98" in *The Seattle Times*, March 22, 2015, page A2.

1960: PAVLICK – KENNEDY

[2569] This large chapter was thought to be complete before I learned in 2014 of this attempt in an essay by James Edward Peters in John Jovich's *Reflections on JFK's Assassination: 250 Famous Americans Remember November 22, 1963*, pages 13-14.

[2570] Quoted from The Spartanburg Herald; Spartanburg, S.C.; Saturday Morning, December 17, 1960, page 1.

[2571] Photo was purchased from AP and very tightly cropped. ©The Associated Press.

[2572] http://en.wikipedia.org/wiki/Richard_Paul_Pavlick on 2014/05/25.

[2573] "JFK: the assassin who failed" by Philip Kerr, *New Statesman*, November 27, 2000.

[2574] Kerr, same article.

[2575] This photo of Pavlick's car showing the trunk and some of its contents was imported, then moderately cropped from http://media.cmgdigital.com/shared/lt/lt_cache/thumbnail/715/img/photos/2013/11/08/f0/04/npall-posttime112411-02.jpg The author believes the photo appeared in The Palm Beach Post. His professional picture researcher tried very hard to purchase it from PARS International, but they were unable to identify as theirs and have no ability to research. Not knowing the answers to their demands for name of photographer and date printed and caption, the author concludes that he has done due diligence attempting to identify the copyright owner, and shows the irreplaceable photo as fair use.

[2576] Quoted as fair use (for brevity) from "Man Accused Of Plotting To Assassinate Kennedy", AP, in The Spartanburg Herald; December 17, 1960; page 1.

[2577] Quoted as fair use (for brevity) from "The man who did not kill JFK" by Bob Greene, CNN Contributor, October 24, 2010, retrieved from http://www.cnn.com/2010/OPINION/10/24/greene.jfk.arrest/index.html on 2014/05/26.

[2578] Quoted as fair use (for brevity) from "The Kennedy Assassin Who Failed" by Dan Lewis for smithsonian.com, December 6, 2012, retrieved from http://www.smithsonianmag.com/history/the-kennedy-assassin-who-failed-153519612/?no-ist= on 2014/05/25.

1963: De La Beckwith – Evers

[2579] Photo purchased from Corbis and very lightly cropped: © Bettmann / Corbis.

[2580] Branch 816.

[2581] Quoted with permission from McMillan, Priscilla Johnson. *Marina and Lee* 406. Permission statement is in endnote [150].

[2582] Photo imported from http://en.wikipedia.org/wiki/Medgar_Evers on 2015/04/16, to which Wikipedia attaches "Non-free media information and use rationale" explaining how the "Non-profit educational clause of the Fair Use doctrine" allows use of the photo. This book is also educational and probably unprofitable, so the author claims the same fair use.

[2583] Quoted with permission after payment, from Branch 825. Copyright notice is in endnote [2567].

[2584] http://en.wikipedia.org/wiki/Medgar_Evers on 2014/04/26.

[2585] Stout, David. "Byron De La Beckwith Dies; Killer of Medgar Evers Was 80", *The New York Times*, January 23, 2001, on Web at http://www.nytimes.com/2001/01/23/us/byron-de-la-beckwith-dies-killer-of-medgar-evers-was-80.html

[2586] Quoted with permission after payment, from Branch 833. Copyright notice is in endnote [2567].

[2587] Fetherling, George. *The Book of Assassins: A Biographical Dictionary from Ancient Times to the Present* 51.

[2588] His life, trial and death is told in http://en.wikipedia.org/wiki/Byron_De_La_Beckwith on 2014/04/26, most of whose facts appear to have come from *The New York Times* obituary by David Stout, cited above.

1968: Ray – King

[2589] Time-Life Books, The Editors of. *Turbulent Years: The 60s*, pages 76-78.

[2590] Quoted with permission from Posner, Gerald. *Killing the Dream: James Earl Ray and the Assassination of Martin Luther King, Jr.*, published by Random House in 1998, page 20n (the footnote on page 20).

[2591] Photo taken on April 3, 1968, was purchased from AP and lightly cropped. ©The Associated Press. From left to right are Hosea Williams, Jesse Jackson, King and Ralph Abernathy.

[2592] Quoted with permission after payment, from Blaine, Gerald, with Lisa McCubbin. *The Kennedy Detail: JFK's Secret Service Agents Break Their Silence* 372. Copyright notice is in endnote [1444].

[2593] Photo of Robert and Ethel Kennedy at the funeral of MLK on April 10, 1968, was taken by photographer Burt Glinn and was purchased from Magnum Photos.

[2594] Photo of the King family was purchased from Corbis and tightly cropped: © Bob Adelman / Corbis.

[2595] Quoted with permission from Posner *Killing the Dream*, published by Random House in 1998, page 13n (which means the footnote on page 13).

[2596] Time-Life Books, The Editors of. *Assassination: True Crime* 151.

[2597] Posner *Killing the Dream* 17-18, with long supporting endnote 12 on page 348; corroborated in Time-Life Books *Assassination: True Crime* 156.

[2598] Posner *Killing the Dream* 326.

[2599] Posner *Killing the Dream* 25-28.

[2600] Posner *Killing the Dream* 331.

[2601] Blair, Clay, Jr. *The Strange Case of James Earl Ray: The Man Who Murdered Martin Luther King* 152 and 231.

[2602] This photo was purchased to show here, with credit: Joseph Louw / The LIFE Images Collection / Getty Images.

[2603] Posner *Killing the Dream* 33-34; and Blair 151, 154 and 160.

[2604] Posner *Killing the Dream* 35.

[2605] Posner *Killing the Dream* 37-39.

[2606] Blair 162.

[2607] Blair 175.

[2608] Photo in FBI Files at the National Archives and Records Administration is in the public domain.

[2609] Posner *Killing the Dream* 40-43.

[2610] Blair 186.

[2611] Posner *Killing the Dream* 43-44.

[2612] Posner *Killing the Dream* 44-47.

[2613] Posner *Killing the Dream* 55-56.

[2614] Sullivan, Robert, editor. *The Most Notorious Crimes in American History* 30.

[2615] Ray, James Earl. *Who Killed Martin Luther King? The True Story by the Alleged Assassin* 132.

[2616] Ray 139; Posner *Killing the Dream* 67-72.

[2617] Quoted from *The Final Assassinations Report: Report of the Select Committee on Assassinations, U.S. House of Representatives* , page 421.

[2618] Ray 9, 10.

[2619] Ray 96.

[2620] Ray, James Earl. *Who Killed Martin Luther King? The True Story by the Alleged Assassin*. Foreword by Jesse Jackson; Preface by Mark Lane.

[2621] Posner *Killing the Dream* 77-79.

[2622] Posner *Killing the Dream* 83-88.

[2623] Posner *Killing the Dream* 92-95.

[2624] Quoted in Blair, Clay, Jr. *The Strange Case of James Earl Ray: The Man Who Murdered Martin Luther King* 36; see also Posner *Killing the Dream* 95. Regarding Blair, his book was published by Bantam Books, now a brand of Penguin Random House, whose permissions department says they do not hold the copyright, do not know who, if anyone, does. The author's copyright agent searched without success to find Blair. Having performed due diligence, the author prints this brief quote as fair use. If any valid copyright holder arises, please see my CREDITS AND PERMISSIONS on page ii.

[2625] Quoted with permission from Ray 23.

[2626] Posner *Killing the Dream* 217-220; Time-Life Books *Assassination: True Crime* 154.

[2627] Posner *Killing the Dream* 333-334.

[2628] Posner *Killing the Dream* 137-138.

[2629] A box on page 333 explains why prudent writers may not quote any words spoken by Dr. Martin Luther King, Jr.

[2630] Quoted as fair use in Wofford, Harris. *Of Kennedys and Kings: Making Sense of the Sixties* 203.

[2631] Clarke, James W. *American Assassins: The Darker Side of Politics* 245-246, 254, 256-257.

[2632] Blair 78.

[2633] Quoted as fair use after due diligence from Blair 88-89. See the citation in endnote [2624] above.

1968: Sirhan – Robert Kennedy

[2634] Quoted as fair use from Wofford, Harris. *Of Kennedys and Kings: Making Sense of the Sixties* 201-202.

[2635] Quoted with permission from Shesol, Jeff. *Mutual Contempt: Lyndon Johnson, Robert Kennedy, and the Feud That Defined a Decade*, page 447.

[2636] Quoted as fair use from Wofford 202.

[2637] Quoted with permission from Shesol 447.

[2638] Quoted with permission after payment, from Schaap, Dick. *R.F.K.* 124.

[2639] Kennedy, Robert F. *To Seek a Newer World*, Bantam edition published 4 days after his announcement and augmented with "MY ANNOUNCEMENT OF CANDIDACY", pages xv-xvi.

[2640] Sorensen, Theodore C. *The Kennedy Legacy* 145.

[2641] Quoted with permission from O'Sullivan, Shane. *Who Killed Bobby? The Unsolved Murder of Robert F. Kennedy*, page 5.

[2642] Quoted with permission from Sorensen *The Kennedy Legacy*, page 148.

[2643] Quoted with permission from O'Sullivan 6.

[2644] The photo of Kennedy and Freckles was taken by photographer Burton Berinsky. The author's professional and highly experienced picture researcher obtained information on contacting the agent for Berinsky photos from the JFK Library, and made repeated attempts over two months to purchase this photo. There was never any reply, so having done due diligence, the photo is shown as fair use, with credit and appreciation to the photographer. Please see CREDITS AND PERMISSIONS on page ii.

[2645] Quoted from Jansen, Godfrey. *Why Robert Kennedy Was Killed: The Story of Two Victims*, page 157. This author's skilled copyright agent expended considerable due diligence trying to contact both Jansen and his publisher, and never had any reply. Under the copyright laws, your author claims the right to fair use after due diligence. Please see CREDITS AND PERMISSIONS on page ii.

[2646] Quoted with permission from Thomas, Evan. *Robert Kennedy: His Life*, page 386. Copyright notice supplied by publisher: "Reprinted with the permission of Simon & Schuster, Inc. from ROBERT KENNEDY: HIS LIFE by Evan Thomas. Copyright © 2000 Evan Thomas."

[2647] Beran, Michael Knox. *The Last Patrician: Bobby Kennedy and the End of American Aristocracy* 205-206.

[2648] Quoted as fair use (for brevity: 9 words) from Marvin, Richard. *The Kennedy Curse*, page 81.

[2649] Quoted with permission from O'Sullivan 11.

[2650] Quoted with permission from O'Sullivan 13.

[2651] Quoted with permission from O'Sullivan 14.

[2652] Quoted as fair use from Jansen 205.

[2653] O'Sullivan 19.

[2654] Partially based on the description in American Heritage's *RFK: His Life and Death*, page 136.

[2655] This photo of Kennedy and kneeling busboy Juan Romero was purchased to show here, with credit: Boris Yaro-Popperfoto / Getty Images.

[2656] Quoted with permission from O'Sullivan, page 1.

[2657] Quoted with permission from Heymann, C. David. *RFK: A Candid Biography of Robert F. Kennedy*, footnote 508. Copyright notice is in endnote [913].

[2658] Quoted as fair use (for brevity: 19 words) from United Press International: Klagsbrun and Whitney, editors. *Assassination: Robert F. Kennedy – 1925-1968*, page 84. The author's copyright agent sent requests to http://about.upi.com/licensing/ and http://about.upi.com/contact/legal, without receiving any reply. This is apparently too small for them to consider.

[2659] Quoted with permission from O'Sullivan 59-60.

[2660] United Press International: Klagsbrun and Whitney 143.

[2661] Quoted with permission from Heymann 505. Copyright notice is in endnote [913].

[2662] Quoted with kind permission, without charge, from Beran 207.

[2663] Photo was purchased from AV Archives at the John F. Kennedy Presidential Library and Museum, Boston.

[2664] Photo was purchased from Corbis and tightly cropped: © Bettmann / Corbis..

[2665] Quoted as fair use from Jansen 153.

[2666] Quoted with permission from Fetherling, George. *The Book of Assassins* 334.

[2667] Quoted with permission from Clarke, James W. *American Assassins: The Darker Side of Politics* 81-82.

[2668] Quoted with permission from Clarke 84, which cites Trial testimony, Sirhan, vol. 17, pp. 4856, 4937.

[2669] Quoted with permission from Clarke 86, which cites Trial testimony, Sirhan, vol. 17, p. 5026.

[2670] Quoted with permission from Clarke 87, which cites Trial testimony, Sirhan, vol. 17, pp. 4931, 4971, 4977.

[2671] Quoted with permission from Clarke 94.

[2672] Quoted with permission from Clarke 88, which cites Trial testimony, Sirhan, vol. 17, pp. 4969, 4971.

[2673] Quoted with permission from Clarke 92, which cites People's Exhibit 71 for notebook, and Kaiser, Robert *RFK Must Die* (see below) p. 219 for quotation.

[2674] Quoted with permission from Clarke 94, which cites Trial testimony, Sirhan, vol. 18, pp. 5131-5143 for Ambassador, and Kaiser, Robert *RFK Must Die* (see below) p. 534 for San Diego.

[2675] Photo of revolver is in the California State Archives, "Los Angeles Police Department Records of the Robert F. Kennedy Assassination Investigation; 19. Photographs. 1968-1969, Microfilm Roll Nos. 16-17."

[2676] Quoted with permission from O'Sullivan 215-216.

[2677] Quoted as fair use from Jansen 200.

[2678] Quoted with permission from Clarke 76-77.

[2679] Kaiser, Robert Blair. *R.F.K. Must Die! A History of the Robert Kennedy Assassination and Its Aftermath*, page 498.

[2680] Quoted with permission from Moldea, Dan E. *The Killing of Robert F. Kennedy: An Investigation of Motive, Means, and Opportunity*, page 123.

[2681] Klaber, William, and Philip H. Melanson. *Shadow Play: The Untold Story of the Robert F. Kennedy Assassination*, pages 317-318.

[2682] Quoted as fair use (for brevity) from http://en.wikipedia.org/wiki/Sirhan_Sirhan on 2012/04/24.

[2683] Quoted as fair use (for brevity) from http://en.wikipedia.org/wiki/Sirhan_Sirhan on 2012/04/24.

[2684] Quoted with permission from Clarke 103-104.

1972: BREMER – WALLACE

[2685] Photo taken by Yoichi Okamoto is shown courtesy of the Lyndon Baines Johnson Library and Museum, Austin, TX, administered by the National Archives and Records Administration.

[2686] Quoted with permission from Lesher, Stephan. *George Wallace: American Populist* 478.

[2687] http://en.wikipedia.org/wiki/Arthur_Bremer on 2012/09/20, which cites "'Loner gunman shoots Democrat maverick'. *The Times* (London). October 5, 2008."

[2688] Quoted with permission from Healey, Thomas S. *The Two Deaths of George Wallace: The Question of Forgiveness*, pages 48-49, which cites "Personal interview, Lawden Yates, Alabama Forensic Labs. Additional material from phone interview with Paul Eschrich of Sporting Arms and Ammunition Manufacturers Institute, Stamford, CT".

[2689] Quoted with permission from Healey 71.

[2690] Quoted with permission from Healey 71.

[2691] Quoted with permission from Fetherling, George. *The Book of Assassins: A Biographical Dictionary from Ancient Times to the Present*, page 74.

[2692] Quoted with permission from Healey 71-72.

[2693] Quoted with permission from Healey 81.

[2694] Quoted with permission from Healey 85-87.

[2695] Quoted with permission from Healey 89 90.

[2696] Quoted with permission from Lesher 479, which cites "Quoted by James Jones, of *Newsweek*, Michael F. Wendland, *Detroit News*, May 16, 1972."

[2697] Quoted with permission from Lesher 480.

[2698] Quoted with permission from Healey 38.

[2699] Quoted with permission from Clarke, James W. *American Assassins: The Darker Side of Politics* 175.

[2700] Quoted with permission from Lesher 481.

[2701] Quoted with permission from Healey 49-50.

[2702] Quoted with permission from Lesher 481.

[2703] Quoted with permission from Healey 46.

[2704] This is a frame from a CBS-TV broadcast. The right to show it here was purchased from CBS News Archives.

[2705] Quoted with permission from Lesher 481.

[2706] Quoted as fair use from Livingstone, Harrison Edward. *High Treason 2: The Great Cover-Up: The Assassination of President John F. Kennedy* 403-406. A statement about this source is in endnote [2018].

[2707] Photo purchased from AP and lightly cropped. ©The Associated Press.

[2708] Quoted with permission from Lesher 482.

[2709] Quoted with permission after payment, from Blaine, Gerald, with Lisa McCubbin. *The Kennedy Detail: JFK's Secret Service Agents Break Their Silence* 376. Copyright notice is in endnote [1444].

[2710] Quoted with permission from Lesher 485.

[2711] Quoted with permission from Lesher 489, which cites "James T. Wooten, 'Wallace Tells Convention He Wants to Help Party,' *New York Times*, July 12, 1972, p. 1."

[2712] Quoted with permission from Lesher 490.

[2713] Quoted with permission from Clarke 174.

[2714] Quoted with permission from Lesher 483-484.

[2715] Quoted with permission from Lesher 484, which cites "Seymour M. Hersh, 'Nixon's Last Cover-Up: The Tapes He Wants the Archives to Suppress,' *New Yorker*, December 14, 1992, p. 76."

[2716] Quoted with permission from Healey 90-91.

[2717] Quoted with permission from Fetherling, George. *The Book of Assassins: A Biographical Dictionary from Ancient Times to the Present*, page 73.

[2718] Quoted with permission from Healey 94-95.

[2719] Quoted with permission from Clarke 187.

[2720] Photo by Joe Holloway Jr. was purchased from AP and lightly cropped. ©The Associated Press.

[2721] Quoted as fair use (for brevity) from http://en.wikipedia.org/wiki/George_Wallace on 2012/09/15, which cites "'Wallace in his own words' *The Huntsville Times*, Huntsville, Alabama, September 14, 1998, p. A9".

[2722] Quoted as fair use (for brevity) from http://en.wikipedia.org/wiki/Arthur_Bremer on 2012/09/20.

[2723] Quoted as fair use (for brevity) from http://en.wikipedia.org/wiki/George_Wallace on 2012/09/15.

[2724] http://en.wikipedia.org/wiki/Arthur_Bremer on 2012/09/20.

1974: BYCK – NIXON

[2725] Quoted as fair use (for brevity) from en.wikipedia.org/wiki/Samuel_Byck on 2012/04/07.

[2726] www.sdpoa.org/absolutenm/articlefiles/300-June%202008.pdf on 2012/04/07.

[2727] en.wikipedia.org/wiki/Samuel_Byck on 2012/04/07.

[2728] Quoted with permission from Clarke 128-129, which cites "Documents, Samuel Byck, Department of Transportation Federal Aviation Administration, Security Summary (SE-1600-20) ASE-74-4".

[2729] Quoted as fair use (for brevity) from en.wikipedia.org/wiki/Samuel_Byck on 2012/04/07. There is a slightly different account in Time-Life Books, The Editors of. *Assassination: True Crime*, page 54.

[2730] en.wikipedia.org/wiki/Samuel_Byck on 2012/04/07.

[2731] Quoted with permission from Clarke 129.

[2732] en.wikipedia.org/wiki/Samuel_Byck on 2012/04/07.

[2733] en.wikipedia.org/wiki/Samuel_Byck on 2012/04/07.

[2734] en.wikipedia.org/wiki/Samuel_Byck on 2012/04/07.

[2735] Clarke 131.

[2736] Clarke 133.

[2737] Clarke 130, for this and next four items.

[2738] Clarke 130-131.

[2739] Clarke 131-135.

[2740] Clarke 131, which cites "Documents, Secret Service, report dated November 21, 1972".

[2741] en.wikipedia.org/wiki/Samuel_Byck on 2012/04/07.

[2742] en.wikipedia.org/wiki/Samuel_Byck on 2012/04/07.

[2743] Said about himself on audio tape: http://www.youtube.com/watch?v=VHAWUby7V-A

[2744] Clarke 134, which cites "Documents, FBI and Secret Service".

[2745] en.wikipedia.org/wiki/Samuel_Byck on 2012/04/07.

[2746] Photo purchased from Corbis and moderately cropped: © Bettmann / Corbis.

[2747] Quoted with permission from Clarke 134, which cites "Tape, February 21, 1974".

[2748] Quoted with permission from Clarke 134, citing tapes of January 30 and February 5, 1974.

[2749] Quoted with permission from Clarke 141-142.

[2750] Quoted as fair use (for brevity) from en.wikipedia.org/wiki/Samuel_Byck on 2012/04/07.

1975: Fromme – Ford

[2751] Quoted with permission from Ford, Gerald R. *A Time to Heal* 309-310.

[2752] At left is the author's scan of *Newsweek*'s cover dated September 15, 1975. *Newsweek* has long since ceased publication, the purchaser of its archives reportedly has not indexed its holdings. After repeated attempts to obtain clearance or purchase rights without any reply, the author claims due diligence and shows the cover as fair use. TIME is a sadly different matter. Permissions to purchase and use their copyrighted material are handled by PARS International, which demanded $460 each for me to show you three covers, small and grayscale, in this book with expected limited print run. That's too pricey for the small benefit. If you would like to see the vividly colored cover, large size, go on the Web to: http://search.time.com/results.html?N=46&Ns=p_date_range|1&Nf=p_date_range%7cBTWN+19750915+19750915

[2753] United States Code, Title 18, Section 1751.

[2754] Bravin, Jess. *Squeaky: The Life and Times of Lynette Alice Fromme* 16 and 318.

[2755] Bravin 318.

[2756] Bravin 382.

[2757] Bravin 332.

[2758] Bravin 17.

[2759] Bravin 29.

[2760] Bravin 34.

[2761] Bravin 43.

[2762] Bravin 34.

[2763] Quoted with kind permission from Bravin 46.

[2764] Quoted as fair use after due diligence from Bugliosi, Vincent, with Curt Gentry. *Helter Skelter: The True Story of the Manson Murders* 567. Bugliosi died in 2015. The author's copyright agent has tried without success to contact Gentry. The book was published by Bantam Books, now a brand of Penguin Random House, whose permissions department says they do not hold the copyright, do not know who, if anyone, does. When the author paid for rights to use quotations from Bugliosi's *Four Days* and *Reclaiming History*, we asked if we could also pay for several quotes from *Helter Skelter*, but were told they did not represent that older book. Having performed due diligence, the author claims the right to quote as fair use. If any valid copyright holder arises, please see Credits and Permissions on page ii.

[2765] Quoted with permission from Bravin 47.

[2766] Quoted with permission from Bravin 48.

[2767] This booking photo from the Ventura County (CA) Sheriff's Department is in the public domain.

[2768] Quoted after due diligence from Bugliosi *Helter Skelter* 198. Statement about this source is in endnote [2764] above.

[2769] Quoted after due diligence from Bugliosi *Helter Skelter* 198. Statement about this source is in endnote [2764] above.

[2770] Bravin 87.

[2771] Quoted after due diligence from Bugliosi *Helter Skelter* 135. Statement about this source is in endnote [2764] above.

[2772] Statement of ranch visitor Danny DeCarlo to LA detectives, quoted in Bugliosi *Helter Skelter* 135. See endnote [2764] above.

[2773] Quoted with permission from Bravin 83, 85.

[2774] Quoted after due diligence from Bugliosi *Helter Skelter* 424. Statement about this source is in endnote [2764] above.

[2775] Photo was imported from http://www.latinoseguridad.com/LatinoSeguridad/Criminales/Manson.shtml. At left are Sandra Good and Ruth Moorehouse. The author made repeated attempts to contact the website with no reply, perhaps because I do not know the Spanish language. Having used due diligence, the author shows the photo as fair use. Please see my Credits and Permissions on page ii.

[2776] Quoted after due diligence from Bugliosi *Helter Skelter* 429. Statement about this source is in endnote [2764] above.

[2777] Quoted with permission from Bravin 121.

[2778] Quoted after due diligence from Bugliosi *Helter Skelter* 442-443. Statement about this source is in endnote [2764] above.

[2779] Quoted with permission from Bravin 121.

[2780] Quoted after due diligence from Bugliosi *Helter Skelter* 660-661. Statement about this source is in endnote [2764] above.

[2781] Bravin 205.

[2782] Quoted with permission from Bravin 191.

[2783] Bravin 194.

[2784] Bravin 183-184.

[2785] Quoted with permission from Bravin 196.

[2786] Quoted with permission from Bravin 198-199.

[2787] Bravin 197.

[2788] Quoted with permission from Bravin 291.

[2789] Quoted with permission after payment, from Blaine, Gerald, with Lisa McCubbin. *The Kennedy Detail: JFK's Secret Service Agents Break Their Silence*, page 381. Copyright notice is in endnote [1444].

[2790] Quoted with permission from Hosty, James P., Jr., with Thomas C. Hosty. *Assignment: Oswald*, page 245.

[2791] Quoted with permission from Bravin 230.

[2792] Quoted with permission from Bravin 248.

[2793] Quoted with permission from Bravin 392.

[2794] Quoted as fair use (for brevity) from Cole, Richard (AP). "Bizarre twist in Unabomb jury phase" *The Seattle Times* 21 Nov. 1997: A7.

[2795] Quoted with permission from Bravin 262.

[2796] Bravin 271.

[2797] Quoted with permission from Bravin 256, which briefly quotes the *Washington Post*, 08 Sep. 1975.

[2798] Quoted with permission from Bravin 264.

[2799] Quoted with permission from Bravin 302, which very briefly quotes Judge MacBride.

[2800] Bravin 346.

[2801] Bravin 331.

[2802] Photo imported, then converted to grayscale, from http://en.wikipedia.org/wiki/Lynette_Fromme on 2014/10/31, where it is captioned "The Colt M1911 .45-caliber pistol used by Fromme in her assassination attempt on Gerald Ford". The photo is shown courtesy of the Gerald R. Ford Presidential Library and Museum, Ann Arbor, MI.

[2803] Bravin 11.

[2804] Quoted in Time-Life Books, The Editors of. *Assassination: True Crime*, page 55, and taken as fair use for three words.

[2805] Quoted with permission after payment, from Thomas, Helen. *Front Row at the White House: My Life and Times*, pages 319-320, for which the copyright notice is in endnote [907].

[2806] Quoted with permission from Bravin 380.

[2807] Quoted with permission from Bravin 384.

[2808] Quoted with permission from Bravin 386.

[2809] Quoted with permission from Bravin 291.

[2810] Quoted with permission from Bravin 387.

[2811] Quoted with permission after payment, from Thomas, Helen. *Front Row*, page 320. This form with key words from the title is used because more than one book by this author is cited in these notes. Copyright notice is in endnote [907].

[2812] Quoted as fair use (for brevity) from Deutsch, Linda (Associated Press). "Manson follower clears hurdle in bid for parole" *The Seattle Times* 5 October 2012: A7.

[2813] http://mostlikelytokill.blogspot.com/2010/05/lynette-alice-squeaky-fromme.html on 2014/10/31.

1975: Moore – Ford

[2814] Photo imported from http://en.wikipedia.org/wiki/Gerald_Ford, then cropped and converted to grayscale. The photo is shown courtesy of the Gerald R. Ford Presidential Library and Museum, Ann Arbor, MI.

[2815] The photo, taken at the front Post St. entrance to the St. Francis Hotel, where the author and his beautiful new bride of only a few hours entered in 1966 to begin their honeymoon, to their surprise and delight in the Governor's Suite (you can learn a lot from endnotes!), is shown courtesy of the Gerald R. Ford Presidential Library and Museum, Ann Arbor, MI.

[2816] Quoted with permission from Ford, Gerald R. *A Time to Heal: The Autobiography of Gerald R. Ford*, pages 310-312.

[2817] Photo purchased from AP, then tightly cropped. ©The Associated Press. The photo was taken in December 1975 as she was driven to court to plead guilty.

[2818] Quoted with permission from Bravin, Jess. *Squeaky: The Life and Times of Lynette Alice Fromme*, page 284.

[2819] Quoted as fair use (for brevity) from http://en.wikipedia.org/wiki/Sara_Jane_Moore on 2014/11/03.

[2820] Quoted with permission from Bravin 284, citing on 415: "*Time*, October 6, 1975."

[2821] Quoted with permission from Bravin 285, citing on 415: "*Los Angeles Times*, September 25, 1975." See also Time-Life Books, The Editors of. *Assassination: True Crime*, page 55.

[2822] *Playboy* June 1976: "The *Real* Reason I Tried to Kill President Ford".

[2823] Quoted with permission from Bravin 285.

[2824] http://www.washingtonpost.com/wp-dyn/content/article/2006/12/30/AR2006123000160_3.html on 2014/11/03.

[2825] Photo taken by Gordon Stone of the *San Francisco Examiner* was purchased from the AP, then very slightly cropped. ©The Associated Press.

[2826] Quoted as fair use (for brevity) from http://en.wikipedia.org/wiki/Oliver_Sipple on 2014/11/03.

[2827] Quoted as fair use (for brevity) from http://www.washingtonpost.com/wp-dyn/content/article/2006/12/30/AR2006123000160_3.html on 2014/11/03.

[2828] Thomas, Helen. *Front Row at the White House: My Life and Times*, page 320, for which copyright notice is in endnote [907].

[2829] Quoted as fair use (for brevity) from "Former President Ford lauded, laid to rest" on Cable News Network, 2007/01/04.

[2830] Quoted as fair use (for brevity) from http://en.wikipedia.org/wiki/Sara_Jane_Moore on 2014/11/03.

[2831] Photo by Richard Drew was purchased from AP, then tightly cropped and converted to grayscale. ©The Associated Press.

[2832] Quoted as fair use (for brevity) from http://en.wikipedia.org/wiki/Sara_Jane_Moore on 2014/11/03, citing "http://today.msnbc.msn.com/id/30978026/ns/today-today_people/" and "http://www.theweek.com/article/index/97054/Video_Sara_Jane_Moore_on_the_Today_show"

[2833] Blaine, Gerald, with Lisa McCubbin. *The Kennedy Detail: JFK's Secret Service Agents Break Their Silence*, page 382.

1981: Hinckley – Reagan

[2834] McCarthy, Dennis V. N., with Philip W. Smith. *Protecting the President: The Inside Story of a Secret Service Agent* 20.

[2835] Photo by Ron Edmonds purchased from AP and moderately cropped. ©The Associated Press.

[2836] Quoted with permission from Abrams, Herbert L. *The President has been Shot: Confusion, Disability, and the 25th Amendment in the Aftermath of the Attempted Assassination of Ronald Reagan*, pages 55-56, which cites "Quoted in 'Transcript of an Interview with the President on His Wounding and Recovery,' *Washington Post*, April 3, 1981, 1."

[2837] Quoted with permission from Abrams 56, which cites "Department of the Treasury, *Management Review*, 59."

[2838] To hear news broadcasts reporting the shooting, at about this time, obtain Garner, Joe. *We Interrupt This Broadcast: The Events That Stopped Our Lives – from the Hindenburg Explosion to the Death of John F. Kennedy Jr.*, pages 104-105, and listen to its enclosed compact disc 2 track 9.

[2839] Quoted with permission from Abrams 57, which cites "Susan Okie, 'Reagan's Risk May Have Been Much Greater Than Believed,' *Washington Post*, April 2, 1981, 1."

[2840] Abrams 58.

[2841] Quoted with the gracious permission of James Reston, Jr., author and copyright owner of *The Accidental Victim: JFK, Lee Harvey Oswald, and the Real Target in Dallas* (printed book), page 171.

[2842] Quoted with permission from Abrams 60.

[2843] Quoted with permission from Abrams 62.

[2844] Quoted with permission from Abrams 65.

[2845] Abrams 64.

[2846] Photo was taken by White House photographer Michael Evans, converted to grayscale and cropped. It is shown courtesy of the Ronald Reagan Presidential Library and Center for Public Affairs, administered by the National Archives and Records Administration.

[2847] http://en.wikipedia.org/wiki/Thomas_Delahanty on 2014/12/19.

[2848] http://en.wikipedia.org/wiki/Tim_McCarthy on 2014/12/19.

[2849] Thomas, Helen. *Front Row at the White House: My Life and Times*, pages 145-146, for which the copyright notice is in endnote [907].

[2850] "James Brady, shot along with Reagan, fought for gun control" obituary by James Barron of *The New York Times* in *The Seattle Times*, 2014/08/05 A2.

[2851] "Reagan aide James Brady's death ruled to be homicide" by Nick Corasaniti of *The New York Times* in *The Seattle Times* 2014/08/09 A2.

[2852] "No new charges in Brady death" by Ben Nuckols of *The Associated Press* in *The Seattle Times* 2015/01/03 A2.

[2853] The Wikipedia article on John Hinckley identifies this as an "FBI mug shot", confirmed by "WFO" (Washington Field Office) on the placard he holds. As such, it is a photo taken by the federal government in the normal course of job duties, so is in the public domain.

[2854] http://en.wikipedia.org/wiki/John_Hinckley,_Jr. on 2014/12/22.

[2855] Quoted as fair use (for brevity) from http://en.wikipedia.org/wiki/John_Hinckley,_Jr. on 2014/12/22, which cites "'Letter written to Jodie Foster by John Hinckley, Jr.'. University of Missouri–Kansas City School of Law."

[2856] Quoted as fair use (for brevity) from Sullivan, Robert, editor. *The Most Notorious Crimes in American History* 43.

[2857] Thomas, Helen. *Front Row*, page 320. This form with key words from the title is used because more than one book by this author is cited in these notes. Copyright notice is in endnote [907].

[2858] Quoted with permission from Healey, Thomas S. *The Two Deaths of George Wallace: The Question of Forgiveness* 54.

[2859] Quoted with permission after payment, from Pipes, Daniel. *Conspiracy: How the Paranoid Style Flourishes and Where It Comes From*, page 168.

[2860] Quoted with permission from oral history of Homicide Detective Gus Rose in Sneed, Larry A. *No More Silence: An Oral History of the Assassination of President Kennedy* 343.

1963: Oswald – Kennedy or Connally?

[2861] Buchanan, Thomas G. *Who Killed Kennedy?*, pages 76-77.

[2862] Quoted with permission from Meagher, Sylvia. *Accessories After The Fact: The Warren Commission, The Authorities, and The Report*, page 242.

[2863] Quoted with permission from Meagher *Accessories* 243.

[2864] Quoted with permission from Meagher *Accessories* 246.

— 11 — Failure

[2865] Quoted with permission after payment, from Stafford, Jean. *A Mother in History* 8.

[2866] Quoted in http://watergate.info/1994/04/27/clinton-remarks-at-nixon-funeral.html on 2014/07/30.

[2867] Quoted with permission after payment, from Bugliosi, Vincent. *Four Days in November: The Assassination of President John F. Kennedy* 348, citing "Kelley Exhibit A, 20 H 441; CE 1988, 24 H 19."; which was reprinted from Bugliosi, Vincent. *Reclaiming History: The Assassination of President John F. Kennedy* 217, with the same citation. Copyright notice for *Four Days* is in endnote [1767].

[2868] Quoted with permission from Wecht, Cyril. *Cause of Death* 54-55, 57. Copyright notice is in endnote [623].

[2869] TESTIMONY OF RUTH HYDE PAINE on *WCH* II 510.

[2870] Quoted with permission after payment, from Bishop, Jim. *The Day Kennedy Was Shot*, page 324.

[2871] Quoted with permission after payment, from Warren, Earl. *The Memoirs of Earl Warren*, page 364. Copyright notice is in endnote [211].

[2872] Quoted with permission after payment, from Warren 365. Copyright notice is in endnote [211].

[2873] Quoted with permission after payment, from Warren 367. Copyright notice is in endnote [211].

[2874] According to the Photo Historian in the USMC History Division, this was probably taken by reserve officer John Edward Marckx, USMC 070952, a member of Oswald's Marine Air Control Squadron 1 on Corregidor at the time John Wayne dropped by for roast beef and salsa(!). The author's patient, skilled, experienced picture researcher has expended considerable time doing due diligence to locate Mr. Marckx, without success, so I claim the right to fair use. Please see CREDITS AND PERMISSIONS on page ii.

— 12 — THE RIFLE

[2875] Dad said he most likely heard this from some fellow duffer-golfer. He thought I might find a use for it, and he was right.

[2876] COMMISSION EXHIBIT (hereinafter CE) 139 on *Hearings Before the President's Commission on the Assassination of President Kennedy* (hereinafter *WCH*) XVI 512; TESTIMONY OF JOSEPH A. MOONEY on *WCH* III 289 (hereinafter in the form *WCH* III 289 (Mooney)); TESTIMONY OF EUGENE BOONE on *WCH* III 292-293; TESTIMONY OF ROBERT A. FRAZIER on *WCH* III 392, 395.

[2877] CE 139 on *WCH* XVI 512; CE 541 on *WCH* XVII 238-241; *WCH* III 393-394 (Robert Frazier).

[2878] CE 139 on *WCH* XVI 512; *WCH* III 395-396 (Robert Frazier).

[2879] CE 139 on *WCH* XVI 512; CE 541 on *WCH* XVII 238-241; *WCH* III 397 (Robert Frazier).

[2880] *WCH* III 397 (Robert Frazier).

[2881] *WCH* III 397 (Robert Frazier).

[2882] *WCH* III 392, 396 (Robert Frazier).

[2883] *WCH* III 392 (Robert Frazier).

[2884] *WCH* III 392 (Robert Frazier); CE 540 on *WCH* XVII 238.

[2885] *WCH* III 392 (Robert Frazier).

[2886] CE 1977 on *WCH* XXIV 2-3; *WCH* III 393-394 (Robert Frazier).

[2887] *WCH* III 392-393 (Robert Frazier); Walter H. B. Smith. *Small Arms of the World* (6th ed. 1960).

[2888] *WCH* III 416 (Robert Frazier).

[2889] *WCH* III 397-398 (Robert Frazier); W. H. B. Smith. *The Book of Rifles* (3rd edition 1963), pages 298-307; W. H. B. Smith. *Mannlicher Rifles and Pistols* (1947), pages 84-87.

[2890] *WCH* III 397-398 (Robert Frazier).

[2891] *WCH* III 397-398 (Robert Frazier).

[2892] TESTIMONY OF JOHN WILL FRITZ on *WCH* IV 205; TESTIMONY OF J. C. DAY on *WCH* IV 258.

[2893] CE 575 on *WCH* XVII 259; *WCH* III 398 (Robert Frazier).

[2894] *WCH* III 398 (Robert Frazier).

[2895] CE 141 on *WCH* XVI 513; *WCH* IV 205-206 (Fritz); *WCH* IV 258 (Day).

[2896] *WCH* III 399 (Robert Frazier).

[2897] *WCH* III 400 (Robert Frazier).

[2898] *WCH* III 437-438 (Robert Frazier); TESTIMONY OF RONALD SIMMONS on *WCH* III 443, 449.

[2899] *WCH* III 400, 416 (Robert Frazier).

[2900] *WCH* III 400-401, 416 (Robert Frazier).

[2901] CE 512 on *WCH* XVII 223; *WCH* III 284 (Mooney).

[2902] CE 510 on *WCH* XVII 221.

[2903] *WCH* III 414-428 (Robert Frazier); TESTIMONY OF JOSEPH D. NICOL on *WCH* III 505-507.

[2904] *WCH* III 401-402 (Robert Frazier); CE 2724 on *WCH* XXVI 103-104.

[2905] CE 546 on *WCH* XVII 242; CE 547 on *WCH* XVII 243; *WCH* III 401-402 (Robert Frazier).

[2906] CE 547 on *WCH* XVII 243; *WCH* III 401-402 (Robert Frazier).

[2907] *WCH* III 402 (Robert Frazier).

[2908] *WCH* III 402 (Robert Frazier).

[2909] CE 399 on *WCH* XVII 49; CE 567 on *WCH* XVII 256; CE 569 on *WCH* XVII 257; CE 2011 2-4 on *WCH* XXIV 412-413; TESTIMONY OF DARRELL C. TOMLINSON on *WCH* VI 129-130.

[2910] *WCH* III 430 (Robert Frazier).

[2911] *WCH* III 430 (Robert Frazier).

[2912] *WCH* III 432, 435 (Robert Frazier).

[2913] *WCH* III 432 (Robert Frazier).

[2914] *WCH* III 435 (Robert Frazier).

[2915] *WCH* III 435, 437 (Robert Frazier); *WCH* III 497 (Nicol).

[2916] *WCH* III 430, 432, 434, 436-437 (Robert Frazier).

[2917] *WCH* III 428-437 (Robert Frazier); *WCH* III 497-502 (Nicol).

[2918] *Report of the President's Commission on the Assassination of President Kennedy* (popularly known as the *Warren Report*, hereinafter expressed as *WR*), pages 553-558.

[2919] Photo scanned from CE 339 on *WCH* XVI 936. Coming from that US Federal government source, it is in the public domain. Photo is in the National Archives.

[2920] Photo purchased to show here: William Allen, photographer, *Dallas Times Herald* Collection / The Sixth Floor Museum at Dealey Plaza.

[2921] Quoted with permission after payment, from Epstein, Edward Jay. *Inquest: The Warren Commission and the Establishment of Truth* (hc), page 155.

[2922] Epstein wrote in *The Assassination Chronicles* (pages 12-13) in 1992 that "One young [Commission] lawyer, Professor Wesley J. Liebeler, even turned over to me his working files, which contained ... most important, the original FBI summary reports—which showed what had been established about the assassination by the FBI before the Warren Commission began its inquiry."

[2923] Quoted with permission after payment, in Epstein *Inquest* 180-183.

[2924] Gerald Posner in *Case Closed: Lee Harvey Oswald and the Assassination of JFK*, in footnote at bottom of page 270 cites "HSCA Vol. I, pp. 446-47; HSCA Vol. VII, p. 372."

[2925] Posner in *Case Closed* cites "*Rush to Judgment*, pp. 95-101."

[2926] Posner in *Case Closed* cites "*They've Killed the President*, p. 76."

[2927] Posner in *Case Closed* cites "WC Vol. III, p. 411; HSCA Vol. VII, pp. 371-72."

[2928] Posner in *Case Closed* cites "*Accessories*, p. 102."

[2929] Posner in *Case Closed* cites "HSCA Vol. VII, p. 371."

[2930] Quoted with permission after payment, from Posner *Case Closed* 270n (which means the footnote at bottom of page 270). Copyright notice is in endnote [1039].

[2931] Quoted with permission from Callahan, Bob. *Who Shot JFK?: A Guide to the Major Conspiracy Theories*, page 34.

[2932] Quoted with permission after payment, from Epstein *Inquest* 141, which cites "*Hearings*, Vol. III, pp. 403-405."

[2933] *WCH* III 405 (Robert Frazier).

[2934] Quoted with permission after payment, from Epstein *Inquest* 142, which cites *WCH* III 406.

[2935] *WCH* III 405 (Robert Frazier).

[2936] *WCH* III 391 (Robert Frazier).

[2937] A poor photocopy on *WCH* XVII 245 shows 3 almost-touching holes shot by agent Killion, but at only 15 yards.

[2938] *WCH* III 411 (Robert Frazier).

[2939] *WCH* III 441-451 (Simmons).

[2940] *WCH* III 444 (Simmons).

[2941] Photo scanned and cropped from CE 1303 on *WCH* XXII 480, top. Coming from that US Federal government source, it is in the public domain.

[2942] *WCH* III 395 (Robert Frazier) for all three exact lengths stated below the two photos of the rifle.

[2943] Photo scanned and cropped from CE 1304–CONTINUED on *WCH* XXII 480, bottom. Coming from that US Federal government source, it is in the public domain.

[2944] Photo scanned and cropped from CE 1304 on *WCH* XXII 480, middle. Coming from that US Federal government source, it is in the public domain.

[2945] TESTIMONY OF SGT. JAMES A. ZAHM on *WCH* XI 307-308.

[2946] *WCH* XI 309-310 (Zahm).

[2947] CE 2694 on *WCH* XXVI 58-68.

[2948] CE 2694—CONTINUED on *WCH* XXVI 62.

[2949] Quoted with permission after payment, from Epstein *Chronicles*, page 586. This was originally in his *Legend: The Secret World of Lee Harvey Oswald*, *Appendix A: The Status of the Evidence: III. The Accuracy of the Rifle*.

[2950] Quoted with permission after payment, from Posner *Case Closed* 335n. Copyright notice is in endnote [1039].

[2951] *WCH* III 400 (Robert Frazier).

[2952] *WCH* III 437-438 (Robert Frazier).

[2953] Quoted with permission after payment, from Posner *Case Closed* 317-318, which cites "Testimony of Lyndal Shaneyfelt, WC Vol. V, p. 153; "The Warren Report," CBS News, Part I, June 25, 1967, p. 14; HSCA Rpt., p. 83". Copyright notice is in endnote [1039].

[2954] *WCH* III 407 (Robert Frazier).

[2955] TESTIMONY OF MAJ. EUGENE D. ANDERSON on *WCH* XI 306.

[2956] Those two distances are based on CE 893 shown on *WR* 102 (also on *WCH* XVIII 89) for 177', and CE 902 shown on *WCH* XVIII 95 for 265'.

[2957] *WCH* XI 310 (Zahm).

[2958] Transcribed by the author from an interview of Robert Oswald by Josh Mankowitz in a segment titled "My Brother's Keeper" on *Dateline NBC*, broadcast by NBC-TV on June 14, 1998, and quoted here with permission after payment. The NBC license agreement is described in endnote [16]. I went through a cumbersome process and eventually paid an unusually large amount to NBC-TV primarily to have this important and irreplaceable testimony from brother Robert.

[2959] *WCH* III 440 (Robert Frazier).

[2960] *WCH* III 503 (Nicol).

[2961] *WCH* V 58-74 (Robert Frazier).

[2962] AFFIDAVIT OF ROBERT A. FRAZIER on *WCH* VII 590.

[2963] AFFIDAVIT OF CORTLANDT CUNNINGHAM on *WCH* VII 591.

[2964] TESTIMONY OF CORTLANDT CUNNINGHAM on *WCH* II 251-253.

[2965] *WCH* III 451-496 (Cunningham).

[2966] *WCH* III 456 (Cunningham).

[2967] *WCH* III 482-487 and 492-496 (Cunningham).

[2968] AFFIDAVIT OF CHARLES L. KILLION on *WCH* VII 591.

[2969] *WCH* III 414 (Robert Frazier).

[2970] *WCH* III 413 (Robert Frazier).

[2971] Quoted with permission from Cronkite, Walter. *A Reporter's Life* 307.

[2972] Quoted with permission from Russo, Gus. *Live by the Sword: The Secret War Against Castro and the Death of JFK*, pages 465-466.

— 13 — THE SHOOTER

[2973] Printed on the back cover of Oswald's "US Marine Corps Scorebook for US Rifle Caliber .30 M-l and US Carbine Caliber .30 M-l-Al", COMMISSION EXHIBIT (hereinafter CE 239, last page, shown on page 679 of volume XVI of the *Hearings Before the President's Commission on the Assassination of President Kennedy* (hereinafter in form *WCH* XVI 679).

[2974] This photo is in Groden, Robert J. *The Search for Lee Harvey Oswald: A Comprehensive Photographic Record* 28, which credits "Jack White JFK Educational Research". That collection is at Special Collections and Archives at the University of Texas at Arlington Libraries. Brenda S. McClurkin there, an expert on Jack White photos, says it is not by him. Therefore, the author and his experienced professional picture researcher conclude it was taken by a Marine Corps photographer in the normal conduct of federal government duties, and is therefore in the public domain. Please see my CREDITS AND PERMISSIONS on page ii.

[2975] The 3 pages are scanned from ANDERSON EXHIBIT NO. 1 on *WCH* XIX 16-18. Coming from that US Federal government source, they are in the public domain. Writing on top of first page appears to be "Major Anderson Deposition / Exhibit *(illegible)*".

[2976] FOLSOM EXHIBIT NO. 1 on *WCH* XIX 656-768.

[2977] TESTIMONY OF ALLISON G. FOLSOM, LT. COL., USMC on *WCH* VIII 303-311.

[2978] *WCH* VIII 311 (Folsom).

[2979] TESTIMONY OF MAJ. EUGENE D. ANDERSON on *WCH* XI 302.

[2980] *WCH* XI 303 (Anderson).

[2981] *WCH* XI 304 (Anderson).

[2982] *WCH* XI 305 (Anderson); this opinion is also stated in *Report of the President's Commission on the Assassination of President Kennedy* (the *Warren Report*, hereinafter expressed as *WR*), page 192.

[2983] *WCH* XI 305 (Anderson).

[2984] *WCH* XI 305-306 (Anderson).

[2985] TESTIMONY OF SGT. JAMES A. ZAHM on *WCH* XI 308; this final opinion is also stated on *WR* 192.

[2986] TESTIMONY OF NELSON DELGADO on *WCH* VIII 234-237.

[2987] TESTIMONY OF ROBERT A. FRAZIER on *WCH* III 413.

[2988] CE 239 on *WCH* XVI 639-679.

[2989] TESTIMONY OF MRS. MARGUERITE OSWALD on *WCH* I 240.

[2990] CE 239, first page, on *WCH* XVI 639.

[2991] CE 239, last page, on *WCH* XVI 679.

[2992] Quoted with permission after payment, from Manchester, William. *The Death of a President* 95n (which means the footnote at the bottom of page 95), for which the permission acknowledgement is in endnote [17].

[2993] Quoted with permission from Russo, Gus. *Live by the Sword: The Secret War Against Castro and the Death of JFK*, 465.

[2994] FBI interview on February 22, 1964, CE 1404, page 1, on *WCH* XXII 785 (left).

[2995] CE 1404, pages 2-3, on *WCH* XXII 785 (right) and 786 (left).

[2996] CE 2694 on *WCH* XXVI 58-68.

[2997] CE 2694, page 6, on *WCH* XXVI 59 (right).

[2998] FBI report of interview of Mr. V. C. Snider on CE 2694, page 4 (there are no pages 1-3), on *WCH* XXVI 58.

[2999] CE 2694, page 10, on *WCH* XXVI 61 (right).

[3000] CE 2694, pages 11-12 and 16-23, on *WCH* XXVI 62 and 64-68.

[3001] CE 2694, pages 14-15, on *WCH* XXVI 63 (right) and 64 (left).

[3002] Quoted with permission from Mailer, Norman. *Oswald's Tale: An American Mystery*, pages 777-778.

[3003] http://en.wikipedia.org/wiki/Wilt_Chamberlain%27s_100-point_game, consulted on 2014/08/25.

[3004] TESTIMONY OF ROBERT OSWALD on *WCH* I 326.

[3005] *WCH* I 327-328 (Robert Oswald).

[3006] Oswald, Robert L., with Myrick and Barbara Land. *Lee: A Portrait of Lee Harvey Oswald by His Brother* 204-211. This source was described in endnote [68].

[3007] Oswald, Robert 205.

[3008] Oswald, Robert 208-209.

— 14 — TOO CLOSE TO CALL

[3009] In remarks at Amherst College on October 26, 1963, quoted on http://www.jfklibrary.org/Research/Ready-Reference/JFK-Speeches/Remarks-at-Amherst-College-October-26-1963.aspx

[3010] TESTIMONY OF MRS. JOHN F. KENNEDY on page 180 of Volume V of *Hearings Before the President's Commission on the Assassination of President Kennedy*. Subsequent citations from testimony will be expressed as in the next line.

[3011] *WCH* V 180 (Mrs. Kennedy). The two unusual "[pause]" notations are in the Warren Commission's transcript.

[3012] Quoted with permission from Huffaker, Bob, Bill Mercer, George Phenix, and Wes Wise. *When The News Went Live: Dallas 1963*, page 67.

[3013] *Report of the President's Commission on the Assassination of President Kennedy* (popularly known as the *Warren Report*) page 111, hereinafter expressed in the form *WR* 111; which cites "CE 1024, statement of Agent Glen A Bennett." CE means COMMISSION EXHIBIT; this CE 1024 is on *WCH* XVIII 760.

[3014] *WR* 111, which cites "CE 2112", which shows the handwritten-on-the-plane original report on *WCH* XXIV 541-542.

[3015] They were married before May 1964 when he testified: TESTIMONY OF JAMES THOMAS TAGUE on *WCH* VII 552.

[3016] Bishop, Jim. *The Day Kennedy Was Shot*, page 167. Subsequent references will be in form Bishop *Kennedy* 167.

[3017] Photo purchased from Corbis: © Bettmann/Corbis.

[3018] This is a blowup of a very small cropped area from the photo above.

[3019] TESTIMONY OF MRS. DONALD BAKER on *WCH* VII 507-515. She was single Miss Virgie Rachley on the day of the shooting.

[3020] Quoted with permission after payment, from Bishop *Kennedy*, page 172.

[3021] *WCH* VII 553 (Tague).

[3022] *WCH* VII 555 (Tague).

[3023] TESTIMONY OF CLYDE A. HAYGOOD on *WCH* VI 298.

[3024] Quoted with permission from Sneed, Larry A. *No More Silence: An Oral History of the Assassination of President Kennedy*, page 110.

[3025] Photo imported from http://news.bbc.co.uk/onthisday/hi/witness/november/22/newsid_3223000/3223926.stm, converted to grayscale and tightly cropped . The photo taken by the Dallas Police Department is not known to be in the Municipal Archives of the City of Dallas, so the author concludes it is in the public domain. Please see CREDITS AND PERMISSIONS on page ii.

[3026] Quoted with permission from Sneed 212.

[3027] Quoted with permission from Sneed 213.

[3028] Quoted with the kind permission of the University Press of Kansas from McKnight, Gerald D. *Breach of Trust: How the Warren Commission Failed the Nation and Why*, pages 98-99.

[3029] Quoted with permission from Prouty, L. Fletcher. *JFK: The CIA, Vietnam, and the Plot to Assassinate John F. Kennedy*, page 299.

[3030] Quoted with permission from Sneed 111.

[3031] Quoted with permission from McKnight 184-185. In a subsequent reference to the same report on 230, McKnight cites "FBIHQ Oswald File, 105-82555-4584, 27-39."

[3032] Quoted with permission from McKnight 231-232, which cites "Hoover to Rankin, 8/12/1964, FBIHQ JFK Assassination File, 62-109060-3657."

[3033] Quoted with permission from Moore, Jim. *Conspiracy of One: The Definitive Book on the Kennedy Assassination* 197-199.

[3034] Quoted with permission from Sneed 111-113.

[3035] *WCH* VII 552 (Tague).

[3036] Quoted with permission after payment, from Epstein, Edward Jay. *The Assassination Chronicles: Inquest, Counterplot and Legend*, page 163.

[3037] *WR* 19.

[3038] Quoted with permission from Holland, Max. *The Kennedy Assassination Tapes*, page 142. Ellipsis and square brackets are Holland's.

3039 Quoted with permission from Holland, footnote 182 on page 142, which cites "'Turn May Have Saved Connally,' *Houston Post,* 23 November 1963; *HSCA Report,* 40."

3040 Quoted with permission from Holland 110.

3041 Quoted with permission from Holland 417.

3042 Quoted with permission from Holland 248-249.

3043 Quoted with permission from Holland 250. The square bracket and ellipsis are Holland's.

3044 Livingstone, Harrison Edward. *Killing the Truth: Deceit and Deception in the JFK Case*, pages 211-212, which cites "This testimony, reprinted with permission, is taken from a mock trial, entitled 'Trial of the Century: United States v. Lee Harvey Oswald.' Copyright © 1992, American Bar Association. The opinions expressed by participants in the mock trial do not necessarily represent those of the American Bar Association or of the speakers in the mock presentation. The individuals quoted here [include] Robert L. Piziali, Ph.D., Failure Analysis Associates, Inc. ..." See also Canal, John A. *Silencing the Lone Assassin*, pages 165-169 for an account of the trial. A statement about Livingstone is in endnote 2018.

3045 Quoted with permission after payment, from Posner *Case Closed: Lee Harvey Oswald and the Assassination of JFK*, pages 333-334, which cites his "Interview with Dr. Robert Piziali, November 9, 1992; testimony of Dr. Piziali, American Bar Association, mock trial of Lee Harvey Oswald, August 10, 1992." Copyright notice is in endnote 1039.

3046 Quoted with permission after payment, from Posner *Case Closed* 334, which cites "Testimony of Dr. Robert Piziali, American Bar Association, mock trial of Lee Harvey Oswald, August 10, 1992." Copyright notice is in endnote 1039.

3047 Quoted from Livingstone *Killing the Truth* 221. A statement about this source is in endnote 2018.

3048 Livingstone *Killing the Truth* 221-228. A statement about this source is in endnote 2018.

3049 Quoted with permission after payment, from Bishop *Kennedy* 253.

3050 Quoted with permission after payment, from Bishop *Kennedy* 681-682.

3051 TESTIMONY OF ROY H. KELLERMAN, SPECIAL AGENT, SECRET SERVICE on *WCH* II 73.

3052 *WCH* II 74-75 (Kellerman).

3053 Quoted with permission from Sneed 216.

3054 *WR* 29, which cites "CE 769 p. 1" being a 9-page account from Special Agent Winston G. Lawson beginning on *WCH* XVII 618, that being entered into evidence from "4 H 320 (Lawson)", which is the TESTIMONY OF WINSTON G. LAWSON, ACCOMPANIED BY FRED B. SMITH, DEPUTY GENERAL COUNSEL, TREASURY DEPARTMENT on *WCH* IV 320.

3055 Quoted with permission after payment, from Blaine, Gerald, with Lisa McCubbin. *The Kennedy Detail: JFK's Secret Service Agents Break Their Silence*, page 355. Copyright notice is in endnote 1444.

3056 Photo imported from http://kennedy-photos.blogspot.com/ "148. Rare View of JFK in Dallas Motorcade.jpg". The author and his experienced picture researcher spent considerable time attempting to identify the photographer and original source of the photo, but can only learn, from The Sixth Floor Museum at Dealey Plaza, that is was taken by a hotel employee from a window of the Adolphus Hotel on Main Street. I claim the right to show it as fair use after due diligence. Please see CREDITS AND PERMISSIONS on page ii.

3057 Photo purchased to show here: Tom C. Dillard Collection, *The Dallas Morning News* / The Sixth Floor Museum at Dealey Plaza.

3058 Quoted with permission after payment, from Bugliosi, Vincent. *Four Days in November: The Assassination of President John F. Kennedy*, page 36, citing "2 H 129, WCT William Robert Greer."; which was reprinted from Bugliosi, Vincent. *Reclaiming History: The Assassination of President John F. Kennedy*, page 25, with the same citation. Copyright notice for *Four Days* is in endnote 1767.

3059 Quoted with permission after payment, from Perret, Geoffrey. *Jack: A Life Like No Other*, pages 397-398. Copyright notice is in endnote 1578.

3060 This photo was imported from http://kennedy-photos.blogspot.com/ JFK In Dallas--11-22-63.jpg James L. Swanson's *End of Days* prints a very similar photo, likely from the same photographer at the same time, crediting "© Tom Dillard Collection, *The Dallas Morning News* / The Sixth Floor Museum at Dealey Plaza". This author's professional picture researcher and the excellent, cooperative Sixth Floor Museum staff say the photo is not in the Tom Dillard collection, which is now in The Sixth Floor Museum. Having done due diligence, I show it as fair use, as allowed by the U.S. copyright law. Please see my CREDITS AND PERMISSIONS statement and pledge on page ii.

3061 Quoted with permission from Hosty, James P., Jr., with Thomas C. Hosty. *Assignment: Oswald*, pages 250-251.

3062 Quoted with permission after payment from Smith, Sally Bedell. *Grace and Power: The Private World of the Kennedy White House*, page 33. Copyright notice is in endnote 1356.

3063 Quoted with permission from Hersh, Seymour M. *The Dark Side of Camelot*, page 12.

3064 Quoted with permission from Hersh 439.

3065 Quoted with permission from Hersh footnote on page 439, which cites on 472: "Hugh Sidey's cited column on Kennedy, 'Upstairs at the White House,' was published in *Time* magazine on May 18, 1987."

[3066] This photo was scanned from Smith, Sally Bedell *Grace and Power*, photo 56 in insert after p. 194, which credits "Earl E.T. Smith Jr. Collection". The author paid Penguin Random House for permission to use several quotations from that book; see the copyright notice in the first citation of the source, endnote [1356]. PRH wrote "We have no rights to the photograph" and "have no information for Earl E.T. Smith Jr. Collection". The author's copyright agent attempted to gain permission to use from Smith's last-known agent, ICM, which did not reply. The author claims due diligence, and as allowed by US copyright law, shows this irreplaceable view of JFK not otherwise seen, as fair use.

[3067] Photo with caption "The author views JFK's corset at the National Archives, February 2013" scanned from Reston, James, Jr. *The Accidental Victim: JFK, Lee Harvey Oswald, and the Real Target in Dallas*, page 183. Mr. Reston, who is in this author's esteem the "Trailblazer" for his pioneering insight into knowing Oswald's real target, owns the copyright for that book, and has generously granted permission to show you that photo here.

[3068] Quoted with the gracious permission of James Reston, Jr., author and copyright owner of *The Accidental Victim*, 182-183.

[3069] Quoted with permission from Sneed 50.

[3070] Quoted with the gracious permission of James Reston, Jr., author and copyright owner of *The Accidental Victim*, 140-141.

[3071] Quoted from Livingstone, Harrison Edward. *Killing Kennedy: And the Hoax of the Century*, page 52. A statement about this source is in endnote [2018].

[3072] Quoted with permission after payment, from Epstein, Edward Jay. *Inquest: The Warren Commission and the Establishment of Truth*, page 122, which cites "Specter Interview."

[3073] Quoted with permission after payment, from Epstein *Inquest* 122, which cites "Specter Interview."

[3074] Quoted with permission after payment, from Epstein *Inquest* 122, which cites "Rankin Interview II."

[3075] Quoted with permission after payment, from Epstein *Inquest* 122, which cites "[*Warren*] *Report*, p. 97."

[3076] *WR* 99 with caption "Photograph taken during reenactment showing C2766 rifle with camera attached." Shown here is the same photo with the same exhibit number, scanned from the higher-clarity image CE 887 on *WCH* XVIII 86. Coming from that US Federal government source, it is in the public domain.

[3077] Photo by Ferd Kaufman was purchased from AP and tightly cropped. ©The Associated Press.

[3078] Quoted from Lifton, David S. *Best Evidence: Disguise and Deception in the Assassination of John F. Kennedy*, published by Macmillan in 1980, page 76*n* (which means the *note* on page 76). The Commission reported on *WR* 106 "the probable angle through the President's body was calculated at 17°43'30", assuming that he was sitting in a vertical position." The author's copyright agent applied for permission to quote, and in reply Sam Moore, Manager of the Penguin Publishing Group Permissions Department, wrote "we would consider this fair use, and as such, no formal permission is necessary." Nonetheless, this author is grateful. Macmillan published both of my Dad's books in the 1940s.

[3079] Photo scanned from CE 903 on *WCH* XVIII 96. Coming from that US Federal government source, it is in the public domain. The photograph is in the National Archives.

[3080] Quoted from Livingstone *Killing the Truth* 46. A statement about this source is in endnote [2018].

[3081] Photo was purchased to show here: Tom C. Dillard Collection, *The Dallas Morning News* / The Sixth Floor Museum at Dealey Plaza.

[3082] Image at left was scanned from CE 893 on *WR* 102, which is also printed on *WCH* XVIII 89. Coming from that US Federal government source, it is in the public domain.

[3083] Image at right was cropped and enlarged from lower-left quadrant of that CE 893. Coming from that US Federal government source, it is in the public domain.

[3084] Image at left was scanned from CE 902 on *WCH* XVIII 95, vertically in middle of page. Coming from that US Federal government source, it is in the public domain. The same exhibit, smaller and with somewhat less clarity, is on *WR* 108. Image at right was cropped and enlarged from lower-left quadrant of that CE 902. Coming from that US Federal government source, it is in the public domain.

[3085] TESTIMONY OF LYNDAL L. SHANEYFELT on *WCH* V 161: "Over the entire run ... Between frame 161 and 313."

[3086] *WR* 49 endnote 147, which cites "5 H 160-161 (Lyndal L. Shaneyfelt)."

[3087] *WR* 555, which cites "3 H 400 ([Robert] Frazier)." where FBI firearms expert Robert A. Frazier explains his tests to determine that.

[3088] Quoted with permission from Specter, Arlen, with Charles Robbins. *Passion for Truth: From Finding JFK's Single Bullet to Questioning Anita Hill to Impeaching Clinton*, page 110.

[3089] Quoted with permission from Sturdivan, Larry M. *The JFK Myths: A Scientific Investigation of the Kennedy Assassination*, page xxiii, from Foreword by Kenneth A. Rahn.

[3090] This photo was taken by the FBI. The scratched and dusty print is in the JFK Assassination collection at the National Archives in College Park, Maryland, and is thus in the public domain. What you see here was somewhat cleaned up by the author's graphics expert — not as much as he wanted to do, but enough to not distort or distract.

[3091] All Moon characteristics here are from http://en.wikipedia.org/wiki/Moon#Appearance_from_Earth on 2014/08/29.

[3092] That Wikipedia article gives the Moon's "angular diameter 29.3 to 34.1 arcminutes" calculated from "Williams, Dr. David R. (2 February 2006). 'Moon Fact Sheet'. NASA (National Space Science Data Center). Retrieved 31 December 2008."

[3093] Quoted with permission from "Connally Gains, Doctors Report; Turn May Have Saved Life—Full Recovery Likely" by John Herbers, *Special to The New York Times* on November 23, 1963, in Semple, Robert B., Jr., editor. *Four Days in November: The Original Coverage of the John F. Kennedy Assassination by the Staff of The New York Times*, page 270.

— 15 — REGARDING KENNEDY

[3094] Quoted in *Congressional Record*, November 25, 1963, p. 22695 (they number pages from the beginning of each year).

[3095] Quoted with permission after payment, from Ford, Gerald R., and John R. Stiles. *Portrait of the Assassin*, page 433.

[3096] Quoted as fair use after due diligence from Brussell, Mae, compiler of "The Last Words of Lee Harvey Oswald", as incorporated into Wallechinsky, David, and Irving Wallace. *The People's Almanac #2*, pages 47-52. Mae Magnin Brussell died in 1988, apparently without leaving descendants or relatives. The *People's Almanac* was published by Bantam Books, now a brand of Penguin Random House, whose permissions department says they do not hold the copyright, do not know who, if anyone, does. Having performed due diligence, the author claims the right to quote as fair use. If any valid copyright holder arises, please see CREDITS AND PERMISSIONS on page ii.

[3097] The same quotation is in Livingstone, Harrison Edward, and Robert J. Groden. *High Treason: The Assassination of JFK & the Case for Conspiracy*, page 138, which cites "O'Toole, George. *The Assassination Tapes: An Electronic Probe Into the Murder of John F. Kennedy and the Dallas Cover-up*. New York: Penthouse Press 1975."; see also Bugliosi, Vincent *Four Days in November: The Assassination of President John F. Kennedy* 207, 210, 249, 259, reprinted from Bugliosi, Vincent *Reclaiming History: The Assassination of President John F. Kennedy* 131, 132, 156, 163 respectively.

[3098] The same quotation is in Livingstone and Groden *High Treason* 138, with same citation as above, see also Bugliosi *Four Days* 300, 310, 348, 349; reprinted from Bugliosi *Reclaiming History* 188, 194, 217-218.

[3099] See also Bugliosi *Four Days* 416, which was reprinted from Bugliosi *Reclaiming History* 259.

[3100] Quoted with permission after payment, from Bishop, Jim. *The Day Kennedy Was Shot*, page 152. Subsequent references will be in form Bishop *Kennedy* 152.

[3101] TESTIMONY OF RUTH HYDE PAINE, *Hearings Before the President's Commission on the Assassination of President Kennedy*, Volume IX, page 371. Second and subsequent testimonies are hereinafter cited in form: *WCH* IX 371 (Ruth Paine).

[3102] Quoted with permission after payment, from Bishop *Kennedy* 563. Subsequent references will be in form Bishop *Kennedy* 563.

[3103] Quoted with permission from Douglass, James W. *JFK and the Unspeakable: Why He Died and Why It Matters*, page 331, which cites "Transcript of Marina Oswald interview, November 24, 1963, at Inn of the Six Flags, Arlington, Texas, pp. 41, 43. Warren Commission Document 344. David S. Lifton, *Document Addendum to the Warren Report* (El Segundo, Calif.: Sightext Publications, 1968), pp. 331, 333."

[3104] Quoted with permission from Hosty, James P., Jr., with Thomas C. Hosty. *Assignment: Oswald*, pages 87-90.

[3105] FBI report, File #DL 89-43 (2) dated 11/28/63 of interview on 11/27/63, in COMMISSION EXHIBIT (hereinafter CE) 1780 on *WCH* XXIII 385.

[3106] FBI report, File #DL 89-43 (5) dated 12/1/63 of interview on 11/30/63, in CE 1794 on *WCH* XXIII 413.

[3107] TESTIMONY OF MRS. LEE HARVEY (Marina) OSWALD on *WCH* I 22.

[3108] *WCH* I 71 (Marina Oswald).

[3109] *WCH* V 605 (Marina Oswald).

[3110] *WCH* I 123 (Marina Oswald).

[3111] *WCH* V 394 (Marina Oswald).

[3112] Quoted with permission after payment, from Ford and Stiles *Portrait*, page 321.

[3113] *WCH* V 606 (Marina Oswald).

[3114] *WCH* V 607 (Marina Oswald).

[3115] *WCH* V 607-608 (Marina Oswald).

[3116] *WCH* V 607 (Marina Oswald).

[3117] Quoted with permission from McMillan, Priscilla Johnson. *Marina and Lee*, 413. Permission statement is in endnote [150].

[3118] Quoted with permission from McMillan 414. Permission statement is in endnote [150].

[3119] Quoted with permission from McMillan 570-571. Permission statement is in endnote [150].

[3120] Quoted with permission from McMillan 581. Permission statement is in endnote [150].

[3121] Quoted with permission from McMillan, Priscilla Johnson. *Marina and Lee*, in the Bantam Books paperback (pocketbook) edition of 1978, on pages ii-iii if the front pages had been numbered. Permission statement is in endnote [150].

[3122] DEPOSITION OF MARINA OSWALD PORTER, August 9, 1978 *Appendix to Hearings before the Select Committee on Assassinations of the U.S. House of Representatives, Ninety-Fifth Congress, Second Session* Volume XII pages 349 and 412-413; hereinafter abbreviated as *HSCAHA*.

[3123] *Hearings before the Select Committee on Assassinations of the U.S. House of Representatives, Ninety-Fifth Congress, Second Session* Volume II pages 209-210; hereinafter abbreviated as *HSCAH*.

[3124] *HSCAH* II 213.

[3125] Quoted with permission from Benson, Michael. *Encyclopedia of the JFK Assassination*, page 61.

[3126] *HSCAH* II 224-225.

[3127] *HSCAH* II 251-252.

[3128] *HSCAH* II 279.

[3129] Quoted from Livingstone, Harrison Edward. *High Treason 2: The Great Cover-Up: The Assassination of President John F. Kennedy*, page 458. A statement about this source is in endnote [2018].

[3130] Quoted with permission from Wecht, Cyril *Cause of Death* 57. Copyright notice is in endnote [623].

[3131] TESTIMONY OF MRS. MARGUERITE OSWALD on *WCH* I 233.

[3132] TESTIMONY OF ROBERT EDWARD LEE OSWALD on *WCH* I 449.

[3133] Quoted from Oswald, Robert. *Lee: A Portrait of Lee Harvey Oswald by His Brother*, page 18. This source was described in endnote [68].

[3134] TESTIMONY OF SAMUEL B. BALLEN on *WCH* IX 54-55.

[3135] *WCH* IX 48 (Ballen).

[3136] TESTIMONY OF JAMES W. BOOKHOUT on *WCH* VII 312.

[3137] *WCH* VII 315 (Bookhout).

[3138] Quoted with kind permission and assistance from the heirs of Thomas Buchanan; from Buchanan, Thomas G. *Who Killed Kennedy?*, page 72 in the revised and expanded American publication by Putnam, not the earlier-smaller British edition.

[3139] TESTIMONY OF MAX E. CLARK on *WCH* VIII 352.

[3140] TESTIMONY OF ILYA A. MAMANTOV on *WCH* IX 122.

[3141] TESTIMONY OF GEORGE S. DE MOHRENSCHILDT on *WCH* IX 265-266.

[3142] Photo purchased from Corbis and very lightly cropped: © Bettmann / Corbis.

[3143] Quoted with the gracious permission of James Reston, Jr., author and copyright owner of *The Lone Star: The Life of John Connally*, page 233.

[3144] *WCH* IX 255 (George De Mohrenschildt).

[3145] *WCH* IX 322 (George De Mohrenschildt).

[3146] *WCH* IX 275 (George De Mohrenschildt).

[3147] Quoted from Livingstone *High Treason 2*, page 457. A statement about this source is in endnote [2018].

[3148] Quoted with permission of the author, James Reston, Jr., from his featured article "Was Connally the Real Target?" in *TIME* magazine 28 Nov. 1988, page 36.

[3149] Unpublished manuscript by George De Mohrenschildt in *Appendix to Hearings before the Select Committee on Assassinations of the U.S. House of Representatives, Ninety-Fifth Congress, Second Session* Volume XII page 113; hereinafter *HSCAHA* XII 113.

[3150] *HSCAHA* XII 146.

[3151] *HSCAHA* XII 132-133.

[3152] *HSCAHA* XII 89.

[3153] *HSCAHA* XII 225-228.

[3154] *HSCAHA* XII 305.

[3155] *HSCAHA* XII 315.

[3156] TESTIMONY OF JEANNE DE MOHRENSCHILDT on *WCH* IX 325.

[3157] *WCH* IX 328 (Jeanne De Mohrenschildt).

[3158] *Report of the President's Commission on the Assassination of President Kennedy* (popularly known as the *Warren Report*) page 8; hereinafter expressed in the form *WR* 8.

[3159] Quoted as fair use (for brevity) from Robinson, Melissa B. (AP) "Notes show Oswald said he didn't kill Kennedy" *The Seattle Times* 21 Nov. 1997: A10.

[3160] Quoted as fair use (for brevity) from Robinson A10.

[3161] *WR* 598.

[3162] *WR* 607. See also TESTIMONY OF J. W. FRITZ on *WCH* IV 225 and Bishop *Kennedy* 303.

[3163] *WCH* IV 225 (Fritz). See also Manchester, William. *The Death of a President* 457.

[3164] *WCH* IV 239-240 (Fritz).

[3165] Quoted as fair use (for brevity) from Robinson A10.

[3166] Quoted as fair use (for brevity) from Robinson A10.

[3167] TESTIMONY OF L. C. GRAVES on *WCH* XIII 4.

[3168] *WCH* VII 257 (Graves).

[3169] *WCH* XIII 5 (Graves).

[3170] TESTIMONY OF PAUL RODERICK GREGORY on *WCH* IX 148.

[3171] *WCH* IX 157-158 (Paul Gregory).

[3172] Quoted with permission after payment, from article by Paul Gregory titled "This Close to a Killer" in *The New York Times* Sunday Magazine page MM36, November 10, 2013. Credit notice supplied by PARS International Corp.: "From The New York Times, 11/10/2013 © 2013 The New York Times. All rights reserved. Used by permission and protected by the Copyright Laws of the United States. The printing, copying, redistribution or retransmission of this Content without express written permission is prohibited."

[3173] CE 832, page 2, on *WCH* XVII 786.

[3174] TESTIMONY OF JAMES PATRICK HOSTY, JR. on *WCH* IV 468.

[3175] *WCH* VII 312 (Bookhout).

[3176] *WCH* IV 468 (Hosty).

[3177] Quoted with permission from Hosty 24.

3178 TESTIMONY OF RAYMOND FRANKLIN KRYSTINIK on *WCH* IX 465.

3179 *WCH* IX 465-466 (Krystinik).

3180 TESTIMONY OF JAMES R. LEAVELLE on *WCH* VII 266-267.

3181 *WCH* VII 267 (Leavelle).

3182 *WCH* IV 234 (Fritz); TESTIMONY OF C. N. DHORITY on *WCH* VII 156; TESTIMONY OF DETECTIVE L. D. MONTGOMERY on *WCH* XIII 27. (Why the Commission used this one officer's title is unknown.)

3183 Quoted from Livingstone, Harrison Edward. *Killing the Truth: Deceit and Deception in the JFK Case*, page 83, which cites "12 HSCA 186, 132; Sylvia Meagher, *Accessories After the Fact*, p. 234." A statement is in endnote [2018].

3184 Quoted as fair use from Livingstone, Harrison Edward. *Killing Kennedy: And the Hoax of the Century*, page 313.

3185 TESTIMONY OF FRANCIS L. MARTELLO on *WCH* X 56, quoting from a memo he prepared for the Secret Service and FBI.

3186 *WCH* X 60 (Martello).

3187 Quoted with permission from McMillan 426. Permission statement is in endnote [150].

3188 *WCH* XIII 26 (Montgomery).

3189 TESTIMONY OF MRS. LILLIAN MURRET on *WCH* VIII 153; see also Bugliosi *Reclaiming History* 946n.

3190 TESTIMONY OF MARILYN DOROTHEA MURRET on *WCH* VIII 173-174.

3191 Quoted with permission from Oglesby, Carl. *Who Killed JFK?*, page 58.

3192 TESTIMONY OF MICHAEL R. PAINE on *WCH* II 395.

3193 *WCH* II 414 (Michael Paine).

3194 *WCH* II 423-424 (Michael Paine).

3195 Quoted as fair use (for brevity: 40 words) from *The Washington Post,* November 28, 1963.

3196 Quoted as fair use (for brevity: 39 words) from *New York World-Telegram and Sun,* November 25, 1963.

3197 TESTIMONY OF JAMES ROWLEY on *WCH* V 472.

3198 Quoted with permission from Zirbel, Craig I. *The Texas Connection*, page 196.

3199 Quoted with permission from Zirbel 231-232.

3200 TESTIMONY OF ADRIAN THOMAS ALBA on *WCH* X 228.

3201 TESTIMONY OF MAX E. CLARK on *WCH* VIII 351.

3202 TESTIMONY OF DECLAN P. FORD on *WCH* II 327.

3203 TESTIMONY OF MRS. KATHERINE FORD on *WCH* II 315.

3204 TESTIMONY OF ALEXANDRA DE MOHRENSCHILDT TAYLOR GIBSON on *WCH* XI 145.

3205 TESTIMONY OF EVERETT D. GLOVER on *WCH* X 30.

3206 TESTIMONY OF ELENA A. HALL on *WCH* VIII 405.

3207 TESTIMONY OF JOHN RAYMOND HALL on *WCH* VIII 411.

3208 TESTIMONY OF ILYA A. MAMANTOV on *WCH* IX.

3209 TESTIMONY OF ANNA N. MELLER on *WCH* VIII 386.

3210 TESTIMONY OF RUTH HYDE PAINE on *WCH* II 507 and *WCH* III 69.

3211 TESTIMONY OF GARY E. TAYLOR on *WCH* IX 95.

3212 Quoted with permission after payment, from Ford and Stiles *Portrait* 226.

— 16 — REGARDING CONNALLY

3213 Spoken to and quoted by George De Mohrenschildt in his unpublished manuscript in *Appendix to Hearings before the Select Committee on Assassinations of the U.S. House of Representatives, Ninety-Fifth Congress, Second Session* Volume XII, page 148; hereinafter *HSCAHA* XII 148. (HSCA = House Committee, H = Hearings, A = Appendix)

3214 Epstein, Edward Jay. *Legend: The Secret World of Lee Harvey Oswald*, page 306.

3215 Quoted with permission after payment, from Epstein *Legend*, page 307 note 9.

3216 Quoted as fair use after due diligence from Brussell, Mae, compiler of "The Last Words of Lee Harvey Oswald" in Wallechinsky, David, and Irving Wallace. *The People's Almanac #2* on pages 47-52; see also Bugliosi *Four Days* 349, which was reprinted from Bugliosi *Reclaiming History* 218. Relative to Brussell, see the citation in endnote [3096].

3217 TESTIMONY OF MRS. LEE HARVEY (Marina) OSWALD, *Hearings Before the President's Commission on the Assassination of President Kennedy*, Volume I, page 72. Testimony is hereinafter cited in this form: *WCH* I 72 (Marina Oswald). Commenting on her statement, see also Ford, Gerald R., and John R. Stiles in *Portrait of the Assassin*, pages 322-323.

3218 *WCH* V 608 (Marina Oswald).

3219 *WCH* V 607 (Marina Oswald).

3220 *WCH* V 609-610 (Marina Oswald).

3221 *WCH* V 611 (Marina Oswald).

3222 *Hearings before the Select Committee on Assassinations of the U.S. House of Representatives, Ninety-Fifth Congress, Second Session* Volume II, pages 279-280; hereinafter *HSCAH* II 279-280.

3223 Quoted with the gracious permission of James Reston, Jr., author and copyright owner of *The Accidental Victim* 61-62; Originally written in Reston, James, Jr. *The Lone Star: The Life of John Connally* (to which he also owns copyright) 236.

3224 TESTIMONY OF MRS. MARGUERITE OSWALD on *WCH* I 224.

3225 TESTIMONY OF ROBERT OSWALD on *WCH* I 450.

3226 Quoted from Oswald, Robert. *Lee: A Portrait of Lee Harvey Oswald by His Brother*, pages 18-19. This source was described in endnote [68].

3227 TESTIMONY OF JAMES W. BOOKHOUT on *WCH* VII 315.

3228 *HSCAHA* XII 145.

3229 *HSCAHA* XII 148.

3230 *HSCAHA* XII 83-84.

3231 This was first written in Reston, James, Jr. *The Lone Star: The Life of John Connally*, page 233.

3232 Quoted with the gracious permission of James Reston, Jr., author and copyright owner of *The Accidental Victim* 30-31.

3233 Quoted with the gracious permission of James Reston, Jr., author and copyright owner of *The Accidental Victim* 35.

3234 TESTIMONY OF ALEXANDRA DE MOHRENSCHILDT TAYLOR GIBSON on *WCH* XI 145.

3235 TESTIMONY OF JAMES ROWLEY on *WCH* V 468.

3236 TESTIMONY OF SAMUEL B. BALLEN on *WCH* IX 45.

3237 TESTIMONY OF MAX E. CLARK on *WCH* VIII 351.

3238 TESTIMONY OF JEANNE DE MOHRENSCHILDT on *WCH* IX 326.

3239 TESTIMONY OF DECLAN P. FORD on *WCH* II 327.

3240 TESTIMONY OF MRS. KATHERINE FORD on *WCH* II 315.

3241 TESTIMONY OF J. W. FRITZ on *WCH* IV 225.

3242 TESTIMONY OF PAUL RODERICK GREGORY on *WCH* IX 149.

3243 TESTIMONY OF ELENA A. HALL on *WCH* VIII 405.

3244 TESTIMONY OF JOHN RAYMOND HALL on *WCH* VIII 411.

3245 TESTIMONY OF ANNA N. MELLER on *WCH* VIII 386.

3246 TESTIMONY OF MARILYN DOROTHEA MURRET on *WCH* VIII 173-174.

3247 TESTIMONY OF MICHAEL R. PAINE on *WCH* II 399.

3248 TESTIMONY OF RUTH HYDE PAINE on *WCH* IX 373.

3249 TESTIMONY OF GARY E. TAYLOR on *WCH* IX 95.

— 17 — POLITICAL PROCLIVITY

3250 Quoted with permission after payment, from Blaine, Gerald, with Lisa McCubbin. *The Kennedy Detail: JFK's Secret Service Agents Break Their Silence*, page 264. Copyright notice is in endnote [1444].

3251 Quoted as fair use (for brevity) from http://en.wikipedia.org/wiki/Political_Spectrum on 2014/01/21.

3252 Quoted with permission from Johnson, Lyndon Baines. *The Vantage Point: Perspectives of the Presidency 1963–1969*, page 6. Copyright and permission notice is in endnote [1559].

3253 Quoted with permission after payment, from Onassis, Jacqueline Kennedy. *Jacqueline Kennedy: Historic Conversations on Life with John F. Kennedy.* Interviews with Arthur M. Schlesinger, Jr., page 89 and footnote 24 by Schlesinger.

3254 Quoted with permission from Dallek, Robert. *An Unfinished Life: John F. Kennedy: 1917 - 1963*, page 693.

3255 TESTIMONY OF MRS. LEE HARVEY (Marina) OSWALD on *WCH* I 16; see also Bugliosi, Vincent. *Reclaiming History: The Assassination of President John F. Kennedy*, page 693.

3256 *The Final Assassinations Report: Report of the Select Committee on Assassinations, U.S. House of Representatives*. Bantam Books, 1979 paperback, page 62.

3257 Quoted with permission after payment, from Bugliosi, Vincent. *Reclaiming History: The Assassination of President John F. Kennedy*, page 947. Copyright notice is in endnote [1788].

3258 *WCH* I 71 (Marina Oswald).

3259 *WCH* V 605 (Marina Oswald).

3260 TESTIMONY OF JEANNE DE MOHRENSCHILDT on *WCH* IX 325.

3261 DEPOSITION OF MARINA OSWALD PORTER, *Appendix to Hearings before the Select Committee on Assassinations of the U.S. House of Representatives, Ninety-Fifth Congress, Second Session* Volume XII pages 349 and 412-413.

3262 Quoted with permission from Oglesby, Carl. *Who Killed JFK?*, page 58.

3263 Quoted from Leslie, Warren. *Dallas Public and Private*, page 152-153. The author's copyright agent learned that the publisher is out of business and the author is deceased, so for this one brief quote, this author claims fair use after due diligence. Please see CREDITS AND PERMISSIONS on page ii.

3264 *WCH* I 16 (Marina Oswald).

3265 *HSCAHA* XII 241.

3266 *HSCAHA* XII 256.

3267 *HSCAHA* XII 241.

3268 *HSCAHA* XII 303

— 18 — CONNALLY WILL RIDE

3269 Quoted from *Report of the President's Commission on the Assassination of President John F. Kennedy*, best known as the *Warren Report*, page 421, which will hereinafter be cited in the form *WR* 421.

[3270] Quoted with permission from Bugliosi, Vincent. *Outrage: The Five Reasons Why O.J. Simpson Got Away with Murder*, page 182.

[3271] Matthews, James P., and Ernest Schwork, editors. *The Complete Kennedy Saga! Four Books In One!* In the third "book" titled *Highlights of the Warren Report*, pages 57-58.

[3272] Quoted from the news clipping in COMMISSION EXHIBIT No. 1361 on page 613 of volume XXII of the *Hearings before the President's Commission on the Assassination of President Kennedy*; hereinafter cited as: CE 1361 on *WCH* XXII 613.

[3273] Quoted with permission from Kaiser, David. *The Road to Dallas: The Assassination of John F. Kennedy*, page 357. Permission notice is in endnote [998].

[3274] Quoted from CE 1363 on *WCH* XXII 615.

[3275] Quoted from CE 1362 on *WCH* XXII 614.

[3276] Portion of the right-hand column of CE 1364 on *WCH* XXII 616.

[3277] TESTIMONY OF BUELL WESLEY FRAZIER on *WCH* II 222.

[3278] Quoted with permission from Mallon, Thomas. *Mrs. Paine's Garage: and the Murder of John F. Kennedy* 71n (meaning the footnote at the bottom of page 71).

— 19 — THE SHOT NOT TAKEN

[3279] Quoted with permission from Dallas motorcycle Officer Stavis "Steve" Ellis, who chose "the four guys that I had to ride immediately to the rear of the President's car", in Sneed, Larry A. *No More Silence: An Oral History of the Assassination of President Kennedy*, page 144.

[3280] Photo is lightly cropped from #PC96 in the collection of the John F. Kennedy Presidential Library and Museum, Boston.

[3281] Quoted from Fay, Paul B., Jr. *The Pleasure of His Company*, pages 97-98. This delightful memoir was published by Harper & Row in 1966 with copyright © 1996 by Paul B. Fay, Jr. For the fact that JFK sat where all of us expect him to be, there can be no better antecedent than "Red" Fay's story of his first ride with his buddy-become-President. I worked diligently for permission to quote these 257 words. My copyright agent applied to Fay's publisher's successor via request #A22354, to which the Permissions Department of HarperCollins Publishers replied they did not hold the copyright, believed it had reverted to the author or estate, and we should apply to Sterling Lord Literistic at 65 Bleecker St. in NYC. He did so by mail, and received no reply. As this book neared ready-to-print, the author found Sterling Lord's elegant Website and entered my request for permission on the most perfect input form I have ever encountered for that purpose. After three weeks with no answer, I did it again. After two more weeks, I phoned them at 212-780-6050, asked for the Permissions Department, where I left a message explaining my business and requesting a callback. They did not respond, so I don't even know if they represent Fay's book. In parallel I searched and found the names of Paul Jr. and Anita's children: Katherine Fay, Sally Cottingham and son Paul B. Fay III, the Principal and CEO of Haas & Haynie, developers with office in South San Francisco. I left repeated phone messages for Paul III, then on the office's general message facility, and also sent an email message to their contact address "info@" stating exactly what I wanted and why. Absolutely none of these requests — there have been eleven altogether — have brought any reply. I must conclude that my need is so unimportant that nobody will respond. I believe "Red" Fay, if alive, would be pleased to approve my use. Therefore, as allowed by U.S. copyright laws, having done due diligence I claim the right to include Red's 257 words and the photo below as fair use. If any Fays come upon this, please see my CREDITS AND PERMISSIONS on page ii.

[3282] The photo was scanned from Fay, the eighth photo in the second section of illustrations, on the sixth page after 118. The book does not state any sources or credits for its photographs. The author claims the right of fair use as in endnote [3281].

[3283] Quoted as fair use from http://en.wikiquote.org/wiki/Donald_Rumsfeld, an encompassing source that lists slightly different words about this same subject at different times. This unusually understandable version is from a press conference at NATO Headquarters in Brussels, Belgium on June 6, 2002.

[3284] Quoted as fair use from http://en.wikiquote.org/wiki/Donald_Rumsfeld (continuation of the preceding).

[3285] Photo purchased from Corbis and moderately cropped: © Bettmann / Corbis.

[3286] All positions are as seen on the DVD produced by the National Geographic Channel, *JFK: The Final Hours*.

[3287] Photo purchased from AP and very slightly cropped. ©The Associated Press.

[3288] Quoted with permission after payment, from Blaine, Gerald, with Lisa McCubbin. *The Kennedy Detail: JFK's Secret Service Agents Break Their Silence*, pages 390 and 392. Copyright notice is in endnote [1444].

[3289] Quoted with permission after payment, from Blaine with McCubbin, page 393. Copyright notice is in endnote [1444].

[3290] Four photos were scanned from Livingstone, Harrison Edward. *Killing the Truth: Deceit and Deception in the JFK Case*, photos 3-6 in the color insert after 624. Livingstone, himself, took the photos from LHO's TSBD window. They are shown as fair use under copyright law after a due diligence search. A statement about this source is in endnote [2018].

[3291] Photo scanned from COMMISSION EXHIBIT No. 875, upper photo on *WCH* XVII 884. Coming from that US Federal government source, it is in the public domain. Hereinafter such a cite will be in the form CE 875 on *WCH* XVII 884.

[3292] Photo scanned from Livingstone, Harrison Edward. *Killing Kennedy: And the Hoax of the Century*, photo 15 in the insert after page 74. Livingstone writes that this is one "of the three unidentified photographs found in the Secret Service records at the National Archives." Through his professional photo researcher, highly experienced at NARA, the author has learned that there are many unidentified, noncataloged and misplaced items in the Archives. Connally's envelope to Oswald in Chapter 4 – MINSK is a classic example, *q.v.* A statement about this source is in endnote [2018].

[3293] Photo scanned and cropped from Sneed, Larry A. *No More Silence: An Oral History of the Assassination of President Kennedy*, University of North Texas Press, copyright 1998 Larry A. Sneed. It is on the seventh page of the photo insert section after page 166, with credit for the photo on page x to "Stavis and Nita Ellis".

[3294] Both photos were purchased to show here: Phil Willis Collection / The Sixth Floor Museum at Dealey Plaza. Both were converted to grayscale (unfortunately, you cannot see the limo's lovely Midnight Blue) and moderately cropped.

[3295] TESTIMONY OF MISS VICTORIA ELIZABETH ADAMS in *Hearings Before the President's Commission on the Assassination of President Kennedy*, volume VI, pages 387-388; subsequent testimonies from a same witness are hereinafter expressed in the form *WCH* VI 387-388 (Victoria Adams).

[3296] Quoted with permission from Benson, Michael. *Encyclopedia of the JFK Assassination*, page 63.

[3297] COMMISSION EXHIBIT (hereinafter CE) 1381, page 26, on *WCH* XXII 644.

[3298] In his 1976 self-published book *Photographic Whitewash: Suppressed Kennedy Assassination Pictures*, Harold Weisberg typed an extensive diatribe about these failures on pages 49-52.

[3299] Quoted as fair use (for brevity: 13 words) from Managing Editor George P. Hunt in *LIFE* magazine, November 24, 1967, page 3. I would have much preferred to include all of his 117 words on the matter, but as was related in chapter 5 where I could not afford to print Connally's article, the price would have been $2,000, much too expensive for this old retiree who has already spent more than $60,000 out-of-pocket to produce this book as this endnote is edited in January 2016.

[3300] Quoted with permission from Benson *Encyclopedia*, page 63.

[3301] These two "grabs" were purchased to show here: Elsie Dorman Collection / The Sixth Floor Museum at Dealey Plaza. They were converted to grayscale and cropped to illustrate the natural view of a person concentrating on the limousine.

[3302] Quoted as fair use (for brevity) from http://whatis.techtarget.com/definition/grayscale

[3303] Distances were calculated by the author for Oswald's obstructed view into the limousine approaching on Houston, scaling the photo of the TSBD displayed in chapter 5, cross-checked with the County Surveyor's elevations in a plot used later.

[3304] Quoted with permission after payment, from Bugliosi, Vincent. *Reclaiming History: The Assassination of President John F. Kennedy*, page 32; which was reprinted as Bugliosi, Vincent. *Four Days in November: The Assassination of President John F. Kennedy*, page 48. Copyright notice for *Reclaiming History* is in endnote [1788].

[3305] Quoted with permission after payment, from Bishop, Jim. *The Day Kennedy Was Shot*, page 167. Subsequent references will be in the form Bishop *Kennedy* 167.

[3306] TESTIMONY OF WILLIAM ROBERT GREER, SPECIAL AGENT, SECRET SERVICE on *WCH* II 117.

[3307] *Assassination of President John F. Kennedy*, a United States Secret Service film, listed in REFERENCES CITED section in "DVD: *JFK: A New World Order*". The documentary film is the second feature on the "Bonus Disk" in the 3-disk set.

[3308] Transcribed as fair use (for brevity) from Jim Underwood, narrator, on the DVD of the U.S. Secret Service film *Assassination of President John F. Kennedy*.

[3309] On the DVD of the film *Assassination of President John F. Kennedy*, in the best complete sequence, the events listed below begin at: 12:24, 12:32, 12:45, 12:55, 13:00, 13:03, 13:05, and the head shot is at 13:09, after which Oswald presumably left the window to hide the rifle and escape down the stairs, so we don't care about the timing of later motorcade events.

[3310] Photo scanned from CE 875, upper photo on *WCH* XVII 873. This and the next three, coming from that US Federal government source, are in the public domain.

[3311] Photo scanned from CE 875, upper photo on *WCH* XVII 878.

[3312] Photo scanned from CE 875, upper photo on *WCH* XVII 876.

[3313] Photo scanned from CE 875, lower photo on *WCH* XVII 876.

[3314] Photo purchased from Corbis: © Robert A. Cumins/Corbis.

[3315] TESTIMONY OF J. EDGAR HOOVER on *WCH* V 105.

[3316] Quoted with permission from Weisberg, Harold. *Whitewash: The Report on the Warren Report*, page 110.

[3317] Quoted with kind permission and assistance from the heirs of Thomas Buchanan; from Buchanan, Thomas G. *Who Killed Kennedy?* page 113 in the revised and expanded American publication by Putnam, not the earlier, smaller British edition.

[3318] Quoted with permission from Weisberg *Whitewash* 110.

[3319] Quoted with permission from Weisberg *Whitewash* 338.

[3320] Quoted with permission after payment, from Thompson, Josiah. *Six Seconds in Dallas: A Micro-Study of the Kennedy Assassination*, page 190.

[3321] Quoted with permission after payment, from Bishop *Kennedy* 170.

[3322] Quoted with the gracious permission of James Reston, Jr., author and copyright owner of *The Lone Star: The Life of John Connally*, page 639, which cites "On 'motor program': Dr. Thomas Gualtieri, an authority on neuropsychiatric disorders and their treatment, interview with author."

[3323] Quoted with permission after payment, from Stafford, Jean. *A Mother in History*, pages 41-42.

[3324] Quoted with permission from Wecht, Cyril *Cause of Death*, page 75. Copyright notice is in endnote [623].

[3325] Quoted with permission from Groden, Robert J. *The Killing of a President: The Complete Photographic Record of the JFK Assassination, the Conspiracy, and the Cover-Up*, page 12. Copyright notice supplied by publisher: "From THE KILLING OF A PRESIDENT by Robert Groden, copyright © 1993 by Robert J. Groden. Used by permission of Viking Books, an imprint of Penguin Publishing Group, a division of Penguin Random House LLC."

[3326] Groden *Killing* 22-39.

[3327] Groden *Killing* 20 and 40.

[3328] Quoted from Livingstone *Killing the Truth* 52-53. A statement about this source is in endnote [2018].

[3329] Quoted from Livingstone *Killing the Truth* 228-229, which cites "This testimony, reprinted with permission, is taken from a mock trial, entitled 'Trial of the Century: United States v. Lee Harvey Oswald.' Copyright © 1992, American Bar Association. The opinions expressed by participants in the mock trial do not necessarily represent those of the American Bar Association or of the speakers in the mock presentation. The individuals quoted here [include] Roger McCarthy, Ph.D., Failure Analysis Associates, Inc., Menlo Park, California." A statement about this source is in endnote [2018].

[3330] Quoted from Livingstone *Killing the Truth* 229. A statement about this source, also for next five cites, is in endnote [2018].

[3331] Quoted from Livingstone *Killing the Truth* 230.

[3332] Quoted from Livingstone *Killing the Truth* 230.

[3333] Quoted from Livingstone *Killing the Truth* 230-231.

[3334] Quoted from Livingstone *Killing Kennedy* 17.

[3335] Quoted from Livingstone *Killing Kennedy* 333-334.

[3336] Livingstone *Killing the Truth* 48, 90.

[3337] Quoted with permission from Groden, Robert J. *The Search for Lee Harvey Oswald: A Comprehensive Photographic Record* 105. Copyright notice supplied by publisher: "From THE SEARCH FOR LEE HARVEY OSWALD by Robert J. Groden, copyright © 1995 by Robert J. Groden. Used by permission of Viking Books, an imprint of Penguin Publishing Group, a division of Penguin Random House LLC."

[3338] Quoted with permission from Groden *Search* 108. Copyright notice is in endnote [3337].

[3339] TESTIMONY OF ROY H. KELLERMAN, SPECIAL AGENT, SECRET SERVICE on *WCH* II 64-65.

[3340] Quoted from http://www.coachbuilt.com/bui/h/hess_eisenhardt/hess_eisenhardt.htm. That website grants permission, provided these notices are printed: "COPYRIGHT NOTICE: Copyright 2003-2005 Coachbuilt.com, Inc. All rights reserved. Permission to use, copy and distribute documents and related graphics available within this World Wide Web ("Web") server ("Server") is granted, provided that: the above copyright notice and below liability notice appear in all copies and that the copyright notice, this permission notice, and the liability notice appear, use of documents and related graphics available from this Server is for informational and non-commercial purposes only, no documents or related graphics available from this Server are modified in any way, no graphics available from this Server are used, copied or distributed separate from accompanying text. Except where expressly provided above, nothing contained herein shall be construed as conferring by implication, estoppel or otherwise any license or right under any patent, copyright, trademark or other intellectual property right of Coachbuilt.com, Inc. or any other third party. All other product or company names mentioned herein are the trademarks of their respective owners. NOTICE OF LIABILITY: Coachbuilt.com, Inc. makes no representations about the suitability of the information contained in the documents and related graphics published on this Server for any purpose. All such documents and graphics are provided 'as is' without warranty of any kind. Coachbuilt.com, Inc. hereby disclaims all warranties and conditions with regard to this information, including all implied warranties and conditions of merchantability, fitness for a particular purpose and non-infringement." Whew!

[3341] Photo was converted to grayscale and tightly cropped from that taken by Cecil Stoughton, White House, and is from the collection of the John F. Kennedy Presidential Library and Museum, Boston. Sharing the handrail with JFK are Willy Brandt, the Governing Mayor of Berlin in middle, and Konrad Adenauer, Chancellor of West Germany at our right. Notice that Kennedy is on the passenger side of the Lincoln limousine in which he will ride and die in Dallas.

[3342] Photo was cropped from that taken by Cecil Stoughton, White House, and is from the collection of the John F. Kennedy Presidential Library and Museum, Boston. Notice that as in Germany, Kennedy is, as always, on the passenger side of the Lincoln limousine in which he will ride in Dallas.

[3343] Photo purchased from Corbis: © Bettmann/Corbis.

[3344] Quoted with permission after payment, from Blaine with McCubbin 25. Copyright notice is in endnote [1444].

[3345] Photo purchased from Corbis: © The Bettmann Premium Collection/Corbis.

[3346] Photo purchased to show here: Tom C. Dillard Collection, *The Dallas Morning News* / The Sixth Floor Museum at Dealey Plaza. The photo was tightly cropped to concentrate on the four passengers in the limousine.

[3347] Photo by Jack A. Weaver, who "made available this Polaroid photograph and it has been forwarded to the FBI Laboratory for enlargement and study." as recorded in a December 12, 1963, FBI report preserved by the Warren Commission as Commission Document (CD) 329. CD's are not displayed in the 26 volumes. If you wish to see this entire document and others from the FBI, look at http://www.maryferrell.org/showDoc.html?docId=10730&relPageId=18

[3348] The clearest presentation I have found is spread across the two pages 252-253 in Thompson, Josiah. *Six Seconds in Dallas: A Micro-Study of the Kennedy Assassination.*

[3349] The photo by Jim Altgens was purchased from AP. ©The Associated Press. It was printed three times. A scan of one print is shown here. Two prints were darkened to show areas that Oswald could not see as the limousine drove toward him; they are on the next page. Thus the three images in the book are equally second-generation, with equal tone.

[3350] Diagram scanned from CE 872 on *WCH* XVII 867. From that US Federal government source, it is in the public domain.

[3351] TESTIMONY OF C. DOUGLAS DILLON on *WCH* V 580.

3352 Quoted with permission from Doyle, Sir Arthur Conan. *Silver Blaze* in *The Complete Sherlock Holmes*, page 340. Gracious permission to quote here and below, without charge, was given to the author's copyright agent by Jon Lellenberg, licensing agent in the U.S. for the Sir Arthur Conan Doyle Literary Estate.

3353 Quoted with permission from Doyle 338-339.

3354 Quoted with permission from Doyle 347.

3355 Quoted with permission from Doyle 349.

3356 Quoted with permission from Specter, Arlen, with Charles Robbins. *Passion for Truth: From Finding JFK's Single Bullet to Questioning Anita Hill to Impeaching Clinton*, page 1.

— 20 — OBSTRUCTION OF BEST EVIDENCE

3357 *The Big Picture: An American Commentary*. HarperCollins, 1991, found with help of BrainyQuote.com, Xplore Inc, 2015: http://www.brainyquote.com/quotes/authors/a/a_whitney_brown.html, accessed on 2015/10/05 (October 5, 2015).

3358 Personal email message from James Reston, Jr. to author Pierre Sundborg on 2015/06/29.

3359 Photo shown courtesy of Jean Martin, Coordinator of Collin College's SAIL program.

3360 Most of the information in this chapter, about what happened to Mike Howard and other law officers on November 21 and later, is from several telephone interviews of Mike by the author between August 15 and October 21, 2015. Mike reviewed prints of this chapter with great care, with able assistance from his wife Martha, and found several small problems (*e.g.*, the color of his raincoat), all of which have been corrected. He has told the author he now finds it to be accurate, to the best of his excellent memory. Where I have made suppositions (*e.g.*, Hoover might have told LBJ of Oswald's Kill List), I label them as being my conjectures, so no blame can possibly accrue to Mike.

3361 This and all subsequent photos in this chapter (all except the Warren Commission's photos of Oswald's notebook) are from the private collection and shown through the courtesy of Mike Howard.

3362 TESTIMONY OF ROBERT EDWARD LEE OSWALD on page 409 of Volume I of *Hearings Before the President's Commission on the Assassination of President Kennedy*, better known as the *Warren Commission Hearings*. Hereinafter, similar references will be in the form *WCH* I 409.

3363 Scanned and cropped to show only — but all of — the printed area on the full page *WCH* XVI 42.

3364 "ED" is a prefix abbreviation for the "Edison" telephone exchange, from before all-number dialing and direct-dial Area codes. Those two letters are on phone button 3, so today you may reach the headquarters of Acme Brick Company at the same number, (817) 332-4101. Acme appears to be prospering at 3024 Acme Brick Plaza in Fort Worth, as may be seen by a search on Bing of the company's name. It is now part of Warren Buffet's Berkshire Hathaway conglomerate.

3365 Scanned and cropped, in the same way as stated in preceding endnote 3363, from *WCH* XVI 43.

3366 This is an enlargement, cropped from the upper half of the image shown in preceding note 3365, from *WCH* XVI 43, top.

— 21 — OTHERS ON THIS TRAIL

3367 Quoted with the gracious permission of James Reston, Jr., from his personal email message "With Gratitude" to this author on 2013/09/17 (September 17, 2013).

3368 FBI report, File #DL 89-43 (5) dated 12/1/63 of the interview on 11/30/63, in COMMISSION EXHIBIT (hereinafter CE) 1794 on page 413 of volume XXIII of *Hearings Before the President's Commission on the Assassination of President Kennedy*, better known as the *Warren Commission Hearings*. Hereinafter, similar references will be in form *WCH* XXIII 413.

3369 Quoted with the gracious permission of James Reston, Jr., author and copyright owner of *The Accidental Victim: JFK, Lee Harvey Oswald, and the Real Target in Dallas*, pages 173-175, which cites "Belin interview on 'USA Today on TV,' February 20, 1988, and interview with author."

3370 TESTIMONY OF GEORGE A. BOUHE on *WCH* VIII 374.

3371 TESTIMONY OF GOV. JOHN BOWDEN CONNALLY, JR. on *WCH* IV 140-141.

3372 TESTIMONY OF JEANNE DE MOHRENSCHILDT *WCH* IX 325.

3373 Quoted with kind permission and assistance from the heirs of Thomas Buchanan; from Buchanan, Thomas G. *Who Killed Kennedy?*, pages 70-72 in the revised, expanded American publication by Putnam; not the earlier, smaller British edition.

3374 TESTIMONY OF J. EDGAR HOOVER, *WCH* V 104.

3375 TESTIMONY OF MRS. LEE HARVEY OSWALD (RESUMED) *WCH* V 588. The translator was probably Peter Gregory, the father and more fluent, because Paul Gregory, his son whom Marina had tutored for $35, was probably away at college.

3376 *WCH* V 607-608 (Marina Oswald). (This is the form of second and subsequent citations from a witness's testimony.)

3377 *WCH* V 609-611 (Marina Oswald).

3378 Quoted with gracious permission after a modest payment, from Epstein, Edward Jay. *Inquest: The Warren Commission and the Establishment of Truth* (hc), page 132, which cites "Chronological File, September 8, 1964. The lawyer who wrote it told me that the memorandum was never officially submitted because the deadline was extended from September 11 to September 20."

3379 Quoted with permission after payment, from Epstein *Inquest* 132.

3380 *Report of the President's Commission on the Assassination of President Kennedy* (the *Warren Report*), pages 387-388.

[3381] Quoted from Matthews, James P., and Ernest Schwork, editors. *The Complete Kennedy Saga! Four Books In One!* No page numbers; this is in the first section at about page 11. The author and his excellent copyright researcher have tried to find the "publisher", Associated Professional Services of Los Angeles, without success. They are not listed on copyright.com, nor do they have any Web presence. Because of that diligence in searching for someone to give permission, and because the quotation is brief, I claim fair use. Please see CREDITS AND PERMISSIONS on page ii.

[3382] Quoted with permission after payment, from Ford, Gerald R., and John R. Stiles. *Portrait of the Assassin*, pages 110-111.

[3383] Myers, Dale K. *With Malice: Lee Harvey Oswald and the Murder of Officer J.D. Tippit*, Second Edition, page 428.

[3384] Quoted with permission after payment, from Newman, Albert H. *The Assassination of John F. Kennedy: The Reasons Why*, page 215.

[3385] Quoted as fair use (for brevity) from Crawford, Ann Fears and Jack Keever. *John B. Connally: Portrait in Power*, footnote 10 on page 300.

[3386] Quoted with permission from Ashman, Charles. *Connally: The Adventures of Big Bad John*, pages 42-43.

[3387] Quoted with permission from Kerr, Andy. *A Journey Amongst the Good and the Great*, page 3.

[3388] Quoted with permission from Kerr 97.

[3389] Quoted with permission from Reston, James (Sr.). *Deadline: A Memoir*, published by Random House in 1991, page 295.

[3390] Quoted with permission from Reston, James (Sr.). *Deadline: A Memoir*, published by Random House in 1991, page 250.

[3391] Quoted with the gracious permission of James Reston, Jr., author and copyright owner of *The Last Apocalypse: Europe at the Year 1000 A.D.*, from the inside of the back cover.

[3392] Quoted with the gracious permission of James Reston, Jr., author and copyright owner of *The Accidental Victim*.

[3393] Personal email message from James Reston, Jr. to the author on 2015/11/05.

[3394] Quoted with the gracious permission of James Reston, Jr., author and copyright owner of *The Last Apocalypse*, page 211.

[3395] Personal email message from Tara L. Zades, Syndication Manager, Time Inc. International Licensing & Development, to the author on 2015/11/20. My guess: They don't give away anything, and if they were to charge for readers' letters, the writers could claim a share, lawyers would get involved, and, as Ronald Reagan famously said, "There you go again!"

[3396] This image was scanned by the author from the dust jacket of his copy of the book. Copyright to *The Lone Star* has reverted to its author, so this is shown with the kind permission of the esteemed "Trailblazer", James Reston, Jr.

[3397] Quoted with the gracious permission of James Reston, Jr., author and copyright owner of *The Lone Star: The Life of John Connally*, the entire chapter 11 – "The Assassin", pages 213-236.

[3398] Quoted with the gracious permission of James Reston, Jr., from *The Lone Star* 252-253.

[3399] Quoted with the gracious permission of James Reston, Jr., author and copyright owner of *Collision at Home Plate: The Lives of Pete Rose and Bart Giamatti* 317.

[3400] Quoted from Livingstone, Harrison Edward. *High Treason 2: The Great Cover-Up: The Assassination of President John F. Kennedy* 443. A statement about this source, applying also to the next five citations, is in endnote [2018].

[3401] Quoted from Livingstone *High Treason 2* 449.

[3402] Quoted from Livingstone *High Treason 2* 444-445.

[3403] Quoted from Livingstone *High Treason 2* 448.

[3404] Quoted from Livingstone *High Treason 2* 449.

[3405] Quoted from Livingstone *High Treason 2* 450.

[3406] Zirbel, Craig I. *The Texas Connection*, pages 275-282.

[3407] Zirbel 114, 121.

[3408] Zirbel 123, 245.

[3409] O'Donnell, Kenneth P., and David F. Powers with Joe McCarthy. *Johnny, We Hardly Knew Ye*, pages 219-223.

[3410] Quoted with permission after payment, from Sorensen, Theodore C. *Kennedy*, page 184.

[3411] Quoted with kind permission, without fee, from White, Theodore H. *The Making of the President 1960*, pages 208-209.

[3412] Zirbel 134-135, 245.

[3413] Zirbel 122.

[3414] Zirbel 245-246.

[3415] Zirbel 161, 246-247.

[3416] Zirbel 162, 249.

[3417] Zirbel 163-164

[3418] Zirbel 165, 248.

[3419] Quoted with permission from Zirbel 248.

[3420] Quoted with permission from Zirbel 165.

[3421] Quoted with permission from Zirbel 248.

[3422] Zirbel 249, 251.

[3423] Zirbel 251.

[3424] Zirbel 252.

[3425] Quoted with permission from Zirbel 33-34.

[3426] Quoted with permission from Zirbel 70-72.

[3427] Zirbel 249.

[3428] White *1960*, page 4.

[3429] Mailer, Norman. *Oswald's Tale: An American Mystery*, page 500.

[3430] Quoted with permission from Zirbel 240.

[3431] Quoted with permission from Connally, John, with Mickey Herskowitz. *In History's Shadow: An American Odyssey*, pages 189-190.

[3432] Quoted with permission from Connally, John, with Herskowitz 367.

[3433] Quoted with permission from Connally, John, with Herskowitz. Ninth photo in photo insert section after 180.

[3434] Quoted with permission from Callahan, Bob. *Who Shot JFK?: A Guide to the Major Conspiracy Theories*, page 35.

[3435] Quoted with permission from Callahan 35-36.

[3436] Quoted with kind permission from Galanor, Stewart. *Cover-Up*, page 52.

[3437] Quoted as fair use (for brevity) from Belzer, Richard. *UFOs, JFK, and Elvis: Conspiracies You Don't Have To Be Crazy To Believe*, from inside-back dustcover.

[3438] Quoted as fair use (for brevity) from Belzer, page 75.

[3439] Quoted as fair use (for brevity) from http://en.wikipedia.org/wiki/William_Rubinstein on 2014/01/04.

[3440] Quoted as fair use (for brevity) from Rubinstein, William. Article "Oswald Shoots JFK: But Who is the Real Target?" in British periodical *History Today*, October 1999, imported from http://www.britannica.com/bcom/magazine/article/0,5744,303923,00.html on 2000/10/19.

[3441] Quoted as fair use (for brevity) from Rubinstein, the same as the previous source.

[3442] Quoted with permission from Connally, Nellie, with Mickey Herskowitz. *From Love Field: Our Final Hours with President John F. Kennedy*, page 122.

[3443] Quoted with permission after payment, from Bugliosi, Vincent. *Reclaiming History: The Assassination of President John F. Kennedy*. Endnote to "Governor Connally's reaction" on page 475 of the printed book, on pages 321-322 of the file Endnotes.pdf on the CD-ROM enclosed in a pocket inside the book's back cover. Copyright notice is in endnote [1788].

[3444] This image was scanned by the author from the dust jacket of his copy of the printed-on-paper book. Copyright to *The Accidental Victim* is its author's, so this is shown with the kind permission of the "Trailblazer", James Reston, Jr.

— 22 — A TRAGIC REALITY

[3445] Quoted as fair use (for brevity: 12 words) from Kennedy, John F. *Profiles in Courage*, page 208.

[3446] Quoted with permission after payment, from Warren, Earl. *The Memoirs of Earl Warren*, page 354. Copyright notice is in endnote [211].

[3447] Quoted with permission from Sneed, Larry A. *No More Silence: An Oral History of the Assassination of President Kennedy*, page 220.

[3448] Quoted with permission from Sneed 218.

[3449] Quoted with permission from the oral history of Captain W.R. "Pinky" Westbrook in Sneed 324.

[3450] This is an enlargement cropped from the upper half of COMMISSION EXHIBIT 18, as printed on page 43 of volume XVI of the *Hearings Before the President's Commission on the Assassination of President Kennedy*, better known as the *Warren Commission Hearings*. Such citations will be hereinafter expressed in the form WCH XVI 43.

[3451] This reconstruction by the author is based on several telephone interviews of Mike Howard between August and November 2015, then on Mike's careful review of prints of this book's chapter 20. Mike has been fastidious, even correcting the shade of his London Fog raincoat to "tan". When he has not been entirely certain of any fact, he carefully said so, then if pressed, offered his opinion or best guess, insisting that the author identify those as such. He's a wonderful source!

[3452] Personal email message from Reston to the author on 2015/11/05.

[3453] This awesome photo was taken by White House photographer Abbie Rowe, an employee of the National Park Service. Your author first saw a smaller print of it in Nellie Connally's book *From Love Field* and knew it belonged here, full-page. My gifted picture researcher, Gina McNeeley, found Mr. Rowe's original negative at the National Archives and Records Administration in College Park, Maryland. NARA does not allow mere mortals to scan their negatives, so she engaged her usual professional firm. Their first scan was terrible — 8 shades of gray. My graphics designer, Mark Drefs, then specified the necessary scan parameters, and a second scan of the negative was satisfactory. But, because of where Mr. Rowe stood, it was much tilted. Mark then cleaned up the scan, sharpened the focus, and counter-tilted to the author's wishes, and I then cropped to a central area framed by columns of bayonets, and was at last satisfied. This is far from being the most expensive photo in the book (many cost $400 to $600) but was the most challenging to get right.

[3454] Quoted with permission from Oglesby, Carl. *Who Killed JFK?*, pages 57-58. The three embedded quotations are from the TESTIMONY OF MRS. LEE HARVEY OSWALD (Marina) on WCH I 16.

[3455] Quoted with permission from Johnson, Lyndon Baines. *The Vantage Point: Perspectives of the Presidency 1963–1969*, page 11. Copyright and permission notice is in endnote [1559].

[3456] Quoted with permission from Bradlee, Benjamin C. *Conversations with Kennedy*, page 12.

[3457] Quoted with kind permission, without fee, from White, Theodore H. *The Making of the President 1960*, page 207.

[3458] Quoted with permission from White. *The Making of the President 1960*, page 207.

[3459] Quoted with permission from Reston, James (Sr.). *Deadline: A Memoir*, published by Random House in 1991, page 285.

[3460] Quoted with the gracious permission of James Reston, Jr., author and copyright owner of *The Accidental Victim: JFK, Lee Harvey Oswald, and the Real Target in Dallas*, page 177.

[3461] Quoted as fair use (for brevity) from "Letter to the Editor" of *The New York Times* by William Manchester, printed on February 5, 1992.

[3462] Quoted with permission from Bugliosi, Vincent. *Outrage: The Five Reasons Why O.J. Simpson Got Away with Murder* 4.

[3463] Quoted with permission after payment, from Manchester, William. *The Death of a President* 645, for which the permission acknowledgement is in endnote [17].

[3464] Quoted as fair use (for brevity) from http://www.brainyquote.com/quotes/quotes/a/alberteins103652.html on 2015/04/16.

[3465] Quoted with permission from Bugliosi *Outrage* 288-289.

[3466] Quoted from Oswald, Robert L., with Myrick and Barbara Land. *Lee: A Portrait of Lee Harvey Oswald by His Brother*, page 220. This source was described in endnote [68].

[3467] Quoted from Oswald, Robert 224. This source was described in endnote [68].

[3468] Quoted from Oswald, Robert 229. This source was described in endnote [68].

[3469] Quoted with permission from "Statement by Marina Oswald Porter", in the 1978 Bantam Books paperback of McMillan, Priscilla Johnson. *Marina and Lee*, on non-numbered page before the title page. Permission statement is in endnote [150].

[3470] This is quoted as fair use after due diligence after author and copyright agent learned the copyright had reverted from the publisher to author Evelyn Lincoln, who died without descendants. *My Twelve Years with John F. Kennedy*, page 309.

[3471] Quoted from President Kennedy's inaugural address on 20 January 1961.

[3472] Quoted as fair use (for brevity) from Feinsilber, Mike (AP). "Records suggest Kennedy planned to withdraw U.S. from S. Vietnam" *The Seattle Times*, 22 November 1997, page A9.

[3473] Photo by deservedly much-honored White House photographer Abbie Rowe, who will take the first photo in this chapter — four Kennedys going up the east stairway of the US Capitol — in less than eight weeks. From the collection of the John F. Kennedy Library and Museum, Boston, it was moderately cropped to show here.

[3474] Image scanned from Groden, Robert J. *The Killing of a President: The Complete Photographic Record of the JFK Assassination, the Conspiracy, and the Cover-Up*, page 1, cropped to remove written note at bottom "Committee Print of Pentagon Papers | 7/15/77". Groden's careful photo credits on his page 223 do not list this image, apparently because it is of a federal government document prepared by the National Security Advisor in the White House, then declassified and released to the public, so is in the public domain.

[3475] That is the number of names of the dead, engraved into the Vietnam Veteran's Memorial on the National Mall, as of 2014.

[3476] The right to show this wonderful, haunting image to appropriately end this book was purchased through Los Angeles law firm Alston & Bird LLP. Copyright by Bill Mauldin (1963). Courtesy of the Bill Mauldin Estate LLC.

— REFERENCES CITED —

[3477] Quoted with permission after payment, from Stafford, Jean. *A Mother in History*, pages 11-12.

[3478] Quoted with permission from Mailer, Norman. *Oswald's Tale: An American Mystery*, page 351.

[3479] *Hearings Before the President's Commission on the Assassination of President Kennedy*, better known as the *Warren Commission Hearings*, volume I, page v, from which page were also quoted the next three items in "quotation marks".

— NOT CITED —

[3480] TESTIMONY OF MRS. MARGUERITE OSWALD in *Warren Commission Hearings*, volume I, pages 131-132. Corroborated in Oswald, Robert L., with Myrick and Barbara Land. *Lee: A Portrait of Lee Harvey Oswald by His Brother*, page 120.

— NOTES AND SOURCES —

[3481] Quoted as fair use (for brevity) from "Casey Stengel Quotes" on http://www.baseball-almanac.com/quotes/quosteng.shtml accessed on 2013/06/03.

INDEX